Java® 9
FOR PROGRAMMERS
FOURTH EDITION
DEITEL® DEVELOPER SERIES

Deitel® Series

Deitel® Developer Series

Android™ 6 for Programmers: An App-Driven
Approach, 3/E
C for Programmers with an Introduction to C11
C++11 for Programmers
C# 6 for Programmers
Java® 9 for Programmers
JavaScript for Programmers
Swift™ for Programmers

How to Program Series

Android™ How to Program, 3/E
C++ How to Program, 10/E
C How to Program, 8/E
Java® How to Program, Early Objects Version, 11/E
Java® How to Program, Late Objects Version, 11/E
Internet & World Wide Web How to Program, 5/E
Visual Basic® 2012 How to Program, 6/E
Visual C#® How to Program, 6/E

Simply Series

Simply Visual Basic® 2010: An App-Driven
Approach, 4/E
Simply C++: An App-Driven Tutorial Approach

VitalSource Web Books

http://bit.ly/DeitelOnVitalSource

Android™ How to Program, 2/E and 3/E
C++ How to Program, 9/E and 10/E
Java® How to Program, 10/E and 11/E
Simply C++: An App-Driven Tutorial Approach
Simply Visual Basic® 2010: An App-Driven
Approach, 4/E
Visual Basic® 2012 How to Program, 6/E
Visual C#® How to Program, 6/E
Visual C#® 2012 How to Program, 5/E

LiveLessons Video Learning Products

http://deitel.com/books/LiveLessons/

Android™ 6 App Development Fundamentals, 3/E
C++ Fundamentals
Java SE 8® Fundamentals, 2/E
Java SE 9® Fundamentals, 3/E
C# 6 Fundamentals
C# 2012 Fundamentals
JavaScript Fundamentals
Swift™ Fundamentals

REVEL™ Interactive Multimedia

REVEL™ for Deitel Java™

To receive updates on Deitel publications, Resource Centers, training courses, partner offers and more, please join the Deitel communities on

- Facebook®—http://facebook.com/DeitelFan
- Twitter®—http://twitter.com/deitel
- LinkedIn®—http://linkedin.com/company/deitel-&-associates
- YouTube™—http://youtube.com/DeitelTV

and register for the free *Deitel® Buzz Online* e-mail newsletter at:

http://www.deitel.com/newsletter/subscribe.html

To communicate with the authors, send e-mail to:

deitel@deitel.com

For information on programming-languages corporate training seminars offered by Deitel & Associates, Inc. worldwide, write to deitel@deitel.com or visit:

http://www.deitel.com/training/

For continuing updates on Pearson/Deitel publications visit:

http://www.deitel.com
http://www.pearsonhighered.com/deitel/

Visit the Deitel Resource Centers, which will help you master programming languages, software development, Android™ and iOS® app development, and Internet- and web-related topics:

http://www.deitel.com/ResourceCenters.html

Java® 9
FOR PROGRAMMERS
FOURTH EDITION
DEITEL® DEVELOPER SERIES

Paul Deitel • Harvey Deitel
Deitel & Associates, Inc.

PRENTICE
HALL

Boston • Columbus • Indianapolis • New York • San Francisco • Amsterdam • Cape Town
Dubai • London • Madrid • Milan • Munich • Paris • Montreal • Toronto • Delhi • Mexico City
São Paulo • Sydney • Hong Kong • Seoul • Singapore • Taipei • Tokyo

Many of the designations used by manufacturers and sellers to distinguish their products are claimed as trademarks. Where those designations appear in this book, and the publisher was aware of a trademark claim, the designations have been printed with initial capital letters or in all capitals. Additional trademarks appear on page vi.

The authors and publisher have taken care in the preparation of this book, but make no expressed or implied warranty of any kind and assume no responsibility for errors or omissions. No liability is assumed for incidental or consequential damages in connection with or arising out of the use of the information or programs contained herein.

For information about buying this title in bulk quantities, or for special sales opportunities (which may include electronic versions; custom cover designs; and content particular to your business, training goals, marketing focus, or branding interests), please contact our corporate sales department at corpsales@pearsoned.com or (800) 382-3419.

For government sales inquiries, please contact governmentsales@pearsoned.com.

For questions about sales outside the U.S., please contact intlcs@pearson.com.

Visit us on the web: informit.com/ph

Library of Congress Control Number: 2017937968

ISBN-13: 978-0-13-477756-6
ISBN-10: 0-13-477756-5

1 17

In memory of Dr. Henry Heimlich:
Barbara Deitel used your Heimlich maneuver to
save Abbey Deitel's life. Our family is forever
grateful to you.

Harvey, Barbara, Paul and Abbey Deitel

Trademarks

Contents

3 Introduction to Classes, Objects, Methods and Strings 35

4 Control Statements: Part 1; Assignment, ++ and -- Operators 56

5   Control Statements: Part 2; Logical Operators   79

6   Methods: A Deeper Look   109

7   Arrays and ArrayLists   135

8   Classes and Objects: A Deeper Look   184

9   Object-Oriented Programming: Inheritance   221

12   JavaFX Graphical User Interfaces: Part 1   319

13   JavaFX GUI: Part 2   347

14 Strings, Characters and Regular Expressions 380

15 Files, Input/Output Streams, NIO and XML Serialization 418

16 Generic Collections 451

17 Lambdas and Streams 488

18 Recursion   537

19 Generic Classes and Methods: A Deeper Look   563

20 JavaFX Graphics, Animation and Video   585

21 Concurrency and Multi-Core Performance   634

24 Java Persistence API (JPA) 820

25 ATM Case Study, Part 1: Object-Oriented Design with the UML 845

28 Additional Java 9 Topics   **975**

Foreword

Throughout my career I've met and interviewed many expert Java developers who've learned from Paul and Harvey, through one or more of their professional books, college textbooks, videos and corporate training. Many Java User Groups have joined together around the Deitels' publications, which are used internationally in professional training programs and university courses. You are joining an elite group.

How do I become an expert Java developer?

This is one of the most common questions I receive at events with Java professionals and talks for university students. Programmers want to become expert developers—and this is a great time to be one. The market is wide open, full of opportunities and fascinating projects.

So, how do you do it? First, let's be clear: Software development is hard, but it opens the door to great opportunities. Accept that it's hard, embrace the complexity, enjoy the ride. There are no limits to how much you can expand your skills. The success or failure of initiatives everywhere depends on expert developers' knowledge and skills.

The push for you to get expert-level skills is what makes *Java® 9 for Programmers* so compelling. It's written by authors who are educators and developers, with nine decades of computing experience between them and with input over the years from some of the world's leading professional Java experts—Java Champions, open-source Java developers, even creators of Java itself. Their collective knowledge and experience will guide you. Even seasoned Java professionals will learn and grow their expertise with the wisdom in these pages.

Java was released in 1995—Paul and Harvey had the first edition of their college textbook *Java How to Program* ready for Fall 1996 classes. Since that groundbreaking book, they've produced ten more editions and many editions of their *Java® for Programmers* professional books, keeping current with the latest developments and idioms in the Java software-engineering community. You hold in your hands the map that will enable you to rapidly develop your Java skills.

The Deitels have broken down the humongous Java world into well-defined, specific goals. With both Java 8 and Java 9 in the same book, you'll have up-to-date skills on the latest Java technologies. I'm impressed with the care that the Deitels always take to accommodate readers at all levels. They ease you into difficult concepts and deal with the challenges that professionals encounter in industry projects. And if you have a question, don't be shy—the Deitels publish their e-mail address—`deitel@deitel.com`—in every book they write to encourage interaction.

One of my favorite chapters is Lambdas and Streams. It covers the topic in detail and the examples shine—many real-world challenges that will help you sharpen your skills.

I love the chapter about JShell—the new Java 9 tool that enables interactive Java. JShell allows you to explore, discover and experiment with new concepts, language features and APIs, make mistakes—accidentally and intentionally—and correct them, and rapidly prototype new code. It will prove to be an important tool for leveraging your learning and productivity. Paul and Harvey give a full treatment of JShell that developers at all levels will be able to put to use immediately.

Perhaps most important: Check out the chapter on the Java Platform Module System—the single most important new software-engineering capability introduced in Java since its inception. Developers building new big systems—and especially developers migrating existing systems to Java 9—will appreciate the Deitel's detailed walkthrough of modularity.

There's lots of additional information about Java 9, the important new Java release. You can jump right in and learn the latest Java features. If you're still working with Java 8, you can ease into Java 9 at your own pace.

Also check out the amazing coverage of JavaFX—Java's latest GUI, graphics and multimedia capabilities. JavaFX is the recommended toolkit for new projects. And be sure to dig in on Paul and Harvey's treatment of concurrency. They explain the basic concepts so clearly that the intermediate and advanced examples and discussions will be easy to master. You will be ready to maximize your applications' performance in an increasingly multi-core world.

Enjoy the book—I wish you great success!

Bruno Sousa
bruno@javaman.com.br
Java Champion
Java Specialist at ToolsCloud
President of SouJava (the Brazilian Java Society)
SouJava representative at the Java Community Process

Preface

Welcome to the Java® programming language and *Java® 9 for Programmers*! This book presents leading-edge computing technologies for software developers. It also will help you prepare for most topics covered by the following Oracle Java Standard Edition 8 (Java SE 8) Certifications (and the Java SE 9 editions, when they appear):

- Oracle Certified Associate, Java SE 8 Programmer
- Oracle Certified Professional, Java SE 8 Programmer

If you haven't already done so, please read the back cover and the additional reviewer comments inside the back cover—these concisely capture the essence of the book. In this Preface we provide more details.

We focus on software engineering best practices. At the heart of the book is the Deitel signature **live-code approach**—we present most concepts in the context of hundreds of complete working programs that have been tested on **Windows®**, **macOS®** and **Linux®**. The code examples are accompanied by live sample executions. All the source code for the book's code examples is available at:

```
http://www.deitel.com/books/Java9FP
```

New and Updated Features

In the following sections, we discuss the key features and updates we've made for *Java® 9 for Programmers*, including:

- Coverage of Java SE 9: The **Java Platform Module System, interactive Java with JShell**, and many other Java 9 topics
- Object-oriented programming emphasizing current idioms
- **JavaFX GUI, graphics (2D and 3D), animation and video** coverage
- **Generics** and **generic collections**
- Deep **lambdas** and **streams** coverage
- **Concurrency** and **multi-core performance**
- Database: **JDBC** and **JPA**
- **Object-oriented design case study** with full Java code implementation

Flexibility Using Java SE 8 or the New Java SE 9

To meet the needs of our diverse audiences, we designed the book for professionals interested in Java SE 8 or Java SE 9, which from this point forward we'll refer to simply as Java 8 and Java 9, respectively. Features first introduced in Java 8 or Java 9 are accompanied by an 8 or 9 icon, respectively, in the margin, like those to the left of this paragraph. The new

Java 9 capabilities are covered in clearly marked chapters and sections. Figures 1.1 and 1.2 list some key Java 8 and Java 9 features that we cover, respectively.

Java 8 features	
Lambdas and streams	Date & Time API (`java.time`)
Type-inference improvements	Parallel array sorting
`@FunctionalInterface` annotation	Java concurrency API improvements
Bulk data operations for Java Collections—	`static` and `default` methods in interfaces
`filter`, `map` and `reduce`	Functional interfaces that define only one
Library enhancements to support lambdas (e.g.,	abstract method and can include `static`
`java.util.stream`, `java.util.function`)	and `default` methods

Fig. 1.1 | Some key features we cover that were introduced in Java 8.

Java 9 features	
New Java Platform Module System chapter	`_` is no longer allowed as an identifier
New JShell chapter	Mentions of:
`private` interface methods	`CompletableFuture` enhancements
Effectively `final` variables can be used in `try`-	Stack Walking API
with-resources statements	JEP 254, Compact Strings
Collection factory methods	Overview of Java 9 security enhancements
HTML5 Javadoc enhancements	Object serialization security enhancements
Regular expressions: New `Matcher` methods	Enhanced deprecation
`Stream` interface enhancements	Features removed from Java in Java 9
JavaFX 9 skin APIs and other enhancements	Features proposed for future removal

Fig. 1.2 | Some key new features we cover that were introduced in Java 9.

Java 9 for Programmers Modular Organization

Java 9 for Programmers features a modular organization. Many Java 9 features are integrated throughout the book. The pure Java 9 chapters (23, 27 and 28) are shown in **bold**:

Part 1: Introduction
Chapter 1, Introduction and Test-Driving a Java Application
Chapter 2, Introduction to Java Applications; Input/Output and Operators
Chapter 3, Introduction to Classes, Objects, Methods and Strings
Chapter 23, Introduction to JShell: Java 9's REPL for Interactive Java

Part 2: Core Programming Topics
Chapter 4, Control Statements: Part 1; Assignment, ++ and −− Operators
Chapter 5, Control Statements: Part 2; Logical Operators
Chapter 6, Methods: A Deeper Look
Chapter 7, Arrays and `ArrayLists`
Chapter 14, Strings, Characters and Regular Expressions
Chapter 15, Files, Input/Output Streams, NIO and XML Serialization

Part 3: Object-Oriented Programming
Chapter 8, Classes and Objects: A Deeper Look
Chapter 9, Object-Oriented Programming: Inheritance
Chapter 10, Object-Oriented Programming: Polymorphism and Interfaces
Chapter 11, Exception Handling: A Deeper Look

Part 4: JavaFX Graphical User Interfaces, Graphics, Animation and Video
Chapter 12, JavaFX Graphical User Interfaces: Part 1
Chapter 13, JavaFX GUI: Part 2
Chapter 20, JavaFX Graphics, Animation and Video

Part 5: Generics, Generic Collections, Lambdas and Streams
Chapter 16, Generic Collections
Chapter 17, Lambdas and Streams
Chapter 18, Recursion
Chapter 19, Generic Classes and Methods: A Deeper Look

Part 6: Concurrency and Multi-Core Performance
Chapter 21, Concurrency and Multi-Core Performance

Part 7: Database-Driven Desktop Development
Chapter 22, Accessing Databases with JDBC
Chapter 24, Java Persistence API (JPA)

Part 8: Modularity and Additional Java 9 Topics
Chapter 27, Java Platform Module System
Chapter 28, Additional Java 9 Topics

Part 9: Object-Oriented Design
Chapter 25, ATM Case Study, Part 1: Object-Oriented Design with the UML
Chapter 26, ATM Case Study Part 2: Implementing an Object-Oriented Design

Introduction and Programming Fundamentals (Parts 1 and 2)

Chapters 1 through 7 provide an example-driven treatment of traditional fundamental programming topics. This book features an early objects approach—see the section "Object-Oriented Programming" later in this Preface. Note in the preceding outline that Part 1 includes the Chapter 23 on Java 9's new JShell.

Flexible Coverage of Java 9: The Module System, JShell and Other Java 9 Topics

Java 9 was still under development when this book was published. In addition to the topics discussed in this section, many Java 9 topics are integrated throughout the book. Check the following website for updates to this content:

```
http://www.deitel.com/books/Java9FP
```

The Java Platform Module System

9   Chapter 27 includes a substantial treatment of the Java Platform Module System (JPMS)—Java 9's most important new software-engineering technology. Modularity—the result of Project Jigsaw—helps professional developers be more productive as they build, maintain and evolve large systems. Figure 1.3 outlines the chapter's topics.

Java Platform Module System chapter outline

Module Declarations
requires, requires transitive, exports and exports...to, uses, provides...with, open, opens and opens...to

Modularized Welcome App
Welcome App's Structure, Class Welcome, module-info.java, Module-Dependency Graph, Compiling a Module, Running an App from a Module's Exploded Folders, Packaging a Module into a Modular JAR File, Running the Welcome App from a Modular JAR File, Aside: Classpath vs. Module Path

Creating and Using a Custom Module
Exporting a Package for Use in Other Modules, Using a Class from a Package in Another Module, Compiling and Running the Example, Packaging the App into Modular JAR Files, Strong Encapsulation and Accessibility

Module-Dependency Graphs: A Deeper Look
java.sql, java.se, Browsing the JDK Module Graph, Error: Module Graph with a Cycle

Migrating Code to Java 9
Unnamed Module, Automatic Modules, jdeps: Java Dependency Analysis

Resources in Modules; Using an Automatic Module
Automatic Modules, Requiring Multiple Modules, Opening a Module for Reflection, Module-Dependency Graph, Compiling the Module, Running a Modularized App

Creating Custom Runtimes with jlink
Listing the JRE's Modules, Custom Runtime Containing Only java.base, Creating a Custom Runtime for the Welcome App, Executing the Welcome App Using a Custom Runtime, Using the Module Resolver on a Custom Runtime

Services and ServiceLoader
Service-Provider Interface, Loading and Consuming Service Providers, uses Module Directive and Service Consumers, Running the App with No Service Providers, Implementing a Service Provider, provides...with Module Directive and Declaring a Service Provider, Running the App with One Service Provider, Implementing a Second Service Provider, Running the App with Two Service Providers

Fig. 1.3 | Java Platform Module System (Chapter 27) outline.

JShell: Java 9's REPL (Read-Eval-Print-Loop) for Interactive Java

9   JShell provides a friendly environment that enables you to quickly explore, discover and experiment with Java's language features and its extensive libraries. JShell replaces the tedious cycle of editing, compiling and executing with its **read-evaluate-print-loop**. Rather than complete programs, you write JShell commands and Java code snippets. When you enter a snippet, JShell *immediately*

- **reads** it,
- **evaluates** it and
- **prints** messages that help you see the effects of your code, then it
- **loops** to perform this process again for the next snippet.

As you work through Chapter 23's scores of examples, you'll see how JShell and its **instant feedback** keep your attention, enhance your performance and speed the learning and software-development processes.

You'll find JShell easy and fun to use. It will help you learn Java features faster and more deeply and will help you quickly verify that these features work as they're supposed to. JShell encourages you to dig in. You'll appreciate how JShell helps you rapidly prototype key code segments and discover and experiment with new APIs.

We chose a modular approach with the JShell content packaged in Chapter 23. The chapter:

1. is **easy to include or omit**.

2. is organized as a series of 16 sections, many of which are designed to be covered after a specific earlier chapter of the book (Fig. 1.4).

3. offers rich coverage of JShell's capabilities. It's **example-intensive**—you should do each of the examples. Get JShell into your fingertips. You'll appreciate how quickly and conveniently you can do things.

4. includes **dozens of Self-Review Exercises, each with an answer**. These exercises can be done after you read Chapter 2 and Section 23.3. As you do each of them, flip the page and check your answer. You'll master the basics of JShell quickly. Then as you do the remaining examples you'll master the vast majority of JShell's capabilities.

JShell discussions	Can be covered after
Section 23.3 introduces **JShell**, including starting a session, executing statements, declaring variables, evaluating expressions, JShell's **type-inference** capabilities and more.	Chapter 2, Introduction to Java Applications; Input/Output and Operators
Section 23.4 discusses command-line input with **Scanner** in JShell.	
Section 23.5 discusses how to declare and use **classes** in JShell, including how to load a Java source-code file containing an existing class declaration.	Chapter 3, Introduction to Classes, Objects, Methods and Strings
Section 23.6 shows how to use JShell's **auto-completion** capabilities to discover a class's capabilities and JShell commands.	
Section 23.7 presents additional JShell auto-completion capabilities for **experimentation and discovery**, including viewing method parameters, documentation and method overloads.	Chapter 6, Methods: A Deeper Look
Section 23.8 shows how to declare and use methods in JShell, including **forward referencing** a method that does not yet exist in the JShell session.	

Fig. 1.4 | Chapter 23 JShell discussions that may be covered after specific earlier chapters. (Part 1 of 2.)

JShell discussions	Can be covered after
Section 23.9 shows how **exceptions** are handled in JShell.	Chapter 7, Arrays and `ArrayLists`
Section 23.10 shows how to add existing **packages** to the classpath and import them for use in JShell.	Chapter 8, Classes and Objects: A Deeper Look

The remaining JShell sections are reference material that can be covered after Section 23.10. Topics include using an external editor, a summary of JShell commands, getting help in JShell, additional features of `/edit` command, `/reload` command, `/drop` command, feedback modes, other JShell features configurable with `/set`, keyboard shortcuts for snippet editing, how JShell reinterprets Java for interactive use and IDE JShell support.

Fig. 1.4 | Chapter 23 JShell discussions that may be covered after specific earlier chapters. (Part 2 of 2.)

9 *Chapter 28: Additional Java 9 Topics*
Chapter 28 reviews the list of Java 9 features discussed throughout the book, then presents live-code examples and discussions of several additional features from Fig. 1.2. The chapter also lists some Java 9 features that are beyond the book's scope, points out features that are being removed in Java 9 and lists features that are proposed for future removal.

Object-Oriented Programming (Part 3)

Object-oriented programming. We introduce object-oriented concepts and terminology in Chapter 1. You'll develop customized classes and objects in Chapter 3.

Early objects real-world case studies. The early classes and objects presentation in Chapters 3–7 features Account, AutoPolicy, Time, Employee, GradeBook and Card shuffling-and-dealing case studies, gradually introducing deeper OO concepts.

Inheritance, Interfaces, Polymorphism and Composition. The deeper treatment of object-oriented programming in Chapters 8–10 features additional real-world case studies, including class Time, an Employee class hierarchy, and a Payable interface implemented in disparate Employee and Invoice classes. We explain the use of current idioms, such as "**programming to an interface not an implementation**" and "**preferring composition to inheritance**" in building industrial-strength applications.

Exception handling. We integrate basic exception handling beginning in Chapter 7 then present a deeper treatment in Chapter 11. Exception handling is important for building **mission-critical** and **business-critical** applications. To use a Java component, you need to know not only how that component behaves when "things go well," but also what exceptions that component "throws" when "things go poorly" and how your code should handle those exceptions.

*Class **Arrays** and **ArrayList**.* Chapter 7 covers class Arrays—which contains methods for performing common array manipulations—and class ArrayList—which implements a dynamically resizable array-like collection.

JavaFX GUI, Graphics (2D and 3D), Animation and Video Coverage (Part 4)

We've significantly updated our JavaFX presentation, replacing our Swing GUI and graphics coverage. In Chapters 12–13, we use JavaFX and **Scene Builder**—a drag-and-drop tool for creating JavaFX GUIs quickly and conveniently—to build several apps demonstrating various JavaFX layouts, controls and event-handling capabilities. In Swing, drag-and-drop tools and their generated code were *IDE dependent*. JavaFX Scene Builder is a standalone tool that you can use separately or with any of the Java IDEs to do **portable drag-and-drop GUI design**. In Chapter 20, we present JavaFX 2D and 3D graphics, animation and video capabilities. Despite the fact that the JavaFX chapters are spread out in the book, **Chapter 20 can be covered immediately after Chapter 13**.

Integrating Swing GUI Components in JavaFX GUIs
With JavaFX, you still can use your favorite Swing capabilities. For example, in Chapter 22, we demonstrate how to display database data in a Swing `JTable` component that's embedded in a JavaFX GUI via a JavaFX 8 `SwingNode`. As you explore Java further, you'll see that you also can incorporate JavaFX capabilities into your Swing GUIs.

Generics and Generic Collections (Part 5)

We begin with generic class `ArrayList` in Chapter 7. Our later discussions (Chapters 16–19) provide a deeper treatment of **generic collections**—showing how to use the built-in collections of the Java API. We discuss **recursion**, which is important for many reasons including implementing tree-like, data-structure classes.

We then show how to implement **generic methods and classes**. Rather than building custom generic data structures, most programmers should use the pre-built generic collections. **Lambdas and streams** (introduced in Chapter 17) are especially useful for working with generic collections.

Flexible Lambdas and Streams Coverage (Chapter 17)

The most significant new features in Java 8 were lambdas and streams. This book has several audiences, including

- those who'd like a significant treatment of lambdas and streams
- those who want a basic introduction with a few simple examples
- those who do not want to use lambdas and streams yet.

For this reason, we've placed most of the lambdas and streams treatment in Chapter 17, which is architected as a series of *easy-to-include-or-omit* sections that are keyed to the book's earlier sections and chapters. We do integrate lambdas and streams into a few examples after Chapter 17, because their capabilities are so compelling.

In Chapter 17, you'll see that lambdas and streams can help you write programs faster, more concisely, more simply, with fewer bugs and that are easier to **parallelize** (to realize performance improvements on **multi-core systems**) than programs written with previous techniques. You'll see that "functional programming" with lambdas and streams complements object-oriented programming.

8

Many of Chapter 17's sections are written so they can be covered earlier in the book (Fig. 1.5). After reading Chapter 17, you'll be able to cleverly reimplement many examples throughout the book.

Lambdas and streams discussions	Can be covered after
Sections 17.2—17.5 introduce basic lambda and streams capabilities that you can use to **replace counting loops**, and discuss the mechanics of how streams are processed.	Chapter 5, Control Statements: Part 2; Logical Operators
Section 17.6 introduces **method references** and additional streams capabilities.	Chapter 6, Methods: A Deeper Look
Section 17.7 introduces streams capabilities that process **one-dimensional arrays**.	Chapter 7, Arrays and `ArrayLists`
Sections 17.8—17.10 demonstrate additional streams capabilities and present various **functional interfaces used in streams processing**.	Section 10.10 which introduces Java 8 interface features for the functional interfaces that support lambdas and streams.
Section 17.11 shows how to use lambdas and streams to **process collections of `String` objects**.	Chapter 14, Strings, Characters and Regular Expressions
Section 17.12 shows how to use lambdas and streams to **process a `List<Employee>`**.	Chapter 16, Generic Collections
Section 17.13 shows how to use lambdas and streams to **process lines of text from a file**.	Chapter 15, Files, Input/Output Streams, NIO and XML Serialization
Section 17.14 introduces streams of random values	All earlier Chapter 17 sections.
Section 17.15 introduces infinite streams	All earlier Chapter 17 sections.
Section 17.16 shows how to use lambdas to implement **JavaFX event-listener interfaces**.	Chapter 12, JavaFX Graphical User Interfaces: Part 1

Chapter 21, Concurrency and Multi-Core Performance, shows that programs using lambdas and streams are often easier to **parallelize** so they can take advantage of **multi-core architectures** to enhance performance. The chapter demonstrates **parallel stream processing** and shows that **Arrays** method **parallelSort** improves performance on **multi-core architectures** when sorting large arrays.

Fig. 1.5 | Java 8 lambdas and streams discussions and examples.

Concurrency and Multi-Core Performance (Part 6)

We were privileged to have as a reviewer of the previous edition of this book (*Java SE 8 for Programmers*) Brian Goetz, co-author of *Java Concurrency in Practice* (Addison-Wesley). We updated Chapter 21, Concurrency and Multi-Core Performance, with Java 8 technology and idiom. We added a **parallelSort** vs. **sort** example that uses the **Java 8 Date/Time API** to time each operation and demonstrate parallelSort's better performance on a **multi-core** system. We included a **Java 8 parallel vs. sequential stream processing** example, again using the Date/Time API to show performance improvements. We added a

Java 8 `CompletableFuture` example that demonstrates sequential and parallel execution of long-running calculations and we discuss **CompletableFuture enhancements** in Chapter 28, Additional Java 9 Topics.

JavaFX concurrency. We now use **JavaFX concurrency** features, including class `Task` to execute long-running tasks in separate threads and display their results in the JavaFX application thread, and the `Platform` class's `runLater` method to schedule a `Runnable` for execution in the JavaFX application thread.

Database: JDBC and JPA (Part 7)

JDBC. Chapter 22 covers the widely used **JDBC** and uses the **Java DB database management system.** The chapter introduces **Structured Query Language (SQL)** and features a case study on developing a JavaFX database-driven address book that demonstrates **prepared statements**. In JDK 9, Oracle no longer bundles Java DB, which is simply an Oracle-branded version of Apache Derby. JDK 9 users can download and use Apache Derby instead (`https://db.apache.org/derby/`).

Java Persistence API. Chapter 24 covers the newer **Java Persistence API (JPA)**—a standard for **object relational mapping (ORM)** that uses JDBC "under the hood." ORM tools can look at a database's **schema** and generate a set of classes that enabled you to interact with a database without having to use JDBC and SQL directly. This speeds database-application development, reduces errors and produces more portable code.

Object-Oriented Design Case Study (Part 9)

Developing an Object-Oriented Design and Java Implementation of an ATM. Chapters 25–26 include a case study on object-oriented design using the UML (Unified Modeling Language™)—a graphical language for modeling object-oriented systems. We design and implement the software for a simple automated teller machine (ATM). We analyze a typical **requirements document** that specifies the system to be built. We determine the **classes** needed to implement that system, the **attributes** the classes need to have, the **behaviors** the classes need to exhibit and specify how the classes must **interact** with one another to meet the system requirements. From the design we produce a **complete Java implementation**. Readers often report having a "light-bulb moment"—the case study helps them "tie it all together" and understand object orientation more deeply.

Teaching Approach

Java 9 for Programmers contains hundreds of complete working code examples. We stress program clarity and concentrate on building well-engineered software.

Syntax Coloring. For readability, we syntax shade all the Java code, similar to the way most Java integrated-development environments and code editors syntax color code. Our syntax-shading conventions are as follows:

```
comments appear like this
keywords appear like this
constants and literal values appear like this
all other code appears in black
```

Code Highlighting. We place transparent light gray rectangles around key code segments.

Using Fonts for Emphasis. We place the key terms and the index's page reference for each defining occurrence in **bold** text for easier reference. We emphasize on-screen components in the **bold sans serif** font (e.g., the **File** menu) and emphasize Java program text in a mono-spaced font (for example, int x = 5;).

Objectives. The chapter objectives provide a high-level overview of the chapter's contents.

Illustrations/Figures. Abundant tables, line drawings, UML diagrams, programs and program outputs are included.

Index. We've included an extensive index. Defining occurrences of key terms are highlighted with a **bold** page number.

Software Development Wisdom

We include hundreds of tips to help you focus on important aspects of software development. These represent the best we've gleaned from a combined nine decades of programming and teaching experience in industry and academia.

Good Programming Practice 1.1
The Good Programming Practices *call attention to techniques that will help you produce programs that are clearer, more understandable and more maintainable.*

Common Programming Error 1.1
Pointing out these Common Programming Errors *reduces the likelihood that you'll make them.*

Error-Prevention Tip 1.1
These tips contain suggestions for exposing bugs and removing them from your programs; many describe aspects of Java that prevent bugs from getting into programs in the first place.

Performance Tip 1.1
These tips highlight opportunities for making your programs run faster or minimizing the amount of memory that they occupy.

Portability Tip 1.1
The Portability Tips *help you write code that will run on a variety of platforms. Such portability is a key aspect of Java's mandate.*

Software Engineering Observation 1.1
The Software Engineering Observations *highlight architectural and design issues that affect the construction of software systems, especially large-scale systems.*

Look-and-Feel Observation
The Look-and-Feel Observations *highlight graphical-user-interface conventions. These observations help you design attractive, user-friendly and effective graphical user interfaces that conform to industry norms.*

JEPs, JSRs and the JCP

Throughout the book we encourage you to research various aspects of Java online. Some acronyms you're likely to see are JEP, JSR and JCP.

JEPs (JDK Enhancement Proposals) are used by Oracle to gather proposals from the Java community for changes to the Java language, APIs and tools, and to help create the roadmaps for future Java Standard Edition (Java SE), Java Enterprise Edition (Java EE) and Java Micro Edition (Java ME) platform versions and the JSRs (Java Specification Requests) that define them. The complete list of JEPs can be found at

```
http://openjdk.java.net/jeps/0
```

JSRs (Java Specification Requests) are the formal descriptions of Java platform features' technical specifications. Each new feature that gets added to Java (Standard Edition, Enterprise Edition or Micro Edition) has a JSR that goes through a review and approval process before the feature is added to Java. Sometimes JSRs are grouped together into an "umbrella" JSR. For example JSR 337 is the umbrella for Java 8 features, and JSR 379 is the umbrella for Java 9 features. The complete list of JSRs can be found at

```
https://www.jcp.org/en/jsr/all
```

The **JCP (Java Community Process)** is responsible for developing JSRs. JCP expert groups create the JSRs, which are publicly available for review and feedback. You can learn more about the JCP at:

```
https://www.jcp.org
```

Secure Java Programming

It's difficult to build industrial-strength systems that stand up to attacks from viruses, worms, and other forms of "malware." Today, via the Internet, such attacks can be instantaneous and global in scope. Building security into software from the beginning of the development cycle can greatly reduce vulnerabilities. We audited our book against the CERT® Oracle Secure Coding Standard for Java

```
http://bit.ly/CERTSecureJava
```

and adhered to various secure coding practices as appropriate for a book at this level.

The CERT Coordination Center (www.cert.org) was created to analyze and respond promptly to attacks. CERT—the Computer Emergency Response Team—is a government-funded organization within the Carnegie Mellon University Software Engineering Institute™. CERT publishes and promotes secure coding standards for various popular programming languages to help software developers implement industrial-strength systems by employing programming practices that prevent system attacks from succeeding.

We'd like to thank Robert C. Seacord. A few years back, when Mr. Seacord was the Secure Coding Manager at CERT and an adjunct professor in the Carnegie Mellon University School of Computer Science, he was a technical reviewer for our book, *C How to Program, 7/e*, where he scrutinized our C programs from a security standpoint, recommending that we adhere to the *CERT C Secure Coding Standard*. This experience also influenced our coding practices in our C++, C# and Java books.

Java® 9 Fundamentals LiveLessons, Third Edition

Our *Java® 9 Fundamentals LiveLessons, 3/e* (summer 2017) video training product shows you what you need to know to start building robust, powerful software with Java. It includes 40+ hours of expert training synchronized with *Java® How to Program, Early Objects, 11/e—Java® 9 for Programmers* is a subset of that book. The videos are available to Safari subscribers at:

```
http://safaribooksonline.com
```

and may be purchased from

```
http://informit.com
```

Professionals like viewing the LiveLessons for reinforcement of core concepts and for additional insights.

Software Used in *Java® 9 for Programmers*

All the software you'll need is available for download. See the **Before You Begin** section that follows this Preface for links to each download. We wrote most of the examples in *Java 9® for Programmers* using the free Java Standard Edition Development Kit (JDK) 8. For the Java 9 content, we used the OpenJDK's early access version of JDK 9. All of the Java 9 programs run on the early access versions of JDK 9. All of the remaining programs run on both JDK 8 and early access versions of JDK 9, and were tested on Windows, macOS and Linux. Several of the later chapters also use the NetBeans IDE

```
http://netbeans.org
```

There are many other free Java IDEs, the most popular of which are Eclipse (from the Eclipse Foundation)

```
http://eclipse.org
```

and IntelliJ Community edition (from JetBrains)

```
https://www.jetbrains.com/idea/
```

Java Documentation Links

Throughout the book, we provide links to Java documentation where you can learn more about various topics that we present. For Java 8 documentation, the links begin with

```
http://docs.oracle.com/javase/8/
```

and for Java 9 documentation, the links currently begin with

```
http://download.java.net/java/jdk9/
```

The Java 9 documentation links will change when Oracle releases Java 9—*possibly* to links beginning with

```
http://docs.oracle.com/javase/9/
```

For any links that change after publication, we'll post updates at

```
http://www.deitel.com/books/Java9FP
```

Java® How to Program, 11/e

If you're an industry professional who also teaches college courses, you may want to consider our two college textbook versions of *Java 9 for Programmers*:

- *Java® How to Program, Early Objects, 11/e*, and
- *Java® How to Program, Late Objects, 11/e*

There are several approaches to teaching introductory course sequences in Java programming. The two most popular are the **early objects approach** and the **late objects approach**. The key difference between them is the order in which we present Chapters 1–7. The books have identical content in Chapter 8 and higher. These textbooks are supported by various instructor supplements. College instructors can request an examination copy of either of these books and obtain access to the supplements from their Pearson representative:

```
http://www.pearsonhighered.com/educator/replocator/
```

Keeping in Touch with the Authors

As you read the book, if you have **questions**, send an e-mail to us at

```
deitel@deitel.com
```

and we'll respond promptly. For **book updates**, visit

```
http://www.deitel.com/books/Java9FP
```

subscribe to the *Deitel® Buzz Online* **newsletter** at

```
http://www.deitel.com/newsletter/subscribe.html
```

and join the **Deitel social networking communities** on

- **LinkedIn**® (`http://linkedin.com/company/deitel-&-associates`)
- **Facebook**® (`http://www.deitel.com/deitelfan`)
- **Twitter**® (`@deitel`)
- **YouTube**® (`http://youtube.com/DeitelTV`)

Acknowledgments

We'd like to thank Barbara Deitel for long hours devoted to technical research on this project. We're fortunate to have worked with the dedicated team of publishing professionals at Pearson. We appreciate the efforts and 22-year mentorship of our friend and professional colleague Mark L. Taub, Editor-in-Chief of the Pearson Technology Group. Mark and his team publish our professional books, LiveLessons video products and Learning Paths in the Safari service (`http://www.safaribooksonline.com`). Kristy Alaura recruited the book's reviewers and managed the review process. Sandra Schroeder and Julie Nahil managed the book's production. We selected the cover art and Chuti Prasertsith designed the cover.

Reviewers

We wish to acknowledge the efforts of our reviewers—a distinguished group of Oracle Java team members, Oracle Java Champions and other industry professionals. They scrutinized the text and the programs and provided countless suggestions for improving the presentation. Any remaining faults in the book are our own.

We appreciate the guidance of JavaFX experts Jim Weaver and Johan Vos (co-authors of *Pro JavaFX 8*), Jonathan Giles and Simon Ritter on the JavaFX chapters.

Reviewers: Lance Anderson (Java Platform Module System and Additional Java 9 Topics chapters; Principle Member of Technical Staff, Oracle), Alex Buckley (Java Platform Module System chapter; Specification Lead, Java Language & VM, Oracle), Robert Field (JShell chapter only; JShell Architect, Oracle), Trisha Gee (JetBrains, Java Champion), Jonathan Giles (Consulting Member of Technical Staff, Oracle), Brian Goetz (JShell and Java Platform Module System chapters; Oracle's Java Language Architect), Maurice Naftalin (JShell chapter only; Java Champion), José Antonio González Seco (Consultant), Bruno Souza (President of SouJava—the Brazilian Java Society, Java Specialist at ToolsCloud, Java Champion and SouJava representative at the Java Community Process), Dr. Venkat Subramaniam (President, Agile Developer, Inc. and Instructional Professor, University of Houston) and Johan Vos (CTO, Cloud Products at Gluon, Java Champion).

A Special Thank You to Robert Field

Robert Field, Oracle's JShell Architect reviewed the new JShell chapter, responding to our numerous emails in which we asked JShell questions, reported bugs we encountered as JShell evolved and suggested improvements. It was a privilege having our content scrutinized by the person responsible for JShell.

A Special Thank You to Brian Goetz

Brian Goetz, Oracle's Java Language Architect and Specification Lead for Java 8's Project Lambda, and co-author of *Java Concurrency in Practice*, did a full-book review of our book *Java® How to Program, Early Objects, 10/e*. He provided us with an extraordinary collection of insights and constructive comments. For *Java® 9 for Programmers*, he did a detailed review of our new JShell and Java Platform Module System chapters and answered our Java questions throughout the project.

Well, there you have it! As you read the book, we'd appreciate your comments, criticisms, corrections and suggestions for improvement. Please send your questions and all other correspondence to:

```
deitel@deitel.com
```

We'll respond promptly. We wish you great success!

Paul and Harvey Deitel

About the Authors

Paul J. Deitel, CEO and Chief Technical Officer of Deitel & Associates, Inc., is a graduate of MIT and has over 35 years of experience in computing. He holds the Java Certified Programmer and Java Certified Developer designations, and is an Oracle Java Champion. Through Deitel & Associates, Inc., he has delivered hundreds of programming courses worldwide to clients, including Cisco, IBM, Siemens, Sun Microsystems (now Oracle), Dell, Fidelity, NASA at the Kennedy Space Center, the National Severe Storm Laboratory, White Sands Missile Range, Rogue Wave Software, Boeing, SunGard Higher Education, Puma, iRobot, Invensys and many more. He and his co-author, Dr. Harvey M. Deitel, are the world's best-selling programming-language professional book/textbook/video authors.

Dr. Harvey M. Deitel, Chairman and Chief Strategy Officer of Deitel & Associates, Inc., has over 55 years of experience in computing. Dr. Deitel earned B.S. and M.S. degrees in Electrical Engineering from MIT and a Ph.D. in Mathematics from Boston University—he studied computing in each of these programs before they spun off Computer Science programs. He has extensive industry and college teaching experience, including earning tenure and serving as the Chairman of the Computer Science Department at Boston College before founding Deitel & Associates, Inc., in 1991 with his son, Paul. The Deitels' publications have earned international recognition, with more than 100 translations published in Japanese, German, Russian, Spanish, French, Polish, Italian, Simplified Chinese, Traditional Chinese, Korean, Portuguese, Greek, Urdu and Turkish. Dr. Deitel has delivered hundreds of programming courses to academic, corporate, government and military clients.

About Deitel® & Associates, Inc.

Deitel & Associates, Inc., founded by Paul Deitel and Harvey Deitel, is an internationally recognized authoring and corporate training organization, specializing in computer programming languages, object technology, mobile app development and Internet and web software technology. The company's training clients include many of the world's largest companies, government agencies, branches of the military, and academic institutions. The company offers instructor-led training courses delivered at client sites worldwide on major programming languages and platforms, including Java®, Android, Swift, iOS, C++, C, Visual C#®, object technology, Internet and web programming and a growing list of additional programming and software development courses.

Through its 42-year publishing partnership with Pearson/Prentice Hall, Deitel & Associates, Inc., publishes leading-edge programming professional books and textbooks in print and e-book formats available from booksellers worldwide, and **LiveLessons** video courses (available at `informit.com` an `safaribooksonline.com`) and Learning Paths (available at `safaribooksonline.com`). Deitel & Associates, Inc. and the authors can be reached at:

> `deitel@deitel.com`

To learn more about Deitel's corporate training curriculum, visit:

> `http://www.deitel.com/training`

To request a proposal for worldwide on-site, instructor-led training, write to

> `deitel@deitel.com`

Individuals wishing to purchase Deitel books and *LiveLessons* video training can do so through `amazon.com`, `informit.com` and other online retailers. Bulk orders by corporations, the government, the military and academic institutions should be placed directly with Pearson. For more information, visit

> `http://www.informit.com/store/sales.aspx`

Before You Begin

This section contains information you should review before using this book. Any updates to the information presented here will be posted at:

```
http://www.deitel.com/books/Java9FP
```

In addition, we provide getting-started videos that demonstrate the instructions in this Before You Begin section.

Font and Naming Conventions

We use fonts to distinguish between on-screen components (such as menu names and menu items) and Java code or commands. Our convention is to emphasize on-screen components in a sans-serif bold **Helvetica** font (for example, **File** menu) and to emphasize Java code and commands in a sans-serif Lucida font (for example, System.out.println()).

Java SE Development Kit (JDK)

The software you'll need for this book is available free for download from the web. Most of the examples were tested with the Java SE Development Kit 8 (also known as JDK 8). The most recent JDK version is available from:

```
http://www.oracle.com/technetwork/java/javase/downloads/index.html
```

The current version of the JDK at the time of this writing is JDK 8 update 121.

Java SE 9

The Java SE 9-specific features that we discuss in optional sections and chapters require JDK 9. At the time of this writing, JDK 9 was available as a Developer Preview. If you're using this book before the final JDK 9 is released, see the section "Installing and Configuring JDK 9 Developer Preview" later in this Before You Begin. We also discuss in that section how you can manage multiple JDK versions on Windows, macOS and Linux.

JDK Installation Instructions

After downloading the JDK installer, be sure to carefully follow the installation instructions for your platform at:

```
https://docs.oracle.com/javase/8/docs/technotes/guides/install/
    install_overview.html
```

You'll need to update the JDK version number in any version-specific instructions. For example, the instructions refer to jdk1.8.0, but the current version at the time of this writing is jdk1.8.0_121. If you're a Linux user, your distribution's software package manager might provide an easier way to install the JDK. For example, you can learn how to install the JDK on Ubuntu here:

```
http://askubuntu.com/questions/464755/how-to-install-openjdk-8-on-
    14-04-lts
```

Setting the PATH Environment Variable

The PATH environment variable designates which directories your computer searches for applications, such as those for compiling and running your Java applications (called javac and java, respectively). *Carefully follow the installation instructions for Java on your platform to ensure that you set the PATH environment variable correctly.* The steps for setting environment variables differ by operating system. Instructions for various platforms are listed at:

```
https://docs.oracle.com/javase/8/docs/technotes/guides/install/
    install_overview.html
```

If you do not set the PATH variable correctly on Windows and some Linux installations, when you use the JDK's tools, you'll receive a message like:

```
'java' is not recognized as an internal or external command,
operable program or batch file.
```

In this case, go back to the installation instructions for setting the PATH and recheck your steps. If you've downloaded a newer version of the JDK, you may need to change the name of the JDK's installation directory in the PATH variable.

JDK Installation Directory and the **bin** Subdirectory

The JDK's installation directory varies by platform. The directories listed below are for Oracle's JDK 8 update 121:

- JDK on Windows:
  C:\Program Files\Java\jdk1.8.0_121

- macOS (formerly called OS X):
  /Library/Java/JavaVirtualMachines/jdk1.8.0_121.jdk/Contents/Home

- Ubuntu Linux:
  /usr/lib/jvm/java-8-oracle

Depending on your platform, the JDK installation folder's name might differ. For Linux, the install location depends on the installer you use and possibly the Linux version as well. We used Ubuntu Linux. The PATH environment variable must point to the JDK installation directory's bin subdirectory.

When setting the PATH, be sure to use the proper JDK-installation-directory name for the specific version of the JDK you installed—as newer JDK releases become available, the JDK-installation-directory name changes with a new *update version number*. For example, at the time of this writing, the most recent JDK 8 release was update 121. For this version, the JDK-installation-directory name typically ends with _121.

CLASSPATH Environment Variable

If you attempt to run a Java program and receive a message like

```
Exception in thread "main" java.lang.NoClassDefFoundError: YourClass
```

then your system has a CLASSPATH environment variable that must be modified. To fix the preceding error, follow the steps in setting the PATH environment variable to locate the CLASSPATH variable, then edit the variable's value to include the local directory—typically represented as a dot (.). On Windows add

```
.;
```

at the beginning of the CLASSPATH's value (with no spaces before or after these characters). On macOS and Linux, add

```
.:
```

Setting the JAVA_HOME Environment Variable

Several chapters require you to set the JAVA_HOME environment variable to your JDK's installation directory. The same steps you used to set the PATH may also be used to set other environment variables, such as JAVA_HOME.

Java Integrated Development Environments (IDEs)

There are many Java integrated development environments that you can use for Java programming. Because the steps for using them differ, we used only the JDK command-line tools for most of the book's examples. We provide getting-started videos that show how to download, install and use three popular IDEs—NetBeans, Eclipse and IntelliJ IDEA.

NetBeans Downloads
You can download the JDK/NetBeans bundle from:

```
http://www.oracle.com/technetwork/java/javase/downloads/index.html
```

The NetBeans version that's bundled with the JDK is for Java SE development. For the standalone NetBeans installer, visit:

```
https://netbeans.org/downloads/
```

For Java Enterprise Edition (Java EE) development, choose the Java EE version, which supports both Java SE and Java EE development.

Eclipse Downloads
You can download the Eclipse IDE from:

```
https://eclipse.org/downloads/eclipse-packages/
```

For Java SE development choose the Eclipse IDE for Java Developers. For Java Enterprise Edition (Java EE) development, choose the Eclipse IDE for Java EE Developers, which supports both Java SE and Java EE development.

IntelliJ IDEA Community Edition Downloads
You can download the free IntelliJ IDEA Community from:

```
https://www.jetbrains.com/idea/download/index.html
```

The free version supports only Java SE development, but there is a paid version that supports other Java technologies.

Scene Builder

Our JavaFX GUI, graphics and multimedia examples (starting in Chapter 12) use the free Scene Builder tool, which enables you to create graphical user interfaces (GUIs) with drag-and-drop techniques. You can download Scene Builder from:

    http://gluonhq.com/labs/scene-builder/

Obtaining the Code Examples

The *Java 9 for Programmers* examples are available for download at

    http://www.deitel.com/books/Java9FP/

Click the **Download Code Examples** link to download a ZIP archive file containing the examples—typically, the file will be saved in you user account's Downloads folder.

Extract the contents of examples.zip using a ZIP extraction tool such as 7-Zip (www.7-zip.org), WinZip (www.winzip.com) or the built-in capabilities of your operating system. Instructions throughout the book assume that the examples are located at:

- C:\examples on Windows
- your user account's Documents/examples subfolder on macOS or Linux

Installing and Configuring JDK 9 Developer Preview

Throughout the book, we introduce various new Java 9 features. The Java 9 features require JDK 9, which at the time of this writing was still early access software available from

    https://jdk9.java.net/download/

This page provides installers for Windows and macOS (formerly Mac OS X). On these platforms, download the appropriate installer, double click it and follow the on-screen instructions. For Linux, the download page provides only a tar.gz archive file. You can download that file, then extract its contents to a folder on your system. *If you have both JDK 8 and JDK 9 installed*, we provide instructions below showing how to specify which JDK to use on Windows, macOS or Linux.

JDK Version Numbers

Prior to Java 9, JDK versions were numbered 1.X.0_*updateNumber* where X was the major Java version. For example,

- Java 8's current JDK version number is jdk1.8.0_121 and
- Java 7's final JDK version number was jdk1.7.0_80.

As of Java 9, the numbering scheme has changed. JDK 9 initially will be known as jdk-9. Eventually, there will be minor version updates that add new features, and security updates that fix security holes in the Java platform. These updates will be reflected in the JDK version numbers. For example, in 9.1.3:

- 9—is the major Java version number
- 1—is the minor version update number and
- 3—is the security update number.

So 9.2.5 would indicate the version of Java 9 for which there have been two minor version updates and five total security updates across all Java 9 major and minor versions. For the new version-numbering scheme's details, see JEP (Java Enhancement Proposal) 223 at

```
http://openjdk.java.net/jeps/223
```

Managing Multiple JDKs on Windows

On Windows, you use the PATH environment variable to tell the operating system where to find a JDK's tools. The instructions at

```
https://docs.oracle.com/javase/8/docs/technotes/guides/install/
    windows_jdk_install.html#BABGDJFH
```

specify how to update the PATH. Replace the JDK version number in the instructions with the JDK version number you wish to use—currently jdk-9. You should check your JDK 9's installation folder name for an updated version number. This setting will automatically be applied to each new **Command Prompt** you open.

If you prefer not to modify your system's PATH—perhaps because you're also using JDK 8—you can open a **Command Prompt** window then set the PATH only for that window. To do so, use the command

```
set PATH=location;%PATH%
```

where *location* is the full path to JDK 9's bin folder and ;%PATH% appends the **Command Prompt** window's original PATH contents to the new PATH. Typically, the command would be

```
set PATH="C:\Program Files\Java\jdk-9\bin";%PATH%
```

Each time you open a new **Command Prompt** window to use JDK 9, you'll have to reissue this command.

Managing Multiple JDKs on macOS

On a Mac, you can determine which JDKs you have installed by opening a **Terminal** window and entering the command

```
/usr/libexec/java_home -V
```

which shows the version numbers, names and locations of your JDKs—note that -V is a capital V, not lowercase. On our system the following is displayed:

```
Matching Java Virtual Machines (2):
    9, x86_64:  "Java SE 9-ea  "/Library/Java/JavaVirtualMachines/
        jdk-9.jdk/Contents/Home
    1.8.0_121, x86_64:  "Java SE 8  "/Library/Java/
        JavaVirtualMachines/jdk1.8.0_121.jdk/Contents/Home
```

the version numbers are 9 and 1.8.0_121. In "Java SE 9-ea" above, "ea" means "early access."
    To set the default JDK version, enter

```
/usr/libexec/java_home -v # --exec javac -version
```

where # is the version number of the specific JDK that should be the default. At the time of this writing, for JDK 8, # should be 1.8.0_121 and, for JDK 9, # should be 9.
    Next, enter the command:

```
export JAVA_HOME=`/usr/libexec/java_home -v #`
```

where # is the version number of the current default JDK. This sets the **Terminal** window's JAVA_HOME environment variable to that JDK's location. This environment variable will be used when launching JShell.

Managing Multiple JDKs on Linux

The way you manage multiple JDK versions on Linux depends on how you install your JDKs. If you use your Linux distribution's tools for installing software (we used apt-get on Ubuntu Linux), then on many Linux distributions you can use the following command to list the installed JDKs:

```
sudo update-alternatives --config java
```

If more than one is installed, the preceding command shows you a numbered list of JDKs—you then enter the number for the JDK you wish to use as the default. For a tutorial showing how to use apt-get to install JDKs on Ubuntu Linux, see

```
https://www.digitalocean.com/community/tutorials/how-to-install-
java-with-apt-get-on-ubuntu-16-04
```

If you installed JDK 9 by downloading the tar.gz file and extracting it to your system, you'll need to specify in a shell window the path to the JDK's bin folder. To do so, enter the following command in your shell window:

```
export PATH="location:$PATH"
```

where *location* is the path to JDK 9's bin folder. This updates the PATH environment variable with the location of JDK 9's commands, like javac and java, so that you can execute the JDK's commands in the shell window.

You're now ready to begin reading *Java 9 for Programmers*. We hope you enjoy the book!

Introduction and Test-Driving a Java Application

Objectives

In this chapter you'll:

- Understand the importance of Java.
- Review object-technology concepts.
- Understand a typical Java program-development environment.
- Test-drive a Java application.
- Review some key recent software technologies.
- See where to get your Java questions answered.

1.1 Introduction

Welcome to Java—one of the world's most widely used computer programming languages and, according to the TIOBE Index (`https://www.tiobe.com/tiobe-index/`), the world's most popular. For many organizations, Java is the preferred language for meeting their enterprise programming needs. It's also widely used for implementing Internet-based applications and software for devices that communicate over a network.

There are billions of personal computers in use and an even larger number of mobile devices with computers at their core. According to Oracle's 2016 JavaOne conference key-note presentation,, there are now 10 million Java developers worldwide and Java runs on 15 billion devices (Fig. 1.1), including two billion vehicles and 350 million medical devices. In addition, the explosive growth of mobile phones, tablets and other devices is creating significant opportunities for programming mobile apps.

Devices		
Access control systems	Airplane systems	ATMs
Automobiles	Blu-ray Disc™ players	Building controls
Cable boxes	Copiers	Credit cards
CT scanners	Desktop computers	e-Readers
Game consoles	GPS navigation systems	Home appliances
Home security systems	Internet-of-Things gateways	Light switches
Logic controllers	Lottery systems	Medical devices
Mobile phones	MRIs	Network switches
Optical sensors	Parking meters	Personal computers
Point-of-sale terminals	Printers	Robots
Routers	Servers	Smart cards
Smart meters	Smartpens	Smartphones
Tablets	Televisions	Thermostats
Transportation passes	TV set-top boxes	Vehicle diagnostic systems

Fig. 1.1 | Some devices that use Java.

Java Standard Edition

Java has evolved so rapidly that the eleventh edition of our sister book *Java How to Program*—based on **Java Standard Edition 8 (Java SE 8)** and the new **Java Standard Edition 9 (Java SE 9)**—was published just 21 years after the first edition. Java Standard Edition contains the capabilities needed to develop desktop and server applications. The book can be used conveniently with *either* Java SE 8 *or* Java SE 9 (released just after this book was published). For those who want to stay with Java 8 for a while, the Java SE 9 features are discussed in modular, easy-to-include-or-omit sections throughout this book.

Prior to Java SE 8, Java supported three programming paradigms:

- *procedural programming,*
- *object-oriented programming* and
- *generic programming.*

Java SE 8 added the beginnings of *functional programming with lambdas and streams.* In Chapter 17, we'll show how to use lambdas and streams to write programs faster, more concisely, with fewer bugs and that are easier to *parallelize* (i.e., perform multiple calculations simultaneously) to take advantage of today's *multi-core* hardware architectures to enhance application performance.

Java Enterprise Edition

Java is used in such a broad spectrum of applications that it has two other editions. The **Java Enterprise Edition (Java EE)** is geared toward developing large-scale, distributed networking applications and web-based applications. In the past, most computer applications ran on "standalone" computers (that is, not networked together). Today's applications can be written with the aim of communicating among the world's computers via the Internet and the web.

Java Micro Edition

The **Java Micro Edition (Java ME)**—a subset of Java SE—is geared toward developing applications for resource-constrained embedded devices, such as smartwatches, television set-top boxes, smart meters (for monitoring electric energy usage) and more. Many of the devices in Fig. 1.1 use Java ME.

1.2 Object Technology Concepts

Today, as demands for new and more powerful software are soaring, building software quickly, correctly and economically remains an elusive goal. *Objects*, or more precisely, the *classes* objects come from, are essentially *reusable* software components. There are date objects, time objects, audio objects, video objects, automobile objects, people objects, etc. Almost any *noun* can be reasonably represented as a software object in terms of *attributes* (e.g., name, color and size) and *behaviors* (e.g., calculating, moving and communicating). Software-development groups can use a modular, object-oriented design-and-implementation approach to be much more productive than with earlier popular techniques like "structured programming"—object-oriented programs are often easier to understand, correct and modify.

1.2.1 Automobile as an Object

To help you understand objects and their contents, let's begin with a simple analogy. Suppose you want to *drive a car and make it go faster by pressing its accelerator pedal*. What must happen before you can do this? Well, before you can drive a car, someone has to *design* it. A car typically begins as engineering drawings, similar to the *blueprints* that describe the design of a house. These drawings include the design for an accelerator pedal. The pedal *hides* from the driver the complex mechanisms that actually make the car go faster, just as the brake pedal "hides" the mechanisms that slow the car, and the steering wheel "hides" the mechanisms that turn the car. This enables people with little or no knowledge of how engines, braking and steering mechanisms work to drive a car easily.

Just as you cannot cook meals in the kitchen of a blueprint, you cannot drive a car's engineering drawings. Before you can drive a car, it must be *built* from the engineering drawings that describe it. A completed car has an *actual* accelerator pedal to make it go faster, but even that's not enough—the car won't accelerate on its own (hopefully!), so the driver must *press* the pedal to accelerate the car.

1.2.2 Methods and Classes

Let's use our car example to introduce some key object-oriented programming concepts. Performing a task in a program requires a **method**. The method houses the program statements that actually perform its tasks. The method hides these statements from its user, just as the accelerator pedal of a car hides from the driver the mechanisms of making the car go faster. In Java, we create a program unit called a **class** to house the set of methods that perform the class's tasks. For example, a class that represents a bank account might contain one method to *deposit* money to an account, another to *withdraw* money from an account and a third to *inquire* what the account's current balance is. A class is similar in concept to a car's engineering drawings, which house the design of an accelerator pedal, steering wheel, and so on.

1.2.3 Instantiation

Just as someone has to *build a car* from its engineering drawings before you can actually drive a car, you must *build an object* of a class before a program can perform the tasks that the class's methods define. The process of doing this is called *instantiation*. An object is then referred to as an **instance** of its class.

1.2.4 Reuse

Just as a car's engineering drawings can be *reused* many times to build many cars, you can *reuse* a class many times to build many objects. Reuse of existing classes when building new classes and programs saves time and effort. Reuse also helps you build more reliable and effective systems, because existing classes and components often have undergone extensive *testing, debugging* and *performance* tuning. Just as the notion of *interchangeable parts* was crucial to the Industrial Revolution, reusable classes are crucial to the software revolution that has been spurred by object technology.

1.2.5 Messages and Method Calls

When you drive a car, pressing its gas pedal sends a *message* to the car to perform a task—that is, to go faster. Similarly, you *send messages to an object*. Each message is implemented as a **method call** that tells a method of the object to perform its task. For example, a program might call a bank-account object's *deposit* method to increase the account's balance.

1.2.6 Attributes and Instance Variables

A car, besides having capabilities to accomplish tasks, also has *attributes*, such as its color, its number of doors, the amount of gas in its tank, its current speed and its record of total miles driven (i.e., its odometer reading). Like its capabilities, the car's attributes are represented as part of its design in its engineering diagrams (which, for example, include an odometer and a fuel gauge). As you drive an actual car, these attributes are carried along with the car. Every car maintains its *own* attributes. For example, each car knows how much gas is in its own gas tank, but *not* how much is in the tanks of *other* cars.

An object, similarly, has attributes that it carries along as it's used in a program. These attributes are specified as part of the object's class. For example, a bank-account object has a *balance attribute* that represents the amount of money in the account. Each bank-account object knows the balance in the account it represents, but *not* the balances of the *other* accounts in the bank. Attributes are specified by the class's **instance variables**.

1.2.7 Encapsulation and Information Hiding

Classes (and their objects) **encapsulate**, i.e., encase, their attributes and methods. A class's (and its object's) attributes and methods are intimately related. Objects may communicate with one another, but they're normally not allowed to know how other objects are implemented—implementation details can be *hidden* within the objects themselves. This **information hiding**, as we'll see, is crucial to good software engineering.

1.2.8 Inheritance

A new class of objects can be created conveniently by **inheritance**—the new class (called the **subclass**) starts with the characteristics of an existing class (called the **superclass**), possibly customizing them and adding unique characteristics of its own. In our car analogy, an object of class "convertible" certainly *is an* object of the more *general* class "automobile," but more *specifically*, the roof can be raised or lowered.

1.2.9 Interfaces

Java also supports **interfaces**—collections of related methods that typically enable you to tell objects *what* to do, but not *how* to do it (we'll see exceptions to this in Java SE 8 and Java SE 9 when we discuss interfaces in Chapter 10). In the car analogy, a "basic-driving-capabilities" interface consisting of a steering wheel, an accelerator pedal and a brake pedal would enable a driver to tell the car *what* to do. Once you know how to use this interface for turning, accelerating and braking, you can drive many types of cars, even though manufacturers may *implement* these systems *differently*.

A class **implements** zero or more interfaces, each of which can have one or more methods, just as a car implements separate interfaces for basic driving functions, controlling the radio, controlling the heating and air conditioning systems, and the like. Just as car manufacturers implement capabilities *differently*, classes may implement an interface's methods *differently*. For example a software system may include a "backup" interface that offers the methods *save* and *restore*. Classes may implement those methods differently, depending on the types of things being backed up, such as programs, text, audios, videos, etc., and the types of devices where these items will be stored.

1.2.10 Object-Oriented Analysis and Design (OOAD)

Soon you'll be writing programs in Java. How will you create the **code** (i.e., the program instructions) for your programs? Perhaps, like many programmers, you'll simply turn on your computer and start typing. This approach may work for small programs (like the ones we present in the early chapters of the book), but what if you were asked to create a software system to control thousands of automated teller machines for a major bank? Or suppose you were asked to work on a team of 1,000 software developers building the next generation of the U.S. air traffic control system? For projects so large and complex, you should not simply sit down and start writing programs.

To create the best solutions, you should follow a detailed **analysis** process for determining your project's **requirements** (i.e., defining *what* the system is supposed to do) and developing a **design** that satisfies them (i.e., specifying *how* the system should do it). Ideally, you'd go through this process and carefully review the design (and have your design reviewed by other software professionals) before writing any code. If this process involves analyzing and designing your system from an object-oriented point of view, it's called an **object-oriented analysis-and-design (OOAD) process**. Java is object oriented. Programming in such a language—called **object-oriented programming (OOP)**—allows you to implement an object-oriented design as a working system.

1.2.11 The UML (Unified Modeling Language)

Although many different OOAD processes exist, a single graphical language for communicating the results of *any* OOAD process has come into wide use. The Unified Modeling Language (UML) is now the most widely used graphical scheme for modeling object-oriented systems. We present our first UML diagrams in Chapters 3 and 4, then use them in our deeper treatment of object-oriented programming through Chapter 11. In our ATM Software Engineering Case Study in Chapters 25–26 we present a simple subset of the UML's features as we guide you through an object-oriented design experience.

1.3 Java

The microprocessor revolution's most important contribution to date is that it enabled the development of personal computers. Microprocessors also have had a profound impact in intelligent consumer-electronic devices, including the recent explosion in the "Internet of Things." Recognizing this early on, Sun Microsystems in 1991 funded an internal corporate research project led by James Gosling, which resulted in a C++-based object-oriented programming language that Sun called Java. Using Java, you can write programs that will run on a great variety of computer systems and computer-controlled devices. This is sometimes called "write once, run anywhere."

Java drew the attention of the business community because of the phenomenal interest in the Internet. It's now used to develop large-scale enterprise applications, to enhance the functionality of web servers (the computers that provide the content we see in our web browsers), to provide applications for consumer devices (cell phones, smartphones, television set-top boxes and more), to develop robotics software and for many other purposes. It's also the key language for developing Android smartphone and tablet apps. Sun Microsystems was acquired by Oracle in 2010.

Java has become the most widely used general-purpose programming language with more than 10 million developers. In this book, you'll study the two most recent versions of Java—Java Standard Edition 8 (Java SE 8) and Java Standard Edition 9 (Java SE 9).

Java Class Libraries

You can create each class and method you need to form your programs. However, most Java programmers take advantage of the rich collections of existing classes and methods in the **Java class libraries**, also known as the **Java APIs** (**Application Programming Interfaces**).

Performance Tip 1.1

Using Java API classes and methods instead of writing your own versions can improve program performance, because they're carefully written to perform efficiently. This also shortens program development time.

Android

Android is the fastest growing mobile and smartphone operating system. There are now approximately 6 million Android app developers worldwide[1] and Java is Android's primary development language (though apps can also be developed in C#, C++ and C). One benefit of developing Android apps is the openness of the platform. The operating system is open source and free.

The Android operating system was developed by Android, Inc., which was acquired by Google in 2005. In 2007, the Open Handset Alliance™

```
http://www.openhandsetalliance.com/oha_members.html
```

was formed to develop, maintain and evolve Android, driving innovation in mobile technology and improving the user experience while reducing costs. According to Statista.com, as of Q3 2016, Android had 87.8% of the global smartphone market share, compared to 11.5% for Apple., The Android operating system is used in numerous smartphones, e-reader devices, tablets, in-store touch-screen kiosks, cars, robots, multimedia players and more.

We present an introduction to Android app development in our book, *Android 6 for Programmers: An App-Driven Approach, Third Edition*. After you learn Java, you'll find it straightforward to begin developing and running Android apps. You can place your apps on Google Play (play.google.com), and if they're successful, you may even be able to launch a business.

---

1. http://www.businessofapps.com/12-million-mobile-developers-worldwide-nearly-half-develop-android-first/.

1.4 A Typical Java Development Environment

We now explain the steps to create and execute a Java application. Normally there are five phases—edit, compile, load, verify and execute. We discuss them in the context of the Java SE 8 Development Kit (JDK). See the *Before You Begin* section *for information on downloading and installing the JDK on Windows, Linux and macOS.*

Phase 1: Creating a Program

Phase 1 consists of editing a file with an *editor program*, normally known simply as an *editor* (Fig. 1.2). Using the editor, you type a Java program (typically referred to as **source code**), make any necessary corrections and save it on a secondary storage device, such as your hard drive. Java source code files are given a name ending with the **.java extension**, indicating that the file contains Java source code.

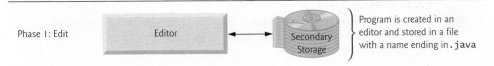

Fig. 1.2 | Typical Java development environment—editing phase.

Two editors widely used on Linux systems are vi and emacs. Windows provides **Notepad**. macOS provides **TextEdit**. Many freeware and shareware editors are also available online, including Notepad++ (http://notepad-plus-plus.org), EditPlus (http://www.editplus.com), TextPad (http://www.textpad.com), jEdit (http://www.jedit.org) and more.

Integrated development environments (IDEs) provide tools that support the software development process, such as editors, debuggers for locating **logic errors** that cause programs to execute incorrectly and more. The most popular Java IDEs are:

- Eclipse (http://www.eclipse.org)
- IntelliJ IDEA (http://www.jetbrains.com)
- NetBeans (http://www.netbeans.org)

On the book's website at

```
http://www.deitel.com/books/java9fp
```

we provide videos that show you how to execute this book's Java applications and how to develop new Java applications with Eclipse, NetBeans and IntelliJ IDEA.

Phase 2: Compiling a Java Program into Bytecodes

In Phase 2, you use the command **javac** (the **Java compiler**) to **compile** a program (Fig. 1.3). For example, to compile a program called Welcome.java, you'd type

```
javac Welcome.java
```

in your system's command window (i.e., the **Command Prompt** in Windows, the **Terminal** application in macOS) or a Linux shell (also called **Terminal** in some Linux versions). If the program compiles, the compiler produces a **.class** file called Welcome.class. IDEs typically provide a menu item, such as **Build** or **Make**, that invokes the javac command for you. If the compiler detects errors, you'll need to go back to Phase 1 and correct them. In Chapter 2, we'll say more about the kinds of errors the compiler can detect.

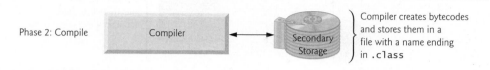

Fig. 1.3 | Typical Java development environment—compilation phase.

Common Programming Error 1.1
When using javac, *if you receive a message such as "bad command or* filename," *"*javac: command not found" *or* "'javac' is not recognized as an internal or external command, operable program or batch file," *then your Java software installation was not completed properly. This indicates that the system's* PATH *environment variable was not set properly. Carefully review the installation instructions in the Before You Begin section of this book. On some systems, after correcting the* PATH, *you may need to reboot your computer or open a new command window for these settings to take effect.*

The Java compiler translates Java source code into **bytecodes** that represent the tasks to execute in the execution phase (Phase 5). The **Java Virtual Machine (JVM)**—a part of the JDK and the foundation of the Java platform—executes bytecodes. A **virtual machine (VM)** is software that simulates a computer but hides the underlying operating system and hardware from the programs that interact with it. If the same VM is implemented on many computer platforms, applications written for that type of VM can be used on all those platforms. The JVM is one of the most widely used virtual machines. Microsoft's .NET uses a similar virtual-machine architecture.

Unlike machine-language instructions, which are *platform dependent*, bytecodes are *platform independent* and thus **portable**—without recompiling the source code, the same bytecodes can execute on any platform containing a JVM that understands the version of Java in which the bytecodes were compiled. The JVM is invoked by the **java** command. For example, to execute a Java application called Welcome, you'd type the command

```
java Welcome
```

in a command window to invoke the JVM, which would then initiate the steps necessary to execute the application. This begins Phase 3. IDEs typically provide a menu item, such as **Run**, that invokes the java command for you.

Phase 3: Loading a Program into Memory
In Phase 3, the JVM places the program in memory to execute it—this is known as **loading** (Fig. 1.4). The JVM's **class loader** takes the .class files containing the program's bytecodes and transfers them to primary memory. It also loads any of the .class files provided by Java that your program uses. The .class files can be loaded from a disk on your system or over a network (e.g., your local college or company network, or the Internet).

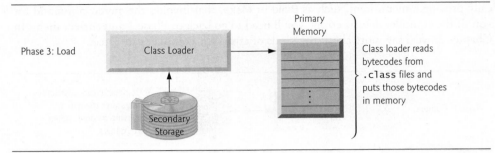

Fig. 1.4 | Typical Java development environment—loading phase.

Phase 4: Bytecode Verification

In Phase 4, as the classes are loaded, the **bytecode verifier** examines their bytecodes to en-sure that they're valid and do not violate Java's security restrictions (Fig. 1.5). Java enforces strong security to make sure that Java programs arriving over the network do not damage your files or your system (as computer viruses and worms might).

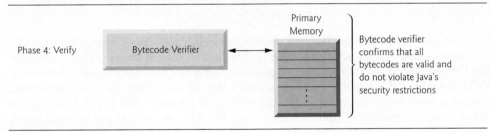

Fig. 1.5 | Typical Java development environment—verification phase.

Phase 5: Execution

In Phase 5, the JVM **executes** the bytecodes to perform the program's specified actions (Fig. 1.6). In early Java versions, the JVM was simply a Java-bytecode *interpreter*. Most pro-grams would execute slowly, because the JVM would interpret and execute one bytecode at a time. Some modern computer architectures can execute several instructions in parallel. To-day's JVMs typically execute bytecodes using a combination of interpretation and **just-in-time (JIT) compilation**. In this process, the JVM analyzes the bytecodes as they're interpret-ed, searching for *hot spots*—bytecodes that execute frequently. For these parts, a **just-in-time (JIT) compiler**, such as Oracle's **Java HotSpot™ compiler**, translates the bytecodes into the computer's machine language. When the JVM encounters these compiled parts again, the faster machine-language code executes. Thus programs actually go through *two* compilation phases—one in which Java code is translated into bytecodes (for portability across JVMs on different computer platforms) and a second in which, during execution, the bytecodes are translated into *machine language* for the computer on which the program executes.

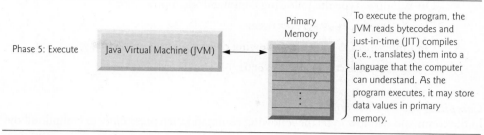

Fig. 1.6 | Typical Java development environment—execution phase.

Problems That May Occur at Execution Time

Programs might not work on the first try. Each of the preceding phases can fail because of various errors that we'll discuss throughout this book. For example, an executing program might try to divide by zero (an illegal operation for whole-number arithmetic in Java). This would cause the Java program to display an error message. If this occurred, you'd return to the edit phase, make the necessary corrections and proceed through the remaining phases again to determine whether the corrections fixed the problem(s). [*Note:* Most programs in Java input or output data. When we say that a program displays a message, we normally mean that it displays that message on your computer's screen.]

1.5 Test-Driving a Java Application

In this section, you'll run and interact with an existing Java **Painter** app, which you'll build in a later chapter. The elements and functionality you'll see are typical of what you'll learn to program in this book. Using the **Painter**'s graphical user interface (GUI), you choose a drawing color and pen size, then drag the mouse to draw circles in the specified color and size. You also can undo each drawing operation or clear the entire drawing. [*Note:* We emphasize screen features like window titles and menus (e.g., the **File** menu) in a **sans-serif font** and emphasize nonscreen elements, such as file names and program code (e.g., `ProgramName.java`), in a `fixed-width sans-serif font`.]

The steps in this section show you how to execute the **Painter** app from a **Command Prompt** (Windows), shell (Linux) or **Terminal** (macOS) window on your system. Throughout the book, we'll refer to these windows simply as *command windows*. We assume that the book's examples are located in `C:\examples` on Windows or in your user account's `Documents/examples` folder on Linux or macOS.

Checking Your Setup

Read the Before You Begin section that follows the Preface to set up Java on your computer and ensure that you've downloaded the book's examples to your hard drive.

Changing to the Completed Application's Directory

Open a command window and use the `cd` command to change to the folder for the **Painter** application:

- On Windows type the following command, then press *Enter*:

  ```
  cd C:\examples\ch01\Painter
  ```

- On Linux/macOS, type the following command, then press *Enter*.

  ```
  cd ~/Documents/examples/ch01/Painter
  ```

Compiling the Application

In the command window, type the following command then press *Enter* to compile all the files for the **Painter** example:

```
javac *.java
```

The * indicates that all files with names that end in .java should be compiled.

Running the Painter Application

Recall from Section 1.4 that the java command, followed by the name of an app's .class file (in this case, Painter), executes the application. Type the command java Painter then press *Enter* to execute the app. Figure 1.7 shows the **Painter** app running on Windows, Linux and macOS, respectively. The app's capabilities are identical across operating systems, so the remaining steps in this section show only Windows screen captures. Java commands are *case sensitive*—that is, uppercase letters are different from lowercase letters. It's important to type Painter with a capital P. Otherwise, the application will *not* execute. Also, if you receive the error message, "Exception in thread "main" java.lang.NoClass-DefFoundError: Painter," your system has a CLASSPATH problem. Please refer to the Before You Begin section for instructions to help you fix this problem.

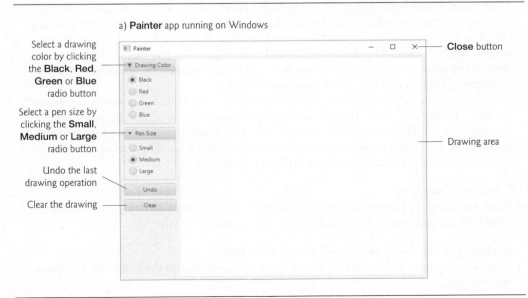

a) **Painter** app running on Windows

Select a drawing color by clicking the **Black**, **Red**, **Green** or **Blue** radio button

Select a pen size by clicking the **Small**, **Medium** or **Large** radio button

Undo the last drawing operation

Clear the drawing

Close button

Drawing area

Fig. 1.7 | **Painter** app executing in Windows, Linux and macOS. (Part 1 of 2.)

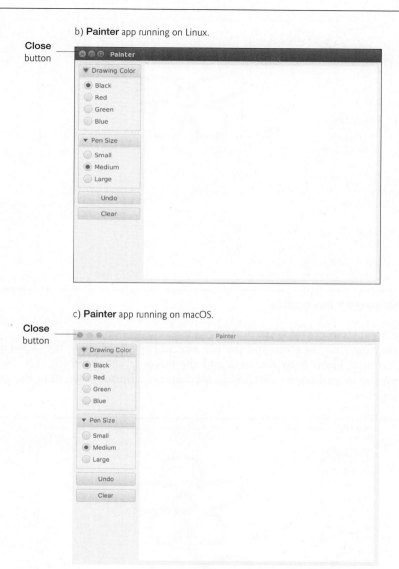

Fig. 1.7 | **Painter** app executing in Windows, Linux and macOS. (Part 2 of 2.)

Drawing the Flower Petals

In this section's remaining steps, you'll draw a red flower with a green stem, green grass and blue rain. We'll begin with the flower petals in a red, medium-sized pen. Change the drawing color to red by clicking the **Red** radio button. Next, drag your mouse on the drawing area to draw flower petals (Fig. 1.8). If you don't like a portion of what you've drawn, you can click the **Undo** button repeatedly to remove the most recent circles that were drawn, or you can begin again by clicking the **Clear** button.

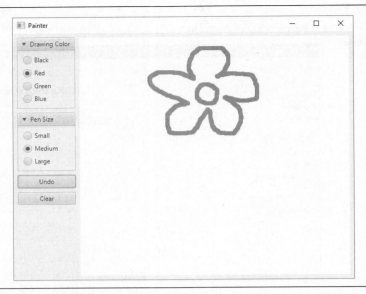

Fig. 1.8 | Drawing the flower petals.

Drawing the Stem, Leaves and Grass

Change the drawing color to green and the pen size to large by clicking the **Green** and **Large** radio buttons. Then, draw the stem and the leaves as shown in Fig. 1.9. Next, change the pen size to medium by clicking the **Medium** radio button, then draw the grass as shown in Fig. 1.9.

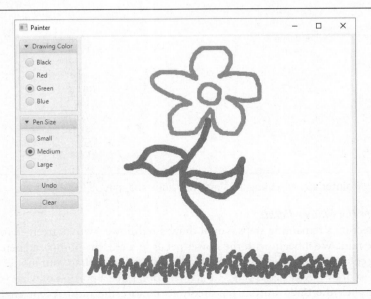

Fig. 1.9 | Drawing the stem and grass.

Drawing the Rain

Change the drawing color to blue and the pen size to small by clicking the **Blue** and **Small** radio buttons. Then, draw some rain as shown in Fig. 1.10.

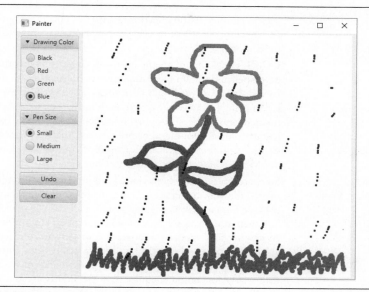

Fig. 1.10 | Drawing the rain.

Exiting the Painter App

At this point, you can close the **Painter** app. To do so, simply click the app's close box (shown for Windows, Linux and macOS in Fig. 1.7).

1.6 Software Technologies

Figure 1.11 lists a number of popular software technologies.

Technology	Description
Agile software development	**Agile software development** is a set of methodologies that try to get software implemented faster and using fewer resources. Check out the Agile Alliance (www.agilealliance.org) and the Agile Manifesto (www.agilemanifesto.org).
Refactoring	**Refactoring** involves reworking programs to make them clearer and easier to maintain while preserving their correctness and functionality. It's widely employed with agile development methodologies. Many IDEs contain built-in *refactoring tools* to do major portions of the reworking automatically.

Fig. 1.11 | Software technologies. (Part 1 of 3.)

Technology	Description
Design patterns	**Design patterns** are proven architectures for constructing flexible and maintainable object-oriented software. The field of design patterns tries to enumerate those recurring patterns, encouraging software designers to *reuse* them to develop better-quality software using less time, money and effort.
LAMP	**LAMP** is an acronym for the open-source technologies that many developers use to build web applications inexpensively—it stands for *Linux*, *Apache*, *MySQL* and *PHP* (or *Perl* or *Python*—two other popular scripting languages). MySQL is an open-source database-management system. PHP is a popular open-source server-side "scripting" language for developing web applications. Apache is the most popular web server software. The equivalent for Windows development is WAMP—*Windows*, *Apache*, *MySQL* and *PHP*.
Software as a Service (SaaS)	Software has generally been viewed as a product; most software still is offered this way. If you want to run an application, you buy a software package from a software vendor—often a CD, DVD or web download. You then install that software on your computer and run it as needed. As new versions appear, you upgrade your software, often at considerable cost in time and money. This process can become cumbersome for organizations that must maintain tens of thousands of systems on a diverse array of computer equipment. With **Software as a Service (SaaS)**, the software runs on servers elsewhere on the Internet. When that server is updated, all clients worldwide see the new capabilities—no local installation is needed. You access the service through a browser. Browsers are quite portable, so you can run the same applications on a wide variety of computers from anywhere in the world. Salesforce.com, Google, Microsoft and many other companies offer SaaS.
Platform as a Service (PaaS)	**Platform as a Service (PaaS)** provides a computing platform for developing and running applications as a service over the web, rather than installing the tools on your computer. Some PaaS providers are Google App Engine, Amazon EC2 and Windows Azure™.
Cloud computing	SaaS and PaaS are examples of cloud computing. You can use software and data stored in the "cloud"—i.e., accessed on remote computers (or servers) via the Internet and available on demand—rather than having it stored locally on your desktop, notebook computer or mobile device. This allows you to increase or decrease computing resources to meet your needs at any given time, which is more cost effective than purchasing hardware to provide enough storage and processing power to meet occasional peak demands. Cloud computing also saves money by shifting to the service provider the burden of managing these apps (such as installing and upgrading the software, security, backups and disaster recovery).
Software Development Kit (SDK)	**Software Development Kits (SDKs)** include the tools and documentation developers use to program applications.

Fig. 1.11 | Software technologies. (Part 2 of 3.)

Technology	Description
Big Data	The amount of data being produced worldwide is enormous and growing quickly. According to IBM, approximately 2.5 quintillion bytes (2.5 *exabytes*) of data are created daily,, and according to Salesforce.com, as of October 2015 90% of the world's data was created in just the prior 12 months!, According to an IDC study, the global data supply will reach 40 *zettabytes* (equal to 40 trillion gigabytes) annually by 2020., Figure 1.4 shows some common byte measurements. **Big data** applications deal with massive amounts of data and this field is growing quickly, creating lots of opportunity for software developers. Millions of IT jobs globally already are supporting big data applications.

Fig. 1.11 | Software technologies. (Part 3 of 3.)

Software is complex. Large, real-world software applications can take many months or even years to design and implement. When large software products are under development, they typically are made available to the user communities as a series of releases, each more complete and polished than the last (Fig. 1.12).

Version	Description
Alpha	*Alpha* software is the earliest release of a software product that's still under active development. Alpha versions are often buggy, incomplete and unstable and are released to a relatively small number of developers for testing new features, getting early feedback, etc. Alpha software also is commonly called *early access* software.
Beta	*Beta* versions are released to a larger number of developers later in the development process after most major bugs have been fixed and new features are nearly complete. Beta software is more stable, but still subject to change.
Release candidates	*Release candidates* are generally *feature complete*, (mostly) bug free and ready for use by the community, which provides a diverse testing environment— the software is used on different systems, with varying constraints and for a variety of purposes.
Final release	Any bugs that appear in the release candidate are corrected, and eventually the final product is released to the general public. Software companies often distribute incremental updates over the Internet.
Continuous beta	Software that's developed using this approach (for example, Google search or Gmail) generally does not have version numbers. It's hosted in the *cloud* (not installed on your computer) and is constantly evolving so that users always have the latest version.

Fig. 1.12 | Software product-release terminology.

1.7 Getting Your Questions Answered

There are many online forums in which you can get your Java questions answered and interact with other Java programmers. Some popular Java and general programming forums include:

- `StackOverflow.com`
- `Coderanch.com`
- The Oracle Java Forum—`https://community.oracle.com/community/java`
- `</dream.in.code>`—`http://www.dreamincode.net/forums/forum/32-java/`

2

Introduction to Java Applications; Input/Output and Operators

Objectives

In this chapter you'll:

- Write simple Java applications.
- Use input and output statements.
- Use Java's primitive types.
- Use arithmetic operators.
- Understand the precedence of arithmetic operators.
- Write decision-making statements.
- Use relational and equality operators.

2.1 Introduction

This chapter introduces Java programming. We begin with examples of programs that display (output) messages on the screen. We then present a program that obtains (inputs) two numbers from a user, calculates their sum and displays the result. You'll perform arithmetic calculations and save their results for later use. The last example demonstrates how to make decisions. The application compares two numbers, then displays messages that show the comparison results. You'll use the JDK command-line tools to compile and run this chapter's programs. If you prefer to use an integrated development environment (IDE), we've also posted getting-started videos at

> http://www.deitel.com/books/java9fp

for the three most popular Java IDEs—Eclipse, NetBeans and IntelliJ IDEA.

2.2 Your First Program in Java: Printing a Line of Text

A Java **application** is a computer program that executes when you use the **java command** to launch the Java Virtual Machine (JVM). Sections 2.2.1—2.2.2 discuss how to compile and run a Java application. First we consider a simple application that displays a line of text. Figure 2.1 shows the program followed by a box that displays its output.

```
1   // Fig. 2.1: Welcome1.java
2   // Text-printing program.
3
4   public class Welcome1 {
5      // main method begins execution of Java application
6      public static void main(String[] args) {
7         System.out.println("Welcome to Java Programming!");
8      } // end method main
9   } // end class Welcome1
```

```
Welcome to Java Programming!
```

Fig. 2.1 | Text-printing program.

The figure includes line numbers—they're *not* part of a Java program. Line 7 does the program's work—displaying the phrase "Welcome to Java Programming!" on the screen.

Commenting Your Programs

By convention, we begin every program with a comment indicating the figure number and the program's filename. The comment in line 1 begins with //, indicating that it's an **end-of-line comment**—it terminates at the end of the line on which the // appears. Line 2, by our convention, is a comment that describes the purpose of the program.

Java also has **traditional comments**, which can be spread over several lines as in

```
/* This is a traditional comment. It
   can be split over multiple lines */
```

These begin with the delimiter /* and end with */. The compiler ignores all text between the delimiters. Java incorporated traditional comments and end-of-line comments from the C and C++ programming languages, respectively.

Java provides comments of a third type—**Javadoc comments**. These are delimited by /** and */. The compiler ignores all text between the delimiters. Javadoc comments enable you to embed program documentation directly in your programs. Such comments are the preferred Java documenting format in industry. The **javadoc utility program** (part of the JDK) reads Javadoc comments and uses them to prepare program documentation in HTML5 web-page format. We use // comments throughout our code, rather than traditional or Javadoc comments, to save space.

Using Blank Lines

Blank lines (like line 3), space characters and tabs can make programs easier to read. Together, they're known as **white space**. The compiler ignores white space.

Declaring a Class

Line 4 begins a **class declaration** for class Welcome1. Every Java program consists of at least one class that you define. The **class keyword** introduces a class declaration and is immediately followed by the **class name** (Welcome1). **Keywords** are reserved for use by Java and are spelled with all lowercase letters. The complete list of keywords is shown in Appendix C.

In Chapters 2–7, every class we define begins with the **public** keyword. For now, we simply require it. You'll learn more about public and non-public classes in Chapter 8.

Filename for a **public** Class

A public class *must* be placed in a file that has a filename of the form *ClassName*.java, so class Welcome1 is stored in the file Welcome1.java.

Common Programming Error 2.1

A compilation error occurs if a public class's filename is not exactly the same name as the class (in terms of both spelling and capitalization) followed by the .java extension.

Class Names and Identifiers

By convention, class names begin with a capital letter and capitalize the first letter of each word they include (e.g., SampleClassName). A class name is an **identifier**—a series of characters consisting of letters, digits, underscores (_) and dollar signs ($) that does *not* begin with a digit and does *not* contain spaces. Some valid identifiers are Welcome1, $value, _value, m_inputField1 and button7. The name 7button is *not* a valid identifier because it begins with a digit, and the name input field is *not* a valid identifier because it contains a space. Normally, an identifier that does not begin with a capital letter is not a class name. Java is **case sensitive**—uppercase and lowercase letters are distinct—so value and Value are different (but both valid) identifiers.

Good Programming Practice 2.1
By convention, every word in a class-name identifier begins with an uppercase letter. For example, the class-name identifier DollarAmount starts its first word, Dollar, with an uppercase D and its second word, Amount, with an uppercase A. This naming convention is known as **camel case***, because the uppercase letters stand out like a camel's humps.*

9 *Underscore (_) in Java 9*
As of Java 9, you can no longer use an underscore (_) by itself as an identifier.

Class Body
A **left brace** (at the end of line 4), {, begins the **body** of every class declaration. A corresponding **right brace** (at line 9), }, must end each class declaration. Lines 5–8 are indented.

Good Programming Practice 2.2
By convention, indent the entire body of each class declaration one "level" between the braces that delimit the class's body. This format emphasizes the class declaration's structure and makes it easier to read. We use three spaces to form a level of indent—many programmers prefer two or four spaces. Whatever you choose, use it consistently.

Declaring a Method
Line 5 is a comment indicating the purpose of lines 6–8 of the program. Line 6 is the starting point of every Java application. The **parentheses** after the identifier main indicate that it's a **method**. Java class declarations normally contain one or more methods. For a Java application, one of the methods *must* be called main and must be defined as in line 6; otherwise, the program will not execute. We'll explain the purpose of keyword static in Section 3.2.5. Keyword **void** indicates that this method will *not* return any information. The String[] args in parentheses is a required part of main's declaration—we discuss this in Chapter 7.

The left brace at the end of line 6 begins the **body of the method declaration**. A corresponding right brace ends it (line 8). Line 7 is indented between the braces.

Good Programming Practice 2.3
Indent the entire body of each method declaration one "level" between the braces that define the method's body. This emphasizes the method's structure and makes it easier to read.

Performing Output with System.out.println
Line 7 displays the characters between the double quotation marks. The quotation marks themselves are *not* displayed. Together, the quotation marks and the characters between them are a **string**—also known as a **character string** or a **string literal**. White-space char-

acters in strings are *not* ignored by the compiler. Strings *cannot* span multiple lines of code—later we'll show how to conveniently deal with long strings.

The **System.out** object—which is predefined for you—is known as the **standard output object**. It allows a program to display information in the **command window** from which the program executes. In Microsoft Windows, the command window is the **Command Prompt**. In UNIX/Linux/macOS, the command window is called a **terminal** or a **shell**. Many programmers call it simply the **command line**.

Method **System.out.println** displays (or prints) a *line* of text in the command window. The string in the parentheses in line 7 is the method's **argument**. When System.out.println completes its task, it positions the output cursor (the location where the next character will be displayed) at the beginning of the next line in the command window. This is similar to what happens when you press the *Enter* key while typing in a text editor—the cursor appears at the beginning of the next line in the document.

The entire line 7, including System.out.println, the argument "Welcome to Java Programming!" in the parentheses and the **semicolon** (;), is called a **statement**. A method typically contains statements that perform its task. Most statements end with a semicolon.

2.2.1 Compiling the Application

We're now ready to compile and execute the program. We assume you're using the Java Development Kit's command-line tools, not an IDE. The following instructions assume that the book's examples are located in c:\examples on Windows or in your user account's Documents/examples folder on Linux/macOS.

Open a command window and change to the directory where the program is stored. Many operating systems use the command cd to change directories (or folders). On Windows, for example,

```
cd c:\examples\ch02\fig02_01
```

changes to the fig02_01 directory. On UNIX/Linux/macOS, the command

```
cd ~/Documents/examples/ch02/fig02_01
```

changes to the fig02_01 directory. To compile the program, type

```
javac Welcome1.java
```

If the program does not contain compilation errors, this command creates the file called Welcome1.class (known as Welcome1's **class file**) containing the platform-independent Java bytecodes that represent our application. When we use the java command to execute the application on a given platform, the JVM will translate these bytecodes into instructions that are understood by the underlying operating system and hardware.

Common Programming Error 2.2

The compiler error message "class Welcome1 is public, should be declared in a file named Welcome1.java" indicates that the filename does not match the name of the public class in the file or that you typed the class name incorrectly when compiling the class.

Each compilation-error message contains the filename and line number where the error occurred. For example, Welcome1.java:6 indicates that an error occurred at line 6 in Welcome1.java. The rest of the message provides information about the syntax error.

2.2.2 Executing the Application

Now that you've compiled the program, type the following command and press *Enter*:

```
java Welcome1
```

to launch the JVM and load the Welcome1.class file. The command *omits* the .class file-name extension; otherwise, the JVM will *not* execute the program. The JVM calls Welcome1's main method. Next, line 7 of main displays "Welcome to Java Programming!". Figure 2.2 shows the program executing in a Microsoft Windows **Command Prompt** window. [*Note:* Many environments show command windows with black backgrounds and white text. We adjusted these settings to make our screen captures more readable.]

Error-Prevention Tip 2.1

When attempting to run a Java program, if you receive a message such as "Exception in thread "main" java.lang.NoClassDefFoundError: Welcome1," your CLASSPATH environment variable has not been set properly. Please carefully review the installation instructions in the Before You Begin section of this book. On some systems, you may need to reboot your computer or open a new command window after configuring the CLASSPATH.

You type this command to execute the application

The program outputs to the screen
Welcome to Java Programming!

Fig. 2.2 | Executing Welcome1 from the **Command Prompt**.

2.3 Modifying Your First Java Program

Let's modify the example in Fig. 2.1 to print text on one line by using multiple statements and to print text on several lines by using a single statement.

Displaying a Single Line of Text with Multiple Statements

Welcome to Java Programming! can be displayed several ways. Class Welcome2, shown in Fig. 2.3, uses two statements (lines 7–8) to produce the output shown in Fig. 2.1. From this point forward, we highlight the new and key features in each code listing. Lines 7–8 in method main display *one* line of text. The first statement uses System.out's method print to display a string. Each print or println statement resumes displaying characters from where the last print or println statement stopped displaying characters. Unlike println, after displaying its argument, print does *not* position the output cursor at the beginning of the next line—the next character the program displays will appear *immediately after* the last character that print displays. So, line 8 positions the first character in its argument (the letter "J") immediately after the last character that line 7 displays (the *space character* before the string's closing double-quote character).

```
 1   // Fig. 2.3: Welcome2.java
 2   // Printing a line of text with multiple statements.
 3
 4   public class Welcome2 {
 5      // main method begins execution of Java application
 6      public static void main(String[] args) {
 7         System.out.print("Welcome to ");
 8         System.out.println("Java Programming!");
 9      } // end method main
10   } // end class Welcome2
```

```
Welcome to Java Programming!
```

Fig. 2.3 | Printing a line of text with multiple statements.

Displaying Multiple Lines of Text with a Single Statement

A single statement can display multiple lines by using **newline characters** (\n), which indicate to System.out's print and println methods when to position the output cursor at the beginning of the next line in the command window. Like blank lines, space characters and tab characters, newline characters are white space characters. The program in Fig. 2.4 outputs four lines of text, using newline characters to determine when to begin each new line. Most of the program is identical to those in Figs. 2.1 and 2.3.

```
 1   // Fig. 2.4: Welcome3.java
 2   // Printing multiple lines of text with a single statement.
 3
 4   public class Welcome3 {
 5      // main method begins execution of Java application
 6      public static void main(String[] args) {
 7         System.out.println("Welcome\nto\nJava\nProgramming!");
 8      } // end method main
 9   } // end class Welcome3
```

```
Welcome
to
Java
Programming!
```

Fig. 2.4 | Printing multiple lines of text with a single statement.

Line 7 displays four lines of text in the command window. Normally, the characters in a string are displayed *exactly* as they appear in the double quotes. However, the paired characters \ and n (repeated three times in the statement) do *not* appear on the screen. The **backslash** (\) is an **escape character**, which has special meaning to System.out's print and println methods. When a backslash appears in a string, Java combines it with the next character to form an **escape sequence**—\n represents the newline character. When a newline character appears in a string being output with System.out, the newline character causes the screen's output cursor to move to the beginning of the next line in the command window.

Figure 2.5 lists several escape sequences and describes how they affect the display of characters in the command window. For the complete list of escape sequences, visit

```
http://docs.oracle.com/javase/specs/jls/se8/html/jls-3.html#jls-3.10.6
```

Escape sequence	Description
\n	Newline. Position the screen cursor at the beginning of the *next* line.
\t	Horizontal tab. Move the screen cursor to the next tab stop.
\r	Carriage return. Position the screen cursor at the beginning of the *current* line—do *not* advance to the next line. Any characters output after the carriage return *overwrite* the characters previously output on that line.
\\	Backslash. Used to print a backslash character.
\"	Double quote. Used to print a double-quote character. For example, `System.out.println("\"in quotes\"");` displays `"in quotes"`.

Fig. 2.5 | Some common escape sequences.

2.4 Displaying Text with `printf`

Method **`System.out.printf`** (f means "formatted") displays *formatted* data. Figure 2.6 uses this to output on two lines the strings `"Welcome to"` and `"Java Programming!"`.

```
1   // Fig. 2.6: Welcome4.java
2   // Displaying multiple lines with method System.out.printf.
3
4   public class Welcome4 {
5      // main method begins execution of Java application
6      public static void main(String[] args) {
7         System.out.printf("%s%n%s%n", "Welcome to", "Java Programming!");
8      } // end method main
9   } // end class Welcome4
```

```
Welcome to
Java Programming!
```

Fig. 2.6 | Displaying multiple lines with method `System.out.printf`.

Line 7 calls method `System.out.printf` to display the program's output. The method call specifies three arguments. When a method requires multiple arguments, they're placed in a **comma-separated list**.

Good Programming Practice 2.4
Place a space after each comma (,) in an argument list to make programs more readable.

Method `printf`'s first argument is a **format string** that may consist of **fixed text** and **format specifiers**. Fixed text is output by `printf` just as it would be by `print` or `println`. Each format specifier is a *placeholder* for a value and specifies the *type of data* to output. Format specifiers also may include optional formatting information.

Format specifiers begin with a percent sign (%) followed by a character that represents the *data type*. For example, the format specifier **%s** is a placeholder for a string. The format string specifies that `printf` should output two strings, each followed by a newline character. At the first format specifier's position, `printf` substitutes the value of the first argument after the format string. At each subsequent format specifier's position, `printf` substitutes the value of the next argument. So this example substitutes "Welcome to" for the first %s and "Java Programming!" for the second %s. The output shows that two lines of text are displayed on two lines.

Instead of using the escape sequence \n, we used the **%n** format specifier, which is a line separator that's *portable* across operating systems. You cannot use %n in the argument to `System.out.print` or `System.out.println`; however, the line separator output by `System.out.println` *after* it displays its argument *is* portable across operating systems.

2.5 Another Application: Adding Integers

Our next application (Fig. 2.7) reads two **integers** typed by a user at the keyboard, computes their sum and displays it. In the sample output, we use bold text to identify the user's input (i.e., **45** and **72**).

```
1    // Fig. 2.7: Addition.java
2    // Addition program that inputs two numbers then displays their sum.
3    import java.util.Scanner; // program uses class Scanner
4
5    public class Addition {
6       // main method begins execution of Java application
7       public static void main(String[] args) {
8          // create a Scanner to obtain input from the command window
9          Scanner input = new Scanner(System.in);
10
11         System.out.print("Enter first integer: "); // prompt
12         int number1 = input.nextInt(); // read first number from user
13
14         System.out.print("Enter second integer: "); // prompt
15         int number2 = input.nextInt(); // read second number from user
16
17         int sum = number1 + number2; // add numbers, then store total in sum
18
19         System.out.printf("Sum is %d%n", sum); // display sum
20      } // end method main
21   } // end class Addition
```

```
Enter first integer: 45
Enter second integer: 72
Sum is 117
```

Fig. 2.7 | Addition program that inputs two numbers, then displays their sum.

2.5.1 import Declarations

A great strength of Java is its rich set of predefined classes that you can *reuse* rather than "reinventing the wheel." These classes are grouped into **packages**—*named groups of related classes*—and are collectively referred to as the **Java class library**, or the **Java Application Programming Interface (Java API)**. Line 3 is an **import declaration** that helps the compiler locate a class that's used in this program. It indicates that the program uses the predefined Scanner class (discussed shortly) from the package named **java.util**. The compiler then ensures that you use the class correctly.

Common Programming Error 2.3

All import declarations must appear before the first class declaration in the file. Placing an import declaration inside or after a class declaration is a syntax error.

Common Programming Error 2.4

Forgetting to include an import declaration for a class that must be imported results in a compilation error containing a message such as "cannot find symbol." When this occurs, check that you provided the proper import declarations and that the names in them are correct, including proper capitalization.

2.5.2 Declaring and Creating a Scanner to Obtain User Input from the Keyboard

All Java variables *must* be declared with a **name** and a **type** *before* they can be used. A variable name can be any valid identifier. Like other statements, declaration statements end with a semicolon (;).

Line 9 of main is a **variable declaration statement** that specifies the *name* (input) and *type* (Scanner) of a variable that's used in this program. A **Scanner** (package java.util) enables a program to read data (e.g., numbers and strings) for use in a program. The data can come from many sources, such as the user at the keyboard or a file on disk. Before using a Scanner, you must create it and specify the *source* of the data.

The = in line 9 indicates that Scanner variable input should be initialized in its declaration with the result of the expression to the right of the equals sign—new Scanner(System.in). This expression uses the **new** keyword to create a Scanner object that reads characters typed by the user at the keyboard. The **standard input object**, **System.in**, enables applications to read *bytes* of data typed by the user. The Scanner translates these bytes into types (like ints) that can be used in a program.

Good Programming Practice 2.5

By convention, variable-name identifiers use the camel-case naming convention with a lowercase first letter—for example, firstNumber.

2.5.3 Prompting the User for Input

Line 11 uses System.out.print to display the message "Enter first integer: ". This message is called a **prompt** because it directs the user to take a specific action. Recall from Section 2.2 that identifiers starting with capital letters typically represent class names. Class System is part of package **java.lang**.

Software Engineering Observation 2.1

By default, package `java.lang` *is imported in every Java program; thus, classes in* `java.lang` *are the only ones in the Java API that do not require an* `import` *declaration.*

2.5.4 Declaring a Variable to Store an Integer and Obtaining an Integer from the Keyboard

The variable declaration statement in line 12 declares that variable `number1` holds data of type `int`—that is, *integer* values, The range of values for an `int` is –2,147,483,648 to +2,147,483,647. The `int` values you use in a program may not contain commas; however, for readability, you can place underscores in numbers. So 60_000_000 represents the `int` value 60,000,000.

Some other types of data are **float** and **double**, for holding real numbers, and **char**, for holding character data. Variables of type `char` represent individual characters, such as an uppercase letter (e.g., A), a digit (e.g., 7), a special character (e.g., * or %) or an escape sequence (e.g., the tab character, \t). The types `int`, `float`, `double` and `char` are called **primitive types**. Primitive-type names are keywords and must appear in all lowercase letters. Appendix D summarizes the characteristics of the eight primitive types (`boolean`, `byte`, `char`, `short`, `int`, `long`, `float` and `double`).

The = in line 12 initializes the `int` variable `number1` with the result of the expression `input.nextInt()`. This uses the `Scanner` object `input`'s `nextInt` method to obtain an integer from the user at the keyboard. At this point the program *waits* for the user to type the number and press the *Enter* key to submit the number to the program.

Our program assumes that the user enters a valid integer value. If not, a logic error will occur and the program will terminate. Chapter 11, Exception Handling: A Deeper Look, discusses how to make your programs more robust by enabling them to handle such errors. This is also known as making your programs *fault tolerant*.

2.5.5 Obtaining a Second Integer

Line 14 prompts the user to enter the second integer. Line 15 declares the `int` variable `number2` and initializes it with a second integer read from the user at the keyboard.

2.5.6 Using Variables in a Calculation

Line 17 declares the `int` variable `sum` and initializes it with the result of `number1 + number2`. In the preceding statement, the addition operator is a **binary operator**. Portions of statements that contain calculations are called **expressions**. An expression is any portion of a statement that has a *value*. The value of the expression `number1 + number2` is the *sum* of the numbers. Similarly, the value of the expression `input.nextInt()` (lines 12 and 15) is the integer typed by the user.

2.5.7 Displaying the Calculation Result

After the calculation has been performed, line 19 uses method `System.out.printf` to display the sum. The format specifier **%d** is a *placeholder* for an `int` value (in this case the value of `sum`)—the letter d stands for "decimal integer." The remaining characters in the format string are all fixed text. So, method `printf` displays "Sum is ", followed by the value of `sum` (in the position of the %d format specifier) and a newline.

Calculations also can be performed *inside* `printf` statements. We could have combined the statements at lines 17 and 19 into one statement by replacing sum in line 19 with `number1 + number2`.

2.5.8 Java API Documentation

For each new Java API class we use, we indicate the package in which it's located. This information helps you locate descriptions of each package and class in the Java API documentation. A web-based version of this documentation can be found at

```
http://docs.oracle.com/javase/8/docs/api/index.html
```

You can download it from the Additional Resources section at

```
http://www.oracle.com/technetwork/java/javase/downloads
```

2.5.9 Declaring and Initializing Variables in Separate Statements

Each variable must have a value *before* you can use the variable in a calculation (or other expression). The variable declaration statement in line 12 both declared `number1` *and* initialized it with a value entered by the user.

Sometimes you declare a variable in one statement, then initialize it in another. For example, line 12 could have been written in two statements as

```
int number1; // declare the int variable number1
number1 = input.nextInt(); // assign the user's input to number1
```

The first statement declares `number1`, but does *not* initialize it. The second statement uses the **assignment operator**, =, to assign `number1` the value entered by the user. Everything to the *right* of the assignment operator, =, is always evaluated *before* the assignment is performed.

2.6 Arithmetic

The **arithmetic operators** are summarized in Fig. 2.8. The **asterisk** (*) indicates multiplication, and the percent sign (**%**) is the **remainder operator**, which we'll discuss shortly. The arithmetic operators in Fig. 2.8 are *binary* operators.

Java operation	Operator	Algebraic expression	Java expression
Addition	+	$f + 7$	`f + 7`
Subtraction	−	$p - c$	`p - c`
Multiplication	*	bm	`b * m`
Division	/	x / y or $\frac{x}{y}$ or $x \div y$	`x / y`
Remainder	%	$r \bmod s$	`r % s`

Fig. 2.8 | Arithmetic operators.

Integer division yields an integer quotient. For example, the expression 7 / 4 evaluates to 1, and the expression 17 / 5 evaluates to 3. Any fractional part in integer division is simply *truncated*—no *rounding* occurs. Java provides the remainder operator, %, which yields the remainder after division. The expression x % y yields the remainder after x is divided by y. Thus, 7 % 4 yields 3, and 17 % 5 yields 2. This operator is most commonly used with integer operands but it can also be used with other arithmetic types.

Rules of Operator Precedence

Java applies the arithmetic operators in a precise sequence determined by the **rules of operator precedence**, which are generally the same as those followed in algebra:

1. Multiplication, division and remainder operations are applied first. If an expression contains several such operations, they're applied from left to right. Multiplication, division and remainder operators have the same level of precedence.

2. Addition and subtraction operations are applied next. If an expression contains several such operations, the operators are applied from left to right. Addition and subtraction operators have the same level of precedence.

These rules enable Java to apply operators in the correct *order*.[1] When we say that operators are applied from left to right, we're referring to their **associativity**. Some associate from right to left. Figure 2.9 summarizes these rules of operator precedence. A complete precedence chart is included in Appendix A.

Operator(s)	Operation(s)	Order of evaluation (precedence)
*	Multiplication	Evaluated first. If there are several operators of this
/	Division	type, they're evaluated from *left to right*.
%	Remainder	
+	Addition	Evaluated next. If there are several operators of this
-	Subtraction	type, they're evaluated from *left to right*.
=	Assignment	Evaluated last.

Fig. 2.9 | Precedence of arithmetic operators.

2.7 Decision Making: Equality and Relational Operators

A **condition** is an expression that can be **true** or **false**. This section introduces Java's **if selection statement**, which allows a program to make a **decision** based on a condition's value. If an if statement's condition is *true*, its body executes. If the condition is *false*, its body does not execute.

Conditions in if statements can be formed by using the **equality operators** (== and !=) and **relational operators** (>, <, >= and <=) summarized in Fig. 2.10. Both equality operators have the same level of precedence, which is *lower* than that of the relational operators. The equality operators associate from *left to right*. The relational operators all have the same level of precedence and also associate from *left to right*.

---

1. Subtle order-of-evaluation issues can occur in expressions. For more information, see Chapter 15 of *The Java® Language Specification* (https://docs.oracle.com/javase/specs/jls/se8/html/jls-15.html).

Algebraic operator	Java equality or relational operator	Sample Java condition	Meaning of Java condition
Equality operators			
=	==	x == y	x is equal to y
≠	!=	x != y	x is not equal to y
Relational operators			
>	>	x > y	x is greater than y
<	<	x < y	x is less than y
≥	>=	x >= y	x is greater than or equal to y
≤	<=	x <= y	x is less than or equal to y

Fig. 2.10 | Equality and relational operators.

Figure 2.11 uses six if statements to compare two integers input by the user. If the condition in any of these if statements is *true*, the statement associated with that if statement executes; otherwise, the statement is skipped. We use a Scanner to input the integers from the user and store them in variables number1 and number2. The program *compares* the numbers and displays the results of the comparisons that are true.

```
1   // Fig. 2.11: Comparison.java
2   // Compare integers using if statements, relational operators
3   // and equality operators.
4   import java.util.Scanner; // program uses class Scanner
5
6   public class Comparison {
7      // main method begins execution of Java application
8      public static void main(String[] args) {
9         // create Scanner to obtain input from command line
10        Scanner input = new Scanner(System.in);
11
12        System.out.print("Enter first integer: "); // prompt
13        int number1 = input.nextInt(); // read first number from user
14
15        System.out.print("Enter second integer: "); // prompt
16        int number2 = input.nextInt(); // read second number from user
17
18        if (number1 == number2)
19           System.out.printf("%d == %d%n", number1, number2);
20        }
21
22        if (number1 != number2) {
23           System.out.printf("%d != %d%n", number1, number2);
24        }
25
```

Fig. 2.11 | Compare integers using if statements, relational operators and equality operators. (Part 1 of 2.)

```
26          if (number1 < number2) {
27              System.out.printf("%d < %d%n", number1, number2);
28          }
29
30          if (number1 > number2) {
31              System.out.printf("%d > %d%n", number1, number2);
32          }
33
34          if (number1 <= number2) {
35              System.out.printf("%d <= %d%n", number1, number2);
36          }
37
38          if (number1 >= number2) {
39              System.out.printf("%d >= %d%n", number1, number2);
40          }
41      } // end method main
42  } // end class Comparison
```

```
Enter first integer: 777
Enter second integer: 777
777 == 777
777 <= 777
777 >= 777
```

```
Enter first integer: 1000
Enter second integer: 2000
1000 != 2000
1000 < 2000
1000 <= 2000
```

```
Enter first integer: 2000
Enter second integer: 1000
2000 != 1000
2000 > 1000
2000 >= 1000
```

Fig. 2.11 | Compare integers using if statements, relational operators and equality operators. (Part 2 of 2.)

Class Comparison's main method (lines 8–41) begins the execution of the program. Line 10 declares Scanner variable input and assigns it a Scanner that inputs data from the standard input (i.e., the keyboard). Lines 12–16 prompt for and read the user's input.

Lines 18–20 compare the values of variables number1 and number2 to test for equality. If the values are equal, the statement in line 19 displays a line of text indicating that the numbers are equal. The if statements starting in lines 22, 26, 30, 34 and 38 compare number1 and number2 using the operators !=, <, >, <= and >=, respectively. If the conditions are true in one or more of those if statements, the corresponding body statement displays an appropriate line of text.

Each if statement in Fig. 2.11 contains a single body statement that's indented. Also notice that we've enclosed each body statement in a pair of braces, { }, creating a **compound statement** or a **block**.

Common Programming Error 2.5

Placing a semicolon immediately after the right parenthesis after the condition in an if statement is often a logic error (although not a syntax error). The semicolon causes the body of the if statement to be empty, so the if statement performs no action, regardless of whether or not its condition is true. Worse yet, the original body statement of the if statement always executes, often causing the program to produce incorrect results.

Operators Discussed So Far

Figure 2.12 shows the operators discussed so far in decreasing order of precedence. All but the assignment operator, =, associate from *left to right*. The assignment operator, =, associates from *right to left*. An assignment expression's value is whatever was assigned to the variable on the = operator's left side—for example, the value of the expression x = 7 is 7. So an expression like x = y = 0 is evaluated as if it had been written as x = (y = 0), which first assigns the value 0 to variable y, then assigns the result of that assignment, 0, to x.

Operators			Associativity	Type
*	/	%	left to right	multiplicative
+	-		left to right	additive
<	<=	> >=	left to right	relational
==	!=		left to right	equality
=			right to left	assignment

Fig. 2.12 | Precedence and associativity of operators discussed.

Good Programming Practice 2.6

When writing expressions containing many operators, refer to the operator precedence chart (Appendix A). Confirm that the operations in the expression are performed in the order you expect. If, in a complex expression, you're uncertain about the order of evaluation, use parentheses to force the order, exactly as you'd do in algebraic expressions.

2.8 Wrap-Up

In this chapter, you learned many important features of Java, including displaying data on the screen in a command window, inputting data from the keyboard, performing calculations and making decisions. As you'll see in Chapter 3, Java applications typically contain just a few lines of code in method main—these statements normally create the objects that perform the work of the application. In Chapter 3, you'll implement your own classes and use objects of those classes in applications.

3

Introduction to Classes, Objects, Methods and Strings

Objectives

In this chapter you'll:

- Declare a class and use it to create an object.
- Implement a class's behaviors as methods.
- Implement a class's attributes as instance variables.
- Call an object's methods to make them perform their tasks.
- Understand what primitive types and reference types are.
- Use a constructor to initialize an object's data.
- Represent and use numbers containing decimal points.

3.1 Introduction[1]

In Chapter 2, you worked with *existing* classes, objects and methods. You used the *predefined* standard output object System.out, *invoking* its methods print, println and printf to display information. You used the *existing* Scanner class to create an object that reads into memory integer data typed by the user at the keyboard. Throughout the book, you'll use many more *preexisting* classes and objects—this is one of the great strengths of Java as an object-oriented programming language.

In this chapter, you'll create your own classes and methods. Each new class you create becomes a new *type* that can be used to declare variables and create objects. You can declare new classes as needed; this is one reason why Java is known as an *extensible* language.

We present a case study on creating and using a simple, real-world bank-account class—Account. Such a class should maintain as *instance variables* attributes, such as its name and balance, and provide *methods* for tasks such as querying the balance (getBalance), making deposits that increase the balance (deposit) and making withdrawals that decrease the balance (withdraw). We'll build the getBalance and deposit methods into the class in the chapter's examples and you can add the withdraw method on your own as an exercise.

In Chapter 2, we used the data type int to represent integers. In this chapter, we introduce data type double to represent an account balance as a number that can contain a *decimal point*—such numbers are called *floating-point numbers*. In Chapter 8, when we get a bit deeper into object technology, we'll begin representing monetary amounts precisely with class BigDecimal (package java.math), as you should do when writing industrial-strength monetary applications. [Alternatively, you could treat monetary amounts as whole numbers of pennies, then break the result into dollars and cents by using division and remainder operations, respectively, and insert a period between the dollars and the cents.]

---

1. This chapter depends on the review of terminology and concepts of object-oriented programming in Section 1.2.

3.2 Instance Variables, *set* Methods and *get* Methods

In this section, you'll create two classes—Account (Fig. 3.1) and AccountTest (Fig. 3.2).
Class AccountTest is an *application class* in which the main method will create and use an
Account object to demonstrate class Account's capabilities.

3.2.1 Account Class with an Instance Variable, and *set* and *get* Methods

Different accounts typically have different names. For this reason, class Account (Fig. 3.1)
contains a name *instance variable*. A class's instance variables maintain data for each object
(that is, each instance) of the class. Later in the chapter we'll add an instance variable named
balance so we can keep track of how much money is in the account. Class Account contains two methods—method setName stores a name in an Account object and method
getName obtains a name from an Account object.

```java
1   // Fig. 3.1: Account.java
2   // Account class that contains a name instance variable
3   // and methods to set and get its value.
4
5   public class Account {
6      private String name; // instance variable
7
8      // method to set the name in the object
9      public void setName(String name) {
10        this.name = name; // store the name
11     }
12
13     // method to retrieve the name from the object
14     public String getName() {
15        return name; // return value of name to caller
16     }
17  }
```

Fig. 3.1 | Account class that contains a name instance variable and methods to *set* and *get* its
value.

Class Declaration
The *class declaration* begins in line 5:

```java
    public class Account {
```

The keyword public (which Chapter 8 explains in detail) is an **access modifier**. For now,
we'll simply declare every class public. Each public class declaration must be stored in a
file having the *same* name as the class and ending with the .java filename extension;
otherwise, a compilation error will occur. Thus, public classes Account and AccountTest
(Fig. 3.2) *must* be declared in the *separate* files Account.java and AccountTest.java,
respectively.

Every class declaration contains the keyword class followed immediately by the
class's name—in this case, Account. Every class's body is enclosed in a pair of left and right
braces as in lines 5 and 17 of Fig. 3.1.

Identifiers and Camel-Case Naming
Recall from Chapter 2 that class names, method names and variable names are all *identifiers* and by convention all use the *camel-case* naming scheme. Also by convention, class names begin with an initial *uppercase* letter, and method names and variable names begin with an initial *lowercase* letter.

Instance Variable **name**
Recall from Section 1.2 that an object has attributes, implemented as instance variables and carried with it throughout its lifetime. Instance variables exist before methods are called on an object, while the methods are executing and after the methods complete execution. Each object (instance) of the class has its *own* copy of the class's instance variables. A class normally contains one or more methods that manipulate the instance variables belonging to particular objects of the class.

Instance variables are declared *inside* a class declaration but *outside* the bodies of the class's methods. Line 6

```
private String name; // instance variable
```

declares instance variable name of type String *outside* the bodies of methods setName (lines 9–11) and getName (lines 14–16). String variables can hold character string values such as "Jane Green". If there are many Account objects, each has its own name. Because name is an instance variable, it can be manipulated by each of the class's methods.

> ### Good Programming Practice 3.1
> *We prefer to list a class's instance variables first in the class's body, so that you see the names and types of the variables before they're used in the class's methods. You can list the class's instance variables anywhere in the class outside its method declarations, but scattering the instance variables can lead to hard-to-read code.*

Access Modifiers **public** *and* **private**
Most instance-variable declarations are preceded with the keyword private (as in line 6). Like public, **private** is an *access modifier*. Variables or methods declared with private are accessible only to methods of the class in which they're declared. So, the variable name can be used only in each Account object's methods (setName and getName in this case). You'll soon see that this presents powerful software engineering opportunities.

setName Method of Class **Account**
Let's walk through the code of setName's method declaration (lines 9–11):

```
public void setName(String name) {
   this.name = name; // store the name
}
```

We refer to the first line of each method declaration (line 9 in this case) as the *method header*. The method's return type (which appears before the method name) specifies the type of data the method returns to its *caller* after performing its task. As you'll soon see, the statement in line 19 of main (Fig. 3.2) *calls* method setName, so main is setName's *caller* in this example. The return type void (line 9 in Fig. 3.1) indicates that setName will perform a task but will *not* return (i.e., give back) any information to its caller. In Chapter 2, you used methods that return information—for example, you used Scanner method nextInt to input an integer typed by the user at the keyboard. When nextInt reads a value from the user, it *returns* that value for use in the program. As you'll see shortly, Account method getName returns a value.

Method setName receives *parameter* name of type String. Parameters are declared in a parameter list, which is located inside the parentheses that follow the method name in the method header. When there are multiple parameters, each is separated from the next by a comma. Each parameter *must* specify a type (in this case, String) followed by a variable name (in this case, name).

Parameters Are Local Variables

In Chapter 2, we declared all of an app's variables in the main method. Variables declared in a particular method's body (such as main) are local variables which can be used *only* in that method. Each method can access its own local variables, not those of other methods. When a method terminates, the values of its local variables are *lost*. A method's parameters also are local variables of the method.

setName Method Body

Every *method body* is delimited by a pair of *braces* (as in lines 9 and 11 of Fig. 3.1) containing one or more statements that perform the method's task(s). In this case, the method body contains a single statement (line 10) that assigns the value of the name *parameter* (a String) to the class's name *instance variable*, thus storing the account name in the object.

If a method contains a local variable with the *same* name as an instance variable (as in lines 9 and 6, respectively), that method's body will refer to the local variable rather than the instance variable. In this case, the local variable is said to *shadow* the instance variable in the method's body. The method's body can use the keyword **this** to refer to the shadowed instance variable explicitly, as shown on the left side of the assignment in line 10. After line 10 executes, the method has completed its task, so it returns to its *caller*.

Good Programming Practice 3.2

We could have avoided the need for keyword this *here by choosing a different name for the parameter in line 9, but using the* this *keyword as shown in line 10 is a widely accepted practice to minimize the proliferation of identifier names.*

getName Method of Class Account

Method getName (lines 14–16)

```
public String getName() {
    return name; // return value of name to caller
}
```

returns a particular Account object's name to the caller. The method has an *empty* parameter list, so it does *not* require additional information to perform its task. The method returns a String. When a method that specifies a return type *other* than void is called and completes its task, it *must* return a result to its caller. A statement that calls method getName on an Account object (such as the ones in lines 14 and 24 of Fig. 3.2) expects to receive the Account's name—a String, as specified in the method declaration's *return type*.

The **return** statement in line 15 of Fig. 3.1 passes the String value of instance variable name back to the caller. For example, when the value is returned to the statement in lines 23–24 of Fig. 3.2, the statement uses that value to output the name.

3.2.2 AccountTest Class That Creates and Uses an Object of Class Account

Next, we'd like to use class Account in an app and *call* each of its methods. A class that contains a main method begins the execution of a Java app. Class Account *cannot* execute by itself because it does *not* contain a main method—if you type java Account in the command window, you'll get an error indicating "Main method not found in class Account." To fix this problem, you must either declare a *separate* class that contains a main method or place a main method in class Account.

Driver Class AccountTest

A person drives a car by telling it what to do (go faster, go slower, turn left, turn right, etc.)—without having to know how the car's internal mechanisms work. Similarly, a method (such as main) "drives" an Account object by calling its methods—without having to know how the class's internal mechanisms work. In this sense, the class containing method main is referred to as a **driver class**.

To help you prepare for the larger programs you'll encounter later in this book and in industry, we define class AccountTest and its main method in the file AccountTest.java (Fig. 3.2). Once main begins executing, it may call other methods in this and other classes; those may, in turn, call other methods, and so on. Class AccountTest's main method creates one Account object and calls its getName and setName methods.

```java
1   // Fig. 3.2: AccountTest.java
2   // Creating and manipulating an Account object.
3   import java.util.Scanner;
4
5   public class AccountTest {
6      public static void main(String[] args) {
7         // create a Scanner object to obtain input from the command window
8         Scanner input = new Scanner(System.in);
9
10        // create an Account object and assign it to myAccount
11        Account myAccount = new Account();
12
13        // display initial value of name (null)
14        System.out.printf("Initial name is: %s%n%n", myAccount.getName());
15
16        // prompt for and read name
17        System.out.println("Please enter the name:");
18        String theName = input.nextLine(); // read a line of text
19        myAccount.setName(theName); // put theName in myAccount
20        System.out.println(); // outputs a blank line
21
22        // display the name stored in object myAccount
23        System.out.printf("Name in object myAccount is:%n%s%n",
24           myAccount.getName());
25     }
26  }
```

Fig. 3.2 | Creating and manipulating an Account object. (Part 1 of 2.)

```
Initial name is: null

Please enter the name:
Jane Green

Name in object myAccount is:
Jane Green
```

Fig. 3.2 | Creating and manipulating an Account object. (Part 2 of 2.)

Scanner *Object for Receiving Input from the User*

Line 8 creates a Scanner object named input for inputting a name from the user. Line 17 prompts the user to enter a name. Line 18 uses the Scanner object's **nextLine** method to read the name from the user and assign it to the *local* variable theName. You type the name and press *Enter* to submit it to the program. Pressing *Enter* inserts a newline character after the characters you typed. Method nextLine reads characters (*including white-space characters*, such as the blank in "Jane Green") until it encounters the newline, then returns a String containing the characters up to, but *not* including, the newline, which is *discarded*.

Class Scanner provides various other input methods, as you'll see throughout the book. A method similar to nextLine—named **next**—reads the *next word*. When you press *Enter* after typing some text, method next reads characters until it encounters a *white-space character* (such as a space, tab or newline), then returns a String containing the characters up to, but *not* including, the white-space character, which is *discarded*. All information after the first white-space character is *not lost*—it can be read by subsequent statements that call the Scanner's methods later in the program.

Instantiating an Object—*Keyword* **new** *and Constructors*

Line 11 creates an Account object and assigns it to variable myAccount of type Account. The variable is initialized with the result of new Account()—a **class instance creation expression**. Keyword **new** creates a new object of the specified class—in this case, Account. The parentheses are *required*. As you'll learn in Section 3.3, those parentheses in combination with a class name represent a call to a **constructor**, which is *similar* to a method but is called implicitly by the new operator to *initialize* an object's instance variables when the object is *created*. In Section 3.3, you'll see how to place an *argument* in the parentheses to specify an *initial value* for an Account object's name instance variable—you'll enhance class Account to enable this. For now, we simply leave the parentheses *empty*. Line 8 contains a class instance creation expression for a Scanner object—the expression initializes the Scanner with System.in, which tells the Scanner where to read the input from (i.e., the keyboard).

Calling Class Account's getName *Method*

Line 14 displays the *initial* name, which is obtained by calling the object's getName method. Just as we can use object System.out to call its methods print, printf and println, we can use object myAccount to call its methods getName and setName. Line 14 calls getName using the myAccount object created in line 11, followed by a **dot separator** (.), then the method name getName and an *empty* set of parentheses because no arguments are being passed. When getName is called:

1. The app transfers program execution from the call (line 14 in main) to method getName's declaration (lines 14–16 of Fig. 3.1). Because getName was called via the myAccount object, getName "knows" which object's instance variable to manipulate.

2. Next, method getName performs its task—that is, it *returns* the name (line 15 of Fig. 3.1). When the return statement executes, program execution continues where getName was called (line 14 in Fig. 3.2).

3. System.out.printf displays the String returned by method getName, then the program continues executing at line 17 in main.

Error-Prevention Tip 3.1

Never use as a format-control a string that was input from the user. When method System.out.printf evaluates the format-control string in its first argument, the method performs tasks based on the conversion specifier(s) in that string. If the format-control string were obtained from the user, a malicious user could supply conversion specifiers that would be executed by System.out.printf, possibly causing a security breach.

null—the Default Initial Value for *String* Variables

The first line of the output shows the name "null." Unlike local variables, which are *not* automatically initialized, *every instance variable has a* **default initial value**—a value provided by Java when you do *not* specify the instance variable's initial value. Thus, *instance variables* are *not* required to be explicitly initialized before they're used in a program—unless they must be initialized to values *other than* their default values. The default value for an instance variable of type String (like name in this example) is null, which we discuss further in Section 3.5 when we consider *reference types*.

Calling Class *Account's* *setName* Method

Line 19 calls myAccounts's setName method. A method call can supply *arguments* whose *values* are assigned to the corresponding method parameters. In this case, the value of main's local variable theName in parentheses is the *argument* that's passed to setName so that the method can perform its task. When setName is called:

1. The app transfers program execution from line 19 in main to setName method's declaration (lines 9–11 of Fig. 3.1), and the *argument value* in the call's parentheses (theName) is assigned to the corresponding *parameter* (name) in the method header (line 9 of Fig. 3.1). Because setName was called via the myAccount object, setName "knows" which object's instance variable to manipulate.

2. Next, method setName performs its task—that is, it assigns the name parameter's value to instance variable name (line 10 of Fig. 3.1).

3. When program execution reaches setName's closing right brace, it returns to where setName was called (line 19 of Fig. 3.2), then continues at line 20 of Fig. 3.2.

The number of *arguments* in a method call *must match* the number of *parameters* in the method declaration's parameter list. Also, the argument types in the method call must be *consistent* with the types of the corresponding parameters in the method's declaration. (As you'll see in Chapter 6, an argument's type and its corresponding parameter's type are *not* required to be *identical.*) In our example, the method call passes one argument of type String (theName)—and the method declaration specifies one parameter of type String (name, declared in line 9 of Fig. 3.1). So in this example the type of the argument in the method call *exactly* matches the type of the parameter in the method header.

Displaying the Name That Was Entered by the User
Line 20 of Fig. 3.2 outputs a blank line. When the second call to method getName (line 24) executes, the name entered by the user in line 18 is displayed. After the statement at lines 23–24 completes execution, the end of method main is reached, so the program terminates.

3.2.3 Compiling and Executing an App with Multiple Classes
You must compile the classes in Figs. 3.1 and 3.2 before you can *execute* the app. This is the first time you've created an app with *multiple* classes. Class AccountTest has a main method; class Account does not. To compile this app, first change to the directory that contains the app's source-code files. Next, type the command

```
javac Account.java AccountTest.java
```

to compile *both* classes at once. If the directory containing the app includes *only* this app's files, you can compile both classes with the command

```
javac *.java
```

The asterisk (*) in *.java indicates *all* files in the *current* directory ending with the file-name extension ".java" should be compiled. If both classes compile correctly—that is, no compilation errors are displayed—you can then run the app with the command

```
java AccountTest
```

3.2.4 Account UML Class Diagram
We'll often use UML class diagrams to help you visualize a class's *attributes* and *operations*. In industry, UML diagrams help systems designers specify a system in a concise, graphical, programming-language-independent manner, before programmers implement the system in a specific programming language. Figure 3.3 presents a **UML class diagram** for class Account of Fig. 3.1.

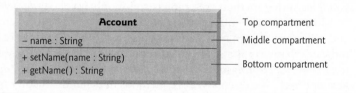

Fig. 3.3 | UML class diagram for class Account of Fig. 3.1.

Top Compartment
In the UML, each class is modeled in a class diagram as a rectangle with three compartments. In this diagram the *top* compartment contains the *class name* Account centered horizontally in boldface type.

Middle Compartment

The *middle* compartment contains the *class's attribute* name, which corresponds to the instance variable of the same name in Java. Instance variable name is private in Java, so the UML class diagram lists a *minus sign (–) access modifier* before the attribute name. Following the attribute name are a *colon* and the *attribute type*, in this case String.

Bottom Compartment

The *bottom* compartment contains the class's **operations**, setName and getName, which correspond to the Java methods. The UML models operations by listing the operation name preceded by an *access modifier*, in this case + getName. This plus sign (+) indicates that get-Name is a *public* operation in the UML (because it's a public method in Java). Operation getName does *not* have any parameters, so the parentheses following the operation name in the class diagram are *empty*, just as they are in the method's declaration in line 14 of Fig. 3.1. Operation setName, also a public operation, has a String parameter called name.

Return Types

The UML indicates the *return type* of an operation by placing a colon and the return type *after* the parentheses following the operation name. Account method getName (Fig. 3.1) has a String return type. Method setName *does not* return a value (because it returns void in Java), so the UML class diagram *does not* specify a return type after the parentheses of this operation.

Parameters

The UML models a parameter a bit differently from Java by listing the parameter name, followed by a colon and the parameter type in the parentheses after the operation name. The UML has its own data types similar to those of Java, but for simplicity, we'll use the Java data types. Account method setName (Fig. 3.1) has a String parameter named name, so Fig. 3.3 lists name : String between the parentheses following the method name.

3.2.5 Additional Notes on Class AccountTest

static Method main

In Chapter 2, each class we declared had one main method. Recall that main is *always* called automatically by the Java Virtual Machine (JVM) when you execute an app. You must call most other methods *explicitly* to tell them to perform their tasks. In Chapter 6, you'll learn that method toString is commonly invoked *implicitly*.

Lines 6–25 of Fig. 3.2 declare method main. A key part of enabling the JVM to locate and call method main to begin the app's execution is the static keyword (line 6), which indicates that main is a static method. A static method is special, because you can call it *without first creating an object of the class in which the method is declared*—in this case class AccountTest. We discuss static methods in detail in Chapter 6.

Notes on import Declarations

Notice the import declaration in Fig. 3.2 (line 3), which indicates to the compiler that the program uses class Scanner. As mentioned in Chapter 2, classes System and String are in package java.lang, which is *implicitly* imported into *every* Java program, so all programs can use that package's classes without explicitly importing them. Most other classes you'll use in Java programs must be imported *explicitly*.

There's a special relationship between classes that are compiled in the *same* directory, like classes `Account` and `AccountTest`. By default, such classes are considered to be in the *same* package—known as the **default package**. Classes in the same package are *implicitly imported* into the source-code files of other classes in that package. Thus, an `import` declaration is *not* required when one class in a package uses another in the same package—such as when class `AccountTest` uses class `Account`.

The `import` declaration in line 3 is *not* required if we refer to class `Scanner` throughout this file as `java.util.Scanner`, which includes the *full package name and class name*. This is known as the class's **fully qualified class name**. For example, line 8 of Fig. 3.2 also could be written as

```
java.util.Scanner input = new java.util.Scanner(System.in);
```

Software Engineering Observation 3.1

The Java compiler does not require import *declarations in a Java source-code file if the fully qualified class name is specified every time a class name is used. Most Java programmers prefer the more concise programming style enabled by* import *declarations.*

3.2.6 Software Engineering with `private` Instance Variables and `public` *set* and *get* Methods

Through the use of *set* and *get* methods, you can validate attempted modifications to `private` data and control how that data is presented to the caller—these are compelling software engineering benefits. We'll discuss this in more detail in Section 3.4.

If the instance variable were `public`, any **client** of the class—that is, any other class that calls the class's methods—could see the data and do whatever it wanted with it, including setting it to an *invalid* value.

You might think that even though a client of the class cannot directly access a `private` instance variable, the client can do whatever it wants with the variable through `public` *set* and *get* methods. You would think that you could peek at the `private` data any time with the `public` *get* method and that you could modify the `private` data at will through the `public` *set* method. But *set* methods can be programmed to validate their arguments and reject any attempts to *set* the data to bad values, such as a negative body temperature, a day in March out of the range 1 through 31, a product code not in the company's product catalog, etc. And a *get* method can present the data in a different form. For example, a `Grade` class might store a grade as an `int` between 0 and 100, but a `getGrade` method might return a letter grade as a `String`, such as `"A"` for grades between 90 and 100, `"B"` for grades between 80 and 89, etc. Tightly controlling the access to and presentation of `private` data can greatly reduce errors, while increasing the robustness and security of your programs.

Declaring instance variables with access modifier `private` is known as *information hiding*. When a program creates (instantiates) an object of class `Account`, variable `name` is *encapsulated* (hidden) in the object and can be accessed only by methods of the object's class.

Software Engineering Observation 3.2

Precede each instance variable and method declaration with an access modifier. Generally, instance variables should be declared private *and methods* public. *Later in the book, we'll discuss why you might want to declare a method* private.

*Conceptual View of an **Account** Object with Encapsulated Data*
You can think of an Account object as shown in Fig. 3.4. The private instance variable name is *hidden inside* the object (represented by the inner circle containing name) and *protected by an outer layer* of public methods (represented by the outer circle containing get-Name and setName). Any client code that needs to interact with the Account object can do so *only* by calling the public methods of the protective outer layer.

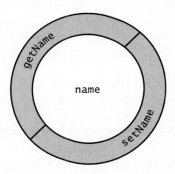

Fig. 3.4 | Conceptual view of an Account object with its encapsulated private instance variable name and protective layer of public methods.

3.3 Account Class: Initializing Objects with Constructors

As mentioned in Section 3.2, when an object of class Account (Fig. 3.1) is created, its String instance variable name is initialized to null by *default*. But what if you want to provide a name when you *create* an Account object?

Each class you declare can optionally provide a *constructor* with parameters that can be used to initialize an object of a class when the object is created. Java *requires* a constructor call for *every* object that's created, so this is the ideal point to initialize an object's instance variables. The next example enhances class Account (Fig. 3.5) with a constructor that can receive a name and use it to initialize instance variable name when an Account object is created (Fig. 3.6).

```
 1   // Fig. 3.5: Account.java
 2   // Account class with a constructor that initializes the name.
 3
 4   public class Account {
 5      private String name; // instance variable
 6
 7      // constructor initializes name with parameter name
 8      public Account(String name) { // constructor name is class name
 9         this.name = name;
10      }
11
```

Fig. 3.5 | Account class with a constructor that initializes the name. (Part 1 of 2.)

```
12      // method to set the name
13      public void setName(String name) {
14          this.name = name;
15      }
16
17      // method to retrieve the name
18      public String getName() {
19          return name;
20      }
21  }
```

Fig. 3.5 | Account class with a constructor that initializes the name. (Part 2 of 2.)

3.3.1 Declaring an Account Constructor for Custom Object Initialization

When you declare a class, you can provide your own constructor to specify *custom initialization* for objects of your class. For example, you might want to specify a name for an Account object when the object is created, as you'll see in line 8 of Fig. 3.6:

```
Account account1 = new Account("Jane Green");
```

In this case, the String argument "Jane Green" is passed to the Account object's constructor and used to initialize the name instance variable. The preceding statement requires that the class provide a constructor that takes only a String parameter. Figure 3.5 contains a modified Account class with such a constructor.

***Account* Constructor Declaration**
Lines 8–10 of Fig. 3.5 declare Account's constructor, which *must* have the *same name* as the class. A constructor's *parameter list* specifies that the constructor requires zero or more pieces of data to perform its task. Line 8 indicates that the constructor has exactly one parameter—a String called name. When you create a new Account object, you'll pass a person's name to the constructor's name parameter. The constructor will then assign the name parameter's value to the *instance variable* name (line 9).

Error-Prevention Tip 3.2
Even though it's possible to do so, do not call methods from constructors. We'll explain this in Chapter 10, Object-Oriented Programming: Polymorphism and Interfaces.

Parameter *name* of Class *Account*'s Constructor and Method setName
Recall from Section 3.2.1 that method parameters are local variables. In Fig. 3.5, the constructor and method setName both have a parameter called name. Although these parameters have the same identifier (name), the parameter in line 8 is a local variable of the constructor that's *not* visible to method setName, and the one in line 13 is a local variable of setName that's *not* visible to the constructor.

3.3.2 Class AccountTest: Initializing Account Objects When They're Created

The AccountTest program (Fig. 3.6) initializes two Account objects using the constructor. Line 8 creates and initializes the Account object account1. Keyword new requests memory from the system to store the Account object, then implicitly calls the class's constructor to *initialize* the object. The call is indicated by the parentheses after the class name, which contain the *argument* "Jane Green" that's used to initialize the new object's name. Line 8 assigns the new object to the variable account1. Line 9 repeats this process, passing the argument "John Blue" to initialize the name for account2. Lines 12–13 use each object's getName method to obtain the names and show that they were indeed initialized when the objects were *created*. The output shows *different* names, confirming that each Account maintains its *own copy* of the instance variable name.

```
1   // Fig. 3.6: AccountTest.java
2   // Using the Account constructor to initialize the name instance
3   // variable at the time each Account object is created.
4
5   public class AccountTest {
6      public static void main(String[] args) {
7         // create two Account objects
8         Account account1 = new Account("Jane Green");
9         Account account2 = new Account("John Blue");
10
11        // display initial value of name for each Account
12        System.out.printf("account1 name is: %s%n", account1.getName());
13        System.out.printf("account2 name is: %s%n", account2.getName());
14     }
15  }
```

```
account1 name is: Jane Green
account2 name is: John Blue
```

Fig. 3.6 | Using the Account constructor to initialize the name instance variable at the time each Account object is created.

Constructors Cannot Return Values
An important difference between constructors and methods is that *constructors cannot return values*, so they *cannot* specify a return type (not even void). Normally, constructors are declared public—later in the book we'll explain when to use private constructors.

Default Constructor
Recall that line 11 of Fig. 3.2

```
Account myAccount = new Account();
```

used new to create an Account object. The *empty* parentheses after "new Account" indicate a call to the class's **default constructor**—in any class that does *not* explicitly declare a constructor, the compiler provides a default constructor (which always has no parameters). When a class has only the default constructor, the class's instance variables are initialized to their *default values*. In Section 8.5, you'll learn that classes can have multiple constructors.

There's No Default Constructor in a Class That Declares a Constructor
If you declare a constructor for a class, the compiler will *not* create a *default constructor* for that class. In that case, you will not be able to create an Account object with the class in-

stance creation expression new Account() as we did in Fig. 3.2—unless the custom constructor you declare takes *no* parameters.

> **Software Engineering Observation 3.3**
> *Unless default initialization of your class's instance variables is acceptable, provide a custom constructor to ensure that your instance variables are properly initialized with meaningful values when each new object of your class is created.*

Adding the Constructor to Class *Account's UML Class Diagram*

The UML class diagram of Fig. 3.7 models class Account of Fig. 3.5, which has a constructor with a String name parameter. As with operations, the UML models constructors in the *third* compartment of a class diagram. To distinguish a constructor from the class's operations, the UML requires that the word "constructor" be enclosed in guillemets (« and ») and placed before the constructor's name. It's customary to list constructors *before* other operations in the third compartment.

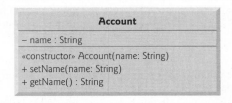

Fig. 3.7 | UML class diagram for Account class of Fig. 3.5.

3.4 Account Class with a Balance; Floating-Point Numbers

We now declare an Account class that maintains the *balance* of a bank account in addition to the name. Most account balances are not integers. So, class Account represents the account balance as a **floating-point number**—a number with a *decimal point*, such as 43.95, 0.0, –129.8873. [In Chapter 8, we'll begin representing monetary amounts precisely with class BigDecimal as you should do when writing industrial-strength monetary applications.]

Java provides two primitive types for storing floating-point numbers in memory— float and double. Variables of type **float** represent **single-precision floating-point numbers** and can hold up to *seven significant digits*. Variables of type **double** represent **double-precision floating-point numbers**. These require *twice* as much memory as float variables and can hold up to *15 significant digits*—about *double* the precision of float variables.

Most programmers represent floating-point numbers with type double. In fact, Java treats all floating-point numbers you type in a program's source code (such as 7.33 and 0.0975) as double values by default. Such values in the source code are known as **floating-point literals**. See Appendix D, Primitive Types, for the precise ranges of values for floats and doubles.

3.4.1 Account Class with a balance Instance Variable of Type double

Our next app contains a version of class Account (Fig. 3.8) that maintains as instance variables the name *and* the balance of a bank account. A typical bank services *many* accounts, each with its *own* balance, so line 7 declares an instance variable `balance` of type `double`. Every instance (i.e., object) of class `Account` contains its *own* copies of *both* the `name` and the `balance`.

```java
1   // Fig. 3.8: Account.java
2   // Account class with a double instance variable balance and a constructor
3   // and deposit method that perform validation.
4
5   public class Account {
6      private String name; // instance variable
7      private double balance; // instance variable
8
9      // Account constructor that receives two parameters
10     public Account(String name, double balance) {
11        this.name = name; // assign name to instance variable name
12
13        // validate that the balance is greater than 0.0; if it's not,
14        // instance variable balance keeps its default initial value of 0.0
15        if (balance > 0.0) { // if the balance is valid
16           this.balance = balance; // assign it to instance variable balance
17        }
18     }
19
20     // method that deposits (adds) only a valid amount to the balance
21     public void deposit(double depositAmount) {
22        if (depositAmount > 0.0) { // if the depositAmount is valid
23           balance = balance + depositAmount; // add it to the balance
24        }
25     }
26
27     // method returns the account balance
28     public double getBalance() {
29        return balance;
30     }
31
32     // method that sets the name
33     public void setName(String name) {
34        this.name = name;
35     }
36
37     // method that returns the name
38     public String getName() {
39        return name;
40     }
41  }
```

Fig. 3.8 | `Account` class with a `double` instance variable `balance` and a constructor and `deposit` method that perform validation.

Account Class Two-Parameter Constructor

The class has a *constructor* and four *methods*. It's common for someone opening an account to deposit money immediately, so the constructor (lines 10–18) now receives a second parameter—`balance` of type `double` that represents the *starting balance*. Lines 15–17 ensure that initialBalance is greater than 0.0. If so, the balance parameter's value is assigned to the instance variable balance. Otherwise, the instance variable balance remains at 0.0—its *default initial value*.

Account Class deposit Method

Method deposit (lines 21–25) does *not* return any data when it completes its task, so its return type is void. The method receives one parameter named depositAmount—a double value that's *added* to the instance variable balance *only* if the parameter value is *valid* (i.e., greater than zero). Line 23 first adds the current balance and depositAmount, forming a *temporary* sum which is *then* assigned to balance, *replacing* its prior value (recall that addition has a *higher* precedence than assignment). It's important to understand that the calculation on the right side of the assignment operator in line 23 does *not* modify the balance—that's why the assignment is necessary.

Account Class getBalance Method

Method getBalance (lines 28–30) allows *clients* of the class (i.e., other classes whose methods call the methods of this class) to obtain the value of a particular Account object's balance. The method specifies return type double and an *empty* parameter list.

Account's Methods Can All Use balance

Once again, lines 15, 16, 23 and 29 use the variable balance even though it was *not* declared in *any* of the methods. We can use balance in these methods because it's an *instance variable* of the class.

3.4.2 AccountTest Class to Use Class Account

Class AccountTest (Fig. 3.9) creates two Account objects (lines 7–8) and initializes them with a *valid* balance of 50.00 and an *invalid* balance of -7.53, respectively—for the purpose of our examples, we assume that balances must be greater than or equal to zero. The calls to method System.out.printf in lines 11–14 output the account names and balances, which are obtained by calling each Account's getName and getBalance methods.

```
 1   // Fig. 3.9: AccountTest.java
 2   // Inputting and outputting floating-point numbers with Account objects.
 3   import java.util.Scanner;
 4
 5   public class AccountTest {
 6      public static void main(String[] args) {
 7         Account account1 = new Account("Jane Green", 50.00);
 8         Account account2 = new Account("John Blue", -7.53);
 9
10         // display initial balance of each object
11         System.out.printf("%s balance: $%.2f%n",
12            account1.getName(), account1.getBalance());
13         System.out.printf("%s balance: $%.2f%n%n",
14            account2.getName(), account2.getBalance());
15
```

Fig. 3.9 | Inputting and outputting floating-point numbers with Account objects. (Part 1 of 2.)

```
16          // create a Scanner to obtain input from the command window
17          Scanner input = new Scanner(System.in);
18
19          System.out.print("Enter deposit amount for account1: "); // prompt
20          double depositAmount = input.nextDouble(); // obtain user input
21          System.out.printf("%nadding %.2f to account1 balance%n%n",
22             depositAmount);
23          account1.deposit(depositAmount); // add to account1's balance
24
25          // display balances
26          System.out.printf("%s balance: $%.2f%n",
27             account1.getName(), account1.getBalance());
28          System.out.printf("%s balance: $%.2f%n%n",
29             account2.getName(), account2.getBalance());
30
31          System.out.print("Enter deposit amount for account2: "); // prompt
32          depositAmount = input.nextDouble(); // obtain user input
33          System.out.printf("%nadding %.2f to account2 balance%n%n",
34             depositAmount);
35          account2.deposit(depositAmount); // add to account2 balance
36
37          // display balances
38          System.out.printf("%s balance: $%.2f%n",
39             account1.getName(), account1.getBalance());
40          System.out.printf("%s balance: $%.2f%n%n",
41             account2.getName(), account2.getBalance());
42      }
43   }
```

```
Jane Green balance: $50.00
John Blue balance: $0.00

Enter deposit amount for account1: 25.53

adding 25.53 to account1 balance

Jane Green balance: $75.53
John Blue balance: $0.00

Enter deposit amount for account2: 123.45

adding 123.45 to account2 balance

Jane Green balance: $75.53
John Blue balance: $123.45
```

Fig. 3.9 | Inputting and outputting floating-point numbers with Account objects. (Part 2 of 2.)

Displaying the Account Objects' Initial Balances
When method getBalance is called for account1 from line 12, the value of account1's balance is returned from line 29 of Fig. 3.8 and displayed by the System.out.printf statement (Fig. 3.9, lines 11–12). Similarly, when method getBalance is called for account2 from line 14, the value of the account2's balance is returned from line 29 of Fig. 3.8 and displayed by the System.out.printf statement (Fig. 3.9, lines 13–14). The

balance of account2 is initially 0.00, because the constructor rejected the attempt to start account2 with a *negative* balance, so the balance retains its default initial value.

Formatting Floating-Point Numbers for Display

Each of the balances is output by printf with the format specifier %.2f. The **%f format specifier** is used to output values of type float or double. The .2 between % and f represents the number of *decimal places* (2) that should be output to the *right* of the decimal point in the floating-point number—also known as the number's **precision**. Any floating-point value output with %.2f will be *rounded* to the *hundredths position*—for example, 123.457 would be rounded to 123.46 and 27.33379 would be rounded to 27.33.

Reading a Floating-Point Value from the User and Making a Deposit

Line 19 (Fig. 3.9) prompts the user to enter a deposit amount for account1. Line 20 declares *local* variable depositAmount to store each deposit amount entered by the user. Unlike *instance* variables (such as name and balance in class Account), *local* variables (like depositAmount in main) are *not* initialized by default, so they normally must be initialized explicitly. As you'll learn momentarily, variable depositAmount's initial value will be determined by the user's input.

> ### Error-Prevention Tip 3.3
> *The Java compiler issues a compilation error if you attempt to use the value of an uninitialized local variable. This helps you avoid dangerous execution-time logic errors. It's always better to get the errors out of your programs at compilation time rather than execution time.*

Line 20 obtains the input from the user by calling Scanner object input's **nextDouble** method, which returns a double value entered by the user. Lines 21–22 display the depositAmount. Line 23 calls object account1's deposit method with the depositAmount as the method's *argument*. When the method is called, the argument's value is assigned to the parameter depositAmount of method deposit (line 21 of Fig. 3.8); then method deposit adds that value to the balance. Lines 26–29 (Fig. 3.9) output the names and balances of both Accounts *again* to show that *only* account1's balance has changed.

Line 31 prompts the user to enter a deposit amount for account2. Line 32 obtains the input from the user by calling Scanner object input's nextDouble method. Lines 33–34 display the depositAmount. Line 35 calls object account2's deposit method with depositAmount as the method's *argument*; then method deposit adds that value to the balance. Finally, lines 38–41 output the names and balances of both Accounts *again* to show that *only* account2's balance has changed.

UML Class Diagram for Class Account

The UML class diagram in Fig. 3.10 concisely models class Account of Fig. 3.8. The diagram models in its *second* compartment the private attributes name of type String and balance of type double.

Class Account's *constructor* is modeled in the *third* compartment with parameters name of type String and initialBalance of type double. The class's four public methods also are modeled in the *third* compartment—operation deposit with a depositAmount parameter of type double, operation getBalance with a return type of double, operation setName with a name parameter of type String and operation getName with a return type of String.

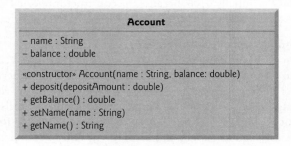

Fig. 3.10 | UML class diagram for `Account` class of Fig. 3.8.

3.5 Primitive Types vs. Reference Types

Java's types are divided into primitive types and **reference types**. In Chapter 2, you worked with variables of type `int`—one of the primitive types. The other primitive types are `boolean`, `byte`, `char`, `short`, `long`, `float` and `double`—these are summarized in Appendix D. All nonprimitive types are *reference types*, so classes, which specify the types of objects, are reference types.

A primitive-type variable can hold exactly *one* value of its declared type at a time. For example, an `int` variable can store one integer at a time. When another value is assigned to that variable, the new value replaces the previous one—which is *lost*.

Recall that local variables are *not* initialized by default. Primitive-type instance variables *are* initialized by default—instance variables of types `byte`, `char`, `short`, `int`, `long`, `float` and `double` are initialized to 0, and variables of type `boolean` are initialized to `false`. You can specify your own initial value for a primitive-type variable by assigning the variable a value in its declaration, as in

```
private int numberOfStudents = 10;
```

Programs use variables of reference types (normally called **references**) to store the *locations* of objects. Such a variable is said to **refer to an object** in the program. *Objects* that are referenced may each contain *many* instance variables. Line 8 of Fig. 3.2:

```
Scanner input = new Scanner(System.in);
```

creates an object of class `Scanner`, then assigns to the variable `input` a *reference* to that Scanner object. Line 11 of Fig. 3.2:

```
Account myAccount = new Account();
```

creates an object of class `Account`, then assigns to the variable `myAccount` a *reference* to that Account object. *Reference-type instance variables, if not explicitly initialized, are initialized by default to the value `null`*—which represents a "reference to nothing." That's why the first call to `getName` in line 14 of Fig. 3.2 returns `null`—the value of `name` has *not* yet been set, so the *default initial value* `null` is returned.

To call methods on an object, you need a reference to the object. In Fig. 3.2, the statements in method `main` use the variable `myAccount` to call methods `getName` (lines 14 and 24) and `setName` (line 19) to interact with the `Account` object. Primitive-type variables do *not* refer to objects, so such variables *cannot* be used to call methods.

3.6 Wrap-Up

In this chapter, you learned how to create your own classes and methods, create objects of those classes and call methods of those objects to perform useful actions. You declared instance variables of a class to maintain data for each object of the class, and you declared your own methods to operate on that data. You called a method to tell it to perform its task, passed information to a method as arguments whose values are assigned to the method's parameters and received the value returned by a method. You saw the difference between a local variable of a method and an instance variable of a class, and that only instance variables are initialized automatically. You used a class's constructor to specify the initial values for an object's instance variables. You saw how to create UML class diagrams that model visually the methods, attributes and constructors of classes. Finally, you used floating-point numbers (numbers with decimal points). [In Chapter 8, we'll begin representing monetary amounts precisely with class `BigDecimal`.] In the next chapter we introduce control statements, which specify the order in which a program's actions are performed.

4

Control Statements: Part 1; Assignment, ++ and -- Operators

Objectives

In this chapter you'll:

- Use the if and if...else selection statements to choose between alternative actions.
- Use the while iteration statement to execute statements in a program repeatedly.
- Use counter-controlled iteration and sentinel-controlled iteration.
- Use the compound assignment operator and the increment and decrement operators.
- See that the primitive data types are portable.

4.1 Introduction

In this chapter, we discuss Java's `if` statement in additional detail and introduce the `if...else` and `while` statements. We present the compound assignment operator and the increment and decrement operators. Finally, we consider the portability of Java's primitive types.

4.2 Control Structures

During the 1960s, it became clear that the indiscriminate use of transfers of control was the root of much difficulty experienced by software development groups. The blame was pointed at the **goto statement** (used in most programming languages of the time), which allows you to specify a transfer of control to one of a wide range of destinations in a program. The term **structured programming** became almost synonymous with "`goto` elimination." [*Note:* Java does *not* have a `goto` statement; however, the word `goto` is *reserved* by Java and should *not* be used as an identifier in programs.]

Bohm and Jacopini's work demonstrated that all programs could be written in terms of only three control structures—the **sequence structure**, the **selection structure** and the **repetition structure**.[1] When we introduce Java's control-structure implementations, we'll refer to them in the terminology of the *Java Language Specification* as "control statements."

4.2.1 Sequence Structure in Java

The sequence structure is built into Java. Unless directed otherwise, the computer executes Java statements one after the other in the order in which they're written—that is, in sequence. The UML **activity diagram** in Fig. 4.1 illustrates a typical sequence structure in which two calculations are performed in order. Java lets you have as many actions as you want in sequence. As we'll soon see, anywhere a single action may be placed, we may place several actions in sequence.

1. C. Bohm, and G. Jacopini, "Flow Diagrams, Turing Machines, and Languages with Only Two Formation Rules," *Communications of the ACM*, Vol. 9, No. 5, May 1966, pp. 336–371.

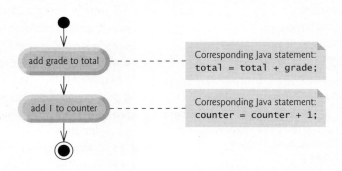

Fig. 4.1 | Sequence-structure activity diagram.

A UML activity diagram models the **workflow** (also called the **activity**) of a portion of a software system. Such workflows may include a portion of an algorithm, like the sequence structure in Fig. 4.1. Activity diagrams are composed of symbols, such as **action-state symbols** (rectangles with their left and right sides replaced with outward arcs), **diamonds** and **small circles**. These symbols are connected by **transition arrows**, which represent the *flow of the activity*—that is, the *order* in which the actions should occur. We use the UML in this chapter and Chapter 5 to show control flow in control statements.

Consider the activity diagram in Fig. 4.1. It contains two **action states**, each containing an **action expression**—"add grade to total" or "add 1 to counter"—that specifies a particular action to perform. Other actions might include calculations or input/output operations. The arrows represent **transitions**, which indicate the order in which the actions represented by the action states occur. The program that implements the activities illustrated by the diagram in Fig. 4.1 first adds grade to total, then adds 1 to counter.

The **solid circle** at the top of the activity diagram represents the **initial state**—the *beginning* of the workflow *before* the program performs the modeled actions. The **solid circle surrounded by a hollow circle** at the bottom of the diagram represents the **final state**—the *end* of the workflow *after* the program performs its actions.

Figure 4.1 also includes rectangles with the upper-right corners folded over. These are UML **notes** (like comments in Java)—explanatory remarks that describe the purpose of symbols in the diagram. Figure 4.1 uses notes to show the Java code associated with each action state. A **dotted line** connects each note with the element it describes. Activity diagrams normally do *not* show the corresponding Java code. We do this here to illustrate how the diagram relates to Java code. For more information on the UML, see our object-oriented design case study (Chapters 25–26) or visit http://www.uml.org.

4.2.2 Selection Statements in Java

Java has three types of **selection statements** (discussed in this chapter and Chapter 5). The *if statement* either performs (selects) an action, if a condition is *true*, or skips it, if the condition is *false*. The *if...else statement* performs an action if a condition is *true* and performs a different action if the condition is *false*. The *switch statement* (Chapter 5) performs one of *many* different actions, depending on the value of an expression.

The if statement is a **single-selection statement** because it selects or ignores a *single* action (or, as we'll soon see, a *single group of actions*). The if...else statement is called a **double-selection statement** because it selects between *two different actions* (or *groups of actions*). The switch statement is called a **multiple-selection statement** because it selects among *many different actions* (or *groups of actions*).

4.2.3 Iteration Statements in Java

Java provides four **iteration statements** (also called **repetition statements** or **looping statements**) that enable programs to perform statements repeatedly as long as a condition (called the **loop-continuation condition**) remains *true*. The iteration statements are while, do...while, for and enhanced for. (Chapter 5 presents the do...while and for statements and Chapter 7 presents the enhanced for statement.) The while and for statements perform the action (or group of actions) in their bodies zero or more times—if the loop-continuation condition is initially *false*, the action (or group of actions) will *not* execute. The do...while statement performs the action (or group of actions) in its body *one or more* times. The words if, else, switch, while, do and for are Java keywords. A complete list of Java keywords appears in Appendix C.

4.2.4 Summary of Control Statements in Java

Java has only three kinds of control structures, which from this point forward we refer to as *control statements*: the *sequence statement*, *selection statements* (three types) and *iteration statements* (four types). Every program is formed by combining as many of these statements as is appropriate for the algorithm the program implements. We can model each control statement as an activity diagram. Like Fig. 4.1, each diagram contains an initial state and a final state that represent a control statement's entry point and exit point, respectively. **Single-entry/single-exit control statements** make it easy to build programs—we simply connect the exit point of one to the entry point of the next. We call this **control-statement stacking**. There's only one other way in which control statements may be connected—**control-statement nesting**—in which one control statement appears *inside* another. Thus, algorithms in Java programs are constructed from only three kinds of control statements, combined in only two ways. This is the essence of simplicity.

4.3 if Single-Selection Statement

Programs use selection statements to choose among alternative courses of action. For example, suppose that the passing grade on an exam is 60. The statement

```
if (studentGrade >= 60) {
    System.out.println("Passed");
}
```

determines whether the *condition* studentGrade >= **60** is *true*. If so, "Passed" is printed, and the next statement in order is performed. If the condition is *false*, the printing statement is ignored, and the next statement in order is performed. The indentation of the second line of this selection statement is optional, but recommended, because it emphasizes the inherent structure of structured programs.

UML Activity Diagram for an `if` *Statement*

Figure 4.2 illustrates the single-selection `if` statement. This figure contains the most important symbol in an activity diagram—the *diamond*, or **decision symbol**, which indicates that a *decision* is to be made. The workflow continues along a path determined by the symbol's associated **guard conditions**, which can be *true* or *false*. Each transition arrow emerging from a decision symbol has a guard condition (specified in square brackets next to the arrow). If a guard condition is *true*, the workflow enters the action state to which the transition arrow points. In Fig. 4.2, if the grade is greater than or equal to 60, the program prints "Passed" then transitions to the activity's final state. If the grade is less than 60, the program immediately transitions to the final state without displaying a message.

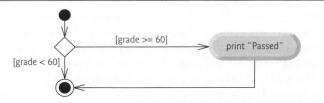

Fig. 4.2 | `if` single-selection statement UML activity diagram.

The `if` statement is a single-entry/single-exit control statement. The activity diagrams for the remaining control statements also contain initial states, transition arrows, action states that indicate actions to perform, decision symbols (with associated guard conditions) that indicate decisions to be made, and final states.

4.4 `if...else` Double-Selection Statement

The `if` single-selection statement performs an indicated action only when the condition is `true`; otherwise, the action is skipped. The **`if...else` double-selection statement** allows you to specify an action to perform when the condition is *true* and another action when the condition is *false*. For example, the statement

```
if (grade >= 60) {
   System.out.println("Passed");
}
else {
   System.out.println("Failed");
}
```

prints "Passed" if the student's grade is greater than or equal to 60, but prints "Failed" if it's less than 60. In either case, after printing occurs, the next statement in sequence is performed.

UML Activity Diagram for an `if...else` *Statement*

Figure 4.3 illustrates the flow of control in the `if...else` statement. Once again, the symbols in the UML activity diagram (besides the initial state, transition arrows and final state) represent action states and decisions.

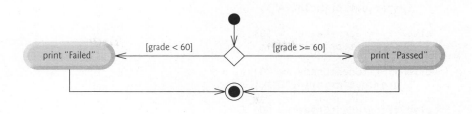

Fig. 4.3 | if...else double-selection statement UML activity diagram.

4.4.1 Nested if...else Statements

A program can test multiple cases by placing if...else statements inside other if...else statements to create **nested if...else statements**. For example, the following nested if...else prints A for exam grades greater than or equal to 90, B for grades 80 to 89, C for grades 70 to 79, D for grades 60 to 69 and F for all other grades:

```java
if (studentGrade >= 90) {
   System.out.println("A");
}
else {
   if (studentGrade >= 80) {
      System.out.println("B");
   }
   else {
      if (studentGrade >= 70) {
         System.out.println("C");
      }
      else {
         if (studentGrade >= 60) {
            System.out.println("D");
         }
         else {
            System.out.println("F");
         }
      }
   }
}
```

Error-Prevention Tip 4.1

In a nested if...else statement, ensure that you test for all possible cases.

If variable studentGrade is greater than or equal to 90, the first four conditions in the nested if...else statement will be true, but only the statement in the if part of the first if...else statement will execute. After that statement executes, the else part of the "outermost" if...else statement is skipped. The preceding nested if...else statement also can be written as

```
        if (studentGrade >= 90) {
            System.out.println("A");
        }
        else if (studentGrade >= 80) {
            System.out.println("B");
        }
        else if (studentGrade >= 70) {
            System.out.println("C");
        }
        else if (studentGrade >= 60) {
            System.out.println("D");
        }
        else {
            System.out.println("F");
        }
```

The two forms are identical except for the spacing and indentation, which the compiler ignores. The latter form avoids deep indentation of the code to the right. Such indentation often leaves little room on a line of source code, forcing lines to be split.

4.4.2 Dangling-else Problem

We always enclose control statement bodies in braces ({ and }). This avoids a logic error called the "dangling-else" problem.

4.4.3 Blocks

The if statement normally expects only *one* statement in its body. To include *several* statements in the body of an if (or the body of an else for an if...else statement), enclose the statements in braces. Statements contained in braces (such as a method's body) form a **block**. A block can be placed anywhere in a method that a single statement can be placed.

The following example includes a block of multiple statements in the else part of an if...else statement:

```
        if (grade >= 60) {
            System.out.println("Passed");
        }
        else {
            System.out.println("Failed");
            System.out.println("You must take this course again.");
        }
```

In this case, if grade is less than 60, the program executes *both* statements in the body of the else and prints

```
Failed
You must take this course again.
```

Note the braces surrounding the two statements in the else clause. These braces are important. Without the braces, the statement

```
System.out.println("You must take this course again.");
```

would be outside the body of the else part of the if...else statement and would execute *regardless* of whether the grade was less than 60.

Just as a block can be placed anywhere a single statement can be placed, it's also possible to have an empty statement. Recall from Section 2.7 that the empty statement is represented by placing a semicolon (;) where a statement would normally be.

Common Programming Error 4.1

Placing a semicolon after the condition in an if or if...else statement leads to a logic error in single-selection if statements and a syntax error in double-selection if...else statements (when the if-part contains an actual body statement).

4.4.4 Conditional Operator (?:)

Java provides the **conditional operator (?:)** that can be used in place of simple if...else statements. This can make your code shorter and clearer. The conditional operator is the only **ternary operator** (i.e., it takes *three* operands). Together, the operands and the ?: symbol form a **conditional expression.** The first operand (to the left of the ?) is a **boolean expression** (i.e., a *condition* that evaluates to a boolean value—**true** or **false**), the second operand (between the ? and :) is the value of the conditional expression if the condition is true and the third operand (to the right of the :) is the value of the conditional expression if the condition is false. For example, the following statement prints the value of println's conditional-expression argument:

```
System.out.println(studentGrade >= 60 ? "Passed" : "Failed");
```

The conditional expression in this statement evaluates to "Passed" if the boolean expression studentGrade >= 60 is true and to "Failed" if it's false. Thus, this statement with the conditional operator performs essentially the same function as the if...else statement shown earlier in this section. The precedence of the conditional operator is low, so the entire conditional expression is normally placed in parentheses. Conditional expressions can be used as parts of larger expressions where if...else statements cannot.

Error-Prevention Tip 4.2

Use expressions of the same type for the second and third operands of the ?: operator to avoid subtle errors.

4.5 while Iteration Statement

An iteration statement specifies that a program should repeat an action while some condition remains *true*. As an example of Java's **while iteration statement**, consider a program segment that finds the first power of 3 larger than 100. After the following while statement executes, product contains the result:

```
int product = 3;

while (product <= 100) {
   product = 3 * product;
}
```

Each iteration of the while statement multiplies product by 3, so product takes on the values 9, 27, 81 and 243 successively. When product becomes 243, the condition product <= 100 becomes false. This terminates the iteration, so the final value of product is 243.

At this point, program execution continues with the next statement after the while statement.

Common Programming Error 4.2

*Not providing in the body of a while statement an action that eventually causes the condition in the while to become false normally results in an **infinite loop**.*

UML Activity Diagram for a while Statement

The UML activity diagram in Fig. 4.4 illustrates the flow of control in the preceding while statement. Once again, the symbols in the diagram (besides the initial state, transition arrows, a final state and three notes) represent an action state and a decision. This diagram introduces the UML's **merge symbol**. The UML represents both the merge symbol and the decision symbol as diamonds. The merge symbol joins two flows of activity into one. In this diagram, the merge symbol joins the transitions from the initial state and from the action state, so they both flow into the decision that determines whether the loop should begin (or continue) executing.

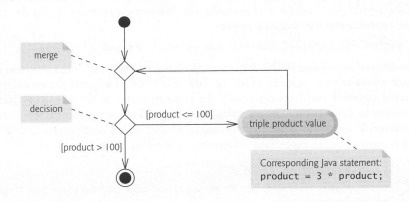

Fig. 4.4 | while iteration statement UML activity diagram.

The decision and merge symbols can be distinguished by the number of "incoming" and "outgoing" transition arrows. A decision symbol has one transition arrow pointing to the diamond and two or more pointing out from it to indicate possible transitions from that point. In addition, each transition arrow pointing out of a decision symbol has a guard condition next to it. A merge symbol has two or more transition arrows pointing to the diamond and only one pointing from the diamond, to indicate multiple activity flows merging to continue the activity. *None* of the transition arrows associated with a merge symbol has a guard condition.

Figure 4.4 clearly shows the iteration of the while statement discussed earlier in this section. The transition arrow emerging from the action state points back to the merge, from which program flow transitions back to the decision that's tested at the beginning of each iteration of the loop. The loop continues to execute until the guard condition product > 100 becomes true. Then the while statement exits (reaches its final state), and control passes to the next statement in sequence in the program.

4.6 Counter-Controlled Iteration

Consider the following problem statement:

> *A class of ten students took a quiz. The grades (integers in the range 0–100) for this quiz are available to you. Determine the class average on the quiz.*

The class average is equal to the sum of the grades divided by the number of students. The program for solving this problem must input each grade, keep track of the total of all grades input, perform the averaging calculation and print the result.

Implementing Counter-Controlled Iteration

ClassAverage's main method (Fig. 4.5) implements counter-controlled class-averaging—it allows the user to enter 10 grades, then calculates and displays the average.

```java
1   // Fig. 4.5: ClassAverage.java
2   // Solving the class-average problem using counter-controlled iteration.
3   import java.util.Scanner; // program uses class Scanner
4
5   public class ClassAverage {
6      public static void main(String[] args) {
7         // create Scanner to obtain input from command window
8         Scanner input = new Scanner(System.in);
9
10        // initialization phase
11        int total = 0;  // initialize sum of grades entered by the user
12        int gradeCounter = 1; // initialize # of grade to be entered next
13
14        // processing phase uses counter-controlled iteration
15        while (gradeCounter <= 10) { // loop 10 times
16           System.out.print("Enter grade: "); // prompt
17           int grade = input.nextInt(); // input next grade
18           total = total + grade; // add grade to total
19           gradeCounter = gradeCounter + 1; // increment counter by 1
20        }
21
22        // termination phase
23        int average = total / 10; // integer division yields integer result
24
25        // display total and average of grades
26        System.out.printf("%nTotal of all 10 grades is %d%n", total);
27        System.out.printf("Class average is %d%n", average);
28     }
29  }
```

```
Enter grade: 67
Enter grade: 78
Enter grade: 89
Enter grade: 67
Enter grade: 87
Enter grade: 98
Enter grade: 93
```

Fig. 4.5 | Solving the class-average problem using counter-controlled iteration. (Part 1 of 2.)

```
Enter grade: 85
Enter grade: 82
Enter grade: 100

Total of all 10 grades is 846
Class average is 84
```

Fig. 4.5 | Solving the class-average problem using counter-controlled iteration. (Part 2 of 2.)

Local Variables in Method `main`

Line 8 declares and initializes `Scanner` variable `input`, which is used to read values entered by the user. Lines 11, 12, 17 and 23 declare local variables `total`, `gradeCounter`, `grade` and `average`, respectively, to be of type `int`. Variable `grade` stores the user input.

These declarations appear in the body of method `main`. Variables declared in a method body are local variables and can be used only from the line of their declaration to the closing right brace of the block in which they're declared. A local variable's declaration must appear *before* the variable is used in that method. A local variable cannot be accessed outside the method in which it's declared. Variable `grade`, declared in the body of the `while` loop, can be used only in that block.

Initialization Phase: Initializing Variables `total` *and* `gradeCounter`

The assignments (in lines 11–12) initialize `total` to 0 and `gradeCounter` to 1. These initializations occur *before* the variables are used in calculations.

Common Programming Error 4.3

Using the value of a local variable before it's initialized results in a compilation error. All local variables must be initialized before their values are used in expressions.

Processing Phase: Reading 10 Grades from the User

Line 15 indicates that the `while` statement should continue looping (also called **iterating**) as long as `gradeCounter`'s value is less than or equal to 10. While this condition remains *true*, the `while` statement repeatedly executes the statements between the braces that delimit its body (lines 15–20).

Line 16 displays the prompt `"Enter grade: "`. Line 17 reads the grade entered by the user and assigns it to variable `grade`. Then line 18 adds the new `grade` entered by the user to the `total` and assigns the result to `total`, which replaces its previous value.

Line 19 adds 1 to `gradeCounter` to indicate that the program processed a grade and is ready to input the next grade. Incrementing `gradeCounter` eventually causes it to exceed 10. Then the loop terminates, because its condition (line 15) becomes *false*.

Termination Phase: Calculating and Displaying the Class Average

When the loop terminates, line 23 performs the averaging calculation and assigns its result to the variable `average`. Line 26 uses `System.out`'s `printf` method to display the text `"Total of all 10 grades is "` followed by variable `total`'s value. Line 27 then uses `printf` to display the text `"Class average is "` followed by variable `average`'s value. When execution reaches line 28, the program terminates.

Notice that this example contains only one class, with method `main` performing all the work. In this chapter and in Chapter 3, you've seen examples consisting of two classes—

one containing instance variables and methods that perform tasks using those variables and one containing method `main`, which creates an object of the other class and calls its methods. Occasionally, when it does not make sense to try to create a reusable class to demonstrate a concept, we'll place the program's statements entirely within a single class's `main` method.

Notes on Integer Division and Truncation

The averaging calculation performed by method `main` produces an integer result. The program's output indicates that the sum of the grade values in the sample execution is 846, which, when divided by 10, should yield the floating-point number 84.6. However, the result of the calculation `total / 10` (line 23 of Fig. 4.5) is the integer 84, because `total` and 10 are both integers. Dividing two integers results in **integer division**—any fractional part of the result is **truncated** (i.e., *lost*). In the next section we'll see how to obtain a floating-point result from the averaging calculation.

> **Common Programming Error 4.4**
> *Assuming that integer division rounds (rather than truncates) can lead to incorrect results. For example, 7 ÷ 4, which yields 1.75 in conventional arithmetic, truncates to 1 in integer arithmetic, rather than rounding to 2.*

A Note about Arithmetic Overflow

In Fig. 4.5, line 18

```
total = total + grade; // add grade to total
```

added each `grade` entered by the user to the `total`. Even this simple statement has a *potential* problem—adding the integers could result in a value that's *too large* to store in an `int` variable. This is known as **arithmetic overflow** and causes *undefined behavior*, which can lead to unintended results, as discussed at

```
http://en.wikipedia.org/wiki/Integer_overflow#Security_ramifications
```

Figure 2.7's `Addition` program had the same issue in line 17, which calculated the sum of two `int` values entered by the user:

```
int sum = number1 + number2; // add numbers, then store total in sum
```

The maximum and minimum values that can be stored in an `int` variable are represented by the constants `Integer.MIN_VALUE` and `Integer.MAX_VALUE`, respectively. There are similar constants for the other integral types and for floating-point types. Each primitive type has a corresponding class type in package `java.lang`. You can see the values of these constants in each class's online documentation. The online documentation for class `Integer` is located at:

```
http://docs.oracle.com/javase/8/docs/api/java/lang/Integer.html
```

It's considered a good practice to ensure, *before* you perform arithmetic calculations like those in line 18 of Fig. 4.5 and line 17 of Fig. 2.7, that they will *not* overflow. The code for doing this is shown on the CERT website:

```
http://www.securecoding.cert.org
```

Just search for guideline "NUM00-J." In industrial-strength code, you should perform checks like these for *all* calculations.

A Deeper Look at Receiving User Input

Whenever a program receives input from the user, various problems might occur. For example, in line 17 of Fig. 4.5

```
int grade = input.nextInt(); // input next grade
```

we assume the user will enter an integer grade in the range 0 to 100. However, the person entering a grade could enter an integer less than 0, an integer greater than 100, an integer outside the range of values that can be stored in an int variable, a number containing a decimal point or a value containing letters or special symbols that's not even an integer.

To ensure that inputs are valid, industrial-strength programs must test for all possible erroneous cases. A program that inputs grades should **validate** the grades by using **range checking** to ensure that they are values from 0 to 100. You can then ask the user to reenter any value that's out of range. If a program requires inputs from a specific set of values (e.g., nonsequential product codes), you can ensure that each input matches a value in the set.

4.7 Sentinel-Controlled Iteration

Let's generalize Section 4.6's class-average problem. Consider the following problem:

> *Develop a class-averaging program that processes grades for an arbitrary number of students each time it's run.*

In the previous class-average example, the problem statement specified the number of students, so the number of grades (10) was known in advance. In this example, no indication is given of how many grades the user will enter during the program's execution. The program must process an arbitrary number of grades.

One way to solve this problem is to use a special value called a **sentinel value** (also called a **signal value**, a **dummy value** or a **flag value**) to indicate "end of data entry." The user enters grades until all legitimate grades have been entered. The user then types the sentinel value to indicate that no more grades will be entered. **Sentinel-controlled iteration** is often called **indefinite iteration** because the number of iterations is *not* known before the loop begins executing.

Clearly, a sentinel value must be chosen that cannot be confused with an acceptable input value. Grades on a quiz are nonnegative integers, so –1 is an acceptable sentinel value for this problem. Thus, a run of the class-average program might process a stream of inputs such as 95, 96, 75, 74, 89 and –1. The program would then compute and print the class average for the grades 95, 96, 75, 74 and 89; since –1 is the sentinel value, it should *not* enter into the averaging calculation.

Implementing Sentinel-Controlled Iteration

In Fig. 4.6, method main implements sentinel-controlled class averaging. Although each grade is an integer, the averaging calculation is likely to produce a number with a *decimal point*—in other words, a real (floating-point) number. The type int cannot represent such a number, so this class uses type double to do so. The while statement (lines 20–27) is followed in sequence by an if...else statement (lines 31–42). Much of the code in this program is identical to that in Fig. 4.5, so we concentrate on the new concepts.

```java
 1  // Fig. 4.6: ClassAverage.java
 2  // Solving the class-average problem using sentinel-controlled iteration.
 3  import java.util.Scanner; // program uses class Scanner
 4
 5  public class ClassAverage {
 6     public static void main(String[] args) {
 7        // create Scanner to obtain input from command window
 8        Scanner input = new Scanner(System.in);
 9
10        // initialization phase
11        int total = 0; // initialize sum of grades
12        int gradeCounter = 0; // initialize # of grades entered so far
13
14        // processing phase
15        // prompt for input and read grade from user
16        System.out.print("Enter grade or -1 to quit: ");
17        int grade = input.nextInt();
18
19        // loop until sentinel value read from user
20        while (grade != -1) {
21           total = total + grade; // add grade to total
22           gradeCounter = gradeCounter + 1; // increment counter
23
24           // prompt for input and read next grade from user
25           System.out.print("Enter grade or -1 to quit: ");
26           grade = input.nextInt();
27        }
28
29        // termination phase
30        // if user entered at least one grade...
31        if (gradeCounter != 0) {
32           // use number with decimal point to calculate average of grades
33           double average = (double) total / gradeCounter;
34
35           // display total and average (with two digits of precision)
36           System.out.printf("%nTotal of the %d grades entered is %d%n",
37              gradeCounter, total);
38           System.out.printf("Class average is %.2f%n", average);
39        }
40        else { // no grades were entered, so output appropriate message
41           System.out.println("No grades were entered");
42        }
43     }
44  }
```

```
Enter grade or -1 to quit: 97
Enter grade or -1 to quit: 88
Enter grade or -1 to quit: 72
Enter grade or -1 to quit: -1

Total of the 3 grades entered is 257
Class average is 85.67
```

Fig. 4.6 | Solving the class-average problem using sentinel-controlled iteration.

Program Logic for Sentinel-Controlled Iteration vs. Counter-Controlled Iteration
Line 12 initializes gradeCounter to 0, because no grades have been entered yet. Remember
that this program uses *sentinel-controlled iteration* to input the grades. To keep an accurate
record of the number of grades entered, the program increments gradeCounter only when
the user enters a valid grade.

Compare the logic for sentinel-controlled iteration used here with that for counter-
controlled iteration in Fig. 4.5. In counter-controlled iteration, the while statement (lines
15–20 of Fig. 4.5) reads a value from the user for the specified number of iterations. In
sentinel-controlled iteration, the program reads the first value (lines 16–17 of Fig. 4.6)
before reaching the while. This value determines whether the program's flow of control
should enter the while's body. If the condition is false, the user entered the sentinel
value, so the while's body does not execute (i.e., no grades were entered). If, on the other
hand, the condition is true, the body executes, and the loop adds the grade value to the
total and increments the gradeCounter (lines 21–22). Next, lines 25–26 *in the loop body*
input another value from the user. Then, program control reaches the while's closing right
brace (line 27), so execution continues by testing the while's condition (line 20), using the
most recent grade input by the user. The value of grade is always input from the user
immediately before the program tests the while condition, so the program can determine
whether the value just input is the sentinel value *before* processing that value (i.e., adds it
to the total). If the sentinel value is input, the loop terminates, and the program does not
add −1 to the total.

Good Programming Practice 4.1

In a sentinel-controlled loop, prompts should remind the user of the sentinel.

After the loop terminates, the if...else statement at lines 31–42 executes. The condition at line 31 determines whether any grades were input. If none were input, the else
part (lines 40–42) of the if...else statement executes and displays the message "No
grades were entered" and the program terminates.

Error-Prevention Tip 4.3

*When performing division (/) or remainder (%) calculations in which the right operand
could be zero, test for this and handle it (e.g., display an error message) rather than allowing the error to occur.*

Explicitly and Implicitly Converting Between Primitive Types
If at least one grade was entered, line 33 of Fig. 4.6 calculates the average of the grades.
Recall from Fig. 4.5 that integer division yields an integer result. Even though variable
average is declared as a double, if we had written the averaging calculation as

```
double average = total / gradeCounter;
```

it would lose the fractional part of the quotient *before* the result of the division is assigned
to average. This occurs because total and gradeCounter are *both* integers, and integer
division yields an integer result.

Most averages are not whole numbers (e.g., 0, −22 and 1024). So, we calculate the class
average in this example as a floating-point number. To perform a floating-point calculation

with integer values, we must *temporarily* treat these values as floating-point numbers in the calculation. Java provides the **unary cast operator** to accomplish this task. Line 33 of Fig. 4.6 uses the **(double)** cast operator to create a *temporary* floating-point copy of its operand total (which appears to the operator's right). Using a cast operator in this manner is called **explicit conversion** or **type casting**. The value stored in total is still an integer.

The calculation now consists of a floating-point value (the temporary double copy of total) divided by the integer gradeCounter. Java can evaluate only arithmetic expressions in which the operands' types are *identical*. To ensure this, Java performs an operation called **promotion** (or **implicit conversion**) on selected operands. For example, in an expression containing int and double values, the int values are promoted to double values for use in the expression. In this example, the value of gradeCounter is promoted to type double, then floating-point division is performed and the result of the calculation is assigned to average. As long as the (double) cast operator is applied to *any* variable in the calculation, the calculation will yield a double result. We say more about primitive types in Section 4.11. You'll see more about the promotion rules in Section 6.6.

Common Programming Error 4.5

A cast operator can be used to convert between primitive numeric types, such as int and double, and between related reference types (as we discuss in Chapter 10, Object-Oriented Programming: Polymorphism and Interfaces). Casting to the wrong type may cause compilation errors or runtime errors.

You form a cast operator by placing parentheses around any type's name. The operator is a **unary operator**—it takes only one operand. Java also has unary plus (+) and minus (–) operators, so you can write expressions like –7 or +5. Cast operators associate from *right to left* and have the same precedence as other unary operators. This precedence is one level higher than that of the **multiplicative operators** *, / and %. (See the operator precedence chart in Appendix A.) We indicate the cast operator with the notation (*type*) in our precedence charts, to indicate that any type name can be used to form a cast operator.

Line 38 of Fig. 4.6 displays the class average. In this example, we display the class average *rounded* to the nearest hundredth. The format specifier %.2f in printf's format control string indicates that variable average's value should be displayed with two digits of precision to the right of the decimal point—indicated by .2 in the format specifier. The three grades entered during the sample execution total 257, which yields the average 85.666666.... Method printf uses the precision in the format specifier to round the value to the specified number of digits. In this program, the average is rounded to the hundredths position and is displayed as 85.67.

Floating-Point Number Precision

Floating-point numbers are not always 100% precise, but they have numerous applications. For example, when we speak of a "normal" body temperature of 98.6, we do not need to be precise to a large number of digits. When we read the temperature on a thermometer as 98.6, it may actually be 98.5999473210643. Calling this number simply 98.6 is fine for most applications involving body temperatures.

Floating-point numbers often arise as a result of division, such as in this example's class-average calculation. In conventional arithmetic, when we divide 10 by 3, the result is 3.3333333..., with the sequence of 3s repeating infinitely. The computer allocates only a fixed amount of space to hold such a value, so clearly the stored floating-point value can be only an approximation.

Owing to the imprecise nature of floating-point numbers, type `double` is preferred over type `float`, because `double` variables can represent floating-point numbers more accurately. For this reason, we primarily use type `double` throughout the book. In some applications, the precision of `float` and `double` variables will be inadequate. For precise floating-point numbers (such as those required by monetary calculations), Java provides class `BigDecimal` (package `java.math`), which we'll discuss in Chapter 8.

Common Programming Error 4.6

Using floating-point numbers in a manner that assumes they're represented precisely can lead to incorrect results.

4.8 Nesting Different Control Statements

We've seen that control statements can be stacked on top of one another (in sequence). In this case study, we examine the only other structured way control statements can be connected—namely, by **nesting** one control statement within another.

Consider the following problem statement:

> *A college offers a course that prepares students for the state licensing exam for real-estate brokers. Last year, ten of the students who completed this course took the exam. The college wants to know how well its students did on the exam. You've been asked to write a program to summarize the results. You've been given a list of these 10 students. Next to each name is written a 1 if the student passed the exam or a 2 if the student failed.*
>
> *Your program should analyze the results of the exam as follows:*
>
> 1. *Input each test result (i.e., a 1 or a 2). Display the message "Enter result" on the screen each time the program requests another test result.*
>
> 2. *Count the number of test results of each type.*
>
> 3. *Display a summary of the test results, indicating the number of students who passed and the number who failed.*
>
> 4. *If more than eight students passed the exam, print "Bonus to instructor!"*

Figure 4.7 solves this problem. Lines 11–13 and 19 of `main` declare the variables that are used to process the examination results.

Error-Prevention Tip 4.4

Initializing local variables when they're declared helps you avoid any compilation errors that might arise from attempts to use uninitialized variables. While Java does not require that local-variable initializations be incorporated into declarations, it does require that local variables have a value before they're used in an expression.

```
1   // Fig. 4.7: Analysis.java
2   // Analysis of examination results using nested control statements.
3   import java.util.Scanner; // class uses class Scanner
```

Fig. 4.7 | Analysis of examination results using nested control statements. (Part 1 of 3.)

```java
4
5   public class Analysis {
6      public static void main(String[] args) {
7         // create Scanner to obtain input from command window
8         Scanner input = new Scanner(System.in);
9
10        // initializing variables in declarations
11        int passes = 0;
12        int failures = 0;
13        int studentCounter = 1;
14
15        // process 10 students using counter-controlled loop
16        while (studentCounter <= 10) {
17           // prompt user for input and obtain value from user
18           System.out.print("Enter result (1 = pass, 2 = fail): ");
19           int result = input.nextInt();
20
21           // if...else is nested in the while statement
22           if (result == 1) {
23              passes = passes + 1;
24           }
25           else {
26              failures = failures + 1;
27           }
28
29           // increment studentCounter so loop eventually terminates
30           studentCounter = studentCounter + 1;
31        }
32
33        // termination phase; prepare and display results
34        System.out.printf("Passed: %d%nFailed: %d%n", passes, failures);
35
36        // determine whether more than 8 students passed
37        if (passes > 8) {
38           System.out.println("Bonus to instructor!");
39        }
40     }
41  }
```

```
Enter result (1 = pass, 2 = fail): 1
Enter result (1 = pass, 2 = fail): 2
Enter result (1 = pass, 2 = fail): 1
Enter result (1 = pass, 2 = fail): 1
Enter result (1 = pass, 2 = fail): 1
Enter result (1 = pass, 2 = fail): 1
Enter result (1 = pass, 2 = fail): 1
Enter result (1 = pass, 2 = fail): 1
Enter result (1 = pass, 2 = fail): 1
Enter result (1 = pass, 2 = fail): 1
Passed: 9
Failed: 1
Bonus to instructor!
```

Fig. 4.7 | Analysis of examination results using nested control statements. (Part 2 of 3.)

```
Enter result (1 = pass, 2 = fail): 1
Enter result (1 = pass, 2 = fail): 2
Enter result (1 = pass, 2 = fail): 1
Enter result (1 = pass, 2 = fail): 2
Enter result (1 = pass, 2 = fail): 1
Enter result (1 = pass, 2 = fail): 2
Enter result (1 = pass, 2 = fail): 2
Enter result (1 = pass, 2 = fail): 1
Enter result (1 = pass, 2 = fail): 1
Enter result (1 = pass, 2 = fail): 1
Passed: 6
Failed: 4
```

Fig. 4.7 | Analysis of examination results using nested control statements. (Part 3 of 3.)

The while statement (lines 16–31) loops 10 times. During each iteration, the loop inputs and processes one exam result. Notice that the if...else statement (lines 22–27) for processing each result is *nested* in the while statement. If the result is 1, the if...else statement increments passes; otherwise, it assumes the result is 2 and increments failures. Line 30 increments studentCounter before the loop condition is tested again at line 16. After 10 values have been input, the loop terminates and line 34 displays the number of passes and failures. The if statement at lines 37–39 determines whether more than eight students passed the exam and, if so, outputs the message "Bonus to instructor!".

Figure 4.7 shows the input and output from two sample executions of the program. During the first, the condition at line 37 of method main is true—more than eight students passed the exam, so the program outputs a message to bonus the instructor.

4.9 Compound Assignment Operators

The **compound assignment operators** enable you to abbreviate assignment expressions. For example, you can abbreviate the statement

```
c = c + 3; // adds 3 to c
```

with the **addition compound assignment operator**, +=, as

```
c += 3; // adds 3 to c more concisely
```

The += operator adds the value of the expression on its right to the value of the variable on its left and stores the result in the variable on the left. Thus, the assignment expression c += 3 adds 3 to c. In general, statements like

variable = *variable* *operator* *expression*;

where *operator* is one of the binary operators +, -, *, / or % (or others we discuss later in the text) and the same variable name is used can be written in the form

variable *operator*= *expression*;

Figure 4.8 shows the arithmetic compound assignment operators, sample expressions using the operators and explanations of what the operators do.

Assignment operator	Sample expression	Explanation	Assigns
Assume: int c = 3, d = 5, e = 4, f = 6, g = 12;			
+=	c += 7	c = c + 7	10 to c
-=	d -= 4	d = d - 4	1 to d
*=	e *= 5	e = e * 5	20 to e
/=	f /= 3	f = f / 3	2 to f
%=	g %= 9	g = g % 9	3 to g

Fig. 4.8 | Arithmetic compound assignment operators.

4.10 Increment and Decrement Operators

Java provides two unary operators (summarized in Fig. 4.9) for adding 1 to or subtracting 1 from the value of a numeric variable. These are the unary **increment operator**, ++, and the unary **decrement operator**, --. A program can increment by 1 the value of a variable called c using the increment operator, ++, rather than the expression c = c + 1 or c += 1. An increment or decrement operator that's prefixed to (placed before) a variable is referred to as the **prefix increment** or **prefix decrement operator**, respectively. An increment or decrement operator that's postfixed to (placed after) a variable is referred to as the **postfix increment** or **postfix decrement operator**, respectively.

Operator	Sample expression	Explanation
++ (prefix increment)	++a	Increment a by 1, then use the new value of a in the expression in which a resides.
++ (postfix increment)	a++	Use the current value of a in the expression in which a resides, then increment a by 1.
-- (prefix decrement)	--b	Decrement b by 1, then use the new value of b in the expression in which b resides.
-- (postfix decrement)	b--	Use the current value of b in the expression in which b resides, then decrement b by 1.

Fig. 4.9 | Increment and decrement operators.

Using the prefix increment (or decrement) operator to add 1 to (or subtract 1 from) a variable is known as **preincrementing** (or **predecrementing**). This causes the variable to be incremented (decremented) by 1; then the new value of the variable is used in the expression in which it appears. Using the postfix increment (or decrement) operator to add 1 to (or subtract 1 from) a variable is known as **postincrementing** (or **postdecrementing**). This causes the current value of the variable to be used in the expression in which it appears; then the variable's value is incremented (decremented) by 1.

Difference Between Prefix Increment and Postfix Increment Operators

Figure 4.10 demonstrates the difference between the prefix increment and postfix increment versions of the ++ increment operator. The decrement operator (––) works similarly.

```java
1   // Fig. 4.10: Increment.java
2   // Prefix increment and postfix increment operators.
3
4   public class Increment {
5      public static void main(String[] args) {
6         // demonstrate postfix increment operator
7         int c = 5;
8         System.out.printf("c before postincrement: %d%n", c); // prints 5
9         System.out.printf("    postincrementing c: %d%n", c++); // prints 5
10        System.out.printf(" c after postincrement: %d%n", c); // prints 6
11
12        System.out.println(); // skip a line
13
14        // demonstrate prefix increment operator
15        c = 5;
16        System.out.printf(" c before preincrement: %d%n", c); // prints 5
17        System.out.printf("     preincrementing c: %d%n", ++c); // prints 6
18        System.out.printf("  c after preincrement: %d%n", c); // prints 6
19     }
20  }
```

```
c before postincrement: 5
    postincrementing c: 5
 c after postincrement: 6

c before preincrement: 5
    preincrementing c: 6
 c after preincrement: 6
```

Fig. 4.10 | Prefix increment and postfix increment operators.

Line 7 initializes the variable c to 5, and line 8 outputs c's initial value. Line 9 outputs the value of the expression c++. This expression postincrements the variable c, so c's *original* value (5) is output, then c's value is incremented (to 6). Thus, line 9 outputs c's initial value (5) again. Line 10 outputs c's new value (6) to prove that the variable's value was indeed incremented in line 9.

Line 15 resets c's value to 5, and line 16 outputs c's value. Line 17 outputs the value of the expression ++c. This expression preincrements c, so its value is incremented; then the *new* value (6) is output. Line 18 outputs c's value again to show that the value of c is still 6 after line 17 executes.

Simplifying Statements with the Compound Assignment, Increment and Decrement Operators

The arithmetic compound assignment operators and the increment and decrement operators can be used to simplify program statements. For example, Fig. 4.7, lines 23, 26 and 30

```java
passes = passes + 1;
failures = failures + 1;
studentCounter = studentCounter + 1;
```

can be written more concisely with compound assignment operators as

```
passes += 1;
failures += 1;
studentCounter += 1;
```

with prefix increment operators as

```
++passes;
++failures;
++studentCounter;
```

or with postfix increment operators as

```
passes++;
failures++;
studentCounter++;
```

When incrementing or decrementing a variable in a statement by itself, the prefix increment and postfix increment forms have the *same* effect, and the prefix decrement and postfix decrement forms have the *same* effect. It's only when a variable appears in the context of a larger expression that preincrementing and postincrementing the variable have different effects (and similarly for predecrementing and postdecrementing).

Common Programming Error 4.7

Attempting to use the increment or decrement operator on an expression other than one to which a value can be assigned is a syntax error. For example, writing ++(x + 1) is a syntax error, because (x + 1) is not a variable.

Operator Precedence and Associativity

Figure 4.11 shows the precedence and associativity of the operators we've introduced. They're shown from top to bottom in decreasing order of precedence. The second column describes the operators' associativity. The conditional operator (?:); the unary operators increment (++), decrement (--), plus (+) and minus (-); the cast operators and the assignment operators =, +=, -=, *=, /= and %= associate from *right to left*. The other operators associate from *left to right*. The third column lists the type of each group of operators.

Operators						Associativity	Type
++	--					right to left	unary postfix
++	--	+	-	(*type*)		right to left	unary prefix
*	/	%				left to right	multiplicative
+	-					left to right	additive
<	<=	>	>=			left to right	relational
==	!=					left to right	equality
?:						right to left	conditional
=	+=	-=	*=	/=	%=	right to left	assignment

Fig. 4.11 | Precedence and associativity of the operators discussed so far.

4.11 Primitive Types

The table in Appendix D lists the eight primitive types in Java. Like C and C++, Java requires all variables to have a type.[2] In C and C++, programmers frequently have to write
separate versions of programs to support different computer platforms, because the primitive types are not guaranteed to be identical from computer to computer. For example,
an int on one machine might be represented by 16 bits (2 bytes) of memory, on a second
machine by 32 bits (4 bytes), and on another machine by 64 bits (8 bytes). In Java, int
values are always 32 bits (4 bytes).

Portability Tip 4.1

The primitive types in Java are portable across all computer platforms that support Java.

Each type in Appendix D is listed with its size in bits (there are eight bits to a byte)
and its range of values. Because the designers of Java want to ensure portability, they use
internationally recognized standards for character formats (Unicode; for more information, visit http://www.unicode.org) and floating-point numbers (IEEE 754; for more
information, visit http://grouper.ieee.org/groups/754/).

Recall from Section 3.2 that variables of primitive types declared outside of a method
as instance variables of a class are *automatically assigned default values unless explicitly initialized*. Instance variables of types char, byte, short, int, long, float and double are all
given the value 0 by default. Instance variables of type boolean are given the value false
by default. Reference-type instance variables are initialized by default to the value null.

4.12 Wrap-Up

Only three types of control structures—sequence, selection and iteration—are needed to
develop any program. This chapter demonstrated the if single-selection statement, the
if...else double-selection statement and the while iteration statement. We used control-
statement stacking to total and compute the average of a set of student grades with count-
er- and sentinel-controlled iteration, and we used control-statement nesting to analyze and
make decisions based on a set of exam results. We introduced Java's compound assignment
operators and its increment and decrement operators. Finally, we discussed the portability
of Java's primitive types. In Chapter 5, we continue our discussion of control statements,
introducing the for, do...while and switch statements. In Chapter 7, we demonstrate the
enhanced for statement.

---

2.   We'll see an exception to this with lambdas in Chapter 17, Lambdas and Streams.

5

Control Statements: Part 2; Logical Operators

Objectives

In this chapter you'll:

- Review the essentials of counter-controlled iteration.
- Use the `for` and `do...while` iteration statements to execute statements in a program repeatedly.
- Understand multiple selection using the `switch` selection statement.
- Implement an object-oriented `AutoPolicy` case study using `String`s in `switch` statements.
- Alter the flow of control with the `break` and `continue` program-control statements.
- Use the logical operators to form complex conditional expressions in control statements.

5.1 Introduction

This chapter introduces all but one of Java's remaining control statements. We demonstrate Java's for, do...while and switch statements. Through a series of short examples using while and for, we explore the essentials of counter-controlled iteration. We use a switch statement to count the number of A, B, C, D and F grade equivalents in a set of numeric grades entered by the user. We introduce the break and continue program-control statements. We discuss Java's logical operators, which enable you to use more complex conditional expressions in control statements.

5.2 Essentials of Counter-Controlled Iteration

This section uses the while iteration statement introduced in Chapter 4 to formalize the elements required to perform counter-controlled iteration, which requires

1. a **control variable** (or loop counter)

2. the **initial value** of the control variable

3. the **increment** by which the control variable is modified each time through the loop (also known as **each iteration of the loop**)

4. the **loop-continuation condition** that determines if looping should continue.

To see these elements of counter-controlled iteration, consider the application of Fig. 5.1, which uses a loop to display the numbers from 1 through 10.

```
1   // Fig. 5.1: WhileCounter.java
2   // Counter-controlled iteration with the while iteration statement.
3
4   public class WhileCounter {
5      public static void main(String[] args) {
6         int counter = 1; // declare and initialize control variable
7
```

Fig. 5.1 | Counter-controlled iteration with the while iteration statement. (Part 1 of 2.)

```
 8            while (counter <= 10) { // loop-continuation condition
 9                System.out.printf("%d  ", counter);
10                ++counter; // increment control variable
11            }
12
13            System.out.println();
14        }
15    }
```

```
1  2  3  4  5  6  7  8  9  10
```

Fig. 5.1 | Counter-controlled iteration with the `while` iteration statement. (Part 2 of 2.)

In Fig. 5.1, the elements of counter-controlled iteration are defined in lines 6, 8 and 10. Line 6 *declares* the control variable (`counter`) as an `int`, *reserves space* for it in memory and sets its *initial value* to 1. Line 9 displays control variable `counter`'s value during each iteration of the loop. Line 10 *increments* the control variable by 1 for each iteration of the loop. The loop-continuation condition in the `while` (line 8) tests whether the value of the control variable is less than or equal to 10 (the final value for which the condition is `true`). The program performs the body of this `while` even when the control variable is 10. The loop terminates when the control variable exceeds 10 (i.e., `counter` becomes 11).

Common Programming Error 5.1

Because floating-point values may be approximate, controlling loops with floating-point variables may result in imprecise counter values and inaccurate termination tests.

Error-Prevention Tip 5.1

Use integers to control counting loops.

5.3 for Iteration Statement

Section 5.2 presented the essentials of counter-controlled iteration. The `while` statement can be used to implement any counter-controlled loop. Java also provides the **for iteration statement**, which specifies the counter-controlled-iteration details in a single line of code. Figure 5.2 reimplements the application of Fig. 5.1 using `for`.

```
 1  // Fig. 5.2: ForCounter.java
 2  // Counter-controlled iteration with the for iteration statement.
 3
 4  public class ForCounter {
 5      public static void main(String[] args) {
 6          // for statement header includes initialization,
 7          // loop-continuation condition and increment
 8          for (int counter = 1; counter <= 10; counter++) {
 9              System.out.printf("%d  ", counter);
10          }
```

Fig. 5.2 | Counter-controlled iteration with the `for` iteration statement. (Part 1 of 2.)

```
11
12          System.out.println();
13      }
14  }
```

```
1   2   3   4   5   6   7   8   9   10
```

Fig. 5.2 | Counter-controlled iteration with the `for` iteration statement. (Part 2 of 2.)

When the `for` statement (lines 8–10) begins executing, the control variable `counter` is *declared* and *initialized* to 1. (Recall from Section 5.2 that the first two elements of counter-controlled iteration are the *control variable* and its *initial value*.) Next, the program checks the *loop-continuation condition*, `counter <= 10`, which is between the two required semicolons. Because the initial value of `counter` is 1, the condition initially is `true`. Therefore, the body statement (line 9) displays control variable `counter`'s value, namely 1. After executing the loop's body, the program increments `counter` in the expression `counter++`, which appears to the right of the second semicolon. Then the loop-continuation test is performed again to determine whether the program should continue with the next iteration of the loop. At this point, the control variable's value is 2, so the condition is still `true` (the *final value* is not exceeded)—thus, the program performs the body statement again (i.e., the next iteration of the loop). This process continues until the numbers 1 through 10 have been displayed and the `counter`'s value becomes 11, causing the loop-continuation test to fail and iteration to terminate (after 10 iterations of the loop body). Then the program performs the first statement after the `for`—in this case, line 12.

Figure 5.2 uses (in line 8) the loop-continuation condition `counter <= 10`. If you incorrectly specified `counter < 10` as the condition, the loop would iterate only nine times. This is a common *logic error* called an **off-by-one error**.

Error-Prevention Tip 5.2
As Chapter 4 mentioned, integers can overflow, causing logic errors. A loop's control variable also could overflow. Write your loop conditions carefully to prevent this.

A Closer Look at the *for* Statement's Header
Figure 5.3 takes a closer look at the `for` statement in Fig. 5.2. The first line—including the keyword `for` and everything in parentheses after `for` (line 8 in Fig. 5.2)—is sometimes called the **for statement header**. The `for` header "does it all"—it specifies each item needed for counter-controlled iteration with a control variable.

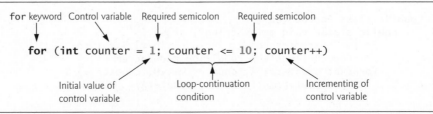

Fig. 5.3 | `for` statement header components.

*General Format of a **for** Statement*

The general format of the for statement is

```
for (initialization; loopContinuationCondition; increment) {
    statements
}
```

where the *initialization* expression names the loop's control variable and *optionally* provides its initial value, *loopContinuationCondition* determines whether the loop should continue executing and *increment* modifies the control variable's value, so that the loop-continuation condition eventually becomes false. The two semicolons in the for header are required. If the loop-continuation condition is initially false, the program does *not* execute the body. Instead, execution proceeds with the statement following the for.

*Representing a **for** Statement with an Equivalent **while** Statement*

The for statement often can be represented with an equivalent while statement as follows:

```
initialization;

while (loopContinuationCondition) {
    statements
    increment;
}
```

In Section 5.8, we show a case in which a for statement cannot be represented with an equivalent while statement. Typically, for statements are used for counter-controlled iteration and while statements for sentinel-controlled iteration. However, while and for can each be used for either iteration type.

*Scope of a **for** Statement's Control Variable*

If the *initialization* expression in the for header declares the control variable (i.e., the control variable's type is specified before the variable name, as in Fig. 5.2), the control variable can be used *only* in that for statement—it will not exist outside it. This restricted use is known as the variable's **scope**, which defines where it can be used in a program. For example, a *local variable* can be used *only* in the method that declares it and *only* from the point of declaration through the next right brace (}), which is often the brace that closes the method body. Scope is discussed in detail in Chapter 6, Methods: A Deeper Look.

Common Programming Error 5.2

When a for statement's control variable is declared in the initialization section of the for's header, using the control variable after the for's body is a compilation error.

*Expressions in a **for** Statement's Header Are Optional*

The three expressions in a for header are optional. If the *loopContinuationCondition* is omitted, Java assumes that it's *always* true, thus creating an *infinite loop*. You might omit the *initialization* expression if the program initializes the control variable *before* the loop. You might omit the *increment* expression if the program calculates the increment with statements in the loop's body or if no increment is needed. The increment expression in a for acts as if it were a standalone statement at the end of the for's body. So, the expressions

```
counter = counter + 1
counter += 1
++counter
counter++
```

are equivalent increment expressions in a for statement. Many programmers prefer counter++ because it's concise and because a for loop evaluates its increment expression *after* its body executes, so the postfix increment form seems more natural. In this case, the variable being incremented does not appear in a larger expression, so preincrementing and postincrementing actually have the *same* effect.

Common Programming Error 5.3
Placing a semicolon immediately to the right of the right parenthesis of a for header makes that for's body an empty statement. This is normally a logic error.

Error-Prevention Tip 5.3
Infinite loops occur when the loop-continuation condition in an iteration statement never becomes false. To prevent this situation in a counter-controlled loop, ensure that the control variable is modified during each iteration of the loop so that the loop-continuation condition will eventually become false. In a sentinel-controlled loop, ensure that the sentinel value is able to be input.

Placing Arithmetic Expressions in a for Statement's Header
The initialization, loop-continuation condition and increment portions of a for statement can contain arithmetic expressions. For example, assume that x = 2 and y = 10. If x and y are not modified in the body of the loop, the statement

```
for (int j = x; j <= 4 * x * y; j += y / x)
```

is equivalent to the statement

```
for (int j = 2; j <= 80; j += 5)
```

The increment of a for statement may also be *negative*, in which case it's a **decrement**, and the loop counts *downward*.

Using a for Statement's Control Variable in the Statement's Body
Programs frequently display the control-variable value or use it in calculations in the loop body, but this use is *not* required. The control variable is commonly used to control iteration *without* being mentioned in the body of the for.

Error-Prevention Tip 5.4
Although the value of the control variable can be changed in the body of a for loop, avoid doing so, because this practice can lead to subtle errors.

UML Activity Diagram for the for Statement
The for statement's UML activity diagram is similar to that of the while statement (Fig. 4.4). Figure 5.4 shows the activity diagram of the for statement in Fig. 5.2. The diagram makes it clear that initialization occurs *once before* the loop-continuation test is evaluated the first time, and that incrementing occurs *each* time through the loop *after* the body statement executes.

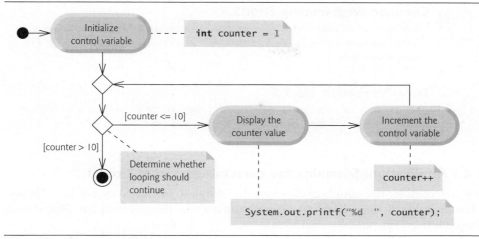

Fig. 5.4 | UML activity diagram for the for statement in Fig. 5.2.

5.4 Examples Using the for Statement

The following examples show techniques for varying the control variable in a for statement. In each case, we write *only* the appropriate for header. Note the change in the relational operator for the loops that *decrement* the control variable.

a) Vary the control variable from 1 to 100 in increments of 1.

```
for (int i = 1; i <= 100; i++)
```

b) Vary the control variable from 100 to 1 in *decrements* of 1.

```
for (int i = 100; i >= 1; i--)
```

c) Vary the control variable from 7 to 77 in increments of 7.

```
for (int i = 7; i <= 77; i += 7)
```

d) Vary the control variable from 20 to 2 in *decrements* of 2.

```
for (int i = 20; i >= 2; i -= 2)
```

e) Vary the control variable over the values 2, 5, 8, 11, 14, 17, 20.

```
for (int i = 2; i <= 20; i += 3)
```

f) Vary the control variable over the values 99, 88, 77, 66, 55, 44, 33, 22, 11, 0.

```
for (int i = 99; i >= 0; i -= 11)
```

Common Programming Error 5.4

Do not use equality operators (!= or ==) in a loop-continuation condition if the loop's control variable increments or decrements by more than 1. For example, consider the for statement header for (int counter = 1; counter != 10; counter += 2). The loop-continuation test counter != 10 never becomes false (resulting in an infinite loop) because counter increments by 2 after each iteration.

Common Programming Error 5.5

Using an incorrect relational operator in the loop-continuation condition of a loop that counts downward (e.g., using i <= 1 instead of i >= 1 in a loop counting down to 1) is usually a logic error.

Error-Prevention Tip 5.5

Counting loops are error prone. In subsequent chapters, we'll introduce lambdas and streams—technologies that you can use to eliminate such errors.

5.4.1 Application: Summing the Even Integers from 2 to 20

We now consider two sample applications that demonstrate simple uses of for. The application in Fig. 5.5 uses a for statement to sum the even integers from 2 to 20 and store the result in an int variable called total.

```java
1   // Fig. 5.5: Sum.java
2   // Summing integers with the for statement.
3
4   public class Sum {
5       public static void main(String[] args) {
6           int total = 0;
7
8           // total even integers from 2 through 20
9           for (int number = 2; number <= 20; number += 2) {
10              total += number;
11          }
12
13          System.out.printf("Sum is %d%n", total);
14      }
15  }
```

```
Sum is 110
```

Fig. 5.5 | Summing integers with the for statement.

The *initialization* and *increment* expressions can be comma-separated lists that enable you to use multiple initialization expressions or multiple increment expressions. For example, *although this is discouraged*, you could merge the for statement's body in lines 9–11 of Fig. 5.5 into the increment portion of the for header by using a comma as follows:

```java
for (int number = 2; number <= 20; total += number, number += 2) {
    ; // empty statement
}
```

Good Programming Practice 5.1

For readability limit the size of control-statement headers to a single line if possible.

5.4.2 Application: Compound-Interest Calculations

Next, let's use the for statement to compute compound interest. Consider the following problem:

> A person invests $1,000 in a savings account yielding 5% interest. Assuming that all the interest is left on deposit, calculate and print the amount of money in the account at the end of each year for 10 years. Use the following formula to determine the amounts:
>
> $a = p\,(1 + r)^n$
>
> where
>
> p is the original amount invested (i.e., the principal)
> r is the annual interest rate (e.g., use 0.05 for 5%)
> n is the number of years
> a is the amount on deposit at the end of the nth year.

The solution to this problem (Fig. 5.6) involves a loop that performs the indicated calculation for each of the 10 years the money remains on deposit. Lines 6, 7 and 15 in main declare double variables principal, rate and amount. Lines 6–7 initialize principal to 1000.0 and rate to 0.05. Line 15 initializes amount to the result of the compound-interest calculation. Java treats floating-point constants like 1000.0 and 0.05 as type double. Similarly, Java treats whole-number constants like 7 and -22 as type int.

```java
1   // Fig. 5.6: Interest.java
2   // Compound-interest calculations with for.
3
4   public class Interest {
5      public static void main(String[] args) {
6         double principal = 1000.0; // initial amount before interest
7         double rate = 0.05; // interest rate
8
9         // display headers
10        System.out.printf("%s%20s%n", "Year", "Amount on deposit");
11
12        // calculate amount on deposit for each of ten years
13        for (int year = 1; year <= 10; ++year) {
14           // calculate new amount on deposit for specified year
15           double amount = principal * Math.pow(1.0 + rate, year);
16
17           // display the year and the amount
18           System.out.printf("%4d%,20.2f%n", year, amount);
19        }
20     }
21  }
```

```
Year     Amount on deposit
   1             1,050.00
   2             1,102.50
   3             1,157.63
   4             1,215.51
```

Fig. 5.6 | Compound-interest calculations with for. (Part 1 of 2.)

```
     5              1,276.28
     6              1,340.10
     7              1,407.10
     8              1,477.46
     9              1,551.33
    10              1,628.89
```

Fig. 5.6 | Compound-interest calculations with for. (Part 2 of 2.)

Formatting Strings with Field Widths and Justification
Line 10 outputs the headers for two columns of output. The first column displays the year and the second column the amount on deposit at the end of that year. We use the format specifier %20s to output the String "Amount on Deposit". The integer 20 between the % and the conversion character s indicates that the value should be displayed with a **field width** of 20—that is, printf displays the value with at least 20 character positions. If the value to be output is less than 20 character positions wide (17 characters in this example), the value is **right justified** in the field by default. If the year value to be output were more than four character positions wide, the field width would be extended to the right to accommodate the entire value—this would push the amount field to the right, upsetting the neat columns of our tabular output. To output values **left justified**, simply precede the field width with the **minus sign (-) formatting flag** (e.g., %-20s).

Performing the Interest Calculations with static Method pow of Class Math
The for statement (lines 13–19) executes its body 10 times, varying control variable year from 1 to 10 in increments of 1. This loop terminates when year becomes 11. (Variable year represents n in the problem statement.)

Classes provide methods that perform common tasks on objects. In fact, most methods must be called on a specific object. For example, to output text in Fig. 5.6, line 10 calls method printf on the System.out object. Some classes also provide methods that perform common tasks and do *not* require you to first create objects of those classes. These are called static methods. For example, Java does not include an exponentiation operator, so the designers of Java's Math class defined static method pow for raising a value to a power. You can call a static method by specifying the *class name* followed by a dot (.) and the method name, as in

   ClassName.*methodName*(*arguments*)

In Chapter 6, you'll learn how to implement static methods in your own classes.

We use static method **pow** of class **Math** to perform the compound-interest calculation in Fig. 5.6. Math.pow(x, y) calculates the value of x raised to the yth power. The method receives two double arguments and returns a double value. Line 15 performs the calculation $a = p(1 + r)^n$, where a is amount, p is principal, r is rate and n is year. Class Math is defined in package java.lang, so you do *not* need to import class Math to use it.

The body of the for statement contains the calculation 1.0 + rate, which appears as an argument to the Math.pow method. In fact, this calculation produces the *same* result each time through the loop, so repeating it in every iteration of the loop is wasteful.

Performance Tip 5.1

In loops, avoid calculations for which the result never changes—such calculations should typically be placed before the loop. Many of today's sophisticated optimizing compilers will place such calculations outside loops in the compiled code.

Formatting Floating-Point Numbers

After each calculation, line 18 outputs the year and the amount on deposit at the end of that year. The year is output in a field width of four characters (as specified by %4d). The amount is output as a floating-point number with the format specifier %,20.2f.

The **comma (,) formatting flag** indicates that the floating-point value should be output with a **grouping separator**. The actual separator used is specific to the user's locale (i.e., country). For example, in the United States, the number will be output using commas to separate every three digits and a decimal point to separate the fractional part of the number, as in 1,234.45. The number 20 in the format specification indicates that the value should be output right justified in a *field width* of 20 characters. The .2 specifies the formatted number's *precision*—in this case, the number is *rounded* to the nearest hundredth and output with two digits to the right of the decimal point.

A Warning about Displaying Rounded Values

We declared variables amount, principal and rate to be of type double in this example. We're dealing with fractional parts of dollars and thus need a type that allows decimal points in its values. Unfortunately, floating-point numbers can cause trouble. Here's a simple explanation of what can go wrong when using double (or float) to represent dollar amounts (assuming that dollar amounts are displayed with two digits to the right of the decimal point): Two double dollar amounts stored in the machine could be 14.234 (which would normally be rounded to 14.23 for display purposes) and 18.673 (which would normally be rounded to 18.67 for display purposes). When these amounts are added, they produce the internal sum 32.907, which would normally be rounded to 32.91 for display purposes. Thus, your output could appear as

```
  14.23
+ 18.67
  32.91
```

but a person adding the individual numbers as displayed would expect the sum to be 32.90. You've been warned!

Error-Prevention Tip 5.6

Do not use variables of type double (or float) to perform precise monetary calculations. The imprecision of floating-point numbers can lead to errors. You can use integers to perform precise monetary calculations. Java also provides class java.math.BigDecimal for this purpose, which we demonstrate in Fig. 8.16.

Error-Prevention Tip 5.7

In a global economy, dealing with currencies, monetary amounts, conversions, rounding and formatting is complex. The new JavaMoney API (http://javamoney.github.io) was developed to meet these challenges. At the time of this writing, it was not yet incorporated into the JDK.

5.5 do...while Iteration Statement

The **do...while iteration statement** is similar to the while statement. A while tests its loop-continuation condition at the *beginning* of the loop, *before* executing the loop's body; if the condition is false, the body *never* executes. A do...while tests its loop-continuation condition *after* executing the loop's body; therefore, *the body always executes at least once.* When a do...while statement terminates, execution continues with the next statement in sequence. Figure 5.7 uses a do...while to output the numbers 1–10.

```java
1   // Fig. 5.7: DoWhileTest.java
2   // do...while iteration statement.
3
4   public class DoWhileTest {
5      public static void main(String[] args) {
6         int counter = 1;
7
8         do {
9            System.out.printf("%d  ", counter);
10           ++counter;
11        } while (counter <= 10);
12
13        System.out.println();
14     }
15  }
```

```
1  2  3  4  5  6  7  8  9  10
```

Fig. 5.7 | do...while iteration statement.

Line 6 declares and initializes control variable counter. Upon entering the do...while statement, line 9 outputs counter's value and line 10 increments counter. Then the program evaluates the loop-continuation test at the *bottom* of the loop (line 11). If the condition is true, the loop continues at the first body statement (line 9). If the condition is false, the loop terminates and the program continues at the next statement after the loop.

UML Activity Diagram for the do...while Iteration Statement
Figure 5.8 contains the UML activity diagram for the do...while statement. This diagram makes it clear that the loop-continuation condition is not evaluated until *after* the loop performs the action state *at least once*. Compare this activity diagram with that of the while statement (Fig. 4.4).

5.6 switch Multiple-Selection Statement

Chapter 4 discussed the if single-selection statement and the if...else double-selection statement. The **switch multiple-selection statement** performs different actions based on the possible values of a **constant integral expression** of type byte, short, int or char (but not long). The expression may also be a String, which we demonstrate in Section 5.7.

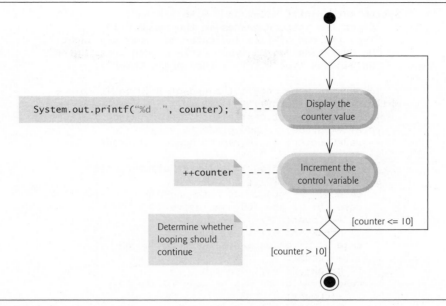

Fig. 5.8 | do...while iteration statement UML activity diagram.

Using a switch Statement to Count A, B, C, D and F Grades

Figure 5.9 calculates the class average of a set of user-entered numeric grades. The program's switch statement determines whether each grade is the equivalent of an A, B, C, D or F and increments the appropriate grade counter. The program also displays a summary of the number of students who received each grade.

```
1   // Fig. 5.9: LetterGrades.java
2   // LetterGrades class uses the switch statement to count letter grades.
3   import java.util.Scanner;
4
5   public class LetterGrades {
6      public static void main(String[] args) {
7         int total = 0; // sum of grades
8         int gradeCounter = 0; // number of grades entered
9         int aCount = 0; // count of A grades
10        int bCount = 0; // count of B grades
11        int cCount = 0; // count of C grades
12        int dCount = 0; // count of D grades
13        int fCount = 0; // count of F grades
14
15        Scanner input = new Scanner(System.in);
16
```

Fig. 5.9 | LetterGrades class uses the switch statement to count letter grades. (Part I of 3.)

```
17          System.out.printf("%s%n%s%n    %s%n    %s%n",
18              "Enter the integer grades in the range 0-100.",
19              "Type the end-of-file indicator to terminate input:",
20              "On UNIX/Linux/macOS type <Ctrl> d then press Enter",
21              "On Windows type <Ctrl> z then press Enter");
22
23          // loop until user enters the end-of-file indicator
24          while (input.hasNext()) {
25              int grade = input.nextInt(); // read grade
26              total += grade; // add grade to total
27              ++gradeCounter; // increment number of grades
28
29              //  increment appropriate letter-grade counter
30              switch (grade / 10) {
31                  case 9:  // grade was between 90
32                  case 10: // and 100, inclusive
33                      ++aCount;
34                      break; // exits switch
35                  case 8: // grade was between 80 and 89
36                      ++bCount;
37                      break; // exits switch
38                  case 7: // grade was between 70 and 79
39                      ++cCount;
40                      break; // exits switch
41                  case 6: // grade was between 60 and 69
42                      ++dCount;
43                      break; // exits switch
44                  default: // grade was less than 60
45                      ++fCount;
46                      break; // optional; exits switch anyway
47              }
48          }
49
50          // display grade report
51          System.out.printf("%nGrade Report:%n");
52
53          // if user entered at least one grade...
54          if (gradeCounter != 0) {
55              // calculate average of all grades entered
56              double average = (double) total / gradeCounter;
57
58              // output summary of results
59              System.out.printf("Total of the %d grades entered is %d%n",
60                  gradeCounter, total);
61              System.out.printf("Class average is %.2f%n", average);
62              System.out.printf("%n%s%n%s%d%n%s%d%n%s%d%n%s%d%n%s%d%n",
63                  "Number of students who received each grade:",
64                  "A: ", aCount,  // display number of A grades
65                  "B: ", bCount,  // display number of B grades
66                  "C: ", cCount,  // display number of C grades
67                  "D: ", dCount,  // display number of D grades
68                  "F: ", fCount); // display number of F grades
69          }
```

Fig. 5.9 | LetterGrades class uses the switch statement to count letter grades. (Part 2 of 3.)

```
70            else { // no grades were entered, so output appropriate message
71               System.out.println("No grades were entered");
72            }
73         }
74   }
```

```
Enter the integer grades in the range 0-100.
Type the end-of-file indicator to terminate input:
   On UNIX/Linux/macOS type <Ctrl> d then press Enter
   On Windows type <Ctrl> z then press Enter
99
92
45
57
63
71
76
85
90
100
^Z

Grade Report:
Total of the 10 grades entered is 778
Class average is 77.80

Number of students who received each grade:
A: 4
B: 1
C: 2
D: 1
F: 2
```

Fig. 5.9 | LetterGrades class uses the switch statement to count letter grades. (Part 3 of 3.)

Like earlier versions of the class-average program, the main method of class Letter-Grades (Fig. 5.9) declares local variables total (line 7) and gradeCounter (line 8) to keep track of the sum of the grades entered by the user and the number of grades entered, respectively. Lines 9–13 declare counter variables for each grade category. Note that the variables in lines 7–13 are explicitly initialized to 0.

Method main has two key parts. Lines 24–48 read an arbitrary number of integer grades from the user using sentinel-controlled iteration, update instance variables total and gradeCounter, and increment an appropriate letter-grade counter for each grade entered. Lines 51–72 output a report containing the total of all grades entered, the average of the grades and the number of students who received each letter grade. Let's examine these parts in more detail.

Reading Grades from the User
Lines 17–21 prompt the user to enter integer grades and to type the end-of-file indicator to terminate the input. The **end-of-file indicator** is a system-dependent keystroke combination which the user enters to indicate that there's *no more data to input*. In Chapter 15, Files, Input/Output Streams, NIO and XML Serialization, you'll see how the end-of-file indicator is used when a program reads its input from a file.

On UNIX/Linux/macOS systems, end-of-file is entered by typing the sequence

<Ctrl> d

on a line by itself. This notation means to simultaneously press both the *Ctrl* key and the *d* key. On Windows systems, end-of-file can be entered by typing

<Ctrl> z

[*Note:* On some systems, you must press *Enter* after typing the end-of-file key sequence. Also, Windows typically displays the characters ^Z on the screen when the end-of-file indicator is typed, as shown in the output of Fig. 5.9.]

Portability Tip 5.1

The keystroke combinations for entering end-of-file are system dependent.

The `while` statement (lines 24–48) obtains the user input. The condition at line 24 calls `Scanner` method **hasNext** to determine whether there's more data to input. This method returns the `boolean` value `true` if there's more data; otherwise, it returns `false`. The returned value is then used as the value of the condition in the `while` statement. Method `hasNext` returns `false` once the user types the end-of-file indicator.

Line 25 inputs a grade value from the user. Line 26 adds `grade` to `total`. Line 27 increments `gradeCounter`. These variables are used to compute the average of the grades. Lines 30–47 use a `switch` statement to increment the appropriate letter-grade counter based on the numeric grade entered.

Processing the Grades

The `switch` statement (lines 30–47) determines which counter to increment. We assume that the user enters a valid grade in the range 0–100. A grade in the range 90–100 represents A, 80–89 represents B, 70–79 represents C, 60–69 represents D and 0–59 represents F. The `switch` statement consists of a block that contains a sequence of **case labels** and an optional **default case**. These are used in this example to determine which counter to increment based on the grade.

When the flow of control reaches the `switch`, the program evaluates the expression in the parentheses (`grade / 10`) following keyword `switch`. This is the `switch`'s **controlling expression**. The program compares this expression's value (which must evaluate to an integral value of type `byte`, `char`, `short` or `int`, or to a `String`) with each `case` label. The controlling expression in line 30 performs integer division, which *truncates the fractional part* of the result. Thus, when we divide a value from 0 to 100 by 10, the result is always a value from 0 to 10. We use several of these values in our `case` labels. For example, if the user enters the integer 85, the controlling expression evaluates to 8. The `switch` compares 8 with each `case` label. If a match occurs (`case 8:` at line 35), the program executes that `case`'s statements. For the integer 8, line 36 increments `bCount`, because a grade in the 80s is a B. The **break statement** (line 37) causes program control to proceed with the first statement after the `switch`—in this program, we reach the end of the `while` loop, so control returns to the loop-continuation condition in line 24 to determine whether the loop should continue executing.

The cases explicitly test for the values 10, 9, 8, 7 and 6. Note the cases at lines 31–32 that test for the values 9 and 10 (both of which represent the grade A). Listing cases consecutively in this manner with no statements between them enables the cases to perform the same set of statements—when the controlling expression evaluates to 9 or 10, the statements in lines 33–34 will execute. The switch statement does *not* provide a mechanism for testing *ranges* of values, so *every* value you need to test must be listed in a separate case label. Each case can have multiple statements. The switch statement differs from other control statements in that it does *not* require braces around multiple statements in a case.

case *without a* break *Statement*
Without break statements, each time a match occurs in the switch, the statements for that case and subsequent cases execute until a break statement or the end of the switch is encountered. This is often referred to as "falling through" to the statements in subsequent cases.

Common Programming Error 5.6

Forgetting a break *statement when one is needed in a* switch *is a logic error.*

The default *Case*
If no match occurs between the controlling expression's value and a case label, the default case (lines 44–46) executes. We use the default case in this example to process all controlling-expression values that are less than 6—that is, all failing grades. If no match occurs and the switch does not contain a default case, program control simply continues with the first statement after the switch.

Error-Prevention Tip 5.8

In a switch *statement, ensure that you test all possible values of the controlling expression.*

Displaying the Grade Report
Lines 51–72 output a report based on the grades entered (as shown in the input/output window in Fig. 5.9). Line 54 determines whether the user entered at least one grade—this helps us avoid dividing by zero. If so, line 56 calculates the average of the grades. Lines 59–68 then output the total of all the grades, the class average and the number of students who received each letter grade. If no grades were entered, line 71 outputs an appropriate message. The output in Fig. 5.9 shows a sample grade report based on 10 grades.

switch *Statement UML Activity Diagram*
Figure 5.10 shows the UML activity diagram for the general switch statement. Most switch statements use a break in each case to terminate the switch statement after processing the case. Figure 5.10 emphasizes this by including break statements in the activity diagram. The diagram makes it clear that the break statement at the end of a case causes control to exit the switch statement immediately.

The break statement is *not* required for the switch's last case (or the optional default case, when it appears last), because execution continues with the next statement after the switch.

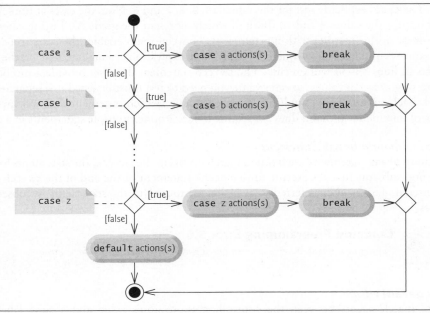

Fig. 5.10 | switch multiple-selection statement UML activity diagram with **break** statements.

Error-Prevention Tip 5.9

Provide a default *case in* switch *statements. This focuses you on the need to process exceptional conditions.*

Good Programming Practice 5.2

Although each case *and the* default *case in a* switch *can occur in any order, place the* default *case last. When the* default *case is last, the* break *for that case is not required.*

Notes on the Expression in Each **case** *of a* **switch**

When using a switch, remember that each case must contain a String or a constant integral expression—that is, any combination of integer constants that evaluates to a constant integer value (e.g., –7, 0 or 221). An integer constant is simply an integer value. In addition, you can use **character constants**—specific characters in single quotes, such as 'A', '7' or '$'—which represent the integer values of characters. (Appendix B shows the integer values of the characters in the ASCII character set, which is a subset of the Unicode® character set used by Java.)

The expression in each case can also be a **constant variable**—a variable containing a value which does not change for the entire program. Such a variable is declared with keyword final (discussed in Chapter 6). Java has a feature called enum types, which we also present in Chapter 6—enum type constants can also be used in case labels.

In Chapter 10, Object-Oriented Programming: Polymorphism and Interfaces, we present a more elegant way to implement switch logic—we use a technique called *polymorphism* to create programs that are often clearer, easier to maintain and easier to extend than programs using switch logic.

5.7 Class AutoPolicy: Strings in switch Statements

Strings can be used as controlling expressions in switch statements, and String literals can be used in case labels. To demonstrate this, we'll implement an app that meets the following requirements:

> *You've been hired by an auto insurance company that serves these northeast states—Connecticut, Maine, Massachusetts, New Hampshire, New Jersey, New York, Pennsylvania, Rhode Island and Vermont. The company would like you to create a program that produces a report indicating for each of their auto insurance policies whether the policy is held in a state with "no-fault" auto insurance—Massachusetts, New Jersey, New York and Pennsylvania.*

The Java app that meets these requirements contains two classes—AutoPolicy (Fig. 5.11) and AutoPolicyTest (Fig. 5.12).

Class *AutoPolicy*
Class AutoPolicy (Fig. 5.11) represents an auto insurance policy. The class contains:

- int instance variable accountNumber (line 4) to store the policy's account number
- String instance variable makeAndModel (line 5) to store the car's make and model (such as a "Toyota Camry")
- String instance variable state (line 6) to store a two-character state abbreviation representing the state in which the policy is held (e.g., "MA" for Massachusetts)
- a constructor (lines 9–14) that initializes the class's instance variables
- methods setAccountNumber and getAccountNumber (lines 17–24) to *set* and *get* an AutoPolicy's accountNumber instance variable
- methods setMakeAndModel and getMakeAndModel (lines 27–34) to *set* and *get* an AutoPolicy's makeAndModel instance variable
- methods setState and getState (lines 37–44) to *set* and *get* an AutoPolicy's state instance variable
- method isNoFaultState (lines 47–61) to return a boolean value indicating whether the policy is held in a no-fault auto insurance state; note the method name—the naming convention for a *get* method that returns a boolean value is to begin the name with "is" rather than "get" (such a method is commonly called a *predicate method*).

```
 1   // Fig. 5.11: AutoPolicy.java
 2   // Class that represents an auto insurance policy.
 3   public class AutoPolicy {
 4      private int accountNumber; // policy account number
 5      private String makeAndModel; // car that the policy applies to
 6      private String state; // two-letter state abbreviation
 7
 8      // constructor
 9      public AutoPolicy(int accountNumber, String makeAndModel,
10         String state) {
```

Fig. 5.11 | Class that represents an auto insurance policy. (Part 1 of 2.)

```java
11            this.accountNumber = accountNumber;
12            this.makeAndModel = makeAndModel;
13            this.state = state;
14      }
15
16      // sets the accountNumber
17      public void setAccountNumber(int accountNumber) {
18            this.accountNumber = accountNumber;
19      }
20
21      // returns the accountNumber
22      public int getAccountNumber() {
23            return accountNumber;
24      }
25
26      // sets the makeAndModel
27      public void setMakeAndModel(String makeAndModel) {
28            this.makeAndModel = makeAndModel;
29      }
30
31      // returns the makeAndModel
32      public String getMakeAndModel() {
33            return makeAndModel;
34      }
35
36      // sets the state
37      public void setState(String state) {
38            this.state = state;
39      }
40
41      // returns the state
42      public String getState() {
43            return state;
44      }
45
46      // predicate method returns whether the state has no-fault insurance
47      public boolean isNoFaultState() {
48            boolean noFaultState;
49
50            // determine whether state has no-fault auto insurance
51            switch (getState()) { // get AutoPolicy object's state abbreviation
52               case "MA": case "NJ": case "NY": case "PA":
53                  noFaultState = true;
54                  break;
55               default:
56                  noFaultState = false;
57                  break;
58            }
59
60            return noFaultState;
61      }
62 }
```

Fig. 5.11 | Class that represents an auto insurance policy. (Part 2 of 2.)

In method isNoFaultState, the switch statement's controlling expression (line 51) is the String returned by AutoPolicy method getState. The switch statement compares the controlling expression's value with the case labels (line 52) to determine whether the policy is held in Massachusetts, New Jersey, New York or Pennsylvania (the no-fault states). If there's a match, then line 53 sets local variable noFaultState to true and the switch statement terminates; otherwise, the default case sets noFaultState to false (line 56). Then method isNoFaultState returns local variable noFaultState's value.

For simplicity, we did not validate an AutoPolicy's data in the constructor or *set* methods, and we assume that state abbreviations are always two uppercase letters. In addition, a real AutoPolicy class would likely contain many other instance variables and methods for data such as the account holder's name, address, etc.

Class *AutoPolicyTest*
Class AutoPolicyTest (Fig. 5.12) creates two AutoPolicy objects (lines 6–9 in main). Lines 12–13 pass each object to static method policyInNoFaultState (lines 18–25), which uses AutoPolicy methods to determine and display whether the object it receives represents a policy in a no-fault auto insurance state.

```java
1   // Fig. 5.12: AutoPolicyTest.java
2   // Demonstrating Strings in switch.
3   public class AutoPolicyTest {
4      public static void main(String[] args) {
5         // create two AutoPolicy objects
6         AutoPolicy policy1 =
7            new AutoPolicy(11111111, "Toyota Camry", "NJ");
8         AutoPolicy policy2 =
9            new AutoPolicy(22222222, "Ford Fusion", "ME");
10
11        // display whether each policy is in a no-fault state
12        policyInNoFaultState(policy1);
13        policyInNoFaultState(policy2);
14     }
15
16     // method that displays whether an AutoPolicy
17     // is in a state with no-fault auto insurance
18     public static void policyInNoFaultState(AutoPolicy policy) {
19        System.out.println("The auto policy:");
20        System.out.printf(
21           "Account #: %d; Car: %s;%nState %s %s a no-fault state%n%n",
22           policy.getAccountNumber(), policy.getMakeAndModel(),
23           policy.getState(),
24           (policy.isNoFaultState() ? "is": "is not"));
25     }
26  }
```

```
The auto policy:
Account #: 11111111; Car: Toyota Camry;
State NJ is a no-fault state
```

Fig. 5.12 | Demonstrating Strings in switch. (Part 1 of 2.)

```
The auto policy:
Account #: 22222222; Car: Ford Fusion;
State ME is not a no-fault state
```

Fig. 5.12 | Demonstrating `Strings` in `switch`. (Part 2 of 2.)

5.8 break and continue Statements

In addition to selection and iteration statements, Java provides statements break (which we discussed in the context of the switch statement) and **continue** (presented in this section and Appendix F) to alter the flow of control. The preceding section showed how break can be used to terminate a switch statement's execution. This section discusses how to use break in iteration statements.

5.8.1 break Statement

The break statement, when executed in a while, for, do...while or switch, causes *immediate* exit from that statement. Execution continues with the first statement after the control statement. Common uses of break are to escape early from a loop or to skip the remainder of a switch (as in Fig. 5.9).

Figure 5.13 demonstrates a break statement exiting a for. When the if statement nested at lines 8–10 in the for statement detects that count is 5, the break statement at line 9 executes. This terminates the for statement, and the program proceeds to line 15 (immediately after the for statement), which displays a message indicating the value of the control variable when the loop terminated. The loop fully executes its body only four times instead of 10.

```
 1   // Fig. 5.13: BreakTest.java
 2   // break statement exiting a for statement.
 3   public class BreakTest {
 4      public static void main(String[] args) {
 5         int count; // control variable also used after loop terminates
 6
 7         for (count = 1; count <= 10; count++) { // loop 10 times
 8            if (count == 5) {
 9               break; // terminates loop if count is 5
10            }
11
12            System.out.printf("%d ", count);
13         }
14
15         System.out.printf("%nBroke out of loop at count = %d%n", count);
16      }
17   }
```

```
1 2 3 4
Broke out of loop at count = 5
```

Fig. 5.13 | break statement exiting a for statement.

5.8.2 continue Statement

The continue statement, when executed in a while, for or do...while, skips the remaining statements in the loop body and proceeds with the *next iteration* of the loop. In while and do...while statements, the program evaluates the loop-continuation test immediately after the continue statement executes. In a for statement, the increment expression executes, then the program evaluates the loop-continuation test.

Figure 5.14 uses continue (line 7) to skip the statement at line 10 when the nested if determines that count's value is 5. When the continue statement executes, program control continues with the increment of the control variable in the for statement (line 5).

```
 1   // Fig. 5.14: ContinueTest.java
 2   // continue statement terminating an iteration of a for statement.
 3   public class ContinueTest {
 4      public static void main(String[] args) {
 5         for (int count = 1; count <= 10; count++) { // loop 10 times
 6            if (count == 5) {
 7               continue; // skip remaining code in loop body if count is 5
 8            }
 9
10            System.out.printf("%d ", count);
11         }
12
13         System.out.printf("%nUsed continue to skip printing 5%n");
14      }
15   }
```

```
1 2 3 4 6 7 8 9 10
Used continue to skip printing 5
```

Fig. 5.14 | continue statement terminating an iteration of a for statement.

In Section 5.3, we stated that while could be used in most cases in place of for. This is *not* true when the increment expression in the while follows a continue statement. In this case, the increment does *not* execute before the program evaluates the iteration-continuation condition, so the while does not execute in the same manner as the for.

Software Engineering Observation 5.1

Some programmers feel that break and continue violate structured programming. The same effects are achievable with structured-programming techniques, so these programmers do not use break or continue.

Software Engineering Observation 5.2

There's a tension between achieving quality software engineering and achieving the best-performing software. Sometimes one of these goals is achieved at the expense of the other. For all but the most performance-intensive situations, apply the following guideline: First, make your code simple and correct; then make it fast and small, but only if necessary.

5.9 Logical Operators

The if, if...else, while, do...while and for statements each require a *condition* to determine how to continue a program's flow of control. So far, we've studied only simple conditions, such as count <= 10, number != sentinelValue and total > 1000. Simple conditions are expressed in terms of the relational operators >, <, >= and <= and the equality operators == and !=, and each expression tests only one condition. To test *multiple* conditions in the process of making a decision, we performed these tests in separate statements or in nested if or if...else statements. Sometimes control statements require more complex conditions to determine a program's flow of control.

Java's **logical operators** enable you to *combine* simple conditions into more complex ones. The logical operators are && (conditional AND), || (conditional OR), & (boolean logical AND), | (boolean logical inclusive OR), ∧ (boolean logical exclusive OR) and ! (logical NOT). [*Note:* The &, | and ∧ operators are also bitwise operators when they're applied to integral operands. We discuss the bitwise operators in Appendix E.]

5.9.1 Conditional AND (&&) Operator

Suppose we wish to ensure at some point in a program that two conditions are *both* true before we choose a certain path of execution. In this case, we can use the && (**conditional AND**) operator, as follows:

```
if (gender == FEMALE && age >= 65) {
    ++seniorFemales;
}
```

This if statement contains two simple conditions. The condition gender == FEMALE compares variable gender to the constant FEMALE to determine whether a person is female. The condition age >= 65 might be evaluated to determine whether a person is a senior citizen. The if statement considers the combined condition

```
gender == FEMALE && age >= 65
```

which is true if and only if *both* simple conditions are true. In this case, the if statement's body increments seniorFemales by 1. If either or both of the simple conditions are false, the program skips the increment.

Similarly, the following condition ensures that a grade is in the range 1–100:

```
grade >= 1 && grade <= 100
```

This condition is true if and only if grade is greater than or equal to 1 *and* grade is less than or equal to 100. Some programmers find that the preceding combined condition is more readable when *redundant* parentheses are added, as in:

```
(grade >= 1) && (grade <= 100)
```

The table in Fig. 5.15 summarizes the && operator, showing all four possible combinations of false and true values for *expression1* and *expression2*. Such tables are called **truth tables**. Java evaluates to false or true all expressions that include relational operators, equality operators or logical operators.

expression1	expression2	expression1 && expression2
false	false	false
false	true	false
true	false	false
true	true	true

Fig. 5.15 | && (conditional AND) operator truth table.

5.9.2 Conditional OR (||) Operator

Now suppose we wish to ensure that *either or both* of two conditions are true before we choose a certain path of execution. In this case, we use the || (**conditional OR**) operator, as in the following program segment:

```
if ((semesterAverage >= 90) || (finalExam >= 90)) {
    System.out.println ("Student grade is A");
}
```

This statement also contains two simple conditions. The condition semesterAverage >= 90 evaluates to determine whether the student deserves an A in the course because of a solid performance throughout the semester. The condition finalExam >= 90 evaluates to determine whether the student deserves an A in the course because of an outstanding performance on the final exam. The if statement then considers the combined condition

```
(semesterAverage >= 90) || (finalExam >= 90)
```

and awards the student an A if *either or both* of the simple conditions are true. The only time the message "Student grade is A" is *not* printed is when *both* of the simple conditions are false. Figure 5.16 is a truth table for operator conditional OR (||). Operator && has a higher precedence than operator ||. Both operators associate from left to right.

expression1	expression2	expression1 || expression2
false	false	false
false	true	true
true	false	true
true	true	true

Fig. 5.16 | || (conditional OR) operator truth table.

5.9.3 Short-Circuit Evaluation of Complex Conditions

The parts of an expression containing && or || operators are evaluated *only* until it's known whether the condition is true or false. Thus, evaluation of the expression

```
(gender == FEMALE) && (age >= 65)
```

stops immediately if gender *is not* equal to FEMALE (that is, the entire expression is false) and continues if gender *is* equal to FEMALE (that is, the entire expression could still be true if the condition age >= 65 is true). This feature of conditional AND and conditional OR expressions is called **short-circuit evaluation**.

Common Programming Error 5.7

In expressions using &&, *a condition—we'll call this the* dependent condition*—may require another condition to be* true *for the dependent condition's evaluation to be meaningful. In this case, the dependent condition should be placed* after *the* && *operator to prevent errors. Consider the expression* (i != 0) && (10 / i == 2). *The dependent condition* (10 / i == 2) *must* appear after the && to prevent the possibility of division by zero.

5.9.4 Boolean Logical AND (&) and Boolean Logical Inclusive OR (|) Operators

The **boolean logical AND (&)** and **boolean logical inclusive OR** (|) operators are identical to the && and || operators, except that the & and | operators *always* evaluate *both* of their operands (i.e., they do *not* perform short-circuit evaluation). So, the expression

```
(gender == 1) & (age >= 65)
```

evaluates age >= 65 *regardless* of whether gender is equal to 1. This is useful if the right operand has a required **side effect**—a modification of a variable's value. For example,

```
(birthday == true) | (++age >= 65)
```

guarantees that the condition ++age >= 65 will be evaluated. Thus, the variable age is incremented, regardless of whether the overall expression is true or false.

Error-Prevention Tip 5.10

For clarity, avoid expressions with side effects (such as assignments) in conditions. They can make code harder to understand and can lead to subtle logic errors.

Error-Prevention Tip 5.11

Every condition must result in a boolean *value; otherwise, a compilation error occurs.*

5.9.5 Boolean Logical Exclusive OR (^)

A simple condition containing the **boolean logical exclusive OR** (^) operator is true *if and only if one of its operands is* true *and the other is* false. If both are true or both are false, the entire condition is false. Figure 5.17 is a truth table for the boolean logical exclusive OR operator (^). This operator is guaranteed to evaluate *both* of its operands.

expression1	expression2	expression1 ^ expression2
false	false	false
false	true	true
true	false	true
true	true	false

Fig. 5.17 | ^ (boolean logical exclusive OR) operator truth table.

5.9.6 Logical Negation (!) Operator

The ! (**logical NOT**, also called **logical negation** or **logical complement**) operator "reverses" the meaning of a condition. Unlike the logical operators &&, ||, &, | and ^, which are *binary* operators that combine two conditions, the logical negation operator is a *unary* operator that has only one condition as an operand. The operator is placed *before* a condition to choose a path of execution if the original condition (without the logical negation operator) is false, as in the program segment

```
if (! (grade == sentinelValue)) {
    System.out.printf("The next grade is %d%n", grade);
}
```

which executes the printf call only if grade is *not* equal to sentinelValue. The parentheses around the condition grade == sentinelValue are needed because the logical negation operator has a *higher* precedence than the equality operator.

In most cases, you can avoid using logical negation by expressing the condition differently with an appropriate relational or equality operator. For example, the previous statement may also be written as follows:

```
if (grade != sentinelValue) {
    System.out.printf("The next grade is %d%n", grade);
}
```

This flexibility can help you express a condition in a more convenient manner. Figure 5.18 is a truth table for the logical negation operator.

expression	!expression
false	true
true	false

Fig. 5.18 | ! (logical NOT) operator truth table.

5.9.7 Logical Operators Example

Figure 5.19 uses logical operators to produce the truth tables discussed in this section. The output shows the boolean expression that was evaluated and its result. We used the **%b format specifier** to display the word "true" or the word "false" based on a boolean expression's value. Lines 7–11 produce the truth table for &&. Lines 14–18 produce the truth table for ||. Lines 21–25 produce the truth table for &. Lines 28–33 produce the truth table for |. Lines 36–41 produce the truth table for ^. Lines 44–45 produce the truth table for !.

```
1   // Fig. 5.19: LogicalOperators.java
2   // Logical operators.
3
4   public class LogicalOperators {
5      public static void main(String[] args) {
```

Fig. 5.19 | Logical operators. (Part 1 of 3.)

```
 6          // create truth table for && (conditional AND) operator
 7          System.out.printf("%s%n%s: %b%n%s: %b%n%s: %b%n%s: %b%n%n",
 8             "Conditional AND (&&)", "false && false", (false && false),
 9             "false && true", (false && true),
10             "true && false", (true && false),
11             "true && true", (true && true));
12
13          // create truth table for || (conditional OR) operator
14          System.out.printf("%s%n%s: %b%n%s: %b%n%s: %b%n%s: %b%n%n",
15             "Conditional OR (||)", "false || false", (false || false),
16             "false || true", (false || true),
17             "true || false", (true || false),
18             "true || true", (true || true));
19
20          // create truth table for & (boolean logical AND) operator
21          System.out.printf("%s%n%s: %b%n%s: %b%n%s: %b%n%s: %b%n%n",
22             "Boolean logical AND (&)", "false & false", (false & false),
23             "false & true", (false & true),
24             "true & false", (true & false),
25             "true & true", (true & true));
26
27          // create truth table for | (boolean logical inclusive OR) operator
28          System.out.printf("%s%n%s: %b%n%s: %b%n%s: %b%n%s: %b%n%n",
29             "Boolean logical inclusive OR (|)",
30             "false | false", (false | false),
31             "false | true", (false | true),
32             "true | false", (true | false),
33             "true | true", (true | true));
34
35          // create truth table for ^ (boolean logical exclusive OR) operator
36          System.out.printf("%s%n%s: %b%n%s: %b%n%s: %b%n%s: %b%n%n",
37             "Boolean logical exclusive OR (^)",
38             "false ^ false", (false ^ false),
39             "false ^ true", (false ^ true),
40             "true ^ false", (true ^ false),
41             "true ^ true", (true ^ true));
42
43          // create truth table for ! (logical negation) operator
44          System.out.printf("%s%n%s: %b%n%s: %b%n", "Logical NOT (!)",
45             "!false", (!false), "!true", (!true));
46       }
47    }
```

```
Conditional AND (&&)
false && false: false
false && true: false
true && false: false
true && true: true

Conditional OR (||)
false || false: false
false || true: true
true || false: true
true || true: true
```

Fig. 5.19 | Logical operators. (Part 2 of 3.)

```
Boolean logical AND (&)
false & false: false
false & true: false
true & false: false
true & true: true

Boolean logical inclusive OR (|)
false | false: false
false | true: true
true | false: true
true | true: true

Boolean logical exclusive OR (^)
false ^ false: false
false ^ true: true
true ^ false: true
true ^ true: false

Logical NOT (!)
!false: true
!true: false
```

Fig. 5.19 | Logical operators. (Part 3 of 3.)

Precedence and Associativity of the Operators Presented So Far

Figure 5.20 shows the precedence and associativity of the Java operators introduced so far. The operators are shown from top to bottom in decreasing order of precedence.

Operators	Associativity	Type
++ --	right to left	unary postfix
++ -- + - ! (*type*)	right to left	unary prefix
* / %	left to right	multiplicative
+ -	left to right	additive
< <= > >=	left to right	relational
== !=	left to right	equality
&	left to right	boolean logical AND
^	left to right	boolean logical exclusive OR
		left to right	boolean logical inclusive OR
&&	left to right	conditional AND
||	left to right	conditional OR
?:	right to left	conditional
= += -= *= /= %=	right to left	assignment

Fig. 5.20 | Precedence/associativity of the operators discussed so far.

5.10 Wrap-Up

In this chapter, we completed our introduction to control statements, which enable you to control the flow of execution in methods. Chapter 4 discussed if, if...else and while. This chapter demonstrated for, do...while and switch. We showed that any algorithm can be developed using combinations of the sequence structure, the three types of selection statements—if, if...else and switch—and the three types of iteration statements—while, do...while and for. In this chapter and Chapter 4, we discussed how you can combine these building blocks. You used the break statement to exit a switch statement and to immediately terminate a loop, and used a continue statement to terminate a loop's current iteration and proceed with the loop's next iteration. This chapter also introduced Java's logical operators, which enable you to use more complex conditional expressions in control statements. In Chapter 6, we examine methods in greater depth.

Methods: A Deeper Look

Objectives

In this chapter you'll learn:

- How **static** methods and fields are associated with classes rather than objects.
- About argument promotion and casting.
- How packages group related classes.
- How to use secure random-number generation to implement game-playing applications.
- How the visibility of declarations is limited to specific regions of programs.
- What method overloading is and how to create overloaded methods.

6.1 Introduction

In this chapter, we study methods in more depth. You'll learn more about static methods, which can be called without the need for an object of the class to exist. We'll take a brief diversion into simulation techniques with random-number generation and develop a version of the dice game called craps that uses most of the programming techniques you've used to this point in the book. In addition, you'll learn how to declare constants.

Many of the classes you'll use or create while developing applications will have more than one method of the same name. This technique, called *overloading*, is used to implement methods that perform similar tasks for arguments of different types or for different numbers of arguments. We continue our discussion of methods in Chapter 18, Recursion.

6.2 Program Units in Java

You write Java programs by combining new methods and classes with predefined ones available in the **Java Application Programming Interface** (also referred to as the **Java API** or **Java class library**) and in various other class libraries. Related classes are typically grouped into *packages* so that they can be *imported* into programs and *reused*. You'll learn how to group your own classes into *packages* in Section 8.17. Java 9 introduces another program unit called *modules*, which we discuss in **Chapter 27, Java Platform Module System**.

The Java API provides a rich collection of predefined classes that contain methods for performing common mathematical calculations, string manipulations, character manipulations, input/output operations, database operations, networking operations, file processing, error checking and more.

Software Engineering Observation 6.1

Familiarize yourself with the rich collection of classes and methods provided by the Java API (http://docs.oracle.com/javase/8/docs/api). Section 6.7 overviews several common packages. Don't reinvent the wheel. When possible, reuse Java API classes and methods. This reduces program development time and avoids introducing programming errors.

Error-Prevention Tip 6.1

Some methods return a value indicating whether the method performed its task successfully. When you call such a method, be sure to check the return value of that method and, if that method was unsuccessful, deal with the issue appropriately.

6.3 static Methods, static Fields and Class Math

Most methods execute in response to method calls *on specific objects*. However, sometimes a method performs a task that does not depend on an object. Such a method applies to the class in which it's declared as a whole and is known as a static method or a **class method**. (In Section 10.10, you'll see that interfaces also may contain static methods.)

Classes often contain static methods to perform common tasks. For example, recall that Math's static method pow raises a value to a power (shown in Fig. 5.6). To declare a method as static, place the keyword static before the return type in the method's declaration. For any class imported into your program, you can call the class's static methods by specifying the class's name, followed by a dot (.) and the method name, as in

> *ClassName.methodName(arguments)*

Math *Class Methods*
We use various Math class methods here to present the concept of static methods. Class Math provides methods that enable you to perform common mathematical calculations. For example, you can calculate the square root of 900.0 with the static method call

```
Math.sqrt(900.0)
```

This expression evaluates to 30.0. Method sqrt takes an argument of type double and returns a result of type double. To output the value of the preceding method call in the command window, you might write the statement

```
System.out.println(Math.sqrt(900.0));
```

In this statement, the value that sqrt returns becomes the argument to method println. There was no need to create a Math object before calling method sqrt. Also *all* Math class methods are static—therefore, each is called by preceding its name with the class name Math and the dot (.) separator.

Software Engineering Observation 6.2

Class Math is part of the java.lang package, which is implicitly imported by the compiler, so it's not necessary to import class Math to use its methods.

Method arguments may be constants, variables or expressions. If c = 13.0, d = 3.0 and f = 4.0, then the statement

```
System.out.println(Math.sqrt(c + d * f));
```

calculates and prints the square root of 13.0 + 3.0 * 4.0 = 25.0—namely, 5.0. Figure 6.1 summarizes several Math class methods. In the figure, *x* and *y* are of type double.

static *Variables*
Recall from Section 3.2 that each object of a class maintains its *own* copy of every instance variable of the class. There are variables for which each object of a class does *not* need its own separate copy (as you'll see momentarily). Such variables are declared static and are also known as **class variables**. When objects of a class containing static variables are created, all the objects of that class share *one* copy of the static variables. Together a class's static variables and instance variables are known as its **fields**. You'll learn more about static fields in Section 8.11.

Method	Description	Example
abs(*x*)	absolute value of *x*	abs(23.7) is 23.7 abs(0.0) is 0.0 abs(-23.7) is 23.7
ceil(*x*)	rounds *x* to the smallest integer not less than *x*	ceil(9.2) is 10.0 ceil(-9.8) is -9.0
cos(*x*)	trigonometric cosine of *x* (*x* in radians)	cos(0.0) is 1.0
exp(*x*)	exponential method e^x	exp(1.0) is 2.71828 exp(2.0) is 7.38906
floor(*x*)	rounds *x* to the largest integer not greater than *x*	floor(9.2) is 9.0 floor(-9.8) is -10.0
log(*x*)	natural logarithm of *x* (base *e*)	log(Math.E) is 1.0 log(Math.E * Math.E) is 2.0
max(*x*, *y*)	larger value of *x* and *y*	max(2.3, 12.7) is 12.7 max(-2.3, -12.7) is -2.3
min(*x*, *y*)	smaller value of *x* and *y*	min(2.3, 12.7) is 2.3 min(-2.3, -12.7) is -12.7
pow(*x*, *y*)	*x* raised to the power *y* (i.e., x^y)	pow(2.0, 7.0) is 128.0 pow(9.0, 0.5) is 3.0
sin(*x*)	trigonometric sine of *x* (*x* in radians)	sin(0.0) is 0.0
sqrt(*x*)	square root of *x*	sqrt(900.0) is 30.0
tan(*x*)	trigonometric tangent of *x* (*x* in radians)	tan(0.0) is 0.0

Fig. 6.1 | Math class methods.

Math Class static Constants PI and E

Class Math declares two constants, **Math.PI** and **Math.E**, that represent *high-precision approximations* to commonly used mathematical constants:

- Math.PI (3.141592653589793) is the ratio of a circle's circumference to its diameter.

- Math.E (2.718281828459045) is the base value for natural logarithms (calculated with class Math's static method log).

These constants are declared in class Math with the modifiers public, final and static. Making them public allows you to use them in your own classes. Any field declared with keyword **final** is *constant*—its value cannot change after the field is initialized. Making these fields static allows them to be accessed via the class name Math and a dot (.) separator, just as class Math's methods are.

Why Is Method main Declared static?

When you execute the Java Virtual Machine (JVM) with the java command, the JVM attempts to invoke the main method of the class you specify—at this point no objects of the class have been created. Declaring main as static allows the JVM to invoke main without creating an instance of the class. When you execute your application, you specify its class name as an argument to the java command, as in

> java *ClassName argument1 argument2 ...*

The JVM loads the class specified by *ClassName* and uses that class name to invoke method main. In the preceding command, *ClassName* is a **command-line argument** to the JVM that tells it which class to execute. Following the *ClassName*, you can also specify a list of Strings (separated by spaces) as command-line arguments that the JVM will pass to your application. Such arguments might be used to specify options (e.g., a filename) to run the application. Every class may contain main—only the main of the class used to execute the application is called. As you'll learn in Chapter 7, Arrays and ArrayLists, your application can access those command-line arguments and use them to customize the application.

6.4 Methods with Multiple Parameters

Methods often require more than one piece of information to perform their tasks. We now consider how to write your own methods with *multiple* parameters.

Figure 6.2 uses a method called maximum to determine and return the largest of three double values. In main, lines 11–15 prompt the user to enter three double values, then read them from the user. Line 18 calls method maximum (declared in lines 25–39) to determine the largest of the three values it receives as arguments. When method maximum returns the result to line 18, the program assigns maximum's return value to local variable result. Then line 21 outputs the maximum value. At the end of this section, we'll discuss the use of operator + in line 21.

```java
1   // Fig. 6.2: MaximumFinder.java
2   // Programmer-declared method maximum with three double parameters.
3   import java.util.Scanner;
4
5   public class MaximumFinder {
6      public static void main(String[] args) {
7         // create Scanner for input from command window
8         Scanner input = new Scanner(System.in);
9
10        // prompt for and input three floating-point values
11        System.out.print(
12           "Enter three floating-point values separated by spaces: ");
13        double number1 = input.nextDouble(); // read first double
14        double number2 = input.nextDouble(); // read second double
15        double number3 = input.nextDouble(); // read third double
16
17        // determine the maximum value
18        double result = maximum(number1, number2, number3);
19
20        // display maximum value
21        System.out.println("Maximum is: " + result);
22     }
23
```

Fig. 6.2 | Programmer-declared method maximum with three double parameters. (Part 1 of 2.)

```
24      // returns the maximum of its three double parameters
25      public static double maximum(double x, double y, double z) {
26          double maximumValue = x; // assume x is the largest to start
27
28          // determine whether y is greater than maximumValue
29          if (y > maximumValue) {
30              maximumValue = y;
31          }
32
33          // determine whether z is greater than maximumValue
34          if (z > maximumValue) {
35              maximumValue = z;
36          }
37
38          return maximumValue;
39      }
40  }
```

```
Enter three floating-point values separated by spaces: 9.35 2.74 5.1
Maximum is: 9.35
```

```
Enter three floating-point values separated by spaces: 5.8 12.45 8.32
Maximum is: 12.45
```

```
Enter three floating-point values separated by spaces: 6.46 4.12 10.54
Maximum is: 10.54
```

Fig. 6.2 | Programmer-declared method maximum with three double parameters. (Part 2 of 2.)

The public and static Keywords

Method maximum's declaration begins with keyword public to indicate that the method is "available to the public"—it can be called from methods of other classes. The keyword static enables the main method (another static method) to call maximum as shown in line 18 without qualifying the method name with the class name MaximumFinder—static methods in the same class can call each other directly. Any other class that uses maximum must fully qualify the method name, as in MaximumFinder.maximum(10, 30, 20).

Method maximum

Consider maximum's declaration (lines 25–39). Line 25 indicates that it returns a double value, that the method's name is maximum and that the method requires three double parameters (x, y and z) to accomplish its task. Multiple parameters are specified as a comma-separated list. When maximum is called from line 18, the parameters x, y and z are initialized with copies of the values of arguments number1, number2 and number3, respectively. There must be one argument in the method call for each parameter in the method declaration. Each argument also must be *consistent* with the corresponding parameter's type. For example, a parameter of type double can receive values like 7.35, 22 or –0.03456, but not `String`s like `"hello"` nor the `boolean` values `true` or `false`. Section 6.6 discusses the argument types that you can provide in a method call for each primitive-type parameter.

To determine the maximum value, we initially assume that parameter x contains the largest value, so line 26 declares local variable `maximumValue` and initializes it with the value of parameter x. Of course, it's possible that parameter y or z contains the actual largest value, so we must compare each of these with `maximumValue`. Lines 29–31 determine whether y is greater than `maximumValue`. If so, line 30 assigns y to `maximumValue`. Lines 34–36 determine whether z is greater than `maximumValue`. If so, line 35 assigns z to `maximumValue`. At this point the largest value resides in `maximumValue`, so line 38 returns that value to line 18. When program control returns to where maximum was called, maximum's parameters x, y and z no longer exist in memory.

Software Engineering Observation 6.3
Methods can return at most one value, but the returned value could be a reference to an object that contains many values in its instance variables.

Software Engineering Observation 6.4
Variables should be declared as fields only if they're required for use in more than one method of the class or if the program should save their values between calls to the class's methods.

Common Programming Error 6.1
Declaring method parameters of the same type as `float x, y` instead of `float x, float y` is a syntax error—a type is required for each parameter in the parameter list.

Implementing Method `maximum` by Reusing Method `Math.max`
The entire body of our maximum method could also be implemented with two calls to `Math.max`, as follows:

```
return Math.max(x, Math.max(y, z));
```

The first call to `Math.max` specifies arguments x and `Math.max(y, z)`. *Before* any method can be called, its arguments must be evaluated to determine their values. If an argument is a method call, the method call must be performed to determine its return value. So, in the preceding statement, `Math.max(y, z)` is evaluated to determine the maximum of y and z. Then the result is passed as the second argument to the other call to `Math.max`, which returns the larger of its two arguments. This is a good example of software reuse—we find the largest of three values by reusing `Math.max`, which finds the larger of two values. Note how concise this code is compared to lines 26–38 of Fig. 6.2.

Assembling Strings with String Concatenation
Java allows you to assemble `String` objects into larger strings by using operators + or +=. This is known as **string concatenation**. When both operands of operator + are `String` objects, operator + creates a new `String` object containing the characters of the left operand followed by those of the right operand—so the expression `"hello " + "there"` creates the `String` `"hello there"`.

In line 21 of Fig. 6.2, the expression

```
"Maximum is: " + result
```

uses operator + with operands of types String and double. *Every primitive value and object in Java can be represented as a String.* When one of the + operator's operands is a String, the other is converted to a String, then the two are *concatenated.* In line 21, the double value is converted to its String representation and placed at the end of "Maximum is: ". If there are any *trailing zeros* in a double value, these will be *discarded* when the number is converted to a String—for example, 9.3500 would be represented as 9.35.

Primitive values used in String concatenation are converted to Strings. A boolean concatenated with a String is converted to the String "true" or "false". *All objects have a toString method that returns a String representation of the object.* (We discuss toString in more detail in subsequent chapters.) When an object is concatenated with a String, the object's toString method is called implicitly and returns the object's String representation. Method toString also can be called explicitly.

You can break large String literals into several smaller Strings and place them on multiple lines of code for readability. In this case, the Strings can be reassembled using concatenation. We discuss the details of Strings in Chapter 14.

Common Programming Error 6.2

It's a syntax error to break a String literal across lines. If necessary, you can split a String into several smaller Strings and use concatenation to form the desired String.

Common Programming Error 6.3

Confusing the + operator used for string concatenation with the + operator used for addition can lead to strange results. Java evaluates the operands of an operator from left to right. For example, if integer variable y has the value 5, the expression "y + 2 = " + y + 2 results in the string "y + 2 = 52", not "y + 2 = 7", because first the value of y (5) is concatenated to the string "y + 2 = ", then the value 2 is concatenated to the new larger string "y + 2 = 5". The expression "y + 2 = " + (y + 2) produces the desired result "y + 2 = 7".

6.5 Notes on Declaring and Using Methods

Calling Methods

There are three ways to call a method:

1. Using a method name by itself to call another method of the *same* class—such as maximum(number1, number2, number3) in line 18 of Fig. 6.2.

2. Using a variable that contains a reference to an object, followed by a dot (.) and the method name to call a non-static method of the referenced object—such as the method call in line 14 of Fig. 3.2, myAccount.getName(), which calls a method of class Account from the main method of AccountTest. Non-static methods are typically called **instance methods**.

3. Using the class name and a dot (.) to call a static method of a class—such as Math.sqrt(900.0) in Section 6.3.

Returning from Methods

There are three ways to return control to the statement that calls a method:

- When the method-ending right brace is reached in a method with return type void.

- When the following statement executes in a method with return type void

  ```
  return;
  ```

- When a method returns a result with a statement of the following form in which the *expression* is evaluated and its result (and control) are returned to the caller:

  ```
  return expression;
  ```

Common Programming Error 6.4
Declaring a method outside the body of a class declaration or inside the body of another method is a syntax error.

Common Programming Error 6.5
Declaring a local variable in a method with the same name as one of the method's parameters is a compilation error.

Common Programming Error 6.6
Forgetting to return a value from a method that should return a value is a compilation error. If a return type other than void is specified, the method must *contain a return statement that returns a value consistent with the method's return type. Returning a value from a method whose return type has been declared void is a compilation error.*

static Members Can Access Only the Class's Other static Members Directly

A static method can call directly (that is, using the method name by itself) *only* other static methods of the same class and can manipulate directly *only* static variables in the same class. To access a class's instance variables and instance methods (that is, its non-static members), a static method must use a reference to an object of that class. Instance methods can access all fields (static variables and instance variables) and methods of the class.

Many objects of a class, each with its own copies of the instance variables, may exist at the same time. Suppose a static method were to invoke a non-static method directly. How would the method know which object's instance variables to manipulate? What would happen if no objects of the class existed at the time the non-static method was invoked?

6.6 Argument Promotion and Casting

Another important feature of method calls is **argument promotion**—converting an *argument's value*, if possible, to the type that the method expects to receive in its corresponding *parameter*. For example, a program can call Math method sqrt with an int argument even though a double argument is expected. The statement

```
System.out.println(Math.sqrt(4));
```

correctly evaluates Math.sqrt(4) and prints the value 2.0. The method declaration's parameter list causes Java to convert the int value 4 to the double value 4.0 *before* passing the value to method sqrt. Such conversions may lead to compilation errors if Java's **promotion rules** are not satisfied. These rules specify which conversions are allowed—that is, which ones can be performed *without losing data*. In the sqrt example above, an int is converted to a double without changing its value. However, converting a double to an int *truncates* the fractional part of the double value—thus, part of the value is lost. Converting large integer types to small integer types (for example, long to int, or int to short) may also result in changed values.

The promotion rules apply to expressions containing values of two or more primitive types and to primitive-type values passed as arguments to methods. Each value is promoted to the "highest" type in the expression. Actually, the expression uses a *temporary copy* of each value—the types of the original values remain unchanged. Figure 6.3 lists the primitive types and the types to which each can be promoted. The valid promotions for a given type are always to a type higher in the table. For example, an int can be promoted to the higher types long, float and double.

Type	Valid promotions
double	None
float	double
long	float or double
int	long, float or double
char	int, long, float or double
short	int, long, float or double (but not char)
byte	short, int, long, float or double (but not char)
boolean	None (boolean values are not considered to be numbers in Java)

Fig. 6.3 | Promotions allowed for primitive types.

Converting values to types lower in the table of Fig. 6.3 will result in different values if the lower type cannot represent the value of the higher type (for example, the int value 2000000 cannot be represented as a short, and any floating-point number with digits after its decimal point cannot be represented in an integer type such as long, int or short). Therefore, in cases where information may be lost due to conversion, the Java compiler requires you to use a *cast operator* (introduced in Section 4.7) to explicitly force the conversion to occur—otherwise a compilation error occurs. This enables you to "take control" from the compiler. You essentially say, "I know this conversion might cause loss of information, but for my purposes here, that's fine." Suppose method square calculates the square of an integer and thus requires an int argument. To call square with a double argument named doubleValue, we would be required to write the method call as

```
square((int) doubleValue)
```

This method call explicitly casts (converts) doubleValue's value to a a temporary integer for use in method square. Thus, if doubleValue's value is 4.5, the method receives the value 4 and returns 16, not 20.25.

Common Programming Error 6.7
Casting a primitive-type value to another primitive type may change the value if the new type is not a valid promotion. For example, casting a floating-point value to an integer value may introduce truncation errors (loss of the fractional part) into the result.

6.7 Java API Packages

As you've seen, Java contains many *predefined* classes that are grouped into categories of related classes called *packages*. Together, these are known as the Java Application Programming Interface (Java API), or the Java class library. A great strength of Java is the Java API's thousands of classes. Some key Java API packages that we use in this book are described in Fig. 6.4, which represents only a small portion of the *reusable components* in the Java API.

Package	Description
java.io	The **Java Input/Output Package** contains classes and interfaces that enable programs to input and output data. (See Chapter 15, Files, Input/Output Streams, NIO and XML Serialization.)
java.lang	The **Java Language Package** contains classes and interfaces (discussed throughout the book) that are required by many Java programs. This package is imported by the compiler into all programs.
java.net	The **Java Networking Package** contains classes and interfaces that enable programs to communicate via computer networks like the Internet.
java.security	The **Java Security Package** contains classes and interfaces for enhancing application security.
java.sql	The **JDBC Package** contains classes and interfaces for working with databases. (See Chapter 22, Accessing Databases with JDBC.)
java.util	The **Java Utilities Package** contains utility classes and interfaces that enable storing and processing of large amounts of data. Many of these classes and interfaces have been updated to support Java SE 8's lambda capabilities. (See Chapter 16, Generic Collections.)
java.util.concurrent	The **Java Concurrency Package** contains utility classes and interfaces for implementing programs that can perform multiple tasks in parallel. (See Chapter 21, Concurrency and Multi-Core Performance.)
javafx packages	JavaFX is Java's preferred GUI, graphics and multimedia technology for the future. We cover JavaFX extensively throughout the book.
Some Java SE 8 Packages Used in This Book	
java.time	The Java SE 8 **Date/Time API Package** contains classes and interfaces for working with dates and times. (See Chapter 21, Concurrency and Multi-Core Performance.)
java.util.function and java.util.stream	These packages contain types for working with Java SE 8's functional programming capabilities. (See Chapter 17, Lambdas and Streams.)

Fig. 6.4 | Java API packages (a subset).

The set of packages available in Java is quite large. In addition to those summarized in Fig. 6.4, Java includes packages for complex graphics, advanced graphical user interfaces, printing, advanced networking, security, database processing, multimedia, accessibility (for people with disabilities), concurrent programming, cryptography, XML processing and many other capabilities. For an overview of the packages in Java, visit

http://docs.oracle.com/javase/8/docs/api/overview-summary.html

You can locate additional information about a predefined Java class's methods in the Java API documentation at

```
http://docs.oracle.com/javase/8/docs/api
```

When you visit this site, click the **Index** link to see an alphabetical listing of all the classes and methods in the Java API. Locate the class name and click its link to see the online description of the class. Click the **METHOD** link to see a table of the class's methods. Each `static` method will be listed with the word "`static`" preceding its return type.

6.8 Case Study: Secure Random-Number Generation

We now take a brief diversion into a popular type of programming application—simulation and game playing. In this and the next section, we develop a game-playing program with multiple methods. The program uses most of the control statements presented thus far in the book and introduces several new programming concepts.

The **element of chance** can be introduced in a program via an object of class **Secure-Random** (package `java.security`). Such objects can produce random `boolean`, `byte`, `float`, `double`, `int`, `long` and Gaussian values. In the next several examples, we use objects of class `SecureRandom` to produce random values.

Moving to Secure Random Numbers
Recent editions of this book used Java's `Random` class to obtain "random" values. This class produced *deterministic* values that could be *predicted* by malicious programmers. Secure-Random objects produce **nondeterministic random numbers** that *cannot* be predicted.

Deterministic random numbers have been the source of many software security breaches. Most programming languages now have library features similar to `SecureRandom` for producing nondeterministic random numbers to help prevent such problems. From this point forward in the text, when we refer to "random numbers" we mean "secure random numbers."

Software Engineering Observation 6.5

For developers concerned with building increasingly secure applications, Java 9 enhances SecureRandom's capabilities as defined by JEP 273.

Creating a *SecureRandom* Object
A new secure random-number generator object can be created as follows:

```
SecureRandom randomNumbers = new SecureRandom();
```

It can then be used to generate random values—we discuss only random `int` values here. For more information on the `SecureRandom` class, see

```
http://docs.oracle.com/javase/8/docs/api/java/security/
SecureRandom.html
```

Obtaining a Random *int* Value
Consider the following statement:

```
int randomValue = randomNumbers.nextInt();
```

SecureRandom method **nextInt** generates a random int value. If it truly produces values *at random*, then every value in the range should have an *equal chance* (or probability) of being chosen each time nextInt is called.

Changing the Range of Values Produced By *nextInt*

The range of values produced by method nextInt generally differs from the range of values required in a particular Java application. For example, a program that simulates coin tossing might require only 0 for "heads" and 1 for "tails." A program that simulates the rolling of a six-sided die might require random integers in the range 1–6. A program that randomly predicts the next type of spaceship (out of four possibilities) that will fly across the horizon in a video game might require random integers in the range 1–4. For cases like these, class SecureRandom provides another version of method nextInt that receives an int argument and returns a value from 0 up to, but not including, the argument's value. For example, for coin tossing, the following statement returns 0 or 1.

```
int randomValue = randomNumbers.nextInt(2);
```

Rolling a Six-Sided Die

To demonstrate random numbers, let's develop a program that simulates 20 rolls of a six-sided die and displays the value of each roll. We begin by using nextInt to produce random values in the range 0–5, as follows:

```
int face = randomNumbers.nextInt(6);
```

The argument 6—called the **scaling factor**—represents the number of unique values that nextInt should produce (in this case six—0, 1, 2, 3, 4 and 5). This manipulation is called **scaling** the range of values produced by SecureRandom method nextInt.

A six-sided die has the numbers 1–6 on its faces, not 0–5. So we **shift** the range of numbers produced by adding a **shifting value**—in this case 1—to our previous result, as in

```
int face = 1 + randomNumbers.nextInt(6);
```

The shifting value (1) specifies the *first* value in the desired range of random integers. The preceding statement assigns face a random integer in the range 1–6.

Rolling a Six-Sided Die 20 Times

Figure 6.5 shows two sample outputs which confirm that the results of the preceding calculation are integers in the range 1–6, and that each run of the program can produce a *different* sequence of random numbers. Line 3 imports class SecureRandom from the java.security package. Line 8 creates the SecureRandom object randomNumbers to produce random values. Line 13 executes 20 times in a loop to roll the die. The if statement (lines 18–20) in the loop starts a new line of output after every five numbers to create a neat, five-column format.

```
1   // Fig. 6.5: RandomIntegers.java
2   // Shifted and scaled random integers.
3   import java.security.SecureRandom; // program uses class SecureRandom
4
```

Fig. 6.5 | Shifted and scaled random integers. (Part 1 of 2.)

```
 5   public class RandomIntegers {
 6      public static void main(String[] args) {
 7         // randomNumbers object will produce secure random numbers
 8         SecureRandom randomNumbers = new SecureRandom();
 9
10         // loop 20 times
11         for (int counter = 1; counter <= 20; counter++) {
12            // pick random integer from 1 to 6
13            int face = 1 + randomNumbers.nextInt(6);
14
15            System.out.printf("%d  ", face); // display generated value
16
17            // if counter is divisible by 5, start a new line of output
18            if (counter % 5 == 0) {
19               System.out.println();
20            }
21         }
22      }
23   }
```

```
1  5  3  6  2
5  2  6  5  2
4  4  4  2  6
3  1  6  2  2
```

```
6  5  4  2  6
1  2  5  1  3
6  3  2  2  1
6  4  2  6  4
```

Fig. 6.5 | Shifted and scaled random integers. (Part 2 of 2.)

Rolling a Six-Sided Die 60,000,000 Times

To show that the numbers produced by nextInt occur with approximately equal likelihood, let's simulate 60,000,000 rolls of a die with the application in Fig. 6.6. Each integer from 1 to 6 should appear approximately 10,000,000 times. Note in line 18 that we used the _ digit separator to make the int value 60_000_000 more readable. Recall that you cannot separate digits with commas. For example, if you replace the int value 60_000_000 with 60,000,000, the JDK 8 compiler generates several compilation errors throughout the for statement's header (line 18). Note that this example might take several seconds to execute—see our note about SecureRandom performance following the example.

```
1   // Fig. 6.6: RollDie.java
2   // Roll a six-sided die 60,000,000 times.
3   import java.security.SecureRandom;
4
5   public class RollDie {
6      public static void main(String[] args) {
```

Fig. 6.6 | Roll a six-sided die 60,000,000 times. (Part 1 of 3.)

```
7      // randomNumbers object will produce secure random numbers
8      SecureRandom randomNumbers = new SecureRandom();
9
10     int frequency1 = 0; // count of 1s rolled
11     int frequency2 = 0; // count of 2s rolled
12     int frequency3 = 0; // count of 3s rolled
13     int frequency4 = 0; // count of 4s rolled
14     int frequency5 = 0; // count of 5s rolled
15     int frequency6 = 0; // count of 6s rolled
16
17     // tally counts for 60,000,000 rolls of a die
18     for (int roll = 1; roll <= 60_000_000; roll++) {
19        int face = 1 + randomNumbers.nextInt(6); // number from 1 to 6
20
21        // use face value 1-6 to determine which counter to increment
22        switch (face) {
23           case 1:
24              ++frequency1; // increment the 1s counter
25              break;
26           case 2:
27              ++frequency2; // increment the 2s counter
28              break;
29           case 3:
30              ++frequency3; // increment the 3s counter
31              break;
32           case 4:
33              ++frequency4; // increment the 4s counter
34              break;
35           case 5:
36              ++frequency5; // increment the 5s counter
37              break;
38           case 6:
39              ++frequency6; // increment the 6s counter
40              break;
41        }
42     }
43
44     System.out.println("Face\tFrequency"); // output headers
45     System.out.printf("1\t%d%n2\t%d%n3\t%d%n4\t%d%n5\t%d%n6\t%d%n",
46        frequency1, frequency2, frequency3, frequency4,
47        frequency5, frequency6);
48  }
49 }
```

Face	Frequency
1	10001086
2	10000185
3	9999542
4	9996541
5	9998787
6	10003859

Fig. 6.6 | Roll a six-sided die 60,000,000 times. (Part 2 of 3.)

Face	Frequency
1	10003530
2	9999925
3	9994766
4	10000707
5	9998150
6	10002922

Fig. 6.6 | Roll a six-sided die 60,000,000 times. (Part 3 of 3.)

As the sample outputs show, scaling and shifting the values produced by nextInt enables the program to simulate rolling a six-sided die. The application uses nested control statements (the switch is nested inside the for) to determine the number of times each side of the die appears. The for statement (lines 18–42) iterates 60,000,000 times. During each iteration, line 19 produces a random value from 1 to 6. That value is then used as the controlling expression (line 22) of the switch statement (lines 22–41). Based on the face value, the switch statement increments one of the six counter variables during each iteration of the loop. This switch statement has no default case, because we have a case for every possible die value that the expression in line 19 could produce. Run the program, and observe the results. As you'll see, every time you run this program, it produces *different* results.

When we study arrays in Chapter 7, we'll show an elegant way to replace the entire switch statement in this program with a *single* statement. Then, when we study Java SE 8's functional programming capabilities in Chapter 17, we'll show how to replace the loop that rolls the dice, the switch statement *and* the statement that displays the results with a *single* statement!

Performance Tip 6.1

Using SecureRandom instead of Random to achieve higher levels of security incurs a significant performance penalty. For "casual" applications, you might want to use class Random from package java.util—simply replace SecureRandom with Random.

Generalized Scaling and Shifting of Random Numbers
Previously, we simulated the rolling of a six-sided die with the statement

```
int face = 1 + randomNumbers.nextInt(6);
```

This statement always assigns to variable face an integer in the range 1 ≤ face ≤ 6. The *width* of this range (i.e., the number of consecutive integers in the range) is 6, and the *starting number* in the range is 1. In the preceding statement, the width of the range is determined by the number 6 that's passed as an argument to SecureRandom method nextInt, and the starting number of the range is the number 1 that's added to randomNumbers.nextInt(6). We can generalize this result as

```
int number = shiftingValue + randomNumbers.nextInt(scalingFactor);
```

where *shiftingValue* specifies the *first number* in the desired range of consecutive integers and *scalingFactor* specifies *how many numbers* are in the range.

It's also possible to choose integers at random from sets of values other than ranges of consecutive integers. For example, to obtain a random value from the sequence 2, 5, 8, 11 and 14, you could use the statement

```
int number = 2 + 3 * randomNumbers.nextInt(5);
```

In this case, `randomNumbers.nextInt(5)` produces values in the range 0–4. Each value produced is multiplied by 3 to produce a number in the sequence 0, 3, 6, 9 and 12. We add 2 to that value to *shift* the range of values and obtain a value from the sequence 2, 5, 8, 11 and 14. We can generalize this result as

```
int number = shiftingValue +
        differenceBetweenValues * randomNumbers.nextInt(scalingFactor);
```

where *shiftingValue* specifies the first number in the desired range of values, *differenceBetweenValues* represents the *constant difference* between consecutive numbers in the sequence and *scalingFactor* specifies how many numbers are in the range.

6.9 Case Study: A Game of Chance; Introducing enum Types

A popular game of chance is a dice game known as craps, which is played in casinos and back alleys throughout the world. The rules of the game are straightforward:

> *You roll two dice. Each die has six faces, which contain one, two, three, four, five and six spots, respectively. After the dice have come to rest, the sum of the spots on the two upward faces is calculated. If the sum is 7 or 11 on the first throw, you win. If the sum is 2, 3 or 12 on the first throw (called "craps"), you lose (i.e., the "house" wins). If the sum is 4, 5, 6, 8, 9 or 10 on the first throw, that sum becomes your "point." To win, you must continue rolling the dice until you "make your point" (i.e., roll that same point value). You lose by rolling a 7 before making your point.*

Figure 6.7 simulates the game of craps, using methods to implement the game's logic. The `main` method (lines 20–66) calls the `rollDice` method (lines 69–80) as necessary to roll the dice and compute their sum. The sample outputs show winning and losing on the first roll, and winning and losing on a subsequent roll.

```java
1   // Fig. 6.7: Craps.java
2   // Craps class simulates the dice game craps.
3   import java.security.SecureRandom;
4
5   public class Craps {
6       // create secure random number generator for use in method rollDice
7       private static final SecureRandom randomNumbers = new SecureRandom();
8
9       // enum type with constants that represent the game status
10      private enum Status {CONTINUE, WON, LOST};
11
12      // constants that represent common rolls of the dice
13      private static final int SNAKE_EYES = 2;
14      private static final int TREY = 3;
```

Fig. 6.7 | Craps class simulates the dice game craps. (Part 1 of 3.)

```
15       private static final int SEVEN = 7;
16       private static final int YO_LEVEN = 11;
17       private static final int BOX_CARS = 12;
18
19       // plays one game of craps
20       public static void main(String[] args) {
21          int myPoint = 0; // point if no win or loss on first roll
22          Status gameStatus; // can contain CONTINUE, WON or LOST
23
24          int sumOfDice = rollDice(); // first roll of the dice
25
26          // determine game status and point based on first roll
27          switch (sumOfDice) {
28             case SEVEN: // win with 7 on first roll
29             case YO_LEVEN: // win with 11 on first roll
30                gameStatus = Status.WON;
31                break;
32             case SNAKE_EYES: // lose with 2 on first roll
33             case TREY: // lose with 3 on first roll
34             case BOX_CARS: // lose with 12 on first roll
35                gameStatus = Status.LOST;
36                break;
37             default: // did not win or lose, so remember point
38                gameStatus = Status.CONTINUE; // game is not over
39                myPoint = sumOfDice; // remember the point
40                System.out.printf("Point is %d%n", myPoint);
41                break;
42          }
43
44          // while game is not complete
45          while (gameStatus == Status.CONTINUE) { // not WON or LOST
46             sumOfDice = rollDice(); // roll dice again
47
48             // determine game status
49             if (sumOfDice == myPoint) { // win by making point
50                gameStatus = Status.WON;
51             }
52             else {
53                if (sumOfDice == SEVEN) { // lose by rolling 7 before point
54                   gameStatus = Status.LOST;
55                }
56             }
57          }
58
59          // display won or lost message
60          if (gameStatus == Status.WON) {
61             System.out.println("Player wins");
62          }
63          else {
64             System.out.println("Player loses");
65          }
66       }
67
```

Fig. 6.7 | Craps class simulates the dice game craps. (Part 2 of 3.)

```
68        // roll dice, calculate sum and display results
69        public static int rollDice() {
70            // pick random die values
71            int die1 = 1 + randomNumbers.nextInt(6); // first die roll
72            int die2 = 1 + randomNumbers.nextInt(6); // second die roll
73
74            int sum = die1 + die2; // sum of die values
75
76            // display results of this roll
77            System.out.printf("Player rolled %d + %d = %d%n", die1, die2, sum);
78
79            return sum;
80        }
81    }
```

```
Player rolled 5 + 6 = 11
Player wins
```

```
Player rolled 5 + 4 = 9
Point is 9
Player rolled 4 + 2 = 6
Player rolled 3 + 6 = 9
Player wins
```

```
Player rolled 1 + 2 = 3
Player loses
```

```
Player rolled 2 + 6 = 8
Point is 8
Player rolled 5 + 1 = 6
Player rolled 2 + 1 = 3
Player rolled 1 + 6 = 7
Player loses
```

Fig. 6.7 | Craps class simulates the dice game craps. (Part 3 of 3.)

Method rollDice

In the rules of the game, the player must roll *two* dice on each roll. We declare method rollDice (lines 69–80) to roll the dice and compute and print their sum. Method roll-Dice is declared once, but it's called from two places (lines 24 and 46) in main, which contains the logic for one complete game of craps. Method rollDice takes no arguments, so it has an empty parameter list. Each time it's called, rollDice returns the sum of the dice, so the return type int is indicated in the method header (line 69). Although lines 71 and 72 look the same (except for the die names), they do not necessarily produce the same result. Each statement produces a *random* value in the range 1–6. Variable randomNumbers (used in lines 71–72) is *not* declared in the method. Instead it's declared as a private static final variable of the class and initialized in line 7. This enables us to create one

SecureRandom object that's reused in each call to rollDice. If there were a program that contained multiple instances of class Craps, they'd all share this one SecureRandom object.

Method main's Local Variables

The game is reasonably involved. The player may win or lose on the first roll, or may win or lose on any subsequent roll. Method main (lines 20–66) uses

- local variable myPoint (line 21) to store the "point" if the player doesn't win or lose on the first roll,
- local variable gameStatus (line 22) to keep track of the overall game status and
- local variable sumOfDice (line 24) to hold the sum of the dice for the most recent roll.

Variable myPoint is initialized to 0 to ensure that the application will compile. If you do not initialize myPoint, the compiler issues an error, because myPoint is not assigned a value in *every* case of the switch statement, and thus the program could try to use myPoint before it's assigned a value. By contrast, gameStatus *is* assigned a value in *every* case of the switch statement (including the default case)—thus, it's guaranteed to be initialized before it's used, so we do not need to initialize it in line 22.

enum Type Status

Local variable gameStatus (line 22) is declared to be of a new type called Status (declared at line 10). Type Status is a private member of class Craps, because Status will be used only in that class. Status is a type called an **enum type**, which, in its simplest form, declares a set of constants represented by identifiers. An enum type is a special kind of class that's introduced by the keyword enum and a type name (in this case, Status). As with classes, braces delimit an enum declaration's body. Inside the braces is a comma-separated list of **enum constants**, each representing a unique value. The identifiers in an enum must be *unique*. You'll learn more about enum types in Chapter 8.

Good Programming Practice 6.1

Use only uppercase letters in the names of enum constants to make them stand out and remind you that they're not variables.

Variables of type Status can be assigned only the three constants declared in the enum (line 10) or a compilation error will occur. When the game is won, the program sets local variable gameStatus to Status.WON (lines 30 and 50). When the game is lost, the program sets local variable gameStatus to Status.LOST (lines 35 and 54). Otherwise, the program sets local variable gameStatus to Status.CONTINUE (line 38) to indicate that the game is not over and the dice must be rolled again.

Good Programming Practice 6.2

Using enum constants (like Status.WON, Status.LOST and Status.CONTINUE) rather than literal values (such as 0, 1 and 2) makes programs easier to read and maintain.

Logic of the main Method

Line 24 in main calls rollDice, which picks two random values from 1 to 6, displays the values of the first die, the second die and their sum, and returns the sum. Method main next enters the switch statement (lines 27–42), which uses the sumOfDice value from line 24 to determine whether the game has been won or lost, or should continue with another roll. The values that result in a win or loss on the first roll are declared as private static final int constants in lines 13–17. The identifier names use casino parlance for these sums. These constants, like enum constants, are declared by convention with all capital letters, to make them stand out in the program. Lines 28–31 determine whether the player won on the first roll with SEVEN (7) or YO_LEVEN (11). Lines 32–36 determine whether the player lost on the first roll with SNAKE_EYES (2), TREY (3), or BOX_CARS (12). After the first roll, if the game is not over, the default case (lines 37–41) sets gameStatus to Status.CONTINUE, saves sumOfDice in myPoint and displays the point.

If we're still trying to "make our point" (i.e., the game is continuing from a prior roll), lines 45–57 execute. Line 46 rolls the dice again. If sumOfDice matches myPoint (line 49), line 50 sets gameStatus to Status.WON, then the loop terminates because the game is complete. If sumOfDice is SEVEN (line 53), line 54 sets gameStatus to Status.LOST, and the loop terminates because the game is complete. When the game completes, lines 60–65 display a message indicating whether the player won or lost, and the program terminates.

The program uses the various program-control mechanisms we've discussed. The Craps class uses two methods—main and rollDice (called twice from main)—and the switch, while, if...else and nested if control statements. Note also the use of multiple case labels in the switch statement to execute the same statements for sums of SEVEN and YO_LEVEN (lines 28–29) and for sums of SNAKE_EYES, TREY and BOX_CARS (lines 32–34).

*Why Some Constants Are Not Defined as **enum** Constants*

You might be wondering why we declared the sums of the dice as private static final int constants rather than as enum constants. The reason is that the program must compare the int variable sumOfDice (line 24) to these constants to determine the outcome of each roll. Suppose we declared enum Sum containing constants representing the five sums used in the game, then used these constants in the switch statement (lines 27–42). Doing so would prevent us from using sumOfDice as the switch statement's controlling expression, because Java does *not* allow you to compare an int to an enum constant. To achieve the same functionality as the current program, we'd have to use a variable currentSum of type Sum as the switch's controlling expression. Unfortunately, Java does not provide an easy way to convert an int value to a particular enum constant. This could be done with a separate switch statement. This would be cumbersome and would not improve the program's readability (thus defeating the purpose of using an enum).

6.10 Scope of Declarations

You've seen declarations of various Java entities, such as classes, methods, variables and parameters. Declarations introduce names that can be used to refer to such Java entities. The **scope** of a declaration is the portion of the program that can refer to the declared entity by its name. Such an entity is said to be "in scope" for that portion of the program. This section introduces several important scope issues.

The basic scope rules are as follows:

1. The scope of a parameter declaration is the body of the method in which the declaration appears.

2. The scope of a local-variable declaration is from the point at which the declaration appears to the end of that block.

3. The scope of a local-variable declaration that appears in the initialization section of a for statement's header is the body of the for statement and the other expressions in the header.

4. A method or field's scope is the entire body of the class. This enables a class's instance methods to use the fields and other methods of the class.

Any block may contain variable declarations. If a local variable or parameter in a method has the same name as a field of the class, the field is *hidden* until the block terminates execution—this is called **shadowing**. To access a shadowed field in a block:

- If the field is an instance variable, precede its name with the this keyword and a dot (.), as in this.x.

- If the field is a static class variable, precede its name with the class's name and a dot (.), as in *ClassName*.x.

It's a compilation error if multiple *local* variables have the same name in the same method.

Figure 6.8 demonstrates field and local-variable scopes. Line 6 declares and initializes the field x to 1. This field is *shadowed* in any block (or method) that declares a local variable named x. Method main declares a local variable x (line 11) and initializes it to 5. This local variable's value is output to show that the field x (whose value is 1) is *shadowed* in main.

```java
1   // Fig. 6.8: Scope.java
2   // Scope class demonstrates field and local-variable scopes.
3
4   public class Scope {
5      // field that is accessible to all methods of this class
6      private static int x = 1;
7
8      // method main creates and initializes local variable x
9      // and calls methods useLocalVariable and useField
10     public static void main(String[] args) {
11        int x = 5; // method's local variable x shadows field x
12
13        System.out.printf("local x in main is %d%n", x);
14
15        useLocalVariable(); // useLocalVariable has local x
16        useField(); // useField uses class Scope's field x
17        useLocalVariable(); // useLocalVariable reinitializes local x
18        useField(); // class Scope's field x retains its value
19
20        System.out.printf("%nlocal x in main is %d%n", x);
21     }
22
23     // create and initialize local variable x during each call
24     public static void useLocalVariable() {
25        int x = 25; // initialized each time useLocalVariable is called
26
```

Fig. 6.8 | Scope class demonstrates field and local-variable scopes. (Part 1 of 2.)

```
27              System.out.printf(
28                  "%nlocal x on entering method useLocalVariable is %d%n", x);
29              ++x; // modifies this method's local variable x
30              System.out.printf(
31                  "local x before exiting method useLocalVariable is %d%n", x);
32          }
33
34          // modify class Scope's field x during each call
35          public static void useField() {
36              System.out.printf(
37                  "%nfield x on entering method useField is %d%n", x);
38              x *= 10; // modifies class Scope's field x
39              System.out.printf(
40                  "field x before exiting method useField is %d%n", x);
41          }
42      }
```

```
local x in main is 5

local x on entering method useLocalVariable is 25
local x before exiting method useLocalVariable is 26

field x on entering method useField is 1
field x before exiting method useField is 10

local x on entering method useLocalVariable is 25
local x before exiting method useLocalVariable is 26

field x on entering method useField is 10
field x before exiting method useField is 100

local x in main is 5
```

Fig. 6.8 | Scope class demonstrates field and local-variable scopes. (Part 2 of 2.)

The program declares two other methods—useLocalVariable (lines 24–32) and useField (lines 35–41)—that take no arguments and return no results. Method main calls each method twice (lines 15–18). Method useLocalVariable declares local variable x (line 25). When useLocalVariable is first called (line 15), it creates local variable x and initializes it to 25, outputs the value of x (lines 27–28), increments x (line 29) and outputs the value of x again (lines 30–31). When useLocalVariable is called a second time (line 17), it *recreates* local variable x and *reinitializes* it to 25, so the output of each useLocalVariable call is identical.

Method useField does not declare any local variables. Therefore, when it refers to x, the field x (line 6) of the class is used. When method useField is first called (line 16), it outputs the value (1) of field x (lines 36–37), multiplies the field x by 10 (line 38) and outputs the value (10) of field x again (lines 39–40) before returning. The next time method useField is called (line 18), the field has its modified value (10), so the method outputs 10, then 100. Finally, in method main, the program outputs the value of local variable x again (line 20) to show that none of the method calls modified main's local variable x, because the methods all referred to variables named x in other scopes.

Principle of Least Privilege

In a general sense, "things" should have the capabilities they need to get their job done, but no more. An example is the scope of a variable. A variable should not be visible when it's not needed.

Good Programming Practice 6.3

Declare variables as close to where they're first used as possible.

6.11 Method Overloading

Methods of the *same* name can be declared in the same class, as long as they have *different* sets of parameters (determined by the number, types and order of the parameters)—this is called **method overloading**. When an overloaded method is called, the compiler selects the appropriate method by examining the number, types and order of the arguments in the call. Method overloading is commonly used to create several methods with the *same* name that perform the *same* or *similar* tasks, but on *different* types or *different* numbers of arguments. For example, Math methods abs, min and max (summarized in Section 6.3) are overloaded with four versions each:

1. One with two double parameters.

2. One with two float parameters.

3. One with two int parameters.

4. One with two long parameters.

Our next example demonstrates declaring and invoking overloaded methods. We demonstrate overloaded constructors in Chapter 8.

6.11.1 Declaring Overloaded Methods

Class MethodOverload (Fig. 6.9) declares two overloaded square methods—one calculates the square of an int (and returns an int) and one calculates the square of a double (and returns a double). Although these methods have the same name and similar parameter lists and bodies, think of them simply as *different* methods. It may help to think of the method names as "square of int" and "square of double," respectively.

```
1   // Fig. 6.9: MethodOverload.java
2   // Overloaded method declarations.
3
4   public class MethodOverload {
5      // test overloaded square methods
6      public static void main(String[] args) {
7         System.out.printf("Square of integer 7 is %d%n", square(7));
8         System.out.printf("Square of double 7.5 is %f%n", square(7.5));
9      }
10
```

Fig. 6.9 | Overloaded method declarations. (Part 1 of 2.)

```
11      // square method with int argument
12      public static int square(int intValue) {
13          System.out.printf("%nCalled square with int argument: %d%n",
14              intValue);
15          return intValue * intValue;
16      }
17
18      // square method with double argument
19      public static double square(double doubleValue) {
20          System.out.printf("%nCalled square with double argument: %f%n",
21              doubleValue);
22          return doubleValue * doubleValue;
23      }
24  }
```

```
Called square with int argument: 7
Square of integer 7 is 49

Called square with double argument: 7.500000
Square of double 7.5 is 56.250000
```

Fig. 6.9 | Overloaded method declarations. (Part 2 of 2.)

Line 7 invokes method square with the argument 7. Literal integer values are treated as type int, so the method call in line 7 invokes the version of square at lines 12–16 that specifies an int parameter. Similarly, line 8 invokes method square with the argument 7.5. Literal floating-point values are treated as type double, so the method call in line 8 invokes the version of square at lines 19–23 that specifies a double parameter. Each method first outputs a line of text to prove that the proper method was called in each case. The values in lines 8 and 20 are displayed with the format specifier %f. We did not specify a precision in either case. By default, floating-point values are displayed with six digits of precision if the precision is *not* specified in the format specifier.

6.11.2 Distinguishing Between Overloaded Methods

The compiler distinguishes overloaded methods by their **signatures**—a combination of the method's *name* and the *number, types* and *order* of its parameters, but *not* its return type. If the compiler looked only at method names during compilation, the code in Fig. 6.9 would be ambiguous—the compiler would not know how to distinguish between the two square methods (lines 12–16 and 19–23). Internally, the compiler uses longer method names that include the original method name, the types of each parameter and the exact order of the parameters to determine whether the methods in a class are *unique* in that class.

For example, in Fig. 6.9, the compiler might (internally) use the logical name "square of int" for the square method that specifies an int parameter and "square of double" for the square method that specifies a double parameter (the actual names the compiler uses are messier). If method1's declaration begins as

```
void method1(int a, float b)
```

then the compiler might use the logical name "`method1` of `int` and `float`." If the parameters are specified as

> `void method1(`**`float`**` a, `**`int`**` b)`

then the compiler might use the logical name "`method1` of `float` and `int`." The *order* of the parameter types is important—the compiler considers the preceding two `method1` headers to be *distinct*.

6.11.3 Return Types of Overloaded Methods

In discussing the logical names of methods used by the compiler, we did not mention the return types of the methods. *Method calls cannot be distinguished only by return type.* When two methods have the *same* signature and *different* return types, the compiler issues an error message indicating that the method is already defined in the class. Overloaded methods *can* have *different* return types if the methods have *different* parameter lists. Also, overloaded methods need *not* have the same number of parameters.

Common Programming Error 6.8

Declaring overloaded methods with identical parameter lists is a compilation error regardless of whether the return types are different.

6.12 Wrap-Up

In this chapter, we covered additional capabilities of methods. You learned the difference between instance methods and `static` methods and how to call `static` methods by preceding the method name with the name of the class in which it appears and the dot (.) separator. You used operators + and += to perform string concatenations. We also discussed Java's promotion rules for converting implicitly between primitive types and ways to perform explicit conversions with cast operators. Next, you learned about some of the commonly used packages in the Java API.

You saw how to declare named constants using both enum types and `private static final` variables. You used class `SecureRandom` to generate random numbers for simulations. You also learned about the scope of fields and local variables in a class. Finally, you learned that multiple methods in one class can be overloaded by providing methods with the same name and different signatures. Such methods are normally used to perform the same or similar tasks using different types or different numbers of parameters.

In Chapter 7, you'll learn how to maintain lists and tables of data in arrays. You'll see a more elegant implementation of the application that rolls a die 60,000,000 times. We'll present two versions of a `GradeBook` case study that stores sets of student grades in a `GradeBook` object. You'll also learn how to access an application's command-line arguments that are passed to method `main` when an application begins execution.

7

Arrays and ArrayLists

Objectives

In this chapter you'll:

- Use arrays to store data in and retrieve data from lists and tables of values.
- Declare arrays, initialize arrays and refer to individual elements of arrays.
- Iterate through arrays with the enhanced **for** statement.
- Pass arrays to methods.
- Declare and manipulate multidimensional arrays.
- Use variable-length argument lists.
- Read command-line arguments into a program.
- Build an object-oriented card-shuffling-and-dealing simulation.
- Build single-array and double-array versions of an object-oriented instructor gradebook class.
- Perform common array manipulations with the methods of class **Arrays**.
- Use class **ArrayList** to manipulate a dynamically resizable array-like data structure.

Outline

7.1 Introduction

Array objects are data structures consisting of related data items of the same type. Arrays make it convenient to process related groups of values. Arrays remain the same length once they're created.

After discussing how arrays are declared, created and initialized, we present practical examples that demonstrate common array manipulations. We introduce Java's *exception-handling* mechanism and use it to allow a program to continue executing when it attempts to access an array element that does not exist. We also present a case study that examines how arrays can help simulate the shuffling and dealing of playing cards in a card-game application. We introduce Java's *enhanced `for` statement*, which allows a program to access the data in an array more conveniently and with less chance of error than does the counter-controlled `for` statement presented in Section 5.3. We build two versions of an instructor `GradeBook` case study that use arrays to maintain sets of student grades *in memory* and analyze student grades. We show how to use *variable-length argument lists* to create methods that can be called with varying numbers of arguments, and we demonstrate how to process *command-line arguments* in method `main`. Next, we present some common array manipulations with `static` methods of class `Arrays` from the `java.util` package.

Although commonly used, arrays have limited capabilities. For example, you must specify an array's size, and if at execution time you wish to modify it, you must do so by creating a new array. At the end of this chapter, we introduce one of Java's prebuilt data structures from the Java API's *collection classes*. These offer greater capabilities than traditional arrays. They're reusable, reliable, powerful and efficient. We focus on the `ArrayList` collection. `ArrayList`s are similar to arrays but provide additional functionality, such as **dynamic resizing** as necessary to accommodate more or fewer elements.

Java SE 8
After reading Chapter 17, Lambdas and Streams, you'll be able to reimplement many of this chapter's examples in a more concise and elegant manner, and in a way that makes them easier to parallelize to improve performance on today's multi-core systems. Recall from the Preface that Chapter 17 is keyed to many earlier sections of the book so that you can conveniently user lambdas and streams if you'd like.

7.2 Arrays

An array is a group of variables (called **elements** or **components**) containing values that all have the *same* type. Arrays are *objects*, so they're considered *reference types*. As you'll soon see, what we typically think of as an array is actually a *reference* to an array object in memory. The *elements* of an array can be either *primitive types* or *reference types* (including arrays, as we'll see in Section 7.11). To refer to a particular element in an array, we specify the *name* of the reference to the array and the *position number* of the element in the array. The position number of the element is called the element's **index** or **subscript**.

Logical Array Representation
Figure 7.1 shows a logical representation of an integer array called c. This array contains 12 *elements*. A program refers to any one of these elements with an **array-access expression** that includes the *name* of the array followed by the *index* of the particular element in **square brackets** (**[]**). The first element in every array has **index zero** and is sometimes called the **zeroth element.** Thus, the elements of array c are c[0], c[1], c[2] and so on. The highest index in array c is 11, which is 1 less than 12—the number of elements in the array. Array names follow the same conventions as other variable names.

An index must be a *nonnegative integer* that's less than the array's size. A program can use an expression as an index. For example, if we assume that variable a is 5 and variable b is 6, then the statement

```
c[a + b] += 2;
```

adds 2 to array element c[11]. An indexed array name is an *array-access expression*, which can be used on the left side of an assignment to place a new value into an array element.

Common Programming Error 7.1
An index must be an `int` *value or a value of a type that can be promoted to* `int`—*namely,* `byte`, `short` *or* `char`, *but not* `long`; *otherwise, a compilation error occurs.*

Let's examine array c in Fig. 7.1 more closely. The **name** of the array is c. Every array object knows its own length and stores it in a `length` **instance variable**. The expression c.`length` returns array c's length. Even though the `length` instance variable of an array is `public`, it cannot be changed because it's a `final` variable. This array's 12 elements are referred to as c[0], c[1], c[2], ..., c[11]. The value of c[0] is -45, the value of c[1] is

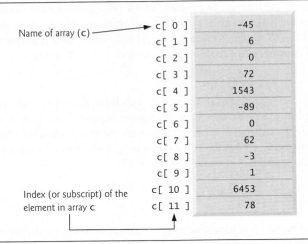

Name of array (c)

Index (or subscript) of the
element in array c

Fig. 7.1 | A 12-element array.

6, the value of c[2] is 0, the value of c[7] is 62 and the value of c[11] is 78. To calculate the sum of the values contained in the first three elements of array c and store the result in variable sum, we would write

```
sum = c[0] + c[1] + c[2];
```

To divide the value of c[6] by 2 and assign the result to the variable x, we would write

```
x = c[6] / 2;
```

7.3 Declaring and Creating Arrays

Array objects occupy space in memory. Like other objects, arrays are created with keyword new. To create an array object, you specify the type of the array elements and the number of elements as part of an **array-creation expression** that uses keyword new. Such an expression returns a *reference* that can be stored in an array variable. The following declaration and array-creation expression create an array object containing 12 int elements and store the array's reference in the array variable named c:

```
int[] c = new int[12];
```

This expression can be used to create the array in Fig. 7.1. When an array is created, each of its elements receives a default value—zero for the numeric primitive-type elements, false for boolean elements and null for references. As you'll soon see, you can provide nondefault element values when you create an array.

Creating the array in Fig. 7.1 can also be performed in two steps as follows:

```
int[] c; // declare the array variable
c = new int[12]; // create the array; assign to array variable
```

In the declaration, the *square brackets* following the type indicate that c is a variable that will refer to an array (i.e., the variable will store an array *reference*). In the assignment statement, the array variable c receives the reference to a new array of 12 int elements.

Common Programming Error 7.2

In an array declaration, specifying the number of elements in the square brackets of the declaration (e.g., `int[12] c;`*) is a syntax error.*

A program can create several arrays in a single declaration. The following declaration reserves 100 elements for b and 27 elements for x:

```
String[] b = new String[100], x = new String[27];
```

When the type of the array and the square brackets are combined at the beginning of the declaration, all the identifiers in the declaration are array variables. In this case, variables b and x refer to `String` arrays. For readability, we prefer to declare only *one* variable per declaration. The preceding declaration is equivalent to:

```
String[] b = new String[100]; // create array b
String[] x = new String[27]; // create array x
```

Good Programming Practice 7.1

For readability, declare only one variable per declaration. Keep each declaration on a separate line, and include a comment describing the variable being declared.

When only one variable is declared in each declaration, the square brackets can be placed either after the type or after the array variable name, as in:

```
String b[] = new String[100]; // create array b
String x[] = new String[27]; // create array x
```

but placing the square brackets after the type is preferred.

Common Programming Error 7.3

Declaring multiple array variables in a single declaration can lead to subtle errors. Consider the declaration `int[] a, b, c;`*. If a, b and c should be declared as array variables, then this declaration is correct—placing square brackets directly following the type indicates that* all *the identifiers in the declaration are array variables. However, if only a is intended to be an array variable, and b and c are intended to be individual* `int` *variables, then this declaration is incorrect—the declaration* `int a[], b, c;` *would achieve the desired result.*

A program can declare arrays of any type. Every element of a primitive-type array contains a value of the array's declared element type. Similarly, in an array of a reference type, every element is a reference to an object of the array's declared element type. For example, every element of an `int` array is an `int` value, and every element of a `String` array is a reference to a `String` object.

7.4 Examples Using Arrays

This section presents several examples that demonstrate declaring arrays, creating arrays, initializing arrays and manipulating array elements.

7.4.1 Creating and Initializing an Array

The application of Fig. 7.2 uses keyword new to create an array of 10 `int` elements, which are initially zero (the default initial value for `int` variables). Line 7 declares array—a reference capable of referring to an array of `int` elements—then initializes the variable with a reference to an array object containing 10 `int` elements. Line 9 outputs the column headings. The first column contains the index (0–9) of each array element, and the second column contains the default initial value (0) of each array element.

```java
1   // Fig. 7.2: InitArray.java
2   // Initializing the elements of an array to default values of zero.
3
4   public class InitArray {
5      public static void main(String[] args) {
6         // declare variable array and initialize it with an array object
7         int[] array = new int[10]; // create the array object
8
9         System.out.printf("%s%8s%n", "Index", "Value"); // column headings
10
11        // output each array element's value
12        for (int counter = 0; counter < array.length; counter++) {
13           System.out.printf("%5d%8d%n", counter, array[counter]);
14        }
15     }
16  }
```

```
Index    Value
    0        0
    1        0
    2        0
    3        0
    4        0
    5        0
    6        0
    7        0
    8        0
    9        0
```

Fig. 7.2 | Initializing the elements of an array to default values of zero.

The for statement (lines 12–14) outputs the index (represented by counter) and value of each array element (represented by array[counter]). Control variable counter is initially 0—index values start at 0, so using **zero-based counting** allows the loop to access every element of the array. The for's loop-continuation condition uses the expression array.length (line 12) to determine the length of the array. In this example, the length of the array is 10, so the loop continues executing as long as the value of control variable counter is less than 10. The highest index value of a 10-element array is 9, so using the less-than operator in the loop-continuation condition guarantees that the loop does not attempt to access an element *beyond* the end of the array (i.e., during the final iteration of the loop, counter is 9). We'll soon see what Java does when it encounters such an *out-of-range index* at execution time.

7.4.2 Using an Array Initializer

You can create an array and initialize its elements with an **array initializer**—a comma-separated list of expressions (called an **initializer list**) enclosed in braces. In this case, the array length is determined by the number of elements in the initializer list. For example,

```java
int[] n = {10, 20, 30, 40, 50};
```

creates a *five*-element array with index values 0–4. Element n[0] is initialized to 10, n[1] is initialized to 20, and so on. When the compiler encounters an array declaration that includes an initializer list, it *counts* the number of initializers in the list to determine the size of the array, then sets up the appropriate new operation "behind the scenes."

The application in Fig. 7.3 initializes an integer array with 10 values (line 7) and displays the array in tabular format. The code for displaying the array elements (lines 12–14) is identical to that in Fig. 7.2 (lines 12–14).

```java
 1   // Fig. 7.3: InitArray.java
 2   // Initializing the elements of an array with an array initializer.
 3
 4   public class InitArray {
 5      public static void main(String[] args) {
 6         // initializer list specifies the initial value for each element
 7         int[] array = {32, 27, 64, 18, 95, 14, 90, 70, 60, 37};
 8
 9         System.out.printf("%s%8s%n", "Index", "Value"); // column headings
10
11         // output each array element's value
12         for (int counter = 0; counter < array.length; counter++) {
13            System.out.printf("%5d%8d%n", counter, array[counter]);
14         }
15      }
16   }
```

```
Index    Value
    0       32
    1       27
    2       64
    3       18
    4       95
    5       14
    6       90
    7       70
    8       60
    9       37
```

Fig. 7.3 | Initializing the elements of an array with an array initializer.

7.4.3 Calculating the Values to Store in an Array

The application in Fig. 7.4 creates a 10-element array and assigns to each element one of the even integers from 2 to 20 (2, 4, 6, ..., 20). Then the application displays the array in tabular format. The for statement at lines 10–12 calculates an array element's value by multiplying the current value of the control variable counter by 2, then adding 2.

```
1   // Fig. 7.4: InitArray.java
2   // Calculating the values to be placed into the elements of an array.
3
4   public class InitArray {
5       public static void main(String[] args) {
6           final int ARRAY_LENGTH = 10; // declare constant
7           int[] array = new int[ARRAY_LENGTH]; // create array
8
9           // calculate value for each array element
10          for (int counter = 0; counter < array.length; counter++) {
11              array[counter] = 2 + 2 * counter;
12          }
13
14          System.out.printf("%s%8s%n", "Index", "Value"); // column headings
15
16          // output each array element's value
17          for (int counter = 0; counter < array.length; counter++) {
18              System.out.printf("%5d%8d%n", counter, array[counter]);
19          }
20      }
21  }
```

```
Index   Value
    0       2
    1       4
    2       6
    3       8
    4      10
    5      12
    6      14
    7      16
    8      18
    9      20
```

Fig. 7.4 | Calculating the values to be placed into the elements of an array.

Line 6 uses the modifier `final` to declare the constant variable `ARRAY_LENGTH` with the value 10. Constant variables must be initialized *before* they're used and *cannot* be modified thereafter. If you attempt to *modify* a `final` variable after it's initialized in its declaration, the compiler issues an error message like

```
cannot assign a value to final variable variableName
```

Good Programming Practice 7.2

*Constant variables also are called **named constants**. They often make programs more readable—a named constant such as `ARRAY_LENGTH` clearly indicates its purpose, whereas a literal value such as 10 could have different meanings based on its context.*

Good Programming Practice 7.3

Constants use all uppercase letters by convention and multiword named constants should have each word separated from the next with an underscore (_) as in `ARRAY_LENGTH`.

Common Programming Error 7.4

Assigning a value to a previously initialized final *variable is a compilation error. Similarly, attempting to access the value of a* final *variable before it's initialized results in a compilation error like, "*variable *variableName* might not have been initialized.*"

7.4.4 Summing the Elements of an Array

Often, array elements represent values for use in a calculation. If, for example, they're exam grades, a professor may wish to total the array elements and use that sum to calculate the class average. The GradeBook examples in Figs. 7.14 and 7.18 use this technique. Figure 7.5 sums the values contained in a 10-element array. The program declares, creates and initializes the array at line 6. Lines 10–12 perform the calculations.

```java
1   // Fig. 7.5: SumArray.java
2   // Computing the sum of the elements of an array.
3
4   public class SumArray {
5      public static void main(String[] args) {
6         int[] array = {87, 68, 94, 100, 83, 78, 85, 91, 76, 87};
7         int total = 0;
8
9         // add each element's value to total
10        for (int counter = 0; counter < array.length; counter++) {
11           total += array[counter];
12        }
13
14        System.out.printf("Total of array elements: %d%n", total);
15     }
16  }
```

```
Total of array elements: 849
```

Fig. 7.5 | Computing the sum of the elements of an array.

7.4.5 Using Bar Charts to Display Array Data Graphically

Many programs present data to users in a graphical manner. For example, numeric values are often displayed as bars in a bar chart. In such a chart, longer bars represent proportionally larger numeric values. One simple way to display numeric data graphically is with a bar chart that shows each numeric value as a bar of asterisks (*).

Professors often like to examine the grade distribution on an exam. A professor might visualize this with a graph of the number of grades in each of several categories. Suppose the grades were 87, 68, 94, 100, 83, 78, 85, 91, 76 and 87. They include one grade of 100, two grades in the 90s, four grades in the 80s, two grades in the 70s, one grade in the 60s and no grades below 60. Figure 7.6 stores this grade distribution data in an array of 11 elements, each corresponding to a category of grades. For example, array[0] indicates the number of grades in the range 0–9, array[7] the number of grades in the range 70–79 and array[10] the number of 100 grades.

```java
1   // Fig. 7.6: BarChart.java
2   // Bar chart printing program.
3
4   public class BarChart {
5      public static void main(String[] args) {
6         int[] array = {0, 0, 0, 0, 0, 0, 1, 2, 4, 2, 1};
7
8         System.out.println("Grade distribution:");
9
10        // for each array element, output a bar of the chart
11        for (int counter = 0; counter < array.length; counter++) {
12           // output bar label ("00-09: ", ..., "90-99: ", "100: ")
13           if (counter == 10) {
14              System.out.printf("%5d: ", 100);
15           }
16           else {
17              System.out.printf("%02d-%02d: ",
18                 counter * 10, counter * 10 + 9);
19           }
20
21           // print bar of asterisks
22           for (int stars = 0; stars < array[counter]; stars++) {
23              System.out.print("*");
24           }
25
26           System.out.println();
27        }
28     }
29  }
```

```
Grade distribution:
00-09:
10-19:
20-29:
30-39:
40-49:
50-59:
60-69: *
70-79: **
80-89: ****
90-99: **
  100: *
```

Fig. 7.6 | Bar chart printing program.

The GradeBook classes later in the chapter (Figs. 7.14 and 7.18) contain code that calculates these grade frequencies based on a set of grades. For now, we manually create the array with the given grade frequencies. The application reads the numbers from the array and graphs the information as a bar chart. It displays each grade range followed by a bar of asterisks indicating the number of grades in that range. To label each bar, lines 13–19 output a grade range (e.g., "70-79: ") based on the current counter value. When counter is 10, line 14 outputs 100 with a field width of 5, followed by a colon and a space, to align the label "100: " with the other bar labels. The nested for statement (lines 22–24) outputs the bars.

Note the loop-continuation condition at line 22 (stars < array[counter]). Each time the program reaches the inner for, the loop counts from 0 up to array[counter], thus using a value in array to determine the number of asterisks to display. In this example, *no* students received a grade below 60, so array[0]–array[5] contain zeroes, and *no* asterisks are displayed next to the first six grade ranges. In line 17, the format specifier %02d indicates that an int value should be formatted as a field of two digits. The **0 flag** in the format specifier displays a leading 0 for values with fewer digits than the field width (2).

7.4.6 Using the Elements of an Array as Counters

Sometimes, programs use counter variables to summarize data, such as the results of a survey. In Fig. 6.6, we used separate counters in our die-rolling program to track the number of occurrences of each side of a six-sided die as the program rolled the die 60,000,000 times. An array version of this application is shown in Fig. 7.7.

```
1   // Fig. 7.7: RollDie.java
2   // Die-rolling program using arrays instead of switch.
3   import java.security.SecureRandom;
4
5   public class RollDie {
6      public static void main(String[] args) {
7         SecureRandom randomNumbers = new SecureRandom();
8         int[] frequency = new int[7]; // array of frequency counters
9
10        // roll die 60,000,000 times; use die value as frequency index
11        for (int roll = 1; roll <= 60_000_000; roll++) {
12           ++frequency[1 + randomNumbers.nextInt(6)];
13        }
14
15        System.out.printf("%s%10s%n", "Face", "Frequency");
16
17        // output each array element's value
18        for (int face = 1; face < frequency.length; face++) {
19           System.out.printf("%4d%10d%n", face, frequency[face]);
20        }
21     }
22  }
```

```
Face Frequency
   1   9995532
   2  10003079
   3  10000564
   4  10000726
   5   9998994
   6  10001105
```

Fig. 7.7 | Die-rolling program using arrays instead of switch.

Figure 7.7 uses the array frequency (line 8) to count the occurrences of each side of the die. *The single statement in line 12 of this program replaces lines 19–41 of Fig. 6.6.* Line 12 uses the random value to determine which frequency element to increment . The calculation in line 12 produces random numbers from 1 to 6, so the array `frequency` must be large enough to store six counters. However, we use a seven-element array in which we ignore `frequency[0]`—it's more logical to have the face value 1 increment `frequency[1]` than `frequency[0]`. Thus, each face value is used as an index for array `frequency`. In line 12, the calculation inside the square brackets evaluates first to determine which element of the array to increment, then the `++` operator adds one to that element. We also replaced lines 45–47 from Fig. 6.6 by looping through array `frequency` to output the results (lines 18–20). When we study Java SE 8's functional programming capabilities in Chapter 17, we'll show how to replace lines 11–13 and 18–20 with a *single* statement!

7.4.7 Using Arrays to Analyze Survey Results

Our next example uses arrays to summarize data collected in a survey. Consider the following problem statement:

> *Twenty students were asked to rate on a scale of 1 to 5 the quality of the food in the student cafeteria, with 1 being "awful" and 5 being "excellent." Place the 20 responses in an integer array and determine the frequency of each rating.*

This is a typical array-processing application (Fig. 7.8). We wish to summarize the number of responses of each type (that is, 1–5). Array `responses` (lines 7–8) is a 20-element integer array containing the students' survey responses. The last value in the array *is intentionally* an incorrect response (14). When a Java program executes, array element indices are checked for validity—all indices must be greater than or equal to 0 and less than the length of the array. Any attempt to access an element outside that range of indices results in a runtime error that's known as an `ArrayIndexOutOfBoundsException`. At the end of this section, we'll discuss the invalid response value, demonstrate array **bounds checking** and introduce Java's *exception-handling* mechanism, which can be used to detect and handle an `ArrayIndexOutOfBoundsException`.

```
1   // Fig. 7.8: StudentPoll.java
2   // Poll analysis program.
3
4   public class StudentPoll {
5      public static void main(String[] args) {
6         // student response array (more typically, input at runtime)
7         int[] responses =
8            {1, 2, 5, 4, 3, 5, 2, 1, 3, 3, 1, 4, 3, 3, 3, 2, 3, 3, 2, 14};
9         int[] frequency = new int[6]; // array of frequency counters
10
11        // for each answer, select responses element and use that value
12        // as frequency index to determine element to increment
13        for (int answer = 0; answer < responses.length; answer++) {
14           try {
15              ++frequency[responses[answer]];
16           }
17           catch (ArrayIndexOutOfBoundsException e) {
18              System.out.println(e); // invokes toString method
```

Fig. 7.8 | Poll analysis program. (Part 1 of 2.)

```
19              System.out.printf("   responses[%d] = %d%n%n",
20                  answer, responses[answer]);
21          }
22      }
23
24      System.out.printf("%s%10s%n", "Rating", "Frequency");
25
26      // output each array element's value
27      for (int rating = 1; rating < frequency.length; rating++) {
28          System.out.printf("%6d%10d%n", rating, frequency[rating]);
29      }
30    }
31 }
```

```
java.lang.ArrayIndexOutOfBoundsException: 14
   responses[19] = 14

Rating Frequency
     1        3
     2        4
     3        8
     4        2
     5        2
```

Fig. 7.8 | Poll analysis program. (Part 2 of 2.)

The frequency Array

We use the *six-element* array frequency (line 9) to count the number of occurrences of each response. Each element (except element 0) is used as a *counter* for one of the possible survey-response values—frequency[1] counts the number of students who rated the food as 1, frequency[2] counts the number of students who rated the food as 2, and so on.

Summarizing the Results

The for statement (lines 13–22) reads the responses from the array responses one at a time and increments one of the counters frequency[1] to frequency[5]; we ignore frequency[0] because the survey responses are limited to the range 1–5. The key statement in the loop appears in line 15. This statement increments the appropriate frequency counter as determined by the value of responses[answer].

Let's step through the first few iterations of the for statement:

*   When answer is 0, responses[answer] is the value of responses[0] (that is, 1—see line 8). So, frequency[responses[answer]] evaluates to frequency[1] and counter frequency[1] is incremented by one. To evaluate the expression, we begin with the value in the *innermost* set of brackets (answer, currently 0). The value of answer is plugged into the expression, and the next set of brackets (responses[answer]) is evaluated. That value is used as the index for the frequency array to determine which counter to increment (in this case, frequency[1]).

*   The next time through the loop answer is 1, responses[answer] is the value of responses[1] (that is, 2—see line 8), so frequency[responses[answer]] is interpreted as frequency[2], causing frequency[2] to be incremented.

- When answer is 2, `responses[answer]` is the value of `responses[2]` (that is, 5—see line 8), so `frequency[responses[answer]]` is interpreted as `frequency[5]`, causing `frequency[5]` to be incremented, and so on.

Regardless of the number of responses processed, only a six-element array (in which we ignore element zero) is required to summarize the results, because all the correct responses are from 1 to 5, and the index values for a six-element array are 0–5. In the program's output, the Frequency column summarizes only 19 of the 20 values in the `responses` array—the last element of the array `responses` contains an (intentionally) incorrect response that was not counted. Section 7.5 discusses what happens when the program in Fig. 7.8 encounters the invalid response (14) in the last element of array `responses`.

7.5 Exception Handling: Processing the Incorrect Response

An **exception** indicates a problem that occurs while a program executes. **Exception handling** helps you create **fault-tolerant programs** that can resolve (or handle) exceptions. In some cases, this allows a program to continue executing as if no problems were encountered. For example, the `StudentPoll` application still displays results (Fig. 7.8), even though one of the responses was out of range. More severe problems might prevent a program from continuing normal execution, instead requiring it to notify the user of the problem, then terminate. When the JVM or a method detects a problem, such as an invalid array index or an invalid method argument, it **throws** an exception—that is, an exception occurs. Methods in your own classes can also throw exceptions, as you'll learn in Chapter 8.

7.5.1 The `try` Statement

To handle an exception, place any code that might throw an exception in a **try statement** (lines 14–21 of Fig. 7.8). The **try block** (lines 14–16) contains the code that might *throw* an exception, and the **catch block** (lines 17–21) contains the code that *handles* the exception if one occurs. You can have *many* catches to handle different *types* of exceptions that might be thrown in the corresponding try block. When line 15 correctly increments a frequency array element, lines 17–21 are ignored. The braces that delimit the bodies of the try and catch blocks are required.

7.5.2 Executing the `catch` Block

When the program encounters the invalid value 14 in the `responses` array, it attempts to add 1 to `frequency[14]`, which is *outside* the bounds of the array—the frequency array has only six elements (with indexes 0–5). Because array bounds checking is performed at execution time, the JVM generates an *exception*—specifically line 15 throws an `ArrayIndexOutOfBoundsException` to notify the program of this problem. At this point the try block terminates and the catch block begins executing—if you declared any local variables in the try block, they're now *out of scope* (and no longer exist), so they're not accessible in the catch block.

The catch block declares an exception parameter (e) of type `ArrayIndexOutOfBounds-Exception`. The catch block can handle exceptions of the specified type. Inside the catch block, you can use the parameter's identifier to interact with a caught exception object.

Error-Prevention Tip 7.1

When writing code to access an array element, ensure that the array index remains greater than or equal to 0 and less than the length of the array. This will prevent ArrayIndexOutOfBoundsExceptions *if your program is correct.*

Software Engineering Observation 7.1

Systems in industry that have undergone extensive testing are still likely to contain bugs. Our preference for industrial-strength systems is to catch and deal with runtime exceptions, such as ArrayIndexOutOfBoundsExceptions, *to ensure that a system either stays up and running or degrades gracefully, and to inform the system's developers of the problem.*

7.5.3 toString Method of the Exception Parameter

When lines 17–21 *catch* the exception, the program displays a message indicating the problem that occurred. Line 18 *implicitly* calls the exception object's toString method to get the error message that's implicitly stored in the exception object and display it. Once the message is displayed in this example, the exception is considered *handled* and the program continues with the next statement after the catch block's closing brace. In this example, the end of the for statement is reached (line 22), so the program continues with the increment of the control variable in line 13. We discuss exception handling again in Chapter 8, and more deeply in Chapter 11.

7.6 Case Study: Card Shuffling and Dealing Simulation

The examples in the chapter thus far have used arrays containing elements of primitive types. Recall from Section 7.2 that the elements of an array can be either primitive types or reference types. This section uses random-number generation and an array of reference-type elements, namely objects representing playing cards, to develop a class that simulates card shuffling and dealing. This class can then be used to implement applications that play specific card games.

We first develop class Card (Fig. 7.9), which represents a playing card that has a face (e.g., "Ace", "Deuce", "Three", ..., "Jack", "Queen", "King") and a suit (e.g., "Hearts", "Diamonds", "Clubs", "Spades"). Next, we develop the DeckOfCards class (Fig. 7.10), which creates a deck of 52 playing cards in which each element is a Card object. We then build a test application (Fig. 7.11) that demonstrates class DeckOfCards's card shuffling and dealing capabilities.

Class Card

Class Card (Fig. 7.9) contains two String instance variables—face and suit—that are used to store references to the face name and suit name for a specific Card. The constructor for the class (lines 9–12) receives two Strings that it uses to initialize face and suit. Method toString (lines 15–17) creates a String consisting of the face of the card, the String " of " and the suit of the card.[1] Card's toString method can be invoked *explicitly* to obtain a string representation of a Card object (e.g., "Ace of Spades"). The toString method of an object is called *implicitly* when the object is used where a String is expected (e.g., when printf outputs the object as a String using the %s format specifier or when the object is concatenated to a `String` using the + operator). For this behavior to occur, `toString` must be declared with the header shown in Fig. 7.9.

```java
1   // Fig. 7.9: Card.java
2   // Card class represents a playing card.
3
4   public class Card {
5      private final String face; // face of card ("Ace", "Deuce", ...)
6      private final String suit; // suit of card ("Hearts", "Diamonds", ...)
7
8      // two-argument constructor initializes card's face and suit
9      public Card(String cardFace, String cardSuit) {
10        this.face = cardFace; // initialize face of card
11        this.suit = cardSuit; // initialize suit of card
12     }
13
14     // return String representation of Card
15     public String toString() {
16        return face + " of " + suit;
17     }
18  }
```

Fig. 7.9 | Card class represents a playing card.

Class *DeckOfCards*

Class `DeckOfCards` (Fig. 7.10) creates and manages an array of `Card` references. The named constant `NUMBER_OF_CARDS` (line 8) specifies the number of `Card`s in a deck (52). Line 10 declares and initializes an instance variable named `deck` that refers to a new array of `Card`s that has `NUMBER_OF_CARDS` (52) elements—the deck array's elements are `null` by default. Recall from Chapter 3 that `null` represents a "reference to nothing," so no `Card` objects exist yet. An array of a *reference* type is declared like any other array. Class `DeckOfCards` also declares `int` instance variable `currentCard` (line 11), representing the sequence number (0–51) of the next `Card` to be dealt from the `deck` array.

```java
1   // Fig. 7.10: DeckOfCards.java
2   // DeckOfCards class represents a deck of playing cards.
3   import java.security.SecureRandom;
4
5   public class DeckOfCards {
6      // random number generator
7      private static final SecureRandom randomNumbers = new SecureRandom();
8      private static final int NUMBER_OF_CARDS = 52; // constant # of Cards
9
```

Fig. 7.10 | DeckOfCards class represents a deck of playing cards. (Part 1 of 2.)

---

1. You'll learn in Chapter 9 that when we provide a custom `toString` method for a class, we are actually "overriding" a version of that method supplied by class `Object` from which all Java classes "inherit." As of Chapter 9, every method we explicitly override will be preceded by the "annotation" `@Override`, which prevents a common programming error.

```
10      private Card[] deck = new Card[NUMBER_OF_CARDS]; // Card references
11      private int currentCard = 0; // index of next Card to be dealt (0-51)
12
13      // constructor fills deck of Cards
14      public DeckOfCards() {
15          String[] faces = {"Ace", "Deuce", "Three", "Four", "Five", "Six",
16              "Seven", "Eight", "Nine", "Ten", "Jack", "Queen", "King"};
17          String[] suits = {"Hearts", "Diamonds", "Clubs", "Spades"};
18
19          // populate deck with Card objects
20          for (int count = 0; count < deck.length; count++) {
21              deck[count] =
22                  new Card(faces[count % 13], suits[count / 13]);
23          }
24      }
25
26      // shuffle deck of Cards with one-pass algorithm
27      public void shuffle() {
28          // next call to method dealCard should start at deck[0] again
29          currentCard = 0;
30
31          // for each Card, pick another random Card (0-51) and swap them
32          for (int first = 0; first < deck.length; first++) {
33              // select a random number between 0 and 51
34              int second = randomNumbers.nextInt(NUMBER_OF_CARDS);
35
36              // swap current Card with randomly selected Card
37              Card temp = deck[first];
38              deck[first] = deck[second];
39              deck[second] = temp;
40          }
41      }
42
43      // deal one Card
44      public Card dealCard() {
45          // determine whether Cards remain to be dealt
46          if (currentCard < deck.length) {
47              return deck[currentCard++]; // return current Card in array
48          }
49          else {
50              return null; // return null to indicate that all Cards were dealt
51          }
52      }
53  }
```

Fig. 7.10 | DeckOfCards class represents a deck of playing cards. (Part 2 of 2.)

DeckOfCards Constructor

The class's constructor uses a for statement (lines 20–23) to fill the deck instance variable with Card objects. The loop initializes control variable count to 0 and loops while count is less than deck.length, causing count to take on each integer value from 0 through 51 (the deck array's indices). Each Card is instantiated and initialized with two Strings—one from the faces array (which contains the Strings "Ace" through "King") and one from the `suits` array (which contains the `Strings` "Hearts", "Diamonds", "Clubs" and "Spades"). The calculation `count % 13` always results in a value from 0 to 12 (the 13 indices of the `faces` array in lines 15–16), and the calculation `count / 13` always results in a value from 0 to 3 (the four indices of the `suits` array in line 17). When the loop completes, `deck` contains the `Cards` with faces "Ace" through "King" in order for each suit (13 "Hearts", then 13 "Diamonds", then 13 "Clubs", then 13 "Spades"). We use arrays of `Strings` to represent the faces and suits in this example. As an exercise, you could modify this example to `enum` constants to represent the faces and suits.

DeckOfCards Method `shuffle`

Method `shuffle` (lines 27–41) shuffles the `Cards` in the deck. The method loops through all 52 `Cards` (array indices 0 to 51). For each `Card`, line 34 selects a random index between 0 and 51 to select another `Card`. Next, lines 37–39 swap the current `Card` and the randomly selected `Card` in the array. The extra variable `temp` (line 37) temporarily stores one of the two `Card` objects being swapped. After the `for` loop terminates, the `Card` objects are randomly ordered. A total of only 52 swaps are made in a single pass of the entire array, and the array of `Card` objects is shuffled!

The swap in lines 37–39 cannot be performed with only the two statements

```
deck[first] = deck[second];
deck[second] = deck[first];
```

If `deck[first]` is the "Ace" of "Spades" and `deck[second]` is the "Queen" of "Hearts", after the first assignment, both array elements contain the "Queen" of "Hearts" and the "Ace" of "Spades" is lost—so, the extra variable `temp` is needed.

[*Note:* It's recommended that you use a so-called *unbiased* shuffling algorithm—like the Fisher-Yates shuffling algorithm—for real card games. Such an algorithm ensures that all possible shuffled card sequences are equally likely to occur.]

DeckOfCards Method `dealCard`

Method `dealCard` (lines 44–52) deals one `Card` in the array. Recall that `currentCard` indicates the index of the next `Card` to be dealt (i.e., the `Card` at the *top* of the deck). Thus, line 46 compares `currentCard` to the length of the `deck` array. If the `deck` is not empty (i.e., `currentCard` is less than 52), line 47 returns the "top" `Card` and postincrements `currentCard` to prepare for the next call to `dealCard`—otherwise, line 50 returns `null`.

Shuffling and Dealing Cards

Figure 7.11 demonstrates class `DeckOfCards`. Line 7 creates a `DeckOfCards` object named `myDeckOfCards`. The `DeckOfCards` constructor creates the deck with the 52 `Card` objects in order by suit and face. Line 8 invokes `myDeckOfCards`'s `shuffle` method to rearrange the `Card` objects. Lines 11–18 deal all 52 `Cards` and print them in four columns of 13 `Cards` each. Line 13 deals one `Card` object by invoking `myDeckOfCards`'s `dealCard` method, then displays the `Card` left justified in a field of 19 characters. When a `Card` is output as a `String`, the `Card`'s `toString` method (Fig. 7.9) is implicitly invoked. Lines 15–17 in Fig. 7.11 start a new line after every four `Cards`.

```
 1   // Fig. 7.11: DeckOfCardsTest.java
 2   // Card shuffling and dealing.
 3
 4   public class DeckOfCardsTest {
 5      // execute application
 6      public static void main(String[] args) {
 7         DeckOfCards myDeckOfCards = new DeckOfCards();
 8         myDeckOfCards.shuffle(); // place Cards in random order
 9
10         // print all 52 Cards in the order in which they are dealt
11         for (int i = 1; i <= 52; i++) {
12            // deal and display a Card
13            System.out.printf("%-19s", myDeckOfCards.dealCard());
14
15            if (i % 4 == 0) { // output a newline after every fourth card
16               System.out.println();
17            }
18         }
19      }
20   }
```

Six of Spades	Eight of Spades	Six of Clubs	Nine of Hearts
Queen of Hearts	Seven of Clubs	Nine of Spades	King of Hearts
Three of Diamonds	Deuce of Clubs	Ace of Hearts	Ten of Spades
Four of Spades	Ace of Clubs	Seven of Diamonds	Four of Hearts
Three of Clubs	Deuce of Hearts	Five of Spades	Jack of Diamonds
King of Clubs	Ten of Hearts	Three of Hearts	Six of Diamonds
Queen of Clubs	Eight of Diamonds	Deuce of Diamonds	Ten of Diamonds
Three of Spades	King of Diamonds	Nine of Clubs	Six of Hearts
Ace of Spades	Four of Diamonds	Seven of Hearts	Eight of Clubs
Deuce of Spades	Eight of Hearts	Five of Hearts	Queen of Spades
Jack of Hearts	Seven of Spades	Four of Clubs	Nine of Diamonds
Ace of Diamonds	Queen of Diamonds	Five of Clubs	King of Spades
Five of Diamonds	Ten of Clubs	Jack of Spades	Jack of Clubs

Fig. 7.11 | Card shuffling and dealing.

Preventing *NullPointerExceptions*

In Fig. 7.10, we created a deck array of 52 Card references—by default, each element of a reference-type array created with new is initialized to null. Similarly, reference-type fields of a class are also initialized to null by default. A NullPointerException occurs when you try to call a method on a null reference. In industrial-strength code, ensuring that references are not null before you use them to call methods prevents NullPointerExceptions.

7.7 Enhanced for Statement

The **enhanced for statement** iterates through the elements of an array *without* using a counter, thus avoiding the possibility of "stepping outside" the array. We show how to use the enhanced for statement with the Java API's prebuilt data structures (called collections) in Section 7.16. The syntax of an enhanced for statement is:

```
for (parameter : arrayName) {
    statement
}
```

where *parameter* has a *type* and an *identifier* (e.g., `int number`), and *arrayName* is the array through which to iterate. The type of the parameter must be *consistent* with the type of the elements in the array. As the next example illustrates, the identifier represents successive element values in the array on successive iterations of the loop.

Figure 7.12 uses the enhanced `for` statement (lines 10–12) to sum the integers in an array of student grades. The enhanced `for`'s parameter is of type `int`, because `array` contains `int` values—the loop selects one `int` value from the array during each iteration. The enhanced `for` statement iterates through successive values in the array one by one. The statement's header can be read as "for each iteration, assign the next element of `array` to `int` variable `number`, then execute the following statement." Thus, for each iteration, identifier `number` represents an `int` value in `array`. Lines 10–12 are equivalent to the following counter-controlled iteration used in lines 10–12 of Fig. 7.5 to total the integers in `array`, except that the counting details are hidden from you in the enhanced `for` statement:

```
for (int counter = 0; counter < array.length; counter++) {
    total += array[counter];
}
```

```
1   // Fig. 7.12: EnhancedForTest.java
2   // Using the enhanced for statement to total integers in an array.
3
4   public class EnhancedForTest {
5      public static void main(String[] args) {
6         int[] array = {87, 68, 94, 100, 83, 78, 85, 91, 76, 87};
7         int total = 0;
8
9         // add each element's value to total
10        for (int number : array) {
11           total += number;
12        }
13
14        System.out.printf("Total of array elements: %d%n", total);
15     }
16  }
```

```
Total of array elements: 849
```

Fig. 7.12 | Using the enhanced `for` statement to total integers in an array.

The enhanced `for` statement can be used *only* to obtain array elements—it *cannot* be used to *modify* elements. If your program needs to modify elements, use the traditional counter-controlled `for` statement.

The enhanced `for` statement can be used in place of the counter-controlled `for` statement whenever code looping through an array does *not* require access to the counter indicating the index of the current array element. For example, totaling the integers in an array requires access only to the element values—the index of each element is irrelevant. However, if a program must use a counter for some reason other than simply to loop through an array (e.g., to print an index number next to each array element value, as in the examples earlier in this chapter), use the counter-controlled for statement.

Error-Prevention Tip 7.2

The enhanced for statement simplifies iterating through an array. This makes the code more readable and eliminates several error possibilities, such as improperly specifying the control variable's initial value, the loop-continuation test and the increment expression.

Java SE 8

The for statement and the enhanced for statement each iterate sequentially from a starting value to an ending value. In Chapter 17, Lambdas and Streams, you'll learn about streams. As you'll see, streams provide an elegant, more concise and less error-prone means for iterating through collections in a manner that enables some iterations to occur in parallel with others to achieve better multi-core system performance.

7.8 Passing Arrays to Methods

This section demonstrates how to pass arrays and individual array elements as arguments to methods. To pass an array argument to a method, specify the name of the array *without any brackets*. For example, if array hourlyTemperatures is declared as

```
double[] hourlyTemperatures = new double[24];
```

then the method call

```
modifyArray(hourlyTemperatures);
```

passes the reference of array hourlyTemperatures to method modifyArray. Every array object "knows" its own length. Thus, when we pass an array object's reference into a method, we need not pass the array length as an additional argument.

For a method to receive an array reference through a method call, the method's parameter list must specify an *array parameter*. For example, the method header for method modifyArray might be written as

```
void modifyArray(double[] b)
```

indicating that modifyArray receives the reference of a double array in parameter b. The method call passes array hourlyTemperature's reference, so when the called method uses the array variable b, it *refers to* the same array object as hourlyTemperatures in the caller.

When an argument to a method is an entire array or an individual array element of a reference type, the called method receives a *copy* of the reference. However, when an argument to a method is an individual array element of a primitive type, the called method receives a copy of the element's *value*. Such primitive values are called **scalars** or **scalar quantities**. To pass an individual array element to a method, use the indexed name of the array element as an argument in the method call.

Figure 7.13 demonstrates the difference between passing an entire array and passing a primitive-type array element to a method. Method main invokes static methods modifyArray (line 18) and modifyElement (line 30). Recall that a static method can invoke other static methods of the same class without using the class name and a dot (.).

```
1   // Fig. 7.13: PassArray.java
2   // Passing arrays and individual array elements to methods.
3
4   public class PassArray {
5      // main creates array and calls modifyArray and modifyElement
6      public static void main(String[] args) {
7         int[] array = {1, 2, 3, 4, 5};
8
9         System.out.printf(
10           "Effects of passing reference to entire array:%n" +
11           "The values of the original array are:%n");
12
13        // output original array elements
14        for (int value : array) {
15           System.out.printf("   %d", value);
16        }
17
18        modifyArray(array); // pass array reference
19        System.out.printf("%n%nThe values of the modified array are:%n");
20
21        // output modified array elements
22        for (int value : array) {
23           System.out.printf("   %d", value);
24        }
25
26        System.out.printf(
27           "%n%nEffects of passing array element value:%n" +
28           "array[3] before modifyElement: %d%n", array[3]);
29
30        modifyElement(array[3]); // attempt to modify array[3]
31        System.out.printf(
32           "array[3] after modifyElement: %d%n", array[3]);
33     }
34
35     // multiply each element of an array by 2
36     public static void modifyArray(int[] array2) {
37        for (int counter = 0; counter < array2.length; counter++) {
38           array2[counter] *= 2;
39        }
40     }
41
42     // multiply argument by 2
43     public static void modifyElement(int element) {
44        element *= 2;
45        System.out.printf(
46           "Value of element in modifyElement: %d%n", element);
47     }
48  }
```

```
Effects of passing reference to entire array:
The values of the original array are:
   1   2   3   4   5
```

Fig. 7.13 | Passing arrays and individual array elements to methods. (Part I of 2.)

```
The values of the modified array are:
   2    4    6    8    10

Effects of passing array element value:
array[3] before modifyElement: 8
Value of element in modifyElement: 16
array[3] after modifyElement: 8
```

Fig. 7.13 | Passing arrays and individual array elements to methods. (Part 2 of 2.)

The enhanced for statement in lines 14–16 outputs array's elements. Line 18 invokes modifyArray (lines 36–40), passing array as an argument. The method receives a copy of array's reference and uses it to multiply each of array's elements by 2. To prove that array's elements were modified, lines 22–24 output the elements again. As the output shows, method modifyArray doubled the value of each element. We could *not* use the enhanced for statement in lines 37–39 because we're modifying the array's elements.

Figure 7.13 next demonstrates that when a copy of an individual primitive-type array element is passed to a method, modifying the *copy* in the called method does *not* affect the original value of that element in the calling method's array. Lines 26–28 output the value of array[3] *before* invoking method modifyElement. Remember that the value of this element is now 8 after it was modified in the call to modifyArray. Line 30 calls method modifyElement and passes array[3] as an argument. Remember that array[3] is actually one int value (8) in array. Therefore, the program passes a copy of array[3]'s value. Method modifyElement (lines 43–47) multiplies the value received as an argument by 2, stores the result in its parameter element, then outputs the value of element (16). Since method parameters, like local variables, cease to exist when the method in which they're declared completes execution, the method parameter element is destroyed when modifyElement terminates. When the program returns control to main, lines 31–32 output the *unmodified* value of array[3] (i.e., 8).

7.9 Pass-By-Value vs. Pass-By-Reference

The preceding example demonstrated how arrays and primitive-type array elements are passed as arguments to methods. We now take a closer look at how arguments in general are passed to methods. Two ways to pass arguments in method calls in many programming languages are **pass-by-value** and **pass-by-reference** (sometimes called **call-by-value** and **call-by-reference**). When an argument is passed by value, a *copy* of the argument's *value* is passed to the called method. The called method works exclusively with the copy. Changes to the called method's copy do *not* affect the original variable's value in the caller.

When an argument is passed by reference, the called method can access the argument's value in the caller directly and modify that data, if necessary. Pass-by-reference improves performance by eliminating the need to copy possibly large amounts of data.

Unlike some other languages, Java does *not* allow you to choose pass-by-value or pass-by-reference—*all arguments are passed by value*. A method call can pass two types of values to a method—copies of primitive values (e.g., values of type int and double) and copies of references to objects. Objects themselves cannot be passed to methods. When a method modifies a primitive-type parameter, changes to the parameter have no effect on the original argument value in the calling method. For example, when line 30 in main of Fig. 7.13 passes array[3] to method modifyElement, the statement in line 44 that doubles the value of parameter element has *no* effect on the value of array[3] in main. This is also true for reference-type parameters. If you modify a reference-type parameter so that it refers to another object, only the parameter refers to the new object—the reference stored in the caller's variable still refers to the original object.

Although an object's reference is passed by value, a method can still interact with the referenced object by calling its public methods using the copy of the object's reference. Since the reference stored in the parameter is a copy of the reference that was passed as an argument, the parameter in the called method and the argument in the calling method refer to the *same* object in memory. For example, in Fig. 7.13, both parameter array2 in method modifyArray and variable array in main refer to the *same* array object in memory. Any changes made using the parameter array2 are carried out on the object that array references in the calling method. In Fig. 7.13, the changes made in modifyArray using array2 affect the contents of the array object referenced by array in main. Thus, with a reference to an object, the called method *can* manipulate the caller's object directly.

Performance Tip 7.1

Passing references to arrays, instead of the array objects themselves, makes sense for performance reasons. Because Java arguments are passed by value, if array objects were passed, a copy of each element would be passed. For large arrays, this would waste time and consume considerable storage for the copies of the elements.

7.10 Case Study: Class GradeBook Using an Array to Store Grades

We now present the first part of our case study on developing a GradeBook class that instructors can use to maintain students' grades on an exam and display a grade report that includes the grades, class average, lowest grade, highest grade and a grade-distribution bar chart. The version of class GradeBook presented in this section stores the grades for one exam in a one-dimensional array. In Section 7.12, we present a version of class GradeBook that uses a two-dimensional array to store students' grades for *several* exams.

Storing Student Grades in an Array in Class *GradeBook*

Class GradeBook (Fig. 7.14) uses an array of ints to store several students' grades on a single exam. Array grades is declared as an instance variable (line 6), so each GradeBook object maintains its *own* set of grades. The constructor (lines 9–12) has two parameters—the name of the course and an array of grades. When an application (e.g., class GradeBookTest in Fig. 7.15) creates a GradeBook object, the application passes an existing int array to the constructor, which assigns the array's reference to instance variable grades (line 11). The grades array's *size* is determined by the length instance variable of the constructor's array parameter. Thus, a GradeBook object can process a *variable* number of grades. The grade values in the argument could have been input from a user, read from a file on disk (as discussed in Chapter 15) or come from a variety of other sources. In class GradeBookTest, we initialize an array with grade values (Fig. 7.15, line 7). Once the grades are stored in *instance variable* grades of class GradeBook, all the class's methods can access the elements of grades.

```java
1    // Fig. 7.14: GradeBook.java
2    // GradeBook class using an array to store test grades.
3
4    public class GradeBook {
5       private String courseName; // name of course this GradeBook represents
6       private int[] grades; // array of student grades
7
8       // constructor
9       public GradeBook(String courseName, int[] grades) {
10          this.courseName = courseName;
11          this.grades = grades;
12       }
13
14       // method to set the course name
15       public void setCourseName(String courseName) {
16          this.courseName = courseName;
17       }
18
19       // method to retrieve the course name
20       public String getCourseName() {
21          return courseName;
22       }
23
24       // perform various operations on the data
25       public void processGrades() {
26          // output grades array
27          outputGrades();
28
29          // call method getAverage to calculate the average grade
30          System.out.printf("%nClass average is %.2f%n", getAverage());
31
32          // call methods getMinimum and getMaximum
33          System.out.printf("Lowest grade is %d%nHighest grade is %d%n%n",
34             getMinimum(), getMaximum());
35
36          // call outputBarChart to print grade distribution chart
37          outputBarChart();
38       }
39
40       // find minimum grade
41       public int getMinimum() {
42          int lowGrade = grades[0]; // assume grades[0] is smallest
43
44          // loop through grades array
45          for (int grade : grades) {
46             // if grade lower than lowGrade, assign it to lowGrade
47             if (grade < lowGrade) {
48                lowGrade = grade; // new lowest grade
49             }
50          }
51
52          return lowGrade;
53       }
```

Fig. 7.14 | GradeBook class using an array to store test grades. (Part 1 of 3.)

```
54
55      // find maximum grade
56      public int getMaximum() {
57         int highGrade = grades[0]; // assume grades[0] is largest
58
59         // loop through grades array
60         for (int grade : grades) {
61            // if grade greater than highGrade, assign it to highGrade
62            if (grade > highGrade) {
63               highGrade = grade; // new highest grade
64            }
65         }
66
67         return highGrade;
68      }
69
70      // determine average grade for test
71      public double getAverage() {
72         int total = 0;
73
74         // sum grades for one student
75         for (int grade : grades) {
76            total += grade;
77         }
78
79         // return average of grades
80         return (double) total / grades.length;
81      }
82
83      // output bar chart displaying grade distribution
84      public void outputBarChart() {
85         System.out.println("Grade distribution:");
86
87         // stores frequency of grades in each range of 10 grades
88         int[] frequency = new int[11];
89
90         // for each grade, increment the appropriate frequency
91         for (int grade : grades) {
92            ++frequency[grade / 10];
93         }
94
95         // for each grade frequency, print bar in chart
96         for (int count = 0; count < frequency.length; count++) {
97            // output bar label ("00-09: ", ..., "90-99: ", "100: ")
98            if (count == 10) {
99               System.out.printf("%5d: ", 100);
100           }
101           else {
102              System.out.printf("%02d-%02d: ", count * 10, count * 10 + 9);
103           }
104
```

Fig. 7.14 | GradeBook class using an array to store test grades. (Part 2 of 3.)

```
105                // print bar of asterisks
106                for (int stars = 0; stars < frequency[count]; stars++) {
107                    System.out.print("*");
108                }
109
110                System.out.println();
111            }
112        }
113
114        // output the contents of the grades array
115        public void outputGrades() {
116            System.out.printf("The grades are:%n%n");
117
118            // output each student's grade
119            for (int student = 0; student < grades.length; student++) {
120                System.out.printf("Student %2d: %3d%n",
121                    student + 1, grades[student]);
122            }
123        }
124    }
```

Fig. 7.14 | GradeBook class using an array to store test grades. (Part 3 of 3.)

Method processGrades (lines 25–38) contains a series of method calls that output a report summarizing the grades. Line 27 calls method outputGrades to print the contents of the array grades. Lines 119–122 in method outputGrades output the students' grades. A counter-controlled for statement *must* be used in this case, because lines 120–121 use counter variable student's value to output each grade next to a particular student number (see the output in Fig. 7.15). Although array indices start at 0, a professor might typically number students starting at 1. Thus, lines 120–121 output student + 1 as the student number to produce grade labels "Student 1: ", "Student 2: ", and so on.

Method processGrades next calls method getAverage (line 30) to obtain the average of the grades in the array. Method getAverage (lines 71–81) uses an enhanced for statement to total the values in array grades before calculating the average. The parameter in the enhanced for's header (e.g., int grade) indicates that for each iteration, the int variable grade takes on a value in the array grades. The averaging calculation in line 80 uses grades.length to determine the number of grades being averaged.

Lines 33–34 in method processGrades call methods getMinimum and getMaximum to determine the lowest and highest grades of any student on the exam, respectively. Each of these methods uses an enhanced for statement to loop through array grades. Lines 45–50 in method getMinimum loop through the array. Lines 47–49 compare each grade to lowGrade; if a grade is less than lowGrade, lowGrade is set to that grade. When line 52 executes, lowGrade contains the lowest grade in the array. Method getMaximum (lines 56–68) works similarly to method getMinimum.

Finally, line 37 in method processGrades calls outputBarChart to print a grade-distribution chart using a technique similar to that in Fig. 7.6. In that example, we manually calculated the number of grades in each category (i.e., 0–9, 10–19, ..., 90–99 and 100) by simply looking at a set of grades. Here, lines 91–93 use a technique similar to that in Figs. 7.7–7.8 to calculate the frequency of grades in each category. Line 88 declares and creates array `frequency` of 11 `int`s to store the frequency of grades in each category. For each `grade` in array `grades`, lines 91–93 increment the appropriate `frequency` array element. To determine which one to increment, line 92 divides the current `grade` by 10 using *integer division*—e.g., if `grade` is 85, line 92 increments `frequency[8]` to update the count of grades in the range 80–89. Lines 96–111 print the bar chart (as shown in Fig. 7.15) based on the values in array `frequency`. Lines 106–108 of Fig. 7.14 use a value in array `frequency` to determine the number of asterisks to display in each bar.

Class *GradeBookTest* That Demonstrates Class *GradeBook*

The application of Fig. 7.15 creates an object of class `GradeBook` using the `int` array `gradesArray` (declared and initialized in line 7). Lines 9–10 pass a course name and `gradesArray` to the `GradeBook` constructor. Lines 11–12 display a welcome message that includes the course name stored in the `GradeBook` object. Line 13 invokes the `GradeBook` object's `processGrades` method. The output summarizes the 10 grades in `myGradeBook`.

 Software Engineering Observation 7.2

A test harness (or test application) is responsible for creating an object of the class being tested and providing it with data. This data could come from any of several sources. Test data can be placed directly into an array with an array initializer, it can come from the user at the keyboard, from a file (as you'll see in Chapter 15), from a database (as you'll see in Chapter 22) or from a network. After passing this data to the class's constructor to instantiate the object, the test harness should call upon the object to test its methods and manipulate its data. Gathering data in the test harness like this allows the class to be more reusable, able to manipulate data from several sources.

```java
1   // Fig. 7.15: GradeBookTest.java
2   // GradeBookTest creates a GradeBook object using an array of grades,
3   // then invokes method processGrades to analyze them.
4   public class GradeBookTest {
5      public static void main(String[] args) {
6         // array of student grades
7         int[] gradesArray = {87, 68, 94, 100, 83, 78, 85, 91, 76, 87};
8
9         GradeBook myGradeBook = new GradeBook(
10           "CS101 Introduction to Java Programming", gradesArray);
11        System.out.printf("Welcome to the grade book for%n%s%n%n",
12           myGradeBook.getCourseName());
13        myGradeBook.processGrades();
14     }
15  }
```

```
Welcome to the grade book for
CS101 Introduction to Java Programming

The grades are:

Student  1:  87
Student  2:  68
```

Fig. 7.15 | `GradeBookTest` creates a `GradeBook` object using an array of grades, then invokes method `processGrades` to analyze them. (Part 1 of 2.)

```
Student  3:  94
Student  4: 100
Student  5:  83
Student  6:  78
Student  7:  85
Student  8:  91
Student  9:  76
Student 10:  87

Class average is 84.90
Lowest grade is 68
Highest grade is 100

Grade distribution:
00-09:
10-19:
20-29:
30-39:
40-49:
50-59:
60-69: *
70-79: **
80-89: ****
90-99: **
  100: *
```

Fig. 7.15 | GradeBookTest creates a GradeBook object using an array of grades, then invokes method processGrades to analyze them. (Part 2 of 2.)

Java SE 8
In Chapter 17, Lambdas and Streams, the example of Fig. 17.9 uses stream methods min, max, count and average to process the elements of an int array elegantly and concisely without having to write iteration statements. In Chapter 21, Concurrency and Multi-Core Performance, the example of Fig. 21.30 uses stream method summaryStatistics to perform all of these operations in one method call.

7.11 Multidimensional Arrays

Multidimensional arrays with two dimensions often represent *tables* of values with data arranged in *rows* and *columns*. To identify a particular table element, you specify *two* indices. *By convention*, the first identifies the element's row and the second its column. Arrays that require two indices to identify each element are called **two-dimensional arrays**. (Multidimensional arrays can have more than two dimensions.) Java does not support multidimensional arrays directly, but it allows you to specify one-dimensional arrays whose elements are also one-dimensional arrays, thus achieving the same effect. Figure 7.16 illustrates a two-dimensional array named a with three rows and four columns (i.e., a three-by-four array). In general, an array with *m* rows and *n* columns is called an *m*-**by-***n* **array**.

Every element in array a is identified in Fig. 7.16 by an *array-access expression* of the form a[*row*][*column*]; a is the name of the array, and *row* and *column* are the indices that uniquely identify each element by row and column index. The element names in *row* 0 all have a *first* index of 0, and the element names in *column* 3 all have a *second* index of 3.

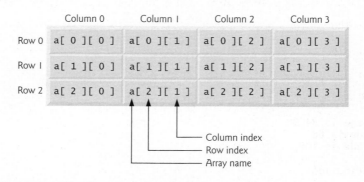

Fig. 7.16 | Two-dimensional array with three rows and four columns.

7.11.1 Arrays of One-Dimensional Arrays

Like one-dimensional arrays, multidimensional arrays can be initialized with array initial-izers in declarations. A two-dimensional array b with two rows and two columns could be declared and initialized with **nested array initializers** as follows:

```
int[][] b = {{1, 2}, {3, 4}};
```

The initial values are *grouped by row* in braces. So 1 and 2 initialize b[0][0] and b[0][1], respectively, and 3 and 4 initialize b[1][0] and b[1][1], respectively. The compiler counts the number of nested array initializers (represented by sets of braces within the out-er braces) to determine the number of *rows* in array b. The compiler counts the initializer values in the nested array initializer for a row to determine the number of *columns* in that row. As we'll see momentarily, this means that *rows can have different lengths*.

Multidimensional arrays are maintained as *arrays of one-dimensional arrays*. Therefore array b in the preceding declaration is actually composed of two separate one-dimensional arrays—one containing the values in the first nested initializer list {1, 2} and one con-taining the values in the second nested initializer list {3, 4}. Thus, array b itself is an array of two elements, each a one-dimensional array of int values.

7.11.2 Two-Dimensional Arrays with Rows of Different Lengths

The manner in which multidimensional arrays are represented makes them quite flexible. In fact, the lengths of the rows in array b are *not* required to be the same. For example,

```
int[][] b = {{1, 2}, {3, 4, 5}};
```

creates integer array b with two elements (determined by the number of nested array ini-tializers) that represent the rows of the two-dimensional array. Each element of b is a *ref-erence* to a one-dimensional array of int variables. The int array for row 0 is a one-dimensional array with *two* elements (1 and 2), and the int array for row 1 is a one-dimen-sional array with *three* elements (3, 4 and 5).

7.11.3 Creating Two-Dimensional Arrays with Array-Creation Expressions

A multidimensional array with the *same* number of columns in every row can be created with an array-creation expression. For example, the following line declares array b and assigns it a reference to a three-by-four array:

```
int[][] b = new int[3][4];
```

In this case, we use the literal values 3 and 4 to specify the number of rows and number of columns, respectively, but this is *not* required. Programs can also use variables to specify array dimensions, because *new creates arrays at execution time—not at compile time*. The elements of a multidimensional array are initialized when the array object is created.

A multidimensional array in which each row has a *different* number of columns can be created as follows:

```
int[][] b = new int[2][];   // create 2 rows
b[0] = new int[5]; // create 5 columns for row 0
b[1] = new int[3]; // create 3 columns for row 1
```

The preceding statements create a two-dimensional array with two rows. Row 0 has *five* columns, and row 1 has *three* columns.

7.11.4 Two-Dimensional Array Example: Displaying Element Values

Figure 7.17 demonstrates initializing two-dimensional arrays with array initializers and using nested for loops to **traverse** the arrays (i.e., manipulate *every* element of each array). Class InitArray's main declares two arrays. The declaration of array1 (line 7) uses nested array initializers of the *same* length to initialize the first row to the values 1, 2 and 3, and the second row to the values 4, 5 and 6. The declaration of array2 (line 8) uses nested initializers of *different* lengths. In this case, the first row is initialized to two elements with the values 1 and 2, respectively. The second row is initialized to one element with the value 3. The third row is initialized to three elements with the values 4, 5 and 6, respectively.

```
1   // Fig. 7.17: InitArray.java
2   // Initializing two-dimensional arrays.
3
4   public class InitArray {
5      // create and output two-dimensional arrays
6      public static void main(String[] args) {
7         int[][] array1 = {{1, 2, 3}, {4, 5, 6}};
8         int[][] array2 = {{1, 2}, {3}, {4, 5, 6}};
9
10        System.out.println("Values in array1 by row are");
11        outputArray(array1); // displays array1 by row
12
13        System.out.printf("%nValues in array2 by row are%n");
14        outputArray(array2); // displays array2 by row
15     }
16
```

Fig. 7.17 | Initializing two-dimensional arrays. (Part I of 2.)

```
17      // output rows and columns of a two-dimensional array
18      public static void outputArray(int[][] array) {
19         // loop through array's rows
20         for (int row = 0; row < array.length; row++) {
21            // loop through columns of current row
22            for (int column = 0; column < array[row].length; column++) {
23               System.out.printf("%d  ", array[row][column]);
24            }
25
26            System.out.println();
27         }
28      }
29   }
```

```
Values in array1 by row are
1  2  3
4  5  6

Values in array2 by row are
1  2
3
4  5  6
```

Fig. 7.17 | Initializing two-dimensional arrays. (Part 2 of 2.)

Lines 11 and 14 call outputArray (lines 18–28) to output the elements of array1 and array2, respectively. The method's parameter—int[][] array—indicates that it receives a two-dimensional array. The nested for statement (lines 20–27) outputs the array's rows. In the loop-continuation condition of the outer for statement, the expression array.length determines the number of rows in the array. In the inner for statement, the expression array[row].length determines the number of columns in the current row of the array. The inner for statement's condition enables the loop to determine the exact number of columns in each row. We demonstrate nested enhanced for statements in Fig. 7.18.

7.11.5 Common Multidimensional-Array Manipulations Performed with for Statements

Many common array manipulations use for statements. As an example, the following for statement sets all the elements in row 2 of array a in Fig. 7.16 to zero:

```
for (int column = 0; column < a[2].length; column++) {
   a[2][column] = 0;
}
```

We specified row 2; therefore, we know that the *first* index is always 2 (0 is the first row, and 1 is the second row). This for loop varies only the *second* index (i.e., the column index). If row 2 of array a contains four elements, then the preceding for statement is equivalent to the assignment statements

```
a[2][0] = 0;
a[2][1] = 0;
a[2][2] = 0;
a[2][3] = 0;
```

The following nested for statement totals the values of all the elements in array a:

```java
int total = 0;
for (int row = 0; row < a.length; row++) {
    for (int column = 0; column < a[row].length; column++) {
        total += a[row][column];
    }
}
```

These nested for statements total the array elements *one row at a time*. The outer for statement begins by setting the row index to 0 so that the first row's elements can be totaled by the inner for statement. The outer for then increments row to 1 so that the second row can be totaled. Then, the outer for increments row to 2 so that the third row can be totaled. The variable total can be displayed when the outer for statement terminates. In the next example, we show how to process a two-dimensional array in a similar manner using nested enhanced for statements.

7.12 Case Study: Class GradeBook Using a Two-Dimensional Array

In Section 7.10, we presented class GradeBook (Fig. 7.14), which used a one-dimensional array to store student grades on a single exam. In most semesters, students take several exams. Professors are likely to want to analyze grades across the entire semester, both for a single student and for the class as a whole.

Storing Student Grades in a Two-Dimensional Array in Class GradeBook

Figure 7.18 contains a GradeBook class that uses a two-dimensional array grades to store the grades of *several* students on *multiple* exams. Each *row* of the array represents a *single* student's grades for the entire course, and each *column* represents the grades of *all* the students who took a particular exam. Class GradeBookTest (Fig. 7.19) passes the array as an argument to the GradeBook constructor. In this example, we use a ten-by-three array for ten students' grades on three exams. Five methods perform array manipulations to process the grades. Each method is similar to its counterpart in the earlier one-dimensional array version of GradeBook (Fig. 7.14). Method getMinimum (lines 39–55 of Fig. 7.18) determines the lowest grade of any student for the semester. Method getMaximum (lines 58–74) determines the highest grade of any student for the semester. Method getAverage (lines 77–87) determines a particular student's semester average. Method outputBarChart (lines 90–121) outputs a grade bar chart for the entire semester's student grades. Method outputGrades (lines 124–148) outputs the array in a tabular format, along with each student's semester average.

```java
1   // Fig. 7.18: GradeBook.java
2   // GradeBook class using a two-dimensional array to store grades.
3
4   public class GradeBook {
5       private String courseName; // name of course this grade book represents
6       private int[][] grades; // two-dimensional array of student grades
7
```

Fig. 7.18 | GradeBook class using a two-dimensional array to store grades. (Part 1 of 4.)

```
 8      // two-argument constructor initializes courseName and grades array
 9      public GradeBook(String courseName, int[][] grades) {
10         this.courseName = courseName;
11         this.grades = grades;
12      }
13
14      // method to set the course name
15      public void setCourseName(String courseName) {
16         this.courseName = courseName;
17      }
18
19      // method to retrieve the course name
20      public String getCourseName() {
21         return courseName;
22      }
23
24      // perform various operations on the data
25      public void processGrades() {
26         // output grades array
27         outputGrades();
28
29         // call methods getMinimum and getMaximum
30         System.out.printf("%n%s %d%n%s %d%n%n",
31            "Lowest grade in the grade book is", getMinimum(),
32            "Highest grade in the grade book is", getMaximum());
33
34         // output grade distribution chart of all grades on all tests
35         outputBarChart();
36      }
37
38      // find minimum grade
39      public int getMinimum() {
40         // assume first element of grades array is smallest
41         int lowGrade = grades[0][0];
42
43         // loop through rows of grades array
44         for (int[] studentGrades : grades) {
45            // loop through columns of current row
46            for (int grade : studentGrades) {
47               // if grade less than lowGrade, assign it to lowGrade
48               if (grade < lowGrade) {
49                  lowGrade = grade;
50               }
51            }
52         }
53
54         return lowGrade;
55      }
56
57      // find maximum grade
58      public int getMaximum() {
59         // assume first element of grades array is largest
60         int highGrade = grades[0][0];
```

Fig. 7.18 | GradeBook class using a two-dimensional array to store grades. (Part 2 of 4.)

```
61
62          // loop through rows of grades array
63          for (int[] studentGrades : grades) {
64             // loop through columns of current row
65             for (int grade : studentGrades) {
66                // if grade greater than highGrade, assign it to highGrade
67                if (grade > highGrade) {
68                   highGrade = grade;
69                }
70             }
71          }
72
73          return highGrade;
74       }
75
76       // determine average grade for particular set of grades
77       public double getAverage(int[] setOfGrades) {
78          int total = 0;
79
80          // sum grades for one student
81          for (int grade : setOfGrades) {
82             total += grade;
83          }
84
85          // return average of grades
86          return (double) total / setOfGrades.length;
87       }
88
89       // output bar chart displaying overall grade distribution
90       public void outputBarChart() {
91          System.out.println("Overall grade distribution:");
92
93          // stores frequency of grades in each range of 10 grades
94          int[] frequency = new int[11];
95
96          // for each grade in GradeBook, increment the appropriate frequency
97          for (int[] studentGrades : grades) {
98             for (int grade : studentGrades) {
99                ++frequency[grade / 10];
100            }
101         }
102
103         // for each grade frequency, print bar in chart
104         for (int count = 0; count < frequency.length; count++) {
105            // output bar label ("00-09: ", ..., "90-99: ", "100: ")
106            if (count == 10) {
107               System.out.printf("%5d: ", 100);
108            }
109            else {
110               System.out.printf("%02d-%02d: ",
111                  count * 10, count * 10 + 9);
112            }
113
```

Fig. 7.18 | GradeBook class using a two-dimensional array to store grades. (Part 3 of 4.)

```
114              // print bar of asterisks
115              for (int stars = 0; stars < frequency[count]; stars++) {
116                  System.out.print("*");
117              }
118
119              System.out.println();
120          }
121      }
122
123      // output the contents of the grades array
124      public void outputGrades() {
125          System.out.printf("The grades are:%n%n");
126          System.out.print("                "); // align column heads
127
128          // create a column heading for each of the tests
129          for (int test = 0; test < grades[0].length; test++) {
130              System.out.printf("Test %d  ", test + 1);
131          }
132
133          System.out.println("Average"); // student average column heading
134
135          // create rows/columns of text representing array grades
136          for (int student = 0; student < grades.length; student++) {
137              System.out.printf("Student %2d", student + 1);
138
139              for (int test : grades[student]) { // output student's grades
140                  System.out.printf("%8d", test);
141              }
142
143              // call method getAverage to calculate student's average grade;
144              // pass row of grades as the argument to getAverage
145              double average = getAverage(grades[student]);
146              System.out.printf("%9.2f%n", average);
147          }
148      }
149  }
```

Fig. 7.18 | GradeBook class using a two-dimensional array to store grades. (Part 4 of 4.)

Methods getMinimum and getMaximum

Methods getMinimum, getMaximum, outputBarChart and outputGrades each loop through array grades by using nested for statements—for example, the nested enhanced for statement (lines 44–52) from the declaration of method getMinimum. The outer enhanced for statement iterates through the two-dimensional array grades, assigning successive rows to parameter studentGrades on successive iterations. The square brackets following the parameter name indicate that studentGrades refers to a one-dimensional int array—namely, a row in array grades containing one student's grades. To find the lowest overall grade, the inner for statement compares the elements of the current one-dimensional array studentGrades to variable lowGrade. For example, on the first iteration of the outer for, row 0 of grades is assigned to parameter studentGrades. The inner enhanced for statement then loops through studentGrades and compares each grade value with lowGrade. If a grade is less than lowGrade, lowGrade is set to that grade. On the second iteration of the outer enhanced for statement, row 1 of grades is assigned to studentGrades, and the elements of this row are compared with variable lowGrade. This repeats until all rows of grades have been traversed. When execution of the nested statement is complete, lowGrade contains the lowest grade in the two-dimensional array. Method getMaximum works similarly to method getMinimum.

Method outputBarChart
Method outputBarChart in Fig. 7.18 is nearly identical to the one in Fig. 7.14. However, to output the overall grade distribution for a whole semester, the method here uses nested enhanced for statements (lines 97–101) to create the one-dimensional array frequency based on all the grades in the two-dimensional array. The rest of the code in each of the two outputBarChart methods that displays the chart is identical.

Method outputGrades
Method outputGrades (lines 124–148) uses nested for statements to output values of the array grades and each student's semester average. The output (Fig. 7.19) shows the result, which resembles the tabular format of a professor's physical grade book. Lines 129–131 of of Fig. 7.18 print the column headings for each test. We use a counter-controlled for statement here so that we can identify each test with a number. Similarly, the for statement in lines 136–147 first outputs a row label using a counter variable to identify each student (line 137). Although array indices start at 0, lines 130 and 137 output test + 1 and student + 1, respectively, to produce test and student numbers starting at 1 (see the output in Fig. 7.19). The inner for statement (lines 139–141 of Fig. 7.18) uses the outer for statement's counter variable student to loop through a specific row of array grades and output each student's test grade. An enhanced for statement can be nested in a counter-controlled for statement, and vice versa. Finally, line 145 obtains each student's semester average by passing the current row of grades (i.e., grades[student]) to method getAverage.

Method getAverage
Method getAverage (lines 77–87) takes one argument—a one-dimensional array of test results for a particular student. When line 145 calls getAverage, the argument is grades[student], which specifies that a particular row of the two-dimensional array grades should be passed to getAverage. For example, based on the array created in Fig. 7.19, the argument grades[1] represents the three values (a one-dimensional array of grades) stored in row 1 of the two-dimensional array grades. Recall that a two-dimensional array is one whose elements are one-dimensional arrays. Method getAverage calculates the sum of the array elements, divides the total by the number of test results and returns the floating-point result as a double value (line 86 of Fig. 7.18).

Class GradeBookTest That Demonstrates Class GradeBook
Figure 7.19 creates an object of class GradeBook using the two-dimensional array of ints named gradesArray (declared and initialized in lines 8–17). Lines 19–20 pass a course name and gradesArray to the GradeBook constructor. Lines 21–22 display a welcome message containing the course name, then line 23 invokes myGradeBook's processGrades method to display a report summarizing the students' grades for the semester.

```
 1    // Fig. 7.19: GradeBookTest.java
 2    // GradeBookTest creates a GradeBook object using a two-dimensional array
 3    // of grades, then invokes method processGrades to analyze them.
 4    public class GradeBookTest {
 5       // main method begins program execution
 6       public static void main(String[] args) {
 7          // two-dimensional array of student grades
 8          int[][] gradesArray = {{87, 96, 70},
 9                                 {68, 87, 90},
10                                 {94, 100, 90},
11                                 {100, 81, 82},
12                                 {83, 65, 85},
13                                 {78, 87, 65},
14                                 {85, 75, 83},
15                                 {91, 94, 100},
16                                 {76, 72, 84},
17                                 {87, 93, 73}};
18
19          GradeBook myGradeBook = new GradeBook(
20             "CS101 Introduction to Java Programming", gradesArray);
21          System.out.printf("Welcome to the grade book for%n%s%n%n",
22             myGradeBook.getCourseName());
23          myGradeBook.processGrades();
24       }
25    }
```

```
Welcome to the grade book for
CS101 Introduction to Java Programming

The grades are:

            Test 1  Test 2  Test 3   Average
Student  1     87      96      70     84.33
Student  2     68      87      90     81.67
Student  3     94     100      90     94.67
Student  4    100      81      82     87.67
Student  5     83      65      85     77.67
Student  6     78      87      65     76.67
Student  7     85      75      83     81.00
Student  8     91      94     100     95.00
Student  9     76      72      84     77.33
Student 10     87      93      73     84.33

Lowest grade in the grade book is 65
Highest grade in the grade book is 100

Overall grade distribution:
00-09:
10-19:
20-29:
30-39:
40-49:
```

Fig. 7.19 | GradeBookTest creates GradeBook object using a two-dimensional array of grades, then invokes method processGrades to analyze them. (Part 1 of 2.)

```
50-59:
60-69: ***
70-79: ******
80-89: ***********
90-99: *******
  100: ***
```

Fig. 7.19 | GradeBookTest creates GradeBook object using a two-dimensional array of grades, then invokes method processGrades to analyze them. (Part 2 of 2.)

7.13 Variable-Length Argument Lists

With **variable-length argument lists**, you can create methods that receive an unspecified number of arguments. A type followed by an **ellipsis (...)** in a method's parameter list indicates that the method receives a variable number of arguments of that type. The ellipsis can occur only *once* in a parameter list, and the ellipsis, together with its type and the parameter name, must be placed at the *end* of the parameter list. While you can use method overloading and array passing to accomplish much of what is accomplished with variable-length argument lists, using an ellipsis in a method's parameter list is more concise.

Figure 7.20 demonstrates method average (lines 6–15), which receives a variable-length sequence of doubles. Java treats the variable-length argument list as an array whose elements are all of the same type. So, the method body can manipulate the parameter numbers as an array of doubles. Lines 10–12 use the enhanced for loop to walk through the array and calculate the total of the doubles in the array. Line 14 accesses numbers.length to obtain the size of the numbers array for use in the averaging calculation. Lines 27, 29 and 31 in main call method average with two, three and four arguments, respectively. Method average has a variable-length argument list (line 6), so it can average as many double arguments as the caller passes. The output shows that each call to method average returns the correct value.

 Common Programming Error 7.5
Placing an ellipsis indicating a variable-length argument list in the middle of a parameter list is a syntax error. An ellipsis may be placed only at the end of the parameter list.

```java
1   // Fig. 7.20: VarargsTest.java
2   // Using variable-length argument lists.
3
4   public class VarargsTest {
5      // calculate average
6      public static double average(double... numbers) {
7         double total = 0.0;
8
9         // calculate total using the enhanced for statement
10        for (double d : numbers) {
11           total += d;
12        }
```

Fig. 7.20 | Using variable-length argument lists. (Part 1 of 2.)

```
13
14          return total / numbers.length;
15      }
16
17      public static void main(String[] args) {
18          double d1 = 10.0;
19          double d2 = 20.0;
20          double d3 = 30.0;
21          double d4 = 40.0;
22
23          System.out.printf("d1 = %.1f%nd2 = %.1f%nd3 = %.1f%nd4 = %.1f%n%n",
24              d1, d2, d3, d4);
25
26          System.out.printf("Average of d1 and d2 is %.1f%n",
27              average(d1, d2));
28          System.out.printf("Average of d1, d2 and d3 is %.1f%n",
29              average(d1, d2, d3));
30          System.out.printf("Average of d1, d2, d3 and d4 is %.1f%n",
31              average(d1, d2, d3, d4));
32      }
33  }
```

```
d1 = 10.0
d2 = 20.0
d3 = 30.0
d4 = 40.0

Average of d1 and d2 is 15.0
Average of d1, d2 and d3 is 20.0
Average of d1, d2, d3 and d4 is 25.0
```

Fig. 7.20 | Using variable-length argument lists. (Part 2 of 2.)

7.14 Using Command-Line Arguments

It's possible to pass arguments from the command line to an application via method main's String[] parameter, which receives an array of Strings. By convention, this parameter is named args. When an application is executed using the java command, Java passes the **command-line arguments** that appear after the class name in the java command to the application's main method as Strings in the array args. The number of command-line arguments is obtained by accessing the array's length attribute. Common uses of command-line arguments include passing options and filenames to applications.

Our next example uses command-line arguments to determine the size of an array, the value of its first element and the increment used to calculate the values of the array's remaining elements. The command

```
java InitArray 5 0 4
```

passes three arguments, 5, 0 and 4, to the application InitArray. Command-line arguments are separated by white space, *not* commas. When this command executes, InitArray's main method receives the three-element array args (i.e., args.length is 3) in which args[0] contains the String "5", args[1] contains the String "0" and args[2] contains the String "4". The program determines how to use these arguments—in Fig. 7.21 we convert the three command-line arguments to int values and use them to initialize an array. When the program executes, if args.length is not 3, the program prints an error message and terminates (lines 7–11). Otherwise, lines 14–31 initialize and display the array based on the values of the command-line arguments.

```java
1   // Fig. 7.21: InitArray.java
2   // Initializing an array using command-line arguments.
3
4   public class InitArray {
5      public static void main(String[] args) {
6         // check number of command-line arguments
7         if (args.length != 3) {
8            System.out.printf(
9               "Error: Please re-enter the entire command, including%n" +
10              "an array size, initial value and increment.%n");
11        }
12        else {
13           // get array size from first command-line argument
14           int arrayLength = Integer.parseInt(args[0]);
15           int[] array = new int[arrayLength];
16
17           // get initial value and increment from command-line arguments
18           int initialValue = Integer.parseInt(args[1]);
19           int increment = Integer.parseInt(args[2]);
20
21           // calculate value for each array element
22           for (int counter = 0; counter < array.length; counter++) {
23              array[counter] = initialValue + increment * counter;
24           }
25
26           System.out.printf("%s%8s%n", "Index", "Value");
27
28           // display array index and value
29           for (int counter = 0; counter < array.length; counter++) {
30              System.out.printf("%5d%8d%n", counter, array[counter]);
31           }
32        }
33     }
34  }
```

```
java InitArray
Error: Please re-enter the entire command, including
an array size, initial value and increment.
```

```
java InitArray 5 0 4
Index    Value
    0        0
    1        4
    2        8
    3       12
    4       16
```

Fig. 7.21 | Initializing an array using command-line arguments. (Part 1 of 2.)

```
java InitArray 8 1 2
Index    Value
    0        1
    1        3
    2        5
    3        7
    4        9
    5       11
    6       13
    7       15
```

Fig. 7.21 | Initializing an array using command-line arguments. (Part 2 of 2.)

Line 14 gets args[0]—a String that specifies the array size—and converts it to an int value that the program uses to create the array in line 15. The static method parseInt of class Integer converts its String argument to an int.

Lines 18–19 convert the args[1] and args[2] command-line arguments to int values and store them in initialValue and increment, respectively. Lines 22–24 calculate the value for each array element.

The output of the first execution shows that the application received an insufficient number of command-line arguments. The second execution uses command-line arguments 5, 0 and 4 to specify the size of the array (5), the value of the first element (0) and the increment of each value in the array (4), respectively. The corresponding output shows that these values create an array containing the integers 0, 4, 8, 12 and 16. The output from the third execution shows that the command-line arguments 8, 1 and 2 produce an array whose 8 elements are the nonnegative odd integers from 1 to 15.

7.15 Class Arrays

Class **Arrays** helps you avoid reinventing the wheel by providing static methods for common array manipulations. These methods include **sort** for *sorting* an array (i.e., arranging elements into ascending order), **binarySearch** for *searching* a *sorted* array (i.e., determining whether an array contains a specific value and, if so, where the value is located), **equals** for *comparing* arrays and **fill** for *placing values into an array*. These methods are overloaded for primitive-type arrays and for arrays of objects. Our focus in this section is on using the built-in capabilities provided by the Java API.

Figure 7.22 uses Arrays methods sort, binarySearch, equals and fill, and shows how to *copy* arrays with class System's static **arraycopy method**. In main, line 9 sorts the elements of array doubleArray. The static method sort of class Arrays orders the array's elements in *ascending* order by default. We discuss how to sort in *descending* order later in the chapter. Overloaded versions of sort allow you to sort a specific range of elements within the array. Lines 10–14 output the sorted array.

Line 18 calls static method fill of class Arrays to populate all 10 elements of filledIntArray with 7s. Overloaded versions of fill allow you to populate a specific range of elements with the same value. Line 19 calls our class's displayArray method (declared at lines 62–68) to output the contents of filledIntArray.

```
1   // Fig. 7.22: ArrayManipulations.java
2   // Arrays class methods and System.arraycopy.
3   import java.util.Arrays;
4
5   public class ArrayManipulations {
6      public static void main(String[] args) {
7         // sort doubleArray into ascending order
8         double[] doubleArray = {8.4, 9.3, 0.2, 7.9, 3.4};
9         Arrays.sort(doubleArray);
10        System.out.printf("%ndoubleArray: ");
11
12        for (double value : doubleArray) {
13           System.out.printf("%.1f ", value);
14        }
15
16        // fill 10-element array with 7s
17        int[] filledIntArray = new int[10];
18        Arrays.fill(filledIntArray, 7);
19        displayArray(filledIntArray, "filledIntArray");
20
21        // copy array intArray into array intArrayCopy
22        int[] intArray = {1, 2, 3, 4, 5, 6};
23        int[] intArrayCopy = new int[intArray.length];
24        System.arraycopy(intArray, 0, intArrayCopy, 0, intArray.length);
25        displayArray(intArray, "intArray");
26        displayArray(intArrayCopy, "intArrayCopy");
27
28        // compare intArray and intArrayCopy for equality
29        boolean b = Arrays.equals(intArray, intArrayCopy);
30        System.out.printf("%n%nintArray %s intArrayCopy%n",
31           (b ? "==" : "!="));
32
33        // compare intArray and filledIntArray for equality
34        b = Arrays.equals(intArray, filledIntArray);
35        System.out.printf("intArray %s filledIntArray%n",
36           (b ? "==" : "!="));
37
38        // search intArray for the value 5
39        int location = Arrays.binarySearch(intArray, 5);
40
41        if (location >= 0) {
42           System.out.printf(
43              "Found 5 at element %d in intArray%n", location);
44        }
45        else {
46           System.out.println("5 not found in intArray");
47        }
48
49        // search intArray for the value 8763
50        location = Arrays.binarySearch(intArray, 8763);
51
```

Fig. 7.22 | Arrays class methods and System.arraycopy. (Part 1 of 2.)

```
52          if (location >= 0) {
53              System.out.printf(
54                  "Found 8763 at element %d in intArray%n", location);
55          }
56          else {
57              System.out.println("8763 not found in intArray");
58          }
59      }
60
61      // output values in each array
62      public static void displayArray(int[] array, String description) {
63          System.out.printf("%n%s: ", description);
64
65          for (int value : array) {
66              System.out.printf("%d ", value);
67          }
68      }
69  }
```

```
doubleArray: 0.2 3.4 7.9 8.4 9.3
filledIntArray: 7 7 7 7 7 7 7 7 7 7
intArray: 1 2 3 4 5 6
intArrayCopy: 1 2 3 4 5 6

intArray == intArrayCopy
intArray != filledIntArray
Found 5 at element 4 in intArray
8763 not found in intArray
```

Fig. 7.22 | Arrays class methods and System.arraycopy. (Part 2 of 2.)

Line 24 copies the elements of intArray into intArrayCopy. The first argument (intArray) passed to System method arraycopy is the array from which elements are to be copied. The second argument (0) is the index that specifies the *starting point* in the range of elements to copy from the array. This value can be any valid array index. The third argument (intArrayCopy) specifies the *destination array* that will store the copy. The fourth argument (0) specifies the index in the destination array *where the first copied element should be stored*. The last argument specifies the *number of elements to copy* from the array in the first argument. In this case, we copy all the elements in the array.

Lines 29 and 34 call static method equals of class Arrays to determine whether all the elements of two arrays are equivalent. If the arrays contain the same elements in the same order, the method returns true; otherwise, it returns false.

Error-Prevention Tip 7.3

When comparing array contents, always use Arrays.equals(array1, array2), which compares the two arrays' contents, rather than array1.equals(array2), which compares whether array1 and array2 refer to the same array object.

Lines 39 and 50 call static method binarySearch of class Arrays to perform a binary search on intArray, using the second argument (5 and 8763, respectively) as the key. If the value is found, binarySearch returns the index of the element; otherwise, binarySearch returns a negative value. The negative value returned is based on the search key's *insertion point*—the index where the key would be inserted in the array if we were performing an insert operation. After binarySearch determines the insertion point, it changes its sign to negative and subtracts 1 to obtain the return value. For example, in Fig. 7.22, the insertion point for the value 8763 is the element with index 6 in the array. Method binarySearch changes the insertion point to –6, subtracts 1 from it and returns the value –7. Subtracting 1 from the insertion point guarantees that method binarySearch returns positive values (>= 0) if and only if the key is found. This return value is useful for inserting elements in a sorted array.

Java SE 8—Class Arrays Method parallelSort

The Arrays class now has several new "parallel" methods that take advantage of multi-core hardware. Arrays method parallelSort can sort large arrays more efficiently on multi-core systems. In Section 21.12, we create a very large array and use features of the Date/Time API to compare how long it takes to sort the array with sort and parallelSort.

7.16 Introduction to Collections and Class ArrayList

The Java API provides several predefined data structures, called **collections**, used to store groups of related objects in memory. These classes provide efficient methods that organize, store and retrieve your data *without* requiring knowledge of how the data is being *stored*. This reduces application-development time.

You've used arrays to store sequences of objects. Arrays do not automatically change their size at execution time to accommodate additional elements. The collection class ArrayList<E> (package java.util) provides a convenient solution to this problem—it can *dynamically* change its size to accommodate more elements. The E (by convention) is a *placeholder*—when declaring a new ArrayList, replace it with the type of elements that you want the ArrayList to hold. For example,

```
ArrayList<String> list;
```

declares list as an ArrayList collection that can store only Strings. Classes with this kind of placeholder that can be used with any type are called **generic classes**. *Only reference types can be used to declare variables and create objects of generic classes.* However, Java provides a mechanism—known as *boxing*—that allows primitive values to be wrapped as objects for use with generic classes. So, for example,

```
ArrayList<Integer> integers;
```

declares integers as an ArrayList that can store only Integers. When you place an int value into an ArrayList<Integer>, the int value is *boxed* (wrapped) as an Integer object, and when you get an Integer object from an ArrayList<Integer>, then assign the object to an int variable, the int value inside the object is *unboxed* (unwrapped).

Additional generic collection classes and generics are discussed in Chapter 16. Figure 7.23 shows some common methods of class ArrayList<E>.

Method	Description
add	Overloaded to add an element to the *end* of the `ArrayList` or at a specific index in the `ArrayList`.
clear	Removes all the elements from the `ArrayList`.
contains	Returns `true` if the `ArrayList` contains the specified element; otherwise, returns `false`.
get	Returns the element at the specified index.
indexOf	Returns the index of the first occurrence of the specified element in the `ArrayList`.
remove	Overloaded. Removes the first occurrence of the specified value or the element at the specified index.
size	Returns the number of elements stored in the `ArrayList`.
trimToSize	Trims the capacity of the `ArrayList` to the current number of elements.

Fig. 7.23 | Some methods of class `ArrayList<E>`.

Demonstrating an ArrayList<String>

Figure 7.24 demonstrates some common `ArrayList` capabilities. Line 8 creates a new empty `ArrayList` of `Strings` with a default initial capacity of 10 elements. The capacity indicates how many items the `ArrayList` can hold *without growing*. `ArrayList` is implemented using a conventional array behind the scenes. When the `ArrayList` grows, it must create a larger internal array and *copy* each element to the new array. This is a time-consuming operation. It would be inefficient for the `ArrayList` to grow each time an element is added. Instead, it grows only when an element is added *and* the number of elements is equal to the capacity—i.e., there's no space for the new element.

```
1   // Fig. 7.24: ArrayListCollection.java
2   // Generic ArrayList<E> collection demonstration.
3   import java.util.ArrayList;
4
5   public class ArrayListCollection {
6      public static void main(String[] args) {
7         // create a new ArrayList of Strings with an initial capacity of 10
8         ArrayList<String> items = new ArrayList<String>();
9
10        items.add("red"); // append an item to the list
11        items.add(0, "yellow"); // insert "yellow" at index 0
12
13        // header
14        System.out.print(
15           "Display list contents with counter-controlled loop:");
16
17        // display the colors in the list
18        for (int i = 0; i < items.size(); i++) {
19           System.out.printf(" %s", items.get(i));
20        }
```

Fig. 7.24 | Generic `ArrayList<E>` collection demonstration. (Part 1 of 2.)

```
21
22          // display colors using enhanced for in the display method
23          display(items,
24              "%nDisplay list contents with enhanced for statement:");
25
26          items.add("green"); // add "green" to the end of the list
27          items.add("yellow"); // add "yellow" to the end of the list
28          display(items, "List with two new elements:");
29
30          items.remove("yellow"); // remove the first "yellow"
31          display(items, "Remove first instance of yellow:");
32
33          items.remove(1); // remove item at index 1
34          display(items, "Remove second list element (green):");
35
36          // check if a value is in the List
37          System.out.printf("\"red\" is %sin the list%n",
38              items.contains("red") ? "" : "not ");
39
40          // display number of elements in the List
41          System.out.printf("Size: %s%n", items.size());
42      }
43
44      // display the ArrayList's elements on the console
45      public static void display(ArrayList<String> items, String header) {
46          System.out.printf(header); // display header
47
48          // display each element in items
49          for (String item : items) {
50              System.out.printf(" %s", item);
51          }
52
53          System.out.println();
54      }
55  }
```

```
Display list contents with counter-controlled loop: yellow red
Display list contents with enhanced for statement: yellow red
List with two new elements: yellow red green yellow
Remove first instance of yellow: red green yellow
Remove second list element (green): red yellow
"red" is in the list
Size: 2
```

Fig. 7.24 | Generic `ArrayList<E>` collection demonstration. (Part 2 of 2.)

The **add** method adds elements to the `ArrayList` (lines 10–11). The add method with *one* argument *appends* its argument to the *end* of the `ArrayList`. The add method with *two* arguments *inserts* a new element at the specified *position*. The first argument is an index. As with arrays, collection indices start at zero. The second argument is the *value* to insert at that *index*. The indices of all subsequent elements are incremented by one. Inserting an element is usually slower than adding an element to the end of the `ArrayList`.

Lines 18–20 display the items in the `ArrayList`. Method **size** returns the number of elements currently in the `ArrayList`. Method **get** (line 19) obtains the element at a specified index. Lines 23–24 display the elements again by invoking method `display` (defined at lines 45–54). Lines 26–27 add two more elements to the `ArrayList`, then line 28 displays the elements again to confirm that the two elements were added to the *end* of the collection.

The **remove** method is used to remove an element with a specific value (line 30). It removes only the first such element. If no such element is in the `ArrayList`, `remove` does nothing. An overloaded version of the method removes the element at the specified index (line 33). When an element is removed, the indices of any elements after the removed element decrease by one.

Line 38 uses the **contains** method to check if an item is in the `ArrayList`. The `contains` method returns `true` if the element is found in the `ArrayList`, and `false` otherwise. The method compares its argument to each element of the `ArrayList` in order, so using `contains` on a large `ArrayList` can be *inefficient*. Line 41 displays the `ArrayList`'s size.

Diamond (<>) Notation for Creating an Object of a Generic Class
Consider line 8 of Fig. 7.24:

```
ArrayList<String> items = new ArrayList<String>();
```

Notice that `ArrayList<String>` appears in the variable declaration *and* in the class instance creation expression. The **diamond (<>) notation** simplifies statements like this. Using <> in a class instance creation expression for an object of a *generic* class tells the compiler to determine what belongs in the angle brackets. The preceding statement can be written as:

```
ArrayList<String> items = new ArrayList<>();
```

When the compiler encounters the diamond (<>) in the class instance creation expression, it uses the declaration of variable `items` to determine the `ArrayList`'s element type (`String`)—this is known as *inferring the element type*.

7.17 Wrap-Up

This chapter began our treatment of Java data structures, exploring the use of arrays to store data in and retrieve data from lists and tables of values. The chapter examples demonstrated how to declare an array, initialize an array and refer to individual elements of an array. The chapter introduced the enhanced `for` statement to iterate through arrays. We used exception handling to test for `ArrayIndexOutOfBoundsExceptions` that occur when a program attempts to access an array element outside the bounds of an array. We also illustrated how to pass arrays to methods and how to declare and manipulate multidimensional arrays. Finally, the chapter showed how to write methods that use variable-length argument lists and how to read arguments passed to a program from the command line.

We introduced the `ArrayList<E>` generic collection, which provides all the functionality and performance of arrays, along with other useful capabilities such as dynamic resizing. We used the `add` methods to add new items to the end of an `ArrayList` and to insert items in an `ArrayList`. The `remove` method was used to remove the first occurrence of a specified item, and an overloaded version of `remove` was used to remove an item at a specified index. We used the `size` method to obtain number of items in the `ArrayList`.

Chapter 16, Generic Collections, introduces the Java Collections Framework, which uses generics to allow you to specify the exact types of objects that a particular data structure will store. Chapter 16 also introduces Java's other predefined data structures and covers additional methods of class `Arrays`. You'll be able to use some of the `Arrays` methods after reading the current chapter, but some of them require knowledge of concepts presented later in the book. Chapter 19 discusses generics, which enable you to create general models of methods and classes that can be declared once, but used with many different data types.

We've now introduced the basic concepts of classes, objects, control statements, methods, arrays and collections. In Chapter 8, we take a deeper look at classes and objects.

8

Classes and Objects: A Deeper Look

Objectives

In this chapter you'll:

- See additional details of creating class declarations.
- Use the **throw** statement to indicate that a problem has occurred.
- Use keyword **this** in a constructor to call another constructor in the same class.
- Use **static** variables and methods.
- Import **static** members of a class.
- Use the **enum** type to create sets of constants with unique identifiers.
- Declare **enum** constants with parameters.
- Use **BigDecimal** for precise monetary calculations.

8.1 Introduction

We now take a deeper look at building classes, controlling access to members of a class and creating constructors. We show how to throw an exception to indicate that a problem has occurred—Section 7.5 discussed catching exceptions. We use the this keyword to enable one constructor to conveniently call another constructor of the same class. We discuss *composition*—a capability that allows a class to have references to objects of other classes as members. We reexamine the use of *set* and *get* methods. Recall that Section 6.9 introduced the basic enum type to declare a set of constants. In this chapter, we discuss the relationship between enum types and classes, demonstrating that an enum type, like a class, can be declared in its own file with constructors, methods and fields. The chapter also discusses static class members and final instance variables in detail. We show a special relationship between classes in the same package. Finally, we demonstrate how to use class Big-Decimal to perform precise monetary calculations. Two additional types of classes—nested classes and anonymous inner classes—are discussed in detail in our later chapters on GUI, graphics and multimedia.

8.2 Time Class Case Study

Our first example consists of two classes—Time1 (Fig. 8.1) and Time1Test (Fig. 8.2). Class Time1 represents the time of day. Class Time1Test's main method creates one object of class Time1 and invokes its methods. The output of this program appears in Fig. 8.2.

Time1 Class Declaration
Class Time1's private int instance variables hour, minute and second (Fig. 8.1, lines 5–7) represent the time in universal-time format (24-hour clock format in which hours are in the range 0–23, and minutes and seconds are each in the range 0–59). Time1 contains public methods setTime (lines 11–22), toUniversalString (lines 25–27) and toString (lines 30–34). These methods are also called the **public services** or the **public interface** that the class provides to its clients.

```java
1    // Fig. 8.1: Time1.java
2    // Time1 class declaration maintains the time in 24-hour format.
3
4    public class Time1 {
5       private int hour; // 0 - 23
6       private int minute; // 0 - 59
7       private int second; // 0 - 59
8
9       // set a new time value using universal time; throw an
10      // exception if the hour, minute or second is invalid
11      public void setTime(int hour, int minute, int second) {
12         // validate hour, minute and second
13         if (hour < 0 || hour >= 24 || minute < 0 || minute >= 60 ||
14            second < 0 || second >= 60) {
15            throw new IllegalArgumentException(
16               "hour, minute and/or second was out of range");
17         }
18
19         this.hour = hour;
20         this.minute = minute;
21         this.second = second;
22      }
23
24      // convert to String in universal-time format (HH:MM:SS)
25      public String toUniversalString() {
26         return String.format("%02d:%02d:%02d", hour, minute, second);
27      }
28
29      // convert to String in standard-time format (H:MM:SS AM or PM)
30      public String toString() {
31         return String.format("%d:%02d:%02d %s",
32            ((hour == 0 || hour == 12) ? 12 : hour % 12),
33            minute, second, (hour < 12 ? "AM" : "PM"));
34      }
35   }
```

Fig. 8.1 | `Time1` class declaration maintains the time in 24-hour format.

Default Constructor

In this example, class `Time1` does *not* declare a constructor, so the compiler supplies a default constructor (as we discussed in Section 3.3.2). Each instance variable implicitly receives the default `int` value. Instance variables also can be initialized when they're declared in the class body, using the same initialization syntax as with a local variable.

Method `setTime` and Throwing Exceptions

Method `setTime` (lines 11–22) is a `public` method that declares three `int` parameters and uses them to set the time. Lines 13–14 test each argument to determine whether the value is outside the proper range. The `hour` value must be greater than or equal to 0 and less than 24, because universal-time format represents hours as integers from 0 to 23 (e.g., 1 PM is hour 13 and 11 PM is hour 23; midnight is hour 0 and noon is hour 12). Similarly, both `minute` and `second` values must be greater than or equal to 0 and less than 60. For values outside these ranges, `setTime` **throws an exception** of type **`IllegalArgumentException`** (lines 15–16), which notifies the client code that an invalid argument was passed to the method. As you learned in Section 7.5, you can use try...catch to catch exceptions and attempt to recover from them, which we'll do in Fig. 8.2. The class instance creation expression in the **throw statement** (Fig. 8.1; line 15) creates a new object of type IllegalArgumentException. The parentheses indicate a call to the IllegalArgumentException constructor. In this case, we call the constructor that allows us to specify a custom error message. After the exception object is created, the throw statement immediately terminates method setTime and the exception is returned to the calling method that attempted to set the time. If the argument values are all valid, lines 19–21 assign them to the hour, minute and second instance variables.

Software Engineering Observation 8.1

For a method like setTime in Fig. 8.1, validate all of the method's arguments before using them to set instance variable values to ensure that the object's data is modified only if all the arguments are valid.

Method *toUniversalString*
Method toUniversalString (lines 25–27) takes no arguments and returns a String in *universal-time format*, consisting of two digits each for the hour, minute and second—recall that you can use the 0 flag in a printf format specification (e.g., "%02d") to display leading zeros for a value that doesn't use all the character positions in the specified field width. For example, if the time were 1:30:07 PM, the method would return 13:30:07. Line 26 uses static method **format** of class String to return a String containing the formatted hour, minute and second values, each with two digits and possibly a leading 0 (specified with the 0 flag). Method format is similar to method System.out.printf except that format *returns* a formatted String rather than displaying it in a command window. The formatted String is returned by method toUniversalString.

Method *toString*
Method toString (lines 30–34) takes no arguments and returns a String in *standard-time format*, consisting of the hour, minute and second values separated by colons and followed by AM or PM (e.g., 11:30:17 AM or 1:27:06 PM). Like method toUniversalString, method toString uses static String method format to format the minute and second as two-digit values, with leading zeros if necessary. Line 32 uses a conditional operator (?:) to determine the value for hour in the String—if the hour is 0 or 12 (AM or PM), it appears as 12; otherwise, it appears as a value from 1 to 11. The conditional operator in line 33 determines whether AM or PM will be returned as part of the String.

Recall that all objects in Java have a toString method that returns a String representation of the object. We chose to return a String containing the time in standard-time format. Method toString is called *implicitly* whenever a Time1 object appears in the code where a String is needed, such as the value to output with a %s format specifier in a call to System.out.printf. You may also call toString *explicitly* to obtain a String representation of a Time object.

Using Class *Time1*
Class Time1Test (Fig. 8.2) uses class Time1. Line 7 declares the Time1 variable time and initializes it with a new Time1 object. Operator new implicitly invokes class Time1's default

constructor, because Time1 does not declare any constructors. To confirm that the Time1 object was initialized properly, line 10 calls the private method displayTime (lines 31– 34), which, in turn, calls the Time1 object's toUniversalString and toString methods to output the time in universal-time format and standard-time format, respectively. Note that toString could have been called implicitly here rather than explicitly. Next, line 14 invokes method setTime of the time object to change the time. Then line 15 calls displayTime again to output the time in both formats to confirm that it was set correctly.

Software Engineering Observation 8.2

*Recall from Chapter 3 that methods declared with access modifier private can be called only by other methods of the class in which the private methods are declared. Such methods are commonly referred to as **utility methods** or **helper methods** because they're typically used to support the operation of the class's other methods.*

```java
 1   // Fig. 8.2: Time1Test.java
 2   // Time1 object used in an app.
 3
 4   public class Time1Test {
 5      public static void main(String[] args) {
 6         // create and initialize a Time1 object
 7         Time1 time = new Time1(); // invokes Time1 constructor
 8
 9         // output string representations of the time
10         displayTime("After time object is created", time);
11         System.out.println();
12
13         // change time and output updated time
14         time.setTime(13, 27, 6);
15         displayTime("After calling setTime", time);
16         System.out.println();
17
18         // attempt to set time with invalid values
19         try {
20            time.setTime(99, 99, 99); // all values out of range
21         }
22         catch (IllegalArgumentException e) {
23            System.out.printf("Exception: %s%n%n", e.getMessage());
24         }
25
26         // display time after attempt to set invalid values
27         displayTime("After calling setTime with invalid values", time);
28      }
29
30      // displays a Time1 object in 24-hour and 12-hour formats
31      private static void displayTime(String header, Time1 t) {
32         System.out.printf("%s%nUniversal time: %s%nStandard time: %s%n",
33            header, t.toUniversalString(), t.toString());
34      }
35   }
```

Fig. 8.2 | Time1 object used in an app. (Part 1 of 2.)

```
After time object is created
Universal time: 00:00:00
Standard time: 12:00:00 AM

After calling setTime
Universal time: 13:27:06
Standard time: 1:27:06 PM

Exception: hour, minute and/or second was out of range

After calling setTime with invalid values
Universal time: 13:27:06
Standard time: 1:27:06 PM
```

Fig. 8.2 | `Time1` object used in an app. (Part 2 of 2.)

Calling *Time1* Method *setTime* with Invalid Values

To illustrate that method `setTime` *validates* its arguments, line 20 calls method `setTime` with *invalid* arguments of 99 for the `hour`, `minute` and `second`. This statement is placed in a `try` block (lines 19–21) in case `setTime` throws an `IllegalArgumentException`, which it will do since the arguments are all invalid. When this occurs, the exception is caught at lines 22–24, and line 23 displays the exception's error message by calling its `getMessage` method. Line 27 outputs the time again in both formats to confirm that `setTime` did *not* change the time when invalid arguments were supplied.

Software Engineering of the *Time1* Class Declaration

Consider several issues of class design with respect to class `Time1`. The instance variables `hour`, `minute` and `second` are each declared `private`. The actual data representation used within the class is of no concern to the class's clients. For example, it would be perfectly reasonable for `Time1` to represent the time internally as the number of seconds since midnight or the number of minutes and seconds since midnight. Clients could use the same `public` methods and get the same results without being aware of this. (As an exercise, you could reimplement class `Time2` to represent the time as the number of seconds since midnight and show that indeed no change is visible to the clients of the class.)

Software Engineering Observation 8.3

Classes simplify programming, because the client can use only a class's `public` methods. Such methods are usually client oriented rather than implementation oriented. Clients are neither aware of, nor involved in, a class's implementation. Clients generally care about what the class does but not how the class does it.

Software Engineering Observation 8.4

Interfaces change less frequently than implementations. When an implementation changes, implementation-dependent code must change accordingly. Hiding the implementation reduces the possibility that other program parts will become dependent on a class's implementation details.

Java SE 8—Date/Time API

This section's example and several of this chapter's later examples demonstrate various class-implementation concepts in classes that represent dates and times. In professional

8

Java development, rather than building your own date and time classes, you'll typically re-use the ones provided by the Java API. Though Java has always had classes for manipulating dates and times, Java SE 8 introduced a new **Date/Time API**—defined by the classes in the package **java.time**. Applications built with Java SE 8 should use the Date/Time API's capabilities, rather than those in earlier Java versions. The new API fixes various issues with the older classes and provides more robust, easier-to-use capabilities for manipulating dates, times, time zones, calendars and more. We use some Date/Time API features in Chapter 21. You can learn more about the Date/Time API's classes at:

> http://docs.oracle.com/javase/8/docs/api/java/time/package-
>   summary.html

8.3 Controlling Access to Members

The access modifiers public and private control access to a class's variables and methods. In Chapter 9, we'll introduce the additional access modifier protected. The primary purpose of public methods is to present to the class's clients a view of the services the class provides (i.e., the class's public interface). Clients need not be concerned with how the class accomplishes its tasks. For this reason, the class's private variables and private methods (i.e., its *implementation details*) are *not* accessible to its clients.

Figure 8.3 demonstrates that private class members are *not* accessible outside the class. Lines 7–9 attempt to access the private instance variables hour, minute and second of the Time1 object time. When this program is compiled, the compiler generates error messages that these private members are not accessible. This program assumes that the Time1 class from Fig. 8.1 is used.

```java
 1  // Fig. 8.3: MemberAccessTest.java
 2  // Private members of class Time1 are not accessible.
 3  public class MemberAccessTest {
 4     public static void main(String[] args) {
 5        Time1 time = new Time1(); // create and initialize Time1 object
 6
 7        time.hour = 7; // error: hour has private access in Time1
 8        time.minute = 15; // error: minute has private access in Time1
 9        time.second = 30; // error: second has private access in Time1
10     }
11  }
```

```
MemberAccessTest.java:7: error: hour has private access in Time1
      time.hour = 7; // error: hour has private access in Time1
          ^
MemberAccessTest.java:8: error: minute has private access in Time1
      time.minute = 15; // error: minute has private access in Time1
          ^
MemberAccessTest.java:9: error: second has private access in Time1
      time.second = 30; // error: second has private access in Time1
          ^
3 errors
```

Fig. 8.3 | Private members of class Time1 are not accessible.

> **Common Programming Error 8.1**
>
> *An attempt by a method that's not a member of a class to access a* private *member of that class generates a compilation error.*

8.4 Referring to the Current Object's Members with the this Reference

Every object can access a *reference to itself* with keyword **this** (sometimes called the **this reference**). When an instance method is called for a particular object, the method's body *implicitly* uses keyword this to refer to the object's instance variables and other methods. This enables the class's code to know which object should be manipulated. As you'll see in Fig. 8.4, you can also use keyword this *explicitly* in an instance method's body. Section 8.5 shows another interesting use of keyword this. Section 8.11 explains why keyword this cannot be used in a static method.

Figure 8.4 demonstrates implicit and explicit use of the this reference. This example is the first in which we declare *two* classes in one file—class ThisTest is declared in lines 4–9, and class SimpleTime in lines 12–41. When you compile a .java file containing more than one class, the compiler produces a separate .class file for every class. In this case, two separate files are produced—SimpleTime.class and ThisTest.class. When one source-code (.java) file contains multiple class declarations, the compiler places the .class files in the *same* directory. Note also in Fig. 8.4 that only class ThisTest is declared public. A source-code file can contain only *one* public class—otherwise, a compilation error occurs. *Non-public classes* can be used only by other classes in the *same package*—recall from Section 3.2.5 that classes compiled into the same directory are in the same package. So, in this example, class SimpleTime can be used only by class ThisTest.

```
1   // Fig. 8.4: ThisTest.java
2   // this used implicitly and explicitly to refer to members of an object.
3
4   public class ThisTest {
5      public static void main(String[] args) {
6         SimpleTime time = new SimpleTime(15, 30, 19);
7         System.out.println(time.buildString());
8      }
9   }
10
11  // class SimpleTime demonstrates the "this" reference
12  class SimpleTime {
13     private int hour;   // 0-23
14     private int minute; // 0-59
15     private int second; // 0-59
16
17     // if the constructor uses parameter names identical to
18     // instance variable names the "this" reference is
19     // required to distinguish between the names
20     public SimpleTime(int hour, int minute, int second) {
21        this.hour = hour; // set "this" object's hour
```

Fig. 8.4 | this used implicitly and explicitly to refer to members of an object. (Part 1 of 2.)

```
22          this.minute = minute; // set "this" object's minute
23          this.second = second; // set "this" object's second
24      }
25
26      // use explicit and implicit "this" to call toUniversalString
27      public String buildString() {
28          return String.format("%24s: %s%n%24s: %s",
29              "this.toUniversalString()", this.toUniversalString(),
30              "toUniversalString()", toUniversalString());
31      }
32
33      // convert to String in universal-time format (HH:MM:SS)
34      public String toUniversalString() {
35          // "this" is not required here to access instance variables,
36          // because method does not have local variables with same
37          // names as instance variables
38          return String.format("%02d:%02d:%02d",
39              this.hour, this.minute, this.second);
40      }
41  }
```

```
this.toUniversalString(): 15:30:19
    toUniversalString(): 15:30:19
```

Fig. 8.4 | `this` used implicitly and explicitly to refer to members of an object. (Part 2 of 2.)

Class `SimpleTime` (lines 12–41) declares three `private` instance variables—hour, minute and second (lines 13–15). The class's constructor (lines 20–24) receives three int arguments to initialize a `SimpleTime` object. Once again, we used parameter names for the constructor that are *identical* to the class's instance-variable names (lines 13–15), so we use the `this` reference to refer to the instance variables in lines 21–23.

Error-Prevention Tip 8.1
Most IDEs will issue a warning if you say x = x; instead of this.x = x;. The statement x = x; is often called a no-op (no operation).

Method `buildString` (lines 27–31) returns a `String` created by a statement that uses the `this` reference explicitly and implicitly. Line 29 uses it *explicitly* to call method `toUniversalString`. Line 30 uses it *implicitly* to call the same method. Both lines perform the same task. You typically will not use `this` explicitly to reference other methods within the current object. Also, line 39 in method `toUniversalString` explicitly uses the `this` reference to access each instance variable. This is *not* necessary here, because the method does *not* have any local variables that shadow the instance variables of the class.

Performance Tip 8.1
There's only one copy of each method per class—every object of the class shares the method's code. Each object, on the other hand, has its own copy of the class's instance variables. The class's non-static methods implicitly use this to determine the specific object of the class to manipulate.

Class ThisTest's main method (lines 5–8) demonstrates class SimpleTime. Line 6 creates an instance of class SimpleTime and invokes its constructor. Line 7 invokes the object's buildString method, then displays the results.

8.5 Time Class Case Study: Overloaded Constructors

As you know, you can declare your own constructor to specify how objects of a class should be initialized. Next, we demonstrate a class with several **overloaded constructors** that enable objects of that class to be initialized in different ways. To overload constructors, simply provide multiple constructor declarations with different signatures.

Class *Time2* with Overloaded Constructors

The Time1 class's default constructor in Fig. 8.1 initialized hour, minute and second to their default 0 values (i.e., midnight in universal time). The default constructor does not enable the class's clients to initialize the time with nonzero values. Class Time2 (Fig. 8.5) contains five overloaded constructors that provide convenient ways to initialize objects. In this program, four of the constructors invoke a fifth, which in turn ensures that the value supplied for hour is in the range 0 to 23, and the values for minute and second are each in the range 0 to 59. The compiler invokes the appropriate constructor by matching the number, types and order of the types of the arguments specified in the constructor call with the number, types and order of the types of the parameters specified in each constructor declaration. Class Time2 also provides *set* and *get* methods for each instance variable.

```java
1   // Fig. 8.5: Time2.java
2   // Time2 class declaration with overloaded constructors.
3
4   public class Time2 {
5      private int hour; // 0 - 23
6      private int minute; // 0 - 59
7      private int second; // 0 - 59
8
9      // Time2 no-argument constructor:
10     // initializes each instance variable to zero
11     public Time2() {
12        this(0, 0, 0); // invoke constructor with three arguments
13     }
14
15     // Time2 constructor: hour supplied, minute and second defaulted to 0
16     public Time2(int hour) {
17        this(hour, 0, 0); // invoke constructor with three arguments
18     }
19
20     // Time2 constructor: hour and minute supplied, second defaulted to 0
21     public Time2(int hour, int minute) {
22        this(hour, minute, 0); // invoke constructor with three arguments
23     }
24
```

Fig. 8.5 | Time2 class declaration with overloaded constructors. (Part 1 of 3.)

```java
25    // Time2 constructor: hour, minute and second supplied
26    public Time2(int hour, int minute, int second) {
27        if (hour < 0 || hour >= 24) {
28            throw new IllegalArgumentException("hour must be 0-23");
29        }
30
31        if (minute < 0 || minute >= 60) {
32            throw new IllegalArgumentException("minute must be 0-59");
33        }
34
35        if (second < 0 || second >= 60) {
36            throw new IllegalArgumentException("second must be 0-59");
37        }
38
39        this.hour = hour;
40        this.minute = minute;
41        this.second = second;
42    }
43
44    // Time2 constructor: another Time2 object supplied
45    public Time2(Time2 time) {
46        // invoke constructor with three arguments
47        this(time.hour, time.minute, time.second);
48    }
49
50    // Set Methods
51    // set a new time value using universal time;
52    // validate the data
53    public void setTime(int hour, int minute, int second) {
54        if (hour < 0 || hour >= 24) {
55            throw new IllegalArgumentException("hour must be 0-23");
56        }
57
58        if (minute < 0 || minute >= 60) {
59            throw new IllegalArgumentException("minute must be 0-59");
60        }
61
62        if (second < 0 || second >= 60) {
63            throw new IllegalArgumentException("second must be 0-59");
64        }
65
66        this.hour = hour;
67        this.minute = minute;
68        this.second = second;
69    }
70
71    // validate and set hour
72    public void setHour(int hour) {
73        if (hour < 0 || hour >= 24) {
74            throw new IllegalArgumentException("hour must be 0-23");
75        }
76
```

Fig. 8.5 | Time2 class declaration with overloaded constructors. (Part 2 of 3.)

```
77          this.hour = hour;
78      }
79
80      // validate and set minute
81      public void setMinute(int minute) {
82          if (minute < 0 || minute >= 60) {
83              throw new IllegalArgumentException("minute must be 0-59");
84          }
85
86          this.minute = minute;
87      }
88
89      // validate and set second
90      public void setSecond(int second) {
91          if (second < 0 || second >= 60) {
92              throw new IllegalArgumentException("second must be 0-59");
93          }
94
95          this.second = second;
96      }
97
98      // Get Methods
99      // get hour value
100     public int getHour() {return hour;}
101
102     // get minute value
103     public int getMinute() {return minute;}
104
105     // get second value
106     public int getSecond() {return second;}
107
108     // convert to String in universal-time format (HH:MM:SS)
109     public String toUniversalString() {
110         return String.format(
111             "%02d:%02d:%02d", getHour(), getMinute(), getSecond());
112     }
113
114     // convert to String in standard-time format (H:MM:SS AM or PM)
115     public String toString() {
116         return String.format("%d:%02d:%02d %s",
117             ((getHour() == 0 || getHour() == 12) ? 12 : getHour() % 12),
118             getMinute(), getSecond(), (getHour() < 12 ? "AM" : "PM"));
119     }
120 }
```

Fig. 8.5 | Time2 class declaration with overloaded constructors. (Part 3 of 3.)

Class *Time2's Constructors—Calling One Constructor from Another via* **this**

Lines 11–13 declare a so-called **no-argument constructor** that's invoked without arguments. Once you declare any constructors in a class, the compiler will *not* provide a *default
constructor*. This no-argument constructor ensures that class Time2's clients can create
Time2 objects with default values. Such a constructor simply initializes the object as specified in the constructor's body. In the body, we introduce a use of this that's allowed only

as the *first* statement in a constructor's body. Line 12 uses this in method-call syntax to invoke the Time2 constructor that takes three parameters (lines 26–42) with values of 0 for the hour, minute and second. Using this as shown here is a popular way to *reuse* initialization code provided by another of the class's constructors rather than defining similar code in the no-argument constructor's body. A constructor that calls another constructor in this manner is known as a **delegating constructor**. We use this syntax in four of the five Time2 constructors to make the class easier to maintain and modify. If we need to change how objects of class Time2 are initialized, only the constructor that the class's other constructors call will need to be modified.

Common Programming Error 8.2

It's a compilation error when this is used in a constructor's body to call another of the class's constructors if that call is not the first statement in the constructor. It's also a compilation error when a method attempts to invoke a constructor directly via this.

Lines 16–18 declare a Time2 constructor with a single int parameter representing the hour, which is passed with 0 for the minute and second to the constructor at lines 26–42. Lines 21–23 declare a Time2 constructor that receives two int parameters representing the hour and minute, which are passed with 0 for the second to the constructor at lines 26–42. Like the no-argument constructor, each of these constructors invokes the three-argument constructor to minimize code duplication. Lines 26–42 declare the Time2 constructor that receives three int parameters representing the hour, minute and second. This constructor validates and initializes the instance variables.

Lines 45–48 declare a Time2 constructor that receives a reference to another Time2 object. The argument object's values are passed to the three-argument constructor to initialize the hour, minute and second. Line 47 directly accesses the hour, minute and second values of the argument time with the expressions time.hour, time.minute and time.second—even though hour, minute and second are declared as private variables of class Time2. This is due to a special relationship between objects of the same class.

Software Engineering Observation 8.5

When one object of a class has a reference to another object of the same class, the first object can access all the second object's data and methods (including those that are private).

Class *Time2's* setTime *Method*
Method setTime (lines 53–69) throws an IllegalArgumentException (lines 55, 59 and 63) if any of the method's arguments is out of range. Otherwise, it sets Time2's instance variables to the argument values (lines 66–68).

Notes Regarding Class *Time2's* Set *and* Get *Methods and Constructors*
Time2's *get* methods are called from other methods of the class. In particular, methods toUniversalString and toString call getHour, getMinute and getSecond in line 111 and lines 117–118, respectively. In each case, these methods could have accessed the class's private data directly without calling the *get* methods. However, consider changing the representation of the time from three int values (requiring 12 bytes of memory) to a single int value representing the total number of seconds that have elapsed since midnight (requiring only four bytes of memory). If we made such a change, only the bodies of the

methods that access the `private` data directly would need to change—in particular, the three-argument constructor, the `setTime` method and the individual *set* and *get* methods for the `hour`, `minute` and `second`. There would be no need to modify the bodies of methods `toUniversalString` or `toString` because they do *not* access the data directly. Designing the class in this manner reduces the likelihood of programming errors when altering the class's implementation.

Similarly, each `Time2` constructor could include a copy of the appropriate statements from the three-argument constructor. Doing so may be slightly more efficient, because the extra constructor calls are eliminated. But, *duplicating* statements makes changing the class's internal data representation more difficult. Having the `Time2` constructors call the constructor with three arguments requires that any changes to the implementation of the three-argument constructor be made only once. Also, the compiler can optimize programs by removing calls to simple methods and replacing them with the expanded code of their declarations—a technique known as **inlining the code**, which improves program performance.

Using Class *Time2's* Overloaded Constructors

Class `Time2Test` (Fig. 8.6) invokes the overloaded `Time2` constructors (lines 6–10 and 21). Line 6 invokes the `Time2` no-argument constructor. Lines 7–10 demonstrate passing arguments to the other `Time2` constructors. Line 7 invokes the single-argument constructor that receives an `int` at lines 16–18 of Fig. 8.5. Line 8 of Fig. 8.6 invokes the two-argument constructor at lines 21–23 of Fig. 8.5. Line 9 of Fig. 8.6 invokes the three-argument constructor at lines 26–42 of Fig. 8.5. Line 10 of Fig. 8.6 invokes the single-argument constructor that takes a `Time2` at lines 45–48 of Fig. 8.5. Next, the app displays the `String` representations of each `Time2` object to confirm that it was initialized properly (lines 13–17 of Fig. 8.6). Line 21 attempts to initialize t6 by creating a new `Time2` object and passing three *invalid* values to the constructor. When the constructor attempts to use the invalid hour value to initialize the object's `hour`, an `IllegalArgumentException` occurs. We catch this exception at line 23 and display its error message, which results in the last line of the output.

```
 1   // Fig. 8.6: Time2Test.java
 2   // Overloaded constructors used to initialize Time2 objects.
 3
 4   public class Time2Test {
 5      public static void main(String[] args) {
 6         Time2 t1 = new Time2(); // 00:00:00
 7         Time2 t2 = new Time2(2); // 02:00:00
 8         Time2 t3 = new Time2(21, 34); // 21:34:00
 9         Time2 t4 = new Time2(12, 25, 42); // 12:25:42
10         Time2 t5 = new Time2(t4); // 12:25:42
11
12         System.out.println("Constructed with:");
13         displayTime("t1: all default arguments", t1);
14         displayTime("t2: hour specified; default minute and second", t2);
15         displayTime("t3: hour and minute specified; default second", t3);
16         displayTime("t4: hour, minute and second specified", t4);
17         displayTime("t5: Time2 object t4 specified", t5);
```

Fig. 8.6 | Overloaded constructors used to initialize `Time2` objects. (Part 1 of 2.)

```
18
19      // attempt to initialize t6 with invalid values
20      try {
21         Time2 t6 = new Time2(27, 74, 99); // invalid values
22      }
23      catch (IllegalArgumentException e) {
24         System.out.printf("%nException while initializing t6: %s%n",
25            e.getMessage());
26      }
27   }
28
29   // displays a Time2 object in 24-hour and 12-hour formats
30   private static void displayTime(String header, Time2 t) {
31      System.out.printf("%s%n   %s%n   %s%n",
32         header, t.toUniversalString(), t.toString());
33   }
34 }
```

```
Constructed with:
t1: all default arguments
   00:00:00
   12:00:00 AM
t2: hour specified; default minute and second
   02:00:00
   2:00:00 AM
t3: hour and minute specified; default second
   21:34:00
   9:34:00 PM
t4: hour, minute and second specified
   12:25:42
   12:25:42 PM
t5: Time2 object t4 specified
   12:25:42
   12:25:42 PM

Exception while initializing t6: hour must be 0-23
```

Fig. 8.6 | Overloaded constructors used to initialize `Time2` objects. (Part 2 of 2.)

8.6 Default and No-Argument Constructors

Every class *must* have at least *one* constructor. If you do not provide any in a class's declaration, the compiler creates a *default constructor* that takes *no* arguments when it's invoked. The default constructor initializes the instance variables to the initial values specified in their declarations or to their default values (zero for primitive numeric types, `false` for `boolean` values and `null` for references).

Recall that if your class declares constructors, the compiler will *not* create a default constructor. In this case, you must declare a no-argument constructor if default initialization is required. Like a default constructor, a no-argument constructor is invoked with empty parentheses. The `Time2` no-argument constructor (lines 11–13 of Fig. 8.5) explicitly initializes a `Time2` object by passing to the three-argument constructor 0 for each parameter. Since 0 is the default value for `int` instance variables, the no-argument constructor in this example could actually be declared with an empty body. In this case, each instance variable would receive its default value when the no-argument constructor is called. If we were to omit the no-argument constructor, clients of this class would not be able to create a Time2 object with the expression new Time2().

Error-Prevention Tip 8.2

Ensure that you do not *include a return type in a constructor definition. Java allows other methods of the class besides its constructors to have the same name as the class and to specify return types. Such methods are* not *constructors and will* not *be called when an object of the class is instantiated.*

Common Programming Error 8.3

A compilation error occurs if a program attempts to initialize an object of a class by passing the wrong number or types of arguments to the class's constructor.

8.7 Notes on *Set* and *Get* Methods

As you know, client code can manipulate a class's private fields *only* through the class's methods. A typical manipulation might be the adjustment of a customer's bank balance (e.g., a private instance variable of a class BankAccount) by a method computeInterest. *Set* methods are also commonly called **mutator methods**, because they typically *change* an object's state—i.e., *modify* the values of instance variables. *Get* methods are also commonly called **accessor methods** or **query methods**.

Set *and* Get *Methods vs.* public *Data*

It would seem that providing *set* and *get* capabilities is essentially the same as making a class's instance variables public. This is one of the subtleties that makes Java so desirable for software engineering. A public instance variable can be read or written by any method that has a reference to an object containing that variable. If an instance variable is declared private, a public *get* method certainly allows other methods to access it, but the *get* method can *control* how the client can access it. For example, a *get* method might control the format of the data it returns, shielding the client code from the actual data representation. A public *set* method can—and should—carefully scrutinize attempts to modify the variable's value and throw an exception if necessary. For example, attempts to *set* the day of the month to 37 or a person's weight to a negative value should be rejected. Thus, although *set* and *get* methods provide access to private data, the access is restricted by the implementation of the methods. This helps promote good software engineering.

Software Engineering Observation 8.6

Classes should never have public *nonconstant data, but declaring data* public static final *enables you to make constants available to clients of your class. For example, class Math offers* public static final *constants* Math.E *and* Math.PI.

Validity Checking in Set *Methods*

The benefits of data integrity do not follow automatically simply because instance variables are declared private—you must provide validity checking. A class's *set* methods could determine that attempts were made to assign invalid data to objects of the class. Typically *set* methods have void return type and use exception handling to indicate attempts to assign invalid data. We discuss exception handling in detail in Chapter 11.

Software Engineering Observation 8.7
When appropriate, provide public methods to change and retrieve the values of private instance variables. This architecture helps hide the implementation of a class from its clients, which improves program modifiability.

Error-Prevention Tip 8.3
Using set and get methods helps you create more robust classes. If only one method performs a particular task, such as setting an instance variable in an object, it's easier to debug and maintain the class. If the instance variable is not being set properly, the code that actually modifies instance variable is localized to one set method. Your debugging efforts can be focused on that one method.

Predicate Methods
Another common use for accessor methods is to test whether a condition is *true* or *false*—such methods are often called **predicate methods.** An example would be class ArrayList's isEmpty method, which returns true if the ArrayList is empty and false otherwise. A program might test isEmpty before attempting to read another item from an ArrayList.

Good Programming Practice 8.1
By convention, predicate method names begin with is rather than get.

8.8 Composition

A class can have references to objects of other classes as members. This is called **composition** and is sometimes referred to as a *has-a* **relationship.** For example, an AlarmClock object needs to know the current time *and* the time when it's supposed to sound its alarm, so it's reasonable to include *two* references to Time objects in an AlarmClock object. A car *has-a* steering wheel, a break pedal, an accelerator pedal and more.

Class Date
This composition example contains classes Date (Fig. 8.7), Employee (Fig. 8.8) and EmployeeTest (Fig. 8.9). Class Date (Fig. 8.7) declares instance variables month, day and year (lines 5–7) to represent a date. The constructor receives three int parameters. Lines 15–18 validate the month—if it's out-of-range, lines 16–17 throw an exception. Lines 21–25 validate the day. If the day is incorrect based on the number of days in the particular month (except February 29th which requires special testing for leap years), lines 23–24 throw an exception. Lines 28–29 perform the leap year testing for February. If the month is February and the day is 29 and the year is not a leap year, lines 30–31 throw an exception. If no exceptions are thrown, then lines 34–36 initialize the Date's instance variables and line 38 output the this reference as a String. Since this is a reference to the current Date object, the object's toString method (lines 42–44) is called *implicitly* to obtain the object's String representation. In this example, we assume that the value for year is correct—an industrial-strength Date class should also validate the year.

```
1    // Fig. 8.7: Date.java
2    // Date class declaration.
3
4    public class Date {
5       private int month; // 1-12
6       private int day; // 1-31 based on month
7       private int year; // any year
8
9       private static final int[] daysPerMonth =
10         {0, 31, 28, 31, 30, 31, 30, 31, 31, 30, 31, 30, 31};
11
12      // constructor: confirm proper value for month and day given the year
13      public Date(int month, int day, int year) {
14         // check if month in range
15         if (month <= 0 || month > 12) {
16            throw new IllegalArgumentException(
17               "month (" + month + ") must be 1-12");
18         }
19
20         // check if day in range for month
21         if (day <= 0 ||
22            (day > daysPerMonth[month] && !(month == 2 && day == 29))) {
23            throw new IllegalArgumentException("day (" + day +
24               ") out-of-range for the specified month and year");
25         }
26
27         // check for leap year if month is 2 and day is 29
28         if (month == 2 && day == 29 && !(year % 400 == 0 ||
29            (year % 4 == 0 && year % 100 != 0))) {
30            throw new IllegalArgumentException("day (" + day +
31               ") out-of-range for the specified month and year");
32         }
33
34         this.month = month;
35         this.day = day;
36         this.year = year;
37
38         System.out.printf("Date object constructor for date %s%n", this);
39      }
40
41      // return a String of the form month/day/year
42      public String toString() {
43         return String.format("%d/%d/%d", month, day, year);
44      }
45   }
```

Fig. 8.7 | Date class declaration.

Class *Employee*

Class Employee (Fig. 8.8) has reference-type instance variables firstName (String), last-Name (String), birthDate (Date) and hireDate (Date), showing that a class can have as instance variables references to objects of other classes. The Employee constructor (lines 11–17) takes four parameters representing the first name, last name, birth date and hire date. The objects referenced by the parameters are assigned to an `Employee` object's instance variables. When `Employee`'s `toString` method is called, it returns a `String` containing the employee's name and the `String` representations of the two `Date` objects. Each of these `String`s is obtained with an *implicit* call to the `Date` class's `toString` method.

```java
1   // Fig. 8.8: Employee.java
2   // Employee class with references to other objects.
3
4   public class Employee {
5      private String firstName;
6      private String lastName;
7      private Date birthDate;
8      private Date hireDate;
9
10     // constructor to initialize name, birth date and hire date
11     public Employee(String firstName, String lastName, Date birthDate,
12        Date hireDate) {
13        this.firstName = firstName;
14        this.lastName = lastName;
15        this.birthDate = birthDate;
16        this.hireDate = hireDate;
17     }
18
19     // convert Employee to String format
20     public String toString() {
21        return String.format("%s, %s  Hired: %s  Birthday: %s",
22           lastName, firstName, hireDate, birthDate);
23     }
24  }
```

Fig. 8.8 | `Employee` class with references to other objects.

Class EmployeeTest

Class `EmployeeTest` (Fig. 8.9) creates two `Date` objects to represent an `Employee`'s birthday and hire date, respectively. Line 8 creates an `Employee` and initializes its instance variables by passing to the constructor two `String`s (representing the `Employee`'s first and last names) and two `Date` objects (representing the birthday and hire date). Line 10 *implicitly* invokes the `Employee`'s `toString` method to display the values of its instance variables and demonstrate that the object was initialized properly.

```java
1   // Fig. 8.9: EmployeeTest.java
2   // Composition demonstration.
3
4   public class EmployeeTest {
5      public static void main(String[] args) {
6         Date birth = new Date(7, 24, 1949);
7         Date hire = new Date(3, 12, 1988);
8         Employee employee = new Employee("Bob", "Blue", birth, hire);
9
```

Fig. 8.9 | Composition demonstration. (Part 1 of 2.)

```
10            System.out.println(employee);
11        }
12    }
```

```
Date object constructor for date 7/24/1949
Date object constructor for date 3/12/1988
Blue, Bob  Hired: 3/12/1988  Birthday: 7/24/1949
```

Fig. 8.9 | Composition demonstration. (Part 2 of 2.)

8.9 enum Types

In Fig. 6.7, we introduced the basic enum type, which defines a set of constants represented as unique identifiers. In that program the enum constants represented the game's status. In this section we discuss the relationship between enum types and classes. Like classes, all enum types are *reference* types. An enum type is declared with an **enum declaration**, which is a comma-separated list of *enum constants*—the declaration may optionally include other components of traditional classes, such as constructors, fields and methods (as you'll see momentarily). Each enum declaration declares an enum class with the following restrictions:

1. enum constants are *implicitly* final.

2. enum constants are *implicitly* static.

3. Any attempt to create an object of an enum type with operator new results in a compilation error.

The enum constants can be used anywhere constants can be used, such as in the case labels of switch statements and to control enhanced for statements.

*Declaring Instance Variables, a Constructor and Methods in an **enum** Type*
Figure 8.10 demonstrates instance variables, a constructor and methods in an enum type. The enum declaration contains two parts—the enum constants and the other members of the enum type.

```
1   // Fig. 8.10: Book.java
2   // Declaring an enum type with a constructor and explicit instance fields
3   // and accessors for these fields
4
5   public enum Book {
6       // declare constants of enum type
7       JHTP("Java How to Program", "2018"),
8       CHTP("C How to Program", "2016"),
9       IW3HTP("Internet & World Wide Web How to Program", "2012"),
10      CPPHTP("C++ How to Program", "2017"),
11      VBHTP("Visual Basic How to Program", "2014"),
12      CSHARPHTP("Visual C# How to Program", "2017");
13
```

Fig. 8.10 | Declaring an enum type with a constructor and explicit instance fields and accessors for these fields. (Part 1 of 2.)

```
14        // instance fields
15        private final String title; // book title
16        private final String copyrightYear; // copyright year
17
18        // enum constructor
19        Book(String title, String copyrightYear) {
20            this.title = title;
21            this.copyrightYear = copyrightYear;
22        }
23
24        // accessor for field title
25        public String getTitle() {
26            return title;
27        }
28
29        // accessor for field copyrightYear
30        public String getCopyrightYear() {
31            return copyrightYear;
32        }
33    }
```

Fig. 8.10 | Declaring an enum type with a constructor and explicit instance fields and accessors for these fields. (Part 2 of 2.)

The first part (lines 7–12) declares six constants. Each is optionally followed by arguments that are passed to the **enum constructor** (lines 19–22). Like the constructors in classes, an enum constructor can specify any number of parameters and can be overloaded. In this example, the enum constructor requires two String parameters—one that specifies the book's title and one that specifies its copyright year. To properly initialize each enum constant, we follow it with parentheses containing two String arguments.

The second part (lines 15–32) declares the enum type's other members—instance variables title and copyrightYear (lines 15–16), a constructor (lines 19–22) and two methods (lines 25–27 and 30–32) that return the book title and copyright year, respectively. Each enum constant in enum type Book is an object of enum type Book that has its own copy of instance variables.

Using **enum type Book**
Figure 8.11 tests the Book enum and illustrates how to iterate through a range of its constants. For every enum, the compiler generates the static method **values** (called in line 10), which returns an array of the enum's constants in the order they were declared. Lines 10–13 display the constants. Line 12 invokes the enum Book's getTitle and getCopyrightYear methods to get the title and copyright year associated with the constant. When an enum constant is converted to a String (e.g., book in line 11), the constant's identifier is used as the String representation (e.g., JHTP for the first enum constant).

```
1    // Fig. 8.11: EnumTest.java
2    // Testing enum type Book.
3    import java.util.EnumSet;
```

Fig. 8.11 | Testing enum type Book. (Part 1 of 2.)

```
4
5    public class EnumTest {
6       public static void main(String[] args) {
7          System.out.println("All books:");
8
9          // print all books in enum Book
10         for (Book book : Book.values()) {
11            System.out.printf("%-10s%-45s%s%n", book,
12               book.getTitle(), book.getCopyrightYear());
13         }
14
15         System.out.printf("%nDisplay a range of enum constants:%n");
16
17         // print first four books
18         for (Book book : EnumSet.range(Book.JHTP, Book.CPPHTP)) {
19            System.out.printf("%-10s%-45s%s%n", book,
20               book.getTitle(), book.getCopyrightYear());
21         }
22      }
23   }
```

```
All books:
JHTP        Java How to Program                           2018
CHTP        C How to Program                              2016
IW3HTP      Internet & World Wide Web How to Program      2012
CPPHTP      C++ How to Program                            2017
VBHTP       Visual Basic How to Program                   2014
CSHARPHTP   Visual C# How to Program                      2017

Display a range of enum constants:
JHTP        Java How to Program                           2018
CHTP        C How to Program                              2016
IW3HTP      Internet & World Wide Web How to Program      2012
CPPHTP      C++ How to Program                            2017
```

Fig. 8.11 | Testing enum type Book. (Part 2 of 2.)

Lines 18–21 use the static method **range** of class **EnumSet** (package java.util) to display a range of the enum Book's constants. Method range takes two parameters—the first and the last enum constants in the range—and returns an EnumSet that contains all the constants between these two constants, inclusive. For example, the expression EnumSet.range(Book.JHTP, Book.CPPHTP) returns an EnumSet containing Book.JHTP, Book.CHTP, Book.IW3HTP and Book.CPPHTP. The enhanced for statement can be used with an EnumSet just as it can with an array, so lines 18–21 use it to display the title and copyright year of every book in the EnumSet. Class EnumSet provides several other static methods for creating sets of enum constants from the same enum type.

Common Programming Error 8.4

In an enum declaration, it's a syntax error to declare enum constants after the enum type's constructors, fields and methods.

8.10 Garbage Collection

Every object uses system resources, such as memory. We need a disciplined way to give resources back to the system when they're no longer needed; otherwise, "resource leaks" might occur that would prevent resources from being reused by your program or possibly by other programs. The JVM performs automatic **garbage collection** to reclaim the *memory* occupied by objects that are no longer used. When there are *no more references* to an object, the object is *eligible* to be collected. Collection typically occurs when the JVM executes its **garbage collector**, which may not happen for a while, or even at all before a program terminates. So, memory leaks that are common in other languages like C and C++ (because memory is *not* automatically reclaimed in those languages) are *less* likely in Java, but some can still happen in subtle ways. Resource leaks other than memory leaks can also occur. For example, an app may open a file on secondary storage to modify its contents—if the app does not close the file, it must terminate before any other app can use the file.

*A Note about Class **Object**'s **finalize** Method*
Every class in Java has the methods of class Object (package java.lang), one of which is method **finalize**. (You'll learn more about class Object in Chapter 9.) You should *never* use method finalize, because it can cause many problems and there's uncertainty as to whether it will *ever* get called before a program terminates.

The original intent of finalize was to allow the garbage collector to perform **termination housekeeping** on an object just before reclaiming the object's memory. Now, it's considered better practice for any class that uses system resources—such as files on secondary storage—to provide a method that programmers can call to release resources when they're no longer needed in a program. AutoClosable objects reduce the likelihood of resource leaks when you use them with the try-with-resources statement. As its name implies, an AutoClosable object is closed automatically, once a try-with-resources statement finishes using the object. We discuss this in more detail in Section 11.12.

Software Engineering Observation 8.8
Many Java API classes (e.g., class Scanner and classes that read files from or write files to secondary storage) provide close or dispose methods that programmers can call to release resources when they're no longer needed in a program.

8.11 static Class Members

Every object has its own copy of all the instance variables of the class. In certain cases, only one copy of a particular variable should be *shared* by all objects of a class. A **static field**—called a **class variable**—is used in such cases. A static variable represents **classwide information**—all objects of the class share the *same* piece of data. The declaration of a static variable begins with the keyword static.

*Motivating **static***
Let's motivate static data with an example. Suppose that we have a video game with Martians and other space creatures. Each Martian tends to be brave and willing to attack other space creatures when the Martian is aware that at least four other Martians are present. If fewer than five Martians are present, each of them becomes cowardly. Thus, each Martian

needs to know the martianCount. We could endow class Martian with martianCount as an *instance variable*. If we do this, then every Martian will have *a separate copy* of the instance variable, and every time we create a new Martian, we'll have to update the instance variable martianCount in every Martian object. This wastes space with the redundant copies, wastes time in updating the separate copies and is error prone. Instead, we declare martianCount to be static, making martianCount classwide data. Every Martian can see the martianCount as if it were an instance variable of class Martian, but only *one* copy of the static martianCount is maintained. This saves space. We save time by having the Martian constructor increment the static martianCount—there's only one copy, so we do not have to increment separate copies for each Martian object.

Software Engineering Observation 8.9

Use a static variable when all objects of a class must use the same copy of the variable.

Class Scope

Static variables have *class scope*—they can be used in all of the class's methods. We can access a class's public static members through a reference to any object of the class, or by qualifying the member name with the class name and a dot (.), as in Math.sqrt(2). A class's private static class members can be accessed by client code only through methods of the class. Actually, *static class members exist even when no objects of the class exist*—they're available as soon as the class is loaded into memory at execution time. To access a public static member when no objects of the class exist (and even when they do), prefix the class name and a dot (.) to the static member, as in Math.PI. To access a private static member when no objects of the class exist, provide a public static method and call it by qualifying its name with the class name and a dot.

Software Engineering Observation 8.10

Static class variables and methods exist, and can be used, even if no objects of that class have been instantiated.

static *Methods Cannot Directly Access Instance Variables and Instance Methods*

A static method *cannot* directly access a class's instance variables and instance methods, because a static method can be called even when no objects of the class have been instantiated. For the same reason, the this reference *cannot* be used in a static method. The this reference must refer to a specific object of the class, and when a static method is called, there might not be any objects of its class in memory.

Common Programming Error 8.5

A compilation error occurs if a static method calls an instance method in the same class by using only the method name. Similarly, a compilation error occurs if a static method attempts to access an instance variable in the same class by using only the variable name.

Common Programming Error 8.6

Referring to this in a static method is a compilation error.

Tracking the Number of Employee Objects That Have Been Created

Our next program declares two classes—Employee (Fig. 8.12) and EmployeeTest (Fig. 8.13). Class Employee declares private static variable count (Fig. 8.12, line 6) and public static method getCount (lines 32–34). The static variable count maintains a count of the number of objects of class Employee that have been created so far. This class variable is initialized to 0 in line 6. If a static variable is *not* initialized, the compiler assigns it a default value—in this case 0, the default value for type int.

```java
1   // Fig. 8.12: Employee.java
2   // static variable used to maintain a count of the number of
3   // Employee objects in memory.
4
5   public class Employee {
6      private static int count = 0; // number of Employees created
7      private String firstName;
8      private String lastName;
9
10     // initialize Employee, add 1 to static count and
11     // output String indicating that constructor was called
12     public Employee(String firstName, String lastName) {
13        this.firstName = firstName;
14        this.lastName = lastName;
15
16        ++count;   // increment static count of employees
17        System.out.printf("Employee constructor: %s %s; count = %d%n",
18           firstName, lastName, count);
19     }
20
21     // get first name
22     public String getFirstName() {
23        return firstName;
24     }
25
26     // get last name
27     public String getLastName() {
28        return lastName;
29     }
30
31     // static method to get static count value
32     public static int getCount() {
33        return count;
34     }
35  }
```

Fig. 8.12 | static variable used to maintain a count of the number of Employee objects in memory.

When Employee objects exist, variable count can be used in any method of an Employee object—this example increments count in the constructor (line 16). The public static method getCount (lines 32–34) returns the number of Employee objects that have been created so far. When no objects of class Employee exist, client code can access variable count by calling method getCount via the class name, as in Employee.getCount().

Good Programming Practice 8.2
Invoke every static method by using the class name and a dot (.) to emphasize that the method being called is a static method.

When objects exist, static method getCount also can be called via any reference to an Employee object. This contradicts the preceding Good Programming Practice and, in fact, the Java SE 9 compiler issues warnings on lines 16–17 of Fig. 8.13.

Class EmployeeTest

EmployeeTest method main (Fig. 8.13) instantiates two Employee objects (lines 11–12). When each Employee object's constructor is invoked, lines 13–14 of Fig. 8.12 assign the Employee's first name and last name to instance variables firstName and lastName. These statements do *not* copy the original String arguments. Strings in Java are **immutable**—they cannot be modified after they're created. Therefore, it's safe to have *many* references to one String object. This is not normally the case for objects of most other classes in Java. If String objects are immutable, you might wonder why we're able to use operators + and += to concatenate String objects. String concatenation actually results in a *new* String object containing the concatenated values. The original String objects are *not* modified.

```
1   // Fig. 8.13: EmployeeTest.java
2   // static member demonstration.
3
4   public class EmployeeTest {
5      public static void main(String[] args) {
6         // show that count is 0 before creating Employees
7         System.out.printf("Employees before instantiation: %d%n",
8            Employee.getCount());
9
10        // create two Employees; count should be 2
11        Employee e1 = new Employee("Susan", "Baker");
12        Employee e2 = new Employee("Bob", "Blue");
13
14        // show that count is 2 after creating two Employees
15        System.out.printf("%nEmployees after instantiation:%n");
16        System.out.printf("via e1.getCount(): %d%n", e1.getCount());
17        System.out.printf("via e2.getCount(): %d%n", e2.getCount());
18        System.out.printf("via Employee.getCount(): %d%n",
19           Employee.getCount());
20
21        // get names of Employees
22        System.out.printf("%nEmployee 1: %s %s%nEmployee 2: %s %s%n",
23           e1.getFirstName(), e1.getLastName(),
24           e2.getFirstName(), e2.getLastName());
25     }
26  }
```

```
Employees before instantiation: 0
Employee constructor: Susan Baker; count = 1
Employee constructor: Bob Blue; count = 2
```

Fig. 8.13 | static member demonstration. (Part 1 of 2.)

```
Employees after instantiation:
via e1.getCount(): 2
via e2.getCount(): 2
via Employee.getCount(): 2

Employee 1: Susan Baker
Employee 2: Bob Blue
```

Fig. 8.13 | static member demonstration. (Part 2 of 2.)

When main terminates, local variables e1 and e2 are discarded—remember that a local variable exists *only* until the block in which it's declared completes execution. Because e1 and e2 were the only references to the Employee objects created in lines 11–12 (Fig. 8.13), these objects become "eligible for garbage collection" as main terminates.

In a typical app, the garbage collector *might* eventually reclaim the memory for any objects that are eligible for collection. If any objects are not reclaimed before the program terminates, the operating system will reclaim the memory used by the program. The JVM does *not* guarantee when, or even whether, the garbage collector will execute. When it does, it's possible that no objects or only a subset of the eligible objects will be collected.

8.12 static Import

In Section 6.3, you learned about the static fields and methods of class Math. We access class Math's static fields and *methods* by preceding each with the class name Math and a dot (.). A **static import** declaration enables you to import the static members of a class or interface so you can access them via their *unqualified names* in your class—that is, the class name and a dot (.) are *not* required when using an imported static member.

static Import Forms
A static import declaration has two forms—one that imports a particular static member (which is known as **single static import**) and one that imports *all* static members of a class (known as **static import on demand**). The following syntax imports a particular static member:

> **import static** *packageName.ClassName.staticMemberName*;

where *packageName* is the package of the class (e.g., java.lang), *ClassName* is the name of the class (e.g., Math) and *staticMemberName* is the name of the static field or method (e.g., PI or abs). In the following syntax, the asterisk (*) indicates that *all* static members of a class should be available for use in the file:

> **import static** *packageName.ClassName.**;

static import declarations import *only* static class members. Regular import statements should be used to specify the classes used in a program.

Demonstrating static Import
Figure 8.14 demonstrates a static import. Line 3 is a static import declaration, which imports *all* static fields and methods of class Math from package java.lang. Lines 7–10 access the Math class's static methods sqrt (line 7) and ceil (line 8) and its static fields

E (line 9) and PI (line 10) *without* preceding the field names or method names with class name Math and a dot.

Common Programming Error 8.7
A compilation error occurs if a program attempts to import two or more classes' static methods that have the same signature or static fields that have the same name.

```java
1   // Fig. 8.14: StaticImportTest.java
2   // Static import of Math class methods.
3   import static java.lang.Math.*;
4
5   public class StaticImportTest {
6      public static void main(String[] args) {
7         System.out.printf("sqrt(900.0) = %.1f%n", sqrt(900.0));
8         System.out.printf("ceil(-9.8) = %.1f%n", ceil(-9.8));
9         System.out.printf("E = %f%n", E);
10        System.out.printf("PI = %f%n", PI);
11     }
12  }
```

```
sqrt(900.0) = 30.0
ceil(-9.8) = -9.0
E = 2.718282
PI = 3.141593
```

Fig. 8.14 | static import of Math class methods.

8.13 final Instance Variables

The *principle of least privilege* is fundamental to good software engineering. In the context of an app's code, it states that code should be granted only the amount of privilege and access that it needs to accomplish its designated task, but no more. This makes your programs more robust by preventing code from accidentally (or maliciously) modifying variable values and calling methods that should *not* be accessible.

Let's see how this principle applies to instance variables. Some need to be *modifiable* and some do not. You can use the keyword final to specify that a variable is *not* modifiable (i.e., it's a *constant*) and that any attempt to modify it is an error. For example,

```java
private final int INCREMENT;
```

declares a final (constant) instance variable INCREMENT of type int. Such variables can be initialized when they're declared. If they're not, they *must* be initialized in every constructor of the class. Initializing constants in constructors enables each object of the class to have a different value for the constant. If a final variable is *not* initialized in its declaration or in every constructor, a compilation error occurs.

Common Programming Error 8.8
Attempting to modify a final instance variable after it's initialized is a compilation error.

Error-Prevention Tip 8.4

Attempts to modify a final instance variable are caught at compilation time rather than causing execution-time errors. It's always preferable to get bugs out at compilation time, if possible, rather than allow them to slip through to execution time (where experience has shown that repair is often many times more expensive).

Software Engineering Observation 8.11

Declaring an instance variable as final helps enforce the principle of least privilege. If an instance variable should not be modified, declare it to be final to prevent modification. For example, in Fig. 8.8, the instance variables firstName, lastName, birthDate and hire-Date are never modified after they're initialized, so they should be declared final. We'll enforce this practice in all programs going forward. Testing, debugging and maintaining programs is easier when every variable that can be final is, in fact, final. You'll see additional benefits of final in Chapter 21, Concurrency and Multi-Core Performance.

Software Engineering Observation 8.12

A final field should also be declared static if it's initialized in its declaration to a value that's the same for all objects of the class. After this initialization, its value can never change. Therefore, we don't need a separate copy of the field for every object of the class. Making the field static enables all objects of the class to share the final field.

8.14 Package Access

If no access modifier (public, protected or private—we discuss protected in Chapter 9) is specified for a method or variable when it's declared in a class, the method or variable is considered to have **package access**. In a program that consists of one class declaration, this has no specific effect. However, if a program uses *multiple* classes from the *same* package (i.e., a group of related classes), these classes can access each other's package-access members directly through references to objects of the appropriate classes, or in the case of static members through the class name. Package access is rarely used.

Figure 8.15 demonstrates package access. The app contains two classes in one source-code file—the PackageDataTest class (lines 5–19) containing main and the PackageData class (lines 22–30). Classes in the same source file are part of the same package. Consequently, class PackageDataTest is allowed to modify the package-access data of Package-Data objects. When you compile this program, the compiler produces two separate .class files—PackageDataTest.class and PackageData.class. The compiler places the two .class files in the same directory. You can also place class PackageData (lines 22–30) in a separate source-code file.

```
1  // Fig. 8.15: PackageDataTest.java
2  // Package-access members of a class are accessible by other classes
3  // in the same package.
4
5  public class PackageDataTest {
```

Fig. 8.15 | Package-access members of a class are accessible by other classes in the same package. (Part 1 of 2.)

```
 6        public static void main(String[] args) {
 7            PackageData packageData = new PackageData();
 8
 9            // output String representation of packageData
10            System.out.printf("After instantiation:%n%s%n", packageData);
11
12            // change package access data in packageData object
13            packageData.number = 77;
14            packageData.string = "Goodbye";
15
16            // output String representation of packageData
17            System.out.printf("%nAfter changing values:%n%s%n", packageData);
18        }
19    }
20
21    // class with package access instance variables
22    class PackageData {
23        int number = 0; // package-access instance variable
24        String string = "Hello"; // package-access instance variable
25
26        // return PackageData object String representation
27        public String toString() {
28            return String.format("number: %d; string: %s", number, string);
29        }
30    }
```

```
After instantiation:
number: 0; string: Hello

After changing values:
number: 77; string: Goodbye
```

Fig. 8.15 | Package-access members of a class are accessible by other classes in the same package. (Part 2 of 2.)

In the PackageData class declaration, lines 23–24 declare the instance variables number and string with no access modifiers—therefore, these are package-access instance variables. Class PackageDataTest's main method creates an instance of the PackageData class (line 7) to demonstrate the ability to modify the PackageData instance variables directly (as shown in lines 13–14). The results of the modification can be seen in the output window.

8.15 Using BigDecimal for Precise Monetary Calculations

In earlier chapters, we demonstrated monetary calculations using values of type double. In Chapter 5, we discussed the fact that some double values are represented *approximately*. Any application that requires precise floating-point calculations—such as those in financial applications—should instead use class **BigDecimal** (from package **java.math**).

*Interest Calculations Using **BigDecimal***
Figure 8.16 reimplements the interest-calculation example of Fig. 5.6 using objects of class BigDecimal to perform the calculations. We also introduce class **NumberFormat** (package **java.text**) for formatting numeric values as *locale-specific* Strings—for example, in the U.S. locale, the value 1234.56, would be formatted as "1,234.56", whereas in many European locales it would be formatted as "1.234,56".

```java
1   // Fig. 8.16: Interest.java
2   // Compound-interest calculations with BigDecimal.
3   import java.math.BigDecimal;
4   import java.text.NumberFormat;
5
6   public class Interest {
7      public static void main(String args[]) {
8         // initial principal amount before interest
9         BigDecimal principal = BigDecimal.valueOf(1000.0);
10        BigDecimal rate = BigDecimal.valueOf(0.05); // interest rate
11
12        // display headers
13        System.out.printf("%s%20s%n", "Year", "Amount on deposit");
14
15        // calculate amount on deposit for each of ten years
16        for (int year = 1; year <= 10; year++) {
17           // calculate new amount for specified year
18           BigDecimal amount =
19              principal.multiply(rate.add(BigDecimal.ONE).pow(year));
20
21           // display the year and the amount
22           System.out.printf("%4d%20s%n", year,
23              NumberFormat.getCurrencyInstance().format(amount));
24        }
25     }
26  }
```

```
Year  Amount on deposit
   1       $1,050.00
   2       $1,102.50
   3       $1,157.62
   4       $1,215.51
   5       $1,276.28
   6       $1,340.10
   7       $1,407.10
   8       $1,477.46
   9       $1,551.33
  10       $1,628.89
```

Fig. 8.16 | Compound-interest calculations with BigDecimal.

*Creating **BigDecimal** Objects*
Lines 9–10 declare and initialize BigDecimal variables principal and rate using the BigDecimal static method **valueOf** that receives a double argument and returns a BigDecimal object that represents the *exact* value specified.

*Performing the Interest Calculations with **BigDecimal***

Lines 18–19 perform the interest calculation using BigDecimal methods **multiply**, **add** and **pow**. The expression in line 19 evaluates as follows:

1. First, the expression rate.add(BigDecimal.ONE) adds 1 to the rate to produce a BigDecimal containing 1.05—this is equivalent to 1.0 + rate in line 15 of Fig. 5.6. The BigDecimal constant **ONE** represents the value 1. Class BigDecimal also provides the commonly used constants **ZERO** (0) and **TEN** (10).

2. Next, BigDecimal method pow is called on the preceding result to raise 1.05 to the power year—this is equivalent to passing 1.0 + rate and year to method Math.pow in line 15 of Fig. 5.6.

3. Finally, we call BigDecimal method multiply on the principal object, passing the preceding result as the argument. This returns a BigDecimal representing the amount on deposit at the end of the specified year.

Since the expression rate.add(BigDecimal.ONE) produces the same value in each iteration of the loop, we could have simply initialized rate to 1.05 in line 10 of Fig. 8.16; however, we chose to mimic the precise calculations we used in line 15 of Fig. 5.6.

*Formatting Currency Values with **NumberFormat***

During each iteration of the loop, line 23 of Fig. 8.16

```
NumberFormat.getCurrencyInstance().format(amount)
```

evaluates as follows:

1. First, the expression uses NumberFormat's static method **getCurrencyInstance** to get a NumberFormat that's preconfigured to format numeric values as locale-specific currency Strings—for example, in the U.S. locale, the numeric value 1628.89 is formatted as $1,628.89. Locale-specific formatting is an important part of **internationalization**—the process of customizing your applications for users' various locales and spoken languages.

2. Next, the expression invokes method NumberFormat method **format** (on the object returned by getCurrencyInstance) to perform the formatting of the amount value. Method format then returns the locale-specific String representation. For the U.S. locale, the result is rounded to two digits to the right of the decimal point.

*Rounding **BigDecimal** Values*

In addition to precise calculations, BigDecimal gives you control over rounding—by default all calculations are exact and *no* rounding occurs. If you do not specify how to round BigDecimal values and a given value cannot be represented exactly—such as the result of 1 divided by 3, which is 0.3333333...—an ArithmeticException occurs.

Though we do not do so in this example, you can specify the *rounding mode* for BigDecimal by supplying a MathContext object (package java.math) to class BigDecimal's constructor when you create a BigDecimal. You may also provide a MathContext to various BigDecimal methods that perform calculations. Class MathContext contains several preconfigured MathContext objects that you can learn about at

```
http://docs.oracle.com/javase/8/docs/api/java/math/MathContext.html
```

By default, each preconfigured `MathContext` uses so-called "banker's rounding" as explained for the `RoundingMode` constant `HALF_EVEN` at:

```
http://docs.oracle.com/javase/8/docs/api/java/math/
RoundingMode.html#HALF_EVEN
```

Scaling *BigDecimal* Values

A `BigDecimal`'s scale is the number of digits to the right of its decimal point. If you need a `BigDecimal` rounded to a specific digit, you can call `BigDecimal` method `setScale`. For example, the following expression returns a `BigDecimal` with two digits to the right of the decimal point and using banker's rounding:

```
amount.setScale(2, RoundingMode.HALF_EVEN)
```

8.16 JavaMoney API

Dealing with currencies, monetary amounts, conversions, rounding and formatting is complex. The new JavaMoney API was developed to meet these challenges. At the time of this writing, it was not yet incorporated into either Java SE or Java EE. You can read about JavaMoney at

```
https://java.net/projects/javamoney/pages/Home
http://jsr354.blogspot.ch
```

and you can obtain the software and documentation at

```
http://javamoney.github.io
```

8.17 Time Class Case Study: Creating Packages

In almost every example, we've imported existing classes. Each Java API class belongs to a package that contains a group of related classes. These packages are defined once, but can be imported into many programs. As applications become more complex, packages help you manage the complexity of application components. Packages also facilitate software reuse by enabling programs to *import* classes from other packages. Packages also provide a convention for unique class names, which helps prevent class-name conflicts (discussed later in this section). This section introduces how to create your own packages.

Steps for Declaring a Reusable Class

Before a class can be imported into multiple applications, it must be placed in a package to make it reusable. The steps for creating a reusable class are:

1. Declare a `public` class. If the class is not `public`, it can be used only by other classes in the same package.

2. Choose a unique package name and add a **package declaration** to the source-code file for the reusable class declaration. In each Java source-code file there can be only one `package` declaration, and it *must* precede all other declarations and statements. [*Note:* If no package statement is provided, the class is placed in the so-called *default package* and is accessible only to other classes in the default package that are located in the same directory. All prior programs in this book having two or more classes have used this default package.]

3. Compile the class so that it's placed in the appropriate package directory.

4. Import the reusable class into a program and use the class.

We'll now discuss each of these steps in detail.

Steps 1 and 2: Creating a `public` Class and Adding the `package` Statement

For *Step 1*, we modified the `public` class `Time1` declared in Fig. 8.1 by adding the following package declaration before the class declaration:

```
package com.deitel.ch08;
```

No modifications have been made to the implementation of the class, so we'll not discuss its implementation details again here.

For *Step 2*, we add a `package` declaration (line 3) that declares a `package` named `com.deitel.ch08`. Placing a `package` declaration at the beginning of a Java source file indicates that the class declared in the file is part of the specified package. Only `package` declarations, `import` declarations and comments can appear outside the braces of a class declaration. A Java source-code file must have the following order:

1. a `package` declaration (if any),

2. `import` declarations (if any), then

3. class declarations.

Only one of the class declarations in a particular file can be `public`. Other classes in the file are placed in the same package and can be used only to support the other classes in that package.

To provide unique package names, start each one with your Internet domain name in reverse order. For example, our domain name is `deitel.com`, so our package names begin with `com.deitel`. After the domain name is reversed, you can choose any other names you want for your package. If you're part of a company with many divisions or a university with many schools, you may want to use the name of your division or school as the next name in the package. We chose to use `ch08` as the next name in our package name to indicate that this class is from Chapter 8.

Step 3: Compiling the Packaged Class

Step 3 is to compile the class so that it's stored in the appropriate package. When a Java file containing a `package` declaration is compiled, the resulting class file is placed in the directory specified by the declaration. The preceding `package` declaration indicates that class `Time1` should be placed in the directory

```
com
    deitel
        ch08
```

The names in the `package` declaration specify the exact location of the package's classes.

When compiling a class in a package, the `javac` command-line option **-d** causes the `javac` compiler to create appropriate directories based on the class's `package` declaration. The option also specifies where the directories should be stored. For example, in a command window, we used the compilation command

```
javac -d . Time1.java
```

to specify that the first directory in our package name should be placed in the current directory. The period (.) after -d in the preceding command represents the current directory on the Windows, UNIX, Linux and macOS operating systems (and several others as well). After executing this command,

- the current directory contains a directory called com,
- com contains a directory called deitel and
- deitel contains a directory called ch08.

In the ch08 directory, you can find the file Time1.class.

The package name is part of the **fully qualified class name**, so class Time1's name is actually com.deitel.ch08.Time1. You can use this fully qualified name in your programs, or you can import the class and use its **simple name** (the class name by itself—Time1) in the program. If another package also contains a Time1 class, the fully qualified class names can be used to distinguish between the classes and prevent a **name conflict** (also called a **name collision**).

Step 4: Importing the Reusable Class

Once Time1 is compiled and stored in its package, the class can be imported into programs (*Step 4*). We modified class Time1Test (Fig. 8.2) by adding the import declaration

```
import com.deitel.ch08.Time1; // import class Time1
```

before the class declaration. Class Time1Test is in the default package because its .java file does not contain a package declaration. Since the two classes are in different packages, the import is required so that class Time1Test can use class Time1.

The preceding import declaration is known as a **single-type-import**—it specifies *one* class to import. When your program uses multiple classes from the same package, you can import those classes with an import declaration of the form:

```
import java.util.*; // import classes from package java.util
```

which uses an asterisk (*) at its end to inform the compiler that all public classes from the package (in this case, java.util) are available for use in the program. This is known as a **type-import-on-demand declaration**. Only the classes from package java.util that are used in the program are loaded by the JVM. The preceding import allows you to use the simple name of any class from the java.util package in the program. Throughout this book, we use single-type-import declarations for clarity.

Common Programming Error 8.9

Using the import declaration import java.; causes a compilation error. You must specify the exact name of the package from which you want to import classes.*

Specifying the Classpath During Compilation

When compiling Time1Test, javac must locate the .class file for Time1 to ensure that class Time1Test uses class Time1 correctly. The compiler uses a special object called a **class loader** to locate the classes it needs. The class loader begins by searching the standard Java classes that are bundled with the JDK. If the class is not found in the standard Java classes, the class loader searches the **classpath**, which contains a list of locations in which classes are stored. The classpath consists of a list of directories or **archive files**, each separated by a **directory separator**—a semicolon (;) on Windows or a colon (:) on Linux/macOS. An archive file is an individual file that contains directories of other files, typically in a compressed format. Archive files normally end with the .jar (Java archive file) file-name extension. The directories and archive files specified in the classpath contain the classes you wish to make available to the Java compiler and the JVM.

By default, the classpath consists only of the current directory. However, the classpath can be modified by

1. providing the **-classpath** option to the javac compiler or

2. setting the **CLASSPATH environment variable**. As you'll see in Chapter 27, Java 9's module path is preferred to the classpath.

For more information on the classpath, visit https://docs.oracle.com/javase/8/docs/technotes/tools/windows/classpath.html.

Common Programming Error 8.10
Specifying an explicit classpath eliminates the current directory from the classpath. This prevents classes in the current directory (including packages in the current directory) from loading properly. If classes must be loaded from the current directory, include a dot (.) in the classpath to specify the current directory.

Software Engineering Observation 8.13
In general, it's a better practice to use the -classpath option of the compiler, rather than the CLASSPATH environment variable, to specify the classpath for a program. This enables each application to have its own classpath.

Error-Prevention Tip 8.5
Specifying the classpath with the CLASSPATH environment variable can cause subtle and difficult-to-locate errors in programs that use different versions of the same package.

To locate the classes in the com.deitel.ch08 package from this example, the class loader looks in the current directory for the first name in the package—com—then navigates the directory structure. Directory com contains the subdirectory deitel and deitel contains the subdirectory ch08. In the ch08 directory is the file Time1.class, which is loaded by the class loader to ensure that the class is used properly in our program.

Specifying the Classpath When Executing an Application
When you execute an application, the JVM must be able to locate the .class files of the classes used in that application. Like the compiler, the java command uses a class loader that searches the standard classes and extension classes first, then searches the classpath (the current directory by default). The classpath can be specified explicitly by using either of the techniques discussed for the compiler. As with the compiler, it's better to specify an individual program's classpath via command-line JVM options. You can specify the classpath in the java command via the **-classpath** or **-cp** command-line options, followed by a list of directories or archive files separated by semicolons (;) on Microsoft Windows or by colons (:) on UNIX/Linux/Mac OS X. Again, if classes must be loaded from the current directory, be sure to include a dot (.) in the classpath to specify the current directory.

8.18 Wrap-Up

In this chapter, we presented additional class concepts. The Time class case study showed a complete class declaration consisting of private data, overloaded public constructors for initialization flexibility, *set* and *get* methods for manipulating the class's data, and methods that returned String representations of a Time object in two different formats. You also learned that every class can declare a toString method that returns a String representation of an object of the class and that method toString can be called implicitly whenever an object of a class appears in the code where a String is expected. We showed how to throw an exception to indicate that a problem has occurred.

You learned that the this reference is used implicitly in a class's instance methods to access the class's instance variables and other instance methods. You also saw explicit uses of the this reference to access the class's members (including shadowed fields) and how to use keyword this in a constructor to call another constructor of the class.

We discussed the differences between default constructors provided by the compiler and no-argument constructors provided by the programmer. You learned that a class can have references to objects of other classes as members—a concept known as composition. You learned more about enum types and how they can be used to create a set of constants for use in a program. You learned about Java's garbage-collection capability and how it (unpredictably) reclaims the memory of objects that are no longer used. The chapter explained the motivation for static fields in a class and demonstrated how to declare and use static fields and methods in your own classes. You also learned how to declare and initialize final variables.

You saw that fields declared without an access modifier are given package access by default. You saw the relationship between classes in the same package that allows each class in a package to access the package-access members of other classes in the package. Finally, we demonstrated how to use class BigDecimal to perform precise monetary calculations. Finally, you saw how to package a class for reuse.

In the next chapter, you'll learn about an important aspect of object-oriented programming in Java—inheritance. You'll see that all classes in Java are related by inheritance, directly or indirectly, to the class called Object. You'll also begin to understand how the relationships between classes enable you to build more powerful apps.

9

Object-Oriented Programming: Inheritance

Objectives

In this chapter you'll:

- Understand inheritance and how to use it to develop new classes based on existing classes.
- Learn the notions of superclasses and subclasses and the relationship between them.
- Use keyword **extends** to create a class that inherits attributes and behaviors from another class.
- Use access modifier **protected** in a superclass to give subclass methods access to these superclass members.
- Access superclass members with **super** from a subclass.
- Learn how constructors are used in inheritance hierarchies.
- Learn about the methods of class **Object**, the direct or indirect superclass of all classes.

9.1 Introduction

This chapter continues our discussion of object-oriented programming (OOP) by introducing **inheritance**, in which a new class is created by acquiring an existing class's members and possibly embellishing them with new or modified capabilities. With inheritance, you can save time during program development by basing new classes on existing proven and debugged high-quality software. This also increases the likelihood that a system will be implemented and maintained effectively.

When creating a class, rather than declaring completely new members, you can designate that the new class should *inherit* the members of an existing class. The existing class is called the **superclass**, and the new class is the **subclass.** (The C++ programming language refers to the superclass as the **base class** and the subclass as the **derived class**.) A subclass can become a superclass for future subclasses.

A subclass can add its own fields and methods. Therefore, a subclass is *more specific* than its superclass and represents a more specialized group of objects. The subclass exhibits the behaviors of its superclass and can modify those behaviors so that they operate appropriately for the subclass. This is why inheritance is sometimes referred to as **specialization**.

The **direct superclass** is the superclass from which the subclass explicitly inherits. An **indirect superclass** is any class above the direct superclass in the **class hierarchy**, which defines the inheritance relationships among classes—as you'll see in Section 9.2, diagrams help you understand these relationships. In Java, the class hierarchy begins with class Object (in package java.lang), which *every* class in Java directly or indirectly **extends** (or "inherits from"). Section 9.6 lists the methods of class Object that are inherited by all other Java classes. Java supports only **single inheritance**, in which each class is derived from exactly *one* direct superclass. Unlike C++, Java does *not* support multiple inheritance (which occurs when a class is derived from more than one direct superclass). Chapter 10, Object-Oriented Programming: Polymorphism and Interfaces, explains how to use Java *interfaces* to realize many of the benefits of multiple inheritance while avoiding the associated problems.

We distinguish between the *is-a* **relationship** and the *has-a* **relationship**. *Is-a* represents inheritance. In an *is-a* relationship, *an object of a subclass can also be treated as an* *object of its superclass*—e.g., a car *is a* vehicle. By contrast, *has-a* represents composition (see Chapter 8). In a *has-a* relationship, *an object contains as members references to other objects*— e.g., a car *has a* steering wheel (and a car object has a reference to a steering-wheel object).

New classes can inherit from classes in **class libraries**. Organizations develop their own class libraries and can take advantage of others available worldwide. Some day, most new software likely will be constructed from **standardized reusable components**, just as automobiles and most computer hardware are constructed today. This will facilitate the rapid development of more powerful, abundant and economical software.

9.2 Superclasses and Subclasses

Often, an object of one class *is an* object of another class as well. For example, a CarLoan *is a* Loan as are HomeImprovementLoans and MortgageLoans. Thus, in Java, class CarLoan can be said to inherit from class Loan. In this context, class Loan is a superclass and class CarLoan is a subclass. A CarLoan *is a* specific type of Loan, but it's incorrect to claim that every Loan *is a* CarLoan—the Loan could be any type of loan. Figure 9.1 lists several simple examples of superclasses and subclasses—superclasses tend to be "more general" and subclasses "more specific."

Superclass	Subclasses
Student	GraduateStudent, UndergraduateStudent
Shape	Circle, Triangle, Rectangle, Sphere, Cube
Loan	CarLoan, HomeImprovementLoan, MortgageLoan
Employee	Faculty, Staff
BankAccount	CheckingAccount, SavingsAccount

Fig. 9.1 | Inheritance examples.

Because every subclass object *is an* object of its superclass, and one superclass can have many subclasses, the set of objects represented by a superclass is often larger than the set of objects represented by any of its subclasses. For example, the superclass Vehicle represents *all* vehicles, including cars, trucks, boats, bicycles and so on. By contrast, subclass Car represents a smaller, more specific subset of vehicles.

University Community Member Hierarchy

Inheritance relationships form treelike *hierarchical* structures. A superclass exists in a hierarchical relationship with its subclasses. Let's develop a sample class hierarchy (Fig. 9.2), also called an **inheritance hierarchy**. A university community has thousands of members, including employees, students and alumni. Employees are either faculty or staff members. Faculty members are either administrators (e.g., deans and department chairpersons) or teachers. The hierarchy could contain many other classes. For example, students can be graduate or undergraduate students. Undergraduate students can be freshmen, sophomores, juniors or seniors.

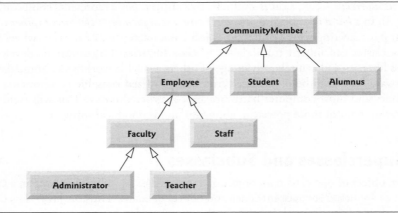

Fig. 9.2 | Inheritance hierarchy UML class diagram for university CommunityMembers.

Each arrow in the hierarchy represents an *is-a* relationship. As we follow the arrows upward in this class hierarchy, we can state, for example, that "an Employee *is a* CommunityMember" and "a Teacher *is a* Faculty member." CommunityMember is the direct superclass of Employee, Student and Alumnus and is an indirect superclass of all the other classes in the diagram. Starting from the bottom, you can follow the arrows and apply the *is-a* relationship up to the topmost superclass. For example, an Administrator *is a* Faculty member, *is an* Employee, *is a* CommunityMember and, of course, *is an* Object.

Shape Hierarchy

Now consider the Shape inheritance hierarchy in Fig. 9.3. This hierarchy begins with superclass Shape, which is extended by subclasses TwoDimensionalShape and ThreeDimensionalShape—Shapes are either TwoDimensionalShapes or ThreeDimensionalShapes. The third level of this hierarchy contains *specific* types of TwoDimensionalShapes and ThreeDimensionalShapes. As in Fig. 9.2, we can follow the arrows from the bottom of the diagram to the topmost superclass in this class hierarchy to identify several *is-a* relationships. For example, a Triangle *is a* TwoDimensionalShape and *is a* Shape, while a Sphere *is a* ThreeDimensionalShape and *is a* Shape. This hierarchy could contain many other classes. For example, ellipses and trapezoids also are TwoDimensionalShapes.

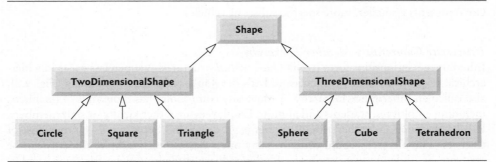

Fig. 9.3 | Inheritance hierarchy UML class diagram for Shapes.

Not every class relationship is an inheritance relationship. In Chapter 8, we discussed the *has-a* relationship, in which classes have members that are references to objects of other classes. Such relationships create classes by *composition* of existing classes. For example, given the classes Employee, BirthDate and TelephoneNumber, it's improper to say that an Employee *is a* BirthDate or that an Employee *is a* TelephoneNumber. However, an Employee *has a* BirthDate, and an Employee *has a* TelephoneNumber.

It's possible to treat superclass objects and subclass objects similarly—their commonalities are expressed in the superclass's members. Objects of all classes that extend a common superclass can be treated as objects of that superclass—such objects have an *is-a* relationship with the superclass. Later in this chapter and in Chapter 10, we consider many examples that take advantage of the *is-a* relationship.

A subclass can customize methods that it inherits from its superclass. To do this, the subclass **overrides** (*redefines*) the superclass method with an appropriate implementation, as we'll see in the chapter's code examples.

9.3 protected Members

Chapter 8 discussed access modifiers public and private. A class's public members are accessible wherever the program has a *reference* to an *object* of that class or one of its *subclasses*. A class's private members are accessible only within the class itself. In this section, we introduce the access modifier **protected**. Using protected access offers an intermediate level of access between public and private. A superclass's protected members can be accessed by members of that superclass, by members of its subclasses and by members of other classes in the *same package*—protected members also have *package access*.

All public and protected superclass members retain their original access modifier when they become members of the subclass—public members of the superclass become public members of the subclass, and protected members of the superclass become protected members of the subclass. A superclass's private members are *not* accessible outside the class itself. Rather, they're *hidden* from its subclasses and can be accessed only through the public or protected methods inherited from the superclass.

Subclass methods can refer to public and protected members inherited from the superclass simply by using the member names. When a subclass method *overrides* an inherited superclass method, the *superclass* version of the method can be accessed from the *subclass* by preceding the superclass method name with keyword **super** and a dot (.) separator. We discuss accessing overridden members of the superclass in Section 9.4.

Software Engineering Observation 9.1
Methods of a subclass cannot directly access private members of their superclass. A subclass can change the state of private superclass instance variables only through non-private methods provided in the superclass and inherited by the subclass.

Software Engineering Observation 9.2
Declaring private instance variables helps you test, debug and correctly modify systems. If a subclass could access its superclass's private instance variables, classes that inherit from that subclass could access the instance variables as well. This would propagate access to what should be private instance variables, and the benefits of information hiding would be lost.

9.4 Relationship Between Superclasses and Subclasses

We now use an inheritance hierarchy containing types of *employees* in a company's payroll application to discuss the relationship between a superclass and its subclass. In this company, *commission employees* (who will be represented as objects of a superclass) are paid a percentage of their sales, while *base-salaried commission employees* (who will be represented as objects of a subclass) receive a base salary *plus* a percentage of their sales.

We divide our discussion of the relationship between these classes into five examples. The first declares class CommissionEmployee, which directly inherits from class Object and declares as private instance variables a first name, last name, social security number, commission rate and gross (i.e., total) sales amount.

The second example declares class BasePlusCommissionEmployee, which also directly inherits from class Object and declares as private instance variables a first name, last name, social security number, commission rate, gross sales amount *and* base salary. We create this class by *writing every line of code* the class requires—we'll soon see that it's much more efficient to create it by inheriting from class CommissionEmployee.

The third example declares a new BasePlusCommissionEmployee class that *extends* class CommissionEmployee (i.e., a BasePlusCommissionEmployee *is a* CommissionEmployee who also has a base salary). This *software reuse lets us write much less code* when developing the new subclass. In this example, class BasePlusCommissionEmployee attempts to access class CommissionEmployee's private members—this results in compilation errors, because the subclass *cannot* access the superclass's private instance variables.

The fourth example shows that if CommissionEmployee's instance variables are declared as protected, the BasePlusCommissionEmployee subclass *can* access that data directly. Both BasePlusCommissionEmployee classes contain identical functionality, but we show how the inherited version is easier to create and manage.

After we discuss the convenience of using protected instance variables, we create the fifth example, which sets the CommissionEmployee instance variables back to private to enforce good software engineering. Then we show how the BasePlusCommissionEmployee subclass can use CommissionEmployee's public methods to manipulate (in a controlled manner) the private instance variables inherited from CommissionEmployee.

9.4.1 Creating and Using a CommissionEmployee Class

We begin by declaring class CommissionEmployee (Fig. 9.4). Line 4 begins the class declaration and indicates that class CommissionEmployee **extends** (i.e., *inherits from*) class **Object** (from package java.lang). This causes class CommissionEmployee to inherit the class Object's methods—class Object does not have any fields. If you don't explicitly specify which class a new class extends, the class extends Object implicitly. For this reason, you typically will not include "extends Object" in your code—we do so in this one example only for demonstration purposes.

```
1   // Fig. 9.4: CommissionEmployee.java
2   // CommissionEmployee class represents an employee paid a
3   // percentage of gross sales.
```

Fig. 9.4 | CommissionEmployee class represents an employee paid a percentage of gross sales. (Part 1 of 3.)

```
 4    public class CommissionEmployee extends Object {
 5        private final String firstName;
 6        private final String lastName;
 7        private final String socialSecurityNumber;
 8        private double grossSales; // gross weekly sales
 9        private double commissionRate; // commission percentage
10
11        // five-argument constructor
12        public CommissionEmployee(String firstName, String lastName,
13            String socialSecurityNumber, double grossSales,
14            double commissionRate) {
15            // implicit call to Object's default constructor occurs here
16
17            // if grossSales is invalid throw exception
18            if (grossSales < 0.0) {
19                throw new IllegalArgumentException("Gross sales must be >= 0.0");
20            }
21
22            // if commissionRate is invalid throw exception
23            if (commissionRate <= 0.0 || commissionRate >= 1.0) {
24                throw new IllegalArgumentException(
25                    "Commission rate must be > 0.0 and < 1.0");
26            }
27
28            this.firstName = firstName;
29            this.lastName = lastName;
30            this.socialSecurityNumber = socialSecurityNumber;
31            this.grossSales = grossSales;
32            this.commissionRate = commissionRate;
33        }
34
35        // return first name
36        public String getFirstName() {return firstName;}
37
38        // return last name
39        public String getLastName() {return lastName;}
40
41        // return social security number
42        public String getSocialSecurityNumber() {return socialSecurityNumber;}
43
44        // set gross sales amount
45        public void setGrossSales(double grossSales) {
46            if (grossSales < 0.0) {
47                throw new IllegalArgumentException("Gross sales must be >= 0.0");
48            }
49
50            this.grossSales = grossSales;
51        }
52
53        // return gross sales amount
54        public double getGrossSales() {return grossSales;}
```

Fig. 9.4 | CommissionEmployee class represents an employee paid a percentage of gross sales. (Part 2 of 3.)

```
55
56     // set commission rate
57     public void setCommissionRate(double commissionRate) {
58         if (commissionRate <= 0.0 || commissionRate >= 1.0) {
59             throw new IllegalArgumentException(
60                 "Commission rate must be > 0.0 and < 1.0");
61         }
62
63         this.commissionRate = commissionRate;
64     }
65
66     // return commission rate
67     public double getCommissionRate() {return commissionRate;}
68
69     // calculate earnings
70     public double earnings() {return commissionRate * grossSales;}
71
72     // return String representation of CommissionEmployee object
73     @Override // indicates that this method overrides a superclass method
74     public String toString() {
75         return String.format("%s: %s %s%n%s: %s%n%s: %.2f%n%s: %.2f",
76             "commission employee", firstName, lastName,
77             "social security number", socialSecurityNumber,
78             "gross sales", grossSales,
79             "commission rate", commissionRate);
80     }
81 }
```

Fig. 9.4 | CommissionEmployee class represents an employee paid a percentage of gross sales. (Part 3 of 3.)

Overview of Class CommissionEmployee's Methods and Instance Variables

Class CommissionEmployee's public services include a constructor (lines 12–33) and methods earnings (line 70) and toString (lines 73–80). Lines 36–42 declare public *get* methods for the class's final instance variables (declared in lines 5–7) firstName, last-Name and socialSecurityNumber. These three instance variables are declared final because they do not need to be modified after they're initialized—this is also why we do not provide corresponding *set* methods. Lines 45–67 declare public *set* and *get* methods for the class's grossSales and commissionRate instance variables (declared in lines 8–9). The class declares its instance variables as private, so objects of other classes cannot directly access these variables.

Class CommissionEmployee's Constructor

Constructors are *not* inherited, so class CommissionEmployee does not inherit class Object's constructor. However, a superclass's constructors are still available to be called by subclasses. In fact, Java requires that *the first task of any subclass constructor is to call its direct superclass's constructor*, either explicitly or implicitly (if no constructor call is specified), to ensure that the instance variables inherited from the superclass are initialized properly. The syntax for calling a superclass constructor explicitly is discussed in Section 9.4.3. In this example, class CommissionEmployee's constructor calls class Object's constructor implicitly. If the code does not include an explicit call to the superclass constructor, Java *implicitly* calls the superclass's default or *no-argument* constructor. The comment in line 15 of Fig. 9.4 indicates where the implicit call to the superclass Object's default constructor is made (you do *not* write the code for this call). Object's default constructor does nothing. Even if a class does not have constructors, the default constructor that the compiler implicitly declares for the class will call the superclass's default or no-argument constructor.

After the implicit call to Object's constructor, lines 18–20 and 23–26 validate the grossSales and commissionRate arguments. If these are valid (that is, the constructor does not throw an IllegalArgumentException), lines 28–32 assign the constructor's arguments to the class's instance variables.

We did not validate the values of arguments firstName, lastName and socialSecurityNumber before assigning them to the corresponding instance variables. We could validate the first and last names—perhaps to ensure that they're of a reasonable length. Similarly, a social security number could be validated using regular expressions (Section 14.7) to ensure that it contains nine digits, with or without dashes (e.g., 123-45-6789 or 123456789).

Class CommissionEmployee's earnings Method

Method earnings (line 70) calculates a CommissionEmployee's earnings. The method multiplies the commissionRate by the grossSales and returns the result.

Class CommissionEmployee's toString Method

Method toString (lines 73–80) is special—it's one of the methods that *every* class inherits directly or indirectly from class Object (summarized in Section 9.6). Method toString returns a String representing an object. It's called implicitly whenever an object must be converted to a String representation, such as when an object is output by printf or output by String method format via the %s format specifier. Class Object's toString method returns a String that includes the name of the object's class and the object's so-called hashcode (see Section 9.6). It's primarily a placeholder that can be *overridden* by a subclass to specify an appropriate String representation of the data in a subclass object.

Method toString of class CommissionEmployee overrides (redefines) class Object's toString method. When invoked, CommissionEmployee's toString method uses String method format to return a String containing information about the CommissionEmployee. To override a superclass method, a subclass must declare a method with the *same signature* (method name, number of parameters, parameter types and order of parameter types) as the superclass method—Object's toString method takes no parameters, so CommissionEmployee declares toString with no parameters.

@Override Annotaton

Line 73 uses the optional **@Override annotation** to indicate that the following method declaration (i.e., toString) should *override* an *existing* superclass method. This annotation helps the compiler catch a few common errors. For example, in this case, you intend to override superclass method toString, which is spelled with a lowercase "t" and an uppercase "S." If you inadvertently use a lowercase "s," the compiler will flag this as an error because the superclass does not contain a method named tostring with a lowercase "s." If you didn't use the @Override annotation, tostring would be an entirely different method that would *not* be called if a CommissionEmployee were used where a String was needed.

Another common overriding error is declaring the wrong number or types of parameters in the parameter list. This creates an *unintentional overload* of the superclass method, rather than overriding the existing method. If you then attempt to call the method (with the correct number and types of parameters) on a subclass object, the superclass's version is invoked—potentially leading to subtle logic errors. When the compiler encounters a method declared with @Override, it compares the method's signature with the superclass's method signatures. If there isn't an exact match, the compiler issues an error message, such as "method does not override or implement a method from a supertype." You can then correct your method's signature so that it matches one in the superclass.

Error-Prevention Tip 9.1

Though the @Override annotation is optional, declare overridden methods with it to ensure at compilation time that you defined their signatures correctly. It's always better to find errors at compile time rather than at runtime. For this reason, the toString methods in Fig. 7.9 and in Chapter 8's examples should have been declared with @Override.

Common Programming Error 9.1

It's a compilation error to override a method with a more restricted access modifier—a public superclass method cannot become a protected or private subclass method; a protected superclass method cannot become a private subclass method. Doing so would break the is-a relationship, which requires that all subclass objects be able to respond to method calls made to public methods declared in the superclass. If a public method could be overridden as a protected or private method, the subclass objects would not be able to respond to the same method calls as superclass objects. Once a method is declared public in a superclass, the method remains public for all that class's direct and indirect subclasses.

Class *CommissionEmployeeTest*

Figure 9.5 tests class CommissionEmployee. Lines 6–7 instantiate a CommissionEmployee object and invoke CommissionEmployee's constructor (lines 12–33 of Fig. 9.4) to initialize it with "Sue" as the first name, "Jones" as the last name, "222-22-2222" as the social security number, 10000 as the gross sales amount ($10,000) and .06 as the commission rate (i.e., 6%). Lines 11–20 use CommissionEmployee's *get* methods to retrieve the object's instance-variable values for output. Lines 22–23 invoke the object's setGrossSales and setCommissionRate methods to change the values of instance variables grossSales and commissionRate. Lines 25–26 output the String representation of the updated CommissionEmployee. When an object is output using the %s format specifier, the object's toString method is invoked *implicitly* to obtain the object's String representation. [*Note:* In this chapter, we do not use the earnings method in each class, but it's used extensively in Chapter 10.]

```
1   // Fig. 9.5: CommissionEmployeeTest.java
2   // CommissionEmployee class test program.
3   public class CommissionEmployeeTest {
4      public static void main(String[] args) {
```

Fig. 9.5 | CommissionEmployee class test program. (Part 1 of 2.)

```
5     // instantiate CommissionEmployee object
6     CommissionEmployee employee = new CommissionEmployee(
7        "Sue", "Jones", "222-22-2222", 10000, .06);
8
9     // get commission employee data
10    System.out.println("Employee information obtained by get methods:");
11    System.out.printf("%n%s %s%n", "First name is",
12       employee.getFirstName());
13    System.out.printf("%s %s%n", "Last name is",
14       employee.getLastName());
15    System.out.printf("%s %s%n", "Social security number is",
16       employee.getSocialSecurityNumber());
17    System.out.printf("%s %.2f%n", "Gross sales is",
18       employee.getGrossSales());
19    System.out.printf("%s %.2f%n", "Commission rate is",
20       employee.getCommissionRate());
21
22    employee.setGrossSales(5000);
23    employee.setCommissionRate(.1);
24
25    System.out.printf("%n%s:%n%n%s%n",
26       "Updated employee information obtained by toString", employee);
27    }
28 }
```

```
Employee information obtained by get methods:

First name is Sue
Last name is Jones
Social security number is 222-22-2222
Gross sales is 10000.00
Commission rate is 0.06

Updated employee information obtained by toString:

commission employee: Sue Jones
social security number: 222-22-2222
gross sales: 5000.00
commission rate: 0.10
```

Fig. 9.5 | CommissionEmployee class test program. (Part 2 of 2.)

9.4.2 Creating and Using a BasePlusCommissionEmployee Class

We now discuss the second part of our introduction to inheritance by declaring and testing (a completely new and independent) class BasePlusCommissionEmployee (Fig. 9.6), which contains a first name, last name, social security number, gross sales amount, commission rate *and* base salary. Class BasePlusCommissionEmployee's public services include a BasePlusCommissionEmployee constructor (lines 13–40) and methods earnings (lines 89–91) and toString (lines 94–102). Lines 43–86 declare public *get* and *set* methods for the class's private instance variables (declared in lines 5–10) firstName, lastName, socialSecurityNumber, grossSales, commissionRate and baseSalary. These variables and methods encapsulate all the necessary features of a base-salaried commission employee. Note the *similarity* between this class and class `CommissionEmployee` (Fig. 9.4)—in this example, we'll not yet exploit that similarity.

```java
1   // Fig. 9.6: BasePlusCommissionEmployee.java
2   // BasePlusCommissionEmployee class represents an employee who receives
3   // a base salary in addition to commission.
4   public class BasePlusCommissionEmployee {
5      private final String firstName;
6      private final String lastName;
7      private final String socialSecurityNumber;
8      private double grossSales; // gross weekly sales
9      private double commissionRate; // commission percentage
10     private double baseSalary; // base salary per week
11
12     // six-argument constructor
13     public BasePlusCommissionEmployee(String firstName, String lastName,
14        String socialSecurityNumber, double grossSales,
15        double commissionRate, double baseSalary) {
16        // implicit call to Object's default constructor occurs here
17
18        // if grossSales is invalid throw exception
19        if (grossSales < 0.0) {
20           throw new IllegalArgumentException("Gross sales must be >= 0.0");
21        }
22
23        // if commissionRate is invalid throw exception
24        if (commissionRate <= 0.0 || commissionRate >= 1.0) {
25           throw new IllegalArgumentException(
26              "Commission rate must be > 0.0 and < 1.0");
27        }
28
29        // if baseSalary is invalid throw exception
30        if (baseSalary < 0.0) {
31           throw new IllegalArgumentException("Base salary must be >= 0.0");
32        }
33
34        this.firstName = firstName;
35        this.lastName = lastName;
36        this.socialSecurityNumber = socialSecurityNumber;
37        this.grossSales = grossSales;
38        this.commissionRate = commissionRate;
39        this.baseSalary = baseSalary;
40     }
41
42     // return first name
43     public String getFirstName() {return firstName;}
44
45     // return last name
46     public String getLastName() {return lastName;}
47
```

Fig. 9.6 | BasePlusCommissionEmployee class represents an employee who receives a base salary in addition to a commission. (Part 1 of 3.)

```
48      // return social security number
49      public String getSocialSecurityNumber() {return socialSecurityNumber;}
50
51      // set gross sales amount
52      public void setGrossSales(double grossSales) {
53          if (grossSales < 0.0) {
54              throw new IllegalArgumentException("Gross sales must be >= 0.0");
55          }
56
57          this.grossSales = grossSales;
58      }
59
60      // return gross sales amount
61      public double getGrossSales() {return grossSales;}
62
63      // set commission rate
64      public void setCommissionRate(double commissionRate) {
65          if (commissionRate <= 0.0 || commissionRate >= 1.0) {
66              throw new IllegalArgumentException(
67                  "Commission rate must be > 0.0 and < 1.0");
68          }
69
70          this.commissionRate = commissionRate;
71      }
72
73      // return commission rate
74      public double getCommissionRate() {return commissionRate;}
75
76      // set base salary
77      public void setBaseSalary(double baseSalary) {
78          if (baseSalary < 0.0) {
79              throw new IllegalArgumentException("Base salary must be >= 0.0");
80          }
81
82          this.baseSalary = baseSalary;
83      }
84
85      // return base salary
86      public double getBaseSalary() {return baseSalary;}
87
88      // calculate earnings
89      public double earnings() {
90          return baseSalary + (commissionRate * grossSales);
91      }
92
93      // return String representation of BasePlusCommissionEmployee
94      @Override
95      public String toString() {
96          return String.format(
97              "%s: %s %s%n%s: %s%n%s: %.2f%n%s: %.2f%n%s: %.2f",
98              "base-salaried commission employee", firstName, lastName,
```

Fig. 9.6 | BasePlusCommissionEmployee class represents an employee who receives a base salary in addition to a commission. (Part 2 of 3.)

```
 99                 "social security number", socialSecurityNumber,
100                 "gross sales", grossSales, "commission rate", commissionRate,
101                 "base salary", baseSalary);
102         }
103     }
```

Fig. 9.6 | BasePlusCommissionEmployee class represents an employee who receives a base salary in addition to a commission. (Part 3 of 3.)

Class BasePlusCommissionEmployee does *not* specify "extends Object" in line 4, so the class *implicitly* extends Object. Also, like class CommissionEmployee's constructor (lines 12–33 of Fig. 9.4), class BasePlusCommissionEmployee's constructor invokes class Object's default constructor *implicitly*, as noted in the comment in line 16 of Fig. 9.6.

Class BasePlusCommissionEmployee's earnings method (lines 89–91) returns the result of adding the BasePlusCommissionEmployee's base salary to the product of the commission rate and the employee's gross sales.

Class BasePlusCommissionEmployee overrides Object method toString to return a String containing the BasePlusCommissionEmployee's information. Once again, we use format specifier %.2f to format the gross sales, commission rate and base salary with two digits of precision to the right of the decimal point (line 97).

Testing Class *BasePlusCommissionEmployee*

Figure 9.7 tests class BasePlusCommissionEmployee. Lines 7–9 create a BasePlusCommissionEmployee object and pass "Bob", "Lewis", "333-33-3333", 5000, .04 and 300 to the constructor as the first name, last name, social security number, gross sales, commission rate and base salary, respectively. Lines 14–25 use BasePlusCommissionEmployee's *get* methods to retrieve the values of the object's instance variables for output. Line 27 invokes the object's setBaseSalary method to change the base salary. Method setBaseSalary (Fig. 9.6, lines 77–83) ensures that instance variable baseSalary is not assigned a negative value. Line 31 of Fig. 9.7 invokes method toString *explicitly* to get the object's String representation.

```
 1   // Fig. 9.7: BasePlusCommissionEmployeeTest.java
 2   // BasePlusCommissionEmployee test program.
 3
 4   public class BasePlusCommissionEmployeeTest {
 5      public static void main(String[] args) {
 6         // instantiate BasePlusCommissionEmployee object
 7         BasePlusCommissionEmployee employee =
 8            new BasePlusCommissionEmployee(
 9            "Bob", "Lewis", "333-33-3333", 5000, .04, 300);
10
11         // get base-salaried commission employee data
12         System.out.printf(
13            "Employee information obtained by get methods:%n");
14         System.out.printf("%s %s%n", "First name is",
15            employee.getFirstName());
```

Fig. 9.7 | BasePlusCommissionEmployee test program. (Part 1 of 2.)

```
16          System.out.printf("%s %s%n", "Last name is",
17             employee.getLastName());
18          System.out.printf("%s %s%n", "Social security number is",
19             employee.getSocialSecurityNumber());
20          System.out.printf("%s %.2f%n", "Gross sales is",
21             employee.getGrossSales());
22          System.out.printf("%s %.2f%n", "Commission rate is",
23             employee.getCommissionRate());
24          System.out.printf("%s %.2f%n", "Base salary is",
25             employee.getBaseSalary());
26
27          employee.setBaseSalary(1000);
28
29          System.out.printf("%n%s:%n%n%s%n",
30             "Updated employee information obtained by toString",
31             employee.toString());
32       }
33    }
```

```
Employee information obtained by get methods:

First name is Bob
Last name is Lewis
Social security number is 333-33-3333
Gross sales is 5000.00
Commission rate is 0.04
Base salary is 300.00

Updated employee information obtained by toString:

base-salaried commission employee: Bob Lewis
social security number: 333-33-3333
gross sales: 5000.00
commission rate: 0.04
base salary: 1000.00
```

Fig. 9.7 | BasePlusCommissionEmployee test program. (Part 2 of 2.)

Notes on Class *BasePlusCommissionEmployee*

Much of class BasePlusCommissionEmployee's code (Fig. 9.6) is *similar*, or *identical*, to that of class CommissionEmployee (Fig. 9.4). For example, private instance variables firstName and lastName and methods getFirstName and getLastName are identical to those of class CommissionEmployee. The classes also both contain private instance variables socialSecurityNumber, commissionRate and grossSales, and corresponding *get* and *set* methods. In addition, the BasePlusCommissionEmployee constructor is *almost* identical to that of class CommissionEmployee, except that BasePlusCommissionEmployee's constructor also sets the baseSalary. The other additions to class BasePlusCommissionEmployee are private instance variable baseSalary and methods setBaseSalary and getBaseSalary. Class BasePlusCommissionEmployee's toString method is *almost* identical to that of class CommissionEmployee except that it also outputs instance variable baseSalary with two digits of precision to the right of the decimal point.

We literally *copied* code from class CommissionEmployee and *pasted* it into class Base-PlusCommissionEmployee, then modified class BasePlusCommissionEmployee to include a base salary and methods that manipulate the base salary. This *"copy-and-paste" approach* is often error prone and time consuming. Worse yet, it spreads copies of the same code throughout a system, creating code-maintenance problems—changes to the code would need to be made in multiple classes. Is there a way to "acquire" the instance variables and methods of one class in a way that makes them part of other classes *without duplicating code*? Next we answer this question, using a more elegant approach to building classes that emphasizes the benefits of inheritance.

Software Engineering Observation 9.3

With inheritance, the instance variables and methods that are the same for all the classes in the hierarchy are declared in a superclass. Changes made to these common features in the superclass are inherited by the subclass. Without inheritance, changes would need to be made to all the source-code files that contain a copy of the code in question.

9.4.3 Creating a CommissionEmployee– BasePlusCommissionEmployee Inheritance Hierarchy

Now we declare class BasePlusCommissionEmployee (Fig. 9.8) to *extend* class Commission-Employee (Fig. 9.4). A BasePlusCommissionEmployee object *is a* CommissionEmployee, because inheritance passes on class CommissionEmployee's capabilities. Class BasePlusCommissionEmployee also has instance variable baseSalary (Fig. 9.8, line 4). Keyword extends (line 3) indicates inheritance. BasePlusCommissionEmployee *inherits* CommissionEmployee's instance variables and methods.

Software Engineering Observation 9.4

At the design stage in an object-oriented system, you'll often find that certain classes are closely related. You should "factor out" common instance variables and methods and place them in a superclass. Then use inheritance to develop subclasses, specializing them with capabilities beyond those inherited from the superclass.

Software Engineering Observation 9.5

Declaring a subclass does not affect its superclass's source code. Inheritance preserves the integrity of the superclass.

```
1   // Fig. 9.8: BasePlusCommissionEmployee.java
2   // private superclass members cannot be accessed in a subclass.
3   public class BasePlusCommissionEmployee extends CommissionEmployee {
4      private double baseSalary; // base salary per week
5
6      // six-argument constructor
7      public BasePlusCommissionEmployee(String firstName, String lastName,
8         String socialSecurityNumber, double grossSales,
9         double commissionRate, double baseSalary) {
```

Fig. 9.8 | private superclass members cannot be accessed in a subclass. (Part 1 of 3.)

```
10              // explicit call to superclass CommissionEmployee constructor
11              super(firstName, lastName, socialSecurityNumber,
12                 grossSales, commissionRate);
13
14              // if baseSalary is invalid throw exception
15              if (baseSalary < 0.0) {
16                 throw new IllegalArgumentException("Base salary must be >= 0.0");
17              }
18
19              this.baseSalary = baseSalary;
20           }
21
22           // set base salary
23           public void setBaseSalary(double baseSalary) {
24              if (baseSalary < 0.0) {
25                 throw new IllegalArgumentException("Base salary must be >= 0.0");
26              }
27
28              this.baseSalary = baseSalary;
29           }
30
31           // return base salary
32           public double getBaseSalary() {return baseSalary;}
33
34           // calculate earnings
35           @Override
36           public double earnings() {
37              // not allowed: commissionRate and grossSales private in superclass
38              return baseSalary + (commissionRate * grossSales);
39           }
40
41           // return String representation of BasePlusCommissionEmployee
42           @Override
43           public String toString() {
44              // not allowed: attempts to access private superclass members
45              return String.format(
46                 "%s: %s %s%n%s: %s%n%s: %.2f%n%s: %.2f%n%s: %.2f",
47                 "base-salaried commission employee", firstName, lastName,
48                 "social security number", socialSecurityNumber,
49                 "gross sales", grossSales, "commission rate", commissionRate,
50                 "base salary", baseSalary);
51           }
52     }
```

```
BasePlusCommissionEmployee.java:38: error: commissionRate has private access
in CommissionEmployee
      return baseSalary + (commissionRate * grossSales);
                           ^
BasePlusCommissionEmployee.java:38: error: grossSales has private access in
CommissionEmployee
      return baseSalary + (commissionRate * grossSales);
                                            ^
```

Fig. 9.8 | private superclass members cannot be accessed in a subclass. (Part 2 of 3.)

```
BasePlusCommissionEmployee.java:47: error: firstName has private access in
CommissionEmployee
         "base-salaried commission employee", firstName, lastName,
                                               ^
BasePlusCommissionEmployee.java:47: error: lastName has private access in
CommissionEmployee
         "base-salaried commission employee", firstName, lastName,
                                                          ^
BasePlusCommissionEmployee.java:48: error: socialSecurityNumber has private
access in CommissionEmployee
         "social security number", socialSecurityNumber,
                                   ^
BasePlusCommissionEmployee.java:49: error: grossSales has private access in
CommissionEmployee
         "gross sales", grossSales, "commission rate", commissionRate,
                        ^
BasePlusCommissionEmployee.java:49: error: commissionRate has private access
inCommissionEmployee
         "gross sales", grossSales, "commission rate", commissionRate,
                                                       ^
```

Fig. 9.8 | `private` superclass members cannot be accessed in a subclass. (Part 3 of 3.)

Only CommissionEmployee's public and protected members are directly accessible in the subclass. The CommissionEmployee constructor is *not* inherited. So, the public BasePlusCommissionEmployee services include its constructor (lines 7–20), public methods inherited from CommissionEmployee, and methods setBaseSalary (lines 23–29), getBaseSalary (line 32), earnings (lines 35–39) and toString (lines 42–51). Methods earnings and toString *override* the corresponding methods in class CommissionEmployee because their superclass versions do not properly calculate a BasePlusCommissionEmployee's earnings or return an appropriate String representation, respectively.

A Subclass's Constructor Must Call Its Superclass's Constructor

Each subclass constructor must implicitly or explicitly call one of its superclass's constructors to initialize the instance variables inherited from the superclass. Lines 11–12 in Base-PlusCommissionEmployee's six-argument constructor (lines 7–20) explicitly call class CommissionEmployee's five-argument constructor (declared at lines 12–33 of Fig. 9.4) to initialize the superclass portion of a BasePlusCommissionEmployee object (i.e., variables firstName, lastName, socialSecurityNumber, grossSales and commissionRate). We do this by using the **superclass constructor call syntax**—keyword super, followed by a set of parentheses containing the superclass constructor arguments, which are used to initialize the superclass instance variables firstName, lastName, socialSecurityNumber, grossSales and commissionRate, respectively. The explicit superclass constructor call in lines 11–12 of Fig. 9.8 must be the *first* statement in the constructor's body.

If BasePlusCommissionEmployee's constructor did not invoke the superclass's constructor explicitly, the compiler would attempt to insert a call to the superclass's default or no-argument constructor. Class CommissionEmployee does not have such a constructor, so the compiler would issue an error. When a superclass contains a no-argument constructor, you can use super() to call that constructor explicitly, but this is rarely done.

Software Engineering Observation 9.6

You learned previously that you should not call a class's instance methods from its constructors and that we'll say why in Chapter 10. Calling a superclass constructor from a subclass constructor does not contradict this advice.

BasePlusCommissionEmployee Methods Earnings and toString

The compiler generates errors for line 38 (Fig. 9.8) because CommissionEmployee's instance variables commissionRate and grossSales are private—subclass BasePlusCommissionEmployee's methods are *not* allowed to access superclass CommissionEmployee's private instance variables. The compiler issues additional errors at lines 47–49 of BasePlusCommissionEmployee's toString method for the same reason. The errors in BasePlusCommissionEmployee could have been prevented by using the *get* methods inherited from class CommissionEmployee. For example, line 38 could have called getCommissionRate and getGrossSales to access CommissionEmployee's private instance variables commissionRate and grossSales, respectively. Lines 47–49 also could have used appropriate *get* methods to retrieve the values of the superclass's instance variables.

9.4.4 CommissionEmployee–BasePlusCommissionEmployee Inheritance Hierarchy Using protected Instance Variables

To enable class BasePlusCommissionEmployee to directly access superclass instance variables firstName, lastName, socialSecurityNumber, grossSales and commissionRate, we can declare those members as protected in the superclass. As we discussed in Section 9.3, a superclass's protected members are accessible by all subclasses of that superclass. In the new CommissionEmployee class, we modified only lines 5–9 of Fig. 9.4 to declare the instance variables with the protected access modifier as follows:

```
protected final String firstName;
protected final String lastName;
protected final String socialSecurityNumber;
protected double grossSales; // gross weekly sales
protected double commissionRate; // commission percentage
```

The rest of the class declaration (which is not shown here) is identical to that of Fig. 9.4.

We could have declared CommissionEmployee's instance variables public to enable subclass BasePlusCommissionEmployee to access them. However, declaring public instance variables is poor software engineering because it allows unrestricted access to the these variables from any class, greatly increasing the chance of errors. With protected instance variables, the subclass gets access to the instance variables, but classes that are not subclasses and classes that are not in the same package cannot access these variables directly—recall that protected class members are also visible to other classes in the same package.

Class *BasePlusCommissionEmployee*

Class BasePlusCommissionEmployee (Fig. 9.9) extends the new version of class CommissionEmployee with protected instance variables. BasePlusCommissionEmployee objects inherit CommissionEmployee's protected instance variables firstName, lastName, socialSecurityNumber, grossSales and commissionRate—all these variables are now protected members of BasePlusCommissionEmployee. As a result, the compiler does not generate errors when compiling line 38 of method `earnings` and lines 46–48 of method `toString`. If another class extends this version of class `BasePlusCommissionEmployee`, the new subclass also can access the `protected` members.

```java
1   // Fig. 9.9: BasePlusCommissionEmployee.java
2   // BasePlusCommissionEmployee inherits protected instance
3   // variables from CommissionEmployee.
4
5   public class BasePlusCommissionEmployee extends CommissionEmployee {
6      private double baseSalary; // base salary per week
7
8      // six-argument constructor
9      public BasePlusCommissionEmployee(String firstName, String lastName,
10        String socialSecurityNumber, double grossSales,
11        double commissionRate, double baseSalary) {
12        super(firstName, lastName, socialSecurityNumber,
13           grossSales, commissionRate);
14
15        // if baseSalary is invalid throw exception
16        if (baseSalary < 0.0) {
17           throw new IllegalArgumentException("Base salary must be >= 0.0");
18        }
19
20        this.baseSalary = baseSalary;
21     }
22
23     // set base salary
24     public void setBaseSalary(double baseSalary) {
25        if (baseSalary < 0.0) {
26           throw new IllegalArgumentException("Base salary must be >= 0.0");
27        }
28
29        this.baseSalary = baseSalary;
30     }
31
32     // return base salary
33     public double getBaseSalary() {return baseSalary;}
34
35     // calculate earnings
36     @Override // indicates that this method overrides a superclass method
37     public double earnings() {
38        return baseSalary + (commissionRate * grossSales);
39     }
40
41     // return String representation of BasePlusCommissionEmployee
42     @Override
43     public String toString() {
44        return String.format(
45           "%s: %s %s%n%s: %s%n%s: %.2f%n%s: %.2f%n%s: %.2f",
46           "base-salaried commission employee", firstName, lastName,
47           "social security number", socialSecurityNumber,
```

Fig. 9.9 | `BasePlusCommissionEmployee` inherits `protected` instance variables from `CommissionEmployee`. (Part 1 of 2.)

```
48          "gross sales", grossSales, "commission rate", commissionRate,
49          "base salary", baseSalary);
50      }
51  }
```

Fig. 9.9 | BasePlusCommissionEmployee inherits protected instance variables from CommissionEmployee. (Part 2 of 2.)

A Subclass Object Contains the Instance Variables of All of Its Superclasses

When you create a BasePlusCommissionEmployee, it contains all instance variables declared in the class hierarchy to that point—that is, those from classes Object (which does not have instance variables), CommissionEmployee and BasePlusCommissionEmployee. Class BasePlusCommissionEmployee does *not* inherit CommissionEmployee's constructor, but *explicitly invokes* it (lines 12–13) to initialize the BasePlusCommissionEmployee instance variables inherited from CommissionEmployee. Similarly, CommissionEmployee's constructor *implicitly* calls class Object's constructor. BasePlusCommissionEmployee's constructor must *explicitly* call CommissionEmployee's constructor because CommissionEmployee does *not* have a no-argument constructor that could be invoked implicitly.

Testing Class *BasePlusCommissionEmployee*

Class BasePlusCommissionEmployeeTest for this example is identical to that of Fig. 9.7 and produces the same output, so we do not show it here. Although the version of class BasePlusCommissionEmployee in Fig. 9.6 does not use inheritance and the version in Fig. 9.9 does, both classes provide the *same* functionality. The source code in Fig. 9.9 (51 lines) is considerably shorter than that in Fig. 9.6 (103 lines), because most of the class's functionality is now inherited from CommissionEmployee—there's now only one copy of the CommissionEmployee functionality. This makes the code easier to maintain, modify and debug, because the code related to a CommissionEmployee exists only in that class.

Notes on Using *protected* Instance Variables

In this example, we declared superclass instance variables as protected so that subclasses could access them. Inheriting protected instance variables enables direct access to the variables by subclasses. In most cases, however, it's better to use private instance variables to encourage proper software engineering. Your code will be easier to maintain, modify and debug.

Using protected instance variables creates several potential problems. First, the subclass object can set an inherited variable's value directly without using a *set* method. Therefore, a subclass object can assign an invalid value to the variable, possibly leaving the object in an inconsistent state. For example, if we were to declare CommissionEmployee's instance variable grossSales as protected, a subclass object (e.g., BasePlusCommissionEmployee) could then assign a negative value to grossSales.

Another problem with using protected instance variables is that subclass methods are more likely to be written so that they depend on the superclass's data implementation. In practice, subclasses should depend only on the superclass services (i.e., non-private methods) and not on the superclass data implementation. With protected instance variables in the superclass, we may need to modify all the subclasses of the superclass if the superclass implementation changes. For example, if for some reason we were to change the names of instance variables firstName and lastName to first and last, then we would have to do so for all occurrences in which a subclass directly references superclass instance variables firstName and lastName. Such a class is said to be **fragile** or **brittle**, because a small change in the superclass can "break" subclass implementation. You should be able to change the superclass implementation while still providing the same services to the subclasses. Of course, if the superclass services change, we must reimplement our subclasses.

A third problem is that a class's protected members are visible to all classes in the same package as the class containing the protected members. This is not always desirable.

Software Engineering Observation 9.7

Use the protected access modifier when a superclass should provide a method only to its subclasses and other classes in the same package, but not to other clients.

Software Engineering Observation 9.8

Declaring superclass instance variables private (as opposed to protected) enables the superclass implementation of these instance variables to change without affecting subclass implementations.

Error-Prevention Tip 9.2

Avoid protected instance variables. Instead, include non-private methods that access private instance variables. This will help ensure that objects of the class maintain consistent states.

9.4.5 CommissionEmployee–BasePlusCommissionEmployee Inheritance Hierarchy Using private Instance Variables

Let's reexamine our hierarchy once more, this time using good software engineering practices.

Class CommissionEmployee

Class CommissionEmployee (Fig. 9.10) declares instance variables firstName, lastName, socialSecurityNumber, grossSales and commissionRate as *private* (lines 5–9) and provides public methods getFirstName, getLastName, getSocialSecurityNumber, setGrossSales, getGrossSales, setCommissionRate, getCommissionRate, earnings and toString for manipulating these values. Methods earnings (lines 70–72) and toString (lines 75–82) use the class's *get* methods to obtain the values of its instance variables. If we decide to change the names of the instance variables, the earnings and toString declarations will *not* require modification—only the bodies of the *get* and *set* methods that directly manipulate the instance variables will need to change. These changes occur solely within the superclass—no changes to the subclass are needed. *Localizing the effects of changes* like this is a good software engineering practice.

```
1   // Fig. 9.10: CommissionEmployee.java
2   // CommissionEmployee class uses methods to manipulate its
3   // private instance variables.
```

Fig. 9.10 | CommissionEmployee class uses methods to manipulate its private instance variables. (Part 1 of 3.)

```
 4   public class CommissionEmployee {
 5      private final String firstName;
 6      private final String lastName;
 7      private final String socialSecurityNumber;
 8      private double grossSales; // gross weekly sales
 9      private double commissionRate; // commission percentage
10
11      // five-argument constructor
12      public CommissionEmployee(String firstName, String lastName,
13         String socialSecurityNumber, double grossSales,
14         double commissionRate) {
15         // implicit call to Object constructor occurs here
16
17         // if grossSales is invalid throw exception
18         if (grossSales < 0.0) {
19            throw new IllegalArgumentException("Gross sales must be >= 0.0");
20         }
21
22         // if commissionRate is invalid throw exception
23         if (commissionRate <= 0.0 || commissionRate >= 1.0) {
24            throw new IllegalArgumentException(
25               "Commission rate must be > 0.0 and < 1.0");
26         }
27
28         this.firstName = firstName;
29         this.lastName = lastName;
30         this.socialSecurityNumber = socialSecurityNumber;
31         this.grossSales = grossSales;
32         this.commissionRate = commissionRate;
33      }
34
35      // return first name
36      public String getFirstName() {return firstName;}
37
38      // return last name
39      public String getLastName() {return lastName;}
40
41      // return social security number
42      public String getSocialSecurityNumber() {return socialSecurityNumber;}
43
44      // set gross sales amount
45      public void setGrossSales(double grossSales) {
46         if (grossSales < 0.0) {
47            throw new IllegalArgumentException("Gross sales must be >= 0.0");
48         }
49
50         this.grossSales = grossSales;
51      }
52
53      // return gross sales amount
54      public double getGrossSales() {return grossSales;}
```

Fig. 9.10 | CommissionEmployee class uses methods to manipulate its private instance variables. (Part 2 of 3.)

```
55
56      // set commission rate
57      public void setCommissionRate(double commissionRate) {
58          if (commissionRate <= 0.0 || commissionRate >= 1.0) {
59              throw new IllegalArgumentException(
60                  "Commission rate must be > 0.0 and < 1.0");
61          }
62
63          this.commissionRate = commissionRate;
64      }
65
66      // return commission rate
67      public double getCommissionRate() {return commissionRate;}
68
69      // calculate earnings
70      public double earnings() {
71          return getCommissionRate() * getGrossSales();
72      }
73
74      // return String representation of CommissionEmployee object
75      @Override
76      public String toString() {
77          return String.format("%s: %s %s%n%s: %s%n%s: %.2f%n%s: %.2f",
78              "commission employee", getFirstName(), getLastName(),
79              "social security number", getSocialSecurityNumber(),
80              "gross sales", getGrossSales(),
81              "commission rate", getCommissionRate());
82      }
83  }
```

Fig. 9.10 | CommissionEmployee class uses methods to manipulate its private instance variables. (Part 3 of 3.)

Class *BasePlusCommissionEmployee*

Subclass BasePlusCommissionEmployee (Fig. 9.11) inherits CommissionEmployee's non-private methods and can access (in a controlled way) the private superclass members via those methods. Class BasePlusCommissionEmployee has several changes that distinguish it from Fig. 9.9. Methods earnings (lines 36–37 of Fig. 9.11) and toString (lines 40–44) each invoke method getBaseSalary to obtain the base salary value, rather than accessing baseSalary directly. If we decide to rename instance variable baseSalary, only the bodies of method setBaseSalary and getBaseSalary will need to change.

```
1   // Fig. 9.11: BasePlusCommissionEmployee.java
2   // BasePlusCommissionEmployee class inherits from CommissionEmployee
3   // and accesses the superclass's private data via inherited
4   // public methods.
5   public class BasePlusCommissionEmployee extends CommissionEmployee {
6       private double baseSalary; // base salary per week
7
```

Fig. 9.11 | BasePlusCommissionEmployee class inherits from CommissionEmployee and accesses the superclass's private data via inherited public methods. (Part 1 of 2.)

```
8      // six-argument constructor
9      public BasePlusCommissionEmployee(String firstName, String lastName,
10        String socialSecurityNumber, double grossSales,
11        double commissionRate, double baseSalary) {
12        super(firstName, lastName, socialSecurityNumber,
13          grossSales, commissionRate);
14
15        // if baseSalary is invalid throw exception
16        if (baseSalary < 0.0) {
17          throw new IllegalArgumentException("Base salary must be >= 0.0");
18        }
19
20        this.baseSalary = baseSalary;
21      }
22
23      // set base salary
24      public void setBaseSalary(double baseSalary) {
25        if (baseSalary < 0.0) {
26          throw new IllegalArgumentException("Base salary must be >= 0.0");
27        }
28
29        this.baseSalary = baseSalary;
30      }
31
32      // return base salary
33      public double getBaseSalary() {return baseSalary;}
34
35      // calculate earnings
36      @Override
37      public double earnings() {return getBaseSalary() + super.earnings();}
38
39      // return String representation of BasePlusCommissionEmployee
40      @Override
41      public String toString() {
42        return String.format("%s %s%n%s: %.2f", "base-salaried",
43          super.toString(), "base salary", getBaseSalary());
44      }
45    }
```

Fig. 9.11 | BasePlusCommissionEmployee class inherits from CommissionEmployee and accesses the superclass's private data via inherited public methods. (Part 2 of 2.)

Class *BasePlusCommissionEmployee's earnings Method*

Method earnings (lines 36–37) overrides class CommissionEmployee's earnings method (Fig. 9.10, lines 70–72) to calculate a base-salaried commission employee's earnings. The new version obtains the portion of the earnings based on commission alone by calling CommissionEmployee's earnings method with super.earnings() (line 37 of Fig. 9.11), then adds the base salary to this value to calculate the total earnings. Note the syntax used to invoke an *overridden* superclass method from a subclass—place the keyword super and a dot (.) separator before the superclass method name. This method invocation is a good software engineering practice—if a method performs all or some of the actions needed by another method, call that method rather than duplicate its code. By having BasePlusCommissionEmployee's earnings method invoke CommissionEmployee's earnings method to calculate part of a BasePlusCommissionEmployee object's earnings, we *avoid duplicating the code* and *reduce code-maintenance problems.*

Common Programming Error 9.2

When a superclass method is overridden in a subclass, the subclass version often calls the superclass version to do a portion of the work. Failure to prefix the superclass method name with the keyword super *and the dot (.) separator when calling the superclass's method causes the subclass method to call itself, potentially creating an error called infinite recursion, which would eventually cause the method-call stack to overflow—a fatal runtime error. Recursion, used correctly, is a powerful capability discussed in Chapter 18.*

Class *BasePlusCommissionEmployee's* `toString` Method

Similarly, BasePlusCommissionEmployee's toString method (Fig. 9.11, lines 40–44) overrides CommissionEmployee's toString method (Fig. 9.10, lines 75–82) to return a String representation that's appropriate for a base-salaried commission employee. The new version creates part of a BasePlusCommissionEmployee object's String representation (i.e., the String "commission employee" and the values of class CommissionEmployee's private instance variables) by calling CommissionEmployee's toString method with the expression super.toString() (Fig. 9.11, line 43). BasePlusCommissionEmployee's toString method then completes the remainder of a BasePlusCommissionEmployee object's String representation (i.e., the value of class BasePlusCommissionEmployee's base salary).

Testing Class *BasePlusCommissionEmployee*

Class BasePlusCommissionEmployeeTest performs the same manipulations on a BasePlusCommissionEmployee object as in Fig. 9.7 and produces the same output, so we do not show it here. Although each BasePlusCommissionEmployee class you've seen behaves identically, the version in Fig. 9.11 is the best engineered. By using inheritance and by calling methods that hide the data and ensure consistency, we've efficiently and effectively constructed a well-engineered class.

9.5 Constructors in Subclasses

As we explained, instantiating a subclass object begins a chain of constructor calls in which the subclass constructor, before performing its own tasks, explicitly uses super to call one of the constructors in its direct superclass or implicitly calls the superclass's default or no-argument constructor. Similarly, if the superclass is derived from another class—true of every class except Object—the superclass constructor invokes the constructor of the next class up the hierarchy, and so on. The last constructor called in the chain is *always* Object's constructor. The original subclass constructor's body finishes executing *last*. Each superclass's constructor manipulates the superclass instance variables that the subclass object inherits. For example, consider again the CommissionEmployee–BasePlusCommissionEmployee hierarchy from Figs. 9.10–9.11. When an app creates a BasePlusCommissionEmployee object, its constructor is called. That constructor calls CommissionEmployee's constructor, which in turn calls Object's constructor. Class Object's constructor has an *empty body*, so it immediately returns control to CommissionEmployee's constructor, which then initializes the CommissionEmployee instance variables that are part of the

BasePlusCommissionEmployee object. When CommissionEmployee's constructor completes execution, it returns control to BasePlusCommissionEmployee's constructor, which initializes the baseSalary.

Software Engineering Observation 9.9

Java ensures that even if a constructor does not assign a value to an instance variable, the variable is still initialized to its default value (e.g., 0 for primitive numeric types, false for booleans, null for references).

9.6 Class Object

As we discussed earlier in this chapter, all classes in Java inherit directly or indirectly from class Object (package java.lang), so its 11 methods (some are overloaded) are inherited by all other classes. Figure 9.12 summarizes Object's methods. We discuss several Object methods throughout this book (as indicated in Fig. 9.12).

Method	Description
equals	This method compares two objects for equality and returns true if they're equal and false otherwise. The method takes any Object as an argument. When objects of a particular class must be compared for equality, the class should override method equals to compare the *contents* of the two objects. For the requirements of implementing this method (which include also overriding method hashCode), refer to the method's documentation at http://docs.oracle.com/javase/8/docs/api/java/lang/Object.html. The default equals implementation uses operator == to determine whether two references *refer to the same object* in memory. Section 14.3.3 demonstrates class String's equals method and differentiates between comparing String objects with == and with equals.
hashCode	Hashcodes are int values used for high-speed storage and retrieval of information stored in a hashtable data structure (see Section 16.10). This method is also called as part of Object's default toString method implementation.
toString	This method (introduced in Section 9.4.1) returns a String representation of an object. The default implementation of this method returns the package name and class name of the object's class typically followed by a hexadecimal representation of the value returned by the object's hashCode method.
wait, notify, notifyAll	Methods notify, notifyAll and the three overloaded versions of wait are related to multithreading, which is discussed in Chapter 21.
getClass	Every object in Java knows its own type at execution time. Method getClass (used in Sections 10.5– and 12.5) returns an object of class Class (package java.lang) that contains information about the object's type, such as its class name (returned by Class method getName).
finalize	This protected method is called by the garbage collector to perform termination housekeeping on an object just before the garbage collector reclaims the object's memory. Recall from Section 8.10 that it's unclear whether, or when, finalize will be called. For this reason, most programmers should avoid method finalize.

Fig. 9.12 | Object methods. (Part 1 of 2.)

Method	Description
clone	This **protected** method, which takes no arguments and returns an **Object** reference, makes a copy of the object on which it's called. The default implementation performs a so-called **shallow copy**—instance-variable values in one object are copied into another object of the same type. For reference types, only the references are copied. A typical overridden **clone** method's implementation would perform a **deep copy** that creates a new object for each reference-type instance variable. *Implementing **clone** correctly is difficult. For this reason, its use is discouraged.* Some industry experts suggest that object serialization should be used instead. We discuss object serialization in Chapter 15. Recall from Chapter 7 that arrays are objects. As a result, like all other objects, arrays inherit the members of class **Object**. Every array has an overridden **clone** method that copies the array. However, if the array stores references to objects, the objects are not copied—a shallow copy is performed.

Fig. 9.12 | Object methods. (Part 2 of 2.)

9.7 Designing with Composition vs. Inheritance

There's much discussion in the software engineering community about the relative merits of composition and inheritance. Each has its own place, but inheritance is often overused and composition is more appropriate in many cases. A mix of composition and inheritance often is a reasonable design approach.[1]

Software Engineering Observation 9.10

In industry, problem solving often requires interaction among many colleagues. Rarely will you be able to get everyone on a project to agree on the "right" approach to a solution. Also, rarely will any particular approach be "perfect." You'll often compare the relative merits of different approaches, as we do in this section.

Inheritance-Based Designs

Inheritance creates *tight coupling* among the classes in a hierarchy—each subclass typically depends on its direct or indirect superclasses' implementations. Changes in superclass implementation can affect the behavior of subclasses, often in subtle ways. Tightly coupled designs are more difficult to modify than those in loosely coupled, composition-based designs (discussed momentarily). Change is the rule rather than the exception—this encourages composition.

In general, you should use inheritance only for true *is-a* relationships in which you can assign a subclass object to a superclass reference. When you invoke a method via a superclass reference to a subclass object, the subclass's corresponding method executes. This is called polymorphic behavior, which we explore in Chapter 10.

---

1. The concepts we present in this section are widely discussed in the software engineering community and derived from many sources, most notably the books: Gamma, Erich et al. *Design Patterns: Elements of Reusable Object-Oriented Software*. Reading, MA: Addison-Wesley, 1995, and Bloch, Joshua. *Effective Java*. Upper Saddle River, NJ: Addison-Wesley, 2008.

Software Engineering Observation 9.11

Some of the difficulties with inheritance occur on large projects where different classes in the hierarchy are controlled by different people. An inheritance hierarchy is less problematic when it's entirely under one person's control.

Composition-Based Designs

Composition is loosely coupled. When you compose a reference as an instance variable of a class, it's part of the class's implementation details that are hidden from the class's client code. If the reference's class type changes, you may need to make changes to the composing class's internal details, but those changes do not affect the client code.

In addition, inheritance is done at compile time. Composition is more flexible—it, too, can be done at compile time, but it also can be done at execution time because non-final references to composed objects can be modified. We call this dynamic composition. This is another aspect of loose coupling—if the reference is of a superclass type, you can replace the referenced object with an object of *any* type that has an *is-a* relationship with the reference's class type.

When you use a composition approach instead of inheritance, you'll typically create a larger number of smaller classes, each focused on one responsibility. Smaller classes generally are easier to test, debug and modify.

Java does not offer multiple inheritance—each class in Java may extend only one class. However, a new class may reuse the capabilities of one or more other classes by composition. As you'll see in Chapter 10, Object-Oriented Programming: Polymorphism and Interfaces, we also can get many of the benefits of multiple inheritance by implementing multiple interfaces.

Performance Tip 9.1

A potential disadvantage of composition is that it typically requires more objects at runtime, which might negatively impact garbage-collection and virtual-memory performance.

Software Engineering Observation 9.12

A public method of a composing class can call a method of a composed object to perform a task for the benefit of the composing class's clients. This is known as forwarding the method call and is a common way to reuse a class's capabilities via composition rather than inheritance.

Software Engineering Observation 9.13

When implementing a new class and choosing whether you should reuse an existing class via inheritance or composition, use composition if the existing class's public methods should not be part of the new class's public interface.

9.8 Wrap-Up

This chapter introduced inheritance—the ability to create classes by acquiring an existing class's members (without copying and pasting the code) and having the ability to embellish them with new capabilities. You learned the notions of superclasses and subclasses and used keyword `extends` to create a subclass that inherits members from a superclass. We showed how to use the `@Override` annotation to prevent unintended overloading by indicating that a method overrides a superclass method. We introduced the access modifier `protected`; subclass methods can directly access `protected` superclass members. You learned how to use `super` to access overridden superclass members. You also saw how constructors are used in inheritance hierarchies. you learned about the methods of class `Object`, the direct or indirect superclass of all Java classes. Finally, we discussed designing classes with composition vs. inheritance.

In Chapter 10, Object-Oriented Programming: Polymorphism and Interfaces, we build on our discussion of inheritance by introducing *polymorphism*—an object-oriented concept that enables us to write programs that conveniently handle, in a more general and convenient manner, objects of a wide variety of classes related by inheritance, by interfaces or both. After studying Chapter 10, you'll be familiar with classes, objects, encapsulation, inheritance and polymorphism—the key technologies of object-oriented programming.

Object-Oriented Programming: Polymorphism and Interfaces

Objectives

In this chapter you'll:

- Learn the concept of polymorphism and how it enables "programming in the general."
- Use overridden methods to effect polymorphism.
- Distinguish between abstract and concrete classes.
- Declare abstract methods to create abstract classes.
- Learn how polymorphism makes systems extensible and maintainable.
- Determine an object's type at execution time.
- Declare and implement interfaces, and become familiar with the Java SE 8 interface enhancements.

10.1 Introduction

We continue our study of object-oriented programming by explaining and demonstrating **polymorphism** with inheritance hierarchies. Polymorphism enables you to "program in the *general*" rather than "program in the *specific*." In particular, polymorphism enables you to write programs that process objects that share the same superclass, either directly or indirectly, as if they were all objects of the superclass; this can simplify programming.

Consider the following example of polymorphism. Suppose we create a program that simulates the movement of several types of animals for a biological study. Classes Fish, Frog and Bird represent the types of animals under investigation. Imagine that each class extends superclass Animal, which contains a method move and maintains an animal's current location as *x-y* coordinates. Each subclass implements method move. Our program maintains an Animal array containing references to objects of the various Animal subclasses. To simulate the animals' movements, the program sends each object the *same* message once per second—namely, move. Each specific type of Animal responds to a move message in its own way—a Fish might swim three feet, a Frog might jump five feet and a Bird might fly ten feet. Each object knows how to modify its *x-y* coordinates appropriately for its *specific* type of movement. Relying on each object to know how to "do the right thing" (i.e., do what's appropriate for that type of object) in response to the *same* method call is the key concept of polymorphism. The *same* message (in this case, move) sent to a *variety* of objects has *many forms* of results—hence the term polymorphism.

Implementing for Extensibility

With polymorphism, we can design and implement systems that are easily *extensible*—new classes can be added with little or no modification to the general portions of the program, as long as the new classes are part of the inheritance hierarchy that the program processes generically. The new classes simply "plug right in." The only parts of a program that must be altered are those that require direct knowledge of the new classes that we add to the hierarchy. For example, if we extend class Animal to create class Tortoise (which might respond to a move message by crawling one inch), we need to write only the Tortoise class and the part of the simulation that instantiates a Tortoise object. The portions of the simulation that tell each Animal to move generically can remain the same.

Chapter Overview

First, we discuss common examples of polymorphism. We then provide a simple example demonstrating polymorphic behavior. We use superclass references to manipulate *both* superclass objects and subclass objects polymorphically.

We then present a case study that revisits the employee hierarchy of Section 9.4.5. We develop a simple payroll application that polymorphically calculates the weekly pay of several different types of employees using each employee's earnings method. Though the earnings of each type of employee are calculated in a *specific* way, polymorphism allows us to process the employees "in the *general*." In the case study, we enlarge the hierarchy to include two new classes—SalariedEmployee (for people paid a fixed weekly salary) and HourlyEmployee (for people paid an hourly salary and "time-and-a-half" for overtime). We declare the common functionality for all the classes in the updated hierarchy in an "abstract" Employee class from which "concrete" classes SalariedEmployee, HourlyEmployee and CommissionEmployee inherit directly and "concrete" class BasePlusCommissionEmployee inherits indirectly. As you'll see, *when we invoke each employee's earnings method off a superclass Employee reference (regardless of the employee's type), the correct earnings subclass calculation is performed,* due to Java's built-in polymorphic capabilities.

Programming in the Specific

Occasionally, when performing polymorphic processing, we need to program "in the *specific*." Our Employee case study demonstrates that a program can determine the *type* of an object at *execution time* and act on that object accordingly. In the case study, we've decided that BasePlusCommissionEmployees should receive 10% raises on their base salaries. So, we use these capabilities to determine whether a particular employee object *is a* BasePlusCommissionEmployee. If so, we increase that employee's base salary by 10%.

Interfaces

The chapter continues with an introduction to Java *interfaces*, which are particularly useful for assigning *common* functionality to possibly *unrelated* classes. This allows objects of these classes to be processed polymorphically—objects of classes that **implement** the *same* interface can respond to all of the interface method calls. To demonstrate creating and using interfaces, we modify our payroll application to create a generalized accounts payable application that can calculate payments due for company employees *and* invoice amounts to be billed for purchased goods.

10.2 Polymorphism Examples

Let's consider several additional examples of polymorphism.

Quadrilaterals

If class Rectangle is derived from class Quadrilateral, then a Rectangle object *is a* more *specific* version of a Quadrilateral. Any operation (e.g., calculating the perimeter or the area) that can be performed on a Quadrilateral can also be performed on a Rectangle. These operations can also be performed on other Quadrilaterals, such as Squares, Parallelograms and Trapezoids. The polymorphism occurs when a program invokes a method through a superclass Quadrilateral variable—at execution time, the correct subclass version of the method is called, based on the type of the reference stored in the superclass variable. You'll see a simple code example that illustrates this process in Section 10.3.

Space Objects in a Video Game

Suppose we design a video game that manipulates objects of classes Martian, Venusian, Plutonian, SpaceShip and LaserBeam. Imagine that each class inherits from the superclass SpaceObject, which contains method draw. Each subclass implements this method. A screen manager maintains a collection (e.g., a SpaceObject array) of references to objects of the various classes. To refresh the screen, the screen manager periodically sends each object the *same* message—namely, draw. However, each object responds its *own* way, based on its class. For example, a Martian object might draw itself in red with green eyes and the appropriate number of antennae. A SpaceShip object might draw itself as a bright silver flying saucer. A LaserBeam object might draw itself as a bright red beam across the screen. Again, the *same* message (in this case, draw) sent to a *variety* of objects has "many forms" of results.

A screen manager might use polymorphism to facilitate adding new classes to a system with minimal modifications to the system's code. Suppose that we want to add Mercurian objects to our video game. To do so, we'd build a class Mercurian that extends SpaceObject and provides its own draw method implementation. When Mercurian objects appear in the SpaceObject collection, the screen-manager code *invokes method draw, exactly as it does for every other object in the collection, regardless of its type.* So the new Mercurian objects simply "plug right in" without any modification of the screen-manager code by the programmer. Thus, without modifying the system (other than to build new classes and modify the code that creates new objects), you can use polymorphism to conveniently include additional types that were not even considered when the system was created.

Software Engineering Observation 10.1

Polymorphism enables you to deal in generalities and let the execution-time environment handle the specifics. You can tell objects to behave in manners appropriate to those objects, without knowing their specific types, as long as they belong to the same inheritance hierarchy.

Software Engineering Observation 10.2

Polymorphism promotes extensibility: Software that invokes polymorphic behavior is independent of the object types to which messages are sent. New object types that can respond to existing method calls can be incorporated into a system without modifying the base system. Only client code that instantiates new objects must be modified to accommodate new types.

10.3 Demonstrating Polymorphic Behavior

Section 9.4 created a class hierarchy, in which class BasePlusCommissionEmployee inherited from CommissionEmployee. The examples in that section manipulated CommissionEmployee and BasePlusCommissionEmployee objects by using references to them to invoke their methods—we aimed superclass variables at superclass objects and subclass variables at subclass objects. These assignments are natural and straightforward—superclass variables are *intended* to refer to superclass objects, and subclass variables are *intended* to refer to subclass objects. However, as you'll soon see, other assignments are possible.

In the next example, we aim a *superclass* reference at a *subclass* object. We then show how invoking a method on a subclass object via a superclass reference invokes the *subclass* functionality—the type of the *referenced object*, *not* the type of the *variable*, determines which method is called. This example demonstrates that *an object of a subclass can be treated as an object of its superclass,* enabling various interesting manipulations. A program can create an array of superclass variables that refer to objects of many subclass types. This is allowed because each subclass object *is an* object of its superclass. For example, we can assign the reference of a BasePlusCommissionEmployee object to a superclass CommissionEmployee variable, because a BasePlusCommissionEmployee *is a* CommissionEmployee—so we can treat a BasePlusCommissionEmployee as a CommissionEmployee.

As you'll learn later in the chapter, you *cannot treat a superclass object as a subclass object,* because a superclass object is *not* an object of any of its subclasses. For example, we cannot assign the reference of a CommissionEmployee object to a subclass BasePlusCommissionEmployee variable, because a CommissionEmployee is *not* a BasePlusCommissionEmployee—a CommissionEmployee does *not* have a baseSalary instance variable and does *not* have methods setBaseSalary and getBaseSalary. The *is-a* relationship applies only *up the hierarchy* from a subclass to its direct (and indirect) superclasses, and *not* vice versa (i.e., not down the hierarchy from a superclass to its subclasses or indirect subclasses).

The Java compiler *does* allow the assignment of a superclass reference to a subclass variable if we explicitly *cast* the superclass reference to the subclass type. Why would we ever want to perform such an assignment? A superclass reference can be used to invoke *only* the methods declared in the superclass—attempting to invoke *subclass-only* methods through a superclass reference results in compilation errors. If a program needs to perform a subclass-specific operation on a subclass object referenced by a superclass variable, the program must first cast the superclass reference to a subclass reference through a technique known as **downcasting**. This enables the program to invoke subclass methods that are *not* in the superclass. We demonstrate the mechanics of downcasting in Section 10.5.

Software Engineering Observation 10.3

Although it's allowed, you should generally avoid downcasting.

The example in Fig. 10.1 demonstrates three ways to use superclass and subclass variables to store references to superclass and subclass objects. The first two are straightforward—as in Section 9.4, we assign a superclass reference to a superclass variable, and a subclass reference to a subclass variable. Then we demonstrate the relationship between subclasses and superclasses (i.e., the *is-a* relationship) by assigning a subclass reference to a superclass variable. This program uses classes CommissionEmployee and BasePlusCommissionEmployee from Fig. 9.10 and Fig. 9.11, respectively.

```java
1   // Fig. 10.1: PolymorphismTest.java
2   // Assigning superclass and subclass references to superclass and
3   // subclass variables.
4
5   public class PolymorphismTest {
6      public static void main(String[] args) {
7         // assign superclass reference to superclass variable
8         CommissionEmployee commissionEmployee = new CommissionEmployee(
9            "Sue", "Jones", "222-22-2222", 10000, .06);
10
11        // assign subclass reference to subclass variable
12        BasePlusCommissionEmployee basePlusCommissionEmployee =
13           new BasePlusCommissionEmployee(
14           "Bob", "Lewis", "333-33-3333", 5000, .04, 300);
15
16        // invoke toString on superclass object using superclass variable
17        System.out.printf("%s %s:%n%n%s%n%n",
18           "Call CommissionEmployee's toString with superclass reference ",
19           "to superclass object", commissionEmployee.toString());
20
21        // invoke toString on subclass object using subclass variable
22        System.out.printf("%s %s:%n%n%s%n%n",
23           "Call BasePlusCommissionEmployee's toString with subclass",
24           "reference to subclass object",
25           basePlusCommissionEmployee.toString());
26
27        // invoke toString on subclass object using superclass variable
28        CommissionEmployee commissionEmployee2 =
29           basePlusCommissionEmployee;
30        System.out.printf("%s %s:%n%n%s%n",
31           "Call BasePlusCommissionEmployee's toString with superclass",
32           "reference to subclass object", commissionEmployee2.toString());
33     }
34  }
```

```
Call CommissionEmployee's toString with superclass reference to superclass
object:

commission employee: Sue Jones
social security number: 222-22-2222
gross sales: 10000.00
commission rate: 0.06

Call BasePlusCommissionEmployee's toString with subclass reference to
subclass object:

base-salaried commission employee: Bob Lewis
social security number: 333-33-3333
gross sales: 5000.00
commission rate: 0.04
base salary: 300.00
```

Fig. 10.1 | Assigning superclass and subclass references to superclass and subclass variables. (Part 1 of 2.)

```
Call BasePlusCommissionEmployee's toString with superclass reference to
subclass object:

base-salaried commission employee: Bob Lewis
social security number: 333-33-3333
gross sales: 5000.00
commission rate: 0.04
base salary: 300.00
```

Fig. 10.1 | Assigning superclass and subclass references to superclass and subclass variables. (Part 2 of 2.)

In Fig. 10.1, lines 8–9 create a CommissionEmployee object and assign its reference to a CommissionEmployee variable. Lines 12–14 create a BasePlusCommissionEmployee object and assign its reference to a BasePlusCommissionEmployee variable. These assignments are natural—for example, a CommissionEmployee variable's primary purpose is to hold a reference to a CommissionEmployee object. Lines 17–19 use commissionEmployee to invoke toString *explicitly*. Because commissionEmployee refers to a CommissionEmployee object, superclass CommissionEmployee's version of toString is called. Similarly, lines 22–25 use basePlusCommissionEmployee to invoke toString *explicitly* on the BasePlusCommissionEmployee object. This invokes subclass BasePlusCommissionEmployee's version of toString.

Lines 28–29 then assign the reference of subclass object basePlusCommissionEmployee to a superclass CommissionEmployee variable, which lines 30–32 use to invoke method toString. *When a superclass variable contains a reference to a subclass object, and that reference is used to call a method, the subclass version of the method is called.* Hence, commissionEmployee2.toString() in line 32 actually calls class BasePlusCommissionEmployee's toString method. The Java compiler allows this "crossover" because an object of a subclass *is an* object of its superclass (but *not* vice versa). When the compiler encounters a method call made through a variable, the compiler determines if the method can be called by checking the variable's class type. If that class contains the proper method declaration (or inherits one), the call is compiled. At execution time, the type of the object to which the variable refers determines the actual method to use. This process, called *dynamic binding*, is discussed in detail in Section 10.5.

10.4 Abstract Classes and Methods

When we think of a class, we assume that programs will create objects of that type. Sometimes it's useful to declare classes—called **abstract classes**—for which you *never* intend to create objects. Because they're used only as superclasses in inheritance hierarchies, we refer to them as **abstract superclasses**. These classes cannot be used to instantiate objects, because, as we'll soon see, abstract classes are *incomplete*. Subclasses must declare the "missing pieces" to become "concrete" classes, from which you can instantiate objects. Otherwise, these subclasses, too, will be abstract. We demonstrate abstract classes in Section 10.5.

Purpose of Abstract Classes

An abstract class's purpose is to provide an appropriate superclass from which other classes can inherit and thus share a common design. In the Shape hierarchy of Fig. 9.3, for example, subclasses inherit the notion of what it means to be a Shape—perhaps common attributes such as location, color and borderThickness, and behaviors such as draw, move, resize and changeColor. Classes that can be used to instantiate objects are called **concrete classes**. Such classes provide implementations of *every* method they declare (some of the implementations can be inherited). For example, we could derive concrete classes Circle, Square and Triangle from abstract superclass TwoDimensionalShape. Similarly, we could derive concrete classes Sphere, Cube and Tetrahedron from abstract superclass ThreeDimensionalShape. Abstract superclasses are *too general* to create real objects—they specify only what is common among subclasses. We need to be more *specific* before we can create objects. For example, if you send the draw message to abstract class TwoDimensionalShape, the class knows that two-dimensional shapes should be *drawable*, but it does not know what *specific* shape to draw, so it cannot implement a real draw method. Concrete classes provide the specifics that make it reasonable to instantiate objects.

Not all hierarchies contain abstract classes. However, you'll often write client code that uses only abstract superclass types to reduce the client code's dependencies on a range of subclass types. For example, you can write a method with a parameter of an abstract superclass type. When called, such a method can receive an object of *any* concrete class that directly or indirectly extends the superclass specified as the parameter's type.

Abstract classes sometimes constitute several levels of a hierarchy. For example, the Shape hierarchy of Fig. 9.3 begins with abstract class Shape. On the next level of the hierarchy are *abstract* classes TwoDimensionalShape and ThreeDimensionalShape. The next level of the hierarchy declares *concrete* classes for TwoDimensionalShapes (Circle, Square and Triangle) and for ThreeDimensionalShapes (Sphere, Cube and Tetrahedron).

Declaring an Abstract Class and Abstract Methods
You make a class abstract by declaring it with keyword **abstract**. An abstract class normally contains one or more **abstract methods**. An abstract method is an *instance method* with keyword abstract in its declaration, as in

```
public abstract void draw(); // abstract method
```

Abstract methods do *not* provide implementations. A class that contains *any* abstract methods must be explicitly declared abstract even if that class contains some concrete (nonabstract) methods. Each concrete subclass of an abstract superclass also must provide concrete implementations of each of the superclass's abstract methods. Constructors and static methods cannot be declared abstract. Constructors are *not* inherited, so an abstract constructor could never be implemented. Though non-private static methods are inherited, they cannot be overridden. Since abstract methods are meant to be overridden so that they can process objects based on their types, it would not make sense to declare a static method as abstract.

Software Engineering Observation 10.4
An abstract class declares common attributes and behaviors (both abstract and concrete) of the classes in a class hierarchy. An abstract class typically contains one or more abstract methods that subclasses must override if they are to be concrete. The instance variables and concrete methods of an abstract class are subject to the normal rules of inheritance.

Common Programming Error 10.1

Attempting to instantiate an object of an abstract class is a compilation error.

Common Programming Error 10.2

Classes must be declared abstract *if they declare* abstract *methods or if they inherit abstract methods and do not provide concrete implementations of them; otherwise, compilation errors occur.*

Using Abstract Classes to Declare Variables

Although we cannot instantiate objects of abstract superclasses, you'll soon see that we *can* use abstract superclasses to declare variables that can hold references to objects of *any* concrete class *derived from* those abstract superclasses. We'll use such variables to manipulate subclass objects *polymorphically*. You also can use abstract superclass names to invoke static methods declared in those abstract superclasses.

Consider another application of polymorphism. A drawing program needs to display many shapes, including types of new shapes that you'll *add* to the system *after* writing the drawing program. The drawing program might need to display shapes, such as Circles, Triangles, Rectangles or others, that derive from abstract class Shape. The drawing program uses Shape variables to manage the objects that are displayed. To draw any object in this inheritance hierarchy, the drawing program uses a superclass Shape variable containing a reference to the subclass object to invoke the object's draw method. This method is declared abstract in superclass Shape, so each concrete subclass *must* implement method draw in a manner specific to that shape—each object in the Shape inheritance hierarchy *knows how to draw itself*. The drawing program does not have to worry about the type of each object or whether the program has ever encountered objects of that type.

Layered Software Systems

Polymorphism is particularly effective for implementing so-called *layered software systems*. In operating systems, for example, each type of physical device could operate quite differently from the others. Even so, commands to read or write data from and to devices may have a certain uniformity. For each device, the operating system uses a piece of software called a *device driver* to control all communication between the system and the device. The write message sent to a device-driver object needs to be interpreted specifically in the context of that driver and how it manipulates devices of a specific type. However, the write call itself really is no different from the write to any other device in the system—place some number of bytes from memory onto that device. An object-oriented operating system might use an abstract superclass to provide an "interface" appropriate for all device drivers. Then, through inheritance from that abstract superclass, subclasses are formed that all behave similarly. The device-driver methods are declared as abstract methods in the abstract superclass. The implementations of these abstract methods are provided in the concrete subclasses that correspond to the specific types of device drivers. New devices are always being developed, often long after the operating system has been released. When you buy a new device, it comes with a device driver provided by the device vendor. The device is immediately operational after you connect it to your computer and install the driver. This is another elegant example of how polymorphism makes systems *extensible*.

10.5 Case Study: Payroll System Using Polymorphism

This section reexamines the CommissionEmployee-BasePlusCommissionEmployee hierarchy that we explored throughout Section 9.4. Now we use an abstract method and polymorphism to perform payroll calculations based on an enhanced employee inheritance hierarchy that meets the following requirements:

> *A company pays its employees on a weekly basis. The employees are of four types: Salaried employees are paid a fixed weekly salary regardless of the number of hours worked, hourly employees are paid by the hour and receive overtime pay (i.e., 1.5 times their hourly salary rate) for all hours worked in excess of 40 hours, commission employees are paid a percentage of their sales and base-salaried commission employees receive a base salary plus a percentage of their sales. For the current pay period, the company has decided to reward base-salaried commission employees by adding 10% to their base salaries. The company wants you to write an application that performs its payroll calculations polymorphically.*

We use abstract class Employee to represent the general concept of an employee. The classes that extend Employee are SalariedEmployee, CommissionEmployee and HourlyEmployee. Class BasePlusCommissionEmployee—which extends CommissionEmployee—represents the last employee type. The UML class diagram in Fig. 10.2 shows the inheritance hierarchy for our polymorphic employee-payroll application. Abstract class name Employee is *italicized*—a convention of the UML.

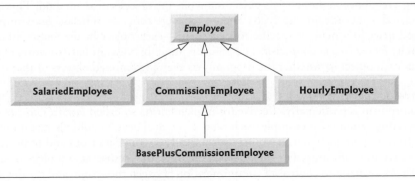

Fig. 10.2 | Employee hierarchy UML class diagram.

Abstract superclass Employee declares the "interface" to the hierarchy—that is, the set of methods that a program can invoke on all Employee objects. We use the term "interface" here in a *general* sense to refer to the various ways programs can communicate with objects of *any* Employee subclass. Be careful not to confuse the general notion of an "interface" with the formal notion of a Java interface, the subject of Section 10.9. Each employee, regardless of the way his or her earnings are calculated, has a first name, a last name and a social security number, so private instance variables firstName, lastName and socialSecurityNumber appear in abstract superclass Employee.

The diagram in Fig. 10.3 shows each of the five classes in the hierarchy down the left side and methods earnings and toString across the top. For each class, the diagram shows the desired results of each method. We do not list superclass Employee's *get* methods because they're *not* overridden in any of the subclasses—each of these methods is inherited and used "as is" by each subclass.

	earnings	toString
Employee	abstract	*firstName lastName* social security number: *SSN*
Salaried- Employee	weeklySalary	salaried employee: *firstName lastName* social security number: *SSN* weekly salary: *weeklySalary*

Hourly-
Employee
	if (hours <= 40) {
	  wage * hours
	}
	else if (hours > 40) {
	  40 * wage +
	  (hours - 40) *
	  wage * 1.5
	}
		hourly employee: *firstName lastName*
		social security number: *SSN*
		hourly wage: *wage*; hours worked: *hours*

Commission- Employee	commissionRate * grossSales	commission employee: *firstName lastName* social security number: *SSN* gross sales: *grossSales*; commission rate: *commissionRate*
BasePlus- Commission- Employee	(commissionRate * grossSales) + baseSalary	base salaried commission employee: *firstName lastName* social security number: *SSN* gross sales: *grossSales*; commission rate: *commissionRate*; base salary: *baseSalary*

Fig. 10.3 | Polymorphic interface for the `Employee` hierarchy classes.

The following sections implement the `Employee` class hierarchy of Fig. 10.2. The first section implements *abstract superclass* `Employee`. The next four sections each implement one of the *concrete* classes. The last section implements a test program that builds objects of all these classes and processes those objects polymorphically.

10.5.1 Abstract Superclass Employee

Class `Employee` (Fig. 10.4) provides methods `earnings` and `toString`, in addition to the *get* methods that return the values of `Employee`'s instance variables. An `earnings` method certainly applies *generically* to all employees. But each earnings calculation depends on the employee's particular class. So we declare `earnings` as abstract in superclass `Employee` because a *specific* default implementation does not make sense for that method—there isn't enough information to determine what amount `earnings` should return.

Each subclass overrides `earnings` with an appropriate implementation. To calculate an employee's earnings, the program assigns to a superclass `Employee` variable a reference to the employee's object, then invokes the `earnings` method on that variable. We maintain an array of `Employee` variables, each holding a reference to an `Employee` object. You *cannot* use class `Employee` directly to create `Employee` *objects*, because `Employee` is an *abstract* class. Due to inheritance, however, all objects of all `Employee` subclasses may be thought of as `Employee` objects. The program will iterate through the array and call method `earnings` for each `Employee` object. Java processes these method calls *polymorphically*. Declaring `earnings` as an `abstract` method in `Employee` enables the calls to `earnings` through `Employee` variables to compile and forces every direct *concrete* subclass of `Employee` to *override* `earnings`.

Method `toString` in class `Employee` returns a `String` containing the first name, last name and social security number of the employee. As we'll see, each subclass of `Employee` *overrides* method `toString` to create a `String` representation of an object of that class that contains the employee's type (e.g., `"salaried employee:"`) followed by the rest of the employee's information.

Let's consider class `Employee`'s declaration (Fig. 10.4). The class includes a constructor that receives the first name, last name and social security number (lines 10–15); *get* methods that return the first name, last name and social security number (lines 18, 21 and 24, respectively); method `toString` (lines 27–31), which returns the `String` representation of an `Employee`; and abstract method `earnings` (line 34), which will be implemented by each of the *concrete* subclasses. The `Employee` constructor does *not* validate its parameters in this example; normally, such validation should be provided.

```java
1   // Fig. 10.4: Employee.java
2   // Employee abstract superclass.
3
4   public abstract class Employee {
5      private final String firstName;
6      private final String lastName;
7      private final String socialSecurityNumber;
8
9      // constructor
10     public Employee(String firstName, String lastName,
11        String socialSecurityNumber) {
12        this.firstName = firstName;
13        this.lastName = lastName;
14        this.socialSecurityNumber = socialSecurityNumber;
15     }
16
17     // return first name
18     public String getFirstName() {return firstName;}
19
20     // return last name
21     public String getLastName() {return lastName;}
22
23     // return social security number
24     public String getSocialSecurityNumber() {return socialSecurityNumber;}
25
26     // return String representation of Employee object
27     @Override
28     public String toString() {
```

Fig. 10.4 | Employee abstract superclass. (Part 1 of 2.)

```
29          return String.format("%s %s%nsocial security number: %s",
30              getFirstName(), getLastName(), getSocialSecurityNumber());
31      }
32
33      // abstract method must be overridden by concrete subclasses
34      public abstract double earnings(); // no implementation here
35  }
```

Fig. 10.4 | Employee abstract superclass. (Part 2 of 2.)

Why did we decide to declare earnings as an abstract method? It simply does not make sense to provide a *specific* implementation of this method in class Employee. We cannot calculate the earnings for a *general* Employee—we first must know the *specific* type of Employee to determine the appropriate earnings calculation. By declaring this method abstract, we indicate that each concrete subclass *must* provide an appropriate earnings implementation and that a program will be able to use superclass Employee variables to invoke method earnings *polymorphically* for any type of Employee.

10.5.2 Concrete Subclass SalariedEmployee

Class SalariedEmployee (Fig. 10.5) extends class Employee (line 4) and overrides *abstract* method earnings (lines 34–35), which makes SalariedEmployee a *concrete* class. The class includes a constructor (lines 8–18) that receives a first name, a last name, a social security number and a weekly salary; a *set* method to assign a new *nonnegative* value to instance variable weeklySalary (lines 21–28); a *get* method to return weeklySalary's value (line 31); a method earnings (lines 34–35) to calculate a SalariedEmployee's earnings; and a method toString (lines 38–42), which returns a String including "salaried employee: " followed by employee-specific information produced by superclass Employee's toString method and SalariedEmployee's getWeeklySalary method. Class SalariedEmployee's constructor passes the first name, last name and social security number to the Employee constructor (line 10) to initialize the private instance variables of the superclass. Once again, we've duplicated the weeklySalary validation code in the constructor and the setWeeklySalary method. Recall that more complex validation could be placed in a static class method that's called from the constructor and the *set* method.

Error-Prevention Tip 10.1

We've said that you should not call a class's instance methods from its constructors—you can call static class methods and make the required call to one of the superclass's constructors. If you follow this advice, you'll avoid the problem of calling the class's overridable methods either directly or indirectly, which can lead to runtime errors. See Section 10.8 for additional details.

```
1   // Fig. 10.5: SalariedEmployee.java
2   // SalariedEmployee concrete class extends abstract class Employee.
3
4   public class SalariedEmployee extends Employee {
```

Fig. 10.5 | SalariedEmployee concrete class extends abstract class Employee. (Part 1 of 2.)

```
 5      private double weeklySalary;
 6
 7      // constructor
 8      public SalariedEmployee(String firstName, String lastName,
 9         String socialSecurityNumber, double weeklySalary) {
10         super(firstName, lastName, socialSecurityNumber);
11
12         if (weeklySalary < 0.0) {
13            throw new IllegalArgumentException(
14               "Weekly salary must be >= 0.0");
15         }
16
17         this.weeklySalary = weeklySalary;
18      }
19
20      // set salary
21      public void setWeeklySalary(double weeklySalary) {
22         if (weeklySalary < 0.0) {
23            throw new IllegalArgumentException(
24               "Weekly salary must be >= 0.0");
25         }
26
27         this.weeklySalary = weeklySalary;
28      }
29
30      // return salary
31      public double getWeeklySalary() {return weeklySalary;}
32
33      // calculate earnings; override abstract method earnings in Employee
34      @Override
35      public double earnings() {return getWeeklySalary();}
36
37      // return String representation of SalariedEmployee object
38      @Override
39      public String toString() {
40         return String.format("salaried employee: %s%n%s: $%,.2f",
41            super.toString(), "weekly salary", getWeeklySalary());
42      }
43   }
```

Fig. 10.5 | SalariedEmployee concrete class extends abstract class Employee. (Part 2 of 2.)

Method earnings overrides Employee's *abstract* method earnings to provide a *concrete* implementation that returns the SalariedEmployee's weekly salary. If we do not implement earnings, class SalariedEmployee must be declared abstract—otherwise, class SalariedEmployee will not compile. Of course, we want SalariedEmployee to be a *concrete* class in this example.

Method toString (lines 38–42) overrides Employee's toString. If class SalariedEmployee did *not* override toString, it would have inherited Employee's version. In that case, SalariedEmployee's toString method would simply return the employee's full name and social security number, which does *not* adequately represent a SalariedEmployee. To produce a complete String representation of a SalariedEmployee, the subclass's `toString` method returns "salaried employee: " followed by the superclass `Employee`-specific information (i.e., first name, last name and social security number) obtained by invoking the *superclass's* `toString` method (line 41)—this is a nice example of *code reuse*. The `String` representation of a `SalariedEmployee` also contains the employee's weekly salary obtained by invoking the class's `getWeeklySalary` method.

10.5.3 Concrete Subclass `HourlyEmployee`

Class `HourlyEmployee` (Fig. 10.6) also extends `Employee` (line 4). The class includes a constructor (lines 9–24) that receives a first name, a last name, a social security number, an hourly wage and the number of hours worked. Lines 27–33 and 39–46 declare *set* methods that assign new values to instance variables `wage` and `hours`, respectively. Method `setWage` ensures that `wage` is *nonnegative*, and method `setHours` ensures that the value of `hours` is between 0 and 168 (the total number of hours in a week) inclusive. Class `HourlyEmployee` also includes *get* methods (lines 36 and 49) to return the values of `wage` and `hours`, respectively; a method `earnings` (lines 52–60) to calculate an `HourlyEmployee`'s earnings; and a method `toString` (lines 63–68), which returns a `String` containing the employee's type ("hourly employee: ") and the employee-specific information. The `HourlyEmployee` constructor, like the `SalariedEmployee` constructor, passes the first name, last name and social security number to the superclass `Employee` constructor (line 11) to initialize the `private` instance variables. In addition, method `toString` calls *superclass* method `toString` (line 66) to obtain the `Employee`-specific information (i.e., first name, last name and social security number)—this is another nice example of *code reuse*.

```
1   // Fig. 10.6: HourlyEmployee.java
2   // HourlyEmployee class extends Employee.
3
4   public class HourlyEmployee extends Employee {
5      private double wage; // wage per hour
6      private double hours; // hours worked for week
7
8      // constructor
9      public HourlyEmployee(String firstName, String lastName,
10        String socialSecurityNumber, double wage, double hours) {
11        super(firstName, lastName, socialSecurityNumber);
12
13        if (wage < 0.0) { // validate wage
14           throw new IllegalArgumentException("Hourly wage must be >= 0.0");
15        }
16
17        if ((hours < 0.0) || (hours > 168.0)) { // validate hours
18           throw new IllegalArgumentException(
19              "Hours worked must be >= 0.0 and <= 168.0");
20        }
21
22        this.wage = wage;
23        this.hours = hours;
24     }
25
```

Fig. 10.6 | `HourlyEmployee` class extends `Employee`. (Part 1 of 2.)

```
26    // set wage
27    public void setWage(double wage) {
28        if (wage < 0.0) { // validate wage
29            throw new IllegalArgumentException("Hourly wage must be >= 0.0");
30        }
31
32        this.wage = wage;
33    }
34
35    // return wage
36    public double getWage() {return wage;}
37
38    // set hours worked
39    public void setHours(double hours) {
40        if ((hours < 0.0) || (hours > 168.0)) { // validate hours
41            throw new IllegalArgumentException(
42                "Hours worked must be >= 0.0 and <= 168.0");
43        }
44
45        this.hours = hours;
46    }
47
48    // return hours worked
49    public double getHours() {return hours;}
50
51    // calculate earnings; override abstract method earnings in Employee
52    @Override
53    public double earnings() {
54        if (getHours() <= 40) { // no overtime
55            return getWage() * getHours();
56        }
57        else {
58            return 40 * getWage() + (getHours() - 40) * getWage() * 1.5;
59        }
60    }
61
62    // return String representation of HourlyEmployee object
63    @Override
64    public String toString() {
65        return String.format("hourly employee: %s%n%s: $%,.2f; %s: %,.2f",
66            super.toString(), "hourly wage", getWage(),
67            "hours worked", getHours());
68    }
69 }
```

Fig. 10.6 | HourlyEmployee class extends Employee. (Part 2 of 2.)

10.5.4 Concrete Subclass CommissionEmployee

Class CommissionEmployee (Fig. 10.7) extends class Employee (line 4). The class includes a constructor (lines 9–25) that takes a first name, a last name, a social security number, a sales amount and a commission rate; *set* methods (lines 28–34 and 40–47) to assign valid new values to instance variables grossSales and commissionRate, respectively; *get* methods (lines 37 and 50) that retrieve the values of these instance variables; method earnings (lines 53–56) to calculate a CommissionEmployee's earnings; and method toString (lines 59–65), which returns "commission employee: " followed by the employee's specific information. The constructor also passes the first name, last name and social security number to *superclass* Employee's constructor (line 12) to initialize Employee's private instance variables. Method toString calls *superclass* method toString (line 62) to obtain the Employee-specific information (i.e., first name, last name and social security number).

```java
1   // Fig. 10.7: CommissionEmployee.java
2   // CommissionEmployee class extends Employee.
3
4   public class CommissionEmployee extends Employee {
5      private double grossSales; // gross weekly sales
6      private double commissionRate; // commission percentage
7
8      // constructor
9      public CommissionEmployee(String firstName, String lastName,
10        String socialSecurityNumber, double grossSales,
11        double commissionRate) {
12        super(firstName, lastName, socialSecurityNumber);
13
14        if (commissionRate <= 0.0 || commissionRate >= 1.0) { // validate
15           throw new IllegalArgumentException(
16              "Commission rate must be > 0.0 and < 1.0");
17        }
18
19        if (grossSales < 0.0) { // validate
20           throw new IllegalArgumentException("Gross sales must be >= 0.0");
21        }
22
23        this.grossSales = grossSales;
24        this.commissionRate = commissionRate;
25     }
26
27     // set gross sales amount
28     public void setGrossSales(double grossSales) {
29        if (grossSales < 0.0) { // validate
30           throw new IllegalArgumentException("Gross sales must be >= 0.0");
31        }
32
33        this.grossSales = grossSales;
34     }
35
36     // return gross sales amount
37     public double getGrossSales() {return grossSales;}
38
39     // set commission rate
40     public void setCommissionRate(double commissionRate) {
41        if (commissionRate <= 0.0 || commissionRate >= 1.0) { // validate
42           throw new IllegalArgumentException(
43              "Commission rate must be > 0.0 and < 1.0");
44        }
```

Fig. 10.7 | CommissionEmployee class extends Employee. (Part 1 of 2.)

```
45
46            this.commissionRate = commissionRate;
47      }
48
49      // return commission rate
50      public double getCommissionRate() {return commissionRate;}
51
52      // calculate earnings; override abstract method earnings in Employee
53      @Override
54      public double earnings() {
55          return getCommissionRate() * getGrossSales();
56      }
57
58      // return String representation of CommissionEmployee object
59      @Override
60      public String toString() {
61          return String.format("%s: %s%n%s: $%,.2f; %s: %.2f",
62              "commission employee", super.toString(),
63              "gross sales", getGrossSales(),
64              "commission rate", getCommissionRate());
65      }
66  }
```

Fig. 10.7 | CommissionEmployee class extends Employee. (Part 2 of 2.)

10.5.5 Indirect Concrete Subclass BasePlusCommissionEmployee

Class BasePlusCommissionEmployee (Fig. 10.8) extends class CommissionEmployee (line 4) and therefore is an *indirect* subclass of class Employee. Class BasePlusCommissionEmployee has a constructor (lines 8–19) that receives a first name, a last name, a social security number, a sales amount, a commission rate and a base salary. It then passes all of these except the base salary to the CommissionEmployee constructor (lines 11–12) to initialize the superclass instance variables. BasePlusCommissionEmployee also contains a *set* method (lines 22–28) to assign a new value to instance variable baseSalary and a *get* method (line 31) to return baseSalary's value. Method earnings (lines 34–35) calculates a BasePlusCommissionEmployee's earnings. Line 35 in method earnings calls *superclass* CommissionEmployee's earnings method to calculate the commission-based portion of the employee's earnings—this is another nice example of *code reuse*. BasePlusCommissionEmployee's toString method (lines 38–43) creates a String representation of a BasePlusCommissionEmployee that contains "base-salaried", followed by the String obtained by invoking *superclass* CommissionEmployee's toString method (line 41), then the base salary. The result is a String beginning with "base-salaried commission employee" followed by the rest of the BasePlusCommissionEmployee's information. Recall that CommissionEmployee's toString obtains the employee's first name, last name and social security number by invoking the toString method of its *superclass* (i.e., Employee)— yet another example of *code reuse*. BasePlusCommissionEmployee's toString method initiates a *chain of method calls* that span all three levels of the Employee hierarchy.

```java
1   // Fig. 10.8: BasePlusCommissionEmployee.java
2   // BasePlusCommissionEmployee class extends CommissionEmployee.
3
4   public class BasePlusCommissionEmployee extends CommissionEmployee {
5      private double baseSalary; // base salary per week
6
7      // constructor
8      public BasePlusCommissionEmployee(String firstName, String lastName,
9         String socialSecurityNumber, double grossSales,
10        double commissionRate, double baseSalary) {
11        super(firstName, lastName, socialSecurityNumber,
12           grossSales, commissionRate);
13
14        if (baseSalary < 0.0) { // validate baseSalary
15           throw new IllegalArgumentException("Base salary must be >= 0.0");
16        }
17
18        this.baseSalary = baseSalary;
19     }
20
21     // set base salary
22     public void setBaseSalary(double baseSalary) {
23        if (baseSalary < 0.0) { // validate baseSalary
24           throw new IllegalArgumentException("Base salary must be >= 0.0");
25        }
26
27        this.baseSalary = baseSalary;
28     }
29
30     // return base salary
31     public double getBaseSalary() {return baseSalary;}
32
33     // calculate earnings; override method earnings in CommissionEmployee
34     @Override
35     public double earnings() {return getBaseSalary() + super.earnings();}
36
37     // return String representation of BasePlusCommissionEmployee object
38     @Override
39     public String toString() {
40        return String.format("%s %s; %s: $%,.2f",
41           "base-salaried", super.toString(),
42           "base salary", getBaseSalary());
43     }
44  }
```

Fig. 10.8 | BasePlusCommissionEmployee class extends CommissionEmployee.

10.5.6 Polymorphic Processing, Operator instanceof and Downcasting

To test our Employee hierarchy, the application in Fig. 10.9 creates an object of each of the four *concrete* classes SalariedEmployee, HourlyEmployee, CommissionEmployee and BasePlusCommissionEmployee. The program manipulates these objects *nonpolymorphically*, via variables of each object's own type, then *polymorphically*, using an array of Employee variables. While processing the objects polymorphically, the program increases the base salary of each BasePlusCommissionEmployee by 10%—this requires *determining the object's type at execution time*. Finally, the program polymorphically determines and outputs the *type* of each object in the Employee array. Lines 7–16 create objects of each of the four concrete Employee subclasses. Lines 20–28 output the String representation and earnings of each of these objects *nonpolymorphically*. Each object's toString method is called *implicitly* by printf when the object is output as a String with the %s format specifier.

```java
1   // Fig. 10.9: PayrollSystemTest.java
2   // Employee hierarchy test program.
3
4   public class PayrollSystemTest {
5      public static void main(String[] args) {
6         // create subclass objects
7         SalariedEmployee salariedEmployee =
8            new SalariedEmployee("John", "Smith", "111-11-1111", 800.00);
9         HourlyEmployee hourlyEmployee =
10           new HourlyEmployee("Karen", "Price", "222-22-2222", 16.75, 40);
11        CommissionEmployee commissionEmployee =
12           new CommissionEmployee(
13           "Sue", "Jones", "333-33-3333", 10000, .06);
14        BasePlusCommissionEmployee basePlusCommissionEmployee =
15           new BasePlusCommissionEmployee(
16           "Bob", "Lewis", "444-44-4444", 5000, .04, 300);
17
18        System.out.println("Employees processed individually:");
19
20        System.out.printf("%n%s%n%s: $%,.2f%n%n",
21           salariedEmployee, "earned", salariedEmployee.earnings());
22        System.out.printf("%s%n%s: $%,.2f%n%n",
23           hourlyEmployee, "earned", hourlyEmployee.earnings());
24        System.out.printf("%s%n%s: $%,.2f%n%n",
25           commissionEmployee, "earned", commissionEmployee.earnings());
26        System.out.printf("%s%n%s: $%,.2f%n%n",
27           basePlusCommissionEmployee,
28           "earned", basePlusCommissionEmployee.earnings());
29
30        // create four-element Employee array
31        Employee[] employees = new Employee[4];
32
33        // initialize array with Employees
34        employees[0] = salariedEmployee;
35        employees[1] = hourlyEmployee;
36        employees[2] = commissionEmployee;
37        employees[3] = basePlusCommissionEmployee;
38
39        System.out.printf("Employees processed polymorphically:%n%n");
40
41        // generically process each element in array employees
42        for (Employee currentEmployee : employees) {
43           System.out.println(currentEmployee); // invokes toString
```

Fig. 10.9 | Employee hierarchy test program. (Part 1 of 3.)

```
44
45          // determine whether element is a BasePlusCommissionEmployee
46          if (currentEmployee instanceof BasePlusCommissionEmployee) {
47             // downcast Employee reference to
48             // BasePlusCommissionEmployee reference
49             BasePlusCommissionEmployee employee =
50                (BasePlusCommissionEmployee) currentEmployee;
51
52             employee.setBaseSalary(1.10 * employee.getBaseSalary());
53
54             System.out.printf(
55                "new base salary with 10%% increase is: $%,.2f%n",
56                employee.getBaseSalary());
57          }
58
59          System.out.printf(
60             "earned $%,.2f%n%n", currentEmployee.earnings());
61       }
62
63       // get type name of each object in employees array
64       for (int j = 0; j < employees.length; j++) {
65          System.out.printf("Employee %d is a %s%n", j,
66             employees[j].getClass().getName());
67       }
68    }
69 }
```

```
Employees processed individually:

salaried employee: John Smith
social security number: 111-11-1111
weekly salary: $800.00
earned: $800.00

hourly employee: Karen Price
social security number: 222-22-2222
hourly wage: $16.75; hours worked: 40.00
earned: $670.00

commission employee: Sue Jones
social security number: 333-33-3333
gross sales: $10,000.00; commission rate: 0.06
earned: $600.00

base-salaried commission employee: Bob Lewis
social security number: 444-44-4444
gross sales: $5,000.00; commission rate: 0.04; base salary: $300.00
earned: $500.00

Employees processed polymorphically:

salaried employee: John Smith
social security number: 111-11-1111
weekly salary: $800.00
earned $800.00
```

Fig. 10.9 | Employee hierarchy test program. (Part 2 of 3.)

```
hourly employee: Karen Price
social security number: 222-22-2222
hourly wage: $16.75; hours worked: 40.00
earned $670.00

commission employee: Sue Jones
social security number: 333-33-3333
gross sales: $10,000.00; commission rate: 0.06
earned $600.00

base-salaried commission employee: Bob Lewis
social security number: 444-44-4444
gross sales: $5,000.00; commission rate: 0.04; base salary: $300.00
new base salary with 10% increase is: $330.00
earned $530.00

Employee 0 is a SalariedEmployee
Employee 1 is a HourlyEmployee
Employee 2 is a CommissionEmployee
Employee 3 is a BasePlusCommissionEmployee
```

Fig. 10.9 | Employee hierarchy test program. (Part 3 of 3.)

Creating the Array of Employees

Line 31 declares employees and assigns it an array of four Employee variables. Lines 34–37 assign to the elements a reference to a SalariedEmployee, an HourlyEmployee, a CommissionEmployee and a BasePlusCommissionEmployee, respectively. These assignments are allowed, because a SalariedEmployee *is an* Employee, an HourlyEmployee *is an* Employee, a CommissionEmployee *is an* Employee and a BasePlusCommissionEmployee *is an* Employee. Therefore, we can assign the references of SalariedEmployee, HourlyEmployee, CommissionEmployee and BasePlusCommissionEmployee objects to *superclass* Employee variables, *even though Employee is an abstract class.*

Polymorphically Processing Employees

Lines 42–61 iterate through array employees and invoke methods toString and earnings with Employee variable currentEmployee, which is assigned the reference to a different Employee in the array on each iteration. The output illustrates that the specific methods for each class are indeed invoked. All calls to method toString and earnings are resolved at *execution* time, based on the *type* of the object to which currentEmployee refers. This process is known as **dynamic binding** or **late binding**. For example, line 43 *implicitly* invokes method toString of the object to which currentEmployee refers. As a result of *dynamic binding*, Java decides which class's toString method to call *at execution time rather than at compile time.* Only the methods of class Employee can be called via an Employee variable (and Employee, of course, includes the methods of class Object). A superclass reference can be used to invoke only methods of the *superclass—the subclass* method implementations are invoked *polymorphically.*

Performing Type-Specific Operations on BasePlusCommissionEmployees

We perform special processing on BasePlusCommissionEmployee objects—as we encounter these objects at execution time, we increase their base salary by 10%. When processing objects *polymorphically*, we typically do not need to worry about the *specifics*, but to adjust the base salary, we *do* have to determine the *specific* type of Employee object at *execution time*. Line 46 uses the **instanceof** operator to determine whether a particular Employee object's type is BasePlusCommissionEmployee. The condition in line 46 is *true* if the object referenced by currentEmployee *is a* BasePlusCommissionEmployee. This would also be *true* for any object of a BasePlusCommissionEmployee subclass because of the *is-a* relationship a subclass has with its superclass. Lines 49–50 *downcast* currentEmployee from type Employee to type BasePlusCommissionEmployee—this cast is allowed only if the object has an *is-a* relationship with BasePlusCommissionEmployee. The condition at line 46 ensures that this is the case. This cast is required if we're to invoke subclass BasePlusCommissionEmployee methods getBaseSalary and setBaseSalary on the current Employee object—as you'll see momentarily, *attempting to invoke a subclass-only method directly on a superclass reference is a compilation error.*

Common Programming Error 10.3

Assigning a superclass variable to a subclass variable is a compilation error.

Common Programming Error 10.4

When downcasting a reference, a ClassCastException *occurs if the referenced object at execution time does not have an* is-a *relationship with the type specified in the cast operator.*

If the instanceof expression in line 46 is true, lines 49–56 perform the special processing required for the BasePlusCommissionEmployee object. Using BasePlusCommissionEmployee variable employee, line 52 invokes subclass-only methods getBaseSalary and setBaseSalary to retrieve and update the employee's base salary with the 10% raise.

Calling earnings Polymorphically

Lines 59–60 invoke method earnings on currentEmployee, which polymorphically calls the appropriate subclass object's earnings method. Obtaining the earnings of the SalariedEmployee, HourlyEmployee and CommissionEmployee polymorphically in lines 59–60 produces the same results as obtaining these employees' earnings individually in lines 20–25. The earnings amount obtained for the BasePlusCommissionEmployee in lines 59–60 is higher than that obtained in lines 26–28, due to the 10% increase in its base salary.

Getting Each Employee's Class Name

Lines 64–67 display each employee's type as a String. Every object *knows its own class* and can access this information through the **getClass** method, which all classes inherit from class Object. Method getClass returns an object of type **Class** (from package java.lang), which contains information about the object's type, including its class name. Line 66 invokes getClass on the current object to get its class. The result of the getClass call is used to invoke **getName** to get the object's class name.

Avoiding Compilation Errors with Downcasting

In the previous example, we avoided several compilation errors by *downcasting* an Employee variable to a BasePlusCommissionEmployee variable in lines 49–50. If you remove the cast operator (BasePlusCommissionEmployee) from line 50 and attempt to assign Employee variable `currentEmployee` directly to `BasePlusCommissionEmployee` variable em-ployee, you'll receive an "`incompatible types`" compilation error. This error indicates that the attempt to assign the reference of superclass object `currentEmployee` to subclass variable `employee` is *not* allowed. The compiler prevents this assignment because a `CommissionEmployee` is *not* a `BasePlusCommissionEmployee`—*the* is-a *relationship applies only between the subclass and its superclasses, not vice versa.*

Similarly, if lines 52 and 56 used superclass variable `currentEmployee` to invoke sub-class-only methods `getBaseSalary` and `setBaseSalary`, we'd receive "`cannot find symbol`" compilation errors at these lines. Attempting to invoke subclass-only methods via a superclass variable is *not* allowed—even though lines 52 and 56 execute only if `instanceof` in line 46 returns `true` to indicate that `currentEmployee` holds a reference to a `BasePlusCommissionEmployee` object. Using a superclass `Employee` variable, we can invoke only methods found in class `Employee`—`earnings`, `toString` and `Employee`'s *get* and *set* methods.

Software Engineering Observation 10.5

Although the actual method that's called depends on the runtime type of the object to which a variable refers, a variable can be used to invoke only those methods that are members of that variable's type, which the compiler verifies.

10.6 Allowed Assignments Between Superclass and Subclass Variables

Now that you've seen a complete application that processes diverse subclass objects *polymorphically*, we summarize what you can and cannot do with superclass and subclass objects and variables. Although a subclass object also *is a* superclass object, the two classes are nevertheless different. As discussed previously, subclass objects can be treated as objects of their superclass. But because the subclass can have additional subclass-only members, assigning a superclass reference to a subclass variable is not allowed without an *explicit cast*—such an assignment would leave the subclass members undefined for the superclass object.

We've discussed three proper ways to assign superclass and subclass references to variables of superclass and subclass types:

1. Assigning a superclass reference to a superclass variable is straightforward.
2. Assigning a subclass reference to a subclass variable is straightforward.
3. Assigning a subclass reference to a superclass variable is safe, because the subclass object *is an* object of its superclass. However, the superclass variable can be used to refer *only* to superclass members. If this code refers to subclass-only members through the superclass variable, the compiler reports errors.

10.7 `final` Methods and Classes

We saw in Sections 6.3– and 6.9 that variables can be declared `final` to indicate that they cannot be modified *after* they're initialized—such variables represent constant values. You also declare method parameters `final` to prevent them from being modified in the method's body. It's also possible to declare methods and classes with the `final` modifier.

Final Methods Cannot Be Overridden

A **final method** in a superclass *cannot* be overridden in a subclass—this guarantees that the final method implementation will be used by all direct and indirect subclasses in the hierarchy. Methods that are declared private are implicitly final, because it's not possible to override them in a subclass. Methods that are declared static are also implicitly final. A final method's declaration can never change, so all subclasses use the same method implementation, and calls to final methods are resolved at compile time—this is known as **static binding**.

Final Classes Cannot Be Superclasses

A **final class** cannot be extended to create a subclass. All methods in a final class are implicitly final. Class String is an example of a final class. If you were allowed to create a subclass of String, objects of that subclass could be used wherever Strings are expected. Since class String cannot be extended, programs that use Strings can rely on the functionality of String objects as specified in the Java API. Making the class final also prevents programmers from creating subclasses that might bypass security restrictions.

We've now discussed declaring variables, methods and classes final, and we've emphasized that if something *can* be final it *should* be final—this is another example of the *principle of least privilege*. When we study concurrency in Chapter 21, you'll see that final variables make it much easier to parallelize your programs for use on today's multicore processors. For more insights on the use of final, visit

> http://docs.oracle.com/javase/tutorial/java/IandI/final.html

Common Programming Error 10.5

Attempting to declare a subclass of a final class is a compilation error.

Software Engineering Observation 10.6

In the Java API, the vast majority of classes are not declared final. This enables inheritance and polymorphism. However, in some cases, it's important to declare classes final—typically for security reasons. Also, unless you carefully design a class for extension, you should declare the class as final to avoid (often subtle) errors.

Software Engineering Observation 10.7

Though final classes cannot be extended, you can reuse them via composition.

10.8 A Deeper Explanation of Issues with Calling Methods from Constructors

We've stated that you should not call overridable methods from constructors. To understand why, recall that when you construct a subclass object, the *subclass* constructor first calls a constructor in its direct *superclass*. At this point, any subclass instance-variable initialization code in the subclass constructor's body has not yet executed. If the *superclass* constructor then calls a method that the subclass overrides, the *subclass's* version executes. This could lead to subtle, difficult-to-detect errors if the subclass method uses instance variables that have not yet been initialized properly, because the subclass constructor hasn't finished executing.

Let's assume that a constructor and a *set* method perform the same validation for a particular instance variable. How should you handle the common code?

- If the validation code is brief, you can duplicate it in the constructor and the *set* method. This is a simple way to eliminate the problem we're considering here.

- For lengthier validation, you can define a static validation method—typically a private static helper method—then call it from the constructor and from the *set* method. It's acceptable to call a static method from a constructor, because static methods are not overridable.

It's also acceptable for a constructor to call a final instance method, provided that the method does not directly or indirectly call any overridable instance methods.

10.9 Creating and Using Interfaces

8

[Note: Java SE 8 interface enhancements are introduced in Section 10.10 and discussed in more detail in Chapter 17. Java SE 9 interface enhancements are introduced in Section 10.11.]
Our next example (Figs. 10.11–10.14) reexamines the payroll system of Section 10.5. Suppose that the company involved wishes to perform several accounting operations in a single accounts payable application—in addition to calculating the earnings that must be paid to each employee, the company must also calculate the payment due on each of several invoices (i.e., bills for goods purchased). Though applied to *unrelated* things—employees and invoices—both operations have to do with obtaining a payment amount. For an employee, the payment is the employee's earnings. For an invoice, the payment is the total cost of the goods listed on the invoice. Can we calculate such *different* things as the payments due for employees and invoices in *a single* application *polymorphically*? Does Java offer a capability requiring that *unrelated* classes implement a set of *common* methods (e.g., a method that calculates a payment amount)? Java **interfaces** offer exactly this capability.

Standardizing Interactions

Interfaces define and standardize the ways in which things such as people and systems can interact with one another. For example, the controls on a radio serve as an interface between radio users and a radio's internal components. The controls allow users to perform only a limited set of operations (e.g., change the station, adjust the volume, choose between AM and FM), and different radios may implement the controls in different ways (e.g., using push buttons, dials, voice commands). The interface specifies *what* operations a radio must permit users to perform but does not specify *how* the operations are performed.

Similarly, in our car analogy from Section 1.2, a "basic-driving-capabilities" interface consisting of a steering wheel, an accelerator pedal and a brake pedal would enable a driver to tell the car *what* to do. Once you know how to use this interface for turning, accelerating and braking, you can drive many types of cars, even though manufacturers may *implement* these systems *differently*. For example, there are many types of braking systems—disc brakes, drum brakes, antilock brakes, hydraulic brakes, air brakes and more. When you press the brake pedal, your car's actual brake system is irrelevant—all that matters is that the car slows down when you press the brake.

Software Objects Communicate Via Interfaces

Software objects also communicate via interfaces. A Java interface describes a set of methods that can be called on an object to tell it, for example, to perform some task or return some piece of information. The next example introduces an interface named `Payable` to describe the functionality of any object that must be "capable of being paid" and thus must offer a method to determine the proper payment amount due. An **interface declaration** begins with the keyword **interface** and contains *only* constants and abstract methods. Unlike classes, all interface members *must* be `public`, and *interfaces may not specify any implementation details*, such as concrete method declarations and instance variables.[1] All methods declared in an interface are implicitly `public abstract` methods, and all fields are implicitly `public`, `static` and `final`.

Using an Interface

To use an interface, a concrete class must specify that it **implements** the interface and must declare each method in the interface with the signature specified in the interface declaration. To specify that a class implements an interface, add the `implements` keyword and the name of the interface to the end of your class declaration's first line, as in:

> **public class** *ClassName* **extends** *SuperclassName* **implements** *InterfaceName*

or

> **public class** *ClassName* **implements** *InterfaceName*

InterfaceName in the preceding snippets may be a comma-separated list of interface names.

Implementing an interface is like signing a *contract* with the compiler that states, "I will declare all the `abstract` methods specified by the interface or I will declare my class `abstract`."

Common Programming Error 10.6

In a concrete class that `implements` an interface, failing to implement any of the interface's `abstract` methods results in a compilation error indicating that the class must be declared `abstract`.

Relating Disparate Types

An interface is often used when *disparate* classes—i.e., classes that are not related by a class hierarchy—need to share common methods and constants. This allows objects of *unrelated* classes to be processed *polymorphically*—objects of classes that implement the *same* interface can respond to the *same* method calls (for methods of that interface). You can create an interface that describes the desired functionality, then implement this interface in any classes that require that functionality. For example, in the accounts payable application developed in this section, we implement interface `Payable` in any class that must be able to calculate a payment amount (e.g., `Employee` and `Invoice`).

Interfaces vs. Abstract Classes

An interface should be used in place of an `abstract` class when there's no default implementation to inherit—that is, no fields and no concrete method implementations. Like `public`

---

1. Sections 10.10—10.11 introduce the Java SE 8 and Java SE 9 interface enhancements that allow method implementations and `private` methods, respectively, in interfaces.

abstract classes, interfaces are typically `public` types. Like a `public` class, a `public` interface must be declared in a file with the same name as the interface and the `.java` filename extension.

Software Engineering Observation 10.8

Many developers feel that interfaces are an even more important modeling technology than classes, especially with the interface enhancements in Java SE 8 (see Section 10.10).

Tagging Interfaces

A *tagging interface* (also called a *marker interface*) is an empty interfaces that have *no* methods or constant values. They're used to add *is-a* relationships to classes. For example, Java has a mechanism called *object serialization*, which can convert objects to byte representations and can convert those byte representations back to objects, using classes `ObjectOutputStream` and `ObjectInputStream`. To enable this mechanism to work with your objects, you simply have to *tag* them as `Serializable` by adding `implements Serializable` to the end of your class declaration's first line. Then all the objects of your class have the *is-a* relationship with `Serializable`—that's all it takes to implement basic object serialization.

10.9.1 Developing a `Payable` Hierarchy

To build an application that can determine payments for employees and invoices alike, we first create interface `Payable`, which contains method `getPaymentAmount` that returns a `double` amount that must be paid for an object of any class that implements the interface. Method `getPaymentAmount` is a general-purpose version of method `earnings` of the `Employee` hierarchy—method `earnings` calculates a payment amount specifically for an `Employee`, while `getPaymentAmount` can be applied to a broad range of possibly unrelated objects. After declaring interface `Payable`, we introduce class `Invoice`, which `implements` interface `Payable`. We then modify class `Employee` such that it also implements interface `Payable`.

Classes `Invoice` and `Employee` both represent things for which the company must be able to calculate a payment amount. Both classes implement the `Payable` interface, so a program can invoke method `getPaymentAmount` on `Invoice` objects and `Employee` objects alike. As we'll soon see, this enables the *polymorphic* processing of `Invoices` and `Employees` required for the company's accounts payable application.

Good Programming Practice 10.1

When declaring a method in an interface, choose a method name that describes the method's purpose in a general manner, because the method may be implemented by many unrelated classes.

UML Diagram Containing an Interface

The UML class diagram in Fig. 10.10 shows the interface and class hierarchy used in our accounts payable application. The hierarchy begins with interface `Payable`. The UML distinguishes an interface from classes by placing the word "interface" in guillemets (« and ») above the interface name. The UML expresses the relationship between a class and an interface through a relationship known as **realization**. A class is said to *realize*, or *implement*, the methods of an interface. A class diagram models a realization as a dashed arrow with a hollow arrowhead pointing from the implementing class to the interface. The diagram in Fig. 10.10 indicates that classes `Invoice` and `Employee` each realize interface `Payable`. As in the class diagram of Fig. 10.2, class `Employee` appears in *italics*, indicating that it's an *abstract class. Concrete* class `SalariedEmployee` extends `Employee`, *inheriting its superclass's realization relationship* with interface `Payable`.

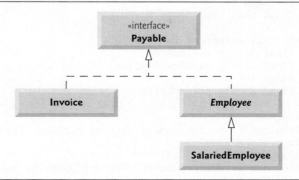

Fig. 10.10 | `Payable` hierarchy UML class diagram.

10.9.2 Interface `Payable`

Interface `Payable`'s declaration begins in Fig. 10.11 at line 4 with the `interface` keyword. The interface contains the `public abstract` method named `getPaymentAmount`. Interface methods are `public` and `abstract` by default, so they do not need to be declared as such. Interface `Payable` has only one method, but interfaces can have *any* number of methods. In addition, method `getPaymentAmount` has no parameters, but interface methods *can* have parameters. Interfaces may also contain `final static` constants.

> **Good Programming Practice 10.2**
> *Use `public` and `abstract` explicitly when declaring interface methods to make your intentions clear. As you'll see in Sections 10.10—10.11, Java SE 8 and Java SE 9 allow other kinds of methods in interfaces.*

```
1   // Fig. 10.11: Payable.java
2   // Payable interface declaration.
3
4   public interface Payable {
5      public abstract double getPaymentAmount(); // no implementation
6   }
```

Fig. 10.11 | `Payable` interface declaration.

10.9.3 Class `Invoice`

Class `Invoice` (Fig. 10.12) represents a simple invoice that contains billing information for only one kind of part. The class declares `private` instance variables `partNumber`, `part-Description`, `quantity` and `pricePerItem` (in lines 5–8) that indicate the part number, a description of the part, the quantity of the part ordered and the price per item. Class Invoice also contains a constructor (lines 11–26), *get* methods (lines 29–38) and a toString method (lines 41–46) that returns a String representation of an Invoice object.

```java
1   // Fig. 10.12: Invoice.java
2   // Invoice class that implements Payable.
3
4   public class Invoice implements Payable {
5       private final String partNumber;
6       private final String partDescription;
7       private final int quantity;
8       private final double pricePerItem;
9
10      // constructor
11      public Invoice(String partNumber, String partDescription, int quantity,
12         double pricePerItem) {
13         if (quantity < 0) { // validate quantity
14            throw new IllegalArgumentException("Quantity must be >= 0");
15         }
16
17         if (pricePerItem < 0.0) { // validate pricePerItem
18            throw new IllegalArgumentException(
19               "Price per item must be >= 0");
20         }
21
22         this.quantity = quantity;
23         this.partNumber = partNumber;
24         this.partDescription = partDescription;
25         this.pricePerItem = pricePerItem;
26      }
27
28      // get part number
29      public String getPartNumber() {return partNumber;}
30
31      // get description
32      public String getPartDescription() {return partDescription;}
33
34      // get quantity
35      public int getQuantity() {return quantity;}
36
37      // get price per item
38      public double getPricePerItem() {return pricePerItem;}
39
40      // return String representation of Invoice object
41      @Override
42      public String toString() {
43         return String.format("%s: %n%s: %s (%s) %n%s: %d %n%s: $%,.2f",
44            "invoice", "part number", getPartNumber(), getPartDescription(),
45            "quantity", getQuantity(), "price per item", getPricePerItem());
46      }
```

Fig. 10.12 | Invoice class that implements Payable. (Part 1 of 2.)

```
47
48        // method required to carry out contract with interface Payable
49        @Override
50        public double getPaymentAmount() {
51            return getQuantity() * getPricePerItem(); // calculate total cost
52        }
53   }
```

Fig. 10.12 | `Invoice` class that implements `Payable`. (Part 2 of 2.)

Line 4 indicates that class `Invoice` implements interface `Payable`. Like all classes, class `Invoice` also *implicitly* extends `Object`. Class `Invoice` implements the one abstract method in interface `Payable`—method `getPaymentAmount` is declared in lines 49–52. The method calculates the total payment required to pay the invoice. The method multiplies the values of `quantity` and `pricePerItem` (obtained through the appropriate *get* methods) and returns the result. This method satisfies the implementation requirement for this method in interface `Payable`—we've *fulfilled* the *interface contract* with the compiler.

A Class Can Extend Only One Other Class But Can Implement Many Interfaces
Java does not allow subclasses to inherit from more than one superclass, but it allows a class to *inherit* from one *superclass* and *implement* as many *interfaces* as it needs. To implement more than one interface, use a comma-separated list of interface names after keyword `implements` in the class declaration, as in:

> **public class** *ClassName* **extends** *SuperclassName* **implements** *FirstInterface*,
> *SecondInterface*, ...

Software Engineering Observation 10.9
All objects of a class that implements multiple interfaces have the is-a *relationship with each implemented interface type.*

Class `ArrayList` (Section 7.16) is one of many Java API classes that implement multiple interfaces. For example, `ArrayList` implements interface `Iterable`, which enables the enhanced `for` statement to iterate over an `ArrayList`'s elements. `ArrayList` also implements interface `List` (Section 16.6), which declares the common methods (such as `add`, `remove` and `contains`) that you can call on any object that represents a lists of items.

10.9.4 Modifying Class `Employee` to Implement Interface `Payable`

We now modify class `Employee` to implement interface `Payable` (Fig. 10.13). This class declaration is identical to that of Fig. 10.4 with two exceptions:

- Line 4 of Fig. 10.13 indicates that class `Employee` now implements `Payable`.
- Line 38 implements interface `Payable`'s `getPaymentAmount` method.

Notice that `getPaymentAmount` simply calls `Employee`'s abstract method `earnings`. At execution time, when `getPaymentAmount` is called on an object of an `Employee` subclass, `getPaymentAmount` calls that subclass's concrete `earnings` method, which knows how to calculate earnings for objects of that subclass type.

```java
 1  // Fig. 10.13: Employee.java
 2  // Employee abstract superclass that implements Payable.
 3
 4  public abstract class Employee implements Payable {
 5     private final String firstName;
 6     private final String lastName;
 7     private final String socialSecurityNumber;
 8
 9     // constructor
10     public Employee(String firstName, String lastName,
11        String socialSecurityNumber) {
12        this.firstName = firstName;
13        this.lastName = lastName;
14        this.socialSecurityNumber = socialSecurityNumber;
15     }
16
17     // return first name
18     public String getFirstName() {return firstName;}
19
20     // return last name
21     public String getLastName() {return lastName;}
22
23     // return social security number
24     public String getSocialSecurityNumber() {return socialSecurityNumber;}
25
26     // return String representation of Employee object
27     @Override
28     public String toString() {
29        return String.format("%s %s%nsocial security number: %s",
30           getFirstName(), getLastName(), getSocialSecurityNumber());
31     }
32
33     // abstract method must be overridden by concrete subclasses
34     public abstract double earnings(); // no implementation here
35
36     // implementing getPaymentAmount here enables the entire Employee
37     // class hierarchy to be used in an app that processes Payables
38     public double getPaymentAmount() {return earnings();}
39  }
```

Fig. 10.13 | Employee abstract superclass that implements Payable.

Subclasses of *Employee* and Interface *Payable*

When a class implements an interface, the same *is-a* relationship as inheritance applies. Class Employee implements Payable, so we can say that an Employee *is a* Payable, and thus any object of an Employee subclass also *is a* Payable. So, if we update the class hierarchy in Section 10.5 with the new Employee superclass in Fig. 10.13, then Salaried-Employees, HourlyEmployees, CommissionEmployees and BasePlusCommissionEmployees are all Payable objects. Just as we can assign the reference of a SalariedEmployee subclass object to a superclass Employee variable, we can assign the reference of a SalariedEmployee object (or any other Employee derived-class object) to a Payable variable. Invoice implements Payable, so an Invoice object also *is a* Payable object, and we can assign the reference of an Invoice object to a Payable variable.

Software Engineering Observation 10.10

Inheritance and interfaces are similar in their implementation of the is-a relationship. An object of a class that implements an interface may be thought of as an object of that interface type. An object of any subclass of a class that implements an interface also can be thought of as an object of the interface type.

Software Engineering Observation 10.11

The is-a *relationship that exists between superclasses and subclasses, and between interfaces and the classes that implement them, holds when passing an object to a method. When a method parameter receives an argument of a superclass or interface type, the method polymorphically processes the object received as an argument.*

Software Engineering Observation 10.12

Using a superclass reference, we can polymorphically invoke any method declared in the superclass and its superclasses (e.g., class Object*). Using an interface reference, we can polymorphically invoke any method declared in the interface, its superinterfaces (one interface can extend another) and in class* Object—*a variable of an interface type must refer to an object to call methods, and all objects have the methods of class* Object.

10.9.5 Using Interface Payable to Process Invoices and Employees Polymorphically

PayableInterfaceTest (Fig. 10.14) illustrates that interface Payable can be used to process a set of Invoices and Employees *polymorphically* in a single application. Lines 7–12 declare and initialize the four-element array payableObjects. Lines 8–9 place the references of Invoice objects in payableObjects' first two elements. Lines 10–11 then place the references of SalariedEmployee objects in payableObjects' last two elements. The elements are allowed to be initialized with Invoices and SalariedEmployees, because an Invoice *is a* Payable, a SalariedEmployee *is an* Employee and an Employee *is a* Payable.

```
1   // Fig. 10.14: PayableInterfaceTest.java
2   // Payable interface test program processing Invoices and
3   // Employees polymorphically.
4   public class PayableInterfaceTest {
5      public static void main(String[] args) {
6         // create four-element Payable array
7         Payable[] payableObjects = new Payable[] {
8            new Invoice("01234", "seat", 2, 375.00),
9            new Invoice("56789", "tire", 4, 79.95),
10           new SalariedEmployee("John", "Smith", "111-11-1111", 800.00),
11           new SalariedEmployee("Lisa", "Barnes", "888-88-8888", 1200.00)
12        };
13
```

Fig. 10.14 | Payable interface test program processing Invoices and Employees polymorphically. (Part 1 of 2.)

```
14          System.out.println(
15              "Invoices and Employees processed polymorphically:");
16
17          // generically process each element in array payableObjects
18          for (Payable currentPayable : payableObjects) {
19              // output currentPayable and its appropriate payment amount
20              System.out.printf("%n%s %npayment due: $%,.2f%n",
21                  currentPayable.toString(), // could invoke implicitly
22                  currentPayable.getPaymentAmount());
23          }
24      }
25  }
```

```
Invoices and Employees processed polymorphically:

invoice:
part number: 01234 (seat)
quantity: 2
price per item: $375.00
payment due: $750.00

invoice:
part number: 56789 (tire)
quantity: 4
price per item: $79.95
payment due: $319.80

salaried employee: John Smith
social security number: 111-11-1111
weekly salary: $800.00
payment due: $800.00

salaried employee: Lisa Barnes
social security number: 888-88-8888
weekly salary: $1,200.00
payment due: $1,200.00
```

Fig. 10.14 | `Payable` interface test program processing `Invoices` and `Employees` polymorphically. (Part 2 of 2.)

Lines 18–23 *polymorphically* process each `Payable` object in `payableObjects`, displaying each object's `String` representation and payment amount. Line 21 invokes method `toString` via a `Payable` interface reference, even though `toString` is not declared in interface `Payable`—*all references (including those of interface types) refer to objects that extend `Object` and therefore have a `toString` method.* (Method `toString` also can be invoked *implicitly* here.) Line 22 invokes `Payable` method `getPaymentAmount` to obtain the payment amount for each object in `payableObjects`, regardless of the actual type of the object. The output reveals that each of the method calls in lines 21–22 invokes the appropriate class's `toString` and `getPaymentAmount` methods.

10.9.6 Some Common Interfaces of the Java API

You'll use interfaces extensively when developing Java applications. The Java API contains numerous interfaces, and many of the Java API methods take interface arguments and return interface values. Figure 10.15 overviews a few of the more popular interfaces of the Java API that we use in later chapters.

Interface	Description
Comparable	Java contains several comparison operators (e.g., <, <=, >, >=, ==, !=) that allow you to compare primitive values. However, these operators *cannot* be used to compare objects. Interface Comparable is used to allow objects of a class that implements the interface to be compared to one another. Interface Comparable is commonly used for ordering objects in a collection such as an ArrayList. We use Comparable in Chapter 16, Generic Collections, and Chapter 19, Generic Classes and Methods: A Deeper Look.
Serializable	An interface used to identify classes whose objects can be written to (i.e., serialized) or read from (i.e., deserialized) some type of storage (e.g., file on disk, database field) or transmitted across a network.
Runnable	Implemented by any class that represents a task to perform. Objects of such a class are often executed in parallel using a technique called *multithreading* (discussed in Chapter 21, Concurrency and Multi-Core Performance). The interface contains one method, run, which specifies the behavior of an object when executed.
GUI event-listener interfaces	You work with graphical user interfaces (GUIs) every day. In your web browser, you might type the address of a website to visit, or you might click a button to return to a previous site. The browser responds to your interaction and performs the desired task. Your interaction is known as an *event*, and the code that the browser uses to respond to an event is known as an *event handler*. In Chapter 12, JavaFX Graphical User Interfaces: Part 1, you'll begin learning how to build GUIs with event handlers that respond to user interactions. Event handlers are declared in classes that implement an appropriate *event-listener interface*. Each event-listener interface specifies one or more methods that must be implemented to respond to user interactions.
AutoCloseable	Implemented by classes that can be used with the try-with-resources statement (Chapter 11, Exception Handling: A Deeper Look) to help prevent resource leaks. We use this interface in Chapter 15, Files, Input/Output Streams, NIO and XML Serialization, and Chapter 22, Accessing Databases with JDBC.

Fig. 10.15 | Common interfaces of the Java API.

10.10 Java SE 8 Interface Enhancements

8

This section introduces interface features that were added in Java SE 8. We discuss these in more detail in later chapters.

10.10.1 default Interface Methods

Prior to Java SE 8, interface methods could be *only* public abstract methods. This meant that an interface specified *what* operations an implementing class must perform but not *how* the class should perform them.

As of Java SE 8, interfaces also may contain public **default** methods with *concrete* default implementations that specify *how* operations are performed when an implementing class does not override the methods. If a class implements such an interface, the class also receives the interface's default implementations (if any). To declare a default method, place the keyword default before the method's return type and provide a concrete method implementation.

Adding Methods to Existing Interfaces
Prior to Java SE 8, adding methods to an interface would break any implementing classes that did not implement the new methods. Recall that if you didn't implement each of an interface's methods, you had to declare your class abstract.

Any class that implements the original interface will *not* break when a default method is added—the class simply receives the new default method. When a class implements a Java SE 8 interface, the class "signs a contract" with the compiler that says, "I will declare all the *abstract* methods specified by the interface or I will declare my class abstract"—the implementing class is not required to override the interface's default methods, but it can if necessary.

Software Engineering Observation 10.13
Java SE 8 default *methods enable you to evolve existing interfaces by adding new methods to those interfaces without breaking code that uses them.*

Interfaces vs. abstract Classes
Prior to Java SE 8, an interface was typically used (rather than an abstract class) when there were no implementation details to inherit—no fields and no method implementations. With default methods, you can instead declare common method implementations in interfaces. This gives you more flexibility in designing your classes, because a class can implement many interfaces, but can extend only one superclass.

10.10.2 static Interface Methods

Prior to Java SE 8, it was common to associate with an interface a class containing static helper methods for working with objects that implemented the interface. In Chapter 16, you'll learn about class Collections which contains many static helper methods for working with objects that implement interfaces Collection, List, Set and more. For example, Collections method sort can sort objects of *any* class that implements interface List. With static interface methods, such helper methods can now be declared directly in interfaces rather than in separate classes.

10.10.3 Functional Interfaces

As of Java SE 8, any interface containing only one abstract method is known as a **functional interface**—these are also called SAM (single abstract method) interfaces. There are many such interfaces throughout the Java APIs. Some functional interfaces that you'll use in this book include:

• ChangeListener (Chapter 12)—You'll implement this interface to define a method that's called when the interacts with a slider graphical user interface control.

- **Comparator** (Chapter 16)—You'll implement this interface to define a method that can compare two objects of a given type to determine whether the first object is less than, equal to or greater than the second.

- **Runnable** (Chapter 21)—You'll implement this interface to define a task that may be run in parallel with other parts of your program.

Functional interfaces are used extensively with Java's lambda capabilities that we introduce in Chapter 17. Lambdas provide a shorthand notation for implementing functional interfaces.

10.11 Java SE 9 `private` Interface Methods

As you know, a class's `private` helper methods may be called only by the class's other methods. As of Java SE 9, you can declare helper methods in *interfaces* via **private interface methods**. An interface's `private` instance methods can be called directly (i.e., without an object reference) only by the interface's other instance methods. An interface's `private` `static` methods can be called by any of the interface's instance or `static` methods.

> **Common Programming Error 10.7**
>
> *Including the* `default` *keyword in a* `private` *interface method's declaration is a compilation error—*`default` *methods must be* `public`*.*

10.12 `private` Constructors

In Section 3.4, we mentioned that constructors are normally declared `public`. Sometimes it's useful to declare one or more of a class's constructors as `private`.

Preventing Object Instantiation

You can prevent client code from creating objects of a class by making the class's constructors `private`. For example, consider class `Math`, which contains only `public` `static` constants and `public` `static` methods. There's no need to create a `Math` object to use the class's constants and methods, so its constructor is `private`.

Sharing Initialization Code in Constructors

One common use of a `private` constructor is sharing initialization code among a class's other constructors. You can use delegating constructors (introduced in Fig. 8.5) to call the `private` constructor that contains the shared initialization code.

Factory Methods

Another common use of `private` constructors is to force client code to use so-called "factory methods" to create objects. A **factory method** is a `public` `static` method that creates and initializes an object of a specified type (possibly of the same class), then returns a reference to it. A key benefit of this architecture is that the method's return type can be an interface or a superclass (either `abstract` or concrete).[2]

---

2. Gamma, Erich et al. *Design Patterns: Elements of Reusable Object-Oriented Software.* Reading, MA: Addison-Wesley, 1995.

10.13 Program to an Interface, Not an Implementation[3]

We've explained implementation inheritance via `extends` in detail. Recall that Java does not allow a class to inherit from more than one superclass.

With interface inheritance, a class `implements` an interface describing various `abstract` methods that the new class must provide. The new class also may inherit some method implementations (allowed in interfaces as of Java SE 8), but no instance variables. Recall that Java allows a class to implement multiple interfaces in addition to extending one class. An interface also may extend one or more other interfaces.

10.13.1 Implementation Inheritance Is Best for Small Numbers of Tightly Coupled Classes

Implementation inheritance is primarily used to declare closely related classes that have many of the same instance variables and method implementations. Every subclass object has the *is-a* relationship with the superclass, so anywhere a superclass object is expected, a subclass object may be provided.

Classes declared with implementation inheritance are tightly coupled—you define the common instance variables and methods once in a superclass, then inherit them into subclasses. Changes to a superclass directly affect all corresponding subclasses. When you use a superclass variable, only a superclass object or one of its subclass objects may be assigned to the variable.

A key disadvantage of implementation inheritance is that the tight coupling among the classes can make it difficult to modify the hierarchy. For example, consider supporting retirement plans in Section 10.5's `Employee` hierarchy. There are many different types of retirement plans (such as 401Ks and IRAs). We might add a `makeRetirementDeposit` method to class `Employee`, then define various subclasses such as `SalariedEmployee-With401K`, `SalariedEmployeeWithIRA`, `HourlyEmployeeWith401K`, `HourlyEmployee-WithIRA`, etc. Each subclass would override `makeRetirementDeposit` as appropriate for a given employee and retirement-plan type. As you can see, you quickly wind up with a proliferation of subclasses, making the hierarchy hard to maintain.

As we mentioned in Chapter 9, small inheritance hierarchies under the control of one person tend to be more manageable than large ones maintained by many people. This is true even with the tight coupling associated with implementation inheritance.

10.13.2 Interface Inheritance Is Best for Flexibility

Interface inheritance often requires more work than implementation inheritance, because you must provide implementations of the interface's `abstract` methods—even if those implementations are similar or identical among classes. However, this gives you additional flexibility by eliminating the tight coupling between classes. When you use a variable of an interface type, you can assign it an object of *any* type that implements the interface, either directly or indirectly. This allows you to add new types to your code easily and to replace existing objects with objects of new and improved implementation classes. The dis-

---

3. Defined in Gamma, Erich et al. *Design Patterns: Elements of Reusable Object-Oriented Software*. Reading, MA: Addison-Wesley, 1995, 17–18, and further emphasized and discussed in Bloch, Joshua. *Effective Java*. Upper Saddle River, NJ: Addison-Wesley, 2008.

cussion of device drivers in the context of `abstract` classes at the end of Section 10.4 is a good example of how interfaces enable systems to be modified easily.

Software Engineering Observation 10.14

Java SE 8's and Java SE 9's `interface` *enhancements (Sections 10.10—10.11)—which allow* `interface`*s to contain* `public` *and* `private` *instance methods and* `static` *methods with implementations—make programming with* `interface`*s appropriate for almost all cases in which you would have used* `abstract` *classes previously. With the exception of fields, you get all the benefits that classes provide, plus classes can implement any number of interfaces but can extend only one class (*`abstract` *or concrete).*

Software Engineering Observation 10.15

Just as superclasses can change, so can interfaces. If the signature of an interface method changes, all corresponding classes would require modification. Experience has shown that interfaces change much less frequently than implementations.

10.13.3 Rethinking the Employee Hierarchy

Let's reconsider Section 10.5's `Employee` hierarchy with composition and an interface. We can say that each type of employee in the hierarchy is an `Employee` that *has a* `CompensationModel`. We can declare `CompensationModel` as an interface with an `abstract` earnings method, then declare implementations of `CompensationModel` that specify the various ways in which an `Employee` gets paid:

- A `SalariedCompensationModel` would contain a `weeklySalary` instance variable and would implement method `earnings` to return the `weeklySalary`.

- An `HourlyCompensationModel` would contain wage and hours instance variables and would implement method `earnings` based on the number of hours worked, with `1.5 * wage` for any hours over 40.

- A `CommissionCompensationModel` would contain grossSales and commission-Rate instance variables and would implement method `earnings` to return grossSales * commissionRate.

- A `BasePlusCommissionCompensationModel` would contain instance variables grossSales, commissionRate and baseSalary and would implement `earnings` to return baseSalary + grossSales * commissionRate.

Each `Employee` object you create can then be initialized with an object of the appropriate `CompensationModel` implementation. Class `Employee`'s earnings method would simply use the class's composed `CompensationModel` instance variable to call the earnings method of the corresponding `CompensationModel` object.

Flexibility if Compensation Models Change

Declaring the `CompensationModel`s as separate classes that implement the same interface provides flexibility for future changes. Let's assume `Employee`s who are paid purely by commission based on gross sales should get an extra 10% commission, but those who have a base salary should not. In Section 10.5's `Employee` hierarchy, making this change to class `CommissionEmployee`'s earnings method (Fig. 10.7) directly affects how `BasePlusCommissionEmployee`s are paid, because `BasePlusCommissionEmployee`'s earnings method calls CommissionEmployee's earnings method. However, changing the CommissionCompensationModel's earnings implementation does not affect class BasePlusCommissionCompensationModel, because these classes are not tightly coupled by inheritance.

Flexibility if Employees Are Promoted

Interface-based composition is more flexible than Section 10.5's class hierarchy if an Employee gets promoted. Class Employee can provide a setCompensationModel method that receives a CompensationModel and assigns it to the Employee's composed CompensationModel variable. When an Employee gets promoted, you'd simply call setCompensationModel to replace the Employee's existing CompensationModel object with an appropriate new one. To promote an employee using Section 10.5's Employee hierarchy, you'd need to change the employee's type by creating a new object of the appropriate class and moving data from the old object into the new one.

Flexibility if Employees Acquire New Capabilities

Using composition and interfaces also is more flexible than Section 10.5's class hierarchy for enhancing class Employee. Let's assume we decide to support retirement plans (such as 401Ks and IRAs). We could say that every Employee *has a* RetirementPlan and define interface RetirementPlan with a makeRetirementDeposit method. Then, we can provide appropriate implementations for various retirement-plan types.

10.14 Wrap-Up

This chapter introduced polymorphism—the ability to process objects that share the same superclass in a class hierarchy as if they were all objects of the superclass. We discussed how polymorphism makes systems extensible and maintainable, then demonstrated how to use overridden methods to effect polymorphic behavior. We introduced abstract classes, which allow you to provide an appropriate superclass from which other classes can inherit. You learned that an abstract class can declare abstract methods that each subclass must implement to become a concrete class and that a program can use variables of an abstract class to invoke the subclasses' implementations of abstract methods polymorphically. You also learned how to determine an object's type at execution time. We explained the notions of final methods and classes. The chapter discussed declaring and implementing an interface as a way for possibly disparate classes to implement common functionality, enabling objects of those classes to be processed polymorphically.

We introduced the interface enhancements in Java SE 8—default methods and static methods—and in Java SE 9—private methods. Next, we discussed the purpose of private constructors. Finally, we discussed programming to an interface vs. programming to an implementation, and how the Employee hierarchy can be reimplemented using a CompensationModel interface.

You should now be familiar with classes, objects, encapsulation, inheritance, interfaces and polymorphism—the most essential aspects of object-oriented programming.

In the next chapter, you'll learn about exceptions, useful for handling errors during a program's execution. Exception handling provides for more robust programs.

Exception Handling: A Deeper Look

Objectives

In this chapter you'll:

- Learn why exception handling is an effective mechanism for responding to runtime problems.
- Use `try` blocks to delimit code in which exceptions might occur.
- Use `throw` to indicate a problem.
- Use `catch` blocks to specify exception handlers.
- Learn when to use exception handling.
- Understand the exception class hierarchy.
- Use the `finally` block to release resources.
- Chain exceptions by catching one exception and throwing another.
- Create user-defined exceptions.
- Use the debugging feature `assert` to state conditions that should be true at a particular point in a method.
- Learn how `try`-with-resources can automatically release a resource when the `try` block terminates.

11.1 Introduction

As you know from Chapters 7–8, an exception indicates a problem during a program's execution. Exception handling enables applications to resolve (or handle) exceptions. In some cases, a program can continue executing as if no problem had been encountered. The features presented in this chapter help you write *robust* and *fault-tolerant* programs that can deal with problems and continue executing or *terminate gracefully*.[1]

First, we handle an exception that occurs when a method attempts to divide an integer by zero. We discuss when to use exception handling and show a portion of the exception-handling class hierarchy. As you'll see, only subclasses of `Throwable` can be used with exception handling. We introduce the `try` statement's `finally` block, which executes whether or not an exception occurs. We then show how to use *chained exceptions* to add application-specific information to an exception and how to create your own exception types. Next, we introduce *preconditions* and *postconditions*, which must be true when your methods are called and when they return, respectively. We then present *assertions*, which you can use at development time to help debug your code. We also discuss catching multiple exceptions with one `catch` handler, and the `try`-with-resources statement that automatically releases a resource after it's used in the `try` block.

This chapter focuses on the exception-handling concepts and presents several mechanical examples that demonstrate various features. Many Java API methods throw exceptions that we handle in our code. Figure 11.1 shows some of the exception types you've already seen and others you'll learn about.

Software Engineering Observation 11.1

Companies often have strict design, coding, testing, debugging and maintenance standards. These often vary among companies. Sometimes their exception-handling standards are sensitive to the type of application, such as real-time systems, high-performance mathematical calculations, big data, network-based distributed systems, etc. This chapter's tips provide observations consistent with these types of industry policies.

---

1. Java exception handling is based in part on the work of Andrew Koenig and Bjarne Stroustrup—A. Koenig and B. Stroustrup, "Exception Handling for C++ (revised)," *Proceedings of the Usenix C++ Conference*, pp. 149–176, San Francisco, April 1990.

Chapter	Sample of exceptions used
Chapter 7	`ArrayIndexOutOfBoundsException`
Chapters 8–10	`IllegalArgumentException`
Chapter 11	`ArithmeticException, InputMismatchException`
Chapter 15	`SecurityException, FileNotFoundException, IOException,` `ClassNotFoundException, IllegalStateException,` `FormatterClosedException, NoSuchElementException`
Chapter 16	`ClassCastException, UnsupportedOperationException,` `NullPointerException`, custom exception types
Chapter 19	`ClassCastException`, custom exception types
Chapter 21	`InterruptedException, IllegalMonitorStateException, Execution-` `Exception, CancellationException`
Chapter 22	`SQLException, IllegalStateException, PatternSyntaxException`

Fig. 11.1 | Various exception types that you'll see throughout this book.

11.2 Example: Divide by Zero without Exception Handling

First we demonstrate what happens when errors arise in an application that does not use exception handling. Figure 11.2 prompts the user for two integers and passes them to method `quotient`, which calculates the integer quotient and returns an `int` result. In this example, you'll see that exceptions are **thrown** (i.e., the exception occurs) by a method when it detects a problem and is unable to handle it.

```java
 1   // Fig. 11.2: DivideByZeroNoExceptionHandling.java
 2   // Integer division without exception handling.
 3   import java.util.Scanner;
 4
 5   public class DivideByZeroNoExceptionHandling {
 6      // demonstrates throwing an exception when a divide-by-zero occurs
 7      public static int quotient(int numerator, int denominator) {
 8         return numerator / denominator; // possible division by zero
 9      }
10
11      public static void main(String[] args) {
12         Scanner scanner = new Scanner(System.in);
13
14         System.out.print("Please enter an integer numerator: ");
15         int numerator = scanner.nextInt();
16         System.out.print("Please enter an integer denominator: ");
17         int denominator = scanner.nextInt();
18
19         int result = quotient(numerator, denominator);
```

Fig. 11.2 | Integer division without exception handling. (Part 1 of 2.)

```
20          System.out.printf(
21              "%nResult: %d / %d = %d%n", numerator, denominator, result);
22      }
23  }
```

```
Please enter an integer numerator: 100
Please enter an integer denominator: 7

Result: 100 / 7 = 14
```

```
Please enter an integer numerator: 100
Please enter an integer denominator: 0
Exception in thread "main" java.lang.ArithmeticException: / by zero
        at DivideByZeroNoExceptionHandling.quotient(
            DivideByZeroNoExceptionHandling.java:8)
        at DivideByZeroNoExceptionHandling.main(
            DivideByZeroNoExceptionHandling.java:19)
```

```
Please enter an integer numerator: 100
Please enter an integer denominator: hello
Exception in thread "main" java.util.InputMismatchException
        at java.util.Scanner.throwFor(Unknown Source)
        at java.util.Scanner.next(Unknown Source)
        at java.util.Scanner.nextInt(Unknown Source)
        at java.util.Scanner.nextInt(Unknown Source)
        at DivideByZeroNoExceptionHandling.main(
            DivideByZeroNoExceptionHandling.java:17)
```

Fig. 11.2 | Integer division without exception handling. (Part 2 of 2.)

Stack Trace

The first sample execution in Fig. 11.2 shows a successful division. In the second execution, the user enters the value 0 as the denominator. Several lines of information are displayed in response to this invalid input. This information is known as a **stack trace**, which includes the name of the exception (java.lang.ArithmeticException) in a descriptive message that indicates the problem and the method-call stack (i.e., the call chain) at the time the problem occurred. The stack trace includes the path of execution that led to the exception method by method. This helps you debug the program. Even if a problem has not occurred, you can see the stack trace any time by calling Thread.dumpStack().

Stack Trace for an ArithmeticException

The first line specifies that an ArithmeticException has occurred. The text after the name of the exception ("/ by zero") indicates that this exception occurred as a result of an attempt to divide by zero. Java does not allow division by zero in integer arithmetic. When this occurs, Java throws an **ArithmeticException**. ArithmeticExceptions can arise from a number of different problems, so the extra data ("/ by zero") provides more specific information.

Starting from the last line of the stack trace, we see that the exception was detected in line 19 of method `main`. Each line of the stack trace contains the class name and method (e.g., `DivideByZeroNoExceptionHandling.main`) followed by the filename and line number (e.g., `DivideByZeroNoExceptionHandling.java:19`). Moving up the stack trace, we see that the exception occurs in line 8, in method `quotient`. The top row of the call chain indicates the **throw point**—the initial point at which the exception occurred. The throw point of this exception is in line 8 of method `quotient`.

Side Note Regarding Floating-Point Arithmetic
Java *does* allow division by zero with floating-point values. Such a calculation results in positive or negative infinity, which is represented as a floating-point value that displays as `"Infinity"` or `"-Infinity"`. If you divide 0.0 by 0.0, the result is NaN (not a number), which is represented as a floating-point value that displays as `"NaN"`. If you need to compare a floating-point value to NaN, use the method `isNaN` of class `Float` (for `float` values) or of class `Double` (for `double` values). Classes `Float` and `Double` are in package `java.lang`.

Stack Trace for an InputMismatchException
In the third execution, the user enters the string `"hello"` as the denominator. Notice again that a stack trace is displayed. This informs us that an `InputMismatchException` has occurred (package `java.util`). Our prior examples that input numeric values assumed that the user would input a proper integer value. However, users sometimes make mistakes and input noninteger values. An **`InputMismatchException`** occurs when `Scanner` method `nextInt` receives a `string` that does not represent a valid integer. Starting from the end of the stack trace, we see that the exception was detected in line 17 of method `main`. Moving up the stack trace, we see that the exception occurred in method `nextInt`. Notice that in place of the filename and line number, we're provided with the text `Unknown Source`. This means that the so-called *debugging symbols* that provide the filename and line number information for that method's class were not available to the JVM—this is typically the case for the classes of the Java API. Many IDEs have access to the Java API source code and will display filenames and line numbers in stack traces.

Program Termination
In the sample executions of Fig. 11.2 when exceptions occur and stack traces are displayed, the program also *exits*. This does not always occur in Java. Sometimes a program may continue even though an exception has occurred and a stack trace has been printed. In such cases, the application may produce unexpected results. For example, a graphical user interface (GUI) application will often continue executing. In Fig. 11.2 both types of exceptions were detected in method `main`. In the next example, we'll see how to *handle* these exceptions so that you can enable the program to run to normal completion.

11.3 Example: Handling ArithmeticExceptions and InputMismatchExceptions

The application in Fig. 11.3, which is based on Fig. 11.2, uses *exception handling* to process any `ArithmeticExceptions` and `InputMismatchExceptions` that arise. The application still prompts the user for two integers and passes them to method `quotient`, which calculates the quotient and returns an `int` result. This version of the application uses exception handling so that if the user makes a mistake, the program catches and handles (i.e., deals with) the exception—in this case, allowing the user to re-enter the input.

```java
1   // Fig. 11.3: DivideByZeroWithExceptionHandling.java
2   // Handling ArithmeticExceptions and InputMismatchExceptions.
3   import java.util.InputMismatchException;
4   import java.util.Scanner;
5
6   public class DivideByZeroWithExceptionHandling
7   {
8      // demonstrates throwing an exception when a divide-by-zero occurs
9      public static int quotient(int numerator, int denominator)
10        throws ArithmeticException {
11        return numerator / denominator; // possible division by zero
12     }
13
14     public static void main(String[] args) {
15        Scanner scanner = new Scanner(System.in);
16        boolean continueLoop = true; // determines if more input is needed
17
18        do {
19           try { // read two numbers and calculate quotient
20              System.out.print("Please enter an integer numerator: ");
21              int numerator = scanner.nextInt();
22              System.out.print("Please enter an integer denominator: ");
23              int denominator = scanner.nextInt();
24
25              int result = quotient(numerator, denominator);
26              System.out.printf("%nResult: %d / %d = %d%n", numerator,
27                 denominator, result);
28              continueLoop = false; // input successful; end looping
29           }
30           catch (InputMismatchException inputMismatchException) {
31              System.err.printf("%nException: %s%n",
32                 inputMismatchException);
33              scanner.nextLine(); // discard input so user can try again
34              System.out.printf(
35                 "You must enter integers. Please try again.%n%n");
36           }
37           catch (ArithmeticException arithmeticException) {
38              System.err.printf("%nException: %s%n", arithmeticException);
39              System.out.printf(
40                 "Zero is an invalid denominator. Please try again.%n%n");
41           }
42        } while (continueLoop);
43     }
44  }
```

```
Please enter an integer numerator: 100
Please enter an integer denominator: 7

Result: 100 / 7 = 14
```

Fig. 11.3 | Handling ArithmeticExceptions and InputMismatchExceptions. (Part 1 of 2.)

```
Please enter an integer numerator: 100
Please enter an integer denominator: 0

Exception: java.lang.ArithmeticException: / by zero
Zero is an invalid denominator. Please try again.

Please enter an integer numerator: 100
Please enter an integer denominator: 7

Result: 100 / 7 = 14
```

```
Please enter an integer numerator: 100
Please enter an integer denominator: hello

Exception: java.util.InputMismatchException
You must enter integers. Please try again.

Please enter an integer numerator: 100
Please enter an integer denominator: 7

Result: 100 / 7 = 14
```

Fig. 11.3 | Handling ArithmeticExceptions and InputMismatchExceptions. (Part 2 of 2.)

The first sample execution in Fig. 11.3 does *not* encounter any problems. In the second execution the user enters a *zero denominator*, and an ArithmeticException exception occurs. In the third execution the user enters the string "hello" as the denominator, and an InputMismatchException occurs. For each exception, the user is informed of the mistake and asked to try again, then is prompted for two new integers. In each sample execution, the program runs to completion successfully.

Class InputMismatchException is imported in line 3. Class ArithmeticException does not need to be imported because it's in package java.lang. Line 16 creates the boolean variable continueLoop, which is true if the user has *not* yet entered valid input. Lines 18–42 repeatedly ask users for input until a *valid* input is received.

Enclosing Code in a *try Block*

Lines 19–29 contain a **try block**, which encloses the code that *might* throw an exception and the code that should *not* execute if an exception occurs (i.e., if an exception occurs, the remaining code in the try block will be skipped). A try block consists of the keyword try followed by a block of code enclosed in curly braces. [*Note:* The term "try block" sometimes refers only to the block of code that follows the try keyword (not including the try keyword itself). For simplicity, we use the term "try block" to refer to the block of code that follows the try keyword, as well as the try keyword.] The statements that read the integers from the keyboard (lines 21 and 23) each use method nextInt to read an int value. Method nextInt throws an InputMismatchException if the value read in is *not* an integer.

The division that can cause an ArithmeticException is not performed in the try block. Rather, the call to method quotient (line 25) invokes the code that attempts the division (line 11); the JVM *throws* an ArithmeticException object when the denominator is zero.

Software Engineering Observation 11.2

Exceptions may surface through explicitly mentioned code in a try block, through deeply nested method calls initiated by code in a try block or from the Java Virtual Machine as it executes Java bytecodes.

Catching Exceptions

The try block in this example is followed by two catch blocks—one that handles an InputMismatchException (lines 30–36) and one that handles an ArithmeticException (lines 37–41). A **catch block** (also called a **catch clause** or **exception handler**) *catches* (i.e., receives) and *handles* an exception. A catch block begins with the keyword catch followed by a parameter in parentheses (called the *exception parameter*, discussed shortly) and a block of code enclosed in curly braces.

At least one catch block or a **finally block** (discussed in Section 11.6) *must* immediately follow the try block. Each catch block specifies in parentheses an **exception parameter** that identifies the exception type the handler can process. When an exception occurs in a try block, the catch block that executes is the *first* one whose type matches the type of the exception that occurred (i.e., the type in the catch block matches the thrown exception type exactly or is a direct or indirect superclass of it). The exception parameter's name enables the catch block to interact with a caught exception object—e.g., to implicitly invoke the caught exception's toString method (as in lines 31–32 and 38), which displays basic information about the exception. Notice that we use the **System.err (standard error stream) object** to output error messages. By default, System.err's print methods, like those of System.out, display data to the *command prompt*.

Line 33 in the first catch block calls Scanner method nextLine. Because an InputMismatchException occurred, the call to method nextInt never successfully read in the user's data—so we read that input with a call to method nextLine. We do not do anything with the input at this point, because we know that it's *invalid*. Each catch block displays an error message and asks the user to try again. After either catch block terminates, the user is prompted for input. We'll soon take a deeper look at how this flow of control works in exception handling.

Common Programming Error 11.1

It's a syntax error to place code between a try block and its corresponding catch blocks.

Multi-catch

It's relatively common for a try block to be followed by several catch blocks to handle various types of exceptions. If the bodies of several catch blocks are identical, you can use the **multi-catch** feature to catch those exception types in a *single* catch handler and perform the same task. The syntax for a *multi-catch* is:

```
catch (Type1 | Type2 | Type3 e)
```

Each exception type is separated from the next with a vertical bar (|). The preceding line of code indicates that *any* of the types (or their subclasses) can be caught in the exception handler. Any number of Throwable types can be specified in a multi-catch. In this case, the exception parameter's type is the common superclass of the specified types.

Uncaught Exceptions

An **uncaught exception** is one for which there are no matching `catch` blocks. You saw uncaught exceptions in the second and third outputs of Fig. 11.2. Recall that when exceptions occurred in that example, the application terminated early (after displaying the exception's *stack trace*). This does not always occur as a result of uncaught exceptions. Java uses a "multithreaded" model of program execution—each **thread** is a *concurrent activity*. One program can have many threads. If a program has only *one* thread, an uncaught exception will cause the program to terminate. If a program has *multiple* threads, an uncaught exception will terminate *only* the thread in which the exception occurred. In such programs, however, certain threads may rely on others, and if one thread terminates due to an uncaught exception, there may be adverse effects on the rest of the program. Chapter 21, Concurrency and Multi-Core Performance, discusses these issues in depth.

Termination Model of Exception Handling

If an exception occurs in a `try` block (such as an `InputMismatchException` being thrown as a result of the code at line 23 of Fig. 11.3), the `try` block *terminates* immediately and program control transfers to the *first* of the following `catch` blocks in which the exception parameter's type matches the thrown exception's type. In Fig. 11.3, the first `catch` block catches `InputMismatchExceptions` (which occur if invalid input is entered) and the second `catch` block catches `ArithmeticExceptions` (which occur if an attempt is made to divide by zero). After the exception is handled, program control does *not* return to the throw point, because the `try` block has *expired* (and its *local variables* have been *lost*). Rather, control resumes after the last `catch` block. This is known as the **termination model of exception handling**. Some languages use the **resumption model of exception handling**, in which, after an exception is handled, control resumes just after the *throw point*.

Notice that we name our exception parameters (`inputMismatchException` and `arithmeticException`) based on their type. Java programmers often simply use the letter e as the name of their exception parameters.

After executing a `catch` block, this program's flow of control proceeds to the first statement after the last `catch` block (line 42 in this case). The condition in the `do...while` statement is `true` (variable `continueLoop` contains its initial value of `true`), so control returns to the beginning of the loop and the user is again prompted for input. This control statement will loop until *valid* input is entered. At that point, program control reaches line 28, which assigns `false` to variable `continueLoop`. The `try` block then *terminates*. If no exceptions are thrown in the `try` block, the `catch` blocks are *skipped* and control continues with the first statement after the `catch` blocks (we'll learn about another possibility when we discuss the `finally` block in Section 11.6). Now the condition for the `do...while` loop is `false`, and method `main` ends.

The `try` block and its corresponding `catch` and/or `finally` blocks form a **try statement**. Do not confuse the terms "try block" and "try statement"—the latter includes the `try` block as well as the following `catch` blocks and/or `finally` block.

As with any other block of code, when a `try` block terminates, *local variables* declared in the block *go out of scope* and are no longer accessible; thus, the local variables of a `try` block are not accessible in the corresponding `catch` blocks. When a `catch` block *terminates*, *local variables* declared within the `catch` block (including the exception parameter of that `catch` block) also *go out of scope* and are *destroyed*. Any remaining `catch` blocks in the `try` statement are *ignored*, and execution resumes at the first line of code after the `try...catch` sequence—this will be a `finally` block, if one is present.

Using the *throws* Clause

In method `quotient` (Fig. 11.3, lines 9–12), line 10 is known as a **throws clause**. It specifies the exceptions the method *might* throw if problems occur. This clause, which must appear after the method's parameter list and before the body, contains a comma-separated list of the exception types. Such exceptions may be thrown by statements in the method's body or by methods called from there. We've added the `throws` clause to this application to indicate that this method might throw an `ArithmeticException`. Method `quotient`'s callers are thus informed that the method might throw an `ArithmeticException`. Some exception types, such as `ArithmeticException`, are not required to be listed in the `throws` clause. For those that are, the method can throw exceptions that have the *is-a* relationship with the classes listed in the `throws` clause. You'll learn more about this in Section 11.5.

Error-Prevention Tip 11.1

Read a method's online API documentation before using it in a program. The documentation specifies exceptions thrown by the method (if any) and indicates reasons why such exceptions may occur. Next, read the online API documentation for the specified exception classes. The documentation for an exception class typically contains potential reasons that such exceptions occur. Finally, provide for handling those exceptions in your program.

When line 11 executes, if the `denominator` is zero, the JVM throws an `Arithmetic-Exception` object. This object will be caught by the `catch` block at lines 37–41, which displays basic information about the exception by *implicitly* invoking the exception's `toString` method, then asks the user to try again.

If the `denominator` is not zero, method `quotient` performs the division and returns the result to the point of invocation of method `quotient` in the `try` block (line 25). Lines 26–27 display the result of the calculation and line 28 sets `continueLoop` to `false`. In this case, the `try` block completes successfully, so the program skips the `catch` blocks and fails the condition at line 42, and method `main` completes execution normally.

When `quotient` throws an `ArithmeticException`, `quotient` *terminates* and does *not* return a value, and `quotient`'s *local variables go out of scope* (and are destroyed). If `quotient` contained local variables that were references to objects and there were no other references to those objects, the objects would be marked for *garbage collection*. Also, when an exception occurs, the `try` block from which `quotient` was called *terminates* before lines 26–28 can execute. Here, too, if local variables were created in the `try` block prior to the exception's being thrown, these variables would go out of scope.

If an `InputMismatchException` is generated by lines 21 or 23, the `try` block *terminates* and execution *continues* with the `catch` block at lines 30–36. In this case, method `quotient` is not called. Then method `main` continues after the last `catch` block.

11.4 When to Use Exception Handling

Exception handling is designed to process **synchronous errors**, which occur when a statement executes. Common examples we'll see throughout the book are *out-of-range array indices*, *arithmetic overflow* (i.e., a value outside the representable range of values), *division by* *zero, invalid method parameters* and *thread interruption* (as we'll see in Chapter 21). Exception handling is not designed to process problems associated with **asynchronous events** (e.g., disk I/O completions, network message arrivals, mouse clicks and keystrokes), which occur in parallel with, and *independent of*, the program's flow of control.

Software Engineering Observation 11.3

Incorporate your exception-handling and error-recovery strategy into your system from the inception of the design process—including these after a system has been implemented can be difficult.

Software Engineering Observation 11.4

Exception handling provides a single, uniform technique for documenting, detecting and recovering from errors. This helps programmers working on large projects understand each other's error-processing code.

Software Engineering Observation 11.5

A great variety of situations can generate exceptions—some exceptions are easier to recover from than others.

Software Engineering Observation 11.6

Sometimes you can prevent an exception by validating data first. For example, before you perform integer division, you can ensure that the denominator is not zero, which prevents the ArithmeticException that occurs when you divide by zero.

11.5 Java Exception Hierarchy

All Java exception classes inherit directly or indirectly from class **Exception**, forming an *inheritance hierarchy*. You can extend this hierarchy with your own exception classes.

Figure 11.4 shows a small portion of the inheritance hierarchy for class **Throwable** (a subclass of Object), which is the superclass of class Exception. Only Throwable objects can be used with the exception-handling mechanism. Class Throwable has two direct subclasses: Exception and Error. Class Exception and its subclasses—for example, RuntimeException (package java.lang) and IOException (package java.io)—represent exceptional situations that can occur in a Java program and that can be caught by the application. Class **Error** and its subclasses represent *abnormal situations* that happen in the JVM. Most *Errors happen infrequently and should not be caught by applications—it's usually not possible for applications to recover from Errors.*

The Java exception hierarchy contains hundreds of classes. Information about Java's exception classes can be found throughout the Java API. You can view Throwable's documentation at

```
http://docs.oracle.com/javase/8/docs/api/java/lang/Throwable.html
```

From there, you can look at this class's subclasses to get more information about Java's Exceptions and Errors.

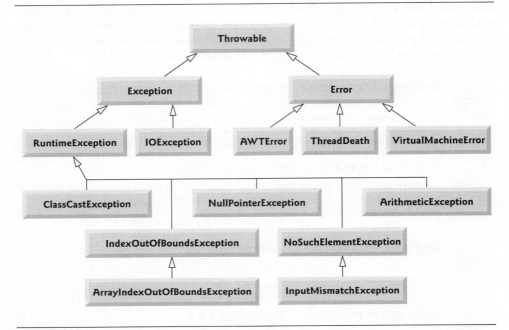

Fig. 11.4 | Portion of class `Throwable`'s inheritance hierarchy.

Checked vs. Unchecked Exceptions

Java distinguishes between **checked exceptions** and **unchecked exceptions**. This distinction is important, because the Java compiler enforces special requirements for *checked* exceptions (discussed momentarily). An exception's type determines whether it's checked or unchecked.

RuntimeExceptions Are Unchecked Exceptions

All exception types that are direct or indirect subclasses of **RuntimeException** (package `java.lang`) are *unchecked* exceptions. These are typically caused by defects in your program's code. Examples of unchecked exceptions include:

- `ArrayIndexOutOfBoundsExceptions` (discussed in Chapter 7)—You can avoid these by ensuring that your array indices are always greater than or equal to 0 and less than the array's `length`.

- `ArithmeticExceptions` (shown in Fig. 11.3)—You can avoid the `Arithmetic-Exception` that occurs when you divide by zero by checking the denominator to determine whether it's 0 *before* performing the calculation.

Classes that inherit directly or indirectly from class `Error` (Fig. 11.4) are *unchecked*, because `Error`s typically are unrecoverable, so your program should not even attempt to deal with them. For example, the documentation for `VirtualMachineError` says that these are "thrown to indicate that the Java Virtual Machine is broken or has run out of resources necessary for it to continue operating." At this point, there's nothing your program can do.

Checked Exceptions

All classes that inherit from class Exception but *not* directly or indirectly from class Run-timeException are considered to be *checked* exceptions. Such exceptions are typically caused by conditions that are not under the control of the program—for example, in file processing, the program can't open a file if it does not exist.

The Compiler and Checked Exceptions

The compiler checks each method call and method declaration to determine whether the method throws a checked exception. If so, the compiler verifies that the checked exception is *caught* or is *declared* in a throws clause—this is known as the **catch-or-declare requirement**. We show how to catch or declare checked exceptions in the next several examples. Recall from Section 11.3 that the throws clause specifies the exceptions a method throws. Such exceptions are not caught in the method's body. To satisfy the *catch* part of the *catch-or-declare requirement*, the code that generates the exception must be wrapped in a try block and must provide a catch handler for the checked-exception type (or one of its superclasses). To satisfy the *declare* part of the catch-or-declare requirement, the method containing the code that generates the exception must provide a throws clause containing the checked-exception type after its parameter list and before its method body. If the catch-or-declare requirement is not satisfied, the compiler will issue an error message. This forces you to think about the problems that may occur when a method that throws checked exceptions is called.

Error-Prevention Tip 11.2
You must deal with checked exceptions. This results in more robust code than would be created if you were able to simply ignore them.

Common Programming Error 11.2
If a subclass method overrides a superclass method, it's an error for the subclass method to list more exceptions in its throws clause than the superclass method does. However, a subclass's throws clause can contain a subset of a superclass's throws clause.

Software Engineering Observation 11.7
If your method calls other methods that throw checked exceptions, those exceptions must be caught or declared. If an exception can be handled meaningfully in a method, the method should catch the exception rather than declare it.

Software Engineering Observation 11.8
Checked exceptions represent problems from which programs often can recover, so programmers are required to deal with them.

The Compiler and Unchecked Exceptions

Unlike checked exceptions, the Java compiler does *not* examine the code to determine whether an unchecked exception is caught or declared. Unchecked exceptions typically can be *prevented* by proper coding. For example, the unchecked ArithmeticException thrown by method quotient (lines 9–12) in Fig. 11.3 can be avoided if the method ensures that the denominator is not zero *before* performing the division. Unchecked exceptions are *not* required to be listed in a method's throws clause—even if they are, it's *not* required that such exceptions be caught by an application.

Software Engineering Observation 11.9

Although the compiler does not enforce the catch-or-declare *requirement for unchecked exceptions, provide appropriate exception-handling code when it's known that such exceptions might occur. For example, a program should process the* NumberFormatException *from* Integer *method* parseInt, *even though* NumberFormatException *is an indirect subclass of* RuntimeException *(and thus an unchecked exception). This makes your programs more robust.*

Catching Subclass Exceptions

If a catch handler is written to catch *superclass* exception objects, it can also catch all objects of that class's *subclasses*. This enables catch to handle related exceptions polymorphically. You can catch each subclass individually if they require different processing.

Only the First Matching catch *Executes*

If *multiple* catch blocks match a particular exception type, only the *first* matching catch block executes when an exception of that type occurs. It's a compilation error to catch the *exact same type* in two different catch blocks associated with a particular try block. However, there can be several catch blocks that match an exception—i.e., several catch blocks whose types are the same as the exception type or a superclass of that type. For example, we could follow a catch block for type ArithmeticException with a catch block for type Exception—both would match ArithmeticExceptions, but only the first matching catch block would execute.

Common Programming Error 11.3

Placing a catch *block for a superclass exception type before other* catch *blocks that catch subclass exception types would prevent those* catch *blocks from executing, so a compilation error occurs.*

Error-Prevention Tip 11.3

Catching subclass types individually is subject to error if you forget to test for one or more of the subclass types explicitly; catching the superclass guarantees that objects of all subclasses will be caught. Positioning a catch *block for the superclass type after all other subclass* catch *blocks ensures that all subclass exceptions are eventually caught.*

Software Engineering Observation 11.10

In industry, throwing or catching type Exception *is discouraged—we use it in this chapter simply to demonstrate exception-handling mechanics. In subsequent chapters, we generally throw and catch more specific exception types.*

11.6 finally Block

Programs that obtain certain resources must return them to the system to avoid so-called **resource leaks.** In programming languages such as C and C++, the most common resource leak is a *memory leak*. Java performs automatic *garbage collection* of memory no longer used by programs, thus avoiding most memory leaks. However, other types of resource leaks can occur. For example, files, database connections and network connections that are not closed properly after they're no longer needed might not be available for use in other programs.

Error-Prevention Tip 11.4

A subtle issue is that Java does not entirely eliminate memory leaks. Java will not garbage-collect an object until there are no remaining references to it. Thus, if you erroneously keep references to unwanted objects, memory leaks can occur.

The optional finally block (sometimes referred to as the **finally clause**) consists of the finally keyword, followed by code enclosed in curly braces. If it's present, it's placed after the last catch block. If there are no catch blocks, the finally block is required and immediately follows the try block.

When the finally Block Executes

The finally block will execute *whether or not* an exception is thrown in the corresponding try block. The finally block also will execute if a try block exits by using a return, break or continue statement or simply by reaching its closing right brace. The one case in which the finally block will *not* execute is if the application *exits early* from a try block by calling method **System.exit**. This method, which we demonstrate in Chapter 15, *immediately* terminates an application.

If an exception that occurs in a try block cannot be caught by one of that try block's catch handlers, the program skips the rest of the try block and control proceeds to the finally block. Then the program passes the exception to the next outer try block—normally in the calling method—where an associated catch block might catch it. This process can occur through many levels of try blocks. Also, the exception could go *uncaught* (as we discussed in Section 11.3).

If a catch block throws an exception, the finally block still executes. Then the exception is passed to the next outer try block—again, normally in the calling method.

Releasing Resources in a finally Block

Because a finally block always executes, it typically contains *resource-release code*. Suppose a resource is allocated in a try block. If no exception occurs, the catch blocks are *skipped* and control proceeds to the finally block, which frees the resource. Control then proceeds to the first statement after the finally block. If an exception occurs in the try block, the try block *terminates*. If the program catches the exception in one of the corresponding catch blocks, it processes the exception, then the finally block *releases the resource* and control proceeds to the first statement after the finally block. If the program doesn't catch the exception, the finally block *still* releases the resource and an attempt is made to catch the exception in a calling method.

Error-Prevention Tip 11.5

The finally block is an ideal place to release resources acquired in a try block (such as opened files), which helps eliminate resource leaks.

Performance Tip 11.1

Always release a resource explicitly and at the earliest possible moment at which it's no longer needed. This makes resources available for reuse as early as possible, thus improving resource utilization and program performance.

Demonstrating the `finally` Block

Figure 11.5 demonstrates that the `finally` block executes even if an exception is *not* thrown in the corresponding `try` block. The program contains static methods main (lines 5–14), throwException (lines 17–35) and doesNotThrowException (lines 38–50). Methods throwException and doesNotThrowException are declared `static`, so main can call them directly without instantiating a `UsingExceptions` object.

```
1   // Fig. 11.5: UsingExceptions.java
2   // try...catch...finally exception handling mechanism.
3
4   public class UsingExceptions {
5      public static void main(String[] args) {
6         try {
7            throwException();
8         }
9         catch (Exception exception) { // exception thrown by throwException
10           System.err.println("Exception handled in main");
11        }
12
13        doesNotThrowException();
14     }
15
16     // demonstrate try...catch...finally
17     public static void throwException() throws Exception {
18        try { // throw an exception and immediately catch it
19           System.out.println("Method throwException");
20           throw new Exception(); // generate exception
21        }
22        catch (Exception exception) { // catch exception thrown in try
23           System.err.println(
24              "Exception handled in method throwException");
25           throw exception; // rethrow for further processing
26
27           // code here would not be reached; would cause compilation errors
28
29        }
30        finally { // executes regardless of what occurs in try...catch
31           System.err.println("Finally executed in throwException");
32        }
33
34        // code here would not be reached; would cause compilation errors
35     }
36
37     // demonstrate finally when no exception occurs
38     public static void doesNotThrowException() {
39        try { // try block does not throw an exception
40           System.out.println("Method doesNotThrowException");
41        }
42        catch (Exception exception) { // does not execute
43           System.err.println(exception);
44        }
```

Fig. 11.5 | try...catch...finally exception-handling mechanism. (Part 1 of 2.)

```
45          finally { // executes regardless of what occurs in try...catch
46             System.err.println("Finally executed in doesNotThrowException");
47          }
48
49          System.out.println("End of method doesNotThrowException");
50       }
51    }
```

```
Method throwException
Exception handled in method throwException
Finally executed in throwException
Exception handled in main
Method doesNotThrowException
Finally executed in doesNotThrowException
End of method doesNotThrowException
```

Fig. 11.5 | try...catch...finally exception-handling mechanism. (Part 2 of 2.)

System.out and System.err are **streams**—sequences of bytes. While System.out (known as the **standard output stream**) displays a program's output, System.err (known as the **standard error stream**) displays a program's errors. Output from these streams can be *redirected* (i.e., sent to somewhere other than the *command prompt*, such as to a *file*). Using two different streams enables you to easily *separate* error messages from other output. For example, data output from System.err could be sent to a log file, while data output from System.out can be displayed on the screen. For simplicity, this chapter will *not* redirect output from System.err but will display such messages to the *command prompt*. You'll learn more about input/output streams in Chapter 15.

*Throwing Exceptions Using the **throw** Statement*
Method main (Fig. 11.5) begins executing, enters its try block and immediately calls method throwException (line 7). Method throwException throws an Exception. The statement at line 20 is known as a **throw statement**—it's executed to indicate that an exception has occurred. So far, you've caught only exceptions thrown by called methods. You can throw exceptions yourself by using the throw statement. Just as with exceptions thrown by the Java API's methods, this indicates to client applications that an error has occurred. A throw statement specifies an object to be thrown. The operand of a throw can be of any class derived from class Throwable.

Software Engineering Observation 11.11
When toString is invoked on any Throwable object, its resulting String includes the descriptive string that was supplied to the constructor, or simply the class name if no string was supplied.

Software Engineering Observation 11.12
An exception can be thrown without containing information about the problem that occurred. In this case, simply knowing that an exception of a particular type occurred may provide sufficient information for the handler to process the problem correctly.

Software Engineering Observation 11.13

Throw exceptions from constructors to indicate that the constructor parameters are not valid—this prevents an object from being created in an invalid state.

Rethrowing Exceptions

Line 25 of Fig. 11.5 **rethrows the exception**. Exceptions are rethrown when a catch block, upon receiving an exception, decides either that it cannot process that exception or that it can only partially process it. Rethrowing an exception defers the exception handling (or perhaps a portion of it) to another catch block associated with an outer try statement. An exception is rethrown by using the **throw keyword**, followed by a reference to the exception object that was just caught. Exceptions cannot be rethrown from a finally block, as the exception parameter (a local variable) from the catch block no longer exists.

When a rethrow occurs, the *next enclosing try block* detects the rethrown exception, and that try block's catch blocks attempt to handle it. In this case, the next enclosing try block is found at lines 6–8 in method main. Before the rethrown exception is handled, however, the finally block (lines 30–32) executes. Then method main detects the rethrown exception in the try block and handles it in the catch block (lines 9–11).

Next, main calls method doesNotThrowException (line 13). No exception is thrown in doesNotThrowException's try block (lines 39–41), so the program skips the catch block (lines 42–44), but the finally block (lines 45–47) nevertheless executes. Control proceeds to the statement after the finally block (line 49). Then control returns to main and the program terminates.

Common Programming Error 11.4

If an exception has not been caught when control enters a finally block and the finally block throws an exception that's not caught in the finally block, the first exception will be lost *and the exception from the finally block will be returned to the calling method.*

Error-Prevention Tip 11.6

Avoid placing in a finally block code that can throw an exception. If such code is required, enclose the code in a try...catch within the finally block.

Common Programming Error 11.5

Assuming that an exception thrown from a catch block will be processed by that catch block or any other catch block associated with the same try statement can lead to logic errors.

Good Programming Practice 11.1

Exception handling removes error-processing code from the main line of a program's code to improve program clarity. Do not place try...catch...finally around every statement that may throw an exception. This decreases readability. Rather, place one try block around a significant portion of your code, follow the try with catch blocks that handle each possible exception and follow the catch blocks with a single finally block (if one is required).

11.7 Stack Unwinding and Obtaining Information from an Exception

When an exception is thrown but *not caught* in a particular method, the method-call stack is "unwound," and an attempt is made to catch the exception in the next outer try block. This process is called **stack unwinding**. Unwinding the method-call stack means that the method in which the exception was not caught *terminates*, all local variables in that method *go out of scope* and control returns to the statement that originally invoked that method. If a try block encloses that statement, an attempt is made to catch the exception. If a try block does not enclose that statement or if the exception is not caught, stack unwinding occurs again. Figure 11.6 demonstrates stack unwinding, and the exception handler in main shows how to access the data in an exception object.

```java
1   // Fig. 11.6: UsingExceptions.java
2   // Stack unwinding and obtaining data from an exception object.
3
4   public class UsingExceptions {
5      public static void main(String[] args) {
6         try {
7            method1();
8         }
9         catch (Exception exception) { // catch exception thrown in method1
10           System.err.printf("%s%n%n", exception.getMessage());
11           exception.printStackTrace();
12
13           // obtain the stack-trace information
14           StackTraceElement[] traceElements = exception.getStackTrace();
15
16           System.out.printf("%nStack trace from getStackTrace:%n");
17           System.out.println("Class\t\tFile\t\t\tLine\tMethod");
18
19           // loop through traceElements to get exception description
20           for (StackTraceElement element : traceElements) {
21              System.out.printf("%s\t", element.getClassName());
22              System.out.printf("%s\t", element.getFileName());
23              System.out.printf("%s\t", element.getLineNumber());
24              System.out.printf("%s%n", element.getMethodName());
25           }
26        }
27     }
28
29     // call method2; throw exceptions back to main
30     public static void method1() throws Exception {
31        method2();
32     }
33
34     // call method3; throw exceptions back to method1
35     public static void method2() throws Exception {
36        method3();
37     }
```

Fig. 11.6 | Stack unwinding and obtaining data from an exception object. (Part 1 of 2.)

```
38
39      // throw Exception back to method2
40      public static void method3() throws Exception {
41          throw new Exception("Exception thrown in method3");
42      }
43  }
```

```
Exception thrown in method3

java.lang.Exception: Exception thrown in method3
        at UsingExceptions.method3(UsingExceptions.java:41)
        at UsingExceptions.method2(UsingExceptions.java:36)
        at UsingExceptions.method1(UsingExceptions.java:31)
        at UsingExceptions.main(UsingExceptions.java:7)

Stack trace from getStackTrace:
Class           File                    Line    Method
UsingExceptions UsingExceptions.java    41      method3
UsingExceptions UsingExceptions.java    36      method2
UsingExceptions UsingExceptions.java    31      method1
UsingExceptions UsingExceptions.java    7       main
```

Fig. 11.6 | Stack unwinding and obtaining data from an exception object. (Part 2 of 2.)

Stack Unwinding

In main, the try block (lines 6–8) calls method1 (declared at lines 30–32), which in turn calls method2 (declared at lines 35–37), which in turn calls method3 (declared at lines 40–42). Line 41 in method3 throws an Exception object—this is the *throw point*. Because the throw statement is *not* enclosed in a try block, *stack unwinding* occurs—method3 terminates at line 41, then returns control to the statement in method2 that invoked method3 (i.e., line 36). Because *no* try block encloses line 36, *stack unwinding* occurs again—method2 terminates at line 36 and returns control to the statement in method1 that invoked method2 (i.e., line 31). Because *no* try block encloses line 31, *stack unwinding* occurs one more time—method1 terminates at line 31 and returns control to the statement in main that invoked method1 (i.e., line 7). The try block at lines 6–8 encloses this statement. The exception has not been handled, so the try block terminates and the first matching catch block (lines 9–26) catches and processes the exception. If there were no matching catch blocks, and the exception is *not declared* in each method that throws it, a compilation error would occur—main does not have a throws clause because main catches the exception. Remember that this is not always the case—for *unchecked* exceptions, the application will compile, but it will run with unexpected results.

Obtaining Data from an Exception Object

All exceptions derive from class Throwable, which has a **printStackTrace** method that outputs to the standard error stream the *stack trace* (discussed in Section 11.2). Often this is helpful in testing and debugging. Class Throwable also provides a **getStackTrace** method that retrieves the stack-trace information that might be printed by printStackTrace. Class Throwable's **getMessage** method (inherited by all Throwable subclasses) returns the descriptive string stored in an exception. Throwable method toString (also inherited by all Throwable subclasses) returns a String containing the name of the exception's class and a descriptive message.

An exception that's not caught in an application causes Java's *default exception handler* to run. This displays the name of the exception, a descriptive message that indicates the problem that occurred and a complete execution stack trace. In an application with a single thread of execution, the application terminates. In an application with multiple threads, the thread that caused the exception terminates. We discuss multithreading in Chapter 21.

The `catch` handler in Fig. 11.6 (lines 9–26) demonstrates `getMessage`, `printStack-Trace` and `getStackTrace`. If we wanted to output the stack-trace information to streams other than the standard error stream, we could use the information returned from `get-StackTrace` and output it to another stream or use one of the overloaded versions of method `printStackTrace`. Sending data to other streams is discussed in Chapter 15.

Line 10 invokes the exception's `getMessage` method to get the *exception description*. Line 11 invokes the exception's `printStackTrace` method to output the *stack trace* that indicates where the exception occurred. Line 14 invokes the exception's `getStackTrace` method to obtain the stack-trace information as an array of **StackTraceElement** objects. Lines 20–25 get each `StackTraceElement` in the array and invoke its methods **get-ClassName**, **getFileName**, **getLineNumber** and **getMethodName** to get the class name, file-name, line number and method name, respectively, for that `StackTraceElement`. Each `StackTraceElement` represents *one* method call on the *method-call stack*.

The program's output shows that the output of `printStackTrace` follows the pattern: *className.methodName(fileName:lineNumber)*, where *className*, *methodName* and *file-Name* indicate the names of the class, method and file in which the exception occurred, respectively, and the *lineNumber* indicates where in the file the exception occurred. You saw this in the output for Fig. 11.2. Method `getStackTrace` enables custom processing of the exception information. Compare the output of `printStackTrace` with the output created from the `StackTraceElement`s to see that both contain the same stack-trace information.

Software Engineering Observation 11.14

Occasionally, you might want to ignore an exception by writing a `catch` handler with an empty body. Before doing so, ensure that the exception doesn't indicate a condition that code higher up the stack might want to know about or recover from.

Java SE 9: Stack-Walking API
`Throwable` methods `printStackTrace` and `getStackTrace` each process the entire method-call stack. When debugging, this can be inefficient—for example, you may be interested only in stack frames corresponding to methods of a specific class. Java SE 9 introduces the **Stack-Walking API** (class **StackWalker** in package `java.lang`), which uses lambdas and streams (introduced in Chapter 17) to access method-call-stack information in a more efficient manner. You can learn more about this API at:

```
http://openjdk.java.net/jeps/259
```

11.8 Chained Exceptions

Sometimes a method responds to an exception by throwing a different exception type that's specific to the current application. If a `catch` block throws a new exception, the original exception's information and stack trace are *lost*. Earlier Java versions provided no mechanism to wrap the original exception information with the new exception's information to provide a complete stack trace showing where the original problem occurred. This made debugging such problems particularly difficult. **Chained exceptions** enable an exception object to maintain the complete stack-trace information from the original exception. Figure 11.7 demonstrates chained exceptions.

```java
1   // Fig. 11.7: UsingChainedExceptions.java
2   // Chained exceptions.
3
4   public class UsingChainedExceptions {
5      public static void main(String[] args) {
6         try {
7            method1();
8         }
9         catch (Exception exception) { // exceptions thrown from method1
10           exception.printStackTrace();
11        }
12     }
13
14     // call method2; throw exceptions back to main
15     public static void method1() throws Exception {
16        try {
17           method2();
18        }
19        catch (Exception exception) { // exception thrown from method2
20           throw new Exception("Exception thrown in method1", exception);
21        }
22     }
23
24     // call method3; throw exceptions back to method1
25     public static void method2() throws Exception {
26        try {
27           method3();
28        }
29        catch (Exception exception) { // exception thrown from method3
30           throw new Exception("Exception thrown in method2", exception);
31        }
32     }
33
34     // throw Exception back to method2
35     public static void method3() throws Exception {
36        throw new Exception("Exception thrown in method3");
37     }
38  }
```

```
java.lang.Exception: Exception thrown in method1
        at UsingChainedExceptions.method1(UsingChainedExceptions.java:17)
        at UsingChainedExceptions.main(UsingChainedExceptions.java:7)
```

Fig. 11.7 | Chained exceptions. (Part 1 of 2.)

```
Caused by: java.lang.Exception: Exception thrown in method2
        at UsingChainedExceptions.method2(UsingChainedExceptions.java:27)
        at UsingChainedExceptions.method1(UsingChainedExceptions.java:17)
        ... 1 more
Caused by: java.lang.Exception: Exception thrown in method3
        at UsingChainedExceptions.method3(UsingChainedExceptions.java:36)
        at UsingChainedExceptions.method2(UsingChainedExceptions.java:27)
        ... 2 more
```

Fig. 11.7 | Chained exceptions. (Part 2 of 2.)

Program Flow of Control

The program has four methods—main (lines 5–12), method1 (lines 15–22), method2 (lines 25–32) and method3 (lines 35–37). Line 7 in main's try block calls method1. Line 17 in method1's try block calls method2. Line 27 in method2's try block calls method3. In method3, line 36 throws a new Exception. Because line 36 is not in a try block, method3 terminates, and the exception is returned to the calling method (method2) at line 27. This statement *is* in a try block; therefore, the try block terminates and the exception is caught at lines 29–31. Line 30 in the catch block throws a new exception. We call the Exception constructor with *two* arguments—the second represents the exception that was the original cause of the problem. In this program, that exception occurred at line 36. Because an exception is thrown from the catch block, method2 terminates and returns the new exception to method1 at line 17. Once again, this statement is in a try block, so the try block terminates and the exception is caught at lines 19–21. Line 20 in the catch block throws a new exception and uses the exception that was caught as the second argument to Exception's constructor. Because an exception is thrown from the catch block, method1 terminates and returns the new exception to main at line 7. The try block in main terminates, and the exception is caught at lines 9–11. Line 10 prints a stack trace.

Throwable *Method* getCause

For any chained exception, you can get the Throwable that initially caused that exception by calling Throwable method **getCause**.

Program Output

Notice in the program output that the first three lines show the most recent exception that was thrown (i.e., the one from method1 at line 20). The next four lines indicate the exception that was thrown from method2 at line 27. Finally, the last four lines represent the exception that was thrown from method3 at line 36. Also notice that, as you read the output in reverse, it shows how many more chained exceptions remain.

11.9 Declaring New Exception Types

Most Java programmers use *existing* classes from the Java API, third-party vendors and freely available class libraries (usually downloadable from the Internet) to build Java applications. The methods of those classes typically are declared to throw appropriate exceptions when problems occur. You write code that processes these existing exceptions to make your programs more robust.

If you build classes that other programmers will use, it's often appropriate to declare your own exception classes that are specific to the problems that can occur when another programmer uses your reusable classes.

A New Exception Type Must Extend an Existing One

A new exception class must extend an existing exception class to ensure that the class can be used with the exception-handling mechanism. An exception class is like any other class; however, a typical new exception class contains no members other than four constructors:

- one that takes no arguments and passes a default error message String to the superclass constructor

- one that receives a customized error message as a String and passes it to the superclass constructor

- one that receives a customized error message as a String and a Throwable (for chaining exceptions) and passes both to the superclass constructor

- one that receives a Throwable (for chaining exceptions) and passes it to the superclass constructor.

Good Programming Practice 11.2

Associating each type of serious execution-time malfunction with an appropriately named Exception class improves program clarity.

Software Engineering Observation 11.15

Most programmers will not need to declare their own exception classes. Before defining your own, study the existing ones in the Java API and try to choose one that already exists. If there is not an appropriate existing class, try to extend a related exception class. For example, if you're creating a new class to represent when a method attempts a division by zero, you might extend class ArithmeticException because division by zero occurs during arithmetic. If the existing classes are not appropriate superclasses for your new exception class, decide whether your new class should be a checked or an unchecked exception class. If clients should be required to handle the exception, the new exception class should be a checked exception (i.e., extend Exception but not RuntimeException). The client application should be able to reasonably recover from such an exception. If the client code should be able to ignore the exception (i.e., the exception is an unchecked one), the new exception class should extend RuntimeException.

Good Programming Practice 11.3

By convention, all exception-class names should end with the word Exception.

11.10 Preconditions and Postconditions

Programmers spend significant amounts of time maintaining and debugging code. To facilitate these tasks and to improve the overall design, you can specify the expected states before and after a method's execution. These states are called preconditions and postconditions, respectively.

Preconditions

A **precondition** must be true when a method is *invoked*. Preconditions describe constraints on method parameters and any other expectations the method has about the current state of a program *just before it begins executing*. If the preconditions are *not* met, then the method's behavior is *undefined*—it may *throw an exception, proceed with an illegal value* or *attempt to recover* from the error. You should not expect consistent behavior if the preconditions are not satisfied.

Postconditions

A **postcondition** is true *after the method successfully returns*. Postconditions describe *constraints on the return value* and any other *side effects* the method may have. When defining a method, you should document all postconditions so that others know what to expect when they call your method, and you should make certain that your method honors all its postconditions if its preconditions are indeed met.

Throwing Exceptions When Preconditions or Postconditions Are Not Met

When their preconditions or postconditions are not met, methods typically throw exceptions. Consider String method charAt, which has one int parameter—an index in the String. As a precondition, method charAt assumes that index is greater than or equal to zero and less than the String's length. If the precondition is met, the postcondition states that the method will return the character at the position specified by the parameter index. Otherwise, the method throws an IndexOutOfBoundsException. We trust that method charAt satisfies its postcondition, provided that we meet the precondition. We need not be concerned with the details of how the method actually retrieves the character at the index.

Typically, a method's preconditions and postconditions are described as part of its specification. When designing your own methods, you typically state the preconditions and postconditions in a comment before the method declaration.

11.11 Assertions

When implementing and debugging a class, it's sometimes useful to state conditions that should be true at a particular point in a method. These conditions, called **assertions**, help ensure a program's validity by catching potential bugs and identifying possible logic errors during development. Preconditions and postconditions are two types of assertions. Preconditions are assertions about a program's state when a method is invoked, and postconditions are assertions about its state after a method finishes.

While assertions can be stated as comments to guide you during program development, Java includes two versions of the **assert** statement for validating assertions programatically. The assert statement evaluates a boolean expression and, if false, throws an **AssertionError** (a subclass of Error). The first form of the assert statement is

```
assert expression;
```

which throws an AssertionError if *expression* is false. The second form is

```
assert expression1 : expression2;
```

which evaluates *expression1* and throws an AssertionError with *expression2* as the error message if *expression1* is false.

You can use assertions to implement *preconditions* and *postconditions* programmatically or to verify any other *intermediate* states that help you ensure that your code is working correctly. Figure 11.8 demonstrates the `assert` statement. Line 9 prompts the user to enter a number between 0 and 10, then line 10 reads the number. Line 13 determines whether the user entered a number within the valid range. If the number is out of range, the `assert` statement reports an error; otherwise, the program proceeds normally.

```
1   // Fig. 11.8: AssertTest.java
2   // Checking with assert that a value is within range
3   import java.util.Scanner;
4
5   public class AssertTest {
6      public static void main(String[] args) {
7         Scanner input = new Scanner(System.in);
8
9         System.out.print("Enter a number between 0 and 10: ");
10        int number = input.nextInt();
11
12        // assert that the value is >= 0 and <= 10
13        assert (number >= 0 && number <= 10) : "bad number: " + number;
14
15        System.out.printf("You entered %d%n", number);
16     }
17  }
```

```
Enter a number between 0 and 10: 5
You entered 5
```

```
Enter a number between 0 and 10: 50
Exception in thread "main" java.lang.AssertionError: bad number: 50
        at AssertTest.main(AssertTest.java:13)
```

Fig. 11.8 | Checking with `assert` that a value is within range.

You use assertions primarily for debugging and identifying logic errors in an application. You must explicitly enable assertions when executing a program, because they reduce performance and are unnecessary for the program's user. To do so, use the java command's -ea command-line option, as in

```
java -ea AssertTest
```

Software Engineering Observation 11.16

Users shouldn't encounter `AssertionError`s—these should be used only during program development. For this reason, you shouldn't catch `AssertionError`s. Instead, allow the program to terminate, so you can see the error message, then locate and fix the source of the problem. You should not use `assert` to indicate runtime problems in production code (as we did in Fig. 11.8 for demonstration purposes)—use the exception mechanism for this purpose.

11.12 try-with-Resources: Automatic Resource Deallocation

Typically *resource-release code* should be placed in a `finally` block to ensure that a resource is released, regardless of whether there were exceptions when the resource was used in the corresponding `try` block. An alternative notation—the **try-with-resources** statement—simplifies writing code in which you obtain one or more resources, use them in a `try` block and release them in a corresponding `finally` block. For example, a file-processing application could process a file with a `try`-with-resources statement to ensure that the file is closed properly when it's no longer needed—we demonstrate this in Chapter 15. Each resource must be an object of a class that implements the **AutoCloseable** interface and thus provides a `close` method.

The general form of a `try`-with-resources statement is

```
try (ClassName theObject = new ClassName()) {
    // use theObject here, then release its resources at
    // the end of the try block
}
catch (Exception e) {
    // catch exceptions that occur while using the resource
}
```

where *ClassName* is a class that implements `AutoCloseable`. This code creates a *ClassName* object, uses it in the `try` block, then calls its `close` method *at the end of the* `try` *block—or, if an exception occurs, at the end of a* `catch` *block*—to release the object's resources. You can create multiple `AutoCloseable` objects in the parentheses following `try` by separating them with a semicolon (;). You'll see examples of the `try`-with-resources statement in Chapters 15 and 22.

Java SE 9: **try-with-Resources Can Use Effectively `final` Variables**

Java SE 8 introduced **effectively `final`** local variables. If the compiler can *infer* that the variable could have been declared `final`, because its enclosing method never modifies the variable after it's declared and initialized, then the variable is effectively `final`. Such variables frequently are used with lambdas (Chapter 17, Lambdas and Streams).

As of Java SE 9, you can create an `AutoCloseable` object and assign it to a local variable that's explicitly declared `final` or that's effectively `final`. Then, you can use it in a `try`-with-resources statement that releases the object's resources at the end of the `try` block.

```
ClassName theObject = new ClassName();

try (theObject) {
    // use theObject here, then release its resources at
    // the end of the try block
}
catch (Exception e) {
    // catch exceptions that occur while using the resource
}
```

As before, you can separate with a semicolon (;) multiple `AutoCloseable` objects in the parentheses following `try`. This simplifies the `try`-with-resources statement's code, especially for cases in which the statement uses and releases multiple `AutoCloseable` objects.

11.13 Wrap-Up

In this chapter, you learned how to use exception handling to deal with errors. You learned that exception handling enables you to remove error-handling code from the "main line" of the program's execution. We showed how to use `try` blocks to enclose code that may throw an exception, and how to use `catch` blocks to deal with exceptions that may arise.

You learned about the termination model of exception handling, which dictates that after an exception is handled, program control does not return to the throw point. We discussed checked vs. unchecked exceptions, and how to specify with the `throws` clause the exceptions that a method might throw.

You learned how to use the `finally` block to release resources whether or not an exception occurs. You also learned how to throw and rethrow exceptions. We showed how to obtain information about an exception using methods `printStackTrace`, `getStack-Trace` and `getMessage`. Next, we presented chained exceptions, which allow you to wrap original exception information with new exception information. Then, we showed how to create your own exception classes.

We introduced preconditions and postconditions to help programmers using your methods understand conditions that must be true when the method is called and when it returns, respectively. When preconditions and postconditions are not met, methods typically throw exceptions. We discussed the `assert` statement and how it can be used to help you debug your programs. In particular, `assert` can be used to ensure that preconditions and postconditions are met.

We also introduced multi-`catch` for processing several types of exceptions in the same `catch` handler and the `try`-with-resources statement for automatically deallocating a resource after it's used in the `try` block. In the next chapter, we take a deeper look at graphical user interfaces (GUIs).

12

JavaFX Graphical User Interfaces: Part 1

Objectives

In this chapter you'll:

- Build JavaFX GUIs and handle events generated by user interactions with them.
- Understand the structure of a JavaFX app window.
- Use JavaFX Scene Builder to create FXML files that describe JavaFX scenes containing `Label`s, `ImageView`s, `TextField`s, `Slider`s and `Button`s without writing any code.
- Arrange GUI components using the `VBox` and `GridPane` layout containers.
- Use a controller class to define event handlers for JavaFX FXML GUI.
- Build two JavaFX apps.

Outline

12.1 Introduction

A **graphical user interface (GUI)** presents a user-friendly mechanism for interacting with an app. A GUI (pronounced "GOO-ee") gives an app a distinctive "look-and-feel." GUIs are built from **GUI components**—also called *controls* or *widgets* (short for window gadgets). A GUI component is an object with which the user interacts via the mouse, the keyboard or another form of input, such as voice recognition.

Look-and-Feel Observation 12.1

Providing different apps with consistent, intuitive user-interface components gives users a sense of familiarity with a new app, so that they can learn it more quickly and use it more productively.

History of GUI in Java

Java's original GUI library was the Abstract Window Toolkit (AWT). Swing was added to the platform in Java SE 1.2. Until recently, Swing was the primary Java GUI technology. Swing will remain part of Java and is still widely used.

JavaFX is Java's GUI, graphics and multimedia API of the future. Sun Microsystems (acquired by Oracle in 2010) announced JavaFX in 2007 as a competitor to Adobe Flash and Microsoft Silverlight. JavaFX 1.0 was released in 2008. Prior to version 2.0, developers wrote JavaFX apps in JavaFX Script, which compiled to Java bytecode, allowing JavaFX apps to run on the Java Virtual Machine. Starting with version 2.0 in 2011, JavaFX was reimplemented as Java libraries that could be used directly in Java apps. Some of the benefits of JavaFX over Swing include:

- JavaFX is easier to use—it provides one API for client functionality, including GUI, graphics and multimedia (images, animation, audio and video). Swing is only for GUIs, so you need to use other APIs for graphics and multimedia apps.

- With Swing, many IDEs provided GUI design tools for dragging and dropping components onto a layout; however, each IDE produced different code (such as different variable and method names). JavaFX Scene Builder (Section 12.2) can be used standalone or integrated with many IDEs and it produces the same code regardless of the IDE.

- Though Swing components could be customized, JavaFX gives you complete control over a JavaFX GUI's look-and-feel (Chapter 13) via Cascading Style Sheets (CSS)—the same technology used to style web pages.

- JavaFX has better threading support, which is important for getting the best application performance on today's multi-core systems.

- JavaFX uses hardware-accelerated rendering via the GPU (graphics processing unit),

- JavaFX supports transformations for repositioning and reorienting JavaFX components, and animations for changing the properties of JavaFX components over time. These can be used to make apps more intuitive and easier to use.

- JavaFX provides multiple upgrade paths for enhancing existing GUIs—Swing GUI capabilities may be embedded into JavaFX apps via class `SwingNode` and JavaFX capabilities may be embedded into Swing apps via class `JFXPanel`.

This chapter introduces JavaFX GUI basics—we present a more detailed treatment of Java FX GUI in the next chapter. Chapter 20 discusses graphics and multimedia.

12.2 JavaFX Scene Builder

Most Java textbooks that introduce GUI programming provide hand-coded GUIs—that is, the authors build the GUIs from scratch in Java code, rather than using a visual GUI design tool. This is due to the fractured Java IDE market—there are many Java IDEs, so authors can't depend on any one IDE being used, and each generates different code.

JavaFX is organized differently. The **Scene Builder** tool is a standalone JavaFX GUI visual layout tool that can also be used with various IDEs, including the most popular ones—Eclipse, IntelliJ IDEA and NetBeans. You can download Scene Builder at:

```
http://gluonhq.com/labs/scene-builder/
```

JavaFX Scene Builder enables you to create GUIs by dragging and dropping GUI components from Scene Builder's library onto a design area, then modifying and styling the GUI—all without writing any code. JavaFX Scene Builder's live editing and preview features allow you to view your GUI as you create and modify it, without compiling and running the app. You can use **Cascading Style Sheets** (CSS) to change the entire look-and-feel of your GUI—a concept sometimes called **skinning**. In Chapter 20, we'll introduce styling with CSS.

FXML (FX Markup Language)

As you create and modify a GUI, JavaFX Scene Builder generates **FXML** (**FX Markup Language**)—an XML vocabulary for defining and arranging JavaFX GUI controls without writing any Java code. XML (eXtensible Markup Language) is a widely used language for describing things—it's readable both by computers and by humans. In JavaFX, FXML concisely describes GUI, graphics and multimedia elements. *You do not need to know FXML or XML to study this chapter.* As you'll see in Section 12.4, JavaFX Scene Builder hides the FXML details from you, so you can focus on defining *what* the GUI should contain without specifying *how* to generate it—this is an example of *declarative programming*.

Software Engineering Observation 12.1

The FXML code is separate from the program logic that's defined in Java source code—this separation of the interface (the GUI) from the implementation (the Java code) makes it easier to debug, modify and maintain JavaFX GUI apps.

12.3 JavaFX App Window Structure

A JavaFX app window consists of several parts (Fig. 12.1).

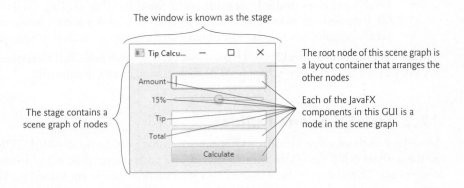

Fig. 12.1 | JavaFX app window parts.

Controls
Controls are GUI components, such as Labels that display text, TextFields that enable a program to receive user input, Buttons that users click to initiate actions, and more.

Stage
The window in which a JavaFX app's GUI is displayed is known as the **stage** and is an instance of class **Stage** (package javafx.stage).

Scene
The stage contains one active **scene** that defines the GUI as a **scene graph**—a tree data structure of an app's visual elements, such as GUI controls, shapes, images, video, text and more. The scene is an instance of class **Scene** (package javafx.scene).

Nodes
Each visual element in the scene graph is a **node**—an instance of a subclass of **Node** (package javafx.scene), which defines common attributes and behaviors for all nodes. With the exception of the first node in the scene graph—the **root node**—each node in the scene graph has one parent. Nodes can have transforms (e.g., moving, rotating and scaling), opacity (whether a node is transparent, partially transparent or opaque), effects (e.g., drop shadows, blurs, reflection and lighting) and more that we'll introduce in Chapter 20.

Layout Containers

Nodes that have children are typically **layout containers** that arrange their child nodes in the scene. You'll use two layout containers (VBox and GridPane) in this chapter and learn several more in Chapters 13 and 20. The nodes arranged in a layout container are a combination of controls and, in more complex GUIs, possibly other layout containers.

Event Handler and Controller Class

When the user interacts with a control, such as clicking a Button or typing text into a TextField, the control generates an event. Programs can respond to these events—known as event handling—to specify what should happen when each user interaction occurs. An **event handler** is a method that responds to a user interaction. An FXML GUI's event handlers are defined in a so-called **controller class** (as you'll see in Section 12.5.5).

12.4 Welcome App—Displaying Text and an Image

In this section, *without writing any code*, you'll build a GUI that displays text in a **Label** and an image in an **ImageView** (Fig. 12.2). You'll use visual-programming techniques to *drag-and-drop* JavaFX components onto Scene Builder's content panel—the design area. Next, you'll use Scene Builder's **Inspector** to configure options, such as the Labels's text and font size, and the ImageView's image. Finally, you'll view the completed GUI using Scene Builder's **Show Preview in Window** option. In Section 12.5's **Tip Calculator** app, we'll discuss the Java code necessary to load and display an FXML GUI.

Fig. 12.2 | Final **Welcome** GUI in a preview window on Microsoft Windows 10.

12.4.1 Opening Scene Builder and Creating the File Welcome.fxml

Open Scene Builder so that you can create the FXML file that defines the GUI. The window initially appears as shown in Fig. 12.3. **Untitled** at the top of the window indicates that Scene Builder has created a new FXML file that you have not yet saved.[1] Select **File > Save** to display the **Save As** dialog, then select a location in which to store the file, name the file Welcome.fxml and click the **Save** button.

The **Library** contains JavaFX **Containers**, **Controls** and other items that can be dragged and dropped on the canvas

You use the content panel to design the GUI

You use the **Inspector** window to configure the currently selected item in the content panel

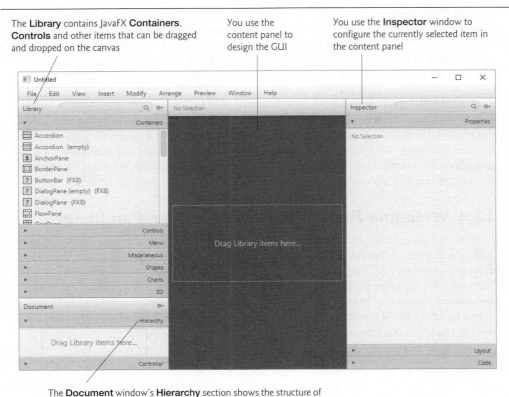

The **Document** window's **Hierarchy** section shows the structure of the GUI and allows you to select and reorganize controls

Fig. 12.3 | JavaFX Scene Builder when you first open it.

12.4.2 Adding an Image to the Folder Containing Welcome.fxml

The image you'll use for this app (bug.png) is located in the images subfolder of this chapter's examples folder. To make it easy to find the image when you're ready to add it to the app, locate the images folder on your file system, then copy bug.png into the folder where you saved Welcome.fxml.

12.4.3 Creating a VBox Layout Container

For this app, you'll place a Label and an ImageView in a **VBox layout container** (package javafx.scene.layout), which will be the scene graph's root node. Layout containers help you arrange and size GUI components. A VBox arranges its nodes *vertically* from top to bottom. We discuss the GridPane layout container in Section 12.5 and several others in Chapter 13. To add a VBox to Scene Builder's content panel so you can begin designing

---

1. We show the Scene Builder screen captures on Microsoft Windows 10, but Scene Builder is nearly identical on Windows, macOS and Linux. The key difference is that the menu bar on macOS is at the top of the screen, whereas the menu bar is part of the window on Windows and Linux.

the GUI, double-click **VBox** in the **Library** window's **Containers** section. (You also can drag-and-drop a VBox from the **Containers** section onto Scene Builder's content panel.)

12.4.4 Configuring the VBox Layout Container

You'll now specify the VBox's alignment, initial size and padding.

Specifying the **VBox's** Alignment

A VBox's **alignment** determines the layout positioning of the VBox's children. In this app, we'd like each child node (the Label and the ImageView) to be centered horizontally in the scene, and we'd like both children to be centered vertically, so that there is an equal amount of space above the Label and below the ImageView. To accomplish this:

1. Select the VBox in Scene Builder's content panel by clicking it. Scene Builder displays many VBox properties in the Scene Builder **Inspector**'s **Properties** section.

2. Click the **Alignment** property's drop-down list and notice the variety of potential alignment values you can use. Click CENTER to set the **Alignment**.

Each property value you specify for a JavaFX object is used to set one of that object's instance variables when JavaFX creates the object at runtime.

Specifying the **VBox's** Preferred Size

The **preferred size** (width and height) of the scene graph's root node is used by the scene to determine its window size when the app begins executing. To set the preferred size:

1. Select the VBox.

2. Expand the **Inspector**'s **Layout** section by clicking the right arrow (▶) next to **Layout**. The section expands and the right arrow changes to a down arrow. Clicking the arrow again would collapse the section.

3. Click the **Pref Width** property's text field, type 450 and press *Enter* to change the preferred width.

4. Click the **Pref Height** property's text field, type 300 and press *Enter* to change the preferred height.

12.4.5 Adding and Configuring a Label

Next, you'll create the Label that displays "Welcome to JavaFX!".

Adding a **Label** to the **VBox**

Expand the Scene Builder **Library** window's **Controls** section by clicking the right arrow (▶) next to **Controls**, then drag-and-drop a **Label** from the **Controls** section onto the VBox in Scene Builder's content panel. (You also can double-click **Label** in the **Containers** section to add the Label.) Scene Builder automatically centers the Label object horizontally and vertically in the VBox, based on the VBox's **Alignment** property.

Changing the **Label's** Text

You can set a Label's text either by double clicking it and typing the new text, or by selecting the Label and setting its **Text** property in the **Inspector**'s **Properties** section. Set the Label's text to "Welcome to JavaFX!".

*Changing the **Label**'s Font*
For this app, we set the Label to display in a large bold font. To do so, select the Label, then in the **Inspector**'s **Properties** section, click the value to the right of the **Font** property. In the window that appears, set the **Style** property to Bold and the **Size** property to 30. The design should now appear as shown in Fig. 12.4.

Scene Builder highlights
the container in which the
selected control appears

Selected control—you can
drag the blue handles at
the sides and corners to
resize the control

Fig. 12.4 | Welcome GUI's design after adding and configuring a Label.

12.4.6 Adding and Configuring an **ImageView**

Finally, you'll add the ImageView that displays bug.png.

*Adding an **ImageView** to the **VBox***
Drag and drop an **ImageView** from the **Library** window's **Controls** section to just below the Label, as shown in Fig. 12.5. You can also double-click **ImageView** in the **Library** window, in which case Scene Builder automatically places the new ImageView object below the Label. You can reorder a VBox's controls by dragging them in the VBox or in the **Document** window's **Hierarchy** section (Fig. 12.3). Scene Builder automatically centers the ImageView horizontally in the VBox. Also notice that the Label and ImageView are centered vertically such that the same amount of space appears above the Label and below the ImageView.

*Setting the **ImageView**'s Image*
Next you'll set the image to display:

1. Select the ImageView, then in the **Inspector**'s **Properties** section click the ellipsis (...) button to the right of the **Image** property. By default, Scene Builder opens a dialog showing the folder in which the FXML file is saved. This is where you placed the image file bug.png in Section 12.4.2.

2. Select the image file, then click **Open**. Scene Builder displays the image and resizes the ImageView to match the image's aspect ratio—that is, the ratio of the image's width to its height.

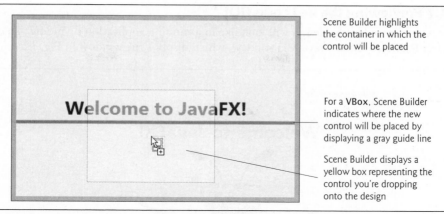

Scene Builder highlights the container in which the control will be placed

For a **VBox**, Scene Builder indicates where the new control will be placed by displaying a gray guide line

Scene Builder displays a yellow box representing the control you're dropping onto the design

Fig. 12.5 | Dragging and dropping the ImageView below the Label.

Changing the *ImageView's Size*

We'd like to display the image at its original size. If you reset the ImageView's default **Fit Width** and **Fit Height** property values—which Scene Builder set when you added the ImageView to the design—Scene Builder will resize the ImageView to the image's exact dimensions. To reset these properties:

1. Expand the **Inspector**'s **Layout** section.

2. Hover the mouse over the **Fit Width** property's value. This displays the button 🔅 to the right property's value. Click the button and select **Reset to Default** to reset the value. This technique can be used with any property value to reset its default.

3. Repeat *Step 2* to reset the **Fit Height** property's value.

You've now completed the GUI. Scene Builder's content panel should now appear as shown in Fig. 12.6. Save the FXML file by selecting **File > Save**.

Fig. 12.6 | Completed **Welcome** GUI in Scene Builder's content panel.

12.4.7 Previewing the Welcome GUI

You can preview what the design will look like in a running application's window. To do so, select **Preview > Show Preview in Window**, which displays the window in Fig. 12.7.

Fig. 12.7 | Previewing the **Welcome** GUI on Microsoft Windows 10—only the window borders will differ on Linux, macOS and earlier Windows versions.

12.5 Tip Calculator App—Introduction to Event Handling

The **Tip Calculator** app (Fig. 12.8(a)) calculates and displays a restaurant bill tip and total. By default, the app calculates the total with a 15% tip. You can specify a tip percentage from 0% to 30% by moving the Slider *thumb*—this updates the tip percentage (Fig. 12.8(b) and (c)). In this section, you'll build a **Tip Calculator** app using several JavaFX components and learn how to respond to user interactions with the GUI.

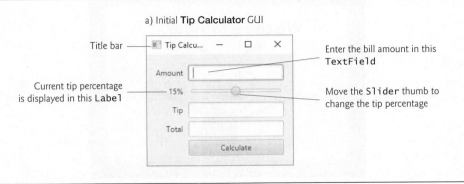

a) Initial **Tip Calculator** GUI

Title bar

Current tip percentage is displayed in this **Label**

Enter the bill amount in this **TextField**

Move the Slider thumb to change the tip percentage

Fig. 12.8 | Entering the bill amount and calculating the tip. (Part 1 of 2.)

b) GUI after you enter the amount 34.56
and click the **Calculate** `Button`

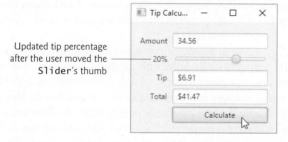

Click the **Calculate** `Button` to
display the tip and total

c) GUI after user moves the `Slider`'s thumb to change the tip
percentage to 20%, then clicks the **Calculate** `Button`

Updated tip percentage
after the user moved the
`Slider`'s thumb

Fig. 12.8 | Entering the bill amount and calculating the tip. (Part 2 of 2.)

You'll begin by test-driving the app, using it to calculate 15% and 20% tips. Then we'll overview the technologies you'll use to create the app. You'll build the app's GUI using the Scene Builder. Finally, we'll present the complete Java code for the app and do a detailed code walkthrough.

12.5.1 Test-Driving the Tip Calculator App

Compile and run the app located in the `TipCalculator` folder with this chapter's examples. The class containing the `main` method is named `TipCalculator`.

Entering a Bill Total

Using your keyboard, enter 34.56, then press the **Calculate** `Button`. The **Tip** and **Total** `TextFields` show the tip amount and the total bill for a 15% tip (Fig. 12.8(b)).

Selecting a Custom Tip Percentage

Use the `Slider` to specify a *custom* tip percentage. Drag the `Slider`'s *thumb* until the percentage reads **20%** (Fig. 12.8(c)), then press the **Calculate** `Button` to display the updated tip and total. As you drag the thumb, the tip percentage in the `Label` to the `Slider`'s left updates continuously. By default, the `Slider` allows you to select values from 0.0 to 100.0, but in this app we'll restrict the `Slider` to selecting whole numbers from 0 to 30.

12.5.2 Technologies Overview

This section introduces the technologies you'll use to build the **Tip Calculator** app.

Class `Application`

The class responsible for launching a JavaFX app is a subclass of **`Application`** (package `javafx.application`). When the subclass's `main` method is called:

1. Method `main` calls class `Application`'s `static` **`launch`** method to begin executing the app.

2. The `launch` method, in turn, causes the JavaFX runtime to create an object of the `Application` subclass and call its **`start`** method.

3. The `Application` subclass's `start` method creates the GUI, attaches it to a `Scene` and places it on the `Stage` that `start` receives as an argument.

Arranging JavaFX Components with a *GridPane*

Recall that layout containers arrange JavaFX components in a `Scene`. A **`GridPane`** (package `javafx.scene.layout`) arranges JavaFX components into *columns* and *rows* in a rectangular grid.

    This app uses a `GridPane` (Fig. 12.9) to arrange views into two columns and five rows. Each cell in a `GridPane` can be empty or can hold one or more JavaFX components, including layout containers that arrange other controls. Each component in a `GridPane` can span *multiple* columns or rows, though we did not use that capability in this GUI. When you drag a `GridPane` onto Scene Builder's content panel, Scene Builder creates the `GridPane` with two columns and three rows by default. You can add and remove columns and rows as necessary. We'll discuss other `GridPane` features as we present the GUI-building steps. To learn more about class `GridPane`, visit:

```
https://docs.oracle.com/javase/8/javafx/api/javafx/scene/layout/
GridPane.html
```

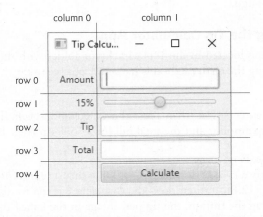

Fig. 12.9 | **Tip Calculator** GUI's `GridPane` labeled by its rows and columns.

Creating and Customizing the GUI with Scene Builder

You'll create `Labels`, `TextFields`, a `Slider` and a `Button` by dragging them onto Scene Builder's content panel, then customize them using the **Inspector** window.

- A **TextField** (package `javafx.scene.control`) can accept text input from the user or display text. You'll use one editable `TextField` to input the bill amount from the user and two *uneditable* `TextFields` to display the tip and total amounts.

- A **Slider** (package `javafx.scene.control`) represents a value in the range 0.0–100.0 by default and allows the user to select a number in that range by moving the `Slider`'s thumb. You'll customize the `Slider` so the user can choose a custom tip percentage *only* from the more limited integer range 0 to 30.

- A **Button** (package `javafx.scene.control`) allows the user to initiate an action—in this app, pressing the **Calculate** `Button` calculates and displays the tip and total amounts.

Formatting Numbers as Locale-Specific Currency and Percentage Strings

You'll use class **NumberFormat** (package **java.text**) to create *locale-specific* currency and percentage strings—an important part of *internationalization*.[2]

Event Handling

Normally, a user interacts with an app's GUI to indicate the tasks that the app should perform. For example, when you write an e-mail, clicking the e-mail app's **Send** button tells the app to send the e-mail to the specified e-mail addresses.

GUIs are **event driven**. When the user interacts with a GUI component, the interaction—known as an **event**—drives the program to perform a task. Some common user interactions that cause an app to perform a task include *clicking* a button, *typing* in a text field, *selecting* an item from a menu, *closing* a window and *moving* the mouse. The code that performs a task in response to an event is called an **event handler**, and the process of responding to events is known as **event handling**.

Before an app can respond to an event for a particular control, you must:

1. Define an event handler that implements an appropriate interface—known as an **event-listener interface**.

2. Indicate that an object of that class should be notified when the event occurs—known as **registering the event handler**.

In this app, you'll respond to two events—when the user moves the `Slider`'s thumb, the app will update the `Label` that displays the current tip percentage, and when the user clicks the **Calculate** `Button`, the app will calculate and display the tip and total bill amount.

You'll see that for certain events—such as when the user clicks a `Button`—you can link a control to its event-handling method by using the **Code** section of Scene Builder's **Inspector** window. In this case, the event-listener interface is implemented for you to call the method that you specify. For events that occur when the value of a control's property

---

2. Recall that the new JavaMoney API (`http://javamoney.github.io`) was developed to meet the challenges of handling currencies, monetary amounts, conversions, rounding and formatting. At the time of this writing, it was not yet incorporated into the JDK.

changes—such as when the user moves a Slider's thumb to change the Slider's value—you'll see that you must create the event handler entirely in code.

Implementing Interface ChangeListener for Handling Slider Thumb Position Changes

You'll implement interface **ChangeListener** (package javafx.beans.value) to respond when the user moves the Slider's thumb. In particular, you'll use the interface's changed method to display the updated tip percentage as the user moves the Slider's thumb.

Model-View-Controller (MVC) Architecture

JavaFX applications in which the GUI is implemented as FXML adhere to the **Model-View-Controller (MVC) design pattern**, which separates an app's data (contained in the **model**) from the app's GUI (the **view**) and the app's processing logic (the **controller**).

The controller implements logic for processing user inputs. The model contains application data, and the view presents the data stored in the model. When a user provides some input, the controller modifies the model with the given input. In the **Tip Calculator**, the model is the bill amount, the tip and the total. When the model changes, the controller updates the view to present the changed data.

In a JavaFX FXML app, a **controller class** defines instance variables for interacting with controls programmatically, as well as event-handling methods that respond to the user's interactions. The controller class may also declare additional instance variables, static variables and methods that support the app's operation. In a simple app like the **Tip Calculator**, the model and controller are often combined into a single class, as we'll do in this example.

FXMLLoader Class

When a JavaFX FXML app begins executing, class **FXMLLoader**'s static method **load** is used to load the FXML file that represents the app's GUI. This method:

- Creates the GUI's scene graph—containing the GUI's layouts and controls—and returns a **Parent** (package javafx.scene) reference to the scene graph's root node.

- Initializes the controller's instance variables for the components that are manipulated programmatically.

- Creates and registers the event handlers for any events specified in the FXML.

We'll discuss these steps in more detail in Sections 12.5.4—12.5.5.

12.5.3 Building the App's GUI

In this section, we'll show the precise steps for creating the **Tip Calculator**'s GUI. The GUI will not look like the one shown in Fig. 12.8 until you've completed the steps.

fx:id Property Values for This App's Controls

If the controller class will manipulate a control or layout programmatically (as we'll do with one Label, all the TextFields and the Slider), you must provide a name for that control or layout. In Section 12.5.4, you'll learn how to declare Java variables for each such component in the FXML, and we'll discuss how those variables are initialized for you. Each object's name is specified via its **fx:id property**. You can set this property's value by selecting a component in your scene, then expanding the **Inspector** window's **Code** section—the **fx:id** property appears at the top of the **Code** section. Figure 12.10 shows the **fx:id** properties of the **Tip Calculator**'s programmatically manipulated controls. For clarity, our naming convention is to use the control's class name in the **fx:id** property.

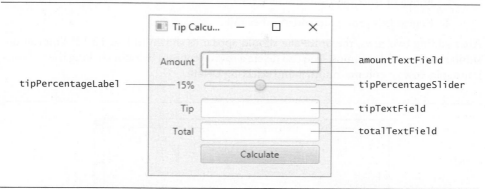

Fig. 12.10 | **Tip Calculator**'s programmatically manipulated controls labeled with their **fx:id**s.

Creating the *TipCalculator.fxml* File
As you did in Section 12.4.1, open Scene Builder to create a new FXML file. Then, select **File > Save** to display the **Save As** dialog, specify the location in which to store the file, name the file TipCalculator.fxml and click the **Save** button.

Step 1: Adding a *GridPane*
Drag a GridPane from the **Library** window's **Containers** section onto Scene Builder's content panel. By default, the GridPane contains two columns and three rows as shown in Fig. 12.11.

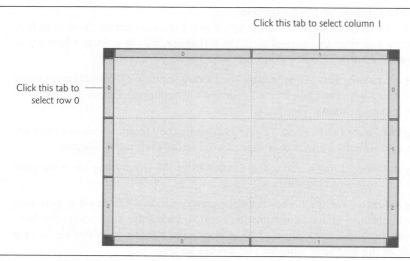

Fig. 12.11 | GridPane with two columns (0 and 1) and three rows (0, 1 and 2).

Step 2: Adding Rows to the *GridPane*
Recall that the GUI in Fig. 12.9 has two columns and five rows. Here you'll add two more rows. To add a row above or below an existing row:

1. Right click any row's row number tab and select either **Grid Pane > Add Row Above** or **Grid Pane > Add Row Below**.

2. Repeat this process to add another row.

After adding two rows, the `GridPane` should appear as shown in Fig. 12.12. You can use similar steps to add columns. You can delete a row or column by right clicking the tab containing its row or column number and selecting **Delete**.

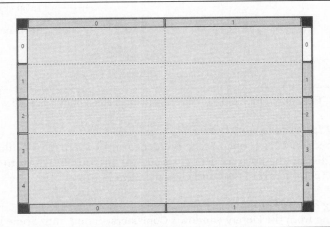

Fig. 12.12 | `GridPane` after adding two more rows.

Step 3: Adding the Controls to the *GridPane*
You'll now add the controls in Fig. 12.9 to the `GridPane`. For each control that has an **fx:id** in Fig. 12.10, when you drag the control onto the `GridPane`, set the control's **fx:id** property in the **Inspector** window's **Code** section. Perform the following steps:

1. *Adding the `Labels`.* Drag `Labels` from the **Library** window's **Controls** section into the first four rows of column 0 (the `GridPane`'s left column). As you add each `Label`, set its text as shown Fig. 12.9.

2. *Adding the `TextFields`.* Drag `TextFields` from the **Library** window's **Controls** section into rows 0, 2 and 3 of column 1 (the `GridPane`'s right column).

3. *Adding a `Slider`.* Drag a horizontal `Slider` from the **Library** window's **Controls** section into row 1 of column 1.

4. *Adding a `Button`.* Drag a `Button` from the **Library** window's **Controls** section into row 4 of column 1. Change the `Button`'s text to **Calculate**. You can set the `Button`'s text by double clicking it, or by selecting the `Button`, then setting its **Text** property in the **Inspector** window's **Properties** section.

The `GridPane` should appear as shown in Fig. 12.13.

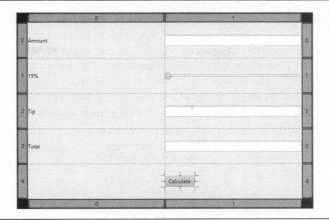

Fig. 12.13 │ GridPane filled with the **Tip Calculator**'s controls.

Step 4: Sizing the *GridPane to Fit Its Contents*

When you begin designing a GUI by adding a layout, Scene Builder automatically sets the layout object's **Pref Width** property to 600 and **Pref Height** property to 400, which is much larger than this GUI's final width and height. For this app, we'd like the layout's size to be computed, based on the layout's contents. To make this change:

1. First, select the GridPane by clicking inside the GridPane, but not on any of the controls you've placed into its columns and rows. Sometimes, it's easier to select the GridPane node in the Scene Builder **Document** window's **Hierarchy** section.

2. In the **Inspector**'s **Layout** section, reset the **Pref Width** and **Pref Height** property values to their defaults (as you did in Section 12.4.4). This sets both properties' values to USE_COMPUTED_SIZE, so the layout calculates its own size.

The layout now appears as shown in Fig. 12.14.

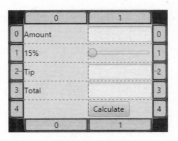

Fig. 12.14 │ GridPane sized to fit its contents.

Step 5: Right-Aligning *GridPane Column 0's Contents*

A GridPane column's contents are left-aligned by default. To right-align the contents of column 0, select it by clicking the tab at the top or bottom of the column, then in the **Inspector**'s **Layout** section, set the **Halignment** (horizontal alignment) property to RIGHT.

*Step 6: Sizing the **GridPane** Columns to Fit Their Contents*
By default, Scene Builder sets each GridPane column's width to 100 pixels and each row's height to 30 pixels to ensure that you can easily drag controls into the GridPane's cells. In this app, we sized each column to fit its contents. To do so, select the column 0 by clicking the tab at the top or bottom of the column, then in the **Inspector**'s **Layout** section, reset the **Pref Width** property to its default size (that is, USE_COMPUTED_SIZE) to indicate that the column's width should be based on its widest child—the **Amount** Label in this case. Repeat this process for column 1. The GridPane should appear as shown in Fig. 12.15.

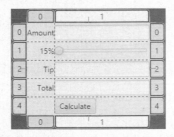

Fig. 12.15 | GridPane with columns sized to fit their contents.

*Step 7: Sizing the **Button***
By default, Scene Builder sets a Button's width based on its text. For this app, we chose to make the Button the same width as the other controls in the GridPane's right column. To do so, select the Button, then in the **Inspector**'s **Layout** section, set the **Max Width** property to MAX_VALUE. This causes the Button's width to grow to fill the column's width.

Previewing the GUI
Preview the GUI by selecting **Preview > Show Preview in Window**. As you can see in Fig. 12.16, there's no space between the Labels in the left column and the controls in the right column. In addition, there's no space around the GridPane, because by default the Stage is sized to fit the Scene's contents. Thus, many of the controls touch the window's borders. You'll fix these issues in the next step.

Fig. 12.16 | GridPane with the TextFields and Button resized.

*Step 8: Configuring the **GridPane**'s Padding and Horizontal Gap Between Its Columns*
The space between a node's contents and its top, right, bottom and left edges is known as the **padding**, which separates the contents from the node's edges. Since the GridPane's size

determines the Stage's window size, the GridPane's padding separates its children from the window's edges. To set the padding, select the GridPane, then in the **Inspector's Layout** section, set the **Padding** property's four values (which represent the **TOP, RIGHT, BOTTOM** and **LEFT**) to 14—the JavaFX recommended distance between a control's edge and the Scene's edge.

You can specify the default amount of space between a GridPane's columns and rows with its **Hgap** (horizontal gap) and **Vgap** (vertical gap) properties, respectively. Because Scene Builder sets each GridPane row's height to 30 pixels—which is greater than the heights of this app's controls—there's already some vertical space between the components. To specify the horizontal gap between the columns, select the GridPane in the **Document** window's **Hierarchy** section, then in the **Inspector's Layout** section, set the **Hgap** property to 8—the recommended distance between controls. If you'd like to precisely control the vertical space between components, you can reset each row's **Pref Height** to its default value, then set the GridPane's **Vgap** property.

Step 9: Making the *tipTextField* and *totalTextField* Uneditable and Not Focusable

The tipTextField and totalTextField are used in this app only to display results, not receive text input. For this reason, they should not be interactive. You can type in a Text-Field only if it's "in **focus**"—that is, it's the control that the user is interacting with. When you click an interactive control, it receives the focus. Similarly, when you press the *Tab* key, the focus transfers from the current focusable control to the next one—this occurs in the order the controls were added to the GUI. Interactive controls—such as TextFields, Sliders and Buttons—are focusable by default. Non-interactive controls—like Labels—are not focusable.

In this app, the tipTextField and totalTextField are neither editable nor focusable. To make these changes, select both TextFields, then in the **Inspector's Properties** section uncheck the **Editable** and **Focus Traversable** properties. To select multiple controls at once, you can click the first (in the **Document** window's **Hierarchy** section or in the content panel), then hold the *Shift* key and click each of the others.

Step 10: Setting the *Slider's* Properties

To complete the GUI, you'll now configure the **Tip Calculator's** Slider. By default, a Slider's range is 0.0 to 100.0 and its initial value is 0.0. This app allows only integer tip percentages in the range 0 to 30 with a default of 15. To make these changes, select the Slider, then in the **Inspector's Properties** section, set the Slider's **Max** property to 30 and the **Value** property to 15. We also set the **Block Increment** property to 5—this is the amount by which the **Value** property increases or decreases when the user clicks between an end of the Slider and the Slider's thumb. Save the FXML file by selecting **File > Save**.

Though we set the **Max**, **Value** and **Block Increment** properties to integer values, the Slider still produces floating-point values as the user moves its thumb. In the app's Java code, we'll restrict the Slider's values to integers when we respond to its events.

Previewing the Final Layout

You've now completed the **Tip Calculator's** design. Select **Preview > Show Preview in Window** to view the final GUI (Fig. 12.17). When we discuss the TipCalculatorController class in Section 12.5.5, we'll show how to specify the **Calculate** Button's event handler in the FXML file.

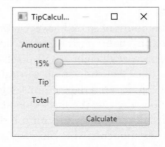

Fig. 12.17 | Final GUI design previewed in Scene Builder.

Specifying the Controller Class's Name
As we mentioned in Section 12.5.2, in a JavaFX FXML app, the app's controller class typically defines instance variables for interacting with controls programmatically, as well as event-handling methods. To ensure that an object of the controller class is created when the app loads the FXML file at runtime, you must specify the controller class's name in the FXML file:

1. Expand Scene Builder **Document** window's **Controller** section (located below the **Hierarchy** section in Fig. 12.3).

2. In the **Controller Class** field, type `TipCalculatorController`—by convention, the controller class's name starts with the same name as the FXML file (`TipCalculator`) and ends with `Controller`.

*Specifying the **Calculate** **Button**'s Event-Handler Method Name*
You can specify in the FXML file the names of the methods that will be called to handle specific control's events. When you select a control, the **Inspector** window's **Code** section shows all the events for which you can specify event handlers in the FXML file. When the user clicks a Button, the method specified in the **On Action** field is called—this method is defined in the controller class you specify in Scene Builder's **Controller** window. Enter `calculateButtonPressed` in the **On Action** field.

Generating a Sample Controller Class
You can have Scene Builder generate the initial controller class containing the variables you'll use to interact with controls programmatically and the empty **Calculate** Button event handler. Scene Builder calls this the "controller skeleton." Select **View > Show Sample Controller Skeleton** to generate the skeleton (Fig. 12.18). As you can see, the sample class has the class name you specified, a variable for each control that has an **fx:id** and an empty **Calculate** Button event handler. We'll discuss the @FXML annotation in Section 12.5.5 To use this skeleton to create your controller class, you can click the **Copy** button, then paste the contents into a file named `TipCalculatorController.java` in the same folder as the `TipCalculator.fxml` file you created in this section.

Fig. 12.18 | Skeleton code generated by Scene Builder.

12.5.4 TipCalculator Class

A simple JavaFX FXML-based app has two Java source-code files. For the **Tip Calculator** app these are:

- TipCalculator.java—This file contains the TipCalculator class (discussed in this section), which declares the main method that loads the FXML file to create the GUI and attaches the GUI to a Scene displayed on the app's Stage.

- TipCalculatorController.java—This file contains the TipCalculatorController class (discussed in Section 12.5.5), where you'll specify the Slider and Button controls' event handlers.

Figure 12.19 presents class TipCalculator. As we discussed in Section 12.5.2, the starting point for a JavaFX app is an Application subclass, so class TipCalculator extends Application (line 9). The main method calls class Application's static launch method (line 23) to initialize the JavaFX runtime and to begin executing the app. This method causes the JavaFX runtime to create an object of the TipCalculator class and calls its start method (lines 10–19), passing the Stage object representing the window in which the app will be displayed. The JavaFX runtime creates the window.

```
1  // Fig. 12.19: TipCalculator.java
2  // Main app class that loads and displays the Tip Calculator's GUI
3  import javafx.application.Application;
4  import javafx.fxml.FXMLLoader;
5  import javafx.scene.Parent;
6  import javafx.scene.Scene;
7  import javafx.stage.Stage;
8
9  public class TipCalculator extends Application {
10     @Override
11     public void start(Stage stage) throws Exception {
12        Parent root =
13           FXMLLoader.load(getClass().getResource("TipCalculator.fxml"));
14
15        Scene scene = new Scene(root); // attach scene graph to scene
16        stage.setTitle("Tip Calculator"); // displayed in window's title bar
17        stage.setScene(scene); // attach scene to stage
18        stage.show(); // display the stage
19     }
20
21     public static void main(String[] args) {
22        // create a TipCalculator object and call its start method
23        launch(args);
24     }
25  }
```

Fig. 12.19 | Main app class that loads and displays the **Tip Calculator**'s GUI.

*Overridden **Application** Method **start***
Method start (lines 11–19) creates the GUI, attaches it to a Scene and places it on the Stage that method start receives as an argument. Lines 12–13 use class FXMLLoader's static method load to create the GUI's scene graph. This method:

- Returns a Parent (package javafx.scene) reference to the scene graph's root node—this is a reference to the GUI's GridPane in this app.

- Creates an object of the TipCalculatorController class that we specified in the FXML file.

- Initializes the controller's instance variables for the components that are manipulated programmatically.

- Attaches the event handlers specified in the FXML to the appropriate controls. This is known as registering the event handlers and enables the controls to call the corresponding methods when the user interacts with the app.

We discuss the initialization of the controller's instance variables and the registration of the event handlers in Section 12.5.5.

*Creating the **Scene***
To display the GUI, you must attach it to a Scene, then attach the Scene to the Stage that method start receives as an argument. To attach the GUI to a Scene, line 15 creates a Scene, passing root (the scene graph's root node) as an argument to the constructor. By default, the Scene's size is determined by the size of the scene graph's root node. Overload-

ed versions of the Scene constructor allow you to specify the Scene's size and fill (a color, gradient or image), which appears in the Scene's background. Line 16 uses Stage method setTitle to specify the text that appears in the Stage window's title bar. Line 17 calls Stage method setScene to place the Scene onto the Stage. Finally, line 18 calls Stage method show to display the Stage window.

12.5.5 TipCalculatorController Class

Figures 12.20–12.23 present the TipCalculatorController class that responds to user interactions with the app's Button and Slider.

*Class **TipCalculatorController**'s import Statements*
Figure 12.20 shows class TipCalculatorController's import statements.

```
 1   // TipCalculatorController.java
 2   // Controller that handles calculateButton and tipPercentageSlider events
 3   import java.math.BigDecimal;
 4   import java.math.RoundingMode;
 5   import java.text.NumberFormat;
 6   import javafx.beans.value.ChangeListener;
 7   import javafx.beans.value.ObservableValue;
 8   import javafx.event.ActionEvent;
 9   import javafx.fxml.FXML;
10   import javafx.scene.control.Label;
11   import javafx.scene.control.Slider;
12   import javafx.scene.control.TextField;
13
```

Fig. 12.20 | TipCalculatorController's import declarations.

The classes and interfaces used by class TipCalculatorController include:

- Class BigDecimal of package java.math (line 3) is used to perform precise monetary calculations. The RoundingMode enum of package java.math (line 4) is used to specify how BigDecimal values are rounded during calculations or when formatting floating-point numbers as Strings.

- Class NumberFormat of package java.text (line 5) provides numeric formatting capabilities, such as locale-specific currency and percentage formats. For example, in the U.S. locale, the monetary value 34.95 is formatted as $34.95 and the percentage 15 is formatted as 15%. Class NumberFormat determines the locale of the system on which your app runs, then formats currency amounts and percentages accordingly.

- You implement interface ChangeListener of package javafx.beans.value (line 6) to respond when the user moves the Slider's thumb. This interface's changed method receives an object that implements interface ObservableValue (line 7)— that is, a value that generates an event when it changes.

- A Button's event handler receives an ActionEvent object (line 8; package javafx.event) indicating which Button the user clicked. As you'll see in Chapter 13, many JavaFX controls support ActionEvents.

- The annotation FXML (line 9; package javafx.fxml) is used in a JavaFX controller class's code to mark instance variables that should refer to JavaFX components in the GUI's FXML file and methods that can respond to the events of JavaFX components in the GUI's FXML file.

- Package javafx.scene.control (lines 10–12) contains many JavaFX control classes, including Label, Slider and TextField.

TipCalculatorController's static Variables and Instance Variables

Lines 16—37 of Fig. 12.21 present class TipCalculatorController's static and instance variables. The NumberFormat objects (lines 16–19) are used to format currency values and percentages, respectively. NumberFormat method getCurrencyInstance returns a NumberFormat object that formats values as currency using the default locale for the system on which the app is running. Similarly, NumberFormat method getPercentInstance returns a NumberFormat object that formats values as percentages using the system's default locale. The BigDecimal object tipPercentage (line 21) stores the current tip percentage and is used in the tip calculation (Fig. 12.22) when the user clicks the **Calculate** Button.

```
14  public class TipCalculatorController {
15     // formatters for currency and percentages
16     private static final NumberFormat currency =
17        NumberFormat.getCurrencyInstance();
18     private static final NumberFormat percent =
19        NumberFormat.getPercentInstance();
20
21     private BigDecimal tipPercentage = new BigDecimal(0.15); // 15% default
22
23     // GUI controls defined in FXML and used by the controller's code
24     @FXML
25     private TextField amountTextField;
26
27     @FXML
28     private Label tipPercentageLabel;
29
30     @FXML
31     private Slider tipPercentageSlider;
32
33     @FXML
34     private TextField tipTextField;
35
36     @FXML
37     private TextField totalTextField;
38
```

Fig. 12.21 | TipCalculatorController's static and instance variables.

@FXML Annotation

Recall from Section 12.5.3 that each control that this app manipulates in its Java source code needs an **fx:id**. Lines 24–37 (Fig. 12.21) declare the controller class's corresponding instance variables. The **@FXML annotation** that precedes each declaration (lines 24, 27, 30, 33 and 36) indicates that the variable name can be used in the FXML file that describes the app's GUI. The variable names that you specify in the controller class must precisely match the **fx:id** values you specified when building the GUI. When the FXMLLoader loads TipCalculator.fxml to create the GUI, it also initializes each of the controller's instance variables that are declared with @FXML to ensure that they refer to the corresponding GUI components in the FXML file.

TipCalculatorController's calculateButtonPressed Event Handler

Figure 12.22 presents class TipCalculatorController's calculateButtonPressed method, which is called when the user clicks the **Calculate** Button. The @FXML annotation (line 40) preceding the method indicates that this method can be used to specify a control's event handler in the FXML file that describes the app's GUI. For a control that generates an ActionEvent (as is the case for many JavaFX controls), the event-handling method must return void and receive one ActionEvent parameter (line 41).

```
39    // calculates and displays the tip and total amounts
40    @FXML
41    private void calculateButtonPressed(ActionEvent event) {
42       try {
43          BigDecimal amount = new BigDecimal(amountTextField.getText());
44          BigDecimal tip = amount.multiply(tipPercentage);
45          BigDecimal total = amount.add(tip);
46
47          tipTextField.setText(currency.format(tip));
48          totalTextField.setText(currency.format(total));
49       }
50       catch (NumberFormatException ex) {
51          amountTextField.setText("Enter amount");
52          amountTextField.selectAll();
53          amountTextField.requestFocus();
54       }
55    }
56
```

Fig. 12.22 | TipCalculatorController's calculateButtonPressed event handler.

Registering the Calculate Button's Event Handler

When the FXMLLoader loads TipCalculator.fxml to create the GUI, it creates and registers an event handler for the **Calculate** Button's ActionEvent. The event handler for this event must implement interface **EventHandler<ActionEvent>**—EventHandler is a generic type, like ArrayList (introduced in Chapter 7). This interface contains a handle method that returns void and receives an ActionEvent parameter. This method's body, in turn, calls method calculateButtonPressed when the user clicks the **Calculate** Button. FXMLLoader performs similar tasks for every event listener you specify via the Scene Builder **Inspector** window's **Code** section.

Calculating and Displaying the Tip and Total Amounts

Lines 43–48 calculate and display the tip and total. Line 43 calls the amountTextField's getText method to get the bill amount typed by the user. This String is passed to Big-Decimal's constructor, which throws a NumberFormatException if its argument is not a number. In that case, line 51 calls amountTextField's setText method to display the message "Enter amount" in the TextField. Line 52 then calls method selectAll to select the TextField's text and line 53 calls requestFocus to give the TextField the focus. Now the user can immediately type a value in the amountTextField without having to first select its text. Methods getText, setText and selectAll are inherited into class TextField from class TextInputControl (package javafx.scene.control), and method request-Focus is inherited into class TextField from class Node (package javafx.scene).

If line 43 does not throw an exception, line 44 calculates the tip by calling method multiply to multiply the amount by the tipPercentage, and line 45 calculates the total by adding the tip to the bill amount. Next lines 47 and 48 use the currency object's format method to create currency-formatted Strings representing the tip and total amounts, which we display in tipTextField and totalTextField, respectively.

TipCalculatorController's *initalize Method*

Figure 12.23 presents class TipCalculatorController's initialize method. This method can be used to configure the controller before the GUI is displayed. Line 60 calls the currency object's setRoundingMode method to specify how currency values should be rounded. The value RoundingMode.HALF_UP indicates that values greater than or equal to .5 should round up—for example, 34.567 would be formatted as 34.57 and 34.564 would be formatted as 34.56.

```
57     // called by FXMLLoader to initialize the controller
58     public void initialize() {
59        // 0-4 rounds down, 5-9 rounds up
60        currency.setRoundingMode(RoundingMode.HALF_UP);
61
62        // listener for changes to tipPercentageSlider's value
63        tipPercentageSlider.valueProperty().addListener(
64           new ChangeListener<Number>() {
65              @Override
66              public void changed(ObservableValue<? extends Number> ov,
67                 Number oldValue, Number newValue) {
68                 tipPercentage =
69                    BigDecimal.valueOf(newValue.intValue() / 100.0);
70                 tipPercentageLabel.setText(percent.format(tipPercentage));
71              }
72           }
73        );
74     }
75  }
```

Fig. 12.23 | TipCalculatorController's initalize method.

Using an Anonymous Inner Class for Event Handling

Each JavaFX control has properties. Some—such as a Slider's value—can generate events when they change. For such events, you must manually register as the event handler an object that implements the ChangeListener interface (package javafx.beans.value).

ChangeListener is a generic type that's specialized with the property's type. The call to valueProperty (line 63) returns a DoubleProperty (package javax.beans.property) that represents the Slider's value. A DoubleProperty is an ObservableValue<Number> that can notify listeners when a value changes. Each class that implements interface ObservableValue provides method addListener (called on line 63) to register an event-handler that implements interface ChangeListener. For a Slider's value, addListener's argument is an object that implements ChangeListener<Number>, because the Slider's value is a numeric value.

If an event handler is not reused, you often define it as an instance of an **anonymous inner class**—a class that's declared without a name and typically appears inside a method. The addListener method's argument is specified in lines 64–72 as one statement that

- declares the event listener's class,

- creates an object of that class and

- registers it as the listener for changes to the tipPercentageSlider's value.

Since an anonymous inner class has no name, you must create an object of the class at the point where it's declared (thus the keyword new in line 64). A reference to that object is then passed to addListener. After the new keyword, the syntax

```
ChangeListener<Number>()
```

in line 64 begins the declaration of an anonymous inner class that implements interface ChangeListener<Number>. This is similar to beginning a class declaration with

```
public class MyHandler implements ChangeListener<Number>
```

The opening left brace at 64 and the closing right brace at line 72 delimit the anonymous inner class's body. Lines 65–71 declare the interface's changed method, which receives a reference to the ObservableValue that changed, a Number containing the Slider's old value before the event occurred and a Number containing the Slider's new value. When the user moves the Slider's thumb, lines 68–69 store the new tip percentage and line 70 updates the tipPercentageLabel. (The notation ? extends Number in line 66 indicates that the ObservableValue's type argument is a Number or a subclass of Number. We explain this notation in more detail in Section 19.7.)

Anonymous Inner Class Notes
An anonymous inner class can access its top-level class's instance variables, static variables and methods—in this case, the anonymous inner class uses the instance variables tipPercentage and tipPercentageLabel, and the static variable percent. However, an anonymous inner class has limited access to the local variables of the method in which it's declared—it can access only the final or effectively final (Java SE 8) local variables declared in the enclosing method's body.

8

Software Engineering Observation 12.2
The event listener for an event must implement the appropriate event-listener interface.

Common Programming Error 12.1
If you forget to register an event-handler object for a particular GUI component's event type, events of that type will be ignored.

8   *Java SE 8: Using a Lambda to Implement the* **ChangeListener**
Recall from Section 10.10 that in Java SE 8 an interface containing one method—such as
ChangeListener in Fig. 12.23—is a functional interface. We'll show how to implement
such interfaces with lambdas in Chapter 17.

12.6 Features Covered in the Other JavaFX Chapters

JavaFX is a robust GUI, graphics and multimedia technology. In Chapters 13 and 20,
you'll:

- Learn additional JavaFX layouts and controls.
- Handle other event types (such as MouseEvents).
- Apply transformations (such as moving, rotating, scaling and skewing) and effects
  (such as drop shadows, blurs, reflection and lighting) to a scene graph's nodes.
- Use CSS to specify the look-and-feel of controls.
- Use JavaFX properties and data binding to enable automatic updating of controls
  as corresponding data changes.
- Use JavaFX graphics capabilities.
- Perform JavaFX animations.
- Use JavaFX multimedia capabilities to play audio and video.

In addition, our JavaFX Resource Center

```
http://www.deitel.com/JavaFX
```

contains links to online resources where you can learn more about JavaFX's capabilities.

12.7 Wrap-Up

In this chapter, we introduced JavaFX. We presented the structure of a JavaFX stage (the
application window). You learned that the stage displays a scene graph, that the scene
graph is composed of nodes and that nodes consist of layouts and controls.

You designed GUIs using visual programming techniques in JavaFX Scene Builder,
which enabled you to create GUIs without writing any Java code. You arranged Label,
ImageView, TextField, Slider and Button controls using the VBox and GridPane layout
containers. You learned how class FXMLLoader uses the FXML created in Scene Builder to
create the GUI.

You implemented a controller class to respond to user interactions with Button and
Slider controls. We showed that certain event handlers can be specified directly in FXML
from Scene Builder, but event handlers for changes to a control's property values must be
implemented directly in the controllers code. You also learned that the FXMLLoader creates
and initializes an instance of an application's controller class, initializes the controller's
instance variables that are declared with the @FXML annotation, and creates and registers
event handlers for any events specified in the FXML.

In the next chapter, you'll use additional JavaFX controls and layouts and use CSS to
style your GUI. You'll also learn more about JavaFX properties and how to use a technique
called data binding to automatically update elements in a GUI with new data.

13

JavaFX GUI: Part 2

Objectives

In this chapter you'll:

- Learn more details of laying out nodes in a scene graph with JavaFX layout panels.
- Continue building JavaFX GUIs with Scene Builder.
- Create and manipulate RadioButtons and ListViews.
- Use BorderPanes and TitledPanes to layout controls.
- Handle mouse events.
- Use property binding and property listeners to perform tasks when a control's property value changes.
- Programmatically create layouts and controls.
- Customize a ListView's cells with a custom cell factory.
- See an overview of other JavaFX capabilities.
- Be introduced to the JavaFX 9 updates in Java SE 9.

13.1 Introduction

This chapter continues our JavaFX presentation that began in Chapter 12. In this chapter, you'll:

- Use additional layouts (TitledPane, BorderPane and Pane) and controls (RadioButton and ListView).

- Handle mouse and RadioButton events.

- Set up event handlers that respond to property changes on controls (such as the value of a Slider).

- Display Rectangles and Circles as nodes in the scene graph.

- Bind a collection of objects to a ListView that displays the collection's contents.

- Customize the appearance of a ListView's cells.

Finally, we overview other JavaFX capabilities and mention Java SE 9's JavaFX changes.

13.2 Laying Out Nodes in a Scene Graph

A layout determines the size and positioning of nodes in the scene graph.

Node Size

In general, a node's size should *not* be defined *explicitly*. Doing so often creates a design that looks pleasing when it first loads, but deteriorates when the app is resized or the content updates. In addition to the width and height properties, most JavaFX nodes have the properties **prefWidth**, **prefHeight**, **minWidth**, **minHeight**, **maxWidth** and **maxHeight** that specify a node's *range* of acceptable sizes as it's laid out within its parent node:

- The minimum size properties specify a node's smallest allowed size in points.

- The maximum size properties specify a node's largest allowed size in points.

- The preferred size properties specify a node's preferred width and height that should be used by the layout in most cases.

Node Position and Layout Panes

A node's position should be defined *relative* to its parent node and the other nodes in its parent. JavaFX **layout panes** are container nodes that arrange their child nodes in a scene graph relative to one another, based on their sizes and positions. Child nodes are controls, other layout panes, shapes and more.

Most JavaFX layout panes use *relative positioning*—if a layout-pane node is resized, it adjusts its children's sizes and positions accordingly, based on their preferred, minimum and maximum sizes. Figure 13.1 describes each of the JavaFX layout panes, including those presented in Chapter 12. In this chapter, we'll use Pane, BorderPane, GridPane and VBox from the `javafx.scene.layout` package.

Layout	Description
AnchorPane	Enables you to set the position of child nodes relative to the pane's edges. Resizing the pane does not alter the layout of the nodes.
BorderPane	Includes five areas—top, bottom, left, center and right—where you can place nodes. The top and bottom regions fill the Border-Pane's width and are vertically sized to their children's preferred heights. The left and right regions fill the BorderPane's height and are horizontally sized to their children's preferred widths. The center area occupies all of the BorderPane's remaining space. You might use the different areas for tool bars, navigation, a main content area, etc.
FlowPane	Lays out nodes consecutively—either horizontally or vertically. When the boundary for the pane is reached, the nodes wrap to a new line in a horizontal FlowPane or a new column in a vertical FlowPane.
GridPane	Creates a flexible grid for laying out nodes in rows and columns.
Pane	The base class for layout panes. This can be used to position nodes at fixed locations—known as absolute positioning.
StackPane	Places nodes in a stack. Each new node is stacked atop the previous node. You might use this to place text on top of images, for example.
TilePane	A horizontal or vertical grid of equally sized tiles. Nodes that are tiled horizontally wrap at the TilePane's width. Nodes that are tiled vertically wrap at the TilePane's height.
HBox	Arranges nodes horizontally in one row.
VBox	Arranges nodes vertically in one column.

Fig. 13.1 | JavaFX layout panes.

13.3 Painter App: RadioButtons, Mouse Events and Shapes

In this section, you'll create a simple **Painter** app (Fig. 13.2) that allows you to drag the mouse to draw. First, we'll overview the technologies you'll use, then we'll discuss creating the app's project and building its GUI. Finally, we'll present the source code for its Painter and PainterController classes.

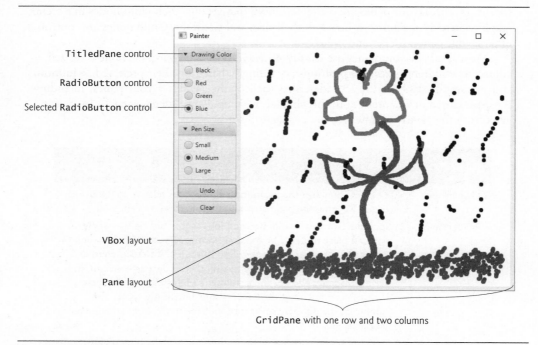

Fig. 13.2 | Painter app.

13.3.1 Technologies Overview

This section introduces the JavaFX features you'll use in the **Painter** app.

RadioButtons and ToggleGroups
RadioButtons function as *mutually exclusive* options. You add multiple RadioButtons to a ToggleGroup to ensure that only one RadioButton in a given group is selected at a time. For this app, you'll use JavaFX Scene Builder's capability for specifying each RadioButton's ToggleGroup in FXML; however, you can also create a ToggleGroup in Java, then use a RadioButton's **setToggleGroup** method to specify its ToggleGroup.

BorderPane Layout Container
A **BorderPane layout container** arranges controls into one or more of the five regions shown in Fig. 13.3. The top and bottom areas have the same width as the BorderPane. The left, center and right areas fill the vertical space between the top and bottom areas.

Each area may contain only one control or one layout container that, in turn, may contain other controls.

Look-and-Feel Observation 13.1
All the areas in a BorderPane *are optional: If the top or bottom area is empty, the left, center and right areas expand vertically to fill that area. If the left or right area is empty, the center expands horizontally to fill that area.*

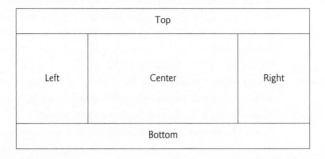

Fig. 13.3 | BorderPane's five areas.

TitledPane Layout Container

A **TitledPane layout container** displays a title at its top and is a collapsible panel containing a layout node, which in turn contains other nodes. You'll use TitledPanes to organize the app's RadioButtons and to help the user understand the purpose of each RadioButton group.

JavaFX Shapes

The **javafx.scene.shape** package contains various classes for creating 2D and 3D shape nodes that can be displayed in a scene graph. In this app, you'll programmatically create **Circle** objects as the user drags the mouse, then attach them to the app's drawing area so that they're displayed in the scene graph.

Pane Layout Container

Each Circle you programmatically create is attached to a **Pane** layout (the drawing area) at a specified *x-y* coordinate measured from the Pane's upper-left corner.

Mouse Event Handling

When you drag the mouse, the app's controller responds by displaying a Circle (in the currently selected color and pen size) at the current mouse position in the Pane. JavaFX nodes support various mouse events, which are summarized in Fig. 13.4. For this app, you'll configure an **onMouseDragged** event handler for the Pane. JavaFX also supports other types of input events. For example, for touchscreen devices there are various touch-oriented events and for keyboards there are various key events. For a complete list of JavaFX node events, see the Node class's properties that begin with the word "on" at:

```
http://docs.oracle.com/javase/8/javafx/api/javafx/scene/Node.html
```

Mouse events	When the event occurs for a given node
onMouseClicked	When the user clicks a mouse button—that is, presses and releases a mouse button without moving the mouse—with the mouse cursor within that node.
onMouseDragEntered	When the mouse cursor enters a node's bounds during a mouse drag— that is, the user is moving the mouse with a mouse button pressed.
onMouseDragExited	When the mouse cursor exits the node's bounds during a mouse drag.
onMouseDragged	When the user begins a mouse drag with the mouse cursor within that node and continues moving the mouse with a mouse button pressed.
onMouseDragOver	When a drag operation that started in a *different* node continues with the mouse cursor over the given node.
onMouseDragReleased	When the user completes a drag operation that began in that node.
onMouseEntered	When the mouse cursor enters that node's bounds.
onMouseExited	When the mouse cursor exits that node's bounds.
onMouseMoved	When the mouse cursor moves within that node's bounds.
onMousePressed	When user presses a mouse button with the mouse cursor within that node's bounds.
onMouseReleased	When user releases a mouse button with the mouse cursor within that node's bounds.

Fig. 13.4 | Mouse events.

Setting a Control's User Data

Each JavaFX control has a **setUserData method** that receives an Object. You can use this to store any object you'd like to associate with that control. With each drawing-color RadioButton, we store the specific Color that the RadioButton represents. With each pen size RadioButton, we store an enum constant for the corresponding pen size. We then use these objects when handling the RadioButton events.

13.3.2 Creating the Painter.fxml File

Create a folder on your system for this example's files, then open Scene Builder and save the new FXML file as Painter.fxml. If you already have an FXML file open, you also can choose **File > New** to create a new FXML file, then save it.

13.3.3 Building the GUI

In this section, we'll discuss the **Painter** app's GUI. Rather than providing the exact steps as we did in Chapter 12, we'll provide general instructions for building the GUI and focus on specific details for new concepts.

 Software Engineering Observation 13.1

As you build a GUI, it's often easier to manipulate layouts and controls via Scene Builder's **Hierarchy** *window than directly in the stage design area.*

fx:id Property Values for This App's Controls

Figure 13.5 shows the **fx:id** properties of the **Painter** app's programmatically manipulated controls. As you build the GUI, you should set the corresponding **fx:id** properties in the FXML document, as we discussed in Chapter 12.

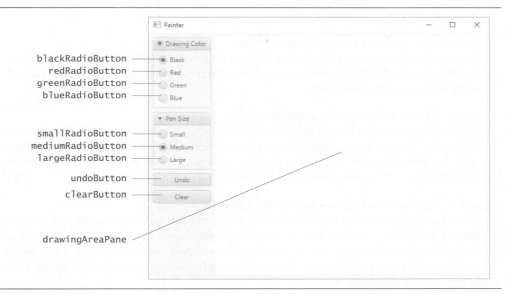

Fig. 13.5 | **Painter** GUI labeled with **fx:id**s for the programmatically manipulated controls.

Step 1: Adding a BorderPane as the Root Layout Node

Drag a `BorderPane` from the Scene Builder **Library** window's **Containers** section onto the content panel.

Step 2: Configuring the BorderPane

We set the `GridPane`'s **Pref Width** and **Pref Height** properties to 640 and 480 respectively. Recall that the stage's size is determined based on the size of the root node in the FXML document. Set the `BorderPane`'s **Padding** property to 8 to inset it from the stage's edges.

Step 3: Adding the VBox and Pane

Drag a `VBox` into the `BorderPane`'s left area and a `Pane` into the center area. As you drag over the `BorderPane`, Scene Builder shows the layout's five areas and highlights the area in which area the item you're dragging will be placed when you release the mouse. Set the `Pane`'s **fx:id** to `drawingAreaPane` as specified in Fig. 13.5.

For the `VBox`, set its **Spacing** property (in the **Inspector**'s **Layout** section) to 8 to add some vertical spacing between the controls that will be added to this container. Set its right **Margin** property to 8 to add some horizontal spacing between the `VBox` and the `Pane` be added to this container. Also reset its **Pref Width** and **Pref Height** properties to their default values (`USE_COMPUTED_SIZE`) and set its **Max Height** property to `MAX_VALUE`. This will enable the `VBox` to be as wide as it needs to be to accommodate its child nodes and occupy the full column height.

Reset the Pane's **Pref Width** and **Pref Height** to their default USE_COMPUTED_SIZE values, and set its **Max Width** and **Max Height** to MAX_VALUE so that it occupies the full width and height of the BorderPane's center area. In the **JavaFX CSS** category of the **Inspector** window's **Properties** section, click the field below **Style** (which is initially empty) and select -fx-background-color to indicate that you'd like to specify the Pane's background color. In the field to the right, specify white.

Step 4: Adding the *TitledPane*s to the *VBox*
From the **Library** window's **Containers** section, drag two **TitledPane (empty)** objects onto the VBox. For the first TitledPane, set its **Text** property to Drawing Color. For the second, set its **Text** property to Pen Size.

Step 5: Customizing the *TitledPane*s
Each TitledPane in the completed GUI contains multiple RadioButtons. We'll use a VBox within each TitledPane to help arrange those controls. Drag a VBox onto each Titled-Pane. For each VBox, set its **Spacing** property to 8 and its **Pref Width** and **Pref Height** to USE_COMPUTED_SIZE so the VBoxes will be sized based on their contents.

Step 6: Adding the *RadioButton*s to the *VBox*
From the **Library** window's **Controls** section, drag four RadioButtons onto the VBox for the **Drawing Color** TitledPane, and three RadioButtons onto the VBox for the **Pen Size** TitledPane, then configure their **Text** properties and **fx:id**s as shown in Fig. 13.5. Select the blackRadioButton and ensure that its **Selected** property is checked, then do the same for the mediumRadioButton.

Step 7: Specifying the *ToggleGroup*s for the *RadioButton*s
Select all four RadioButtons in the first TitledPane's VBox, then set the **Toggle Group** property to colorToggleGroup. When the FXML file is loaded, a ToggleGroup object by that name will be created and these four RadioButtons will be associated with it to ensure that only one is selected at a time. Repeat this step for the three RadioButtons in the second TitledPane's VBox, but set the **Toggle Group** property to sizeToggleGroup.

Step 8: Changing the *TitledPane*s' Preferred Width and Height
For each TitledPane, set its **Pref Width** and **Pref Height** to USE_COMPUTED_SIZE so the TitledPanes will be sized based on their contents.

Step 9: Adding the *Button*s
Add two Buttons below the TitledPanes, then configure their **Text** properties and **fx:id**s as shown in Fig. 13.5. Set each Button's **Max Width** property to MAX_VALUE so that they fill the VBox's width.

Step 10: Setting the Width the *VBox*
We'd like the VBox to be only as wide as it needs to be to display the controls in that column. To specify this, select the VBox in the **Document** window's **Hierarchy** section. Set the column's **Min Width** and **Pref Width** to USE_COMPUTED_SIZE, then set the **Max Width** to USE_PREF_SIZE (which indicates that the maximum width should be the preferred width). Also, reset the **Max Height** to its default USE_COMPUTED_SIZE value. The GUI is now complete and should appear as shown in Fig. 13.5.

Step 11: Specifying the Controller Class's Name
As we mentioned in Section 12.5.2, in a JavaFX FXML app, the app's controller class typically defines instance variables for interacting with controls programmatically, as well as event-handling methods. To ensure that an object of the controller class is created when the app loads the FXML file at runtime, you must specify the controller class's name in the FXML file:

1. Expand Scene Builder's **Controller** window (located below the **Hierarchy** window).

2. In the **Controller Class** field, type `PainterController`.

Step 12: Specifying the Event-Handler Method Names
Next, you'll specify in the **Inspector** window's **Code** section the names of the methods that will be called to handle specific control's events:

- For the `drawingAreaPane`, specify `drawingAreaMouseDragged` as the **On Mouse Dragged** event handler (located under the **Mouse** heading in the **Code** section). This method will draw a circle in the specified color and size for each mouse-dragged event.

- For the four **Drawing Color** `RadioButtons`, specify `colorRadioButtonSelected` as each `RadioButton`'s **On Action** event handler. This method will set the current drawing color, based on the user's selection.

- For the three **Pen Size** `RadioButtons`, specify `sizeRadioButtonSelected` as each `RadioButton`'s **On Action** event handler. This method will set the current pen size, based on the user's selection.

- For the **Undo** Button, specify `undoButtonPressed` as the **On Action** event handler. This method will remove the last circle the user drew on the screen.

- For the **Clear** Button, specify `clearButtonPressed` as the **On Action** event handler. This method will clear the entire drawing.

Step 13: Generating a Sample Controller Class
As you saw in Section 12.5, Scene Builder generates the initial controller-class skeleton for you when you select **View > Show Sample Controller Skeleton**. You can copy this code into a `PainterController.java` file and store the file in the same folder as `Painter.fxml`. We show the completed `PainterController` class in Section 13.3.5.

13.3.4 Painter Subclass of Application

Figure 13.6 shows class `Painter` subclass of `Application` that launches the app, which performs the same tasks to start the **Painter** app as described for the **Tip Calculator** app in Section 12.5.4.

```
1   // Fig. 13.5: Painter.java
2   // Main application class that loads and displays the Painter's GUI.
3   import javafx.application.Application;
4   import javafx.fxml.FXMLLoader;
```

Fig. 13.6 | Main application class that loads and displays the **Painter**'s GUI.

```
 5   import javafx.scene.Parent;
 6   import javafx.scene.Scene;
 7   import javafx.stage.Stage;
 8
 9   public class Painter extends Application {
10      @Override
11      public void start(Stage stage) throws Exception {
12         Parent root =
13            FXMLLoader.load(getClass().getResource("Painter.fxml"));
14
15         Scene scene = new Scene(root);
16         stage.setTitle("Painter"); // displayed in window's title bar
17         stage.setScene(scene);
18         stage.show();
19      }
20
21      public static void main(String[] args) {
22         launch(args);
23      }
24   }
```

Fig. 13.6 | Main application class that loads and displays the **Painter**'s GUI.

13.3.5 PainterController Class

Figure 13.7 shows the final version of class `PainterController` with this app's new features highlighted. Recall from Chapter 12 that the controller class defines instance variables for interacting with controls programmatically, as well as event-handling methods. The controller class may also declare additional instance variables, `static` variables and methods that support the app's operation.

```
 1   // Fig. 13.6: PainterController.java
 2   // Controller for the Painter app
 3   import javafx.event.ActionEvent;
 4   import javafx.fxml.FXML;
 5   import javafx.scene.control.RadioButton;
 6   import javafx.scene.control.ToggleGroup;
 7   import javafx.scene.input.MouseEvent;
 8   import javafx.scene.layout.Pane;
 9   import javafx.scene.paint.Color;
10   import javafx.scene.paint.Paint;
11   import javafx.scene.shape.Circle;
12
13   public class PainterController {
14      // enum representing pen sizes
15      private enum PenSize {
16         SMALL(2),
17         MEDIUM(4),
18         LARGE(6);
```

Fig. 13.7 | Controller for the **Painter** app. (Part 1 of 3.)

```
19
20        private final int radius;
21
22        PenSize(int radius) {this.radius = radius;} // constructor
23
24        public int getRadius() {return radius;}
25    };
26
27    // instance variables that refer to GUI components
28    @FXML private RadioButton blackRadioButton;
29    @FXML private RadioButton redRadioButton;
30    @FXML private RadioButton greenRadioButton;
31    @FXML private RadioButton blueRadioButton;
32    @FXML private RadioButton smallRadioButton;
33    @FXML private RadioButton mediumRadioButton;
34    @FXML private RadioButton largeRadioButton;
35    @FXML private Pane drawingAreaPane;
36    @FXML private ToggleGroup colorToggleGroup;
37    @FXML private ToggleGroup sizeToggleGroup;
38
39    // instance variables for managing Painter state
40    private PenSize radius = PenSize.MEDIUM; // radius of circle
41    private Paint brushColor = Color.BLACK; // drawing color
42
43    // set user data for the RadioButtons
44    public void initialize() {
45        // user data on a control can be any Object
46        blackRadioButton.setUserData(Color.BLACK);
47        redRadioButton.setUserData(Color.RED);
48        greenRadioButton.setUserData(Color.GREEN);
49        blueRadioButton.setUserData(Color.BLUE);
50        smallRadioButton.setUserData(PenSize.SMALL);
51        mediumRadioButton.setUserData(PenSize.MEDIUM);
52        largeRadioButton.setUserData(PenSize.LARGE);
53    }
54
55    // handles drawingArea's onMouseDragged MouseEvent
56    @FXML
57    private void drawingAreaMouseDragged(MouseEvent e) {
58        Circle newCircle = new Circle(e.getX(), e.getY(),
59            radius.getRadius(), brushColor);
60        drawingAreaPane.getChildren().add(newCircle);
61    }
62
63    // handles color RadioButton's ActionEvents
64    @FXML
65    private void colorRadioButtonSelected(ActionEvent e) {
66        // user data for each color RadioButton is the corresponding Color
67        brushColor =
68            (Color) colorToggleGroup.getSelectedToggle().getUserData();
69    }
70
```

Fig. 13.7 | Controller for the **Painter** app. (Part 2 of 3.)

```
71      // handles size RadioButton's ActionEvents
72      @FXML
73      private void sizeRadioButtonSelected(ActionEvent e) {
74         // user data for each size RadioButton is the corresponding PenSize
75         radius =
76            (PenSize) sizeToggleGroup.getSelectedToggle().getUserData();
77      }
78
79      // handles Undo Button's ActionEvents
80      @FXML
81      private void undoButtonPressed(ActionEvent event) {
82         int count = drawingAreaPane.getChildren().size();
83
84         // if there are any shapes remove the last one added
85         if (count > 0) {
86            drawingAreaPane.getChildren().remove(count - 1);
87         }
88      }
89
90      // handles Clear Button's ActionEvents
91      @FXML
92      private void clearButtonPressed(ActionEvent event) {
93         drawingAreaPane.getChildren().clear(); // clear the canvas
94      }
95   }
```

Fig. 13.7 | Controller for the **Painter** app. (Part 3 of 3.)

PenSize enum
Lines 15–25 define the nested enum type PenSize, which specifies three pen sizes—SMALL, MEDIUM and LARGE. Each has a corresponding radius that will be used when creating a Circle object to display in response to a mouse-drag event.

Java allows you to declare classes, interfaces and enums as **nested types** inside other classes. Except for the anonymous inner class introduced in Section 12.5.5, all the classes, interfaces and enums we've discussed were **top level**—that is, they *were* not declared *inside* another type. The enum type PenSize is declared here as a private nested type because it's used only by class PainterController. We'll say more about nested types later in the book.

Instance Variables
Lines 28–37 declare the @FXML instance variables that the controller uses to programmatically interact with the GUI. Recall that the names of these variables must match the corresponding **fx:id** values that you specified in Painter.fxml; otherwise, the FXMLLoader will not be able to connect the GUI components to the instance variables. Two of the @FXML instance variables are ToggleGroups—in the RadioButton event handlers, we'll use these to determine which RadioButton was selected. Lines 40–41 define two additional instance variables that store the current drawing Color and the current PenSize, respectively.

Method initialize
Recall that when the FXMLLoader creates a controller-class object, FXMLLoader determines whether the class contains an initialize method with no parameters and, if so, calls that

method to initialize the controller. Lines 44–53 define method initialize to specify each RadioButton's corresponding user data object—either a Color or a PenSize. You'll use these objects in the RadioButtons' event handlers.

drawingAreaMouseDragged Event Handler

Lines 56–61 define drawingAreaMouseDragged, which responds to drag events in the drawingAreaPane. Each mouse event handler you define must have one **MouseEvent** parameter (package **javafx.scene.input**). When the event occurs, this parameter contains information about the event, such as its location, whether any mouse buttons were pressed, which node the user interacted with and more. You specified drawingAreaMouse-Dragged in Scene Builder as the drawingAreaPane's **On Mouse Dragged** event handler.

Lines 58–59 create a new Circle object using the constructor that takes as arguments the center point's *x*-coordinate, the center point's *y*-coordinate, the Circle's radius and the Circle's Color.

Next, line 60 attaches the new Circle to the drawingAreaPane. Each layout pane has a **getChildren** method that returns an **ObservableList<Node>** collection containing the layout's child nodes. An ObservableList provides methods for adding and removing elements. You'll learn more about ObservableList later in this chapter. Line 60 uses the ObservableList's add method to add a new Node to the drawingAreaPane—all JavaFX shapes inherit indirectly from class Node in the javafx.scene package.

colorRadioButtonSelected Event Handler

Lines 64–69 define colorRadioButtonSelected, which responds to the ActionEvents of the **Drawing Color** RadioButtons—these occur each time a new color RadioButton is selected. You specified this event handler in Scene Builder as the **On Action** event handler for all four **Drawing Color** RadioButtons.

Lines 67–68 set the current drawing Color. ColorToggleGroup method **getSelect-edToggle** returns the Toggle that's currently selected. Class RadioButton is one of several controls (others are RadioButtonMenuItem and ToggleButton) that implement interface **Toggle**. We then use the Toggle's **getUserData** method to get the user data Object that was associated with the corresponding RadioButton in method initialize. For the color RadioButtons, this Object is aways a Color, so we cast the Object to a Color and assign it to brushColor.

sizeRadioButtonSelected Event Handler

Lines 72–77 define sizeRadioButtonSelected, which responds to the pen size RadioButtons' ActionEvents. You specified this event handler as the **On Action** event handler for all three **Pen Size** RadioButtons. Lines 75–76 set the current PenSize, using the same approach as setting the current color in method colorRadioButtonSelected.

undoButtonPressed Event Handler

Lines 80–88 define undoButtonPressed, which responds to an ActionEvent from the undoButton by removing the last Circle displayed. You specified this event handler in Scene Builder as the undoButton's **On Action** event handler.

To undo the last Circle, we remove the last child from the drawingAreaPane's collection of child nodes. First, line 82 gets the number of elements in that collection. Then, if that's greater than 0, line 86 removes the node at the last index in the collection.

clearButtonPressed *Event Handler*

Lines 91–94 define `clearButtonPressed`, which responds to the `ActionEvent` from the `clearButton` by clearing `drawingAreaPane`'s collection of child nodes. You specified this event handler in Scene Builder as the `clearButton`'s **On Action** event handler. Line 93 clears the collection of child nodes to erase the entire drawing.

13.4 Color Chooser App: Property Bindings and Property Listeners

In this section, we present a **Color Chooser** app (Fig. 13.8) that demonstrates property bindings and property listeners.

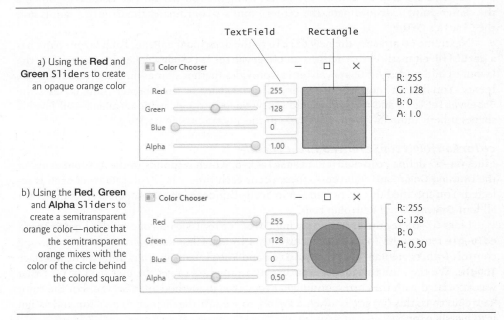

Fig. 13.8 | **Color Chooser** app with opaque and semitransparent orange colors.

13.4.1 Technologies Overview

In this section, we introduce the technologies you'll use to build the **Color Chooser**.

RGBA Colors

The app uses the **RGBA color system** to display a rectangle of color based on the values of four `Slider`s. In RGBA, every color is represented by its red, green and blue color values, each ranging from 0 to 255, where 0 denotes no color and 255 full color. For example, a color with a red value of 0 would contain no red component. The alpha value (A)—which ranges from 0.0 to 1.0—represents a color's *opacity*, with 0.0 being completely *transparent* and 1.0 completely *opaque*. The two colors in Fig. 13.8's sample outputs have the same RGB values, but the color displayed in Fig. 13.8(b) is *semitransparent*. You'll use a `Color` object that's created with RGBA values to fill a `Rectangle` that displays the `Color`.

Properties of a Class

JavaFX makes extensive use of properties. A **property** is defined by creating *set* and *get* methods with specific naming conventions. In general, the pair of methods that define a read/write property have the form:

```
public final void setPropertyName(Type propertyName)
public final Type getPropertyName()
```

Typically, such methods manipulate a corresponding *private* instance variable that has the same name as the property, but this is not required. For example, methods setHour and getHour together represent a property named hour and typically would manipulate a private hour instance variable. If the property represents a boolean value, its *get* method name typically begins with "is" rather than "get"—for example, ArrayList method isEmpty.

Software Engineering Observation 13.2

Methods that define properties should be declared final to prevent subclasses from overriding the methods, which could lead to unexpected results in client code.

Property Bindings

JavaFX properties are implemented in a manner that makes them *observable*—when a property's value changes, other objects can respond accordingly. This is similar to event handling. One way to respond to a property change is via a **property binding**, which enables a property of one object to be updated when a property of another object changes. For example, you'll use property bindings to enable a TextField to display the corresponding Slider's current value when the user moves that Slider's thumb. Property bindings are not limited to JavaFX controls. Package **javafx.beans.property** contains many classes that you can use to define bindable properties in your own classes.

Property Listeners

Property listeners are similar to property bindings. A **property listener** is an event handler that's invoked when a property's value changes. In the event handler, you can respond to the property change in a manner appropriate for your app. In this app, when a Slider's value changes, a property listener will store the value in a corresponding instance variable, create a new Color based on the values of all four Sliders and set that Color as the fill color of a Rectangle object that displays the current color. For more information on properties, property bindings and property listeners, visit:

```
http://docs.oracle.com/javase/8/javafx/properties-binding-tutorial/
binding.htm
```

13.4.2 Building the GUI

In this section, we'll discuss the **Color Chooser** app's GUI. Rather than providing the exact steps as we did in Chapter 12, we'll provide general instructions for building the GUI and focus on specific details for new concepts. As you build the GUI, recall that it's often easier to manipulate layouts and controls via the Scene Builder **Document** window's **Hierarchy** section than directly in the stage design area. Before proceeding, open Scene Builder and create an FXML file named ColorChooser.fxml.

fx:id Property Values for This App's Controls

Figure 13.9 shows the **fx:id** properties of the **Color Choooser** app's programmatically manipulated controls. As you build the GUI, you should set the corresponding **fx:id** properties in the FXML document, as you learned in Chapter 12.

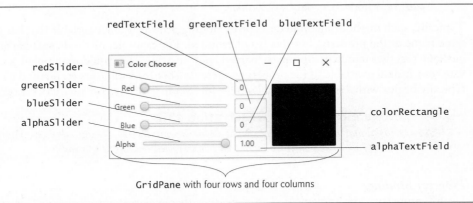

Fig. 13.9 | **Color Chooser** app's programmatically manipulated controls labeled with their **fx:id**s.

Step 1: Adding a GridPane

Drag a GridPane from the **Library** window's **Containers** section onto Scene Builder's content panel.

Step 2: Configuring the GridPane

This app's GridPane requires four rows and four columns. Use the techniques you've learned previously to add two columns and one row to the GridPane. Set the GridPane's **Hgap** and **Padding** properties to 8 to inset the GridPane from the stage's edges and to provide space between its columns.

Step 3: Adding the Controls

Using Fig. 13.9 as a guide, add the Labels, Sliders, TextFields, a Circle and a Rectangle to the GridPane—Circle and Rectangle are located in the Scene Builder **Library**'s **Shapes** section. When adding the Circle and Rectangle, place both into the rightmost column's first row. Be sure to add the Circle *before* the Rectangle so that it will be located *behind* the rectangle in the layout. Set the text of the Labels and TextFields as shown and set all the appropriate **fx:id** properties as you add each control.

Step 4: Configuring the Sliders

For the red, green and blue Sliders, set the **Max** properties to 255 (the maximum amount of a given color in the RGBA color scheme). For the alpha Slider, set its **Max** property to 1.0 (the maximum opacity in the RGBA color scheme).

Step 5: Configuring the TextFields

Set all of the TextField's **Pref Width** properties to 50.

Step 6: Configuring the `Rectangle`
Set the `Rectangle`'s **Width** and **Height** properties to 100, then set its **Row Span** property to Remainder so that it spans all four rows.

Step 7: Configuring the `Circle`
Set the `Circle`'s **Radius** property to 40, then set its **Row Span** property to Remainder so that it spans all four rows.

Step 8: Configuring the Rows
Set all four columns' **Pref Height** properties to USE_COMPUTED_SIZE so that the rows are only as tall as their content.

Step 9: Configuring the Columns
Set all four columns' **Pref Width** properties to USE_COMPUTED_SIZE so that the columns are only as wide as their content. For the leftmost column, set the **Halignment** property to RIGHT. For the rightmost column, set the **Halignment** property to CENTER.

Step 10: Configuring the `GridPane`
Set the `GridPane`'s **Pref Width** and **Pref Height** properties to USE_COMPUTED_SIZE so that it sizes itself, based on its contents. Your GUI should now appear as shown in Fig. 13.9.

Step 11: Specifying the Controller Class's Name
To ensure that an object of the controller class is created when the app loads the FXML file at runtime, specify `ColorChooserController` as the controller class's name in the FXML file as you've done previously.

Step 12: Generating a Sample Controller Class
Select **View > Show Sample Controller Skeleton**, then copy this code into a `ColorChooser-Controller.java` file and store the file in the same folder as `ColorChooser.fxml`. We show the completed `ColorChooserController` class in Section 13.4.4.

13.4.3 ColorChooser Subclass of Application
Figure 13.6 shows the `ColorChooser` subclass of `Application` that launches the app. This class loads the FXML and displays the app as in the prior JavaFX examples.

```
1    // Fig. 13.8: ColorChooser.java
2    // Main application class that loads and displays the ColorChooser's GUI.
3    import javafx.application.Application;
4    import javafx.fxml.FXMLLoader;
5    import javafx.scene.Parent;
6    import javafx.scene.Scene;
7    import javafx.stage.Stage;
8
9    public class ColorChooser extends Application {
10       @Override
11       public void start(Stage stage) throws Exception {
12          Parent root =
13             FXMLLoader.load(getClass().getResource("ColorChooser.fxml"));
```

Fig. 13.10 | Application class that loads and displays the **Color Chooser**'s GUI. (Part 1 of 2.)

```
14
15        Scene scene = new Scene(root);
16        stage.setTitle("Color Chooser");
17        stage.setScene(scene);
18        stage.show();
19    }
20
21    public static void main(String[] args) {
22        launch(args);
23    }
24 }
```

Fig. 13.10 | Application class that loads and displays the **Color Chooser**'s GUI. (Part 2 of 2.)

13.4.4 ColorChooserController Class

Figure 13.11 shows the final version of class ColorChooserController with this app's new features highlighted.

```
1  // Fig. 13.9: ColorChooserController.java
2  // Controller for the ColorChooser app
3  import javafx.beans.value.ChangeListener;
4  import javafx.beans.value.ObservableValue;
5  import javafx.fxml.FXML;
6  import javafx.scene.control.Slider;
7  import javafx.scene.control.TextField;
8  import javafx.scene.paint.Color;
9  import javafx.scene.shape.Rectangle;
10
11 public class ColorChooserController {
12    // instance variables for interacting with GUI components
13    @FXML private Slider redSlider;
14    @FXML private Slider greenSlider;
15    @FXML private Slider blueSlider;
16    @FXML private Slider alphaSlider;
17    @FXML private TextField redTextField;
18    @FXML private TextField greenTextField;
19    @FXML private TextField blueTextField;
20    @FXML private TextField alphaTextField;
21    @FXML private Rectangle colorRectangle;
22
23    // instance variables for managing
24    private int red = 0;
25    private int green = 0;
26    private int blue = 0;
27    private double alpha = 1.0;
28
29    public void initialize() {
30       // bind TextField values to corresponding Slider values
31       redTextField.textProperty().bind(
32          redSlider.valueProperty().asString("%.0f"));
```

Fig. 13.11 | Controller for the ColorChooser app. (Part 1 of 2.)

```
33        greenTextField.textProperty().bind(
34           greenSlider.valueProperty().asString("%.0f"));
35        blueTextField.textProperty().bind(
36           blueSlider.valueProperty().asString("%.0f"));
37        alphaTextField.textProperty().bind(
38           alphaSlider.valueProperty().asString("%.2f"));
39
40        // listeners that set Rectangle's fill based on Slider changes
41        redSlider.valueProperty().addListener(
42           new ChangeListener<Number>() {
43              @Override
44              public void changed(ObservableValue<? extends Number> ov,
45                 Number oldValue, Number newValue) {
46                 red = newValue.intValue();
47                 colorRectangle.setFill(Color.rgb(red, green, blue, alpha));
48              }
49           }
50        );
51        greenSlider.valueProperty().addListener(
52           new ChangeListener<Number>() {
53              @Override
54              public void changed(ObservableValue<? extends Number> ov,
55                 Number oldValue, Number newValue) {
56                 green = newValue.intValue();
57                 colorRectangle.setFill(Color.rgb(red, green, blue, alpha));
58              }
59           }
60        );
61        blueSlider.valueProperty().addListener(
62           new ChangeListener<Number>() {
63              @Override
64              public void changed(ObservableValue<? extends Number> ov,
65                 Number oldValue, Number newValue) {
66                 blue = newValue.intValue();
67                 colorRectangle.setFill(Color.rgb(red, green, blue, alpha));
68              }
69           }
70        );
71        alphaSlider.valueProperty().addListener(
72           new ChangeListener<Number>() {
73              @Override
74              public void changed(ObservableValue<? extends Number> ov,
75                 Number oldValue, Number newValue) {
76                 alpha = newValue.doubleValue();
77                 colorRectangle.setFill(Color.rgb(red, green, blue, alpha));
78              }
79           }
80        );
81     }
82  }
```

Fig. 13.11 | Controller for the ColorChooser app. (Part 2 of 2.)

Instance Variables
Lines 13–27 declare the controller's instance variables. Variables red, green, blue and alpha store the current values of the redSlider, greenSlider, blueSlider and alphaSlider, respectively. These values are used to update the colorRectangle's fill color each time the user moves a Slider's thumb.

Method `initialize`
Lines 29–81 define method `initialize`, which initializes the controller after the GUI is created. In this app, `initialize` configures the property bindings and property listeners.

Property-to-Property Bindings
Lines 31–38 set up property bindings between a Slider's value and the corresponding TextField's text so that changing a Slider updates the corresponding TextField. Consider lines 31–32, which bind the redSlider's valueProperty to the redTextField's textProperty:

```
redTextField.textProperty().bind(
    redSlider.valueProperty().asString("%.0f"));
```

Each TextField has a text property that's returned by its **textProperty** method as a **StringProperty** (package javafx.beans.property). StringProperty method **bind** receives an **ObservableValue** as an argument. When the ObservableValue changes, the bound property updates accordingly. In this case the ObservableValue is the result of the expression redSlider.valueProperty().asString("%.0f"). Slider's valueProperty method returns the Slider's value property as a **DoubleProperty**—an observable double value. Because the TextField's text property must be bound to a String, we call DoubleProperty method **asString**, which returns a **StringBinding** object (an ObservableValue) that produces a String representation of the DoubleProperty. This version of asString receives a format-control String specifying the DoubleProperty's format.

Property Listeners
To perform an arbitrary task when a property's value changes, register a property listener. Lines 41–80 register property listeners for the Sliders' value properties. Consider lines 41–50, which register the ChangeListener that executes when the user moves the redSlider's thumb. As we did in Section 12.5 for the **Tip Calculator**'s Slider, we use an anonymous inner class to define the listener. Each ChangeListener stores the int value of the newValue parameter in a corresponding instance variable, then calls the colorRectangle's setFill method to change its color, using Color method rgb to create the new Color object.

13.5 Cover Viewer App: Data-Driven GUIs with JavaFX Collections

Often an app needs to edit and display data. JavaFX provides a comprehensive model for allowing GUIs to interact with data. In this section, you'll build the **Cover Viewer** app (Fig. 13.12), which binds a list of Book objects to a ListView. When the user selects an item in the ListView, the corresponding Book's cover image is displayed in an ImageView.

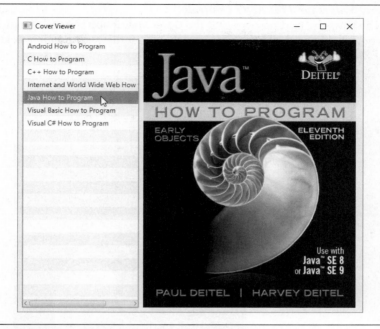

Fig. 13.12 | **Cover Viewer** with *Java How to Program* selected.

13.5.1 Technologies Overview

This app uses a ListView control to display a collection of book titles. Though you can individually add items to a ListView, in this app you'll bind an **ObservableList** object to the ListView. If you make changes to an ObservableList, its observer (the ListView in this app) will automatically be notified of those changes. Package **javafx.collections** defines ObservableList (similar to an ArrayList) and other observable collection interfaces. The package also contains class **FXCollections**, which provides static methods for creating and manipulating observable collections. You'll use a property listener to display the correct image when the user selects an item from the ListView—in this case, the property that changes is the selected item.

13.5.2 Adding Images to the App's Folder

From this chapter's examples folder, copy the images folder (which contains the large and small subfolders) into the folder where you'll save this app's FXML file, and the source-code files CoverViewer.java and CoverViewerController.java. Though you'll use only the large images in this example, you'll copy this app's folder to create the next example, which uses both sets of images.

13.5.3 Building the GUI

In this section, we'll discuss the **Cover Viewer** app's GUI. As you've done previously, create a new FXML file, then save it as CoverViewer.fxml.

fx:id Property Values for This App's Controls
Figure 13.13 shows the **fx:id** properties of the **Cover Viewer** app's programmatically manipulated controls. As you build the GUI, you should set the corresponding **fx:id** properties in the FXML document.

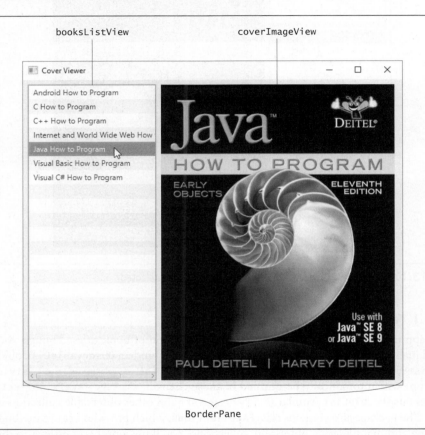

Fig. 13.13 | **Cover Viewer** app's programmatically manipulated controls labeled with their **fx:id**s.

Adding and Configuring the Controls
Using the techniques you learned previously, create a BorderPane. In the left area, place a ListView control, and in the center area, place an ImageView control.

For the ListView, set the following properties:

- **Margin**—8 (for the right margin) to separate the ListView from the ImageView
- **Pref Width**—200
- **Max Height**—MAX_VALUE
- **Min Width**, **Min Height**, **Pref Height** and **Max Width**—USE_COMPUTED_SIZE

For the ImageView, set the **Fit Width** and **Fit Height** properties to 370 and 480, respectively. To size the BorderPane based on its contents, set its **Pref Width** and **Pref Height** to USE_COMPUTED_SIZE. Also, set the **Padding** property to 8 to inset the BorderPane from the stage.

Specifying the Controller Class's Name
To ensure that an object of the controller class is created when the app loads the FXML file at runtime, specify `CoverViewerController` as the controller class's name in the FXML file as you've done previously.

Generating a Sample Controller Class
Select **View > Show Sample Controller Skeleton**, then copy this code into a `CoverViewer-Controller.java` file and store the file in the same folder as `CoverViewer.fxml`. We show the completed `CoverViewerController` class in Section 13.5.5.

13.5.4 CoverViewer Subclass of Application

Figure 13.14 shows class `CoverViewer` subclass of `Application`.

```
1   // Fig. 13.13: CoverViewer.java
2   // Main application class that loads and displays the CoverViewer's GUI.
3   import javafx.application.Application;
4   import javafx.fxml.FXMLLoader;
5   import javafx.scene.Parent;
6   import javafx.scene.Scene;
7   import javafx.stage.Stage;
8
9   public class CoverViewer extends Application {
10     @Override
11     public void start(Stage stage) throws Exception {
12        Parent root =
13           FXMLLoader.load(getClass().getResource("CoverViewer.fxml"));
14
15        Scene scene = new Scene(root);
16        stage.setTitle("Cover Viewer");
17        stage.setScene(scene);
18        stage.show();
19     }
20
21     public static void main(String[] args) {
22        launch(args);
23     }
24  }
```

Fig. 13.14 | Main application class that loads and displays the **Cover Viewer**'s GUI.

13.5.5 CoverViewerController Class

Figure 13.15 shows the final version of class `CoverViewerController` with the app's new features highlighted.

```
1   // Fig. 13.14: CoverViewerController.java
2   // Controller for Cover Viewer application
3   import javafx.beans.value.ChangeListener;
```

Fig. 13.15 | Controller for **Cover Viewer** application. (Part 1 of 2.)

```
4  import javafx.beans.value.ObservableValue;
5  import javafx.collections.FXCollections;
6  import javafx.collections.ObservableList;
7  import javafx.fxml.FXML;
8  import javafx.scene.control.ListView;
9  import javafx.scene.image.Image;
10 import javafx.scene.image.ImageView;
11
12 public class CoverViewerController {
13    // instance variables for interacting with GUI
14    @FXML private ListView<Book> booksListView;
15    @FXML private ImageView coverImageView;
16
17    // stores the list of Book Objects
18    private final ObservableList<Book> books =
19       FXCollections.observableArrayList();
20
21    // initialize controller
22    public void initialize() {
23       // populate the ObservableList<Book>
24       books.add(new Book("Android How to Program",
25          "/images/small/androidhtp.jpg", "/images/large/androidhtp.jpg"));
26       books.add(new Book("C How to Program",
27          "/images/small/chtp.jpg", "/images/large/chtp.jpg"));
28       books.add(new Book("C++ How to Program",
29          "/images/small/cpphtp.jpg", "/images/large/cpphtp.jpg"));
30       books.add(new Book("Internet and World Wide Web How to Program",
31          "/images/small/iw3htp.jpg", "/images/large/iw3htp.jpg"));
32       books.add(new Book("Java How to Program",
33          "/images/small/jhtp.jpg", "/images/large/jhtp.jpg"));
34       books.add(new Book("Visual Basic How to Program",
35          "/images/small/vbhtp.jpg", "/images/large/vbhtp.jpg"));
36       books.add(new Book("Visual C# How to Program",
37          "/images/small/vcshtp.jpg", "/images/large/vcshtp.jpg"));
38       booksListView.setItems(books); // bind booksListView to books
39
40       // when ListView selection changes, show large cover in ImageView
41       booksListView.getSelectionModel().selectedItemProperty().
42          addListener(
43             new ChangeListener<Book>() {
44                @Override
45                public void changed(ObservableValue<? extends Book> ov,
46                   Book oldValue, Book newValue) {
47                   coverImageView.setImage(
48                      new Image(newValue.getLargeImage()));
49                }
50             }
51          );
52    }
53 }
```

Fig. 13.15 | Controller for **Cover Viewer** application. (Part 2 of 2.)

@FXML *Instance Variables*

Lines 14–15 declare the controller's @FXML instance variables. Notice that ListView is a generic class. In this case, the ListView displays Book objects. Class Book contains three String instance variables with corresponding *set* and *get* methods:

- title—the book's title.
- thumbImage—the path to the book's thumbnail image (used in the next example).
- largeImage—the path to the book's large cover image.

The class also provides a toString method that returns the Book's title and a constructor that initializes the three instance variables. You should copy class Book from this chapter's examples folder into the folder that contains CoverViewer.fxml, CoverViewer.java and CoverViewerController.java.

Instance Variable **books**

Lines 18–19 define the books instance variable as an ObservableList<Book> and initialize it by calling FXCollections static method **observableArrayList**. This method returns an empty collection object (similar to an ArrayList) that implements the Observable-List interface.

Initializing the **books** *ObservableList*

Lines 24–37 in method initialize create and add Book objects to the books collection. Line 38 passes this collection to ListView method **setItems**, which binds the ListView to the ObservableList. This *data binding* allows the ListView to display the Book objects automatically. By default, the ListView displays each Book's String representation. (In the next example, you'll customize this.)

Listening for **ListView** *Selection Changes*

To synchronize the book cover that's being displayed with the currently selected book, we listen for changes to the ListView's selected item. By default a ListView supports single selection—one item at a time may be selected. ListViews also support multiple selection. The type of selection is managed by the ListView's **MultipleSelectionModel** (a subclass of **SelectionModel** from package javafx.scene.control), which contains observable properties and various methods for manipulating the corresponding ListView's items.

To respond to selection changes, you register a listener for the MultipleSelection-Model's selectedItem property (lines 41–51). ListView method **getSelectionModel** returns a MultipleSelectionModel object. In this example, MultipleSelectionModel's **selectedItemProperty** method returns a **ReadOnlyObjectProperty<Book>**, and the corresponding ChangeListener receives as its oldValue and newValue parameters the previously selected and newly selected Book objects, respectively.

Lines 47–48 use newValue's large image path to initialize a new **Image** (package javafx.scene.image)—this loads the image from that path. We then pass the new Image to the coverImageView's **setImage** method to display the Image.

13.6 Cover Viewer App: Customizing ListView Cells

In the preceding example, the ListView displayed a Book's String representation (i.e., its title). In this example, you'll create a custom ListView cell factory to create cells that display each book as its thumbnail image and title using a VBox, an ImageView and a Label (Fig. 13.16).

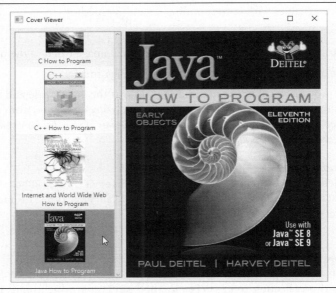

Fig. 13.16 | Cover Viewer app with *Java How to Program* selected.

13.6.1 Technologies Overview

ListCell *Generic Class for Custom* ListView *Cell Formats*
As you saw in Section 13.5, ListView cells display the String representations of a List-View's items by default. To create a custom cell format, you must first define a subclass of the **ListCell** generic class (package javafx.scene.control) that specifies how to create a ListView cell. As the ListView displays items, it gets ListCells from its cell factory. You'll use the ListView's **setCellFactory** method to replace the default cell factory with one that returns objects of the ListCell subclass. You'll override this class's **updateItem** method to specify the cells' custom layout and contents.

Programmatically Creating Layouts and Controls
So far, you've created GUIs visually using JavaFX Scene Builder. In this app, you'll also create a portion of the GUI programmatically—in fact, everything we've shown you in Scene Builder also can be accomplished in Java code directly. In particular, you'll create and configure a VBox layout containing an ImageView and a Label. The VBox represents the custom ListView cell format.

13.6.2 Copying the CoverViewer App

This app's FXML layout and classes Book and CoverViewer are identical to those in Section 13.5, and the CoverViewerController class has only one new statement. For this example, we'll show a new class that implements the custom ListView cell factory and the one new statement in class CoverViewerController. Rather than creating a new app from scratch, copy the CoverViewer app from the previous example into a new folder named CoverViewerCustomListView.

13.6.3 ImageTextCell Custom Cell Factory Class

Class ImageTextCell (Fig. 13.17) defines the custom ListView cell layout for this version of the **Cover Viewer** app. The class extends ListCell<Book> because it defines a customized presentation of a Book in a ListView cell.

```
1   // Fig. 13.16: ImageTextCell.java
2   // Custom ListView cell factory that displays an Image and text
3   import javafx.geometry.Pos;
4   import javafx.scene.control.Label;
5   import javafx.scene.control.ListCell;
6   import javafx.scene.image.Image;
7   import javafx.scene.image.ImageView;
8   import javafx.scene.layout.VBox;
9   import javafx.scene.text.TextAlignment;
10
11  public class ImageTextCell extends ListCell<Book> {
12     private VBox vbox = new VBox(8.0); // 8 points of gap between controls
13     private ImageView thumbImageView = new ImageView(); // initially empty
14     private Label label = new Label();
15
16     // constructor configures VBox, ImageView and Label
17     public ImageTextCell() {
18        vbox.setAlignment(Pos.CENTER); // center VBox contents horizontally
19
20        thumbImageView.setPreserveRatio(true);
21        thumbImageView.setFitHeight(100.0); // thumbnail 100 points tall
22        vbox.getChildren().add(thumbImageView); // attach to Vbox
23
24        label.setWrapText(true); // wrap if text too wide to fit in label
25        label.setTextAlignment(TextAlignment.CENTER); // center text
26        vbox.getChildren().add(label); // attach to VBox
27
28        setPrefWidth(USE_PREF_SIZE); // use preferred size for cell width
29     }
30
31     // called to configure each custom ListView cell
32     @Override
33     protected void updateItem(Book item, boolean empty) {
34        // required to ensure that cell displays properly
35        super.updateItem(item, empty)
36
37        if (empty || item == null) {
38           setGraphic(null); // don't display anything
39        }
40        else {
41           // set ImageView's thumbnail image
42           thumbImageView.setImage(new Image(item.getThumbImage()));
43           label.setText(item.getTitle()); // configure Label's text
```

Fig. 13.17 | Custom ListView cell factory that displays an image and text.

```
44                    setGraphic(vbox); // attach custom layout to ListView cell
45            }
46        }
47    }
```

Fig. 13.17 | Custom ListView cell factory that displays an image and text.

Constructor

The constructor (lines 17–29) configures the instance variables we use to build the custom presentation. Line 18 indicates that the VBox's children should be centered. Lines 20–22 configure the ImageView and attach it to the VBox's collection of children. Line 20 indicates that the ImageView should preserve the image's aspect ratio, and line 21 indicates that the ImageView should be 100 points tall. Line 22 attaches the ImageView to the VBox.

Lines 24–26 configure the Label and attach it to the VBox's collection of children. Line 24 indicates that the Label should wrap its text if its too wide to fit in the Label's width, and line 25 indicates that the text should be centered in the Label. Line 26 attaches the Label to the VBox. Finally, line 28 indicates that the cell should use its preferred width, which is determined from the width of its parent ListView.

Method updateItem

Method updateItem (lines 32–46) configures the Label's text and the ImageView's Image then displays the custom presentation in the ListView. This method is called by the List-View's cell factory when a ListView cell is required—that is, when the ListView is first displayed and when ListView cells are about to scroll onto the screen. The method receives the Book to display and a boolean indicating whether the cell that's about to be created is empty. You must call the superclass's version of updateItem (line 35) to ensure that the custom cells display correctly.

If the cell is empty or the item parameter is null, then there is no Book to display and line 38 calls the ImageTextCell's inherited **setGraphic** method with null. This method receives as its argument the Node that should be displayed in the cell. Any JavaFX Node can be provided, giving you tremendous flexibility for customizing a cell's appearance.

If there is a Book to display, lines 40–45 configure the ImageTextCell's the Label and ImageView. Line 42 configures the Book's Image and sets it to display in the ImageView. Line 43 sets the Label's text to the Book's title. Finally, line 38 uses method setGraphic to set the ImageTextCell's VBox as the custom cell's presentation.

Performance Tip 13.1

For the best ListView performance, it's considered best practice to define the custom presentation's controls as instance variables in the ListCell subclass and configure them in the subclass's constructor. This minimizes the amount of work required in each call to method updateItem.

13.6.4 CoverViewerController Class

Once you've defined the custom cell layout, updating the CoverViewerController to use it requires that you set the ListView's cell factory. Insert the following code as the last statement in the CoverViewerController's initialize method:

```
booksListView.setCellFactory(
    new Callback<ListView<Book>, ListCell<Book>>() {
        @Override
        public ListCell<Book> call(ListView<Book> listView) {
            return new ImageTextCell();
        }
    }
);
```

and add an import for `javafx.util.Callback`.

The argument to `ListView` method `setCellFactory` is an implementation of the functional interface **CallBack** (package **javafx.util**). This generic interface provides a `call` method that receives one argument and returns a value. In this case, we implement interface `Callback` with an object of an anonymous inner class. In `Callback`'s angle brackets the first type (`ListView<Book>`) is the parameter type for the interface's `call` method and the second (`ListCell<Book>`) is the `call` method's return type. The parameter represents the `ListView` in which the custom cells will appear. The `call` method call simply creates and returns an object of the `ImageTextCell` class.

Each time the `ListView` requires a new cell, the anonymous inner class's `call` method will be invoked to get a new `ImageTextCell`. Then the `ImageTextCell`'s `update` method will be called to create the custom cell presentation. Note that by using a Java SE 8 lambda (Chapter 17) rather than an anonymous inner class, you can replace the entire statement that sets the cell factory with a single line of code.

13.7 Additional JavaFX Capabilities

This section overviews various additional JavaFX capabilities that are available in JavaFX 8 and JavaFX 9.

TableView Control

Section 13.5 demonstrated how to bind data to a `ListView` control. You often load such data from a database (Chapter 22, Accessing Databases with JDBC, and Chapter 24, Java Persistence API (JPA)). JavaFX's `TableView` control (package `javafx.scene.control`) displays tabular data in rows and columns, and supports user interactions with that data.

Accessibility

In a Java SE 8 update, JavaFX added *accessibility* features to help people with visual impairments use their devices. For example, the screen readers in various operating systems can speak screen text or text that you provide to help users with visual impairments understand the purpose of a control. Visually impaired users must enable their operating systems' screen-reading capabilities. JavaFX controls also support:

- GUI navigation via the keyboard—for example, the user can press the *Tab* key to jump from one control to the next. If a screen reader also is enabled, as the user moves the focus from control to control, the screen reader will speak appropriate information about each control (discussed below).

- A high-contrast mode to make controls more readable—as with screen readers, visually impaired users must enable this feature in their operating systems.

See your operating system's documentation for information on enabling its screen reader and high-contrast mode.

Every JavaFX `Node` subclass also has the following accessibility-related properties:

- `accessibleTextProperty`—A `String` that a screen reader speaks for a control. For example, a screen reader normally speaks the text displayed on a `Button`, but setting this property for a `Button` causes the screen reader to speak this property's text instead. You also can set this property to provide accessibility text for controls that do not have text, such as `ImageView`s.

- `accessibleHelpProperty`—A more detailed control description `String` than that provided by the `accessibleTextProperty`. This property's text should help the user understand the purpose of the control in the context of your app.

- `accessibleRoleProperty`—A value from the `enum` `AccessibleRole` (package `javafx.scene`). A screen reader uses this property value to determine the attributes and actions supported for a given control.

- `accessibleRoleDescriptionProperty`—A `String` text description of a control that a screen reader typically speaks followed by the control's contents (such as the text on a `Button`) or the value of the `accessibleTextProperty`.

In addition, you can add `Label`s to a GUI that describe other controls. In such cases, you should set each `Label`'s `labelFor` property to the specific control the `Label` describes. For example, a `TextField` in which the user can enter a phone number might be preceded by a `Label` containing the text `"Phone Number"`. If the `Label`'s `labelFor` property references the `TextField`, then a screen reader will read the `Label`'s text as well when describing the `TextField` to the user.

Third-Party JavaFX Libraries

JavaFX continues to become more popular. There are various open-source, third-party libraries, which define additional JavaFX capabilities that you can incorporate into your own apps. Some popular JavaFX libraries include:

- ControlsFX (`http://www.controlsfx.org/`) provides common dialogs, additional controls, validation capabilities, `TextField` enhancements, a `Spread-SheetView`, `TableView` enhancements and more. You can find the API documentation at `http://docs.controlsfx.org/` and various code samples at `http://code.controlsfx.org`. We use one of the open-source ControlsFX dialogs in Chapter 20.

- JFXtras (`http://jfxtras.org/`) also provides many additional JavaFX controls, including date/time pickers, controls for maintaining an agenda, a calendar control, additional window features and more.

- Medusa provides many JavaFX gauges that look like clocks, speedometers and more. You can view samples at `https://github.com/HanSolo/Medusa/blob/master/README.md`.

Creating Custom JavaFX Controls

You can create custom controls by extending existing JavaFX control classes to customize them or by extending JavaFX's `Control` class directly.

JavaFXPorts: JavaFX for Mobile and Embedded Devices

A key Java benefit is writing apps that can run on any device with a Java Virtual Machine (JVM), including notebook computers, desktop computers, servers, mobile devices and embedded devices (such as those used in the Internet of Things). Oracle officially supports JavaFX only for desktop apps. Gluon's open-source JavaFXPorts project brings the desktip version of JavaFX to mobile devices (iOS and Android) and devices like the inexpensive Raspberry Pi (https://www.raspberrypi.org/), which can be used as a standalone computer or for embedded-device applications. For more information on JavaFXPorts, visit

```
http://javafxports.org/
```

In addition, Gluon Mobile provides a mobile-optimized JavaFX implementation for iOS and Android. For more information, see

```
http://gluonhq.com/products/mobile/
```

Scenic View for Debugging JavaFX Scenes and Nodes

Scenic View is a debugging tool for JavaFX scenes and nodes. You embed **Scenic View** directly into your apps or run it as a standalone app. You can inspect your JavaFX scenes and nodes, and modify them dynamically to see how changes affect their presentation on the screen—without having to edit your code, recompile it and re-run it for each change. For more information, visit

```
http://www.scenic-view.org
```

JavaFX Resources and JavaFX in the Real World

Visit

```
http://bit.ly/JavaFXResources
```

for a lengthy and growing list of JavaFX resources that includes links to:

- articles
- tutorials (free and for purchase)
- key blogs and websites
- YouTube® videos
- books (for purchase)
- many libraries, tools, projects and frameworks
- slide shows from JavaFX presentations and
- various real-world examples of JavaFX in use.

13.8 JavaFX 9: Java SE 9 JavaFX Updates

This section overviews several JavaFX 9 changes and enhancements.

Java SE 9 Modularization

Java SE 9's biggest new software-engineering feature is the module system. This applies to JavaFX 9 as well. The key JavaFX 9 modules are:

9

- `javafx.base`—Contains the packages required by all JavaFX 9 apps. All the other JavaFX 9 modules depend on this one.

- `javafx.controls`—Contains the packages for controls, layouts and charts, including the various controls we demonstrated in this chapter and Chapter 12.

- `javafx.fxml`—Contains the packages for working with FXML, including the FXML features we demonstrated in this chapter and Chapter 12.

- `javafx.graphics`—Contains the packages for working with graphics, animation, CSS (for styling nodes), text and more (Chapter 20, JavaFX Graphics, Animation and Video).

- `javafx.media`—Contains the packages for incorporating audio and video (Chapter 20, JavaFX Graphics, Animation and Video).

- `javafx.swing`—Contains the packages for integrating Swing GUI components into JavaFX 9 apps.

- `javafx.web`—Contains the package for integrating web content.

In your apps, if you use modularization and JDK 9, only the modules required by your app will be loaded at runtime. Otherwise, your app will continue to work as it did previously, provided that you did not use so-called internal APIs—that is, undocumented Java APIs that are not meant for public use. In the modularized JDK 9, such APIs are automatically *private* and inaccessible to your apps—any code that depends on pre-Java-SE-9 internal APIs will not compile. We discuss modularization in more detail in Chapter 27, Java Platform Module System.

New Public Skinning APIs

In Chapter 20, JavaFX Graphics, Animation and Video, we demonstrate how to format JavaFX objects using a technology called *Cascading Style Sheets (CSS)* that was originally developed for styling the elements in web pages. As you'll see, CSS allows you to specify *presentation* (e.g., fonts, spacing, sizes, colors, positioning) separately from the GUI's *structure* and *content* (layout containers, shapes, text, GUI components, etc.). If a JavaFX GUI's presentation is determined entirely by a style sheet (which specifies the rules for styling the GUI), you can simply swap in a new style sheet—sometimes called a **skin**—to change the GUI's appearance. This is commonly called **skinning**.

Each JavaFX control also has a skin class that determines its default appearance. In JavaFX 8, skin classes are defined as internal APIs, but many developers create custom skins by extending these skin classes. In JavaFX 9, the skin classes are now public APIs in the package `javafx.scene.control.skin`. You can extend the appropriate skin class to customize the look-and-feel for a given type of control. You then create an object of your custom skin class and set it for a control via its `setSkin` method.

GTK+ 3 Support on Linux

GTK+ (GIMP Toolkit—`http://gtk.org`) is a GUI toolkit that JavaFX uses behind the scenes to render GUIs and graphics on Linux. In Java SE 9, JavaFX now supports GTK+ 3—the latest version of GTK+.

High-DPI Screen Support

In a Java SE 8 update, JavaFX added support for High DPI (dots-per-inch) screens on Windows and macOS. Java SE 9 adds Linux High-DPI support, as well as capabilities to programmatically manipulate the scale at which JavaFX apps are rendered on Windows, macOS and Linux.

Updated GStreamer

JavaFX implements its audio and video multimedia capabilities using the open-source GStreamer framework (https://gstreamer.freedesktop.org). JavaFX 9 incorporates a more recent version of GStreamer with various bug fixes and performance enhancements.

Updated WebKit

JavaFX's WebView control enables you to embed web content in your JavaFX apps. WebView is based on the open source WebKit framework (http://www.webkit.org)—a web browser engine that supports loading and rendering web pages. JavaFX 9 incorporates an updated version of WebKit.

13.9 Wrap-Up

In this chapter, we continued our presentation of JavaFX. We discussed JavaFX layout panes in more detail and used BorderPane, TitledPane and Pane to arrange controls.

You learned about the many mouse events supported by JavaFX nodes, and we used the onMouseDragged event in a simple **Painter** app that displayed Circles as the user dragged the mouse across a Pane. The **Painter** app allowed the user to choose the current color and pen size from groups of mutually exclusive RadioButtons. You used Toggle-Groups to manage the relationship between the RadioButtons in each group. You also learned how to provide a so-called user data Object for a control. When a RadioButton was selected, you obtained it from the ToggleGroup, then accessed the RadioButton's user data Object to determine the drawing color or pen size.

We discussed property binding and property listeners, then used them to implement a **Color Chooser** app. You bound a TextField's text to a Slider's value to automatically update the TextField when the user moved the Slider's thumb. You also used a property listener to allow the app's controller to update the color of a Rectangle when a Slider's value changed.

In our **Cover Viewer** app, we showed how to bind an ObservableList collection to a ListView control to populate it with the collection's elements. By default, each object in the collection was displayed as a String in the ListView. You configured a property listener to display an image in an ImageView when the user selected an item in the ListView. We modified the **Cover Viewer** app to use a custom ListView cell factory to specify the exact layout of a ListView cell's contents. Finally, we introduced several other JavaFX capabilities and the Java SE 9 changes to JavaFX.

In the next chapter, we discuss class String and its methods. We introduce regular expressions for pattern matching in strings and demonstrate how to validate user input with regular expressions.

14

Strings, Characters and Regular Expressions

Objectives

In this chapter you'll:

- Create and manipulate immutable character-string objects of class `String`.

- Create and manipulate mutable character-string objects of class `StringBuilder`.

- Create and manipulate objects of class `Character`.

- Break a `String` object into tokens using `String` method `split`.

- Use regular expressions to validate `String` data entered into an application.

14.1 Introduction

This chapter introduces Java's string- and character-processing capabilities. The techniques discussed here are appropriate for validating program input, displaying information to users and performing other text-based manipulations. They're also appropriate for developing text editors, word processors, page-layout software and other kinds of text-processing software. We've presented several string-processing capabilities in earlier chapters. This chapter discusses in detail the capabilities of classes String, StringBuilder and Character from the java.lang package—these classes provide the foundation for string and character manipulation in Java.

The chapter also discusses regular expressions that provide applications with the capability to validate input. The functionality is located in the String class along with classes Matcher and Pattern located in the java.util.regex package.

14.2 Fundamentals of Characters and Strings

Characters are the fundamental building blocks of Java source programs. Every program is composed of a sequence of characters that—when grouped together meaningfully—are interpreted by the Java compiler as a series of instructions used to accomplish a task. A program may contain **character literals**. A character literal is an integer value represented as a character in single quotes. For example, `'z'` represents the integer value of z, and `'\t'` represents the integer value of a tab character. The value of a character literal is the integer value of the character in the **Unicode character set**. Appendix B presents the integer equivalents of the characters in the ASCII character set, which is a subset of Unicode (unicode.org).

Recall from Section 2.2 that a string is a sequence of characters treated as a single unit. A string may include letters, digits and various **special characters**, such as +, -, *, / and $.

A string is an object of class String. **String literals** (stored in memory as String objects) are written as a sequence of characters in double quotation marks, as in:

```
"John Q. Doe"           (a name)
"9999 Main Street"      (a street address)
"Waltham, Massachusetts" (a city and state)
"(201) 555-1212"        (a telephone number)
```

A string literal may be assigned to a String reference. The declaration

```
String color = "blue";
```

initializes String variable color to refer to a String object that contains the string "blue".

Performance Tip 14.1

To conserve memory, Java treats all string literals with the same contents as a single String object that has many references to it.

14.3 Class String

Class String is used to represent strings in Java. The next several subsections cover many of class String's capabilities.

Performance Tip 14.2

As of Java SE 9, Java uses a more compact String representation. This significantly reduces the amount of memory used to store Strings containing only Latin-1 characters— that is, those with the character codes 0–255. For more information, see JEP 254's proposal at http://openjdk.java.net/jeps/254.

14.3.1 String Constructors

Class String provides constructors for initializing String objects in a variety of ways. Four of the constructors are demonstrated in the main method of Fig. 14.1.

```
1   // Fig. 14.1: StringConstructors.java
2   // String class constructors.
3
4   public class StringConstructors {
5      public static void main(String[] args) {
6         char[] charArray = {'b', 'i', 'r', 't', 'h', ' ', 'd', 'a', 'y'};
7         String s = new String("hello");
8
9         // use String constructors
10        String s1 = new String();
11        String s2 = new String(s);
12        String s3 = new String(charArray);
13        String s4 = new String(charArray, 6, 3);
14
```

Fig. 14.1 | String class constructors. (Part 1 of 2.)

```
15          System.out.printf(
16              "s1 = %s%ns2 = %s%ns3 = %s%ns4 = %s%n", s1, s2, s3, s4);
17      }
18  }
```

```
s1 =
s2 = hello
s3 = birth day
s4 = day
```

Fig. 14.1 | String class constructors. (Part 2 of 2.)

Line 10 instantiates a new String using class String's no-argument constructor and assigns its reference to s1. The new String object contains no characters (i.e., the **empty string**, which can also be represented as "") and has a length of 0. Line 11 instantiates a new String object using class String's constructor that takes a String object as an argument and assigns its reference to s2. The new String object contains the same sequence of characters as the String object s that's passed as an argument to the constructor.

Performance Tip 14.3

It's not necessary to copy an existing String object. String objects are immutable, because class String does not provide methods that allow the contents of a String object to be modified after it is created. In fact, it's rarely necessary to call String constructors.

Line 12 instantiates a new String object and assigns its reference to s3 using class String's constructor that takes a char array as an argument. The new String object contains a copy of the characters in the array.

Line 13 instantiates a new String object and assigns its reference to s4 using class String's constructor that takes a char array and two integers as arguments. The second argument specifies the starting position (the *offset*) from which characters in the array are accessed. Remember that the first character is at position 0. The third argument specifies the number of characters (the count) to access in the array. The new String object is formed from the accessed characters. If the offset or the count specified as an argument results in accessing an element outside the bounds of the character array, a StringIndex-OutOfBoundsException is thrown.

14.3.2 String Methods length, charAt and getChars

String methods **length**, **charAt** and **getChars** return the length of a String, obtain the character at a specific location in a String and retrieve a set of characters from a String as a char array, respectively. Figure 14.2 demonstrates each of these methods.

```
1  // Fig. 14.2: StringMiscellaneous.java
2  // This application demonstrates the length, charAt and getChars
3  // methods of the String class.
4
```

Fig. 14.2 | String methods length, charAt and getChars. (Part 1 of 2.)

```
5   public class StringMiscellaneous {
6      public static void main(String[] args) {
7         String s1 = "hello there";
8         char[] charArray = new char[5];
9
10        System.out.printf("s1: %s", s1);
11
12        // test length method
13        System.out.printf("%nLength of s1: %d", s1.length());
14
15        // loop through characters in s1 with charAt and display reversed
16        System.out.printf("%nThe string reversed is: ");
17
18        for (int count = s1.length() - 1; count >= 0; count--) {
19           System.out.printf("%c ", s1.charAt(count));
20        }
21
22        // copy characters from string into charArray
23        s1.getChars(0, 5, charArray, 0);
24        System.out.printf("%nThe character array is: ");
25
26        for (char character : charArray) {
27           System.out.print(character);
28        }
29
30        System.out.println();
31     }
32  }
```

```
s1: hello there
Length of s1: 11
The string reversed is: e r e h t   o l l e h
The character array is: hello
```

Fig. 14.2 | String methods length, charAt and getChars. (Part 2 of 2.)

Line 13 uses String method length to determine the number of characters in String s1. Like arrays, strings know their own length. However, unlike arrays, you access a String's length via class String's length method.

Lines 18–20 print the characters of the String s1 in reverse order (and separated by spaces). String method charAt (line 19) returns the character at a specific position in the String. Method charAt receives an integer argument that's used as the index and returns the character at that position. Like arrays, the first element of a String is at position 0.

Line 23 uses String method getChars to copy the characters of a String into a character array. The first argument is the starting index from which characters are to be copied. The second argument is the index that's one past the last character to be copied from the String. The third argument is the character array into which the characters are to be copied. The last argument is the starting index where the copied characters are placed in the target character array. Next, lines 26–28 print the char array contents one character at a time.

14.3.3 Comparing Strings

You'll often sort and search collections. Frequently, the information being sorted or searched consists of Strings that must be compared to place them into order or to determine whether a string appears in an array (or other collection). Class String provides methods for *comparing* strings, as demonstrated in the next two examples.

To understand what it means for one string to be greater than or less than another, consider the process of alphabetizing a series of last names. No doubt, you'd place "Jones" before "Smith" because the first letter of "Jones" comes before the first letter of "Smith" in the alphabet. But the alphabet is more than just a list of 26 letters—it's an *ordered* list of characters. Each letter occurs in a specific position within the list. Z is more than just a letter of the alphabet—it's specifically the twenty-sixth letter of the alphabet.

How does the computer know that one letter "comes before" another? All characters are represented in the computer as numeric codes (see Appendix B). When the computer compares Strings, it actually compares the numeric codes of the characters in the Strings.

Figure 14.3 demonstrates String methods **equals**, **equalsIgnoreCase**, **compareTo** and **regionMatches** and using the equality operator == to compare String objects.

```java
1   // Fig. 14.3: StringCompare.java
2   // String methods equals, equalsIgnoreCase, compareTo and regionMatches.
3
4   public class StringCompare {
5      public static void main(String[] args) {
6         String s1 = new String("hello"); // s1 is a copy of "hello"
7         String s2 = "goodbye";
8         String s3 = "Happy Birthday";
9         String s4 = "happy birthday";
10
11        System.out.printf(
12           "s1 = %s%ns2 = %s%ns3 = %s%ns4 = %s%n%n", s1, s2, s3, s4);
13
14        // test for equality
15        if (s1.equals("hello")) {  // true
16           System.out.println("s1 equals \"hello\"");
17        }
18        else {
19           System.out.println("s1 does not equal \"hello\"");
20        }
21
22        // test for equality with ==
23        if (s1 == "hello") { // false; they are not the same object
24           System.out.println("s1 is the same object as \"hello\"");
25        }
26        else {
27           System.out.println("s1 is not the same object as \"hello\"");
28        }
29
```

Fig. 14.3 | String methods equals, equalsIgnoreCase, compareTo and regionMatches. (Part 1 of 3.)

```
30          // test for equality (ignore case)
31          if (s3.equalsIgnoreCase(s4)) { // true
32              System.out.printf("%s equals %s with case ignored%n", s3, s4);
33          }
34          else {
35              System.out.println("s3 does not equal s4");
36          }
37
38          // test compareTo
39          System.out.printf(
40              "%ns1.compareTo(s2) is %d", s1.compareTo(s2));
41          System.out.printf(
42              "%ns2.compareTo(s1) is %d", s2.compareTo(s1));
43          System.out.printf(
44              "%ns1.compareTo(s1) is %d", s1.compareTo(s1));
45          System.out.printf(
46              "%ns3.compareTo(s4) is %d", s3.compareTo(s4));
47          System.out.printf(
48              "%ns4.compareTo(s3) is %d%n%n", s4.compareTo(s3));
49
50          // test regionMatches (case sensitive)
51          if (s3.regionMatches(0, s4, 0, 5)) {
52              System.out.println("First 5 characters of s3 and s4 match");
53          }
54          else {
55              System.out.println(
56                  "First 5 characters of s3 and s4 do not match");
57          }
58
59          // test regionMatches (ignore case)
60          if (s3.regionMatches(true, 0, s4, 0, 5)) {
61              System.out.println(
62                  "First 5 characters of s3 and s4 match with case ignored");
63          }
64          else {
65              System.out.println(
66                  "First 5 characters of s3 and s4 do not match");
67          }
68      }
69  }
```

```
s1 = hello
s2 = goodbye
s3 = Happy Birthday
s4 = happy birthday

s1 equals "hello"
s1 is not the same object as "hello"
Happy Birthday equals happy birthday with case ignored
```

Fig. 14.3 | String methods equals, equalsIgnoreCase, compareTo and regionMatches.
(Part 2 of 3.)

```
s1.compareTo(s2) is 1
s2.compareTo(s1) is -1
s1.compareTo(s1) is 0
s3.compareTo(s4) is -32
s4.compareTo(s3) is 32

First 5 characters of s3 and s4 do not match
First 5 characters of s3 and s4 match with case ignored
```

Fig. 14.3 | String methods `equals`, `equalsIgnoreCase`, `compareTo` and `regionMatches`. (Part 3 of 3.)

String Method `equals`

Line 15 uses method `equals` (an `Object` method overridden in `String`) to compare `String` s1 and the `String` literal `"hello"` for equality. For `Strings`, the method determines whether the contents of the two `Strings` are *identical*. If so, it returns `true`; otherwise, it returns `false`. The preceding condition is `true` because `String` s1 was initialized with the literal `"hello"`. Method `equals` uses a **lexicographical comparison**—it compares the integer Unicode values that represent each character in each `String`. Thus, if the `String` `"hello"` is compared to the string `"HELLO"`, the result is `false`, because the integer representation of a lowercase letter is *different* from that of the corresponding uppercase letter.

Comparing *Strings* with the *==* Operator

The condition at line 23 uses the equality operator `==` to compare `String` s1 for equality with the `String` literal `"hello"`. When primitive-type values are compared with `==`, the result is `true` if *both values are identical*. When references are compared with `==`, the result is `true` if *both references refer to the same object in memory*. To compare the actual contents (or state information) of objects for equality, a method must be invoked. In the case of `Strings`, that method is `equals`. The condition evaluates to `false` at line 23 because the reference s1 was initialized with the statement

```
s1 = new String("hello");
```

which creates a new `String` object with a copy of string literal `"hello"` and assigns the new object to variable s1. If s1 had been initialized with the statement

```
s1 = "hello";
```

which directly assigns the string literal `"hello"` to variable s1, the condition would be `true`. Remember that Java treats all string literal objects with the same contents as one `String` object to which there can be many references. Thus, the `"hello"` literals in lines 6, 15 and 23 all refer to the same `String` object.

Common Programming Error 14.1

Comparing references with == can lead to logic errors, because == compares the references to determine whether they refer to the same object, not whether two objects have the same contents. When two separate objects that contain the same values are compared with ==, the result will be `false`. When comparing objects to determine whether they have the same contents, use method `equals`.

String Method `equalsIgnoreCase`

When sorting Strings, you might compare them for equality with method equalsIgnoreCase, which performs a case-insensitive comparison. Thus, "hello" and "HELLO" compare as equal. Line 31 uses String method equalsIgnoreCase to compare String s3—Happy Birthday—for equality with String s4—happy birthday. The result of this comparison is true because the comparison ignores case.

String Method `compareTo`

Lines 39–48 use method compareTo to compare Strings. Class String implements interface Comparable which declares method compareTo. Line 40 compares String s1 to String s2. Method compareTo returns 0 if the Strings are equal, a negative number if the String that invokes compareTo is less than the String that's passed as an argument and a positive number if the String that invokes compareTo is greater than the String that's passed as an argument. Method compareTo uses a *lexicographical* comparison—it compares the numeric values of corresponding characters in each String.

String Method `regionMatches`

The condition at line 51 uses a version of String method regionMatches to compare portions of two Strings for equality. The first argument to this version of the method is the starting index in the String that invokes the method. The second argument is a comparison String. The third argument is the starting index in the comparison String. The last argument is the number of characters to compare between the two Strings. The method returns true only if the specified number of characters are lexicographically equal.

Finally, the condition at line 60 uses a five-argument version of String method regionMatches to compare portions of two Strings for equality. When the first argument is true, the method ignores the case of the characters being compared. The remaining arguments are identical to those described for the four-argument regionMatches method.

String Methods `startsWith` and `endsWith`

Figure 14.4 demonstrates String methods **startsWith** and **endsWith**. Method main creates array strings containing "started", "starting", "ended" and "ending". The remainder of method main consists of three for statements that test the elements of the array to determine whether they start with or end with a particular set of characters.

```java
1   // Fig. 14.4: StringStartEnd.java
2   // String methods startsWith and endsWith.
3
4   public class StringStartEnd {
5      public static void main(String[] args) {
6         String[] strings = {"started", "starting", "ended", "ending"};
7
8         // test method startsWith
9         for (String string : strings) {
10           if (string.startsWith("st")) {
11              System.out.printf("\"%s\" starts with \"st\"%n", string);
12           }
13        }
```

Fig. 14.4 | String methods startsWith and endsWith. (Part 1 of 2.)

```
14
15          System.out.println();
16
17          // test method startsWith starting from position 2 of string
18          for (String string : strings) {
19              if (string.startsWith("art", 2)) {
20                  System.out.printf(
21                      "\"%s\" starts with \"art\" at position 2%n", string);
22              }
23          }
24
25          System.out.println();
26
27          // test method endsWith
28          for (String string : strings) {
29              if (string.endsWith("ed")) {
30                  System.out.printf("\"%s\" ends with \"ed\"%n", string);
31              }
32          }
33      }
34  }
```

```
"started" starts with "st"
"starting" starts with "st"

"started" starts with "art" at position 2
"starting" starts with "art" at position 2

"started" ends with "ed"
"ended" ends with "ed"
```

Fig. 14.4 | String methods startsWith and endsWith. (Part 2 of 2.)

Lines 9–13 use the version of method startsWith that takes a String argument. The condition in the if statement (line 10) determines whether each String in the array starts with the characters "st". If so, the method returns true and the application prints that String. Otherwise, the method returns false and nothing happens.

Lines 18–23 use the startsWith method that takes a String and an integer as arguments. The integer specifies the index at which the comparison should begin in the String. The condition in the if statement (line 19) determines whether each String in the array has the characters "art" beginning with the third character in each String. If so, the method returns true and the application prints the String.

The third for statement (lines 28–32) uses method endsWith, which takes a String argument. The condition at line 29 determines whether each String in the array ends with the characters "ed". If so, the method returns true and the application prints the String.

14.3.4 Locating Characters and Substrings in Strings

Often it's useful to search a string for a character or set of characters. For example, if you're creating your own word processor, you might want to provide a capability for searching through documents. Figure 14.5 demonstrates the many versions of String methods **indexOf** and **lastIndexOf** that search for a specified character or substring in a String.

```java
1   // Fig. 14.5: StringIndexMethods.java
2   // String searching methods indexOf and lastIndexOf.
3
4   public class StringIndexMethods {
5      public static void main(String[] args) {
6         String letters = "abcdefghijklmabcdefghijklm";
7
8         // test indexOf to locate a character in a string
9         System.out.printf(
10           "'c' is located at index %d%n", letters.indexOf('c'));
11        System.out.printf(
12           "'a' is located at index %d%n", letters.indexOf('a', 1));
13        System.out.printf(
14           "'$' is located at index %d%n%n", letters.indexOf('$'));
15
16        // test lastIndexOf to find a character in a string
17        System.out.printf("Last 'c' is located at index %d%n",
18           letters.lastIndexOf('c'));
19        System.out.printf("Last 'a' is located at index %d%n",
20           letters.lastIndexOf('a', 25));
21        System.out.printf("Last '$' is located at index %d%n%n",
22           letters.lastIndexOf('$'));
23
24        // test indexOf to locate a substring in a string
25        System.out.printf("\"def\" is located at index %d%n",
26           letters.indexOf("def"));
27        System.out.printf("\"def\" is located at index %d%n",
28           letters.indexOf("def", 7));
29        System.out.printf("\"hello\" is located at index %d%n%n",
30           letters.indexOf("hello"));
31
32        // test lastIndexOf to find a substring in a string
33        System.out.printf("Last \"def\" is located at index %d%n",
34           letters.lastIndexOf("def"));
35        System.out.printf("Last \"def\" is located at index %d%n",
36           letters.lastIndexOf("def", 25));
37        System.out.printf("Last \"hello\" is located at index %d%n",
38           letters.lastIndexOf("hello"));
39     }
40  }
```

```
'c' is located at index 2
'a' is located at index 13
'$' is located at index -1

Last 'c' is located at index 15
Last 'a' is located at index 13
Last '$' is located at index -1

"def" is located at index 3
"def" is located at index 16
"hello" is located at index -1
```

Fig. 14.5 | String-searching methods `indexOf` and `lastIndexOf`. (Part 1 of 2.)

```
Last "def" is located at index 16
Last "def" is located at index 16
Last "hello" is located at index -1
```

Fig. 14.5 | String-searching methods `indexOf` and `lastIndexOf`. (Part 2 of 2.)

All the searches in this example are performed on the String `letters` (initialized with `"abcdefghijklmabcdefghijklm"`). Lines 9–14 use method `indexOf` to locate the first occurrence of a character in a String. If the method finds the character, it returns the character's index in the String—otherwise, it returns -1. There are two versions of `indexOf` that search for characters in a String. The expression in line 10 uses the version of method `indexOf` that takes an integer representation of the character to find. The expression at line 12 uses another version of method `indexOf`, which takes two integer arguments—the character and the starting index at which the search of the String should begin.

Lines 17–22 use method `lastIndexOf` to locate the last occurrence of a character in a String. The method searches from the end of the String toward the beginning. If it finds the character, it returns the character's index in the String—otherwise, it returns −1. There are two versions of `lastIndexOf` that search for characters in a String. The expression at line 18 uses the version that takes the integer representation of the character. The expression at line 20 uses the version that takes two integer arguments—the integer representation of the character and the index from which to begin searching *backward*.

Lines 25–38 demonstrate versions of methods `indexOf` and `lastIndexOf` that each take a String as the first argument. These versions perform identically to those described earlier except that they search for sequences of characters (or substrings) that are specified by their String arguments. If the substring is found, these methods return the index in the String of the first character in the substring.

14.3.5 Extracting Substrings from Strings

Class String provides two `substring` methods to enable a new String object to be created by copying part of an existing String object. Each method returns a new String object. Both methods are demonstrated in Fig. 14.6.

```
I   // Fig. 14.6: SubString.java
2   // String class substring methods.
3
4   public class SubString {
5      public static void main(String[] args) {
6         String letters = "abcdefghijklmabcdefghijklm";
7
8         // test substring methods
9         System.out.printf("Substring from index 20 to end is \"%s\"%n",
10           letters.substring(20));
11        System.out.printf("%s \"%s\"%n",
12           "Substring from index 3 up to, but not including, 6 is",
13           letters.substring(3, 6));
14     }
15  }
```

Fig. 14.6 | String class substring methods. (Part 1 of 2.)

```
Substring from index 20 to end is "hijklm"
Substring from index 3 up to, but not including, 6 is "def"
```

Fig. 14.6 | String class substring methods. (Part 2 of 2.)

The expression letters.substring(20) at line 10 uses the substring method that takes one integer argument. The argument specifies the starting index in the original String letters from which characters are to be copied. The substring returned contains a copy of the characters from the starting index to the end of the String. Specifying an index outside the bounds of the String causes a **StringIndexOutOfBoundsException**.

Line 13 uses the substring method that takes two integer arguments—the starting index from which to copy characters in the original String and the index one beyond the last character to copy (i.e., copy up to, but *not including*, that index in the String). The substring returned contains a copy of the specified characters from the original String. An index outside the bounds of the String causes a StringIndexOutOfBoundsException.

14.3.6 Concatenating Strings

String method **concat** (Fig. 14.7) concatenates two String objects (similar to using the + operator) and returns a new String containing the characters from both original Strings. The expression s1.concat(s2) at line 11 forms a String by appending the characters in s2 to the those in s1. The original Strings to which s1 and s2 refer are *not modified*.

```java
1   // Fig. 14.7: StringConcatenation.java
2   // String method concat.
3
4   public class StringConcatenation {
5      public static void main(String[] args) {
6         String s1 = "Happy ";
7         String s2 = "Birthday";
8
9         System.out.printf("s1 = %s%ns2 = %s%n%n",s1, s2);
10        System.out.printf(
11           "Result of s1.concat(s2) = %s%n", s1.concat(s2));
12        System.out.printf("s1 after concatenation = %s%n", s1);
13     }
14  }
```

```
s1 = Happy
s2 = Birthday

Result of s1.concat(s2) = Happy Birthday
s1 after concatenation = Happy
```

Fig. 14.7 | String method concat.

14.3.7 Miscellaneous String Methods

Class String provides several methods that return Strings or character arrays containing modified copies of an original String's contents. These methods—none of which modify the String on which they're called—are demonstrated in Fig. 14.8.

```
 1   // Fig. 14.8: StringMiscellaneous2.java
 2   // String methods replace, toLowerCase, toUpperCase, trim and toCharArray.
 3
 4   public class StringMiscellaneous2 {
 5      public static void main(String[] args) {
 6         String s1 = "hello";
 7         String s2 = "GOODBYE";
 8         String s3 = "   spaces   ";
 9
10         System.out.printf("s1 = %s%ns2 = %s%ns3 = %s%n%n", s1, s2, s3);
11
12         // test method replace
13         System.out.printf(
14            "Replace 'l' with 'L' in s1: %s%n%n", s1.replace('l', 'L'));
15
16         // test toLowerCase and toUpperCase
17         System.out.printf("s1.toUpperCase() = %s%n", s1.toUpperCase());
18         System.out.printf("s2.toLowerCase() = %s%n%n", s2.toLowerCase());
19
20         // test trim method
21         System.out.printf("s3 after trim = \"%s\"%n%n", s3.trim());
22
23         // test toCharArray method
24         char[] charArray = s1.toCharArray();
25         System.out.print("s1 as a character array = ");
26
27         for (char character : charArray) {
28            System.out.print(character);
29         }
30
31         System.out.println();
32      }
33   }
```

```
s1 = hello
s2 = GOODBYE
s3 =    spaces

Replace 'l' with 'L' in s1: heLLo

s1.toUpperCase() = HELLO
s2.toLowerCase() = goodbye

s3 after trim = "spaces"

s1 as a character array = hello
```

Fig. 14.8 | String methods replace, toLowerCase, toUpperCase, trim and
toCharArray.

Line 14 uses String method replace to return a new String object in which every
occurrence in s1 of character 'l' (lowercase el) is replaced with character 'L'. Method
replace leaves the original String unchanged. If there are no occurrences of the first argu-

ment in the String, method replace returns the original String. An overloaded version of method replace enables you to replace substrings rather than individual characters.

Line 17 uses String method **toUpperCase** to generate a new String with uppercase letters where corresponding lowercase letters exist in s1. The method returns a new String object containing the converted String and leaves the original String unchanged. If there are no characters to convert, method toUpperCase returns the original String.

Line 18 uses String method **toLowerCase** to return a new String object with lower-case letters where corresponding uppercase letters exist in s2. The original String remains unchanged. If there are no characters in the original String to convert, toLowerCase returns the original String.

Line 21 uses String method **trim** to generate a new String object that removes all white-space characters that appear at the beginning and/or end of the String on which trim operates. The method returns a new String object containing the String without leading or trailing white space. The original String remains unchanged. If there are no white-space characters at the beginning and end, trim returns the original String.

Line 24 uses String method **toCharArray** to create a new character array containing a copy of the characters in s1. Lines 27–29 output each char in the array.

14.3.8 String Method valueOf

As we've seen, every object in Java has a toString method that enables a program to obtain the object's *string representation*. Unfortunately, this technique cannot be used with primitive types because they do not have methods. Class String provides static methods that take an argument of any type and convert it to a String object. Figure 14.9 demonstrates the String class **valueOf** methods.

```
1   // Fig. 14.9: StringValueOf.java
2   // String valueOf methods.
3
4   public class StringValueOf {
5      public static void main(String[] args) {
6         char[] charArray = {'a', 'b', 'c', 'd', 'e', 'f'};
7         boolean booleanValue = true;
8         char characterValue = 'Z';
9         int integerValue = 7;
10        long longValue = 10000000000L; // L suffix indicates long
11        float floatValue = 2.5f; // f indicates that 2.5 is a float
12        double doubleValue = 33.333; // no suffix, double is default
13        Object objectRef = "hello"; // assign string to an Object reference
14
15        System.out.printf(
16           "char array = %s%n", String.valueOf(charArray));
17        System.out.printf("part of char array = %s%n",
18           String.valueOf(charArray, 3, 3));
19        System.out.printf(
20           "boolean = %s%n", String.valueOf(booleanValue));
21        System.out.printf(
22           "char = %s%n", String.valueOf(characterValue));
```

Fig. 14.9 | String valueOf methods. (Part 1 of 2.)

```
23          System.out.printf("int = %s%n", String.valueOf(integerValue));
24          System.out.printf("long = %s%n", String.valueOf(longValue));
25          System.out.printf("float = %s%n", String.valueOf(floatValue));
26          System.out.printf(
27             "double = %s%n", String.valueOf(doubleValue));
28          System.out.printf("Object = %s", String.valueOf(objectRef));
29       }
30    }
```

```
char array = abcdef
part of char array = def
boolean = true
char = Z
int = 7
long = 10000000000
float = 2.5
double = 33.333
Object = hello
```

Fig. 14.9 | String valueOf methods. (Part 2 of 2.)

The expression String.valueOf(charArray) at line 16 uses the character array char-Array to create a new String object. The expression String.valueOf(charArray, 3, 3) at line 18 uses a portion of the character array charArray to create a new String object. The second argument specifies the starting index from which the characters are used. The third argument specifies the number of characters to be used.

There are seven other versions of method valueOf, which take arguments of type boolean, char, int, long, float, double and Object, respectively. These are demonstrated in lines 19–28. The version of valueOf that takes an Object as an argument can do so because all Objects can be converted to Strings with method toString.

[*Note:* Lines 10–11 use literal values 10000000000L and 2.5f as the initial values of long variable longValue and float variable floatValue, respectively. By default, Java treats integer literals as type int and floating-point literals as type double. Appending the letter L to the literal 10000000000 and appending the letter f to the literal 2.5 indicates to the compiler that 10000000000 should be treated as a long and 2.5 as a float. An uppercase L or lowercase l can be used to denote a variable of type long and an uppercase F or lowercase f can be used to denote a variable of type float.]

14.4 Class StringBuilder

We now discuss the features of class **StringBuilder** for creating and manipulating *dynamic* string information—that is, *modifiable* strings. Every StringBuilder is capable of storing a number of characters specified by its *capacity*. If a StringBuilder's capacity is exceeded, the capacity expands to accommodate the additional characters.

Performance Tip 14.4
Java can perform certain optimizations involving String objects (such as referring to one String object from multiple variables) because it knows these objects will not change. Strings (not StringBuilders) should be used if the data will not change.

Performance Tip 14.5

In programs that frequently perform string concatenation, or other string modifications, it's often more efficient to implement the modifications with class StringBuilder.

Software Engineering Observation 14.1

*StringBuilders are not thread safe. If multiple threads require access to the same dynamic string information, use class **StringBuffer** in your code. Classes StringBuilder and StringBuffer provide identical capabilities, but class StringBuffer is thread safe. For more details on threading, see Chapter 21.*

14.4.1 StringBuilder Constructors

Class StringBuilder provides four constructors. We demonstrate three of these in Fig. 14.10. Line 6 uses the no-argument StringBuilder constructor to create a String-Builder with no characters in it and an initial capacity of 16 characters (the default for a StringBuilder). Line 7 uses the StringBuilder constructor that takes an integer argument to create a StringBuilder with no characters in it and the initial capacity specified by the integer argument (i.e., 10). Line 8 uses the StringBuilder constructor that takes a String argument to create a StringBuilder containing the characters in the String argument. The initial capacity is the number of characters in the String argument plus 16. Lines 10–12 implicitly use the method toString of class StringBuilder to output the StringBuilders with the printf method. In Section 14.4.4, we discuss how Java uses StringBuilder objects to implement the + and += operators for string concatenation.

```java
1   // Fig. 14.10: StringBuilderConstructors.java
2   // StringBuilder constructors.
3
4   public class StringBuilderConstructors {
5      public static void main(String[] args) {
6         StringBuilder buffer1 = new StringBuilder();
7         StringBuilder buffer2 = new StringBuilder(10);
8         StringBuilder buffer3 = new StringBuilder("hello");
9
10        System.out.printf("buffer1 = \"%s\"%n", buffer1);
11        System.out.printf("buffer2 = \"%s\"%n", buffer2);
12        System.out.printf("buffer3 = \"%s\"%n", buffer3);
13     }
14  }
```

```
buffer1 = ""
buffer2 = ""
buffer3 = "hello"
```

Fig. 14.10 | StringBuilder constructors.

14.4.2 StringBuilder Methods length, capacity, setLength and ensureCapacity

Class StringBuilder's **length** and **capacity** method return the number of characters currently in a StringBuilder and the number of characters that can be stored without allocating more memory, respectively. Method **ensureCapacity** guarantees that a String-Builder has at least the specified capacity. Method **setLength** increases or decreases the length of a StringBuilder. Figure 14.11 demonstrates these methods.

```java
 1    // Fig. 14.11: StringBuilderCapLen.java
 2    // StringBuilder length, setLength, capacity and ensureCapacity methods.
 3
 4    public class StringBuilderCapLen {
 5       public static void main(String[] args) {
 6          StringBuilder buffer = new StringBuilder("Hello, how are you?");
 7
 8          System.out.printf("buffer = %s%nlength = %d%ncapacity = %d%n%n",
 9             buffer.toString(), buffer.length(), buffer.capacity());
10
11          buffer.ensureCapacity(75);
12          System.out.printf("New capacity = %d%n%n", buffer.capacity());
13
14          buffer.setLength(10));
15          System.out.printf("New length = %d%nbuffer = %s%n",
16             buffer.length(), buffer.toString());
17       }
18    }
```

```
buffer = Hello, how are you?
length = 19
capacity = 35

New capacity = 75

New length = 10
buffer = Hello, how
```

Fig. 14.11 | StringBuilder length, setLength, capacity and ensureCapacity methods.

The application contains one StringBuilder called buffer. Line 6 uses the String-Builder constructor that takes a String argument to initialize the StringBuilder with "Hello, how are you?". Lines 8–9 print the contents, length and capacity of the String-Builder. Note in the output window that the capacity of the StringBuilder is initially 35. Recall that the StringBuilder constructor that takes a String argument initializes the capacity to the length of the string passed as an argument plus 16.

Line 11 uses method ensureCapacity to expand the capacity of the StringBuilder to a minimum of 75 characters. Actually, if the original capacity is less than the argument, the method ensures a capacity that's the greater of the number specified as an argument and twice the original capacity plus 2. The StringBuilder's current capacity remains unchanged if it's more than the specified capacity.

Performance Tip 14.6

Dynamically increasing the capacity of a StringBuilder can take a relatively long time. Executing a large number of these operations can degrade the performance of an application. If a StringBuilder is going to increase greatly in size, possibly multiple times, setting its capacity high at the beginning will increase performance.

Line 14 uses method setLength to set the length of the StringBuilder to 10. If the specified length is less than the current number of characters in the StringBuilder, its contents are truncated to the specified length (i.e., the characters in the StringBuilder after the specified length are discarded). If the specified length is greater than the number of characters currently in the StringBuilder, null characters (characters with the numeric representation 0) are appended until the total number of characters in the StringBuilder is equal to the specified length.

14.4.3 StringBuilder Methods charAt, setCharAt, getChars and reverse

Class StringBuilder provides methods **charAt**, **setCharAt**, **getChars** and **reverse** to manipulate the characters in a StringBuilder (Fig. 14.12). Method charAt (line 10) takes an integer argument and returns the character in the StringBuilder at that index. Method getChars (line 13) copies characters from a StringBuilder into the character array passed as an argument. This method takes four arguments—the starting index from which characters should be copied in the StringBuilder, the index one past the last character to be copied from the StringBuilder, the character array into which the characters are to be copied and the starting location in the character array where the first character should be placed. Method setCharAt (lines 20 and 21) takes an integer and a character argument and sets the character at the specified position in the StringBuilder to the character argument. Method reverse (line 24) reverses the contents of the StringBuilder. Attempting to access a character that's outside the bounds of a StringBuilder results in a StringIndexOutOfBoundsException.

```
1   // Fig. 14.12: StringBuilderChars.java
2   // StringBuilder methods charAt, setCharAt, getChars and reverse.
3
4   public class StringBuilderChars {
5      public static void main(String[] args) {
6         StringBuilder buffer = new StringBuilder("hello there");
7
8         System.out.printf("buffer = %s%n", buffer.toString());
9         System.out.printf("Character at 0: %s%nCharacter at 4: %s%n%n",
10           buffer.charAt(0), buffer.charAt(4));
11
12        char[] charArray = new char[buffer.length()];
13        buffer.getChars(0, buffer.length(), charArray, 0);
14        System.out.print("The characters are: ");
15
16        for (char character : charArray) {
17           System.out.print(character);
18        }
19
20        buffer.setCharAt(0, 'H');
21        buffer.setCharAt(6, 'T');
22        System.out.printf("%n%nbuffer = %s", buffer.toString());
23
```

Fig. 14.12 | StringBuilder methods charAt, setCharAt, getChars and reverse. (Part 1 of 2.)

```
24        buffer.reverse();
25        System.out.printf("%n%nbuffer = %s%n", buffer.toString());
26     }
27  }
```

```
buffer = hello there
Character at 0: h
Character at 4: o

The characters are: hello there

buffer = Hello There

buffer = erehT olleH
```

Fig. 14.12 | StringBuilder methods charAt, setCharAt, getChars and reverse. (Part 2 of 2.)

14.4.4 StringBuilder append Methods

Class StringBuilder provides *overloaded* **append** methods (Fig. 14.13) to allow values of various types to be appended to the end of a StringBuilder. Versions are provided for each of the primitive types and for character arrays, Strings, Objects, and more. (Remember that method toString produces a string representation of any Object.) Each method takes its argument, converts it to a string and appends it to the StringBuilder. The call System.getProperty("line.separator") returns a platform-independent newline.

```
1   // Fig. 14.13: StringBuilderAppend.java
2   // StringBuilder append methods.
3
4   public class StringBuilderAppend
5   {
6      public static void main(String[] args)
7      {
8         Object objectRef = "hello";
9         String string = "goodbye";
10        char[] charArray = {'a', 'b', 'c', 'd', 'e', 'f'};
11        boolean booleanValue = true;
12        char characterValue = 'Z';
13        int integerValue = 7;
14        long longValue = 10000000000L;
15        float floatValue = 2.5f;
16        double doubleValue = 33.333;
17
18        StringBuilder lastBuffer = new StringBuilder("last buffer");
19        StringBuilder buffer = new StringBuilder();
20
21        buffer.append(objectRef)
22            .append(System.getProperty("line.separator"))
23            .append(string)
```

Fig. 14.13 | StringBuilder append methods. (Part 1 of 2.)

```
24                      .append(System.getProperty("line.separator"))
25                      .append(charArray)
26                      .append(System.getProperty("line.separator"))
27                      .append(charArray, 0, 3)
28                      .append(System.getProperty("line.separator"))
29                      .append(booleanValue)
30                      .append(System.getProperty("line.separator"))
31                      .append(characterValue);
32                      .append(System.getProperty("line.separator"))
33                      .append(integerValue)
34                      .append(System.getProperty("line.separator"))
35                      .append(longValue)
36                      .append(System.getProperty("line.separator"))
37                      .append(floatValue)
38                      .append(System.getProperty("line.separator"))
39                      .append(doubleValue)
40                      .append(System.getProperty("line.separator"))
41                      .append(lastBuffer);
42
43          System.out.printf("buffer contains%n%s%n", buffer.toString());
44      }
45   }
```

```
buffer contains
hello
goodbye
abcdef
abc
true
Z
7
10000000000
2.5
33.333
last buffer
```

Fig. 14.13 | StringBuilder append methods. (Part 2 of 2.)

The compiler can use StringBuilder and the append methods to implement the + and += String concatenation operators. For example, assuming the declarations

```
String string1 = "hello";
String string2 = "BC";
int value = 22;
```

the statement

```
String s = string1 + string2 + value;
```

concatenates "hello", "BC" and 22. The concatenation can be performed as follows:

```
String s = new StringBuilder().append("hello").append("BC").
   append(22).toString();
```

First, the preceding statement creates an *empty* StringBuilder, then appends to it the strings "hello" and "BC" and the integer 22. Next, StringBuilder's toString method converts the StringBuilder to a String object to be assigned to String s. The statement

```
s += "!";
```

can be performed as follows (this may differ by compiler):

```
s = new StringBuilder().append(s).append("!").toString();
```

This creates an empty StringBuilder, then appends to it the current contents of s followed by "!". Next, StringBuilder's method toString (which must be called *explicitly* here) returns the StringBuilder's contents as a String, and the result is assigned to s.

14.4.5 StringBuilder Insertion and Deletion Methods

StringBuilder provides overloaded **insert** methods to insert values of various types at any position in a StringBuilder. Versions are provided for the primitive types and for character arrays, Strings, Objects and CharSequences. Each method takes its second argument and inserts it at the index specified by the first argument. If the first argument is less than 0 or greater than the StringBuilder's length, a StringIndexOutOfBounds-Exception occurs. Class StringBuilder also provides methods **delete** and **deleteCharAt** to delete characters at any position in a StringBuilder. Method delete takes two arguments—the starting index and the index one past the end of the characters to delete. All characters beginning at the starting index up to but *not* including the ending index are deleted. Method deleteCharAt takes one argument—the index of the character to delete. Invalid indices cause both methods to throw a StringIndexOutOfBoundsException. Figure 14.14 demonstrates methods insert, delete and deleteCharAt.

```
1   // Fig. 14.14: StringBuilderInsertDelete.java
2   // StringBuilder methods insert, delete and deleteCharAt.
3
4   public class StringBuilderInsertDelete {
5      public static void main(String[] args) {
6         Object objectRef = "hello";
7         String string = "goodbye";
8         char[] charArray = {'a', 'b', 'c', 'd', 'e', 'f'};
9         boolean booleanValue = true;
10        char characterValue = 'K';
11        int integerValue = 7;
12        long longValue = 10000000;
13        float floatValue = 2.5f; // f suffix indicates that 2.5 is a float
14        double doubleValue = 33.333;
15
16        StringBuilder buffer = new StringBuilder();
17
18        buffer.insert(0, objectRef);
19        buffer.insert(0, "  "); // each of these contains two spaces
```

Fig. 14.14 | StringBuilder methods insert, delete and deleteCharAt. (Part 1 of 2.)

```
20          buffer.insert(0, string);
21          buffer.insert(0, "  ");
22          buffer.insert(0, charArray);
23          buffer.insert(0, "  ");
24          buffer.insert(0, charArray, 3, 3);
25          buffer.insert(0, "  ");
26          buffer.insert(0, booleanValue);
27          buffer.insert(0, "  ");
28          buffer.insert(0, characterValue);
29          buffer.insert(0, "  ");
30          buffer.insert(0, integerValue);
31          buffer.insert(0, "  ");
32          buffer.insert(0, longValue);
33          buffer.insert(0, "  ");
34          buffer.insert(0, floatValue);
35          buffer.insert(0, "  ");
36          buffer.insert(0, doubleValue);
37
38          System.out.printf(
39             "buffer after inserts:%n%s%n%n", buffer.toString());
40
41          buffer.deleteCharAt(10); // delete 5 in 2.5
42          buffer.delete(2, 6); // delete .333 in 33.333
43
44          System.out.printf(
45             "buffer after deletes:%n%s%n", buffer.toString());
46       }
47    }
```

```
buffer after inserts:
33.333  2.5  10000000  7  K  true  def  abcdef  goodbye  hello

buffer after deletes:
33  2.  10000000  7  K  true  def  abcdef  goodbye  hello
```

Fig. 14.14 | StringBuilder methods insert, delete and deleteCharAt. (Part 2 of 2.)

14.5 Class Character

Java provides eight **type-wrapper classes**—Boolean, Character, Double, Float, Byte, Short, Integer and Long—that enable primitive-type values to be treated as objects. In this section, we present class Character—the type-wrapper class for primitive type char.

Most Character methods are static methods designed for convenience in processing individual char values. These methods take at least a character argument and perform either a test or a manipulation of the character. Class Character also contains a constructor that receives a char argument to initialize a Character object. Most of the methods of class Character are presented in the next three examples. For more information on class Character (and all the type-wrapper classes), see the java.lang package in the Java API documentation.

Figure 14.15 demonstrates static methods that test characters to determine whether they're a specific character type and the static methods that perform case conversions on characters. You can enter any character and apply the methods to the character.

```java
1   // Fig. 14.15: StaticCharMethods.java
2   // Character static methods for testing characters and converting case.
3   import java.util.Scanner;
4
5   public class StaticCharMethods {
6      public static void main(String[] args) {
7         Scanner scanner = new Scanner(System.in); // create scanner
8         System.out.println("Enter a character and press Enter");
9         String input = scanner.next();
10        char c = input.charAt(0); // get input character
11
12        // display character info
13        System.out.printf("is defined: %b%n", Character.isDefined(c));
14        System.out.printf("is digit: %b%n", Character.isDigit(c));
15        System.out.printf("is first character in a Java identifier: %b%n",
16           Character.isJavaIdentifierStart(c));
17        System.out.printf("is part of a Java identifier: %b%n",
18           Character.isJavaIdentifierPart(c));
19        System.out.printf("is letter: %b%n", Character.isLetter(c));
20        System.out.printf(
21           "is letter or digit: %b%n", Character.isLetterOrDigit(c));
22        System.out.printf(
23           "is lower case: %b%n", Character.isLowerCase(c));
24        System.out.printf(
25           "is upper case: %b%n", Character.isUpperCase(c));
26        System.out.printf(
27           "to upper case: %s%n", Character.toUpperCase(c));
28        System.out.printf(
29           "to lower case: %s%n", Character.toLowerCase(c));
30     }
31  }
```

```
Enter a character and press Enter
A
is defined: true
is digit: false
is first character in a Java identifier: true
is part of a Java identifier: true
is letter: true
is letter or digit: true
is lower case: false
is upper case: true
to upper case: A
to lower case: a
```

Fig. 14.15 | Character static methods for testing characters and converting case. (Part 1 of 2.)

```
Enter a character and press Enter
8
is defined: true
is digit: true
is first character in a Java identifier: false
is part of a Java identifier: true
is letter: false
is letter or digit: true
is lower case: false
is upper case: false
to upper case: 8
to lower case: 8
```

```
Enter a character and press Enter
$
is defined: true
is digit: false
is first character in a Java identifier: true
is part of a Java identifier: true
is letter: false
is letter or digit: false
is lower case: false
is upper case: false
to upper case: $
to lower case: $
```

Fig. 14.15 | Character `static` methods for testing characters and converting case. (Part 2 of 2.)

Line 13 uses `Character` method **isDefined** to determine whether character c is defined in the Unicode character set. If so, the method returns `true`; otherwise, it returns `false`. Line 14 uses `Character` method **isDigit** to determine whether character c is a defined Unicode digit. If so, the method returns `true`, and otherwise, `false`.

Line 16 uses `Character` method **isJavaIdentifierStart** to determine whether c is a character that can be the first character of an identifier in Java—that is, a letter, an underscore (_) or a dollar sign ($). If so, the method returns `true`, and otherwise, `false`. Line 18 uses `Character` method **isJavaIdentifierPart** to determine whether character c is a character that can be used in an identifier in Java—that is, a digit, a letter, an underscore (_) or a dollar sign ($). If so, the method returns `true`, and otherwise, `false`.

Line 19 uses `Character` method **isLetter** to determine whether character c is a letter. If so, the method returns `true`, and otherwise, `false`. Line 21 uses `Character` method **isLetterOrDigit** to determine whether character c is a letter or a digit. If so, the method returns `true`, and otherwise, `false`.

Line 23 uses `Character` method **isLowerCase** to determine whether c is a lowercase letter. If so, the method returns `true`, and otherwise, `false`. Line 25 uses **isUpperCase** to determine whether c is an uppercase letter. If so, the method returns `true`, and otherwise, `false`. Line 27 uses `Character` method **toUpperCase** to convert the character c to its uppercase equivalent. The method returns the converted character if the character has an uppercase equivalent, and otherwise, the method returns its original argument. Line 29 uses `Character` method **toLowerCase** to convert the character c to its lowercase equivalent. The method returns the converted character if the character has a lowercase equivalent, and otherwise, the method returns its original argument.

Figure 14.16 demonstrates static Character methods **digit** and **forDigit**, which convert characters to digits and digits to characters, respectively, in different number systems. Common number systems include decimal (base 10), octal (base 8), hexadecimal (base 16) and binary (base 2). The base of a number is also known as its **radix**.

```java
// Fig. 14.16: StaticCharMethods2.java
// Character class static conversion methods.
import java.util.Scanner;

public class StaticCharMethods2 {
   public static void main(String[] args) {
      Scanner scanner = new Scanner(System.in);

      // get radix
      System.out.println("Please enter a radix:");
      int radix = scanner.nextInt();

      // get user choice
      System.out.printf("Please choose one:%n1 -- %s%n2 -- %s%n",
         "Convert digit to character", "Convert character to digit");
      int choice = scanner.nextInt();

      // process request
      switch (choice) {
         case 1: // convert digit to character
            System.out.println("Enter a digit:");
            int digit = scanner.nextInt();
            System.out.printf("Convert digit to character: %s%n",
               Character.forDigit(digit, radix));
            break;
         case 2: // convert character to digit
            System.out.println("Enter a character:");
            char character = scanner.next().charAt(0);
            System.out.printf("Convert character to digit: %s%n",
               Character.digit(character, radix));
            break;
      }
   }
}
```

```
Please enter a radix:
16
Please choose one:
1 -- Convert digit to character
2 -- Convert character to digit
2
Enter a character:
A
Convert character to digit: 10
```

Fig. 14.16 | Character class static conversion methods. (Part 1 of 2.)

```
Please enter a radix:
16
Please choose one:
1 -- Convert digit to character
2 -- Convert character to digit
1
Enter a digit:
13
Convert digit to character: d
```

Fig. 14.16 | Character class static conversion methods. (Part 2 of 2.)

Line 24 uses method forDigit to convert the integer digit into a character in the number system specified by the integer radix (the base of the number). For example, the decimal integer 13 in base 16 (the radix) has the character value 'd'. Lowercase and uppercase letters represent the *same* value in number systems. Line 30 uses method digit to convert variable character into an integer in the number system specified by the integer radix (the base of the number). For example, the character 'A' is the base 16 (the radix) representation of the base 10 value 10. The radix must be between 2 and 36, inclusive.

Figure 14.17 demonstrates the constructor and several instance methods of class Character—**charValue**, toString and equals. Lines 5–6 instantiate two Character objects by assigning the character constants 'A' and 'a', respectively, to the Character variables. Java automatically converts these char literals into Character objects—a process known as *autoboxing* that we discuss in more detail in Section 16.4. Line 9 uses Character method charValue to return the char value stored in Character object c1. Line 9 also gets a string representation of Character object c2 using method toString. The condition in line 11 uses method equals to determine whether the object c1 has the same contents as the object c2 (i.e., the characters inside each object are equal).

```
 1  // Fig. 14.17: OtherCharMethods.java
 2  // Character class instance methods.
 3  public class OtherCharMethods {
 4     public static void main(String[] args) {
 5        Character c1 = 'A';
 6        Character c2 = 'a';
 7
 8        System.out.printf(
 9           "c1 = %s%nc2 = %s%n%n", c1.charValue(), c2.toString());
10
11        if (c1.equals(c2)) {
12           System.out.println("c1 and c2 are equal%n");
13        }
14        else {
15           System.out.println("c1 and c2 are not equal%n");
16        }
17     }
18  }
```

Fig. 14.17 | Character class instance methods. (Part 1 of 2.)

```
c1 = A
c2 = a

c1 and c2 are not equal
```

Fig. 14.17 | Character class instance methods. (Part 2 of 2.)

14.6 Tokenizing Strings

When you read a sentence, your mind breaks it into **tokens**—individual words and punctuation marks that convey meaning to you. Compilers also perform tokenization. They break up statements into individual pieces like keywords, identifiers, operators and other programming-language elements. We now study class String's **split** method, which breaks a String into its component tokens. Tokens are separated from one another by **delimiters**, typically white-space characters such as space, tab, newline and carriage return. Other characters can also be used as delimiters to separate tokens. The application in Fig. 14.18 demonstrates String's split method.

When the user presses the *Enter* key, the input sentence is stored in variable sentence. Line 14 invokes String method split with the String argument " ", which returns an array of Strings. The space character in the argument String is the delimiter that method split uses to locate the tokens in the String. As you'll learn in the next section, the argument to method split can be a regular expression for more complex tokenizing. Lines 15–16 display the length of the array tokens—i.e., the number of tokens in sentence. Lines 18–20 output each token on a separate line.

```
1   // Fig. 14.18: TokenTest.java
2   // Tokenizing with String method split
3   import java.util.Scanner;
4
5   public class TokenTest {
6      // execute application
7      public static void main(String[] args) {
8         // get sentence
9         Scanner scanner = new Scanner(System.in);
10        System.out.println("Enter a sentence and press Enter");
11        String sentence = scanner.nextLine();
12
13        // process user sentence
14        String[] tokens = sentence.split(" ");
15        System.out.printf("Number of elements: %d%nThe tokens are:%n",
16           tokens.length);
17
18        for (String token : tokens) {
19           System.out.println(token);
20        }
21     }
22  }
```

Fig. 14.18 | Tokenizing with String method split. (Part 1 of 2.)

```
Enter a sentence and press Enter
This is a sentence with seven tokens
Number of elements: 7
The tokens are:
This
is
a
sentence
with
seven
tokens
```

Fig. 14.18 | Tokenizing with `String` method `split`. (Part 2 of 2.)

14.7 Regular Expressions, Class Pattern and Class Matcher

A **regular expression** is a `String` that describes a *search pattern* for *matching* characters in other `String`s. Such expressions are useful for *validating input* and ensuring that data is in a particular format. For example, a ZIP code must consist of five digits, and a last name must contain only letters, spaces, apostrophes and hyphens. One application of regular expressions is to facilitate the construction of a compiler. Often, a large and complex regular expression is used to *validate the syntax of a program*. If the program code does *not* match the regular expression, the compiler knows that there's a syntax error in the code.

Class `String` provides several methods for performing regular-expression operations, the simplest of which is the matching operation. `String` method **matches** receives a `String` that specifies the regular expression and matches the contents of the `String` object on which it's called to the regular expression. The method returns a `boolean` indicating whether the match succeeded.

A regular expression consists of literal characters and special symbols. Figure 14.19 specifies some **predefined character classes** that can be used with regular expressions. A character class is an *escape sequence* that represents a group of characters. A digit is any numeric character. A **word character** is any letter (uppercase or lowercase), any digit or the underscore character. A white-space character is a space, a tab, a carriage return, a newline or a form feed. Each character class matches a single character in the `String` we're attempting to match with the regular expression.

Character	Matches	Character	Matches
\d	any digit	\D	any nondigit
\w	any word character	\W	any nonword character
\s	any white-space character	\S	any non-whitespace character

Fig. 14.19 | Predefined character classes.

Regular expressions are not limited to these predefined character classes. The expressions employ various operators and other forms of notation to match complex patterns.

We examine several of these techniques in the application in Figs. 14.20 and 14.21, which *validates user input* via regular expressions. [*Note:* This application is not designed to match all possible valid user input.]

```java
1   // Fig. 14.20: ValidateInput.java
2   // Validating user information using regular expressions.
3
4   public class ValidateInput {
5      // validate first name
6      public static boolean validateFirstName(String firstName) {
7         return firstName.matches("[A-Z][a-zA-Z]*");
8      }
9
10     // validate last name
11     public static boolean validateLastName(String lastName) {
12        return lastName.matches("[a-zA-z]+(['-][a-zA-Z]+)*");
13     }
14
15     // validate address
16     public static boolean validateAddress(String address) {
17        return address.matches(
18           "\\d+\\s+([a-zA-Z]+|[a-zA-Z]+\\s[a-zA-Z]+)");
19     }
20
21     // validate city
22     public static boolean validateCity(String city) {
23        return city.matches("([a-zA-Z]+|[a-zA-Z]+\\s[a-zA-Z]+)");
24     }
25
26     // validate state
27     public static boolean validateState(String state) {
28        return state.matches("([a-zA-Z]+|[a-zA-Z]+\\s[a-zA-Z]+)");
29     }
30
31     // validate zip
32     public static boolean validateZip(String zip) {
33        return zip.matches("\\d{5}");
34     }
35
36     // validate phone
37     public static boolean validatePhone(String phone) {
38        return phone.matches("[1-9]\\d{2}-[1-9]\\d{2}-\\d{4}");
39     }
40   }
```

Fig. 14.20 | Validating user information using regular expressions.

```java
1   // Fig. 14.21: Validate.java
2   // Input and validate data from user using the ValidateInput class.
3   import java.util.Scanner;
```

Fig. 14.21 | Input and validate data from user using the ValidateInput class. (Part 1 of 3.)

```
 4
 5   public class Validate {
 6      public static void main(String[] args) {
 7         // get user input
 8         Scanner scanner = new Scanner(System.in);
 9         System.out.println("Please enter first name:");
10         String firstName = scanner.nextLine();
11         System.out.println("Please enter last name:");
12         String lastName = scanner.nextLine();
13         System.out.println("Please enter address:");
14         String address = scanner.nextLine();
15         System.out.println("Please enter city:");
16         String city = scanner.nextLine();
17         System.out.println("Please enter state:");
18         String state = scanner.nextLine();
19         System.out.println("Please enter zip:");
20         String zip = scanner.nextLine();
21         System.out.println("Please enter phone:");
22         String phone = scanner.nextLine();
23
24         // validate user input and display error message
25         System.out.printf("%nValidate Result:");
26
27         if (!ValidateInput.validateFirstName(firstName)) {
28            System.out.println("Invalid first name");
29         }
30         else if (!ValidateInput.validateLastName(lastName)) {
31            System.out.println("Invalid last name");
32         }
33         else if (!ValidateInput.validateAddress(address)) {
34            System.out.println("Invalid address");
35         }
36         else if (!ValidateInput.validateCity(city)) {
37            System.out.println("Invalid city");
38         }
39         else if (!ValidateInput.validateState(state)) {
40            System.out.println("Invalid state");
41         }
42         else if (!ValidateInput.validateZip(zip)) {
43            System.out.println("Invalid zip code");
44         }
45         else if (!ValidateInput.validatePhone(phone)) {
46            System.out.println("Invalid phone number");
47         }
48         else {
49            System.out.println("Valid input.  Thank you.");
50         }
51      }
52   }
```

Fig. 14.21 | Input and validate data from user using the ValidateInput class. (Part 2 of 3.)

```
Please enter first name:
Jane
Please enter last name:
Doe
Please enter address:
123 Some Street
Please enter city:
Some City
Please enter state:
SS
Please enter zip:
123
Please enter phone:
123-456-7890

Validate Result:
Invalid zip code
```

```
Please enter first name:
Jane
Please enter last name:
Doe
Please enter address:
123 Some Street
Please enter city:
Some City
Please enter state:
SS
Please enter zip:
12345
Please enter phone:
123-456-7890

Validate Result:
Valid input.  Thank you.
```

Fig. 14.21 | Input and validate data from user using the `ValidateInput` class. (Part 3 of 3.)

Figure 14.20 validates user input. Line 7 validates the first name. To match a set of characters that does not have a predefined character class, use square brackets, []. For example, the pattern "[aeiou]" matches a single character that's a vowel. Character ranges are represented by placing a dash (-) between two characters. In the example, "[A-Z]" matches a single uppercase letter. If the first character in the brackets is "^", the expression accepts any character other than those indicated. However, "[^Z]" is not the same as "[A-Y]", which matches uppercase letters A–Y—"[^Z]" matches *any character other than* capital Z, including lowercase letters and nonletters such as the newline character. Ranges in character classes are determined by the letters' integer values. In this example, "[A-Za-z]" matches all uppercase and lowercase letters. The range "[A-z]" matches all letters and also matches those characters (such as [and \) with an integer value between uppercase Z and lowercase a (for more information on integer values of characters see Appendix B). Like predefined character classes, character classes delimited by square brackets match a single character in the search object.

In line 7, the asterisk after the second character class indicates that any number of letters can be matched. In general, when the regular-expression operator "*" appears in a regular expression, the application attempts to match zero or more occurrences of the subexpression immediately preceding the "*". Operator "+" attempts to match one or more occurrences of the subexpression immediately preceding "+". So both "A*" and "A+" will match "AAA" or "A", but only "A*" will match an empty string.

If method validateFirstName returns true (line 27 of Fig. 14.21), the application attempts to validate the last name (line 30) by calling validateLastName (lines 11–13 of Fig. 14.20). The regular expression to validate the last name matches any number of letters split by apostrophes or hyphens.

Line 33 of Fig. 14.21 calls method validateAddress (lines 16–19 of Fig. 14.20) to validate the address. The first character class matches any digit one or more times (\\d+). Two \ characters are used, because \ normally starts an escape sequence in a string. So \\d in a String represents the regular-expression pattern \d. Then we match one or more white-space characters (\\s+). The character "|" matches the expression to its left or to its right. For example, "Hi (John|Jane)" matches both "Hi John" and "Hi Jane". The parentheses are used to group parts of the regular expression. In this example, the left side of | matches a single word, and the right side matches two words separated by any amount of white space. So the address must contain a number followed by one or two words. Therefore, "10 Broadway" and "10 Main Street" are both valid addresses in this example. The city (lines 22–24 of Fig. 14.20) and state (lines 27–29 of Fig. 14.20) methods also match any word of at least one character or, alternatively, any two words of at least one character if the words are separated by a single space, so both Waltham and West Newton would match.

Quantifiers

The asterisk (*) and plus (+) are formally called **quantifiers**. Figure 14.22 lists all the quantifiers. We've already discussed how the asterisk (*) and plus (+) quantifiers work. All quantifiers affect only the subexpression immediately preceding the quantifier. Quantifier question mark (?) matches zero or one occurrences of the expression that it quantifies. A set of braces containing one number ({n}) matches exactly n occurrences of the expression it quantifies. We demonstrate this quantifier to validate the zip code in Fig. 14.20 at line 33. Including a comma after the number enclosed in braces matches at least n occurrences of the quantified expression. The set of braces containing two numbers ({n,m}) matches between n and m occurrences of the expression that it qualifies. Quantifiers may be applied to patterns enclosed in parentheses to create more complex regular expressions.

Quantifier	Matches
*	Matches zero or more occurrences of the pattern.
+	Matches one or more occurrences of the pattern.
?	Matches zero or one occurrences of the pattern.
{n}	Matches exactly n occurrences.
{$n,$}	Matches at least n occurrences.
{n,m}	Matches between n and m (inclusive) occurrences.

Fig. 14.22 | Quantifiers used in regular expressions.

All of the quantifiers are **greedy**. This means that they'll match as many occurrences as they can as long as the match is still successful. However, if any of these quantifiers is followed by a question mark (?), the quantifier becomes **reluctant** (sometimes called **lazy**). It then will match as few occurrences as possible as long as the match is still successful.

The zip code (line 33 in Fig. 14.20) matches a digit five times. This regular expression uses the digit character class and a quantifier with the digit 5 between braces. The phone number (line 38 in Fig. 14.20) matches three digits (the first one cannot be zero) followed by a dash followed by three more digits (again the first one cannot be zero) followed by four more digits.

String method matches checks whether an entire String conforms to a regular expression. For example, we want to accept "Smith" as a last name, but not "9@Smith#". If only a substring matches the regular expression, method matches returns false.

14.7.1 Replacing Substrings and Splitting Strings

Sometimes it's useful to replace parts of a string or to split a string into pieces. For this purpose, class String provides methods **replaceAll**, **replaceFirst** and **split**. These methods are demonstrated in Fig. 14.23.

```
 1  // Fig. 14.23: RegexSubstitution.java
 2  // String methods replaceFirst, replaceAll and split.
 3  import java.util.Arrays;
 4
 5  public class RegexSubstitution {
 6     public static void main(String[] args) {
 7        String firstString = "This sentence ends in 5 stars *****";
 8        String secondString = "1, 2, 3, 4, 5, 6, 7, 8";
 9
10        System.out.printf("Original String 1: %s%n", firstString);
11
12        // replace '*' with '^'
13        firstString = firstString.replaceAll("\\*", "^");
14
15        System.out.printf("^ substituted for *: %s%n", firstString);
16
17        // replace 'stars' with 'carets'
18        firstString = firstString.replaceAll("stars", "carets");
19
20        System.out.printf(
21           "\"carets\" substituted for \"stars\": %s%n", firstString);
22
23        // replace words with 'word'
24        System.out.printf("Every word replaced by \"word\": %s%n%n",
25           firstString.replaceAll("\\w+", "word"));
26
27        System.out.printf("Original String 2: %s%n", secondString);
28
```

Fig. 14.23 | String methods replaceFirst, replaceAll and split. (Part 1 of 2.)

```
29            // replace first three digits with 'digit'
30            for (int i = 0; i < 3; i++) {
31                secondString = secondString.replaceFirst("\\d", "digit");
32            }
33
34            System.out.printf(
35                "First 3 digits replaced by \"digit\" : %s%n", secondString);
36
37            System.out.print("String split at commas: ");
38            String[] results = secondString.split(",\\s*"); // split on commas
39            System.out.println(Arrays.toString(results));
40        }
41    }
```

```
Original String 1: This sentence ends in 5 stars *****
^ substituted for *: This sentence ends in 5 stars ^^^^^
"carets" substituted for "stars": This sentence ends in 5 carets ^^^^^
Every word replaced by "word": word word word word word word ^^^^^

Original String 2: 1, 2, 3, 4, 5, 6, 7, 8
First 3 digits replaced by "digit" : digit, digit, digit, 4, 5, 6, 7, 8
String split at commas: [digit, digit, digit, 4, 5, 6, 7, 8]
```

Fig. 14.23 | String methods replaceFirst, replaceAll and split. (Part 2 of 2.)

Method replaceAll replaces text in a String with new text (the second argument) wherever the original String matches a regular expression (the first argument). Line 13 replaces every instance of "*" in firstString with "^". The regular expression ("*") precedes character * with two backslashes. Normally, * is a quantifier indicating that a regular expression should match *any number of occurrences* of a preceding pattern. However, in line 13, we want to find all occurrences of the literal character *—to do this, we must escape character * with character \. Escaping a special regular-expression character with \ instructs the matching engine to find the actual character. Since the expression is stored in a Java String and \ is a special character in Java Strings, we must include an additional \. So the Java String "*" represents the regular-expression pattern * which matches a single * character in the search string. In line 18, every match for the regular expression "stars" in firstString is replaced with "carets". Line 25 uses replaceAll to replace all words in the string with "word".

Method replaceFirst (line 31) replaces the first occurrence of a pattern match. Java Strings are immutable; therefore, method replaceFirst returns a new String in which the appropriate characters have been replaced. This line takes the original String and replaces it with the String returned by replaceFirst. By iterating three times we replace the first three instances of a digit (\d) in secondString with the text "digit".

Method split divides a String into several substrings. The original is broken in any location that matches a specified regular expression. Method split returns an array of Strings containing the substrings between matches for the regular expression. In line 38, we use method split to tokenize a String of comma-separated integers. The argument is the regular expression that locates the delimiter. In this case, we use the regular expression ",\s*" to separate the substrings wherever a comma occurs—again, the Java String ",\\s*" represents the regular expression ,\s*. By matching any white-space characters, we eliminate extra spaces from the resulting substrings. The commas and white-space characters are not returned as part of the substrings. Line 39 uses Arrays method toString to display the contents of array results in square brackets and separated by commas.

14.7.2 Classes Pattern and Matcher

In addition to the regular-expression capabilities of class String, Java provides other classes in package java.util.regex that help developers manipulate regular expressions. Class **Pattern** represents a regular expression. Class **Matcher** contains both a regular-expression pattern and a CharSequence in which to search for the pattern.

CharSequence (package java.lang) is an *interface* that allows read access to a sequence of characters. The interface requires that the methods charAt, length, subSequence and toString be declared. Both String and StringBuilder implement interface CharSequence, so an instance of either of these classes can be used with class Matcher.

Common Programming Error 14.2

A regular expression can be tested against an object of any class that implements interface CharSequence, but the regular expression must be a String. Attempting to create a regular expression as a StringBuilder is an error.

If a regular expression will be used only once, static Pattern method **matches** can be used. This method takes a String that specifies the regular expression and a CharSequence on which to perform the match. This method returns a boolean indicating whether the search object (the second argument) *matches* the regular expression.

If a regular expression will be used more than once (in a loop, for example), it's more efficient to use static Pattern method **compile** to create a specific Pattern object for that regular expression. This method receives a String representing the regular expression and returns a new Pattern object, which can then be used to call method **matcher**. This method receives a CharSequence to search and returns a Matcher object.

Matcher provides method **matches**, which performs the same task as Pattern method matches, but receives no arguments—the search pattern and search object are encapsulated in the Matcher object. Class Matcher provides other methods, including **find**, **lookingAt**, **replaceFirst** and **replaceAll**.

Figure 14.24 presents a simple example that employs regular expressions. This program matches birthdays against a regular expression. The expression matches only birthdays that do not occur in April and that belong to people whose names begin with "J".

```
1   // Fig. 14.24: RegexMatches.java
2   // Classes Pattern and Matcher.
3   import java.util.regex.Matcher;
4   import java.util.regex.Pattern;
5
6   public class RegexMatches {
7      public static void main(String[] args) {
8         // create regular expression
9         Pattern expression =
10           Pattern.compile("J.*\\d[0-35-9]-\\d\\d-\\d\\d");
```

Fig. 14.24 | Classes Pattern and Matcher. (Part 1 of 2.)

```
11
12          String string1 = "Jane's Birthday is 05-12-75\n" +
13              "Dave's Birthday is 11-04-68\n" +
14              "John's Birthday is 04-28-73\n" +
15              "Joe's Birthday is 12-17-77";
16
17          // match regular expression to string and print matches
18          Matcher matcher = expression.matcher(string1);
19
20          while (matcher.find()) {
21              System.out.println(matcher.group());
22          }
23      }
24  }
```

```
Jane's Birthday is 05-12-75
Joe's Birthday is 12-17-77
```

Fig. 14.24 | Classes Pattern and Matcher. (Part 2 of 2.)

Lines 9–10 create a Pattern by invoking its static method compile. The dot character "." in the regular expression (line 10) matches any single character except a newline. Line 18 creates the Matcher object for the compiled regular expression and the matching sequence (string1). Lines 20–22 use a while loop to *iterate* through the String. Matcher method find (line 20) attempts to match a piece of the search object to the search pattern. Each call to find starts at the point where the last call ended, so multiple matches can be found. Matcher method lookingAt performs the same way, except that it always starts from the beginning of the search object and will always find the *first* match if there is one.

Common Programming Error 14.3

Method matches (from class String, Pattern or Matcher) will return true only if the entire search object matches the regular expression. Methods find and lookingAt (from class Matcher) will return true if a portion of the search object matches the regular expression.

Line 21 uses Matcher method **group**, which returns the String from the search object that matches the search pattern. The String that's returned is the one that was last matched by a call to find or lookingAt. The output in Fig. 14.24 shows the two matches that were found in string1.

8 *Java SE 8*

As you'll see in Section 17.13, you can combine regular-expression processing with Java SE 8 lambdas and streams to implement powerful String- and file processing applications.

9 *Java SE 9: New Matcher Methods*

Java SE 9 adds several new Matcher method overloads—appendReplacement, appendTail, replaceAll, results and replaceFirst. Methods appendReplacement and appendTail simply receive StringBuilders rather than StringBuffers. Methods replaceAll, results and replaceFirst are meant for use with lambdas and streams. We'll show these three methods in Chapter 17.

14.8 Wrap-Up

In this chapter, you learned about more String methods for selecting portions of Strings and manipulating Strings. You learned about the Character class and some of the methods it declares to handle chars. The chapter also discussed the capabilities of the String-Builder class for creating Strings. The end of the chapter discussed regular expressions, which provide a powerful capability to search and match portions of Strings that fit a particular pattern. In the next chapter, you'll learn about file processing, including how persistent data is stored and retrieved.

15

Files, Input/Output Streams, NIO and XML Serialization

Objectives

In this chapter you'll:

- Create, read, write and update files.
- Retrieve information about files and directories using features of the NIO.2 APIs.
- Learn the differences between text files and binary files.
- Use class **Formatter** to output text to a file.
- Use class **Scanner** to input text from a file.
- Use sequential file processing to develop a real-world credit-inquiry program.
- Write objects to and read objects from a file using XML serialization and the JAXB (Java Architecture for XML Binding) APIs.
- Use a **JFileChooser** dialog to allow users to select files or directories on disk.
- Optionally use **java.io** interfaces and classes to perform byte-based and character-based input and output.

15.1 Introduction

Data stored in variables and arrays is *temporary*—it's lost when a local variable goes out of scope or when the program terminates. For long-term retention of data, even after the programs that create the data terminate, computers use **files**. You use files every day for tasks such as writing a document or creating a spreadsheet. Computers store files on **secondary storage devices**, including hard disks, flash drives, DVDs and more. Data maintained in files is **persistent data**—it exists beyond the duration of program execution. In this chapter, we explain how Java programs create, update and process files.

We begin by discussing Java's architecture for handling files programmatically. Next we explain that data can be stored in *text files* and *binary files*—and the differences between them. We demonstrate retrieving information about files and directories using classes `Paths` and `Files` and interfaces `Path` and `DirectoryStream` (package `java.nio.file`), then discuss writing to and reading from files. We create and manipulate text files. As you'll learn, however, it's awkward to read data from text files back into object form. Many object-oriented languages (including Java) provide convenient ways to write objects to and read objects from files (known as *serialization* and *deserialization*). To demonstrate this, we recreate some of our sequential programs that used text files, this time by storing objects in and retrieving objects from files. We discuss databases in Chapter 22, Accessing Databases with JDBC, and Chapter 24, Java Persistence API (JPA).

15.2 Files and Streams

Java views each file as a sequential **stream of bytes** (Fig. 15.1).[1] Every operating system provides a mechanism to determine the end of a file, such as an **end-of-file marker** or a count of the total bytes in the file that's recorded in a system-maintained administrative data structure. A Java program processing a stream of bytes simply receives an indication from the operating system when it reaches the end of the stream—the program does *not* need to know how the underlying platform represents files or streams. In some cases, the

---

1. Java's NIO APIs also include classes and interfaces that implement so-called channel-based architecture for high-performance I/O. These topics are beyond the scope of this book.

end-of-file indication occurs as an exception. In others, the indication is a return value from a method invoked on a stream-processing object.

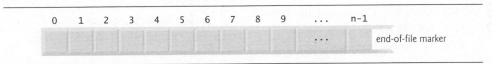

Fig. 15.1 | Java's view of a file of n bytes.

Byte-Based and Character-Based Streams
File streams can be used to input and output data as bytes or characters.

- **Byte-based streams** output and input data in its *binary* format—a char is two bytes, an int is four bytes, a double is eight bytes, etc.

- **Character-based streams** output and input data as a *sequence of characters* in which every character is two bytes—the number of bytes for a given value depends on the number of characters in that value. For example, the value 2000000000 requires 20 bytes (10 characters at two bytes per character) but the value 7 requires only two bytes (1 character at two bytes per character).

Files created using byte-based streams are **binary files**, while files created using character-based streams are **text files**. Text files can be read by text editors, while binary files are read by programs that understand the file's specific content and its ordering. A numeric value in a binary file can be used in calculations, whereas the character 5 is simply a character that can be used in a string of text, as in "Sarah Miller is 15 years old".

Standard Input, Standard Output and Standard Error Streams
A Java program **opens** a file by creating an object and associating a stream of bytes or characters with it. The object's constructor interacts with the operating system to *open* the file. Java can also associate streams with different devices. When a Java program begins executing, it creates three stream objects that are associated with devices—System.in, System.out and System.err. The System.in (standard input stream) object normally enables a program to input bytes from the keyboard. The System.out (standard output stream) object normally enables a program to output character data to the screen. The System.err (standard error stream) object normally enables a program to output character-based error messages to the screen. Each stream can be **redirected**. For System.in, this capability enables the program to read bytes from a different source. For System.out and System.err, it enables the output to be sent to a different location, such as a file on disk. Class System provides methods **setIn**, **setOut** and **setErr** to redirected the standard input, output and error streams, respectively.

The java.io and java.nio Packages
Java programs perform stream-based processing with classes and interfaces from package **java.io** and the subpackages of **java.nio**—Java's New I/O APIs that were first introduced in Java SE 6 and have been enhanced since. There are also other packages throughout the Java APIs containing classes and interfaces based on those in the java.io and java.nio packages.

Character-based input and output can be performed with classes `Scanner` and **Formatter**, as you'll see in Section 15.4. You've used class `Scanner` extensively to input data from the keyboard. `Scanner` also can read data from a file. Class `Formatter` enables formatted data to be output to any text-based stream in a manner similar to method `System.out.printf`. All these features can be used to format text files as well.

Java SE 8 Adds Another Type of Stream

Chapter 17, Lambdas and Streams, introduces a new type of stream that's used to process collections of elements (like arrays and `ArrayList`s), rather than the streams of bytes we discuss in this chapter's file-processing examples. In Section 17.13, we use the `Files` method `lines` to create one of these new streams containing the lines of text in a file.

15.3 Using NIO Classes and Interfaces to Get File and Directory Information

Interfaces `Path` and `DirectoryStream` and classes `Paths` and `Files` (all from package `java.nio.file`) are useful for retrieving information about files and directories on disk:

- **Path** interface—Objects of classes that implement `Path` represent the location of a file or directory. `Path` objects do not open files or provide any file-processing capabilities. Class **File** (package `java.io`) also is used commonly for this purpose.

- **Paths** class—Provides `static` methods used to get a `Path` object representing a file or directory location.

- **Files** class—Provides `static` methods for common file and directory manipulations, such as copying files; creating and deleting files and directories; getting information about files and directories; reading the contents of files; getting objects that allow you to manipulate the contents of files and directories; and more.

- **DirectoryStream** interface—Objects of classes that implement this interface enable a program to iterate through the contents of a directory.

Creating Path Objects

You'll use class `static` method **get** of class `Paths` to convert a `String` representing a file's or directory's location into a `Path` object. You can then use the methods of interface `Path` and class `Files` to determine information about the specified file or directory. We discuss several such methods momentarily. For complete lists of their methods, visit:

```
http://docs.oracle.com/javase/8/docs/api/java/nio/file/Path.html
http://docs.oracle.com/javase/8/docs/api/java/nio/file/Files.html
```

Absolute vs. Relative Paths

A file or directory's path specifies its location on disk. The path includes some or all of the directories leading to the file or directory. An **absolute path** contains *all* directories, starting with the **root directory**, that lead to a specific file or directory. Every file or directory on a particular disk drive has the *same* root directory in its path. A **relative path** is "relative" to another directory—for example, a path relative to the directory in which the application began executing.

*Getting **Path** Objects from URIs*
An overloaded version of Files static method get uses a URI object to locate the file or directory. A **Uniform Resource Identifier (URI)** is a more general form of the **Uniform Resource Locators (URLs)** that are used to locate websites. For example, the URL http:/ /www.deitel.com/ is the URL for the Deitel & Associates website. URIs for locating files vary across operating systems. On Windows platforms, the URI

```
file://C:/data.txt
```

identifies the file data.txt stored in the root directory of the C: drive. On UNIX/Linux platforms, the URI

```
file:/home/student/data.txt
```

identifies the file data.txt stored in the home directory of the user student.

Example: Getting File and Directory Information
Figure 15.2 prompts the user to enter a file or directory name, then uses classes Paths, Path, Files and DirectoryStream to output information about that file or directory.

```java
1  // Fig. 15.2: FileAndDirectoryInfo.java
2  // File class used to obtain file and directory information.
3  import java.io.IOException;
4  import java.nio.file.DirectoryStream;
5  import java.nio.file.Files;
6  import java.nio.file.Path;
7  import java.nio.file.Paths;
8  import java.util.Scanner;
9
10 public class FileAndDirectoryInfo {
11    public static void main(String[] args) throws IOException {
12       Scanner input = new Scanner(System.in);
13
14       System.out.println("Enter file or directory name:");
15
16       // create Path object based on user input
17       Path path = Paths.get(input.nextLine());
18
19       if (Files.exists(path)) { // if path exists, output info about it
20          // display file (or directory) information
21          System.out.printf("%n%s exists%n", path.getFileName());
22          System.out.printf("%s a directory%n",
23             Files.isDirectory(path) ? "Is" : "Is not");
24          System.out.printf("%s an absolute path%n",
25             path.isAbsolute() ? "Is" : "Is not");
26          System.out.printf("Last modified: %s%n",
27             Files.getLastModifiedTime(path));
28          System.out.printf("Size: %s%n", Files.size(path));
29          System.out.printf("Path: %s%n", path);
30          System.out.printf("Absolute path: %s%n", path.toAbsolutePath());
31
```

Fig. 15.2 | File class used to obtain file and directory information. (Part 1 of 2.)

```
32              if (Files.isDirectory(path)) { // output directory listing
33                  System.out.printf("%nDirectory contents:%n");
34
35                  // object for iterating through a directory's contents
36                  DirectoryStream<Path> directoryStream =
37                      Files.newDirectoryStream(path);
38
39                  for (Path p : directoryStream) {
40                      System.out.println(p);
41                  }
42              }
43          }
44          else { // not file or directory, output error message
45              System.out.printf("%s does not exist%n", path);
46          }
47      } // end main
48  } // end class FileAndDirectoryInfo
```

```
Enter file or directory name:
c:\examples\ch15

ch15 exists
Is a directory
Is an absolute path
Last modified: 2013-11-08T19:50:00.838256Z
Size: 4096
Path: c:\examples\ch15
Absolute path: c:\examples\ch15

Directory contents:
C:\examples\ch15\fig15_02
C:\examples\ch15\fig15_12_13
C:\examples\ch15\SerializationApps
C:\examples\ch15\TextFileApps
```

```
Enter file or directory name:
C:\examples\ch15\fig15_02\FileAndDirectoryInfo.java

FileAndDirectoryInfo.java exists
Is not a directory
Is an absolute path
Last modified: 2013-11-08T19:59:01.848255Z
Size: 2952
Path: C:\examples\ch15\fig15_02\FileAndDirectoryInfo.java
Absolute path: C:\examples\ch15\fig15_02\FileAndDirectoryInfo.java
```

Fig. 15.2 | `File` class used to obtain file and directory information. (Part 2 of 2.)

The program begins by prompting the user for a file or directory (line 14). Line 17 inputs the filename or directory name and passes it to `Paths` static method `get`, which converts the `String` to a `Path`. Line 19 invokes `Files` static method **exists**, which receives a `Path` and determines whether it exists (either as a file or as a directory) on disk.

If the name does not exist, control proceeds to line 45, which displays a message containing the Path's String representation followed by "does not exist." Otherwise, lines 21–42 execute:

- Path method **getFileName** (line 21) gets the String name of the file or directory without any location information.

- Files static method **isDirectory** (line 23) receives a Path and returns a boolean indicating whether that Path represents a directory on disk.

- Path method **isAbsolute** (line 25) returns a boolean indicating whether that Path represents an absolute path to a file or directory.

- Files static method **getLastModifiedTime** (line 27) receives a Path and returns a FileTime (package java.nio.file.attribute) indicating when the file was last modified. The program outputs the FileTime's default String representation.

- Files static method **size** (line 28) receives a Path and returns a long representing the number of bytes in the file or directory. For directories, the value returned is platform specific.

- Path method **toString** (called implicitly at line 29) returns a String representing the Path.

- Path method **toAbsolutePath** (line 30) converts the Path on which it's called to an absolute path.

If the Path represents a directory (line 32), lines 36–37 use Files static method **new-DirectoryStream** to get a DirectoryStream<Path> containing Path objects for the directory's contents. Lines 39–41 display the String representation of each Path in the DirectoryStream<Path>. Note that DirectoryStream is a generic type like ArrayList (Section 7.16).

The first output of this program demonstrates a Path for the folder containing this chapter's examples. The second output demonstrates a Path for this example's source-code file. In both cases, we specified an absolute path.

Error-Prevention Tip 15.1

Once you've confirmed that a Path exists, it's still possible that the methods demonstrated in Fig. 15.2 will throw IOExceptions. For example, the file or directory represented by the Path could be deleted from the system after the call to Files method exists and before the other statements in lines 21–42 execute. Industrial strength file- and directory-processing programs require extensive exception handling to deal with such possibilities.

Separator Characters

A **separator character** is used to separate directories and files in a path. On a Windows computer, the *separator character* is a backslash (\). On a Linux or macOS system, it's a forward slash (/). Java processes both characters identically in a pathname. For example, if we were to use the path

```
c:\Program Files\Java\jdk1.6.0_11\demo/jfc
```

which employs each separator character, Java would still process the path properly.

Good Programming Practice 15.1

When building Strings *that represent path information, use* File.separator *to obtain the local computer's proper separator character rather than explicitly using / or \. This constant is a* String *consisting of one character—the proper separator for the system.*

Common Programming Error 15.1

Using \ as a directory separator rather than \\ in a string literal is a logic error. A single \ indicates that the \ followed by the next character represents an escape sequence. Use \\ to insert a \ in a string literal.

15.4 Sequential Text Files

Next, we create and manipulate *sequential files* in which records are stored in order by the record-key field. We begin with *text files*, enabling the reader to quickly create and edit human-readable files. We discuss creating, writing data to, reading data from and updating sequential text files. We also include a credit-inquiry program that retrieves data from a file. The programs in Sections 15.4.1—15.4.3 are all in the chapter's TextFileApps directory so that they can manipulate the same text file, which is also stored in that directory.

15.4.1 Creating a Sequential Text File

Java imposes no structure on a file—notions such as records do not exist as part of the Java language. Therefore, you must structure files to meet the requirements of your applications. In the example that follows, we see how to impose a *keyed* record structure on a file.

The program in this section creates a simple sequential file that might be used in an accounts receivable system to keep track of the amounts owed to a company by its credit clients. For each client, the program obtains from the user an account number and the client's name and balance (i.e., the amount the client owes the company for goods and services received). Each client's data constitutes a "record" for that client. This application uses the account number as the *record key*—the file's records will be created and maintained in account-number order. The program assumes that the user enters the records in account-number order. In a comprehensive accounts receivable system (based on sequential files), a *sorting* capability would be provided so that the user could enter the records in *any* order. The records would then be sorted and written to the file.

Class *CreateTextFile*

Class CreateTextFile (Fig. 15.3) uses a Formatter to output formatted Strings, using the same formatting capabilities as method System.out.printf. A Formatter object can output to various locations, such as to a command window or to a file, as we do in this example. The Formatter object is instantiated in the try-with-resources statement (line 13; introduced in Section 11.12)—recall that try-with-resources will close its resource(s) when the try block terminates successfully or due to an exception. The constructor we use here takes one argument—a String containing the name of the file, including its path. If a path is not specified, as is the case here, the JVM assumes that the file is in the directory from which the program was executed. For text files, we use the .txt file extension. If the file does *not* exist, it will be *created*. If an *existing* file is opened, its contents are **truncated**— all the data in the file is *discarded*. If no exception occurs, the file is open for writing and the resulting Formatter object can be used to write data to the file.

```
1   // Fig. 15.3: CreateTextFile.java
2   // Writing data to a sequential text file with class Formatter.
3   import java.io.FileNotFoundException;
4   import java.lang.SecurityException;
5   import java.util.Formatter;
6   import java.util.FormatterClosedException;
7   import java.util.NoSuchElementException;
8   import java.util.Scanner;
9
10  public class CreateTextFile {
11     public static void main(String[] args) {
12        // open clients.txt, output data to the file then close clients.txt
13        try (Formatter output = new Formatter("clients.txt")) {
14           Scanner input = new Scanner(System.in);
15           System.out.printf("%s%n%s%n? ",
16              "Enter account number, first name, last name and balance.",
17              "Enter end-of-file indicator to end input.");
18
19           while (input.hasNext()) { // loop until end-of-file indicator
20              try {
21                 // output new record to file; assumes valid input
22                 output.format("%d %s %s %.2f%n", input.nextInt(),
23                    input.next(), input.next(), input.nextDouble());
24              }
25              catch (NoSuchElementException elementException) {
26                 System.err.println("Invalid input. Please try again.");
27                 input.nextLine(); // discard input so user can try again
28              }
29
30              System.out.print("? ");
31           }
32        }
33        catch (SecurityException | FileNotFoundException |
34           FormatterClosedException e) {
35           e.printStackTrace();
36        }
37     }
38  }
```

```
Enter account number, first name, last name and balance.
Enter end-of-file indicator to end input.
? 100 Bob Blue 24.98
? 200 Steve Green -345.67
? 300 Pam White 0.00
? 400 Sam Red -42.16
? 500 Sue Yellow 224.62
? ^Z
```

Fig. 15.3 | Writing data to a sequential text file with class Formatter.

Lines 33–36 are a multi-catch which handles several exceptions:

- the **SecurityException** that occurs if the user does not have permission to write data to the file opened in line 13

- the **FileNotFoundException** that occurs if the file does not exist and a new file cannot be created, or if there's an error *opening* the file in line 13, and

- the **FormatterClosedException** that occurs if the Formatter object is closed when you attempt to use it in lines 22–23 to write into a file.

For these exceptions, we display a stack trace, then the program terminates.

Writing Data to the File

Lines 15–17 prompt the user to enter the various fields for each record or the end-of-file key sequence when data entry is complete. Figure 15.4 lists the key combinations for entering end-of-file for various computer systems' command windows—some IDEs do not support these for console-based input (so you might have to execute the programs from command windows). Line 19 uses Scanner method hasNext to determine whether the end-of-file key combination has been entered. The loop executes until hasNext encounters end-of-file.

Operating system	Key combination
macOS and Linux	*<Enter> <Ctrl> d*
Windows	*<Ctrl> z*

Fig. 15.4 | End-of-file key combinations.

Lines 22–23 use a Scanner to read data from the user, then output the data as a record using the Formatter. Each Scanner input method throws a **NoSuchElementException** (handled in lines 25–28) if the data is in the wrong format (e.g., a String when an int is expected) or if there's no more data to input.

If no exception occurs, the record's information is output using method **format**, which can perform identical formatting to System.out.printf. Method format writes a formatted String to the Formatter object's output destination—the file clients.txt. The format string "%d %s %s %.2f%n" indicates that the current record will be stored as an integer (the account number) followed by a String (the first name), another String (the last name) and a floating-point value (the balance). Each piece of information is separated from the next by a space, and the double value (the balance) is output with two digits to the right of the decimal point (as indicated by the .2 in %.2f). The data in the text file can be viewed with a text editor or retrieved later by a program designed to read the file (Section 15.4.2). [*Note:* You can also output data to a text file using class **java.io.PrintWriter**, which provides format and printf methods for outputting formatted data.]

When the user enters the end-of-file key combination, the try-with-resources statement closes the Formatter and the underlying output file by calling Formatter method **close**. If a program does not explicitly call method close, the operating system normally will close the file when program execution terminates—this is an example of operating-system "housekeeping." However, you should always explicitly close a file when it's no longer needed.

Sample Output
The sample data for this application is shown in Fig. 15.5. In the sample output, the user enters information for five accounts, then enters end-of-file to signal that data entry is complete. The sample output does not show how the data records actually appear in the file. In the next section, to verify that the file was created successfully, we present a program that reads the file and prints its contents. Because this is a text file, you can also verify the information simply by opening the file in a text editor.

Sample data			
100	Bob	Blue	24.98
200	Steve	Green	-345.67
300	Pam	White	0.00
400	Sam	Red	-42.16
500	Sue	Yellow	224.62

Fig. 15.5 | Sample data for the program in Fig. 15.3.

15.4.2 Reading Data from a Sequential Text File

Data is stored in files so that it may be retrieved for processing when needed. Section 15.4.1 demonstrated how to create a file for sequential access. This section shows how to read data sequentially from a text file. We demonstrate how class Scanner can be used to input data from a file rather than the keyboard. The application (Fig. 15.6) reads records from the file "clients.txt" created by the application of Section 15.4.1 and displays the record's contents. Line 14 creates the Scanner that will be used to retrieve input from the file.

```
1   // Fig. 15.6: ReadTextFile.java
2   // This program reads a text file and displays each record.
3   import java.io.IOException;
4   import java.lang.IllegalStateException;
5   import java.nio.file.Files;
6   import java.nio.file.Path;
7   import java.nio.file.Paths;
8   import java.util.NoSuchElementException;
9   import java.util.Scanner;
10
11  public class ReadTextFile {
12     public static void main(String[] args) {
13        // open clients.txt, read its contents and close the file
14        try(Scanner input = new Scanner(Paths.get("clients.txt"))) {
15           System.out.printf("%-10s%-12s%-12s%10s%n", "Account",
16              "First Name", "Last Name", "Balance");
17
```

Fig. 15.6 | Sequential file reading using a Scanner. (Part 1 of 2.)

```
18          // read record from file
19          while (input.hasNext()) { // while there is more to read
20              // display record contents
21              System.out.printf("%-10d%-12s%-12s%10.2f%n", input.nextInt(),
22                  input.next(), input.next(), input.nextDouble());
23          }
24      }
25      catch (IOException | NoSuchElementException |
26          IllegalStateException e) {
27          e.printStackTrace();
28      }
29  }
30 }
```

```
Account    First Name   Last Name      Balance
100        Bob          Blue            24.98
200        Steve        Green         -345.67
300        Pam          White            0.00
400        Sam          Red            -42.16
500        Sue          Yellow         224.62
```

Fig. 15.6 | Sequential file reading using a Scanner. (Part 2 of 2.)

The try-with-resources statement opens the file for reading by instantiating a Scanner object (line 14). We pass a Path object to the constructor, which specifies that the Scanner object will read from the file "clients.txt" located in the directory from which the application executes. If the file cannot be found, an IOException occurs. The exception is handled in lines 25–28.

Lines 15–16 display headers for the columns in the application's output. Lines 19–23 read and display the file's content until the *end-of-file marker* is reached—in which case, method hasNext will return false at line 19. Lines 21–22 use Scanner methods nextInt, next and nextDouble to input an int (the account number), two Strings (the first and last names) and a double value (the balance). Each record is one line of data in the file. If the information in the file is not properly formed (e.g., there's a last name where there should be a balance), a NoSuchElementException occurs when the record is input. If the Scanner was closed before the data was input, an **IllegalStateException** occurs. These exceptions are handled in lines 25–28. Note in the format string in line 21 that the account number, first name and last name are left aligned, while the balance is right aligned and output with two digits of precision. Each iteration of the loop inputs one line of text from the text file, which represents one record. When the loop terminates and line 24 is reached, the try-with-resources statement implicitly calls the Scanner's **close** method to close Scanner and the file.

15.4.3 Case Study: A Credit-Inquiry Program

To retrieve data sequentially from a file, programs start from the beginning of the file and read *all* the data consecutively until the desired information is found. It might be necessary to process the file sequentially several times (from the beginning of the file) during the execution of a program. Class Scanner does *not* allow repositioning to the beginning of the file. If it's necessary to read the file again, the program must *close* the file and *reopen* it.

The program in Figs. 15.7–15.8 allows a credit manager to obtain lists of customers with *zero balances* (i.e., customers who do not owe any money), customers with *credit balances* (i.e., customers to whom the company owes money) and customers with *debit balances* (i.e., customers who owe the company money for goods and services received). A credit balance is a *negative* amount, a debit balance a *positive* amount.

MenuOption enum

We begin by creating an enum type (Fig. 15.7) to define the different menu options the credit manager will have—this is required if you need to provide specific values for the enum constants. The options and their values are listed in lines 5–8.

```
1   // Fig. 15.7: MenuOption.java
2   // enum type for the credit-inquiry program's options.
3   public enum MenuOption {
4      // declare contents of enum type
5      ZERO_BALANCE(1),
6      CREDIT_BALANCE(2),
7      DEBIT_BALANCE(3),
8      END(4);
9
10     private final int value; // current menu option
11
12     // constructor
13     private MenuOption(int value) {this.value = value;}
14  }
```

Fig. 15.7 | enum type for the credit-inquiry program's menu options.

CreditInquiry Class

Figure 15.8 contains the functionality for the credit-inquiry program. The program displays a text menu and allows the credit manager to enter one of three options to obtain credit information:

- Option 1 (ZERO_BALANCE) displays accounts with zero balances.
- Option 2 (CREDIT_BALANCE) displays accounts with credit (negative) balances.
- Option 3 (DEBIT_BALANCE) displays accounts with debit (positive) balances.
- Option 4 (END) terminates program execution.

```
1   // Fig. 15.8: CreditInquiry.java
2   // This program reads a file sequentially and displays the
3   // contents based on the type of account the user requests
4   // (credit balance, debit balance or zero balance).
5   import java.io.IOException;
6   import java.lang.IllegalStateException;
7   import java.nio.file.Paths;
8   import java.util.NoSuchElementException;
9   import java.util.Scanner;
```

Fig. 15.8 | Credit-inquiry program. (Part 1 of 4.)

```
10
11   public class CreditInquiry {
12      private final static MenuOption[] choices = MenuOption.values();
13
14      public static void main(String[] args) {
15         Scanner input = new Scanner(System.in);
16
17         // get user's request (e.g., zero, credit or debit balance)
18         MenuOption accountType = getRequest(input);
19
20         while (accountType != MenuOption.END) {
21            switch (accountType) {
22               case ZERO_BALANCE:
23                  System.out.printf("%nAccounts with zero balances:%n");
24                  break;
25               case CREDIT_BALANCE:
26                  System.out.printf("%nAccounts with credit balances:%n");
27                  break;
28               case DEBIT_BALANCE:
29                  System.out.printf("%nAccounts with debit balances:%n");
30                  break;
31            }
32
33            readRecords(accountType);
34            accountType = getRequest(input); // get user's request
35         }
36      }
37
38      // obtain request from user
39      private static MenuOption getRequest(Scanner input) {
40         int request = 4;
41
42         // display request options
43         System.out.printf("%nEnter request%n%s%n%s%n%s%n%s%n",
44            " 1 - List accounts with zero balances",
45            " 2 - List accounts with credit balances",
46            " 3 - List accounts with debit balances",
47            " 4 - Terminate program");
48
49         try {
50            do { // input user request
51               System.out.printf("%n? ");
52               request = input.nextInt();
53            } while ((request < 1) || (request > 4));
54         }
55         catch (NoSuchElementException noSuchElementException) {
56            System.err.println("Invalid input. Terminating.");
57         }
58
59         return choices[request - 1]; // return enum value for option
60      }
61
```

Fig. 15.8 | Credit-inquiry program. (Part 2 of 4.)

```
62      // read records from file and display only records of appropriate type
63      private static void readRecords(MenuOption accountType) {
64          // open file and process contents
65          try (Scanner input = new Scanner(Paths.get("clients.txt"))) {
66              while (input.hasNext()) { // more data to read
67                  int accountNumber = input.nextInt();
68                  String firstName = input.next();
69                  String lastName = input.next();
70                  double balance = input.nextDouble();
71
72                  // if proper account type, display record
73                  if (shouldDisplay(accountType, balance)) {
74                      System.out.printf("%-10d%-12s%-12s%10.2f%n", accountNumber,
75                          firstName, lastName, balance);
76                  }
77                  else {
78                      input.nextLine(); // discard the rest of the current record
79                  }
80              }
81          }
82          catch (NoSuchElementException | IllegalStateException |
83              IOException e) {
84              System.err.println("Error processing file. Terminating.");
85              System.exit(1);
86          }
87      }
88
89      // use record type to determine if record should be displayed
90      private static boolean shouldDisplay(
91          MenuOption option, double balance) {
92          if ((option == MenuOption.CREDIT_BALANCE) && (balance < 0)) {
93              return true;
94          }
95          else if ((option == MenuOption.DEBIT_BALANCE) && (balance > 0)) {
96              return true;
97          }
98          else if ((option == MenuOption.ZERO_BALANCE) && (balance == 0)) {
99              return true;
100         }
101
102         return false;
103     }
104 }
```

```
Enter request
 1 - List accounts with zero balances
 2 - List accounts with credit balances
 3 - List accounts with debit balances
 4 - Terminate program

? 1
```

Fig. 15.8 | Credit-inquiry program. (Part 3 of 4.)

```
Accounts with zero balances:
300         Pam         White              0.00

Enter request
 1 - List accounts with zero balances
 2 - List accounts with credit balances
 3 - List accounts with debit balances
 4 - Terminate program

? 2

Accounts with credit balances:
200         Steve       Green            -345.67
400         Sam         Red               -42.16

Enter request
 1 - List accounts with zero balances
 2 - List accounts with credit balances
 3 - List accounts with debit balances
 4 - Terminate program

? 3

Accounts with debit balances:
100         Bob         Blue              24.98
500         Sue         Yellow           224.62

Enter request
 1 - List accounts with zero balances
 2 - List accounts with credit balances
 3 - List accounts with debit balances
 4 - Terminate program

? 4
```

Fig. 15.8 | Credit-inquiry program. (Part 4 of 4.)

The record information is collected by reading through the file and determining if each record satisfies the criteria for the selected account type. Line 18 in main calls method getRequest (lines 39–60) to display the menu options, translates the number typed by the user into a MenuOption and stores the result in MenuOption variable accountType. Lines 20–35 loop until the user specifies that the program should terminate. Lines 21–31 display a header for the current set of records to be output to the screen. Line 33 calls method readRecords (lines 63–87), which loops through the file and reads every record.

Method readRecords uses a try-with-resources statement to create a Scanner that opens the file for reading (line 65). The file will be opened for reading with a new Scanner object each time readRecords is called, so that we can again read from the beginning of the file. Lines 67–70 read a record. Line 73 calls method shouldDisplay (lines 90–103) to determine whether the current record satisfies the account type requested. If should-Display returns true, the program displays the account information. When the *end-of-file marker* is reached, the loop terminates and the try-with-resources statement closes the Scanner and the file. Once all the records have been read, control returns to main and get-Request is called again (line 34) to retrieve the user's next menu option.

15.4.4 Updating Sequential Files

The data in many sequential files cannot be modified without the risk of destroying other data in the file. For example, if the name "White" needs to be changed to "Worthington", the old name cannot simply be overwritten, because the new name requires more space. The record for White was written to the file as

```
300 Pam White 0.00
```

If the record is rewritten beginning at the same location in the file using the new name, the record will be

```
300 Pam Worthington 0.00
```

The new record is larger (has more characters) than the original record. "Worthington" would overwrite the "0.00" in the current record, and the characters beyond the second "o" in "Worthington" will overwrite the beginning of the next sequential record in the file. The problem here is that fields in a text file—and hence records—can vary in size. For example, 7, 14, –117, 2074 and 27383 are all ints stored in the same number of bytes (4) internally, but they're different-sized fields when written to a file as text. Therefore, records in a sequential file are not usually updated in place—instead, the entire file is rewritten. To make the preceding name change, the records before 300 Pam White 0.00 would be copied to a new file, the new record (which can be of a different size than the one it replaces) would be written and the records after 300 Pam White 0.00 would be copied to the new file. Rewriting the entire file is uneconomical to update just one record, but reasonable if a substantial number of records need to be updated.

15.5 XML Serialization

In Section 15.4, we demonstrated how to write the individual fields of a record into a file as text, and how to read those fields from a file. Sometimes we want to write an entire object to or read an entire object from a file or over a network connection (e.g., when using web services). As we mentioned in Chapter 12, XML (eXtensible Markup Language) is a widely used language for describing data. XML is one format commonly used to represent objects. Another common format called JSON (JavaScript Object Notation) also is used to transmit objects over the Internet. We chose XML in this section rather than JSON, because the APIs for manipulating objects as XML are built into Java SE, whereas the APIs for manipulating objects as JSON are part of Java EE (Enterprise Edition).

In this section, we'll manipulate objects using **JAXB** (**Java Architecture for XML Binding**). As you'll see, the JAXB enables you to perform **XML serialization**—which JAXB refers to as **marshaling**. A **serialized object** is represented by XML that includes the object's data. After a serialized object has been written into a file, it can be read from the file and **deserialized**—that is, the XML that represents the object and its data can be used to recreate the object in memory.

15.5.1 Creating a Sequential File Using XML Serialization

The serialization we show in this section is performed with character-based streams, so the result will be a text file that you can view in standard text editors. We begin by creating and writing serialized objects to a file.

Declaring Class **Account**

We begin by defining class `Account` (Fig. 15.9), which encapsulates the client record information used by the serialization examples. All the classes for this example and the one in Section 15.5.2 are located in the `SerializationApps` directory with the chapter's examples. Class `Account` contains `private` instance variables `account`, `firstName`, `lastName` and `balance` (lines 4–7) and *set* and *get* methods for accessing these instance variables. Though the *set* methods do not validate the data in this example, generally they should.

```
1  // Fig. 15.9: Account.java
2  // Account class for storing records as objects.
3  public class Account {
4     private int accountNumber;
5     private String firstName;
6     private String lastName;
7     private double balance;
8
9     // initializes an Account with default values
10    public Account() {this(0, "", "", 0.0);}
11
12    // initializes an Account with provided values
13    public Account(int accountNumber, String firstName,
14       String lastName, double balance) {
15       this.accountNumber = accountNumber;
16       this.firstName = firstName;
17       this.lastName = lastName;
18       this.balance = balance;
19    }
20
21    // get account number
22    public int getAccountNumber() {return accountNumber;}
23
24    // set account number
25    public void setAccountNumber(int accountNumber)
26       {this.accountNumber = accountNumber;}
27
28    // get first name
29    public String getFirstName() {return firstName;}
30
31    // set first name
32    public void setFirstName(String firstName)
33       {this.firstName = firstName;}
34
35    // get last name
36    public String getLastName() {return lastName;}
37
38    // set last name
39    public void setLastName(String lastName) {this.lastName = lastName;}
40
41    // get balance
42    public double getBalance() {return balance;}
43
```

Fig. 15.9 | `Account` class for storing records as objects. (Part 1 of 2.)

```
44       // set balance
45       public void setBalance(double balance) {this.balance = balance;}
46  }
```

Fig. 15.9 | Account class for storing records as objects. (Part 2 of 2.)

Plain Old Java Objects

JAXB works with **POJOs (plain old Java objects)**—no special superclasses or interfaces are required for XML-serialization support. By default, JAXB serializes only an object's public instance variables and public *read–write* properties. Recall from Section 13.4.1 that a read–write property is defined by creating *get* and *set* methods with specific naming conventions. In class Account, methods getAccountNumber and setAccountNumber (lines 22–26) define a read–write property named accountNumber. Similarly, the *get* and *set* methods in lines 29–45 define the read–write properties firstName, lastName and balance. The class must also provide a public default or no-argument constructor to recreate the objects when they're read from the file.

Declaring Class Accounts

As you'll see in Fig. 15.11, this example stores Account objects in a List<Account>, then serializes the entire List into a file with one operation. To serialize a List, it must be defined as an instance variable of a class. For that reason, we encapsulate the List<Account> in class Accounts (Fig. 15.10).

```
1   // Fig. 15.10: Accounts.java
2   // Maintains a List<Account>
3   import java.util.ArrayList;
4   import java.util.List;
5   import javax.xml.bind.annotation.XmlElement;
6
7   public class Accounts {
8       // @XmlElement specifies XML element name for each object in the List
9       @XmlElement(name="account")
10      private List<Account> accounts = new ArrayList<>(); // stores Accounts
11
12      // returns the List<Accounts>
13      public List<Account> getAccounts() {return accounts;}
14  }
```

Fig. 15.10 | Account class for serializable objects.

Lines 9–10 declare and initialize the List<Account> instance variable accounts. JAXB enables you to customize many aspects of XML serialization, such as serializing a private instance variable or a read-only property. The annotation **@XMLElement** (line 9; package **javax.xml.bind.annotation**) indicates that the private instance variable should be serialized. We'll discuss the annotation's name argument shortly. The annotation is required because the instance variable is not public and there's no corresponding public read–write property.

Writing XML Serialized Objects to a File

The program of Fig. 15.11 serializes an Accounts object to a text file. The program is similar to the one in Section 15.4, so we focus only on the new features. Line 9 imports the **JAXB class** from package javax.xml.bind. This package contains many related classes that implement the XML serializations we perform, but the JAXB class contains easy-to-use static methods that perform the most common operations.

```java
 1   // Fig. 15.11: CreateSequentialFile.java
 2   // Writing objects to a file with JAXB and BufferedWriter.
 3   import java.io.BufferedWriter;
 4   import java.io.IOException;
 5   import java.nio.file.Files;
 6   import java.nio.file.Paths;
 7   import java.util.NoSuchElementException;
 8   import java.util.Scanner;
 9   import javax.xml.bind.JAXB;
10
11   public class CreateSequentialFile {
12      public static void main(String[] args) {
13         // open clients.xml, write objects to it then close file
14         try(BufferedWriter output =
15            Files.newBufferedWriter(Paths.get("clients.xml"))) {
16
17            Scanner input = new Scanner(System.in);
18
19            // stores the Accounts before XML serialization
20            Accounts accounts = new Accounts();
21
22            System.out.printf("%s%n%s%n? ",
23               "Enter account number, first name, last name and balance.",
24               "Enter end-of-file indicator to end input.");
25
26            while (input.hasNext()) { // loop until end-of-file indicator
27               try {
28                  // create new record
29                  Account record = new Account(input.nextInt(),
30                     input.next(), input.next(), input.nextDouble());
31
32                  // add to AccountList
33                  accounts.getAccounts().add(record);
34               }
35               catch (NoSuchElementException elementException) {
36                  System.err.println("Invalid input. Please try again.");
37                  input.nextLine(); // discard input so user can try again
38               }
39
40               System.out.print("? ");
41            }
42
43            // write AccountList's XML to output
44            JAXB.marshal(accounts, output);
45         }
```

Fig. 15.11 | Writing objects to a file with JAXB and BufferedWriter. (Part 1 of 2.)

```
46          catch (IOException ioException) {
47              System.err.println("Error opening file. Terminating.");
48          }
49      }
50  }
```

```
Enter account number, first name, last name and balance.
Enter end-of-file indicator to end input.
? 100 Bob Blue 24.98
? 200 Steve Green -345.67
? 300 Pam White 0.00
? 400 Sam Red -42.16
? 500 Sue Yellow 224.62
? ^Z
```

Fig. 15.11 | Writing objects to a file with JAXB and BufferedWriter. (Part 2 of 2.)

To open the file, lines 14–15 call Files static method **newBufferedWriter**, which receives a Path specifying the file to open for writing ("clients.xml") and—if the file exists—returns a **BufferedWriter** that class JAXB will use to write text to the file. Existing files that are opened for output in this manner are *truncated*. The standard filename extension for XML files is .xml. Lines 14–15 throw an **IOException** if a problem occurs while opening the file—such as, when the program does not have permission to access the file or when a read-only file is opened for writing. If so, the program displays an error message (lines 46–48), then terminates. Otherwise, variable output can be used to write to the file.

Line 20 creates the Accounts object that contains the List<Account>. Lines 26–41 input each record, create an Account object (lines 29–30) and add to the List (line 33).

When the user enters the end-of-file indicator to terminate input, line 44 uses class JAXB's static method **marshal** to serialize as XML the Accounts object containing the List<Account>. The first argument is the object to serialize. The second argument to this particular overload of method marshal is a Writer (package java.io) that's used to output the XML—BufferedWriter is a subclass of Writer. The BufferedWriter obtained in lines 14–15 outputs the XML to a file.

Note that only one statement is required to write the *entire* Accounts object and all of the objects in its List<Account>. In the sample execution for the program in Fig. 15.11, we entered information for five accounts—the same information shown in Fig. 15.5.

The XML Output
Figure 15.12 shows the contents of the file clients.xml. Though you do not need to know XML to work with this example, note that the XML is human readable. When JAXB serializes an object of a class, it uses the class's name with a lowercase first letter as the corresponding XML element name, so the accounts element (lines 2–33) represents the Accounts object.

Recall that line 9 in class Accounts (Fig. 15.10) preceded the List<Account> instance variable with the annotation

```
@XmlElement(name="account")
```

In addition to enabling JAXB to serialize the instance variable, this annotation specifies the XML element name ("account") used to represent each of the List's Account objects in the serialized output. For example, lines 3–8 in Fig. 15.12 represent the Account for Bob Blue. If we did not specify the annotation's name argument, the instance variable's name (accounts) would have been used as the XML element name. Many other aspects of JAXB XML serialization are customizable. For more details, see

https://docs.oracle.com/javase/tutorial/jaxb/intro/

```
 1  <?xml version="1.0" encoding="UTF-8" standalone="yes"?>
 2  <accounts>
 3      <account>
 4          <accountNumber>100</accountNumber>
 5          <balance>24.98</balance>
 6          <firstName>Bob</firstName>
 7          <lastName>Blue</lastName>
 8      </account>
 9      <account>
10          <accountNumber>200</accountNumber>
11          <balance>-345.67</balance>
12          <firstName>Steve</firstName>
13          <lastName>Green</lastName>
14      </account>
15      <account>
16          <accountNumber>300</accountNumber>
17          <balance>0.0</balance>
18          <firstName>Pam</firstName>
19          <lastName>White</lastName>
20      </account>
21      <account>
22          <accountNumber>400</accountNumber>
23          <balance>-42.16</balance>
24          <firstName>Sam</firstName>
25          <lastName>Red</lastName>
26      </account>
27      <account>
28          <accountNumber>500</accountNumber>
29          <balance>224.62</balance>
30          <firstName>Sue</firstName>
31          <lastName>Yellow</lastName>
32      </account>
33  </accounts>
```

Fig. 15.12 | Contents of clients.xml.

Each of class Account's property has a corresponding XML element with the same name as the property. For example, lines 4–7 are the XML elements for Bob Blue's accountNumber, balance, firstName and lastName—JAXB placed the XML elements in alphabetical order, though this is not required or guaranteed. Within each of these elements is the corresponding property's value—100 for the accountNumber, 24.98 for the balance, Bob for the firstName and Blue for the lastName. Lines 9–32 represent the other four Account objects that we input into the program in the sample execution.

15.5.2 Reading and Deserializing Data from a Sequential File

The preceding section showed how to create a file containing XML serialized objects. In this section, we discuss how to *read serialized data* from a file. Figure 15.13 reads objects from the file created by the program in Section 15.5.1, then displays the contents. The program opens the file for input by calling Files static method **newBufferedReader**, which receives a Path specifying the file to open and, if the file exists and no exceptions occur, returns a **BufferedReader** for reading from the file.

```
 1   // Fig. 15.13: ReadSequentialFile.java
 2   // Reading a file of XML serialized objects with JAXB and a
 3   // BufferedReader and displaying each object.
 4   import java.io.BufferedReader;
 5   import java.io.IOException;
 6   import java.nio.file.Files;
 7   import java.nio.file.Paths;
 8   import javax.xml.bind.JAXB;
 9
10   public class ReadSequentialFile {
11      public static void main(String[] args) {
12         // try to open file for deserialization
13         try(BufferedReader input =
14            Files.newBufferedReader(Paths.get("clients.xml"))) {
15            // unmarshal the file's contents
16            Accounts accounts = JAXB.unmarshal(input, Accounts.class);
17
18            // display contents
19            System.out.printf("%-10s%-12s%-12s%10s%n", "Account",
20               "First Name", "Last Name", "Balance");
21
22            for (Account account : accounts.getAccounts()) {
23               System.out.printf("%-10d%-12s%-12s%10.2f%n",
24                  account.getAccountNumber(), account.getFirstName(),
25                  account.getLastName(), account.getBalance());
26            }
27         }
28         catch (IOException ioException) {
29            System.err.println("Error opening file.");
30         }
31      }
32   }
```

```
Account   First Name  Last Name     Balance
100       Bob         Blue            24.98
200       Steve       Green         -345.67
300       Pam         White            0.00
400       Sam         Red            -42.16
500       Sue         Yellow         224.62

No more records
```

Fig. 15.13 | Reading a file of XML serialized objects with JAXB and a BufferedReader and displaying each object.

Line 16 uses JAXB static method **unmarshal** to read the contents of clients.xml and convert the XML into an Accounts object. The overload of unmarshal used here reads XML from a Reader (package java.io) and creates an object of the type specified as the second argument—BufferedReader is a subclass of Reader. The BufferedReader obtained in lines 13–14 reads text from a file. Method unmarshal's second argument is a Class<T> object (package java.lang) representing the type of the object to create from the XML—the notation Accounts.class is a Java compiler shorthand for

```
new Class<Accounts>
```

Once again, note that one statement reads the entire file and recreates the Accounts object. If no exceptions occur, lines 19–26 display the contents of the Accounts object.

15.6 FileChooser and DirectoryChooser Dialogs

JavaFX classes **FileChooser** and **DirectoryChooser** (package javafx.stage) display dialogs that enable the user to select a file or directory, respectively. To demonstrate these dialogs, we enhance the example in Section 15.3. The example (Figs. 15.14–15.15) contains a JavaFX graphical user interface, but still displays the same data as the earlier example.

Creating the JavaFX GUI
The GUI (Fig. 15.15(a)) consists of a 600-by-400 BorderPane with the fx:id borderPane:

- In the BorderPane's top, we placed a **ToolBar** layout (from the Scene Builder **Library**'s **Containers** section), which arranges its controls horizontally (by default) or vertically. Typically, you place ToolBars at your GUI's edges, such as in a BorderPane's top, right, bottom or left areas.

- In the BorderPane's center, we placed a **TextArea** control with the fx:id textArea. We set the control's **Text** property to "Select file or directory" and enabled its **Wrap Text** property to ensure that long lines of text wrap to the next line. If there are more lines of text to display than vertical lines in the TextArea, the control will show a vertical scrollbar. (When **Wrap Text** is not enabled, the TextArea also shows a horizontal scrollbar if the text is too wide to display.)

By default, the ToolBar you drag onto your layout has one Button. You can drag other controls onto the ToolBar and, if necessary, remove the default Button. We added a second Button. For the first Button, we set:

- the **Text** property to "Select File",
- the **fx:id** property to selectFileButton and
- the **On Action** event handler to selectFileButtonPressed.

For the second Button, we set:

- the **Text** property to "Select Directory",
- the **fx:id** property to selectDirectoryButton and
- the **On Action** event handler to selectDirectoryButtonPressed.

Finally, we specified FileChooserTestController as the FXML's controller.

Class That Launches the App

Class FileChooserTest (Fig. 15.14) launches the JavaFX application, using the same techniques you learned in Chapters 12–13.

```java
33   // Fig. 15.14: FileChooserTest.java
34   // App to test classes FileChooser and DirectoryChooser.
35   import javafx.application.Application;
36   import javafx.fxml.FXMLLoader;
37   import javafx.scene.Parent;
38   import javafx.scene.Scene;
39   import javafx.stage.Stage;
40
41   public class FileChooserTest extends Application {
42      @Override
43      public void start(Stage stage) throws Exception {
44         Parent root =
45            FXMLLoader.load(getClass().getResource("FileChooserTest.fxml"));
46
47         Scene scene = new Scene(root);
48         stage.setTitle("File Chooser Test"); // displayed in title bar
49         stage.setScene(scene);
50         stage.show();
51      }
52
53      public static void main(String[] args) {
54         launch(args);
55      }
56   }
```

Fig. 15.14 | App to test classes FileChooser and DirectoryChooser.

Controller Class

Class FileChooserTestController (Fig. 15.15) responds to the Buttons' events. Both event handlers call method analyzePath (defined in lines 70–110) to determine whether a Path is a file or directory, display information about the Path and, if it's a directory, list its contents.

```java
1    // Fig. 15.15: FileChooserTestController.java
2    // Displays information about a selected file or folder.
3    import java.io.File;
4    import java.io.IOException;
5    import java.nio.file.DirectoryStream;
6    import java.nio.file.Files;
7    import java.nio.file.Path;
8    import java.nio.file.Paths;
9    import javafx.event.ActionEvent;
10   import javafx.fxml.FXML;
11   import javafx.scene.control.Button;
12   import javafx.scene.control.TextArea;
```

Fig. 15.15 | Displays information about a selected file or folder. (Part 1 of 5.)

```
13    import javafx.scene.layout.BorderPane;
14    import javafx.stage.DirectoryChooser;
15    import javafx.stage.FileChooser;
16
17    public class FileChooserTestController {
18        @FXML private BorderPane borderPane;
19        @FXML private Button selectFileButton;
20        @FXML private Button selectDirectoryButton;
21        @FXML private TextArea textArea;
22
23        // handles selectFileButton's events
24        @FXML
25        private void selectFileButtonPressed(ActionEvent e) {
26            // configure dialog allowing selection of a file
27            FileChooser fileChooser = new FileChooser();
28            fileChooser.setTitle("Select File");
29
30            // display files in folder from which the app was launched
31            fileChooser.setInitialDirectory(new File("."));
32
33            // display the FileChooser
34            File file = fileChooser.showOpenDialog(
35                borderPane.getScene().getWindow());
36
37            // process selected Path or display a message
38            if (file != null) {
39                analyzePath(file.toPath());
40            }
41            else {
42                textArea.setText("Select file or directory");
43            }
44        }
45
46        // handles selectDirectoryButton's events
47        @FXML
48        private void selectDirectoryButtonPressed(ActionEvent e) {
49            // configure dialog allowing selection of a directory
50            DirectoryChooser directoryChooser = new DirectoryChooser();
51            directoryChooser.setTitle("Select Directory");
52
53            // display folder from which the app was launched
54            directoryChooser.setInitialDirectory(new File("."));
55
56            // display the FileChooser
57            File file = directoryChooser.showDialog(
58                borderPane.getScene().getWindow());
59
60            // process selected Path or display a message
61            if (file != null) {
62                analyzePath(file.toPath());
63            }
```

Fig. 15.15 | Displays information about a selected file or folder. (Part 2 of 5.)

```
64          else {
65              textArea.setText("Select file or directory");
66          }
67       }
68
69       // display information about file or directory user specifies
70       public void analyzePath(Path path) {
71          try {
72              // if the file or directory exists, display its info
73              if (path != null && Files.exists(path)) {
74                  // gather file (or directory) information
75                  StringBuilder builder = new StringBuilder();
76                  builder.append(String.format("%s:%n", path.getFileName()));
77                  builder.append(String.format("%s a directory%n",
78                      Files.isDirectory(path) ? "Is" : "Is not"));
79                  builder.append(String.format("%s an absolute path%n",
80                      path.isAbsolute() ? "Is" : "Is not"));
81                  builder.append(String.format("Last modified: %s%n",
82                      Files.getLastModifiedTime(path)));
83                  builder.append(String.format("Size: %s%n", Files.size(path)));
84                  builder.append(String.format("Path: %s%n", path));
85                  builder.append(String.format("Absolute path: %s%n",
86                      path.toAbsolutePath()));
87
88                  if (Files.isDirectory(path)) { // output directory listing
89                      builder.append(String.format("%nDirectory contents:%n"));
90
91                      // object for iterating through a directory's contents
92                      DirectoryStream<Path> directoryStream =
93                          Files.newDirectoryStream(path);
94
95                      for (Path p : directoryStream) {
96                          builder.append(String.format("%s%n", p));
97                      }
98                  }
99
100                 // display file or directory info
101                 textArea.setText(builder.toString());
102             }
103             else { // Path does not exist
104                 textArea.setText("Path does not exist");
105             }
106          }
107          catch (IOException ioException) {
108              textArea.setText(ioException.toString());
109          }
110       }
111    }
```

Fig. 15.15 | Displays information about a selected file or folder. (Part 3 of 5.)

a) Initial app window.

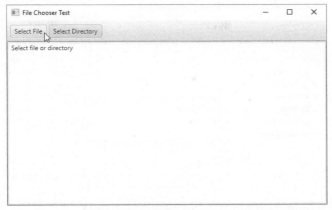

b) Selecting `FileChooserTest.java` from the `FileChooser` dialog displayed when the user clicked the **Select File** Button.

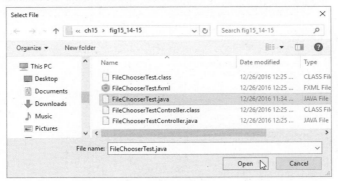

c) Displaying information about the file `FileChooserTest.java`.

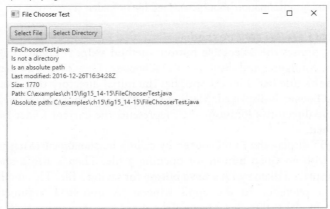

Fig. 15.15 | Displays information about a selected file or folder. (Part 4 of 5.)

d) Selecting fig15_14-15 from the DirectoryChooser dialog displayed when the user clicked the **Select Directory** Button.

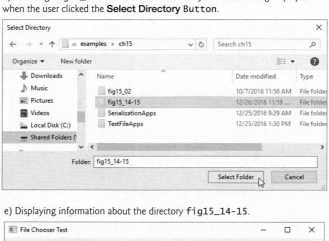

e) Displaying information about the directory fig15_14-15.

Fig. 15.15 | Displays information about a selected file or folder. (Part 5 of 5.)

Method selectFileButtonPressed

When the user presses the **Select File** button, method selectFileButtonPressed (lines 24–44) creates, configures and displays a FileChooser. Line 28 sets the text displayed in the FileChooser's title bar. Line 31 specifies the initial directory that should be opened when the FileChooser is displayed. Method setInitialDirectory receives a File object representing the directory's location—"." represents the current folder from which the app was launched.

Lines 34–35 display the FileChooser by calling its **showOpenDialog** method to display a dialog with an **Open** button for opening a file. There's also a **showSaveDialog** method that displays a dialog with a **Save** button for saving a file. This method receives as its argument a reference to the app's Window. A non-null argument makes the FileChooser a modal dialog that prevents the user from interacting with the rest of the app until the dialog is dismissed—when the user selects a file or clicks **Cancel**. To obtain the app's Window, we use the borderPane's getScene method to get a reference to its parent Scene, then use the Scene's getWindow method to get a reference to the Window containing the Scene.

Method showOpenDialog returns a File representing the selected file's location, or null if the user clicks the **Cancel** button. If the File is not null, line 39 calls analyzePath to display the selected file's information—File method **toPath** returns a Path object representing the location. Otherwise, line 42 displays a message in the TextArea telling the user to select a file or directory. The screen captures in Fig. 15.15(b) and (c) show the FileChooser dialog with the FileChooserTest.java file selected and, after the user presses the **Open** button, the file's information displayed.

Method selectDirectoryButtonPressed
When the user presses the **Select Directory** button, method selectDirectoryButton-Pressed (lines 47–67) creates, configures and displays a DirectoryChooser. The method performs the same tasks as method selectFileButtonPressed. The key difference is line 57, which calls DirectoryChooser method **showDialog** to display the dialog—there are not separate open and save dialogs for selecting folders. Method showDialog returns a File representing the location of the selected directory, or null if the user clicks **Cancel**. If the File is not null, line 62 calls analyzePath to display information about the selected directory. Otherwise, line 65 displays a message in the TextArea telling the user to select a file or directory. The screen captures in Fig. 15.15(d) and (e) show the FileChooser dialog with the fig15_14-15 directory selected and, after the user presses the **Open** button, the directory's information displayed.

15.7 (Optional) Additional java.io Classes

This section overviews additional interfaces and classes (from package java.io).

15.7.1 Interfaces and Classes for Byte-Based Input and Output

InputStream and OutputStream are abstract classes that declare methods for performing byte-based input and output, respectively.

Pipe Streams
Pipes are synchronized communication channels between threads. We discuss threads in Chapter 21. Java provides **PipedOutputStream** (a subclass of OutputStream) and **Piped-InputStream** (a subclass of InputStream) to establish pipes between two threads in a program. One thread sends data to another by writing to a PipedOutputStream. The target thread reads information from the pipe via a PipedInputStream.

Filter Streams
A **FilterInputStream** filters an InputStream, and a FilterOutputStream filters an OutputStream. **Filtering** means simply that the filter stream provides additional functionality, such as aggregating bytes into meaningful primitive-type units. FilterInputStream and FilterOutputStream are typically used as superclasses, so some of their filtering capabilities are provided by their subclasses.

A **PrintStream** (a subclass of FilterOutputStream) performs text output to the specified stream. Actually, we've been using PrintStream output throughout the text to this point—System.out and System.err are PrintStream objects.

Data Streams

Reading data as raw bytes is fast, but crude. Usually, programs read data as aggregates of bytes that form `int`s, `float`s, `double`s and so on. Java programs can use several classes to input and output data in aggregate form.

Interface `DataInput` describes methods for reading primitive types from an input stream. Classes **`DataInputStream`** and RandomAccessFile each implement this interface to read sets of bytes and view them as primitive-type values. Interface `DataInput` includes methods such as readBoolean, readByte, readChar, readDouble, readFloat, readFully (for byte arrays), readInt, readLong, readShort, readUnsignedByte, readUnsigned-Short, readUTF (for reading Unicode characters encoded by Java) and skipBytes.

Interface `DataOutput` describes a set of methods for writing primitive types to an output stream. Classes **`DataOutputStream`** (a subclass of FilterOutputStream) and Ran-domAccessFile each implement this interface to write primitive-type values as bytes. Interface `DataOutput` includes overloaded versions of method write (for a byte or for a byte array) and methods writeBoolean, writeByte, writeBytes, writeChar, writeChars (for Unicode Strings), writeDouble, writeFloat, writeInt, writeLong, writeShort and writeUTF (to output text modified for Unicode).

Buffered Streams

Buffering is an I/O-performance-enhancement technique. With a **`BufferedOutput-Stream`** (a subclass of class FilterOutputStream), each output statement does *not* necessarily result in an actual physical transfer of data to the output device (which is a slow operation compared to processor and main memory speeds). Rather, each output operation is directed to a region in memory called a **buffer** that's large enough to hold the data of many output operations. Then, actual transfer to the output device is performed in one large **physical output operation** each time the buffer fills. The output operations directed to the output buffer in memory are often called **logical output operations**. With a Buff-eredOutputStream, a partially filled buffer can be forced out to the device at any time by invoking the stream object's **flush** method.

Using buffering can greatly increase the performance of an application. Typical I/O operations are extremely slow compared with the speed of accessing data in computer memory. Buffering reduces the number of I/O operations by first combining smaller outputs together in memory. The number of actual physical I/O operations is small compared with the number of I/O requests issued by the program. Thus, the program that's using buffering is more efficient.

Performance Tip 15.1

Buffered I/O can yield significant performance improvements over unbuffered I/O.

With a **`BufferedInputStream`** (a subclass of class FilterInputStream), many "logical" chunks of data from a file are read as one large **physical input operation** into a memory buffer. As a program requests each new chunk of data, it's taken from the buffer. (This procedure is sometimes referred to as a **logical input operation**.) When the buffer is empty, the next actual physical input operation from the input device is performed to read in the next group of "logical" chunks of data. Thus, the number of actual physical input operations is small compared with the number of read requests issued by the program.

*Memory-Based **byte** Array Steams*

Java stream I/O includes capabilities for inputting from byte arrays in memory and outputting to byte arrays in memory. A ByteArrayInputStream (a subclass of InputStream) reads from a byte array in memory. A ByteArrayOutputStream (a subclass of OutputStream) outputs to a byte array in memory. One use of byte-array I/O is *data validation*. A program can input an entire line at a time from the input stream into a byte array. Then a validation routine can scrutinize the contents of the byte array and correct the data if necessary. Finally, the program can proceed to input from the byte array, "knowing" that the input data is in the proper format. Outputting to a byte array is a nice way to take advantage of the powerful output-formatting capabilities of Java streams. For example, data can be stored in a byte array, using the same formatting that will be displayed at a later time, and the byte array can then be output to a file to preserve the formatting.

Sequencing Input from Multiple Streams

A SequenceInputStream (a subclass of InputStream) logically concatenates several InputStreams—the program sees the group as one continuous InputStream. When the program reaches the end of one input stream, that stream closes, and the next stream in the sequence opens.

15.7.2 Interfaces and Classes for Character-Based Input and Output

In addition to the byte-based streams, Java provides the **Reader** and **Writer** abstract classes, which are character-based streams like those you used for text-file processing in Section 15.4. Most of the byte-based streams have corresponding character-based concrete Reader or Writer classes.

*Character-Based Buffering **Readers** and **Writers***

Classes BufferedReader (a subclass of abstract class Reader) and BufferedWriter (a subclass of abstract class Writer) enable buffering for character-based streams. Remember that character-based streams use Unicode characters—such streams can process data in any language that the Unicode character set represents.

*Memory-Based **char** Array **Readers** and **Writers***

Classes **CharArrayReader** and **CharArrayWriter** read and write, respectively, a stream of characters to a char array. A **LineNumberReader** (a subclass of BufferedReader) is a buffered character stream that keeps track of the number of lines read—newlines, returns and carriage-return–line-feed combinations increment the line count. Keeping track of line numbers can be useful if the program needs to inform the reader of an error on a specific line.

*Character-Based File, Pipe and String **Readers** and **Writers***

An InputStream can be converted to a Reader via class **InputStreamReader**. Similarly, an OutputStream can be converted to a Writer via class **OutputStreamWriter**. Class FileReader (a subclass of InputStreamReader) and class FileWriter (a subclass of OutputStreamWriter) read characters from and write characters to a file, respectively. Class **PipedReader** and class **PipedWriter** implement piped-character streams for transferring data between threads. Class **StringReader** and **StringWriter** read characters from and write characters to Strings, respectively. A PrintWriter writes characters to a stream.

15.8 Wrap-Up

In this chapter, you learned how to manipulate persistent data. We compared byte-based and character-based streams, and introduced several classes from packages java.io and java.nio.file. You used classes Files and Paths and interfaces Path and Directory-Stream to retrieve information about files and directories. You used sequential file processing to manipulate records that are stored in order by the record-key field. You used XML serialization to store and retrieve entire objects. The chapter concluded with a small example of using a JFileChooser dialog to allow users to easily select files from a GUI. The next chapter discusses Java's classes for manipulating collections of data—such as class ArrayList, which we introduced in Section 7.16.

16

Generic Collections

Objectives

In this chapter you'll:

- Learn what collections are.
- Use class **Arrays** for array manipulations.
- Learn the type-wrapper classes that enable programs to process primitive data values as objects.
- Understand the boxing and unboxing that occurs automatically between objects of the type-wrapper classes and their corresponding primitive types.
- Use prebuilt generic data structures from the collections framework.
- Use various algorithms of the **Collections** class to process collections.
- Use iterators to "walk through" a collection.
- Learn about synchronization and modifiability wrappers.
- Learn about Java SE 9's new factory methods for creating small immutable **List**s, **Set**s and **Map**s.

16.1 Introduction

In Section 7.16, we introduced the generic `ArrayList` collection—a dynamically resizable array-like data structure that stores references to objects of a type that you specify when you create the `ArrayList`. In this chapter, we continue our discussion of the Java **collections framework**, which contains many other *prebuilt* generic data-structures.

Some examples of collections are your favorite songs stored on your smartphone or media player, your contacts list, the cards you hold in a card game and the members of your favorite sports team.

We discuss the collections-framework interfaces that declare the capabilities of each collection type, various classes that implement these interfaces, methods that process collection objects, and **iterators** that "walk through" collections.

8 *Java SE 8*

After reading Chapter 17, Lambdas and Streams, you'll be able to reimplement many of Chapter 16's examples in a more concise and elegant manner, and in a way that makes them easier to parallelize to improve performance on today's multi-core systems. In Chapter 21, Concurrency and Multi-Core Performance, you'll learn how to improve performance on multi-core systems using Java's *concurrent collections* and *parallel stream* operations.

9 *Java SE 9*

Section 16.14 introduces Java SE 9's new *convenience factory methods*, which help you create small immutable collections that cannot be modified once they're created.

16.2 Collections Overview

A **collection** is a data structure—actually, an object—that can hold references to other objects. Usually, collections contain references to objects of any type that has the *is-a* relationship with the collection's element type. The collections-framework interfaces declare the operations to be performed generically on various types of collections. Figure 16.1 lists some of the collections-framework interfaces. Several implementations of these interfaces are provided within the framework. You may also provide your own implementations.

Interface	Description
`Collection`	The root interface in the collections hierarchy from which interfaces `Set`, `Queue` and `List` are derived.
`Set`	A collection that does *not* contain duplicates.
`List`	An ordered collection that *can* contain duplicate elements.
`Map`	A collection that associates keys to values and *cannot* contain duplicate keys. `Map` does not derive from `Collection`.
`Queue`	Typically a *first-in, first-out* collection that models a *waiting line*; other orders can be specified.

Fig. 16.1 | Some collections-framework interfaces.

Object-Based Collections

The collections-framework classes and interfaces are members of package `java.util`. In early Java versions, the collections framework classes stored and manipulated *only* `Object` references, enabling you to store *any* object in a collection, because all classes directly or indirectly derive from class `Object`. Programs normally need to process *specific* types of objects. As a result, the `Object` references obtained from a collection needed to be *downcast* to an appropriate type to allow the program to process the objects correctly. As we discussed in Chapter 10, downcasting generally should be avoided.

Generic Collections

To eliminate this problem, the collections framework was enhanced with the *generics* capabilities that we introduced with generic `ArrayList`s in Chapter 7 and that we discuss in more detail in Chapter 19, Generic Classes and Methods: A Deeper Look. Generics enable you to specify the *exact type* that will be stored in a collection and give you the benefits of *compile-time type checking*—the compiler issues error messages if you use inappropriate types in your collections. Once you specify the type stored in a generic collection, any reference you retrieve from the collection will have that type. This eliminates the need for explicit type casts that can throw `ClassCastException`s if the referenced object is *not* of the appropriate type. In addition, the generic collections are *backward compatible* with Java code that was written before generics were introduced.

Good Programming Practice 16.1
Avoid reinventing the wheel—rather than building your own data structures, use the interfaces and collections from the Java collections framework, which have been carefully tested and tuned to meet most application requirements.

Choosing a Collection

The documentation for each collection discusses its memory requirements and its methods' performance characteristics for operations such as adding and removing elements, searching for elements, sorting elements and more. Before choosing a collection, review the online documentation for the collection category you're considering (Set, List, Map, Queue, etc.), then choose the implementation that best meets your application's needs.

16.3 Type-Wrapper Classes

Each primitive type (listed in Appendix D) has a corresponding **type-wrapper class** (in package java.lang). These classes are called **Boolean**, **Byte**, **Character**, **Double**, **Float**, **Integer**, **Long** and **Short**. These enable you to manipulate primitive-type values as objects. This is important, because the data structures in the java.util package manipulate and share *objects*—they cannot manipulate variables of primitive types. However, they can manipulate objects of the type-wrapper classes, because every class ultimately derives from Object.

Each of the numeric type-wrapper classes—Byte, Short, Integer, Long, Float and Double—extends class Number. Also, the type-wrapper classes are final classes, so you cannot extend them. Primitive types do not have methods, so the methods related to a primitive type are located in the corresponding type-wrapper class (e.g., method parseInt, which converts a String to an int value, is located in class Integer).

16.4 Autoboxing and Auto-Unboxing

Java provides boxing and unboxing conversions that automatically convert between primitive-type values and type-wrapper objects. A **boxing conversion** converts a value of a primitive type to an object of the corresponding type-wrapper class. An **unboxing conversion** converts an object of a type-wrapper class to a value of the corresponding primitive type. These conversions—called **autoboxing** and **auto-unboxing**—are performed automatically. Consider the following statements:

```
Integer[] integerArray = new Integer[5]; // create integerArray
integerArray[0] = 10; // assign Integer 10 to integerArray[0]
int value = integerArray[0]; // get int value of Integer
```

In this case, autoboxing occurs when assigning an int value (10) to integerArray[0], because integerArray stores references to Integer objects, not int values. Auto-unboxing occurs when assigning integerArray[0] to int variable value, because variable value stores an int value, not a reference to an Integer object. Boxing conversions also occur in conditions, which can evaluate to primitive boolean values or Boolean objects. Many of the examples in Chapters 16–17 use these conversions to store primitive values in and retrieve them from data structures.

16.5 Interface Collection and Class Collections

Interface Collection contains **bulk operations** (i.e., operations performed on an *entire* collection) for operations such as *adding*, *clearing* and *comparing* objects (or elements) in a collection. A Collection can also be converted to an array. In addition, interface Collection provides a method that returns an **Iterator** object, which allows a program to walk through the collection and remove elements from it during the iteration. We discuss class

Iterator in Section 16.6.1. Other methods of interface Collection enable a program to determine a collection's *size* and whether a collection is *empty*.

Software Engineering Observation 16.1

Collection *is used commonly as a parameter type in methods to allow polymorphic processing of all objects that implement interface* Collection.

Software Engineering Observation 16.2

Most collection implementations provide a constructor that takes a Collection *argument, thereby allowing a new collection to be constructed containing the elements of the specified collection.*

Class **Collections** provides static convenience methods that *search*, *sort* and perform other operations on collections. Section 16.7 discusses Collections methods in detail. We also cover Collections' **wrapper methods** that enable you to treat a collection as a *synchronized collection* (Section 16.11) or an *unmodifiable collection* (Section 16.12). Synchronized collections are for use with multithreading (discussed in Chapter 21), which enables programs to perform operations *in parallel*. When two or more threads of a program *share* a collection, problems might occur. As an analogy, consider a traffic intersection. If all cars were allowed to access the intersection at the same time, collisions might occur. For this reason, traffic lights are provided to control access to the intersection. Similarly, we can *synchronize* access to a collection to ensure that only *one* thread manipulates the collection at a time. The synchronization wrapper methods of class Collections return synchronized versions of collections that can be shared among threads in a program. Chapter 21 also discusses some classes from the java.util.concurrent package, which provides more robust collections for use in multithreaded applications. Unmodifiable collections are useful when clients of a class need to *view* a collection's elements, but they should *not* be allowed to *modify* the collection by adding and removing elements.

16.6 Lists

A List (sometimes called a **sequence**) is a Collection of elements in sequence that can contain duplicate elements. Like array indices, List indices are zero based (i.e., the first element's index is zero). In addition to the methods inherited from Collection, List provides methods for manipulating elements via their indices, manipulating a specified range of elements, searching for elements and obtaining a **ListIterator** to access the elements.

Interface List is implemented by several classes, including **ArrayList** and **LinkedList**. Autoboxing occurs when you add primitive-type values to objects of these classes, because they store only references to objects. Class ArrayList is a resizable-array implementations of List. Inserting an element between existing elements of an ArrayList is an *inefficient* operation—all elements after the new one must be moved out of the way, which could be an expensive operation in a collection with a large number of elements. A LinkedList enables *efficient* insertion (or removal) of elements in the middle of a collection, but is much less efficient than an ArrayList for jumping to a specific element in the collection.

The following two subsections demonstrate the List and Collection capabilities. Section 16.6.1 removes elements from an ArrayList with an Iterator. Section 16.6.2 uses ListIterator and several List- and LinkedList-specific methods.

16.6.1 ArrayList and Iterator

Figure 16.2 uses an ArrayList (introduced in Section 7.16) to demonstrate several capabilities of interface Collection. The program places two Color arrays in ArrayLists and uses an Iterator to remove elements in the second ArrayList collection from the first.

```java
 1   // Fig. 16.2: CollectionTest.java
 2   // Collection interface demonstrated via an ArrayList object.
 3   import java.util.List;
 4   import java.util.ArrayList;
 5   import java.util.Collection;
 6   import java.util.Iterator;
 7
 8   public class CollectionTest {
 9      public static void main(String[] args) {
10         // add elements in colors array to list
11         String[] colors = {"MAGENTA", "RED", "WHITE", "BLUE", "CYAN"};
12         List<String> list = new ArrayList<String>();
13
14         for (String color : colors) {
15            list.add(color); // adds color to end of list
16         }
17
18         // add elements in removeColors array to removeList
19         String[] removeColors = {"RED", "WHITE", "BLUE"};
20         List<String> removeList = new ArrayList<String>();
21
22         for (String color : removeColors) {
23            removeList.add(color);
24         }
25
26         // output list contents
27         System.out.println("ArrayList: ");
28
29         for (int count = 0; count < list.size(); count++) {
30            System.out.printf("%s ", list.get(count));
31         }
32
33         // remove from list the colors contained in removeList
34         removeColors(list, removeList);
35
36         // output list contents
37         System.out.printf("%n%nArrayList after calling removeColors:%n");
38
39         for (String color : list) {
40            System.out.printf("%s ", color);
41         }
42      }
```

Fig. 16.2 | Collection interface demonstrated via an ArrayList object. (Part 1 of 2.)

```
43
44     // remove colors specified in collection2 from collection1
45     private static void removeColors(Collection<String> collection1,
46        Collection<String> collection2) {
47        // get iterator
48        Iterator<String> iterator = collection1.iterator();
49
50        // loop while collection has items
51        while (iterator.hasNext()) {
52           if (collection2.contains(iterator.next())) {
53              iterator.remove(); // remove current element
54           }
55        }
56     }
57  }
```

```
ArrayList:
MAGENTA RED WHITE BLUE CYAN

ArrayList after calling removeColors:
MAGENTA CYAN
```

Fig. 16.2 | Collection interface demonstrated via an ArrayList object. (Part 2 of 2.)

Lines 11 and 19 declare and initialize String arrays colors and removeColors. Lines 12 and 20 create ArrayList<String> objects and assign their references to List<String> variables list and removeList, respectively. Recall that ArrayList is a *generic* class, so we can specify a *type argument* (String in this case) to indicate the type of the elements in each list. Because you specify the type to store in a collection at compile time, generic collections provide compile-time *type safety* that allows the compiler to catch attempts to use invalid types. For example, you cannot store Employees in a collection of Strings.

Lines 14–16 populate list with Strings stored in array colors, and lines 22–24 populate removeList with Strings stored in array removeColors using **List method add**, which adds elements to the end of the List. Lines 29–31 output each element of list. Line 29 calls **List method size** to get the number of elements in the ArrayList. Line 30 uses **List method get** to retrieve individual element values. Lines 29–31 also could have used the enhanced for statement.

Line 34 calls method removeColors (lines 45–56), passing list and removeList as arguments. Method removeColors deletes the Strings in removeList from the Strings in list. Lines 39–41 print list's elements after removeColors completes its task.

Method removeColors declares two Collection<String> parameters (lines 45–46)—any two Collections containing Strings can be passed as arguments. The method accesses the elements of the first Collection (collection1) via an Iterator. Line 48 calls **Collection method iterator** to get an Iterator for the Collection. Interfaces Collection and Iterator are generic types. The loop-continuation condition (line 51) calls **Iterator method hasNext** to determine whether there are more elements to iterate through. Method hasNext returns true if another element exists and false otherwise.

The if condition in line 52 calls **Iterator method next** to obtain a reference to the next element, then uses method **contains** of the second Collection (collection2) to determine whether collection2 contains the element returned by next. If so, line 53 calls **Iterator method remove** to remove the element from the Collection collection1.

Common Programming Error 16.1

If a collection is modified by one of its methods after an iterator is created for that collection, the iterator immediately becomes invalid—any operation performed with the iterator fails immediately and throws a ConcurrentModificationException. For this reason, iterators are said to be "fail fast." Fail-fast iterators help ensure that a modifiable collection is not manipulated by two or more threads at the same time, which could corrupt the collection. In Chapter 21, Concurrency and Multi-Core Performance, you'll learn about concurrent collections (package java.util.concurrent) that can be safely manipulated by multiple concurrent threads.

Software Engineering Observation 16.3

We refer to the ArrayLists in this example via List variables. This makes our code more flexible and easier to modify—if we later determine that LinkedLists would be more appropriate, only the lines where we created the ArrayList objects (lines 12 and 20) need to be modified. In general, when you create a collection object, refer to that object with a variable of the corresponding collection interface type. Similarly, implementing method removeColors to receive Collection references enables the method to be used with any collection that implements the interface Collection.

Type Inference with the <> Notation

Lines 12 and 20 specify the type stored in the ArrayList (that is, String) on the left and right sides of the initialization statements. You also can use *type inferencing* with <>— known as the **diamond notation**—in statements that declare and create generic type variables and objects. For example, line 12 can be written as:

```
List<String> list = new ArrayList<>();
```

In this case, Java uses the type in angle brackets on the left of the declaration (that is, String) as the type stored in the ArrayList created on the right side of the declaration. We'll use this syntax for the remaining examples in this chapter.

16.6.2 LinkedList

Figure 16.3 demonstrates various operations on LinkedLists. The program creates two LinkedLists of Strings. The elements of one List are added to the other. Then all the Strings are converted to uppercase, and a range of elements is deleted.

```
1   // Fig. 16.3: ListTest.java
2   // Lists, LinkedLists and ListIterators.
3   import java.util.List;
4   import java.util.LinkedList;
5   import java.util.ListIterator;
6
7   public class ListTest {
8      public static void main(String[] args) {
```

Fig. 16.3 | Lists, LinkedLists and ListIterators. (Part 1 of 3.)

```java
 9          // add colors elements to list1
10          String[] colors =
11             {"black", "yellow", "green", "blue", "violet", "silver"};
12          List<String> list1 = new LinkedList<>();
13
14          for (String color : colors) {
15             list1.add(color);
16          }
17
18          // add colors2 elements to list2
19          String[] colors2 =
20             {"gold", "white", "brown", "blue", "gray", "silver"};
21          List<String> list2 = new LinkedList<>();
22
23          for (String color : colors2) {
24             list2.add(color);
25          }
26
27          list1.addAll(list2); // concatenate lists
28          list2 = null; // release resources
29          printList(list1); // print list1 elements
30
31          convertToUppercaseStrings(list1); // convert to uppercase string
32          printList(list1); // print list1 elements
33
34          System.out.printf("%nDeleting elements 4 to 6...");
35          removeItems(list1, 4, 7); // remove items 4-6 from list
36          printList(list1); // print list1 elements
37          printReversedList(list1); // print list in reverse order
38       }
39
40       // output List contents
41       private static void printList(List<String> list) {
42          System.out.printf("%nlist:%n");
43
44          for (String color : list) {
45             System.out.printf("%s ", color);
46          }
47
48          System.out.println();
49       }
50
51       // locate String objects and convert to uppercase
52       private static void convertToUppercaseStrings(List<String> list) {
53          ListIterator<String> iterator = list.listIterator();
54
55          while (iterator.hasNext()) {
56             String color = iterator.next(); // get item
57             iterator.set(color.toUpperCase()); // convert to upper case
58          }
59       }
60
```

Fig. 16.3 | Lists, LinkedLists and ListIterators. (Part 2 of 3.)

```
61      // obtain sublist and use clear method to delete sublist items
62      private static void removeItems(List<String> list,
63         int start, int end) {
64         list.subList(start, end).clear(); // remove items
65      }
66
67      // print reversed list
68      private static void printReversedList(List<String> list) {
69         ListIterator<String> iterator = list.listIterator(list.size());
70
71         System.out.printf("%nReversed List:%n");
72
73         // print list in reverse order
74         while (iterator.hasPrevious()) {
75            System.out.printf("%s ", iterator.previous());
76         }
77      }
78   }
```

```
list:
black yellow green blue violet silver gold white brown blue gray silver

list:
BLACK YELLOW GREEN BLUE VIOLET SILVER GOLD WHITE BROWN BLUE GRAY SILVER

Deleting elements 4 to 6...
list:
BLACK YELLOW GREEN BLUE WHITE BROWN BLUE GRAY SILVER

Reversed List:
SILVER GRAY BLUE BROWN WHITE BLUE GREEN YELLOW BLACK
```

Fig. 16.3 | Lists, LinkedLists and ListIterators. (Part 3 of 3.)

Lines 12 and 21 create LinkedLists list1 and list2 of type String. LinkedList is a generic class that has one type parameter, for which we specify the type argument String in this example. Lines 14–16 and 23–25 call List method add to *append* elements from arrays colors and colors2 to the *ends* of list1 and list2, respectively.

Line 27 calls **List method addAll** to *append all elements* of list2 to the end of list1. Line 28 sets list2 to null, because list2 is no longer needed. Line 29 calls method printList (lines 41–49) to output list1's contents. Line 31 calls method convertToUppercaseStrings (lines 52–59) to convert each String element to uppercase, then line 32 calls printList again to display the modified Strings. Line 35 calls method removeItems (lines 62–65) to remove the range of elements starting at index 4 up to, but not including, index 7 of the list. Line 37 calls method printReversedList (lines 68–77) to print the list in reverse order.

Method *convertToUppercaseStrings*

Method convertToUppercaseStrings (lines 52–59) changes lowercase String elements in its List argument to uppercase Strings. Line 53 calls **List method listIterator** to get the List's **bidirectional iterator** (i.e., one that can traverse a List *backward* or *for-*

ward). `ListIterator` is also a generic class. In this example, the `ListIterator` references `String` objects, because method `listIterator` is called on a `List` of `String`s. Line 55 calls method `hasNext` to determine whether the `List` *contains another element*. Line 56 gets the next `String` in the `List`. Line 57 calls **`String` method `toUpperCase`** to get an uppercase version of the `String` and calls **`ListIterator` method `set`** to replace the current `String` to which `iterator` refers with the `String` returned by method `toUpperCase`. Like method `toUpperCase`, **`String` method `toLowerCase`** returns a lowercase version of the `String`.

Method `removeItems`

Method `removeItems` (lines 62–65) *removes a range of items* from the list. Line 64 calls **`List` method `subList`** to obtain a portion of the `List` (called a **sublist**). This is called a **range-view method**, which enables the program to view a portion of the list. The sublist is simply a view into the `List` on which `subList` is called. Method `subList` takes as arguments the beginning and ending index for the sublist. The ending index is *not* part of the range of the sublist. In this example, line 35 passes 4 for the beginning index and 7 for the ending index to `subList`. The sublist returned is the set of elements with indices 4 through 6. Next, the program calls **`List` method `clear`** on the sublist to remove the elements of the sublist from the `List`. Any changes made to a sublist are also made to the original `List`.

Method `printReversedList`

Method `printReversedList` (lines 68–77) prints the list backward. Line 69 calls `List` method `listIterator` with the starting position as an argument (in our case, the last element in the list) to get a *bidirectional iterator* for the list. **`List` method `size`** returns the number of items in the `List`. The `while` condition (line 74) calls **`ListIterator`'s `hasPrevious` method** to determine whether there are more elements while traversing the list *backward*. Line 75 calls **`ListIterator`'s `previous` method** to get the previous element from the list and outputs it to the standard output stream.

Views into Collections and *Arrays Method* `asList`

Class `Arrays` provides `static` method **`asList`** to *view* an array (sometimes called the **backing array**) as a **`List`** collection. A `List` view allows you to manipulate the array as if it were a list. This is useful for adding the elements in an array to a collection and for sorting array elements. The next example demonstrates how to create a `LinkedList` with a `List` view of an array, because we cannot pass the array to a `LinkedList` constructor. Sorting array elements with a `List` view is demonstrated in Fig. 16.7. Any modifications made through the `List` view change the array, and any modifications made to the array change the `List` view. The only operation permitted on the view returned by `asList` is *set*, which changes the value of the view and the backing array. Any other attempts to change the view (such as adding or removing elements) result in an **`UnsupportedOperationException`**.

Viewing Arrays as `List`s and Converting `List`s to Arrays

Figure 16.4 uses `Arrays` method `asList` to view an array as a `List` and uses **`List` method `toArray`** to get an array from a `LinkedList` collection. The program calls method `asList` to create a `List` view of an array, which is used to initialize a `LinkedList` object, then adds a series of `String`s to the `LinkedList` and calls method `toArray` to obtain an array containing references to the `String`s.

```
1   // Fig. 16.4: UsingToArray.java
2   // Viewing arrays as Lists and converting Lists to arrays.
3   import java.util.LinkedList;
4   import java.util.Arrays;
5
6   public class UsingToArray {
7       public static void main(String[] args) {
8           String[] colors = {"black", "blue", "yellow"};
9           LinkedList<String> links = new LinkedList<>(Arrays.asList(colors));
10
11          links.addLast("red"); // add as last item
12          links.add("pink"); // add to the end
13          links.add(3, "green"); // add at 3rd index
14          links.addFirst("cyan"); // add as first item
15
16          // get LinkedList elements as an array
17          colors = links.toArray(new String[links.size()]);
18
19          System.out.println("colors: ");
20
21          for (String color : colors) {
22              System.out.println(color);
23          }
24      }
25  }
```

```
colors:
cyan
black
blue
yellow
green
red
pink
```

Fig. 16.4 | Viewing arrays as Lists and converting Lists to arrays.

Line 9 constructs a LinkedList of Strings containing the elements of array colors. Arrays method asList returns a List view of the array, then uses that to initialize the LinkedList with its constructor that receives a Collection as an argument (a List *is a* Collection). Line 11 calls **LinkedList method addLast** to add "red" to the end of links. Lines 12–13 call **LinkedList method add** to add "pink" as the last element and "green" as the element at index 3 (i.e., the fourth element). Method addLast works identically to the single-argument add method. Line 14 calls **LinkedList method addFirst** to add "cyan" as the new first item in the LinkedList. The add operations are permitted because they operate on the LinkedList object, not the view returned by asList. [*Note:* When "cyan" is added as the first element, "green" becomes the fifth element in the LinkedList.]

Line 17 calls interface List's toArray method to get a String array from links. The array is a copy of the list's elements—modifying the array's contents does *not* modify the list. The array passed to method toArray is of the type that you'd like method toArray to return. If the number of elements in that array is greater than or equal to the number of elements in the LinkedList, toArray copies the list's elements into its array argument and returns that array. If the LinkedList has more elements than the number of elements in the array passed to toArray, toArray *allocates a new array* of the same type it receives as an argument, *copies* the list's elements into the new array and returns the new array.

Common Programming Error 16.2

Passing an array that contains data as toArray's argument can cause logic errors. If the array's number of elements is smaller than the number of elements in the list on which toArray is called, a new array is allocated to store the list's elements—without preserving the array argument's elements. If the array's number of elements is greater than the number of elements in the list, the array's elements (starting at index zero) are overwritten with the list's elements. The first element of the remainder of the array is set to null to indicate the end of the list.

16.7 Collections Methods

Class Collections provides several high-performance algorithms for manipulating collection elements. The algorithms (Fig. 16.5) are implemented as static methods. The methods sort, binarySearch, reverse, shuffle, fill and copy operate on Lists. Methods min, max, addAll, frequency and disjoint operate on Collections.

Software Engineering Observation 16.4

The collections framework methods are polymorphic. That is, each can operate on objects that implement specific interfaces, regardless of the underlying implementations.

Method	Description
sort	Sorts the elements of a List.
binarySearch	Locates an object in a List, using the efficient binary search algorithm.
reverse	Reverses the elements of a List.
shuffle	Randomly orders a List's elements.
fill	Sets every List element to refer to a specified object.
copy	Copies references from one List into another.
min	Returns the smallest element in a Collection.
max	Returns the largest element in a Collection.
addAll	Appends all elements in an array to a Collection.
frequency	Calculates how many collection elements are equal to the specified element.
disjoint	Determines whether two collections have no elements in common.

Fig. 16.5 | Some Collections methods.

16.7.1 Method sort

Method sort sorts the elements of a List. The elements' type must implement interface **Comparable**. The order is determined by the natural order of the elements' type as implemented by a compareTo method. For example, the natural order for numeric values is ascending order, and the natural order for Strings is based on their lexicographical ordering (Section 14.3). Method compareTo is declared in interface Comparable and is sometimes called the **natural comparison method**. The sort call may specify as a second argument a **Comparator** object that determines an alternative ordering of the elements.

Sorting in Ascending Order

Figure 16.6 uses Collections method sort to order the elements of a List in *ascending* order (line 15). Line 12 creates list as a List of Strings. Lines 13 and 16 each use an *implicit* call to the list's toString method to output the list contents in the format shown in the output.

```java
1   // Fig. 16.6: Sort1.java
2   // Collections method sort.
3   import java.util.List;
4   import java.util.Arrays;
5   import java.util.Collections;
6
7   public class Sort1 {
8      public static void main(String[] args) {
9         String[] suits = {"Hearts", "Diamonds", "Clubs", "Spades"};
10
11        // Create and display a list containing the suits array elements
12        List<String> list = Arrays.asList(suits);
13        System.out.printf("Unsorted array elements: %s%n", list);
14
15        Collections.sort(list); // sort ArrayList
16        System.out.printf("Sorted array elements: %s%n", list);
17     }
18  }
```

```
Unsorted array elements: [Hearts, Diamonds, Clubs, Spades]
Sorted array elements: [Clubs, Diamonds, Hearts, Spades]
```

Fig. 16.6 | Collections method sort.

Sorting in Descending Order

Figure 16.7 sorts the same list of strings used in Fig. 16.6 in *descending* order. The example introduces the Comparator interface, which is used for sorting a Collection's elements in a different order. Line 16 calls Collections's method sort to order the List in descending order. The static **Collections method reverseOrder** returns a Comparator object that orders the collection's elements in reverse order. Because the collection being sorted is a List<String>, reverseOrder returns a Comparator<String>.

```java
1   // Fig. 16.7: Sort2.java
2   // Using a Comparator object with method sort.
3   import java.util.List;
```

Fig. 16.7 | Collections method sort with a Comparator object. (Part 1 of 2.)

```
 4    import java.util.Arrays;
 5    import java.util.Collections;
 6
 7    public class Sort2 {
 8       public static void main(String[] args) {
 9          String[] suits = {"Hearts", "Diamonds", "Clubs", "Spades"};
10
11          // Create and display a list containing the suits array elements
12          List<String> list = Arrays.asList(suits); // create List
13          System.out.printf("Unsorted array elements: %s%n", list);
14
15          // sort in descending order using a comparator
16          Collections.sort(list, Collections.reverseOrder());
17          System.out.printf("Sorted list elements: %s%n", list);
18       }
19    }
```

```
Unsorted array elements: [Hearts, Diamonds, Clubs, Spades]
Sorted list elements: [Spades, Hearts, Diamonds, Clubs]
```

Fig. 16.7 | Collections method sort with a Comparator object. (Part 2 of 2.)

Sorting with a *Comparator*

Figure 16.8 creates a custom Comparator class, named TimeComparator, that implements interface Comparator to compare two Time2 objects. Class Time2, declared in Fig. 8.5, represents times with hours, minutes and seconds.

```
 1    // Fig. 16.8: TimeComparator.java
 2    // Custom Comparator class that compares two Time2 objects.
 3    import java.util.Comparator;
 4
 5    public class TimeComparator implements Comparator<Time2> {
 6       @Override
 7       public int compare(Time2 time1, Time2 time2) {
 8          int hourDifference = time1.getHour() - time2.getHour();
 9
10          if (hourDifference != 0) { // test the hour first
11             return hourDifference;
12          }
13
14          int minuteDifference = time1.getMinute() - time2.getMinute();
15
16          if (minuteDifference != 0) { // then test the minute
17             return minuteDifference;
18          }
19
20          int secondDifference = time1.getSecond() - time2.getSecond();
21          return secondDifference;
22       }
23    }
```

Fig. 16.8 | Custom Comparator class that compares two Time2 objects.

Class TimeComparator implements interface Comparator, a generic type that takes one type argument (in this case Time2). A class that implements Comparator must declare a compare method that receives two arguments and returns a *negative* integer if the first argument is *less than* the second, 0 if the arguments are *equal* or a *positive* integer if the first argument is *greater than* the second. Method compare (lines 6–22) performs comparisons between Time2 objects. Line 8 calculates the difference between the hours of the two Time2 objects. If the hours are different (line 10), then we return this value. If this value is *positive*, then the first hour is greater than the second and the first time is greater than the second. If this value is *negative*, then the first hour is less than the second and the first time is less than the second. If this value is zero, the hours are the same and we must test the minutes (and maybe the seconds) to determine which time is greater.

Figure 16.9 sorts a list using the custom Comparator class TimeComparator. Line 9 creates an ArrayList of Time2 objects. Recall that both ArrayList and List are generic types and accept a type argument that specifies the element type of the collection. Lines 11–15 create five Time2 objects and add them to this list. Line 21 calls method sort, passing it an object of our TimeComparator class (Fig. 16.8).

```java
1   // Fig. 16.9: Sort3.java
2   // Collections method sort with a custom Comparator object.
3   import java.util.List;
4   import java.util.ArrayList;
5   import java.util.Collections;
6
7   public class Sort3 {
8      public static void main(String[] args) {
9         List<Time2> list = new ArrayList<>(); // create List
10
11         list.add(new Time2(6, 24, 34));
12         list.add(new Time2(18, 14, 58));
13         list.add(new Time2(6, 5, 34));
14         list.add(new Time2(12, 14, 58));
15         list.add(new Time2(6, 24, 22));
16
17         // output List elements
18         System.out.printf("Unsorted array elements:%n%s%n", list);
19
20         // sort in order using a comparator
21         Collections.sort(list, new TimeComparator());
22
23         // output List elements
24         System.out.printf("Sorted list elements:%n%s%n", list);
25      }
26   }
```

```
Unsorted array elements:
[6:24:34 AM, 6:14:58 PM, 6:05:34 AM, 12:14:58 PM, 6:24:22 AM]
Sorted list elements:
[6:05:34 AM, 6:24:22 AM, 6:24:34 AM, 12:14:58 PM, 6:14:58 PM]
```

Fig. 16.9 | Collections method sort with a custom Comparator object.

16.7.2 Method `shuffle`

Method **shuffle** randomly orders a List's elements. Chapter 7 presented a card shuffling and dealing simulation that shuffled a deck of cards with a loop. Figure 16.10 uses method shuffle to shuffle a deck of Card objects that might be used in a card-game simulator.

Class Card (lines 8–32) represents a card in a deck of cards. Each Card has a face and a suit. Lines 9–11 declare two enum types—Face and Suit—which represent the face and the suit of the card, respectively. Method toString (lines 29–31) returns a String containing the face and suit of the Card separated by the string " of ". When an enum constant is converted to a String, the constant's identifier is used as the String representation. Normally we would use all uppercase letters for enum constants. In this example, we chose to use capital letters for only the first letter of each enum constant because we want the card to be displayed with initial capital letters for the face and the suit (e.g., "Ace of Spades").

```
 1   // Fig. 16.10: DeckOfCards.java
 2   // Card shuffling and dealing with Collections method shuffle.
 3   import java.util.List;
 4   import java.util.Arrays;
 5   import java.util.Collections;
 6
 7   // class to represent a Card in a deck of cards
 8   class Card {
 9      public enum Face {Ace, Deuce, Three, Four, Five, Six,
10         Seven, Eight, Nine, Ten, Jack, Queen, King }
11      public enum Suit {Clubs, Diamonds, Hearts, Spades}
12
13      private final Face face;
14      private final Suit suit;
15
16      // constructor
17      public Card(Face face, Suit suit) {
18         this.face = face;
19         this.suit = suit;
20      }
21
22      // return face of the card
23      public Face getFace() {return face;}
24
25      // return suit of Card
26      public Suit getSuit() {return suit;}
27
28      // return String representation of Card
29      public String toString() {
30         return String.format("%s of %s", face, suit);
31      }
32   }
33
34   // class DeckOfCards declaration
35   public class DeckOfCards {
36      private List<Card> list; // declare List that will store Cards
```

Fig. 16.10 | Card shuffling and dealing with Collections method shuffle. (Part 1 of 2.)

```
37
38      // set up deck of Cards and shuffle
39      public DeckOfCards() {
40         Card[] deck = new Card[52];
41         int count = 0; // number of cards
42
43         // populate deck with Card objects
44         for (Card.Suit suit : Card.Suit.values()) {
45            for (Card.Face face : Card.Face.values()) {
46               deck[count] = new Card(face, suit);
47               ++count;
48            }
49         }
50
51         list = Arrays.asList(deck); // get List
52         Collections.shuffle(list);  // shuffle deck
53      }
54
55      // output deck
56      public void printCards() {
57         // display 52 cards in four columns
58         for (int i = 0; i < list.size(); i++) {
59            System.out.printf("%-19s%s", list.get(i),
60               ((i + 1) % 4 == 0) ? System.lineSeparator() : "");
61         }
62      }
63
64      public static void main(String[] args) {
65         DeckOfCards cards = new DeckOfCards();
66         cards.printCards();
67      }
68   }
```

Deuce of Clubs	Six of Spades	Nine of Diamonds	Ten of Hearts
Three of Diamonds	Five of Clubs	Deuce of Diamonds	Seven of Clubs
Three of Spades	Six of Diamonds	King of Clubs	Jack of Hearts
Ten of Spades	King of Diamonds	Eight of Spades	Six of Hearts
Nine of Clubs	Ten of Diamonds	Eight of Diamonds	Eight of Hearts
Ten of Clubs	Five of Hearts	Ace of Clubs	Deuce of Hearts
Queen of Diamonds	Ace of Diamonds	Four of Clubs	Nine of Hearts
Ace of Spades	Deuce of Spades	Ace of Hearts	Jack of Diamonds
Seven of Diamonds	Three of Hearts	Four of Spades	Four of Diamonds
Seven of Spades	King of Hearts	Seven of Hearts	Five of Diamonds
Eight of Clubs	Three of Clubs	Queen of Clubs	Queen of Spades
Six of Clubs	Nine of Spades	Four of Hearts	Jack of Clubs
Five of Spades	King of Spades	Jack of Spades	Queen of Hearts

Fig. 16.10 | Card shuffling and dealing with `Collections` method `shuffle`. (Part 2 of 2.)

Lines 44–49 populate the deck array with cards that have unique face and suit combinations. Both Face and Suit are public static enum types of class Card. To use these enum types outside of class Card, you must qualify each enum's type name with the name of the class in which it resides (i.e., Card) and a dot (.) separator. Hence, lines 44 and 45 use Card.Suit and Card.Face to declare the control variables of the for statements. Recall that method `values` of an enum type returns an array that contains all the constants of the enum type. Lines 44–49 use enhanced `for` statements to construct 52 new `Card`s.

The shuffling occurs in line 52, which calls `static` `Collections` method `shuffle` to shuffle the `Card`s. Method `shuffle` requires a `List` argument, so we must obtain a `List` view of the array before we can shuffle it. Line 51 invokes `static` method `asList` of class `Arrays` to get a `List` view of the `deck` array.

Method `printCards` (lines 56–62) displays the deck of cards in four columns. In each iteration of the loop, lines 59–60 output a card left-justified in a 19-character field followed by either a newline or an empty string based on the number of cards output so far. If the number of cards is divisible by 4, a newline is output; otherwise, the empty string is output. Note that line 60 uses `System` method **lineSeparator** to get the platform-independent newline character to output after every four cards.

16.7.3 Methods `reverse`, `fill`, `copy`, `max` and `min`

Class `Collections` provides methods for *reversing*, *filling* and *copying* `Lists`. **Collections method reverse** reverses the order of the elements in a `List`, and **method fill** *overwrites* elements in a `List` with a specified value. The `fill` operation is useful for reinitializing a `List`. **Method copy** takes two arguments—a destination `List` and a source `List`. Each element in the source `List` is copied to the destination `List`. The destination `List` must be at least as long as the source `List`; otherwise, an `IndexOutOfBoundsException` occurs. If the destination `List` is longer, the elements not overwritten are unchanged.

Each method we've seen so far operates on `Lists`. Methods **min** and **max** each operate on any `Collection`. Method `min` returns the smallest element in a `Collection`, and method `max` returns the largest element in a `Collection`. Both of these methods can be called with a `Comparator` object as a second argument to perform *custom comparisons* of objects, such as the `TimeComparator` in Fig. 16.9. Figure 16.11 demonstrates methods `reverse`, `fill`, `copy`, `max` and `min`.

```
1   // Fig. 16.11: Algorithms1.java
2   // Collections methods reverse, fill, copy, max and min.
3   import java.util.List;
4   import java.util.Arrays;
5   import java.util.Collections;
6
7   public class Algorithms1 {
8      public static void main(String[] args) {
9         // create and display a List<Character>
10        Character[] letters = {'P', 'C', 'M'};
11        List<Character> list = Arrays.asList(letters); // get List
12        System.out.println("list contains: ");
13        output(list);
14
15        // reverse and display the List<Character>
16        Collections.reverse(list); // reverse order the elements
17        System.out.printf("%nAfter calling reverse, list contains:%n");
18        output(list);
19
```

Fig. 16.11 | Collections methods reverse, fill, copy, max and min. (Part 1 of 2.)

```
20          // create copyList from an array of 3 Characters
21          Character[] lettersCopy = new Character[3];
22          List<Character> copyList = Arrays.asList(lettersCopy);
23
24          // copy the contents of list into copyList
25          Collections.copy(copyList, list);
26          System.out.printf("%nAfter copying, copyList contains:%n");
27          output(copyList);
28
29          // fill list with Rs
30          Collections.fill(list, 'R');
31          System.out.printf("%nAfter calling fill, list contains:%n");
32          output(list);
33      }
34
35      // output List information
36      private static void output(List<Character> listRef) {
37          System.out.print("The list is: ");
38
39          for (Character element : listRef) {
40              System.out.printf("%s ", element);
41          }
42
43          System.out.printf("%nMax: %s", Collections.max(listRef));
44          System.out.printf(" Min: %s%n", Collections.min(listRef));
45      }
46  }
```

```
list contains:
The list is: P C M
Max: P  Min: C

After calling reverse, list contains:
The list is: M C P
Max: P  Min: C

After copying, copyList contains:
The list is: M C P
Max: P  Min: C

After calling fill, list contains:
The list is: R R R
Max: R  Min: R
```

Fig. 16.11 | Collections methods reverse, fill, copy, max and min. (Part 2 of 2.)

Line 11 creates List<Character> variable list and initializes it with a List view of the Character array letters. Lines 12–13 output the current contents of the List. Line 16 calls Collections method reverse to reverse the order of list. Method reverse takes one List argument. Since list is a List view of the array letters, the array's elements are now in reverse order. The reversed contents are output in lines 17–18. Line 25 uses Collections method copy to copy list's elements into copyList. Changes to copyList do not change letters, because copyList is a separate List that's not a List view of the array letters. Method copy requires two List arguments—the destination List and the source List. Line 30 calls Collections method fill to place the character 'R' in each list element. Because list is a List view of the array letters, this operation changes each element in letters to 'R'. Method fill requires a List for the first argument and an object of the List's element type for the second argument—in this case, the object is the *boxed* Character version of 'R'. Lines 43–44 in method output call Collections methods max and min to find the largest and the smallest element of a Collection, respectively. Recall that interface List extends interface Collection, so a List *is a* Collection.

16.7.4 Method binarySearch

The high-speed binary search algorithm is built into the Java collections framework as a static **Collections** method **binarySearch**. This method locates an object in a List (e.g., a LinkedList or an ArrayList). If the object is found, its index is returned. If the object is not found, binarySearch returns a negative value. Method binarySearch determines this negative value by first calculating the insertion point and making its sign negative. Then, binarySearch subtracts 1 from the insertion point to obtain the return value, which guarantees that method binarySearch returns positive numbers (>= 0) if and only if the object is found. If multiple elements in the list match the search key, there's no guarantee which one will be located first. Figure 16.12 uses method binarySearch to search for a series of strings in an ArrayList.

```java
1   // Fig. 16.12: BinarySearchTest.java
2   // Collections method binarySearch.
3   import java.util.List;
4   import java.util.Arrays;
5   import java.util.Collections;
6   import java.util.ArrayList;
7
8   public class BinarySearchTest {
9      public static void main(String[] args) {
10        // create an ArrayList<String> from the contents of colors array
11        String[] colors = {"red", "white", "blue", "black", "yellow",
12           "purple", "tan", "pink"};
13        List<String> list = new ArrayList<>(Arrays.asList(colors));
14
15        Collections.sort(list); // sort the ArrayList
16        System.out.printf("Sorted ArrayList: %s%n", list);
17
18        // search list for various values
19        printSearchResults(list, "black");
20        printSearchResults(list, "red");
21        printSearchResults(list, "pink");
22        printSearchResults(list, "aqua"); // below lowest
23        printSearchResults(list, "gray"); // does not exist
24        printSearchResults(list, "teal"); // does not exist
25     }
26
```

Fig. 16.12 | Collections method binarySearch. (Part 1 of 2.)

```
27      // perform search and display result
28      private static void printSearchResults(
29          List<String> list, String key) {
30
31          System.out.printf("%nSearching for: %s%n", key);
32          int result = Collections.binarySearch(list, key);
33
34          if (result >= 0) {
35              System.out.printf("Found at index %d%n", result);
36          }
37          else {
38              System.out.printf("Not Found (%d)%n",result);
39          }
40      }
41  }
```

```
Sorted ArrayList: [black, blue, pink, purple, red, tan, white, yellow]

Searching for: black
Found at index 0

Searching for: red
Found at index 4

Searching for: pink
Found at index 2

Searching for: aqua
Not Found (-1)

Searching for: gray
Not Found (-3)

Searching for: teal
Not Found (-7)
```

Fig. 16.12 | Collections method binarySearch. (Part 2 of 2.)

Line 13 initializes list with an ArrayList containing a copy of the elements in array colors. Collections method binarySearch expects its List argument's elements to be sorted in *ascending* order, so line 15 uses Collections method sort to sort the list. If the List argument's elements are *not* sorted, binarySearch's result is *undefined*. Line 16 outputs the sorted list. Lines 19–24 call method printSearchResults (lines 28–41) to perform searches and output the results. Line 32 calls Collections method binarySearch to search list for the specified key. Method binarySearch takes a List as the first argument and the search key as the second argument. Lines 34–39 output the results of the search. An overloaded version of binarySearch takes a Comparator object as its third argument, which specifies how binarySearch should compare the search key to the List's elements.

16.7.5 Methods addAll, frequency and disjoint

Class Collections also provides the methods addAll, frequency and disjoint. **Collections method addAll** takes two arguments—a Collection into which to *insert* the new element(s) and an array (or variable-length argument list) that provides elements to be inserted. **Collections method frequency** takes two arguments—a Collection to be searched and an Object to be searched for in the collection. Method frequency returns the number of times that the second argument appears in the collection. **Collections method disjoint** takes two Collections and returns true if they have *no elements in common*. Figure 16.13 demonstrates the use of methods addAll, frequency and disjoint.

```java
 1   // Fig. 16.13: Algorithms2.java
 2   // Collections methods addAll, frequency and disjoint.
 3   import java.util.ArrayList;
 4   import java.util.List;
 5   import java.util.Arrays;
 6   import java.util.Collections;
 7
 8   public class Algorithms2 {
 9      public static void main(String[] args) {
10         // initialize list1 and list2
11         String[] colors = {"red", "white", "yellow", "blue"};
12         List<String> list1 = Arrays.asList(colors);
13         ArrayList<String> list2 = new ArrayList<>();
14
15         list2.add("black"); // add "black" to the end of list2
16         list2.add("red"); // add "red" to the end of list2
17         list2.add("green"); // add "green" to the end of list2
18
19         System.out.print("Before addAll, list2 contains: ");
20
21         // display elements in list2
22         for (String s : list2) {
23            System.out.printf("%s ", s);
24         }
25
26         Collections.addAll(list2, colors); // add colors Strings to list2
27
28         System.out.printf("%nAfter addAll, list2 contains: ");
29
30         // display elements in list2
31         for (String s : list2) {
32            System.out.printf("%s ", s);
33         }
34
35         // get frequency of "red"
36         int frequency = Collections.frequency(list2, "red");
37         System.out.printf("%nFrequency of red in list2: %d%n", frequency);
38
39         // check whether list1 and list2 have elements in common
40         boolean disjoint = Collections.disjoint(list1, list2);
41
42         System.out.printf("list1 and list2 %s elements in common%n",
43            (disjoint ? "do not have" : "have"));
44      }
45   }
```

Fig. 16.13 | Collections methods addAll, frequency and disjoint. (Part 1 of 2.)

```
Before addAll, list2 contains: black red green
After addAll, list2 contains: black red green red white yellow blue
Frequency of red in list2: 2
list1 and list2 have elements in common
```

Fig. 16.13 | Collections methods addAll, frequency and disjoint. (Part 2 of 2.)

Line 12 initializes list1 with elements in array colors, and lines 15–17 add Strings "black", "red" and "green" to list2. Line 26 invokes method addAll to add elements in array colors to list2. Line 36 gets the frequency of String "red" in list2 using method frequency. Line 40 invokes method disjoint to test whether Collections list1 and list2 have elements in common, which they do in this example.

16.8 Class PriorityQueue and Interface Queue

Recall that a queue is a collection that represents a waiting line—typically, *insertions* are made at the back of a queue and *deletions* are made from the front. In Chapter 21, Concurrency and Multi-Core Performance, we'll use concurrent queues. In this section, we investigate Java's **Queue** interface and **PriorityQueue** class from package java.util. Interface Queue extends interface Collection and provides additional operations for *inserting*, *removing* and *inspecting* elements in a queue. PriorityQueue, which implements the Queue interface, orders elements by their natural ordering as specified by Comparable elements' compareTo method or by a Comparator object that's supplied to the constructor.

Class PriorityQueue provides functionality that enables *insertions in sorted order* into the underlying data structure and *deletions* from the *front* of the underlying data structure. When adding elements to a PriorityQueue, the elements are inserted in priority order such that the *highest-priority element* (i.e., the largest value) will be the first element removed from the PriorityQueue.

The common PriorityQueue operations are **offer** to *insert* an element at the appropriate location based on priority order, **poll** to *remove* the highest-priority element of the priority queue (i.e., the head of the queue), **peek** to get a reference to the highest-priority element of the priority queue (without removing that element), **clear** to *remove all elements* in the priority queue and **size** to get the number of elements in the priority queue.

Figure 16.14 demonstrates class PriorityQueue. Line 8 creates a PriorityQueue that stores Doubles with an *initial capacity* of 11 elements and orders the elements according to the object's natural ordering (the defaults for a PriorityQueue). PriorityQueue is a generic class. Line 8 instantiates a PriorityQueue with a type argument Double. Class PriorityQueue provides several additional constructors. One of these takes an int and a Comparator object to create a PriorityQueue with the *initial capacity* specified by the int and the *ordering* by the Comparator. Lines 11–13 use method offer to add elements to the priority queue. Method offer throws a NullPointerException if the program attempts to add a null object to the queue. The loop in lines 18–21 uses method size to determine whether the priority queue is *empty* (line 18). While there are more elements, line 19 uses PriorityQueue method peek to retrieve the *highest-priority element* in the queue for output (*without* actually removing it from the queue). Line 20 removes the highest-priority element in the queue with method poll, which returns the removed element.

```
 1   // Fig. 16.14: PriorityQueueTest.java
 2   // PriorityQueue test program.
 3   import java.util.PriorityQueue;
 4
 5   public class PriorityQueueTest {
 6      public static void main(String[] args) {
 7         // queue of capacity 11
 8         PriorityQueue<Double> queue = new PriorityQueue<>();
 9
10         // insert elements to queue
11         queue.offer(3.2);
12         queue.offer(9.8);
13         queue.offer(5.4);
14
15         System.out.print("Polling from queue: ");
16
17         // display elements in queue
18         while (queue.size() > 0) {
19            System.out.printf("%.1f ", queue.peek()); // view top element
20            queue.poll(); // remove top element
21         }
22      }
23   }
```

```
Polling from queue: 3.2 5.4 9.8
```

Fig. 16.14 | PriorityQueue test program.

16.9 Sets

A Set is a collection of unique elements (i.e., no duplicates). The collections framework contains several Set implementations, including **HashSet** and **TreeSet**. HashSet stores its elements (unordered) in a *hash table*, and TreeSet stores its elements (ordered) in a *tree*. Hash tables are presented in Section 16.10. Figure 16.15 uses a HashSet to *remove duplicate strings* from a List. Recall that both List and Collection are generic types, so line 14 creates a List that contains String objects, and line 18 passes the collection to method printNonDuplicates (lines 22–33), which takes a Collection argument. Line 24 constructs a HashSet<String> from the Collection<String> argument. By definition, Sets do *not* contain duplicates, so when the HashSet is constructed, it *removes any duplicates* in the Collection. Lines 28–30 output elements in the Set.

```
 1   // Fig. 16.15: SetTest.java
 2   // HashSet used to remove duplicate values from array of strings.
 3   import java.util.List;
 4   import java.util.Arrays;
 5   import java.util.HashSet;
 6   import java.util.Set;
 7   import java.util.Collection;
```

Fig. 16.15 | HashSet used to remove duplicate values from an array of strings. (Part 1 of 2.)

```
8
9  public class SetTest {
10    public static void main(String[] args) {
11       // create and display a List<String>
12       String[] colors = {"red", "white", "blue", "green", "gray",
13          "orange", "tan", "white", "cyan", "peach", "gray", "orange"};
14       List<String> list = Arrays.asList(colors);
15       System.out.printf("List: %s%n", list);
16
17       // eliminate duplicates then print the unique values
18       printNonDuplicates(list);
19    }
20
21    // create a Set from a Collection to eliminate duplicates
22    private static void printNonDuplicates(Collection<String> values) {
23       // create a HashSet
24       Set<String> set = new HashSet<>(values);
25
26       System.out.printf("%nNonduplicates are: ");
27
28       for (String value : set) {
29          System.out.printf("%s ", value);
30       }
31
32       System.out.println();
33    }
34 }
```

```
List: [red, white, blue, green, gray, orange, tan, white, cyan, peach, gray,
orange]

Nonduplicates are: tan green peach cyan red orange gray white blue
```

Fig. 16.15 | HashSet used to remove duplicate values from an array of strings. (Part 2 of 2.)

Sorted Sets

The collections framework also includes the **SortedSet interface** (which extends Set) for sets that maintain their elements in *sorted* order—either the *elements' natural order* (e.g., numbers are in *ascending* order) or an order specified by a Comparator. Class TreeSet implements SortedSet. The program in Fig. 16.16 places Strings into a TreeSet. The Strings are sorted as they're added to the TreeSet. This example also demonstrates *range-view* methods, which enable a program to view a portion of a collection.

```
1  // Fig. 16.16: SortedSetTest.java
2  // Using SortedSets and TreeSets.
3  import java.util.Arrays;
4  import java.util.SortedSet;
5  import java.util.TreeSet;
6
```

Fig. 16.16 | Using SortedSets and TreeSets. (Part 1 of 2.)

```java
7   public class SortedSetTest {
8       public static void main(String[] args) {
9           // create TreeSet from array colors
10          String[] colors = {"yellow", "green", "black", "tan", "grey",
11             "white", "orange", "red", "green"};
12          SortedSet<String> tree = new TreeSet<>(Arrays.asList(colors));
13
14          System.out.print("sorted set: ");
15          printSet(tree);
16
17          // get headSet based on "orange"
18          System.out.print("headSet (\"orange\"):  ");
19          printSet(tree.headSet("orange"));
20
21          // get tailSet based upon "orange"
22          System.out.print("tailSet (\"orange\"):  ");
23          printSet(tree.tailSet("orange"));
24
25          // get first and last elements
26          System.out.printf("first: %s%n", tree.first());
27          System.out.printf("last : %s%n", tree.last());
28      }
29
30      // output SortedSet using enhanced for statement
31      private static void printSet(SortedSet<String> set) {
32          for (String s : set) {
33              System.out.printf("%s ", s);
34          }
35
36          System.out.println();
37      }
38  }
```

```
sorted set: black green grey orange red tan white yellow
headSet ("orange"):  black green grey
tailSet ("orange"):  orange red tan white yellow
first: black
last : yellow
```

Fig. 16.16 | Using SortedSets and TreeSets. (Part 2 of 2.)

Line 12 creates a TreeSet<String> that contains the elements of array colors, then assigns the new TreeSet<String> to SortedSet<String> variable tree. Line 15 outputs the initial set of strings using method printSet (lines 31–37), which we discuss momentarily. Line 19 calls **TreeSet method headSet** to get a subset of the TreeSet in which every element is less than "orange". The view returned from headSet is then output with printSet. If any changes are made to the subset, they'll *also* be made to the original TreeSet, because the subset returned by headSet is a view of the TreeSet.

Line 23 calls **TreeSet method tailSet** to get a subset in which each element is greater than or equal to "orange", then outputs the result. Any changes made through the tailSet view are made to the original TreeSet. Lines 26–27 call **SortedSet methods first** and **last** to get the smallest and largest elements of the set, respectively.

Method `printSet` (lines 31–37) accepts a `SortedSet` as an argument and prints it. Lines 32–34 print each element of the `SortedSet` using the enhanced `for` statement.

16.10 Maps

Maps associate *keys* to *values*. The keys in a `Map` must be *unique*, but the associated values need not be. If a `Map` contains both unique keys and unique values, it's said to implement a **one-to-one mapping**. If only the keys are unique, the `Map` is said to implement a **many-to-one mapping**—many keys can map to one value.

Maps differ from `Set`s in that `Map`s contain keys and values, whereas `Set`s contain only values. Two classes that implement interface `Map` are **HashMap** and **TreeMap**. HashMaps store elements in hash tables, and TreeMaps store elements in trees. This section discusses hash tables and provides an example that uses a `HashMap` to store key–value pairs. **Interface SortedMap** extends `Map` and maintains its keys in *sorted* order—either the elements' *natural* order or an order specified by a `Comparator`. Class `TreeMap` implements `SortedMap`.

Map Implementation with Hash Tables

When a program creates objects, it may need to store and retrieve them efficiently. Storing and retrieving information with arrays is efficient if some aspect of your data directly matches a numerical key value and if the *keys are unique* and tightly packed. If you have 100 employees with nine-digit social security numbers and you want to store and retrieve employee data by using the social security number as a key, the task will require an array with over 800 million elements, because nine-digit Social Security numbers must begin with 001–899 (excluding 666) as per the Social Security Administration's website

```
http://www.socialsecurity.gov/employer/randomization.html
```

This is impractical for virtually all applications that use social security numbers as keys. A program having so large an array could achieve high performance for both storing and retrieving employee records by simply using the social security number as the array index.

Numerous applications have this problem—namely, that either the keys are of the wrong type (e.g., not positive integers that correspond to array subscripts) or they're of the right type, but *sparsely* spread over a *huge range*. What is needed is a high-speed scheme for converting keys such as social security numbers, inventory part numbers and the like into unique array indices. Then, when an application needs to store something, the scheme can convert the application's key rapidly into an index, and the record can be stored at that slot in the array. Retrieval is accomplished the same way: Once the application has a key for which it wants to retrieve a data record, the application simply applies the conversion to the key—this produces the array index where the data is stored and retrieved.

The scheme we describe here is the basis of a technique called **hashing**. Why the name? When we convert a key into an array index, we literally scramble the bits, forming a kind of "mishmashed," or hashed, number. The number actually has no real significance beyond its usefulness in storing and retrieving a particular data record.

A glitch in the scheme is called a **collision**—this occurs when two different keys "hash into" the same cell (or element) in the array. We cannot store two values in the same space, so we need to find an alternative home for all values beyond the first that hash to a particular array index. There are many schemes for doing this. One is to "hash again" (i.e., to apply another hashing transformation to the key to provide the next candidate cell in the array). The hashing process is designed to *distribute* the values throughout the table, so the assumption is that an available cell will be found with just a few hashes.

Another scheme uses one hash to locate the first candidate cell. If that cell is occupied, successive cells are searched in order until an available cell is found. Retrieval works the same way: The key is hashed once to determine the initial location and check whether it contains the desired data. If it does, the search is finished. If it does not, successive cells are searched linearly until the desired data is found.

The most popular solution to hash-table collisions is to have each cell of the table be a hash "bucket," typically a linked list of all the key–value pairs that hash to that cell. This is the solution that Java's HashMap class (from package java.util) uses. HashMap implements the Map interface.

A hash table's **load factor** affects the performance of hashing schemes. The load factor is the ratio of the number of occupied cells in the hash table to the total number of cells in the hash table. The closer this ratio gets to 1.0, the greater the chance of collisions.

Performance Tip 16.1

The load factor in a hash table is a classic example of a memory-space/execution-time trade-off: By increasing the load factor, we get better memory utilization, but the program runs slower, due to increased hashing collisions. By decreasing the load factor, we get better program speed, because of reduced hashing collisions, but we get poorer memory utilization, because a larger portion of the hash table remains empty.

Class HashMap enables you to use hashing without having to implement hash-table mechanisms—a classic example of reuse. This concept is profoundly important in our study of object-oriented programming. As discussed in earlier chapters, classes encapsulate and hide complexity (i.e., implementation details) and offer user-friendly interfaces. Properly crafting classes to exhibit such behavior is one of the most valued skills in the field of object-oriented programming. Figure 16.17 uses a HashMap to count the number of occurrences of each word in a string.

Line 12 creates an empty HashMap with a *default initial capacity* (16 elements) and a default load factor (0.75)—these defaults are built into the implementation of HashMap. When the number of occupied slots in the HashMap becomes greater than the capacity times the load factor, the capacity is doubled automatically. HashMap is a generic class that takes two type arguments—the type of key (i.e., String) and the type of value (i.e., Integer). Recall that the type arguments passed to a generic class must be reference types, hence the second type argument is Integer, not int.

```
1   // Fig. 16.17: WordTypeCount.java
2   // Program counts the number of occurrences of each word in a String.
3   import java.util.Map;
4   import java.util.HashMap;
5   import java.util.Set;
6   import java.util.TreeSet;
7   import java.util.Scanner;
```

Fig. 16.17 | Program counts the number of occurrences of each word in a String. (Part 1 of 3.)

```
8
9   public class WordTypeCount {
10      public static void main(String[] args) {
11         // create HashMap to store String keys and Integer values
12         Map<String, Integer> myMap = new HashMap<>();
13
14         createMap(myMap); // create map based on user input
15         displayMap(myMap); // display map content
16      }
17
18      // create map from user input
19      private static void createMap(Map<String, Integer> map) {
20         Scanner scanner = new Scanner(System.in); // create scanner
21         System.out.println("Enter a string:"); // prompt for user input
22         String input = scanner.nextLine();
23
24         // tokenize the input
25         String[] tokens = input.split(" ");
26
27         // processing input text
28         for (String token : tokens) {
29            String word = token.toLowerCase(); // get lowercase word
30
31            // if the map contains the word
32            if (map.containsKey(word)) { // is word in map?
33               int count = map.get(word); // get current count
34               map.put(word, count + 1); // increment count
35            }
36            else {
37               map.put(word, 1); // add new word with a count of 1 to map
38            }
39         }
40      }
41
42      // display map content
43      private static void displayMap(Map<String, Integer> map) {
44         Set<String> keys = map.keySet(); // get keys
45
46         // sort keys
47         TreeSet<String> sortedKeys = new TreeSet<>(keys);
48
49         System.out.printf("%nMap contains:%nKey\t\tValue%n");
50
51         // generate output for each key in map
52         for (String key : sortedKeys) {
53            System.out.printf("%-10s%10s%n", key, map.get(key));
54         }
55
56         System.out.printf(
57            "%nsize: %d%nisEmpty: %b%n", map.size(), map.isEmpty());
58      }
59   }
```

Fig. 16.17 | Program counts the number of occurrences of each word in a `String`. (Part 2 of 3.)

```
Enter a string:
this is a sample sentence with several words this is another sample
sentence with several different words

Map contains:
Key             Value
a               1
another         1
different       1
is              2
sample          2
sentence        2
several         2
this            2
with            2
words           2

size: 10
isEmpty: false
```

Fig. 16.17 | Program counts the number of occurrences of each word in a `String`. (Part 3 of 3.)

Line 14 calls method `createMap` (lines 19–40), which uses a `Map` to store the number of occurrences of each word in the sentence. Line 22 obtains the user input, and line 25 tokenizes it. For each token, lines 28–39 convert the token to lowercase letters (line 29), then call **Map method `containsKey`** (line 32) to determine whether the word is in the map (and thus has occurred previously in the string). If the `Map` does *not* contain the word, line 37 uses **Map method `put`** to create a new entry, with the word as the key and an `Integer` object containing 1 as the value. Autoboxing occurs when the program passes integer 1 to method `put`, because the map stores the number of occurrences as an `Integer`. If the word does exist in the map, line 33 uses **Map method `get`** to obtain the key's associated value (the count) in the map. Line 34 increments that value and uses `put` to replace the key's associated value. Method `put` returns the key's prior associated value, or `null` if the key was not in the map.

Error-Prevention Tip 16.1

Always use immutable keys with a `Map`. The key determines where the corresponding value is placed. If the key has changed since the insert operation, when you subsequently attempt to retrieve that value, it might not be found. In this chapter's examples, we use `String`s as keys and `String`s are immutable.

Method `displayMap` (lines 43–58) displays all the entries in the map. It uses **HashMap method `keySet`** (line 44) to get a set of the keys. The keys have type `String` in the map, so method `keySet` returns a generic type `Set` with type parameter specified to be `String`. Line 47 creates a `TreeSet` of the keys, in which the keys are sorted. Lines 52–54 access each key and its value in the map. Line 53 displays each key and its value using format specifier `%-10s` to *left align* each key and format specifier `%10s` to *right align* each value. The keys are displayed in *ascending* order. Line 57 calls **Map method `size`** to get the number of key–value pairs in the `Map`, and calls **Map method `isEmpty`**, which returns a `boolean` indicating whether the `Map` is empty.

16.11 Synchronized Collections

In Chapter 21, we discuss *multithreading*. The collections in the collections framework are *unsynchronized* by default, so they can operate efficiently when multithreading is not required. Because they're unsynchronized, however, concurrent access to a Collection by multiple threads could cause indeterminate results or fatal errors—as we demonstrate in Chapter 21. To prevent potential threading problems, **synchronization wrappers** are provided for collections that might be accessed by multiple threads. A **wrapper** object receives method calls, adds thread synchronization (to prevent concurrent access to the collection) and *delegates* the calls to the wrapped collection object. The Collections class provides static methods for wrapping collections as synchronized versions. Method headers for some synchronization wrappers are listed in Fig. 16.18. Details on these methods are available at http://docs.oracle.com/javase/8/docs/api/java/util/Collections.html. Each method takes a collection and returns its *synchronized view*. For example, the following code creates a synchronized List (list2) that stores String objects:

```
List<String> list1 = new ArrayList<>();
List<String> list2 = Collections.synchronizedList(list1);
```

More robust collections for concurrent access are provided in the java.util.concurrent package, which we introduce in Chapter 21.

---

public static method headers

```
<T> Collection<T> synchronizedCollection(Collection<T> c)

<T> List<T> synchronizedList(List<T> aList)

<T> Set<T> synchronizedSet(Set<T> s)

<T> SortedSet<T> synchronizedSortedSet(SortedSet<T> s)

<K, V> Map<K, V> synchronizedMap(Map<K, V> m)

<K, V> SortedMap<K, V> synchronizedSortedMap(SortedMap<K, V> m)
```

Fig. 16.18 | Some synchronization wrapper methods.

16.12 Unmodifiable Collections

The Collections class provides a set of static methods that create **unmodifiable wrappers** for collections. Unmodifiable wrappers throw UnsupportedOperationExceptions if attempts are made to modify the collection. In an unmodifiable collection, the references stored in the collection are not modifiable, but the objects they refer *are modifiable* unless they belong to an immutable class like String. Headers for some of these methods are listed in Fig. 16.19. Details about these methods are available at http://docs.oracle.com/javase/8/docs/api/java/util/Collections.html. All these methods take a generic type and return an unmodifiable view of the generic type. For example, the following code creates an unmodifiable List (list2) that stores String objects:

```
List<String> list1 = new ArrayList<>();
List<String> list2 = Collections.unmodifiableList(list1);
```

Software Engineering Observation 16.5

You can use an unmodifiable wrapper to create a collection that offers read-only access to others, while allowing read–write access to yourself. You do this simply by giving others a reference to the unmodifiable wrapper while retaining for yourself a reference to the original collection.

---

public static method headers

```
<T> Collection<T> unmodifiableCollection(Collection<T> c)

<T> List<T> unmodifiableList(List<T> aList)

<T> Set<T> unmodifiableSet(Set<T> s)

<T> SortedSet<T> unmodifiableSortedSet(SortedSet<T> s)

<K, V> Map<K, V> unmodifiableMap(Map<K, V> m)

<K, V> SortedMap<K, V> unmodifiableSortedMap(SortedMap<K, V> m)
```

Fig. 16.19 | Some unmodifiable wrapper methods.

16.13 Abstract Implementations

The collections framework provides various abstract implementations of Collection interfaces from which you can quickly "flesh out" complete customized implementations. These abstract implementations include a thin Collection implementation called an **AbstractCollection**, a List implementation that allows *array-like access* to its elements called an **AbstractList**, a Map implementation called an **AbstractMap**, a List implementation that allows *sequential access* (from beginning to end) to its elements called an **AbstractSequentialList**, a Set implementation called an **AbstractSet** and a Queue implementation called **AbstractQueue**. You can learn more about these classes at http://docs.oracle.com/javase/8/docs/api/java/util/package-summary.html. To write a *custom* implementation, you can extend the abstract implementation that best meets your needs, implement each of the class's abstract methods and override the class's concrete methods as necessary.

16.14 Java SE 9: Convenience Factory Methods for Immutable Collections[1]

Java SE 9 adds new static *convenience factory methods* to interfaces List, Set and Map that enable you to create small *immutable* collections—they cannot be modified once they are created (JEP 269). We introduced factory methods in Section 10.12—the word *factory* indicates that these methods create objects. They're *convenient* because you simply pass the elements as arguments to a convenience factory method, which creates the collection and adds the elements to the collection for you.

---

1.   If any changes occur to the new Java SE 9 content in this section, we'll post updates on the book's website at http://www.deitel.com/books/Java9FP. This example requires JDK 9 to execute.

The collections returned by the unmodifiable wrappers we discussed in Section 16.12 create *immutable views* of *mutable collections*—the reference to the original mutable collection can still be used to modify the collection. The convenience factory methods instead return custom collection objects that are truly immutable and optimized to store small collections. In Chapters 17 and 23, we explain how using lambdas and streams with immutable entities can help you create "parallelizable" code that will run more efficiently on today's multi-core architectures. Figure 16.20 demonstrates these convenience factory methods for a List, a Set and two Maps.

Common Programming Error 16.3

Calling any method that attempts to modify a collection returned by the List, Set or Map convenience factory methods results in an UnsupportedOperationException.

Software Engineering Observation 16.6

In Java, collection elements are always references to objects. The objects referenced by an immutable collection may still be mutable.

```java
1   // Fig. 16.20: FactoryMethods.java
2   // Java SE 9 collection factory methods.
3   import java.util.List;
4   import java.util.Map;
5   import java.util.Set;
6
7   public class FactoryMethods {
8      public static void main(String[] args) {
9         // create a List
10        List<String> colorList = List.of("red", "orange", "yellow",
11           "green", "blue", "indigo", "violet");
12        System.out.printf("colorList: %s%n%n", colorList);
13
14        // create a Set
15        Set<String> colorSet = Set.of("red", "orange", "yellow",
16           "green", "blue", "indigo", "violet");
17        System.out.printf("colorSet: %s%n%n", colorSet);
18
19        // create a Map using method "of"
20        Map<String, Integer> dayMap = Map.of("Monday", 1, "Tuesday", 2,
21           "Wednesday", 3, "Thursday", 4, "Friday", 5, "Saturday", 6,
22           "Sunday", 7);
23        System.out.printf("dayMap: %s%n%n", dayMap);
24
25        // create a Map using method "ofEntries" for more than 10 pairs
26        Map<String, Integer> daysPerMonthMap = Map.ofEntries(
27           Map.entry("January", 31),
28           Map.entry("February", 28),
29           Map.entry("March", 31),
30           Map.entry("April", 30),
31           Map.entry("May", 31),
32           Map.entry("June", 30),
```

Fig. 16.20 | Java SE 9 collection factory methods. (Part 1 of 2.)

```
33              Map.entry("July", 31),
34              Map.entry("August", 31),
35              Map.entry("September", 30),
36              Map.entry("October", 31),
37              Map.entry("November", 30),
38              Map.entry("December", 31)
39          );
40          System.out.printf("monthMap: %s%n", daysPerMonthMap);
41      }
42  }
```

```
colorList: [red, orange, yellow, green, blue, indigo, violet]

colorSet: [yellow, green, red, blue, violet, indigo, orange]

dayMap: {Tuesday=2, Wednesday=3, Friday=5, Thursday=4, Saturday=6, Monday=1,
Sunday=7}

monthMap: {April=30, February=28, September=30, July=31, October=31,
November=30, December=31, March=31, January=31, June=30, May=31, August=31}
```

```
colorList: [red, orange, yellow, green, blue, indigo, violet]

colorSet: [violet, yellow, orange, green, blue, red, indigo]

dayMap: {Saturday=6, Tuesday=2, Wednesday=3, Sunday=7, Monday=1, Thursday=4,
Friday=5}

monthMap: {February=28, August=31, July=31, November=30, April=30, May=31,
December=31, September=30, January=31, March=31, June=30, October=31}
```

Fig. 16.20 | Java SE 9 collection factory methods. (Part 2 of 2.)

List Interface's Convenience Factory Method of

Lines 10–11 use the List convenience factory method **of** to create an immutable List<String>. Method of has overloads for Lists of zero to 10 elements and an additional overload that can receive any number of elements. Line 12 displays the String representation of the List's contents—recall that this automatically iterates through the List's elements to create the String. Also, the returned List's elements are guaranteed to be in the *same* order as method of's arguments.

Performance Tip 16.2

The collections returned by the convenience factory methods are optimized for up to 10 elements (for Lists and Sets) or key–value pairs (for Maps).

Software Engineering Observation 16.7

Method of is overloaded for zero to 10 elements because research showed that these handle the vast majority of cases in which immutable collections are needed.

Performance Tip 16.3

Method of's overloads for zero to 10 elements eliminate the extra overhead of processing variable-length argument lists. This improves the performance of applications that create small immutable collections.

Common Programming Error 16.4

The collections returned by the convenience factory methods are not allowed to contain `null` values—these methods throw a `NullPointerException` if any argument is `null`.

Set Interface's Convenience Factory Method of

Lines 15–16 use the `Set` convenience factory method **of** to create an immutable `Set<String>`. As with `List`'s method of, `Set`'s method of has overloads for `Set`s of zero to 10 elements and an additional overload that can receive any number of elements. Line 17 displays the `String` representation of the `Set`'s contents. Note that we showed two sample outputs of this program and that the order of the `Set`'s elements is *different* in each output. According to the `Set` interface's documentation, the iteration order is *unspecified* for `Set`s returned by the convenience factory methods—as the outputs show, that order can change between executions.

Common Programming Error 16.5

`Set`'s method of throws an `IllegalArgumentException` if any of its arguments are duplicates.

Map Interface's Convenience Factory Method of

Lines 20–22 use `Map`'s convenience factory method **of** to create an immutable `Map<String, Integer>`. As with `List` and `Set`, `Map`'s method of has overloads for `Map`s of zero to 10 key–value pairs. Each pair of arguments (for example, "Monday" and 1 in line 20) represents one key–value pair. For `Map`s with more than 10 key–value pairs, interface `Map` provides the method ofEntries (which we discuss momentarily). Line 23 displays the `String` representation of the `Map`'s contents. According to the `Map` interface's documentation, the iteration order is *unspecified* for the keys in `Map`s returned by the convenience factory methods—as the outputs show, that order can change between program executions.

Common Programming Error 16.6

`Map`'s methods of and ofEntries each throw an `IllegalArgumentException` if any of the keys are duplicates.

Map Interface's Convenience Factory Method ofEntries

Lines 26–39 use the `Map` convenience factory method **ofEntries** to create an immutable `Map<String, Integer>`. Each of this method's variable number of arguments is the result of a call to `Map`'s **static** method **entry**, which creates and returns a **Map.Entry** object representing one key–value pair. Line 40 displays the `String` representation of the `Map`'s contents. The outputs confirm once again that the iteration order of a `Map`'s keys can change between program executions.

16.15 Wrap-Up

This chapter introduced the Java collections framework. You learned the collection hierarchy and how to use the collections-framework interfaces to program with collections polymorphically. You used classes `ArrayList` and `LinkedList`, which both implement the `List` interface. We presented Java's built-in interface and class for manipulating queues. You used several predefined methods for manipulating collections. You learned how to use the `Set` interface and class `HashSet` to manipulate an unordered collection of unique values. We continued our presentation of sets with the `SortedSet` interface and class `TreeSet` for manipulating a sorted collection of unique values. You then learned about Java's interfaces and classes for manipulating key–value pairs—`Map`, `SortedMap`, `HashMap` and `TreeMap`. We discussed the `Collections` class's `static` methods for obtaining unmodifiable and synchronized views of collections. Finally, we introduced Java SE 9's new convenience factory methods for creating immutable `List`s, `Set`s and `Map`s. For additional information, visit `http://docs.oracle.com/javase/8/docs/technotes/guides/collections`.

In Chapter 17, Lambdas and Streams, you'll use Java SE 8's functional programming capabilities to simplify collection operations. In Chapter 21, Concurrency and Multi-Core Performance, you'll learn how to improve performance on multi-core systems using Java's concurrent collections and parallel-stream operations.

Lambdas and Streams

Objectives

In this chapter you'll:

- Learn various functional-programming techniques and how they complement object-oriented programming.
- Use lambdas and streams to simplify tasks that process sequences of elements.
- Learn what streams are and how stream pipelines are formed from stream sources, intermediate operations and terminal operations.
- Create streams representing ranges of int values and random int values.
- Implement functional interfaces with lambdas.
- Perform on IntStreams intermediate operations filter, map, mapToObj and sorted, and terminal operations forEach, count, min, max, sum, average and reduce.
- Perform on Streams intermediate operations distinct, filter, map, mapToDouble and sorted, and terminal operations collect, forEach, findFirst and reduce.
- Process infinite streams.
- Implement event handlers with lambdas.

17.1 Introduction[1]

The way you think about Java programming is about to change profoundly. Prior to Java SE 8, Java supported three programming paradigms—*procedural programming, object-ori-*

---

1. We were privileged to have Brian Goetz, Oracle's Java Language Architect and Specification Lead for Java SE 8's Project Lambda, and co-author of *Java Concurrency in Practice*, do a detailed review of our sister book *Java How to Program, 10/e*. He thoroughly scrutinized the version of this chapter that appeared in that edition and provided many additional suggestions that are reflected in this new edition of *Java 9 for Programmers*. Any remaining faults in the book are our own.

ented programming and *generic programming*. Java SE 8 added *lambdas* and *streams*[2]—key technologies of *functional programming*.

In this chapter, we'll use lambdas and streams to write certain kinds of programs faster, simpler, more concisely and with fewer bugs than with previous techniques. In Chapter 21, Concurrency and Multi-Core Performance, you'll see that such programs can be easier to *parallelize* (i.e., perform multiple operations simultaneously) so that you can take advantage of multi-core architectures to enhance performance—a key goal of lambdas and streams.

Software Engineering Observation 17.1

*You'll see in Chapter 21, Concurrency and Multi-Core Performance, that it's hard to create parallel tasks that operate correctly if those tasks modify a program's state (that is, its variables' values). So the techniques that you'll learn in this chapter focus on **immutability**—not modifying the data source being processed or any other program state.*

This chapter presents many examples of lambdas and streams (Fig. 17.1), beginning with several showing better ways to implement tasks you programmed in Chapter 5. The first several examples are presented in a manner that allows them to be covered in the context of earlier chapters. For this reason, some terminology is discussed later in this chapter. Figure 17.2 shows additional lambdas and streams coverage in later chapters.

Section	May be covered after
Sections 17.2—17.4 introduce basic lambda and streams capabilities that process ranges of integers and eliminate the need for counter-controlled repetition.	Chapter 5, Control Statements: Part 2; Logical Operators
Section 17.6 introduces method references and uses them with lambdas and streams to process ranges of integers	Chapter 6, Methods: A Deeper Look
Section 17.7 presents lambda and streams capabilities that process one-dimensional arrays.	Chapter 7, Arrays and `ArrayLists`
Sections 17.8—17.9 discuss key functional interfaces and additional lambda concepts, and tie these into the chapter's earlier examples. Section 10.10 introduced Java SE 8's enhanced interface features (`default` methods, `static` methods and the concept of functional interfaces) that support functional-programming techniques in Java.	Chapter 10, Object-Oriented Programming: Polymorphism and Interfaces
Section 17.16 shows how to use a lambda to implement a JavaFX event-listener functional interface.	Chapter 12, JavaFX Graphical User Interfaces: Part 1

Fig. 17.1 | This chapter's lambdas and streams discussions and examples. (Part 1 of 2.)

---

2. The streams we discuss in this chapter are not the same as the input/output streams we discuss in Chapter 15, Files, Input/Output Streams, NIO and XML Serialization, in which a program reads a stream of bytes from or writes a stream of bytes to a file. Section 17.13 uses lambdas and streams to manipulate the contents of a file.

Section	May be covered after
Section 17.11 shows how to use lambdas and streams to process collections of `String` objects.	Chapter 14, Strings, Characters and Regular Expressions
Section 17.13 shows how to use lambdas and streams to process lines of text from a file—the example in this section also uses some regular expression capabilities from Chapter 14.	Chapter 15, Files, Input/Output Streams, NIO and XML Serialization

Fig. 17.1 | This chapter's lambdas and streams discussions and examples. (Part 2 of 2.)

Coverage	Chapter
Shows that functional programs are easier to parallelize so that they can take advantage of multi-core architectures to enhance performance. Demonstrates parallel stream processing. Shows that `Arrays` method `parallelSort` can improve performance on multi-core vs. single-core architectures when sorting large arrays.	Chapter 21, Concurrency and Multi-Core Performance
Uses streams to process database query results.	Chapter 24, Java Persistence API (JPA)

Fig. 17.2 | Later lambdas and streams coverage.

17.2 Streams and Reduction

[This section demonstrates how streams can be used to simplify programming tasks that you learned in Chapter 5, Control Statements: Part 2; Logical Operators.]

In counter-controlled iteration, you typically determine *what* you want to accomplish then specify precisely *how* to accomplish it using a `for` loop. In this section, we'll investigate that approach, then show you a better way to accomplish the same tasks.

17.2.1 Summing the Integers from 1 through 10 with a `for` Loop

Let's assume that *what* you want to accomplish is to sum the integers from 1 through 10. In Chapter 5, you saw that you can do this with a counter-controlled loop:

```
int total = 0;

for (int number = 1; number <= 10; number++) {
    total += number;
}
```

This loop specifies precisely *how* to perform the task—with a `for` statement that processes each value of control variable `number` from 1 through 10, adding `number`'s current value to `total` once per loop iteration and incrementing `number` after each addition operation. This is known as **external iteration**, because *you* specify all the iteration details.

17.2.2 External Iteration with for Is Error Prone

Let's consider potential problems with the preceding code. As implemented, the loop requires two variables (total and number) that the code *mutates* (that is, modifies) during each loop iteration. Every time you write code that modifies a variable, it's possible to introduce an error into your code. There are several opportunities for error in the preceding code. For example, you could:

- initialize the variable total incorrectly
- initialize the for loop's control variable number incorrectly
- use the wrong loop-continuation condition
- increment control variable number incorrectly or
- incorrectly add each value of number to the total.

In addition, as the tasks you perform get more complicated, understanding *how* the code works gets in the way of understanding *what* it does. This makes the code harder to read, debug and modify, and more likely to contain errors.

17.2.3 Summing with a Stream and Reduction

Now let's take a different approach, specifying *what* to do rather than *how* to do it. In Fig. 17.3, we specify only *what* we want to accomplish—that is, sum the integers from 1 through 10—then simply let Java's **IntStream** class (package **java.util.stream**) deal with *how* to do it. The key to this program is the following expression in lines 9–10

```
IntStream.rangeClosed(1, 10)
        .sum()
```

which can be read as, "for the stream of int values in the range 1 through 10, calculate the sum" or more simply "sum the numbers from 1 through 10." In this code, notice that there is neither a counter-control variable nor a variable to store the total—this is because IntStream conveniently defines rangeClosed and sum.

```
1   // Fig. 17.3: StreamReduce.java
2   // Sum the integers from 1 through 10 with IntStream.
3   import java.util.stream.IntStream;
4
5   public class StreamReduce {
6      public static void main(String[] args) {
7         // sum the integers from 1 through 10
8         System.out.printf("Sum of 1 through 10 is: %d%n",
9            IntStream.rangeClosed(1, 10)
10                    .sum());
11     }
12  }
```

```
Sum of 1 through 10 is: 55
```

Fig. 17.3 | Sum the integers from 1 through 10 with IntStream.

Streams and Stream Pipelines

The chained method calls in lines 9–10 create a **stream pipeline**. A **stream** is a sequence of elements on which you perform tasks, and the stream pipeline moves the stream's elements through a sequence of tasks (or *processing steps*).

Good Programming Practice 17.1

When using chained method calls, align the dots (.) vertically for readability as we did in lines 9–10 of Fig. 17.3.

Specifying the Data Source

A stream pipeline typically begins with a method call that creates the stream—this is known as the *data source*. Line 9 specifies the data source with the method call

```
IntStream.rangeClosed(1, 10)
```

which creates an IntStream representing an ordered range of int values.

Here, we use the static method **rangeClosed** to create an IntStream containing the ordered sequence of int elements 1, 2, 3, 4, 5, 6, 7, 8, 9 and 10. The method is named rangeClosed, because it produces a *closed range* of values—that is, a range of elements that includes *both* of the method's arguments (1 and 10). IntStream also provides method **range**, which produces a *half-open range* of values from its first argument up to, but not including, its second argument—for example,

```
IntStream.range(1, 10)
```

produces an IntStream containing the ordered sequence of int elements 1, 2, 3, 4, 5, 6, 7, 8 and 9, but *not* 10.

Calculating the Sum of the IntStream's Elements

Next, line 10 completes the stream pipeline with the processing step

```
.sum()
```

This invokes the IntStream's **sum** instance method, which returns the sum of all the ints in the stream—in this case, the sum of the integers from 1 through 10.

The processing step performed by method sum is known as a **reduction**—it reduces the stream of values to a *single* value (the sum). This is one of several predefined IntStream reductions—Section 17.7 presents the predefined reductions count, min, max, average and summaryStatistics, as well as the reduce method for defining your own reductions.

Processing the Stream Pipeline

A **terminal operation** initiates a stream pipeline's processing and produces a result. Int-Stream method sum is a terminal operation that produces the sum of the stream's elements. Similarly, the reductions count, min, max, average, summaryStatistics and reduce are all terminal operations. You'll see other terminal operations throughout this chapter. Section 17.3.3 discusses terminal operations in more detail.

17.2.4 Internal Iteration

The key to the preceding example is that it specifies *what* we want the task to accomplish—calculating the sum of the integers from 1 through 10—rather than *how* to accomplish it. This is an example of **declarative programming** (specifying *what*) vs. **imperative programming** (specifying *how*). We broke the goal into two simple tasks—producing the numbers in a closed range (1–10) and calculating their sum. Internally, the IntStream (that is, the data source itself) already knows how to perform each of these tasks. We did *not* need to specify *how* to iterate through the elements or declare and use *any* mutable variables. This is known as **internal iteration**, because IntStream handles all the iteration details—a key aspect of **functional programming**. Unlike external iteration with the for statement, the primary potential for error in line 9 of Fig. 17.3 is specifying the incorrect starting and/or ending values as arguments. Once you're used to it, stream pipeline code also can be easier to read.

Software Engineering Observation 17.2

Functional-programming techniques enable you to write higher-level code, because many of the details are implemented for you by the Java streams library. Your code becomes more concise, which improves productivity and can help you rapidly prototype programs.

Software Engineering Observation 17.3

Functional-programming techniques eliminate large classes of errors, such as off-by-one errors (because iteration details are hidden from you by the libraries) and incorrectly modifying variables (because you focus on immutability and thus do not modify data). This makes it easier to write correct programs.

17.3 Mapping and Lambdas

[This section demonstrates how streams can be used to simplify programming tasks that you learned in Chapter 5, Control Statements: Part 2; Logical Operators.]

The preceding example specified a stream pipeline containing only a data source and a terminal operation that produced a result. Most stream pipelines also contain **intermediate operations** that specify tasks to perform on a stream's elements before a terminal operation produces a result.

In this example, we introduce a common intermediate operation called **mapping**, which transforms a stream's elements to new values. The result is a stream with the same number of elements containing the transformation's results. Sometimes the mapped elements are of different types from the original stream's elements.

To demonstrate mapping, let's revisit the program of Fig. 5.5 in which we calculated the sum of the even integers from 2 through 20 using external iteration, as follows:

```
int total = 0;

for (int number = 2; number <= 20; number += 2) {
   total += number;
}
```

Figure 17.4 reimplements this task using streams and internal iteration.

```
 1   // Fig. 17.4: StreamMapReduce.java
 2   // Sum the even integers from 2 through 20 with IntStream.
 3   import java.util.stream.IntStream;
 4
 5   public class StreamMapReduce {
 6      public static void main(String[] args) {
 7         // sum the even integers from 2 through 20
 8         System.out.printf("Sum of the even ints from 2 through 20 is: %d%n",
 9            IntStream.rangeClosed(1, 10)              // 1...10
10               .map((int x) -> {return x * 2;}) // multiply by 2
11               .sum());                         // sum
12      }
13   }
```

```
Sum of the even ints from 2 through 20 is: 110
```

Fig. 17.4 | Sum the even integers from 2 through 20 with `IntStream`.

The stream pipeline in lines 9–11 performs three chained method calls:

- Line 9 creates the data source—an `IntStream` containing the elements 1, 2, 3, 4, 5, 6, 7, 8, 9 and 10.

- Line 10, which we'll discuss in detail momentarily, performs a processing step that maps each element (x) in the stream to that element multiplied by 2. The result is a stream of the even integers 2, 4, 6, 8, 10, 12, 14, 16, 18 and 20.

- Line 11 reduces the stream's elements to a single value—the sum of the elements. This is the terminal operation that initiates the pipeline's processing, then sums the stream's elements.

The new feature here is the mapping operation in line 10, which in this case multiplies each stream element by 2. `IntStream` method **map** receives as its argument (line 10)

```
(int x) -> {return x * 2;}
```

which you'll see in the next section is an alternate notation for "a *method* that receives an `int` parameter x and returns that value multiplied by 2." For each element in the stream, map calls this method, passing to it the current stream element. The method's return value becomes part of the new stream that map returns.

17.3.1 Lambda Expressions

As you'll see throughout this chapter, many intermediate and terminal stream operations receive methods as arguments. Method map's argument in line 10

```
(int x) -> {return x * 2;}
```

is called a **lambda expression** (or simply a **lambda**), which represents an *anonymous method*—that is, a *method without a name*. Though a lambda expression's syntax does not look like the methods you've seen previously, the left side does look like a method parameter list and the right side does look like a method body. We explain the syntax details shortly.

Lambda expressions enable you to create methods that can be treated as data. You can:

- pass lambdas as arguments to other methods (like map, or even other lambdas)
- assign lambda expressions to variables for later use and
- return lambda expressions from methods.

You'll see that these are powerful capabilities.

Software Engineering Observation 17.4

Lambdas and streams enable you to combine many benefits of functional-programming techniques with the benefits of object-oriented programming.

17.3.2 Lambda Syntax

A lambda consists of a *parameter list* followed by the **arrow token** (->) and a body, as in:

```
(parameterList) -> {statements}
```

The lambda in line 10

```
(int x) -> {return x * 2;}
```

receives an int, multiplies its value by 2 and returns the result. In this case, the body is a *statement block* that may contain statements enclosed in curly braces. The compiler *infers* from the lambda that it returns an int, because the parameter x is an int and the literal 2 is an int—multiplying an int by an int yields an int result. As in a method declaration, lambdas specify parameters in a comma-separated list. The preceding lambda is similar to the method

```
int multiplyBy2(int x) {
    return x * 2;
}
```

but the lambda does not have a name and the compiler infers its return type. There are several variations of the lambda syntax.

Eliminating a Lambda's Parameter Type(s)
A lambda's parameter type(s) usually may be omitted, as in:

```
(x) -> {return x * 2;}
```

in which case, the compiler infers the parameter and return types by the lambda's context—we'll say more about this later. If for any reason the compiler cannot infer the parameter or return types (e.g., if there are multiple type possibilities), it generates an error.

Simplifying the Lambda's Body
If the body contains only one expression, the return keyword, curly braces and semicolon may be omitted, as in:

```
(x) -> x * 2
```

In this case, the lambda *implicitly* returns the expression's value.

Simplifying the Lambda's Parameter List
If the parameter list contains only one parameter, the parentheses may be omitted, as in:

```
x -> x * 2
```

Lambdas with Empty Parameter Lists
To define a lambda with an empty parameter list, use empty parentheses to the left of the arrow token (->), as in:

```
() -> System.out.println("Welcome to lambdas!")
```

Method References
In addition, to the preceding lambda-syntax variations, there are specialized shorthand forms of lambdas that are known as *method references*, which we introduce in Section 17.6.

17.3.3 Intermediate and Terminal Operations

In the stream pipeline shown in lines 9–11, map is an intermediate operation and sum is a terminal operation. Method map is one of many intermediate operations that specify tasks to perform on a stream's elements.

Lazy and Eager Operations
Intermediate operations use **lazy evaluation**—each intermediate operation results in a new stream object, but does not perform any operations on the stream's elements until a terminal operation is called to produce a result. This allows library developers to optimize stream-processing performance. For example, if you have 1,000,000 Person objects and you're looking for the *first* one with the last name "Jones", rather than processing all 1,000,000 elements, stream processing can terminate as soon as the first matching Person object is found.

Performance Tip 17.1
Lazy evaluation helps improve performance by ensuring that operations are performed only if necessary.

Terminal operations are **eager**—they perform the requested operation when they're called. We say more about lazy and eager operations as we encounter them throughout the chapter. You'll see how lazy operations can improve performance in Section 17.5, which discusses how a stream pipeline's intermediate operations are applied to each stream element. Figures 17.5 and 17.6 show some common intermediate and terminal operations, respectively.

Common intermediate stream operations	
filter	Returns a stream containing only the elements that satisfy a condition (known as a *predicate*). The new stream often has fewer elements than the original stream.
distinct	Returns a stream containing only the unique elements—duplicates are eliminated.
limit	Returns a stream with the specified number of elements from the beginning of the original stream.

Fig. 17.5 | Common intermediate stream operations. (Part 1 of 2.)

Common intermediate stream operations	
map	Returns a stream in which each of the original stream's elements is mapped to a new value (possibly of a different type)—for example, mapping numeric values to the squares of the numeric values or mapping numeric grades to letter grades (A, B C, D or F). The new stream has the same number of elements as the original stream.
sorted	Returns a stream in which the elements are in sorted order. The new stream has the same number of elements as the original stream. We'll show how to specify both ascending and descending order.

Fig. 17.5 | Common intermediate stream operations. (Part 2 of 2.)

Common terminal stream operations	
forEach	Performs processing on every element in a stream (for example, display each element).
Reduction operations—*Take all values in the stream and return a single value*	
average	Returns the *average* of the elements in a numeric stream.
count	Returns the *number of elements* in the stream.
max	Returns the *maximum* value in a stream.
min	Returns the *minimum* value in a stream.
reduce	Reduces the elements of a collection to a *single value* using an associative accumulation function (for example, a lambda that adds two elements and returns the sum).

Fig. 17.6 | Common terminal stream operations.

17.4 Filtering

[This section demonstrates how streams can be used to simplify programming tasks that you learned in Chapter 5, Control Statements: Part 2; Logical Operators.]

Another common intermediate stream operation is *filtering* elements to select those that match a condition—known as a *predicate*. For example, the following code selects the even integers in the range 1–10, multiplies each by 3 and sums the results:

```
int total = 0;

for (int x = 1; x <= 10; x++) {
   if (x % 2 == 0) { // if x is even
      total += x * 3;
   }
}
```

Figure 17.7 reimplements this loop using streams.

```
 1    // Fig. 17.7: StreamFilterMapReduce.java
 2    // Triple the even ints from 2 through 10 then sum them with IntStream.
 3    import java.util.stream.IntStream;
 4
 5    public class StreamFilterMapReduce {
 6       public static void main(String[] args) {
 7          // sum the triples of the even integers from 2 through 10
 8          System.out.printf(
 9             "Sum of the triples of the even ints from 2 through 10 is: %d%n",
10             IntStream.rangeClosed(1, 10)
11                .filter(x -> x % 2 == 0)
12                .map(x -> x * 3)
13                .sum());
14       }
15    }
```

```
Sum of the triples of the even ints from 2 through 10 is: 90
```

Fig. 17.7 | Triple the even ints from 2 through 10 then sum them with IntStream.

The stream pipeline in lines 10–13 performs four chained method calls:

- Line 10 creates the data source—an IntStream for the closed range 1 through 10.

- Line 11, which we'll discuss in detail momentarily, filters the stream's elements by selecting only the elements that are divisible by 2 (that is, the even integers), producing a stream of the even integers from 2, 4, 6, 8 and 10.

- Line 12 maps each element (x) in the stream to that element times 3, producing a stream of the even integers from 6, 12, 18, 24 and 30.

- Line 13 reduces the stream to the sum of its elements (90).

The new feature here is the filtering operation in line 11. IntStream method **filter** receives as its argument a method that takes one parameter and returns a boolean result. If the result is true for a given element, that element is included in the resulting stream.
The lambda in line 11:

```
x -> x % 2 == 0
```

determines whether its int argument is divisible by 2 (that is, the remainder after dividing by 2 is 0) and, if so, returns true; otherwise, the lambda returns false. For each element in the stream, filter calls the method that it receives as an argument, passing to the method the current stream element. If the method's return value is true, the corresponding element becomes part of the intermediate stream that filter returns.

Line 11 creates an intermediate stream representing only the elements that are divisible by 2. Next, line 12 uses map to create an intermediate stream representing the even integers (2, 4, 6, 8 and 10) that are multiplied by 3 (6, 12, 18, 24 and 30). Line 13 initiates the stream processing with a call to the *terminal* operation sum. At this point, the combined processing steps are applied to each element, then sum returns the total of the elements that remain in the stream. We discuss this further in the next section.

Error-Prevention Tip 17.1

The order of the operations in a stream pipeline matters. For example, filtering *the even numbers from 1–10 yields 2, 4, 6, 8, 10, then* mapping *them to twice their values yields 4, 8, 12, 16 and 20. On the other hand,* mapping *the numbers from 1–10 to twice their values yields 2, 4, 6, 8, 10, 12, 14, 16, 18 and 20, then* filtering *the even numbers gives all of those values, because they're all even before the* filter *operation is performed.*

The stream pipeline shown in this example could have been implemented by using only map and sum.

17.5 How Elements Move Through Stream Pipelines

Section 17.3 mentioned that each intermediate operation results in a new stream. Each new stream is simply an object representing the processing steps that have been specified to that point in the pipeline. Chaining intermediate-operation method calls adds to the set of processing steps to perform on each stream element. The last stream object in the stream pipeline contains all the processing steps to perform on each stream element.

When you initiate a stream pipeline with a terminal operation, the intermediate operations' processing steps are applied for a given stream element *before* they are applied to the next stream element. So the stream pipeline in Fig. 17.7 operates as follows:

> *For each element*
> > *If the element is an even integer*
> > > *Multiply the element by 3 and add the result to the total*

To prove this, consider a modified version of Fig. 17.7's stream pipeline in which each lambda displays the intermediate operation's name and the current stream element's value:

```
IntStream.rangeClosed(1, 10)
    .filter(
        x -> {
            System.out.printf("%nfilter: %d%n", x);
            return x % 2 == 0;
        })
    .map(
        x -> {
            System.out.println("map: " + x);
            return x * 3;
        })
    .sum()
```

The modified pipeline's output below (we added the comments) clearly shows that each even integer's map step is applied *before* the next stream element's filter step:

```
filter: 1 // odd so no map step is performed for this element

filter: 2 // even so a map step is performed next
map: 2

filter: 3 // odd so no map step is performed for this element

filter: 4 // even so a map step is performed next
map: 4
```

```
filter: 5 // odd so no map step is performed for this element

filter: 6 // even so a map step is performed next
map: 6

filter: 7 // odd so no map step is performed for this element

filter: 8 // even so a map step is performed next
map: 8

filter: 9 // odd so no map step is performed for this element

filter: 10 // even so a map step is performed next
map: 10
```

For the odd elements, the map step was *not* performed. When a filter step returns false, the element's remaining processing steps are *ignored* because that element is not included in the results. (This version of Fig. 17.7 is located in a subfolder with that example.)

17.6 Method References

[This section demonstrates how streams can be used to simplify programming tasks that you learned in Chapter 6, Methods: A Deeper Look.]

For a lambda that simply calls another method, you can replace the lambda with that method's name—known as a **method reference**. The compiler converts a method reference into an appropriate lambda expression.

Like Fig. 6.5, Fig. 17.8 uses SecureRandom to obtain random numbers in the range 1–6. The program uses streams to create the random values and method references to help display the results. We walk through the code in Sections 17.6.1—17.6.4.

```
1   // Fig. 17.8: RandomIntegers.java
2   // Shifted and scaled random integers.
3   import java.security.SecureRandom;
4   import java.util.stream.Collectors;
5
6   public class RandomIntegers {
7      public static void main(String[] args) {
8         SecureRandom randomNumbers = new SecureRandom();
9
10        // display 10 random integers on separate lines
11        System.out.println("Random numbers on separate lines:");
12        randomNumbers.ints(10, 1, 7)
13                    .forEach(System.out::println);
14
15        // display 10 random integers on the same line
16        String numbers =
17           randomNumbers.ints(10, 1, 7)
18                       .mapToObj(String::valueOf)
19                       .collect(Collectors.joining(" "));
```

Fig. 17.8 | Shifted and scaled random integers. (Part 1 of 2.)

```
20            System.out.printf("%nRandom numbers on one line: %s%n", numbers);
21
22      }
23   }
```

```
Random numbers on separate lines:
4
3
4
5
1
5
5
3
6
5

Random numbers on one line: 4 6 2 5 6 4 3 2 4 1
```

Fig. 17.8 | Shifted and scaled random integers. (Part 2 of 2.)

17.6.1 Creating an IntStream of Random Values

Class SecureRandom's **ints** method returns an IntStream of random numbers. In the stream pipeline of lines 12–13

```
randomNumbers.ints(10, 1, 7)
```

creates an IntStream data source with the specified number of random int values (10) in the range starting with the first argument (1) up to, but not including, the second argument (7). So, line 12 produces an IntStream of 10 random integers in the range 1–6.

17.6.2 Performing a Task on Each Stream Element with forEach and a Method Reference

Next, line 13 of the stream pipeline uses IntStream method **forEach** (a terminal operation) to perform a task on each stream element. Method forEach receives as its argument a method that takes one parameter and performs a task using the parameter's value.

The argument to forEach

```
System.out::println
```

in this case is a method reference—a shorthand notation for a lambda that calls the specified method. A method reference of the form

```
objectName::instanceMethodName
```

is a **bound instance method reference**—"bound" means the *specific* object to the left of the :: (System.out) *must* be used to call the instance method to the right of the :: (println).

The compiler converts System.out::println into a one-parameter lambda like

```
x -> System.out.println(x)
```

that passes the lambda's argument—the current stream element (represented by x)—to the `System.out` object's `println` instance method, which implicitly outputs the `String` representation of the argument. The stream pipeline of lines 12–13 is equivalent to the following for loop:

```
for (int i = 1; i <= 10; i++) {
    System.out.println(1 + randomNumbers.nextInt(6));
}
```

17.6.3 Mapping Integers to String Objects with `mapToObj`

The stream pipeline in lines 16–19

```
String numbers =
    randomNumbers.ints(10, 1, 7)
                .mapToObj(String::valueOf)
                .collect(Collectors.joining(" "));
```

creates a `String` containing 10 random integers in the range 1–6 separated by spaces. The pipeline performs three chained method calls:

- Line 17 creates the data source—an `IntStream` of 10 random integers from 1–6.

- Line 18 maps each `int` to its `String` representation, resulting in an intermediate stream of `Strings`. The `IntStream` method `map` that we've used previously returns another `IntStream`. To map to `Strings`, we use instead the `IntStream` method **`mapToObj`**, which enables you to map from `ints` to a stream of reference-type elements. Like `map`, `mapToObject` expects a one-parameter method that returns a result. In this example, `mapToObj`'s argument is a **static method reference** of the form *ClassName*::*staticMethodName*. The compiler converts `String::valueOf` (which returns its argument's `String` representation) into a one-parameter lambda that calls `valueOf`, passing the current stream element as an argument, as in

```
x -> String.valueOf(x)
```

- Line 19, which we discuss in more detail in Section 17.6.4, uses the `Stream` terminal operation **`collect`** to concatenate all the `Strings`, separating each from the next with a space. Method `collect` is a form of reduction because it returns one object—in this case, a `String`.

Line 20 then displays the resulting `String`.

17.6.4 Concatenating Strings with `collect`

Consider line 19 of Fig. 17.8. The `Stream` terminal operation `collect` uses a *collector* to gather the stream's elements into a single object—often a collection. This is similar to a reduction, but `collect` returns an object containing the stream's elements, whereas `reduce` returns a single value of the stream's element type. In this example, we use a pre-defined collector returned by the `static` **`Collectors`** method **`joining`**. This collector creates a concatenated `String` representation of the stream's elements, appending each element to the `String` separated from the previous element by the `joining` method's argument (in this case, a space). Method `collect` then returns the resulting `String`. We discuss other collectors throughout this chapter.

17.7 IntStream Operations

[This section demonstrates how lambdas and streams can be used to simplify programming tasks like those you learned in Chapter 7, Arrays and ArrayLists.]

Figure 17.9 demonstrates additional IntStream operations on streams created from arrays. The IntStream techniques shown in this and the prior examples also apply to **LongStreams** and **DoubleStreams** for long and double values, respectively. We walk through the code in Sections 17.7.1—17.7.4.

```java
 1   // Fig. 17.9: IntStreamOperations.java
 2   // Demonstrating IntStream operations.
 3   import java.util.Arrays;
 4   import java.util.stream.Collectors;
 5   import java.util.stream.IntStream;
 6
 7   public class IntStreamOperations {
 8      public static void main(String[] args) {
 9         int[] values = {3, 10, 6, 1, 4, 8, 2, 5, 9, 7};
10
11         // display original values
12         System.out.print("Original values: ");
13         System.out.println(
14            IntStream.of(values)
15                     .mapToObj(String::valueOf)
16                     .collect(Collectors.joining(" ")));
17
18         // count, min, max, sum and average of the values
19         System.out.printf("%nCount: %d%n", IntStream.of(values).count());
20         System.out.printf("Min: %d%n",
21            IntStream.of(values).min().getAsInt());
22         System.out.printf("Max: %d%n",
23            IntStream.of(values).max().getAsInt());
24         System.out.printf("Sum: %d%n", IntStream.of(values).sum());
25         System.out.printf("Average: %.2f%n",
26            IntStream.of(values).average().getAsDouble());
27
28         // sum of values with reduce method
29         System.out.printf("%nSum via reduce method: %d%n",
30            IntStream.of(values)
31                     .reduce(0, (x, y) -> x + y));
32
33         // product of values with reduce method
34         System.out.printf("Product via reduce method: %d%n",
35            IntStream.of(values)
36                     .reduce((x, y) -> x * y).getAsInt());
37
38         // sum of squares of values with map and sum methods
39         System.out.printf("Sum of squares via map and sum: %d%n%n",
40            IntStream.of(values)
41                     .map(x -> x * x)
42                     .sum());
```

Fig. 17.9 | Demonstrating IntStream operations. (Part 1 of 2.)

```
43
44          // displaying the elements in sorted order
45          System.out.printf("Values displayed in sorted order: %s%n",
46              IntStream.of(values)
47                      .sorted()
48                      .mapToObj(String::valueOf)
49                      .collect(Collectors.joining(" ")));
50      }
51  }
```

```
Original values: 3 10 6 1 4 8 2 5 9 7

Count: 10
Min: 1
Max: 10
Sum: 55
Average: 5.50

Sum via reduce method: 55
Product via reduce method: 3628800
Sum of squares via map and sum: 385

Values displayed in sorted order: 1 2 3 4 5 6 7 8 9 10
```

Fig. 17.9 | Demonstrating `IntStream` operations. (Part 2 of 2.)

17.7.1 Creating an IntStream and Displaying Its Values

IntStream static method **of** (line 14) receives an `int` array argument and returns an Int-Stream for processing the array's values. The stream pipeline in lines 14–16

```
IntStream.of(values)
        .mapToObj(String::valueOf)
        .collect(Collectors.joining(" ")));
```

displays the stream's elements. First, line 14 creates an `IntStream` for the `values` array, then lines 15–16 use the `mapToObj` and `collect` methods as shown Fig. 17.8 to obtain a `String` representation of the stream's elements separated by spaces. We use this technique several times in this example and subsequent examples to display stream elements.

This example repeatedly creates an `IntStream` from the array `values` using:

```
IntStream.of(values)
```

You might think that we could simply store the stream and reuse it. However, once a stream pipeline is processed with a terminal operation, *the stream cannot be reused*, because it does not maintain a copy of the original data source.

17.7.2 Terminal Operations count, min, max, sum and average

Class `IntStream` provides various terminal operations for common stream reductions on streams of `int` values:

- **count** (line 19) returns the number of elements in the stream.
- **min** (line 21) returns an **OptionalInt** (package `java.util`) possibly containing the smallest `int` in the stream. For any stream, it's possible that there are *no ele-*

ments in the stream. Returning OptionalInt enables method min to return the minimum value if the stream contains *at least one element*. In this example, we know the stream has 10 elements, so we call class OptionalInt's **getAsInt** method to obtain the minimum value. If there were no *elements*, the OptionalInt would not contain an int and getAsInt would throw a NoSuchElementException. To prevent this, you can instead call method **orElse**, which returns the OptionalInt's value if there is one, or the value you pass to orElse, otherwise.

- **max** (line 23) returns an OptionalInt possibly containing the largest int in the stream. Again, we call the OptionalInt's getAsInt method to get the largest value, because we know this stream contains elements.

- **sum** (line 24) returns the sum of all the ints in the stream.

- **average** (line 26) returns an **OptionalDouble** (package java.util) possibly containing the average of the ints in the stream as a value of type double. In this example, we know the stream has elements, so we call class OptionalDouble's **getAsDouble** method to obtain the average. If there were no *elements*, the OptionalDouble would not contain the average and getAsDouble would throw a NoSuchElementException. As with OptionalInt, to prevent this exception, you can instead call method **orElse**, which returns the OptionalDouble's value if there is one, or the value you pass to orElse, otherwise.

Class IntStream also provides method **summaryStatistics** that performs the count, min, max, sum and average operations *in one pass* of an IntStream's elements and returns the results as an **IntSummaryStatistics** object (package java.util). This provides a significant performance boost over reprocessing an IntStream repeatedly for each individual operation. This object has methods for obtaining each result and a toString method that summarizes all the results. For example, the statement:

```
System.out.println(IntStream.of(values).summaryStatistics());
```

produces:

```
IntSummaryStatistics{count=10, sum=55, min=1, average=5.500000,
max=10}
```

for the array values in Fig. 17.9.

17.7.3 Terminal Operation reduce

So far, we've presented various predefined IntStream reductions. You can define your own reductions via an IntStream's **reduce** method—in fact, each terminal operation discussed in Section 17.7.2 is a specialized implementation of reduce. The stream pipeline in lines 30–31

```
IntStream.of(values)
         .reduce(0, (x, y) -> x + y)
```

shows how to total an IntStream's values using reduce, rather than sum.

The first argument to reduce (0) is the operation's **identity value**—a value that, when combined with any stream element (using the lambda in the reduce's second argument), produces the element's original value. For example, when summing the elements, the identity value is 0, because any int value added to 0 results in the original int value. Similarly, when getting the product of the elements the identity value is 1, because any int value multiplied by 1 results in the original int value.

Method reduce's second argument is a method that receives two int values (representing the left and right operands of a binary operator), performs a calculation with the values and returns the result. The lambda

```
(x, y) -> x + y
```

adds the values. A lambda with two or more parameters *must* enclose them in parentheses.

Error-Prevention Tip 17.2

The operation specified by a reduce's argument must be associative—that is, the order in which reduce applies the operation to the stream's elements must not matter. This is important, because reduce is allowed to apply its operation to the stream elements in any order. A non-associative operation could yield different results based on the processing order. For example, subtraction is not an associative operation—the expression 7 − (5 − 3) yields 5 whereas the expression (7 − 5) − 3 yields −1. Associative reduce operations are critical for parallel streams (Chapter 21) that split operations across multiple cores for better performance.

Based on the stream's elements

```
3 10 6 1 4 8 2 5 9 7
```

the reduction's evaluation proceeds as follows:

```
0 + 3 --> 3
3 + 10 --> 13
13 + 6 --> 19
19 + 1 --> 20
20 + 4 --> 24
24 + 8 --> 32
32 + 2 --> 34
34 + 5 --> 39
39 + 9 --> 48
48 + 7 --> 55
```

Notice that the first calculation uses the identity value (0) as the left operand and each subsequent calculation uses the result of the prior calculation as the left operand. The reduction process continues producing a running total of the IntStream's values until they've all been used, at which point the final sum is returned.

Calculating the Product of the Values with Method reduce
The stream pipeline in lines 35–36

```
IntStream.of(values)
         .reduce((x, y) -> x * y).getAsInt()
```

uses the one-argument version of method reduce, which returns an OptionalInt that, if the stream has elements, contains the product of the IntStream's values; otherwise, the OptionalInt does not contain a result.

Based on the stream's elements

```
3 10 6 1 4 8 2 5 9 7
```

the reduction's evaluation proceeds as follows:

```
3 * 10 --> 30
30 * 6 --> 180
180 * 1 --> 180
180 * 4 --> 720
720 * 8 --> 5,760
5,760 * 2 --> 11,520
11,520 * 5 --> 57,600
57,600 * 9 --> 518,400
518,400 * 7 --> 3,628,800
```

This process continues producing a running product of the IntStream's values until they've all been used, at which point the final product is returned.

We could have used the two-parameter reduce method, as in:

```
IntStream.of(values)
        .reduce(1, (x, y) -> x * y)
```

However, if the stream were empty, this version of reduce would return the identity value (1), which would not be the expected result for an empty stream.

Summing the Squares of the Values

Now consider summing the squares of the stream's elements. When implementing your stream pipelines, it's helpful to break down the processing steps into easy-to-understand tasks. Summing the squares of the stream's elements requires two distinct tasks:

- squaring the value of each stream element
- summing the resulting values.

Rather than defining this with a reduce method call, the stream pipeline in lines 40–42

```
IntStream.of(values)
        .map(x -> x * x)
        .sum());
```

uses the map and sum methods to compose the sum-of-squares operation. First map produces a new IntStream containing the original element's squares, then sum totals the resulting stream's elements.

17.7.4 Sorting IntStream Values

In Section 7.15, you learned how to sort arrays with the sort static method of class Arrays. You also may sort the elements of a stream. The stream pipeline in lines 46–49

```
IntStream.of(values)
        .sorted()
        .mapToObj(String::valueOf)
        .collect(Collectors.joining(" ")));
```

sorts the stream's elements and displays each value followed by a space. IntStream intermediate operation **sorted** orders the elements of the stream into *ascending* order by default. Like filter, sorted is a *lazy* operation that's performed only when a terminal operation initiates the stream pipeline's processing.

17.8 Functional Interfaces

[This section requires the interface concepts introduced in Sections 10.9—10.10.]
Section 10.10 introduced Java SE 8's enhanced interface features—`default` methods and
`static` methods—and discussed the concept of a *functional interface*—an interface that
contains exactly one `abstract` method (and may also contain `default` and `static` methods). Such interfaces are also known as *single abstract method* (SAM) interfaces. Functional
interfaces are used extensively in functional-style Java programming. Functional programmers work with so-called *pure functions* that have *referential transparency*—that is, they:

- depend only on their parameters
- have no side-effects and
- do not maintain any state.

In Java, pure functions are methods that implement functional interfaces—typically defined as lambdas, like those you've seen so far in this chapter's examples. State changes occur by passing data from method to method. No data is shared.

> **Software Engineering Observation 17.5**
>
> *Pure functions are safer because they do not modify a program's state (variables). This also makes them less error prone and thus easier to test, modify and debug.*

Functional Interfaces in Package `java.util.function`

Package `java.util.function` contains several functional interfaces. Figure 17.10 shows
the six basic generic functional interfaces, several of which you've already used in this chapter's examples. Throughout the table, `T` and `R` are generic type names that represent the
type of the object on which the functional interface operates and the return type of a method, respectively. Many other functional interfaces in package `java.util.function` are
specialized versions of those in Fig. 17.10. Most are for use with `int`, `long` and `double`
primitive values. There are also generic customizations of `Consumer`, `Function` and `Predicate` for binary operations—that is, methods that take two arguments. For each `IntStream` method we've shown that receives a lambda, the method's parameter is actually an
`int`-specialized version of one of these interfaces.

Interface	Description
`BinaryOperator<T>`	Represents a method that takes two parameters of the same type and returns a value of that type. Performs a task using the parameters (such as a calculation) and returns the result. The lambdas you passed to `IntStream` method `reduce` (Section 17.7) implemented `IntBinaryOperator`—an `int` specific version of `BinaryOperator`.
`Consumer<T>`	Represents a one-parameter method that returns `void`. Performs a task using its parameter, such as outputting the object, invoking a method of the object, etc. The lambda you passed to `IntStream` method `forEach` (Section 17.6) implemented interface `IntConsumer`—an `int`-specialized version of `Consumer`. Later sections present several more examples of `Consumers`.

Fig. 17.10 | The six basic generic functional interfaces in package `java.util.function`.

Interface	Description
Function<T,R>	Represents a one-parameter method that performs a task on the parameter and returns a result—possibly of a different type than the parameter. The lambda you passed to IntStream method mapToObj (Section 17.6) implemented interface IntFunction—an int-specialized version of Function. Later sections present several more examples of Functions.
Predicate<T>	Represents a one-parameter method that returns a boolean result. Determines whether the parameter satisfies a condition. The lambda you passed to IntStream method filter (Section 17.4) implemented interface IntPredicate—an int-specialized version of Predicate. Later sections present several more examples of Predicates.
Supplier<T>	Represents a no-parameter method that returns a result. Often used to create a collection object in which a stream operation's results are placed. You'll see several examples of Suppliers starting in Section 17.13.
UnaryOperator<T>	Represents a one-parameter method that returns a result of the same type as its parameter. The lambdas you passed in Section 17.3 to IntStream method map implemented IntUnaryOperator—an int-specialized version of UnaryOperator. Later sections present several more examples of UnaryOperators.

Fig. 17.10 | The six basic generic functional interfaces in package `java.util.function`.

17.9 Lambdas: A Deeper Look

Type Inference and a Lambda's Target Type

Lambda expressions can be used anywhere functional interfaces are expected. The Java compiler can usually *infer* the types of a lambda's parameters and the type returned by a lambda from the context in which the lambda is used. This is determined by the lambda's **target type**—the functional-interface type that's expected where the lambda appears in the code. For example, in the call to IntStream method map from stream pipeline in Fig. 17.4

```
IntStream.rangeClosed(1, 10)
        .map((int x) -> {return x * 2;})
        .sum()
```

the target type is IntUnaryOperator, which represents a method that takes one int parameter and returns an int result. In this case, the lambda parameter's type is explicitly declared to be int and the compiler *infers* the lambda's return type as int, because that's what an IntUnaryOperator requires.

The compiler also can *infer* a lambda parameter's type. For example, in the call to IntStream method filter from stream pipeline in Fig. 17.7

```
IntStream.rangeClosed(1, 10)
        .filter(x -> x % 2 == 0)
        .map(x -> x * 3)
        .sum()
```

the target type is IntPredicate, which represents a method that takes one int parameter and returns a boolean result. In this case, the compiler *infers* the lambda parameter x's type as int, because that's what an IntPredicate requires. We generally let the compiler *infer* the lambda parameter's type in our examples.

Scope and Lambdas

Unlike methods, lambdas do not have their own scope. So, for example, you cannot shadow an enclosing method's local variables with lambda parameters that have the same names. A compilaton error occurs in this case, because the method's local variables and the lambda parameters are in the *same* scope.

Capturing Lambdas and final Local Variables

A lambda that refers to a local variable from the enclosing method (known as the lambda's *lexical scope*) is a **capturing lambda**. For such a lambda, the compiler captures the local variable's value and stores it with the lambda to ensure that the lambda can use the value when the lambda *eventually* executes. This is important, because you can pass a lambda to another method that executes the lambda *after* its lexical scope *no longer exists*.

Any local variable that a lambda references in its lexical scope must be final. Such a variable either can be explicitly declared final or it can be *effectively final* (Java SE 8). For an effectively final variable, the compiler *infers* that the local variable could have been declared final, because its enclosing method never modifies the variable after it's declared and initialized.

17.10 Stream<Integer> Manipulations

[This section requires the interface concepts introduced in Sections 10.9—10.10.]
So far, we've processed IntStreams. A **Stream** performs tasks on reference-type objects. IntStream is simply an int-optimized Stream that provides methods for common int operations. Figure 17.11 performs *filtering* and *sorting* on a Stream<Integer>, using techniques similar to those in prior examples, and shows how to place a stream pipeline's results into a new collection for subsequent processing. We'll work with Streams of other reference types in subsequent examples.

```java
 1   // Fig. 17.11: ArraysAndStreams.java
 2   // Demonstrating lambdas and streams with an array of Integers.
 3   import java.util.Arrays;
 4   import java.util.List;
 5   import java.util.stream.Collectors;
 6
 7   public class ArraysAndStreams {
 8      public static void main(String[] args) {
 9         Integer[] values = {2, 9, 5, 0, 3, 7, 1, 4, 8, 6};
10
11         // display original values
12         System.out.printf("Original values: %s%n", Arrays.asList(values));
13
```

Fig. 17.11 | Demonstrating lambdas and streams with an array of Integers. (Part 1 of 2.)

```
14          // sort values in ascending order with streams
15          System.out.printf("Sorted values: %s%n",
16             Arrays.stream(values)
17                .sorted()
18                .collect(Collectors.toList()));
19
20          // values greater than 4
21          List<Integer> greaterThan4 =
22             Arrays.stream(values)
23                .filter(value -> value > 4)
24                .collect(Collectors.toList());
25          System.out.printf("Values greater than 4: %s%n", greaterThan4);
26
27          // filter values greater than 4 then sort the results
28          System.out.printf("Sorted values greater than 4: %s%n",
29             Arrays.stream(values)
30                .filter(value -> value > 4)
31                .sorted()
32                .collect(Collectors.toList()));
33
34          // greaterThan4 List sorted with streams
35          System.out.printf(
36             "Values greater than 4 (ascending with streams): %s%n",
37             greaterThan4.stream()
38                .sorted()
39                .collect(Collectors.toList()));
40       }
41    }
```

```
Original values: [2, 9, 5, 0, 3, 7, 1, 4, 8, 6]
Sorted values: [0, 1, 2, 3, 4, 5, 6, 7, 8, 9]
Values greater than 4: [9, 5, 7, 8, 6]
Sorted values greater than 4: [5, 6, 7, 8, 9]
Values greater than 4 (ascending with streams): [5, 6, 7, 8, 9]
```

Fig. 17.11 | Demonstrating lambdas and streams with an array of Integers. (Part 2 of 2.)

Throughout this example, we use the Integer array values (line 9) that's initialized with int values—the compiler *boxes* each int into an Integer object. Line 12 displays the contents of values before we perform any stream processing. Arrays method **asList** creates a List<Integer> view of the values array. The generic interface List (discussed in more detail in Chapter 16) is implemented by collections like ArrayList (Chapter 7). Line 12 displays the List<Integer>'s default String representation, which consists of square brackets ([and]) containing a comma-separated list of elements—we use this String representation throughout the example. We walk through the remainder of the code in Sections 17.10.1—17.10.5.

17.10.1 Creating a Stream<Integer>

Class Arrays **stream** method can be used to create a Stream from an array of objects—for example, line 16 produces a Stream<Integer>, because stream's argument is an array of Integers. Interface **Stream** (package java.util.stream) is a generic interface for performing stream operations on any *reference* type. The types of objects that are processed are determined by the Stream's source.

Class Arrays also provides overloaded versions of method stream for creating Int-Streams, LongStreams and DoubleStreams from int, long and double arrays or from ranges of elements in the arrays.

17.10.2 Sorting a Stream and Collecting the Results

The stream pipeline in lines 16–18

```
Arrays.stream(values)
       .sorted()
       .collect(Collectors.toList())
```

uses stream techniques to sort the values array and collect the results in a List<Integer>. First, line 16 creates a Stream<Integer> from values. Next, line 17 calls Stream method sorted to sort the elements—this results in an intermediate Stream<Integer> with the values in *ascending* order. (Section 17.11.3 discusses how to sort in descending order.)

Creating a New Collection Containing a Stream Pipeline's Results

When processing streams, you often create *new* collections containing the results so that you can perform operations on them later. To do so, you can use Stream's terminal operation **collect** (Fig. 17.11, line 18). As the stream pipeline is processed, method collect performs a **mutable reduction operation** that creates a List, Map or Set and modifies it by placing the stream pipeline's results into the collection. You may also use the mutable reduction operation **toArray** to place the results in a new array of the Stream's element type.

The version of method collect in line 18 receives as its argument an object that implements interface **Collector** (package java.util.stream), which specifies how to perform the mutable reduction. Class Collectors (package java.util.stream) provides static methods that return predefined Collector implementations. Collectors method **toList** (line 18) returns a Collector that places the Stream<Integer>'s elements into a List<Integer> collection. In lines 15–18, the resulting List<Integer> is displayed with an *implicit* call to its toString method.

A mutable reduction optionally performs a final data transformation. For example, in Fig. 17.8, we called IntStream method collect with the object returned by Collectors method joining. Behind the scenes, this Collector used a **StringJoiner** (package java.util) to concatenate the stream elements' String representations, then called the StringJoiner's toString method to transform the result into a String. We show additional Collectors in Section 17.12. For more predefined Collectors, visit:

```
https://docs.oracle.com/javase/8/docs/api/java/util/stream/
    Collectors.html
```

17.10.3 Filtering a Stream and Storing the Results for Later Use

The stream pipline in lines 21–24 of Fig. 17.11

```
List<Integer> greaterThan4 =
    Arrays.stream(values)
          .filter(value -> value > 4)
          .collect(Collectors.toList());
```

creates a Stream<Integer>, filters the stream to locate all the values greater than 4 and collects the results into a List<Integer>. Stream method filter's lambda argument implements the functional interface Predicate (package java.util.function), which represents a one-parameter method that returns a boolean indicating whether the parameter value satisfies the predicate.

We assign the stream pipeline's resulting List<Integer> to variable greaterThan4, which is used in line 25 to display the values greater than 4 and used again in lines 37–39 to perform additional operations on only the values greater than 4.

17.10.4 Filtering and Sorting a Stream and Collecting the Results

The stream pipeline in lines 29–32

```
Arrays.stream(values)
    .filter(value -> value > 4)
    .sorted()
    .collect(Collectors.toList())
```

displays the values greater than 4 in sorted order. First, line 29 creates a Stream<Integer>. Then line 30 filters the elements to locate all the values greater than 4. Next, line 31 indicates that we'd like the results sorted. Finally, line 32 collects the results into a List<Integer>, which is then displayed as a String.

Performance Tip 17.2

Call filter before sorted so that the stream pipeline sorts only the elements that will be in the stream pipeline's result.

17.10.5 Sorting Previously Collected Results

The stream pipeline in lines 37–39

```
greaterThan4.stream()
        .sorted()
        .collect(Collectors.toList()));
```

uses the greaterThan4 collection created in lines 21–24 to show additional processing on the results of a prior stream pipeline. List method **stream** creates the stream. Then we sort the elements and collect the results into a new List<Integer> and display its String representation.

17.11 Stream<String> Manipulations

[This section demonstrates how lambdas and streams can be used to simplify programming tasks that you learned in Chapter 14, Strings, Characters and Regular Expressions.]

So far, we've manipulated only streams of int values and Integer objects. Figure 17.12 performs similar stream operations on a Stream<String>. In addition, we demonstrate *case-insensitive sorting* and sorting in *descending* order. Throughout this example, we use the String array strings (lines 9–10) that's initialized with color names—some with an initial uppercase letter. Line 13 displays the contents of strings *before* we perform any stream processing. We walk through the rest of the code in Sections 17.11.1—17.11.3.

```
 1   // Fig. 17.12: ArraysAndStreams2.java
 2   // Demonstrating lambdas and streams with an array of Strings.
 3   import java.util.Arrays;
 4   import java.util.Comparator;
 5   import java.util.stream.Collectors;
 6
 7   public class ArraysAndStreams2 {
 8      public static void main(String[] args) {
 9         String[] strings =
10            {"Red", "orange", "Yellow", "green", "Blue", "indigo", "Violet"};
11
12         // display original strings
13         System.out.printf("Original strings: %s%n", Arrays.asList(strings));
14
15         // strings in uppercase
16         System.out.printf("strings in uppercase: %s%n",
17            Arrays.stream(strings)
18               .map(String::toUpperCase)
19               .collect(Collectors.toList()));
20
21         // strings less than "n" (case insensitive) sorted ascending
22         System.out.printf("strings less than n sorted ascending: %s%n",
23            Arrays.stream(strings)
24               .filter(s -> s.compareToIgnoreCase("n") < 0)
25               .sorted(String.CASE_INSENSITIVE_ORDER)
26               .collect(Collectors.toList()));
27
28         // strings less than "n" (case insensitive) sorted descending
29         System.out.printf("strings less than n sorted descending: %s%n",
30            Arrays.stream(strings)
31               .filter(s -> s.compareToIgnoreCase("n") < 0)
32               .sorted(String.CASE_INSENSITIVE_ORDER.reversed())
33               .collect(Collectors.toList()));
34      }
35   }
```

```
Original strings: [Red, orange, Yellow, green, Blue, indigo, Violet]
strings in uppercase: [RED, ORANGE, YELLOW, GREEN, BLUE, INDIGO, VIOLET]
strings less than n sorted ascending: [Blue, green, indigo]
strings less than n sorted descending: [indigo, green, Blue]
```

Fig. 17.12 | Demonstrating lambdas and streams with an array of Strings.

17.11.1 Mapping Strings to Uppercase

The stream pipeline in lines 17–19

```
Arrays.stream(strings)
      .map(String::toUpperCase)
      .collect(Collectors.toList()));
```

displays the Strings in uppercase letters. To do so, line 17 creates a Stream<String> from the array strings, then line 18 maps each String to its uppercase version by calling String instance method toUpperCase on each stream element.

`Stream` method `map` receives an object that implements the `Function` functional interface, representing a one-parameter method that performs a task with its parameter then returns the result. In this case, we pass to `map` an **unbound instance method reference** of the form *ClassName*::*instanceMethodName* (`String::toUpperCase`). "Unbound" means that the method reference does not indicate the specific object on which the method will be called—the compiler converts this to a one-parameter lambda that invokes the instance method on the lambda's parameter, which must have type *ClassName*. In this case, the compiler converts `String::toUpperCase` into a lambda like

```
s -> s.toUpperCase()
```

which returns the uppercase version of the lambda's argument. Line 19 `collects` the results into a `List<String>` that we output as a `String`.

17.11.2 Filtering `Strings` Then Sorting Them in Case-Insensitive Ascending Order

The stream pipeline in lines 23–26

```
Arrays.stream(strings)
      .filter(s -> s.compareToIgnoreCase("n") < 0)
      .sorted(String.CASE_INSENSITIVE_ORDER)
      .collect(Collectors.toList())
```

filters and sort the `Strings`. Line 23 creates a `Stream<String>` from the array `strings`, then line 24 calls `Stream` method `filter` to locate all the `Strings` that are less than `"n"`, using a *case-insensitive* comparison in the `Predicate` lambda. Line 25 sorts the results and line 26 collects them into a `List<String>` that we output as a `String`.

In this case, line 25 invokes the version of `Stream` method `sorted` that receives a `Comparator` as an argument. A `Comparator` defines a `compare` method that returns a negative value if the first value being compared is less than the second, 0 if they're equal and a positive value if the first value is greater than the second. By default, method `sorted` uses the *natural order* for the type—for `Strings`, the natural order is case sensitive, which means that `"Z"` is less than `"a"`. Passing the predefined `Comparator String.CASE_INSENSITIVE_ORDER` performs a *case-insensitive* sort.

17.11.3 Filtering `Strings` Then Sorting Them in Case-Insensitive Descending Order

The stream pipeline in lines 30–33

```
Arrays.stream(strings)
      .filter(s -> s.compareToIgnoreCase("n") < 0)
      .sorted(String.CASE_INSENSITIVE_ORDER.reversed())
      .collect(Collectors.toList()));
```

performs the same tasks as lines 23–26, but sorts the `Strings` in *descending* order. Functional interface `Comparator` contains `default` method **reversed**, which reverses an existing Comparator's ordering. When you apply `reversed` to `String.CASE_INSENSITIVE_ORDER`, `sorted` performs a case-insensitive sort and places the `Strings` in *descending* order

17.12 Stream<Employee> Manipulations

[This section demonstrates how lambdas and streams can be used to simplify programming tasks that you learned in Chapter 16, Generic Collections.]

The previous examples in this chapter performed stream manipulations on primitive types (like int) and Java class library types (like Integer and String). Of course, you also may perform operations on collections of programmer-defined types.

The example in Figs. 17.13–17.21 demonstrates various lambda and stream capabilities using a Stream<Employee>. Class Employee (Fig. 17.13) represents an employee with a first name, last name, salary and department and provides methods for getting these values. In addition, the class provides a getName method (lines 39–41) that returns the combined first and last name as a String, and a toString method (lines 44–48) that returns a formatted String containing the employee's first name, last name, salary and department. We walk through the rest of the code in Sections 17.12.1—17.12.7

```java
1   // Fig. 17.13: Employee.java
2   // Employee class.
3   public class Employee {
4      private String firstName;
5      private String lastName;
6      private double salary;
7      private String department;
8
9      // constructor
10     public Employee(String firstName, String lastName,
11        double salary, String department) {
12        this.firstName = firstName;
13        this.lastName = lastName;
14        this.salary = salary;
15        this.department = department;
16     }
17
18     // get firstName
19     public String getFirstName() {
20        return firstName;
21     }
22
23     // get lastName
24     public String getLastName() {
25        return lastName;
26     }
27
28     // get salary
29     public double getSalary() {
30        return salary;
31     }
32
```

Fig. 17.13 | Employee class for use in Figs. 17.14–17.21. (Part 1 of 2.)

```
33    // get department
34    public String getDepartment() {
35        return department;
36    }
37
38    // return Employee's first and last name combined
39    public String getName() {
40        return String.format("%s %s", getFirstName(), getLastName());
41    }
42
43    // return a String containing the Employee's information
44    @Override
45    public String toString() {
46        return String.format("%-8s %-8s %8.2f   %s",
47            getFirstName(), getLastName(), getSalary(), getDepartment());
48    }
49 }
```

Fig. 17.13 | Employee class for use in Figs. 17.14–17.21. (Part 2 of 2.)

17.12.1 Creating and Displaying a List<Employee>

Class ProcessingEmployees (Figs. 17.14–17.21) is split into several figures so we can keep the discussions of the example's lambda and streams operations close to the corresponding code. Each figure also contains the portion of the program's output that correspond to code shown in that figure.

Figure 17.14 creates an array of Employees (lines 15–22) and gets its List view (line 25). Line 29 creates a Stream<Employee>, then uses Stream method forEach to display each Employee's String representation. Stream method forEach expects as its argument an object that implements the Consumer functional interface, which represents an action to perform on each element of the stream—the corresponding method receives one argument and returns void. The bound instance method reference System.out::println is converted by the compiler into a one-parameter lambda that passes the lambda's argument—an Employee—to the System.out object's println instance method, which implicitly calls class Employee's toString method to get the String representation. Figure 17.14's output shows the results of displaying each Employee's String representation (line 29)—in this case, Stream method forEach passes each Employee to the System.out object's println method, which calls the Employee's toString method.

```
1    // Fig. 17.14: ProcessingEmployees.java
2    // Processing streams of Employee objects.
3    import java.util.Arrays;
4    import java.util.Comparator;
5    import java.util.List;
6    import java.util.Map;
7    import java.util.TreeMap;
8    import java.util.function.Function;
9    import java.util.function.Predicate;
```

Fig. 17.14 | Processing streams of Employee objects. (Part 1 of 2.)

```
10  import java.util.stream.Collectors;
11
12  public class ProcessingEmployees {
13     public static void main(String[] args) {
14        // initialize array of Employees
15        Employee[] employees = {
16           new Employee("Jason", "Red", 5000, "IT"),
17           new Employee("Ashley", "Green", 7600, "IT"),
18           new Employee("Matthew", "Indigo", 3587.5, "Sales"),
19           new Employee("James", "Indigo", 4700.77, "Marketing"),
20           new Employee("Luke", "Indigo", 6200, "IT"),
21           new Employee("Jason", "Blue", 3200, "Sales"),
22           new Employee("Wendy", "Brown", 4236.4, "Marketing")};
23
24        // get List view of the Employees
25        List<Employee> list = Arrays.asList(employees);
26
27        // display all Employees
28        System.out.println("Complete Employee list:");
29        list.stream().forEach(System.out::println);
30
```

```
Complete Employee list:
Jason     Red       5000.00    IT
Ashley    Green     7600.00    IT
Matthew   Indigo    3587.50    Sales
James     Indigo    4700.77    Marketing
Luke      Indigo    6200.00    IT
Jason     Blue      3200.00    Sales
Wendy     Brown     4236.40    Marketing
```

Fig. 17.14 | Processing streams of Employee objects. (Part 2 of 2.)

Java SE 9: Creating an Immutable List<Employee> with List Method of
In Fig. 17.14, we first created an array of Employees (lines 15–22), then obtained a List
view of the array (line 25). Recall from Chapter 16 that in Java SE 9, you can populate an
immutable List directly via List static method of, as in:

```
List<Employee> list = List.of(
   new Employee("Jason", "Red", 5000, "IT"),
   new Employee("Ashley", "Green", 7600, "IT"),
   new Employee("Matthew", "Indigo", 3587.5, "Sales"),
   new Employee("James", "Indigo", 4700.77, "Marketing"),
   new Employee("Luke", "Indigo", 6200, "IT"),
   new Employee("Jason", "Blue", 3200, "Sales"),
   new Employee("Wendy", "Brown", 4236.4, "Marketing"));
```

17.12.2 Filtering Employees with Salaries in a Specified Range

So far, we've used lambdas only by passing them directly as arguments to stream methods.
Figure 17.15 demonstrates storing a lambda in a variable for later use. Lines 32–33 declare
a variable of the functional interface type Predicate<Employee> and initialize it with a

one-parameter lambda that returns a boolean (as required by Predicate). The lambda returns true if an Employee's salary is in the range 4000 to 6000. We use the stored lambda in lines 40 and 47 to filter Employees.

```
31        // Predicate that returns true for salaries in the range $4000-$6000
32        Predicate<Employee> fourToSixThousand =
33           e -> (e.getSalary() >= 4000 && e.getSalary() <= 6000);
34
35        // Display Employees with salaries in the range $4000-$6000
36        // sorted into ascending order by salary
37        System.out.printf(
38           "%nEmployees earning $4000-$6000 per month sorted by salary:%n");
39        list.stream()
40           .filter(fourToSixThousand)
41           .sorted(Comparator.comparing(Employee::getSalary))
42           .forEach(System.out::println);
43
44        // Display first Employee with salary in the range $4000-$6000
45        System.out.printf("%nFirst employee who earns $4000-$6000:%n%s%n",
46           list.stream()
47              .filter(fourToSixThousand)
48              .findFirst()
49              .get());
50
```

```
Employees earning $4000-$6000 per month sorted by salary:
Wendy     Brown      4236.40    Marketing
James     Indigo     4700.77    Marketing
Jason     Red        5000.00    IT

First employee who earns $4000-$6000:
Jason     Red        5000.00    IT
```

Fig. 17.15 | Filtering Employees with salaries in the range $4000–$6000.

The stream pipeline in lines 39–42 performs the following tasks:

- Line 39 creates a Stream<Employee>.

- Line 40 filters the stream using the Predicate named fourToSixThousand.

- Line 41 sorts *by salary* the Employees that remain in the stream. To create a salary Comparator, we use the Comparator interface's static method comparing, which receives a Function that performs a task on its argument and returns the result. The unbound instance method reference Employee::getSalary is converted by the compiler into a one-parameter lambda that calls getSalary on its Employee argument. The Comparator returned by method comparing calls its Function argument on each of two Employee objects, then returns a negative value if the first Employee's salary is less than the second, 0 if they're equal and a positive value if the first Employee's salary is greater than the second. Stream method sorted uses these values to order the Employees.

- Finally, line 42 performs the terminal forEach operation that processes the stream pipeline and outputs the Employees sorted by salary.

Short-Circuit Stream Pipeline Processing

In Section 5.9, you studied short-circuit evaluation with the logical AND (&&) and logical OR (||) operators. One of the nice performance features of lazy evaluation is the ability to perform *short-circuit evaluation*—that is, to stop processing the stream pipeline as soon as the desired result is available. Line 48 of Fig. 17.15 demonstrates Stream method **find-First**—a *short-circuiting terminal operation* that processes the stream pipeline and terminates processing as soon as the *first* object from the stream's intermediate operation(s) is found. Based on the original list of Employees, the stream pipeline in lines 46–49

```
list.stream()
    .filter(fourToSixThousand)
    .findFirst()
    .get()
```

which filters Employees with salaries in the range $4000–$6000—proceeds as follows:

- The Predicate fourToSixThousand is applied to the first Employee (Jason Red). His salary ($5000.00) is in the range $4000–$6000, so the Predicate returns true and processing of the stream terminates *immediately*, having processed only one of the eight objects in the stream.

- Method findFirst then returns an Optional (in this case, an Optional<Employee>) containing the object that was found, if any. The call to Optional method get (line 49) returns the matching Employee object in this example. Even if the stream contained millions of Employee objects, the filter operation would be performed only until a match was found.

We knew from this example's Employees that this pipeline would find at least one Employee with a salary in the range 4000–6000. So, we called Optional method get without first checking whether the Optional contained a result. If findFirst yields an empty Optional, this would cause a NoSuchElementException.

 Error-Prevention Tip 17.3

For a stream operation that returns an Optional<T>, store the result in a variable of that type, then use the object's isPresent method to confirm that there is a result, before calling the Optional's get method. This prevents NoSuchElementExceptions.

Method findFirst is one of several search-related terminal operations. Figure 17.16 shows several similar Stream methods.

Search-related terminal stream operations	
findAny	Similar to findFirst, but finds and returns *any* stream element based on the prior intermediate operations. Immediately terminates processing of the stream pipeline once such an element is found. Typically, findFirst is used with sequential streams and findAny is used with parallel streams (Section 21.13).
anyMatch	Determines whether *any* stream elements match a specified condition. Returns true if at least one stream element matches and false otherwise. Immediately terminates processing of the stream pipeline if an element matches.

Fig. 17.16 | Search-related terminal stream operations. (Part 1 of 2.)

Search-related terminal stream operations	
allMatch	Determines whether *all* of the elements in the stream match a specified condition. Returns true if so and false otherwise. Immediately terminates processing of the stream pipeline if any element does not match.

Fig. 17.16 | Search-related terminal stream operations. (Part 2 of 2.)

17.12.3 Sorting Employees By Multiple Fields

Figure 17.17 shows how to use streams to sort objects by *multiple* fields. In this example, we sort Employees by last name, then, for Employees with the same last name, we also sort them by first name. To do so, we begin by creating two Functions that each receive an Employee and return a String:

- byFirstName (line 52) is assigned a method reference for Employee instance method getFirstName

- byLastName (line 53) is assigned a method reference for Employee instance method getLastName

Next, we use these Functions to create a Comparator (lastThenFirst; lines 56–57) that first compares two Employees by last name, then compares them by first name. We use Comparator method comparing to create a Comparator that calls Function byLastName on an Employee to get its last name. On the resulting Comparator, we call Comparator method **thenComparing** to create a *composed* Comparator that first compares Employees by last name and, *if the last names are equal*, then compares them by first name. Lines 62–64 use this new lastThenFirst Comparator to sort the Employees in *ascending* order, then display the results. We reuse the Comparator in lines 69–71, but call its reversed method to indicate that the Employees should be sorted in *descending* order by last name, then first name. Lines 52–57 may be expressed more concisely as:

```
Comparator<Employee> lastThenFirst =
    Comparator.comparing(Employee::getLastName)
              .thenComparing(Employee::getFirstName);
```

```
51      // Functions for getting first and last names from an Employee
52      Function<Employee, String> byFirstName = Employee::getFirstName;
53      Function<Employee, String> byLastName = Employee::getLastName;
54
55      // Comparator for comparing Employees by first name then last name
56      Comparator<Employee> lastThenFirst =
57         Comparator.comparing(byLastName).thenComparing(byFirstName);
58
59      // sort employees by last name, then first name
60      System.out.printf(
61         "%nEmployees in ascending order by last name then first:%n");
62      list.stream()
63         .sorted(lastThenFirst)
64         .forEach(System.out::println);
```

Fig. 17.17 | Sorting Employees by last name then first name. (Part 1 of 2.)

```
65
66            // sort employees in descending order by last name, then first name
67            System.out.printf(
68               "%nEmployees in descending order by last name then first:%n");
69            list.stream()
70               .sorted(lastThenFirst.reversed())
71               .forEach(System.out::println);
72
```

```
Employees in ascending order by last name then first:
Jason     Blue       3200.00    Sales
Wendy     Brown      4236.40    Marketing
Ashley    Green      7600.00    IT
James     Indigo     4700.77    Marketing
Luke      Indigo     6200.00    IT
Matthew   Indigo     3587.50    Sales
Jason     Red        5000.00    IT

Employees in descending order by last name then first:
Jason     Red        5000.00    IT
Matthew   Indigo     3587.50    Sales
Luke      Indigo     6200.00    IT
James     Indigo     4700.77    Marketing
Ashley    Green      7600.00    IT
Wendy     Brown      4236.40    Marketing
Jason     Blue       3200.00    Sales
```

Fig. 17.17 | Sorting `Employees` by last name then first name. (Part 2 of 2.)

Aside: Composing Lambda Expressions

Many functional interfaces in the package `java.util.function` package provide `default` methods that enable you to compose functionality. For example, consider the interface `IntPredicate`, which contains three `default` methods:

- **and**—performs a *logical AND* with *short-circuit evaluation* between the `IntPredicate` on which it's called and the `IntPredicate` it receives as an argument.

- **negate**—*reverses* the boolean value of the `IntPredicate` on which it's called.

- **or**—performs a *logical OR* with *short-circuit evaluation* between the `IntPredicate` on which it's called and the `IntPredicate` it receives as an argument.

You can use these methods and `IntPredicate` objects to compose more complex conditions. For example, consider the following two `IntPredicate`s that are each initialized with lambdas:

```
IntPredicate even = value -> value % 2 == 0;
IntPredicate greaterThan5 = value -> value > 5;
```

To locate all the even integers greater than 5 in an `IntStream`, you could pass to `IntStream` method `filter` the following composed `IntPredicate`:

```
even.and(greaterThan5)
```

Like `IntPredicate`, functional interface `Predicate` represents a method that returns a `boolean` indicating whether its argument satisfies a condition. `Predicate` also contains methods **and** and **or** for combining predicates, and **negate** for reversing a predicate's boolean value.

17.12.4 Mapping Employees to Unique-Last-Name Strings

You previously used map operations to perform calculations on int values, to convert ints to Strings and to convert Strings to uppercase letters. Figure 17.18 maps objects of one type (Employee) to objects of a different type (String). The stream pipeline in lines 75–79 performs the following tasks:

- Line 75 creates a Stream<Employee>.

- Line 76 maps the Employees to their last names using the unbound instance-method reference Employee::getName as method map's Function argument. The result is a Stream<String> containing only the Employees' last names.

- Line 77 calls Stream method **distinct** on the Stream<String> to eliminate any duplicate Strings—the resulting stream contains only unique last names.

- Line 78 sorts the unique last names.

- Finally, line 79 performs a terminal forEach operation that processes the stream pipeline and outputs the unique last names in sorted order.

Lines 84–87 sort the Employees by last name then, first name, then map the Employees to Strings with Employee instance method getName (line 86) and display the sorted names in a terminal forEach operation.

```
73        // display unique employee last names sorted
74        System.out.printf("%nUnique employee last names:%n");
75        list.stream()
76           .map(Employee::getLastName)
77           .distinct()
78           .sorted()
79           .forEach(System.out::println);
80
81        // display only first and last names
82        System.out.printf(
83           "%nEmployee names in order by last name then first name:%n");
84        list.stream()
85           .sorted(lastThenFirst)
86           .map(Employee::getName)
87           .forEach(System.out::println);
88
```

```
Unique employee last names:
Blue
Brown
Green
Indigo
Red
```

Fig. 17.18 | Mapping Employee objects to last names and whole names. (Part 1 of 2.)

```
Employee names in order by last name then first name:
Jason Blue
Wendy Brown
Ashley Green
James Indigo
Luke Indigo
Matthew Indigo
Jason Red
```

Fig. 17.18 | Mapping Employee objects to last names and whole names. (Part 2 of 2.)

17.12.5 Grouping Employees By Department

Previously, we've used the terminal stream operation collect to concatenate stream elements into a String representation and to place stream elements into List collections. Figure 17.19 uses Stream method collect (line 93) to group Employees by department.

```
89          // group Employees by department
90          System.out.printf("%nEmployees by department:%n");
91          Map<String, List<Employee>> groupedByDepartment =
92             list.stream()
93                .collect(Collectors.groupingBy(Employee::getDepartment));
94          groupedByDepartment.forEach(
95             (department, employeesInDepartment) -> {
96                System.out.printf("%n%s%n", department);
97                employeesInDepartment.forEach(
98                   employee -> System.out.printf("   %s%n", employee));
99             }
100         );
101
```

```
Employees by department:

Sales
    Matthew    Indigo    3587.50    Sales
    Jason      Blue      3200.00    Sales

IT
    Jason      Red       5000.00    IT
    Ashley     Green     7600.00    IT
    Luke       Indigo    6200.00    IT

Marketing
    James      Indigo    4700.77    Marketing
    Wendy      Brown     4236.40    Marketing
```

Fig. 17.19 | Grouping Employees by department.

Recall that collect's argument is a Collector that specifies how to summarize the data into a useful form. In this case, we use the Collector returned by Collectors static method **groupingBy**, which receives a Function that classifies the objects in the stream.

The values returned by this Function are used as the keys in a Map collection. The corresponding values, by default, are Lists containing the stream elements in a given category.

When method collect is used with this Collector, the result is a Map<String, List<Employee>> in which each String key is a department and each List<Employee> contains the Employees in that department. We assign this Map to variable groupedByDepartment, which we use in lines 94–100 to display the Employees grouped by department. Map method **forEach** performs an operation on each of the Map's key–value pairs—in this case, the keys are departments and the values are collections of the Employees in a given department. The argument to this method is an object that implements functional interface **BiConsumer**, which represents a two-parameter method that does not return a result. For a Map, the first parameter represents the key and the second represents the corresponding value.

17.12.6 Counting the Number of Employees in Each Department

Figure 17.20 once again demonstrates Stream method collect and Collectors static method groupingBy, but in this case we count the number of Employees in each department. The technique shown here enables us to combine grouping and reduction into a single operation.

```
102        // count number of Employees in each department
103        System.out.printf("%nCount of Employees by department:%n");
104        Map<String, Long> employeeCountByDepartment =
105           list.stream()
106              .collect(Collectors.groupingBy(Employee::getDepartment,
107                 Collectors.counting()));
108        employeeCountByDepartment.forEach(
109           (department, count) -> System.out.printf(
110              "%s has %d employee(s)%n", department, count));
111
```

```
Count of Employees by department:
Sales has 2 employee(s)
IT has 3 employee(s)
Marketing has 2 employee(s)
```

Fig. 17.20 | Counting the number of Employees in each department.

The stream pipeline in lines 104–107 produces a Map<String, Long> in which each String key is a department name and the corresponding Long value is the number of Employees in that department. In this case, we use a version of Collectors static method groupingBy that receives two arguments:

- the first is a Function that classifies the objects in the stream and
- the second is another Collector (known as the **downstream Collector**) that's used to collect the objects classified by the Function.

We use a call to Collectors static method counting as the second argument. This resulting Collector reduces the elements in a given classification to a count of those elements, rather than collecting them into a List. Lines 108–110 then output the key–value pairs from the resulting Map<String, Long>.

17.12.7 Summing and Averaging Employee Salaries

Previously, we showed that streams of primitive-type elements can be mapped to streams of objects with method mapToObj (found in classes IntStream, LongStream and DoubleStream). Similarly, a Stream of objects may be mapped to an IntStream, LongStream or DoubleStream. Figure 17.21 demonstrates Stream method **mapToDouble** (lines 116, 123 and 129), which maps objects to double values and returns a DoubleStream. In this case, we map Employee objects to their salaries so that we can calculate the *sum* and *average*.

Method mapToDouble receives an object that implements the functional interface **ToDoubleFunction** (package java.util.function), which represents a one-parameter method that returns a double value. Lines 116, 123 and 129 each pass to mapToDouble the unbound instance-method reference Employee::getSalary, which returns the current Employee's salary as a double. The compiler converts this method reference into a one-parameter lambda that calls getSalary on its Employee argument.

```
112          // sum of Employee salaries with DoubleStream sum method
113          System.out.printf(
114             "%nSum of Employees' salaries (via sum method): %.2f%n",
115             list.stream()
116                .mapToDouble(Employee::getSalary)
117                .sum());
118
119          // calculate sum of Employee salaries with Stream reduce method
120          System.out.printf(
121             "Sum of Employees' salaries (via reduce method): %.2f%n",
122             list.stream()
123                .mapToDouble(Employee::getSalary)
124                .reduce(0, (value1, value2) -> value1 + value2));
125
126          // average of Employee salaries with DoubleStream average method
127          System.out.printf("Average of Employees' salaries: %.2f%n",
128             list.stream()
129                .mapToDouble(Employee::getSalary)
130                .average()
131                .getAsDouble());
132       }
133    }
```

```
Sum of Employees' salaries (via sum method): 34524.67
Sum of Employees' salaries (via reduce method): 34525.67
Average of Employees' salaries: 4932.10
```

Fig. 17.21 | Summing and averaging Employee salaries.

Lines 115–117 create a Stream<Employee>, map it to a DoubleStream, then invoke DoubleStream method sum to total the Employees' salaries. Lines 122–124 also sum the

Employees' salaries, but do so using DoubleStream method reduce rather than sum—note that the lambda in line 124 could be replaced with the static method reference

```
Double::sum
```

Class Double's sum method receives two doubles and returns their sum.

Finally, lines 128–131 calculate the average of the Employees' salaries using DoubleStream method average, which returns an OptionalDouble in case the DoubleStream does not contain any elements. Here, we know the stream has elements, so we simply call OptionalDouble method getAsDouble to get the result.

17.13 Creating a Stream<String> from a File

Figure 17.22 uses lambdas and streams to summarize the number of occurrences of each word in a file, then display a summary of the words in alphabetical order grouped by starting letter. This is commonly called a concordance:

```
http://en.wikipedia.org/wiki/Concordance_(publishing)
```

Concordances are often used to analyze published works. For example, concordances of William Shakespeare's and Christopher Marlowe's works (among others) have been used to question whether they are the same person. Figure 17.23 shows the program's output. Line 14 of Fig. 17.22 creates a regular expression Pattern that we'll use to split lines of text into their individual words. The Pattern \s+ represents one or more consecutive white-space characters—recall that because \ indicates an escape sequence in a String, we must specify each \ in a regular expression as \\. As written, this program assumes that the file it reads contains no punctuation, but you could use regular-expression techniques from Section 14.7 to remove punctuation.

```
1   // Fig. 17.22: StreamOfLines.java
2   // Counting word occurrences in a text file.
3   import java.io.IOException;
4   import java.nio.file.Files;
5   import java.nio.file.Paths;
6   import java.util.Map;
7   import java.util.TreeMap;
8   import java.util.regex.Pattern;
9   import java.util.stream.Collectors;
10
11  public class StreamOfLines {
12     public static void main(String[] args) throws IOException {
13        // Regex that matches one or more consecutive whitespace characters
14        Pattern pattern = Pattern.compile("\\s+");
15
16        // count occurrences of each word in a Stream<String> sorted by word
17        Map<String, Long> wordCounts =
18           Files.lines(Paths.get("Chapter2Paragraph.txt"))
19              .flatMap(line -> pattern.splitAsStream(line))
20              .collect(Collectors.groupingBy(String::toLowerCase,
21                 TreeMap::new, Collectors.counting()));
```

Fig. 17.22 | Counting word occurrences in a text file. (Part 1 of 2.)

```
22
23        // display the words grouped by starting letter
24        wordCounts.entrySet()
25           .stream()
26           .collect(
27              Collectors.groupingBy(entry -> entry.getKey().charAt(0),
28                 TreeMap::new, Collectors.toList()))
29           .forEach((letter, wordList) -> {
30              System.out.printf("%n%C%n", letter);
31              wordList.stream().forEach(word -> System.out.printf(
32                 "%13s: %d%n", word.getKey(), word.getValue()));
33           });
34     }
35  }
```

Fig. 17.22 | Counting word occurrences in a text file. (Part 2 of 2.)

A		I		R	
	a: 2		inputs: 1		result: 1
	and: 3		instruct: 1		results: 2
	application: 2		introduces: 1		run: 1
	arithmetic: 1				
		J		S	
B			java: 1		save: 1
	begin: 1		jdk: 1		screen: 1
					show: 1
C		L			sum: 1
	calculates: 1		last: 1		
	calculations: 1		later: 1	T	
	chapter: 1		learn: 1		that: 3
	chapters: 1				the: 7
	commandline: 1	M			their: 2
	compares: 1		make: 1		then: 2
	comparison: 1		messages: 2		this: 2
	compile: 1				to: 4
	computer: 1	N			tools: 1
D			numbers: 2		two: 2
	decisions: 1				
	demonstrates: 1	O		U	
	display: 1		obtains: 1		use: 2
	displays: 2		of: 1		user: 1
			on: 1		
E			output: 1	W	
	example: 1				we: 2
	examples: 1	P			with: 1
			perform: 1		
F			present: 1	Y	
	for: 1		program: 1		you'll: 2
	from: 1		programming: 1		
			programs: 2		
H					
	how: 2				

Fig. 17.23 | Output of Fig. 17.22 arranged in three columns.

Summarizing the Occurrences of Each Word in the File
The stream pipeline in lines 17–21

```
Map<String, Long> wordCounts =
    Files.lines(Paths.get("Chapter2Paragraph.txt"))
        .flatMap(line -> pattern.splitAsStream(line))
        .collect(Collectors.groupingBy(String::toLowerCase,
            TreeMap::new, Collectors.counting()));
```

summarizes the contents of the text file "Chapter2Paragraph.txt" (which is located in the folder with the example) into a Map<String, Long> in which each String key is a word in the file and the corresponding Long value is the number of occurrences of that word. The pipeline performs the following tasks:

8

- Line 18 calls Files method **lines** (added in Java SE 8) which returns a Stream<String> that reads lines of text from a file and returns each line as a String. Class Files (package java.nio.file) is one of many classes throughout the Java APIs which provide methods that return Streams.

- Line 19 uses Stream method **flatMap** to break each line of text into its separate words. Method flatMap receives a Function that maps an object into a stream of elements. In this case, the object is a String containing words and the result is a Stream<String> for the individual words. The lambda in line 19 passes the

8

String representing a line of text to Pattern method **splitAsStream** (added in Java SE 8), which uses the regular expression specified in the Pattern (line 14) to tokenize the String into its individual words. The result of line 19 is a Stream<String> for the individual words in all the lines of text. (This lambda could be replaced with the method reference pattern::splitAsStream.)

- Lines 20–21 use Stream method collect to count the frequency of each word and place the words and their counts into a TreeMap<String, Long>—a TreeMap because maintains its keys in sorted order. Here, we use a version of Collectors method groupingBy that receives three arguments—a classifier, a Map factory and a downstream Collector. The classifier is a Function that returns objects for use as keys in the resulting Map—the method reference String::toLowerCase converts each word to lowercase. The Map factory is an object that implements interface Supplier and returns a new Map collection—here we use the **constructor reference** TreeMap::new, which returns a TreeMap that maintains its keys in sorted order. The compiler converts a constructor reference into a parameterless lambda that returns a new TreeMap. Collectors.counting() is the downstream Collector that determines the number of occurrences of each key in the stream. The TreeMap's key type is determined by the classifier Function's return type (String), and the TreeMap's value type is determined by the downstream collector—Collectors.counting() returns a Long.

Displaying the Summary Grouped by Starting Letter
Next, the stream pipeline in lines 24–33 groups the key–value pairs in the Map wordCounts by the keys' first letter:

```
wordCounts.entrySet()
       .stream()
       .collect(
           Collectors.groupingBy(entry -> entry.get-
Key().charAt(0),
               TreeMap::new, Collectors.toList()))
       .forEach((letter, wordList) -> {
           System.out.printf("%n%C%n", letter);
           wordList.stream().forEach(word -> System.out.printf(
               "%13s: %d%n", word.getKey(), word.getValue()));
       });
```

This produces a new Map in which each key is a Character and the corresponding value is a List of the key–value pairs in wordCounts in which the key starts with the Character. The statement performs the following tasks:

- First we need to get a Stream for processing the key–value pairs in wordCounts. Interface Map does not contain any methods that return Streams. So, line 24 calls Map method entrySet on wordCounts to get a Set of **Map.Entry** objects that each contain one key–value pair from wordCounts. This produces an object of type Set<Map.Entry<String, Long>>.

- Line 25 calls Set method stream to get a Stream<Map.Entry<String, Long>>.

- Lines 26–28 call Stream method collect with three arguments—a classifier, a Map factory and a downstream Collector. The classifier Function in this case gets the key from the Map.Entry then uses String method charAt to get the key's first character—this becomes a Character key in the resulting Map. Once again, we use the constructor reference TreeMap::new as the Map factory to create a TreeMap that maintains its keys in sorted order. The downstream Collector (Collectors.toList()) places the Map.Entry objects into a List collection. The result of collect is a Map<Character, List<Map.Entry<String, Long>>>.

- Finally, to display the summary of the words and their counts by letter (i.e., the concordance), lines 29–33 pass a lambda to Map method forEach. The lambda (a BiConsumer) receives two parameters—letter and wordList represent the Character key and the List value, respectively, for each key–value pair in the Map produced by the preceding collect operation. The body of this lambda has two statements, so it *must* be enclosed in curly braces. The statement in line 30 displays the Character key on its own line. The statement in lines 31–32 gets a Stream<Map.Entry<String, Long>> from the wordList, then calls Stream method forEach to display the key and value from each Map.Entry object.

17.14 **Streams of Random Values**

Figure 6.6 summarized 60,000,000 rolls of a six-sided die using *external iteration* (a for loop) and a switch statement that determined which counter to increment. We then displayed the results using separate statements that performed external iteration. In Fig. 7.7, we reimplemented Fig. 6.6, replacing the entire switch statement with a single statement that incremented counters in an array—that version of rolling the die still used external iteration to produce and summarize 60,000,000 random rolls and to display the final results. Both prior versions of this example used mutable variables to control the external iteration and to summarize the results. Figure 17.24 reimplements those programs with a *single statement* that does it all, using lambdas, streams, internal iteration and *no mutable variables* to roll the die 60,000,000 times, calculate the frequencies and display the results.

Performance Tip 17.3

The techniques that SecureRandom *uses to produce secure random numbers are significantly slower than those used by* Random *(package* java.util*). For this reason, Fig. 17.24 may appear to freeze when you run it—on our computers, it took over one minute to complete. To save time, you can speed this example's execution by using class* Random. *However, industrial-strength applications should use secure random numbers.*

```
1   // Fig. 17.24: RandomIntStream.java
2   // Rolling a die 60,000,000 times with streams
3   import java.security.SecureRandom;
4   import java.util.function.Function;
5   import java.util.stream.Collectors;
6
7   public class RandomIntStream {
8      public static void main(String[] args) {
9         SecureRandom random = new SecureRandom();
10
11        // roll a die 60,000,000 times and summarize the results
12        System.out.printf("%-6s%s%n", "Face", "Frequency");
13        random.ints(60_000_000, 1, 7)
14           .boxed()
15           .collect(Collectors.groupingBy(Function.identity(),
16              Collectors.counting()))
17           .forEach((face, frequency) ->
18              System.out.printf("%-6d%d%n", face, frequency));
19     }
20  }
```

```
Face  Frequency
1     9992993
2     10000363
3     10002272
4     10003810
5     10000321
6     10000241
```

Fig. 17.24 | Rolling a die 60,000,000 times with streams.

Class SecureRandom has overloaded methods ints, **longs** and **doubles**, which it inherits from class Random (package java.util). These methods return an IntStream, a LongStream or a DoubleStream, respectively, that represent streams of random numbers. Each method has four overloads. We describe the ints overloads here—methods longs and doubles perform the same tasks for streams of long and double values, respectively:

- ints()—creates an IntStream for an *infinite stream* (Section 17.15) of random int values.

- `ints(long)`—creates an `IntStream` with the specified number of random `ints`.

- `ints(int, int)`—creates an `IntStream` for an *infinite stream* of random `int` values in the half-open range starting with the first argument and up to, but not including, the second argument.

- `ints(long, int, int)`—creates an `IntStream` with the specified number of random `int` values in the range starting with the first argument and up to, but not including, the second argument.

Line 13 uses the last overloaded version of `ints` (which we introduced in Section 17.6) to create an `IntStream` of 60,000,000 random integer values in the range 1–6.

Converting an *IntStream* to a *Stream<Integer>*

We summarize the roll frequencies in this example by collecting them into a `Map<Integer, Long>` in which each `Integer` key is a side of the die and each `Long` value is the frequency of that side. Unfortunately, Java does not allow primitive values in collections, so to summarize the results in a `Map`, we must first convert the `IntStream` to a `Stream<Integer>`. We do this by calling `IntStream` method **boxed**.

Summarizing the Die Frequencies

Lines 15–16 call `Stream` method `collect` to summarize the results into a `Map<Integer, Long>`. The first argument to `Collectors` method `groupingBy` (line 15) calls `static` method **identity** from interface `Function`, which creates a `Function` that simply returns its argument. This allows the actual random values to be used as the `Map`'s keys. The second argument to method `groupingBy` counts the number of occurrences of each key.

Displaying the Results

Lines 17–18 call the resulting `Map`'s `forEach` method to display the summary of the results. This method receives an object that implements the `BiConsumer` functional interface as an argument. Recall that for `Maps`, the first parameter represents the key and the second represents the corresponding value. The lambda in lines 17–18 uses parameter `face` as the key and `frequency` as the value, and displays the face and frequency.

17.15 Infinite Streams

A data structure, such as an array or a collection, always represents a finite number of elements—all the elements are stored in memory, and memory is finite. Of course, any stream created from a finite data structure will have a finite number of elements, as has been the case in this chapter's prior examples.

Lazy evaluation makes it possible to work with **infinite streams** that represent an unknown, potentially infinite, number of elements. For example, you could define a method `nextPrime` that produces the next prime number in sequence every time you call it. You could then use this to define an infinite stream that *conceptually* represents all prime numbers. However, because streams are lazy until you perform a terminal operation, you can use intermediate operations to restrict the total number of elements that are actually calculated when a terminal operation is performed. Consider the following pseudocode stream pipeline:

> *Create an infinite stream representing all prime numbers*
> *If the prime number is less than 10,000*
> *Display the prime number*

Even though we begin with an infinite stream, only the finite set of primes less than 10,000 would be displayed.

You create infinite streams with the stream-interfaces methods iterate and generate. For the purpose of this discussion, we'll use the IntStream version of these methods.

IntStream Method `iterate`
Consider the following infinite stream pipeline:

```
IntStream.iterate(1, x -> x + 1)
        .forEach(System.out::println);
```

IntStream method **iterate** generates an ordered sequence of values starting with the seed value (1) in its first argument. Each subsequent element is produced by applying to the preceding value in the sequence the IntUnaryOperator specified as iterate's second argument. The preceding pipeline generates the infinite sequence 1, 2, 3, 4, 5, ..., but this pipeline has a problem. We did not specify how many elements to produce, so this is the equivalent of an infinite loop.

Limiting an Infinite Stream's Number of Elements
One way to limit the total number of elements that an infinite stream produces is the short-circuiting terminal operation **limit**, which specifies the maximum number of elements to process from a stream. In the case of an infinite stream, limit terminates the infinite generation of elements. So, the following stream pipeline

```
IntStream.iterate(1, x -> x + 1)
        .limit(10)
        .forEach(System.out::println);
```

begins with an infinite stream, but limits the total number of elements produced to 10, so it displays the numbers from 1 through 10. Similarly, the pipeline

```
IntStream.iterate(1, x -> x + 1)
        .map(x -> x * x)
        .limit(10)
        .sum()
```

starts with an infinite stream, but sums only the squares of the integers from 1 through 10.

Error-Prevention Tip 17.4
Ensure that stream pipelines using methods that produce infinite streams limit the number of elements to produce.

IntStream Method `generate`
You also may create unordered infinite streams using method **generate**, which receives an IntSupplier representing a method that takes no arguments and returns an int. For example, if you have a SecureRandom object named random, the following stream pipeline generates and displays 10 random integers:

```
IntStream.generate(() -> random.nextInt())
        .limit(10)
        .forEach(System.out::println);
```

This is equivalent to using SecureRandom's no-argument ints method (Section 17.14):

```
SecureRandom.ints()
        .limit(10)
        .forEach(System.out::println);
```

17.16 Lambda Event Handlers

In Section 12.5.5, you learned how to implement an event handler using an anonymous inner class. Event-listener interfaces with one abstract method—like ChangeListener—are functional interfaces. For such interfaces, you can implement event handlers with lambdas. For example, the following Slider event handler from Fig. 12.23:

```
tipPercentageSlider.valueProperty().addListener(
    new ChangeListener<Number>() {
        @Override
        public void changed(ObservableValue<? extends Number> ov,
            Number oldValue, Number newValue) {
            tipPercentage =
                BigDecimal.valueOf(newValue.intValue() / 100.0);
            tipPercentageLabel.setText(percent.format(tipPercentage));
        }
    }
);
```

can be implemented more concisely with a lambda as

```
tipPercentageSlider.valueProperty().addListener(
    (ov, oldValue, newValue) -> {
        tipPercentage =
            BigDecimal.valueOf(newValue.intValue() / 100.0);
        tipPercentageLabel.setText(percent.format(tipPercentage));
    });
```

For a simple event handler, a lambda significantly reduces the amount of code you need to write.

17.17 Additional Notes on Java SE 8 Interfaces

Java SE 8 Interfaces Allow Inheritance of Method Implementations
Functional interfaces *must* contain only one abstract method, but may also contain default methods and static methods that are fully implemented in the interface declarations. For example, the Function interface—which is used extensively in functional programming—has methods apply (abstract), compose (default), andThen (default) and identity (static).

When a class implements an interface with default methods and does *not* override them, the class inherits the default methods' implementations. An interface's designer can now evolve an interface by adding new default and static methods without breaking existing code that implements the interface. For example, interface Comparator

(Section 16.7.1) now contains many `default` and `static` methods, but older classes that implement this interface will still compile and operate properly in Java SE 8.

Recall that one class can implement many interfaces. If a class implements two or more unrelated interfaces that provide a `default` method with the same signature, the implementing class *must* override that method; otherwise, a compilation error occurs.

Java SE 8: @FunctionalInterface Annotation

You can create your own functional interfaces by ensuring that each contains only one `abstract` method and zero or more `default` and/or `static` methods. Though not required, you can declare that an interface is a functional interface by preceding it with the **@FunctionalInterface annotation**. The compiler will then ensure that the interface contains only one `abstract` method; otherwise, it will generate a compilation error.

17.18 Wrap-Up

In this chapter, you worked with lambdas, streams and functional interfaces. We presented many examples, often showing simpler ways to implement tasks that you programmed in earlier chapters.

You learned how to process elements in an `IntStream`—a stream of `int` values. You created an `IntStream` representing a closed range of `int`s, then used intermediate and terminal stream operations to create and process a stream pipeline that produced a result. We used lambdas to create anonymous methods that implemented functional interfaces and passed these lambdas to methods in stream pipelines to specify the processing steps for the streams' elements. We also created `IntStreams` from existing arrays of `int` values.

We discussed how a stream's intermediate processing steps are applied to each element before moving onto the next. We showed how to use a `forEach` terminal operation to perform an operation on each stream element. We used reduction operations to count the number of stream elements, determine the minimum and maximum values, and sum and average the values. You also used method `reduce` to create your own reduction operations.

You used intermediate operations to filter elements that matched a predicate and map elements to new values—in each case, these operations produced intermediate streams on which you could perform additional processing. You also learned how to sort elements in ascending and descending order and how to sort objects by multiple fields.

We demonstrated how to store a stream pipeline's results in a collection by using various predefined `Collector` implementations provided by class `Collectors`. You also learned how to use a `Collector` to group elements into categories.

You learned that various classes can create stream data sources. For example, you used `Files` method `lines` to get a `Stream<String>` that read lines of text from a file and used `SecureRandom` method `ints` to get an `IntStream` of random values. You also learned how to convert an `IntStream` into a `Stream<Integer>` (via method `boxed`) so that you could use `Stream` method `collect` to summarize the frequencies of the `Integer` values and store the results in a `Map`.

We introduced infinite streams and showed how to limit the number of elements they generate. You saw how to implement an event-handling functional interface using a lambda. Finally, we presented some additional information about Java SE 8 interfaces and streams. In the next chapter, we discuss recursive programming in which methods call themselves either directly or indirectly.

18

Recursion

Objectives

In this chapter you'll:

- Learn the concept of recursion.
- Write and use recursive methods.
- Determine the base case and recursion step in a recursive algorithm.
- Learn how recursive method calls are handled by the system.
- Learn the differences between recursion and iteration, and when to use each.
- Learn what fractals are and how to draw them using recursion and JavaFX's **Canvas** and **GraphicsContext** classes.
- Learn what recursive backtracking is and why it's an effective problem-solving technique.

18.1 Introduction

The programs we've discussed so far are generally structured as methods that call one another in a hierarchical manner. For some problems, it's useful to have a method *call itself*—this is known as a **recursive method**. Such a method can call itself either *directly* or *indirectly through another method*. Here, we consider recursion conceptually, then present several examples of recursive methods.

18.2 Recursion Concepts

Recursive problem-solving approaches have a number of elements in common. When a recursive method is called to solve a problem, it actually is capable of solving only the *simplest case(s)*, or **base case(s)**. If the method is called with a *base case*, it returns a result. If the method is called with a more complex problem, it divides the problem into two conceptual pieces—a piece that the method knows how to do and a piece that it does not know how to do. To make recursion feasible, the latter piece must resemble the original problem, but be a slightly simpler or smaller version of it. Because this new problem resembles the original problem, the method calls a fresh *copy* of itself to work on the smaller problem—this is referred to as a **recursive call** and is also called the **recursion step**. The recursion step normally includes a `return` statement, because its result will be combined with the portion of the problem the method knew how to solve to form a result that will be passed back to the original caller. This concept of separating the problem into two smaller portions is a form of the *divide-and-conquer* approach.

The recursion step executes while the original method call is still active (i.e., it has not finished executing). It can result in many more recursive calls as the method divides each new subproblem into two conceptual pieces. For the recursion to eventually terminate, each time the method calls itself with a simpler version of the original problem, the sequence of smaller and smaller problems must *converge on a base case*. When the method recognizes the base case, it returns a result to the previous copy of the method. A sequence of returns ensues until the original method call returns the final result to the caller. We'll illustrate this process with a concrete example in Section 18.3.

A recursive method may call another method, which may in turn make a call back to the recursive method. This is known as an **indirect recursive call** or **indirect recursion**. For example, method A calls method B, which makes a call back to method A. This is still recursion, because the second call to method A is made while the first call to method A is active—

that is, the first call to method A has not yet finished executing (because it's waiting on method B to return a result to it) and has not returned to method A's original caller.

Recursive Directory Structures

To better understand the concept of recursion, let's look at an example that's quite familiar to computer users—the recursive definition of a file-system directory on a computer. A computer normally stores related files in a directory. A directory can be empty, can contain files and/or can contain other directories (usually referred to as subdirectories). Each of these subdirectories, in turn, may also contain both files and directories. If we want to list each file in a directory (including all the files in the directory's subdirectories), we need to create a method that first lists the initial directory's files, then makes recursive calls to list the files in each of that directory's subdirectories. The base case occurs when a directory is reached that does not contain any subdirectories. At this point, all the files in the original directory have been listed and no further recursion is necessary.

18.3 Example Using Recursion: Factorials

Let's write a recursive program to perform a popular mathematical calculation. Consider the *factorial* of a positive integer n, written $n!$ (pronounced "n factorial"), which is the product

$$n \cdot (n - 1) \cdot (n - 2) \cdot \ldots \cdot 1$$

with 1! equal to 1 and 0! defined to be 1. For example, 5! is the product $5 \cdot 4 \cdot 3 \cdot 2 \cdot 1$, which is equal to 120.

The factorial of integer number (where number ≥ 0) can be calculated *iteratively* (non-recursively) using a for statement as follows:

```
factorial = 1;
for (int counter = number; counter >= 1; counter--) {
    factorial *= counter;
}
```

A recursive declaration of the factorial calculation for integers greater than 1 is arrived at by observing the following relationship:

$$n! = n \cdot (n - 1)!$$

For example, 5! is clearly equal to $5 \cdot 4!$, as shown by the following equations:

$$5! = 5 \cdot 4 \cdot 3 \cdot 2 \cdot 1$$
$$5! = 5 \cdot (4 \cdot 3 \cdot 2 \cdot 1)$$
$$5! = 5 \cdot (4!)$$

The evaluation of 5! would proceed as shown in Fig. 18.1. Figure 18.1(a) shows how the succession of recursive calls proceeds until 1! (the base case) is evaluated to be 1, which terminates the recursion. Figure 18.1(b) shows the values returned from each recursive call to its caller until the final value is calculated and returned.

Figure 18.2 uses recursion to calculate and print the factorials of the integers 0 through 21. The recursive method `factorial` (lines 6–13) first tests to determine whether a *terminating condition* (line 7) is true. If number is less than or equal to 1 (the base case), `factorial` returns 1, no further recursion is necessary and the method returns. (A precondition of calling method `factorial` in this example is that its argument must be nonneg-

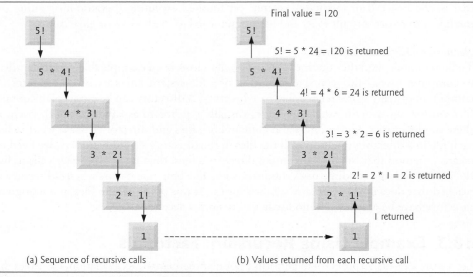

Final value = 120

5!

5! = 5 * 24 = 120 is returned

5 * 4!

4! = 4 * 6 = 24 is returned

4 * 3!

3! = 3 * 2 = 6 is returned

3 * 2!

2! = 2 * 1 = 2 is returned

2 * 1!

1 returned

1

(a) Sequence of recursive calls   (b) Values returned from each recursive call

Fig. 18.1 | Recursive evaluation of 5!.

ative.) If number is greater than 1, line 11 expresses the problem as the product of number and a recursive call to factorial evaluating the factorial of number - 1, which is a slightly smaller problem than the original calculation, factorial(number).

Common Programming Error 18.1

*Omitting the base case or writing the recursion step incorrectly so that it does not converge on the base case can cause **infinite recursion**, where recursive calls are continuously made until memory is exhausted or the method-call stack overflows. This error is analogous to the problem of an infinite loop in an iterative (nonrecursive) solution.*

```java
 1   // Fig. 18.2: FactorialCalculator.java
 2   // Recursive factorial method.
 3
 4   public class FactorialCalculator {
 5      // recursive method factorial (assumes its parameter is >= 0)
 6      public static long factorial(long number) {
 7         if (number <= 1) { // test for base case
 8            return 1; // base cases: 0! = 1 and 1! = 1
 9         }
10         else { // recursion step
11            return number * factorial(number - 1);
12         }
13      }
14
15      public static void main(String[] args) {
16         // calculate the factorials of 0 through 21
17         for (int counter = 0; counter <= 21; counter++) {
```

Fig. 18.2 | Recursive factorial method. (Part 1 of 2.)

```
18              System.out.printf("%d! = %d%n", counter, factorial(counter));
19        }
20      }
21    }
```

```
0! = 1
1! = 1
2! = 2
3! = 6
4! = 24
5! = 120
...
12! = 479001600 ——— 12! causes overflow for int variables
...
20! = 2432902008176640000
21! = -4249290049419214848 ——— 21! causes overflow for long variables
```

Fig. 18.2 | Recursive factorial method. (Part 2 of 2.)

Method main (lines 15–20) displays the factorials of 0–21.[1] The call to the factorial method occurs in line 18. Method factorial receives a parameter of type long and returns a result of type long. The program's output shows that factorial values become large quickly. We use type long (which can represent relatively large integers) so the program can calculate factorials greater than 12!. Unfortunately, the factorial method produces large values so quickly that we exceed the largest long value when we attempt to calculate 21!, as you can see in the last line of the program's output.

Due to the limitations of integral types, float or double variables may ultimately be needed to calculate factorials of larger numbers. This points to a weakness in some programming languages—namely, that they aren't easily *extended with new types* to handle unique application requirements. As we saw in Chapter 9, Java is an *extensible* language that allows us to create arbitrarily large integers if we wish. In fact, package java.math provides classes **BigInteger** and BigDecimal explicitly for arbitrary precision calculations that cannot be performed with primitive types. You can learn more about these classes at

```
http://docs.oracle.com/javase/8/docs/api/java/math/BigInteger.html
http://docs.oracle.com/javase/8/docs/api/java/math/BigDecimal.html
```

Calculating Factorials with Lambdas and Streams
If you've read Chapter 17, consider how you might calculate factorials using lambdas and streams, rather than recursion.

18.4 Reimplementing Class FactorialCalculator Using BigInteger

Figure 18.3 reimplements class FactorialCalculator using BigInteger variables. To demonstrate larger values than what long variables can store, we calculate the factorials of the numbers 0–50. Line 3 imports class BigInteger from package java.math. The new

---

1. The for loops in the main methods of this chapter's examples could be implemented with lambdas and streams by using IntStream and its rangeClosed and forEach methods.

factorial method (lines 7–15) receives a `BigInteger` as an argument and returns a `BigInteger`.

```java
1   // Fig. 18.3: FactorialCalculator.java
2   // Recursive factorial method.
3   import java.math.BigInteger;
4
5   public class FactorialCalculator {
6      // recursive method factorial (assumes its parameter is >= 0)
7      public static BigInteger factorial(BigInteger number) {
8         if (number.compareTo(BigInteger.ONE) <= 0) { // test base case
9            return BigInteger.ONE; // base cases: 0! = 1 and 1! = 1
10        }
11        else { // recursion step
12           return number.multiply(
13              factorial(number.subtract(BigInteger.ONE)));
14        }
15     }
16
17     public static void main(String[] args) {
18        // calculate the factorials of 0 through 50
19        for (int counter = 0; counter <= 50; counter++) {
20           System.out.printf("%d! = %d%n", counter,
21              factorial(BigInteger.valueOf(counter)));
22        }
23     }
24  }
```

```
0! = 1
1! = 1
2! = 2
3! = 6
...
21! = 51090942171709440000 ──── 21! and larger values no longer cause overflow
22! = 1124000727777607680000
...
47! = 258623241511168180642964355153611979969197632389120000000000
48! = 12413915592536072670862289047373375038521486354677760000000000
49! = 608281864034267560872252163321295376887552831379210240000000000
50! = 30414093201713378043612608166064768844377641568960512000000000000
```

Fig. 18.3 | Factorial calculations with a recursive method.

Since `BigInteger` is *not* a primitive type, we can't use the arithmetic, relational and equality operators with `BigInteger`s; instead, we must use `BigInteger` methods to perform these tasks. Line 8 tests for the base case using `BigInteger` method **compareTo**. This method compares the `BigInteger` number that calls the method to the method's `BigInteger` argument. The method returns -1 if the `BigInteger` that calls the method is less than the argument, 0 if they're equal or 1 if the `BigInteger` that calls the method is greater than the argument. Line 8 compares the `BigInteger` number with the `BigInteger` constant **ONE**, which represents the integer value 1. If compareTo returns -1 or 0, then number is less than or equal to 1 (the base case) and the method returns the constant

BigInteger.ONE. Otherwise, lines 12–13 perform the recursion step using BigInteger methods **multiply** and **subtract** to implement the calculations required to multiply number by the factorial of number - 1. The program's output shows that BigInteger handles the large values produced by the factorial calculation.

Calculating Factorials with Lambdas and Streams
If you've read Chapter 17, consider how you might calculate factorials using lambdas and streams, rather than recursion.

18.5 Example Using Recursion: Fibonacci Series

The **Fibonacci series,**

> 0, 1, 1, 2, 3, 5, 8, 13, 21, ...

begins with 0 and 1 and has the property that each subsequent Fibonacci number is the sum of the previous two. This series occurs in nature and describes a form of spiral. The ratio of successive Fibonacci numbers converges on a constant value of 1.618..., a number that has been called the **golden ratio** or the **golden mean.** Humans tend to find the golden mean aesthetically pleasing. Architects often design windows, rooms and buildings whose length and width are in the ratio of the golden mean. Postcards are often designed with a golden-mean length-to-width ratio.

The Fibonacci series may be defined recursively as follows:

> fibonacci(0) = 0
> fibonacci(1) = 1
> fibonacci(n) = fibonacci($n - 1$) + fibonacci($n - 2$)

There are *two base cases* for the Fibonacci calculation: fibonacci(0) is defined to be 0, and fibonacci(1) to be 1. Figure 18.4 calculates the ith Fibonacci number recursively, using method fibonacci (lines 9–18). Method main (lines 20–26) tests fibonacci, displaying the Fibonacci values of 0–40. The variable counter created in the for header (line 22) indicates which Fibonacci number to calculate for each iteration of the loop. Fibonacci numbers tend to become large quickly (though not as quickly as factorials). Therefore, we use type BigInteger as the parameter type and the return type of method fibonacci.

```java
1  // Fig. 18.4: FibonacciCalculator.java
2  // Recursive fibonacci method.
3  import java.math.BigInteger;
4
5  public class FibonacciCalculator {
6     private static BigInteger TWO = BigInteger.valueOf(2);
7
8     // recursive declaration of method fibonacci
9     public static BigInteger fibonacci(BigInteger number) {
10        if (number.equals(BigInteger.ZERO) ||
11           number.equals(BigInteger.ONE)) { // base cases
12           return number;
13        }
```

Fig. 18.4 | Recursive fibonacci method. (Part 1 of 2.)

```
14          else { // recursion step
15              return fibonacci(number.subtract(BigInteger.ONE)).add(
16                  fibonacci(number.subtract(TWO)));
17          }
18      }
19
20      public static void main(String[] args) {
21          // displays the fibonacci values from 0-40
22          for (int counter = 0; counter <= 40; counter++) {
23              System.out.printf("Fibonacci of %d is: %d%n", counter,
24                  fibonacci(BigInteger.valueOf(counter)));
25          }
26      }
27  }
```

```
Fibonacci of 0 is: 0
Fibonacci of 1 is: 1
Fibonacci of 2 is: 1
Fibonacci of 3 is: 2
Fibonacci of 4 is: 3
Fibonacci of 5 is: 5
Fibonacci of 6 is: 8
Fibonacci of 7 is: 13
Fibonacci of 8 is: 21
Fibonacci of 9 is: 34
Fibonacci of 10 is: 55
...
Fibonacci of 37 is: 24157817
Fibonacci of 38 is: 39088169
Fibonacci of 39 is: 63245986
Fibonacci of 40 is: 102334155
```

Fig. 18.4 | Recursive fibonacci method. (Part 2 of 2.)

The call to method fibonacci (line 24) from main is *not* a recursive call, but all subsequent calls to fibonacci performed from lines 15–16 *are* recursive, because at that point the calls are initiated by method fibonacci itself. Each time fibonacci is called, it immediately tests for the *base cases*—number equal to 0 or number equal to 1 (lines 10–11). We use BigInteger constants **ZERO** and ONE to represent the values 0 and 1, respectively. If the condition in lines 10–11 is true, fibonacci simply returns number, because fibonacci(0) is 0 and fibonacci(1) is 1. Interestingly, if number is greater than 1, the recursion step generates *two* recursive calls (lines 15–16), each for a slightly smaller problem than the original call to fibonacci. Lines 15–16 use BigInteger methods **add** and subtract to help implement the recursive step. We also use a constant of type BigInteger named TWO that we defined at line 6.

Analyzing the Calls to Method *Fibonacci*

Figure 18.5 shows how method fibonacci evaluates fibonacci(3). At the bottom of the figure we're left with the values 1, 0 and 1—the results of evaluating the *base cases*. The first two return values (from left to right), 1 and 0, are returned as the values for the calls fibonacci(1) and fibonacci(0). The sum 1 plus 0 is returned as the value of fibonacci(2). This is added to the result (1) of the call to fibonacci(1), producing the value 2. This final value is then returned as the value of fibonacci(3).

Figure 18.5 raises some interesting issues about *the order in which Java compilers evaluate the operands of operators*. This order is different from that in which operators are applied to their operands—namely, the order dictated by the rules of operator precedence. From Figure 18.5, it appears that while fibonacci(3) is being evaluated, two recursive calls will be made—fibonacci(2) and fibonacci(1). But in what order will they be made? *The Java language specifies that the order of evaluation of the operands is from left to right.* Thus, the call fibonacci(2) is made first and the call fibonacci(1) second.

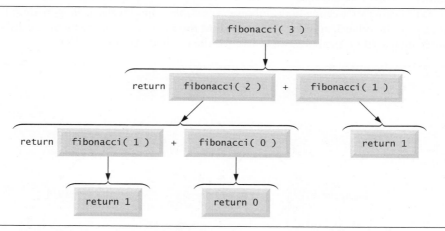

Fig. 18.5 | Set of recursive calls for fibonacci(3).

Complexity Issues

A word of caution is in order about recursive programs like the one we use here to generate Fibonacci numbers. Each invocation of the fibonacci method that does not match one of the *base cases* (0 or 1) results in *two more recursive calls* to the fibonacci method. Hence, this set of recursive calls rapidly gets out of hand. Calculating the Fibonacci value of 20 with the program in Fig. 18.4 requires 21,891 calls to the fibonacci method; calculating the Fibonacci value of 30 requires 2,692,537 calls! As you try to calculate larger Fibonacci values, you'll notice that each consecutive Fibonacci number you use the application to calculate results in a substantial increase in calculation time and in the number of calls to the fibonacci method. For example, the Fibonacci value of 31 requires 4,356,617 calls, and the Fibonacci value of 32 requires 7,049,155 calls! As you can see, the number of calls to fibonacci increases quickly—1,664,080 additional calls between Fibonacci values of 30 and 31 and 2,692,538 additional calls between Fibonacci values of 31 and 32! The difference in the number of calls made between Fibonacci values of 31 and 32 is more than 1.5 times the difference in the number of calls for Fibonacci values between 30 and 31. Problems of this nature can humble even the world's most powerful computers.

Performance Tip 18.1

Avoid Fibonacci-style recursive programs, because they result in an exponential "explosion" of method calls.

Calculating Fibonacci Numbers with Lambdas and Streams

8 If you've read Chapter 17, consider how you might calculate Fibonacci numbers using lambdas and streams, rather than recursion.

18.6 Recursion and the Method-Call Stack

In Chapter 6, the *stack* data structure was introduced in the context of understanding how Java performs method calls. We discussed both the *method-call stack* and *stack frames*. In this section, we'll use these concepts to demonstrate how the program-execution stack handles *recursive* method calls.

Let's begin by returning to the Fibonacci example—specifically, calling method fibonacci with the value 3, as in Fig. 18.5. To show the *order* in which the method calls' stack frames are placed on the stack, we've lettered the method calls in Fig. 18.6.

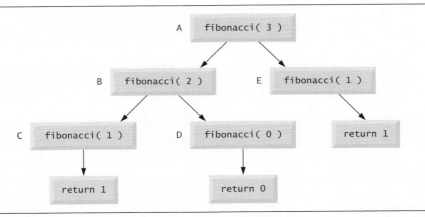

Fig. 18.6 | Method calls made within the call fibonacci(3).

When the first method call (A) is made, a *stack frame* containing the value of the local variable number (3, in this case) is *pushed* onto the *program-execution stack*. This stack, including the stack frame for method call A, is illustrated in part (a) of Fig. 18.7. [*Note:* We use a simplified stack here. An actual program-execution stack and its stack frames would be more complex than in Fig. 18.7, containing such information as where the method call is to *return* to when it has completed execution.]

Within method call A, method calls B and E are made. The original method call has not yet completed, so its stack frame remains on the stack. The first method call to be made from within A is method call B, so the stack frame for method call B is pushed onto the stack on top of the one for method call A. Method call B must execute and complete before method call E is made.

Within method call B, method calls C and D will be made. Method call C is made first, and its stack frame is pushed onto the stack [part (b) of Fig. 18.7]. Method call B has not yet finished, and its stack frame is still on the method-call stack. When method call C executes, it makes no further method calls, but simply returns the value 1. When this method returns, its stack frame is popped off the top of the stack. The method call at the top of the stack is now B, which continues to execute by performing method call D. The stack

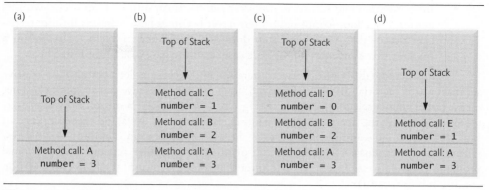

Fig. 18.7 | Method calls on the program-execution stack.

frame for method call D is pushed onto the stack [part (c) of Fig. 18.7]. Method call D completes without making any more method calls and returns the value 0. The stack frame for this method call is then popped off the stack.

Now, both method calls made from within method call B have returned. Method call B continues to execute, returning the value 1. Method call B completes, and its stack frame is popped off the stack. At this point, the stack frame for method call A is at the top of the stack and the method continues its execution. This method makes method call E, whose stack frame is now pushed onto the stack [part (d) of Fig. 18.7]. Method call E completes and returns the value 1. The stack frame for this method call is popped off the stack, and once again method call A continues to execute.

At this point, method call A will not make any other method calls and can finish its execution, returning the value 2 to A's caller (`fibonacci(3)` = 2). A's stack frame is popped off the stack. The executing method is always the one whose stack frame is at the top of the stack, and the stack frame for that method contains the values of its local variables.

18.7 Recursion vs. Iteration

We've studied methods `factorial` and `fibonacci`, which can easily be implemented either recursively or iteratively. In this section, we compare the two approaches and discuss why you might choose one approach over the other in a particular situation.

Both iteration and recursion are *based on a control statement*: Iteration uses an iteration statement (e.g., `for`, `while` or `do...while`), whereas recursion uses a selection statement (e.g., `if`, `if...else` or `switch`):

- Both iteration and recursion involve *iteration*: Iteration explicitly uses an iteration statement, whereas recursion achieves iteration through repeated method calls.

- Iteration and recursion each involve a *termination test*: Iteration terminates when the loop-continuation condition fails, whereas recursion terminates when a base case is reached.

- Iteration with counter-controlled iteration and recursion both *gradually approach termination*: Iteration keeps modifying a counter until the counter assumes a value that makes the loop-continuation condition fail, whereas recursion keeps producing smaller versions of the original problem until the base case is reached.

• Both iteration and recursion *can occur infinitely*: An infinite loop occurs with iteration if the loop-continuation test never becomes false, whereas infinite recursion occurs if the recursion step does not reduce the problem each time in a manner that converges on the base case, or if the base case is not tested.

To illustrate the differences between iteration and recursion, let's examine an iterative solution to the factorial problem (Fig. 18.8, lines 10–12). Here we use an iteration statement, rather than a selection statement (Fig. 18.2, lines 7–12). Both solutions use a termination test. In the recursive solution (Fig. 18.2), line 7 tests for the *base case*. In Fig. 18.8's iterative solution, line 10 tests the loop-continuation condition—if the test fails, the loop terminates. Finally, instead of producing smaller versions of the original problem, the iterative solution uses a counter that is modified until the loop-continuation condition becomes false.

```java
 1   // Fig. 18.8: FactorialCalculator.java
 2   // Iterative factorial method.
 3
 4   public class FactorialCalculator {
 5      // iterative declaration of method factorial
 6      public long factorial(long number) {
 7         long result = 1;
 8
 9         // iteratively calculate factorial
10         for (long i = number; i >= 1; i--) {
11            result *= i;
12         }
13
14         return result;
15      }
16
17      public static void main(String[] args) {
18         // calculate the factorials of 0 through 10
19         for (int counter = 0; counter <= 10; counter++) {
20            System.out.printf("%d! = %d%n", counter, factorial(counter));
21         }
22      }
23   }
```

```
0! = 1
1! = 1
2! = 2
3! = 6
4! = 24
5! = 120
6! = 720
7! = 5040
8! = 40320
9! = 362880
10! = 3628800
```

Fig. 18.8 | Iterative factorial method.

Recursion has many *negatives*. It repeatedly invokes the mechanism, and consequently the *overhead, of method calls*. This iteration can be *expensive* in terms of both processor time and memory space. Each recursive call causes another *copy* of the method (actually, only the method's variables, stored in the stack frame) to be created—this set of copies *can consume considerable memory space*. Since iteration occurs within a method, repeated method calls and extra memory assignment are avoided.

Software Engineering Observation 18.1

Any problem that can be solved recursively can be solved iteratively and vice versa. A recursive approach is preferred over an iterative approach when the recursive approach more naturally mirrors the problem and results in a program that's easier to understand and debug. A recursive approach can often be implemented with fewer lines of code. Another reason to choose a recursive approach is that an iterative one might not be apparent.

Performance Tip 18.2

When performance is crucial, you might want to try various iterative and recursive approaches to see which achieve your goal.

Common Programming Error 18.2

Accidentally having a nonrecursive method call itself either directly or indirectly through another method can cause infinite recursion.

18.8 Towers of Hanoi

Earlier in this chapter we studied methods that can be easily implemented both recursively and iteratively. Now, we present a problem whose recursive solution demonstrates the elegance of recursion, and whose iterative solution may not be as apparent.

The **Towers of Hanoi** is one of the classic problems every budding computer scientist must grapple with. Legend has it that in a temple in the Far East, priests are attempting to move a stack of golden disks from one diamond peg to another (Fig. 18.9). The initial stack has 64 disks threaded onto one peg and arranged from bottom to top by decreasing size. The priests are attempting to move the stack from one peg to another under the constraints that exactly one disk is moved at a time and at no time may a larger disk be placed above a smaller disk. Three pegs are provided, one being used for temporarily holding disks. Supposedly, the world will end when the priests complete their task, so there's little incentive for us to facilitate their efforts.

Let's assume that the priests are attempting to move the disks from peg 1 to peg 3. We wish to develop an algorithm that prints the precise sequence of peg-to-peg disk transfers.

If we try to find an iterative solution, we'll likely find ourselves hopelessly "knotted up" in managing the disks. Instead, attacking this problem recursively quickly yields a solution. Moving *n* disks can be viewed in terms of moving only *n* – 1 disks (hence the recursion) as follows:

1. Move *n* – 1 disks from peg 1 to peg 2, using peg 3 as a temporary holding area.

2. Move the last disk (the largest) from peg 1 to peg 3.

3. Move *n* – 1 disks from peg 2 to peg 3, using peg 1 as a temporary holding area.

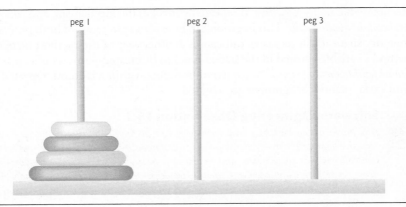

Fig. 18.9 | Towers of Hanoi for the case with four disks.

The process ends when the last task involves moving $n = 1$ disk (i.e., the base case). This task is accomplished by moving the disk, without using a temporary holding area.

In Fig. 18.10, method solveTowers (lines 5–22) solves the Towers of Hanoi, given the total number of disks (in this case 3), the starting peg, the ending peg, and the temporary holding peg as parameters.

```
1   // Fig. 18.10: TowersOfHanoi.java
2   // Towers of Hanoi solution with a recursive method.
3   public class TowersOfHanoi {
4      // recursively move disks between towers
5      public static void solveTowers(int disks, int sourcePeg,
6         int destinationPeg, int tempPeg) {
7         // base case -- only one disk to move
8         if (disks == 1) {
9            System.out.printf("%n%d --> %d", sourcePeg, destinationPeg);
10           return;
11        }
12
13        // recursion step -- move (disk - 1) disks from sourcePeg
14        // to tempPeg using destinationPeg
15        solveTowers(disks - 1, sourcePeg, tempPeg, destinationPeg);
16
17        // move last disk from sourcePeg to destinationPeg
18        System.out.printf("%n%d --> %d", sourcePeg, destinationPeg);
19
20        // move (disks - 1) disks from tempPeg to destinationPeg
21        solveTowers(disks - 1, tempPeg, destinationPeg, sourcePeg);
22     }
23
24     public static void main(String[] args) {
25        int startPeg = 1; // value 1 used to indicate startPeg in output
26        int endPeg = 3; // value 3 used to indicate endPeg in output
27        int tempPeg = 2; // value 2 used to indicate tempPeg in output
28        int totalDisks = 3; // number of disks
```

Fig. 18.10 | Towers of Hanoi solution with a recursive method. (Part 1 of 2.)

```
29
30            // initial nonrecursive call: move all disks.
31            solveTowers(totalDisks, startPeg, endPeg, tempPeg);
32        }
33   }
```

```
1 --> 3
1 --> 2
3 --> 2
1 --> 3
2 --> 1
2 --> 3
1 --> 3
```

Fig. 18.10 | Towers of Hanoi solution with a recursive method. (Part 2 of 2.)

The base case (lines 8–11) occurs when only one disk needs to be moved from the starting peg to the ending peg. The recursion step (lines 15–21) moves disks - 1 disks (line 15) from the first peg (sourcePeg) to the temporary holding peg (tempPeg). When all but one of the disks have been moved to the temporary peg, line 18 moves the largest disk from the start peg to the destination peg. Line 21 finishes the rest of the moves by calling the method solveTowers to recursively move disks - 1 disks from the temporary peg (tempPeg) to the destination peg (destinationPeg), this time using the first peg (sourcePeg) as the temporary peg. Line 31 in main calls the recursive solveTowers method, which outputs the steps to the command prompt.

18.9 Fractals

A **fractal** is a geometric figure that can be generated from a pattern repeated recursively (Fig. 18.11). The figure is modified by recursively applying the pattern to each segment of the original figure. Although such figures had been studied before the 20th century, it was the mathematician Benoit Mandelbrot who in the 1970s introduced the term "fractal," along with the specifics of how a fractal is created and the practical applications of fractals. Mandelbrot's fractal geometry provides mathematical models for many complex forms found in nature, such as mountains, clouds and coastlines. Fractals have many uses in mathematics and science. They can be used to better understand systems or patterns that appear in nature (e.g., ecosystems), in the human body (e.g., in the folds of the brain), or in the universe (e.g., galaxy clusters). Not all fractals resemble objects in nature. Drawing fractals has become a popular art form. Fractals have a **self-similar property**—when subdivided into parts, each resembles a reduced-size copy of the whole. Many fractals yield an exact copy of the original when a portion of the fractal is magnified—such a fractal is said to be **strictly self-similar**.

18.9.1 Koch Curve Fractal

As an example, let's look at the strictly self-similar **Koch Curve** fractal (Fig. 18.11). It's formed by removing the middle third of each line in the drawing and replacing it with two lines that form a point, such that if the middle third of the original line remained, an equilateral triangle would be formed. Formulas for creating fractals often involve removing all or part of the previous fractal image. This pattern has already been determined for this fractal—we focus here on how to use those formulas in a recursive solution.

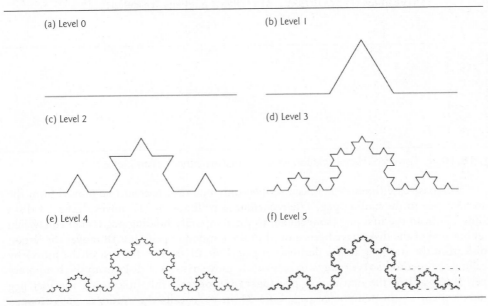

Fig. 18.11 | Koch Curve fractal.

We start with a straight line (Fig. 18.11(a)) and apply the pattern, creating a triangle from the middle third (Fig. 18.11(b)). We then apply the pattern again to each straight line, resulting in Fig. 18.11(c). Each time the pattern is applied, we say that the fractal is at a new **level**, or **depth** or **order** is also used). Fractals can be displayed at many levels—e.g., a fractal at level 3 has had three iterations of the pattern applied (Fig. 18.11(d)). After only a few iterations, this fractal begins to look like a portion of a snowflake (Fig. 18.11(e and f)). Since this is a strictly self-similar fractal, each portion of it contains an exact copy of the fractal. In Fig. 18.11(f), we've highlighted a portion of the fractal with a dashed box. If the image in this box were increased in size, it would look exactly like the entire fractal of part (f).

A similar fractal, the **Koch Snowflake**, is similar to the Koch Curve but begins with a triangle rather than a line. The same pattern is applied to each side of the triangle, resulting in an image that looks like an enclosed snowflake.

18.9.2 (Optional) Case Study: Lo Feather Fractal

We now demonstrate using recursion to draw fractals by writing a program to create a strictly self-similar fractal. We call this the "Lo feather fractal," named for Sin Han Lo, a Deitel & Associates colleague who created it. The fractal will eventually resemble one-half of a feather (see the outputs in Fig. 18.19). The base case, or fractal level of 0, begins as a line between two points, A and B (Fig. 18.12). To create the next higher level, we find the midpoint (C) of the line. To calculate the location of point C, use the following formula:

```
xC = (xA + xB) / 2;
yC = (yA + yB) / 2;
```

[*Note:* The x and y to the left of each letter refer to the *x*-coordinate and *y*-coordinate of that point, respectively. For example, xA refers to the *x*-coordinate of point A, while yC re-fers to the *y*-coordinate of point C. In our diagrams we denote the point by its letter, fol-lowed by two numbers representing the *x*- and *y*-coordinates.]

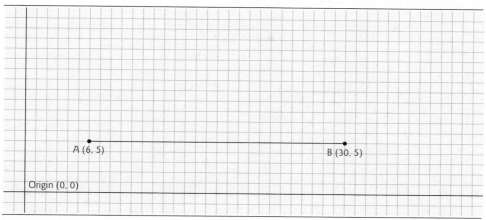

Fig. 18.12 | "Lo feather fractal" at level 0.

To create this fractal, we also must find a point D that lies left of segment AC and cre-ates an isosceles right triangle ADC. To calculate point D's location, use the formulas:

```
xD = xA + (xC - xA) / 2 - (yC - yA) / 2;
yD = yA + (yC - yA) / 2 + (xC - xA) / 2;
```

We now move from level 0 to level 1 as follows: First, add points C and D (as in Fig. 18.13). Then, remove the original line and add segments DA, DC and DB. The remaining lines will curve at an angle, causing our fractal to look like a feather.

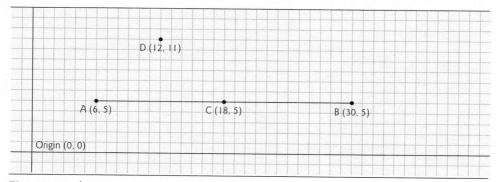

Fig. 18.13 | Determining points C and D for level 1 of the "Lo feather fractal."

For the next level of the fractal, this algorithm is repeated on each of the three lines in level 1. For each line, the formulas above are applied, where the former point D is now con-sidered to be point A, while the other end of each line is considered to be point B. Figure 18.14 contains the line from level 0 (now a dashed line) and the three added lines from level 1. We've changed point D to be point A, and the original points A, C and B to B1, B2 and B3, respectively. The preceding formulas have been used to find the new points C and D on each line. These points are also numbered 1–3 to keep track of which point is associated with each line. The points C1 and D1, for example, represent points C and D associated with the line formed from points A to B1.

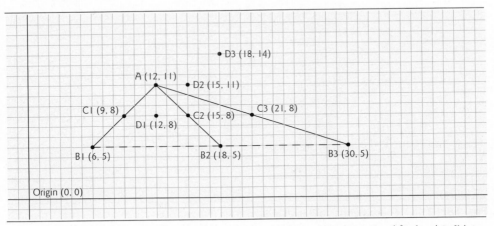

Fig. 18.14 | "Lo feather fractal" at level 1, with C and D points determined for level 2. [*Note:* The fractal at level 0 is included as a dashed line as a reminder of where the line was located in relation to the current fractal.]

To achieve level 2, the three lines in Fig. 18.14 are removed and replaced with new lines from the C and D points just added. Figure 18.15 shows the new lines (the lines from level 2 are shown as dashed lines for your convenience).

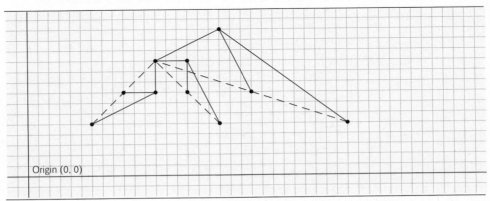

Fig. 18.15 | "Lo feather fractal" at level 2, with dashed lines from level 1 provided.

Figure 18.16 shows level 2 without the dashed lines from level 1. Once this process has been repeated several times, the fractal will begin to look like one-half of a feather, as shown in the output of Fig. 18.19.

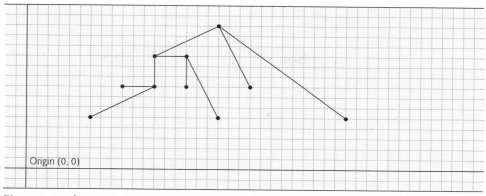

Origin (0, 0)

Fig. 18.16 | "Lo feather fractal" at level 2.

18.9.3 (Optional) Fractal App GUI

In this section and the next, we build a JavaFX **Fractal** app that displays the Lo Fractal—we do not show the example's `Application` subclass, because it performs the same tasks we demonstrated in Chapters 12–13 to load and display the app's FXML.

Figure 18.17 shows the GUI with the **fx:id** values for the controls we access programmatically. Like the **Painter** app in Section 13.3, this app uses a `BorderPane` layout with a with a white background color:

- In the top area, we placed a `ToolBar` (located in the Scene Builder **Library**'s **Containers** section). A `ToolBar` layout arranges its controls horizontally (by default) or vertically. Typically, you place `ToolBar`s at your GUI's edges, such as in a `BorderPane`'s top, left, bottom or right areas.

- In the center, we placed a 400-by-480 pixel `Canvas` (from the Scene Builder **Library**'s **Miscellaneous** section). **Canvas** is a `Node` subclass in which you can draw graphics using a **GraphicsContext** (both in the package `javafx.scene.canvas`). We show you how to draw a line in a specific color in this example and discuss classes `Canvas` and `GraphicsContext` in detail in Section 20.10.

To size the `BorderPane` layout to its contents, we reset its **Pref Width** and **Pref Height** property values (as you learned in Chapter 13) to `USE_COMPUTED_SIZE`.

ToolBar and Its Additional Controls

By default, the `ToolBar` you drag onto your layout has one `Button`. You can drag additional controls onto the `ToolBar` and, if necessary, remove the default `Button`. We added a `ColorPicker` control (with **fx:id** `colorPicker`), another `Button` and a `Label` (with **fx:id** `levelLabel`). For the two `Button`s and the `Label`, we set their text as shown in Fig. 18.17.

ColorPicker

A **ColorPicker** provides a predefined color-selecting GUI that, by default, enables the user to choose colors by color swatches (small squares of sample colors). Initially, the selected color is **White**. We'll programmatically set this to **Blue** in the app's controller. Figure 18.18 shows the `ColorPicker`'s default GUI and the **Custom Colors** GUI that appears when you click the `ColorPicker`'s **Custom Color...** link. The **Custom Colors** GUI enables you to select any custom color.

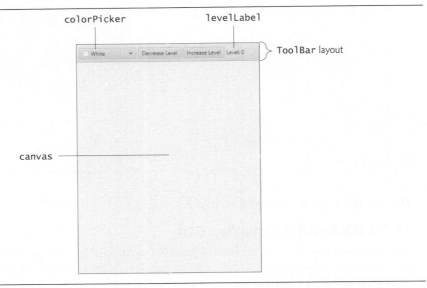

Fig. 18.17 | **Fractal** GUI labeled with **fx:id**s for the programmatically manipulated controls.

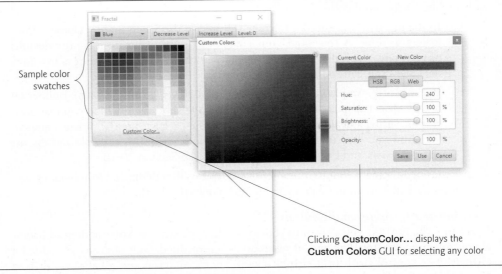

Fig. 18.18 | ColorPicker's predefined GUI.

Event Handlers

When the user selects a color in the default GUI or customizes a color and presses **Save** in the **Custom Colors** GUI, an ActionEvent occurs. In Scene Builder, for the ColorPicker's **On Action** event handler, we specified colorSelected. In addition, for the **Decrease Level** and **Increase Level** Button's **On Action** events handlers, we specified decreaseLevelButtonPressed and increaseLevelButtonPressed, respectively.

18.9.4 (Optional) FractalController Class

Figure 18.19 presents class FractalController, which defines the app's event handlers and the methods for drawing the Lo Fractal recursively. The outputs show the development of the fractal from levels 0–5, then for levels 8 and 11. If we focus on one of the arms of this fractal, it will be identical to the whole image. This property defines the fractal to be strictly self-similar.

```java
1   // Fig. 18.19: FractalController.java
2   // Drawing the "Lo feather fractal" using recursion.
3   import javafx.event.ActionEvent;
4   import javafx.fxml.FXML;
5   import javafx.scene.canvas.Canvas;
6   import javafx.scene.canvas.GraphicsContext;
7   import javafx.scene.control.ColorPicker;
8   import javafx.scene.control.Label;
9   import javafx.scene.paint.Color;
10  import javafx.scene.shape.Line;
11
12  public class FractalController {
13     // constants
14     private static final int MIN_LEVEL = 0;
15     private static final int MAX_LEVEL = 15;
16
17     // instance variables that refer to GUI components
18     @FXML private Canvas canvas;
19     @FXML private ColorPicker colorPicker;
20     @FXML private Label levelLabel;
21
22     // other instance variables
23     private Color currentColor = Color.BLUE;
24     private int level = MIN_LEVEL; // initial fractal level
25     private GraphicsContext gc; // used to draw on Canvas
26
27     // initialize the controller
28     public void initialize() {
29        levelLabel.setText("Level: " + level);
30        colorPicker.setValue(currentColor); // start with purple
31        gc = canvas.getGraphicsContext2D(); // get the GraphicsContext
32        drawFractal();
33     }
34
35     // sets currentColor when user chooses a new Color
36     @FXML
37     void colorSelected(ActionEvent event) {
38        currentColor = colorPicker.getValue(); // get new Color
39        drawFractal();
40     }
41
```

Fig. 18.19 | Drawing the "Lo feather fractal" using recursion. (Part 1 of 4.)

```
42      // decrease level and redraw fractal
43      @FXML
44      void decreaseLevelButtonPressed(ActionEvent event) {
45         if (level > MIN_LEVEL) {
46            --level;
47            levelLabel.setText("Level: " + level);
48            drawFractal();
49         }
50      }
51
52      // increase level and redraw fractal
53      @FXML
54      void increaseLevelButtonPressed(ActionEvent event) {
55         if (level < MAX_LEVEL) {
56            ++level;
57            levelLabel.setText("Level: " + level);
58            drawFractal();
59         }
60      }
61
62      // clear Canvas, set drawing color and draw the fractal
63      private void drawFractal() {
64         gc.clearRect(0, 0, canvas.getWidth(), canvas.getHeight());
65         gc.setStroke(currentColor);
66         drawFractal(level, 40, 40, 350, 350);
67      }
68
69      // draw fractal recursively
70      public void drawFractal(int level, int xA, int yA, int xB, int yB) {
71         // base case: draw a line connecting two given points
72         if (level == 0) {
73            gc.strokeLine(xA, yA, xB, yB);
74         }
75         else { // recursion step: determine new points, draw next level
76            // calculate midpoint between (xA, yA) and (xB, yB)
77            int xC = (xA + xB) / 2;
78            int yC = (yA + yB) / 2;
79
80            // calculate the fourth point (xD, yD) which forms an
81            // isosceles right triangle between (xA, yA) and (xC, yC)
82            // where the right angle is at (xD, yD)
83            int xD = xA + (xC - xA) / 2 - (yC - yA) / 2;
84            int yD = yA + (yC - yA) / 2 + (xC - xA) / 2;
85
86            // recursively draw the Fractal
87            drawFractal(level - 1, xD, yD, xA, yA);
88            drawFractal(level - 1, xD, yD, xC, yC);
89            drawFractal(level - 1, xD, yD, xB, yB);
90         }
91      }
92   }
```

Fig. 18.19 | Drawing the "Lo feather fractal" using recursion. (Part 2 of 4.)

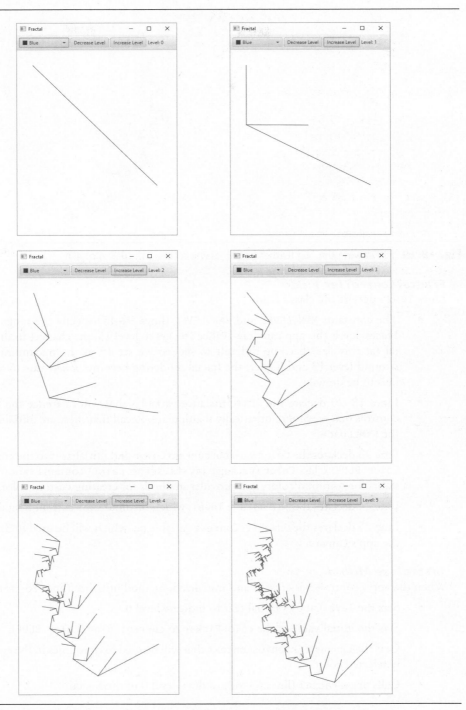

Fig. 18.19 | Drawing the "Lo feather fractal" using recursion. (Part 3 of 4.)

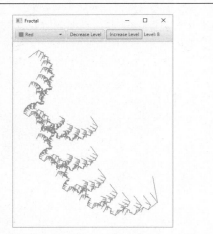 

Fig. 18.19 | Drawing the "Lo feather fractal" using recursion. (Part 4 of 4.)

FractalController Fields

Lines 14–25 declare the class's fields:

- The constants MIN_LEVEL and MAX_LEVEL (lines 14–15) specify the range of Lo Fractal levels this app can draw. Once you get to level 15, the changes in the fractal (at this size) become difficult to see, so we set 15 as the maximum level. Around level 13 and higher, the fractal rendering becomes *slower* due to the details to be drawn.

- Lines 18–20 declare the @FXML instance variables that will reference the GUI's controls that we programmatically manipulate. Recall that these are initialized by the FXMLLoader.

- Line 23 declares the Color variable currentColor and initialize it to the constant Color.BLUE. Class **Color** (package javafx.scene.paint) contains various constants for common colors and provides methods for creating custom colors.

- Line 24 declares the int variable level, which maintains the current fractal level.

- Line 25 declares the GraphicsContext variable gc, which will be used to draw on the app's Canvas.

initialize Method

When the app's controller is created and initialized, method initialize (lines 28–33):

- Sets the levelLabel's initial text to indicate level 0.

- Sets the initial value of the colorPicker to currentColor (Color.BLUE).

- Gets the canvas's GraphicsContext that will be used to draw lines in the currently selected color.

- Calls drawFractal (lines 63–67) to draw level 0 of the fractal.

colorSelected *Event Handler*
When the user choses a new color, the colorPicker's colorSelected event handler (lines 36–40) uses ColorPicker method **getValue** to get the currently selected color, then calls drawFractal (lines 63–67) to redraw the fractal in the new color and current level.

decreaseLevelButtonPressed *and* increaseLevelButtonPressed *Event Handlers*
When the user presses the **Decrease Level** or **Increase Level** Buttons, the corresponding event handler (lines 43–50 or 53–60) executes. These event handlers decrease or increase the level, set the levelLabel's text accordingly and call drawFractal (lines 63–67) to redraw the fractal for the new level and currentColor. Attempting to decrease the level below MIN_LEVEL or above MAX_LEVEL does nothing in this app.

drawFractal *Method with No Arguments*
Each time method drawFractal is called, it uses GraphicsContext method **clearRect** to clear any prior drawing. This method clears a rectangular area by setting the contents of the specified area to the Canvas's background color. The method's four arguments are the *x*- and *y*-coordinates of the rectangle's upper-left corner and the width and height of the rectangle. In this case, we clear the entire Canvas—methods **getWidth** and **getHeight** return the Canvas's width and height, respectively.

Next, line 65 calls GraphicsContext method **setStroke** to set the drawing color to the currentColor. Then line 66 makes the first call to the overloaded *recursive* method drawFractal (lines 70–91) to draw the fractal.

drawFractal *Method with Five Arguments*
Lines 70–91 define the recursive method that creates the fractal. This method takes five parameters: the level of the Lo Fractal to draw and four integers that specify the *x*- and *y*-coordinates of two points. The base case for this method (line 72) occurs when level equals 0, at which time line 73 uses GraphicsContext method **strokeLine** to draw a line between the two points the current call to drawFractal received as arguments.

In the recursive step (lines 75–90), lines 77–84 calculate

- (xC, yC)—the midpoint between (xA, yA) and (xB, yB), and
- (xD, yD)—the point that creates a right isosceles triangle with (xA, yA) and (xC, yC).

Then, lines 87–89 make three recursive calls on three different sets of points.

Since no lines will be drawn until the base case is reached, the distance between two points decreases on each recursive call. As the level of recursion increases, the fractal becomes smoother and more detailed. The shape of this fractal stabilizes as the level approaches 12—that is, the shape of the fractal remains approximately the same and the additional details become hard to perceive. Fractals will stabilize at different levels based on their shape and size.

18.10 Recursive Backtracking

Our recursive methods all have a similar architecture—if the base case is reached, return a result; if not, make one or more recursive calls. This section explores a more complex recursive technique that finds a path through a maze, returning true if there's a possible solution. The solution involves moving through the maze one step at a time, where moves can be made by going down, right, up or left (diagonal moves are not permitted). From the current location in the maze (starting with the entry point), the following steps are taken: For each possible direction, the move is made in that direction and a recursive call is made to solve the remainder of the maze from the new location. When a dead end is reached (i.e., we cannot take any more steps forward without hitting a wall), we *back up* to the previous location and try to go in a different direction. If no other direction can be taken, we back up again. This process continues until we find a point in the maze where a move *can* be made in another direction. Once such a location is found, we move in the new direction and continue with another recursive call to solve the rest of the maze.

To back up to the previous location in the maze, our recursive method simply returns false, moving up the method-call chain to the previous recursive call (which references the previous location in the maze). Using recursion to return to an earlier decision point is known as **recursive backtracking**. If one set of recursive calls does not result in a solution to the problem, the program *backs up* to the previous decision point and makes a different decision, often resulting in another set of recursive calls. In this example, the previous decision point is the previous location in the maze, and the decision to be made is the direction that the next move should take. One direction has led to a *dead end*, so the search continues with a *different* direction. The recursive backtracking solution to the maze problem uses recursion to return only *partway* up the method-call chain, then try a different direction. If the backtracking reaches the entry location of the maze and the paths in all directions have been attempted, the maze does not have a solution.

18.11 Wrap-Up

In this chapter, you learned how to create recursive methods—i.e., methods that call themselves. You learned that recursive methods typically divide a problem into two conceptual pieces—a piece that the method knows how to do (the base case) and a piece that the method does not know how to do (the recursion step). The recursion step is a slightly smaller version of the original problem and is performed by a recursive method call. You saw some popular recursion examples, including calculating factorials and producing values in the Fibonacci series. You then learned how recursion works "under the hood," including the order in which recursive method calls are pushed on or popped off the program-execution stack. Next, you compared recursive and iterative approaches. You learned how to use recursion to solve more complex problems—the Towers of Hanoi and displaying fractals. The chapter concluded with an introduction to recursive backtracking, a technique for solving problems that involves backing up through recursive calls to try different possible solutions. In the next chapter, you'll learn how to implement your own generic methods and types.

Generic Classes and Methods: A Deeper Look

Objectives

In this chapter you'll:

- Create generic methods that perform identical tasks on arguments of different types.
- Create a generic `Stack` class that can be used to store objects of any class or interface type.
- Learn about compile-time translation of generic methods and classes.
- Learn how to overload generic methods with non-generic or generic methods.
- Use wildcards when precise type information about a parameter is not required in the method body.

19.1 Introduction

You've used existing generic methods and classes in Chapters 7 and 16. In this chapter, you'll learn how to write your own.

It would be nice if we could write a single sort method to sort the elements in an Integer array, a String array or an array of any type that supports ordering (i.e., its elements can be compared). It would also be nice if we could write a single Stack class that could be used as a Stack of integers, a Stack of floating-point numbers, a Stack of Strings or a Stack of any other type. It would be even nicer if we could detect type mismatches at *compile time*—known as **compile-time type safety**. For example, if a Stack should store only integers, an attempt to push a String onto that Stack should issue a *compilation* error. This chapter discusses **generics**—specifically **generic methods** and **generic classes**—which provide the means to create the type-safe general models mentioned above.

19.2 Motivation for Generic Methods

Overloaded methods are often used to perform *similar* operations on *different* types of data. To motivate generic methods, let's begin with an example (Fig. 19.1) containing overloaded printArray methods (lines 20–27, 30–37 and 40–47) that print the String representations of the elements of an Integer array, a Double array and a Character array, respectively. We could have used arrays of primitive types int, double and char. We're using arrays of the type-wrapper classes to set up our generic method example, because *only reference types can be used to specify generic types in generic methods and classes.*

```
1   // Fig. 19.1: OverloadedMethods.java
2   // Printing array elements using overloaded methods.
3
4   public class OverloadedMethods {
5      public static void main(String[] args) {
6         // create arrays of Integer, Double and Character
7         Integer[] integerArray = {1, 2, 3, 4, 5, 6};
8         Double[] doubleArray = {1.1, 2.2, 3.3, 4.4, 5.5, 6.6, 7.7};
9         Character[] characterArray = {'H', 'E', 'L', 'L', 'O'};
10
11        System.out.printf("Array integerArray contains: ");
12        printArray(integerArray); // pass an Integer array
13        System.out.printf("Array doubleArray contains: ");
```

Fig. 19.1 | Printing array elements using overloaded methods. (Part I of 2.)

```
14          printArray(doubleArray); // pass a Double array
15          System.out.printf("Array characterArray contains: ");
16          printArray(characterArray); // pass a Character array
17      }
18
19      // method printArray to print Integer array
20      public static void printArray(Integer[] inputArray) {
21          // display array elements
22          for (Integer element : inputArray) {
23              System.out.printf("%s ", element);
24          }
25
26          System.out.println();
27      }
28
29      // method printArray to print Double array
30      public static void printArray(Double[] inputArray) {
31          // display array elements
32          for (Double element : inputArray) {
33              System.out.printf("%s ", element);
34          }
35
36          System.out.println();
37      }
38
39      // method printArray to print Character array
40      public static void printArray(Character[] inputArray) {
41          // display array elements
42          for (Character element : inputArray) {
43              System.out.printf("%s ", element);
44          }
45
46          System.out.println();
47      }
48  }
```

```
Array integerArray contains: 1 2 3 4 5 6
Array doubleArray contains: 1.1 2.2 3.3 4.4 5.5 6.6 7.7
Array characterArray contains: H E L L O
```

Fig. 19.1 | Printing array elements using overloaded methods. (Part 2 of 2.)

The program begins by declaring and initializing three arrays—six-element Integer array integerArray (line 7), seven-element Double array doubleArray (line 8) and five-element Character array characterArray (line 9). Then lines 11–16 display the contents of each array.

When the compiler encounters a method call, it attempts to locate a method declaration with the same name and with parameters that match the argument types in the call. In this example, each printArray call matches one of the printArray method declarations. For example, line 12 calls printArray with integerArray as its argument. The compiler determines the argument's type (i.e., Integer[]) and attempts to locate a printArray method that specifies an Integer[] parameter (lines 20–27), then sets up a call to that method. Similarly, when the compiler encounters the call at line 14, it determines the argument's type (i.e., `Double[]`), then attempts to locate a `printArray` method that specifies a `Double[]` parameter (lines 30–37), then sets up a call to that method. Finally, when the compiler encounters the call at line 16, it determines the argument's type (i.e., `Character[]`), then attempts to locate a `printArray` method that specifies a `Character[]` parameter (lines 40–47), then sets up a call to that method.

Common Features in the Overloaded *printArray* Methods

Study each `printArray` method. The array element type appears in each method's header (lines 20, 30 and 40) and `for`-statement header (lines 22, 32 and 42). If we were to replace the element types in each method with a generic name—`T` by convention—then all three methods would look like the one in Fig. 19.2. It appears that if we can replace the array element type in each of the three methods with a *single generic type*, then we should be able to declare *one* `printArray` method that can display the `String` representations of the elements of *any* array that contains objects. The method in Fig. 19.2 is similar to the generic `printArray` method declaration you'll see in Section 19.3. The one shown here *will not compile*—we use this simply to show that the three `printArray` methods of Fig. 19.1 are identical except for the types they process.

```
1   public static void printArray(T[] inputArray) {
2       // display array elements
3       for (T element : inputArray)  {
4           System.out.printf("%s ", element);
5       }
6
7       System.out.println();
8   }
```

Fig. 19.2 | `printArray` method in which actual type names are replaced with a generic type name (in this case `T`).

19.3 Generic Methods: Implementation and Compile-Time Translation

If the operations performed by several overloaded methods are *identical* for each argument type, the overloaded methods can be more conveniently coded using a generic method. You can write a single generic method declaration that can be called with arguments of different types. Based on the types of the arguments passed to the generic method, the compiler handles each method call appropriately. At *compilation time*, the compiler ensures the *type safety* of your code, preventing many runtime errors.

Figure 19.3 reimplements Fig. 19.1 using a generic `printArray` method (lines 20–27 of Fig. 19.3). The `printArray` calls in lines 12, 14 and 16 are identical to those of Fig. 19.1, and the outputs of the two applications are identical. This demonstrates the expressive power of generics.

```java
 1   // Fig. 19.3: GenericMethodTest.java
 2   // Printing array elements using generic method printArray.
 3
 4   public class GenericMethodTest {
 5      public static void main(String[] args) {
 6         // create arrays of Integer, Double and Character
 7         Integer[] integerArray = {1, 2, 3, 4, 5};
 8         Double[] doubleArray = {1.1, 2.2, 3.3, 4.4, 5.5, 6.6, 7.7};
 9         Character[] characterArray = {'H', 'E', 'L', 'L', 'O'};
10
11         System.out.printf("Array integerArray contains: ");
12         printArray(integerArray); // pass an Integer array
13         System.out.printf("Array doubleArray contains: ");
14         printArray(doubleArray); // pass a Double array
15         System.out.printf("Array characterArray contains: ");
16         printArray(characterArray); // pass a Character array
17      }
18
19      // generic method printArray
20      public static <T> void printArray(T[] inputArray) {
21         // display array elements
22         for (T element : inputArray) {
23            System.out.printf("%s ", element);
24         }
25
26         System.out.println();
27      }
28   }
```

```
Array integerArray contains: 1 2 3 4 5
Array doubleArray contains: 1.1 2.2 3.3 4.4 5.5 6.6 7.7
Array characterArray contains: H E L L O
```

Fig. 19.3 | Printing array elements using generic method `printArray`.

Type Parameter Section of a Generic Method

All generic method declarations have a **type-parameter section** (line 20; <T> in this example) delimited by **angle brackets** that precedes the method's return type. Each type-parameter section contains one or more **type parameters**, separated by commas. A type parameter, also known as a **type variable**, is an identifier that specifies a generic type name. The type parameters can be used to declare the return type, parameters and local variables in a generic method declaration, and they act as placeholders for the types of the arguments passed to the generic method, which are known as **actual type arguments**. A generic method's body is declared like that of any other method. *Type parameters can represent only reference types*—not primitive types (like `int`, `double` and `char`). Also, the type-parameter names throughout the method declaration must match those declared in the type-parameter section. For example, line 22 declares `element` as type T, which matches the type parameter (T) declared in line 20. A type parameter can be declared only once in the type-parameter section but can appear more than once in the method's parameter list. For example, the type-parameter name T appears twice in the following method's parameter list:

```
public static <T> T maximum(T value1, T value2)
```

Type-parameter names need not be unique among different generic methods. In method printArray, T appears in the same two locations where the overloaded printArray methods of Fig. 19.1 specified Integer, Double or Character as the array element type. The remainder of printArray is identical to the versions presented in Fig. 19.1.

Good Programming Practice 19.1

The letters T (for "type"), E (for "element"), K (for "key") and V (for "value") are commonly used as type parameters. For other common ones, see http://docs.oracle.com/javase/tutorial/java/generics/types.html.

Testing the Generic *printArray* Method

As in Fig. 19.1, the program in Fig. 19.3 begins by declaring and initializing six-element Integer array integerArray (line 7), seven-element Double array doubleArray (line 8) and five-element Character array characterArray (line 9). Then each array is output by calling printArray (lines 12, 14 and 16)—once with argument integerArray, once with argument doubleArray and once with argument characterArray.

When the compiler encounters line 12, it first determines argument integerArray's type (i.e., Integer[]) and attempts to locate a method named printArray that specifies a single Integer[] parameter. There's no such method in this example. Next, the compiler determines whether there's a generic method named printArray that specifies a single array parameter and uses a type parameter to represent the array element type. The compiler determines that printArray (lines 20–27) is a match and sets up a call to the method. The same process is repeated for the calls to method printArray at lines 14 and 16.

Common Programming Error 19.1

If the compiler cannot match a method call to a nongeneric or a generic method declaration, a compilation error occurs.

Common Programming Error 19.2

If the compiler doesn't find a method declaration that matches a method call exactly, but does find two or more methods that can satisfy the method call, a compilation error occurs. For the complete details of resolving calls to overloaded and generic methods, see http://docs.oracle.com/javase/specs/jls/se8/html/jls-15.html#jls-15.12.

In addition to setting up the method calls, the compiler also determines whether the operations in the method body can be applied to elements of the type stored in the array argument. The only operation performed on the array elements in this example is to output their String representation. Line 23 performs an *implicit toString call* on every element. *To work with generics, every element of the array must be an object of a class or interface type.* Since all objects have a toString method, the compiler is satisfied that line 23 performs a *valid* operation for any object in printArray's array argument. The toString methods of classes Integer, Double and Character return the String representations of the underlying int, double or char value, respectively.

Erasure at Compilation Time

When the compiler translates generic method `printArray` into Java bytecodes, it removes the type-parameter section and *replaces the type parameters with actual types*. This process is known as **erasure**. By default all generic types are replaced with type `Object`. So the compiled version of method `printArray` appears as shown in Fig. 19.4—there's only *one* copy of this code, which is used for all `printArray` calls in the example. This is quite different from similar mechanisms in other programming languages, such as C++'s templates, in which a *separate copy of the source code* is generated and compiled for *every* type passed as an argument to the method. As you'll see in Section 19.4, the translation and compilation of generics is a bit more involved than what we've discussed in this section.

By declaring `printArray` as a generic method in Fig. 19.3, we eliminated the need for the overloaded methods of Fig. 19.1 and created a reusable method that can output the `String` representations of the elements in any array that contains objects. However, this particular example could have simply declared the `printArray` method as shown in Fig. 19.4, using an `Object` array as the parameter. This would have yielded the same results, because any `Object` can be output as a `String`. In a generic method, the benefits become more apparent when you place restrictions on the type parameters, as we demonstrate in the next section.

```
1   public static void printArray(Object[] inputArray) {
2       // display array elements
3       for (Object element : inputArray) {
4           System.out.printf("%s ", element);
5       }
6
7       System.out.println();
8   }
```

Fig. 19.4 | Generic method `printArray` after the compiler performs erasure.

19.4 Additional Compile-Time Translation Issues: Methods That Use a Type Parameter as the Return Type

Let's consider a generic method in which type parameters are used in the return type and in the parameter list (Fig. 19.5). The application uses a generic method `maximum` to determine and return the largest of its three arguments of the same type. Unfortunately, *the relational operator > cannot be used with reference types*. However, it's possible to compare two objects of the same class if that class implements the generic **interface `Comparable<T>`** (from package `java.lang`). All the type-wrapper classes for primitive types implement this interface. **Generic interfaces** enable you to specify, with a single interface declaration, a set of related types. `Comparable<T>` objects have a **compareTo method**. For example, two Integer objects, `integer1` and `integer2`, can be compared with the expression:

```
integer1.compareTo(integer2)
```

When you declare a class that implements `Comparable<T>`, you must define method `compareTo` such that it compares the contents of two objects of that class and returns the comparison results. Method `compareTo` *must* return

- 0 if the objects are equal,
- a negative integer if object1 is less than object2 or
- a positive integer if object1 is greater than object2.

For example, class Integer's compareTo method compares the int values stored in two Integer objects. A benefit of implementing interface Comparable<T> is that Comparable<T> objects can be used with the sorting and searching methods of class Collections (package java.util). We discussed those methods in Chapter 16. In this example, we'll use method compareTo in method maximum to help determine the largest value.

```java
1   // Fig. 19.5: MaximumTest.java
2   // Generic method maximum returns the largest of three objects.
3
4   public class MaximumTest {
5      public static void main(String[] args) {
6         System.out.printf("Maximum of %d, %d and %d is %d%n", 3, 4, 5,
7            maximum(3, 4, 5));
8         System.out.printf("Maximum of %.1f, %.1f and %.1f is %.1f%n",
9            6.6, 8.8, 7.7, maximum(6.6, 8.8, 7.7));
10        System.out.printf("Maximum of %s, %s and %s is %s%n", "pear",
11           "apple", "orange", maximum("pear", "apple", "orange"));
12     }
13
14     // determines the largest of three Comparable objects
15     public static <T extends Comparable<T>> T maximum(T x, T y, T z) {
16        T max = x; // assume x is initially the largest
17
18        if (y.compareTo(max) > 0) {
19           max = y; // y is the largest so far
20        }
21
22        if (z.compareTo(max) > 0) {
23           max = z; // z is the largest
24        }
25
26        return max; // returns the largest object
27     }
28  }
```

```
Maximum of 3, 4 and 5 is 5
Maximum of 6.6, 8.8 and 7.7 is 8.8
Maximum of pear, apple and orange is pear
```

Fig. 19.5 | Generic method maximum with an upper bound on its type parameter.

Generic Method maximum and Specifying a Type Parameter's Upper Bound

Generic method maximum (lines 15–27) uses type parameter T as its return type (line 15), as the type of method parameters x, y and z (line 15), and as the type of local variable max (line 16). The type-parameter section specifies that T extends Comparable<T>—only objects of classes that implement interface Comparable<T> can be used with this method. Comparable<T> is known as the type parameter's **upper bound**. By default, Object is the upper bound, meaning that an object of any type can be used. Type-parameter declarations that bound the parameter always use keyword extends regardless of whether the type parameter extends a class or implements an interface. The upper bound may be a comma-separated list that contains zero or one class and zero or more interfaces.

Method maximum's type parameter is more restrictive than the one specified for print-Array in Fig. 19.3, which was able to output arrays containing any type of object. The Comparable<T> restriction is important, because not all objects can be compared. However, Comparable<T> objects are guaranteed to have a compareTo method.

Method maximum uses the same algorithm that we used in Section 6.4 to determine the largest of its three arguments. The method assumes that its first argument (x) is the largest and assigns it to local variable max (line 16 of Fig. 19.5). Next, the if statement at lines 18–20 determines whether y is greater than max. The condition invokes y's compareTo method with the expression y.compareTo(max), which returns a negative integer, 0 or a positive integer, to determine y's relationship to max. If the return value of the compareTo is greater than 0, then y is greater and is assigned to variable max. Similarly, the if statement at lines 22–24 determines whether z is greater than max and, if so, assigns z to max. Then line 26 returns max to the caller.

Calling Method maximum

In main, line 7 calls maximum with the integers 3, 4 and 5. When the compiler encounters this call, it first looks for a maximum method that takes three arguments of type int. There's no such method, so the compiler looks for a generic method that can be used and finds generic method maximum. However, recall that the arguments to a generic method must be of a *reference type*. So the compiler autoboxes the three int values as Integer objects and specifies that the three Integer objects will be passed to maximum. Class Integer (package java.lang) implements the Comparable<Integer> interface such that method compareTo compares the int values in two Integer objects. Therefore, Integers are valid arguments to method maximum. When the Integer representing the maximum is returned, we attempt to output it with the %d format specifier, which outputs an int primitive-type value. So maximum's return value is output as an int value.

A similar process occurs for the three double arguments passed to maximum in line 9. Each double is autoboxed as a Double object and passed to maximum. Again, this is allowed because class Double (package java.lang) implements the Comparable<Double> interface. The Double returned by maximum is output with the format specifier %.1f, which outputs a double primitive-type value. So maximum's return value is auto-unboxed and output as a double. The call to maximum in line 11 receives three Strings, which are also Comparable<String> objects. We intentionally placed the largest value in a different position in each method call (lines 7, 9 and 11) to show that the generic method always finds the maximum value, regardless of its position in the argument list.

Erasure and the Upper Bound of a Type Parameter

When the compiler translates method maximum into bytecodes, it uses erasure to replace the type parameters with actual types. In Fig. 19.3, all generic types were replaced with type Object. Actually, all type parameters are replaced with the *upper bound* of the type parameter, which is specified in the type-parameter section. Figure 19.6 simulates the erasure of method maximum's types by showing the method's source code after the type-parameter section is removed and type parameter T is replaced with the upper bound, Comparable, throughout the method declaration. The erasure of Comparable<T> is simply Comparable.

```
 1   public static Comparable maximum(Comparable x, Comparable y,
 2      Comparable z) {
 3
 4      Comparable max = x; // assume x is initially the largest
 5
 6      if (y.compareTo(max) > 0) {
 7         max = y; // y is the largest so far
 8      }
 9
10      if (z.compareTo(max) > 0) {
11         max = z; // z is the largest
12      }
13
14      return max; // returns the largest object
15   }
```

Fig. 19.6 | Generic method `maximum` after erasure is performed by the compiler.

After erasure, method `maximum` specifies that it returns type `Comparable`. However, the calling method does not expect to receive a `Comparable`. It expects to receive an object of the same type that was passed to `maximum` as an argument—`Integer`, `Double` or `String` in this example. When the compiler replaces the type-parameter information with the upper-bound type in the method declaration, it also inserts *explicit cast operations* in front of each method call to ensure that the returned value is of the type expected by the caller. Thus, the call to `maximum` in line 7 (Fig. 19.5) is preceded by an `Integer` cast, as in

```
(Integer) maximum(3, 4, 5)
```

the call to `maximum` in line 9 is preceded by a `Double` cast, as in

```
(Double) maximum(6.6, 8.8, 7.7)
```

and the call to `maximum` in line 11 is preceded by a `String` cast, as in

```
(String) maximum("pear", "apple", "orange")
```

In each case, the type of the cast for the return value is *inferred* from the types of the method arguments in the particular method call, because, according to the method declaration, the return type and the argument types match. Without generics, you'd be responsible for implementing the cast operation.

19.5 Overloading Generic Methods

A generic method may be overloaded like any other method. A class can provide two or more generic methods that specify the same method name but different method parameters. For example, generic method `printArray` of Fig. 19.3 could be overloaded with another `printArray` generic method with the additional parameters `lowSubscript` and `highSubscript` to specify the portion of the array to output.

A generic method can also be overloaded by nongeneric methods. When the compiler encounters a method call, it searches for the method declaration that best matches the method name and the argument types specified in the call—an error occurs if two or more overloaded methods both could be considered best matches. For example, generic method printArray of Fig. 19.3 could be overloaded with a version that's specific to Strings, which outputs the Strings in neat, tabular format.

19.6 Generic Classes

A data structure, such as a stack, can be understood *independently* of the element type it manipulates. Generic classes provide a means for describing the concept of a stack (or any other class) in a *type-independent* manner. We can then instantiate *type-specific* objects of the generic class. Generics provide a nice opportunity for software reusability.

Once you have a generic class, you can use a simple, concise notation to indicate the type(s) that should be used in place of the class's type parameter(s). At compilation time, the compiler ensures the *type safety* of your code and uses the *erasure* techniques described in Sections 19.3—19.4 to enable your client code to interact with the generic class.

One generic Stack class, for example, could be the basis for creating many logical Stack classes (e.g., "Stack of Double," "Stack of Integer," "Stack of Character," "Stack of Employee"). These classes are known as **parameterized classes** or **parameterized types** because they accept one or more type parameters. Recall that type parameters represent only *reference types*, which means the Stack generic class cannot be instantiated with primitive types. However, we can instantiate a Stack that stores objects of Java's type-wrapper classes and allow Java to use *autoboxing* to convert the primitive values into objects. Recall that autoboxing occurs when a value of a primitive type (e.g., int) is pushed onto a Stack that contains wrapper-class objects (e.g., Integer). *Auto-unboxing* occurs when an object of the wrapper class is popped off the Stack and assigned to a primitive-type variable.

Implementing a Generic Stack Class

Figure 19.7 declares a generic Stack class for demonstration purposes—the java.util package already contains a generic Stack class. A generic class declaration looks like a non-generic one, but the class name is followed by *a type-parameter section* (line 6). In this case, type parameter E represents the *element* type the Stack will manipulate. As with generic methods, the type-parameter section of a generic class can have one or more type parameters separated by commas. Type parameter E is used throughout the Stack class declaration to represent the element type. This example implements a Stack as an ArrayList.

```java
1   // Fig. 19.7: Stack.java
2   // Stack generic class declaration.
3   import java.util.ArrayList;
4   import java.util.NoSuchElementException;
5
6   public class Stack<E> {
7      private final ArrayList<E> elements; // ArrayList stores stack elements
8
9      // no-argument constructor creates a stack of the default size
10     public Stack() {
11        this(10); // default stack size
12     }
```

Fig. 19.7 | Stack generic class declaration. (Part 1 of 2.)

```
13
14      // constructor creates a stack of the specified number of elements
15      public Stack(int capacity) {
16          int initCapacity = capacity > 0 ? capacity : 10; // validate
17          elements = new ArrayList<E>(initCapacity); // create ArrayList
18      }
19
20      // push element onto stack
21      public void push(E pushValue) {
22          elements.add(pushValue); // place pushValue on Stack
23      }
24
25      // return the top element if not empty; else throw exception
26      public E pop() {
27          if (elements.isEmpty()) { // if stack is empty
28              throw new NoSuchElementException("Stack is empty, cannot pop");
29          }
30
31          // remove and return top element of Stack
32          return elements.remove(elements.size() - 1);
33      }
34  }
```

Fig. 19.7 | Stack generic class declaration. (Part 2 of 2.)

Class Stack declares variable elements as an ArrayList<E> (line 7). This ArrayList will store the Stack's elements. As you know, an ArrayList can grow dynamically, so objects of our Stack class can also grow dynamically. The Stack class's no-argument constructor (lines 10–12) invokes the one-argument constructor (lines 15–18) to create a Stack in which the underlying ArrayList has a capacity of 10 elements. The one-argument constructor can also be called directly to create a Stack with a specified initial capacity. Line 16 validates the constructor's argument. Line 17 creates the ArrayList of the specified capacity (or 10 if the capacity was invalid).

Method push (lines 21–23) uses ArrayList method add to append the pushed item to the end of the ArrayList elements. The last element in the ArrayList represents the stack's *top*.

Method pop (lines 26–33) first determines whether an attempt is being made to pop an element from an empty Stack. If so, line 28 throws a NoSuchElementException (package java.util). Otherwise, line 32 returns the Stack's top element by removing the underlying ArrayList's last element.

As with generic methods, when a generic class is compiled, the compiler performs *erasure* on the class's type parameters and replaces them with their upper bounds. For class Stack (Fig. 19.7), no upper bound is specified, so the default upper bound, Object, is used. The scope of a generic class's type parameter is the entire class. However, type parameters *cannot* be used in a class's static variable declarations.

Testing the Generic Stack Class

Now, let's consider the application (Fig. 19.8) that uses the Stack generic class (Fig. 19.7). Lines 11–12 in Fig. 19.8 create and initialize variables of type Stack<Double> (pronounced "Stack of Double") and Stack<Integer> (pronounced "Stack of Integer"). The types Double and Integer are known as the Stack's **type arguments**. The compiler uses them to replace the type parameters so that it can perform type checking and insert cast operations as necessary. We'll discuss the cast operations in more detail shortly. Lines 11–12 instantiate doubleStack with a capacity of 5 and integerStack with a capacity of 10 (the default). Lines 15–16 and 19–20 call methods testPushDouble (lines 24–33), testPopDouble (lines 36–52), testPushInteger (lines 55–64) and testPopInteger (lines 67–83), respectively, to demonstrate the two Stacks in this example.

```java
1   // Fig. 19.8: StackTest.java
2   // Stack generic class test program.
3   import java.util.NoSuchElementException;
4
5   public class StackTest {
6      public static void main(String[] args) {
7         double[] doubleElements = {1.1, 2.2, 3.3, 4.4, 5.5};
8         int[] integerElements = {1, 2, 3, 4, 5, 6, 7, 8, 9, 10};
9
10        // Create a Stack<Double> and a Stack<Integer>
11        Stack<Double> doubleStack = new Stack<>(5);
12        Stack<Integer> integerStack = new Stack<>();
13
14        // push elements of doubleElements onto doubleStack
15        testPushDouble(doubleStack, doubleElements);
16        testPopDouble(doubleStack); // pop from doubleStack
17
18        // push elements of integerElements onto integerStack
19        testPushInteger(integerStack, integerElements);
20        testPopInteger(integerStack); // pop from integerStack
21     }
22
23     // test push method with double stack
24     private static void testPushDouble(
25        Stack<Double> stack, double[] values) {
26        System.out.printf("%nPushing elements onto doubleStack%n");
27
28        // push elements to Stack
29        for (double value : values) {
30           System.out.printf("%.1f ", value);
31           stack.push(value); // push onto doubleStack
32        }
33     }
34
35     // test pop method with double stack
36     private static void testPopDouble(Stack<Double> stack) {
37        // pop elements from stack
38        try {
39           System.out.printf("%nPopping elements from doubleStack%n");
40           double popValue; // store element removed from stack
41
```

Fig. 19.8 | Stack generic class test program. (Part 1 of 3.)

```
42          // remove all elements from Stack
43          while (true) {
44             popValue = stack.pop(); // pop from doubleStack
45             System.out.printf("%.1f ", popValue);
46          }
47       }
48       catch(NoSuchElementException noSuchElementException) {
49          System.err.println();
50          noSuchElementException.printStackTrace();
51       }
52    }
53
54    // test push method with integer stack
55    private static void testPushInteger(
56       Stack<Integer> stack, int[] values) {
57       System.out.printf("%nPushing elements onto integerStack%n");
58
59       // push elements to Stack
60       for (int value : values) {
61          System.out.printf("%d ", value);
62          stack.push(value); // push onto integerStack
63       }
64    }
65
66    // test pop method with integer stack
67    private static void testPopInteger(Stack<Integer> stack) {
68       // pop elements from stack
69       try {
70          System.out.printf("%nPopping elements from integerStack%n");
71          int popValue; // store element removed from stack
72
73          // remove all elements from Stack
74          while (true) {
75             popValue = stack.pop(); // pop from intStack
76             System.out.printf("%d ", popValue);
77          }
78       }
79       catch(NoSuchElementException noSuchElementException) {
80          System.err.println();
81          noSuchElementException.printStackTrace();
82       }
83    }
84 }
```

```
Pushing elements onto doubleStack
1.1 2.2 3.3 4.4 5.5
Popping elements from doubleStack
5.5 4.4 3.3 2.2 1.1
java.util.NoSuchElementException: Stack is empty, cannot pop
        at Stack.pop(Stack.java:28)
        at StackTest.testPopDouble(StackTest.java:44)
        at StackTest.main(StackTest.java:16)
```

Fig. 19.8 | Stack generic class test program. (Part 2 of 3.)

```
Pushing elements onto integerStack
1 2 3 4 5 6 7 8 9 10
Popping elements from integerStack
10 9 8 7 6 5 4 3 2 1
java.util.NoSuchElementException: Stack is empty, cannot pop
        at Stack.pop(Stack.java:28)
        at StackTest.testPopInteger(StackTest.java:75)
        at StackTest.main(StackTest.java:20)
```

Fig. 19.8 | Stack generic class test program. (Part 3 of 3.)

Methods `testPushDouble` and `testPopDouble`

Method `testPushDouble` (lines 24–33) invokes method push (line 31) to place the double values 1.1, 2.2, 3.3, 4.4 and 5.5 from array doubleElements onto doubleStack. *Autoboxing* occurs in line 31 when the program tries to push a primitive double value onto the doubleStack, which stores only references to Double objects.

Method `testPopDouble` (lines 36–52) invokes Stack method pop (line 44) in an infinite loop (lines 43–46) to remove all the values from the stack. The output shows that the values indeed pop off in last-in, first-out order (the defining characteristic of stacks). When the loop attempts to pop a sixth value, the doubleStack is empty, so pop throws a NoSuchElementException, which causes the program to proceed to the catch block (lines 48–51). The stack trace indicates the exception that occurred and shows that method pop generated the exception at line 28 of the file Stack.java (Fig. 19.7). The trace also shows that pop was called by StackTest method testPopDouble at line 44 (Fig. 19.8) of StackTest.java and that method testPopDouble was called from method main at line 16 of StackTest.java. This information enables you to determine the methods that were on the method-call stack at the time the exception occurred. Because the program catches the exception, the exception is considered to have been handled and the program can continue executing.

Auto-unboxing occurs in line 44 when the program assigns the Double object popped from the stack to a double primitive variable. Recall from Section 19.4 that the compiler inserts casts to ensure that the proper types are returned from generic methods. After erasure, Stack method pop returns type Object, but the client code in testPopDouble expects to receive a double when method pop returns. So the compiler inserts a Double cast, as in

```
popValue = (Double) stack.pop();
```

The value assigned to popValue will be *unboxed* from the Double object returned by pop.

Methods `testPushInteger` and `testPopInteger`

Method `testPushInteger` (lines 55–64) invokes Stack method push to place values onto integerStack until it's full. Method `testPopInteger` (lines 67–83) invokes Stack method pop to remove values from integerStack. Once again, the values are popped in last-in, first-out order. During *erasure*, the compiler recognizes that the client code in method testPopInteger expects to receive an int when method pop returns. So the compiler inserts an Integer cast, as in

```
popValue = (Integer) stack.pop();
```

The value assigned to popValue will be unboxed from the Integer object returned by pop.

Creating Generic Methods to Test Class **Stack<E>**

The code in methods testPushDouble and testPushInteger is *almost identical* for pushing values onto a Stack<Double> or a Stack<Integer>, respectively, and the code in methods testPopDouble and testPopInteger is almost identical for popping values from a Stack<Double> or a Stack<Integer>, respectively. This presents another opportunity to use generic methods. Figure 19.9 declares generic method testPush (lines 24–33) to perform the same tasks as testPushDouble and testPushInteger in Fig. 19.8—that is, push values onto a Stack<E>. Similarly, generic method testPop (Fig. 19.9, lines 36–52) performs the same tasks as testPopDouble and testPopInteger in Fig. 19.8—that is, pop values off a Stack<E>. The output of Fig. 19.9 precisely matches that of Fig. 19.8.

```java
 1   // Fig. 19.9: StackTest2.java
 2   // Passing generic Stack objects to generic methods.
 3   import java.util.NoSuchElementException;
 4
 5   public class StackTest2 {
 6      public static void main(String[] args) {
 7         Double[] doubleElements = {1.1, 2.2, 3.3, 4.4, 5.5};
 8         Integer[] integerElements = {1, 2, 3, 4, 5, 6, 7, 8, 9, 10};
 9
10         // Create a Stack<Double> and a Stack<Integer>
11         Stack<Double> doubleStack = new Stack<>(5);
12         Stack<Integer> integerStack = new Stack<>();
13
14         // push elements of doubleElements onto doubleStack
15         testPush("doubleStack", doubleStack, doubleElements);
16         testPop("doubleStack", doubleStack); // pop from doubleStack
17
18         // push elements of integerElements onto integerStack
19         testPush("integerStack", integerStack, integerElements);
20         testPop("integerStack", integerStack); // pop from integerStack
21      }
22
23      // generic method testPush pushes elements onto a Stack
24      public static <E> void testPush(String name , Stack<E> stack,
25         E[] elements) {
26         System.out.printf("%nPushing elements onto %s%n", name);
27
28         // push elements onto Stack
29         for (E element : elements) {
30            System.out.printf("%s ", element);
31            stack.push(element); // push element onto stack
32         }
33      }
34
35      // generic method testPop pops elements from a Stack
36      public static <E> void testPop(String name, Stack<E> stack) {
37         // pop elements from stack
38         try {
39            System.out.printf("%nPopping elements from %s%n", name);
40            E popValue; // store element removed from stack
```

Fig. 19.9 | Passing generic Stack objects to generic methods. (Part 1 of 2.)

```
41
42                 // remove all elements from Stack
43                 while (true) {
44                     popValue = stack.pop();
45                     System.out.printf("%s ", popValue);
46                 }
47             }
48         catch(NoSuchElementException noSuchElementException) {
49             System.out.println();
50             noSuchElementException.printStackTrace();
51         }
52     }
53 }
```

```
Pushing elements onto doubleStack
1.1 2.2 3.3 4.4 5.5
Popping elements from doubleStack
5.5 4.4 3.3 2.2 1.1
java.util.NoSuchElementException: Stack is empty, cannot pop
        at Stack.pop(Stack.java:28)
        at StackTest2.testPop(StackTest2.java:44)
        at StackTest2.main(StackTest2.java:16)

Pushing elements onto integerStack
1 2 3 4 5 6 7 8 9 10
Popping elements from integerStack
10 9 8 7 6 5 4 3 2 1
java.util.NoSuchElementException: Stack is empty, cannot pop
        at Stack.pop(Stack.java:28)
        at StackTest2.testPop(StackTest2.java:44)
        at StackTest2.main(StackTest2.java:20)
```

Fig. 19.9 | Passing generic Stack objects to generic methods. (Part 2 of 2.)

Lines 11–12 create the Stack<Double> and Stack<Integer> objects, respectively. Lines 15–16 and 19–20 invoke generic methods testPush and testPop to test the Stack objects. Type parameters can represent only reference types, so to be able to pass arrays doubleElements and integerElements to generic method testPush, the arrays declared in lines 7–8 must be declared with the wrapper types Double and Integer. When these arrays are initialized with primitive values, the compiler *autoboxes* each primitive value.

Generic method testPush (lines 24–33) uses type parameter E (specified at line 24) to represent the data type stored in the Stack<E>. The generic method takes three arguments—a String that represents the name of the Stack<E> object for output purposes, a reference to an object of type Stack<E> and an array of type E—the type of elements that will be pushed onto Stack<E>. The compiler enforces *consistency* between the type of the Stack and the elements that will be pushed onto the Stack when push is invoked, which is the real value of the generic method call. Generic method testPop (lines 36–52) takes two arguments—a String that represents the name of the Stack<E> object for output purposes and a reference to an object of type Stack<E>.

19.7 Wildcards in Methods That Accept Type Parameters

In this section, we introduce a powerful generics concept known as **wildcards**. Let's consider an example that motivates wildcards (Fig. 19.10). Suppose that you'd like to implement a generic method sum that totals the numbers in a collection, such as a List. You'd begin by inserting the numbers in the collection. Because generic classes can be used only with class or interface types, the numbers would be *autoboxed* as objects of the type-wrapper classes. For example, any int value would be *autoboxed* as an Integer object, and any double value would be *autoboxed* as a Double object. We'd like to be able to total all the numbers in the List regardless of their type. For this reason, we'll declare the List with the type argument Number, which is the superclass of both Integer and Double. In addition, method sum will receive a parameter of type List<Number> and total its elements.

```java
1   // Fig. 19.10: TotalNumbers.java
2   // Totaling the numbers in a List<Number>.
3   import java.util.ArrayList;
4   import java.util.List;
5
6   public class TotalNumbers {
7      public static void main(String[] args) {
8         // create, initialize and output List of Numbers containing
9         // both Integers and Doubles, then display total of the elements
10        Number[] numbers = {1, 2.4, 3, 4.1}; // Integers and Doubles
11        List<Number> numberList = new ArrayList<>();
12
13        for (Number element : numbers) {
14           numberList.add(element); // place each number in numberList
15        }
16
17        System.out.printf("numberList contains: %s%n", numberList);
18        System.out.printf("Total of the elements in numberList: %.1f%n",
19           sum(numberList));
20     }
21
22     // calculate total of List elements
23     public static double sum(List<Number> list) {
24        double total = 0; // initialize total
25
26        // calculate sum
27        for (Number element : list) {
28           total += element.doubleValue();
29        }
30
31        return total;
32     }
33  }
```

```
numberList contains: [1, 2.4, 3, 4.1]
Total of the elements in numberList: 10.5
```

Fig. 19.10 | Totaling the numbers in a List<Number>.

Line 10 declares and initializes an array of Numbers. Because the initializers are primitive values, Java *autoboxes* each primitive value as an object of its corresponding wrapper type. The int values 1 and 3 are *autoboxed* as Integer objects, and the double values 2.4 and 4.1 are *autoboxed* as Double objects. Line 11 creates an ArrayList object that stores Numbers and assigns it to List variable numberList.

Lines 13–15 traverse array numbers and place each element in numberList. Line 17 outputs the List's contents by implicitly invoking the List's toString method. Lines 18–19 display the sum of the elements that is returned by the call to method sum.

Method sum (lines 23–32) receives a List of Numbers and calculates the total of its Numbers. The method uses double values to perform the calculations and returns the result as a double. Lines 27–29 total the List's elements. The for statement assigns each Number to variable element, then uses **Number method doubleValue** to obtain the Number's underlying primitive value as a double. The result is added to total. When the loop terminates, line 31 returns the total.

Implementing Method **sum** with a Wildcard Type Argument in Its Parameter

Recall that the purpose of method sum in Fig. 19.10 was to total any type of Numbers stored in a List. We created a List of Numbers that contained both Integer and Double objects. The output of Fig. 19.10 demonstrates that method sum worked properly. Given that method sum can total the elements of a List of Numbers, you might expect that the method would also work for Lists that contain elements of only one numeric type, such as List<Integer>. So we modified class TotalNumbers to create a List of Integers and pass it to method sum. When we compile the program, the compiler issues the following error message:

```
TotalNumbersErrors.java:19: error: incompatible types:
List<Integer> cannot be converted to List<Number>
```

Although Number is the superclass of Integer, the compiler doesn't consider the type List<Number> to be a supertype of List<Integer>. If it were, then every operation we could perform on a List<Number> would also work on a List<Integer>. Consider the fact that you can add a Double object to a List<Number> because a Double *is a* Number, but you cannot add a Double object to a List<Integer> because a Double *is not an* Integer. Thus, the subtype relationship does not hold.

How do we create a more flexible version of method sum that can total the elements of any List containing elements of any subclass of Number? This is where **wildcard type arguments** are important. Wildcards enable you to specify method parameters, return values, variables or fields, and so on, that act as supertypes or subtypes of parameterized types. In Fig. 19.11, method sum's parameter is declared in line 52 with the type:

```
List<? extends Number>
```

A wildcard type argument is denoted by a question mark (**?**), which represents an "unknown type." In this case, the wildcard extends class Number, which means that the wildcard has an upper bound of Number. Thus, the unknown-type argument must be either Number or a subclass of Number. With the wildcard type argument, method sum can receive an argument a List containing any type of Number, such as a List<Integer> (line 20), List<Double> (line 34) or List<Number> (line 48).

```java
1   // Fig. 19.11: WildcardTest.java
2   // Wildcard test program.
3   import java.util.ArrayList;
4   import java.util.List;
5
6   public class WildcardTest {
7      public static void main(String[] args) {
8         // create, initialize and output List of Integers, then
9         // display total of the elements
10        Integer[] integers = {1, 2, 3, 4, 5};
11        List<Integer> integerList = new ArrayList<>();
12
13        // insert elements in integerList
14        for (Integer element : integers) {
15           integerList.add(element);
16        }
17
18        System.out.printf("integerList contains: %s%n", integerList);
19        System.out.printf("Total of the elements in integerList: %.0f%n%n",
20           sum(integerList));
21
22        // create, initialize and output List of Doubles, then
23        // display total of the elements
24        Double[] doubles = {1.1, 3.3, 5.5};
25        List<Double> doubleList = new ArrayList<>();
26
27        // insert elements in doubleList
28        for (Double element : doubles) {
29           doubleList.add(element);
30        }
31
32        System.out.printf("doubleList contains: %s%n", doubleList);
33        System.out.printf("Total of the elements in doubleList: %.1f%n%n",
34           sum(doubleList));
35
36        // create, initialize and output List of Numbers containing
37        // both Integers and Doubles, then display total of the elements
38        Number[] numbers = {1, 2.4, 3, 4.1}; // Integers and Doubles
39        List<Number> numberList = new ArrayList<>();
40
41        // insert elements in numberList
42        for (Number element : numbers) {
43           numberList.add(element);
44        }
45
46        System.out.printf("numberList contains: %s%n", numberList);
47        System.out.printf("Total of the elements in numberList: %.1f%n",
48           sum(numberList));
49     }
50
```

Fig. 19.11 | Wildcard test program. (Part 1 of 2.)

```
51      // total the elements; using a wildcard in the List parameter
52      public static double sum(List<? extends Number> list) {
53         double total = 0; // initialize total
54
55         // calculate sum
56         for (Number element : list) {
57            total += element.doubleValue();
58         }
59
60         return total;
61      }
62   }
```

```
integerList contains: [1, 2, 3, 4, 5]
Total of the elements in integerList: 15

doubleList contains: [1.1, 3.3, 5.5]
Total of the elements in doubleList: 9.9

numberList contains: [1, 2.4, 3, 4.1]
Total of the elements in numberList: 10.5
```

Fig. 19.11 | Wildcard test program. (Part 2 of 2.)

Lines 10–20 create and initialize a List<Integer>, output its elements and total them by calling method sum (line 20). Lines 24–34 and 38–48 perform the same operations for a List<Double> and a List<Number> that contains Integers and Doubles.

In method sum (lines 52–61), although the List argument's element types are not directly known by the method, they're known to be at least of type Number, because the wildcard was specified with the upper bound Number. For this reason line 57 is allowed, because all Number objects have a doubleValue method.

Wildcard Restrictions

Because the wildcard (?) in the method's header (line 52) does not specify a type-parameter name, you cannot use it as a type name throughout the method's body (i.e., you cannot replace Number with ? in line 56). You could, however, declare method sum as follows:

```
public static <T extends Number> double sum(List<T> list)
```

which allows the method to receive a List that contains elements of any Number subclass. You could then use the type parameter T throughout the method body.

If the wildcard is specified without an upper bound, then only the methods of type Object can be invoked on values of the wildcard type. Also, methods that use wildcards in their parameter's type arguments cannot be used to add elements to a collection referenced by the parameter.

Common Programming Error 19.3

Using a wildcard in a method's type-parameter section or using a wildcard as an explicit type of a variable in the method body is a syntax error.

19.8 Wrap-Up

This chapter introduced generics. You saw how to declare generic methods and classes with type parameters specified in type-parameter sections. We showed how to specify the upper bound for a type parameter and how the Java compiler uses erasure and casts to support multiple types with generic methods and classes. You also saw how to use wildcards in a generic method or a generic class. In the next chapter, we demonstrate various JavaFX graphics, animation and multimedia capabilities.

20

JavaFX Graphics, Animation and Video

Objectives

In this chapter you'll:

- Use JavaFX graphics and multimedia capabilities to make your apps "come alive" with graphics, animations, audio and video.
- Use external Cascading Style Sheets to customize the look of Nodes while maintaining their functionality.
- Customize fonts attributes such as font family, size and style.
- Display two-dimensional shape nodes of types Line, Rectangle, Circle, Ellipse, Arc, Path, Polyline and Polygon.
- Customize the stroke and fill of shapes with solid colors, images and gradients.
- Use Transforms to reposition and reorient nodes.
- Display and control video playback with Media, MediaPlayer and MediaView.
- Animate Node properties with Transition and Timeline animations.
- Use an AnimationTimer to create frame-by-frame animations.
- Draw graphics on a Canvas node.
- Display 3D shapes.

20.1 Introduction

In this chapter, we continue our discussion of JavaFX from Chapters 12 and 13. Here, we present various JavaFX graphics and multimedia capabilities. You'll:

- Use external Cascading Style Sheets (CSS) to customize the appearance of JavaFX nodes.

- Customize fonts and font attributes used to display text.

- Display two-dimensional shapes, including lines, rectangles, circles, ellipses, arcs, polylines, polygons and custom paths.

- Apply transforms to Nodes, such as rotating a Node around a particular point, scaling, translating (moving) and more.

- Display video and control its playback (e.g., play, pause, stop, and skip to specific time).

- Animate JavaFX Nodes with Transition and Timeline animations that change Node property values over time. As you'll see, the built-in Transition animations change specific JavaFX Node properties (such as a Node's stroke and fill colors), but Timeline animations can be used to change *any* modifiable Node property.

- Create frame-by-frame animations with an AnimationTimer.

- Draw two-dimensional graphics on a Canvas Node.

- Display three-dimensional shapes, including boxes, cylinders and spheres.

Throughout this chapter, we do not show each example's Application subclass, because it performs the same tasks we demonstrated in Chapters 12 and 13. Also, some examples do not have controller classes because they simply display JavaFX controls or graphics to demonstrate CSS capabilities.

20.2 Controlling Fonts with Cascading Style Sheets (CSS)

In Chapters 12–13, you built JavaFX GUIs using Scene Builder. You specified a particular JavaFX object's appearance by selecting the object in Scene Builder, then setting its property values in the **Properties** inspector. With this approach, if you want to change the GUI's appearance, you must edit each object. If you have a large GUI in which you want to make the same changes to multiple objects, this can be time consuming and error prone.

In this chapter, we format JavaFX objects using a technology called **Cascading Style Sheets (CSS)** that's typically used to style the elements in web pages. CSS allows you to specify *presentation* (e.g., fonts, spacing, sizes, colors, positioning) separately from the GUI's *structure* and *content* (layout containers, shapes, text, GUI components, etc.). If a JavaFX GUI's presentation is determined entirely by CSS rules, you can simply swap in a new style sheet to change the GUI's appearance.

In this section, you'll use CSS to specify the font properties of several Labels and the spacing and padding properties for the VBox layout that contains the Labels. You'll place **CSS rules** that specify the font properties, spacing and padding in a separate file that ends with the **.css filename extension**, then reference that file from the FXML. As you'll see,

- before referencing the CSS file from the FXML, Scene Builder displays the GUI without styling, and
- after referencing the CSS file from the FXML, Scene Builder renders the GUI with the CSS rules applied to the appropriate objects.

For a complete reference that shows

- all the JavaFX CSS properties,
- the JavaFX Node types to which the attributes can be applied, and
- the allowed values for each attribute

visit:

```
https://docs.oracle.com/javase/8/javafx/api/javafx/scene/doc-files/
   cssref.html
```

20.2.1 CSS That Styles the GUI

Figure 20.1 presents this app's CSS rules that specify the VBox's and each Label's style. This file is located in the same folder as the rest of the example's files.

```
1   /* Fig. 20.1: FontsCSS.css */
2   /* CSS rules that style the VBox and Labels */
3
4   .vbox {
5       -fx-spacing: 10;
6       -fx-padding: 10;
7   }
8
9   #label1 {
10      -fx-font: bold 14pt Arial;
11  }
```

Fig. 20.1 | CSS rules that style the VBox and Labels. (Part 1 of 2.)

```
12
13   #label2 {
14       -fx-font: 16pt "Times New Roman";
15   }
16
17   #label3 {
18       -fx-font: bold italic 16pt "Courier New";
19   }
20
21   #label4 {
22       -fx-font-size: 14pt;
23       -fx-underline: true;
24   }
25
26   #label5 {
27       -fx-font-size: 14pt;
28   }
29
30   #label5 .text {
31       -fx-strikethrough: true;
32   }
```

Fig. 20.1 | CSS rules that style the VBox and Labels. (Part 2 of 2.)

.vbox CSS Rule—Style Class Selectors

Lines 4–7 define the .vbox CSS rule that will be applied to this app's VBox object (lines 8–18 of Fig. 20.2). Each CSS rule begins with a **CSS selector** which specifies the JavaFX objects that will be styled according to the rule. In the .vbox CSS rule, .vbox is a **style class selector**. The CSS properties in this rule are applied to any JavaFX object that has a styleClass property with the value "vbox". In CSS, a style class selector begins with a dot (.) and is followed by its **class name** (not to be confused with a Java class). By convention, selector names typically have all lowercase letters, and multi-word names separate each word from the next with a dash (-).

Each CSS rule's body is delimited by a set of required braces ({}) containing the CSS properties that are applied to objects matching the CSS selector. Each JavaFX CSS property name begins with -fx-[1] followed by the name of the corresponding JavaFX object's property in all lowercase letters. So, **-fx-spacing** in line 5 of Fig. 20.1 defines the value for a JavaFX object's spacing property, and **-fx-padding** in line 6 defines the value for a JavaFX object's padding property. The value of each property is specified to the right of the required colon (:). In this case, we set -fx-spacing to 10 to place 10 pixels of vertical space between objects in the VBox, and -fx-padding to 10 to separate the VBox's contents from the VBox's edges by 10 pixels at the top, right, bottom and left edges. You also can specify the -fx-padding with four values separated by spaces. For example,

```
-fx-padding: 10 5 10 5
```

1. According to the JavaFX CSS Reference Guide at https://docs.oracle.com/javase/8/javafx/api/javafx/scene/doc-files/cssref.html, JavaFX CSS property names are designed to be processed in style sheets that may also contain HTML CSS. For this reason, JavaFX's CSS property names are prefixed with "-fx-" to ensure that they have distinct names from their HTML CSS counterparts.

specifies 10 pixels for the top padding, 5 for the right, 10 for the bottom and 5 for the left. We show how to apply the .vbox CSS rule to the VBox object in Section 20.2.2.

#label1 *CSS Rule—ID Selectors*

Lines 9–11 define the #label1 CSS rule. Selectors that begin with # are known as **ID selectors**—they are applied to objects with the specified ID. In this case, the #label1 selector matches the object with the fx:id label1—that is, the Label object in line 12 of Fig. 20.2. The #label1 CSS rule specifies the CSS property

```
-fx-font: bold 14pt Arial;
```

This rule sets an object's font property. The object to which this rule applies displays its text in a bold, 14-point, Arial font. The -fx-font property can specify all aspects of a font, including its style, weight, size and font family—the size and font family are required. There are also properties for setting each font component: -fx-font-style, -fx-font-weight, -fx-font-size and -fx-font-family. These are applied to a JavaFX object's similarly named properties. For more information on specifying CSS font attributes, see

```
https://docs.oracle.com/javase/8/javafx/api/javafx/scene/doc-files/
    cssref.html#typefont
```

For a complete list of CSS selector types and how you can combine them, see

```
https://www.w3.org/TR/css3-selectors/
```

#label2 *CSS Rule*

Lines 13–15 define the #label2 CSS rule that will be applied to the Label with the fx:id label2. The CSS property

```
-fx-font: 16pt "Times New Roman";
```

specifies only the required font size (16pt) and font family ("Times New Roman") components—font family names with multiple words must be enclosed in double quotes.

#label3 *CSS Rule*

Lines 17–19 define the #label3 CSS rule that will be applied to the Label with the fx:id label3. The CSS property

```
-fx-font: bold italic 16pt "Courier New";
```

specifies all the font components—weight (bold), style (italic), size (16pt) and font family ("Courier New").

#label4 *CSS Rule*

Lines 21–24 define the #label4 CSS rule that will be applied to the Label with the fx:id label4. The CSS property

```
-fx-font-size: 14pt;
```

specifies the font size 14pt—all other aspects of this Label's font are inherited from the Label's parent container. The CSS property

```
-fx-underline: true;
```

indicates that the text in the Label should be *underlined*—the default value for this property is false.

#label5 CSS Rule

Lines 26–28 define the #label5 CSS rule that will be applied to the Label with the fx:id label5. The CSS property

```
-fx-font-size: 14pt;
```

specifies the font size 14pt.

#label5 .text CSS Rule

Lines 30–32 define the #label5 .text CSS rule that will be applied to the Text object within the Label that has the fx:id value "label5". The selector in this case is a combination of an ID selector and a style class selector. Each Label contains a Text object with the CSS class .text. When applying this CSS rule, JavaFX first locates the object with the ID label5, then within that object looks for a nested object that specifies the class text.

The CSS property

```
-fx-strikethrough: true;
```

indicates that the text in the Label should be displayed with a line through it—the default value for this property is false.

20.2.2 FXML That Defines the GUI—Introduction to XML Markup[2]

Figure 20.2 shows the contents of FontCSS.fxml—the FontCSS app's FXML GUI, which consists of a VBox layout element (lines 8–18) containing five Label elements (lines 12–16). When you first drag five Labels onto the VBox and configure their text (Fig. 20.2(a)), all the Labels initially have the same appearance in Scene Builder. Also, initially there's no spacing between and around the Labels in the VBox.

```
I   <?xml version="1.0" encoding="UTF-8"?>
2   <!-- Fig. 20.2: FontCSS.fxml -->
3   <!-- FontCSS GUI that is styled via external CSS -->
4
5   <?import javafx.scene.control.Label?>
6   <?import javafx.scene.layout.VBox?>
7
8   <VBox styleClass="vbox" stylesheets="@FontCSS.css"
9       xmlns="http://javafx.com/javafx/8.0.60"
10      xmlns:fx="http://javafx.com/fxml/1">
11      <children>
12          <Label fx:id="label1" text="Arial 14pt bold" />
13          <Label fx:id="label2" text="Times New Roman 16pt plain" />
14          <Label fx:id="label3" text="Courier New 16pt bold and italic" />
```

Fig. 20.2 | FontCSS GUI that is styled via external CSS. (Part 1 of 2.)

2. In many of this chapter's examples, after creating a GUI in Scene Builder, we used a text editor to format the FXML, remove unnecessary properties that were inserted by Scene Builder and properties that we specified via CSS rules. For this reason, when you build these examples from scratch, your FXML may differ from what's shown in this chapter. You also can set a property to its default value in Scene Builder to remove it from the FXML.

```
15          <Label fx:id="label4" text="Default font 14pt with underline" />
16          <Label fx:id="label5" text="Default font 14pt with strikethrough" />
17       </children>
18    </VBox>
```

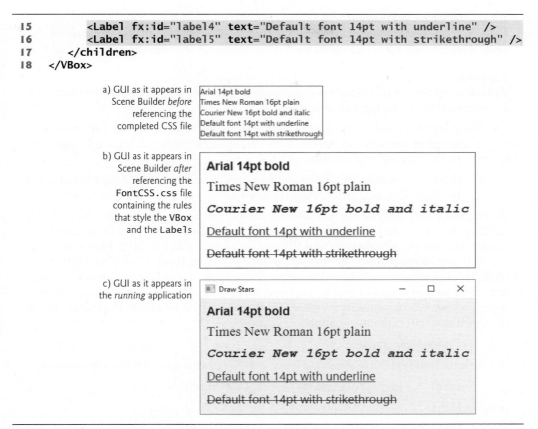

a) GUI as it appears in Scene Builder *before* referencing the completed CSS file

b) GUI as it appears in Scene Builder *after* referencing the FontCSS.css file containing the rules that style the VBox and the Labels

c) GUI as it appears in the *running* application

Fig. 20.2 | FontCSS GUI that is styled via external CSS. (Part 2 of 2.)

XML Declaration

Each FXML document begins with an **XML declaration** (line 1), which must be the first line in the file and indicates that the document contains XML markup. For FXML documents, line 1 must appear as shown in Fig. 20.2. The XML declaration's **version attribute** specifies the XML syntax version (1.0) used in the document. The **encoding attribute** specifies the format of the document's character—XML documents typically contain Unicode characters in UTF-8 format (https://en.wikipedia.org/wiki/UTF-8).

Attributes

Each XML attribute has the format

    name="*value*"

The *name* and *value* are separated by = and the *value* placed in quotation marks (""). Multiple *name*=*value* pairs are separated by whitespace.

Comments

Lines 2–3 are XML comments, which begin with <!-- and end with -->, and can be placed almost anywhere in an XML document. XML comments can span to multiple lines.

FXML import Declarations

Lines 5–6 are FXML **import declarations** that specify the fully qualified names of the JavaFX types used in the document. Such declarations are delimited by <?import and ?>.

Elements

XML documents contain **elements** that specify the document's structure. Most elements are delimited by a **start tag** and an **end tag**:

- A start tag consists of **angle brackets** (< and >) containing the element's name followed by zero or more attributes. For example, the VBox element's start tag (lines 8–10) contains four attributes.

- An end tag consists of the element name preceded by a **forward slash** (/) in angle brackets—for example, </VBox> in line 18.

An element's start and end tags enclose the element's contents. In this case, lines 11–17 declare other elements that describe the VBox's contents. Every XML document must have exactly one **root element** that contains all the other elements. In Fig. 20.2, VBox is the root.

A layout element always contains a **children** element (lines 11–17) containing the child Nodes that are arranged by that layout. For a VBox, the children element contains the child Nodes in the order they're displayed on the screen from top to bottom. The elements in lines 12–16 represent the VBox's five Labels. These are **empty elements** that use the shorthand start-tag-only notation:

<ElementName attributes **/>**

in which the empty element's start tag ends with /> rather than >. The empty element:

```
<Label fx:id="label1" text="Arial 14pt bold" />
```

is equivalent to

```
<Label fx:id="label1" text="Arial 14pt bold">
</Label>
```

which does not have content between the start and end tags. Empty elements often have attributes (such as fx:id and text for each Label element).

XML Namespaces

In lines 9–10, the VBox attributes

```
xmlns="http://javafx.com/javafx/8.0.60"
xmlns:fx="http://javafx.com/fxml/1"
```

specify the XML namespaces used in FXML markup. An XML **namespace** specifies a collection of element and attribute names that you can use in the document. The attribute

```
xmlns="http://javafx.com/javafx/8.0.60"
```

specifies the default namespace. FXML import declarations (like those in lines 5–6) add names to this namespace for use in the document. The attribute

```
xmlns:fx="http://javafx.com/fxml/1"
```

specifies JavaFX's fx namespace. Elements and attributes from this namespace (such as the fx:id attribute) are used internally by the FXMLLoader class. For example, for each FXML element that specifies an `fx:id`, the `FXMLLoader` initializes a corresponding variable in the controller class. The `fx:` in `fx:id` is a **namespace prefix** that specifies the namespace (`fx`) that defines the attribute (`id`). Every element or attribute name in Fig. 20.2 that does not begin with `fx:` is part of the default namespace.

20.2.3 Referencing the CSS File from FXML

For the `Label`s to appear with the fonts shown in Fig. 20.2(b), we must reference the `FontCSS.css` file from the FXML. This enables Scene Builder to apply the CSS rules to the GUI. To reference the CSS file:

1. Select the `VBox` in the Scene Builder.

2. In the **Properties** inspector, click the **+** button under the **Stylesheets** heading.

3. In the dialog that appears, select the `FontCSS.css` file and click **Open**.

This adds the `stylesheets` attribute (line 8)

```
stylesheets="@FontCSS.css"
```

to the `VBox`'s opening tag (lines 8–10). The `@` symbol—called the local resolution operator in FXML—indicates that the file `FontCSS.css` is located relative to the FXML file on disk. No path information is specified here, so the CSS file and the FXML file must be in the same folder.

20.2.4 Specifying the VBox's Style Class

The preceding steps apply the font styles to the `Label`s, based on their ID selectors, but do not apply the spacing and padding to the `VBox`. Recall that for the `VBox` we defined a CSS rule using a *style class selector* with the name `.vbox`. To apply the CSS rule to the `VBox`:

1. Select the `VBox` in the Scene Builder.

2. In the **Properties** inspector, under the **Style Class** heading, specify the value `vbox` *without* the dot, then press *Enter* to complete the setting.

This adds the `styleClass` attribute

```
styleClass="vbox"
```

to the `VBox`'s opening tag (line 8). At this point the GUI appears as in Fig. 20.2(b). You can now run the app to see the output in Fig. 20.2(c).

20.2.5 Programmatically Loading CSS

In the `FontCSS` app, the FXML referenced the CSS style sheet directly (line 8). It's also possible to load CSS files dynamically and add them to a `Scene`'s collection of style sheets. You might do this, for example, in an app that enables users to choose their preferred look-and-feel, such as a light background with dark text vs. a dark background with light text.

To load a stylesheet dynamically, add the following statement to the `Application` subclass's `start` method:

```
scene.getStylesheets().add(
    getClass().getResource("FontCSS.css").toExternalForm());
```

In the preceding statement:

- Inherited Object method getClass obtains a Class object representing the app's Application subclass.

- Class method getResource returns a URL representing the location of the file FontCSS.css. Method getResource looks for the file in the same location from which the Application subclass was loaded.

- URL method toExternalForm returns the URL's String representation. This is passed to the add method of the Scene's collection of style sheets—this adds the style sheet to the scene.

20.3 Displaying Two-Dimensional Shapes

JavaFX has two ways to draw shapes:

- Add **Shape** and **Shape3D** (package **javafx.scene.shape**) subclass objects to a container in the JavaFX stage then manipulate them like other JavaFX Nodes.

- Add a **Canvas** object (package **javafx.scene.canvas**) to a container in the JavaFX stage, then draw on it using various GraphicsContext methods.

The BasicShapes example presented in this section shows you how to display two-dimensional Shapes of types **Line**, **Rectangle**, **Circle**, **Ellipse** and **Arc**. Like other Node types, you can drag shapes from the Scene Builder **Library**'s **Shapes** category onto the design area, then configure them via the **Inspector**'s **Properties**, **Layout** and **Code** sections—of course, you also may create objects of any JavaFX Node type programmatically.

20.3.1 Defining Two-Dimensional Shapes with FXML

Figure 20.3 shows the completed FXML for the BasicShapes app, which references the BasicShapes.css file (line 13) that we present in Section 20.3.2. For this app we dragged two Lines, a Rectangle, a Circle, an Ellipse and an Arc onto a Pane layout and configured their dimensions and positions in Scene Builder.

```
1  <?xml version="1.0" encoding="UTF-8"?>
2  <!-- Fig. 20.3: BasicShapes.fxml -->
3  <!-- Defining Shape objects and styling via CSS -->
4
5  <?import javafx.scene.layout.Pane?>
6  <?import javafx.scene.shape.Arc?>
7  <?import javafx.scene.shape.Circle?>
8  <?import javafx.scene.shape.Ellipse?>
9  <?import javafx.scene.shape.Line?>
10 <?import javafx.scene.shape.Rectangle?>
11
12 <Pane id="Pane" prefHeight="110.0" prefWidth="630.0"
13    stylesheets="@BasicShapes.css" xmlns="http://javafx.com/javafx/8.0.60"
14    xmlns:fx="http://javafx.com/fxml/1">
15    <children>
16       <Line fx:id="line1" endX="100.0" endY="100.0"
17          startX="10.0" startY="10.0" />
```

Fig. 20.3 | Defining Shape objects and styling via CSS. (Part 1 of 2.)

```
18          <Line fx:id="line2" endX="10.0" endY="100.0"
19              startX="100.0" startY="10.0" />
20          <Rectangle fx:id="rectangle" height="90.0" layoutX="120.0"
21              layoutY="10.0" width="90.0" />
22          <Circle fx:id="circle" centerX="270.0" centerY="55.0"
23              radius="45.0" />
24          <Ellipse fx:id="ellipse" centerX="430.0" centerY="55.0"
25              radiusX="100.0" radiusY="45.0" />
26          <Arc fx:id="arc" centerX="590.0" centerY="55.0" length="270.0"
27              radiusX="45.0" radiusY="45.0" startAngle="45.0" type="ROUND" />
28      </children>
29  </Pane>
```

a) GUI in Scene Builder with CSS applied—Ellipse's image fill does not show.

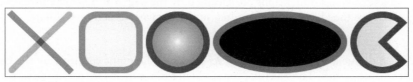

b) GUI in running app—Ellipse's image fill displays correctly.

Fig. 20.3 | Defining Shape objects and styling via CSS. (Part 2 of 2.)

For each property you can set in Scene Builder, there is a corresponding attribute in FXML. For example, the Pane object's **Pref Height** property in Scene Builder corresponds to the prefHeight attribute (line 12) in FXML. When you build this GUI in Scene Builder, use the FXML attribute values shown in Fig. 20.3. Note that as you drag each shape onto your design, Scene Builder automatically configures certain properties, such as the **Fill** and **Stroke** colors for the Rectangle, Circle, Ellipse and Arc. For each such property that does not have a corresponding attribute shown in Fig. 20.3, you can remove the attribute either by setting the property to its default value in Scene Builder or by manually editing the FXML.

Lines 6–10 import the shape classes used in the FXML. We also specified fx:id values (lines 16 and 18) for the two Lines—we use these values in CSS rules with ID selectors to define separate styles for each Line. We removed the shapes' fill, stroke and stroke-Type properties that Scene Builder autogenerated. The default fill for a shape is black. The default stroke is a one-pixel black line. The default strokeType is centered—based on the stroke's thickness, half the thickness appears inside the shape's bounds and half outside. You also may display a shape's stroke completely inside or outside the shape's bounds. We specify the strokes and fills with the styles in Section 20.3.2.

Line Objects

Lines 16–17 and 18–19 define two Lines. Each connects two endpoints specified by the properties **startX**, **startY**, **endX** and **endY**. The *x*- and *y*-coordinates are measured from the top-left corner of the Pane, with *x*-coordinates increasing left to right and *y*-coordinates increasing top to bottom. If you specify a Line's **layoutX** and **layoutY** properties, then the startX, startY, endX and endY properties are measured from that point.

Rectangle Object

Lines 20–21 define a Rectangle object. A Rectangle is displayed based on its layoutX, layoutY, **width** and **height** properties:

- A Rectangle's upper-left corner is positioned at the coordinates specified by the layoutX and layoutY properties, which are inherited from class Node.

- A Rectangle's dimensions are specified by the width and height properties—in this case they have the same value, so the Rectangle defines a square.

Circle Object

Lines 22–23 define a Circle object with its center at the point specified by the **centerX** and **centerY** properties. The **radius** property determines the Circle's size (two times the radius) around its center point.

Ellipse Object

Lines 24–25 define an Ellipse object. Like a Circle, an Ellipse's center is specified by the **centerX** and **centerY** properties. You also specify **radiusX** and **radiusY** properties that help determine the Ellipse's width (left and right of the center point) and height (above and below the center point).

Arc Object

Lines 26–27 define an Arc object. Like an Ellipse, an Arc's center is specified by the **centerX** and **centerY** properties, and the **radiusX** and **radiusY** properties determine the Arc's width and height. For an Arc, you also specify:

- **length**—The arc's length in degrees (0–360). Positive values sweep counterclockwise.

- **startAngle**—The angle in degrees at which the arc should begin.

- **type**—How the arc should be closed. ROUND indicates that the starting and ending points of the arc should be connected to the center point by straight lines. You also may choose OPEN, which does not connect the start and end points, or CHORD, which connects the start and end points with a straight line.

20.3.2 CSS That Styles the Two-Dimensional Shapes

Figure 20.4 shows the CSS for the BasicShapes app. In this CSS file, we define two CSS rules with ID selectors (#line1 and #line2) to style the app's two Line objects. The remaining rules use **type selectors**, which apply to all objects of a given type. You specify a type selector by using the JavaFX class name.

```
 1   /* Fig. 20.4: BasicShapes.css */
 2   /* CSS that styles various two-dimensional shapes */
 3
 4   Line, Rectangle, Circle, Ellipse, Arc {
 5       -fx-stroke-width: 10;
 6   }
 7
 8   #line1 {
 9       -fx-stroke: red;
10   }
11
12   #line2 {
13       -fx-stroke: rgba(0%, 50%, 0%, 0.5);
14       -fx-stroke-line-cap: round;
15   }
16
17   Rectangle {
18       -fx-stroke: red;
19       -fx-arc-width: 50;
20       -fx-arc-height: 50;
21       -fx-fill: yellow;
22   }
23
24   Circle {
25       -fx-stroke: blue;
26       -fx-fill: radial-gradient(center 50% 50%, radius 60%, white, red);
27   }
28
29   Ellipse {
30       -fx-stroke: green;
31       -fx-fill: image-pattern("yellowflowers.png");
32   }
33
34   Arc {
35       -fx-stroke: purple;
36       -fx-fill: linear-gradient(to right, cyan, white);
37   }
```

Fig. 20.4 | CSS that styles various two-dimensional shapes.

Specifying Common Attributes for Various Objects

The CSS rule in lines 4–6 defines the **-fx-stroke-width** CSS property for all the shapes in the app—this property specifies the thickness of the Lines and the border thickness of all the other shapes. To apply this rule to multiple shapes we use CSS type selectors in a comma-separated list. So, line 4 indicates that the rule in lines 4–6 should be applied to all objects of types Line, Rectangle, Circle, Ellipse and Arc in the GUI.

Styling the Lines

The CSS rule in lines 8–10 sets the **-fx-stroke** to the solid color red. This rule applies to the Line with the fx:id "line1". This rule is in addition to the rule at lines 4–6, which sets the stroke width for all Lines (and all the other shapes). When JavaFX renders an object, it combines all the CSS rules that apply to the object to determine its appearance. This rule applies to the `Line` with the `fx:id` "line1". Colors may be specified as

- named colors (such as "red", "green" and "blue"),

- colors defined by their red, green, blue and alpha (transparency) components,

- colors defined by their hue, saturation, brightness and alpha components,

and more. For details on all the ways to specify color in CSS, see

```
https://docs.oracle.com/javase/8/javafx/api/javafx/scene/doc-files/
    cssref.html#typecolor
```

The CSS rule in lines 12–15 applies to the `Line` with the `fx:id` "line2". For this rule, we specified the `-fx-stroke` property's color using the CSS function **rgba**, which defines a color based on its red, green, blue and alpha (transparency) components. Here we used the version of rgba that receives percentages from 0% to 100% specifying the amount of red, green and blue in the color, and a value from 0.0 (transparent) to 1.0 (opaque) for the alpha component. Line 13 produces a semitransparent green line. You can see the interaction between the two `Line`s' colors at the intersection point in Fig. 20.3's output windows. The **-fx-stroke-line-cap** CSS property (line 14) indicates that the ends of the `Line` should be *rounded*—the rounding effect becomes more noticeable with thicker strokes.

Styling the `Rectangle`
For `Rectangle`s, `Circle`s, `Ellipse`s and `Arc`s you can specify both the `-fx-stroke` for the shapes' borders and the **-fx-fill**, which specifies the color or pattern that appears inside the shape. The rule in lines 17–22 uses a CSS type selector to indicate that all `Rectangle`s should have red borders (line 18) and yellow fill (line 21). Lines 19–20 define the `Rectangle`'s **-fx-arc-width** and **-fx-arc-height** properties, which specify the width and height of an ellipse that's divided in half horizontally and vertically, then used to round the `Rectangle`'s corners. Because these properties have the same value (50) in this app, the four corners are each one quarter of a circle with a diameter of 50.

Styling the `Circle`
The CSS rule at lines 24–27 applies to all `Circle` objects. Line 25 sets the `Circle`'s stroke to blue. Line 26 sets the `Circle`'s fill with a **gradient**—colors that transition gradually from one color to the next. You can transition between as many colors as you like and specify the points at which to change colors, called **color stops**. You can use gradients for any property that specifies a color. In this case, we use the CSS function **radial-gradient** in which the color changes gradually from a center point outward. The fill

```
-fx-fill: radial-gradient(center 50% 50%, radius 60%, white, red);
```

indicates that the gradient should begin from a center point at 50% 50%—the middle of the shape horizontally and the middle of the shape vertically. The radius specifies the distance from the center at which an even mixture of the two colors appears. This radial gradient begins with the color white in the center and ends with red at the outer edge of the `Circle`'s fill. We'll discuss a linear gradient momentarily.

Styling the `Ellipse`
The CSS rule at lines 29–32 applies to all `Ellipse` objects. Line 30 specifies that an `Ellipse` should have a green stroke. Line 31 specifies that the `Ellipse`'s fill should be the

image in the file `yellowflowers.png`, which is located in this app's folder. This image is provided in the `images` folder with the chapter's examples—if you're building this app from scratch, copy the video into the app's folder on your system. To specify an image as fill, you use the CSS function **image-pattern**. [*Note:* At the time of this writing, Scene Builder does not display a shape's fill correctly if it's specified with a CSS `image-pattern`. You must run the example to see the fill, as shown in Fig. 20.3(b).]

Styling the Arc
The CSS rule at lines 34–37 applies to all `Arc` objects. Line 35 specifies that an `Arc` should have a `purple` stroke. In this case, line 36

```
-fx-fill: linear-gradient(to right, cyan, white);
```

fills the `Arc` with a **linear gradient**—such gradients gradually transition from one color to the next horizontally, vertically or diagonally. You can transition between as many colors as you like and specify the points at which to change colors. To create a linear gradient, you use the CSS function **linear-gradient**. In this case, `to right` indicates that the gradient should start from the shape's left edge and transition through colors to the shape's right edge. We specified only two colors here—`cyan` at the left edge and `white` at the right edge—but two or more colors can be specified in the comma-separated list. For more information on all the options for configuring radial gradients, linear gradients and image patterns, see

```
https://docs.oracle.com/javase/8/javafx/api/javafx/scene/doc-files/
    cssref.html#typepaint
```

20.4 Polylines, Polygons and Paths

There are several kinds of JavaFX shapes that enable you to create custom shapes:

- **Polyline**—draws a series of connected lines defined by a set of points.
- **Polygon**—draws a series of connected lines defined by a set of points and connects the last point to the first point.
- **Path**—draws a series of connected **PathElements** by moving to a given point, then drawing lines, arcs and curves.

In the `PolyShapes` app, you select which shape you want to display by selecting one of the `RadioButtons` in the left column. You specify a shape's points by clicking throughout the `AnchoredPane` in which the shapes are displayed.

For this example, we do not show the `PolyShapes` subclass of `Application` (located in the example's `PolyShapes.java` file), because it loads the FXML and displays the GUI, as demonstrated in Chapters 12 and 13.

20.4.1 GUI and CSS

This app's GUI (Fig. 20.5) is similar to that of the `Painter` app in Section 13.3. For that reason, we show only the key GUI elements' `fx:id` property values, rather than the complete FXML—each `fx:id` property value ends with the GUI element's type. In this GUI:

- The three `RadioButtons` are part of a `ToggleGroup` with the `fx:id` "`toggleGroup`". The **Polyline** `RadioButton` should be **Selected** by default. We also set each `RadioButton`'s **On Action** event handler to `shapeRadioButtonSelected`.

- We dragged a `Polyline`, a `Polygon` and a `Path` from the Scene Builder **Library**'s **Shapes** section onto the `Pane` that displays the shapes, and set their `fx:id`s to `polyline`, `polygon` and `path`, respectively. We set each shape's `visible` property to `false` by selecting the shape, then unchecking **Visible** in the **Properties** inspector. We display only the shape with the selected `RadioButton` at runtime.

- We set the `Pane`'s **On Mouse Clicked** event handler to `drawingAreaMouseClicked`.

- We set the **Clear** `Button`'s **On Action** event handler to `clearButtonPressed`.

- We set the controller class to `PolyShapesController`.

- Finally, we edited the FXML to remove the `Path` object's `<elements>` and the `Polyline` and `Polygon` objects' `<points>`, as we'll set these programmatically in response to the user's mouse-click events.

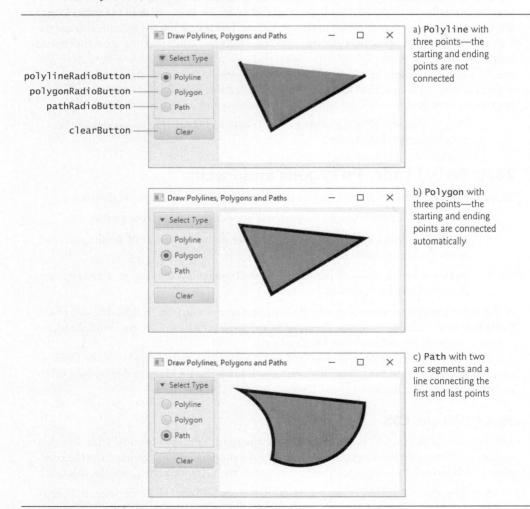

Fig. 20.5 | Polylines, Polygons and Paths.

The PolyShapes.css file defines the properties -fx-stroke, -fx-stroke-width and -fx-fill that are applied to all three shapes in this example:

```
Polyline, Polygon, Path {
    -fx-stroke: black;
    -fx-stroke-width: 5;
    -fx-fill: red;
}
```

20.4.2 PolyShapesController Class

Figure 20.6 shows this app's PolyShapesController class, which responds to the user's interactions. The enum ShapeType (line 17) defines three constants that we use to determine which shape to display. Lines 20–26 declare the variables that correspond to the GUI components and shapes with fx:ids in the FXML. The shapeType variable (line 29) stores whichever shape type is currently selected in the GUI's RadioButtons—by default, the Polyline will be displayed. As you'll soon see, the sweepFlag variable is used to determine whether an arc in a Path is drawn with a negative or positive sweep angle.

```java
1   // Fig. 20.6: PolyShapesController.java
2   // Drawing Polylines, Polygons and Paths.
3   import javafx.event.ActionEvent;
4   import javafx.fxml.FXML;
5   import javafx.scene.control.RadioButton;
6   import javafx.scene.control.ToggleGroup;
7   import javafx.scene.input.MouseEvent;
8   import javafx.scene.shape.ArcTo;
9   import javafx.scene.shape.ClosePath;
10  import javafx.scene.shape.MoveTo;
11  import javafx.scene.shape.Path;
12  import javafx.scene.shape.Polygon;
13  import javafx.scene.shape.Polyline;
14
15  public class PolyShapesController {
16     // enum representing shape types
17     private enum ShapeType {POLYLINE, POLYGON, PATH};
18
19     // instance variables that refer to GUI components
20     @FXML private RadioButton polylineRadioButton;
21     @FXML private RadioButton polygonRadioButton;
22     @FXML private RadioButton pathRadioButton;
23     @FXML private ToggleGroup toggleGroup;
24     @FXML private Polyline polyline;
25     @FXML private Polygon polygon;
26     @FXML private Path path;
27
28     // instance variables for managing state
29     private ShapeType shapeType = ShapeType.POLYLINE;
30     private boolean sweepFlag = true; // used with arcs in a Path
31
```

Fig. 20.6 | Drawing Polylines, Polygons and Paths. (Part 1 of 3.)

```
32      // set user data for the RadioButtons and display polyline object
33      public void initialize() {
34          // user data on a control can be any Object
35          polylineRadioButton.setUserData(ShapeType.POLYLINE);
36          polygonRadioButton.setUserData(ShapeType.POLYGON);
37          pathRadioButton.setUserData(ShapeType.PATH);
38
39          displayShape(); // sets polyline's visibility to true when app loads
40      }
41
42      // handles drawingArea's onMouseClicked event
43      @FXML
44      private void drawingAreaMouseClicked(MouseEvent e) {
45          polyline.getPoints().addAll(e.getX(), e.getY());
46          polygon.getPoints().addAll(e.getX(), e.getY());
47
48          // if path is empty, move to first click position and close path
49          if (path.getElements().isEmpty()) {
50              path.getElements().add(new MoveTo(e.getX(), e.getY()));
51              path.getElements().add(new ClosePath());
52          }
53          else { // insert a new path segment before the ClosePath element
54              // create an arc segment and insert it in the path
55              ArcTo arcTo = new ArcTo();
56              arcTo.setX(e.getX());
57              arcTo.setY(e.getY());
58              arcTo.setRadiusX(100.0);
59              arcTo.setRadiusY(100.0);
60              arcTo.setSweepFlag(sweepFlag);
61              sweepFlag = !sweepFlag;
62              path.getElements().add(path.getElements().size() - 1, arcTo);
63          }
64      }
65
66      // handles color RadioButton's ActionEvents
67      @FXML
68      private void shapeRadioButtonSelected(ActionEvent e) {
69          // user data for each color RadioButton is a ShapeType constant
70          shapeType =
71              (ShapeType) toggleGroup.getSelectedToggle().getUserData();
72          displayShape(); // display the currently selected shape
73      }
74
75      // displays currently selected shape
76      private void displayShape() {
77          polyline.setVisible(shapeType == ShapeType.POLYLINE);
78          polygon.setVisible(shapeType == ShapeType.POLYGON);
79          path.setVisible(shapeType == ShapeType.PATH);
80      }
81
82      // resets each shape
83      @FXML
84      private void clearButtonPressed(ActionEvent event) {
```

Fig. 20.6 | Drawing Polylines, Polygons and Paths. (Part 2 of 3.)

```
85              polyline.getPoints().clear();
86              polygon.getPoints().clear();
87              path.getElements().clear();
88          }
89      }
```

Fig. 20.6 | Drawing `Polylines`, `Polygons` and `Paths`. (Part 3 of 3.)

Method *initialize*

Recall from Section 13.3.1 that you can associate any `Object` with each JavaFX control via its `setUserData` method. For the shape `RadioButtons` in this app, we store the specific `ShapeType` that the `RadioButton` represents (lines 35–37). We use these values when handling the `RadioButton` events to set the `shapeType` instance variable. Line 39 then calls method `displayShape` to display the currently selected shape (the `Polyline` by default). Initially, the shape is not visible because it does not yet have any points.

Method *drawingAreaMouseClicked*

When the user clicks the app's `Pane`, method `drawingAreaMouseClicked` (lines 43–64) modifies all three shapes to incorporate the new point at which the user clicked. `Polylines` and `Polygons` store their points as a collection of `Double` values in which the first two values represent the first point's location, the next two values represent the second point's location, etc. Line 45 gets the `polyline` object's collection of points, then adds the new click point to the collection by calling its `addAll` method and passing the `MouseEvent`'s *x*- and *y*-coordinate values. This adds the new point's information to the end of the collection. Line 46 performs the same task for the `polygon` object.

Lines 49–63 manipulate the `path` object. A `Path` is represented by a collection of **PathElements**. The subclasses of `PathElement` used in this example are:

- **MoveTo**—Moves to a specific position without drawing anything.

- **ArcTo**—Draws an arc from the previous `PathElement`'s endpoint to the specified location. We'll discuss this in more detail momentarily.

- **ClosePath**—Closes the path by drawing a straight line from the end point of the last `PathElement` to the start point of the first `PathElement`.

Other PathElements not covered here include `LineTo`, `HLineTo`, `VLineTo`, `CubicCurveTo` and `QuadCurveTo`.

When the user clicks the `Pane`, line 49 checks whether the `Path` contains elements. If not, line 50 moves the starting point of the `path` to the mouse-click location by adding a `MoveTo` element to the path's `PathElements` collection. Then line 51 adds a new `Close-Path` element to complete the path. For each subsequent mouse-click event, lines 55–60 create an `ArcTo` element and line 62 inserts it before the `ClosePath` element by calling the `PathElements` collection's add method that receives an index as its first argument.

Lines 56–57 set the `ArcTo` element's end point to the `MouseEvent`'s coordinates. The arc is drawn as a piece of an ellipse for which you specify the horizontal radius and vertical radius (lines 58–59). Line 60 sets the `ArcTo`'s `sweepFlag`, which determines whether the arc sweeps in the positive angle direction (`true`; counter clockwise) or the negative angle direction (`false`; clockwise). By default an `ArcTo` element is drawn as the shortest arc between the last PathElement's end point and the point specified by the ArcTo element. To sweep the arc the long way around the ellipse, set the ArcTo's largeArcFlag to true. For each mouse click, line 61 reverses the value of our controller class's sweepFlag instance variable so that the ArcTo elements toggle between positive and negative angles for variety.

Method shapeRadioButtonSelected

When the user clicks a shape RadioButton, lines 70–71 set the controller's shapeType instance variable, then line 72 calls method displayShape to display the selected shape. Try creating a Polyline of several points, then changing to the Polygon and Path to see how the points are used in each shape.

Method displayShape

Lines 77–79 simply set the visibility of the three shapes, based on the current shapeType. The currently selected shape's visibility is set to true to display the shape, and the other shapes' visibility is set to false to hide those shapes.

Method clearButtonPressed

When the user clicks the **Clear** Button, lines 85–86 clear the polyline's and polygon's collections of points, and line 87 clears the path's collection of PathElements. The user can then begin drawing a new shape by clicking the Pane.

20.5 Transforms

A **transform** can be applied to any UI element to *reposition* or *reorient* the element. The built-in JavaFX transforms are subclasses of **Transform**. Some of these subclasses include:

- **Translate**—*moves* an object to a new location.
- **Rotate**—*rotates* an object around a point and by a specified rotation angle.
- **Scale**—*scales* an object's size by the specified amounts.

The next example draws stars using the Polygon control and uses Rotate transforms to create a circle of randomly colored stars. The FXML for this app consists of an empty 300-by-300 Pane layout with the fx:id "pane". We also set the controller class to DrawStars-Controller. Figure 20.7 shows the app's controller and a sample output.

Method initialize (lines 14–37) defines the stars, applies the transforms and attaches the stars to the app's pane. Lines 16–18 define the points of a star as an array of type Double—the collection of points stored in a Polygon is implemented with a generic collection, so you must use type Double rather than double (recall that primitive types cannot be used in Java generics). Each pair of values in the array represents the *x*- and *y*-coordinates of one point in the Polygon. We defined ten points in the array.

```
1   // Fig. 20.7: DrawStarsController.java
2   // Create a circle of stars using Polygons and Rotate transforms
3   import java.security.SecureRandom;
4   import javafx.fxml.FXML;
5   import javafx.scene.layout.Pane;
```

Fig. 20.7 | Create a circle of stars using Polygons and Rotate transforms. (Part 1 of 2.)

```
 6   import javafx.scene.paint.Color;
 7   import javafx.scene.shape.Polygon;
 8   import javafx.scene.transform.Transform;
 9
10   public class DrawStarsController {
11      @FXML private Pane pane;
12      private static final SecureRandom random = new SecureRandom();
13
14      public void initialize() {
15         // points that define a five-pointed star shape
16         Double[] points = {205.0,150.0, 217.0,186.0, 259.0,186.0,
17            223.0,204.0, 233.0,246.0, 205.0,222.0, 177.0,246.0, 187.0,204.0,
18            151.0,186.0, 193.0,186.0};
19
20         // create 18 stars
21         for (int count = 0; count < 18; ++count) {
22            // create a new Polygon and copy existing points into it
23            Polygon newStar = new Polygon();
24            newStar.getPoints().addAll(points);
25
26            // create random Color and set as newStar's fill
27            newStar.setStroke(Color.GREY);
28            newStar.setFill(Color.rgb(random.nextInt(255),
29               random.nextInt(255), random.nextInt(255),
30               random.nextDouble()));
31
32            // apply a rotation to the shape
33            newStar.getTransforms().add(
34               Transform.rotate(count * 20, 150, 150));
35            pane.getChildren().add(newStar);
36         }
37      }
38   }
```

Fig. 20.7 | Create a circle of stars using `Polygon`s and `Rotate` transforms. (Part 2 of 2.)

During each iteration of the loop, lines 23–34 create a `Polygon` using the points in the `points` array and apply a different `Rotate` transform. This results in the circle of `Poly`-gons in the screen capture. To generate the random colors for each star, we use a `Secure-`

Random object to create three random values from 0–255 for the red, green and blue components of the color, and one random value from 0.0–1.0 for the color's alpha transparency value. We pass those values to class Color's static rgb method to create a Color.

To apply a rotation to the new Polygon, we add a Rotate transform to the Polygon's collection of Transforms (lines 33–34). To create the Rotate transform object, we invoke class Transform's static method **rotate** (line 34), which returns a Rotate object. The method's first argument is the rotation angle. Each iteration of the loop assigns a new rotation-angle value by using the control variable multiplied by 20 as the rotate method's first argument. The method's next two arguments are the *x*- and *y*-coordinates of the point of rotation around which the Polygon rotates. The center of the circle of stars is the point *(150, 150)*, because we rotated all 18 stars around that point. Adding each Polygon as a new child element of the pane object allows the Polygon to be rendered on screen.

20.6 Playing Video with Media, MediaPlayer and MediaViewer

Many of today's most popular apps are multimedia intensive. JavaFX provides audio and video multimedia capabilities via the classes of package **javafx.scene.media**:

- For simple audio playback you can use class **AudioClip**.

- For audio playback with more playback controls and for video playback you can use classes **Media**, **MediaPlayer** and **MediaView**.

In this section, you'll build a basic video player. We'll explain classes Media, MediaPlayer and MediaView as we encounter them in the project's controller class (Section 20.6.2). The video used in this example is from NASA's multimedia library[3] and was downloaded from

```
http://www.nasa.gov/centers/kennedy/multimedia/HD-index.html
```

The video file sts117.mp4 is provided in the video folder with this chapter's examples. When building the app from scratch, copy the video onto the app's folder.

Media Formats

For video, JavaFX supports MPEG-4 (also called MP4) and Flash Video formats. We downloaded a Windows WMV version of the video file used in this example, then converted it to MP4 via a free online video converter.[4]

ControlsFX Library's ExceptionDialog

ExceptionDialog is one of many additional JavaFX controls available through the open-source project ControlsFX at

```
http://controlsfx.org
```

We use an ExceptionDialog in this app to display a message to the user if an error occurs during media playback.

You can download the latest version of ControlsFX from the preceding web page, then extract the contents of the ZIP file. Place the extracted ControlsFX JAR file (named

---

3. For NASA's terms of use, visit http://www.nasa.gov/multimedia/guidelines/.
4. There are many free online and downloadable video-format conversion tools. We used the one at https://convertio.co/video-converter/.

controlsfx-8.40.12.jar at the time of this writing) in your project's folder—a JAR file is a compressed archive like a ZIP file, but contains Java class files and their corresponding resources. We included a copy of the JAR file with the final example.

Compiling and Running the App with ControlsFX
To compile this app, you must specify the JAR file as part of the app's classpath. To do so, use the javac command's -classpath option, as in:

```
javac -classpath .;controlsfx-8.40.12.jar *.java
```

Similary, to run the app, use the java command's -cp option, as in

```
java -cp .;controlsfx-8.40.12.jar VideoPlayer
```

In the preceding commands, Linux and macOS users should use a colon (:) rather than a semicolon(;). The classpath in each command specifies the current folder containing the app's files—this is represented by the dot (.)—and the name of the JAR file containing the ControlsFX classes (including ExceptionDialog).

20.6.1 VideoPlayer GUI

Figure 20.8 shows the completed VideoPlayer.fxml file and two sample screen captures of the final running VideoPlayer app. The GUI's layout is a BorderPane consisting of

- a MediaView (located in the Scene Builder **Library**'s **Controls** section) with the fx:id mediaView and

- a ToolBar (located in the Scene Builder **Library**'s **Containers** section) containing one Button with the fx:id playPauseButton and the text "Play". The controller method playPauseButtonPressed responds when the Button is pressed.

We placed the MediaView in the BorderPane's center region (lines 25–27) so that it occupies all available space in the BorderPane, and we placed the ToolBar in the BorderPane's bottom region (lines 15–24). By default, Scene Builder adds one Button to the ToolBar when you drag the ToolBar onto your layout. You can then add other controls to the ToolBar as necessary. We set the controller class to VideoPlayerController.

```
 1  <?xml version="1.0" encoding="UTF-8"?>
 2  <!-- Fig. 20.8: VideoPlayer.fxml -->
 3  <!-- VideoPlayer GUI with a MediaView and a Button -->
 4
 5  <?import javafx.scene.control.Button?>
 6  <?import javafx.scene.control.ToolBar?>
 7  <?import javafx.scene.layout.BorderPane?>
 8  <?import javafx.scene.media.MediaView?>
 9
10  <BorderPane prefHeight="400.0" prefWidth="600.0"
11     style="-fx-background-color: black;"
12     xmlns="http://javafx.com/javafx/8.0.60"
13     xmlns:fx="http://javafx.com/fxml/1"
14     fx:controller="VideoPlayerController">
```

Fig. 20.8 | VideoPlayer GUI with a MediaView and a Button. Video courtesy of NASA—see http://www.nasa.gov/multimedia/guidelines/ for usage guidelines. (Part 1 of 2.)

```
15      <bottom>
16        <ToolBar prefHeight="40.0" prefWidth="200.0"
17          BorderPane.alignment="CENTER">
18          <items>
19            <Button fx:id="playPauseButton"
20              onAction="#playPauseButtonPressed" prefHeight="25.0"
21              prefWidth="60.0" text="Play" />
22          </items>
23        </ToolBar>
24      </bottom>
25      <center>
26        <MediaView fx:id="mediaView" BorderPane.alignment="CENTER" />
27      </center>
28    </BorderPane>
```

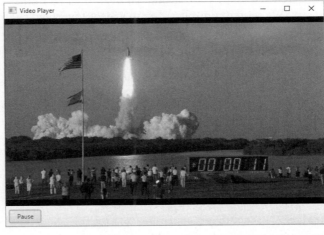

Fig. 20.8 | VideoPlayer GUI with a MediaView and a Button. Video courtesy of NASA—see http://www.nasa.gov/multimedia/guidelines/ for usage guidelines. (Part 2 of 2.)

20.6.2 VideoPlayerController Class

Figure 20.9 shows the completed VideoPlayerController class, which configures video playback and responds to state changes from the MediaPlayer and the events when the user presses the playPauseButton. The controller uses classes Media, MediaPlayer and MediaView as follows:

- A Media object specifies the location of the media to play and provides access to various information about the media, such as its duration, dimensions and more.

- A MediaPlayer object loads a Media object and controls playback. In addition, a MediaPlayer transitions through its various states (*ready*, *playing*, *paused*, etc.) during media loading and playback. As you'll see, you can provide Runnables that execute in response to these state transitions.

- A MediaView object displays the Media being played by a given MediaPlayer object.

```java
 1  // Fig. 20.9: VideoPlayerController.java
 2  // Using Media, MediaPlayer and MediaView to play a video.
 3  import java.net.URL;
 4  import javafx.beans.binding.Bindings;
 5  import javafx.beans.property.DoubleProperty;
 6  import javafx.event.ActionEvent;
 7  import javafx.fxml.FXML;
 8  import javafx.scene.control.Button;
 9  import javafx.scene.media.Media;
10  import javafx.scene.media.MediaPlayer;
11  import javafx.scene.media.MediaView;
12  import javafx.util.Duration;
13  import org.controlsfx.dialog.ExceptionDialog;
14
15  public class VideoPlayerController {
16     @FXML private MediaView mediaView;
17     @FXML private Button playPauseButton;
18     private MediaPlayer mediaPlayer;
19     private boolean playing = false;
20
21     public void initialize() {
22        // get URL of the video file
23        URL url = VideoPlayerController.class.getResource("sts117.mp4");
24
25        // create a Media object for the specified URL
26        Media media = new Media(url.toExternalForm());
27
28        // create a MediaPlayer to control Media playback
29        mediaPlayer = new MediaPlayer(media);
30
31        // specify which MediaPlayer to display in the MediaView
32        mediaView.setMediaPlayer(mediaPlayer);
33
```

Fig. 20.9 | Using Media, MediaPlayer and MediaView to play a video. (Part 1 of 2.)

```
34          // set handler to be called when the video completes playing
35          mediaPlayer.setOnEndOfMedia(
36             new Runnable() {
37                public void run() {
38                   playing = false;
39                   playPauseButton.setText("Play");
40                   mediaPlayer.seek(Duration.ZERO);
41                   mediaPlayer.pause();
42                }
43             }
44          );
45
46          // set handler that displays an ExceptionDialog if an error occurs
47          mediaPlayer.setOnError(
48             new Runnable() {
49                public void run() {
50                   ExceptionDialog dialog =
51                      new ExceptionDialog(mediaPlayer.getError());
52                   dialog.showAndWait();
53                }
54             }
55          );
56
57          // set handler that resizes window to video size once ready to play
58          mediaPlayer.setOnReady(
59             new Runnable() {
60                public void run() {
61                   DoubleProperty width = mediaView.fitWidthProperty();
62                   DoubleProperty height = mediaView.fitHeightProperty();
63                   width.bind(Bindings.selectDouble(
64                      mediaView.sceneProperty(), "width"));
65                   height.bind(Bindings.selectDouble(
66                      mediaView.sceneProperty(), "height"));
67                }
68             }
69          );
70       }
71
72       // toggle media playback and the text on the playPauseButton
73       @FXML
74       private void playPauseButtonPressed(ActionEvent e) {
75          playing = !playing;
76
77          if (playing) {
78             playPauseButton.setText("Pause");
79             mediaPlayer.play();
80          }
81          else {
82             playPauseButton.setText("Play");
83             mediaPlayer.pause();
84          }
85       }
86    }
```

Fig. 20.9 | Using Media, MediaPlayer and MediaView to play a video. (Part 2 of 2.)

Instance Variables

Lines 16–19 declare the controller's instance variables. When the app loads, the media-View variable (line 16) is assigned a reference to the MediaView object declared in the app's FXML. The mediaPlayer variable (line 18) is configured in method initialize to load the video specified by a Media object and used by method playPauseButtonPressed (lines 73–85) to play and pause the video.

*Creating a **Media** Object Representing the Video to Play*

Method initialize configures media playback and registers event handlers for Media-Player events. Line 23 gets a URL representing the location of the sts117.mp4 video file. The notation

```
VideoPlayerController.class
```

creates a Class object representing the VideoPlayerController class. This is equivalent to calling inherited method getClass(). Next line 26 creates a Media object representing the video. The argument to the Media constructor is a String representing the video's location, which we obtain with URL method toExternalForm. The URL String can represent a local file on your computer or can be a location on the web. The Media constructor throws various exceptions, including MediaExceptions if the media cannot be found or is not of a supported media format.

*Creating a **MediaPlayer** Object to Load the Video and Control Playback*

To load the video and prepare it for playback, you must associate it with a MediaPlayer object (line 29). Playing multiple videos requires a separate MediaPlayer for each Media object. However, a given Media object can be associated with multiple MediaPlayers. The MediaPlayer constructor throws a NullPointerException if the Media is null or a MediaException if a problem occurs during construction of the MediaPlayer object.

*Attaching the **MediaPlayer** Object to the **MediaView** to Display the Video*

A MediaPlayer does not provide a view in which to display video. For this purpose, you must associate a MediaPlayer with a MediaView. When the MediaView already exists—such as when it's created in FXML—you call the MediaView's **setMediaPlayer** method (line 32) to perform this task. When creating a MediaView object programmatically, you can pass the MediaPlayer to the MediaView's constructor. A MediaView is like any other Node in the scene graph, so you can apply CSS styles, transforms and animations (Sections 20.7—20.9) to it as well.

*Configuring Event Handlers for **MediaPlayer** Events*

A MediaPlayer transitions through various states. Some common states include *ready*, *playing* and *paused*. For these and other states, you can execute a task as the MediaPlayer enters the corresponding state. In addition, you can specify tasks that execute when the end of media playback is reached or when an error occurs during playback. To perform a task for a given state, you specify an object that implements the **Runnable** interface (package java.lang). This interface contains a no-parameter run method that returns void.

For example, lines 35–44 call the MediaPlayer's **setOnEndOfMedia** method, passing an object of an anonymous inner class that implements interface Runnable to execute when video playback completes. Line 38 sets the boolean instance variable playing to false and line 39 changes the text on the playPauseButton to "Play" to indicate that the user can click the Button to play the video again. Line 40 calls MediaPlayer method **seek** to move to the beginning of the video and line 41 pauses the video.

Lines 47–55 call the MediaPlayer's **setOnError** method to specify a task to perform if the MediaPlayer enters the *error* state, indicating that an error occurred during playback. In this case, we display an ExceptionDialog containing the MediaPlayer's error message. Calling the ExceptionDialog's showAndWait method indicates that the app must wait for the user to dismiss the dialog before continuing.

Binding the *MediaViewer's* Size to the Scene's Size
Lines 58–69 call the MediaPlayer's **setOnReady** method to specify a task to perform if the MediaPlayer enters the *ready* state. We use property bindings to bind the MediaView's width and height properties to the scene's width and height properties so that the MediaView resizes with app's window. A Node's sceneProperty returns a ReadOnlyObjectProperty<Scene> that you can use to access to the Scene in which the Node is displayed. The ReadOnlyObjectProperty<Scene> represents an object that has many properties. To bind to a specific properties of that object, you can use the methods of class **Bindings** (package javafx.beans.binding) to select the corresponding properties. The Scene's width and height are each DoubleProperty objects. Bindings method **selectDouble** gets a reference to a DoubleProperty. The method's first argument is the object that contains the property and the second argument is the name of the property to which you'd like to bind.

Method *playPauseButtonPressed*
The event handler playPauseButtonPressed (lines 73–85) toggles video playback. When playing is true, line 78 sets the playPauseButton's text to "Pause" and line 79 calls the MediaPlayer's **play** method; otherwise, line 82 sets the playPauseButton's text to "Play" and line 83 calls the MediaPlayer's **pause** method.

8 Using Java SE 8 Lambdas to Implement the **Runnabl**es
Each of the anonymous inner classes in this controller's initialize method can be implemented more concisely using lambdas as shown in Section 17.16.

20.7 Transition Animations

Animations in JavaFX apps transition a Node's property values from one value to another in a specified amount of time. Most properties of a Node can be animated. This section focuses on several of JavaFX's predefined **Transition** animations from the **javafx.animations** package. By default, the subclasses that define Transition animations change the values of specific Node properties. For example, a FadeTransition changes the value of a Node's opacity property (which specifies whether the Node is opaque or transparent) over time, whereas a PathTransition changes a Node's location by moving it along a Path over time. Though we show sample screen captures for all the animation examples, the best way to experience each is to run the examples yourself.

20.7.1 TransitionAnimations.fxml
Figure 20.10 shows this app's GUI and screen captures of the running application. When you click the startButton (lines 17–19), its startButtonPressed event handler in the

app's controller creates a sequence of Transition animations for the Rectangle (lines 15–16) and plays them. The Rectangle is styled with the following CSS from the file TransitionAnimations.css:

```css
Rectangle {
    -fx-stroke-width: 10;
    -fx-stroke: red;
    -fx-arc-width: 50;
    -fx-arc-height: 50;
    -fx-fill: yellow;
}
```

which produces a rounded rectangle with a 10-pixel red border and yellow fill.

```xml
 1   <?xml version="1.0" encoding="UTF-8"?>
 2   <!-- Fig. 20.10: TransitionAnimations.fxml -->
 3   <!-- FXML for a Rectangle and Button -->
 4
 5   <?import javafx.scene.control.Button?>
 6   <?import javafx.scene.layout.Pane?>
 7   <?import javafx.scene.shape.Rectangle?>
 8
 9   <Pane id="Pane" prefHeight="200.0" prefWidth="180.0"
10      stylesheets="@TransitionAnimations.css"
11      xmlns="http://javafx.com/javafx/8.0.60"
12      xmlns:fx="http://javafx.com/fxml/1"
13      fx:controller="TransitionAnimationsController">
14      <children>
15         <Rectangle fx:id="rectangle" height="90.0" layoutX="45.0"
16            layoutY="45.0" width="90.0" />
17         <Button fx:id="startButton" layoutX="38.0" layoutY="161.0"
18            mnemonicParsing="false"
19            onAction="#startButtonPressed" text="Start Animations" />
20      </children>
21   </Pane>
```

 a) Initial Rectangle

Fig. 20.10 | FXML for a Rectangle and Button. (Part 1 of 3.)

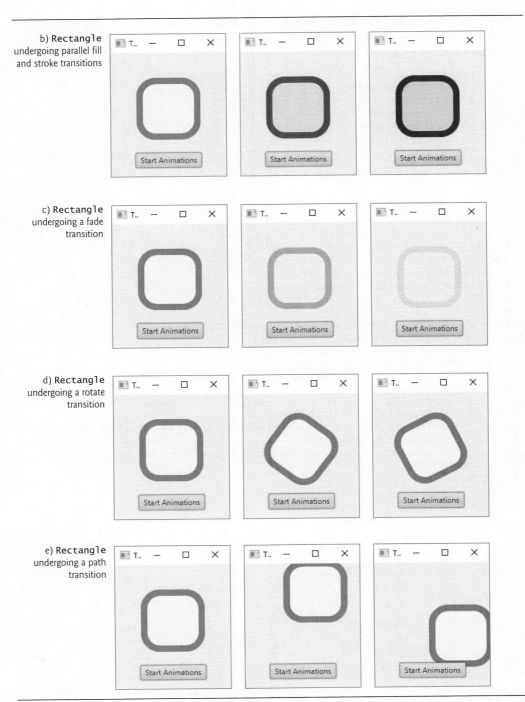

Fig. 20.10 | FXML for a `Rectangle` and `Button`. (Part 2 of 3.)

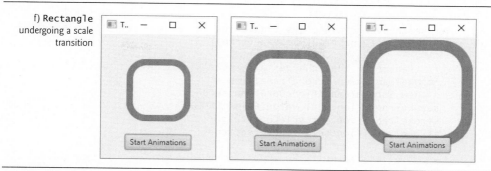

f) Rectangle undergoing a scale transition

Fig. 20.10 | FXML for a `Rectangle` and `Button`. (Part 3 of 3.)

20.7.2 TransitionAnimationsController Class

Figure 20.11 shows this app's controller class, which defines the `startButton`'s event handler (lines 25–87). This event handler defines several animations that are played in sequence.

```java
// Fig. 20.11: TransitionAnimationsController.java
// Applying Transition animations to a Rectangle.
import javafx.animation.FadeTransition;
import javafx.animation.FillTransition;
import javafx.animation.Interpolator;
import javafx.animation.ParallelTransition;
import javafx.animation.PathTransition;
import javafx.animation.RotateTransition;
import javafx.animation.ScaleTransition;
import javafx.animation.SequentialTransition;
import javafx.animation.StrokeTransition;
import javafx.event.ActionEvent;
import javafx.fxml.FXML;
import javafx.scene.paint.Color;
import javafx.scene.shape.LineTo;
import javafx.scene.shape.MoveTo;
import javafx.scene.shape.Path;
import javafx.scene.shape.Rectangle;
import javafx.util.Duration;

public class TransitionAnimationsController {
    @FXML private Rectangle rectangle;

    // configure and start transition animations
    @FXML
    private void startButtonPressed(ActionEvent event) {
        // transition that changes a shape's fill
        FillTransition fillTransition =
            new FillTransition(Duration.seconds(1));
        fillTransition.setToValue(Color.CYAN);
        fillTransition.setCycleCount(2);
```

Fig. 20.11 | Applying `Transition` animations to a `Rectangle`. (Part 1 of 3.)

```
32
33      // each even cycle plays transition in reverse to restore original
34      fillTransition.setAutoReverse(true);
35
36      // transition that changes a shape's stroke over time
37      StrokeTransition strokeTransition =
38         new StrokeTransition(Duration.seconds(1));
39      strokeTransition.setToValue(Color.BLUE);
40      strokeTransition.setCycleCount(2);
41      strokeTransition.setAutoReverse(true);
42
43      // parallelizes multiple transitions
44      ParallelTransition parallelTransition =
45         new ParallelTransition(fillTransition, strokeTransition);
46
47      // transition that changes a node's opacity over time
48      FadeTransition fadeTransition =
49         new FadeTransition(Duration.seconds(1));
50      fadeTransition.setFromValue(1.0); // opaque
51      fadeTransition.setToValue(0.0); // transparent
52      fadeTransition.setCycleCount(2);
53      fadeTransition.setAutoReverse(true);
54
55      // transition that rotates a node
56      RotateTransition rotateTransition =
57         new RotateTransition(Duration.seconds(1));
58      rotateTransition.setByAngle(360.0);
59      rotateTransition.setCycleCount(2);
60      rotateTransition.setInterpolator(Interpolator.EASE_BOTH);
61      rotateTransition.setAutoReverse(true);
62
63      // transition that moves a node along a Path
64      Path path = new Path(new MoveTo(45, 45), new LineTo(45, 0),
65         new LineTo(90, 0), new LineTo(90, 90), new LineTo(0, 90));
66      PathTransition translateTransition =
67         new PathTransition(Duration.seconds(2), path);
68      translateTransition.setCycleCount(2);
69      translateTransition.setInterpolator(Interpolator.EASE_IN);
70      translateTransition.setAutoReverse(true);
71
72      // transition that scales a shape to make it larger or smaller
73      ScaleTransition scaleTransition =
74         new ScaleTransition(Duration.seconds(1));
75      scaleTransition.setByX(0.75);
76      scaleTransition.setByY(0.75);
77      scaleTransition.setCycleCount(2);
78      scaleTransition.setInterpolator(Interpolator.EASE_OUT);
79      scaleTransition.setAutoReverse(true);
80
```

Fig. 20.11 | Applying Transition animations to a Rectangle. (Part 2 of 3.)

```
81          // transition that applies a sequence of transitions to a node
82          SequentialTransition sequentialTransition =
83            new SequentialTransition (rectangle, parallelTransition,
84               fadeTransition, rotateTransition, translateTransition,
85               scaleTransition);
86          sequentialTransition.play(); // play the transition
87       }
88    }
```

Fig. 20.11 | Applying Transition animations to a Rectangle. (Part 3 of 3.)

FillTransition

Lines 28–34 configure a one-second **FillTransition** that changes a shape's fill color. Line 30 specifies the color (CYAN) to which the fill will transition. Line 31 sets the animations cycle count to 2—this specifies the number of iterations of the transition to perform over the specified duration. Line 34 specifies that the animation should automatically play itself in reverse once the initial transition is complete. For this animation, during the first cycle the fill color changes from the original fill color to CYAN, and during the second cycle the animation transitions back to the original fill color.

StrokeTransition

Lines 37–41 configure a one-second **StrokeTransition** that changes a shape's stroke color. Line 39 specifies the color (BLUE) to which the stroke will transition. Line 40 sets the animations cycle count to 2, and line 41 specifies that the animation should automatically play itself in reverse once the initial transition is complete. For this animation, during the first cycle the stroke color changes from the original stroke color to BLUE, and during the second cycle the animation transitions back to the original stroke color.

ParallelTransition

Lines 44–45 configure a **ParallelTransition** that performs multiple transitions at the same time (that is, in parallel). The ParallelTransition constructor receives a variable number of Transitions as a comma-separated list. In this case, the FillTransition and StrokeTransition will be performed in parallel on the app's Rectangle.

FadeTransition

Lines 48–53 configure a one-second **FadeTransition** that changes a Node's opacity. Line 50 specifies the initial opacity—1.0 is fully opaque. Line 51 specifies the final opacity—0.0 is fully transparent. Once again, we set the cycle count to 2 and specified that the animation should auto-reverse itself.

RotateTransition

Lines 56–61 configure a one-second **RotateTransition** that rotates a Node. You can rotate a Node by a specified number of degrees (line 58) or you can use other RotateTransition methods to specify a start angle and end angle. Each Transition animation uses an **Interpolator** to calculate new property values throughout the animation's duration. The default is a **LINEAR** Interpolator which evenly divides the property value changes over the animation's duration. For the RotateTransition, line 60 uses the Interpolator

EASE_BOTH, which changes the rotation slowly at first (known as "easing in"), speeds up the rotation in the middle of the animation, then slows the rotation again to complete the animation (known as "easing out"). For a list of all the predefined Interpolators, see

https://docs.oracle.com/javase/8/javafx/api/javafx/animation/
Interpolator.html

PathTransition

Lines 64–70 configure a two-second **PathTransition** that changes a shape's position by moving it along a Path. Lines 64–65 create the Path, which is specified as the second argument to the PathTransition constructor. A **LineTo** object draws a straight line from the previous PathElement's endpoint to the specified location. Line 69 specifies that this animation should use the Interpolator **EASE_IN**, which changes the position slowly at first, before performing the animation at full speed.

ScaleTransition

Lines 73–79 configure a one-second **ScaleTransition** that changes a Node's size. Line 75 specifies that the object will be scaled 75% larger along the *x*-axis (i.e., horizontally), and line 76 specifies that the object will be scaled 75% larger along the *y*-axis (i.e., vertically). Line 78 specifies that this animation should use the Interpolator **EASE_OUT**, which begins scaling the shape at full speed, then slows down as the animation completes.

SequentialTransition

Lines 82–86 configure a **SequentialTransition** that performs a sequence of transitions—as each completes, the next one in the sequence begins executing. The SequentialTransition constructor receives the Node to which the sequence of animations will be applied, followed by a comma-separated list of Transitions to perform. In fact, every transition animation class has a constructor that enables you to specify a Node. For this example, we did not specify Nodes when creating the other transitions, because they're all applied by the SequentialTransition to the Rectangle. Every Transition has a **play** method (line 86) that begins the animation. Calling play on the SequentialTransition automatically calls play on each animation in the sequence.

20.8 Timeline Animations

In this section, we continue our animation discussion with a **Timeline** animation that bounces a Circle object around the app's Pane over time. A Timeline animation can change any Node property that's modifiable. You specify how to change property values with one or more **KeyFrame** objects that the Timeline animation performs in sequence. For this app, we'll specify a single KeyFrame that modifies a Circle's location, then we'll play that KeyFrame indefinitely. Figure 20.12 shows the app's FXML, which defines a Circle object with a five-pixel black border and the fill color DODGERBLUE.

```
1   <?xml version="1.0" encoding="UTF-8"?>
2   <!-- Fig. 20.12: TimelineAnimation.fxml -->
3   <!-- FXML for a Circle that will be animated by the controller -->
```

Fig. 20.12 | FXML for a Circle that will be animated by the controller. (Part 1 of 2.)

```
4
5   <?import javafx.scene.layout.Pane?>
6   <?import javafx.scene.shape.Circle?>
7
8   <Pane id="Pane" fx:id="pane" prefHeight="400.0"
9       prefWidth="600.0" xmlns:fx="http://javafx.com/fxml/1"
10      xmlns="http://javafx.com/javafx/8.0.60"
11      fx:controller="TimelineAnimationController">
12      <children>
13          <Circle fx:id="c" fill="DODGERBLUE" layoutX="142.0" layoutY="143.0"
14              radius="40.0" stroke="BLACK" strokeType="INSIDE"
15              strokeWidth="5.0" />
16      </children>
17  </Pane>
```

Fig. 20.12 | FXML for a Circle that will be animated by the controller. (Part 2 of 2.)

The application's controller (Fig. 20.13) configures then plays the Timeline animation in the initialize method. Lines 22–45 define the animation, line 48 specifies that
the animation should cycle indefinitely (until the program terminates or the animation's
stop method is called) and line 49 plays the animation.

```
1   // Fig. 20.13: TimelineAnimationController.java
2   // Bounce a circle around a window using a Timeline animation
3   import java.security.SecureRandom;
4   import javafx.animation.KeyFrame;
5   import javafx.animation.Timeline;
6   import javafx.event.ActionEvent;
7   import javafx.event.EventHandler;
8   import javafx.fxml.FXML;
9   import javafx.geometry.Bounds;
10  import javafx.scene.layout.Pane;
11  import javafx.scene.shape.Circle;
12  import javafx.util.Duration;
13
14  public class TimelineAnimationController {
15      @FXML Circle c;
16      @FXML Pane pane;
17
18      public void initialize() {
19          SecureRandom random = new SecureRandom();
20
21          // define a timeline animation
22          Timeline timelineAnimation = new Timeline(
23              new KeyFrame(Duration.millis(10),
24                  new EventHandler<ActionEvent>() {
25                      int dx = 1 + random.nextInt(5);
26                      int dy = 1 + random.nextInt(5);
27
```

Fig. 20.13 | Bounce a circle around a window using a Timeline animation. (Part 1 of 3.)

```
28              // move the circle by the dx and dy amounts
29              @Override
30              public void handle(final ActionEvent e) {
31                  c.setLayoutX(c.getLayoutX() + dx);
32                  c.setLayoutY(c.getLayoutY() + dy);
33                  Bounds bounds = pane.getBoundsInLocal();
34
35                  if (hitRightOrLeftEdge(bounds)) {
36                      dx *= -1;
37                  }
38
39                  if (hitTopOrBottom(bounds)) {
40                      dy *= -1;
41                  }
42              }
43          }
44      )
45  );
46
47  // indicate that the timeline animation should run indefinitely
48  timelineAnimation.setCycleCount(Timeline.INDEFINITE);
49  timelineAnimation.play();
50 }
51
52 // determines whether the circle hit the left or right of the window
53 private boolean hitRightOrLeftEdge(Bounds bounds) {
54     return (c.getLayoutX() <= (bounds.getMinX() + c.getRadius())) ||
55         (c.getLayoutX() >= (bounds.getMaxX() - c.getRadius()));
56 }
57
58 // determines whether the circle hit the top or bottom of the window
59 private boolean hitTopOrBottom(Bounds bounds) {
60     return (c.getLayoutY() <= (bounds.getMinY() + c.getRadius())) ||
61         (c.getLayoutY() >= (bounds.getMaxY() - c.getRadius()));
62 }
63 }
```

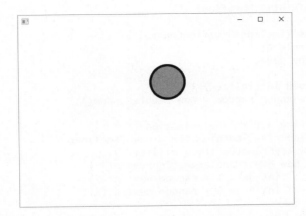

Fig. 20.13 | Bounce a circle around a window using a `Timeline` animation. (Part 2 of 3.)

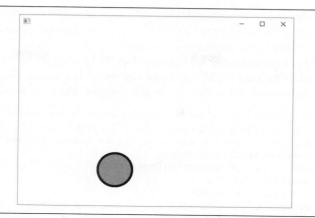

Fig. 20.13 | Bounce a circle around a window using a `Timeline` animation. (Part 3 of 3.)

Creating the `Timeline`

The `Timeline` constructor used in lines 22–45 can receive a comma-separated list of Key-Frames as arguments—in this case, we pass a single `KeyFrame`. Each `KeyFrame` issues an `ActionEvent` at a particular time in the animation. The app can respond to the event by changing a Node's property values. The `KeyFrame` constructor used here specifies that, after 10 milliseconds, the `ActionEvent` will occur. Because we set the `Timeline`'s cycle count to `Timeline.INDEFINITE`, the `Timeline` will perform this `KeyFrame` every 10 milliseconds. Lines 24–43 define the `EventHandler` for the `KeyFrame`'s `ActionEvent`.

`KeyFrame`'s `EventHandler`

In the `KeyFrame`'s `EventHandler` we define instance variables dx and dy (lines 25–26) and initialize them with randomly chosen values that will be used to change the `Circle`'s x- and y-coordinates each time the `KeyFrame` plays. The `EventHandler`'s handle method (lines 29–42) adds these values to the `Circle`'s x- and y-coordinates (lines 31–32). Next, lines 35–41 perform bounds checking to determine whether the `Circle` has collided with any of the Pane's edges. If the `Circle` hits the left or right edge, line 36 multiplies the value of dx by -1 to reverse the `Circle`'s horizontal direction. If the `Circle` hits the top or bottom edge, line 40 multiplies the value of dx by -1 to reverse the horizontal direction.

20.9 Frame-by-Frame Animation with AnimationTimer

A third way to implement JavaFX animations is via an **AnimationTimer** (package `javafx.animation`), which enables you to define frame-by-frame animations. You specify how your objects should move in a given frame, then JavaFX aggregates all of the drawing operations and displays the frame. This can be used with objects in the scene graph or to draw shapes in a Canvas. JavaFX calls the **handle** method of every `AnimationTimer` before it draws an animation frame.

For smooth animation, JavaFX tries to display animation frames at 60 frames per second. This frame rate varies based on the animation's complexity, the processor speed and how busy the processor is at a given time. For this reason, method handle receives a time stamp in nanoseconds (billionths of a second) that you can use to determine the elapsed time since the last animation frame, then you can scale the movements of your objects accordingly. This enables you to define animations that operate at the same overall speed, regardless of the frame rate on a given device.

Figure 20.14 reimplements the animation in Fig. 20.13 using an AnimationTimer. The FXML is identical (other than the filename and controller class name). Much of the code is identical to Fig. 20.13—we've highlighted the key changes, which we discuss below.

```java
 1   // Fig. 20.14: BallAnimationTimerController.java
 2   // Bounce a circle around a window using an AnimationTimer subclass.
 3   import java.security.SecureRandom;
 4   import javafx.animation.AnimationTimer;
 5   import javafx.fxml.FXML;
 6   import javafx.geometry.Bounds;
 7   import javafx.scene.layout.Pane;
 8   import javafx.scene.shape.Circle;
 9   import javafx.util.Duration;
10
11   public class BallAnimationTimerController {
12       @FXML private Circle c;
13       @FXML private Pane pane;
14
15       public void initialize() {
16           SecureRandom random = new SecureRandom();
17
18           // define a timeline animation
19           AnimationTimer timer = new AnimationTimer() {
20               int dx = 1 + random.nextInt(5);
21               int dy = 1 + random.nextInt(5);
22               int velocity = 60; // used to scale distance changes
23               long previousTime = System.nanoTime(); // time since app launch
24
25               // specify how to move Circle for current animation frame
26               @Override
27               public void handle(long now) {
28                   double elapsedTime = (now - previousTime) / 1000000000.0;
29                   previousTime = now;
30                   double scale = elapsedTime * velocity;
31
32                   Bounds bounds = pane.getBoundsInLocal();
33                   c.setLayoutX(c.getLayoutX() + dx * scale);
34                   c.setLayoutY(c.getLayoutY() + dy * scale);
35
36                   if (hitRightOrLeftEdge(bounds)) {
37                       dx *= -1;
38                   }
39
40                   if (hitTopOrBottom(bounds)) {
41                       dy *= -1;
42                   }
43               }
44           };
```

Fig. 20.14 | Bounce a circle around a window using an AnimationTimer subclass. (Part 1 of 2.)

```
45
46          timer.start();
47       }
48
49       // determines whether the circle hit left/right of the window
50       private boolean hitRightOrLeftEdge(Bounds bounds) {
51          return (c.getLayoutX() <= (bounds.getMinX() + c.getRadius())) ||
52             (c.getLayoutX() >= (bounds.getMaxX() - c.getRadius()));
53       }
54
55       // determines whether the circle hit top/bottom of the window
56       private boolean hitTopOrBottom(Bounds bounds) {
57          return (c.getLayoutY() <= (bounds.getMinY() + c.getRadius())) ||
58             (c.getLayoutY() >= (bounds.getMaxY() - c.getRadius()));
59       }
60    }
```

Fig. 20.14 | Bounce a circle around a window using an `AnimationTimer` subclass. (Part 2 of 2.)

Extending *abstract* Class *AnimationTimer*

Class `AnimationTimer` is an `abstract` class, so you must create a subclass. In this example, lines 19–44 create an anonymous inner class that extends `AnimationTimer`. Lines 20–23 define the anonymous inner class's instance variables:

- As in Fig. 20.13, `dx` and `dy` incrementally change the `Circle`'s position and are chosen randomly so the `Circle` moves at different speeds during each execution.

- Variable `velocity` is used as a multiplier to determine the actual distance moved in each animation frame—we discuss this again momentarily.

- Variable `previousTime` represents the time stamp (in nanoseconds) of the previous animation frame—this will be used to determine the elapsed time between frames. We initialized `previousTime` to `System.nanoTime()`, which returns the number of nanoseconds since the JVM launched the app. Each call to `handle` also receives as its argument the number of nanoseconds since the JVM launched the app.

Overriding Method *handle*

Lines 26–43 override `AnimationTimer` method `handle`, which specifies what to do during each animation frame:

- Line 28 calculates the `elapsedTime` in *seconds* since the last animation frame. If method `handle` truly is called 60 times per second, the elapsed time between frames will be approximately 0.0167 seconds—that is, 1/60 of a second.

- Line 29 stores the time stamp in `previousTime` for use in the *next* animation frame.

- When we change the `Circle`'s `layoutX` and `layoutY` (lines 33–34), we multiply `dx` and `dy` by the `scale` (line 30). In Fig. 20.13, the `Circle`'s speed was determined by moving between one and five pixels along the *x*- and *y*-axes every 10 milliseconds—the larger the values, the faster the `Circle` moved. If we scale `dx` or `dy` by just `elapsedTime`, we'd move the `Circle` only small fractions of `dx` and `dy` during each frame—approximately 0.0167 seconds (1/60 of a second) to 0.083 seconds (5/60 of a second), based on their randomly chosen values. For this reason, we multiply the elapsedTime by the velocity (60) to scale the movement in each frame. This results in values that are approximately one to five pixels, as in Fig. 20.13.

20.10 Drawing on a Canvas

So far, you've displayed and manipulated JavaFX two-dimensional shape objects that reside in the scene graph. In this section, we demonstrate similar drawing capabilities using the javafx.scene.canvas package, which contains two classes:

- Class **Canvas** is a subclass of Node in which you can draw graphics.
- Class **GraphicsContext** performs the drawing operations on a Canvas.

As you'll see, a GraphicsContext object enables you to specify the same drawing characteristics that you've previously used on Shape objects. However, with a GraphicsContext, you must set these characteristics and draw the shapes programmatically. To demonstrate various Canvas capabilities, Fig. 20.15 re-implements Section 20.3's BasicShapes example. Here, you'll see various JavaFX classes and enums (from packages javafx.scene.image, javafx.scene.paint and javafx.scene.shape) that JavaFX's CSS capabilities use behind the scenes to style Shapes.

Performance Tip 20.1

A Canvas typically is preferred for performance-oriented graphics, such as those in games with moving elements.

```
1  // Fig. 20.15: CanvasShapesController.java
2  // Drawing on a Canvas.
3  import javafx.fxml.FXML;
4  import javafx.scene.canvas.Canvas;
5  import javafx.scene.canvas.GraphicsContext;
6  import javafx.scene.image.Image;
7  import javafx.scene.paint.Color;
8  import javafx.scene.paint.CycleMethod;
9  import javafx.scene.paint.ImagePattern;
10 import javafx.scene.paint.LinearGradient;
11 import javafx.scene.paint.RadialGradient;
12 import javafx.scene.paint.Stop;
13 import javafx.scene.shape.ArcType;
14 import javafx.scene.shape.StrokeLineCap;
15
16 public class CanvasShapesController {
17    // instance variables that refer to GUI components
18    @FXML private Canvas drawingCanvas;
19
20    // draw on the Canvas
21    public void initialize() {
22       GraphicsContext gc = drawingCanvas.getGraphicsContext2D();
23       gc.setLineWidth(10); // set all stroke widths
24
```

Fig. 20.15 | Drawing on a Canvas. (Part 1 of 2.)

```
25        // draw red line
26        gc.setStroke(Color.RED);
27        gc.strokeLine(10, 10, 100, 100);
28
29        // draw green line
30        gc.setGlobalAlpha(0.5); // half transparent
31        gc.setLineCap(StrokeLineCap.ROUND);
32        gc.setStroke(Color.GREEN);
33        gc.strokeLine(100, 10, 10, 100);
34
35        gc.setGlobalAlpha(1.0); // reset alpha transparency
36
37        // draw rounded rect with red border and yellow fill
38        gc.setStroke(Color.RED);
39        gc.setFill(Color.YELLOW);
40        gc.fillRoundRect(120, 10, 90, 90, 50, 50);
41        gc.strokeRoundRect(120, 10, 90, 90, 50, 50);
42
43        // draw circle with blue border and red/white radial gradient fill
44        gc.setStroke(Color.BLUE);
45        Stop[] stopsRadial =
46           {new Stop(0, Color.RED), new Stop(1, Color.WHITE)};
47        RadialGradient radialGradient = new RadialGradient(0, 0, 0.5, 0.5,
48           0.6, true, CycleMethod.NO_CYCLE, stopsRadial);
49        gc.setFill(radialGradient);
50        gc.fillOval(230, 10, 90, 90);
51        gc.strokeOval(230, 10, 90, 90);
52
53        // draw ellipse with green border and image fill
54        gc.setStroke(Color.GREEN);
55        gc.setFill(new ImagePattern(new Image("yellowflowers.png")));
56        gc.fillOval(340, 10, 200, 90);
57        gc.strokeOval(340, 10, 200, 90);
58
59        // draw arc with purple border and cyan/white linear gradient fill
60        gc.setStroke(Color.PURPLE);
61        Stop[] stopsLinear =
62           {new Stop(0, Color.CYAN), new Stop(1, Color.WHITE)};
63        LinearGradient linearGradient = new LinearGradient(0, 0, 1, 0,
64           true, CycleMethod.NO_CYCLE, stopsLinear);
65        gc.setFill(linearGradient);
66        gc.fillArc(560, 10, 90, 90, 45, 270, ArcType.ROUND);
67        gc.strokeArc(560, 10, 90, 90, 45, 270, ArcType.ROUND);
68     }
69  }
```

Fig. 20.15 | Drawing on a Canvas. (Part 2 of 2.)

Obtaining the **GraphicsContext**

To draw on a Canvas, you first obtain its GraphicsContext by calling Canvas method **getGraphicsContext2D** (line 22).

Setting the Line Width for All the Shapes

When you set a GraphicsContext's drawing characteristics, they're applied (as appropriate) to all subsequent shapes you draw. For example, line 23 calls **setLineWidth** to specify the GraphicsContext's line thickness (10). All subsequent GraphicsContext method calls that draw lines or shape borders will use this setting. This is similar to the -fx-stroke-width CSS attribute we specified for all shapes in Fig. 20.4.

Drawing Lines

Lines 26–33 draw the red and green lines:

- GraphicsContext's **setStroke** method (lines 26 and 32) specifies the **Paint** object (package javafx.scene.paint) used to draw the line. The Paint can be any of the subclasses **Color**, **ImagePattern**, **LinearGradient** or **RadialGradient** (all from package javafx.scene.paint). We demonstrate each of these in this example—Color for the lines and Color, ImagePattern, LinearGradient or RadialGradient as the fills for other shapes.

- GraphicsContext's **strokeLine** method (lines 27 and 33) draws a line using the current Paint object that's set as the stroke. The four arguments are the *x-y* coordinates of the start and end points, respectively.

- GraphicsContext's **setLineCap** method (line 31) sets line cap, like the CSS property -fx-stroke-line-cap in Fig. 20.4. The argument to this method must be constant from the enum **StrokeLineCap** (package javafx.scene.shape). Here we round the line ends.

- GraphicsContext's **setGlobalAlpha** method (line 30) sets the alpha transparency of all subsequent shapes you draw. For the green line we used 0.5, which is 50% transparent. After drawing the green line, we reset this to the default 1.0 (line 35), so that subsequent shapes are fully opaque.

Drawing a Rounded Rectangle

Lines 38–41 draw a rounded rectangle with a red border:

- Line 38 sets the border color to Color.RED.

- GraphicsContext's **setFill** method (lines 39, 49, 55 and 65) specifies the Paint object that fills a shape. Here we fill the rectangle with Color.YELLOW.

- GraphicsContext's **fillRoundRect** method draws a *filled* rectangle with rounded corners using the current Paint object set as the fill. The method's first four arguments represent the rectangle's upper-left *x*-coordinate, upper-left *y*-coordinate, width and height, respectively. The last two arguments represent the arc width and arc height that are used to round the corners. These work identically to the CSS properties -fx-arc-width and -fx-arc-height properties in Fig. 20.4. GraphicsContext also provides a **fillRect** method that draws a rectangle without rounded corners.

- GraphicsContext's **strokeRoundRect** method has the same arguments as fill-RoundRect, but draws a hollow rectangle with rounded corners. GraphicsContext also provides **strokeRect**, which draws a rectangle without rounded corners.

Drawing a Circle with a RadialGradient Fill

Lines 44–51 draw a circle with a blue border and a red-white, radial-gradient fill. Line 44 sets the border color to Color.BLUE. Lines 45–48 configure the RadialGradient—these lines perform the same tasks as the CSS function radial-gradient in Fig. 20.4.

First, lines 45–46 create an array of **Stop** objects (package javafx.scene.paint) representing the color stops. Each Stop has an offset from 0.0 to 1.0 representing the offset (as a percentage) from the gradient's start point and a Color. Here the Stops indicate that the radial gradient will transition from red at the gradient's start point to white at its end point.

The RadialGradient constructor (lines 47–48) receives as arguments:

- the focus angle, which specifies the direction of the radial gradient's focal point from the gradient's center,
- the distance of the focal point as a percentage (0.0–1.0),
- the center point's x and y location as percentages (0.0–1.0) of the width and height for the shape being filled,
- a boolean indicating whether the gradient should scale to fill its shape,
- a constant from the **CycleMethod** enum (package javafx.scene.paint) indicating how the color stops are applied, and
- an array of Stop objects—this can also be a comma-separated list of Stops or a List<Stop> object.

This creates a red-white radial gradient that starts with solid red at the center of the shape and—at 60% of the radial gradient's radius—transitions to white. Line 49 sets the fill to the new radialGradient, then lines 50–51 call GraphicsContext's **fillOval** and **strokeOval** methods to draw a filled oval and hollow oval, respectively. Each method receives as arguments the upper-left x-coordinate, upper-left y-coordinate, width and height of the rectangular area (that is, the bounding box) in which the oval should be drawn. Because the width and height are the same, these calls draw circles.

Drawing an Oval with an ImagePattern Fill

Lines 54–57 draw an oval with a green border and containing an image:

- Line 54 sets the border color to Color.GREEN.
- Line 55 sets the fill to an ImagePattern—a subclass of Paint that loads an Image, either from the local system or from a URL specified as a String. ImagePattern is the class used by the CSS function image-pattern in Fig. 20.4.
- Lines 56–57 draw a filled oval and a hollow oval, respectively.

Drawing an Arc with a LinearGradient Fill

Lines 60–67 draw an arc with a purple border and filled with a cyan-white linear gradient:

- Line 60 sets the border color to Color.PURPLE.

- Lines 61–64 configure the LinearGradient, which is the class used by CSS function linear-gradient in Fig. 20.4. The constructor's first four arguments are the endpoint coordinates that represent the direction and angle of the gradient— if the *x*-coordinates are the same, the gradient is vertical; if the *y*-coordinates are the same, the gradient is horizontal and all other linear gradients follow a diagonal line. When these values are specified in the range 0.0 to 1.0 and the constructor's fifth argument is true, the gradient is scaled to fill the shape. The next argument is the CycleMethod. The last argument is an array of Stop objects—again, this can be a comma-separated list of Stops or a List<Stop> object.

Lines 66–67 call GraphicsContext's **fillArc** and **strokeArc** methods to draw a filled arc and hollow arc, respectively. Each method receives as arguments

- the upper-left *x*-coordinate, upper-left *y*-coordinate, width and height of the rectangular area (that is, the bounding box) in which the oval should be drawn,

- the start angle and sweep of the arc in degrees, and

- a constant from the **ArcType** enum (package javafx.scene.shape)

Additional GraphicsContext Features
There are many additional GraphicsContext features, which you can explore at

```
https://docs.oracle.com/javase/8/javafx/api/javafx/scene/canvas/
GraphicsContext.html
```

Some of the capabilities that we did not discuss here include:

- Drawing and filling text—similar to the font features in Section 20.2.

- Drawing and filling polylines, polygons and paths—similar to the corresponding Shape subclasses in Section 20.4.

- Applying effects and transforms—similar to the transforms in Section 20.5.

- Drawing images.

- Manipulating the individual pixels of a drawing in a Canvas via a PixelWriter.

- Saving and restoring graphics characteristics via the save and restore methods.

20.11 Three-Dimensional Shapes

Throughout this chapter, we've demonstrated many two-dimensional graphics capabilities. In Java SE 8, JavaFX added several three-dimensional shapes and corresponding capabilities. The three-dimensional shapes are subclasses of **Shape3D** from the package javafx.scene.shape. In this section, you'll use Scene Builder to create a **Box**, a **Cylinder** and a **Sphere** and specify several of their properties. Then, in the app's controller, you'll create so-called *materials* that apply color and images to the 3D shapes.

FXML for the Box, Cylinder and Sphere
Figure 20.16 shows the completed FXML that we created with Scene Builder:

- Lines 16–21 define the Box object.

- Lines 22–27 define the `Cylinder` object.
- Lines 28–29 define the `Sphere` object.

We dragged objects of each of these Shape3D subclasses from the Scene Builder **Library**'s **Shapes** section onto the design area and gave them the **fx:id** values box, cylinder and sphere, respectively. We also set the controller to `ThreeDimensionalShapesController`.[5]

```
 1  <?xml version="1.0" encoding="UTF-8"?>
 2  <!-- ThreeDimensionalShapes.fxml -->
 3  <!-- FXML that displays a Box, Cylinder and Sphere -->
 4
 5  <?import javafx.geometry.Point3D?>
 6  <?import javafx.scene.layout.Pane?>
 7  <?import javafx.scene.shape.Box?>
 8  <?import javafx.scene.shape.Cylinder?>
 9  <?import javafx.scene.shape.Sphere?>
10
11  <Pane prefHeight="200.0" prefWidth="510.0"
12      xmlns="http://javafx.com/javafx/8.0.60"
13      xmlns:fx="http://javafx.com/fxml/1"
14      fx:controller="ThreeDimensionalShapesController">
15      <children>
16          <Box fx:id="box" depth="100.0" height="100.0" layoutX="100.0"
17              layoutY="100.0" rotate="30.0" width="100.0">
18              <rotationAxis>
19                  <Point3D x="1.0" y="1.0" z="1.0" />
20              </rotationAxis>
21          </Box>
22          <Cylinder fx:id="cylinder" height="100.0" layoutX="265.0"
23              layoutY="100.0" radius="50.0" rotate="-45.0">
24              <rotationAxis>
25                  <Point3D x="1.0" y="1.0" z="1.0" />
26              </rotationAxis>
27          </Cylinder>
28          <Sphere fx:id="sphere" layoutX="430.0" layoutY="100.0"
29              radius="60.0" />
30      </children>
31  </Pane>
```

Fig. 20.16 | FXML that displays a `Box`, `Cylinder` and `Sphere`. (Part 1 of 2.)

---

5. At the time of this writing, when you drag three-dimensional shapes onto the Scene Builder design area, their dimensions are set to small values by default—a Box's **Width**, **Height** and **Depth** are set to 2, a Cylinder's **Height** and **Radius** are set to 2 and 0.77, and a Sphere's **Radius** is set to 0.77. You may need to select them in the **Hierarchy** pane to set their properties.

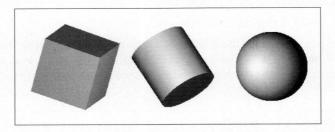

Fig. 20.16 | FXML that displays a Box, Cylinder and Sphere. (Part 2 of 2.)

All three shapes initially are gray. The shading you see in Scene Builder comes from the scene's default lighting. Though we do not use them in this example, package javafx.scene's AmbientLight and PointLight classes can be used to add your own lighting effects. You can also use camera objects to view the scene from different angles and distances. These are located in the Scene Builder **Library**'s **3D** section. For more information on lighting and cameras, see

```
https://docs.oracle.com/javase/8/javafx/graphics-tutorial/javafx-
    3d-graphics.htm
```

Box Properties
Configure the Box's properties in Scene Builder as follows:

- Set **Width**, **Height** and **Depth** to 100, making a cube. The depth is measured along the z-axis which runs perpendicular to your screen—when you move objects along the z-axis they get bigger as they're brought toward you and smaller as they're moved away from you.

- Set **Layout X** and **Layout Y** to 100 to specify the location of the cube.

- Set **Rotate** to 30 to specify the rotation angle in degrees. Positive values rotate counter-clockwise.

- For **Rotation Axis**, set the **X**, **Y** and **Z** values to 1 to indicate that the **Rotate** angle should be used to rotate the cube 30 degrees around *each* axis.

To see how the **Rotate** angle and **Rotation Axis** values affect the Box's rotation, try setting two of the three **Rotation Axis** values to 0, then changing the **Rotate** angle.

Cylinder Properties
Configure the Cylinder's properties in Scene Builder as follows:

- Set **Height** to 100.0 and **Radius** to 50.

- Set **Layout X** and **Layout Y** to 265 and 100, respectively.

- Set **Rotate** to -45 to specify the rotation angle in degrees. Negative values rotate clockwise.

- For **Rotation Axis**, set the **X**, **Y** and **Z** values to 1 to indicate that the **Rotate** angle should be applied to all three axes.

Sphere Properties

Configure the Sphere's properties in Scene Builder as follows:

- Set **Radius** to 60.

- Set **Layout X** and **Layout Y** to 430 and 100, respectively.

ThreeDimensionalShapesController Class

Figure 20.17 shows this app's controller and final output. The colors and images you see on the final shapes are created by applying so-called materials to the shapes. JavaFX class **PhongMaterial** (package javafx.scene.paint) is used to define materials. The name "Phong" is a 3D graphics term—*phong shading* is technique for applying color and shading to 3D surfaces. For more details on this technique, visit

> https://en.wikipedia.org/wiki/Phong_shading

```
1   // Fig. 20.17: ThreeDimensionalShapesController.java
2   // Setting the material displayed on 3D shapes.
3   import javafx.fxml.FXML;
4   import javafx.scene.paint.Color;
5   import javafx.scene.paint.PhongMaterial;
6   import javafx.scene.image.Image;
7   import javafx.scene.shape.Box;
8   import javafx.scene.shape.Cylinder;
9   import javafx.scene.shape.Sphere;
10
11  public class ThreeDimensionalShapesController {
12      // instance variables that refer to 3D shapes
13      @FXML private Box box;
14      @FXML private Cylinder cylinder;
15      @FXML private Sphere sphere;
16
17      // set the material for each 3D shape
18      public void initialize() {
19          // define material for the Box object
20          PhongMaterial boxMaterial = new PhongMaterial();
21          boxMaterial.setDiffuseColor(Color.CYAN);
22          box.setMaterial(boxMaterial);
23
24          // define material for the Cylinder object
25          PhongMaterial cylinderMaterial = new PhongMaterial();
26          cylinderMaterial.setDiffuseMap(new Image("yellowflowers.png"));
27          cylinder.setMaterial(cylinderMaterial);
28
29          // define material for the Sphere object
30          PhongMaterial sphereMaterial = new PhongMaterial();
31          sphereMaterial.setDiffuseColor(Color.RED);
32          sphereMaterial.setSpecularColor(Color.WHITE);
33          sphereMaterial.setSpecularPower(32);
34          sphere.setMaterial(sphereMaterial);
35      }
36  }
```

Fig. 20.17 | Setting the material displayed on 3D shapes. (Part 1 of 2.)

Fig. 20.17 | Setting the material displayed on 3D shapes. (Part 2 of 2.)

PhongMaterial *for the* Box

Lines 20–22 configure and set the Box object's PhongMaterial. Method **setDiffuseColor** sets the color that's applied to the Box's surfaces (that is, sides). The scene's lighting effects determine the shades of the color applied to each visible surface. These shades change, based on the angle from which the light shines on the objects.

PhongMaterial *for the* Cylinder

Lines 25–27 configure and set the Cylinder object's PhongMaterial. Method **setDiffuseMap** sets the Image that's applied to the Cylinder's surfaces. Again, the scene's lighting affects how the image is shaded on the surfaces. When you run the program, notice that the image is darker at the left and right edges (where less light reaches) and barely visible on the bottom (where almost no light reaches).

PhongMaterial *for the* Sphere

Lines 30–34 configure and set the Sphere object's PhongMaterial. We set the diffuse color to red. Method **setSpecularColor** sets the color of a bright spot that makes a 3D shape appear shiny. Method **setSpecularPower** determines the intensity of that spot. Try experimenting with different specular powers to see changes in the bright spot's intensity.

20.12 Wrap-Up

In this chapter, we completed our discussion of JavaFX that began in Chapters 12 and 13. Here, we presented various JavaFX graphics and multimedia capabilities.

We used external Cascading Style Sheets (CSS) to customize the appearance of JavaFX Nodes, including Labels and objects of various Shape subclasses. We displayed two-dimensional shapes, including lines, rectangles, circles, ellipses, arcs, polylines, polygons and custom paths.

We showed how to apply a transform to a Node, rotating 18 Polygon objects around a specific point to create a circle of star shapes. We created a simple video player using class Media to specify the video's location, class MediaPlayer to load the video and control its playback and class MediaView to display the video.

We animated Nodes with Transition and Timeline animations that change Node properties to new values over time. We used built-in Transition animations to change specific JavaFX Node properties (such as a Node's stroke and fill colors, opacity, angle of rotation and scale). We used Timeline animations with KeyFrames to bounce a Circle around a window, and showed that such animations can be used to change any modifiable Node property. We also showed how to create frame-by-frame animations with AnimationTimer.

Next, we presented various capabilities for drawing on a Canvas Node using a GraphicsContext object. You saw that GraphicsContext supports many of the same drawing characteristics and shapes that you can implement with Shape Nodes. Finally, we showed the three-dimensional shapes Box, Cylinder and Sphere, and demonstrated how to use materials to apply color and images to them. For more information on JavaFX, visit the FX Experience blog at

```
http://fxexperience.com/
```

In the next chapter, we discuss Java's concurrent programming capabilities, which enable you to take advantage of today's multi-core processors.

Concurrency and Multi-Core Performance

Objectives

In this chapter you'll:

- Understand concurrency, parallelism and multithreading.
- Learn the thread life cycle.
- Use `ExecutorService` to launch concurrent threads that execute `Runnable`s.
- Use `synchronized` methods to coordinate access to shared mutable data.
- Understand producer/consumer relationships.
- Use JavaFX's concurrency APIs to update GUIs in a thread-safe manner.
- Compare the performance of `Arrays` methods `sort` and `parallelSort` on a multi-core system.
- Use parallel streams for better performance on multi-core systems.
- Use `CompletableFuture`s to execute long calculations asynchronously and get the results in the future.

21.1 Introduction

[*Note: Sections marked "Advanced" are intended for readers who wish a deeper treatment of concurrency and may be skipped by readers preferring only basic coverage.*] It would be nice if we could focus our attention on performing only one task at a time and doing it well. That's usually difficult to do in a complex world in which there's so much going on at once. This chapter presents Java's capabilities for creating and managing multiple tasks. As we'll demonstrate, this can greatly improve program performance and responsiveness.

When we say that two tasks are operating **concurrently**, we mean that they're both *making progress* at once. Until the early 2000s, most computers had only a single processor. Operating systems on such computers execute tasks concurrently by rapidly switching between them, doing a small portion of each before moving on to the next, so that all tasks keep progressing. For example, it's common for personal computers to compile a program, send a file to a printer, receive electronic mail messages over a network and more, concurrently. Since its inception, Java has supported concurrency.

When we say that two tasks are operating **in parallel**, we mean that they're executing *simultaneously*. In this sense, parallelism is a subset of concurrency. The human body performs a great variety of operations in parallel. Respiration, blood circulation, digestion, thinking and walking, for example, can occur in parallel, as can all the senses—sight, hearing, touch, smell and taste. It's believed that this parallelism is possible because the human brain is thought to contain billions of "processors." Today's multi-core computers have multiple processors that can perform tasks in parallel.

Java Concurrency

Java makes concurrency available to you through the language and APIs. Java programs can have multiple **threads of execution**, each with its own method-call stack and program counter, allowing it to execute concurrently with other threads while sharing with them application-wide resources such as memory and file handles. This capability is called **multithreading**.

Performance Tip 21.1

A problem with single-threaded applications that can lead to poor responsiveness is that lengthy activities must complete before others can begin. In a multithreaded application, threads can be distributed across multiple cores (if available) so that multiple tasks execute in parallel and the application can operate more efficiently. Multithreading can also increase performance on single-processor systems—when one thread cannot proceed (because, for example, it's waiting for the result of an I/O operation), another can use the processor.

Concurrent Programming Uses

We'll discuss many applications of **concurrent programming**. For example, when streaming an audio or video over the Internet, the user may not want to wait until the entire audio or video downloads before starting the playback. To solve this problem, multiple threads can be used—one to download the audio or video (later in the chapter we'll refer to this as a *producer*), and another to play it (later in the chapter we'll refer to this as a *consumer*). These activities proceed concurrently. To avoid choppy playback, the threads are **synchronized** (that is, their actions are coordinated) so that the player thread doesn't begin until there's a sufficient amount of the audio or video in memory to keep the player thread busy. Producer and consumer threads *share memory*—we'll show how to coordinate these threads to ensure correct execution. The Java Virtual Machine (JVM) creates threads to run programs and threads to perform housekeeping tasks such as garbage collection.

Concurrent Programming Is Difficult

Writing multithreaded programs can be tricky. Although the human mind can perform functions concurrently, people find it difficult to jump between parallel trains of thought. To see why multithreaded programs can be difficult to write and understand, try the following experiment: Open three books to page 1, and try reading the books concurrently. Read a few words from the first book, then a few from the second, then a few from the third, then loop back and read the next few words from the first book, and so on. After this experiment, you'll appreciate many of the challenges of multithreading—switching between the books, reading briefly, remembering your place in each book, moving the book you're reading closer so that you can see it and pushing the books you're not reading aside—and, amid all this chaos, trying to comprehend the content of the books!

Use the Prebuilt Classes of the Concurrency APIs Whenever Possible

Programming concurrent applications is difficult and error prone. If you must use synchronization in a program, follow these guidelines:

1. *The vast majority of programmers should use existing collection classes and interfaces from the concurrency APIs that manage synchronization for you—such as the Array-BlockingQueue class (an implementation of interface BlockingQueue) we discuss in*

Section 21.6. Two other concurrency API classes that you'll use frequently are `LinkedBlockingQueue` and `ConcurrentHashMap` (each summarized in Fig. 21.22). The concurrency API classes are written by experts, have been thoroughly tested and debugged, operate efficiently and help you avoid common traps and pitfalls. Section 21.10 overviews Java's prebuilt concurrent collections.

2. For advanced programmers who want to control synchronization, use the `synchronized` keyword and `Object` methods `wait`, `notify` and `notifyAll`, which we discuss in the optional Section 21.7.

3. Only the most advanced programmers should use `Locks` and `Conditions`, which we introduce in the optional Section 21.9, and classes like `LinkedTransferQueue`—an implementation of interface `TransferQueue`—which we summarize in Fig. 21.22.

You might want to read our discussions of the more advanced features mentioned in items 2 and 3, even though you most likely will not use them. We explain these because:

- They provide a solid basis for understanding how concurrent applications synchronize access to shared memory.

- By showing you the complexity involved in using these low-level features, we hope to impress upon you the message: *Use the simpler prebuilt concurrency capabilities whenever possible.*

21.2 Thread States and Life Cycle

At any time, a thread is said to be in one of several **thread states**—illustrated in the UML state diagram in Fig. 21.1. Several of the terms in the diagram are defined in later sections. We include this discussion to help you understand what's going on "under the hood" in a Java multithreaded environment. Java hides most of this detail from you, greatly simplifying the task of developing multithreaded applications.

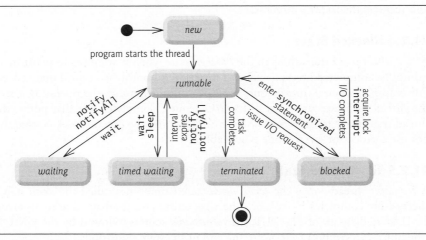

Fig. 21.1 | Thread life-cycle UML state diagram.

21.2.1 *New* and *Runnable* States

A new thread begins its life cycle in the *new* state. It remains in this state until the program starts the thread, which places it in the *runnable* state. A thread in the *runnable* state is considered to be executing its task.

21.2.2 *Waiting* State

Sometimes a *runnable* thread transitions to the **waiting** state while it waits for another thread to perform a task. A *waiting* thread transitions back to the *runnable* state only when another thread notifies it to continue executing.

21.2.3 *Timed Waiting* State

A *runnable* thread can enter the **timed waiting** state for a specified interval of time. It transitions back to the *runnable* state when that time interval expires or when the event it's waiting for occurs. *Timed waiting* threads and *waiting* threads cannot use a processor, even if one is available. A *runnable* thread can transition to the *timed waiting* state if it provides an optional wait interval when it's waiting for another thread to perform a task. Such a thread returns to the *runnable* state when it's notified by another thread or when the timed interval expires—whichever comes first. Another way to place a thread in the *timed waiting* state is to put a *runnable* thread to sleep—a **sleeping thread** remains in the *timed waiting* state for a designated period of time (called a **sleep interval**), after which it returns to the *runnable* state. Threads sleep when they momentarily do not have work to perform. For example, a word processor may contain a thread that periodically backs up (i.e., writes a copy of) the current document to disk for recovery purposes. If the thread did not sleep between successive backups, it would require a loop in which it continually tested whether it should write a copy of the document to disk. This loop would consume processor time without performing productive work, thus reducing system performance. In this case, it's more efficient for the thread to specify a sleep interval (equal to the period between successive backups) and enter the *timed waiting* state. This thread is returned to the *runnable* state when its sleep interval expires, at which point it writes a copy of the document to disk and reenters the *timed waiting* state.

21.2.4 *Blocked* State

A *runnable* thread transitions to the **blocked** state when it attempts to perform a task that cannot be completed immediately and it must temporarily wait until that task completes. For example, when a thread issues an input/output request, the operating system blocks the thread from executing until that I/O request completes—at that point, the *blocked* thread transitions to the *runnable* state, so it can resume execution. A *blocked* thread cannot use a processor, even if one is available.

21.2.5 *Terminated* State

A *runnable* thread enters the **terminated** state (sometimes called the **dead** state) when it successfully completes its task or otherwise terminates (perhaps due to an error). In the UML state diagram of Fig. 21.1, the *terminated* state is followed by the UML final state (the bull's-eye symbol) to indicate the end of the state transitions.

21.2.6 Operating-System View of the *Runnable* State

At the operating system level, Java's *runnable* state typically encompasses *two separate* states (Fig. 21.2). The operating system hides these states from the JVM, which sees only the *runnable* state. When a thread first transitions to the *runnable* state from the *new* state, it's in the **ready** state. A *ready* thread enters the **running** state (i.e., begins executing) when the operating system assigns it to a processor—also known as **dispatching the thread**. In most operating systems, each thread is given a small amount of processor time—called a **quantum** or **timeslice**—with which to perform its task. When its quantum expires, the thread returns to the *ready* state, and the operating system assigns another thread to the processor. Transitions between the *ready* and *running* states are handled solely by the operating system. The JVM does not "see" the transitions—it simply views the thread as being *runnable* and leaves it up to the operating system to transition the thread between *ready* and *running*. The process that an operating system uses to determine which thread to dispatch is called **thread scheduling** and is dependent on thread priorities.

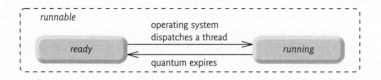

Fig. 21.2 | Operating system's internal view of Java's *runnable* state.

21.2.7 Thread Priorities and Thread Scheduling

Every Java thread has a **thread priority** that helps determine the order in which threads are scheduled. Each new thread inherits the priority of the thread that created it. Informally, higher-priority threads are more important to a program and should be allocated processor time before lower-priority threads. *Nevertheless, thread priorities cannot guarantee the order in which threads execute.*

It's recommended that you do not explicitly create and use `Thread`s to implement concurrency, but rather use the `Executor` interface (described in Section 21.3). The `Thread` class does contain some useful `static` methods, which you *will* use later in the chapter.

Most operating systems support timeslicing, which enables threads of equal priority to share a processor. Without timeslicing, each thread in a set of equal-priority threads runs to completion (unless it leaves the *runnable* state and enters the *waiting* or *timed waiting* state, or gets interrupted by a higher-priority thread) before other threads of equal priority get a chance to execute. With timeslicing, even if a thread has *not* finished executing when its quantum expires, the processor is taken away from the thread and given to the next thread of equal priority, if one is available.

An *operating system's* **thread scheduler** determines which thread runs next. One simple thread-scheduler implementation keeps the highest-priority thread *running* at all times and, if there's more than one highest-priority thread, ensures that all such threads execute for a quantum each in **round-robin** fashion. This process continues until all threads run to completion.

Software Engineering Observation 21.1

Java provides higher-level concurrency utilities to hide much of this complexity and make multithreaded programming less error prone. Thread priorities are used behind the scenes to interact with the operating system, but most programmers who use Java multithreading will not be concerned with setting and adjusting thread priorities.

Portability Tip 21.1

Thread scheduling is platform dependent—the behavior of a multithreaded program could vary across different Java implementations.

21.2.8 Indefinite Postponement and Deadlock

When a higher-priority thread enters the *ready* state, the operating system generally pre-empts the *running* thread (an operation known as **preemptive scheduling**). Depending on the operating system, a steady influx of higher-priority threads could postpone—possibly indefinitely—the execution of lower-priority threads. Such **indefinite postponement** is sometimes referred to more colorfully as **starvation**. Operating systems employ a technique called *aging* to prevent starvation—as a thread waits in the *ready* state, the operating system gradually increases the thread's priority to ensure that the thread will eventually run.

Another problem related to indefinite postponement is called **deadlock**. This occurs when a waiting thread (let's call this thread1) cannot proceed because it's waiting (either directly or indirectly) for another thread (let's call this thread2) to proceed, while simultaneously thread2 cannot proceed because it's waiting (either directly or indirectly) for thread1 to proceed. The two threads are waiting for each other, so the actions that would enable each thread to continue execution can never occur.

21.3 Creating and Executing Threads with the Executor Framework

This section demonstrates how to perform concurrent tasks in an application by using Executors and Runnable objects.

Creating Concurrent Tasks with the Runnable Interface

You implement the **Runnable** interface (of package java.lang) to specify a task that can execute concurrently with other tasks. The Runnable interface declares the single method **run**, which contains the code that defines the task that a Runnable object should perform.

Executing Runnable Objects with an Executor

To allow a Runnable to perform its task, you must execute it. An **Executor** object executes Runnables. It does this by creating and managing a group of threads called a **thread pool**. When an Executor begins executing a Runnable, the Executor calls the Runnable object's run method.

The Executor interface declares a single method named **execute** which accepts a Runnable as an argument. The Executor assigns every Runnable passed to its execute method to one of the available threads in the thread pool. If there are no available threads, the Executor creates a new thread or waits for a thread to become available and assigns that thread the Runnable that was passed to method execute.

Using an Executor has many advantages over creating threads yourself. Executors can *reuse existing threads* to eliminate the overhead of creating a new thread for each task and can improve performance by *optimizing the number of threads* to ensure that the processor stays busy, without creating so many threads that the application runs out of resources.

Software Engineering Observation 21.2

Though it's possible to create threads explicitly, it's recommended that you use the Executor interface to manage the execution of Runnable objects.

Using Class *Executors* to Obtain an *ExecutorService*

The **ExecutorService interface** (of package java.util.concurrent) *extends* Executor and declares various methods for managing the life cycle of an Executor. You obtain an ExecutorService object by calling one of the static methods declared in class **Executors** (of package java.util.concurrent). We use interface ExecutorService and a method of class Executors in our example (Fig. 21.4), which executes three tasks.

Implementing the *Runnable* Interface

Class PrintTask (Fig. 21.3) implements Runnable (line 5), *so that multiple PrintTasks can execute concurrently*. Variable sleepTime (line 7) stores a random integer value from 0 to 5 seconds created in the PrintTask constructor (line 15). Each thread running a Print-Task sleeps for the amount of time specified by sleepTime, then outputs its task's name and a message indicating that it's done sleeping.

```java
1   // Fig. 21.3: PrintTask.java
2   // PrintTask class sleeps for a random time from 0 to 5 seconds
3   import java.security.SecureRandom;
4
5   public class PrintTask implements Runnable {
6      private static final SecureRandom generator = new SecureRandom();
7      private final int sleepTime; // random sleep time for thread
8      private final String taskName;
9
10     // constructor
11     public PrintTask(String taskName) {
12        this.taskName = taskName;
13
14        // pick random sleep time between 0 and 5 seconds
15        sleepTime = generator.nextInt(5000); // milliseconds
16     }
17
18     // method run contains the code that a thread will execute
19     @Override
20     public void run() {
21        try { // put thread to sleep for sleepTime amount of time
22           System.out.printf("%s going to sleep for %d milliseconds.%n",
23              taskName, sleepTime);
24           Thread.sleep(sleepTime); // put thread to sleep
25        }
```

Fig. 21.3 | PrintTask class sleeps for a random time from 0 to 5 seconds. (Part 1 of 2.)

```
26              catch (InterruptedException exception) {
27                  exception.printStackTrace();
28                  Thread.currentThread().interrupt(); // re-interrupt the thread
29              }
30
31              // print task name
32              System.out.printf("%s done sleeping%n", taskName);
33          }
34      }
```

Fig. 21.3 | `PrintTask` class sleeps for a random time from 0 to 5 seconds. (Part 2 of 2.)

A `PrintTask` executes when a thread calls the `PrintTask`'s run method. Lines 22–23 display a message indicating the currently executing task's name and that the task is going to sleep for `sleepTime` milliseconds. Line 24 invokes `static Thread` method **sleep** to place the thread in the *timed waiting* state for the specified amount of time. At this point, the thread loses the processor, and the system allows another thread to execute. When the thread awakens, it reenters the *runnable* state. When the `PrintTask` is assigned to a processor again, line 32 outputs a message indicating that the task is done sleeping, then method run terminates. The `catch` at lines 26–29 is required because method `sleep` might throw a *checked* **InterruptedException** if a sleeping thread's **interrupt** method is called.

Let the Thread Handle *InterruptedExceptions*
It's considered good practice to let the executing thread handle `InterruptedExceptions`. Normally, you'd do this by declaring that method run throws the exception, rather than catching the exception. However, recall from Chapter 11 that when you override a method, the `throws` clause may contain only the same or a subset of the exception types declared in the original method's `throws` clause. `Runnable` method run does not have a `throws` clause, so we cannot provide one in line 20. To ensure that the executing thread receives the `InterruptedException`, line 28 first obtains a reference to the currently executing `Thread` by calling `static` method **currentThread**, then uses that `Thread`'s interrupt method to deliver the `InterruptedException` to the current thread.[1]

Using the *ExecutorService* to Manage Threads That Execute *PrintTasks*
Figure 21.4 uses an `ExecutorService` object to manage threads that execute `PrintTasks` (as defined in Fig. 21.3). Lines 9–11 in Fig. 21.4 create and name three `PrintTasks` to execute. Line 16 uses `Executors` method **newCachedThreadPool** to obtain an `ExecutorService` that creates new threads if no existing threads are available to reuse. These threads are used by the `ExecutorService` to execute the `Runnables`.

```
1   // Fig. 21.4: TaskExecutor.java
2   // Using an ExecutorService to execute Runnables.
3   import java.util.concurrent.Executors;
```

Fig. 21.4 | Using an `ExecutorService` to execute `Runnables`. (Part 1 of 2.)

---

1. For detailed information on handling thread interruptions, see Chapter 7 of *Java Concurrency in Practice* by Brian Goetz, et al., Addison-Wesley Professional, 2006.

```
4    import java.util.concurrent.ExecutorService;
5
6    public class TaskExecutor {
7       public static void main(String[] args) {
8          // create and name each runnable
9          PrintTask task1 = new PrintTask("task1");
10         PrintTask task2 = new PrintTask("task2");
11         PrintTask task3 = new PrintTask("task3");
12
13         System.out.println("Starting Executor");
14
15         // create ExecutorService to manage threads
16         ExecutorService executorService = Executors.newCachedThreadPool();
17
18         // start the three PrintTasks
19         executorService.execute(task1); // start task1
20         executorService.execute(task2); // start task2
21         executorService.execute(task3); // start task3
22
23         // shut down ExecutorService--it decides when to shut down threads
24         executorService.shutdown();
25
26         System.out.printf("Tasks started, main ends.%n%n");
27      }
28   }
```

```
Starting Executor
Tasks started, main ends

task1 going to sleep for 4806 milliseconds
task2 going to sleep for 2513 milliseconds
task3 going to sleep for 1132 milliseconds
task3 done sleeping
task2 done sleeping
task1 done sleeping
```

```
Starting Executor
task1 going to sleep for 3161 milliseconds.
task3 going to sleep for 532 milliseconds.
task2 going to sleep for 3440 milliseconds.
Tasks started, main ends.

task3 done sleeping
task1 done sleeping
task2 done sleeping
```

Fig. 21.4 | Using an ExecutorService to execute Runnables. (Part 2 of 2.)

Lines 19–21 each invoke the ExecutorService's execute method, which executes its Runnable argument (in this case a PrintTask) at some time in the future. The specified task may execute in one of the threads in the ExecutorService's thread pool, in a new thread created to execute it, or in the thread that called the execute method—the ExecutorService manages these details. Method execute returns immediately from each invocation—the program does *not* wait for each PrintTask to finish. Line 24 calls ExecutorService method **shutdown**, which prevents the ExecutorService from accepting new tasks, but *continues executing tasks that have already been submitted.* Once all of the previously submitted tasks have completed, the ExecutorService terminates. Line 26 outputs a message indicating that the tasks were started and the main thread is finishing its execution.

Main Thread

The code in main executes in the **main thread**, which is created by the JVM. The code in the run method of PrintTask (lines 19–33 of Fig. 21.3) executes whenever the Executor starts each PrintTask—again, sometime after they're passed to the ExecutorService's execute method (Fig. 21.4, lines 19–21). When main terminates, the program itself continues running until the submitted tasks complete.

Sample Outputs

The sample outputs show each task's name and sleep time as the thread goes to sleep. The thread with the shortest sleep time *in most cases* awakens first, indicates that it's done sleeping and terminates. In Section 21.8, we discuss multithreading issues that could prevent the thread with the shortest sleep time from awakening first. In the first output, the main thread terminates *before* any of the PrintTasks output their names and sleep times. This shows that the main thread runs to completion before any of the PrintTasks gets a chance to run. In the second output, all of the PrintTasks output their names and sleep times *before* the main thread terminates. This shows that the PrintTasks started executing before the main thread terminated. Also, notice in the second example output, task3 goes to sleep before task2, even though we passed task2 to the ExecutorService's execute method before task3. This illustrates the fact that *we cannot predict the order in which the tasks will start executing, even if we know the order in which they were created and started.*

Waiting for Previously Scheduled Tasks to Terminate

After scheduling tasks to execute, you'll typically want to *wait for the tasks to complete*—for example, so that you can use the tasks' results. After calling method shutdown, you can call ExecutorService method awaitTermination to wait for scheduled tasks to complete. We demonstrate this in Fig. 21.7. We purposely did not call awaitTermination in Fig. 21.4 to demonstrate that a program can continue executing after the main thread terminates.

21.4 Thread Synchronization

When multiple threads share an object and it's *modified* by one or more of them, indeterminate results may occur (as we'll see in the examples) unless access to the shared object is managed properly. If one thread is in the process of updating a shared object and another thread also tries to update it, it's uncertain which thread's update takes effect. Similarly, if one thread is in the process of updating a shared object and another thread tries to read it, it's uncertain whether the reading thread will see the old value or the new one. In such cases, the program's behavior cannot be trusted—sometimes the program will produce the correct results, and sometimes it won't, and there won't be any indication that the shared object was manipulated incorrectly.

The problem can be solved by giving only one thread at a time *exclusive access* to code that accesses the shared object. During that time, other threads desiring to access the object are kept waiting. When the thread with exclusive access finishes accessing the object, one of the waiting threads is allowed to proceed. This process, called **thread synchronization**, coordinates access to shared data by multiple concurrent threads. By synchronizing threads in this manner, you can ensure that each thread accessing a shared object *excludes* all other threads from doing so simultaneously—this is called **mutual exclusion**.

21.4.1 Immutable Data

Actually, thread synchronization is necessary *only* for shared **mutable data**, i.e., data that may *change* during its lifetime. With shared **immutable data** that will *not* change, it's not possible for a thread to see old or incorrect values as a result of another thread's manipulation of that data.

When you share *immutable data* across threads, declare the corresponding data fields `final` to indicate that the variables's values will *not* change after they're initialized. This prevents accidental modification of the shared data, which could compromise thread safety. *Labeling object references as `final` indicates that the reference will not change, but it does not guarantee that the referenced object is immutable—this depends entirely on the object's properties.* But, it's still good practice to mark references that will not change as `final`.

Software Engineering Observation 21.3

Always declare data fields that you do not expect to change as `final`. Primitive variables that are declared as `final` can safely be shared across threads. An object reference that's declared as `final` ensures that the object it refers to will be fully constructed and initialized before it's used by the program, and prevents the reference from pointing to another object.

21.4.2 Monitors

A common way to perform synchronization is to use Java's built-in **monitors**. Every object has a monitor and a **monitor lock** (or **intrinsic lock**). The monitor ensures that its object's monitor lock is held by a maximum of only one thread at any time. Monitors and monitor locks can thus be used to enforce mutual exclusion. If an operation requires the executing thread to *hold a lock* while the operation is performed, a thread must *acquire the lock* before proceeding with the operation. Other threads attempting to perform an operation that requires the same lock will be *blocked* until the first thread *releases the lock*, at which point the *blocked* threads may attempt to acquire the lock and proceed with the operation.

To specify that a thread must hold a monitor lock to execute a block of code, the code should be placed in a **synchronized statement**. Such code is said to be **guarded** by the monitor lock; a thread must **acquire the lock** to execute the guarded statements. The monitor allows only one thread at a time to execute statements within `synchronized` statements that lock on the same object, as only one thread at a time can hold the monitor lock. The `synchronized` statements are declared using the **synchronized keyword**:

```
synchronized (object) {
    statements
}
```

where *object* is the object whose monitor lock will be acquired; *object* is normally this if it's the object in which the synchronized statement appears. If several synchronized statements in different threads are trying to execute on an object at the same time, only one of them may be active on the object—all the other threads attempting to enter a synchronized statement on the same object are placed in the *blocked* state.

When a synchronized statement finishes executing, the object's monitor lock is released and one of the *blocked* threads attempting to enter a synchronized statement can be allowed to acquire the lock to proceed. Java also allows **synchronized methods**. Before executing, a synchronized instance method must acquire the lock on the object that's used to call the method. Similarly, a static synchronized method must acquire the lock on a Class object that represents the class in which the method is declared. A Class object is the execution-time representation of a class that the JVM has loaded into memory.

Software Engineering Observation 21.4

Using a synchronized block to enforce mutual exclusion is an example of the design pattern known as the Java Monitor Pattern (see Section 4.2.1 of Java Concurrency in Practice by Brian Goetz, et al., Addison-Wesley Professional, 2006).

21.4.3 Unsynchronized Mutable Data Sharing

First, we illustrate the dangers of sharing an object across threads *without* proper synchronization. In this example (Figs. 21.5–21.7), two Runnables maintain references to a single integer array. Each Runnable writes three values to the array, then terminates. This may seem harmless, but we'll see that it can result in errors if the array is manipulated without synchronization.

Class SimpleArray

We'll *share* a SimpleArray object (Fig. 21.5) across multiple threads. SimpleArray will enable those threads to place int values into array (declared at line 8). Line 9 initializes variable writeIndex, which determines the array element that should be written to next. The constructor (line 12) creates an integer array of the desired size.

```
1   // Fig. 21.5: SimpleArray.java
2   // Class that manages an integer array to be shared by multiple threads.
3   import java.security.SecureRandom;
4   import java.util.Arrays;
5
6   public class SimpleArray { // CAUTION: NOT THREAD SAFE!
7      private static final SecureRandom generator = new SecureRandom();
8      private final int[] array; // the shared integer array
9      private int writeIndex = 0; // shared index of next element to write
10
11     // construct a SimpleArray of a given size
12     public SimpleArray(int size) {array = new int[size];}
13
```

Fig. 21.5 | Class that manages an integer array to be shared by multiple threads. (*Caution:* The example of Figs. 21.5–21.7 is *not* thread safe.) (Part 1 of 2.)

```
14        // add a value to the shared array
15        public void add(int value) {
16            int position = writeIndex; // store the write index
17
18            try {
19                // put thread to sleep for 0-499 milliseconds
20                Thread.sleep(generator.nextInt(500));
21            }
22            catch (InterruptedException ex) {
23                Thread.currentThread().interrupt(); // re-interrupt the thread
24            }
25
26            // put value in the appropriate element
27            array[position] = value;
28            System.out.printf("%s wrote %2d to element %d.%n",
29                Thread.currentThread().getName(), value, position);
30
31            ++writeIndex; // increment index of element to be written next
32            System.out.printf("Next write index: %d%n", writeIndex);
33        }
34
35        // used for outputting the contents of the shared integer array
36        @Override
37        public String toString() {
38            return Arrays.toString(array);
39        }
40    }
```

Fig. 21.5 | Class that manages an integer array to be shared by multiple threads. (*Caution:* The example of Figs. 21.5–21.7 is *not* thread safe.) (Part 2 of 2.)

Method add (lines 15–33) places a new value into the array. Line 16 stores the current writeIndex value. Line 20 puts the thread that invokes add to sleep for a random interval from 0 to 499 milliseconds. We do this for demonstration purposes to make the problems associated with *unsynchronized access to shared mutable data* more obvious. After the thread is done sleeping, line 27 inserts the value passed to add into the array at the element specified by position. Lines 28–29 display the executing thread's name, the value that was added and the value's index in the array. In line 29, the expression

```
Thread.currentThread().getName()
```

first obtains a reference to the currently executing Thread, then uses its getName method to obtain its name. Line 31 increments writeIndex so that the next call to add will insert a value in the array's next element. Lines 36–39 override method toString to create a String representation of the array's contents.

Class ArrayWriter

Class ArrayWriter (Fig. 21.6) implements the interface Runnable to define a task for inserting values in a SimpleArray object. The constructor (lines 9–12) receives an int representing the first value this task will insert in a SimpleArray object and a reference to the SimpleArray object to manipulate. Line 17 invokes SimpleArray method add. The task completes after lines 16–18 add three consecutive integers beginning with startValue.

```
 1   // Fig. 21.6: ArrayWriter.java
 2   // Adds integers to an array shared with other Runnables
 3   import java.lang.Runnable;
 4
 5   public class ArrayWriter implements Runnable {
 6      private final SimpleArray sharedSimpleArray;
 7      private final int startValue;
 8
 9      public ArrayWriter(int value, SimpleArray array) {
10         startValue = value;
11         sharedSimpleArray = array;
12      }
13
14      @Override
15      public void run() {
16         for (int i = startValue; i < startValue + 3; i++) {
17            sharedSimpleArray.add(i); // add an element to the shared array
18         }
19      }
20   }
```

Fig. 21.6 | Adds integers to an array shared with other Runnables. (*Caution:* The example of Figs. 21.5–21.7 is *not* thread safe.)

Class *SharedArrayTest*

Class SharedArrayTest (Fig. 21.7) executes two ArrayWriter tasks that add values to a single SimpleArray object. Line 10 constructs a six-element SimpleArray object. Lines 13–14 create two new ArrayWriter tasks, one that places the values 1 through 3 in the SimpleArray object, and one that places the values 11 through 13. Lines 17–19 create an ExecutorService and execute the two ArrayWriters. Line 21 invokes the Executor-Service's shutDown method to prevent it from accepting additional tasks and to enable the application to terminate when the currently executing tasks complete execution.

```
 1   // Fig. 21.7: SharedArrayTest.java
 2   // Executing two Runnables to add elements to a shared SimpleArray.
 3   import java.util.concurrent.Executors;
 4   import java.util.concurrent.ExecutorService;
 5   import java.util.concurrent.TimeUnit;
 6
 7   public class SharedArrayTest {
 8      public static void main(String[] arg) {
 9         // construct the shared object
10         SimpleArray sharedSimpleArray = new SimpleArray(6);
11
12         // create two tasks to write to the shared SimpleArray
13         ArrayWriter writer1 = new ArrayWriter(1, sharedSimpleArray);
14         ArrayWriter writer2 = new ArrayWriter(11, sharedSimpleArray);
```

Fig. 21.7 | Executing two Runnables to add elements to a shared array—the italicized text is our commentary, which is not part of the program's output. (*Caution:* The example of Figs. 21.5–21.7 is *not* thread safe.) (Part 1 of 2.)

```
15
16          // execute the tasks with an ExecutorService
17          ExecutorService executorService = Executors.newCachedThreadPool();
18          executorService.execute(writer1);
19          executorService.execute(writer2);
20
21          executorService.shutdown();
22
23          try {
24             // wait 1 minute for both writers to finish executing
25             boolean tasksEnded =
26                executorService.awaitTermination(1, TimeUnit.MINUTES);
27
28             if (tasksEnded) {
29                System.out.printf("%nContents of SimpleArray:%n");
30                System.out.println(sharedSimpleArray); // print contents
31             }
32             else {
33                System.out.println(
34                   "Timed out while waiting for tasks to finish.");
35             }
36          }
37          catch (InterruptedException ex) {
38             ex.printStackTrace();
39          }
40       }
41    }
```

```
pool-1-thread-1 wrote  1 to element 0. — pool-1-thread-1 wrote 1 to element 0
Next write index: 1
pool-1-thread-1 wrote  2 to element 1.
Next write index: 2
pool-1-thread-1 wrote  3 to element 2.
Next write index: 3
pool-1-thread-2 wrote 11 to element 0. — pool-1-thread-2 overwrote element 0's value
Next write index: 4
pool-1-thread-2 wrote 12 to element 4.
Next write index: 5
pool-1-thread-2 wrote 13 to element 5.
Next write index: 6

Contents of SimpleArray:
[11, 2, 3, 0, 12, 13]
```

Fig. 21.7 | Executing two Runnables to add elements to a shared array—the italicized text is our commentary, which is not part of the program's output. (*Caution:* The example of Figs. 21.5– 21.7 is *not* thread safe.) (Part 2 of 2.)

ExecutorService *Method* awaitTermination

Recall that ExecutorService method shutdown returns immediately. Thus any code that appears *after* the call to ExecutorService method shutdown in line 21 *will continue executing as long as the main thread is still assigned to a processor*. We'd like to output the SimpleArray object to show you the results *after* the threads complete their tasks. So, we need the program to wait for the threads to complete before main outputs the SimpleArray object's contents. Interface ExecutorService provides the **awaitTermination** method for this purpose. This method returns control to its caller either when all tasks executing in the ExecutorService complete or when the specified timeout elapses. If all tasks are completed before awaitTermination times out, this method returns true; otherwise it returns false. The two arguments to awaitTermination represent a timeout value and a unit of measure specified with a constant from class TimeUnit (in this case, TimeUnit.MINUTES).

Method awaitTermination throws an InterruptedException if the calling thread is interrupted while waiting for other threads to terminate. Because we catch this exception in the application's main method, there's no need to re-interrupt the main thread, as this program will terminate as soon as main terminates.

In this example, if *both* tasks complete before awaitTermination times out, line 30 displays the SimpleArray object's contents. Otherwise, lines 33–34 display a message indicating that the tasks did not finish executing before awaitTermination timed out.

Sample Program Output
Figure 21.7's output shows the problems (highlighted in the output) that can be caused by *failure to synchronize access to shared mutable data*. The value 1 was written to element 0, then *overwritten* later by the value 11. Also, when writeIndex was incremented to 3, *nothing was written to that element*, as indicated by the 0 in that element of the array.

Recall that we call Thread method sleep between operations on the shared mutable data to emphasize the *unpredictability of thread scheduling* and to increase the likelihood of producing erroneous output. Even if these operations were allowed to proceed at their normal pace, you could still see errors in the program's output. However, modern processors can handle SimpleArray method add's operations so quickly that you might not see the errors caused by the two threads executing this method concurrently, even if you tested the program dozens of times.

One of the challenges of multithreaded programming is spotting the errors—they may occur so infrequently and unpredictably that a broken program does not produce incorrect results during testing, creating the illusion that the program is correct. This is all the more reason to use predefined collections that handle the synchronization for you.

21.4.4 Synchronized Mutable Data Sharing—Making Operations Atomic

Figure 21.7's output errors can be attributed to the fact that the shared SimpleArray is not **thread safe**—it's susceptible to errors if it's *accessed concurrently by multiple threads*. The problem lies in method add, which stores the writeIndex value, places a new value in that element, then increments writeIndex. This would not present a problem in a single-threaded program. However, if one thread obtains the writeIndex value, there's no guarantee that another thread will not come along and increment writeIndex *before* the first thread has had a chance to place a value in the array. If this happens, the first thread will be writing to the array based on a **stale value** of writeIndex—that is, a value that's no longer valid. Another possibility is that one thread might obtain the writeIndex value *after* another thread adds an element to the array but *before* writeIndex is incremented. In this case, too, the first thread would use an invalid writeIndex value.

SimpleArray is *not thread safe because it allows any number of threads to read and modify shared mutable data concurrently*, which can cause errors. To make SimpleArray thread safe, we must ensure that no two threads can access its shared mutable data at the same time. While one thread is in the process of storing writeIndex, adding a value to the array, and incrementing writeIndex, *no other thread* may read or change the value of write-Index or modify the contents of the array at any point during these three operations. In other words, we want these three operations—storing writeIndex, writing to the array, incrementing writeIndex—to be an **atomic operation**, which cannot be divided into smaller suboperations. (As you'll see in later examples, read operations on shared mutable data should also be atomic.) We can simulate atomicity by ensuring that only one thread carries out the three operations at a time. Any other threads that need to perform the operation must *wait* until the first thread has finished the add operation in its entirety.

Atomicity can be achieved using the synchronized keyword. By placing our three suboperations in a synchronized statement or synchronized method, we allow only one thread at a time to acquire the lock and perform the operations. When that thread has completed all of the operations in the synchronized block and releases the lock, another thread may acquire the lock and begin executing the operations. This ensures that a thread executing the operations will see the actual values of the shared mutable data and that *these values will not change unexpectedly in the middle of the operations as a result of another thread's modifying them.*

Software Engineering Observation 21.5

Place all accesses to mutable data that may be shared by multiple threads inside synchronized statements or synchronized methods that synchronize on the same lock. When performing multiple operations on shared mutable data, hold the lock for the entirety of the operation to ensure that the operation is effectively atomic.

Class *SimpleArray with Synchronization*
Figure 21.8 displays class SimpleArray with the proper synchronization. Notice that it's identical to the SimpleArray class of Fig. 21.5, except that add is now a synchronized method (line 18 of Fig. 21.8). So, only one thread at a time can execute this method. We reuse classes ArrayWriter (Fig. 21.6) and SharedArrayTest (Fig. 21.7) from the previous example, so we do not show them again here.

```
1   // Fig. 21.8: SimpleArray.java
2   // Class that manages an integer array to be shared by multiple
3   // threads with synchronization.
4   import java.security.SecureRandom;
5   import java.util.Arrays;
6
7   public class SimpleArray {
8       private static final SecureRandom generator = new SecureRandom();
9       private final int[] array; // the shared integer array
10      private int writeIndex = 0; // index of next element to be written
11
```

Fig. 21.8 | Class that manages an integer array to be shared by multiple threads with synchronization. (Part I of 2.)

```
12    // construct a SimpleArray of a given size
13    public SimpleArray(int size) {
14        array = new int[size];
15    }
16
17    // add a value to the shared array
18    public synchronized void add(int value) {
19        int position = writeIndex; // store the write index
20
21        try {
22            // in real applications, you shouldn't sleep while holding a lock
23            Thread.sleep(generator.nextInt(500)); // for demo only
24        }
25        catch (InterruptedException ex) {
26            Thread.currentThread().interrupt();
27        }
28
29        // put value in the appropriate element
30        array[position] = value;
31        System.out.printf("%s wrote %2d to element %d.%n",
32            Thread.currentThread().getName(), value, position);
33
34        ++writeIndex; // increment index of element to be written next
35        System.out.printf("Next write index: %d%n", writeIndex);
36    }
37
38    // used for outputting the contents of the shared integer array
39    @Override
40    public synchronized String toString() {
41        return Arrays.toString(array);
42    }
43 }
```

```
pool-1-thread-1 wrote  1 to element 0.
Next write index: 1
pool-1-thread-2 wrote 11 to element 1.
Next write index: 2
pool-1-thread-2 wrote 12 to element 2.
Next write index: 3
pool-1-thread-2 wrote 13 to element 3.
Next write index: 4
pool-1-thread-1 wrote  2 to element 4.
Next write index: 5
pool-1-thread-1 wrote  3 to element 5.
Next write index: 6

Contents of SimpleArray:
[1, 11, 12, 13, 2, 3]
```

Fig. 21.8 | Class that manages an integer array to be shared by multiple threads with synchronization. (Part 2 of 2.)

Line 18 declares method add as synchronized, making all of the operations in this method behave as a single, atomic operation. Line 19 performs the first suboperation—

storing the value of `writeIndex`. Line 30 performs the second suboperation, writing a value to the element at the index `position`. Line 34 performs the third suboperation, incrementing `writeIndex`. When the method finishes executing at line 36, the executing thread implicitly *releases* the `SimpleArray` object's lock, making it possible for another thread to begin executing the `add` method.

In the `synchronized` `add` method, we print messages to the console indicating the progress of threads as they execute this method, in addition to performing the actual operations required to insert a value in the array. We do this so that the messages will be printed in the correct order, allowing us to see whether the method is properly synchronized by comparing these outputs with those of the previous, unsynchronized example. We continue to output messages from `synchronized` blocks in later examples for *demonstration purposes only*; typically, however, I/O *should not* be performed in `synchronized` blocks, because it's important to minimize the amount of time that an object is "locked." [***Note:*** **Line 23 in this example calls Thread method sleep (for demo purposes only) to emphasize the unpredictability of thread scheduling. You should never call sleep while holding a lock in a real application.**]

> **Performance Tip 21.2**
>
> *Keep the duration of* synchronized *statements as short as possible while maintaining the needed synchronization. This minimizes the wait time for blocked threads. Avoid performing I/O, lengthy calculations and operations that do not require synchronization while holding a lock.*

21.5 Producer/Consumer Relationship without Synchronization

In a **producer/consumer relationship**, the **producer** portion of an application generates data and *stores it in a shared object*, and the **consumer** portion of the application *reads data from the shared object*. The producer/consumer relationship separates the task of identifying work to be done from the tasks involved in actually carrying out the work.

Examples of Producer/Consumer Relationship
One example of a common producer/consumer relationship is **print spooling**. Although a printer might not be available when you want to print from an application (i.e., the producer), you can still "complete" the print task, as the data is temporarily placed on disk until the printer becomes available. Similarly, when the printer (i.e., a consumer) is available, it doesn't have to wait until a current user wants to print. The spooled print jobs can be printed as soon as the printer becomes available. Another example of the producer/consumer relationship is an application that copies data onto DVDs by placing data in a fixed-size buffer, which is emptied as the DVD drive "burns" the data onto the DVD.

Synchronization and State Dependence
In a multithreaded producer/consumer relationship, a **producer thread** generates data and places it in a shared object called a **buffer**. A **consumer thread** reads data from the buffer. This relationship requires *synchronization* to ensure that values are produced and consumed properly. All operations on *mutable* data that's shared by multiple threads (e.g., the data in the buffer) must be guarded with a lock to prevent corruption, as discussed in

Section 21.4. Operations on the buffer data shared by a producer and consumer thread are also **state dependent**—the operations should proceed only if the buffer is in the correct state. If the buffer is in a *not-full state*, the producer may produce; if the buffer is in a *not-empty state*, the consumer may consume. All operations that access the buffer must use synchronization to ensure that data is written to the buffer or read from the buffer only if the buffer is in the proper state. If the producer attempting to put the next data into the buffer determines that it's full, the producer thread must *wait* until there's space to write a new value. If a consumer thread finds the buffer empty or finds that the previous data has already been read, the consumer must also *wait* for new data to become available. Other examples of state dependence are that you can't drive your car if its gas tank is empty and you can't put more gas into the tank if it's already full.

Logic Errors from Lack of Synchronization

Consider how logic errors can arise if we do not synchronize access among multiple threads manipulating shared mutable data. Our next example (Figs. 21.9–21.13) implements a producer/consumer relationship *without the proper synchronization*. A producer thread writes the numbers 1 through 10 into a shared buffer—a single memory location shared between two threads (a single int variable called buffer in line 5 of Fig. 21.12 in this example). The consumer thread reads this data from the shared buffer and displays the data. The program's output shows the values that the producer writes (produces) into the shared buffer and the values that the consumer reads (consumes) from the shared buffer.

Each value the producer thread writes to the shared buffer must be consumed *exactly once* by the consumer thread. However, the threads in this example are not synchronized. Therefore, *data can be lost or garbled if the producer places new data into the shared buffer before the consumer reads the previous data*. Also, data can be incorrectly *duplicated* if the consumer consumes data again before the producer produces the next value. To show these possibilities, the consumer thread in the following example keeps a total of all the values it reads. The producer thread produces values from 1 through 10. If the consumer reads each value produced once and only once, the total will be 55. However, if you execute this program several times, you'll see that the total is not always 55 (as shown in the outputs in Fig. 21.13). To emphasize the point, the producer and consumer threads in the example each sleep for random intervals of up to three seconds between performing their tasks. Thus, we do not know when the producer thread will attempt to write a new value, or when the consumer thread will attempt to read a value.

Interface `Buffer`

The program consists of interface Buffer (Fig. 21.9) and classes Producer (Fig. 21.10), Consumer (Fig. 21.11), UnsynchronizedBuffer (Fig. 21.12) and SharedBufferTest (Fig. 21.13). Interface Buffer (Fig. 21.9) declares methods blockingPut (line 5) and blockingGet (line 8) that a Buffer (such as UnsynchronizedBuffer) must implement to enable the Producer thread to place a value in the Buffer and the Consumer thread to retrieve a value from the Buffer, respectively. In subsequent examples, methods blockingPut and blockingGet will call methods that throw InterruptedExceptions—typically this indicates that a method temporarily could be blocked from performing a task. We declare each method with a throws clause here so that we don't have to modify this interface for the later examples.

```
1   // Fig. 21.9: Buffer.java
2   // Buffer interface specifies methods called by Producer and Consumer.
3   public interface Buffer {
4      // place int value into Buffer
5      public void blockingPut(int value) throws InterruptedException;
6
7      // return int value from Buffer
8      public int blockingGet() throws InterruptedException;
9   }
```

Fig. 21.9 | Buffer interface specifies methods called by Producer and Consumer. (*Caution:* The example of Figs. 21.9–21.13 is *not* thread safe.)

Class *Producer*

Class Producer (Fig. 21.10) implements the Runnable interface, allowing it to be executed as a task in a separate thread. The constructor (lines 10–12) initializes the Buffer reference sharedLocation with an object created in main (line 13 of Fig. 21.13) and passed to the constructor. As we'll see, this is an UnsynchronizedBuffer object that implements interface Buffer *without synchronizing access to the shared object*.

```
1   // Fig. 21.10: Producer.java
2   // Producer with a run method that inserts the values 1 to 10 in buffer.
3   import java.security.SecureRandom;
4
5   public class Producer implements Runnable {
6      private static final SecureRandom generator = new SecureRandom();
7      private final Buffer sharedLocation; // reference to shared object
8
9      // constructor
10     public Producer(Buffer sharedLocation) {
11        this.sharedLocation = sharedLocation;
12     }
13
14     // store values from 1 to 10 in sharedLocation
15     @Override
16     public void run() {
17        int sum = 0;
18
19        for (int count = 1; count <= 10; count++) {
20           try { // sleep 0 to 3 seconds, then place value in Buffer
21              Thread.sleep(generator.nextInt(3000)); // random sleep
22              sharedLocation.blockingPut(count); // set value in buffer
23              sum += count; // increment sum of values
24              System.out.printf("\t%2d%n", sum);
25           }
26           catch (InterruptedException exception) {
27              Thread.currentThread().interrupt();
28           }
29        }
```

Fig. 21.10 | Producer with a run method that inserts the values 1 to 10 in buffer. (*Caution:* The example of Figs. 21.9–21.13 is *not* thread safe.) (Part 1 of 2.)

```
30
31          System.out.printf(
32              "Producer done producing%nTerminating Producer%n");
33      }
34  }
```

Fig. 21.10 | Producer with a run method that inserts the values 1 to 10 in buffer. (*Caution:* The example of Figs. 21.9–21.13 is *not* thread safe.) (Part 2 of 2.)

The Producer thread in this program executes the tasks specified in the method run (Fig. 21.10, lines 15–33). Each iteration of its loop invokes Thread method sleep (line 21) to place the Producer thread into the *timed waiting* state for a random time interval between 0 and 3 seconds. When the thread awakens, line 22 passes the value of control variable count to the Buffer object's blockingPut method to set the shared buffer's value. Lines 23–24 keep a total of all the values produced so far and output that value. When the loop completes, lines 31–32 display a message indicating that the Producer has finished producing data and is terminating. Next, method run terminates, which indicates that the Producer completed its task. Any method called from a Runnable's run method (e.g., Buffer method blockingPut) executes as part of that task's thread of execution. This fact becomes important in Sections 21.6—21.8 when we add synchronization to the producer/consumer relationship.

Class *Consumer*

Class Consumer (Fig. 21.11) also implements interface Runnable, allowing the Consumer to execute concurrently with the Producer. Lines 10–12 initialize Buffer reference sharedLocation with an object that implements the Buffer interface (created in main, Fig. 21.13) and passed to the constructor as the parameter sharedLocation. As we'll see, this is the same UnsynchronizedBuffer object that's used to initialize the Producer object—thus, the two threads share the same object. The Consumer thread in this program performs the tasks specified in method run. Lines 19–29 in Fig. 21.11 iterate 10 times. Each iteration invokes Thread method sleep (line 22) to put the Consumer thread into the *timed waiting* state for up to 3 seconds. Next, line 23 uses the Buffer's blockingGet method to retrieve the value in the shared buffer, then adds the value to variable sum. Line 24 displays the total of all the values consumed so far. When the loop completes, lines 31–32 display the sum of the consumed values. Then method run terminates, which indicates that the Consumer completed its task. Once both threads enter the *terminated* state, the program ends.

```
1   // Fig. 21.11: Consumer.java
2   // Consumer with a run method that loops, reading 10 values from buffer.
3   import java.security.SecureRandom;
4
5   public class Consumer implements Runnable {
6       private static final SecureRandom generator = new SecureRandom();
7       private final Buffer sharedLocation; // reference to shared object
8
```

Fig. 21.11 | Consumer with a run method that loops, reading 10 values from buffer. (*Caution:* The example of Figs. 21.9–21.13 is *not* thread safe.) (Part 1 of 2.)

```
 9        // constructor
10        public Consumer(Buffer sharedLocation) {
11            this.sharedLocation = sharedLocation;
12        }
13
14        // read sharedLocation's value 10 times and sum the values
15        @Override
16        public void run() {
17            int sum = 0;
18
19            for (int count = 1; count <= 10; count++) {
20                // sleep 0 to 3 seconds, read value from buffer and add to sum
21                try {
22                    Thread.sleep(generator.nextInt(3000));
23                    sum += sharedLocation.blockingGet();
24                    System.out.printf("\t\t\t%2d%n", sum);
25                }
26                catch (InterruptedException exception) {
27                    Thread.currentThread().interrupt();
28                }
29            }
30
31            System.out.printf("%n%s %d%n%s%n",
32                "Consumer read values totaling", sum, "Terminating Consumer");
33        }
34    }
```

Fig. 21.11 | Consumer with a run method that loops, reading 10 values from buffer. (*Caution:* The example of Figs. 21.9–21.13 is *not* thread safe.) (Part 2 of 2.)

We Call *Thread Method* sleep *Only for Demonstration Purposes*

We call method sleep in method run of the Producer and Consumer classes to emphasize the fact that, *in multithreaded applications, it's unpredictable when each thread will perform its task and for how long it will perform the task when it has a processor.* Normally, these thread-scheduling issues are beyond the control of the Java developer. In this program, our thread's tasks are quite simple—the Producer writes the values 1 to 10 to the buffer, and the Consumer reads 10 values from the buffer and adds each value to variable sum. Without the sleep method call, and if the Producer executes first, given today's phenomenally fast processors, the Producer would likely complete its task before the Consumer got a chance to execute. If the Consumer executed first, it would likely consume garbage data ten times, then terminate before the Producer could produce the first real value.

Class UnsynchronizedBuffer *Does Not Synchronize Access to the Buffer*

Class UnsynchronizedBuffer (Fig. 21.12) implements interface Buffer (line 4), but does *not* synchronize access to the buffer's state—we purposely do this to demonstrate the problems that occur when multiple threads access *shared* mutable data *without* synchronization. Line 5 declares instance variable buffer and initializes it to -1. This value is used to demonstrate the case in which the Consumer attempts to consume a value *before* the Producer ever places a value in buffer. Again, methods blockingPut (lines 8–12) and blockingGet (lines 15–19) do *not* synchronize access to the buffer instance variable. Method blockingPut simply assigns its argument to buffer (line 11), and method blockingGet simply returns the value of buffer (line 18). As you'll see in Fig. 21.13, Unsynchronized-Buffer object is shared between the Producer and the Consumer.

```
 1   // Fig. 21.12: UnsynchronizedBuffer.java
 2   // UnsynchronizedBuffer maintains the shared integer that is accessed by
 3   // a producer thread and a consumer thread.
 4   public class UnsynchronizedBuffer implements Buffer {
 5      private int buffer = -1; // shared by producer and consumer threads
 6
 7      // place value into buffer
 8      @Override
 9      public void blockingPut(int value) throws InterruptedException {
10         System.out.printf("Producer writes\t%2d", value);
11         buffer = value;
12      }
13
14      // return value from buffer
15      @Override
16      public int blockingGet() throws InterruptedException {
17         System.out.printf("Consumer reads\t%2d", buffer);
18         return buffer;
19      }
20   }
```

Fig. 21.12 | UnsynchronizedBuffer maintains the shared integer that is accessed by a producer thread and a consumer thread. (*Caution:* The example of Fig. 21.9–Fig. 21.13 is *not* thread safe.)

Class *SharedBufferTest*
In class SharedBufferTest (Fig. 21.13), line 10 creates an ExecutorService to execute the Producer and Consumer Runnables. Line 13 creates an UnsynchronizedBuffer and assigns it to Buffer variable sharedLocation. This object stores the data that the Producer and Consumer threads will share. Lines 22–23 create and execute the Producer and Consumer. The Producer and Consumer constructors are each passed the same Buffer object (sharedLocation), so each object refers to the same Buffer. These lines also implicitly launch the threads and call each Runnable's run method. Finally, line 25 calls method shutdown so that the application can terminate when the threads executing the Producer and Consumer complete their tasks and line 26 waits for the scheduled tasks to complete. When main terminates, the main thread of execution enters the *terminated* state.

```
 1   // Fig. 21.13: SharedBufferTest.java
 2   // Application with two threads manipulating an unsynchronized buffer.
 3   import java.util.concurrent.ExecutorService;
 4   import java.util.concurrent.Executors;
 5   import java.util.concurrent.TimeUnit;
 6
```

Fig. 21.13 | Application with two threads manipulating an unsynchronized buffer—the italicized text in the output is our commentary, which is not part of the program's output. (*Caution:* The example of Figs. 21.9–21.13 is *not* thread safe.) (Part 1 of 3.)

```
7   public class SharedBufferTest {
8      public static void main(String[] args) throws InterruptedException {
9         // create new thread pool
10        ExecutorService executorService = Executors.newCachedThreadPool();
11
12        // create UnsynchronizedBuffer to store ints
13        Buffer sharedLocation = new UnsynchronizedBuffer();
14
15        System.out.println(
16           "Action\t\tValue\tSum of Produced\tSum of Consumed");
17        System.out.printf(
18           "------\t\t-----\t--------------\t--------------%n%n");
19
20        // execute the Producer and Consumer, giving each
21        // access to the sharedLocation
22        executorService.execute(new Producer(sharedLocation));
23        executorService.execute(new Consumer(sharedLocation));
24
25        executorService.shutdown(); // terminate app when tasks complete
26        executorService.awaitTermination(1, TimeUnit.MINUTES);
27     }
28  }
```

Action	Value	Sum of Produced	Sum of Consumed	
------	-----	---------------	---------------	
Producer writes	1	1		
Producer writes	2	3		— *1 lost*
Producer writes	3	6		— *2 lost*
Consumer reads	3		3	
Producer writes	4	10		
Consumer reads	4		7	
Producer writes	5	15		
Producer writes	6	21		— *5 lost*
Producer writes	7	28		— *6 lost*
Consumer reads	7		14	
Consumer reads	7		21	— *7 read again*
Producer writes	8	36		
Consumer reads	8		29	
Consumer reads	8		37	— *8 read again*
Producer writes	9	45		
Producer writes	10	55		— *9 lost*
Producer done producing				
Terminating Producer				
Consumer reads	10		47	
Consumer reads	10		57	— *10 read again*
Consumer reads	10		67	— *10 read again*
Consumer reads	10		77	— *10 read again*
Consumer read values totaling 77				
Terminating Consumer				

Fig. 21.13 | Application with two threads manipulating an unsynchronized buffer—the italicized text in the output is our commentary, which is not part of the program's output. (*Caution:* The example of Figs. 21.9–21.13 is *not* thread safe.) (Part 2 of 3.)

```
Action          Value   Sum of Produced Sum of Consumed
------          -----   --------------- ---------------

Consumer reads  -1                      -1 — reads -1 bad data
Producer writes 1       1
Consumer reads  1                       0
Consumer reads  1                       1 — 1 read again
Consumer reads  1                       2 — 1 read again
Consumer reads  1                       3 — 1 read again
Consumer reads  1                       4 — 1 read again
Producer writes 2       3
Consumer reads  2                       6
Producer writes 3       6
Consumer reads  3                       9
Producer writes 4       10
Consumer reads  4                       13
Producer writes 5       15
Producer writes 6       21                 — 5 lost
Consumer reads  6                       19

Consumer read values totaling 19
Terminating Consumer
Producer writes 7       28                 — 7 never read
Producer writes 8       36                 — 8 never read
Producer writes 9       45                 — 9 never read
Producer writes 10      55                 — 9 never read

Producer done producing
Terminating Producer
```

Fig. 21.13 | Application with two threads manipulating an unsynchronized buffer—the italicized text in the output is our commentary, which is not part of the program's output. (*Caution:* The example of Figs. 21.9–21.13 is *not* thread safe.) (Part 3 of 3.)

Recall that the Producer should execute first, and every value it produces should be consumed exactly once by the Consumer. However, in the first output of Fig. 21.13, notice that the Producer writes 1, 2 and 3 before the Consumer reads its first value (3). Therefore, the values 1 and 2 are *lost*. Later, 5, 6 and 9 are *lost*, while 7 and 8 are *read twice* and 10 is read four times. So the first output produces an incorrect total of 77, instead of the correct total of 55. (Lines in the output where the Producer or Consumer acted out of order are highlighted.) In the second output, the Consumer reads the value -1 *before* the Producer ever writes a value. The Consumer reads the value 1 *five times* before the Producer writes the value 2. Meanwhile, 5, 7, 8, 9 and 10 are all *lost*—the last four because the Consumer terminates *before* the Producer. The result is an incorrect consumer total of 19.

Error-Prevention Tip 21.1

Access to a shared object by concurrent threads must be controlled carefully or a program may produce incorrect results.

To solve the problems of *lost* and *duplicated* data, Section 21.6 presents an example in which we use an ArrayBlockingQueue (from package java.util.concurrent) to synchronize access to the shared object, guaranteeing that each and every value will be processed once and only once.

21.6 Producer/Consumer Relationship: ArrayBlockingQueue

The best way to synchronize producer and consumer threads is to use classes from Java's `java.util.concurrent` package that *encapsulate the synchronization for you.* Java includes the class **ArrayBlockingQueue**—a fully implemented, *thread-safe buffer class* that implements interface **BlockingQueue**. This interface declares methods **put** and **take**. Method put places an element at the end of the BlockingQueue, waiting if the queue is full. Method take removes an element from the head of the BlockingQueue, waiting if the queue is empty. These methods make class ArrayBlockingQueue a good choice for implementing a shared buffer. Because method put blocks until there's room in the buffer to write data, and method take blocks until there's new data to read, the producer must produce a value first, the consumer correctly consumes only after the producer writes a value and the producer correctly produces the next value (after the first) only after the consumer reads the previous (or first) value. ArrayBlockingQueue stores the shared mutable data in an array, the size of which is specified as ArrayBlockingQueue's constructor argument. An Array-BlockingQueue is fixed in size and will not expand to accommodate extra elements.

Class *BlockingBuffer*
Figures 21.14–21.15 demonstrate a Producer and a Consumer accessing an ArrayBlock-ingQueue. Class BlockingBuffer (Fig. 21.14) uses an ArrayBlockingQueue object that stores an Integer (line 6). Line 9 creates the ArrayBlockingQueue and passes 1 to the constructor so that the object holds a single value to mimic the UnsynchronizedBuffer example in Fig. 21.12. We discuss *multiple-element buffers* in Section 21.8. Because our BlockingBuffer class uses the *thread-safe* ArrayBlockingQueue class to manage all of its shared state (the shared buffer in this case), BlockingBuffer is itself *thread safe,* even though we have not implemented the synchronization ourselves.

```java
 1   // Fig. 21.14: BlockingBuffer.java
 2   // Creating a synchronized buffer using an ArrayBlockingQueue.
 3   import java.util.concurrent.ArrayBlockingQueue;
 4
 5   public class BlockingBuffer implements Buffer {
 6      private final ArrayBlockingQueue<Integer> buffer; // shared buffer
 7
 8      public BlockingBuffer() {
 9         buffer = new ArrayBlockingQueue<Integer>(1);
10      }
11
12      // place value into buffer
13      @Override
14      public void blockingPut(int value) throws InterruptedException {
15         buffer.put(value); // place value in buffer
16         System.out.printf("%s%2d\t%s%d%n", "Producer writes ", value,
17            "Buffer cells occupied: ", buffer.size());
18      }
19
```

Fig. 21.14 | Creating a synchronized buffer using an `ArrayBlockingQueue`. (Part 1 of 2.)

```
20        // return value from buffer
21        @Override
22        public int blockingGet() throws InterruptedException {
23            int readValue = buffer.take(); // remove value from buffer
24            System.out.printf("%s %2d\t%s%d%n", "Consumer reads ",
25                readValue, "Buffer cells occupied: ", buffer.size());
26
27            return readValue;
28        }
29    }
```

Fig. 21.14 | Creating a synchronized buffer using an `ArrayBlockingQueue`. (Part 2 of 2.)

`BlockingBuffer` implements interface `Buffer` (Fig. 21.9) and uses classes `Producer` (Fig. 21.10 modified to remove line 24) and `Consumer` (Fig. 21.11 modified to remove line 24) from the example in Section 21.5. This approach demonstrates encapsulated synchronization—*the threads accessing the shared object are unaware that their buffer accesses are now synchronized.* The synchronization is handled entirely in the `blockingPut` and `blockingGet` methods of `BlockingBuffer` by calling the synchronized `ArrayBlockingQueue` methods `put` and `take`, respectively. Thus, the `Producer` and `Consumer` `Runnable`s are properly synchronized simply by calling the shared object's `blockingPut` and `blockingGet` methods.

Line 15 in method `blockingPut` (Fig. 21.14) calls the `ArrayBlockingQueue` object's `put` method. This method call blocks if necessary until there's room in the `buffer` to place the `value`. Method `blockingGet` calls the `ArrayBlockingQueue` object's `take` method (line 23). This method call *blocks* if necessary until there's an element in the `buffer` to remove. Lines 16–17 and 24–25 use the `ArrayBlockingQueue` object's **size** method to display the total number of elements currently in the `ArrayBlockingQueue`.

Class *BlockingBufferTest*

Class `BlockingBufferTest` (Fig. 21.15) contains the `main` method that launches the application. Line 11 creates an `ExecutorService`, and line 14 creates a `BlockingBuffer` object and assigns its reference to the `Buffer` variable `sharedLocation`. Lines 16–17 execute the `Producer` and `Consumer` `Runnable`s. Line 19 calls method `shutdown` to end the application when the threads finish executing the `Producer` and `Consumer` tasks, and line 20 waits for the scheduled tasks to complete.

```
1    // Fig. 21.15: BlockingBufferTest.java
2    // Two threads manipulating a blocking buffer that properly
3    // implements the producer/consumer relationship.
4    import java.util.concurrent.ExecutorService;
5    import java.util.concurrent.Executors;
6    import java.util.concurrent.TimeUnit;
7
8    public class BlockingBufferTest {
9        public static void main(String[] args) throws InterruptedException {
```

Fig. 21.15 | Two threads manipulating a blocking buffer that properly implements the producer/consumer relationship. (Part 1 of 2.)

```
10        // create new thread pool
11        ExecutorService executorService = Executors.newCachedThreadPool();
12
13        // create BlockingBuffer to store ints
14        Buffer sharedLocation = new BlockingBuffer();
15
16        executorService.execute(new Producer(sharedLocation));
17        executorService.execute(new Consumer(sharedLocation));
18
19        executorService.shutdown();
20        executorService.awaitTermination(1, TimeUnit.MINUTES);
21     }
22  }
```

```
Producer writes   1      Buffer cells occupied: 1
Consumer reads    1      Buffer cells occupied: 0
Producer writes   2      Buffer cells occupied: 1
Consumer reads    2      Buffer cells occupied: 0
Producer writes   3      Buffer cells occupied: 1
Consumer reads    3      Buffer cells occupied: 0
Producer writes   4      Buffer cells occupied: 1
Consumer reads    4      Buffer cells occupied: 0
Producer writes   5      Buffer cells occupied: 1
Consumer reads    5      Buffer cells occupied: 0
Producer writes   6      Buffer cells occupied: 1
Consumer reads    6      Buffer cells occupied: 0
Producer writes   7      Buffer cells occupied: 1
Consumer reads    7      Buffer cells occupied: 0
Producer writes   8      Buffer cells occupied: 1
Consumer reads    8      Buffer cells occupied: 0
Producer writes   9      Buffer cells occupied: 1
Consumer reads    9      Buffer cells occupied: 0
Producer writes  10      Buffer cells occupied: 1

Producer done producing
Terminating Producer
Consumer reads   10      Buffer cells occupied: 0

Consumer read values totaling 55
Terminating Consumer
```

Fig. 21.15 | Two threads manipulating a blocking buffer that properly implements the producer/consumer relationship. (Part 2 of 2.)

While methods `put` and `take` of `ArrayBlockingQueue` are properly synchronized, `BlockingBuffer` methods `blockingPut` and `blockingGet` (Fig. 21.14) are not declared to be synchronized. Thus, the statements performed in method `blockingPut`—the `put` operation (Fig. 21.14, line 15) and the output (lines 16–17)—are *not atomic*; nor are the statements in method `blockingGet`—the `take` operation (line 23) and the output (lines 24–25). So there's no guarantee that each output will occur immediately after the corresponding `put` or `take` operation, and the outputs may appear out of order. Even if they do, the `ArrayBlockingQueue` object is properly synchronizing access to the data, as evidenced by the fact that the sum of values read by the consumer is always correct.

21.7 (Advanced) Producer/Consumer Relationship with synchronized, wait, notify and notifyAll

[*Note:* This section is intended for *advanced* programmers who want to control synchronization.[2]] The previous example showed how multiple threads can share a single-element buffer in a thread-safe manner by using the ArrayBlockingQueue class that encapsulates the synchronization necessary to protect the shared mutable data. We now explain how you can implement a shared buffer yourself using the synchronized keyword and methods of class Object. *Using an ArrayBlockingQueue generally results in more-maintainable, better-performing code.*

After identifying the shared mutable data and the *synchronization policy* (i.e., associating the data with a lock that guards it), the next step in synchronizing access to the buffer is to implement methods blockingGet and blockingPut as synchronized methods. This requires that a thread obtain the *monitor lock* on the Buffer object before attempting to access the buffer data, but it does not automatically ensure that threads proceed with an operation only if the buffer is in the proper state. We need a way to allow our threads to *wait*, depending on whether certain conditions are true. In the case of placing a new item in the buffer, the condition that allows the operation to proceed is that the *buffer is not full*. In the case of fetching an item from the buffer, the condition that allows the operation to proceed is that the *buffer is not empty*. If the condition in question is true, the operation may proceed; if it's false, the thread must *wait* until it becomes true. When a thread is waiting on a condition, it's removed from contention for the processor and placed into the *waiting* state and the lock it holds is released.

Methods wait, notify and notifyAll

Object methods wait, notify and notifyAll can be used with conditions to make threads *wait* when they cannot perform their tasks. If a thread obtains the *monitor lock* on an object, then determines that it cannot continue with its task on that object until some condition is satisfied, the thread can call Object method **wait** on the synchronized object; this *releases the monitor lock* on the object, and the thread waits in the *waiting* state while the other threads try to enter the object's synchronized statement(s) or method(s). When a thread executing a synchronized statement (or method) completes or satisfies the condition on which another thread may be waiting, it can call Object method **notify** on the synchronized object to allow a waiting thread to transition to the *runnable* state again. At this point, the thread that was transitioned from the *waiting* state to the *runnable* state can attempt to *reacquire the monitor lock* on the object. Even if the thread is able to reacquire the monitor lock, it still might not be able to perform its task at this time—in which case the thread will reenter the *waiting* state and implicitly *release the monitor lock*. If a thread calls **notifyAll** on the synchronized object, then *all* the threads waiting for the monitor lock become eligible to *reacquire the lock* (that is, they all transition to the *runnable* state).

Remember that only *one* thread at a time can obtain the monitor lock on the object—other threads that attempt to acquire the same monitor lock will be *blocked* until the mon-

---

2. For detailed information on wait, notify and notifyAll, see Chapter 14 of *Java Concurrency in Practice* by Brian Goetz, et al., Addison-Wesley Professional, 2006.

itor lock becomes available again (i.e., until no other thread is executing in a synchronized statement on that object).

Common Programming Error 21.1

It's an error if a thread issues a wait, a notify or a notifyAll on an object without having acquired a lock for it. This causes an **IllegalMonitorStateException**.

Error-Prevention Tip 21.2

It's a good practice to use notifyAll to notify waiting threads to become runnable. Doing so avoids the possibility that your program would forget about waiting threads, which would otherwise starve.

Figures 21.16 and 21.17 demonstrate a Producer and a Consumer accessing a shared buffer with synchronization. In this case, the Producer always produces a value *first*, the Consumer correctly consumes only *after* the Producer produces a value and the Producer correctly produces the next value only after the Consumer consumes the previous (or first) value. We reuse interface Buffer and classes Producer and Consumer from the example in Section 21.5, except that line 24 is removed from class Producer and class Consumer.

Class *SynchronizedBuffer*

The synchronization is handled in class SynchronizedBuffer's blockingPut and blockingGet methods (Fig. 21.16). Thus, the Producer's and Consumer's run methods simply call the shared object's synchronized blockingPut and blockingGet methods. Again, we output messages from the synchronized methods for demonstration purposes only—I/O *should not* be performed in synchronized blocks, because it's important to minimize the amount of time that an object is "locked."

```
 1   // Fig. 21.16: SynchronizedBuffer.java
 2   // Synchronizing access to shared mutable data using Object
 3   // methods wait and notifyAll.
 4   public class SynchronizedBuffer implements Buffer {
 5      private int buffer = -1; // shared by producer and consumer threads
 6      private boolean occupied = false;
 7
 8      // place value into buffer
 9      @Override
10      public synchronized void blockingPut(int value)
11         throws InterruptedException {
12         // while there are no empty locations, place thread in waiting state
13         while (occupied) {
14            // output thread information and buffer information, then wait
15            System.out.println("Producer tries to write."); // for demo only
16            displayState("Buffer full. Producer waits."); // for demo only
17            wait();
18         }
19
20         buffer = value; // set new buffer value
```

Fig. 21.16 | Synchronizing access to shared mutable data using Object methods wait and notifyAll. (Part 1 of 2.)

```
21
22        // indicate producer cannot store another value
23        // until consumer retrieves current buffer value
24        occupied = true;
25
26        displayState("Producer writes " + buffer); // for demo only
27
28        notifyAll(); // tell waiting thread(s) to enter runnable state
29     } // end method blockingPut; releases lock on SynchronizedBuffer
30
31     // return value from buffer
32     @Override
33     public synchronized int blockingGet() throws InterruptedException {
34        // while no data to read, place thread in waiting state
35        while (!occupied) {
36           // output thread information and buffer information, then wait
37           System.out.println("Consumer tries to read."); // for demo only
38           displayState("Buffer empty. Consumer waits."); // for demo only
39           wait();
40        }
41
42        // indicate that producer can store another value
43        // because consumer just retrieved buffer value
44        occupied = false;
45
46        displayState("Consumer reads " + buffer); // for demo only
47
48        notifyAll(); // tell waiting thread(s) to enter runnable state
49
50        return buffer;
51     } // end method blockingGet; releases lock on SynchronizedBuffer
52
53     // display current operation and buffer state; for demo only
54     private synchronized void displayState(String operation) {
55        System.out.printf("%-40s%d\t\t%b%n%n", operation, buffer, occupied);
56     }
57  }
```

Fig. 21.16 | Synchronizing access to shared mutable data using `Object` methods `wait` and `notifyAll`. (Part 2 of 2.)

Fields and Methods of Class *SynchronizedBuffer*

Class SynchronizedBuffer contains fields buffer (line 5) and occupied (line 6)—you must synchronize access to *both* fields to ensure that class SynchronizedBuffer is thread safe. Methods blockingPut (lines 9–29) and blockingGet (lines 32–51) are declared as synchronized—only *one* thread can call either of these methods at a time on a particular SynchronizedBuffer object. Field occupied is used to determine whether it's the Producer's or the Consumer's turn to perform a task. This field is used in conditional expressions in both the blockingPut and blockingGet methods. If occupied is false, then buffer is empty, so the Consumer cannot read the value of buffer, but the Producer can place a value into buffer. If occupied is true, the Consumer can read a value from buffer, but the Producer cannot place a value into buffer.

Method **blockingPut** *and the* **Producer** *Thread*

When the Producer thread's run method invokes synchronized method blockingPut, the thread attempts to acquire the SynchronizedBuffer object's monitor lock. If the monitor lock is available, the Producer thread *implicitly* acquires the lock. Then the loop at lines 13–18 first determines whether occupied is true. If so, buffer is *full* and we want to wait until the buffer is empty, so line 15 outputs a message indicating that the Producer thread is trying to write a value, and line 16 invokes method displayState (lines 54–56) to output another message indicating that buffer is *full* and that the Producer thread is *waiting* until there's space. Line 17 invokes method wait (inherited from Object by SynchronizedBuffer) to place the thread that called method blockingPut (i.e., the Producer thread) in the *waiting* state for the SynchronizedBuffer object. The call to wait causes the calling thread to *implicitly* release the lock on the SynchronizedBuffer object. This is important because the thread cannot currently perform its task and because other threads (in this case, the Consumer) should be allowed to access the object to allow the condition (occupied) to change. Now another thread can attempt to acquire the SynchronizedBuffer object's lock and invoke the object's blockingPut or blockingGet method.

The Producer thread remains in the *waiting* state until another thread *notifies* the Producer that it may proceed—at which point the Producer returns to the *runnable* state and attempts to implicitly reacquire the lock on the SynchronizedBuffer object. If the lock is available, the Producer thread reacquires it, and method blockingPut continues executing with the next statement after the wait call. Because wait is called in a loop, the loop-continuation condition is tested again to determine whether the thread can proceed. If not, then wait is invoked again—otherwise, method blockingPut continues with the next statement after the loop.

Line 20 in method blockingPut assigns the value to the buffer. Line 24 sets occupied to true to indicate that the buffer now contains a value (i.e., a consumer can read the value, but a Producer cannot yet put another value there). Line 26 invokes method displayState to output a message indicating that the Producer is writing a new value into the buffer. Line 28 invokes method notifyAll (inherited from Object). If any threads are *waiting* on the SynchronizedBuffer object's monitor lock, those threads enter the *runnable* state and can now attempt to *reacquire the lock*. Method notifyAll returns immediately, and method blockingPut then returns to the caller (i.e., the Producer's run method). When method blockingPut returns, it *implicitly releases the monitor lock* on the SynchronizedBuffer object.

Method **blockingGet** *and the* **Consumer** *Thread*

Methods blockingGet and blockingPut are implemented similarly. When the Consumer thread's run method invokes synchronized method blockingGet, the thread attempts to *acquire the monitor lock* on the SynchronizedBuffer object. If the lock is available, the Consumer thread acquires it. Then the while loop at lines 35–40 determines whether occupied is false. If so, the buffer is empty, so line 37 outputs a message indicating that the Consumer thread is trying to read a value, and line 38 invokes method displayState to output a message indicating that the buffer is *empty* and that the Consumer thread is *waiting*. Line 39 invokes method wait to place the thread that called method blockingGet (i.e., the Consumer) in the *waiting* state for the SynchronizedBuffer object. Again, the call to wait causes the calling thread to *implicitly release the lock* on the SynchronizedBuffer object, so another thread can attempt to acquire the SynchronizedBuffer object's lock and invoke the object's `blockingPut` or `blockingGet` method. If the lock on the SynchronizedBuffer is not available (e.g., if the Producer has not yet returned from method `blockingPut`), the Consumer is *blocked* until the lock becomes available.

The Consumer thread remains in the *waiting* state until it's *notified* by another thread that it may proceed—at which point the Consumer thread returns to the *runnable* state and attempts to *implicitly reacquire the lock* on the SynchronizedBuffer object. If the lock is available, the Consumer reacquires it, and method `blockingGet` continues executing with the next statement after `wait`. Because `wait` is called in a loop, the loop-continuation condition is tested again to determine whether the thread can proceed with its execution. If not, `wait` is invoked again—otherwise, method `blockingGet` continues with the next statement after the loop. Line 44 sets `occupied` to `false` to indicate that `buffer` is now empty (i.e., a Consumer cannot read the value, but a Producer can place another value in `buffer`), line 46 calls method `displayState` to indicate that the consumer is reading and line 48 invokes method `notifyAll`. If any threads are in the *waiting* state for the lock on this SynchronizedBuffer object, they enter the *runnable* state and can now attempt to *reacquire the lock*. Method `notifyAll` returns immediately, then method `blockingGet` returns the value of `buffer` to its caller. When method `blockingGet` returns (line 50), the lock on the SynchronizedBuffer object is *implicitly released*.

Error-Prevention Tip 21.3

Always invoke method `wait` in a loop that tests the condition the task is waiting on. It's possible that a thread will reenter the runnable state (via a timed wait or another thread calling `notifyAll`) before the condition is satisfied. Testing the condition again ensures that the thread will not erroneously execute if it was notified early.

Method `displayState` Is Also `synchronized`

Notice that method `displayState` is a synchronized method. This is important because it, too, reads the SynchronizedBuffer's shared mutable data. Though only one thread at a time may acquire a given object's lock, one thread may acquire the same object's lock *multiple* times—this is known as a **reentrant lock** and enables one synchronized method to invoke another on the same object.

Testing Class `SynchronizedBuffer`

Class `SharedBufferTest2` (Fig. 21.17) is similar to class `SharedBufferTest` (Fig. 21.13). Line 10 creates an ExecutorService to run the Producer and Consumer tasks. Line 13 creates a SynchronizedBuffer object and assigns its reference to Buffer variable sharedLocation. This object stores the data that will be shared between the Producer and Consumer. Lines 15–16 display the column heads for the output. Lines 19–20 execute a Producer and a Consumer. Finally, line 22 calls method `shutdown` to end the application when the Producer and Consumer complete their tasks, and line 23 waits for the scheduled tasks to complete. When method `main` ends, the main thread of execution terminates.

```
1   // Fig. 21.17: SharedBufferTest2.java
2   // Two threads correctly manipulating a synchronized buffer.
3   import java.util.concurrent.ExecutorService;
```

Fig. 21.17 | Two threads correctly manipulating a synchronized buffer. (Part 1 of 3.)

```
4    import java.util.concurrent.Executors;
5    import java.util.concurrent.TimeUnit;
6
7    public class SharedBufferTest2 {
8       public static void main(String[] args) throws InterruptedException {
9          // create a newCachedThreadPool
10         ExecutorService executorService = Executors.newCachedThreadPool();
11
12         // create SynchronizedBuffer to store ints
13         Buffer sharedLocation = new SynchronizedBuffer();
14
15         System.out.printf("%-40s%s\t\t%s%n%-40s%s%n%n", "Operation",
16            "Buffer", "Occupied", "---------", "------\t\t--------");
17
18         // execute the Producer and Consumer tasks
19         executorService.execute(new Producer(sharedLocation));
20         executorService.execute(new Consumer(sharedLocation));
21
22         executorService.shutdown();
23         executorService.awaitTermination(1, TimeUnit.MINUTES);
24      }
25   }
```

Operation	Buffer	Occupied
---------	------	--------
Consumer tries to read. Buffer empty. Consumer waits.	-1	false
Producer writes 1	1	true
Consumer reads 1	1	false
Consumer tries to read. Buffer empty. Consumer waits.	1	false
Producer writes 2	2	true
Consumer reads 2	2	false
Producer writes 3	3	true
Consumer reads 3	3	false
Producer writes 4	4	true
Producer tries to write. Buffer full. Producer waits.	4	true
Consumer reads 4	4	false
Producer writes 5	5	true
Consumer reads 5	5	false
Producer writes 6	6	true

Fig. 21.17 | Two threads correctly manipulating a synchronized buffer. (Part 2 of 3.)

```
Producer tries to write.
Buffer full. Producer waits.          6                true

Consumer reads 6                      6                false

Producer writes 7                     7                true

Producer tries to write.
Buffer full. Producer waits.          7                true

Consumer reads 7                      7                false

Producer writes 8                     8                true

Consumer reads 8                      8                false

Consumer tries to read.
Buffer empty. Consumer waits.         8                false

Producer writes 9                     9                true

Consumer reads 9                      9                false

Consumer tries to read.
Buffer empty. Consumer waits.         9                false

Producer writes 10                    10               true

Consumer reads 10                     10               false


Producer done producing
Terminating Producer

Consumer read values totaling 55
Terminating Consumer
```

Fig. 21.17 | Two threads correctly manipulating a synchronized buffer. (Part 3 of 3.)

Study the outputs in Fig. 21.17. Observe that *every integer produced is consumed exactly once—no values are lost, and no values are consumed more than once.* The synchronization ensures that the Producer produces a value only when the buffer is *empty* and the Consumer consumes only when the buffer is *full*. The Producer always goes first, the Consumer *waits* if the Producer has not produced since the Consumer last consumed, and the Producer waits if the Consumer has not yet consumed the value that the Producer most recently produced. Execute this program several times to confirm that every integer produced is consumed exactly *once*. In the sample output, note the highlighted lines indicating when the Producer and Consumer must *wait* to perform their respective tasks.

21.8 (Advanced) Producer/Consumer Relationship: Bounded Buffers

The program in Section 21.7 uses thread synchronization to guarantee that two threads manipulate data in a shared buffer correctly. However, the application may not perform optimally. If the two threads operate at different speeds, one of them will spend more (or most) of its time waiting. For example, in the program in Section 21.7 we shared a single integer variable between the two threads. If the Producer thread produces values *faster* than the Consumer can consume them, then the Producer thread *waits* for the Consumer, because there are no other locations in the buffer in which to place the next value. Similarly, if the Consumer consumes values *faster* than the Producer produces them, the Consumer *waits* until the Producer places the next value in the shared buffer. Even when we have threads that operate at the *same* relative speeds, those threads may occasionally become "out of sync" over a period of time, causing one of them to *wait* for the other.

Performance Tip 21.3

We cannot make assumptions about the relative speeds of concurrent threads— *interactions that occur with the operating system, the network, the user and other components can cause the threads to operate at different and ever-changing speeds. When this happens, threads wait. When threads wait excessively, programs become less efficient, interactive programs become less responsive and applications suffer longer delays.*

Bounded Buffers

To minimize the amount of waiting time for threads that share resources and operate at the same average speeds, we can implement a **bounded buffer** that provides a fixed number of buffer cells into which the Producer can place values, and from which the Consumer can retrieve those values. (In fact, the ArrayBlockingQueue class in Section 21.6 is a bounded buffer.) If the Producer temporarily produces values faster than the Consumer can consume them, the Producer can write additional values into the extra buffer cells, if any are available. This capability enables the Producer to perform its task even though the Consumer is not ready to retrieve the current value being produced. Similarly, if the Consumer temporarily consumes faster than the Producer produces new values, the Consumer can read additional values (if there are any) from the buffer. This enables the Consumer to keep busy even though the Producer is not ready to produce additional values. An example of the producer/consumer relationship that uses a bounded buffer is video streaming, which we discussed in Section 21.1.

Even a *bounded buffer* is inappropriate if the Producer and the Consumer operate consistently at different speeds. If the Consumer always executes faster than the Producer, then a buffer containing one location is enough. If the Producer always executes faster, only a buffer with an "infinite" number of locations would be able to absorb the extra production. However, if the Producer and Consumer execute at about the same average speed, a bounded buffer helps to smooth the effects of any occasional speeding up or slowing down in either thread's execution.

The key to using a *bounded buffer* with a Producer and Consumer that operate at about the same speed is to provide the buffer with enough locations to handle the anticipated "extra" production. If, over a period of time, we determine that the Producer often produces as many as three more values than the Consumer can consume, we can provide a buffer of at least three cells to handle the extra production. Making the buffer too small would cause threads to wait longer.

[*Note:* As we mention in Fig. 21.22, ArrayBlockingQueue can work with multiple producers and multiple consumers. For example, a factory that produces its product very fast will need to have many more delivery trucks (i.e., consumers) to remove those products quickly from the warehousing area (i.e., the bounded buffer) so that the factory can continue to produce products at full capacity.]

Performance Tip 21.4

Even when using a bounded buffer, it's possible that a producer thread could fill the buffer, which would force the producer to wait until a consumer consumed a value to free an element in the buffer. Similarly, if the buffer is empty at any given time, a consumer thread must wait until the producer produces another value. The key to using a bounded buffer is to optimize the buffer size to minimize the amount of thread wait time, while not wasting space.

Bounded Buffers Using `ArrayBlockingQueue`

The simplest way to implement a bounded buffer is to use an `ArrayBlockingQueue` for the buffer so that *all of the synchronization details are handled for you*. This can be done by modifying the example from Section 21.6 to pass the desired size for the bounded buffer into the `ArrayBlockingQueue` constructor. Rather than repeat our previous `ArrayBlocking-Queue` example with a different size, we instead present an example that illustrates how you can build a bounded buffer yourself. Again, using an `ArrayBlockingQueue` will result in more-maintainable and better-performing code.

Implementing Your Own Bounded Buffer as a Circular Buffer

The program in Figs. 21.18 and 21.19 demonstrates a Producer and a Consumer accessing a *bounded buffer with synchronization*. Again, we reuse interface Buffer and classes Producer and Consumer from the example in Section 21.5, except that line 24 is removed from class Producer and class Consumer. We implement the bounded buffer (Fig. 21.18) as a **circular buffer** that uses a shared array of three elements. A circular buffer writes into and reads from the array elements in order, beginning at the first cell and moving toward the last. When a Producer or Consumer reaches the last element, it returns to the first and begins writing or reading, respectively, from there. In this version of the producer/consumer relationship, the Consumer consumes a value only when the array is not empty and the Producer produces a value only when the array is not full. Once again, the output statements used in this class's synchronized methods are for *demonstration purposes only*.

```
 1   // Fig. 21.18: CircularBuffer.java
 2   // Synchronizing access to a shared three-element bounded buffer.
 3   public class CircularBuffer implements Buffer {
 4      private final int[] buffer = {-1, -1, -1}; // shared buffer
 5
 6      private int occupiedCells = 0; // count number of buffers used
 7      private int writeIndex = 0; // index of next element to write to
 8      private int readIndex = 0; // index of next element to read
 9
10      // place value into buffer
11      @Override
12      public synchronized void blockingPut(int value)
13         throws InterruptedException {
```

Fig. 21.18 | Synchronizing access to a shared three-element bounded buffer. (Part 1 of 3.)

```
14
15          // wait until buffer has space available, then write value;
16          // while no empty locations, place thread in blocked state
17          while (occupiedCells == buffer.length) {
18             System.out.printf("Buffer is full. Producer waits.%n");
19             wait(); // wait until a buffer cell is free
20          }
21
22          buffer[writeIndex] = value; // set new buffer value
23
24          // update circular write index
25          writeIndex = (writeIndex + 1) % buffer.length;
26
27          ++occupiedCells; // one more buffer cell is full
28          displayState("Producer writes " + value);
29          notifyAll(); // notify threads waiting to read from buffer
30       }
31
32       // return value from buffer
33       @Override
34       public synchronized int blockingGet() throws InterruptedException {
35          // wait until buffer has data, then read value;
36          // while no data to read, place thread in waiting state
37          while (occupiedCells == 0) {
38             System.out.printf("Buffer is empty. Consumer waits.%n");
39             wait(); // wait until a buffer cell is filled
40          }
41
42          int readValue = buffer[readIndex]; // read value from buffer
43
44          // update circular read index
45          readIndex = (readIndex + 1) % buffer.length;
46
47          --occupiedCells; // one fewer buffer cells are occupied
48          displayState("Consumer reads " + readValue);
49          notifyAll(); // notify threads waiting to write to buffer
50
51          return readValue;
52       }
53
54       // display current operation and buffer state
55       public synchronized void displayState(String operation) {
56          // output operation and number of occupied buffer cells
57          System.out.printf("%s%s%d)%n%s", operation,
58             " (buffer cells occupied: ", occupiedCells, "buffer cells:  ");
59
60          for (int value : buffer) {
61             System.out.printf(" %2d  ", value); // output values in buffer
62          }
63
64          System.out.printf("%n                    ");
65
```

Fig. 21.18 | Synchronizing access to a shared three-element bounded buffer. (Part 2 of 3.)

```
66          for (int i = 0; i < buffer.length; i++) {
67              System.out.print("---- ");
68          }
69
70          System.out.printf("%n                    ");
71
72          for (int i = 0; i < buffer.length; i++) {
73              if (i == writeIndex && i == readIndex) {
74                  System.out.print(" WR"); // both write and read index
75              }
76              else if (i == writeIndex) {
77                  System.out.print(" W  "); // just write index
78              }
79              else if (i == readIndex) {
80                  System.out.print("  R "); // just read index
81              }
82              else {
83                  System.out.print("    "); // neither index
84              }
85          }
86
87          System.out.printf("%n%n");
88      }
89  }
```

Fig. 21.18 | Synchronizing access to a shared three-element bounded buffer. (Part 3 of 3.)

Line 4 initializes array `buffer` as a three-element `int` array that represents the circular buffer. Variable `occupiedCells` (line 6) counts the number of elements in `buffer` that contain data to be read. When `occupiedCells` is 0, the circular buffer is *empty* and the Consumer must *wait*—when `occupiedCells` is 3 (the size of the circular buffer), the circular buffer is *full* and the Producer must *wait*. Variable `writeIndex` (line 7) indicates the next location in which a value can be placed by a Producer. Variable `readIndex` (line 8) indicates the position from which the next value can be read by a Consumer. Circular-Buffer's instance variables are *all* part of the class's shared mutable data, thus access to all of these variables must be synchronized to ensure that a `CircularBuffer` is thread safe.

CircularBuffer Method `blockingPut`

`CircularBuffer` method `blockingPut` (lines 11–30) performs the same tasks as in Fig. 21.16, with a few modifications. The loop at lines 17–20 of Figs. 21.18 determines whether the Producer must *wait* (i.e., all buffer cells are *full*). If so, line 18 indicates that the Producer is *waiting* to perform its task. Then line 19 invokes method `wait`, causing the Producer thread to *release* the `CircularBuffer`'s *lock* and *wait* until there's space for a new value to be written into the buffer. When execution continues at line 22 after the `while` loop, the value written by the Producer is placed in the circular buffer at location `writeIndex`. Then line 25 updates `writeIndex` for the next call to `CircularBuffer` method `blockingPut`. This line is the key to the buffer's *circularity*. When `writeIndex` is incremented *past the end of the buffer*, the line sets it to 0. Line 27 increments `occupiedCells`, because there's now one more value in the buffer that the Consumer can read. Next, line 28 invokes method `displayState` (lines 55–88) to update the output with the value produced, the number of occupied buffer cells, the contents of the buffer cells and the current `writeIndex` and `readIndex`. Line 29 invokes method `notifyAll` to transition *waiting* threads to the *runnable* state, so that a waiting `Consumer` thread (if there is one) can now try again to read a value from the buffer.

CircularBuffer Method `blockingGet`

`CircularBuffer` method `blockingGet` (lines 33–52) also performs the same tasks as it did in Fig. 21.16, with a few minor modifications. The loop at lines 37–40 (Fig. 21.18) determines whether the `Consumer` must wait (i.e., all buffer cells are *empty*). If the `Consumer` must *wait*, line 38 updates the output to indicate that the `Consumer` is *waiting* to perform its task. Then line 39 invokes method `wait`, causing the current thread to *release the lock* on the `CircularBuffer` and *wait* until data is available to read. When execution eventually continues at line 42 after a `notifyAll` call from the `Producer`, `readValue` is assigned the value at location `readIndex` in the circular buffer. Then line 45 updates `readIndex` for the next call to `CircularBuffer` method `blockingGet`. This line and line 25 implement the *circularity* of the buffer. Line 47 decrements `occupiedCells`, because there's now one more position in the buffer in which the `Producer` thread can place a value. Line 48 invokes method `displayState` to update the output with the consumed value, the number of occupied buffer cells, the contents of the buffer cells and the current `writeIndex` and `readIndex`. Line 49 invokes method `notifyAll` to allow any `Producer` threads *waiting to write* into the `CircularBuffer` object to attempt to write again. Then line 51 returns the consumed value to the caller.

CircularBuffer Method `displayState`

Method `displayState` (lines 55–88) outputs the application's state. Lines 60–62 output the values of the buffer cells, using a `"%2d"` format specifier to print the contents of each buffer with a leading space if it's a single digit. Lines 72–85 output the current `writeIndex` and `readIndex` with the letters W and R, respectively. Once again, `displayState` is a synchronized method because it accesses class `CircularBuffer`'s shared mutable data.

Testing Class `CircularBuffer`

Class `CircularBufferTest` (Fig. 21.19) contains the `main` method that launches the application. Line 10 creates the `ExecutorService`, and line 13 creates a `CircularBuffer` object and assigns its reference to `CircularBuffer` variable `sharedLocation`. Line 16 invokes the `CircularBuffer`'s `displayState` method to show the initial state of the buffer. Lines 19–20 execute the `Producer` and `Consumer` tasks. Line 22 calls method `shutdown` to end the application when the threads complete the `Producer` and `Consumer` tasks, and line 23 waits for the tasks to complete.

```
1    // Fig. 21.19: CircularBufferTest.java
2    // Producer and Consumer threads correctly manipulating a circular buffer.
3    import java.util.concurrent.ExecutorService;
4    import java.util.concurrent.Executors;
5    import java.util.concurrent.TimeUnit;
6
7    public class CircularBufferTest {
```

Fig. 21.19 | Producer and Consumer threads correctly manipulating a circular buffer. (Part 1 of 4.)

```
 8      public static void main(String[] args) throws InterruptedException {
 9          // create new thread pool
10          ExecutorService executorService = Executors.newCachedThreadPool();
11
12          // create CircularBuffer to store ints
13          CircularBuffer sharedLocation = new CircularBuffer();
14
15          // display the initial state of the CircularBuffer
16          sharedLocation.displayState("Initial State");
17
18          // execute the Producer and Consumer tasks
19          executorService.execute(new Producer(sharedLocation));
20          executorService.execute(new Consumer(sharedLocation));
21
22          executorService.shutdown();
23          executorService.awaitTermination(1, TimeUnit.MINUTES);
24      }
25  }
```

```
Initial State (buffer cells occupied: 0)
buffer cells:     -1    -1    -1
                  ---- ---- ----
                   WR

Producer writes 1 (buffer cells occupied: 1)
buffer cells:      1    -1    -1
                  ---- ---- ----
                   R    W

Consumer reads 1 (buffer cells occupied: 0)
buffer cells:      1    -1    -1
                  ---- ---- ----
                        WR

Buffer is empty. Consumer waits.
Producer writes 2 (buffer cells occupied: 1)
buffer cells:      1     2    -1
                  ---- ---- ----
                        R    W

Consumer reads 2 (buffer cells occupied: 0)
buffer cells:      1     2    -1
                  ---- ---- ----
                              WR

Producer writes 3 (buffer cells occupied: 1)
buffer cells:      1     2     3
                  ---- ---- ----
                   W          R

Consumer reads 3 (buffer cells occupied: 0)
buffer cells:      1     2     3
                  ---- ---- ----
                   WR
```

Fig. 21.19 | Producer and Consumer threads correctly manipulating a circular buffer. (Part 2 of 4.)

```
Producer writes 4 (buffer cells occupied: 1)
buffer cells:    4    2    3
                ---- ---- ----
                 R    W

Producer writes 5 (buffer cells occupied: 2)
buffer cells:    4    5    3
                ---- ---- ----
                 R         W

Consumer reads 4 (buffer cells occupied: 1)
buffer cells:    4    5    3
                ---- ---- ----
                      R    W

Producer writes 6 (buffer cells occupied: 2)
buffer cells:    4    5    6
                ---- ---- ----
                 W    R

Producer writes 7 (buffer cells occupied: 3)
buffer cells:    7    5    6
                ---- ---- ----
                      WR

Consumer reads 5 (buffer cells occupied: 2)
buffer cells:    7    5    6
                ---- ---- ----
                 W    R

Producer writes 8 (buffer cells occupied: 3)
buffer cells:    7    8    6
                ---- ---- ----
                      WR

Consumer reads 6 (buffer cells occupied: 2)
buffer cells:    7    8    6
                ---- ---- ----
                 R         W

Consumer reads 7 (buffer cells occupied: 1)
buffer cells:    7    8    6
                ---- ---- ----
                 R         W

Producer writes 9 (buffer cells occupied: 2)
buffer cells:    7    8    9
                ---- ---- ----
                 W    R

Consumer reads 8 (buffer cells occupied: 1)
buffer cells:    7    8    9
                ---- ---- ----
                 W         R
```

Fig. 21.19 | Producer and Consumer threads correctly manipulating a circular buffer. (Part 3 of 4.)

```
Consumer reads 9 (buffer cells occupied: 0)
buffer cells:    7    8    9
                ---- ---- ----
                 WR

Producer writes 10 (buffer cells occupied: 1)
buffer cells:   10    8    9
                ---- ---- ----
                 R    W


Producer done producing
Terminating Producer
Consumer reads 10 (buffer cells occupied: 0)
buffer cells:   10    8    9
                ---- ---- ----
                      WR


Consumer read values totaling: 55
Terminating Consumer
```

Fig. 21.19 | Producer and Consumer threads correctly manipulating a circular buffer. (Part 4 of 4.)

Each time the Producer writes a value or the Consumer reads a value, the program outputs a message indicating the action performed (a read or a write), the contents of buffer, and the location of writeIndex and readIndex. In the output of Fig. 21.19, the Producer first writes the value 1. The buffer then contains the value 1 in the first cell and the value –1 (the default value that we use for output purposes) in the other two cells. The write index is updated to the second cell, while the read index stays at the first cell. Next, the Consumer reads 1. The buffer contains the same values, but the read index has been updated to the second cell. The Consumer then tries to read again, but the buffer is empty and the Consumer is forced to wait. Only once in this execution of the program was it necessary for either thread to wait.

21.9 (Advanced) Producer/Consumer Relationship: The Lock and Condition Interfaces

Though the synchronized keyword provides for most basic thread-synchronization needs, Java provides other tools to assist in developing concurrent programs. In this section, we discuss the Lock and Condition interfaces. These interfaces give you more precise control over thread synchronization, but are more complicated to use. *Only the most advanced programmers should use these interfaces.*

Interface Lock and Class ReentrantLock

Any object can contain a reference to an object that implements the **Lock** interface (of package java.util.concurrent.locks). A thread calls the Lock's **lock** method (analogous to entering a synchronized block) to acquire the lock. Once a Lock has been obtained by one thread, the Lock object will not allow another thread to obtain the Lock until the first thread releases the Lock (by calling the Lock's **unlock** method—analogous to exiting a synchronized block). If several threads are trying to call method lock on the same Lock object at the same time, only one of these threads can obtain the lock—all the others are placed in the *waiting* state for that lock. When a thread calls method unlock, the lock on the object is released and a waiting thread attempting to lock the object proceeds.

Error-Prevention Tip 21.4

Place calls to Lock method unlock in a finally block. If an exception is thrown, unlock must still be called or deadlock could occur.

Class **ReentrantLock** (of package java.util.concurrent.locks) is a basic implementation of the Lock interface. The constructor for a ReentrantLock takes a boolean argument that specifies whether the lock has a **fairness policy**. If the argument is true, the ReentrantLock's fairness policy is "the longest-waiting thread will acquire the lock when it's available." Such a fairness policy guarantees that *indefinite postponement* (also called *starvation*) cannot occur. If the fairness policy argument is set to false, there's no guarantee as to which waiting thread will acquire the lock when it's available.

Software Engineering Observation 21.6

Using a ReentrantLock with a fairness policy avoids indefinite postponement.

Performance Tip 21.5

In most cases, a non-fair lock is preferable, because using a fair lock can decrease program performance.

Condition Objects and Interface Condition

If a thread that owns a Lock determines that it cannot continue with its task until some condition is satisfied, the thread can wait on a **condition object**. Using Lock objects allows you to explicitly declare the condition objects on which a thread may need to wait. For example, in the producer/consumer relationship, producers can wait on *one* object and consumers can wait on *another*. This is not possible when using the synchronized keywords and an object's built-in monitor lock.

Condition objects are associated with a specific Lock and are created by calling a Lock's **newCondition** method, which returns an object that implements the **Condition** interface (package java.util.concurrent.locks). To wait on a Condition, the thread can call its **await** method (analogous to Object method wait). This immediately releases the associated Lock and places the thread in the *waiting* state for that Condition. Other threads can then try to obtain the Lock.

When a *runnable* thread completes a task and determines that the *waiting* thread can now continue, the *runnable* thread can call Condition method **signal** (analogous to Object method notify) to allow a thread in that Condition's *waiting* state to return to the *runnable* state. At this point, the thread that transitioned from the *waiting* state to the *runnable* state can attempt to reacquire the Lock. Even if it's able to *reacquire* the Lock, the thread still might not be able to perform its task at this time—in which case the thread can call the Condition's await method to *release* the Lock and reenter the *waiting* state.

If multiple threads are in a Condition's *waiting* state when signal is called, the default implementation of Condition signals the longest-waiting thread to transition to the *runnable* state. If a thread calls `Condition` method **`signalAll`** (analogous to `Object` method `notifyAll`), then all the threads waiting for that condition transition to the *runnable* state and become eligible to reacquire the `Lock`. Only one of those threads can obtain the `Lock` on the object—the others will wait until the `Lock` becomes available again. If the `Lock` has a *fairness policy*, the longest-waiting thread acquires the `Lock`. When a thread is finished with a shared object, it must call method `unlock` to release the `Lock`.

Error-Prevention Tip 21.5

When multiple threads manipulate a shared object using locks, ensure that if one thread calls method `await` to enter the waiting *state for a condition object, a separate thread eventually will call* `Condition` *method* `signal` *to transition the thread waiting on the condition object back to the* runnable *state. If multiple threads may be waiting on the condition object, a separate thread can call* `Condition` *method* `signalAll` *as a safeguard to ensure that all the waiting threads have another opportunity to perform their tasks. If this is not done, starvation might occur.*

Common Programming Error 21.2

An `IllegalMonitorStateException` *occurs if a thread issues an* `await`, *a* `signal`, *or a* `signalAll` *on a* `Condition` *object that was created from a* `ReentrantLock` *without having acquired the lock for that* `Condition` *object.*

Lock and Condition vs. the synchronized Keyword

In some applications, using `Lock` and `Condition` objects may be preferable to using the `synchronized` keyword. Locks allow you to *interrupt* waiting threads or to specify a *timeout* for waiting to acquire a lock, which is not possible using the `synchronized` keyword. Also, a `Lock` is *not* constrained to be acquired and released in the *same* block of code, which is the case with the `synchronized` keyword. `Condition` objects allow you to specify multiple conditions on which threads may *wait*. Thus, it's possible to indicate to waiting threads that a specific condition object is now true by calling `signal` or `signalAll` on that `Condition` object. With `synchronized`, there's no way to explicitly state the condition on which threads are waiting, and thus there's no way to notify threads waiting on one condition that they may proceed without also signaling threads waiting on any other conditions. There are other possible advantages to using `Lock` and `Condition` objects, but generally it's best to use the `synchronized` keyword unless your application requires advanced synchronization capabilities.

Software Engineering Observation 21.7

Think of `Lock` *and* `Condition` *as an advanced version of* `synchronized`. `Lock` *and* `Condition` *support timed waits, interruptible waits and multiple* `Condition` *queues per* `Lock`—*if you do not need one of these features, you do not need* `Lock` *and* `Condition`.

Error-Prevention Tip 21.6

Using interfaces `Lock` *and* `Condition` *is error prone—*`unlock` *is not guaranteed to be called, whereas the monitor in a* `synchronized` *statement will always be released when the statement completes execution. Of course, you can guarantee that* `unlock` *will be called if it's placed in a* `finally` *block, as we do in Fig. 21.20.*

Using Locks and Conditions to Implement Synchronization

We now implement the producer/consumer relationship using Lock and Condition objects to coordinate access to a shared single-element buffer (Figs. 21.20 and 21.21). In this case, each produced value is correctly consumed exactly once. Again, we reuse interface Buffer and classes Producer and Consumer from the example in Section 21.5, except that line 24 is removed from class Producer and class Consumer.

Class SynchronizedBuffer

Class SynchronizedBuffer (Fig. 21.20) contains five fields. Line 10 initializes Lock instance variable accessLock with a new ReentrantLock. We did not specify a *fairness policy* in this example, because at any time only a single Producer or Consumer will be waiting to acquire the Lock. Lines 13–14 create two Conditions using Lock method newCondition:

- Condition canWrite contains a queue for a Producer thread waiting while the buffer is *full* (i.e., there's data in the buffer that the Consumer has not read yet). If the buffer is *full*, the Producer calls method await on this Condition. When the Consumer reads data from a *full* buffer, it calls method signal on this Condition.

- Condition canRead contains a queue for a Consumer thread waiting while the buffer is *empty* (i.e., there's no data in the buffer for the Consumer to read). If the buffer is *empty*, the Consumer calls method await on this Condition. When the Producer writes to the *empty* buffer, it calls method signal on this Condition.

The int variable buffer (line 16) holds the shared mutable data. The boolean variable occupied (line 17) keeps track of whether the buffer currently holds data (that the Consumer should read).

```java
 1   // Fig. 21.20: SynchronizedBuffer.java
 2   // Synchronizing access to a shared integer using the Lock and Condition
 3   // interfaces
 4   import java.util.concurrent.locks.Lock;
 5   import java.util.concurrent.locks.ReentrantLock;
 6   import java.util.concurrent.locks.Condition;
 7
 8   public class SynchronizedBuffer implements Buffer {
 9      // Lock to control synchronization with this buffer
10      private final Lock accessLock = new ReentrantLock();
11
12      // conditions to control reading and writing
13      private final Condition canWrite = accessLock.newCondition();
14      private final Condition canRead = accessLock.newCondition();
15
16      private int buffer = -1; // shared by producer and consumer threads
17      private boolean occupied = false; // whether buffer is occupied
18
19      // place int value into buffer
20      @Override
21      public void blockingPut(int value) throws InterruptedException {
22         accessLock.lock(); // lock this object
```

Fig. 21.20 | Synchronizing access to a shared integer using the Lock and Condition interfaces. (Part 1 of 3.)

```
23
24          // output thread information and buffer information, then wait
25          try {
26             // while buffer is not empty, place thread in waiting state
27             while (occupied) {
28                System.out.println("Producer tries to write.");
29                displayState("Buffer full. Producer waits.");
30                canWrite.await(); // wait until buffer is empty
31             }
32
33             buffer = value; // set new buffer value
34
35             // indicate producer cannot store another value
36             // until consumer retrieves current buffer value
37             occupied = true;
38
39             displayState("Producer writes " + buffer);
40
41             // signal any threads waiting to read from buffer
42             canRead.signalAll();
43          }
44          finally {
45             accessLock.unlock(); // unlock this object
46          }
47       }
48
49       // return value from buffer
50       @Override
51       public int blockingGet() throws InterruptedException {
52          int readValue = 0; // initialize value read from buffer
53          accessLock.lock(); // lock this object
54
55          // output thread information and buffer information, then wait
56          try {
57             // if there is no data to read, place thread in waiting state
58             while (!occupied) {
59                System.out.println("Consumer tries to read.");
60                displayState("Buffer empty. Consumer waits.");
61                canRead.await(); // wait until buffer is full
62             }
63
64             // indicate that producer can store another value
65             // because consumer just retrieved buffer value
66             occupied = false;
67
68             readValue = buffer; // retrieve value from buffer
69             displayState("Consumer reads " + readValue);
70
71             // signal any threads waiting for buffer to be empty
72             canWrite.signalAll();
73          }
```

Fig. 21.20 | Synchronizing access to a shared integer using the Lock and Condition interfaces. (Part 2 of 3.)

```
74              finally {
75                  accessLock.unlock(); // unlock this object
76              }
77
78              return readValue;
79          }
80
81          // display current operation and buffer state
82          private void displayState(String operation) {
83              try {
84                  accessLock.lock(); // lock this object
85                  System.out.printf("%-40s%d\t\t%b%n%n", operation, buffer,
86                      occupied);
87              }
88              finally {
89                  accessLock.unlock(); // unlock this object
90              }
91          }
92      }
```

Fig. 21.20 | Synchronizing access to a shared integer using the Lock and Condition interfaces. (Part 3 of 3.)

Method blockingPut calls method lock on the SynchronizedBuffer's accessLock (line 22). If the lock is *available* (i.e., no other thread has acquired it), this thread now owns the lock and the thread continues. If the lock is *unavailable* (i.e., it's held by another thread), method lock waits until the lock is released. After the lock is acquired, lines 25–43 execute. Line 27 determines whether buffer is full. If it is, lines 28–29 display a message indicating that the thread will *wait*. Line 30 calls Condition method await on the canWrite condition object, which temporarily releases the SynchronizedBuffer's Lock and *waits* for a signal from the Consumer that buffer is available for writing. When buffer is available, the method proceeds, writing to buffer (line 33), setting occupied to true (line 37) and displaying a message indicating that the producer wrote a value (line 39). Line 42 calls Condition method signal on the condition object canRead to notify the waiting Consumer (if there is one) that the buffer has new data. Line 45 calls method unlock from a finally block to *release* the lock and allow the Consumer to proceed.

Line 53 of method blockingGet calls method lock to *acquire* the Lock. This method *waits* until the Lock is *available*. Once the Lock is *acquired*, line 58 determines whether the buffer is *empty*. If so, line 61 calls method await on condition object canRead. Recall that method signal is called on variable canRead in the blockingPut method (line 42). When the Condition object is *signaled*, the blockingGet method continues. Lines 66–69 set occupied to false, store the value of buffer in readValue and output the readValue. Then line 72 *signals* the condition object canWrite. This awakens the Producer if it's indeed *waiting* for the buffer to be *emptied*. Line 75 calls method unlock from a finally block to *release* the lock, and line 78 returns readValue to the caller.

Common Programming Error 21.3

Forgetting to signal a waiting thread is a logic error. The thread will remain in the waiting state, preventing it from proceeding. This can lead to indefinite postponement or deadlock.

Class *SharedBufferTest2*

Class SharedBufferTest2 (Fig. 21.21) is identical to that of Fig. 21.17. Study the outputs in Fig. 21.21. *Observe that every integer produced is consumed exactly once—no values are lost, and no values are consumed more than once.* The Lock and Condition objects ensure that the Producer and Consumer cannot perform their tasks unless it's their turn. The Producer *must* go first, the Consumer *must wait* if the Producer has not produced since the Consumer last consumed and the Producer *must wait* if the Consumer has not yet consumed the value that the Producer most recently produced. Execute this program several times to confirm that every integer produced is consumed exactly once. In the sample output, note the highlighted lines indicating when the Producer and Consumer must *wait* to perform their respective tasks.

```java
 1   // Fig. 21.21: SharedBufferTest2.java
 2   // Two threads manipulating a synchronized buffer.
 3   import java.util.concurrent.ExecutorService;
 4   import java.util.concurrent.Executors;
 5   import java.util.concurrent.TimeUnit;
 6
 7   public class SharedBufferTest2 {
 8      public static void main(String[] args) throws InterruptedException {
 9         // create new thread pool
10         ExecutorService executorService = Executors.newCachedThreadPool();
11
12         // create SynchronizedBuffer to store ints
13         Buffer sharedLocation = new SynchronizedBuffer();
14
15         System.out.printf("%-40s%s\t\t%s%n%-40s%s%n%n", "Operation",
16            "Buffer", "Occupied", "---------", "------\t\t--------");
17
18         // execute the Producer and Consumer tasks
19         executorService.execute(new Producer(sharedLocation));
20         executorService.execute(new Consumer(sharedLocation));
21
22         executorService.shutdown();
23         executorService.awaitTermination(1, TimeUnit.MINUTES);
24      }
25   }
```

Operation	Buffer	Occupied
---------	------	--------
Producer writes 1	1	true
Producer tries to write. Buffer full. Producer waits.	1	true
Consumer reads 1	1	false
Producer writes 2	2	true
Producer tries to write. Buffer full. Producer waits.	2	true

Fig. 21.21 | Two threads manipulating a synchronized buffer. (Part 1 of 2.)

Consumer reads 2	2	false
Producer writes 3	3	true
Consumer reads 3	3	false
Producer writes 4	4	true
Consumer reads 4	4	false
Consumer tries to read. Buffer empty. Consumer waits.	4	false
Producer writes 5	5	true
Consumer reads 5	5	false
Consumer tries to read. Buffer empty. Consumer waits.	5	false
Producer writes 6	6	true
Consumer reads 6	6	false
Producer writes 7	7	true
Consumer reads 7	7	false
Producer writes 8	8	true
Consumer reads 8	8	false
Producer writes 9	9	true
Consumer reads 9	9	false
Producer writes 10	10	true
Producer done producing Terminating Producer Consumer reads 10	10	false
Consumer read values totaling 55 Terminating Consumer		

Fig. 21.21 | Two threads manipulating a synchronized buffer. (Part 2 of 2.)

21.10 Concurrent Collections

In Chapter 16, we introduced various collections from the Java Collections API. We also mentioned that you can obtain *synchronized* versions of those collections to allow only one thread at a time to access a collection that might be shared among several threads. The collections from the `java.util.concurrent` package are specifically designed and optimized for sharing collections among multiple threads.

Figure 21.22 lists the many concurrent collections in package `java.util.concurrent`. The entries for `ConcurrentHashMap` and `LinkedBlockingQueue` are shown in **bold** because these are by far the most frequently used concurrent collections. Like the collections introduced in Chapter 16, the concurrent collections were enhanced in Java SE 8 to

8

support lambdas. However, rather than providing methods to support streams, the concurrent collections provide their own implementations of various stream-like operations—e.g., ConcurrentHashMap has methods forEach, reduce and search—that are designed and optimized for concurrent collections that are shared among threads. For more information on the concurrent collections, visit

```
http://docs.oracle.com/javase/8/docs/api/java/util/concurrent/
    package-summary.html
```

Collection	Description
ArrayBlockingQueue	A fixed-size queue that supports the producer/consumer relationship—possibly with many producers and consumers.
ConcurrentHashMap	**A hash-based map (similar to the HashMap introduced in Chapter 16) that allows an arbitrary number of reader threads and a limited number of writer threads. This and the LinkedBlockingQueue are by far the most frequently used concurrent collections.**
ConcurrentLinkedDeque	A concurrent linked-list implementation of a double-ended queue.
ConcurrentLinkedQueue	A concurrent linked-list implementation of a queue that can grow dynamically.
ConcurrentSkipListMap	A concurrent map that is sorted by its keys.
ConcurrentSkipListSet	A sorted concurrent set.
CopyOnWriteArrayList	A thread-safe ArrayList. Each operation that modifies the collection first creates a new copy of the contents. Used when the collection is traversed much more frequently than the collection's contents are modified.
CopyOnWriteArraySet	A set that's implemented using CopyOnWriteArrayList.
DelayQueue	A variable-size queue containing Delayed objects. An object can be removed only after its delay has expired.
LinkedBlockingDeque	A double-ended blocking queue implemented as a linked list that can optionally be fixed in size.
LinkedBlockingQueue	**A blocking queue implemented as a linked list that can optionally be fixed in size. This and the ConcurrentHashMap are by far the most frequently used concurrent collections.**
LinkedTransferQueue	A linked-list implementation of interface TransferQueue. Each producer has the option of waiting for a consumer to take an element being inserted (via method transfer) or simply placing the element into the queue (via method put). Also provides overloaded method tryTransfer to immediately transfer an element to a waiting consumer or to do so within a specified timeout period. If the transfer cannot be completed, the element is not placed in the queue. Typically used in applications that pass messages between threads.
PriorityBlockingQueue	A variable-length priority-based blocking queue (like a PriorityQueue).
SynchronousQueue	[For experts.] A blocking queue implementation that does not have an internal capacity. Each insert operation by one thread must wait for a remove operation from another thread and vice versa.

Fig. 21.22 | Concurrent collections summary (package java.util.concurrent).

21.11 Multithreading in JavaFX

JavaFX applications present a unique set of challenges for multithreaded programming. All JavaFX applications have a single thread, called the **JavaFX application thread**, to handle interactions with the application's controls. Typical interactions include *rendering controls* or *processing user actions* such as mouse clicks. All tasks that require interaction with an application's GUI are placed in an *event queue* and are executed sequentially by the JavaFX application thread.

JavaFX's scene graph is not thread safe—its nodes cannot be manipulated by multiple threads without the risk of incorrect results that might corrupt the scene graph. Unlike the other examples presented in this chapter, thread safety in JavaFX applications is achieved not by synchronizing thread actions, but by *ensuring that programs manipulate the scene graph from only the JavaFX application thread.* This technique is called **thread confinement**. Allowing just one thread to access non-thread-safe objects eliminates the possibility of corruption due to multiple threads accessing these objects concurrently.

It's acceptable to perform brief tasks on the JavaFX application thread in sequence with GUI component manipulations—like calculating tips and totals in Chapter 12's **Tip Calculator** app. If an application must perform a lengthy task in response to a user interaction, the JavaFX application thread cannot render controls or respond to events while the thread is tied up in that task. This causes the GUI to become unresponsive. It's preferable to handle long-running tasks in separate threads, freeing the JavaFX application thread to continue managing other GUI interactions. Of course, you must update the GUI with the computation's results from the JavaFX application thread, rather than from the worker thread that performed the computation.[3]

Platform Method runLater

JavaFX provides multiple mechanisms for updating the GUI from other threads. One is to call the `static` method **runLater** of class **Platform** (package `javafx.application`). This method receives a `Runnable` and schedules it on the JavaFX application thread for execution at some point in the future. Such `Runnable`s should perform only small updates, so the GUI remains responsive.

Class Task and Interface Worker

Long-running or compute-intensive tasks should be performed on separate worker threads, not the JavaFX application thread. Package **javafx.concurrent** provides interface `Worker` and classes `Task` and `ScheduledService` for this purpose:

- A **Worker** is a task that should execute using one or more separate threads.

- Class **Task** is a `Worker` implementation that enables you to perform a task (such as a long-running computation) in a worker thread and update the GUI from the JavaFX application thread based on the task's results. `Task` implements several interfaces, including `Runnable`, so a `Task` object can be scheduled to execute in a

---

3. Like JavaFX, Swing uses a single thread for handling interactions and displaying the GUI. Swing's similar capabilities to the JavaFX concurrency features discussed in this section are located in package `javax.swing`. Class `SwingUtilities` method `invokeLater` schedules a `Runnable` for later execution in the so-called event-dispatch thread. Class `SwingWorker` performs a long-running task in a worker thread and can display results in the GUI from the event-dispatch thread.

separate thread. Class Task also provides methods that are guaranteed to update its properties in the JavaFX application thread—as you'll see, this enables programs to bind a Task's properties to GUI controls for automatic updating. Once a Task completes, it cannot be restarted—performing the Task again requires a new Task object. We'll demonstrate Tasks in the next two examples.

- Class **ScheduledService** is a Worker implementation that creates and manages a Task. Unlike a Task, a ScheduledService can be reset and restarted. It also can be configured to automatically restart both after successful completion and if it fails due to an exception.

21.11.1 Performing Computations in a Worker Thread: Fibonacci Numbers

In the next example, the user enters a number *n* and the program gets the *n*th Fibonacci number, which we calculate using the recursive algorithm discussed in Section 18.5. Since the algorithm is time consuming for large values, we use a Task object to perform the recursive calculation in a worker thread. The GUI also provides a separate set of components that displays the next Fibonacci number in the sequence with each click of a Button. This set of components performs its short computation directly in the event dispatch thread. The program is capable of producing up to the 92nd Fibonacci number—subsequent values are outside the range that can be represented by a long. Recall that you can use class BigInteger to represent arbitrarily large integer values.

Creating a Task
Class FibonacciTask (Fig. 21.23) extends Task<Long> (line 5) to perform the recursive Fibonacci calculation in a *worker thread*. The instance variable n (line 6) represents the Fibonacci number to calculate. Overridden Task method **call** (lines 14–20) computes the *n*th Fibonacci number and returns the result. The Task's type parameter Long (line 5) determines call's return type (line 15). Inherited Task method **updateMessage** (called in lines 16 and 18) updates the Task's message property in the *JavaFX application thread*. As you'll see in Fig. 21.25, this enables us to bind JavaFX controls to FibonacciTask's message property to display messages while the task is executing.

```
 1   // Fig. 21.23: FibonacciTask.java
 2   // Task subclass for calculating Fibonacci numbers in the background
 3   import javafx.concurrent.Task;
 4
 5   public class FibonacciTask extends Task<Long> {
 6      private final int n; // Fibonacci number to calculate
 7
 8      // constructor
 9      public FibonacciTask(int n) {
10         this.n = n;
11      }
12
```

Fig. 21.23 | Task subclass for calculating Fibonacci numbers in the background. (Part 1 of 2.)

```
13      // long-running code to be run in a worker thread
14      @Override
15      protected Long call() {
16          updateMessage("Calculating...");
17          long result = fibonacci(n);
18          updateMessage("Done calculating.");
19          return result;
20      }
21
22      // recursive method fibonacci; calculates nth Fibonacci number
23      public long fibonacci(long number) {
24          if (number == 0 || number == 1) {
25              return number;
26          }
27          else {
28              return fibonacci(number - 1) + fibonacci(number - 2);
29          }
30      }
31  }
```

Fig. 21.23 | Task subclass for calculating Fibonacci numbers in the background. (Part 2 of 2.)

When the worker thread enters the *running* state, FibonacciTask's call method begins executing. First, line 16 calls the inherited updateMessage method to update the FibonacciTask's message property, indicating that the task is calculating. Next, line 17 invokes recursive method fibonacci (lines 23–30) with instance variable n's value as the argument. When fibonacci returns, line 18 updates FibonacciTask's message property again to indicate that the calculation completed, then line 19 returns the result to the JavaFX application thread.

FibonacciNumbers GUI

Figure 21.24 shows the app's GUI (defined in FibonacciNumbers.fxml) labeled with its **fx:id**s. Here we point out only the key elements and the event-handling methods you'll see in class FibonacciNumbersController (Fig. 21.25). For the complete layout details, open FibonacciNumbers.fxml in Scene Builder. The GUI's primary layout is a VBox containing two TitledPanes. The controller class defines two event handlers:

- goButtonPressed is called when the **Go** Button is pressed—this launches the worker thread to calculate a Fibonacci number recursively.

- nextNumberButtonPressed is called when the **Next Number** Button is pressed—this calculates the next Fibonacci number in the sequence. Initially the app displays the Fibonacci of 0 (which is 0).

We do not show the JavaFX Application subclass (located in FibonacciNumbers.java), because it performs the same tasks you've seen previously to load the app's FXML GUI and initialize the controller.

Class FibonacciNumbersController

Class FibonacciNumbersController (Fig. 21.25) displays a window containing two sets of controls:

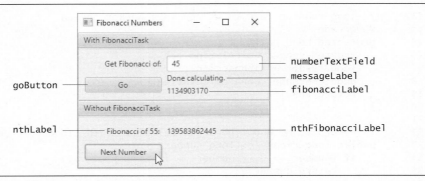

Fig. 21.24 | `FibonacciNumbers` GUI with its **fx:id**s.

- The **With FibonacciTask** `TitledPane` provides controls that enable the user to enter a Fibonacci number to calculate and launch a `FibonacciTask` in a worker thread. `Label`s in this `TitledPane` display the `FibonacciTask`'s message property value as it's updated and the final result of the `FibonacciTask` once it's available.

- The **Without FibonacciTask** `TitledPane` provides the **Next Number** `Button` that enables the user to calculate the next Fibonacci number in sequence. `Label`s in this `TitledPane` display which Fibonacci number is being calculated (that is, `"Fibonacci of n"`) and the corresponding Fibonacci value.

Instance variables n1 and n2 (lines 20–21) contain the previous two Fibonacci numbers in the sequence and are initialized to 0 and 1, respectively. Instance variable `number` (initialized to 1 in line 22) keeps track of which Fibonacci value will be calculated and displayed next when the user clicks the **Next Number** `Button`—so the first time this `Button` is clicked, the Fibonacci of 1 is displayed.

```
 1   // Fig. 21.25: FibonacciNumbersController.java
 2   // Using a Task to perform a long calculation
 3   // outside the JavaFX application thread.
 4   import java.util.concurrent.Executors;
 5   import java.util.concurrent.ExecutorService;
 6   import javafx.event.ActionEvent;
 7   import javafx.fxml.FXML;
 8   import javafx.scene.control.Button;
 9   import javafx.scene.control.Label;
10   import javafx.scene.control.TextField;
11
12   public class FibonacciNumbersController {
13      @FXML private TextField numberTextField;
14      @FXML private Button goButton;
15      @FXML private Label messageLabel;
16      @FXML private Label fibonacciLabel;
17      @FXML private Label nthLabel;
18      @FXML private Label nthFibonacciLabel;
```

Fig. 21.25 | Using a `Task` to perform a long calculation outside the JavaFX application thread. (Part 1 of 3.)

```
19
20      private long n1 = 0; // initialize with Fibonacci of 0
21      private long n2 = 1; // initialize with Fibonacci of 1
22      private int number = 1; // current Fibonacci number to display
23
24      // starts FibonacciTask to calculate in background
25      @FXML
26      void goButtonPressed(ActionEvent event) {
27          // get Fibonacci number to calculate
28          try {
29              int input = Integer.parseInt(numberTextField.getText());
30
31              // create, configure and launch FibonacciTask
32              FibonacciTask task = new FibonacciTask(input);
33
34              // display task's messages in messageLabel
35              messageLabel.textProperty().bind(task.messageProperty());
36
37              // clear fibonacciLabel when task starts
38              task.setOnRunning((succeededEvent) -> {
39                  goButton.setDisable(true);
40                  fibonacciLabel.setText("");
41              });
42
43              // set fibonacciLabel when task completes successfully
44              task.setOnSucceeded((succeededEvent) -> {
45                  fibonacciLabel.setText(task.getValue().toString());
46                  goButton.setDisable(false);
47              });
48
49              // create ExecutorService to manage threads
50              ExecutorService executorService =
51                  Executors.newFixedThreadPool(1); // pool of one thread
52              executorService.execute(task); // start the task
53              executorService.shutdown();
54          }
55          catch (NumberFormatException e) {
56              numberTextField.setText("Enter an integer");
57              numberTextField.selectAll();
58              numberTextField.requestFocus();
59          }
60      }
61
62      // calculates next Fibonacci value
63      @FXML
64      void nextNumberButtonPressed(ActionEvent event) {
65          // display the next Fibonacci number
66          nthLabel.setText("Fibonacci of " + number + ": ");
67          nthFibonacciLabel.setText(String.valueOf(n2));
68          long temp = n1 + n2;
69          n1 = n2;
```

Fig. 21.25 | Using a Task to perform a long calculation outside the JavaFX application thread. (Part 2 of 3.)

```
70          n2 = temp;
71          ++number;
72      }
73   }
```

a) Begin calculating Fibonacci of 45 in the background

b) Calculating other Fibonacci values while Fibonacci of 45 continues calculating

c) Fibonacci of 45 calculation finishes

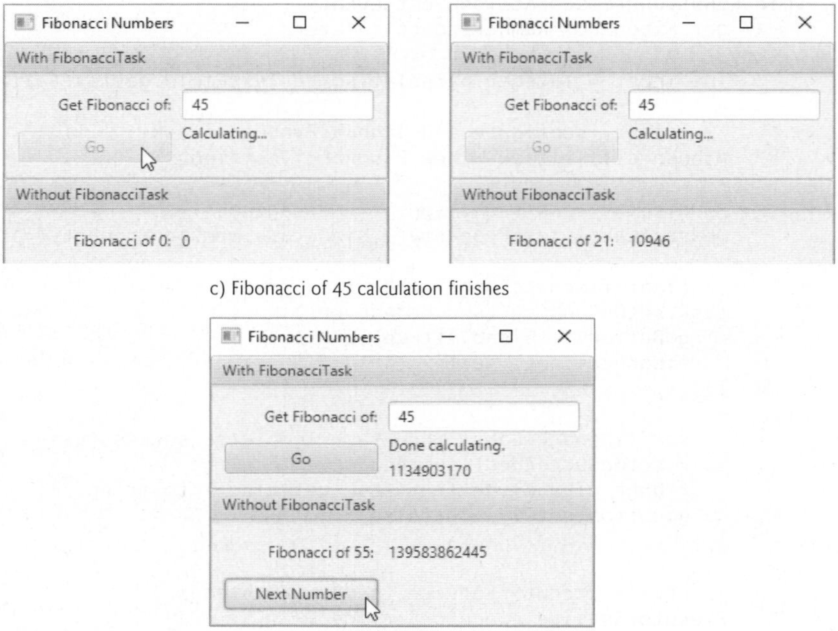

Fig. 21.25 | Using a Task to perform a long calculation outside the JavaFX application thread. (Part 3 of 3.)

Method *goButtonPressed*

When the user clicks the **Go** Button, method goButtonPressed (lines 25–60) executes. Line 29 gets the value entered in the numberTextField and attempts to parse it as an integer. If this fails, lines 56–58 prompt the user to enter an integer, select the text in the numberTextField and give the numberTextField the focus, so the user can immediately enter a new value in the numberTextField.

Line 32 creates a new FibonacciTask object, passing the constructor the user-entered value. Line 35 binds the messageLabel's text property (a StringProperty) to the FibonacciTask's message property (a ReadOnlyStringProperty)—when FibonacciTask updates this property, the messageLabel displays the new value.

All Workers transition through various states. Class Task—an implementation of Worker—enables you to register listeners for several of these states:

- Lines 38–41 use Task method **setOnRunning** to register a listener (implemented as a lambda) that's invoked when the Task enters the *running* state—that is, when the Task has been assigned a processor and begins executing its call method. In this case, we disable the goButton so the user cannot launch another Fibonacci-Task until the current one completes, then we clear the fibonacciLabel (so an old result is not displayed when a new FibonacciTask begins).

- Lines 44–47 use Task method **setOnSucceeded** to register a listener (implemented as a lambda) that's invoked when the Task enters the *succeeded* state—that is, when the Task successfully runs to completion. In this case, we call the Task's **getValue** method (from interface Worker) to obtain the result, which we convert to a String, then display in the fibonacciLabel. Then we enable the goButton so the user can start a new FibonacciTask.

You also can register listeners for a Task's *canceled*, *failed* and *scheduled* states.

Finally, lines 50–53 use an ExecutorService to launch the FibonacciTask (line 52), which schedules it for execution in a separate worker thread. Method execute does not wait for the FibonacciTask to finish executing. It returns immediately, allowing the GUI to continue processing other events while the computation is performed.

Method *nextNumberButtonPressed*

If the user clicks the **Next Number** Button, method nextNumberButtonPressed (lines 63–72) executes. Lines 66–67 update the nthLabel to show which Fibonacci number is being displayed, then update nthFibonacciLabel to display n2's value. Next, lines 68–71 add the previous two Fibonacci numbers stored in n1 and n2 to determine the next number in the sequence (which will be displayed on the next call to nextNumberButtonPressed), update n1 and n2 to their new values and increment number.

The code for these calculations is in method nextNumberButtonPressed, so they're performed on the *JavaFX application thread*. Handling such short computations in this thread does not cause the GUI to become unresponsive, as with the recursive algorithm for calculating the Fibonacci of a large number. Because the longer Fibonacci computation is performed in a separate worker thread, it's possible to click the **Next Number** Button to get the next Fibonacci number while the recursive computation is still in progress.

21.11.2 Processing Intermediate Results: Sieve of Eratosthenes

Class Task provides additional methods and properties that enable you to update a GUI with a Task's intermediate results as the Task continues executing in a Worker thread. The next example uses the following Task methods and properties:

- Method **updateProgress** updates a Task's **progress** property, which represents the percentage completion.

- Method **updateValue** updates a Task's **value** property, which holds each intermediate value.

Like updateMessage, updateProgress and updateValue are guaranteed to update the corresponding properties in the JavaFX application thread.

A *Task to Find Prime Numbers*

Figure 21.26 presents class PrimeCalculatorTask, which extends Task<Integer> to compute the first *n* prime numbers in a *worker thread*. As you'll see in the FindPrimesController (Fig. 21.28), we'll bind this Task's progress property to a ProgressBar control so the app can provide a visual indication of the portion of the Task that has been completed.

The controller also registers a listener for the value property's changes—we'll store each prime value in an ObservableList that's bound to a ListView.

```java
 1   // Fig. 21.26: PrimeCalculatorTask.java
 2   // Calculates the first n primes, publishing them as they are found.
 3   import java.util.Arrays;
 4   import javafx.concurrent.Task;
 5
 6   public class PrimeCalculatorTask extends Task<Integer> {
 7      private final boolean[] primes; // boolean array for finding primes
 8
 9      // constructor
10      public PrimeCalculatorTask(int max) {
11         primes = new boolean[max];
12         Arrays.fill(primes, true); // initialize all primes elements to true
13      }
14
15      // long-running code to be run in a worker thread
16      @Override
17      protected Integer call() {
18         int count = 0; // the number of primes found
19
20         // starting at index 2 (the first prime number), cycle through and
21         // set to false elements with indices that are multiples of i
22         for (int i = 2; i < primes.length; i++) {
23            if (isCancelled()) { // if calculation has been canceled
24               updateMessage("Cancelled");
25               return 0;
26            }
27            else {
28               try {
29                  Thread.sleep(10); // slow the thread
30               }
31               catch (InterruptedException ex) {
32                  updateMessage("Interrupted");
33                  return 0;
34               }
35
36               updateProgress(i + 1, primes.length);
37
38               if (primes[i]) { // i is prime
39                  ++count;
40                  updateMessage(String.format("Found %d primes", count));
41                  updateValue(i); // intermediate result
42
43                  // eliminate multiples of i
44                  for (int j = i + i; j < primes.length; j += i) {
45                     primes[j] = false; // i is not prime
46                  }
47               }
48            }
49         }
```

Fig. 21.26 | Calculates the first *n* primes, publishing them as they are found. (Part 1 of 2.)

```
50
51          return 0;
52      }
53  }
```

Fig. 21.26 | Calculates the first *n* primes, publishing them as they are found. (Part 2 of 2.)

Constructor
The constructor (lines 10–13) receives an integer indicating the upper limit of the prime numbers to locate, creates the `boolean` array `primes` and initializes its elements to `true`.

Sieve of Eratosthenes
`PrimeCalculatorTask` uses the `primes` array and the **Sieve of Eratosthenes** algorithm to find all primes less than `max`. The Sieve of Eratosthenes takes a list of integers and, beginning with the first prime number, filters out all multiples of that prime. It then moves to the next prime, which will be the next number that's not yet filtered out, and eliminates all of its multiples. It continues until the end of the list is reached and all nonprimes have been filtered out. Algorithmically, we begin with element 2 of the `boolean` array and set the cells corresponding to all values that are multiples of 2 to `false` to indicate that they're divisible by 2 and thus not prime. We then move to the next array element, check whether it's `true`, and if so set all of its multiples to `false` to indicate that they're divisible by the current index. When the whole array has been traversed in this way, all indices that contain `true` are prime, as they have no divisors.

Overridden Task Method `call`
In method `call` (lines 16–52), the control variable `i` for the loop (lines 22–49) represents the current index for implementing the Sieve of Eratosthenes. Line 23 calls the inherited Task method **`isCancelled`** to determine whether the user has clicked the **Cancel** button. If so, line 24 updates the Task's `message` property, then line 25 returns 0 to terminate the Task immediately.

If the calculation isn't canceled, line 29 puts the currently executing thread to sleep for 10 milliseconds. We discuss the reason for this shortly. Line 36 calls Task's `update-Progress` method to update the `progress` property in the JavaFX application thread. The percentage completion is determined by dividing the method's first argument by its second argument.

Next, line 38 tests whether the current `primes` element is `true` (and thus prime). If so, line 39 increments the `count` of prime numbers found so far and line 40 updates the Task's `message` property with a `String` containing the `count`. Then, line 41 passes the index `i` to method `updateValue`, which updates Task's `value` property in the JavaFX application thread—as you'll see in the controller, we process this *intermediate result* and display it the GUI. When the entire array has been traversed, line 51 returns 0, which we ignore in the controller, because it is not a prime number.

Because the computation progresses quickly, publishing values often, updates can pile up on the JavaFX application thread, causing it to ignore some updates. This is why for demonstration purposes we put the worker thread to *sleep* for 10 milliseconds during each iteration of the loop. The calculation is slowed just enough to allow the JavaFX application thread to keep up with the updates and enable the GUI to remain responsive.

FindPrimes GUI

Figure 21.27 shows the app's GUI (defined in FindPrimes.fxml) labeled with its **fx:id**s. Here we point out only the key elements and the event-handling methods you'll see in class FindPrimesController (Fig. 21.28). For the complete layout details, open Find-Primes.fxml in Scene Builder. The GUI's primary layout is a BorderPane containing two ToolBars in the top and bottom areas. The controller class defines two event handlers:

- getPrimesButtonPressed is called when the **Get Primes** Button is pressed—this launches the worker thread to find prime numbers less than the value input by the user.

- cancelButtonPressed is called when the **Cancel** Button is pressed—this terminates the worker thread.

We do not show the JavaFX Application subclass (located in FindPrimes.java), because it performs the same tasks you've seen previously to load the app's FXML GUI and initialize the controller.

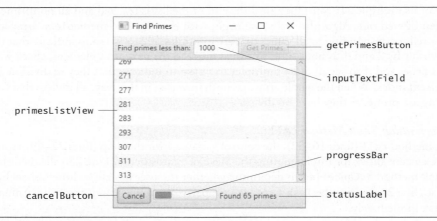

Fig. 21.27 | FindPrimes GUI with its **fx:id**s.

Class FindPrimesController

Class FindPrimesController (Fig. 21.28) creates an ObservableList<Integer> (lines 24–25) and binds it to the app's primesListView (line 30). The controller also provides the event handlers for the **Get Primes** and **Cancel** Buttons.

```
1   // Fig. 21.28: FindPrimesController.java
2   // Displaying prime numbers as they're calculated; updating a ProgressBar
3   import java.util.concurrent.Executors;
4   import java.util.concurrent.ExecutorService;
5   import javafx.collections.FXCollections;
6   import javafx.collections.ObservableList;
7   import javafx.event.ActionEvent;
```

Fig. 21.28 | Displaying prime numbers as they're calculated and updating a ProgressBar. (Part 1 of 4.)

```
8   import javafx.fxml.FXML;
9   import javafx.scene.control.Button;
10  import javafx.scene.control.Label;
11  import javafx.scene.control.ListView;
12  import javafx.scene.control.ProgressBar;
13  import javafx.scene.control.TextField;
14
15  public class FindPrimesController {
16     @FXML private TextField inputTextField;
17     @FXML private Button getPrimesButton;
18     @FXML private ListView<Integer> primesListView;
19     @FXML private Button cancelButton;
20     @FXML private ProgressBar progressBar;
21     @FXML private Label statusLabel;
22
23     // stores the list of primes received from PrimeCalculatorTask
24     private ObservableList<Integer> primes =
25        FXCollections.observableArrayList();
26     private PrimeCalculatorTask task; // finds prime numbers
27
28     // binds primesListView's items to the ObservableList primes
29     public void initialize() {
30        primesListView.setItems(primes);
31     }
32
33     // start calculating primes in the background
34     @FXML
35     void getPrimesButtonPressed(ActionEvent event) {
36        primes.clear();
37
38        // get Fibonacci number to calculate
39        try {
40           int input = Integer.parseInt(inputTextField.getText());
41           task = new PrimeCalculatorTask(input); // create task
42
43           // display task's messages in statusLabel
44           statusLabel.textProperty().bind(task.messageProperty());
45
46           // update progressBar based on task's progressProperty
47           progressBar.progressProperty().bind(task.progressProperty());
48
49           // store intermediate results in the ObservableList primes
50           task.valueProperty().addListener(
51              (observable, oldValue, newValue) -> {
52                 if (newValue != 0) { // task returns 0 when it terminates
53                    primes.add(newValue);
54                    primesListView.scrollTo(
55                       primesListView.getItems().size());
56                 }
57              });
58
```

Fig. 21.28 | Displaying prime numbers as they're calculated and updating a `ProgressBar`. (Part 2 of 4.)

```
59          // when task begins,
60          // disable getPrimesButton and enable cancelButton
61          task.setOnRunning((succeededEvent) -> {
62             getPrimesButton.setDisable(true);
63             cancelButton.setDisable(false);
64          });
65
66          // when task completes successfully,
67          // enable getPrimesButton and disable cancelButton
68          task.setOnSucceeded((succeededEvent) -> {
69             getPrimesButton.setDisable(false);
70             cancelButton.setDisable(true);
71          });
72
73          // create ExecutorService to manage threads
74          ExecutorService executorService =
75             Executors.newFixedThreadPool(1);
76          executorService.execute(task); // start the task
77          executorService.shutdown();
78       }
79       catch (NumberFormatException e) {
80          inputTextField.setText("Enter an integer");
81          inputTextField.selectAll();
82          inputTextField.requestFocus();
83       }
84    }
85
86    // cancel task when user presses Cancel Button
87    @FXML
88    void cancelButtonPressed(ActionEvent event) {
89       if (task != null) {
90          task.cancel(); // terminate the task
91          getPrimesButton.setDisable(false);
92          cancelButton.setDisable(true);
93       }
94    }
95 }
```

Fig. 21.28 | Displaying prime numbers as they're calculated and updating a ProgressBar. (Part 3 of 4.)

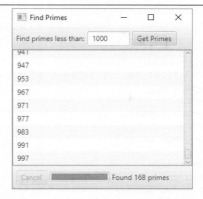

Fig. 21.28 | Displaying prime numbers as they're calculated and updating a ProgressBar. (Part 4 of 4.)

Method getPrimesButtonPressed

When the user presses the **Get Primes** Button, method getPrimesButtonPressed creates a PrimeCalculatorTask (line 41), then configures various property bindings and event listeners:

- Line 44 binds the statusLabel's text property to the task's message property to update the statusLabel automatically as new primes are found.

- Line 47 binds the progressBar's progress property to the task's progress property to update the progressBar automatically with the percentage completion.

- Lines 50–57 register a ChangeListener (using a lambda) that gets invoked each time the task's value property changes. If the newValue of the property is not 0 (indicating that the task terminated), line 53 adds the newValue to the ObservableList<Integer> named primes—recall that this is bound to the primesListView, which displays the list's elements. Next, lines 54–55 scroll the ListView to its last element so the user can see the new values being displayed.

- Lines 61–71 register listeners for the task's *running* and *succeeded* state changes. We use these to enable and disable the app's Buttons based on the task's state.

- Lines 74–77 launch the task in a separate thread.

Method cancelButtonPressed

When the user presses the **Cancel** Button, method cancelButtonPressed calls the PrimeCalculatorTask's inherited **cancel** method (line 90) to terminate the task, then enables the getPrimesButton and disables the cancelButton.

21.12 sort/parallelSort Timings with the Java SE 8 Date/Time API

In Section 7.15, we used class Arrays's static method sort to sort an array and we introduced static method parallelSort for sorting large arrays more efficiently on multicore systems. Figure 21.29 uses both methods to sort 100,000,000 element arrays of random int values so that we can demonstrate parallelSort's performance improvement of over sort on a multi-core system (we ran this example on a quad-core system).[4]

```java
1   // Fig. 21.29: SortComparison.java
2   // Comparing performance of Arrays methods sort and parallelSort.
3   import java.time.Duration;
4   import java.time.Instant;
5   import java.text.NumberFormat;
6   import java.util.Arrays;
7   import java.util.Random;
8
9   public class SortComparison {
10     public static void main(String[] args) {
11        Random random = new Random();
12
13        // create array of random ints, then copy it
14        int[] array1 = random.ints(100_000_000).toArray();
15        int[] array2 = array1.clone();
16
17        // time the sorting of array1 with Arrays method sort
18        System.out.println("Starting sort");
19        Instant sortStart = Instant.now();
20        Arrays.sort(array1);
21        Instant sortEnd = Instant.now();
22
23        // display timing results
24        long sortTime = Duration.between(sortStart, sortEnd).toMillis();
25        System.out.printf("Total time in milliseconds: %d%n%n", sortTime);
26
27        // time the sorting of array2 with Arrays method parallelSort
28        System.out.println("Starting parallelSort");
29        Instant parallelSortStart = Instant.now();
30        Arrays.parallelSort(array2);
31        Instant parallelSortEnd = Instant.now();
32
33        // display timing results
34        long parallelSortTime =
35           Duration.between(parallelSortStart, parallelSortEnd).toMillis();
36        System.out.printf("Total time in milliseconds: %d%n%n",
37           parallelSortTime);
38
39        // display time difference as a percentage
40        String percentage = NumberFormat.getPercentInstance().format(
41           (double) (sortTime - parallelSortTime) / parallelSortTime);
42        System.out.printf("sort took %s more time than parallelSort%n",
43           percentage);
44     }
45  }
```

Fig. 21.29 | Comparing performance of Arrays methods sort and parallelSort. (Part 1 of 2.)

4. To create the 100,000,000 element array in this example, we used Random rather than SecureRandom, because Random executes significantly faster.

```
Starting sort
Total time in milliseconds: 8883

Starting parallelSort
Total time in milliseconds: 2143

sort took 315% more time than parallelSort
```

Fig. 21.29 | Comparing performance of `Arrays` methods `sort` and `parallelSort`. (Part 2 of 2.)

Creating the Arrays
Line 14 uses `Random` method `ints` to create an `IntStream` of 100,000,000 random `int` values, then calls `IntStream` method `toArray` to place the values into an array. Line 15 calls method `clone` to make a copy of `array1` so that the calls to both `sort` and `parallelSort` work with the same set of values.

Timing Arrays Method sort with Date/Time API Classes Instant and Duration
Lines 19 and 21 each call class `Instant`'s `static` method **now** to get the current time before and after the call to `sort`. To determine the difference between two `Instant`s, line 24 uses class `Duration`'s `static` method **between**, which returns a `Duration` object containing the time difference. Next, we call `Duration` method **toMillis** to get the difference in milliseconds.

Timing Arrays Method parallelSort with Date/Time API Classes Instant and Duration
Lines 29–31 time the call to `Arrays` method `parallelSort`. Then, lines 34–35 calculate the difference between the `Instant`s.

Displaying the Percentage Difference Between the Sorting Times
Lines 40–41 use a `NumberFormat` (package `java.text`) to format the ratio of the sort times as a percentage. `NumberFormat` `static` method **getPercentInstance** returns a `NumberFormat` that's used to format a number as a percentage. `NumberFormat` method `format` performs the formatting. As you can see in the sample output, the `sort` method took over *300% more time* than `parallelSort` to sort the 100,000,000 random `int` values.[5]

Other Parallel Array Operations
In addition to method `parallelSort`, class `Arrays` now contains methods `parallelSetAll` and `parallelPrefix`, which perform the following tasks:

- **parallelSetAll**—Fills an array with values produced by a generator function that receives an `int` and returns a value of type `int`, `long`, `double` or the array's element type. Depending on which overload of method `parallelSetAll` is used, the generator function is an implementation of `IntUnaryOperator` (for `int` arrays), `IntToLongFunction` (for `long` arrays), `IntToDoubleFunction` (for double arrays) or `IntFunction<T>` (for arrays of any non-primitive type).

---

5. Depending on your computer's setup, number of cores, whether your operating system is running in a virtual machine, etc., you could see significantly different performance.

- **parallelPrefix**—Applies a `BinaryOperator` to the current and previous array elements and stores the result in the current element. For example, consider:

```
int[] values = {1, 2, 3, 4, 5};
Arrays.parallelPrefix(values, (x, y) -> x + y);
```

This call to `parallelPrefix` uses a `BinaryOperator` that *adds* two values. After the call completes, the array contains 1, 3, 6, 10 and 15. Similarly, the following call to `parallelPrefix`, uses a `BinaryOperator` that *multiplies* two values. After the call completes, the array contains 1, 2, 6, 24 and 120:

```
int[] values = {1, 2, 3, 4, 5};
Arrays.parallelPrefix(values, (x, y) -> x * y);
```

21.13 Java SE 8: Sequential vs. Parallel Streams

In Chapter 17, you learned about Java SE 8 lambdas and streams. We mentioned that streams are easy to *parallelize*, enabling programs to benefit from enhanced performance on multi-core systems. Using the timing capabilities introduced in Section 21.12, Fig. 21.30 demonstrates both *sequential* and *parallel* stream operations on a 50,000,000-element array of random `long` values (created at line 15) to compare the performance.

```
 1   // Fig. 21.30: StreamStatisticsComparison.java
 2   // Comparing performance of sequential and parallel stream operations.
 3   import java.time.Duration;
 4   import java.time.Instant;
 5   import java.util.Arrays;
 6   import java.util.LongSummaryStatistics;
 7   import java.util.stream.LongStream;
 8   import java.util.Random;
 9
10   public class StreamStatisticsComparison {
11      public static void main(String[] args) {
12         Random random = new Random();
13
14         // create array of random long values
15         long[] values = random.longs(50_000_000, 1, 1001).toArray();
16
17         // perform calculations separately
18         Instant separateStart = Instant.now();
19         long count = Arrays.stream(values).count();
20         long sum = Arrays.stream(values).sum();
21         long min = Arrays.stream(values).min().getAsLong();
22         long max = Arrays.stream(values).max().getAsLong();
23         double average = Arrays.stream(values).average().getAsDouble();
24         Instant separateEnd = Instant.now();
25
26         // display results
27         System.out.println("Calculations performed separately");
28         System.out.printf("   count: %,d%n", count);
```

Fig. 21.30 | Comparing performance of sequential and parallel stream operations. (Part 1 of 3.)

```
29              System.out.printf("          sum: %,d%n", sum);
30              System.out.printf("          min: %,d%n", min);
31              System.out.printf("          max: %,d%n", max);
32              System.out.printf("      average: %f%n", average);
33              System.out.printf("Total time in milliseconds: %d%n%n",
34                  Duration.between(separateStart, separateEnd).toMillis());
35
36              // time summaryStatistics operation with sequential stream
37              LongStream stream1 = Arrays.stream(values);
38              System.out.println("Calculating statistics on sequential stream");
39              Instant sequentialStart = Instant.now();
40              LongSummaryStatistics results1 = stream1.summaryStatistics();
41              Instant sequentialEnd = Instant.now();
42
43              // display results
44              displayStatistics(results1);
45              System.out.printf("Total time in milliseconds: %d%n%n",
46                  Duration.between(sequentialStart, sequentialEnd).toMillis());
47
48              // time sum operation with parallel stream
49              LongStream stream2 = Arrays.stream(values).parallel();
50              System.out.println("Calculating statistics on parallel stream");
51              Instant parallelStart = Instant.now();
52              LongSummaryStatistics results2 = stream2.summaryStatistics();
53              Instant parallelEnd = Instant.now();
54
55              // display results
56              displayStatistics(results1);
57              System.out.printf("Total time in milliseconds: %d%n%n",
58                  Duration.between(parallelStart, parallelEnd).toMillis());
59          }
60
61      // display's LongSummaryStatistics values
62      private static void displayStatistics(LongSummaryStatistics stats) {
63              System.out.println("Statistics");
64              System.out.printf("        count: %,d%n", stats.getCount());
65              System.out.printf("          sum: %,d%n", stats.getSum());
66              System.out.printf("          min: %,d%n", stats.getMin());
67              System.out.printf("          max: %,d%n", stats.getMax());
68              System.out.printf("      average: %f%n", stats.getAverage());
69          }
70  }
```

```
Calculations performed separately
    count: 50,000,000
      sum: 25,025,212,218
      min: 1
      max: 1,000
  average: 500.504244
Total time in milliseconds: 710
```

Fig. 21.30 | Comparing performance of sequential and parallel stream operations. (Part 2 of 3.)

```
Calculating statistics on sequential stream
Statistics
    count: 50,000,000
      sum: 25,025,212,218
      min: 1
      max: 1,000
  average: 500.504244
Total time in milliseconds: 305

Calculating statistics on parallel stream
Statistics
    count: 50,000,000
      sum: 25,025,212,218
      min: 1
      max: 1,000
  average: 500.504244
Total time in milliseconds: 143
```

Fig. 21.30 | Comparing performance of sequential and parallel stream operations. (Part 3 of 3.)

Performing Stream Operations with Separate Passes of a Sequential Stream
Section 17.7 demonstrated various numerical operations on IntStreams. Lines 18–24 of Fig. 21.30 perform and time the count, sum, min, max and average stream operations each performed individually on a LongStream returned by Arrays method stream. Lines 27–34 then display the results and the total time required to perform all five operations.

Performing Stream Operations with a Single Pass of a Sequential Stream
Lines 37–46 demonstrate the performance improvement you get by using LongStream method summaryStatistics to determine the count, sum, minimum value, maximum value and average in one pass of a *sequential* LongStream—all streams are sequential by default. This operation took approximately 43% of the time required to perform the five operations separately.

Performing Stream Operations with a Single Pass of a Parallel Stream
Lines 49–50 demonstrate the performance improvement you get by using LongStream method summaryStatistics on a *parallel* LongStream. To obtain a parallel stream that can take advantage of multi-core processors, simply invoke method parallel on an existing stream. As you can see from the sample output, performing the operations on a parallel stream decreased the total time required even further—taking approximately 47% of the calculation time for the sequential LongStream and just 20% of the time required to perform the five operations separately.

21.14 (Advanced) Interfaces Callable and Future

Interface Runnable provides only the most basic functionality for multithreaded programming. In fact, this interface has limitations. Suppose a Runnable is performing a long calculation and the application wants to retrieve the result of that calculation. The run method cannot return a value, so *shared mutable data* would be required to pass the value back to the calling thread. As you now know, this would require thread synchronization. The **Callable** interface (of package java.util.concurrent) fixes this limitation. The interface declares a single method named **call** which returns a value representing the result of the `Callable`'s task—such as the result of a long-running calculation.

An application that creates a `Callable` likely wants to run it concurrently with other `Runnable`s and `Callable`s. `ExecutorService` method **submit** executes its `Callable` argument and returns an object of type **Future** (of package java.util.concurrent), which represents the `Callable`'s future result. The `Future` interface **get** method *blocks* the calling thread, and waits for the `Callable` to complete and return its result. The interface also provides methods that enable you to cancel a `Callable`'s execution, determine whether the `Callable` was canceled and determine whether the `Callable` completed its task.

Executing Aysnchronous Tasks with `CompletableFuture`

Java SE 8 introduced class **CompletableFuture** (package java.util.concurrent), which implements the `Future` interface and enables you to *asynchronously* execute `Runnable`s that perform tasks or `Supplier`s that return values. Interface **Supplier**, like interface `Callable`, is a functional interface with a single method (in this case, get) that receives no arguments and returns a result. Class `CompletableFuture` provides many additional capabilities for advanced programmers, such as creating `CompletableFuture`s without executing them immediately, composing one or more `CompletableFuture`s so that you can wait for any or all of them to complete, executing code after a `CompletableFuture` completes and more.

Figure 21.31 performs two long-running calculations sequentially, then performs them again asynchronously using `CompletableFuture`s to demonstrate the performance improvement from asynchronous execution on a multi-core system. For demonstration purposes, our long-running calculation is performed by a recursive fibonacci method (lines 69–76; similar to the one presented in Section 18.5). For larger Fibonacci values, the recursive implementation can require *significant* computation time—in practice, it's much faster to calculate Fibonacci values using a loop.

```java
1   // Fig. 21.31: FibonacciDemo.java
2   // Fibonacci calculations performed synchronously and asynchronously
3   import java.time.Duration;
4   import java.text.NumberFormat;
5   import java.time.Instant;
6   import java.util.concurrent.CompletableFuture;
7   import java.util.concurrent.ExecutionException;
8
9   // class that stores two Instants in time
10  class TimeData {
11      public Instant start;
12      public Instant end;
13
14      // return total time in seconds
15      public double timeInSeconds() {
16          return Duration.between(start, end).toMillis() / 1000.0;
17      }
18  }
19
```

Fig. 21.31 | Fibonacci calculations performed synchronously and asynchronously. (Part 1 of 3.)

```
20  public class FibonacciDemo {
21      public static void main(String[] args)
22          throws InterruptedException, ExecutionException {
23
24          // perform synchronous fibonacci(45) and fibonacci(44) calculations
25          System.out.println("Synchronous Long Running Calculations");
26          TimeData synchronousResult1 = startFibonacci(45);
27          TimeData synchronousResult2 = startFibonacci(44);
28          double synchronousTime =
29              calculateTime(synchronousResult1, synchronousResult2);
30          System.out.printf(
31              "   Total calculation time = %.3f seconds%n", synchronousTime);
32
33          // perform asynchronous fibonacci(45) and fibonacci(44) calculations
34          System.out.printf("%nAsynchronous Long Running Calculations%n");
35          CompletableFuture<TimeData> futureResult1 =
36              CompletableFuture.supplyAsync(() -> startFibonacci(45));
37          CompletableFuture<TimeData> futureResult2 =
38              CompletableFuture.supplyAsync(() -> startFibonacci(44));
39
40          // wait for results from the asynchronous operations
41          TimeData asynchronousResult1 = futureResult1.get();
42          TimeData asynchronousResult2 = futureResult2.get();
43          double asynchronousTime =
44              calculateTime(asynchronousResult1, asynchronousResult2);
45          System.out.printf(
46              "   Total calculation time = %.3f seconds%n", asynchronousTime);
47
48          // display time difference as a percentage
49          String percentage = NumberFormat.getPercentInstance().format(
50              (synchronousTime - asynchronousTime) / asynchronousTime);
51          System.out.printf("%nSynchronous calculations took %s" +
52              " more time than the asynchronous ones%n", percentage);
53      }
54
55      // executes function fibonacci asynchronously
56      private static TimeData startFibonacci(int n) {
57          // create a TimeData object to store times
58          TimeData timeData = new TimeData();
59
60          System.out.printf("  Calculating fibonacci(%d)%n", n);
61          timeData.start = Instant.now();
62          long fibonacciValue = fibonacci(n);
63          timeData.end = Instant.now();
64          displayResult(n, fibonacciValue, timeData);
65          return timeData;
66      }
67
68      // recursive method fibonacci; calculates nth Fibonacci number
69      private static long fibonacci(long n) {
70          if (n == 0 || n == 1) {
71              return n;
72          }
```

Fig. 21.31 | Fibonacci calculations performed synchronously and asynchronously. (Part 2 of 3.)

```
73          else {
74             return fibonacci(n - 1) + fibonacci(n - 2);
75          }
76       }
77
78       // display fibonacci calculation result and total calculation time
79       private static void displayResult(
80          int n, long value, TimeData timeData) {
81
82          System.out.printf("  fibonacci(%d) = %d%n", n, value);
83          System.out.printf(
84             "  Calculation time for fibonacci(%d) = %.3f seconds%n",
85             n, timeData.timeInSeconds());
86       }
87
88       // display fibonacci calculation result and total calculation time
89       private static double calculateTime(
90          TimeData result1, TimeData result2) {
91
92          TimeData bothThreads = new TimeData();
93
94          // determine earlier start time
95          bothThreads.start = result1.start.compareTo(result2.start) < 0 ?
96             result1.start : result2.start;
97
98          // determine later end time
99          bothThreads.end = result1.end.compareTo(result2.end) > 0 ?
100            result1.end : result2.end;
101
102         return bothThreads.timeInSeconds();
103      }
104 }
```

```
Synchronous Long Running Calculations
  Calculating fibonacci(45)
  fibonacci(45) = 1134903170
  Calculation time for fibonacci(45) = 4.395 seconds
  Calculating fibonacci(44)
  fibonacci(44) = 701408733
  Calculation time for fibonacci(44) = 2.722 seconds
  Total calculation time = 7.122 seconds

Asynchronous Long Running Calculations
  Calculating fibonacci(45)
  Calculating fibonacci(44)
  fibonacci(44) = 701408733
  Calculation time for fibonacci(44) = 2.707 seconds
  fibonacci(45) = 1134903170
  Calculation time for fibonacci(45) = 4.403 seconds
  Total calculation time = 4.403 seconds

Synchronous calculations took 62% more time than the asynchronous ones
```

Fig. 21.31 | Fibonacci calculations performed synchronously and asynchronously. (Part 3 of 3.)

Class *TimeData*

Class TimeData (lines 10–18) stores two Instants representing the start and end time of a task, and provides method timeInSeconds to calculate the total time between them. We use TimeData objects throughout this example to calculate the time required to perform Fibonacci calculations.

Method *startFibonacci* *for Performing and Timing Fibonacci Calculations*

Method startFibonacci (lines 56–66) is called several times in main (lines 26, 27, 36 and 38) to initiate Fibonacci calculations and to calculate the time each calculation requires. The method receives the Fibonacci number to calculate and performs the following tasks:

- Line 58 creates a TimeData object to store the calculation's start and end times.
- Line 60 displays the Fibonacci number to be calculated.
- Line 61 stores the current time before method fibonacci is called.
- Line 62 calls method fibonacci to perform the calculation.
- Line 63 stores the current time after the call to fibonacci completes.
- Line 64 displays the result and the total time required for the calculation.
- Line 65 returns the TimeData object for use in method main.

Performing Fibonacci Calculations Synchronously

Method main first demonstrates synchronous Fibonacci calculations. Line 26 calls start-Fibonacci(45) to initiate the fibonacci(45) calculation and store the TimeData object containing the calculation's start and end times. When this call completes, line 27 calls startFibonacci(44) to initiate the fibonacci(44) calculation and store its TimeData. Next, lines 28–29 pass both TimeData objects to method calculateTime (lines 89–103), which returns the total calculation time in seconds. Lines 30–31 display the total calculation time for the synchronous Fibonacci calculations.

Performing Fibonacci Calculations Asynchronously

Lines 35–38 in main launch the asynchronous Fibonacci calculations in separate threads. CompletableFuture static method **supplyAsync** executes an asynchronous task that returns a value. The method receives as its argument an object that implements interface Supplier—in this case, we use lambdas with empty parameter lists to invoke start-Fibonacci(45) (line 36) and startFibonacci(44) (line 38). The compiler infers that supplyAsync returns a CompletableFuture<TimeData> because method startFibonacci returns type TimeData. Class CompletableFuture also provides static method **runAsync** to execute an asynchronous task that does not return a result—this method receives a Runnable.

Getting the Asynchronous Calculations' Results

Class CompletableFuture implements interface Future, so we can obtain the asynchronous tasks' results by calling Future method get (lines 41–42). These are *blocking* calls—they cause the main thread to *wait* until the asynchronous tasks complete and return their results. In our case, the results are TimeData objects. Once both tasks return, lines 43–44 pass both TimeData objects to method calculateTime (lines 89–103) to get the total calculation time in seconds. Then, lines 45–46 display the total calculation time for the asynchronous Fibonacci calculations. Finally, lines 49–52 calculate and display the percentage difference in execution time for the synchronous and asynchronous calculations.

Program Outputs
On our quad-core computer, the synchronous calculations took a total of 7.122 seconds. Though the individual asynchronous calculations took approximately the same amount of time as the corresponding synchronous calculations, the total time for the asynchronous calculations was only 4.403 seconds, because the two calculations were actually performed *in parallel*. As you can see in the output, the synchronous calculations took 62% more time to complete, so asynchronous execution provided a significant performance improvement.

21.15 (Advanced) Fork/Join Framework

Java's concurrency APIs include the Fork/Join framework, which helps programmers parallelize algorithms. The framework is beyond the scope of this book. Experts tell us that most Java programmers will nevertheless benefit by the Fork/Join framework's use "behind the scenes" in the Java API and other third-party libraries. For example, the parallel capabilities of Java SE 8 streams are implemented using this framework.

8

The Fork/Join framework is particularly well suited to divide-and-conquer-style algorithms, such as the recursive merge sort. Recall that the recursive merge-sort algorithm sorts an array by *splitting* it into two equal-sized subarrays, *sorting* each subarray, then *merging* them into one larger array. Each subarray is sorted by performing the same algorithm on the subarray. For algorithms like merge sort, the Fork/Join framework can be used to create concurrent tasks so that they can be distributed across multiple processors and be truly performed in parallel—the details of assigning the tasks to different processors are handled for you by the framework. To learn more about Fork/Join, see the following Oracle tutorial and other online tutorials:

```
https://docs.oracle.com/javase/tutorial/essential/concurrency/
    forkjoin.html
```

21.16 Wrap-Up

In this chapter, we presented Java's concurrency capabilities for enhancing application performance on multi-core systems. You learned the differences between concurrent and parallel execution. We discussed that Java makes concurrency available to you through multithreading. You also learned that the JVM itself creates threads to run a program, and that it also can create threads to perform housekeeping tasks such as garbage collection.

We discussed the life cycle of a thread and the states that a thread may occupy during its lifetime. Next, we presented the interface Runnable, which is used to specify a task that can execute concurrently with other tasks. This interface's run method is invoked by the thread executing the task. Then we showed how to use the Executor interface to manage the execution of Runnable objects via thread pools, which can reuse existing threads to eliminate the overhead of creating a new thread for each task and can improve performance by optimizing the number of threads to ensure that the processor stays busy.

You learned that when multiple threads share an object and one or more of them modify that object, indeterminate results may occur unless access to the shared object is managed properly. We showed you how to solve this problem via thread synchronization, which coordinates access to shared mutable data by multiple concurrent threads. You learned several techniques for performing synchronization—first with the built-in class ArrayBlockingQueue (which handles *all* the synchronization details for you), then with Java's built-in monitors and the synchronized keyword, and finally with interfaces Lock and Condition.

We discussed the fact that JavaFX GUIs are not thread safe, so all interactions with and modifications to the GUI must be performed in the JavaFX application thread. We also discussed the problems associated with performing long-running calculations in that thread. Then we showed how you can use class Task to perform long-running calculations in worker threads. You learned how to use a Task's properties to display the results of a Task in a GUI when the calculation completed and how to display intermediate results while the calculation was still in process.

We revisited the Arrays class's sort and parallelSort methods to demonstrate the benefit of using a parallel sorting algorithm on a multi-core processor. We used the Java SE 8 Date/Time API's Instant and Duration classes to time the sort operations.

You learned that Java SE 8 streams are easy to parallelize, enabling programs to benefit from enhanced performance on multi-core systems, and that to obtain a parallel stream, you simply invoke method parallel on an existing stream.

We discussed the Callable and Future interfaces, which enable you to execute tasks that return results and to obtain those results, respectively. We then presented an example of performing long-running tasks synchronously and asynchronously using Java SE 8's CompletableFuture class. In the next chapter, we introduce database-application development with Java's JDBC API.

Accessing Databases with JDBC

Objectives

In this chapter you'll:

- Learn relational database concepts.
- Use Structured Query Language (SQL) to retrieve data from and manipulate data in a database.
- Use the JDBC™ API's classes and interfaces to manipulate databases.
- Use JDBC's automatic JDBC driver discovery.
- Embed a Swing GUI control into a JavaFX scene graph via a `SwingNode`.
- Use Swing's `JTable` and a `TableModel` to populate a `JTable` with a `ResultSet`'s data.
- Sort and filter a `JTable`'s contents.
- Use the `RowSet` interface from package `javax.sql` to simplify connecting to and interacting with databases.
- Create precompiled SQL statements with parameters via `PreparedStatement`s.
- Learn how transaction processing makes database applications more robust.

22.1 Introduction

A **database** is an organized collection of data. There are many different strategies for organizing data to facilitate easy access and manipulation. A **database management system** (**DBMS**) provides mechanisms for storing, organizing, retrieving and modifying data for many users. Database management systems allow for the access and storage of data without concern for the internal representation of data.

Structured Query Language
Today's most popular database systems are *relational databases* (Section 22.2). A language called **SQL**—pronounced "sequel," or as its individual letters—is the international standard language used almost universally with relational databases to perform **queries** (i.e., to request information that satisfies given criteria) and to manipulate data. [*Note:* As you learn about SQL, you'll see some authors writing "a SQL statement" (which assumes the pronunciation "sequel") and others writing "an SQL statement" (which assumes that the individual letters are pronounced). In this book we pronounce SQL as "sequel."]

Popular Relational Database Management Systems
Some popular proprietary **relational database management systems** (**RDBMSs**) are Microsoft SQL Server, Oracle, Sybase and IBM DB2, PostgreSQL, MariaDB and MySQL are popular *open-source* DBMSs that can be downloaded and used *freely* by anyone. JDK 8

comes with a pure-Java RDBMS called Java DB—the Oracle-branded version of Apache Derby™.

JDBC

Java programs interact with databases using the **Java Database Connectivity (JDBC™) API**. A **JDBC driver** enables Java applications to connect to a database in a particular DBMS and allows you to manipulate that database using the JDBC API.

> **Software Engineering Observation 22.1**
>
> *The JDBC API is portable—the same code can manipulate databases in various RDBMSs.*

Most popular database management systems provide JDBC drivers. In this chapter, we introduce JDBC and use it to manipulate Java DB databases. The techniques we demonstrate here can be used to manipulate other databases that have JDBC drivers. If not, third-party vendors provide JDBC drivers for many DBMSs.

Java Persistence API (JPA)

In Chapter 24, we introduce Java Persistence API (JPA). In that chapter, you'll learn how to autogenerate Java classes that represent the tables in a database and the relationships between them—known as object-relational mapping—then use objects of those classes to interact with a database. As you'll see, storing data in and retrieving data from a database will be handled for you—many of the JDBC techniques you learn in this chapter typically are hidden from you by JPA.

JDK 9 Note

As of JDK 9, Oracle no longer bundles Java DB with the JDK. If you're using JDK 9 with this chapter, follow the download and installation instructions for Apache Derby at

```
http://db.apache.org/derby/papers/DerbyTut/
        install_software.html#derby
```

before proceeding with this chapter's examples.

22.2 Relational Databases

A **relational database** is a logical representation of data that allows the data to be accessed without consideration of its physical structure. A relational database stores data in **tables**. Figure 22.1 illustrates a sample table that might be used in a personnel system. The table name is Employee, and its primary purpose is to store the attributes of employees. Tables are composed of **rows**, each describing a single entity—in Fig. 22.1, an employee. Rows are composed of **columns** in which values are stored. This table consists of six rows. The Number column of each row is the table's **primary key**—a column (or group of columns) with a value that is *unique* for each row. This guarantees that each row can be identified by its primary key. Good examples of primary-key columns are a social security number, an employee ID number and a part number in an inventory system, as values in each of these columns are guaranteed to be unique. The rows in Fig. 22.1 are displayed in order by primary key. In this case, the rows are listed in ascending order by primary key, but they could be listed in descending order or in no particular order at all.

Fig. 22.1 | Employee table sample data.

Each column represents a different data attribute. Rows are unique (by primary key) within a table, but particular column values may be duplicated between rows. For example, three different rows in the Employee table's Department column contain number 413.

Selecting Data Subsets

Different users of a database are often interested in different data and different relationships among the data. Most users require only subsets of the rows and columns. Queries specify which subsets of the data to select from a table. You use SQL to define queries. For example, you might select data from the Employee table to create a result that shows where each department is located, presenting the data sorted in increasing order by department number. This result is shown in Fig. 22.2. SQL is discussed in Section 22.4.

Department	Location
413	New Jersey
611	Orlando
642	Los Angeles

Fig. 22.2 | Distinct Department and Location data from the Employees table.

22.3 A books Database

We introduce relational databases in the context of this chapter's books database, which you'll use in several examples. Before we discuss SQL, we discuss the *tables* of the books database. We use this database to introduce various database concepts, including how to use SQL to obtain information from the database and to manipulate the data. We provide a script to create the database. You can find the script in the examples directory for this chapter. Section 22.5 explains how to use this script.

Authors Table

The database consists of three tables: Authors, AuthorISBN and Titles. The Authors table (described in Fig. 22.3) consists of three columns that maintain each author's unique ID number, first name and last name. Figure 22.4 contains sample data from the Authors table.

Column	Description
AuthorID	Author's ID number in the database. In the books database, this integer column is defined as **autoincremented**—for each row inserted in this table, the AuthorID value is increased by 1 automatically to ensure that each row has a unique AuthorID. This column represents the table's primary key. Autoincremented columns are so-called identity columns. The SQL script we provide for this database uses the SQL **IDENTITY** keyword to mark the AuthorID column as an identity column. For more information on using the IDENTITY keyword and creating databases, see the Java DB Developer's Guide at http://docs.oracle.com/javadb/10.10.1.2/devguide/derbydev.pdf.
FirstName	Author's first name (a string).
LastName	Author's last name (a string).

Fig. 22.3 | Authors table from the books database.

AuthorID	FirstName	LastName
1	Paul	Deitel
2	Harvey	Deitel
3	Abbey	Deitel
4	Dan	Quirk
5	Michael	Morgano

Fig. 22.4 | Sample data from the Authors table.

Titles *Table*

The Titles table described in Fig. 22.5 consists of four columns that maintain information about each book in the database, including its ISBN, title, edition number and copyright year. Figure 22.6 contains the data from the Titles table.

Column	Description
ISBN	ISBN of the book (a string). The table's primary key. ISBN is an abbreviation for "International Standard Book Number"—a numbering scheme that publishers use to give every book a unique identification number.
Title	Title of the book (a string).
EditionNumber	Edition number of the book (an integer).
Copyright	Copyright year of the book (a string).

Fig. 22.5 | Titles table from the books database.

ISBN	Title	EditionNumber	Copyright
0132151006	Internet & World Wide Web How to Program	5	2012
0133807800	Java How to Program	10	2015
0132575655	Java How to Program, Late Objects Version	10	2015
013299044X	C How to Program	7	2013
0132990601	Simply Visual Basic 2010	4	2013
0133406954	Visual Basic 2012 How to Program	6	2014
0133379337	Visual C# 2012 How to Program	5	2014
0136151574	Visual C++ 2008 How to Program	2	2008
0133378713	C++ How to Program	9	2014
0133570924	Android How to Program	2	2015
0133570924	Android for Programmers: An App-Driven Approach, Volume 1	2	2014
0132121360	Android for Programmers: An App-Driven Approach	1	2012

Fig. 22.6 | Sample data from the `Titles` table of the `books` database.

AuthorISBN *Table*

The `AuthorISBN` table (described in Fig. 22.7) consists of two columns that maintain ISBNs for each book and their corresponding authors' ID numbers. This table associates authors with their books. The `AuthorID` column is a **foreign key**—a column in this table that matches the primary-key column in another table (that is, `AuthorID` in the `Authors` table). The `ISBN` column is also a foreign key—it matches the primary-key column (that is, `ISBN`) in the `Titles` table. A database might consist of many tables. A goal when designing a database is to *minimize* the amount of *duplicated* data among the database's tables. Foreign keys, which are specified when a database table is created in the database, link the data in *multiple* tables. Together the `AuthorID` and `ISBN` columns in this table form a *composite primary key*. Every row in this table *uniquely* matches *one* author to *one* book's ISBN. Figure 22.8 contains the data from the `AuthorISBN` table of the `books` database. [*Note:* To save space, we split the table into two columns, each containing the `AuthorID` and `ISBN` columns.]

Column	Description
AuthorID	The author's ID number, a foreign key to the `Authors` table.
ISBN	The ISBN for a book, a foreign key to the `Titles` table.

Fig. 22.7 | `AuthorISBN` table from the `books` database.

Every foreign-key value must appear as another table's primary-key value so the DBMS can ensure that the foreign key value is valid—this is known as the **Rule of Referential Integrity**. For example, the DBMS ensures that the `AuthorID` value for a particular

AuthorID	ISBN	AuthorID	ISBN
1	0132151006	2	0133379337
2	0132151006	1	0136151574
3	0132151006	2	0136151574
1	0133807800	4	0136151574
2	0133807800	1	0133378713
1	0132575655	2	0133378713
2	0132575655	1	0133764036
1	013299044X	2	0133764036
2	013299044X	3	0133764036
1	0132990601	1	0133570924
2	0132990601	2	0133570924
3	0132990601	3	0133570924
1	0133406954	1	0132121360
2	0133406954	2	0132121360
3	0133406954	3	0132121360
1	0133379337	5	0132121360

Fig. 22.8 | Sample data from the AuthorISBN table of books.

row of the AuthorISBN table is valid by checking that there is a row in the Authors table with that AuthorID as the primary key.

Foreign keys also allow *related* data in *multiple* tables to be *selected* from those tables—this is known as **joining** the data. There is a **one-to-many relationship** between a primary key and a corresponding foreign key (for example, one author can write many books and one book can be written by many authors). This means that a foreign key can appear *many* times in its own table but only *once* (as the primary key) in another table. For example, the ISBN 0132151006 can appear in several rows of AuthorISBN (because this book has several authors) but only once in Titles, where ISBN is the primary key.

Entity-Relationship (ER) Diagram

There's a one-to-many relationship between a primary key and a corresponding foreign key (e.g., one author can write many books). A foreign key can appear many times in its own table, but only once (as the primary key) in another table. Figure 22.9 is an **entity-relationship (ER) diagram** for the books database. This diagram shows the *database tables* and the *relationships* among them. The first compartment in each box contains the table's name, and the remaining compartments contain the table's columns. The names in italic are primary keys. *A table's primary key uniquely identifies each row in the table.* Every row must have a primary-key value, and that value must be unique in the table. This is known as the **Rule of Entity Integrity**. Again, for the AuthorISBN table, the primary key is the combination of both columns—this is known as a composite primary key.

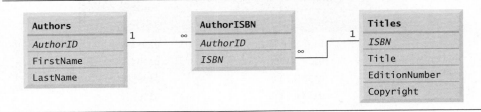

Fig. 22.9 | Table relationships in the books database.

The connecting lines represent *relationships* among the tables. Consider the line between the Authors and AuthorISBN tables. On the Authors end, there's a 1, and on the AuthorISBN end, an infinity symbol (∞). This indicates a *one-to-many relationship*—for *each* author in the Authors table, there can be an *arbitrary number* of ISBNs for books written by that author in the AuthorISBN table (that is, an author can write *any* number of books). The relationship line links the AuthorID column in the Authors table (where AuthorID is the primary key) to the AuthorID column in the AuthorISBN table (where AuthorID is a foreign key)—the line between the tables links the primary key to the matching foreign key.

The line between the Titles and AuthorISBN tables illustrates a *one-to-many relationship*—one book can be written by many authors. Note that the line between the tables links the primary key ISBN in table Titles to the corresponding foreign key in table AuthorISBN. The relationships in Fig. 22.9 illustrate that the sole purpose of the AuthorISBN table is to provide a **many-to-many relationship** between the Authors and Titles tables—an author can write *many* books, and a book can have *many* authors.

22.4 SQL

We now discuss SQL in the context of our books database. You'll be able to use the SQL discussed here in the examples later in the chapter. The next several subsections demonstrate SQL queries and statements using the SQL keywords in Fig. 22.10. Other SQL keywords are beyond this text's scope.

SQL keyword	Description
SELECT	Retrieves data from one or more tables.
FROM	Tables involved in the query. Required in every SELECT.
WHERE	Criteria for selection that determine the rows to be retrieved, deleted or updated. Optional in a SQL statement.
GROUP BY	Criteria for grouping rows. Optional in a SELECT query.
ORDER BY	Criteria for ordering rows. Optional in a SELECT query.
INNER JOIN	Merge rows from multiple tables.
INSERT	Insert rows into a specified table.
UPDATE	Update rows in a specified table.
DELETE	Delete rows from a specified table.

Fig. 22.10 | SQL query keywords.

22.4.1 Basic SELECT Query

Let's consider several SQL queries that extract information from database books. A SQL query "selects" rows and columns from one or more tables in a database. Such selections are performed by queries with the **SELECT** keyword. The basic form of a SELECT query is

> **SELECT** * **FROM** *tableName*

in which the **asterisk (*)** *wildcard character* indicates that all columns from the *tableName* table should be retrieved. For example, to retrieve all the data in the Authors table, use

> **SELECT** * **FROM** Authors

Most programs do not require all the data in a table. To retrieve only specific columns, replace the * with a comma-separated list of column names. For example, to retrieve only the columns AuthorID and LastName for all rows in the Authors table, use the query

> **SELECT** AuthorID, LastName **FROM** Authors

This query returns the data listed in Fig. 22.11.

AuthorID	LastName	AuthorID	LastName
1	Deitel	4	Quirk
2	Deitel	5	Morgano
3	Deitel		

Fig. 22.11 | Sample AuthorID and LastName data from the Authors table.

Software Engineering Observation 22.2

In general, you process results by knowing in advance the column order—for example, selecting AuthorID and LastName from Authors ensures that the columns will appear in the result in that exact order. Selecting columns by name avoids returning unneeded columns and protects against changes in the actual database column order. Programs can then process result columns by specifying the column number in the result (starting from number 1 for the first column).

Common Programming Error 22.1

If you assume that the columns are always returned in the same order from a query that uses the asterisk (*), the program may process the results incorrectly. If the column order in the table(s) changes or if additional columns are added at a later time, the order of the columns in the result will change accordingly.

22.4.2 WHERE Clause

In most cases, it's necessary to locate rows in a database that satisfy certain **selection criteria**. Only rows that satisfy the selection criteria (formally called **predicates**) are selected. SQL uses the optional **WHERE clause** in a query to specify the selection criteria for the query. The basic form of a query with selection criteria is

> **SELECT** *columnName1*, *columnName2*, ... **FROM** *tableName* **WHERE** *criteria*

For example, to select the `Title`, `EditionNumber` and `Copyright` columns from table `Titles` for which the `Copyright` date is greater than 2013, use the query

```
SELECT Title, EditionNumber, Copyright
   FROM Titles
   WHERE Copyright > '2013'
```

Strings in SQL are delimited by single (') rather than double (") quotes. Figure 22.12 shows the result of the preceding query.

Title	EditionNumber	Copyright
Java How to Program	10	2015
Java How to Program, Late Objects Version	10	2015
Visual Basic 2012 How to Program	6	2014
Visual C# 2012 How to Program	5	2014
C++ How to Program	9	2014
Android How to Program	2	2015
Android for Programmers: An App-Driven Approach, Volume 1	2	2014

Fig. 22.12 | Sampling of titles with copyrights after 2013 from table `Titles`.

Pattern Matching: Zero or More Characters
The `WHERE` clause criteria can contain the operators <, >, <=, >=, =, <> (not equal) and `LIKE`. Operator **LIKE** is used for **pattern matching** with wildcard characters **percent (%)** and **underscore (_)**. Pattern matching allows SQL to search for strings that match a given pattern.

A pattern that contains a percent character (%) searches for strings that have zero or more characters at the percent character's position in the pattern. For example, the next query locates the rows of all the authors whose last name starts with the letter D:

```
SELECT AuthorID, FirstName, LastName
   FROM Authors
   WHERE LastName LIKE 'D%'
```

This query selects the two rows shown in Fig. 22.13—three of the five authors have a last name starting with the letter D (followed by zero or more characters). The % symbol in the `WHERE` clause's `LIKE` pattern indicates that any number of characters can appear after the letter D in the `LastName`. The pattern string is surrounded by single-quote characters.

AuthorID	FirstName	LastName
1	Paul	Deitel
2	Harvey	Deitel
3	Abbey	Deitel

Fig. 22.13 | Authors whose last name starts with D from the `Authors` table.

Portability Tip 22.1

See the documentation for your database system to determine whether SQL is case sensitive on your system and to determine the syntax for SQL keywords, such as the LIKE *operator.*

Pattern Matching: Any Character

An underscore (_) in the pattern string indicates a single wildcard character at that position in the pattern. For example, the following query locates the rows of all the authors whose last names start with any character (specified by _), followed by the letter o, followed by any number of additional characters (specified by %):

```
SELECT AuthorID, FirstName, LastName
   FROM Authors
   WHERE LastName LIKE '_o%'
```

The preceding query produces the row shown in Fig. 22.14, because only one author in our database has a last name that contains the letter o as its second letter.

AuthorID	FirstName	LastName
5	Michael	Morgano

Fig. 22.14 | The only author from the Authors table whose last name contains o as the second letter.

22.4.3 ORDER BY Clause

The rows in the result of a query can be sorted into ascending or descending order by using the optional **ORDER BY clause**. The basic form of a query with an ORDER BY clause is

```
SELECT columnName1, columnName2, ... FROM tableName ORDER BY column ASC
SELECT columnName1, columnName2, ... FROM tableName ORDER BY column DESC
```

where ASC specifies ascending order (lowest to highest), DESC specifies descending order (highest to lowest) and *column* specifies the column on which the sort is based. For example, to obtain the list of authors in ascending order by last name (Fig. 22.15), use the query

```
SELECT AuthorID, FirstName, LastName
   FROM Authors
   ORDER BY LastName ASC
```

AuthorID	FirstName	LastName
1	Paul	Deitel
2	Harvey	Deitel
3	Abbey	Deitel
5	Michael	Morgano
4	Dan	Quirk

Fig. 22.15 | Sample data from table Authors in ascending order by LastName.

Sorting in Descending Order

The default sorting order is ascending, so ASC is optional. To obtain the same list of authors in descending order by last name (Fig. 22.16), use the query

```
SELECT AuthorID, FirstName, LastName
   FROM Authors
   ORDER BY LastName DESC
```

AuthorID	FirstName	LastName
4	Dan	Quirk
5	Michael	Morgano
1	Paul	Deitel
2	Harvey	Deitel
3	Abbey	Deitel

Fig. 22.16 | Sample data from table Authors in descending order by LastName.

Sorting By Multiple Columns

Multiple columns can be used for sorting with an ORDER BY clause of the form

```
ORDER BY column1 sortingOrder, column2 sortingOrder, ...
```

where *sortingOrder* is either ASC or DESC. The *sortingOrder* does not have to be identical for each column. The query

```
SELECT AuthorID, FirstName, LastName
   FROM Authors
   ORDER BY LastName, FirstName
```

sorts all the rows in ascending order by last name, then by first name. If any rows have the same last-name value, they're returned sorted by first name (Fig. 22.17).

AuthorID	FirstName	LastName
3	Abbey	Deitel
2	Harvey	Deitel
1	Paul	Deitel
5	Michael	Morgano
4	Dan	Quirk

Fig. 22.17 | Sample data from Authors in ascending order by LastName and FirstName.

Combining the *WHERE* and *ORDER BY* Clauses

The WHERE and ORDER BY clauses can be combined in one query, as in

```
SELECT ISBN, Title, EditionNumber, Copyright
   FROM Titles
   WHERE Title LIKE '%How to Program'
   ORDER BY Title ASC
```

which returns the ISBN, Title, EditionNumber and Copyright of each book in the Titles table that has a Title ending with "How to Program" and sorts them in ascending order by Title. The query results are shown in Fig. 22.18.

ISBN	Title	EditionNumber	Copyright
0133764036	Android How to Program	2	2015
013299044X	C How to Program	7	2013
0133378713	C++ How to Program	9	2014
0132151006	Internet & World Wide Web How to Program	5	2012
0133807800	Java How to Program	10	2015
0133406954	Visual Basic 2012 How to Program	6	2014
0133379337	Visual C# 2012 How to Program	5	2014
0136151574	Visual C++ 2008 How to Program	2	2008

Fig. 22.18 | Sampling of books from table Titles whose titles end with How to Program in ascending order by Title.

22.4.4 Merging Data from Multiple Tables: INNER JOIN

Database designers often split related data into separate tables to ensure that a database does not store data redundantly. For example, in the books database, the AuthorISB table stores the relationship data between authors and their corresponding titles. If we did not separate this information into individual tables, we'd need to include author information with each entry in the Titles table. This would result in the database's storing *duplicate* author information for authors who wrote multiple books. Often, it's necessary to merge data from multiple tables into a single result. Referred to as joining the tables, this is specified by an **INNER JOIN** operator, which merges rows from two tables by matching values in columns that are common to the tables. The basic form of an INNER JOIN is:

```
SELECT columnName1, columnName2, ...
FROM table1
INNER JOIN table2
    ON table1.columnName = table2.columnName
```

The **ON clause** of the INNER JOIN specifies the columns from each table that are compared to determine which rows are merged—one is a primary key and the other is a foreign key in the tables being joined. For example, the following query produces a list of authors accompanied by the ISBNs for books written by each author:

```
SELECT FirstName, LastName, ISBN
FROM Authors
INNER JOIN AuthorISBN
    ON Authors.AuthorID = AuthorISBN.AuthorID
ORDER BY LastName, FirstName
```

The query merges the FirstName and LastName columns from table Authors with the ISBN column from table AuthorISBN, sorting the results in ascending order by LastName and FirstName. Note the use of the syntax *tableName.columnName* in the ON clause. This syntax, called a **qualified name**, specifies the columns from each table that should be compared to join the tables. The "*tableName.*" syntax is required if the columns have the same name in both tables. The same syntax can be used in any SQL statement to distinguish columns in different tables that have the same name. In some systems, table names qualified with the database name can be used to perform cross-database queries. As always, the query can contain an ORDER BY clause. Figure 22.19 shows the results of the preceding query, ordered by LastName and FirstName.

Common Programming Error 22.2

Failure to qualify names for columns that have the same name in two or more tables is an error. In such cases, the statement must precede those column names with their table names and a dot (e.g., Authors.AuthorID*).*

FirstName	LastName	ISBN	FirstName	LastName	ISBN
Abbey	Deitel	0132121360	Harvey	Deitel	013299044X
Abbey	Deitel	0133570924	Harvey	Deitel	0132575655
Abbey	Deitel	0133764036	Paul	Deitel	0133406954
Abbey	Deitel	0133406954	Paul	Deitel	0132990601
Abbey	Deitel	0132990601	Paul	Deitel	0132121360
Abbey	Deitel	0132151006	Paul	Deitel	0133570924
Harvey	Deitel	0132121360	Paul	Deitel	0133764036
Harvey	Deitel	0133570924	Paul	Deitel	0133378713
Harvey	Deitel	0133807800	Paul	Deitel	0136151574
Harvey	Deitel	0132151006	Paul	Deitel	0133379337
Harvey	Deitel	0133764036	Paul	Deitel	013299044X
Harvey	Deitel	0133378713	Paul	Deitel	0132575655
Harvey	Deitel	0136151574	Paul	Deitel	0133807800
Harvey	Deitel	0133379337	Paul	Deitel	0132151006
Harvey	Deitel	0133406954	Michael	Morgano	0132121360
Harvey	Deitel	0132990601	Dan	Quirk	0136151574

Fig. 22.19 | Sampling of authors and ISBNs for the books they have written in ascending order by LastName and FirstName.

22.4.5 INSERT Statement

The **INSERT** statement inserts a row into a table. The basic form of this statement is

```
INSERT INTO tableName (columnName1, columnName2, ..., columnNameN)
    VALUES (value1, value2, ..., valueN)
```

where *tableName* is the table in which to insert the row. The *tableName* is followed by a comma-separated list of column names in parentheses (this list is not required if the INSERT operation specifies a value for every column of the table in the correct order). The list of column names is followed by the SQL keyword **VALUES** and a comma-separated list of values in parentheses. The values specified here must match the columns specified after the table name in both order and type (e.g., if *columnName1* is supposed to be the FirstName column, then *value1* should be a string in single quotes representing the first name). Always explicitly list the columns when inserting rows. If the table's column order changes or a new column is added, using only VALUES may cause an error. The INSERT statement

```
INSERT INTO Authors (FirstName, LastName)
    VALUES ('Sue', 'Red')
```

inserts a row into the Authors table. The statement indicates that values are provided for the FirstName and LastName columns. The corresponding values are 'Sue' and 'Smith'. We do not specify an AuthorID in this example because AuthorID is an autoincremented column in the Authors table. For every row added to this table, the DBMS assigns a unique AuthorID value that is the next value in the autoincremented sequence (i.e., 1, 2, 3 and so on). In this case, Sue Red would be assigned AuthorID number 6. Figure 22.20 shows the Authors table after the INSERT operation. [*Note:* Not every database management system supports autoincremented columns. Check the documentation for your DBMS for alternatives to autoincremented columns.]

Common Programming Error 22.3

SQL delimits strings with single quotes ('). A string containing a single quote (e.g., O'Malley) must have two single quotes in the position where the single quote appears (e.g., 'O''Malley'). The first acts as an escape character for the second. Not escaping single-quote characters in a string that's part of a SQL statement is a SQL syntax error.

Common Programming Error 22.4

It's normally an error to specify a value for an autoincrement column.

AuthorID	FirstName	LastName
1	Paul	Deitel
2	Harvey	Deitel
3	Abbey	Deitel
4	Dan	Quirk
5	Michael	Morgano
6	Sue	Red

Fig. 22.20 | Sample data from table Authors after an INSERT operation.

22.4.6 UPDATE Statement

An **UPDATE** statement modifies data in a table. Its basic form is

```
UPDATE tableName
    SET columnName1 = value1, columnName2 = value2, …, columnNameN = valueN
    WHERE criteria
```

where *tableName* is the table to update. The *tableName* is followed by keyword **SET** and a comma-separated list of *columnName* = *value* pairs. The optional WHERE clause provides criteria that determine which rows to update. Though not required, the WHERE clause is typically used, unless a change is to be made to every row. The UPDATE statement

```
UPDATE Authors
    SET LastName = 'Black'
    WHERE LastName = 'Red' AND FirstName = 'Sue'
```

updates a row in the Authors table. The statement indicates that LastName will be assigned the value Black for the row where LastName is Red and FirstName is Sue. [*Note:* If there are multiple matching rows, this statement will modify *all* such rows to have the last name "Black."] If we know the AuthorID in advance of the UPDATE operation (possibly because we searched for it previously), the WHERE clause can be simplified as follows:

```
WHERE AuthorID = 6
```

Figure 22.21 shows the Authors table after the UPDATE operation has taken place.

AuthorID	FirstName	LastName
1	Paul	Deitel
2	Harvey	Deitel
3	Abbey	Deitel
4	Dan	Quirk
5	Michael	Morgano
6	Sue	Black

Fig. 22.21 | Sample data from table Authors after an UPDATE operation.

22.4.7 DELETE Statement

A SQL **DELETE** statement removes rows from a table. Its basic form is

```
DELETE FROM tableName WHERE criteria
```

where *tableName* is the table from which to delete. The optional WHERE clause specifies the criteria used to determine which rows to delete. If this clause is omitted, all the table's rows are deleted. The DELETE statement

```
DELETE FROM Authors
    WHERE LastName = 'Black' AND FirstName = 'Sue'
```

deletes the row for Sue Black in the Authors table. If we know the AuthorID in advance of the DELETE operation, the WHERE clause can be simplified as follows:

```
WHERE AuthorID = 6
```

Figure 22.22 shows the Authors table after the DELETE operation has taken place.

AuthorID	FirstName	LastName
1	Paul	Deitel
2	Harvey	Deitel
3	Abbey	Deitel
4	Dan	Quirk
5	Michael	Morgano

Fig. 22.22 | Sample data from table `Authors` after a `DELETE` operation.

22.5 Setting Up a Java DB Database[1]

This chapter's examples use the pure Java database **Java DB**, which is installed with Oracle's JDK on Windows, macOS and Linux. Before you can execute this chapter's applications, you must set up in Java DB the `books` database that's used in Sections 22.6—22.8 and the `addressbook` database that's used in Section 22.9. For this chapter, you'll use Java DB's embedded version—the database you manipulate in each example must be located in that example's folder. This chapter's examples are located in two subfolders of the `ch24` examples folder—`books_examples` and `addressbook_example`. Java DB may also act as a server that can receive database requests over a network, but that is beyond this chapter's scope.

JDK Installation Folders
The Java DB software is located in the `db` subdirectory of your JDK's installation directory. The directories listed below are for Oracle's JDK 8 update 121:

- 32-bit JDK on Windows: `C:\Program Files (x86)\Java\jdk1.8.0_121`

- 64-bit JDK on Windows: `C:\Program Files\Java\jdk1.8.0_121`

- macOS:
  `/Library/Java/JavaVirtualMachines/jdk1.8.0_121.jdk/Contents/Home`

- Ubuntu Linux: `/usr/lib/jvm/java-8-oracle`

For Linux, the install location depends on the installer you use and possibly the version of Linux that you use. We used Ubuntu Linux for testing purposes.

Depending on your platform, the JDK installation folder's name might differ if you're using a different JDK version. In the following instructions, you should update the JDK installation folder's name based on the JDK version you're using.

Java DB Configuration
Java DB comes with several files that enable you to configure and run it. Before executing these files from a command window, you must set the environment variable `JAVA_HOME` to refer to the JDK's exact installation directory listed above (or the location where you installed the JDK if it differs from those listed above). See the Before You Begin section of this book for information on setting environment variables.

---

1. If you're using JDK 9 with this chapter, see the note in Section 22.1 about downloading and installing Apache Derby. You'll also need to update the instructions in Section 22.5, based on Apache Derby's installation folder on your computer.

22.5.1 Creating the Chapter's Databases on Windows

After setting the JAVA_HOME environment variable, perform the following steps:

1. Run Notepad as an administrator. To do this on Windows 7, select **Start > All Programs > Accessories**, right click Notepad and select **Run as administrator**. On Windows 10, search for Notepad, right click it in the search results and select **Advanced** in the app bar, then select **Run as administrator**.

2. From Notepad, open the batch file setEmbeddedCP.bat that is located in the JDK installation folder's db\bin folder.

3. Locate the line

   ```
   @rem set DERBY_INSTALL=
   ```

   and change it to

   ```
   @set DERBY_INSTALL=%JAVA_HOME%\db
   ```

   Save your changes and close this file.

4. Open a Command Prompt and change to the JDK installation folder's db\bin folder. Then, type setEmbeddedCP.bat and press *Enter* to set the environment variables required by Java DB.

5. Use the cd command to change to the subfolder books_examples in this chapter's examples folder. This folder contains books.sql to create the database.

6. Execute the following command (with the quote marks) to start the Java DB command-line tool—the double quotes are necessary because the path that the environment variable %JAVA_HOME% represents contains a space.

   ```
   "%JAVA_HOME%\db\bin\ij"
   ```

7. At the ij> prompt type the following command and press *Enter* to create the books database in the current directory and to create the user deitel with the password deitel for accessing the database (each command you enter at the ij> prompt must be terminated with a semicolon):

   ```
   connect 'jdbc:derby:books;create=true;user=deitel;
       password=deitel';
   ```

8. To create the database table and insert sample data in it, we've provided the file books.sql in this example's directory. To execute this SQL script, type

   ```
   run 'books.sql';
   ```

9. Change directories to the addressbook_example subfolder of the ch24 examples folder, which contains the SQL script addressbook.sql that builds the addressbook database. Repeat *Steps 6–9*. In each step, replace books with addressbook.

10. To terminate the Java DB command-line tool, type

    ```
    exit;
    ```

You're now ready to execute this chapter's examples.

22.5.2 Creating the Chapter's Databases on macOS

After setting the `JAVA_HOME` environment variable, perform the following steps:

1. Open a Terminal, then type:

   ```
   DERBY_HOME=/Library/Java/JavaVirtualMachines/jdk1.8.0_121/
       Contents/Home/db
   ```

   and press *Enter*. Then type

   ```
   export DERBY_HOME
   ```

   and press *Enter*. This specifies where Java DB is located on your Mac.

2. In the Terminal window, change directories to the JDK installation folder's `db/bin` folder. Then, type `./setEmbeddedCP` and press *Enter* to set the environment variables required by Java DB.

3. In the Terminal window, use the `cd` command to change to the `books_examples` directory. This directory contains a SQL script `books.sql` that builds the `books` database.

4. Execute the following command to start the command-line tool for interacting with Java DB:

   ```
   $JAVA_HOME/db/bin/ij
   ```

5. Perform *Steps 7–9* of Section 22.5.1 to create the `books` database.

You're now ready to execute this chapter's examples.

22.5.3 Creating the Chapter's Databases on Linux

After setting the `JAVA_HOME` environment variable, perform the following steps:

1. Open a shell window.

2. Perform the steps in Section 22.5.2, but in *Step 1*, set `DERBY_HOME` to

   ```
   DERBY_HOME=YourLinuxJDKInstallationFolder/db
   ```

   On our Ubuntu Linux system, this was:

   ```
   DERBY_HOME=/usr/lib/jvm/java-7-oracle/db
   ```

You're now ready to execute this chapter's examples.

22.6 Connecting to and Querying a Database

The example of Fig. 22.23 performs a simple query on the `books` database that retrieves the entire `Authors` table and displays the data. The program illustrates connecting to the database, querying the database and processing the result. The discussion that follows presents the key JDBC aspects of the program. Lines 3–8 import the JDBC interfaces and classes from package `java.sql` used in this program. Method `main` connects to the `books` database, queries the database, displays the query result and closes the database connection. Line 12 declares a `String` constant for the database URL. This identifies the name of the database to connect to, as well as information about the protocol used by the JDBC driver (discussed shortly). Lines 13–14 declare a `String` constant representing the SQL query that will select the authorID, firstName and lastName columns from the database's authors table.

```java
1   // Fig. 24.23: DisplayAuthors.java
2   // Displaying the contents of the Authors table.
3   import java.sql.Connection;
4   import java.sql.Statement;
5   import java.sql.DriverManager;
6   import java.sql.ResultSet;
7   import java.sql.ResultSetMetaData;
8   import java.sql.SQLException;
9
10  public class DisplayAuthors {
11     public static void main(String args[]) {
12        final String DATABASE_URL = "jdbc:derby:books";
13        final String SELECT_QUERY =
14           "SELECT authorID, firstName, lastName FROM authors";
15
16        // use try-with-resources to connect to and query the database
17        try (
18           Connection connection = DriverManager.getConnection(
19              DATABASE_URL, "deitel", "deitel");
20           Statement statement = connection.createStatement();
21           ResultSet resultSet = statement.executeQuery(SELECT_QUERY)) {
22
23           // get ResultSet's meta data
24           ResultSetMetaData metaData = resultSet.getMetaData();
25           int numberOfColumns = metaData.getColumnCount();
26
27           System.out.printf("Authors Table of Books Database:%n%n");
28
29           // display the names of the columns in the ResultSet
30           for (int i = 1; i <= numberOfColumns; i++) {
31              System.out.printf("%-8s\t", metaData.getColumnName(i));
32           }
33           System.out.println();
34
35           // display query results
36           while (resultSet.next()) {
37              for (int i = 1; i <= numberOfColumns; i++) {
38                 System.out.printf("%-8s\t", resultSet.getObject(i));
39              }
40              System.out.println();
41           }
42        }
43        catch (SQLException sqlException) {
44           sqlException.printStackTrace();
45        }
46     }
47  }
```

Fig. 22.23 | Displaying the contents of the Authors table. (Part I of 2.)

```
Authors Table of Books Database:

AUTHORID        FIRSTNAME       LASTNAME
1               Paul            Deitel
2               Harvey          Deitel
3               Abbey           Deitel
4               Dan             Quirk
5               Michael         Morgano
```

Fig. 22.23 | Displaying the contents of the Authors table. (Part 2 of 2.)

22.6.1 Automatic Driver Discovery

JDBC supports **automatic driver discovery**—it loads the database driver into memory for you. To ensure that the program can locate the driver class, you must include the class's location in the program's classpath when you execute the program. You did this for Java DB in Section 22.5 when you executed the setEmbeddedCP.bat or setEmbeddedCP file on your system—that step configured a CLASSPATH environment variable in the command window for your platform. After doing so, you can run this application simply using the command

```
java DisplayAuthors
```

22.6.2 Connecting to the Database

The JDBC interfaces we use in this example extend the AutoCloseable interface, so you can use objects that implement these interfaces with the try-with-resources statement (lines 17–45). Lines 18–21 create this example's AutoCloseable objects, which are closed when the try block terminates (line 42) or if an exception occurs during the try block's execution. Each object created in the parentheses following keyword try must be separated from the next by a semicolon (;).

Lines 18–19 create a **Connection** object that manages the connection between the Java program and the database. Connection objects enable programs to create SQL statements that manipulate databases. The program initializes connection with the result of a call to the **DriverManager** class's static method **getConnection**. The method's arguments are:

- a String that specifies the database URL,
- a String that specifies the username, and
- a String that specifies the password.

This method attempts to connect to the database specified by its URL argument—if it cannot, it throws a **SQLException** (package java.sql). The username and password for the books database were set in Section 22.5 when you created the database. If you used a different username and password there, you'll need to replace the username (second argument) and password (third argument) passed to method getConnection in lines 18–19.

The URL locates the database. In this chapter's examples, the database is on the local computer, but it could reside on a network. The URL jdbc:derby:books specifies:

- the protocol for communication (jdbc),

- the **subprotocol** for communication (derby), and
- the database name (books).

The subprotocol derby indicates that the program uses a Java DB/Apache Derby-specific subprotocol to connect to the database—recall that Java DB is simply the Oracle branded version of Apache Derby. Figure 22.24 lists the JDBC driver names and database URL formats of several popular RDBMSs.

Software Engineering Observation 22.3

Most database management systems require the user to log in before accessing the database contents. DriverManager method getConnection is overloaded with versions that enable the program to supply the username and password to gain access.

RDBMS	Database URL format
MySQL	jdbc:mysql://*hostname*:*portNumber*/*databaseName*
ORACLE	jdbc:oracle:thin:@*hostname*:*portNumber*:*databaseName*
DB2	jdbc:db2:*hostname*:*portNumber*/*databaseName*
PostgreSQL	jdbc:postgresql://*hostname*:*portNumber*/*databaseName*
Java DB/Apache Derby	jdbc:derby:*dataBaseName* (embedded; used in this chapter)
	jdbc:derby://*hostname*:*portNumber*/*databaseName* (network)
Microsoft SQL Server	jdbc:sqlserver://*hostname*:*portNumber*;databaseName=*dataBaseName*
Sybase	jdbc:sybase:Tds:*hostname*:*portNumber*/*databaseName*

Fig. 22.24 | Popular JDBC database URL formats.

22.6.3 Creating a Statement for Executing Queries

Line 20 of Fig. 22.23 invokes Connection method **createStatement** to obtain an object that implements interface Statement (package java.sql). You use a **Statement** object to submit SQL statements to the database.

22.6.4 Executing a Query

Line 21 uses the Statement object's **executeQuery** method to submit a query that selects all the author information from the Authors table. This method returns an object that implements interface **ResultSet** and contains the query results.

22.6.5 Processing a Query's ResultSet

Lines 24–41 process the ResultSet. Line 24 obtains the ResultSet's **ResultSetMetaData** object (package java.sql). The **metadata** describes the ResultSet's contents. Programs can use metadata programmatically to obtain information about the ResultSet's column names and types. Line 25 uses ResultSetMetaData method **getColumnCount** to retrieve the number of columns in the ResultSet. Lines 30–32 display the column names.

Software Engineering Observation 22.4

Metadata enables programs to process ResultSet contents dynamically when detailed information about the ResultSet is not known in advance.

Lines 36–41 display the data in each ResultSet row. First, the program positions the ResultSet cursor (which points to the row being processed) to the first row. Method **next** (line 36) returns boolean value true if it's able to position to the next row; otherwise, the method returns false to indicate that the end of the ResultSet has been reached.

Common Programming Error 22.5

Initially, a ResultSet cursor is positioned before the first row. A SQLException occurs if you attempt to access a ResultSet's contents before positioning the ResultSet cursor to the first row with method next.

If the ResultSet has rows, lines 37–39 extract and display the contents of each column in the current row. Each column can be extracted as a specific Java type—Result-SetMetaData method **getColumnType** returns a constant integer from class **Types** (package java.sql) indicating a given column's type. Programs can use these values in a switch statement to invoke ResultSet methods that return the column values as appropriate Java types. For example, if the a column's type is Types.INTEGER, ResultSet method **getInt** gets the column value as an int. For simplicity, this example treats each value as an Object. We retrieve each column value with ResultSet method **getObject** (line 38), then display the Object's String representation. ResultSet *get* methods typically receive as an argument either a column number (as an int) or a column name (as a String) indicating which column's value to obtain. Unlike array indices, ResultSet *column numbers start at 1.*

Common Programming Error 22.6

Specifying column index 0 when obtaining values from a ResultSet causes a SQL-Exception—the first column index in a ResultSet is always 1.

Performance Tip 22.1

If a query specifies the exact columns to select from the database, the ResultSet contains the columns in the specified order. For this scenario, using the column number to obtain the column's value is more efficient than using the column name. The column number provides direct access to the specified column. Using the column name requires a search of the column names to locate the appropriate column.

Error-Prevention Tip 22.1

Using column names to obtain values from a ResultSet produces code that is less error prone than obtaining values by column number—you don't need to remember the column order. Also, if the column order changes, your code does not have to change.

When the end of the try block is reached (line 42), the close method is called on the ResultSet, Statement and Connection objects that were obtained at the beginning of the try-with-resources statement.

Common Programming Error 22.7

A SQLException occurs if you attempt to manipulate a ResultSet after closing the Statement that created it. The ResultSet is discarded when the Statement is closed.

Software Engineering Observation 22.5

Each Statement object can open only one ResultSet object at a time. When a Statement returns a new ResultSet, the Statement closes the prior ResultSet. To use multiple ResultSets in parallel, separate Statement objects must return the ResultSets.

22.7 Querying the books Database

Next, we present a DisplayQueryResults app that allows you to enter a SQL query and see its results. The GUI uses a combination of JavaFX and Swing controls. We display the query results in a Swing **JTable** (package javax.swing), which can be populated dynamically from a ResultSet via a **TableModel** (package javax.swing.table). A TableModel provides methods that a JTable can call to access a ResultSet's data. Though JavaFX's TableView control provides data-binding capabilities (like those in Chapter 13), the combination of JTable and TableModel is more powerful for displaying ResultSet data.

22.7.1 ResultSetTableModel Class

Class ResultSetTableModel (Fig. 22.25) is a TableModel that performs the connection to the database and maintains the ResultSet. The class extends class **AbstractTableModel** (package javax.swing.table), which implements interface TableModel. ResultSetTableModel overrides TableModel methods **getColumnClass**, **getColumnCount**, **getColumnName**, **getRowCount** and **getValueAt**, based on the current ResultSet. The default implementations of TableModel methods isCellEditable and setValueAt (provided by AbstractTableModel) are not overridden, because this example does not support editing the JTable cells. The default implementations of TableModel methods **addTableModelListener** and **removeTableModelListener** (provided by AbstractTableModel) are not overridden, because the AbstractTableModel implementations of these methods properly add and remove listeners for the events that occur when a TableModel changes.

```
 1   // Fig. 24.25: ResultSetTableModel.java
 2   // A TableModel that supplies ResultSet data to a JTable.
 3   import java.sql.Connection;
 4   import java.sql.Statement;
 5   import java.sql.DriverManager;
 6   import java.sql.ResultSet;
 7   import java.sql.ResultSetMetaData;
 8   import java.sql.SQLException;
 9   import javax.swing.table.AbstractTableModel;
10
11   // ResultSet rows and columns are counted from 1 and JTable
12   // rows and columns are counted from 0. When processing
13   // ResultSet rows or columns for use in a JTable, it is
```

Fig. 22.25 | A TableModel that supplies ResultSet data to a JTable. (Part 1 of 5.)

```
14    // necessary to add 1 to the row or column number to manipulate
15    // the appropriate ResultSet column (i.e., JTable column 0 is
16    // ResultSet column 1 and JTable row 0 is ResultSet row 1).
17    public class ResultSetTableModel extends AbstractTableModel {
18       private final Connection connection;
19       private final Statement statement;
20       private ResultSet resultSet;
21       private ResultSetMetaData metaData;
22       private int numberOfRows;
23
24       // keep track of database connection status
25       private boolean connectedToDatabase = false;
26
27       // constructor initializes resultSet and obtains its metadata object;
28       // determines number of rows
29       public ResultSetTableModel(String url, String username,
30          String password, String query) throws SQLException {
31          // connect to database
32          connection = DriverManager.getConnection(url, username, password);
33
34          // create Statement to query database
35          statement = connection.createStatement(
36             ResultSet.TYPE_SCROLL_INSENSITIVE, ResultSet.CONCUR_READ_ONLY);
37
38          // update database connection status
39          connectedToDatabase = true;
40
41          // set query and execute it
42          setQuery(query);
43       }
44
45       // get class that represents column type
46       public Class getColumnClass(int column) throws IllegalStateException {
47          // ensure database connection is available
48          if (!connectedToDatabase) {
49             throw new IllegalStateException("Not Connected to Database");
50          }
51
52          // determine Java class of column
53          try {
54             String className = metaData.getColumnClassName(column + 1);
55
56             // return Class object that represents className
57             return Class.forName(className);
58          }
59          catch (Exception exception) {
60             exception.printStackTrace();
61          }
62
63          return Object.class; // if problems occur above, assume type Object
64       }
65
```

Fig. 22.25 | A TableModel that supplies ResultSet data to a JTable. (Part 2 of 5.)

```
66      // get number of columns in ResultSet
67      public int getColumnCount() throws IllegalStateException {
68          // ensure database connection is available
69          if (!connectedToDatabase) {
70              throw new IllegalStateException("Not Connected to Database");
71          }
72
73          // determine number of columns
74          try {
75              return metaData.getColumnCount();
76          }
77          catch (SQLException sqlException) {
78              sqlException.printStackTrace();
79          }
80
81          return 0; // if problems occur above, return 0 for number of columns
82      }
83
84      // get name of a particular column in ResultSet
85      public String getColumnName(int column) throws IllegalStateException {
86          // ensure database connection is available
87          if (!connectedToDatabase) {
88              throw new IllegalStateException("Not Connected to Database");
89          }
90
91          // determine column name
92          try {
93              return metaData.getColumnName(column + 1);
94          }
95          catch (SQLException sqlException) {
96              sqlException.printStackTrace();
97          }
98
99          return ""; // if problems, return empty string for column name
100     }
101
102     // return number of rows in ResultSet
103     public int getRowCount() throws IllegalStateException {
104         // ensure database connection is available
105         if (!connectedToDatabase) {
106             throw new IllegalStateException("Not Connected to Database");
107         }
108
109         return numberOfRows;
110     }
111
112     // obtain value in particular row and column
113     public Object getValueAt(int row, int column)
114         throws IllegalStateException {
115
```

Fig. 22.25 | A TableModel that supplies ResultSet data to a JTable. (Part 3 of 5.)

```
116          // ensure database connection is available
117          if (!connectedToDatabase) {
118              throw new IllegalStateException("Not Connected to Database");
119          }
120
121          // obtain a value at specified ResultSet row and column
122          try {
123              resultSet.absolute(row + 1);
124              return resultSet.getObject(column + 1);
125          }
126          catch (SQLException sqlException) {
127              sqlException.printStackTrace();
128          }
129
130          return ""; // if problems, return empty string object
131      }
132
133      // set new database query string
134      public void setQuery(String query)
135          throws SQLException, IllegalStateException {
136
137          // ensure database connection is available
138          if (!connectedToDatabase) {
139              throw new IllegalStateException("Not Connected to Database");
140          }
141
142          // specify query and execute it
143          resultSet = statement.executeQuery(query);
144
145          // obtain metadata for ResultSet
146          metaData = resultSet.getMetaData();
147
148          // determine number of rows in ResultSet
149          resultSet.last(); // move to last row
150          numberOfRows = resultSet.getRow(); // get row number
151
152
153          fireTableStructureChanged(); // notify JTable that model has changed
154      }
155
156      // close Statement and Connection
157      public void disconnectFromDatabase() {
158          if (connectedToDatabase) {
159              // close Statement and Connection
160              try {
161                  resultSet.close();
162                  statement.close();
163                  connection.close();
164              }
165              catch (SQLException sqlException) {
166                  sqlException.printStackTrace();
167              }
```

Fig. 22.25 | A TableModel that supplies ResultSet data to a JTable. (Part 4 of 5.)

```
168            finally { // update database connection status
169               connectedToDatabase = false;
170            }
171         }
172      }
173   }
```

Fig. 22.25 | A TableModel that supplies ResultSet data to a JTable. (Part 5 of 5.)

ResultSetTableModel Constructor

The ResultSetTableModel constructor (lines 29–43) accepts four String arguments—the URL of the database, the username, the password and the default query to perform. The constructor throws any exceptions that occur back to the application that created the ResultSetTableModel object, so that the application can determine how to handle the exception (e.g., report an error and terminate the application). Line 32 establishes a connection to the database. Lines 35–36 invoke Connection method createStatement to create a Statement object. This example uses a version of createStatement that takes two arguments—the result set type and the result set concurrency. The **result set type** (Fig. 22.26) specifies whether the ResultSet's cursor is able to scroll in both directions or forward only and whether the ResultSet is sensitive to changes made to the underlying data.

Portability Tip 22.2

Some JDBC drivers do not support scrollable ResultSets. In such cases, the driver typically returns a ResultSet in which the cursor can move only forward. For more information, see your database driver documentation.

Common Programming Error 22.8

Attempting to move the cursor backward through a ResultSet when the database driver does not support backward scrolling causes a SQLFeatureNotSupportedException.

ResultSet constant	Description
TYPE_FORWARD_ONLY	Specifies that a ResultSet's cursor can move only in the forward direction (i.e., from the first to the last row in the ResultSet).
TYPE_SCROLL_INSENSITIVE	Specifies that a ResultSet's cursor can scroll in either direction and that the changes made to the underlying data during ResultSet processing are not reflected in the ResultSet unless the program queries the database again.
TYPE_SCROLL_SENSITIVE	Specifies that a ResultSet's cursor can scroll in either direction and that the changes made to the underlying data during ResultSet processing are reflected immediately in the ResultSet.

Fig. 22.26 | ResultSet constants for specifying ResultSet type.

ResultSets that are sensitive to changes reflect those changes immediately after they're made with methods of interface ResultSet. If a ResultSet is insensitive to changes, the query that produced the ResultSet must be executed again to reflect any changes made. The **result set concurrency** (Fig. 22.27) specifies whether the ResultSet can be updated with ResultSet's update methods. This example uses a ResultSet that is scrollable, insensitive to changes and read-only. Line 42 (Fig. 22.25) invokes method setQuery (lines 134–154) to perform the default query.

Portability Tip 22.3
Some JDBC drivers do not support updatable ResultSets. In such cases, the driver typically returns a read-only ResultSet. For more information, see your database driver documentation.

Common Programming Error 22.9
Attempting to update a ResultSet when the database driver does not support updatable ResultSets causes SQLFeatureNotSupportedExceptions.

ResultSet static concurrency constant	Description
CONCUR_READ_ONLY	Specifies that a ResultSet can't be updated—changes to the ResultSet contents cannot be reflected in the database with ResultSet's update methods.
CONCUR_UPDATABLE	Specifies that a ResultSet can be updated (i.e., changes to its contents can be reflected in the database with ResultSet's update methods).

Fig. 22.27 | ResultSet constants for specifying result properties.

ResultSetTableModel Method getColumnClass
Method getColumnClass (lines 46–64) returns a Class object that represents the superclass of all objects in a particular column. The JTable uses this information to configure the default cell renderer and cell editor for that column in the JTable. Line 54 uses ResultSetMetaData method **getColumnClassName** to obtain the fully qualified class name for the specified column. Line 57 loads the class and returns the corresponding Class object. If an exception occurs, the catch in lines 59–61 prints a stack trace and line 63 returns Object.class—the Class instance that represents class Object—as the default type. [*Note:* Line 54 uses the argument column + 1. Like arrays, JTable row and column numbers are counted from 0. However, ResultSet row and column numbers are counted from 1. Thus, when processing ResultSet rows or columns for use in a JTable, it's necessary to add 1 to the row or column number to manipulate the appropriate ResultSet row or column.]

ResultSetTableModel Method getColumnCount
Method getColumnCount (lines 67–82) returns the number of columns in the model's underlying ResultSet. Line 75 uses ResultSetMetaData method **getColumnCount** to obtain

the number of columns in the ResultSet. If an exception occurs, the catch in lines 77–79 prints a stack trace and line 81 returns 0 as the default number of columns.

ResultSetTableModel Method *getColumnName*

Method getColumnName (lines 85–100) returns the name of the column in the model's underlying ResultSet. Line 93 uses ResultSetMetaData method **getColumnName** to obtain the column name from the ResultSet. If an exception occurs, the catch in lines 95–97 prints a stack trace and line 99 returns the empty string as the default column name.

ResultSetTableModel Method *getRowCount*

Method getRowCount (lines 103–110) returns the number of rows in the model's underlying ResultSet. When method setQuery (lines 134–154) performs a query, it stores the number of rows in variable numberOfRows.

ResultSetTableModel Method *getValueAt*

Method getValueAt (lines 113–131) returns the Object in a particular row and column of the model's underlying ResultSet. Line 123 uses ResultSet method **absolute** to position the ResultSet cursor to a specific row. Line 124 uses ResultSet method getObject to obtain the Object in a specific column of the current row. If an exception occurs, the catch in lines 126–128 prints a stack trace and line 130 returns an empty string as the default value.

ResultSetTableModel Method *setQuery*

Method setQuery (lines 134–154) executes the query it receives as an argument to obtain a new ResultSet (line 143). Line 146 gets the ResultSetMetaData for the new ResultSet. Line 149 uses ResultSet method **last** to position the ResultSet cursor at the last row in the ResultSet. [*Note:* This can be slow if the table contains many rows.] Line 150 uses ResultSet method **getRow** to obtain the row number for the current row in the ResultSet. Line 153 invokes method **fireTableStructureChanged** (inherited from class AbstractTableModel) to notify any JTable using this ResultSetTableModel object as its model that the structure of the model has changed. This causes the JTable to repopulate its rows and columns with the new ResultSet data. Method setQuery throws any exceptions that occur in its body back to the application that invoked setQuery.

ResultSetTableModel Method *disconnectFromDatabase*

Method disconnectFromDatabase (lines 157–172) implements an appropriate termination method for class ResultSetTableModel. A class designer should provide a public method that clients of the class must invoke explicitly to free resources that an object has used. In this case, method disconnectFromDatabase closes the ResultSet, Statement and Connection (lines 161–163). Clients of the ResultSetTableModel class should always invoke this method when ResultSetTableModel is no longer needed. Before the method releases resources, line 158 verifies whether the app is currently connected to the database. If not, the method returns. Method disconnectFromDatabase sets connectedToDatabase to false (line 169) to ensure that clients do not use an instance of ResultSetTableModel after that instance has already been terminated. The other methods in class ResultSetTableModel each throw an IllegalStateException if connectedToDatabase is false.

22.7.2 DisplayQueryResults App's GUI

Figure 22.28 shows the app's GUI (defined in DisplayQueryResults.fxml) labeled with its **fx:ids**. You've built many FXML GUIs in prior chapters, so we point out only the key elements and the event-handler methods implemented in class DisplayQueryResults-Controller (Fig. 22.29). For the complete layout details, open the file DisplayQuery-Results.fxml in Scene Builder or view the FXML in a text editor. The GUI's primary layout is a BorderPane with the **fx:id** borderPane—we use this in the controller class to dynamically add a SwingNode containing the JTable to the BorderPane's center (Section 22.7.3). The BorderPane's top and bottom areas contain GridPanes with the app's other controls. The controller class defines two event-handling methods:

- submitQueryButtonPressed is called when the **Submit Query** Button is clicked.

- applyFilterButtonPressed is called when the the **Apply Filter** Button is clicked.

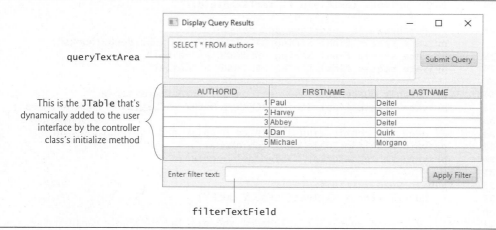

Fig. 22.28 | DisplayQueryResults app's GUI.

22.7.3 DisplayQueryResultsController Class

Class DisplayQueryResultsController (Fig. 22.29) completes the GUI, interacts with the ResultSetTableModel via a JTable object and responds to the GUI's events. We do not show the JavaFX Application subclass here (located in DisplayQueryResults.java), because it performs the same tasks you've seen previously to load the app's FXML GUI and initialize the controller.

```
1   // Fig. 22.29: DisplayQueryResultsController.java
2   // Controller for the DisplayQueryResults app
3   import java.sql.SQLException;
4   import java.util.regex.PatternSyntaxException;
5
6   import javafx.embed.swing.SwingNode;
7   import javafx.event.ActionEvent;
```

Fig. 22.29 | Controller for the DisplayQueryResults app. (Part 1 of 4.)

```
 8   import javafx.fxml.FXML;
 9   import javafx.scene.control.Alert;
10   import javafx.scene.control.Alert.AlertType;
11   import javafx.scene.control.TextArea;
12   import javafx.scene.control.TextField;
13   import javafx.scene.layout.BorderPane;
14
15   import javax.swing.JScrollPane;
16   import javax.swing.JTable;
17   import javax.swing.RowFilter;
18   import javax.swing.table.TableModel;
19   import javax.swing.table.TableRowSorter;
20
21   public class DisplayQueryResultsController {
22      @FXML private BorderPane borderPane;
23      @FXML private TextArea queryTextArea;
24      @FXML private TextField filterTextField;
25
26      // database URL, username and password
27      private static final String DATABASE_URL = "jdbc:derby:books";
28      private static final String USERNAME = "deitel";
29      private static final String PASSWORD = "deitel";
30
31      // default query retrieves all data from Authors table
32      private static final String DEFAULT_QUERY = "SELECT * FROM authors";
33
34      // used for configuring JTable to display and sort data
35      private ResultSetTableModel tableModel;
36      private TableRowSorter<TableModel> sorter;
37
38      public void initialize() {
39         queryTextArea.setText(DEFAULT_QUERY);
40
41         // create ResultSetTableModel and display database table
42         try {
43            // create TableModel for results of DEFAULT_QUERY
44            tableModel = new ResultSetTableModel(DATABASE_URL,
45               USERNAME, PASSWORD, DEFAULT_QUERY);
46
47            // create JTable based on the tableModel
48            JTable resultTable = new JTable(tableModel);
49
50            // set up row sorting for JTable
51            sorter = new TableRowSorter<TableModel>(tableModel);
52            resultTable.setRowSorter(sorter);
53
54            // configure SwingNode to display JTable, then add to borderPane
55            SwingNode swingNode = new SwingNode();
56            swingNode.setContent(new JScrollPane(resultTable));
57            borderPane.setCenter(swingNode);
58         }
59         catch (SQLException sqlException) {
```

Fig. 22.29 | Controller for the DisplayQueryResults app. (Part 2 of 4.)

```
 60            displayAlert(AlertType.ERROR, "Database Error",
 61               sqlException.getMessage());
 62            tableModel.disconnectFromDatabase(); // close connection
 63            System.exit(1); // terminate application
 64         }
 65      }
 66
 67      // query the database and display results in JTable
 68      @FXML
 69      void submitQueryButtonPressed(ActionEvent event) {
 70         // perform a new query
 71         try {
 72            tableModel.setQuery(queryTextArea.getText());
 73         }
 74         catch (SQLException sqlException) {
 75            displayAlert(AlertType.ERROR, "Database Error",
 76               sqlException.getMessage());
 77
 78            // try to recover from invalid user query
 79            // by executing default query
 80            try {
 81               tableModel.setQuery(DEFAULT_QUERY);
 82               queryTextArea.setText(DEFAULT_QUERY);
 83            }
 84            catch (SQLException sqlException2) {
 85               displayAlert(AlertType.ERROR, "Database Error",
 86                  sqlException2.getMessage());
 87               tableModel.disconnectFromDatabase(); // close connection
 88               System.exit(1); // terminate application
 89            }
 90         }
 91      }
 92
 93      // apply specified filter to results
 94      @FXML
 95      void applyFilterButtonPressed(ActionEvent event) {
 96         String text = filterTextField.getText();
 97
 98         if (text.length() == 0) {
 99            sorter.setRowFilter(null);
100         }
101         else {
102            try {
103               sorter.setRowFilter(RowFilter.regexFilter(text));
104            }
105            catch (PatternSyntaxException pse) {
106               displayAlert(AlertType.ERROR, "Regex Error",
107                  "Bad regex pattern");
108            }
109         }
110      }
111
```

Fig. 22.29 | Controller for the DisplayQueryResults app. (Part 3 of 4.)

```
112        // display an Alert dialog
113        private void displayAlert(
114           AlertType type, String title, String message) {
115           Alert alert = new Alert(type);
116           alert.setTitle(title);
117           alert.setContentText(message);
118           alert.showAndWait();
119        }
120   }
```

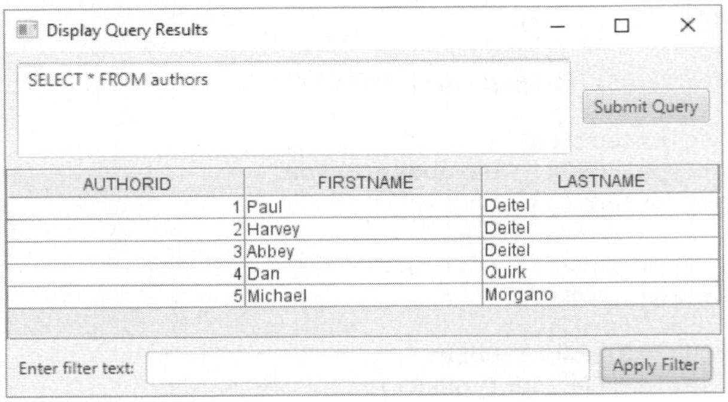

a) Displaying all authors from the **Authors** table.

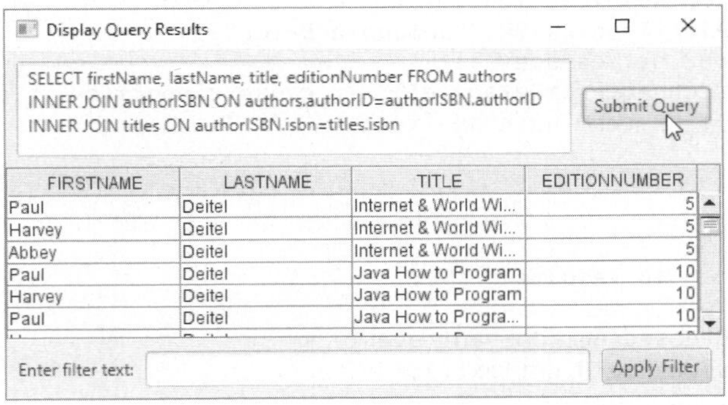

b) Displaying the authors' first and last names joined with the titles and edition numbers of the books they've authored.

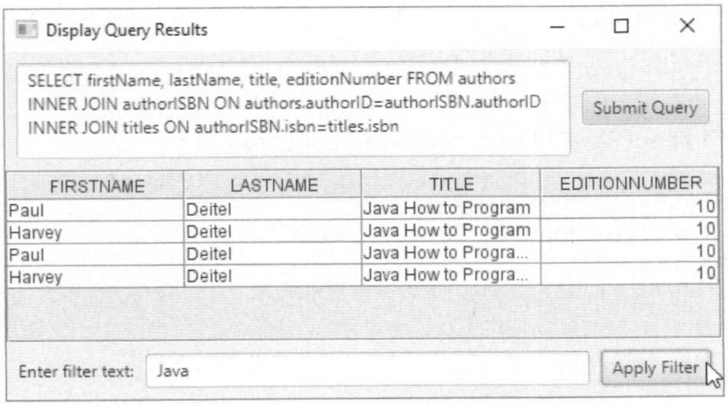

c) Filtering the results of the previous query to show only the books with Java in the title.

Fig. 22.29 | Controller for the `DisplayQueryResults` app. (Part 4 of 4.)

static Fields

Lines 27–29 and 32 declare the URL, username, password and default query that are passed to the ResultSetTableModel constructor to make the initial connection to the database and perform the default query.

Method `initialize`

When the FXMLLoader calls the controller's initialize method, lines 44–45 create a ResultSetTableModel object, assign it to instance variable tableModel (declared at line 35) and complete the GUI. Line 48 creates the JTable object that will display the ResultSetTableModel's ResultSet. Here we use the JTable constructor that receives a TableModel object. This constructor registers the JTable as a listener for TableModelEvents generated by the ResultSetTableModel. When such events occur—for example, when you enter a new query and press **Submit Query**—the JTable automatically updates itself, based on the ResultSetTableModel's current ResultSet. If an exception occurs when the ResultSetTableModel attempts to perform the default query, lines 59–64 catch the exception, display an Alert dialog (by calling method displayAlert in lines 113–119), close the connection and terminate the app.

JTables allow users to sort rows by the data in a specific column. Line 51 creates a **TableRowSorter** (from package **javax.swing.table**) and assigns it to instance variable sorter (declared at line 36). The TableRowSorter uses our ResultSetTableModel to sort rows in the JTable. When the user clicks a particular JTable column's title, the TableRowSorter interacts with the underlying TableModel to reorder the rows based on that column's data. Line 52 uses JTable method **setRowSorter** to specify the TableRowSorter for resultTable.

Lines 55–57 create and configure a **SwingNode**. This Java SE 8 class enables you to embed Swing GUI controls in JavaFX GUIs. The argument to SwingNode method **setContent** is a JComponent—the superclass of all Swing GUI controls. In this case, we pass a new **JScrollPane** object—a subclass of JComponent—that we initialize with the JTable. A JScrollPane provides scrollbars for Swing GUI components that have more content to display than can fit in their area on the screen. For a JTable, depending on its number of rows and columns, the JScrollPane automatically provides vertical and horizontal scrollbars as necessary. Line 57 attaches the SwingNode to the BoderPane's center area.

Software Engineering Observation 22.6

Class SwingNode enables you to reuse existing Swing GUIs or specific Swing controls by embedding them in new JavaFX apps.

Method `submitQueryButtonPressed`

When the user clicks the **Submit Query** Button, method submitQueryButtonPressed (lines 68–91) invokes ResultSetTableModel method setQuery (line 72) to execute the new query. If the user's query fails (for example, because of a syntax error in the user's input), lines 81–82 execute the default query. If the default query also fails, there could be a more serious error, so line 87 ensures that the database connection is closed and line 88 terminates the program. The screen captures in Fig. 22.29 show the results of two queries. Figure 22.29(a) shows the default query that retrieves all the data from table Authors of database books. Figure 22.29(b) shows a query that selects each author's first name and last name from the Authors table and combines that information with the titles and edition numbers of all that author's books from the `Titles` table. Try entering your own queries in the text area and clicking the **Submit Query** button to execute the query.

Method `applyFilterButtonPressed`

`JTable`s can show subsets of the data from the underlying `TableModel`—this is known as filtering the data. When the user enters text in the `filterTextField` and presses the **Apply Filter** Button, method `applyFilterButtonPressed` (lines 94–110) executes. Line 96 obtains the filter text. If the user did not specify filter text, line 99 uses `JTable` method **setRowFilter** to remove any prior filter by setting the filter to `null`. Otherwise, line 103 uses `setRowFilter` to specify a **RowFilter** (from package `javax.swing`) based on the user's input. Class `RowFilter` provides several methods for creating filters. The `static` method **regexFilter** receives a `String` containing a regular expression pattern as its argument and an optional set of indices that specify which columns to filter. If no indices are specified, then all the columns are searched. In this example, the regular expression pattern is the text the user typed. Once the filter is set, the data displayed in the `JTable` is updated based on the filtered `TableModel`. Figure 22.29(c) shows the results of the query in Fig. 22.29(b) filtered to show only records that contain the word `"Java"`.

Method `displayAlert`

When an exception occurs, the app calls method `displayAlert` (lines 113–119) to create and display an **Alert** dialog (package `javafx.scene.control`) containing a message. Line 115 creates the dialog, passing its `AlertType` to the constructor. The `AlertType.ERROR` constant displays an error-message dialog with a red icon containing an **X** to indicate an error. Line 116 sets the title that appears in the dialog's title bar. Line 117 sets the message that appears inside the dialog. Finally, line 118 calls `Alert` method `showAndWait`, which makes this a modal dialog. The user must close the dialog before interacting with the rest of the app.

22.8 RowSet Interface

In the preceding examples, you learned how to query a database by explicitly establishing a `Connection` to the database, preparing a `Statement` for querying the database and executing the query. In this section, we demonstrate the **RowSet interface**, which configures the database connection and prepares query statements automatically. The interface `RowSet` provides several *set* methods that allow you to specify the properties needed to establish a connection (such as the database URL, username and password of the database) and create a `Statement` (such as a query). `RowSet` also provides several *get* methods that return these properties.

Connected and Disconnected *RowSets*

There are two types of `RowSet` objects—connected and disconnected. A **connected RowSet** object connects to the database once and remains connected while the object is in use. A **disconnected RowSet** object connects to the database, executes a query to retrieve the data from the database and then closes the connection. A program may change the data in a disconnected `RowSet` while it's disconnected. Modified data then can be updated in the database after a disconnected `RowSet` reestablishes the connection with the database.

Package **`javax.sql.rowset`** contains two subinterfaces of `RowSet`—`JdbcRowSet` and `CachedRowSet`. **JdbcRowSet**, a connected `RowSet`, acts as a wrapper around a `ResultSet`

object and allows you to scroll through and update the rows in the ResultSet. Recall that
by default, a ResultSet object is nonscrollable and read only—you must explicitly set the
result-set type constant to TYPE_SCROLL_INSENSITIVE and set the result-set concurrency
constant to CONCUR_UPDATABLE to make a ResultSet object scrollable and updatable. A
JdbcRowSet object is scrollable and updatable by default. **CachedRowSet**, a disconnected
RowSet, caches the data of a ResultSet in memory and disconnects from the database.
Like JdbcRowSet, a CachedRowSet object is scrollable and updatable by default. A
CachedRowSet object is also *serializable*, so it can be passed between Java applications
through a network, such as the Internet. However, CachedRowSet has a limitation—the
amount of data that can be stored in memory is limited. Package javax.sql.rowset contains three other subinterfaces of RowSet.

Portability Tip 22.4

*A RowSet can provide scrolling capability for drivers that do not support scrollable Re-
sultSets.*

Using a RowSet

Figure 22.30 reimplements the example of Fig. 22.23 using a RowSet. Rather than establish the connection and create a Statement explicitly, Fig. 22.30 uses a JdbcRowSet object
to create a Connection and a Statement automatically.

```
1   // Fig. 24.30: JdbcRowSetTest.java
2   // Displaying the contents of the Authors table using JdbcRowSet.
3   import java.sql.ResultSetMetaData;
4   import java.sql.SQLException;
5   import javax.sql.rowset.JdbcRowSet;
6   import javax.sql.rowset.RowSetProvider;
7
8   public class JdbcRowSetTest {
9      // JDBC driver name and database URL
10     private static final String DATABASE_URL = "jdbc:derby:books";
11     private static final String USERNAME = "deitel";
12     private static final String PASSWORD = "deitel";
13
14     public static void main(String args[]) {
15        // connect to database books and query database
16        try (JdbcRowSet rowSet =
17           RowSetProvider.newFactory().createJdbcRowSet()) {
18
19           // specify JdbcRowSet properties
20           rowSet.setUrl(DATABASE_URL);
21           rowSet.setUsername(USERNAME);
22           rowSet.setPassword(PASSWORD);
23           rowSet.setCommand("SELECT * FROM Authors"); // set query
24           rowSet.execute(); // execute query
25
26           // process query results
27           ResultSetMetaData metaData = rowSet.getMetaData();
28           int numberOfColumns = metaData.getColumnCount();
```

Fig. 22.30 | Displaying the contents of the Authors table using JdbcRowSet. (Part I of 2.)

```
29              System.out.printf("Authors Table of Books Database:%n%n");
30
31              // display rowset header
32              for (int i = 1; i <= numberOfColumns; i++) {
33                  System.out.printf("%-8s\t", metaData.getColumnName(i));
34              }
35              System.out.println();
36
37              // display each row
38              while (rowSet.next()) {
39                  for (int i = 1; i <= numberOfColumns; i++) {
40                      System.out.printf("%-8s\t", rowSet.getObject(i));
41                  }
42                  System.out.println();
43              }
44          }
45          catch (SQLException sqlException) {
46              sqlException.printStackTrace();
47              System.exit(1);
48          }
49      }
50  }
```

```
Authors Table of Books Database:

AUTHORID        FIRSTNAME       LASTNAME
1               Paul            Deitel
2               Harvey          Deitel
3               Abbey           Deitel
4               Dan             Quirk
5               Michael         Morgano
```

Fig. 22.30 | Displaying the contents of the Authors table using JdbcRowSet. (Part 2 of 2.)

Class **RowSetProvider** (package javax.sql.rowset) provides static method **new-Factory** which returns an object that implements the **RowSetFactory** interface (package javax.sql.rowset). This object can be used to create various types of RowSets. Lines 16–17 in the try-with-resources statement use RowSetFactory method **createJdbcRowSet** to obtain a JdbcRowSet object.

Lines 20–22 set the RowSet properties that the DriverManager uses to establish a database connection. Line 20 invokes JdbcRowSet method **setUrl** to specify the database URL. Line 21 invokes JdbcRowSet method **setUsername** to specify the username. Line 22 invokes JdbcRowSet method **setPassword** to specify the password. Line 23 invokes Jdbc-RowSet method **setCommand** to specify the SQL query that will populate the RowSet. Line 24 invokes JdbcRowSet method **execute** to execute the SQL query. Method execute performs four actions—it establishes a Connection to the database, prepares the query Statement, executes the query and stores the ResultSet returned by the query. The Connection, Statement and ResultSet are encapsulated in the JdbcRowSet object.

The remaining code is almost identical to Fig. 22.23, except that line 27 (Fig. 22.30) obtains a ResultSetMetaData object from the JdbcRowSet, line 38 uses the JdbcRowSet's next method to get the next row of the result and line 40 uses the JdbcRowSet's getObject method to obtain a column's value. When the end of the try block is reached, the try-with-resources statement invokes JdbcRowSet method **close** to close the RowSet's encapsulated ResultSet, Statement and Connection. In a CachedRowSet, invoking close also releases the resources held by that RowSet. The application's output is identical to Fig. 22.23.

22.9 PreparedStatements

A **PreparedStatement** enables you to create compiled SQL statements that execute more efficiently than Statements. PreparedStatements also can specify parameters, making them more flexible than Statements—you can execute the same query repeatedly with different parameter values. For example, in the books database, you might want to locate all book titles for an author with a specific last and first name, and you might want to execute that query for several authors. With a PreparedStatement, that query is defined as:

```
PreparedStatement authorBooks = connection.prepareStatement(
   "SELECT LastName, FirstName, Title " +
   "FROM Authors INNER JOIN AuthorISBN " +
      "ON Authors.AuthorID=AuthorISBN.AuthorID " +
   "INNER JOIN Titles " +
      "ON AuthorISBN.ISBN=Titles.ISBN " +
   "WHERE LastName = ? AND FirstName = ?");
```

The two question marks (?) in the preceding SQL statement's last line are placeholders for values that will be passed to the database as part of the query. Before executing a Prepared-Statement, the program must specify the values by using the PreparedStatement interface's *set* methods.

For the preceding query, both parameters are strings that can be set with Prepared-Statement method **setString** as follows:

```
authorBooks.setString(1, "Deitel");
authorBooks.setString(2, "Paul");
```

Method setString's first argument represents the parameter number being set, and the second argument is that parameter's value. Parameter numbers are *counted from 1*, starting with the first question mark (?). When the program executes the preceding Prepared-Statement with the parameter values set above, the SQL passed to the database is

```
SELECT LastName, FirstName, Title
FROM Authors INNER JOIN AuthorISBN
   ON Authors.AuthorID=AuthorISBN.AuthorID
INNER JOIN Titles
   ON AuthorISBN.ISBN=Titles.ISBN
WHERE LastName = 'Deitel' AND FirstName = 'Paul'
```

Method setString automatically escapes String parameter values as necessary. For example, if the last name is O'Brien, the statement

```
authorBooks.setString(1, "O'Brien");
```

escapes the ' character in O'Brien by replacing it with two single-quote characters, so that the ' appears correctly in the database.

Performance Tip 22.2

PreparedStatements are more efficient than Statements when executing SQL statements multiple times and with different parameter values.

Error-Prevention Tip 22.2

Use PreparedStatements with parameters for queries that receive String values as arguments to ensure that the Strings are quoted properly in the SQL statement.

Error-Prevention Tip 22.3

PreparedStatements help prevent SQL injection attacks, which typically occur in SQL statements that include user input improperly. To avoid this security issue, use Prepared-Statements in which user input can be supplied only via parameters—indicated with ? when creating a PreparedStatement. Once you've created such a PreparedStatement, you can use its set methods to specify the user input as arguments for those parameters.

Interface PreparedStatement provides *set* methods for each supported SQL type. It's important to use the *set* method that's appropriate for the parameter's SQL type in the database—SQLExceptions occur when a program attempts to convert a parameter value to an incorrect type.

22.9.1 AddressBook App That Uses PreparedStatements

We now present an AddressBook JavaFX app that enables you to browse existing entries, add new entries and search for entries with a last name that begins with the specified characters. Our addressbook Java DB database (created in Section 22.5) contains an Addresses table with the columns AddressID, FirstName, LastName, Email and PhoneNumber. The column AddressID is an auto-incremented identity column in the Addresses table.

22.9.2 Class Person

Our AddressBook loads data into Person objects (Fig. 22.31). Each represents one entry in the addressbook database. The class contains instance variables for the address ID, first name, last name, email address and phone number, as well as *set* and *get* methods for manipulating these fields and a toString method that returns the Person's name in the format

```
last name, first name
```

```
1   // Fig. 22.31: Person.java
2   // Person class that represents an entry in an address book.
3   public class Person {
4       private int addressID;
5       private String firstName;
6       private String lastName;
7       private String email;
8       private String phoneNumber;
```

Fig. 22.31 | Person class that represents an entry in an address book. (Part 1 of 2.)

```
 9
10      // constructor
11      public Person() {}
12
13      // constructor
14      public Person(int addressID, String firstName, String lastName,
15         String email, String phoneNumber) {
16         setAddressID(addressID);
17         setFirstName(firstName);
18         setLastName(lastName);
19         setEmail(email);
20         setPhoneNumber(phoneNumber);
21      }
22
23      // sets the addressID
24      public void setAddressID(int addressID) {this.addressID = addressID;}
25
26      // returns the addressID
27      public int getAddressID() {return addressID;}
28
29      // sets the firstName
30      public void setFirstName(String firstName) {
31         this.firstName = firstName;
32      }
33
34      // returns the first name
35      public String getFirstName() {return firstName;}
36
37      // sets the lastName
38      public void setLastName(String lastName) {this.lastName = lastName;}
39
40      // returns the last name
41      public String getLastName() {return lastName;}
42
43      // sets the email address
44      public void setEmail(String email) {this.email = email;}
45
46      // returns the email address
47      public String getEmail() {return email;}
48
49      // sets the phone number
50      public void setPhoneNumber(String phoneNumber) {
51         this.phoneNumber = phoneNumber;
52      }
53
54      // returns the phone number
55      public String getPhoneNumber() {return phoneNumber;}
56
57      // returns the string representation of the Person's name
58      @Override
59      public String toString()
60         {return getLastName() + ", " + getFirstName();}
61   }
```

Fig. 22.31 | Person class that represents an entry in an address book. (Part 2 of 2.)

22.9.3 Class PersonQueries

Class PersonQueries (Fig. 22.32) manages the **Address Book** application's database connection and creates the PreparedStatements for interacting with the database. Lines 17–19 declare three PreparedStatement variables. The constructor (lines 22–47) connects to the database at lines 24–25.

```java
 1   // Fig. 22.32: PersonQueries.java
 2   // PreparedStatements used by the Address Book application.
 3   import java.sql.Connection;
 4   import java.sql.DriverManager;
 5   import java.sql.PreparedStatement;
 6   import java.sql.ResultSet;
 7   import java.sql.SQLException;
 8   import java.util.List;
 9   import java.util.ArrayList;
10
11   public class PersonQueries {
12      private static final String URL = "jdbc:derby:AddressBook";
13      private static final String USERNAME = "deitel";
14      private static final String PASSWORD = "deitel";
15
16      private Connection connection; // manages connection
17      private PreparedStatement selectAllPeople;
18      private PreparedStatement selectPeopleByLastName;
19      private PreparedStatement insertNewPerson;
20
21      // constructor
22      public PersonQueries() {
23         try {
24            connection =
25               DriverManager.getConnection(URL, USERNAME, PASSWORD);
26
27            // create query that selects all entries in the AddressBook
28            selectAllPeople = connection.prepareStatement(
29               "SELECT * FROM Addresses ORDER BY LastName, FirstName");
30
31            // create query that selects entries with last names
32            // that begin with the specified characters
33            selectPeopleByLastName = connection.prepareStatement(
34               "SELECT * FROM Addresses WHERE LastName LIKE ? " +
35               "ORDER BY LastName, FirstName");
36
37            // create insert that adds a new entry into the database
38            insertNewPerson = connection.prepareStatement(
39               "INSERT INTO Addresses " +
40               "(FirstName, LastName, Email, PhoneNumber) " +
41               "VALUES (?, ?, ?, ?)");
42         }
43         catch (SQLException sqlException) {
44            sqlException.printStackTrace();
```

Fig. 22.32 | PreparedStatements used by the **Address Book** application. (Part 1 of 3.)

```
45              System.exit(1);
46         }
47      }
48
49      // select all of the addresses in the database
50      public List<Person> getAllPeople() {
51         // executeQuery returns ResultSet containing matching entries
52         try (ResultSet resultSet = selectAllPeople.executeQuery()) {
53            List<Person> results = new ArrayList<Person>();
54
55            while (resultSet.next()) {
56               results.add(new Person(
57                  resultSet.getInt("AddressID"),
58                  resultSet.getString("FirstName"),
59                  resultSet.getString("LastName"),
60                  resultSet.getString("Email"),
61                  resultSet.getString("PhoneNumber")));
62            }
63
64            return results;
65         }
66         catch (SQLException sqlException) {
67            sqlException.printStackTrace();
68         }
69
70         return null;
71      }
72
73      // select person by last name
74      public List<Person> getPeopleByLastName(String lastName) {
75         try {
76            selectPeopleByLastName.setString(1, lastName); // set last name
77         }
78         catch (SQLException sqlException) {
79            sqlException.printStackTrace();
80            return null;
81         }
82
83         // executeQuery returns ResultSet containing matching entries
84         try (ResultSet resultSet = selectPeopleByLastName.executeQuery()) {
85            List<Person> results = new ArrayList<Person>();
86
87            while (resultSet.next()) {
88               results.add(new Person(
89                  resultSet.getInt("addressID"),
90                  resultSet.getString("FirstName"),
91                  resultSet.getString("LastName"),
92                  resultSet.getString("Email"),
93                  resultSet.getString("PhoneNumber")));
94            }
95
96            return results;
97      }
```

Fig. 22.32 | PreparedStatements used by the **Address Book** application. (Part 2 of 3.)

```
 98              catch (SQLException sqlException) {
 99                 sqlException.printStackTrace();
100                 return null;
101              }
102           }
103
104       // add an entry
105       public int addPerson(String firstName, String lastName,
106          String email, String phoneNumber) {
107
108          // insert the new entry; returns # of rows updated
109          try {
110             // set parameters
111             insertNewPerson.setString(1, firstName);
112             insertNewPerson.setString(2, lastName);
113             insertNewPerson.setString(3, email);
114             insertNewPerson.setString(4, phoneNumber);
115
116             return insertNewPerson.executeUpdate();
117          }
118          catch (SQLException sqlException) {
119             sqlException.printStackTrace();
120             return 0;
121          }
122       }
123
124       // close the database connection
125       public void close() {
126          try {
127             connection.close();
128          }
129          catch (SQLException sqlException) {
130             sqlException.printStackTrace();
131          }
132       }
133    }
```

Fig. 22.32 | PreparedStatements used by the **Address Book** application. (Part 3 of 3.)

Creating *PreparedStatements*

Lines 28–29 invoke Connection method **prepareStatement** to create the Prepared-Statement selectAllPeople that selects all the rows in the Addresses table and sorts them by last name, then by first name. Lines 33–35 create the PreparedStatement selectPeopleByLastName with a parameter. This statement uses the SQL LIKE operator to search the Addresses table by last name. The ? character specifies the last-name parameter—as you'll see, the text we set as this parameter's value will end with %, so that the database will return entries for last names that start with the characters entered by the user. Lines 38–41 create the PreparedStatement insertNewPerson with four parameters that represent the first name, last name, email address and phone number for a new entry. Again, notice the ? characters used to represent these parameters.

PersonQueries *Method* getAllPeople

Method getAllPeople (lines 50–71) executes PreparedStatement selectAllPeople (line 52) by calling method **executeQuery**, which returns a ResultSet containing the rows that match the query (in this case, all the rows in the Addresses table). Lines 55–62 place the query results in an ArrayList<Person>, which is returned to the caller at line 64.

PersonQueries *Method* getPeopleByLastName

Method getPeopleByLastName (lines 74–102) uses PreparedStatement method set-String to set the parameter of selectPeopleByLastName (line 76). Then, line 84 executes the query and lines 87–94 place the query results in an ArrayList<Person>. Line 96 returns the ArrayList to the caller.

PersonQueries *Methods* addPerson *and* Close

Method addPerson (lines 105–122) uses PreparedStatement method setString (lines 111–114) to set the parameters for the insertNewPerson PreparedStatement. Line 116 uses PreparedStatement method **executeUpdate** to update the database by inserting the new record. This method returns an integer indicating the number of rows that were updated (or inserted) in the database. Method close (lines 125–132) simply closes the database connection.

22.9.4 AddressBook GUI

Figure 22.33 shows the app's GUI (defined in AddressBook.fxml) labeled with its **fx:id**s. Here we point out only the key elements and their event-handler methods, which you'll see in class AddressBookController (Fig. 22.34). For the complete layout details, open AddressBook.fxml in Scene Builder. The GUI's primary layout is a BorderPane. The controller class defines three event-handling methods:

- addEntryButtonPressed is called when the **Add Entry** Button is pressed.
- findButtonPressed is called when the **Find** Button is pressed.
- browseAllButtonPressed is called when the **Browse All** Button is pressed.

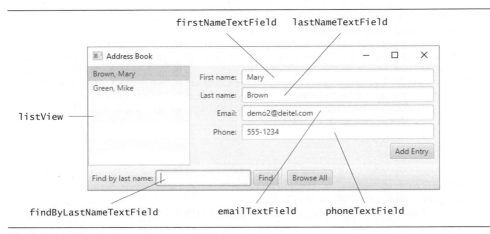

Fig. 22.33 | AddressBook GUI with its **fx:id**s.

22.9.5 Class AddressBookController

The AddressBookController (Fig. 22.34) class uses a PersonQueries object to interact with the database. We do not show the JavaFX Application subclass here (located in AddressBook.java), because it performs the same tasks you've seen previously to load the app's FXML GUI and initialize the controller.

```java
 1   // Fig. 22.34: AddressBookController.java
 2   // Controller for the AddressBook app
 3   import java.util.List;
 4   import javafx.application.Platform;
 5   import javafx.collections.FXCollections;
 6   import javafx.collections.ObservableList;
 7   import javafx.event.ActionEvent;
 8   import javafx.fxml.FXML;
 9   import javafx.scene.control.Alert;
10   import javafx.scene.control.Alert.AlertType;
11   import javafx.scene.control.ListView;
12   import javafx.scene.control.TextField;
13
14   public class AddressBookController {
15      @FXML private ListView<Person> listView; // displays contact names
16      @FXML private TextField firstNameTextField;
17      @FXML private TextField lastNameTextField;
18      @FXML private TextField emailTextField;
19      @FXML private TextField phoneTextField;
20      @FXML private TextField findByLastNameTextField;
21
22      // interacts with the database
23      private final PersonQueries personQueries = new PersonQueries();
24
25      // stores list of Person objects that results from a database query
26      private final ObservableList<Person> contactList =
27         FXCollections.observableArrayList();
28
29      // populate listView and set up listener for selection events
30      public void initialize() {
31         listView.setItems(contactList); // bind to contactsList
32         getAllEntries(); // populates contactList, which updates listView
33
34         // when ListView selection changes, display selected person's data
35         listView.getSelectionModel().selectedItemProperty().addListener(
36            (observableValue, oldValue, newValue) -> {
37               displayContact(newValue);
38            }
39         );
40      }
41
42      // get all the entries from the database to populate contactList
43      private void getAllEntries() {
44         contactList.setAll(personQueries.getAllPeople());
```

Fig. 22.34 | Controller for the AddressBook app. (Part 1 of 4.)

```
45              selectFirstEntry();
46          }
47
48          // select first item in listView
49          private void selectFirstEntry() {
50              listView.getSelectionModel().selectFirst();
51          }
52
53          // display contact information
54          private void displayContact(Person person) {
55              if (person != null) {
56                  firstNameTextField.setText(person.getFirstName());
57                  lastNameTextField.setText(person.getLastName());
58                  emailTextField.setText(person.getEmail());
59                  phoneTextField.setText(person.getPhoneNumber());
60              }
61              else {
62                  firstNameTextField.clear();
63                  lastNameTextField.clear();
64                  emailTextField.clear();
65                  phoneTextField.clear();
66              }
67          }
68
69          // add a new entry
70          @FXML
71          void addEntryButtonPressed(ActionEvent event) {
72              int result = personQueries.addPerson(
73                  firstNameTextField.getText(), lastNameTextField.getText(),
74                  emailTextField.getText(), phoneTextField.getText());
75
76              if (result == 1) {
77                  displayAlert(AlertType.INFORMATION, "Entry Added",
78                      "New entry successfully added.");
79              }
80              else {
81                  displayAlert(AlertType.ERROR, "Entry Not Added",
82                      "Unable to add entry.");
83              }
84
85              getAllEntries();
86          }
87
88          // find entries with the specified last name
89          @FXML
90          void findButtonPressed(ActionEvent event) {
91              List<Person> people = personQueries.getPeopleByLastName(
92                  findByLastNameTextField.getText() + "%");
93
94              if (people.size() > 0) { // display all entries
95                  contactList.setAll(people);
96                  selectFirstEntry();
97              }
```

Fig. 22.34 | Controller for the AddressBook app. (Part 2 of 4.)

```
98          else {
99              displayAlert(AlertType.INFORMATION, "Lastname Not Found",
100                 "There are no entries with the specified last name.");
101         }
102     }
103
104     // browse all the entries
105     @FXML
106     void browseAllButtonPressed(ActionEvent event) {
107         getAllEntries();
108     }
109
110     // display an Alert dialog
111     private void displayAlert(
112         AlertType type, String title, String message) {
113         Alert alert = new Alert(type);
114         alert.setTitle(title);
115         alert.setContentText(message);
116         alert.showAndWait();
117     }
118 }
```

a) Initial **Address Book** screen showing entries.

b) Viewing the entry for **Green, Mike**.

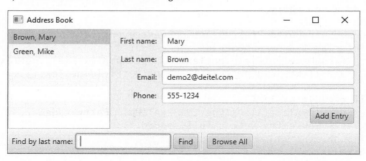

Fig. 22.34 | Controller for the AddressBook app. (Part 3 of 4.)

c) Adding a new entry for **Sue Green**.

d) Searching for last names that start with **Gr**.

e) Returning to the complete list by clicking **Browse All**.

Fig. 22.34 | Controller for the AddressBook app. (Part 4 of 4.)

Instance Variables
Line 23 creates the PersonQueries object. We use the same techniques to populate the ListView that we used in Section 13.5, so lines 26–27 create an ObservableList<Person> named contactList to store the Person objects returned by the PersonQueries object.

Method `initialize`
When the FXMLLoader initializes the controller, method initialize (lines 30–40) performs the following tasks:

- Line 31 binds the contactList to the ListView, so that each time this Observ-ableList<Person> changes, the ListView will update its list of items.

- Line 32 calls method getAllEntries (declared in lines 43–46) to get all the entries from the database and place them in the contactList.

- Lines 35–39 register a ChangeListener that displays the selected contact when the user selects a new item in the ListView. In this case, we used a lambda expression to create the event handler (Fig. 13.15 showed a similar ChangeListener defined as an anonymous inner class).

Methods getAllEntries and selectFirstEntry

When the app first executes, when the user clicks the **Browse All** Button and when the user adds a new entry to the database, method getEntries (lines 43–46) calls PersonQueries method getAllPeople (line 44) to obtain all the entries. The resulting List<Person> is passed to ObservableList method setAll to replace the contactList's contents. At this point, the ListView updates its list of items based on the new contents of contactList.

Next line 45 selects the first item in the ListView by calling method select-FirstEntry (lines 49–51). Line 50 selects the ListView's first item to display that contact's data.

Method displayContact

When an item is selected in the ListView, the ChangeListener registered in method initialize calls displayContact (lines 54–67) to display the selected Person's data. If the argument is null, the method clears the TextField's contents.

Method addEntryButtonPressed

To add a new entry into the database, you can enter the first name, last name, email and phone number (the AddressID will *autoincrement*) in the TextFields that display contact information, then press the **Add Entry** Button. Method addEntryButtonPressed (lines 70–86) calls PersonQueries method addPerson (lines 72–74) to add the new entry to the database. Line 85 calls getAllEntries to obtain the updated database contents and display them in the ListView.

Method findButtonPressed

When the user presses the **Find** Button, method findButtonPressed (lines 89–102) is called. Lines 91–92 call PersonQueries method getPeopleByLastName to search the database. Note that line 92 appends a % to the text input by the user. This enables the corresponding SQL query, which contains a LIKE operator, to locate last names that begin with the characters the user typed in the findByLastNameTextField. If there are several such entries, they're all displayed in the ListView when the contactList is updated (line 95) and the first one is selected (line 96).

Method browseAllButtonPressed

When the user presses the **Browse All** Button, method browseAllButtonPressed (lines 105–108) simply calls method getAllEntries to get all the database entries and display them in the ListView.

22.10 Stored Procedures

Many database-management systems can store individual or sets of SQL statements in a database, so that programs accessing that database can invoke them. Such named collections of SQL statements are called **stored procedures**. JDBC enables programs to invoke stored procedures using objects that implement the interface `CallableStatement`. `CallableStatement`s can receive arguments specified with the methods inherited from interface `PreparedStatement`. In addition, `CallableStatement`s can specify **output parameters** in which a stored procedure can place return values. Interface `CallableStatement` includes methods to specify which parameters in a stored procedure are output parameters. The interface also includes methods to obtain the values of output parameters returned from a stored procedure.

Portability Tip 22.5

Although the syntax for creating stored procedures differs across database management systems, the interface `CallableStatement` provides a uniform interface for specifying input and output parameters for stored procedures and for invoking stored procedures.

Portability Tip 22.6

According to the Java API documentation for interface `CallableStatement`, for maximum portability between database systems, programs should process the update counts (which indicate how many rows were updated) or `ResultSet`s returned from a `CallableStatement` before obtaining the values of any output parameters.

22.11 Transaction Processing

Many database applications require guarantees that a series of database insertions, updates and deletions executes properly before the application continues processing the next database operation. For example, when you transfer money electronically between bank accounts, several factors determine if the transaction is successful. You begin by specifying the source account and the amount you wish to transfer from that account to a destination account. Next, you specify the destination account. The bank checks the source account to determine whether its funds are sufficient to complete the transfer. If so, the bank withdraws the specified amount and, if all goes well, deposits it into the destination account to complete the transfer. What happens if the transfer fails after the bank withdraws the money from the source account? In a proper banking system, the bank redeposits the money in the source account. How would you feel if the money was subtracted from your source account and the bank *did not* deposit the money in the destination account?

Transaction processing enables a program that interacts with a database to *treat a database operation (or set of operations) as a single operation*. Such an operation also is known as an **atomic operation** or a **transaction**. At the end of a transaction, a decision can be made either to **commit the transaction** or **roll back the transaction**. Committing the transaction finalizes the database operation(s); all insertions, updates and deletions performed as part of the transaction cannot be reversed without performing a new database operation. Rolling back the transaction leaves the database in its state prior to the database operation. This is useful when a portion of a transaction fails to complete properly. In our bank-account-transfer discussion, the transaction would be rolled back if the deposit could not be made into the destination account.

Java provides transaction processing via methods of interface Connection. Method **setAutoCommit** specifies whether each SQL statement commits after it completes (a true argument) or whether several SQL statements should be grouped as a transaction (a false argument). If the argument to setAutoCommit is false, the program must follow the last SQL statement in the transaction with a call to Connection method **commit** (to commit the changes to the database) or Connection method **rollback** (to return the database to its state prior to the transaction). Interface Connection also provides method **getAuto-Commit** to determine the autocommit state for the Connection.

22.12 Wrap-Up

In this chapter, you learned basic database concepts, how to query and manipulate data in a database using SQL and how to use JDBC to allow Java applications to interact with Java DB databases. You learned about the SQL commands SELECT, INSERT, UPDATE and DE-LETE, as well as clauses such as WHERE, ORDER BY and INNER JOIN.

You created and configured databases in Java DB by using predefined SQL scripts. You learned the steps for obtaining a Connection to the database, creating a Statement to interact with the database's data, executing the statement and processing the results. You incorporated a Swing JTable component into a JavaFX GUI via a SwingNode and used a TableModel to bind ResultSet data to the JTable.

Next, you used a RowSet to simplify the process of connecting to a database and creating statements. You used PreparedStatements to create precompiled SQL statements. We also provided overviews of CallableStatements and transaction processing. In the next chapter, you'll learn about JShell—Java 9's REPL (read-evaluate-print loop) that enables you to quickly explore, discover and experiment with Java language and API features.

23

Introduction to JShell: Java 9's REPL for Interactive Java

Objectives

In this chapter you'll:

- See how using JShell can enhance the learning and software development processes by enabling you to explore, discover and experiment with Java language and API features.
- Start a JShell session.
- Execute code snippets.
- Declare variables explicitly.
- Evaluate expressions.
- Edit existing code snippets.
- Declare and use a class.
- Save snippets to a file.
- Open a file of JShell snippets and evaluate them.
- Auto-complete code and JShell commands.
- Display method parameters and overloads.
- Discover and explore with the Java API documentation in JShell.
- Declare and use methods.
- Forward reference a method that has not yet been declared.
- See how JShell wraps exceptions.
- Import custom packages for use in a JShell session.
- Control JShell's feedback level.

23.1 Introduction

As educators, it's a joy to write this chapter on what may be the most important pedagogic improvement in Java since its inception more than two decades ago. The Java community—by far the largest programming language community in the world—has grown to more than 10 million developers. But along the way, not much has been done to improve the learning process for programmers new to Java. That changes dramatically in Java 9 with the introduction of **JShell**—Java's **REPL** (**read-evaluate-print loop**).[1]

---

1. We'd like to thank Robert Field at Oracle—the head of the JShell/REPL effort. We interacted with Mr. Field extensively as we developed Chapter 23. He answered our many questions. We reported JShell bugs and made suggestions for improvement.

Now Java has a rich REPL implementation. And with the new JShell APIs, third parties will build JShell and related interactive-development tools into the major IDEs like Eclipse, IntelliJ, NetBeans and others.

What is JShell?

What's the magic? It's simple. JShell provides a fast and friendly environment that enables you to quickly explore, discover and experiment with Java language features and its extensive libraries. REPLs like the one in JShell have been around for decades. In the 1960s, one of the earliest REPLs made convenient interactive development possible in the LISP programming language. Students of that era, like one of your authors, Harvey Deitel, found it fast and fun to use.

JShell replaces the tedious cycle of editing, compiling and executing with its read-evaluate-print loop. Rather than complete programs, you write **JShell commands** and Java code snippets. When you enter a snippet, JShell *immediately* **reads** it, **evaluates** it and **prints** the results that help you see the effects of your code. Then it **loops** to perform this process again for the next snippet. As you work through Chapter 23's scores of examples and exercises, you'll see how JShell and its instant feedback keep your attention, enhance your performance and speed the learning and software development processes.

Code Comes Alive

As you know, we emphasize the value of the live-code teaching approach in our books, focusing on *complete*, working programs. JShell brings this right down to the individual snippet level. Your code literally comes alive as you enter each line. Of course, you'll still make occasional errors as you enter your snippets. JShell reports compilation errors to you on a snippet-by-snippet basis. You can use this capability, for example, to test the items in our Common Programming Error tips and see the errors as they occur.

Kinds of Snippets

Snippets can be expressions, individual statements, multi-line statements and larger entities, like methods and classes. JShell supports all but a few Java features, but there are some differences designed to facilitate JShell's explore–discover–experiment capabilities. In JShell, methods do not need to be in classes, expressions and statements do not need to be in methods, and you do not need a `main` method (other differences are in Section 23.14). Eliminating this infrastructure saves you considerable time, especially compared to the lengthy repeated edit, compile and execute cycles of complete programs. And because JShell automatically displays the results of evaluating your expressions and statements, you do not need as many print statements as we use throughout this book's traditional Java code examples.

Discovery with Auto-Completion

We include a detailed treatment of **auto-completion**—a key discovery feature that speeds the coding process. After you type a portion of a name (class, method, variable, etc.) and press the *Tab* key, JShell completes the name for you or provides a list of all possible names that begin with what you've typed so far. You can then easily display method parameters and even the documentation that describes those methods.

Rapid Prototyping
Professional developers will commonly use JShell for rapid prototyping but not for full-out software development. Once you develop and test a small chunk of code, you can then paste it in to your larger project.

How This Chapter Is Organized
For those who want to use JShell, the chapter has been designed as a series of units, paced to certain earlier chapters of the book. Each unit begins with a statement like: "This section may be read after Chapter 2." So you'd begin by reading through Chapter 2, then read the corresponding section of this chapter—and similarly for subsequent chapters.

The Chapter 2 JShell Exercises
As you work your way through this chapter, execute each snippet and command in JShell to confirm that the features work as advertised. Sections 23.3–23.4 are designed to be read after Chapter 2. Once you read these sections, we recommend that you do Chapter 23's dozens of self-review exercises. JShell encourages you to "learn by doing," so the exercises have you write and test code snippets that exercise many of Chapter 2's Java features.

The self-review exercises are small and to the point, and the answers are provided to help you quickly get comfortable with JShell's capabilities. When you're done you'll have a great sense of what JShell is all about. Please tell us what you think of this new Java tool. Thanks!

Instead of rambling on about the advantages of JShell, we're going to let JShell itself convince you. If you have any questions as you work through the following examples and exercises, just write to us at `deitel@deitel.com` and we'll always respond promptly.

23.2 Installing JDK 9

Java 9 and its JShell are early access technologies that are still under development. This introduction to JShell is based on the JDK 9 Developer Preview (early access build 163). To use JShell, you must first install JDK 9, which is available in early access form at

```
https://jdk9.java.net/download/
```

The Before You Begin section that follows the Preface discusses the JDK version numbering schemes, then shows how to manage multiple JDK installations on your particular platform.

23.3 Introduction to JShell

[*Note:* This section may be read after studying Chapter 2, Introduction to Java Applications; Input/Output and Operators.]

In Chapter 2, to create a Java application, you:

1. created a class containing a `main` method.
2. declared in `main` the statements that will execute when you run the program.
3. compiled the program and fixed any compilation errors that occurred. This step had to be repeated until the program compiled without errors.
4. ran the program to see the results.

By automatically compiling and executing code as you complete each expression or statement, JShell eliminates the overhead of

- creating a class containing the code you wish to test,
- compiling the class and
- executing the class.

Instead, you can focus on interactively discovering and experimenting with Java's language and API features. If you enter code that does not compile, JShell immediately reports the errors. You can then use JShell's editing features to quickly fix and re-execute the code.

23.3.1 Starting a JShell Session

To start a JShell session in:

- Microsoft Windows, open a **Command Prompt** then type **jshell** and press *Enter*.
- macOS (formerly OS X), open a **Terminal** window then type the following command and press *Enter*.

```
$JAVA_HOME/bin/jshell
```

- Linux, open a shell window then type jshell and press *Enter*.

The preceding commands execute a new JShell session and display the following message and the **jshell>** prompt:

```
|  Welcome to JShell -- Version 9-ea
|  For an introduction type: /help intro

jshell>
```

In the first line above, "Version 9-ea" indicates that you're using the **ea** (that is, early access) version of JDK 9. JShell precedes informational messages with vertical bars (|). You are now ready to enter Java code or JShell commands.

9

23.3.2 Executing Statements

[*Note:* As you work through this chapter, type the same code and JShell commands that we show at each jshell> prompt to ensure that what you see on your screen will match what we show in the sample outputs.]

JShell has two input types:

- Java code (which the JShell documentation refers to as **snippets**) and
- JShell commands.

In this section and Section 23.3.3, we begin with Java code snippets. Subsequent sections introduce JShell commands.

You can type any expression or statement at the jshell> prompt then press *Enter* to execute the code and see its results immediately. Consider the program of Fig. 2.1, which we show again in Fig. 23.1. To demonstrate how System.out.println works, this program required many lines of code and comments, which you had to write, compile and execute. Even without the comments, five code lines were still required (lines 4 and 6–9).

```
1   // Fig. 23.1: Welcome1.java
2   // Text-printing program.
3
4   public class Welcome1 {
5      // main method begins execution of Java application
6      public static void main(String[] args) {
7         System.out.println("Welcome to Java Programming!");
8      } // end method main
9   } // end class Welcome1
```

```
Welcome to Java Programming!
```

Fig. 23.1 | Text-printing program.

In JShell, you can execute the statement in line 7 without creating all the infrastructure of class Welcome1 and its main method:

```
jshell> System.out.println("Welcome to Java Programming!")
Welcome to Java Programming!

jshell>
```

In this case, JShell displays the snippet's command-line output below the initial jshell> prompt and the statement you entered. Per our convention, we show user inputs in bold.

Notice that we did not enter the preceding statement's semicolon (;). JShell adds *only* terminating semicolons.[2] You need to add a semicolon if the end of the statement is not the end of the line—for example, if the statement is inside braces ({ and }). Also, if there is more than one statement on a line then you need a semicolon between statements, but not after the last statement.

The blank line before the second jshell> prompt is the result of the newline displayed by method println and the newline that JShell always displays before each jshell> prompt. Using print rather than println eliminates the blank line:

```
jshell> System.out.print("Welcome to Java Programming!")
Welcome to Java Programming!
jshell>
```

JShell keeps track of everything you type, which can be useful for re-executing prior statements and modifying statements to update the tasks they perform.

23.3.3 Declaring Variables Explicitly

Almost anything you can declare in a typical Java source-code file also can be declared in JShell (Section 23.14 discusses some of the features you cannot use). For example, you can explicitly declare a variable as follows:

```
jshell> int number1
number1 ==> 0

jshell>
```

2. Not requiring semicolons is one example of how JShell reinterprets standard Java for convenient interactive use. We discuss several of these throughout the chapter and summarize them in Section 23.14.

When you enter a variable declaration, JShell displays the variable's name (in this case, number1) followed by ==> (which means, "has the value") and the variable's initial value (0). If you do not specify an initial value explicitly, the variable is initialized to its type's default value—in this case, 0 for an int variable.

A variable can be initialized in its declaration—let's redeclare number1:

```
jshell> int number1 = 30
number1 ==> 30

jshell>
```

JShell displays

```
number1 ==> 30
```

to indicate that number1 now has the value 30. When you declare a new variable with the *same name* as another variable in the current JShell session, JShell replaces the first declaration with the new one.[3] Because number1 was declared previously, we could have simply assigned number1 a value, as in

```
jshell> number1 = 45
number1 ==> 45

jshell>
```

Compilation Errors in JShell

You must declare variables before using them in JShell. The following declaration of int variable sum attempts to use a variable named number2 that we have not yet declared, so JShell reports a compilation error, indicating that the compiler was unable to find a variable named number2:

```
jshell> int sum = number1 + number2
|  Error:
|  cannot find symbol
|    symbol:   variable number2
|  int sum = number1 + number2;
|                      ^-----^

jshell>
```

The error message uses the notation ^-----^ to highlight the error in the statement. No error is reported for the previously declared variable number1. Because this snippet has a compilation error, it's invalid. However, JShell still maintains the snippet as part of the JShell session's history, which includes valid snippets, invalid snippets and commands that you've typed. As you'll soon see, you can recall this invalid snippet and execute it again later. JShell's **/history** command displays the current session's history—that is, *everything* you've typed:

---

3. Redeclaring an existing variable is another example of how JShell reinterprets standard Java for interactive use. This behavior is different from how the Java compiler handles a new declaration of an existing variable—such a "double declaration" generates a compilation error.

```
jshell> /history

System.out.println("Welcome to Java Programming!")
System.out.print("Welcome to Java Programming!")
int number1
int number1 = 45
number1 = 45
int sum = number1 + number2
/history

jshell>
```

Fixing the Error

JShell makes it easy to fix a prior error and re-execute a snippet. Let's fix the preceding error by first declaring number2 with the value 72:

```
jshell> int number2 = 72
number2 ==> 72

jshell>
```

Subsequent snippets can now use number2—in a moment, you'll re-execute the snippet that declared and initialized sum with number1 + number2.

Recalling and Re-executing a Previous Snippet

Now that both number1 and number2 are declared, we can declare the int variable sum. You can use the up and down arrow keys to navigate backward and forward through the snippets and JShell commands you've entered previously. Rather than retyping sum's declaration, you can press the up arrow key three times to recall the declaration that failed previously. JShell recalls your prior inputs in reverse order—the last line of text you typed is recalled first. So, the first time you press the up arrow key, the following appears at the jshell> prompt:

```
jshell> int number2 = 72
```

The second time you press the up arrow key, the /history command appears:

```
jshell> /history
```

The third time you press the up arrow key, sum's prior declaration appears:

```
jshell> int sum = number1 + number2
```

Now you can press *Enter* to re-execute the snippet that declares and initializes sum:

```
jshell> int sum = number1 + number2
sum ==> 117

jshell>
```

JShell adds the values of number1 (45) and number2 (72), stores the result in the new sum variable, then shows sum's value (117).

23.3.4 Listing and Executing Prior Snippets

You can view a list of all previous valid Java code snippets with JShell's **/list** command— JShell displays the snippets in the order you entered them:

```
jshell> /list

    1 : System.out.println("Welcome to Java Programming!")
    2 : System.out.print("Welcome to Java Programming!")
    4 : int number1 = 30;
    5 : number1 = 45
    6 : int number2 = 72;
    7 : int sum = number1 + number2;

jshell>
```

Each valid snippet is identified by a sequential **snippet ID**. The snippet with ID 3 is *missing* above, because we replaced that original snippet

```
    int number1
```

with the one that has the ID 4 in the preceding /list. Note that /list may not display everything that /history does. As you recall, if you omit a terminating semicolon, JShell inserts it for you behind the scenes. When you say /list, *only* the declarations (snippets 4, 6 and 7) actually show the semicolons that JShell inserted.

Snippet 1 above is just an expression. If we type it with a terminating semicolon, it's an **expression statement**.

Executing Snippets By ID Number

You can execute any prior snippet by typing */id*, where *id* is the snippet's ID. For example, when you enter /1:

```
jshell> /1
System.out.println("Welcome to Java Programming!")
Welcome to Java Programming!

jshell>
```

JShell displays the first snippet we entered, executes it and shows the result.[4] You can re-execute the last snippet you typed (whether it was valid or invalid) with /!:

```
jshell> /!
System.out.println("Welcome to Java Programming!")
Welcome to Java Programming!

jshell>
```

JShell assigns an ID to every valid snippet you execute, so even though

```
    System.out.println("Welcome to Java Programming!")
```

already exists in this session as snippet 1, JShell creates a new snippet with the next ID in sequence (in this case, 8 and 9 for the last two snippets). Executing the /list command shows that snippets 1, 8 and 9 are identical:

---

4. At the time of this writing, you cannot use the */id* command to execute a *range* of previous snippets; however, the JShell command /reload can re-execute *all* existing snippets (Section 23.12.3).

```
jshell> /list

   1 : System.out.println("Welcome to Java Programming!")
   2 : System.out.print("Welcome to Java Programming!")
   4 : int number1 = 30;
   5 : number1 = 45
   6 : int number2 = 72;
   7 : int sum = number1 + number2;
   8 : System.out.println("Welcome to Java Programming!")
   9 : System.out.println("Welcome to Java Programming!")

jshell>
```

23.3.5 Evaluating Expressions and Declaring Variables Implicitly

When you enter an expression in JShell, it evaluates the expression, implicitly creates a variable and assigns the expression's value to the variable. **Implicit variables** are named $#, where # is the new snippet's ID.[5] For example:

```
jshell> 11 + 5
$10 ==> 16

jshell>
```

evaluates the expression 11 + 5 and assigns the resulting value (16) to the implicitly de-clared variable $10, because there were nine prior valid snippets (even though one was de-leted because we redeclared the variable number1). JShell *infers* that the type of $10 is int, because the expression 11 + 5 adds two int values, producing an int. Expressions may also include one or more method calls. The list of snippets is now:

```
jshell> /list

   1 : System.out.println("Welcome to Java Programming!")
   2 : System.out.print("Welcome to Java Programming!")
   4 : int number1 = 30;
   5 : number1 = 45
   6 : int number2 = 72;
   7 : int sum = number1 + number2;
   8 : System.out.println("Welcome to Java Programming!")
   9 : System.out.println("Welcome to Java Programming!")
  10 : 11 + 5

jshell>
```

Note that the implicitly declared variable $10 appears in the list simply as 10 without the $.

23.3.6 Using Implicitly Declared Variables

Like any other declared variable, you can use an implicitly declared variable in an expres-sion. For example, the following assigns to the *existing* variable sum the result of adding number1 (45) and $10 (16):

---

5.   Implicitly declared variables are another example of how JShell reinterprets standard Java for inter-active use. In regular Java programs you must explicitly declare *every* variable.

```
jshell> sum = number1 + $10
sum ==> 61

jshell>
```

The list of snippets is now:

```
jshell> /list

   1 : System.out.println("Welcome to Java Programming!")
   2 : System.out.print("Welcome to Java Programming!")
   4 : int number1 = 30;
   5 : number1 = 45
   6 : int number2 = 72;
   7 : int sum = number1 + number2;
   8 : System.out.println("Welcome to Java Programming!")
   9 : System.out.println("Welcome to Java Programming!")
  10 : 11 + 5
  11 : sum = number1 + $10

jshell>
```

23.3.7 Viewing a Variable's Value

You can view a variable's value at any time simply by typing its name and pressing *Enter*:

```
jshell> sum
sum ==> 61

jshell>
```

JShell treats the variable name as an expression and simply evaluates its value.

23.3.8 Resetting a JShell Session

You can remove all prior code from a JShell session by entering the **/reset** command:

```
jshell> /reset
|  Resetting state.

jshell> /list

jshell>
```

The subsequent /list command shows that all prior snippets were removed. Confirmation messages displayed by JShell, such as

```
|  Resetting state.
```

are helpful when you're first becoming familiar with JShell. In Section 23.12.5, we'll show how you can change the JShell *feedback mode*, making it more or less verbose.

23.3.9 Writing Multiline Statements

Next, we write an if statement that determines whether 45 is less than 72. First, let's store 45 and 72 in implicitly declared variables, as in:

```
jshell> 45
$1 ==> 45

jshell> 72
$2 ==> 72

jshell>
```

Next, begin typing the `if` statement:

```
jshell> if ($1 < $2) {
   ...>
```

JShell knows that the `if` statement is incomplete, because we typed the opening left brace, but did not provide a body or a closing right brace. So, JShell displays the **continuation prompt** `...>` at which you can enter more of the control statement. The following completes and evaluates the `if` statement:

```
jshell> if ($1 < $2) {
   ...>    System.out.printf("%d < %d%n", $1, $2);
   ...> }
45 < 72

jshell>
```

In this case, a second continuation prompt appeared because the `if` statement was still missing its terminating right brace (}). Note that the statement-terminating semicolon (;) at the end of the `System.out.printf` statement in the `if`'s body is required. We manually indented the `if`'s body statement—JShell does *not* add spacing or braces for you as IDEs generally do. Also, JShell assigns each multiline code snippet—such as an `if` statement— only one snippet ID. The list of snippets is now:

```
jshell> /list

   1 : 45
   2 : 72
   3 : if ($1 < $2) {
           System.out.printf("%d < %d%n", $1, $2);
       }

jshell>
```

23.3.10 Editing Code Snippets

Sometimes you might want to create a new snippet, based on an existing snippet in the current JShell session. For example, suppose you want to create an `if` statement that determines whether $1 is *greater than* $2. The statement that performs this task

```
if ($1 > $2) {
    System.out.printf("%d > %d%n", $1, $2);
}
```

is nearly identical to the `if` statement in Section 23.3.9, so it would be easier to edit the existing statement rather than typing the new one from scratch. When you edit a snippet, JShell saves the edited version as a new snippet with the next snippet ID in sequence.

Editing a Single-Line Snippet

To edit a single-line snippet, locate it with the up-arrow key, make your changes within the snippet then press *Enter* to evaluate it. See Section 23.13 for some keyboard shortcuts that can help you edit single-line snippets.

Editing a Multiline Snippet

For a larger snippet that's spread over several lines—such as a `if` statement that contains one or more statements—you can edit the entire snippet by using JShell's **/edit** command to open the snippet in the **JShell Edit Pad** (Fig. 23.2). The command

```
/edit
```

opens **JShell Edit Pad** and displays *all* valid code snippets you've entered so far. To edit a specific snippet, include the snippet's ID, as in

```
/edit id
```

So, the command:

```
/edit 3
```

displays the `if` statement from Section 23.3.9 in **JShell Edit Pad** (Fig. 23.2)—no snippet IDs are shown in this window. **JShell Edit Pad**'s window is *modal*—that is, while it's open, you cannot enter code snippets or commands at the JShell prompt.

Fig. 23.2 | **JShell Edit Pad** showing the `if` statement from Section 23.3.9.

JShell Edit Pad supports only basic editing capabilities. You can:

- click to insert the cursor at a specific position to begin typing,
- move the cursor via the arrow keys on your keyboard,
- drag the mouse to select text,
- use the *Delete* (*Backspace*) key to delete text,
- cut, copy and paste text using your operating system's keyboard shortcuts, and
- enter text, including new snippets separate from the one(s) you're editing.

In the first and second lines of the `if` statement, select each less than operator (<) and change it to a greater than operator (>), then click **Accept** to create a new `if` statement containing the edited code. When you click **Accept**, JShell also immediately evaluates the new `if` statement and displays its results (if any)—because `$1` (45) is *not* greater than `$2` (72) the System.out.printf statement does not execute,[6] so no additional output is shown in JShell.

---

6. We could have made this an `if...else` statement to show output when the condition is *false*, but this section is meant to be used with Chapter 2 where we introduce only the single-selection `if` statement.

If you want to return immediately to the JShell prompt, rather than clicking **Accept**, you could click **Exit** to execute the edited snippet and close **JShell Edit Pad**. Clicking **Cancel** closes **JShell Edit Pad** and discards any changes you made since the last time you clicked **Accept**, or since **JShell Edit Pad** was launched if have not yet clicked **Accept**.

When you change or create multiple snippets then click **Accept** or **Exit**, JShell compares the **JShell Edit Pad** contents with the previously saved snippets. It then executes every modified or new snippet.

Adding a New Snippet Via JShell Edit Pad

To show that **JShell Edit Pad** does, in fact, execute snippets immediately when you click **Accept**, let's change $1's value to 100 by entering the following statement following the `if` statement after the other code in **JShell Edit Pad**:

```
$1 = 100
```

and clicking **Accept** (Fig. 23.3). Each time you modify a variable's value, JShell immediately displays the variable's name and new value:

```
jshell> /edit 3
$1 ==> 100
```

Click **Exit** to close **JShell Edit Pad** and return to the `jshell>` prompt.

Fig. 23.3 | Entering a new statement following the `if` statement in **JShell Edit Pad**.

The following lists the current snippets—notice that each multiline `if` statement has only one ID:

```
jshell> /list

    1 : 45
    2 : 72
    3 : if ($1 < $2) {
            System.out.printf("%d < %d%n", $1, $2);
        }
    4 : if ($1 > $2) {
            System.out.printf("%d > %d%n", $1, $2);
        }
    5 : $1 = 100

jshell>
```

Executing the New if Statement Again

The following re-executes the new `if` statement (ID **4**) with the updated $1 value:

```
jshell> /4
if ($1 > $2) {
    System.out.printf("%d > %d%n", $1, $2);
}
100 > 72

jshell>
```

The condition $1 > $2 is now `true`, so the `if` statement's body executes. The list of snippets is now

```
jshell> /list

   1 : 45
   2 : 72
   3 : if ($1 < $2) {
           System.out.printf("%d < %d%n", $1, $2);
       }
   4 : if ($1 > $2) {
           System.out.printf("%d > %d%n", $1, $2);
       }
   5 : $1 = 100
   6 : if ($1 > $2) {
           System.out.printf("%d > %d%n", $1, $2);
       }

jshell>
```

23.3.11 Exiting JShell

To terminate the current JShell session, use the **/exit** command or type the keyboard shortcut *Ctrl + d* (or *control + d*). This returns you to the command-line prompt in your **Command Prompt** (in Windows), **Terminal** (in macOS) or shell (in Linux—sometimes called **Terminal**, depending on your Linux distribution).

23.4 Command-Line Input in JShell

[*Note:* This section may be read after studying Chapter 2, Introduction to Java Applications; Input/Output and Operators and the preceding sections in this chapter.]

In Chapter 2, we showed command-line input using a `Scanner` object:

```
Scanner input = new Scanner(System.in);

System.out.print("Enter first integer: ");
int number1 = input.nextInt();
```

We created a `Scanner`, prompted the user for input, then used `Scanner` method `nextInt` to read a value. Recall that the program then waited for you to type an integer and press *Enter* before proceeding to the next statement. The on-screen interaction appeared as:

```
Enter first integer: 45
```

This section shows what that interaction looks like in JShell.

*Creating a **Scanner***

Start a new JShell session or /reset the current one, then create a Scanner object:

```
jshell> Scanner input = new Scanner(System.in)
input ==> java.util.Scanner[delimiters=\p{javaWhitespace}+] ...
   \E][infinity string=\Q∞\E]

jshell>
```

You do not need to import Scanner. JShell automatically imports the java.util package and several others—we show the complete list in Section 23.10. When you create an object, JShell displays its text representation. The notation to the right of input ==> is the Scanner's text representation (which you can simply ignore).

Prompting for Input and Reading a Value

Next, prompt the user for input:

```
jshell> System.out.print("Enter first integer: ")
Enter first integer:
jshell>
```

The statement's output is displayed immediately, followed by the next jshell> prompt. Now enter the input statement:

```
jshell> int number1 = input.nextInt()
_
```

At this point, JShell waits for your input. The input cursor is positioned below the jshell> prompt and snippet you just entered—indicated by the underscore (_) above—rather than next to the prompt "Enter first integer:" as it was in Chapter 2. Now type an integer and press *Enter* to assign it to number1—the last snippet's execution is now complete, so the next jshell> prompt appears.:

```
jshell> int number1 = input.nextInt()
45
number1 ==> 45

jshell>
```

Though you can use Scanner for command-line input in JShell, in most cases it's unnecessary. The goal of the preceding interactions was simply to store an integer value in the variable number1. You can accomplish that in JShell with the simple assignment

```
jshell> int number1 = 45
number1 ==> 45

jshell>
```

For this reason, you'll typically use assignments, rather than command-line input in JShell. We introduced Scanner here, because sometimes you'll want to copy code you developed in JShell into a conventional Java program.

23.5 Declaring and Using Classes

[*Note:* This section may be read after studying Chapter 3, Introduction to Classes, Objects, Methods and Strings.]

In Section 23.3, we demonstrated basic JShell capabilities. In this section, we create a class and manipulate an object of that class. We'll use the version of class `Account` presented in Fig. 3.1.

23.5.1 Creating a Class in JShell

Start a new JShell session (or `/reset` the current one), then declare class `Account`—we ignored the comments from Fig. 3.1:

```
jshell> public class Account {
   ...>     private String name;
   ...>
   ...>     public void setName(String name) {
   ...>         this.name = name;
   ...>     }
   ...>
   ...>     public String getName() {
   ...>         return name;
   ...>     }
   ...> }
|  created class Account

jshell>
```

JShell recognizes when you enter the class's closing brace—then displays

```
|  created class Account
```

and issues the next `jshell>` prompt. Note that the semicolons throughout class `Account`'s body are required.

To save time, rather than typing a class's code as shown above, you can load an existing source code file into JShell, as shown in Section 23.5.6. Though you can specify access modifiers like `public` on your classes (and other types), JShell ignores all access modifiers on the top-level types except for `abstract` (discussed in Chapter 10).

Viewing Declared Classes

To view the names of the classes you've declared so far, enter the **/types** command:[7]

```
jshell> /types
|    class Account

jshell>
```

23.5.2 Explicitly Declaring Reference-Type Variables

The following creates the `Account` variable `account`:

```
jshell> Account account
account ==> null

jshell>
```

The default value of a reference-type variable is `null`.

---

7. `/types` actually displays all types you declare, including classes, interfaces and enums.

23.5.3 Creating Objects

You can create new objects. The following creates an `Account` variable named `account` and initializes it with a new object:

```
jshell> account = new Account()
account ==> Account@56ef9176

jshell>
```

The strange notation

```
    Account@56ef9176
```

is the default text representation of the new `Account` object. If a class provides a custom text representation, you'll see that instead. We show how to provide a custom text representation for objects of a class in Section 7.6. We discuss the default text representation of objects in Section 9.6. The value after the @ symbol is the object's *hashcode*. We discuss hashcodes in Section 16.10.

Declaring an Implicit Account Variable Initialized with an Account Object

If you create an object with only the expression `new Account()`, JShell assigns the object to an implicit variable of type `Account`, as in:

```
jshell> new Account()
$4 ==> Account@1ed4004b

jshell>
```

Note that this object's hashcode (`1ed4004b`) is different from the prior `Account` object's hashcode (`56ef9176`)—these typically are different, but that's not guaranteed.

Viewing Declared Variables

You can view all the variables you've declared so far with the JShell **/vars** command:

```
jshell> /vars
|    Account account = Account@56ef9176
|    Account $4 = Account@1ed4004b

jshell>
```

For each variable, JShell shows the type and variable name followed by an equal sign and the variable's text representation.

23.5.4 Manipulating Objects

Once you have an object, you can call its methods. In fact, you already did this with the `System.out` object by calling its `println`, `print` and `printf` methods in earlier snippets.

The following sets the account object's name:

```
jshell> account.setName("Amanda")

jshell>
```

The method `setName` has the return type `void`, so it does not return a value and JShell does not show any additional output.

The following gets the account object's name:

```
jshell> account.getName()
$6 ==> "Amanda"

jshell>
```

Method `getName` returns a `String`. When you invoke a method that returns a value, JShell stores the value in an implicitly declared variable. In this case, `$6`'s type is *inferred* to be `String`. Of course, you could have assigned the result of the preceding method call to an explicitly declared variable.

Using the Return Value of a Method in a Statement

If you invoke a method as part of a larger statement, the return value is used in that statement, rather than stored. For example, the following uses `println` to display the `account` object's name:

```
jshell> System.out.println(account.getName())
Amanda

jshell>
```

23.5.5 Creating a Meaningful Variable Name for an Expression

You can give a meaningful variable name to a value that JShell previously assigned to an implicit variable. For example, with the following snippet recalled

```
jshell> account.getName()
```

type

Shift + Tab v

The + notation means that you should you press *both* the *Shift* and *Tab* keys together, then release those keys and press *v*. JShell infers the expression's type and begins a variable declaration for you—`account.getName()` returns a `String`, so JShell inserts `String` and an equal sign (=) before the expression, as in

```
jshell> account.getName()
jshell> String _= account.getName()
```

JShell also positions the cursor (indicated by the _ above) immediately before the = so you can simply type the variable name, as in

```
jshell> String name = account.getName()
name ==> "Amanda"

jshell>
```

When you press *Enter*, JShell evaluates the new snippet and stores the value in the specified variable.

23.5.6 Saving and Opening Code-Snippet Files

You can save all of a session's valid code snippets to a file, which you can then load into a JShell session as needed.

Saving Snippets to a File

To save just the *valid* snippets, use the **/save** command, as in:

```
/save filename
```

By default, the file is created in the folder from which you launched JShell. To store the file in a different location, specify the complete path of the file.

Loading Snippets from a File

Once you save your snippets, they can be reloaded with the **/open** command:

```
/open filename
```

which executes each snippet in the file.

Using /open to Load Java Source-Code Files

You also can open existing Java source code files using /open. For example, let's assume you'd like to experiment with class Account from Fig. 3.1 (as you did in Section 23.5.1). Rather than typing its code into JShell, you can save time by loading the class from the source file Account.java. In a command window, you'd change to the folder containing Account.java, execute JShell, then use the following command to load the class declaration into JShell:

```
/open Account.java
```

To load a file from another folder, you can specify the full pathname of the file to open. In Section 23.10, we'll show how to use existing compiled classes in JShell.

23.6 Discovery with JShell Auto-Completion

[*Note:* This section may be read after studying Chapter 3, Introduction to Classes, Objects, Methods and Strings, and completing Section 23.5.]

JShell can help you write code. When you partially type the name of an existing class, variable or method then press the *Tab* key, JShell does one of the following:

- If no other name matches what you've typed so far, JShell enters the rest of the name for you.
- If there are multiple names that begin with the same letters, JShell displays a list of those names to help you decide what to type next—then you can type the next letter(s) and press *Tab* again to complete the name.
- If no names match what you typed so far, JShell does nothing and your operating system's alert sound plays as feedback.

Auto-completion is normally an IDE feature, but with JShell it's IDE independent.

Let's first list the snippets we've entered since the last /reset (from Section 23.5):

```
jshell> /list

   1 : public class Account {
          private String name;

          public void setName(String name) {
             this.name = name;
          }

          public String getName() {
             return name;
          }
       }
   2 : Account account;
   3 : account = new Account()
   4 : new Account()
   5 : account.setName("Amanda")
   6 : account.getName()
   7 : System.out.println(account.getName())
   8 : String name = account.getName();

jshell>
```

23.6.1 Auto-Completing Identifiers

The only variable declared so far that begins with lowercase "a" is account, which was declared in snippet 2. Auto-completion is case sensitive, so "a" does not match the class name Account. If you type "a" at the jshell> prompt:

```
jshell> a
```

then press *Tab*, JShell auto-completes the name:

```
jshell> account
```

If you then enter a dot:

```
jshell> account.
```

then press *Tab*, JShell does not know what method you want to call, so it displays a list of everything—in this case, all the methods—that can appear to the right of the dot:

```
jshell> account.
equals(          getClass()       getName()        hashCode()       notify()
notifyAll()      setName(         toString()       wait(

jshell> account.
```

and follows the list with a new jshell> prompt that includes what you've typed so far. The list includes the methods we declared in class Account (snippet 1) *and* several methods that all Java classes have (as we discuss in Chapter 9). In the list of method names

- those followed by "()" are methods that do not require arguments and
- those followed only by "(" are methods that either require at least one argument or that are so-called *overloaded methods*—multiple methods with the same name, but different parameter lists (discussed in Section 6.11).

Let's assume you want to use `Account`'s `setName` method to change the name stored in the account object to `"John"`. There's only one method that begins with "s", so you can type s then *Tab* to auto-complete `setName`:

```
jshell> account.setName(
```

JShell automatically inserts the method call's opening left parenthesis. Now you can complete the snippet as in:

```
jshell> account.setName("John")

jshell>
```

23.6.2 Auto-Completing JShell Commands

Auto-completion also works for JShell commands. If you type / then press *Tab*, JShell displays the list of JShell commands:

```
jshell> /
/!            /?            /drop         /edit         /env          /exit
/help         /history      /imports      /list         /methods      /open
/reload       /reset        /save         /set          /types        /vars

<press tab again to see synopsis>

jshell> /
```

If you then type h and press *Tab*, JShell displays only the commands that start with /h:

```
jshell> /h
/help         /history

<press tab again to see synopsis>

jshell> /h
```

Finally, if you type "i" and press *Tab*, JShell auto-completes `/history`. Similarly, if you type /l then press *Tab*, JShell auto-completes the command as `/list`, because only that command starts with /l.

23.7 Exploring a Class's Members and Viewing Documentation

[*Note:* This section may be read after studying Chapter 6, Methods: A Deeper Look, and the preceding portions of Chapter 23.]

The preceding section introduced basic auto-completion capabilities. When using JShell for experimentation and discovery, you'll often want to learn more about a class before using it. In this section, we'll show you how to:

- view the parameters required by a method so that you can call it correctly
- view the documentation for a method
- view the documentation for a field of a class
- view the documentation for a class, and
- view the list of overloads for a given method.

To demonstrate these features, let's explore class Math. Start a new JShell session or /reset the current one.

23.7.1 Listing Class Math's static Members

As we discussed in Chapter 6, class Math contains only static members—static methods for various mathematical calculations and the static constants PI and E. To view a complete list, type "Math." then press *Tab*:

```
jshell> Math.
E                  IEEEremainder(  PI               abs(
acos(              addExact(       asin(            atan(
atan2(             cbrt(           ceil(            class
copySign(          cos(            cosh(            decrementExact(
exp(               expm1(          floor(           floorDiv(
floorMod(          fma(            getExponent(     hypot(
incrementExact(    log(            log10(           log1p(
max(               min(            multiplyExact(   multiplyFull(
multiplyHigh(      negateExact(    nextAfter(       nextDown(
nextUp(            pow(            random()         rint(
round(             scalb(          signum(          sin(
sinh(              sqrt(           subtractExact(   tan(
tanh(              toDegrees(      toIntExact(      toRadians(
ulp(

jshell> Math.
```

As you know, JShell auto-completion displays a list of everything that can appear to the right of the dot (.). Here we typed a class name and a dot (.), so JShell shows only the class's static members. The names that are not followed by any parentheses (E and PI) are the class's static variables. All the other names are the class's static methods:

- Any method names followed by ()—only random in this case—do not require any arguments.

- Any method names followed by only an opening left parenthesis, (, require at least one argument or are overloaded.

You can easily view the value of the constants PI and E:

```
jshell> Math.PI
$1 ==> 3.141592653589793

jshell> Math.E
$2 ==> 2.718281828459045

jshell>
```

23.7.2 Viewing a Method's Parameters

Let's assume you wish to test Math's pow method (introduced in Section 5.4.2), but you do not know the parameters it requires. You can type

```
Math.p
```

then press *Tab* to auto-complete the name pow:

```
jshell> Math.pow(
```

Since there are no other methods that begin with "pow", JShell also inserts the left parenthesis to indicate the beginning of a method call. Next, you can type *Tab* to view the method's parameters:

```
jshell> Math.pow(
double Math.pow(double a, double b)

<press tab again to see documentation>

jshell> Math.pow(
```

JShell displays the method's return type, name and complete parameter list followed by the next `jshell>` prompt containing what you've typed so far. As you can see, the method requires two `double` parameters.

23.7.3 Viewing a Method's Documentation

JShell integrates the Java API documentation so you can view documentation conveniently in JShell, rather than requiring you to use a separate web browser. Suppose you'd like to learn more about pow before completing your code snippet. You can press *Tab* again to view the method's Java documentation (known as its javadoc)—we cut out some of the documentation text and replaced it with a vertical ellipsis (…) to save space (try the steps in your own JShell session to see the complete text):

```
jshell> Math.pow(
double Math.pow(double a, double b)
Returns the value of the first argument raised to the power of the
second argument.Special cases:
  * If the second argument is positive or negative zero, then the
    result is 1.0.
...
<press tab again to see next page>
```

For long documentation, JShell displays part of it, then shows the message

```
<press tab again to see next page>
```

You can press *Tab* to view the next page of documentation. The next `jshell>` prompt shows the portion of the snippet you've typed so far:

```
jshell> Math.pow(
```

23.7.4 Viewing a `public` Field's Documentation

You can use the *Tab* feature to learn more about a class's `public` fields. For example, if you enter `Math.PI` followed by *Tab*, JShell displays

```
jshell> Math.PI
PI

Signatures:
Math.PI:double

<press tab again to see documentation>
```

which shows `Math.PI`'s type and indicates that you can use *Tab* again to view the documentation. Doing so displays:

```
jshell> Math.PI
Math.PI:double
The double value that is closer than any other to pi, the ratio of
the circumference of a circle to its diameter.

jshell> Math.PI
```

and the next jshell> prompt shows the portion of the snippet you've typed so far.

23.7.5 Viewing a Class's Documentation

You also can type a class name then *Tab* to view the class's fully qualified name. For example, typing Math then *Tab* shows:

```
jshell> Math
Math            MathContext

Signatures:
java.lang.Math

<press tab again to see documentation>

jshell> Math
```

indicating that class Math is in the package java.lang. Typing *Tab* again shows the beginning of the class's documentation:

```
jshell> Math
java.lang.Math
The class Math contains methods for performing basic numeric opera-
tions such as the elementary exponential, logarithm, square root,
and trigonometric functions. Unlike some of the numeric methods of
...

<press tab again to see next page>
```

In this case, there is more documentation to view, so you can press *Tab* to view it. Whether or not you view the remaining documentation, the jshell> prompt shows the portion of the snippet you've typed so far:

```
jshell> Math
```

23.7.6 Viewing Method Overloads

Many classes have *overloaded* methods. When you press *Tab* to view an overloaded method's parameters, JShell displays the complete list of overloads, showing the parameters for every overload. For example, method Math.abs has four overloads:

```
jshell> Math.abs(
$1    $2

Signatures:
int Math.abs(int a)
long Math.abs(long a)
float Math.abs(float a)
double Math.abs(double a)

<press tab again to see documentation>

jshell> Math.abs(
```

When you press *Tab* again to view the documentation, JShell shows you the *first* overload's documentation:

```
jshell> Math.abs(
int Math.abs(int a)
Returns the absolute value of an int value.If the argument is not
negative, the argument is returned. If the argument is negative,
the negation of the argument is returned.
...

<press tab again to see next page>
```

You can then press *Tab* to view the documentation for the next overload in the list. Again, whether or not you view the remaining documentation, the jshell> prompt shows the portion of the snippet you've typed so far.

23.7.7 Exploring Members of a Specific Object

The exploration features shown in Sections 23.7.1—23.7.6 also apply to the members of a specific object. Let's create and explore a String object:

```
jshell> String dayName = "Monday"
dayName ==> "Monday"

jshell>
```

To view the methods you can call on the dayName object, type "dayName." and press *Tab*:

```
jshell> dayName.
charAt(               chars()               codePointAt(
codePointBefore(      codePointCount(       codePoints()
compareTo(            compareToIgnoreCase(  concat(
contains(             contentEquals(        endsWith(
equals(               equalsIgnoreCase(     getBytes(
getChars(             getClass()            hashCode()
indexOf(              intern()              isEmpty()
lastIndexOf(          length()              matches(
notify()              notifyAll()           offsetByCodePoints(
regionMatches(        replace(              replaceAll(
replaceFirst(         split(                startsWith(
subSequence(          substring(            toCharArray()
toLowerCase(          toString()            toUpperCase(
trim()                wait(

jshell> dayName.
```

Exploring toUpperCase

Let's investigate the toUpperCase method. Continue by typing "toU" and pressing *Tab* to auto-complete its name:

```
jshell> dayName.toUpperCase(
toUpperCase(

jshell> dayName.toUpperCase(
```

Then, type *Tab* to view its parameters:

```
jshell> dayName.toUpperCase(
Signatures:
String String.toUpperCase(Locale locale)
String String.toUpperCase()

<press tab again to see documentation>

jshell> dayName.toUpperCase(
```

This method has two overloads. You can now use *Tab* to read about each overload, or simply choose the one you wish to use, by specifying the appropriate arguments (if any). In this case, we'll use the no-argument version to create a new String containing MONDAY, so we simply enter the closing right parenthesis of the method call and press *Enter*:

```
jshell> dayName.toUpperCase()
$2 ==> "MONDAY"

jshell>
```

Exploring substring

Let's assume you want to create the new String "DAY"—a subset of the implicit variable $2's characters. For this purpose class String provides the overloaded method substring. First type "$2.subs" and press *Tab* to auto-complete its the method's name:

```
jshell> $2.substring(
substring(

jshell>
```

Next, use *Tab* to view the method's overloads:

```
jshell> $2.substring(
Signatures:
String String.substring(int beginIndex)
String String.substring(int beginIndex, int endIndex)

<press tab again to see documentation>

jshell> $2.substring(
```

Next, use *Tab* again to view the first overload's documentation:

```
jshell> $2.substring(
String String.substring(int beginIndex)
Returns a string that is a substring of this string.The substring
begins with the character at the specified index and extends to the
end of this string.
...
<press tab again to see next page>
```

As you can see from the documentation, this overload of the method enables you to obtain a substring starting from a specific character index (that is, position) and continuing through the end of the String. The first character in the String is at index 0. This is the version of the method we wish to use to obtain "DAY" from "MONDAY", so we can return to our code snippet at the jshell> prompt:

```
jshell> $2.substring(
```

Finally, we can complete our call to substring and press *Enter* to view the results:

```
jshell> $2.substring(3)
$3 ==> "DAY"

jshell>
```

23.8 Declaring Methods

[*Note:* This section may be read after studying Chapter 6, Methods: A Deeper Look, and the preceding portions of Chapter 23.]

You can use JShell to prototype methods. For example, let's assume we'd like to write code that displays the cubes of the values from 1 through 10. For the purpose of this discussion, we're going to define two methods:

- Method `displayCubes` will iterate 10 times, calling method `cube` each time.

- Method `cube` will receive one int value and return the cube of that value.

23.8.1 Forward Referencing an Undeclared Method—Declaring Method displayCubes

Let's begin with method `displayCubes`. Start a new JShell session or `/reset` the current one, then enter the following method declaration:

```
void displayCubes() {
    for (int i = 1; i <= 10; i++) {
        System.out.println("Cube of " + i + " is " + cube(i));
    }
}
```

When you complete the method declaration, JShell displays:

```
|  created method displayCubes(), however, it cannot be invoked
until method cube(int) is declared

jshell>
```

Again, we *manually* added the indentation. Note that after you type the method body's opening left brace, JShell displays continuation prompts (...>) before each subsequent line until you complete the method declaration by entering its closing right brace. Also, although JShell says "`created method displayCubes()`", it indicates that you cannot call this method until "`cube(int) is declared`". This is *not* fatal in JShell—it recognizes that `displayCubes` depends on an undeclared method (`cube`)—this is known as **forward referencing** an undeclared method. Once you define `cube`, you can call `displayCubes`.

23.8.2 Declaring a Previously Undeclared Method

Next, let's declare method `cube`, but *purposely make a logic error* by returning the square rather than the cube of its argument:

```
jshell> int cube(int x) {
   ...>     return x * x;
   ...> }
|  created method cube(int)

jshell>
```

At this point, you can use JShell's **/methods** command to see the complete list of methods that are declared in the current JShell session:

```
jshell> /methods
|    void displayCubes()
|    int cube(int)

jshell>
```

Note that JShell displays each method's return type to the right of the parameter list.

23.8.3 Testing cube and Replacing Its Declaration

Now that method cube is declared, let's test it with the argument 2:

```
jshell> cube(2)
$3 ==> 4

jshell>
```

The method correctly returns the 4 (that is, 2 * 2), based on how the method is implemented. However, our the method's purpose was to calculate the cube of the argument, so the result should have been 8 (2 * 2 * 2). You can edit cube's snippet to correct the problem. Because cube was declared as a multiline snippet, the easiest way to edit the declaration is using **JShell Edit Pad**. You could use /list to determine cube's snippet ID then use /edit followed by the ID to open the snippet. You also edit the method by specifying its name, as in:

```
jshell> /edit cube
```

In the **JShell Edit Pad** window, change cube's body to:

```
    return x * x * x;
```

then press **Exit**. JShell displays:

```
jshell> /edit cube
|  modified method cube(int)

jshell>
```

23.8.4 Testing Updated Method cube and Method displayCubes

Now that method cube is properly declared, let's test it again with the arguments 2 and 10:

```
jshell> cube(2)
$5 ==> 8

jshell> cube(10)
$6 ==> 1000

jshell>
```

The method properly returns the cubes of 2 (that is, 8) and 10 (that is, 1000), and stores the results in the implicit variables $5 and $6.

Now let's test `displayCubes`. If you type `"di"` and press *Tab*, JShell auto-completes the name, including the parentheses of the method call, because `displayCubes` receives no parameters. The following shows the results of the call:

```
jshell> displayCubes()
Cube of 1 is 1
Cube of 2 is 8
Cube of 3 is 27
Cube of 4 is 64
Cube of 5 is 125
Cube of 6 is 216
Cube of 7 is 343
Cube of 8 is 512
Cube of 9 is 729
Cube of 10 is 1000

jshell>
```

23.9 Exceptions

[*Note:* This section may be read after studying Chapter 7, Arrays and `ArrayLists`, and the preceding sections of Chapter 23.]

In Section 7.5, we introduced Java's exception-handling mechanism, showing how to catch an exception that occurred when we attempted to use an out-of-bounds array index. In JShell, catching exceptions is not required—it automatically catches each exception and displays information about it, then displays the next JShell prompt, so you can continue your session. This is particularly important for *checked exceptions* (Section 11.5) that are required to be caught in regular Java programs—as you know, catching an exception requires wrapping the code in a `try...catch` statement. By automatically, catching all exceptions, JShell makes it easier for you to *experiment* with methods that throw checked exceptions.

In the following new JShell session, we declare an array of `int` values, then demonstrate both valid and invalid array-access expressions:

```
jshell> int[] values = {10, 20, 30}
values ==> int[3] { 10, 20, 30 }

jshell> values[1]
$2 ==> 20

jshell> values[10]
|   java.lang.ArrayIndexOutOfBoundsException thrown: 10
|         at (#3:1)

jshell>
```

The snippet `values[10]` attempts to access an out-of-bounds element—recall that this results in an `ArrayIndexOutOfBoundsException`. Even though we did not wrap the code in a `try...catch`, JShell catches the exception and displays the its `String` representation. This includes the exception's type and an error message (in this case, the invalid index 10), followed by a so-called stack trace indicating where the problem occurred. The notation

```
|           at (#3:1)
```

indicates that the exception occurred at line 1 of the code snippet with the ID 3. A stack trace indicates the methods that were on the method-call stack at the time the exception occurred. A typical stack trace contains several "at" lines like the one shown here—one per stack frame. After displaying the stack trace, JShell shows the next jshell> prompt. Chapter 11 discusses stack traces in detail.

23.10 Importing Classes and Adding Packages to the CLASSPATH

[*Note:* This section may be read after studying Chapter 8, Classes and Objects: A Deeper Look and the preceding sections of Chapter 23.]

When working in JShell, you can import types from Java 9's packages. In fact, several packages are so commonly used by Java developers that JShell automatically imports them for you. (You can change this with JShell's /set start command—see Section 23.12.)

You can use JShell's **/imports** command to see the current session's list of import declarations. The following listing shows the packages that are auto-imported when you begin a new JShell session:

```
jshell> /imports
|    import java.io.*
|    import java.math.*
|    import java.net.*
|    import java.nio.file.*
|    import java.util.*
|    import java.util.concurrent.*
|    import java.util.function.*
|    import java.util.prefs.*
|    import java.util.regex.*
|    import java.util.stream.*

jshell>
```

The java.lang package's contents are always available in JShell, just as in any Java source-code file.

In addition to the Java API's packages, you can import your own or third-party packages to use their types in JShell. First, you use JShell's **/env -class-path** command to add the packages to JShell's CLASSPATH, which specifies where the additional packages are located. You can then use import declarations to experiment with the packages' contents in JShell.

Using Our Time1 Class

In Chapter 8, we declared a Time1 class and placed it in the package com.deitel.ch08. Here, we'll add that package to JShell's CLASSPATH, import our Time1 class, then use it in JShell. If you have a current JShell session open, use /exit to terminate it. Then, change directories to the ch08 examples folder's and packagingTime1 subfolder then start a new JShell session.

Adding the Location of a Package to the CLASSPATH

The packagingTime1 folder contains a folder named com, which is the first of a nested set of folders that represent the compiled classes in our package com.deitel.ch08. The following uses adds this package to the CLASSPATH:

```
jshell> /env -class-path .
|  Setting new options and restoring state.

jshell>
```

The dot (.) indicates the current folder from which you launched JShell. You also can specify complete paths to other folders on your system or the paths of JAR (Java archive) files that contain packages of compiled classes.

Importing a Class from the Package

Now, you can import the Time1 class for use in JShell. The following shows importing our Time1 class and the complete list of imports in the current session:

```
jshell> import com.deitel.ch08.Time1

jshell> /imports
|    import java.io.*
|    import java.math.*
|    import java.net.*
|    import java.nio.file.*
|    import java.util.*
|    import java.util.concurrent.*
|    import java.util.function.*
|    import java.util.prefs.*
|    import java.util.regex.*
|    import java.util.stream.*
|    import com.deitel.ch08.Time1

jshell>
```

Using the Imported Class

Finally, you can use class Time. Below we create a Time1 object and show that JShell's auto-complete capability can display the list of available Time1 methods. Next, we use auto-completion to show the parameter types for setTime then call it to set the time. Then we display the object's String representation (which implicitly calls toString) and explicitly call the toString and toUniversalString methods:

```
jshell> Time1 time = new Time1()
time ==> 12:00:00 AM

jshell> time.
equals(        getClass()        hashCode()        notify()
notifyAll()    setTime(          toString()        toUniversalString()
wait(

jshell> time.setTime(
Signatures:
void Time1.setTime(int, int, int)

<press tab again to see documentation>
```

```
jshell> time.setTime(13, 27, 6)

jshell> time
time ==> 1:27:06 PM

jshell> time.toString()
$5 ==> "1:27:06 PM"

jshell> time.toUniversalString()
$6 ==> "13:27:06"

jshell>
```

23.11 Using an External Editor

Section 23.3.10 demonstrated **JShell Edit Pad** for editing code snippets. This tool provides only simple editing functionality. Many programmers prefer to use more powerful text editors. Using JShell's **/set editor** command, you can specify your preferred text editor. For example, we have a text editor named EditPlus, located on our Windows system at

```
C:\Program Files\EditPlus\editplus.exe
```

The JShell command

```
jshell> /set editor C:\Program Files\EditPlus\editplus.exe
|  Editor set to: C:\Program Files\EditPlus\editplus.exe

jshell>
```

sets EditPlus as the snippet editor for the current JShell session. The /set editor command's argument is *operating-system specific*. For example, on Ubuntu Linux, you can use the built-in gedit text editor with the command

```
/set editor gedit
```

and on macOS,[8] you can use the built-in TextEdit application with the command

```
/set editor -wait open -a TextEdit
```

Editing Snippets with a Custom Text Editor
When you're using a custom editor, each time you save snippet edits JShell immediately re-evaluates any snippets that have changed and shows their results (but not the snippets themselves) in the JShell output. The following shows a new JShell session in which we set a custom editor, then performed JShell interactions—we explain momentarily the two lines of output that follow the /edit command:

---

8. On macOS, the -wait option is required so that JShell does not simply open the external editor, then return immediately to the next jshell> prompt.

```
jshell> /set editor C:\Program Files\EditPlus\editplus.exe
|  Editor set to: C:\Program Files\EditPlus\editplus.exe

jshell> int x = 10
x ==> 10

jshell> int y = 10
y ==> 20

jshell> /edit
y ==> 20
10 + 20 = 30
jshell> /list

    1 : int x = 10;
    3 : int y = 20;
    4 : System.out.print(x + " + " + y + " = " + (x + y))

jshell>
```

First we declared the int variables x and y, then we launched the external editor to edit our snippets. Initially, the editor shows the snippets that declare x and y (Fig. 23.4).

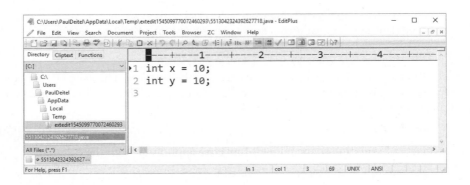

Fig. 23.4 | External editor showing code snippets to edit.

Next, we edited y's declaration, giving it the new value 20, then we added a new snippet to display both values and their sum (Fig. 23.5).

When we saved the edits in our text editor, JShell replaced y's original declaration with the updated one and showed

```
y ==> 20
```

to indicate that y's value changed. Then, JShell executed the new System.out.print snippet and showed its results

```
10 + 20 = 30
```

Finally, when we closed the external editor and pressed *Enter* in the command window, JShell displayed the next jshell> prompt.

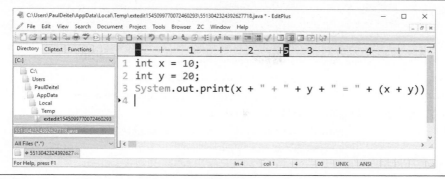

Fig. 23.5 | External editor showing code snippets to edit.

Retaining the Editor Setting

You can retain your editor setting for future JShell sessions as follows:

```
/set editor -retain commandToLaunchYourEditor
```

Restoring the JShell Edit Pad As the Default Editor

If you do not retain your custom editor, subsequent JShell sessions will use **JShell Edit Pad**. If you do retain the custom editor, you can restore **JShell Edit Pad** as the default with

```
/set editor -retain -default
```

23.12 Summary of JShell Commands

Figure 23.6 shows the basic JShell commands. Many of these commands have been presented throughout this chapter. Others are discussed in this section.

Command	Description
/help or /?	Displays JShell's list of commands.
/help intro	Displays a brief introduction to JShell.
/help shortcuts	Displays a description of several JShell shortcut keys.
/list	By default, lists the valid snippets you've entered in the current session. To list all snippets, use /list -all.
/!	Recalls and re-evaluates the last snippet.
/id	Recalls and re-evaluates the snippet with the specified id.
/-n	Recalls and re-evaluates a prior snippet—for n, 1 is the last snippet, 2 is the second-to-last, etc.
/edit	By default, opens a **JShell Edit Pad** window containing the valid snippets you've entered in the current session. See Section 23.11 to learn how to configure an external editor.
/save	Saves the current session's valid snippets to a specified file.

Fig. 23.6 | Jshell commands. (Part 1 of 2.)

Command	Description
/open	Opens a specified file of code snippets, loads the snippets into the current session and evaluates the loaded snippets.
/vars	Displays the current session's variables and their corresponding values.
/methods	Displays the signatures of the current session's declared methods.
/types	Displays types declared in the current session.
/imports	Displays the current session's import declarations.
/exit	Terminates the current JShell session.
/reset	Resets the current JShell session, deleting all code snippets.
/reload	Reloads a JShell session and executes the valid snippets (Section 23.12.3).
/drop	Deletes a specified snippet from the current session (Section 23.12.4).
/env	Makes changes to the JShell environment, such as adding packages or modules so you can use their types in JShell.
/history	Lists everything you've typed in the current JShell session, including all snippets (valid, invalid or overwritten) and JShell commands—the /list command shows only snippets, not JShell commands.
/set	Sets various JShell configuration options, such as the editor used in response to the /edit command, the text used for the JShell prompts, the imports to specify when a session starts, etc. (Sections 23.12.5—23.12.6).

Fig. 23.6 | Jshell commands. (Part 2 of 2.)

23.12.1 Getting Help in JShell

JShell's help documentation is incorporated directly via the **/help** or **/?** commands—/? is simply a shorthand for /help. For a quick introduction to JShell, type:

```
/help intro
```

To display JShell's list of commands, type

```
/help
```

For more information on a given command's options, type

```
/help command
```

For example

```
/help /list
```

displays the /list command's more detailed help documentation. Similarly

```
/help /set start
```

displays more detailed help documentation for the /set command's start option. For a list of the shortcut key combinations in JShell, type

```
/help shortcuts
```

23.12.2 /edit Command: Additional Features

We've discussed using /edit to load all valid snippets, a snippet with a specified ID or a method with a specified name into **JShell Edit Pad**. You can specify the identifier for any variable, method or type declaration that you'd like to edit. For example, if the current JShell session contains the declaration of a class named Account, the following loads that class into **JShell Edit Pad**:

```
/edit Account
```

23.12.3 /reload Command

At the time of this writing, you cannot use the /id command to execute a range of previous snippets. However, JShell's **/reload** command can re-execute all valid snippets in the current session. Consider the session from Sections 23.3.9—23.3.10:

```
jshell> /list

   1 : 45
   2 : 72
   3 : if ($1 < $2) {
           System.out.printf("%d < %d%n", $1, $2);
       }
   4 : if ($1 > $2) {
           System.out.printf("%d > %d%n", $1, $2);
       }
   5 : $1 = 100;
   6 : if ($1 > $2) {
           System.out.printf("%d > %d%n", $1, $2);
       }

jshell>
```

The following reloads that session one snippet at a time:

```
jshell> /reload
|  Restarting and restoring state.
-: 45
-: 72
-: if ($1 < $2) {
       System.out.printf("%d < %d%n", $1, $2);
   }
45 < 72
-: if ($1 > $2) {
       System.out.printf("%d > %d%n", $1, $2);
   }
-: $1 = 100
-: if ($1 > $2) {
       System.out.printf("%d > %d%n", $1, $2);
   }
100 > 72

jshell>
```

Each reloaded snippet is preceded by -: and in the case of the if statements, the output (if any) is shown immediately following each if statement. If you prefer not to see the snippets as they reload, you can use the /reload command's -quiet option:

```
jshell> /reload -quiet
|  Restarting and restoring state.
45 < 72
100 > 72

jshell>
```

In this case, only the results of output statements are displayed. Then, you can view the snippets that were reloaded with the /list command.

23.12.4 /drop Command

You can eliminate a snippet from the current session with JShell's **/drop** command followed by a snippet ID or an identifier. The following new JShell session declares a variable x and a method cube, then drops x via its snippet ID and drops cube via its identifier:

```
jshell> int x = 10
x ==> 10

jshell> int cube(int y) {return y * y * y;}
|  created method cube(int)

jshell> /list

   1 : int x = 10;
   2 : int cube(int y) {return y * y * y;}

jshell> /drop 1
|  dropped variable x

jshell> /drop cube
|  dropped method cube(int)

jshell> /list

jshell>
```

23.12.5 Feedback Modes

JShell has several feedback modes that determine what gets displayed after each interaction. To change the feedback mode, use JShell's **/set feedback** command:

```
/set feedback mode
```

where *mode* is concise, normal (the default), silent or verbose. All of the prior JShell interactions in this chapter used the normal mode.

Feedback Mode **verbose**

Below is a new JShell session in which we used verbose mode, which beginning programmers might prefer:

```
jshell> /set feedback verbose
|  Feedback mode: verbose

jshell> int x = 10
x ==> 10
|  created variable x : int

jshell> int cube(int y) {return y * y * y;}
|  created method cube(int)

jshell> cube(x)
$3 ==> 1000
|  created scratch variable $3 : int

jshell> x = 5
x ==> 5
|  assigned to x : int

jshell> cube(x)
$5 ==> 125
|  created scratch variable $5 : int

jshell>
```

Notice the additional feedback indicating that

- variable x was created,

- variable $3 was created on the first call to cube—JShell refers to the implicit variable as a *scratch variable*,

- an int was assigned to the variable x, and

- scratch variable $5 was created on the second call to cube.

Feedback Mode concise

Next, we /reset the session then set the feedback mode to concise and repeat the preceding session:

```
jshell> /set feedback concise
jshell> int x = 10
jshell> int cube(int y) {return y * y * y;}
jshell> cube(x)
$3 ==> 1000
jshell> x = 5
jshell> cube(x)
$5 ==> 125
jshell>
```

As you can see, the only feedback displayed is the result of each call to cube. If an error occurs, its feedback also will be displayed.

Feedback Mode silent

Next, we /reset the session then set the feedback mode to silent and repeat the preceding session:

```
jshell> /set feedback silent
-> int x = 10
-> int cube(int y) {return y * y * y;}
-> cube(x)
-> x = 5
-> cube(x)
-> /set feedback normal
|  Feedback mode: normal

jshell>
```

In this case, the `jshell>` prompt becomes `->` and only error feedback will be displayed. You might use this mode if you've copied code from a Java source file and want to paste it into JShell, but do not want to see the feedback for each line.

23.12.6 Other JShell Features Configurable with /set

So far, we've demonstrated the `/set` command's capabilities for setting an external snippet editor and setting feedback modes. The `/set` command provides extensive capabilities for creating custom feedback modes via the commands:

- `/set mode`
- `/set prompt`
- `/set truncation`
- `/set format`

The `/set mode` command creates a user-defined custom feedback mode. Then you can use the other three commands to customize all aspects of JShell's feedback. The details of these commands are beyond the scope of this chapter. For more information, see JShell's help documentation for each of the preceding commands.

Customizing JShell Startup
Section 23.10 showed the set of common packages JShell `imports` at the start of each session. Using JShell's **/set start** command

```
/set start filename
```

you can provide a file of Java snippets and JShell commands that will be used in the current session when it restarts due to a `/reset` or `/reload` command. You can also remove all startup snippets with

```
/set start -none
```

or return to the default startup snippets with

```
/set start -default
```

In all three cases, the setting applies only to the current session unless you also include the `-retain` option. For example, the following command indicates that all subsequent JShell sessions should load the specified file of startup snippets and commands:

```
/set start -retain filename
```

You can restore the defaults for future sessions with

```
/set start -retain -default
```

23.13 Keyboard Shortcuts for Snippet Editing

In addition to the commands in Fig. 23.6, JShell supports many keyboard shortcuts for editing code, such as quickly jumping to the beginning or end of a line, or jumping between words in a line. JShell's command-line features are implemented by a library named JLine 2, which provides command-line editing and history capabilites. Figure 23.7 shows a sample of the shortcuts available.

Shortcut	Description
Ctrl + a	Move cursor to beginning of line.
Ctrl + e	Move cursor to end of line.
Alt + b	Move the cursor backwards by one word.
Alt + f	Move the cursor forwards by one word.
Ctrl + r	Perform a search for the last command or snippet containing the characters you type after typing *Ctrl + r*.
Ctrl + t	Reverse the two characters to the left of the cursor.
Ctrl + k	Cut everything from the cursor to the end of the line.
Ctrl + u	Cut everything from the beginning of the line up to, but not including the character at the cursor position.
Ctrl + w	Cut the word before the cursor.
Alt + d	Cut the word after the cursor.

Fig. 23.7 | Some keyboard shortcuts for editing the current snippet at the `jshell>` prompt.

23.14 How JShell Reinterprets Java for Interactive Use

In JShell:

- A `main` method is not required.
- Semicolons are not required on standalone statements.
- Variables do not need to be declared in classes or in methods.
- Methods do not need to be declared inside a class's body.
- Statements do not need to be written inside methods.
- Redeclaring a variable, method or type simply drops the prior declaration and replaces it with the new one, whereas the Java compiler normally would report an error.
- You do not need to catch exceptions, though you can if you need to test exception handling.
- JShell ignores top-level access modifiers (`public`, `private`, `protected`, `static`, `final`)—only `abstract` (Chapter 10) is allowed as a class modifier.
- The `synchronized` keyword (Chapter 21, Concurrency and Multi-Core Performance) is ignored.
- `package` statements and Java 9 `module` statements are not allowed.

9

23.15 IDE JShell Support

At the time of this writing, work is just beginning on JShell support in popular IDEs such as NetBeans, IntelliJ IDEA and Eclipse. NetBeans currently has an early access plug-in that enables you to work with JShell in both Java 8 and Java 9—even though JShell is a Java 9 feature. Some vendors will use JShell's APIs to provide developers with JShell environments that show both the code users type and the results of running that code side-by-side. Some features you might see in IDE JShell support include:

- Source-code syntax coloring for better code readability.
- Automatic source-code indentation and insertion of closing braces (}), parentheses (()) and brackets (]) to save programmers time.
- Debugger integration.
- Project integration, such as being able to automatically use classes in the same project from a JShell session.

23.16 Wrap-Up

In this chapter, you used JShell—Java 9's new interactive REPL for exploration, discovery and experimentation. We showed how to start a JShell session and work with various types of code snippets, including statements, variables, expressions, methods and classes—all without having to declare a class containing a main method to execute the code.

You saw that you can list the valid snippets in the current session, and recall and execute prior snippets and commands using the up and down arrow keys. You also saw that you can list the current session's variables, methods, types and imports. We showed how to clear the current JShell session to remove all existing snippets and how to save snippets to a file then reload them.

We demonstrated JShell's auto-completion capabilities for code and commands, and showed how you can explore a class's members and view documentation directly in JShell. We explored class Math, demonstrating how to list its static members, how to view a method's parameters and overloads, view a method's documentation and view a public field's documentation. We also explored the methods of a String object.

You declared methods and forward referenced an undeclared method that you declared later in the session, then saw that you could go back and execute the first method. We also showed that you can replace a method declaration with a new method—in fact, you can replace any declaration of a variable, method or type.

We showed that JShell catches all exceptions and simply displays a stack trace followed by the next jshell> prompt, so you can continue the session. You imported an existing compiled class from a package, then used that class in a JShell session.

Next, we summarized and demonstrated various other JShell commands. We showed how to configure a custom snippet editor, view JShell's help documentation, reload a session, drop snippets from a session, configure feedback modes and more. We listed some additional keyboard shortcuts for editing the current snippet at the jshell> prompt. Finally, we discussed how JShell reinterprets Java for interactive use and IDE support for JShell. In the next chapter, we introduce the Java Persistence API (JPA), which can greatly simplify how your apps interact with databases.

Self-Review Exercises

We encourage you to use JShell to do Exercises 23.1—23.43 after reading Sections 23.3—23.4. We've included the answers for all these exercises to help you get comfortable with JShell/REPL quickly.

23.1 Confirm that when you use `System.out.println` to display a `String` literal, such as `"Happy Birthday!"`, the quotes (`""`) are not displayed. End your statement with a semicolon.

23.2 Repeat Exercise 23.1, but remove the semicolon at the end of your statement to demonstrate that semicolons in this position are optional in JShell.

23.3 Confirm that JShell does not execute a `//` end-of-line comment.

23.4 Show that an executable statement enclosed in a multiline comment—delimited by `/*` and `*/`—does not execute.

23.5 Show what happens when the following code is entered in JShell:

```
/* incomplete multi-line comment
System.out.println("Welcome to Java Programming!")
/* complete multi-line
comment */
```

23.6 Show that indenting code with spaces does not affect statement execution.

23.7 Declare each of the following variables as type `int` in JShell to determine which are valid and which are invalid?
a) `first`
b) `first number`
c) `first1`
d) `1first`

23.8 Show that braces do not have to occur in matching pairs inside a string literal.

23.9 Show what happens when you type each of the following code snippets into JShell:
a) `System.out.println("seems OK")`
b) `System.out.println("missing something?)`
c) `System.out.println"missing something else?")`

23.10 Demonstrate that after a `System.out.print` the next print results appear on the same line right after the previous one's. [*Hint:* To demonstrate this, reset the current session, enter two `System.out.print` statements, then use the following two commands to save the snippets to a file, then reload and re-execute them:

```
/save mysnippets
/open mysnippets
```

The `/open` command loads the `mysnippets` file's contents then executes them.]

23.11 Demonstrate that after a `System.out.println`, the next text that prints displays its text at the left of the next line. [*Hint:* To demonstrate this, reset the current session, enter a `System.out.println` statement followed by another print statement, then use the following two commands to save the snippets to a file, then reload and re-execute them:

```
/save mysnippets
/open mysnippets
```

The `/open` command loads the `mysnippets` file's contents then executes them.]

23.12 Demonstrate that you can reset a JShell session to remove all prior snippets and start from scratch without having to exit JShell and start a new session.

23.13 Using `System.out.println`, demonstrate that the escape sequence \n causes a newline to be issued to the output. Use the string

```
"Welcome\nto\nJShell!"
```

23.14 Demonstrate that the escape sequence \t causes a tab to be issued to the output. Note that your output will depend on how tabs are set on your system. Use the string

```
"before\tafter\nbefore\t\tafter"
```

23.15 Demonstrate what happens when you include a single backslash (\) in a string. Be sure that the character after the backslash does not create a valid escape sequence.

23.16 Display a string containing \\\\ (recall that \\ is an escape sequence for a backslash). How many backslashes are displayed?

23.17 Use the escape sequence \" to display a quoted string.

23.18 What happens when the following code executes in JShell:

```
System.out.println("Happy Birthday!\rSunny")
```

23.19 Consider the following statement

```
System.out.printf("%s%n%s%n", "Welcome to ", "Java Programming!")
```

Make the following intentional errors (separately) to see what happens.
    a) Omit the parentheses around the argument list.
    b) Omit the commas.
    c) Omit one of the %s%n sequences.
    d) Omit one of the strings (i.e., the second or the third argument).
    e) Replace the first %s with %d.
    f) Replace the string "Welcome to " with the integer 23.

23.20 What happens when you enter the /imports command in a new JShell session?

23.21 Import class `Scanner` then create a `Scanner` object `input` for reading from `System.in`. What happens when you execute the statement:

```
int number = input.nextInt()
```

and the user enters the string "hello"?

23.22 In a new or /reset JShell session, repeat Exercise 23.21 without importing class `Scanner` to demonstrate that the package `java.util` is already imported in JShell.

23.23 Demonstrate what happens when you don't precede a `Scanner` input operation with a meaningful prompting message telling the user what to input. Enter the following statements:

```
Scanner input = new Scanner(System.in)
int value = input.nextInt()
```

23.24 Demonstrate that you can't place an `import` statement in a class.

23.25 Demonstrate that identifiers are case sensitive by declaring variables `id` and `ID` of types `String` and `int`, respectively. Also use the /list command to show the two snippets representing the separate variables.

23.26 Demonstrate that initialization statements like

```
String month = "April"
int age = 65
```

indeed initialize their variables with the indicated values.

23.27 Demonstrate what happens when you:
a) Add 1 to the largest possible int value 2,147,483,647.
b) Subtract 1 from the smallest possible integer −2,147,483,648.

23.28 Demonstrate that large integers like 1234567890 are equivalent to their counterparts with the underscore separators, namely 1_234_567_890:
a) 1234567890 == 1_234_567_890
b) Print each of these values and show that you get the same result.
c) Divide each of these values by 2 and show that you get the same result.

23.29 Placing spaces around operators in an arithmetic expression does not affect the value of that expression. In particular, the following expressions are equivalent:

```
17+23
17 + 23
```

Demonstrate this with an if statement using the condition

```
(17+23) == (17 + 23)
```

23.30 Demonstrate that the parentheses around the argument number1 + number2 in the following statement are unnecessary:

```
System.out.printf("Sum is %d%n", (number1 + number2))
```

23.31 Declare the int variable x and initialize it to 14, then demonstrate that the subsequent assignment x = 27 is destructive.

23.32 Demonstrate that printing the value of the following variable is non-destructive:

```
int y = 29
```

23.33 Using the declarations:

```
int b = 7
int m = 9
```

a) Demonstrate that attempting to do algebraic multiplication by placing the variable names next to one another as in bm doesn't work in Java.
b) Demonstrate that the Java expression b * m indeed multiplies the two operands.

23.34 Use the following expressions to demonstrate that integer division yields an integer result:
a) 8 / 4
b) 7 / 5

23.35 Demonstrate what happens when you attempt each of the following integer divisions:
a) 0 / 1
b) 1 / 0
c) 0 / 0

23.36 Demonstrate that the values of the following expressions:
a) (3 + 4 + 5) / 5
b) 3 + 4 + 5 / 5

are different and thus the parentheses in the first expression are required if you want to divide the entire quantity 3 + 4 + 5 by 5.

23.37 Calculate the value of the following expression:

```
5 / 2 * 2 + 4 % 3 + 9 - 3
```

manually being careful to observe the rules of operator precedence. Confirm the result in JShell.

23.38 Test each of the two equality and four relational operators on the two values 7 and 7. For example, 7 == 7, 7 < 7, etc.

23.39 Repeat Exercise 23.38 using the values 7 and 9.

23.40 Repeat Exercise 23.38 using the values 11 and 9.

23.41 Demonstrate that accidentally placing a semicolon after the right parenthesis of the condition in an if statement can be a logic error.

```
if (3 == 5); {
    System.out.println("3 is equal to 5");
}
```

23.42 Given the following declarations:

```
int x = 1
int y = 2
int z = 3
int a
```

what are the values of a, x, y and z after the following statement executes?

```
a = x = y = z = 10
```

23.43 Manually determine the value of the following expression then use JShell to check your work:

```
(3 * 9 * (3 + (9 * 3 / (3))))
```

Answers to Self-Review Exercises

23.1

```
jshell> System.out.println("Happy Birthday!");
Happy Birthday!

jshell>
```

23.2

```
jshell> System.out.println("Happy Birthday!")
Happy Birthday!

jshell>
```

23.3

```
jshell> // comments are not executable

jshell>
```

23.4

```
jshell> /* opening line of multi-line comment
   ...>     System.out.println("Welcome to Java Programming!")
   ...>     closing line of multi-line comment */

jshell>
```

23.5 There is no compilation error, because the second /* is considered to be part of the first multi-line comment.

```
jshell> /* incomplete multi-line comment
   ...> System.out.println("Welcome to Java Programming!")
   ...> /* complete multi-line
   ...> comment */

jshell>
```

23.6

```
jshell> System.out.println("A")
A

jshell>     System.out.println("A") // indented 3 spaces
A

jshell>          System.out.println("A") // indented 6 spaces
A

jshell>
```

23.7   a) valid. b) invalid (space not allowed). c) valid. d) invalid (can't begin with a digit).

```
jshell> int first
first ==> 0

jshell> int first number
|  Error:
|  ';' expected
|  int first number
|           ^

jshell> int first1
first1 ==> 0

jshell> int 1first
|  Error:
|  '.class' expected
|  int 1first
|      ^
|  Error:
|  not a statement
|  int 1first
|        ^--^
|  Error:
|  unexpected type
|    required: value
|    found:    class
|  int 1first
|  ^--^
|  Error:
|  missing return statement
|  int 1first
|> ^---------^

jshell>
```

23.8

```
jshell> "Unmatched brace { in a string is OK"
$1 ==> "Unmatched brace { in a string is OK"

jshell>
```

23.9

```
jshell> System.out.println("seems OK")
seems OK

jshell> System.out.println("missing something?)
|  Error:
|  unclosed string literal
|  System.out.println("missing something?)
|                     ^

jshell> System.out.println"missing something else?")
|  Error:
|  ';' expected
|  System.out.println"missing something else?")
|                    ^
|  Error:
|  cannot find symbol
|    symbol:   variable println
|  System.out.println"missing something else?")
|  ^----------------^

jshell>
```

23.10

```
jshell> System.out.print("Happy ")
Happy
jshell> System.out.print("Birthday")
Birthday
jshell> /save mysession

jshell> /open mysession
Happy Birthday
jshell>
```

23.11

```
jshell> System.out.println("Happy ")
Happy
jshell> System.out.println("Birthday")
Birthday
jshell> /save mysession

jshell> /open mysession
Happy
Birthday
jshell>
```

23.12

```
jshell> int x = 10
x ==> 10

jshell> int y = 20
y ==> 20
```

(continued...)

```
jshell> x + y
$3 ==> 30

jshell> /reset
|  Resetting state.

jshell> /list

jshell>
```

23.13

```
jshell> System.out.println("Welcome\nto\nJShell!")
Welcome
to
JShell!

jshell>
```

23.14

```
jshell> System.out.println("before\tafter\nbefore\t\tafter")
before    after
before            after

jshell>
```

23.15

```
jshell> System.out.println("Bad escap\e")
|  Error:
|  illegal escape character
|  System.out.println("Bad escap\e")
|                              ^

jshell>
```

23.16 Two.

```
jshell> System.out.println("Displaying backslashes \\\\")
Displaying backslashes \\

jshell>
```

23.17

```
jshell> System.out.println("\"This is a string in quotes\"")
"This is a string in quotes"

jshell>
```

23.18

```
jshell> System.out.println("Happy Birthday!\rSunny")
Sunny Birthday!

jshell>
```

23.19   a)

```
jshell> System.out.printf"%s%n%s%n", "Welcome to ", "Java
Programming!"
|  Error:
|  ';' expected
|  System.out.printf"%s%n%s%n", "Welcome to ", "Java Programming!"
|                   ^
|  Error:
|  cannot find symbol
|    symbol:   variable printf
|  System.out.printf"%s%n%s%n", "Welcome to ", "Java Programming!"
|  ^--------------^

jshell>
```

b)

```
jshell> System.out.printf("%s%n%s%n" "Welcome to " "Java
Programming!")
|  Error:
|  ')' expected
|  System.out.printf("%s%n%s%n" "Welcome to " "Java Programming!")
|                               ^

jshell>
```

c)

```
jshell> System.out.printf("%s%n", "Welcome to ", "Java Programming!")
Welcome to
$6 ==> java.io.PrintStream@6d4b1c02

jshell>
```

d)

```
jshell> System.out.printf("%s%n%s%n", "Welcome to ")
Welcome to
|  java.util.MissingFormatArgumentException thrown: Format
specifier '%s'
|        at Formatter.format (Formatter.java:2524)
|        at PrintStream.format (PrintStream.java:974)
|        at PrintStream.printf (PrintStream.java:870)
|        at (#7:1)

jshell>
```

e)

```
jshell> System.out.printf("%d%n%s%n", "Welcome to ", "Java
Programming!")
|  java.util.IllegalFormatConversionException thrown: d !=
java.lang.String
|        at Formatter$FormatSpecifier.failConversion
(Formatter.java:4275)
|        at Formatter$FormatSpecifier.printInteger
(Formatter.java:2790)
|        at Formatter$FormatSpecifier.print (Formatter.java:2744)
```

(continued...)

```
|        at Formatter.format (Formatter.java:2525)
|        at PrintStream.format (PrintStream.java:974)
|        at PrintStream.printf (PrintStream.java:870)
|        at (#8:1)

jshell>
```

f)

```
jshell> System.out.printf("%s%n%s%n", 23, "Java Programming!")
23
Java Programming!
$9 ==> java.io.PrintStream@6d4b1c02

jshell>
```

23.20

```
jshell> /imports
|    import java.io.*
|    import java.math.*
|    import java.net.*
|    import java.nio.file.*
|    import java.util.*
|    import java.util.concurrent.*
|    import java.util.function.*
|    import java.util.prefs.*
|    import java.util.regex.*
|    import java.util.stream.*

jshell>
```

23.21

```
jshell> import java.util.Scanner

jshell> Scanner input = new Scanner(System.in)
input ==> java.util.Scanner[delimiters=\p{javaWhitespace}+] ...
\E][infinity string=\Q∞\E]

jshell> int number = input.nextInt()
hello
|   java.util.InputMismatchException thrown:
|        at Scanner.throwFor (Scanner.java:860)
|        at Scanner.next (Scanner.java:1497)
|        at Scanner.nextInt (Scanner.java:2161)
|        at Scanner.nextInt (Scanner.java:2115)
|        at (#2:1)

jshell>
```

23.22

```
jshell> Scanner input = new Scanner(System.in)
input ==> java.util.Scanner[delimiters=\p{javaWhitespace}+] ...
\E][infinity string=\Q∞\E]
```

(continued...)

```
jshell> int number = input.nextInt()
hello
|  java.util.InputMismatchException thrown:
|        at Scanner.throwFor (Scanner.java:860)
|        at Scanner.next (Scanner.java:1497)
|        at Scanner.nextInt (Scanner.java:2161)
|        at Scanner.nextInt (Scanner.java:2115)
|        at (#2:1)

jshell>
```

23.23 JShell appears to hang while it waits for the user to type a value and press *Enter*.

```
jshell> Scanner input = new Scanner(System.in)
input ==> java.util.Scanner[delimiters=\p{javaWhitespace}+] ...
\E][infinity string=\Q∞\E]

jshell> int value = input.nextInt()
```

23.24

```
jshell> class Demonstration {
   ...>     import java.util.Scanner;
   ...> }
|  Error:
|  illegal start of type
|     import java.util.Scanner;
|     ^
|  Error:
|  <identifier> expected
|     import java.util.Scanner;
|                             ^

jshell> import java.util.Scanner

jshell> class Demonstration {
   ...> }
|  created class Demonstration

jshell>
```

23.25

```
jshell> /reset
|  Resetting state.

jshell> String id = "Natasha"
id ==> "Natasha"

jshell> int ID = 413
ID ==> 413

jshell> /list
```

(continued...)

```
      1 : String id = "Natasha";
      2 : int ID = 413;

jshell>
```

23.26

```
jshell> String month = "April"
month ==> "April"

jshell> System.out.println(month)
April

jshell> int age = 65
age ==> 65

jshell> System.out.println(age)
65

jshell>
```

23.27

```
jshell> 2147483647 + 1
$9 ==> -2147483648

jshell> -2147483648 - 1
$10 ==> 2147483647

jshell>
```

23.28

```
jshell> 1234567890 == 1_234_567_890
$4 ==> true

jshell> System.out.println(1234567890)
1234567890

jshell> System.out.println(1_234_567_890)
1234567890

jshell> 1234567890 / 2
$5 ==> 617283945

jshell> 1_234_567_890 / 2
$6 ==> 617283945

jshell>
```

23.29

```
jshell> (17+23) == (17 + 23)
$7 ==> true

jshell>
```

23.30

```
jshell> int number1 = 10
number1 ==> 10

jshell> int number2 = 20
number2 ==> 20

jshell> System.out.printf("Sum is %d%n", (number1 + number2))
Sum is 30
$10 ==> java.io.PrintStream@1794d431

jshell> System.out.printf("Sum is %d%n", number1 + number2)
Sum is 30
$11 ==> java.io.PrintStream@1794d431

jshell>
```

23.31

```
jshell> int x = 14
x ==> 14

jshell> x = 27
x ==> 27

jshell>
```

23.32

```
jshell> int y = 29
y ==> 29

jshell> System.out.println(y)
29

jshell> y
y ==> 29
```

23.33

```
jshell> int b = 7
b ==> 7

jshell> int m = 9
m ==> 9

jshell> bm
|  Error:
|  cannot find symbol
|    symbol:   variable bm
|  bm
|  ^^

jshell> b * m
$3 ==> 63

jshell>
```

23.34 a) 2. b) 1.

```
jshell> 8 / 4
$4 ==> 2

jshell> 7 / 5
$5 ==> 1

jshell>
```

23.35

```
jshell> 0 / 1
$6 ==> 0

jshell> 1 / 0
|   java.lang.ArithmeticException thrown: / by zero
|         at (#7:1)

jshell> 0 / 0
|   java.lang.ArithmeticException thrown: / by zero
|         at (#8:1)

jshell>
```

23.36

```
jshell> (3 + 4 + 5) / 5
$9 ==> 2

jshell> 3 + 4 + 5 / 5
$10 ==> 8

jshell>
```

23.37

```
jshell> 5 / 2 * 2 + 4 % 3 + 9 - 3
$11 ==> 11

jshell>
```

23.38

```
jshell> 7 == 7
$12 ==> true

jshell> 7 != 7
$13 ==> false

jshell> 7 < 7
$14 ==> false

jshell> 7 <= 7
$15 ==> true

jshell> 7 > 7
$16 ==> false
```

(continued...)

```
jshell> 7 >= 7
$17 ==> true

jshell>
```

23.39

```
jshell> 7 == 9
$18 ==> false

jshell> 7 != 9
$19 ==> true

jshell> 7 < 9
$20 ==> true

jshell> 7 <= 9
$21 ==> true

jshell> 7 > 9
$22 ==> false

jshell> 7 >= 9
$23 ==> false

jshell>
```

23.40

```
jshell> 11 == 9
$24 ==> false

jshell> 11 != 9
$25 ==> true

jshell> 11 < 9
$26 ==> false

jshell> 11 <= 9
$27 ==> false

jshell> 11 > 9
$28 ==> true

jshell> 11 >= 9
$29 ==> true

jshell>
```

23.41

```
jshell> if (3 == 5); {
   ...>     System.out.println("3 is equal to 5");
   ...> }
3 is equal to 5

jshell>
```

23.42

```
jshell> int x = 1
x ==> 1

jshell> int y = 2
y ==> 2

jshell> int z = 3
z ==> 3

jshell> int a
a ==> 0

jshell> a = x = y = z = 10
a ==> 10

jshell> x
x ==> 10

jshell> y
y ==> 10

jshell> z
z ==> 10

jshell>
```

23.43

```
jshell> (3 * 9 * (3 + (9 * 3 / (3))))
$42 ==> 324

jshell>
```

24

Java Persistence API (JPA)

Objectives

In this chapter you'll:

- Learn the fundamentals of JPA.
- Use classes, interfaces and annotations from the `javax.persistence` package.
- Use the NetBeans IDE's tools to create a Java DB database.
- Use the NetBeans IDE's object-relational-mapping tools to autogenerate JPA entity classes.
- Use autogenerated entity classes to query databases and access data from multiple database tables.
- Use JPA transaction processing capabilities to modify database data.
- Use Java 8 lambdas and streams to manipulate the results of JPA queries.

Outline

24.1 Introduction

Chapter 22 used JDBC to connect to relational databases and Structured Query Language (SQL) to query and manipulate relational databases. Recall that we created `Strings` containing the SQL for every query, insert, update and delete operation. We also created our own classes for managing interactions with databases. If you're not already familiar with relational databases, SQL and JDBC, you should read Chapter 22 first as this chapter assumes you're already familiar with the concepts we presented there. This chapter uses the Java EE version of NetBeans 8.2. You can download the current NetBeans versions[1] from

```
https://netbeans.org/downloads/
```

In this chapter, we introduce the Java Persistence API (JPA). One of JPA's key capabilities is mapping Java classes to relational database tables and objects of those classes to rows in the tables. This is known as **object-relational mapping**. You'll use the NetBeans IDE's object-relational mapping tools to select a database and autogenerate classes that use JPA to interact with that database. Your programs can then use those classes to query the database, insert new records, update existing records and delete records. You will not have to create mappings between your Java code and database tables (as you did with JDBC), and you'll be able to perform complex database manipulations directly in Java.

Though you'll manipulate Java DB databases in this chapter, the JPA can be used with any database management system that supports JDBC. At the end of the chapter, we provide links to online JPA resources where you can learn more.

---

1. As NetBeans and Java EE evolve, the steps in this chapter may change. NetBeans.org provides prior NetBeans versions for download at `http://services.netbeans.org/downloads/dev.php`.

24.2 JPA Technology Overview

When using JPA in this chapter, you'll interact with an existing database via classes that the NetBeans IDE generates from the database's schema. Though we do not do so in this chapter, it's also possible for you to create such classes from scratch and use JPA annotations that enable those classes to create corresponding tables in a database.

24.2.1 Generated Entity Classes

In Section 24.3.5, you'll use the **NetBeans Entity Classes from Database...** option to add to your project classes that represent the database tables. Together, these classes and the corresponding settings are known as a **persistence unit**. The discussion in this section is based on the books database that we introduced in Section 22.3.

For the books database, the NetBeans IDE's object-relational mapping tools create two classes in the data model—Authors and Titles. Each class—known as an **entity class**—represents the corresponding table in the database and objects of these classes—known as **entities**—represent the rows in the corresponding tables. These classes contain:

- Instance variables representing the table's columns—These are named with all lowercase letters by default and have Java types that are compatible with their database types. Each instance variable is preceded by JPA annotations with information about the corresponding database column, such as whether the instance variable is the table's primary key, whether the column's value in the table is auto-generated, whether the column's value is optional and the column's name.

- Constructors for initializing objects of the class—The resulting entity objects represent rows in the corresponding table. Programs can use entity objects to manipulate the corresponding data in the database.

- *Set* and *get* methods that enable client code to access each instance variable.

- Overridden methods of class Object—hashCode, equals and toString.

24.2.2 Relationships Between Tables in the Entity Classes

We did not mention the books database's AuthorISBN table. Recall from Section 22.3 that this table links:

- each author in the Authors table to that author's books in the Titles table, and
- each book in the Titles table to the book's authors in the Authors table.

This is known as a **join table**, because it's used to join information from multiple other tables. The object-relational mapping tools do *not* create a class for the AuthorISBN table. Instead, relationships between tables are taken into account by the generated entity classes:

- The Authors class contains the titlesList instance variable—a List of Title objects representing books written by that author.

- The Titles class contains the authorsList instance variable—a List of Author objects representing that book's authors.

Like the other instance variables, these List variable declarations are preceded by JPA annotations, such as the join table's name, the Authors and AuthorISBN columns that link authors to their books, the `Titles` and `AuthorISBN` columns that link titles to their authors, and the type of the relationship. In the book's database there is a *many-to-many relationship*, because each author can write many books and each book can have many authors. We'll show key features of these autogenerated classes later in the chapter. Section 24.4 demonstrates queries that use the relationships among the books database's tables to display joined data.

24.2.3 The `javax.persistence` Package

The package **`javax.persistence`** contains the JPA interfaces and classes used to interact with the databases in this chapter.

EntityManager Interface
An object that implements the **`EntityManager`** interface manages the interactions between the program and the database. In Sections 24.3—24.4, you'll use an `EntityManager` to create query objects for obtaining entities from the books database. In Section 24.5, you'll use an `EntityManager` to both query the addressbook database and to create transactions for inserting new entities into the database.

EntityManagerFactory Interface and the `Persistence` Class
To obtain an `EntityManager` for a given database, you'll use an object that implements the **`EntityManagerFactory`** interface. As you'll see, the `Persistence` class's `static` method **`createEntityManagerFactory`** returns an `EntityManagerFactory` for the persistence unit you specify as a `String` argument.

In this chapter, you'll use application-managed `EntityManagers`—that is, ones you obtain from an `EntityManagerFactory` in your app. When you use JPA in Java EE apps, you'll obtain container-managed `EntityManagers` from the Java EE server (i.e., the container) on which your app executes.

TypedQuery Class, Dynamic Queries and Named Queries
An object that implements the **`TypedQuery`** generic interface performs queries and returns a collection of matching entities—in this chapter, you'll specify that the queries should return `List` objects, though you can choose `Collection`, `List` or `Set` when you generate the entity classes.

To create queries, you'll use `EntityManager` methods. In Section 24.3, you'll create a query with the `EntityManager`'s **`createQuery`** method. This method's first argument is a `String` written in the **Java Persistence Query Language (JPQL)**—as you'll see, JPQL is similar to SQL (Section 22.4). JPQL queries entity objects, rather than relational database tables. When you define a query in your own code, it's known as a *dynamic query*. In Sections 24.4—24.5, you'll use autogenerated *named queries* that you can access via the `EntityManager` method **`createNamedQuery`**.

24.3 Querying a Database with JPA

In this section, we demonstrate how to create the books database's JPA entity classes, then use JPA and those classes to *connect* to the books database, *query* it and *display* the results of the query. As you'll see, NetBeans provides tools that simplify accessing data via JPA.

This section's example performs a simple query that retrieves the books database's `Authors` table. We then use lambdas and streams to display the table's contents. The steps you'll perform are:

- Create a Java DB database and populate it from the `books.sql` file provided with this chapter's examples.

- Create the Java project.

- Add the JPA reference implementation's libraries to the project.

- Add the Java DB library to the project so that the app can access the driver required to connect to the Java DB database over a network—though we'll use the network-capable version of Java DB here, the database will still reside on your local computer.

- Create the persistence unit containing the entity classes for querying the database.

- Create the Java app that uses JPA to obtain the `Authors` table's data.

24.3.1 Creating the Java DB Database

In this section, you'll use the SQL script (`books.sql`) provided with this chapter's examples to create the `books` database in NetBeans. Chapter 22 demonstrated several database apps that used the embedded version of Java DB. This chapter's examples use the network server version.

Creating the Database

Perform the following steps to create the `books` database:

1. In the upper-left corner of the NetBeans IDE, click the **Services** tab. (If the Services tab is not displayed, select **Services** from the **Window** menu.)

2. Expand the **Databases** node then right click **Java DB**. If **Java DB** is not already running the **Start Server** option will be enabled. In this case, Select **Start Server** to launch the Java DB server. You may need to wait a moment for the server to begin executing.[2]

3. Right click the **Java DB** node, then select **Create Database....**

4. In the **Create Java DB Database** dialog, set **Database Name** to books, **User Name** to `deitel`, and **Password** and **Confirm Password** to `deitel`.[3]

5. Click **OK**.

The preceding steps create the database using Java DB's *server version* that can receive database connections over a network. A new node named

```
jdbc:derby://localhost:1527/books
```

---

2. If the **Start Server** option is disabled, select **Properties...** and ensure that the **Java DB Installation** option is set to the JDK's **db** folder location.

3. We used `deitel` as the user name and password for simplicity—ensure that you use secure passwords in real applications.

appears in the **Services** tab's **Database** node. This is the JDBC URL that's used to connect to the database.

24.3.2 Populating the books Database with Sample Data

You'll now populate the database with sample data using the `books.sql` script that's provided with this chapter's examples. To do so, perform the following steps:

1. Select **File > Open File...** to display the **Open** dialog.

2. Navigate to this chapter's examples folder, select `books.sql` and click **Open**.

3. In NetBeans, right click in the SQL script and select **Run File**.

4. In the **Select Database Connection** dialog, select the JDBC URL for the database you created in Section 24.3.1 and click **OK**.

The IDE will connect to the database and run the SQL script to populate the database. The SQL script attempts to remove the database's tables if they already exist. If they do not, you'll receive error messages when the three DROP TABLE commands in the SQL script execute, but the tables will still be created properly.

You can confirm that the database was populated properly by viewing each table's data in NetBeans. To do so:

1. In the NetBeans **Services** tab, expand the **Databases** node, then expand the node `jdbc:derby://localhost:1527/books`.

2. Expand the **DEITEL** node, then the **Tables** node.

3. Right click one of the tables and select **View Data...**.

The books database is now set up and ready for connections.

24.3.3 Creating the Java Project

For the examples in this section and Section 24.4, we'll create one project that contains the books database's JPA entity classes and two Java apps that use them. To create the project:

1. In the upper-left corner of NetBeans, select the **Projects** tab.

2. Select **File > New Project...**.

3. In the **New Project** dialog, select the **Java** category, then **Java Application** and click **Next >**.

4. For the **Project Name**, specify `BooksDatabaseExamples`, then choose where you wish to store the project on your computer.

5. Ensure that the **Create Main Class** option is checked. By default, NetBeans uses the project name as the class name and puts the class in a package named `books-databaseexamples` (the project name in all lowercase letters). We changed the class name for this first example to `DisplayAuthors`. Also, to indicate that the classes in this package are from this book's JPA chapter, we replaced the package name with

```
com.deitel.jhtp.jpa
```

6. Click **Finish** to create the project.

24.3.4 Adding the JPA and Java DB Libraries

For certain types of projects (such as server-side Java EE applications), NetBeans automatically includes JPA support, but not for simple **Java Application** projects. In addition, NetBeans projects do not include database drivers by default. In this section, you'll add the JPA libraries and Java DB driver library to the project so that you can use JPA's features to interact with the Java DB database you created in Sections 24.3.1—24.3.2.

EclipseLink—The JPA Reference Implementation
Each Java Enterprise Edition (Java EE) API—such as JPA—has a *reference implementation* that you can use to experiment with the API's features and implement applications. The JPA reference implementation—which is included with the NetBeans Java EE version—is **EclipseLink** (http://www.eclipse.org/eclipselink).

Adding Libraries
To add JPA and Java DB support to your project:

1. In the NetBeans **Projects** tab, expand the **BooksDatabaseExamples** node.

2. Right click the project's **Libraries** node and select **Add Library…**.

3. In the **Add Library** dialog, hold the *Ctrl* key—*command* (⌘) in OS X—and select **EclipseLink (JPA 2.1)**, **Java DB Driver** and **Persistence (JPA 2.1)**, then click **Add Library**.

24.3.5 Creating the Persistence Unit for the books Database

In this section, you'll create the persistence unit containing the entity classes Authors and Titles using the NetBeans object-relational mapping tools. To do so:

1. In the NetBeans **Projects** tab, right click the **BooksDatabaseExamples** node, then select **New > Entity Classes from Database…**.

2. In the **New Entity Classes from Database** dialog's **Database Tables** step, select the books database's URL from the **Database Connection** drop-down list. Then, click the **Add All >>** button and click **Next >**.

3. The **Entity Classes** step enables you to customize the entity class names and the package. Keep the default names, ensure that **Generate Named Query Annotations for Persistent Fields**, **Generate JAXB Annotations** and **Create Persistence Unit** are checked then click **Next >**.

4. In the **Mapping Options** step, change the **Collection Type** to java.util.List and keep the other default settings —for queries that return multiple authors or titles, the results will be placed in List objects.

5. Click **Finish**.

The IDE creates the persistence unit containing the Authors and Titles classes and adds their source-code files Authors.java and Titles.java to the project's package node (com.deitel.jhtp.jpa) in the **Source Packages** folder. As part of the persistence unit, the IDE also creates a META-INF package in the **Source Packages** folder. This contains the persistence.xml file, which specifies persistence unit settings. These include the books database's JDBC URL and the persistence unit's name, which you'll use to obtain an

EntityManager to manage the books database interactions. By default, the persistence unit's name is the project name followed by PU—BooksDatabaseExamplesPU. It's also possible to have multiple persistence units, but that's beyond this chapter's scope.

24.3.6 Querying the Authors Table

Figure 24.1 performs a simple books database query that retrieves the Authors table and displays its data. The program illustrates using JPA to connect to the database and query it. You'll use a dynamic query created in main to get the data from the database—in the next example, you'll use auto-generated queries in the persistence unit to perform the same query and others. In Section 24.5, you'll learn how to modify a database through a JPA persistence unit. *Reminder:* Before you run this example, ensure that the Java DB database server is running; otherwise, you'll get runtime exceptions indicating that the app cannot connect to the database server. For details on starting the Java DB server, see Section 24.3.1.

```java
 1   // Fig. 24.1: DisplayAuthors.java
 2   // Displaying the contents of the authors table.
 3   package com.deitel.jhtp.jpa;
 4
 5   import javax.persistence.EntityManager;
 6   import javax.persistence.EntityManagerFactory;
 7   import javax.persistence.Persistence;
 8   import javax.persistence.TypedQuery;
 9
10   public class DisplayAuthors
11   {
12      public static void main(String[] args)
13      {
14         // create an EntityManagerFactory for the persistence unit
15         EntityManagerFactory entityManagerFactory =
16            Persistence.createEntityManagerFactory(
17               "BooksDatabaseExamplesPU");
18
19         // create an EntityManager for interacting with the persistence unit
20         EntityManager entityManager =
21            entityManagerFactory.createEntityManager();
22
23         // create a dynamic TypedQuery<Authors> that selects all authors
24         TypedQuery<Authors> findAllAuthors = entityManager.createQuery(
25            "SELECT author FROM Authors AS author", Authors.class);
26
27         // display List of Authors
28         System.out.printf("Authors Table of Books Database:%n%n");
29         System.out.printf("%-12s%-13s%s%n",
30            "Author ID", "First Name", "Last Name");
31
32         // get all authors, create a stream and display each author
33         findAllAuthors.getResultList().stream()
34            .forEach((author) ->
35               {
```

Fig. 24.1 | Displaying contents of the authors table. (Part 1 of 2.)

```
36                    System.out.printf("%-12d%-13s%s%n", author.getAuthorid(),
37                       author.getFirstname(), author.getLastname());
38              }
39          );
40      }
41  }
```

```
Authors Table of Books Database:

Author ID    First Name    Last Name
1            Paul          Deitel
2            Harvey        Deitel
3            Abbey         Deitel
4            Dan           Quirk
5            Michael       Morgano
```

Fig. 24.1 | Displaying contents of the authors table. (Part 2 of 2.)

Importing the JPA Interfaces and Class Used in This Example

Lines 5–8 import the JPA interfaces and class from package javax.persistence used in this program:

- EntityManager interface—An object of this type manages the data flow between the program and the database.

- EntityManagerFactory interface—An object of this type creates the persistence unit's EntityManager.

- Persistence class—A static method of this class creates the specified persistence unit's EntityManagerFactory.

- TypedQuery interface—The EntityManager returns an object of this type when you create a query. You then execute the query to get data from the database.

Creating the EntityManagerFactory Object

Lines 15–17 create the persistence unit's EntityManagerFactory object. The Persistence class's static method createEntityManagerFactory receives the persistence unit's name—BooksDatabaseExamplesPU. In Section 24.3.5, NetBeans created this name in persistence.xml, based on the project's name.

Creating the EntityManager

Lines 20–21 use the EntityManagerFactory's **createEntityManager** method to create an application-managed EntityManager that handles the interactions between the app and the database. These include querying the database, storing new entities into the database, updating existing entries in the database and removing entities from the database. You'll use the EntityManager in this example to create a query.

Creating a TypedQuery That Retrieves the Authors Table

Lines 24–25 use EntityManager's createQuery method to create a TypedQuery that returns all of the Authors entities in the Authors table—each Authors entity represents one row in the table. The first argument to createQuery is a String written in the Java Persistence Query Language (JPQL). The second argument specifies a `Class` object representing the type of objects the query returns—`Authors.class` is shorthand notation for a creating a `Class` object representing `Authors`. Recall that when creating the entity classes, we specified that query results should be returned as `Lists`. When this query executes, it returns a `List<Authors>` that you can then use in your code to manipulate the `Authors` table. You can learn more about JPQL in the Java EE 7 tutorial at:

```
https://docs.oracle.com/javaee/7/tutorial/persistence-
   querylanguage.htm
```

Displaying the Query Results

Lines 33–39 execute the query and use lambdas and streams to display each `Authors` object. To perform the query created in lines 24–25, line 33 calls its **getResultsList** method, which returns a `List<Authors>`. Next, we create a `Stream` from that `List` and invoke the `Stream`'s `forEach` method to display each `Authors` object in the `List`. The lambda expression passed to `forEach` uses the `Authors` class's autogenerated *get* methods to obtain the author ID, first name and last name from each `Authors` object.

24.3.7 JPA Features of Autogenerated Class Authors

In this section, we overview various JPA annotations that were inserted into the autogenerated entity class `Authors`. Class `Titles` contains similar annotations. You can see the complete list of JPA annotations and their full descriptions at:

```
http://docs.oracle.com/javaee/7/api/index.html?javax/persistence/
   package-summary.html
```

JPA Annotations for Class Authors

If you look through the source code for autogenerated class `Authors` (or class `Titles`), you'll notice that the class does not contain any code that interacts with a database. Instead, you'll see various JPA annotations that the NetBeans IDE's object-relational-mapping tools autogenerate. When you compile the entity classes, the compiler looks at the annotations and adds JPA capabilities that help manage the interactions with the database—this is known as *injecting* capabilities. For the entity classes, the annotations include:

- **@Entity**—Specifies that the class is an entity class.
- **@Table**—Specifies the entity class's corresponding database table.
- **@NamedQueries/@NamedQuery**—An @NamedQueries annotation specifies a collection of @NamedQuery annotations that declare various named queries. You can define your own @NamedQuery annotations in addition to the ones that the object-relational-mapping tools can autogenerate.

JPA Annotations for Class Authors' Instance Variables

JPA annotations also specify information about an entity class's instance variables:

- **@Id**—Used to indicate the instance variable that corresponds to the database table's primary key. For composite primary keys, multiple instance variables would be annotated with @Id.
- **@GeneratedValue**—Indicates that the column value in the database is autogenerated.

- **@Basic**—Specifies whether the column is optional and whether the corresponding data should load *lazily* (i.e., only when the data is accessed through the entity object) or *eagerly* (i.e., loaded immediately when the entity object is created).

- **@Column**—Specifies the database column to which the instance variable corresponds.

- **@JoinTable/@JoinColumn**—These specify relationships between tables. In the Authors class, this helps JPA determine how to populate an Authors entity's titlesList.

- **@ManyToMany**—Specifies the relationship between entities. For the Authors and Titles entity classes, there is a many-to-many relationship—each author can write many books and each book can have many authors. There are also annotations for **@ManyToOne**, **@OneToMany** and **@OneToOne** relationships.

24.4 Named Queries; Accessing Data from Multiple Tables

The next example demonstrates two named queries that were autogenerated when you created the books database's persistence unit in Section 24.3.5. For discussion purposes we split the program into Figs. 24.2 and 24.3, each showing the corresponding portion of the program's output. Once again, we use lambdas and streams capabilities to display the results. As you'll see, we use the relationships between the Authors and Titles entities to display information from both database tables.

24.4.1 Using a Named Query to Get the List of Authors, then Display the Authors with Their Titles

Figure 24.2 uses the techniques you learned in Section 24.3 to display each author followed by that author's list of titles. To add DisplayQueryResults.java to your project:

1. Right click the project's name in the NetBeans **Projects** tab and select **New > Java Class...**.

2. In the **New Java Class** dialog, enter DisplayQueryResults for the **Class Name**, select com.deitel.jhtp.jpa as the **Package** and click **Finish**.

The IDE opens the new file and you can now enter the code in Figs. 24.2 and 24.3. To run this file, right click its name in the project, then select **Run File**. You can also right click the project and select **Properties** then set this class as the **Main Class** in the project's **Run** settings. Then, when you run the project, this file's main method will execute.

```
1   // Fig. 24.2: DisplayQueryResults.java
2   // Display the results of various queries.
3
4   package com.deitel.jhtp.jpa;
5
```

Fig. 24.2 | Using a NamedQuery to get the list of Authors, then display the Authors with their titles. (Part 1 of 3.)

```
 6   import java.util.Comparator;
 7   import javax.persistence.EntityManager;
 8   import javax.persistence.EntityManagerFactory;
 9   import javax.persistence.Persistence;
10   import javax.persistence.TypedQuery;
11
12   public class DisplayQueryResults
13   {
14      public static void main(String[] args)
15      {
16         // create an EntityManagerFactory for the persistence unit
17         EntityManagerFactory entityManagerFactory =
18            Persistence.createEntityManagerFactory(
19               "BooksDatabaseExamplesPU");
20
21         // create an EntityManager for interacting with the persistence unit
22         EntityManager entityManager =
23            entityManagerFactory.createEntityManager();
24
25         // TypedQuery that returns all authors
26         TypedQuery<Authors> findAllAuthors =
27            entityManager.createNamedQuery("Authors.findAll", Authors.class);
28
29         // display titles grouped by author
30         System.out.printf("Titles grouped by author:%n");
31
32         // get the List of Authors then display the results
33         findAllAuthors.getResultList().stream()
34            .sorted(Comparator.comparing(Authors::getLastname)
35               .thenComparing(Authors::getFirstname))
36            .forEach((author) ->
37               {
38                  System.out.printf("%n%s %s:%n",
39                     author.getFirstname(), author.getLastname());
40
41                  for (Titles title : author.getTitlesList())
42                  {
43                     System.out.printf("\t%s%n", title.getTitle());
44                  }
45               }
46         );
47
```

```
Titles grouped by author:

Abbey Deitel:
        Internet & World Wide Web How to Program
        Simply Visual Basic 2010
        Visual Basic 2012 How to Program
        Android How to Program
        Android for Programmers: An App-Driven Approach, 2/e, Volume 1
        Android for Programmers: An App-Driven Approach
```

Fig. 24.2 | Using a NamedQuery to get the list of Authors, then display the Authors with their titles. (Part 2 of 3.)

```
Harvey Deitel:
        Internet & World Wide Web How to Program
        Java How to Program
        Java How to Program, Late Objects Version
        C How to Program
        Simply Visual Basic 2010
        Visual Basic 2012 How to Program
        Visual C# 2012 How to Program
        Visual C++ How to Program
        C++ How to Program
        Android How to Program
        Android for Programmers: An App-Driven Approach, 2/e, Volume 1
        Android for Programmers: An App-Driven Approach

Paul Deitel:
        Internet & World Wide Web How to Program
        Java How to Program
        Java How to Program, Late Objects Version
        C How to Program
        Simply Visual Basic 2010
        Visual Basic 2012 How to Program
        Visual C# 2012 How to Program
        Visual C++ How to Program
        C++ How to Program
        Android How to Program
        Android for Programmers: An App-Driven Approach, 2/e, Volume 1
        Android for Programmers: An App-Driven Approach

Michael Morgano:
        Android for Programmers: An App-Driven Approach

Dan Quirk:
        Visual C++ How to Program
```

Fig. 24.2 | Using a NamedQuery to get the list of Authors, then display the Authors with their titles. (Part 3 of 3.)

Creating a TypedQuery That Retrieves the Authors Table

One of the default options when you created the books database's persistence unit was **Generate Named Query Annotations for Persistent Fields**—you can view these named queries before the class definitions in Authors.java and Titles.java. For class Authors, the object-relational mapping tool autogenerated the following queries:

- "Authors.findAll"—Returns the List of all Authors entities.
- "Authors.findByAuthorid"—Returns the Authors entity with the specified authorid value.
- "Authors.findByFirstname"—Returns the List of all Authors entities with the specified firstname value.
- "Authors.findByLastname"—Returns the List of all Authors entities with the specified lastname value.

You'll see how to provide arguments to queries in Section 24.5. Like the dynamic query you defined in Fig. 24.1, each of these queries is defined using the Java Persistence Query Language (JPQL).

Lines 17–23 get the EntityManager for this program, just as we did in Fig. 24.1. Lines 26–27 use EntityManager's createNamedQuery method to create a TypedQuery that returns the result of the "Authors.findAll" query. The first argument is a String containing the query's name and the second is the Class object representing the entity type that the query returns.

Processing the Results

Lines 33–46 execute the query and use Java 8 lambdas and streams to display each Authors entity's name followed by the list of that author's titles. Line 33 calls the TypedQuery's getResultsList method to perform the query. We create a Stream that sorts the Authors entities by last name then first name. Next, we invoke the Stream's forEach method to display each Authors entity's name and list of titles. The lambda expression passed to forEach uses the Authors class's autogenerated *get* methods to obtain the first name and last name from each Authors entity. Line 41 calls the autogenerated Authors method get-TitlesList to get the current author's List<Titles>, then lines 41–44 display the String returned by each Titles entity's autogenerated getTitle method.

24.4.2 Using a Named Query to Get the List of Titles, then Display Each with Its Authors

In Fig. 24.3, lines 49–50 use EntityManager method createNamedQuery to create a TypedQuery that returns the result of the "Titles.findAll" query. Then, lines 56–68 display each title followed by that title's list of author names. Line 56 calls the TypedQuery's getResultsList method to perform the query. We create a Stream that sorts the Titles entities by title. Next, we invoke the Stream's forEach method to display each Titles entity's title and the corresponding list of authors. Once again, the lambda expression uses the autogenerated Titles and Authors methods to access the entity data that's displayed.

```
48        // TypedQuery that returns all titles
49        TypedQuery<Titles> findAllTitles =
50           entityManager.createNamedQuery("Titles.findAll", Titles.class);
51
52        // display titles grouped by author
53        System.out.printf("%nAuthors grouped by title:%n%n");
54
55        // get the List of Titles then display the results
56        findAllTitles.getResultList().stream()
57           .sorted(Comparator.comparing(Titles::getTitle))
58           .forEach((title) ->
59              {
60                 System.out.println(title.getTitle());
61
```

Fig. 24.3 | Using a NamedQuery to get the list of Titles, then display each with its Authors. (Part I of 3.)

```
62                     for (Authors author : title.getAuthorsList())
63                     {
64                         System.out.printf("\t%s %s%n",
65                             author.getFirstname(), author.getLastname());
66                     }
67                 }
68             );
69         }
70     }
```

```
Authors grouped by title:

Android How to Program
        Paul Deitel
        Harvey Deitel
        Abbey Deitel
Android for Programmers: An App-Driven Approach
        Paul Deitel
        Harvey Deitel
        Abbey Deitel
        Michael Morgano
Android for Programmers: An App-Driven Approach, 2/e, Volume 1
        Paul Deitel
        Harvey Deitel
        Abbey Deitel
C How to Program
        Paul Deitel
        Harvey Deitel
C++ How to Program
        Paul Deitel
        Harvey Deitel
Internet & World Wide Web How to Program
        Paul Deitel
        Harvey Deitel
        Abbey Deitel
Java How to Program
        Paul Deitel
        Harvey Deitel
Java How to Program, Late Objects Version
        Paul Deitel
        Harvey Deitel
Simply Visual Basic 2010
        Paul Deitel
        Harvey Deitel
        Abbey Deitel
Visual Basic 2012 How to Program
        Paul Deitel
        Harvey Deitel
        Abbey Deitel
Visual C# 2012 How to Program
        Paul Deitel
        Harvey Deitel
```

Fig. 24.3 | Using a NamedQuery to get the list of Titles, then display each with its Authors. (Part 2 of 3.)

```
Visual C++ How to Program
        Paul Deitel
        Harvey Deitel
        Dan Quirk
```

Fig. 24.3 | Using a NamedQuery to get the list of Titles, then display each with its Authors. (Part 3 of 3.)

24.5 Address Book: Using JPA and Transactions to Modify a Database

We now reimplement the address book app from Section 22.9 using JPA. As before, you can browse existing entries, add new entries and search for entries with a specific last name. Recall that the AddressBook Java DB database contains an Addresses table with the columns addressID, FirstName, LastName, Email and PhoneNumber. The column addressID is an identity column in the Addresses table.

24.5.1 Transaction Processing

Many database applications require guarantees that a series of database insertions, updates and deletions executes properly before the application continues processing the next database operation. For example, when you transfer money electronically between bank accounts, several factors determine whether the transaction is successful. You begin by specifying the source account and the amount you wish to transfer to a destination account. Next, you specify the destination account. The bank checks the source account to determine whether its funds are sufficient to complete the transfer. If so, the bank withdraws the specified amount and, if all goes well, deposits it into the destination account to complete the transfer. What happens if the transfer fails after the bank withdraws the money from the source account? In a proper banking system, the bank redeposits the money in the source account. How would you feel if the money was subtracted from your source account and the bank *did not* deposit the money in the destination account?

Transaction processing enables a program that interacts with a database to treat a set of operations as a *single* operation, known as an **atomic operation** or a **transaction**. At the end of a transaction, a decision can be made either to **commit the transaction** or **roll back the transaction**:

- Committing the transaction finalizes the database operation(s); all insertions, updates and deletions performed as part of the transaction cannot be reversed without performing a new database operation.

- Rolling back the transaction leaves the database in its state prior to the database operation. This is useful when a portion of a transaction fails to complete properly. In our bank-account-transfer discussion, the transaction would be rolled back if the deposit could not be made into the destination account.

JPA provides transaction processing via methods of interfaces EntityManager and **EntityTransaction**. EntityManager method **getTransaction** returns an EntityTransaction for managing a transaction. EntityTransaction method **begin** starts a transaction. Next, you perform your database's operations using the EntityManager. If the operations execute successfully, you call `EntityTransaction` method **commit** to commit the changes to the database. If any operation fails, you call `EntityTransaction` method **rollback** to return the database to its state prior to the transaction. You'll use these techniques in Section 24.5.4. (In a Java EE project, the server can perform these tasks for you.)

24.5.2 Creating the AddressBook Database, Project and Persistence Unit

Use the techniques you learned in Sections 24.3.1—24.3.5 to perform the following steps:

Step 1: Creating the *addressbook* Database
Using the steps presented in Section 24.3.1, create the `addressbook` database.

Step 2: Populating the Database
Using the steps presented in Section 24.3.2, populate the `addressbook` database with the sample data in the `addressbook.sql` file that's provided with this chapter's examples.

Step 3: Creating the AddressBook Project
This app has a JavaFX GUI. For prior JavaFX apps, we created an FXML file that described the app's GUI, a subclass of `Application` that launched the app and a controller class that handled the app's GUI events and provided other app logic. NetBeans provides a **JavaFX FXML Application** project template that creates the FXML file and Java source-code files for the `Application` subclass and controller class. To use this template:

1. Select **File > New Project...** to open the **New Project** dialog.
2. Under **Categories:** select **JavaFX** and under **Projects:** select **JavaFX FXML Application**, then click **Next >**.
3. For the **Project Name** specify `AddressBook`.
4. For the FXML name, specify `AddressBook`.
5. In the **Create Application Class** textfield, replace the default package name and class name with `com.deitel.jhtp.jpa.AddressBook`.
6. Click `Finish` to create the project.

NetBeans places in the app's package the files `AddressBook.fxml`, `AddressBook.java` and `AddressBookController.java`. If you double-click the FXML file in NetBeans, it will automatically open in Scene Builder (if you have it installed) so that you can design your GUI.

For this app, rather than recreating `AddressBook` GUI, we replaced the default FXML that NetBeans generated in `AddressBook.fxml` with the contents of `AddressBook.fxml` from Section 22.9's example (right click the FXML file in NetBeans and select **Edit** to view its source code). We then changed the controller class's name from `AddressBookController` to

```
com.deitel.jhtp.jpa.AddressBookController
```

because the controller class in this example is in the package `com.deitel.jhtp.jpa`.

Also, in the autogenerated `AddressBook` subclass of `Application` (located in `AddressBook.java`), we added the following statement to set the `stage`'s title bar `String`:

```
stage.setTitle("Address Book");
```

Step 4: Adding the JPA and Java DB Libraries
Using the steps presented in Section 24.3.4, add the required JPA and JavaDB libraries to the project's **Libraries** folder.

*Step 5: Creating the **AddressBook** Database's Persistence Unit*
Using the steps presented in Section 24.3.5, create the AddressBook database's persistence unit, which will be named AddressBookPU by default.

24.5.3 Addresses Entity Class

When you created the AddressBook database's persistence unit, NetBeans autogenerated the Addresses entity class (in Addresses.java) with several named queries. In this app, you'll use the queries:

- "Addresses.findAll"—Returns a List<Addresses> containing Addresses entities for all the contacts.

- "Addresses.findByLastname"—Returns a List<Addresses> containing an Addresses entity for each contact with the specified last name.

Ordering the Named Query Results
By default, the JPQL for the autogenerated named queries does not order the query results. In Section 22.9, we used the SQL's ORDER BY clause to arrange query results into ascending order by last name then first name. JPQL also has an ORDER BY clause. To order the query results in this app, we opened Addresses.java and added

```
ORDER BY a.lastname, a.firstname
```

to the query strings for the "Addresses.findAll" and "Addresses.findByLastname" named queries—again these are specified in the @NamedQuery annotations just before the Addresses class's declaration.

*ToString Method of Class **Addresses***
In this app, we use the List<Addresses> returned by each query to populate an ObservableList that's bound to the app's ListView. Recall that, by default, a ListView's cells display the String representation of the ObservableList's elements. To ensure that each Addresses object in the ListView is displayed in the format *Last Name, First Name*, we modified the Addresses class's autogenerated toString method. To do so, open Addresses.java and replace its return statement with

```
return getLastname() + ", " + getFirstname();
```

24.5.4 AddressBookController Class

The AddressBookController class (Fig. 24.4) uses the persistence unit you created in Section 24.5.2 to interact with addressbook database. Much of the code in Fig. 24.4 is identical to the code in Fig. 22.34. For the discussion in this section, we focus on the highlighted JPA features.

```java
 1   // Fig. 24.4: AddressBookController.java
 2   // Controller for a simple address book
 3   package com.deitel.jhtp.jpa;
 4
 5   import java.util.List;
 6   import javafx.collections.FXCollections;
 7   import javafx.collections.ObservableList;
 8   import javafx.event.ActionEvent;
 9   import javafx.fxml.FXML;
10   import javafx.scene.control.Alert;
11   import javafx.scene.control.Alert.AlertType;
12   import javafx.scene.control.ListView;
13   import javafx.scene.control.TextField;
14   import javax.persistence.EntityManager;
15   import javax.persistence.EntityManagerFactory;
16   import javax.persistence.EntityTransaction;
17   import javax.persistence.Persistence;
18   import javax.persistence.TypedQuery;
19
20   public class AddressBookController {
21      @FXML private ListView<Addresses> listView;
22      @FXML private TextField firstNameTextField;
23      @FXML private TextField lastNameTextField;
24      @FXML private TextField emailTextField;
25      @FXML private TextField phoneTextField;
26      @FXML private TextField findByLastNameTextField;
27
28      // create an EntityManagerFactory for the persistence unit
29      private final EntityManagerFactory entityManagerFactory =
30         Persistence.createEntityManagerFactory("AddressBookPU");
31
32      // create an EntityManager for interacting with the persistence unit
33      private final EntityManager entityManager =
34         entityManagerFactory.createEntityManager();
35
36      // stores list of Addresses objects that results from a database query
37      private final ObservableList<Addresses> contactList =
38         FXCollections.observableArrayList();
39
40      // populate listView and set up listener for selection events
41      public void initialize() {
42         listView.setItems(contactList); // bind to contactsList
43
44         // when ListView selection changes, display selected person's data
45         listView.getSelectionModel().selectedItemProperty().addListener(
46            (observableValue, oldValue, newValue) -> {
47               displayContact(newValue);
48            }
49         );
50         getAllEntries(); // populates contactList, which updates listView
51      }
52
```

Fig. 24.4 | A simple address book. (Part 1 of 5.)

```java
53      // get all the entries from the database to populate contactList
54      private void getAllEntries() {
55         // query that returns all contacts
56         TypedQuery<Addresses> findAllAddresses =
57            entityManager.createNamedQuery(
58               "Addresses.findAll", Addresses.class);
59
60         contactList.setAll(findAllAddresses.getResultList());
61         selectFirstEntry();
62      }
63
64      // select first item in listView
65      private void selectFirstEntry() {
66         listView.getSelectionModel().selectFirst();
67      }
68
69      // display contact information
70      private void displayContact(Addresses contact) {
71         if (contact != null) {
72            firstNameTextField.setText(contact.getFirstname());
73            lastNameTextField.setText(contact.getLastname());
74            emailTextField.setText(contact.getEmail());
75            phoneTextField.setText(contact.getPhonenumber());
76         }
77         else {
78            firstNameTextField.clear();
79            lastNameTextField.clear();
80            emailTextField.clear();
81            phoneTextField.clear();
82         }
83      }
84
85      // add a new entry
86      @FXML
87      void addEntryButtonPressed(ActionEvent event) {
88         Addresses address = new Addresses();
89         address.setFirstname(firstNameTextField.getText());
90         address.setLastname(lastNameTextField.getText());
91         address.setPhonenumber(phoneTextField.getText());
92         address.setEmail(emailTextField.getText());
93
94         // get an EntityTransaction to manage insert operation
95         EntityTransaction transaction = entityManager.getTransaction();
96
97         try
98         {
99            transaction.begin(); // start transaction
100            entityManager.persist(address); // store new entry
101            transaction.commit(); // commit changes to the database
102            displayAlert(AlertType.INFORMATION, "Entry Added",
103               "New entry successfully added.");
104         }
```

Fig. 24.4 | A simple address book. (Part 2 of 5.)

```
105        catch (Exception e) // if transaction failed
106        {
107            transaction.rollback(); // undo database operations
108            displayAlert(AlertType.ERROR, "Entry Not Added",
109                "Unable to add entry: " + e);
110        }
111
112        getAllEntries();
113    }
114
115    // find entries with the specified last name
116    @FXML
117    void findButtonPressed(ActionEvent event) {
118        // query that returns all contacts
119        TypedQuery<Addresses> findByLastname =
120            entityManager.createNamedQuery(
121                "Addresses.findByLastname", Addresses.class);
122
123        // configure parameter for query
124        findByLastname.setParameter(
125            "lastname", findByLastNameTextField.getText() + "%");
126
127        // get all addresses
128        List<Addresses> people = findByLastname.getResultList();
129
130        if (people.size() > 0) { // display all entries
131            contactList.setAll(people);
132            selectFirstEntry();
133        }
134        else {
135            displayAlert(AlertType.INFORMATION, "Lastname Not Found",
136                "There are no entries with the specified last name.");
137        }
138    }
139
140    // browse all the entries
141    @FXML
142    void browseAllButtonPressed(ActionEvent event) {
143        getAllEntries();
144    }
145
146    // display an Alert dialog
147    private void displayAlert(
148        AlertType type, String title, String message) {
149        Alert alert = new Alert(type);
150        alert.setTitle(title);
151        alert.setContentText(message);
152        alert.showAndWait();
153    }
154 }
```

Fig. 24.4 | A simple address book. (Part 3 of 5.)

a) Initial **Address Book** screen showing entries.

b) Viewing the entry for **Green, Mike**.

c) Adding a new entry for **Sue Green**.

d) Searching for last names that start with **Gr**.

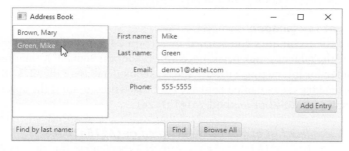

Fig. 24.4 | A simple address book. (Part 4 of 5.)

e) Returning to the complete list by clicking **Browse All**.

Fig. 24.4 | A simple address book. (Part 5 of 5.)

Obtaining the *EntityManager*

Lines 29–34 use the techniques you learned in Section 24.3.6 to obtain an EntityManagerFactory for the AddressBook persistence unit ("AddressBookPU"), then use it to get the EntityManager for interacting with the addressbook database. Lines 37–38 define an ObservableList<Addresses> named contactList that's used to bind the app's query results to the ListView (line 42 of method initialize).

Obtaining the Complete List of Contacts—Method *getAllEntries*

Lines 56–58 in method getAllEntries create a TypedQuery for the named query "Addresses.findAll", which returns a List<Addresses> containing all the Addresses entities in the database. Line 60 calls the TypedQuery's getResultList method and uses the resulting List<Addresses> to populate the contactList, which was previously bound to the ListView. Each time the complete contacts list is loaded, line 61 calls method selectFirstEntry to display the first Addresses entity's details. Due to the listener registered in lines 45–49, this in turn calls method displayContact to display the selected Addresses entity if there is one; otherwise, displayContact clears the TextFields that display a contact's details.

Adding an Entry to the Database—Method *addEntryButtonPressed*

When you enter new data in this app's GUI, then click the **Add Entry** button—a new row should be added to the Addresses table in the database. To create a new entity in the database, you must first create an instance of the entity class (line 88) and set its instance variables (lines 89–92), then use a transaction to insert the data in the database (lines 95–110). Notice that we do not specify a value for the Addresses entity's addressid instance variable—this value is autogenerated by the database when you add a new entry.

Lines 95–110 use the techniques discussed in Section 24.5.1 to perform the insert operation. Line 95 uses EntityManager method getTransaction to get the EntityTransaction used to manage the transaction. In the try block, line 99 uses EntityTransaction method begin to start the transaction. Next, line 100 calls EntityManager method **persist** to insert the new entity into the database. If this operation executes successfully, line 101 calls EntityTransaction method commit to complete the transaction and commit the changes to the database. If the persist operation fails, line 107 in the catch block calls EntityTransaction method rollback to return the database to its state prior to the transaction.[4]

Finding by Last Name—Method *findButtonPressed*
Lines 119–121 in method findButtonPressed create a TypedQuery for the named query "Addresses.findByLastname", which returns a List<Addresses> containing all the entities with the specified last name. If you open the autogenerated Addresses class in your project, you'll see that the query requires a parameter, as specified in the following JPQL that we copied from the Addresses.java file:

```
SELECT a FROM Addresses a WHERE a.lastname = :lastname
```

The notation :lastname represents a parameter named lastname. The autogenerated query locates only exact matches, as indicated by the JPQL equals (=) operator. For this app, we changed = to the JPQL LIKE operator so we can locate last names that begin with the letters typed by the user in the findByLastNameTextField.

Before executing the query, you set arguments for each query parameter by calling TypedQuery method **setParameter** (lines 124–125) with the JPQL parameter name as the first argument and the corresponding value as the second argument. As in SQL, line 125 appends % to the contents of findByLastNameTextField to indicate that we're searching for last names that begin with the user's input, possibly followed by more characters.

When you execute the query (line 128), it returns a List containing any matching entities in database. If the number of results is greater than 0, lines 131–132 display the search results in the ListView and select the first matching result to display its details. Otherwise, 135–136 display an Alert dialog indicating there were no entries with the specified last name.

24.5.5 Other JPA Operations
Though we did not do so in this example, you also can update an existing entity in the database or delete an existing entity from the database.

Updating an Existing Entity
You update an existing entity by modifying its entity object in the context of a transaction. Once you commit the transaction, the changes to the entity are saved to the database.

Deleting an Existing Entity
To remove an entity from the database, call EntityManager method **remove** in the context of a transaction, passing the entity object to delete as an argument. When you commit the transaction the entity is deleted from the database. This operation will fail if the entity is referenced elsewhere in the database.

24.6 Web Resources
Here are a few key online JPA resources.

---

4. For simplicity, we performed this example's database operations on the JavaFX application thread. Any potentially long-running database operations should be performed in separate threads using the techniques in Section 21.11.

`https://docs.oracle.com/javaee/7/tutorial/persistence-intro.htm`
The *Introduction to the Java Persistence API* chapter of the *Java EE 7 Tutorial*.

`https://docs.oracle.com/javaee/7/tutorial/persistence-querylanguage.htm`
The *Java Persistence Query Language* chapter of the *Java EE 7 Tutorial*.

`http://docs.oracle.com/javaee/7/api/javax/persistence/package-summary.html`
The `javax.persistence` package documentation.

`https://platform.netbeans.org/tutorials/nbm-crud.html`
A NetBeans tutorial for creating a JPA-based app.

24.7 Wrap-Up

In this chapter, we introduced the Java Persistence API (JPA). We used the NetBeans IDE to create and populate a Java DB database, using Java DB's network server version, rather than the embedded version demonstrated in Chapter 22. We created NetBeans projects and added the libraries for JPA and the Java DB driver. Next, we used the NetBeans object-relational mapping tools to autogenerate entity classes from an existing database's schema. We then used those classes to interact with the database.

We queried the databases with both dynamic queries created in code and named queries that were autogenerated by NetBeans. We used the relationships between JPA entities to access data from multiple database tables.

Next, we used JPA transactions to insert new data in a database. We also discussed other JPA operations that you can perform in the context of transactions, such as updating existing entities in and deleting entities from a database. Finally, we listed several online JPA resources from which you can learn more about JPA. In the next chapter, we begin our two-chapter object-oriented design and implementation case study.

ATM Case Study, Part 1: Object-Oriented Design with the UML

Objectives

In this chapter you'll learn:

- A simple object-oriented design methodology.
- What a requirements document is.
- To identify classes and class attributes from a requirements document.
- To identify objects' states, activities and operations from a requirements document.
- To determine the collaborations among objects in a system.
- To work with the UML's use case, class, state, activity, communication and sequence diagrams to graphically model an object-oriented system.

25.1 Case Study Introduction

Now we begin the *optional* portion of our object-oriented design and implementation case study. In this chapter and Chapter 26, you'll design and implement an object-oriented automated teller machine (ATM) software system. The case study provides you with a concise, carefully paced, complete design and implementation experience. In Sections 25.2––25.7 and 26.2–26.3, you'll perform the steps of an object-oriented design (OOD) process using the UML while relating these steps to the object-oriented concepts discussed in Chapters 2–10. In this chapter, you'll work with six popular types of UML diagrams to graphically represent the design. In Chapter 26, you'll tune the design with inheritance, then fully implement the ATM as a Java application (Section 26.4). This is not an exercise; rather, it's an end-to-end learning experience that concludes with a detailed walkthrough of the complete Java code that implements our design.

These chapters can be studied as a continuous unit after you've completed the introduction to object-oriented programming in Chapters 8–11. Or, you can pace the sections one at a time after Chapters 2–8 and 10. Each section of the case study begins with a note telling you the chapter after which it can be covered.

25.2 Examining the Requirements Document

[*Note:* This section m after Chapter 2.]
We begin our design process by presenting a **requirements document** that specifies the purpose of the ATM system and *what* it must do. Throughout the case study, we refer often to this requirements document.

Requirements Document
A local bank intends to install a new automated teller machine (ATM) to allow users (i.e., bank customers) to perform basic financial transactions (Fig. 25.1). Each user can have only one account at the bank. ATM users should be able to view their account balance, withdraw cash (i.e., take money out of an account) and deposit funds (i.e., place money into an account). The user interface of the automated teller machine contains:

- a screen that displays messages to the user
- a keypad that receives numeric input from the user
- a cash dispenser that dispenses cash to the user and
- a deposit slot that receives deposit envelopes from the user.

The cash dispenser begins each day loaded with 500 $20 bills. [*Note:* Owing to the limited scope of this case study, certain elements of the ATM described here do not accurately mimic those of a real ATM. For example, a real ATM typically contains a device that reads a user's account number from an ATM card, whereas this ATM asks the user to type the account number on the keypad. A real ATM also usually prints a receipt at the end of a session, but all output from this ATM appears on the screen.]

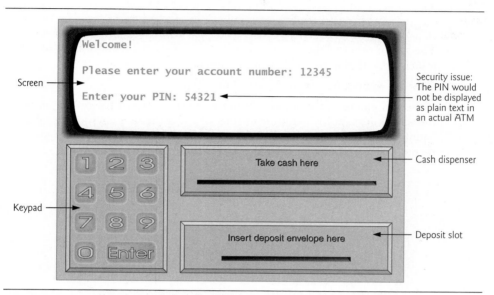

Fig. 25.1 | Automated teller machine user interface.

The bank wants you to develop software to perform the financial transactions initiated by bank customers through the ATM. The bank will integrate the software with the ATM's hardware at a later time. The software should encapsulate the functionality of the hardware devices (e.g., cash dispenser, deposit slot) within software components, but it need not concern itself with how these devices perform their duties. The ATM hardware has not been developed yet, so instead of writing your software to run on the ATM, you should develop a first version to run on a personal computer. This version should use the computer's monitor to simulate the ATM's screen, and the computer's keyboard to simulate the ATM's keypad.

An ATM session consists of authenticating a user (i.e., proving the user's identity) based on an account number and personal identification number (PIN), followed by creating and executing financial transactions. To authenticate a user and perform transactions, the ATM must interact with the bank's account information database (i.e., an organized collection of data stored on a computer; database access was presented in Chapter 22). For each bank account, the database stores an account number, a PIN and a balance indicating the amount of money in the account. [*Note:* We assume that the bank plans to build only one ATM, so we need not worry about multiple ATMs accessing this database at the same time. Furthermore, we assume that the bank does not make any changes to the information in the database while a user is accessing the ATM. Also, any business system like an ATM faces complex and challenging security issues that are beyond the scope of this case study. We make the simplifying assumption, however, that the bank trusts the ATM to access and manipulate the information in the database without significant security measures.]

Upon first approaching the ATM (assuming no one is currently using it), the user should experience the following sequence of events (shown in Fig. 25.1):

1. The screen displays Welcome! and prompts the user to enter an account number.

2. The user enters a five-digit account number using the keypad.

3. The screen prompts the user to enter the PIN (personal identification number) associated with the specified account number.

4. The user enters a five-digit PIN using the keypad.[1]

5. If the user enters a valid account number and the correct PIN for that account, the screen displays the main menu (Fig. 25.2). If the user enters an invalid account number or an incorrect PIN, the screen displays an appropriate message, then the ATM returns to *Step 1* to restart the authentication process.

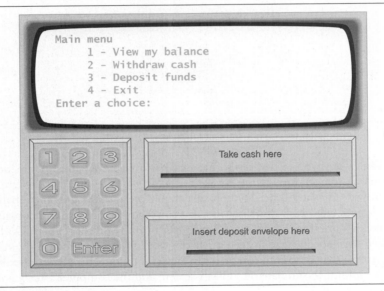

Fig. 25.2 | ATM main menu.

After the ATM authenticates the user, the main menu (Fig. 25.2) should contain a numbered option for each of the three types of transactions: balance inquiry (option 1), withdrawal (option 2) and deposit (option 3). It also should contain an option to allow the user to exit the system (option 4). The user then chooses either to perform a transaction (by entering 1, 2 or 3) or to exit the system (by entering 4).

---

1. In this simple, command-line, text-based ATM, as you type the PIN, it appears on the screen. This is an obvious security breach—you would not want someone looking over your shoulder at an ATM and seeing your PIN displayed on the screen.

If the user enters 1 to make a balance inquiry, the screen displays the user's account balance. To do so, the ATM must retrieve the balance from the bank's database. The following steps describe what occurs when the user enters 2 to make a withdrawal:

1. The screen displays a menu (Fig. 25.3) containing standard withdrawal amounts: $20 (option 1), $40 (option 2), $60 (option 3), $100 (option 4) and $200 (option 5). The menu also contains an option to allow the user to cancel the transaction (option 6).

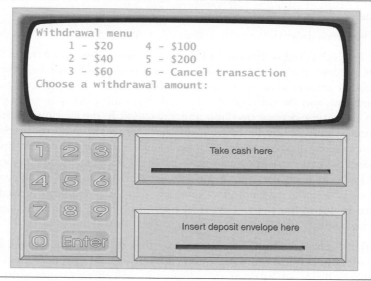

Fig. 25.3 | ATM withdrawal menu.

2. The user enters a menu selection using the keypad.

3. If the withdrawal amount chosen is greater than the user's account balance, the screen displays a message stating this and telling the user to choose a smaller amount. The ATM then returns to *Step 1*. If the withdrawal amount chosen is less than or equal to the user's account balance (i.e., an acceptable amount), the ATM proceeds to *Step 4*. If the user chooses to cancel the transaction (option 6), the ATM displays the main menu and waits for user input.

4. If the cash dispenser contains enough cash, the ATM proceeds to *Step 5*. Otherwise, the screen displays a message indicating the problem and telling the user to choose a smaller withdrawal amount. The ATM then returns to *Step 1*.

5. The ATM debits the withdrawal amount from the user's account in the bank's database (i.e., subtracts the withdrawal amount from the user's account balance).

6. The cash dispenser dispenses the desired amount of money to the user.

7. The screen displays a message reminding the user to take the money.

The following steps describe the actions that occur when the user enters 3 (when viewing the main menu of Fig. 25.2) to make a deposit:

1. The screen prompts the user to enter a deposit amount or type 0 (zero) to cancel.

2. The user enters a deposit amount or 0 using the keypad. [*Note:* The keypad does not contain a decimal point or a dollar sign, so the user cannot type a real dollar amount (e.g., $27.25). Instead, the user must enter a deposit amount as a number of cents (e.g., 2725). The ATM then divides this number by 100 to obtain a number representing a dollar amount (e.g., 2725 ÷ 100 = 27.25).]

3. If the user specifies a deposit amount, the ATM proceeds to *Step 4*. If the user chooses to cancel the transaction (by entering 0), the ATM displays the main menu and waits for user input.

4. The screen displays a message telling the user to insert a deposit envelope.

5. If the deposit slot receives a deposit envelope within two minutes, the ATM credits the deposit amount to the user's account in the bank's database (i.e., adds the deposit amount to the user's account balance). [*Note:* This money is *not* immediately available for withdrawal. The bank first must physically verify the amount of cash in the deposit envelope, and any checks in the envelope must clear (i.e., money must be transferred from the check writer's account to the check recipient's account). When either of these events occurs, the bank appropriately updates the user's balance stored in its database. This occurs independently of the ATM system.] If the deposit slot does not receive a deposit envelope within this time period, the screen displays a message that the system has canceled the transaction due to inactivity. The ATM then displays the main menu and waits for user input.

After the system successfully executes a transaction, it should return to the main menu so that the user can perform additional transactions. If the user exits the system, the screen should display a thank you message, then display the welcome message for the next user.

Analyzing the ATM System
The preceding statement is a simplified example of a requirements document. Typically, such a document is the result of a detailed process of **requirements gathering**, which might include interviews with possible users of the system and specialists in fields related to the system. For example, a systems analyst who is hired to prepare a requirements document for banking software (e.g., the ATM system described here) might interview banking experts to gain a better understanding of what the software must do. The analyst would use the information gained to compile a list of **system requirements** to guide systems designers as they design the system.

The process of requirements gathering is a key task of the first stage of the software life cycle. The **software life cycle** specifies the stages through which software goes from the time it's first conceived to the time it's retired from use. These stages typically include: analysis, design, implementation, testing and debugging, deployment, maintenance and retirement. Several software life-cycle models exist, each with its own preferences and specifications for when and how often software engineers should perform each of these stages. **Waterfall models** perform each stage once in succession, whereas **iterative models** may *repeat* one or more stages several times throughout a product's life cycle.

The analysis stage focuses on defining the problem to be solved. When designing any system, one must *solve the problem right*, but of equal importance, one must *solve the right problem.* Systems analysts collect the requirements that indicate the specific problem to solve. Our requirements document describes the requirements of our ATM system in sufficient detail that you need not go through an extensive analysis stage—it's been done for you.

To capture what a proposed system should do, developers often employ a technique known as **use case modeling**. This process identifies the **use cases** of the system, each representing a different capability that the system provides to its clients. For example, ATMs typically have several use cases, such as "View Account Balance," "Withdraw Cash," "Deposit Funds," "Transfer Funds Between Accounts" and "Buy Postage Stamps." The simplified ATM system we build in this case study allows only the first three.

Each use case describes a typical scenario for which the user uses the system. You've already read descriptions of the ATM system's use cases in the requirements document; the lists of steps required to perform each transaction type (i.e., balance inquiry, withdrawal and deposit) actually described the three use cases of our ATM—"View Account Balance," "Withdraw Cash" and "Deposit Funds," respectively.

Use Case Diagrams

We now introduce the first of several UML diagrams in the case study. We create a **use case diagram** to model the interactions between a system's clients (in this case study, bank customers) and its use cases. The goal is to show the kinds of interactions users have with a system without providing the details—these are provided in other UML diagrams (which we present throughout this case study). Use case diagrams are often accompanied by informal text that gives more detail—like the text that appears in the requirements document. Use case diagrams are produced during the analysis stage of the software life cycle. In larger systems, use case diagrams are indispensable tools that help system designers remain focused on satisfying the users' needs.

Figure 25.4 shows the use case diagram for our ATM system. The stick figure represents an **actor**, which defines the roles that an external entity—such as a person or another system—plays when interacting with the system. For our automated teller machine, the actor is a User who can view an account balance, withdraw cash and deposit funds from the ATM. The User is not an actual person, but instead comprises the roles that a real person—when playing the part of a User—can play while interacting with the ATM. A use case diagram can include multiple actors. For example, the use case diagram for a real bank's ATM system might also include an actor named Administrator who refills the cash dispenser each day.

Our requirements document supplies the actors—"ATM users should be able to view their account balance, withdraw cash and deposit funds." Therefore, the actor in each of the three use cases is the user who interacts with the ATM. An external entity—a real person—plays the part of the user to perform financial transactions. Figure 25.4 shows one actor, whose name, User, appears below the actor in the diagram. The UML models each use case as an oval connected to an actor with a solid line.

Software engineers (more precisely, systems designers) must analyze the requirements document or a set of use cases and design the system before programmers implement it in a particular programming language. During the analysis stage, systems designers focus on understanding the requirements document to produce a high-level specification that describes *what* the system is supposed to do. The output of the design stage—a **design specification**—should specify clearly *how* the system should be constructed to satisfy these requirements. In the next several sections, we perform the steps of a simple object-oriented

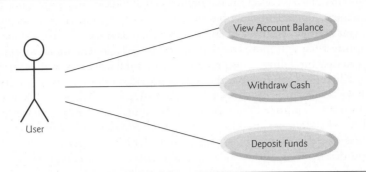

Fig. 25.4 | Use case diagram for the ATM system from the User's perspective.

design (OOD) process on the ATM system to produce a design specification containing a collection of UML diagrams and supporting text.

The UML is designed for use with any OOD process. Many such processes exist, the best known of which is the Rational Unified Process™ (RUP) developed by Rational Software Corporation, now part of IBM. RUP is a rich process intended for designing "industrial strength" applications. For this case study, we present our own simplified design process.

Designing the ATM System

We now begin the design stage of our ATM system. A **system** is a set of components that interact to solve a problem. For example, to perform the ATM system's designated tasks, our ATM system has a user interface (Fig. 25.1), and contains software that executes financial transactions and interacts with a database of bank account information. **System structure** describes the system's objects and their interrelationships. **System behavior** describes how the system changes as its objects interact with one another.

Every system has both structure and behavior—designers must specify both. There are several types of system structures and behaviors. For example, the interactions among objects in the system differ from those between the user and the system, yet both constitute a portion of the system behavior.

The UML 2 standard specifies 13 diagram types for documenting the system models. Each models a distinct characteristic of a system's structure or behavior—six diagrams relate to system structure, the remaining seven to system behavior. We list here only the six diagram types used in our case study—one models system structure; the other five model system behavior.

1. **Use case diagrams**, such as the one in Fig. 25.4, model the interactions between a system and its external entities (actors) in terms of use cases (system capabilities, such as "View Account Balance," "Withdraw Cash" and "Deposit Funds").

2. **Class diagrams**, which you'll study in Section 25.3, model the classes, or "building blocks," used in a system. Each noun or "thing" described in the requirements document is a candidate to be a class in the system (e.g., Account, Keypad). Class diagrams help us specify the *structural relationships* between parts of the system. For example, the ATM system class diagram will specify that the ATM is physically *composed of* a screen, a keypad, a cash dispenser and a deposit slot.

3. **State machine diagrams**, which you'll study in Section 25.5, model the ways in which an object changes state. An object's **state** is indicated by the values of all its attributes at a given time. When an object changes state, it may behave differently in the system. For example, after validating a user's PIN, the ATM transitions from the "user not authenticated" state to the "user authenticated" state, at which point it allows the user to perform financial transactions (e.g., view account balance, withdraw cash, deposit funds).

4. **Activity diagrams**, which you'll also study in Section 25.5, model an object's **activity**—is workflow (sequence of events) during program execution. An activity diagram models the *actions* the object performs and specifies the *order* in which it performs them. For example, an activity diagram shows that the ATM must obtain the balance of the user's account (from the bank's account information database) *before* the screen can display the balance to the user.

5. **Communication diagrams** (called **collaboration diagrams** in earlier versions of the UML) model the interactions among objects in a system, with an emphasis on *what* interactions occur. You'll learn in Section 25.7 that these diagrams show which objects must interact to perform an ATM transaction. For example, the ATM must communicate with the bank's account information database to retrieve an account balance.

6. **Sequence diagrams** also model the interactions among the objects in a system, but unlike communication diagrams, they emphasize *when* interactions occur. You'll learn in Section 25.7 that these diagrams help show the order in which interactions occur in executing a financial transaction. For example, the screen prompts the user to enter a withdrawal amount before cash is dispensed.

In Section 25.3, we continue designing our ATM system by identifying the classes from the requirements document. We accomplish this by extracting key *nouns and noun phrases* from the requirements document. Using these classes, we develop our first draft of the class diagram that models the structure of our ATM system.

Web Resource

We've created an extensive UML Resource Center that contains many links to additional information, including introductions, tutorials, blogs, books, certification, conferences, developer tools, documentation, e-books, FAQs, forums, groups, UML in Java, podcasts, security, tools, downloads, training courses, videos and more. Browse our UML Resource Center at www.deitel.com/UML/.

Self-Review Exercises for Section 25.2

25.1   Suppose we enabled a user of our ATM system to transfer money between two bank accounts. Modify the use case diagram of Fig. 25.4 to reflect this change.

25.2   _____ model the interactions among objects in a system with an emphasis on *when* these interactions occur.
   a) Class diagrams
   b) Sequence diagrams
   c) Communication diagrams
   d) Activity diagrams

25.3   Which of the following choices lists stages of a typical software life cycle in sequential order?
   a) design, analysis, implementation, testing
   b) design, analysis, testing, implementation
   c) analysis, design, testing, implementation
   d) analysis, design, implementation, testing

25.3 Identifying the Classes in a Requirements Document

[*Note:* **This section may be read after Chapter 3.**]
Now we begin designing the ATM system. In this section, we identify the classes that are needed to build the system by analyzing the *nouns* and *noun phrases* that appear in the requirements document. We introduce UML class diagrams to model these classes. This is an important first step in defining the system's structure.

Identifying the Classes in a System

We begin our OOD process by identifying the classes required to build the ATM system. We'll eventually describe these classes using UML class diagrams and implement these classes in Java. First, we review the requirements document of Section 25.2 and identify key nouns and noun phrases to help us identify classes that comprise the ATM system. We may decide that some of these are actually attributes of other classes in the system. We may also conclude that some of the nouns do not correspond to parts of the system and thus should not be modeled at all. Additional classes may become apparent to us as we proceed through the design process.

Figure 25.5 lists the nouns and noun phrases found in the requirements document. We list them from left to right in the order in which we first encounter them. We list only the singular form of each.

Nouns and noun phrases in the ATM requirements document			
bank	money / funds	account number	ATM
screen	PIN	user	keypad
bank database	customer	cash dispenser	balance inquiry
transaction	$20 bill / cash	withdrawal	account
deposit slot	deposit	balance	deposit envelope

Fig. 25.5 | Nouns and noun phrases in the ATM requirements document.

We create classes only for the nouns and noun phrases that have significance in the ATM system. We don't model "bank" as a class, because the bank is not a part of the ATM system—the bank simply wants us to build the ATM. "Customer" and "user" also represent outside entities—they're important because they *interact* with our ATM system, but we do not need to model them as classes in the ATM software. Recall that we modeled an ATM user (i.e., a bank customer) as the actor in the use case diagram of Fig. 25.4.

We do not model "$20 bill" or "deposit envelope" as classes. These are physical objects in the real world, but they're not part of what is being automated. We can adequately represent the presence of bills in the system using an attribute of the class that models the cash dispenser. (We assign attributes to the ATM system's classes in Section 25.4.) For example, the cash dispenser maintains a count of the number of bills it contains. The requirements document does not say anything about what the system should do with deposit envelopes after it receives them. We can assume that simply acknowledging the receipt of an envelope—an operation performed by the class that models the deposit slot—is sufficient to represent the presence of an envelope in the system. We assign operations to the ATM system's classes in Section 25.6.

In our simplified ATM system, representing various amounts of "money," including an account's "balance," as attributes of classes seems most appropriate. Likewise, the nouns "account number" and "PIN" represent significant pieces of information in the ATM system. They're important attributes of a bank account. They do not, however, exhibit behaviors. Thus, we can most appropriately model them as attributes of an account class.

Though the requirements document frequently describes a "transaction" in a general sense, we do not model the broad notion of a financial transaction at this time. Instead, we model the three types of transactions (i.e., "balance inquiry," "withdrawal" and "deposit") as individual classes. These classes possess specific attributes needed for executing the transactions they represent. For example, a withdrawal needs to know the amount of the withdrawal. A balance inquiry, however, does not require any additional data other than the account number. Furthermore, the three transaction classes exhibit unique behaviors. A withdrawal includes dispensing cash to the user, whereas a deposit involves receiving deposit envelopes from the user. In Section 26.3, we "factor out" common features of all transactions into a general "transaction" class using the object-oriented concept of inheritance.

We determine the classes for our system based on the remaining nouns and noun phrases from Fig. 25.5. Each of these refers to one or more of the following:

- ATM
- screen
- keypad
- cash dispenser
- deposit slot
- account
- bank database
- balance inquiry
- withdrawal
- deposit

The elements of this list are likely to be classes that we'll need to implement our system.

We can now model the classes in our system based on the list we've created. We capitalize class names in the design process—a UML convention—as we'll do when we write the actual Java code that implements our design. If the name of a class contains more than one word, we run the words together and capitalize each word (e.g., `MultipleWordName`). Using this convention, we create classes `ATM`, `Screen`, `Keypad`, `CashDispenser`, `Deposit-Slot`, `Account`, `BankDatabase`, `BalanceInquiry`, `Withdrawal` and `Deposit`. We construct our system using these classes as building blocks. Before we begin building the system, however, we must gain a better understanding of how the classes relate to one another.

Modeling Classes

The UML enables us to model, via **class diagrams**, the classes in the ATM system and their interrelationships. Figure 25.6 represents class ATM. Each class is modeled as a rectangle with three compartments. The top one contains the name of the class centered horizontally in boldface. The middle compartment contains the class's attributes. (We discuss attributes in Sections 25.4—25.5.) The bottom compartment contains the class's operations (discussed in Section 25.6). In Fig. 25.6, the middle and bottom compartments are empty because we've not yet determined this class's attributes and operations.

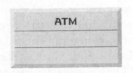

Fig. 25.6 | Representing a class in the UML using a class diagram.

Class diagrams also show the relationships between the classes of the system. Figure 25.7 shows how our classes ATM and Withdrawal relate to one another. For the moment, for simplicity, we choose to model only this subset of classes. We present a more complete class diagram later in this section. Notice that the rectangles representing classes in this diagram are not subdivided into compartments. The UML allows the suppression of class attributes and operations in this manner to create more readable diagrams, when appropriate. Such a diagram is said to be an **elided diagram**—one in which some information, such as the contents of the second and third compartments, is *not* modeled. We'll place information in these compartments in Sections 25.4—25.6.

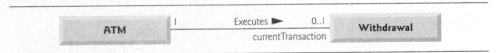

Fig. 25.7 | Class diagram showing an association among classes.

In Fig. 25.7, the solid line that connects the two classes represents an **association**—a relationship between classes. The numbers near each end of the line are **multiplicity** values, which indicate how many objects of each class participate in the association. In this case, following the line from left to right reveals that, at any given moment, one ATM object participates in an association with either zero or one Withdrawal objects—zero if the current user is not currently performing a transaction or has requested a different type of transaction, and one if the user has requested a withdrawal. The UML can model many types of multiplicity. Figure 25.8 lists and explains the multiplicity types.

An association can be named. For example, the word Executes above the line connecting classes ATM and Withdrawal in Fig. 25.7 indicates the name of that association. This part of the diagram reads "one object of class ATM executes zero or one objects of class Withdrawal." Association names are *directional*, as indicated by the filled arrowhead—so

Symbol	Meaning
0	None
1	One
m	An integer value
0..1	Zero or one
m, n	m or n
$m..n$	At least m, but not more than n
*	Any nonnegative integer (zero or more)
0..*	Zero or more (identical to *)
1..*	One or more

Fig. 25.8 | Multiplicity types.

it would be improper, for example, to read the preceding association from right to left as "zero or one objects of class Withdrawal execute one object of class ATM."

The word currentTransaction at the Withdrawal end of the association line in Fig. 25.7 is a **role name**, identifying the role the Withdrawal object plays in its relationship with the ATM. A role name adds meaning to an association between classes by identifying the role a class plays in the context of an association. A class can play several roles in the same system. For example, in a school personnel system, a person may play the role of "professor" when relating to students. The same person may take on the role of "colleague" when participating in an association with another professor, and "coach" when coaching student athletes. In Fig. 25.7, the role name currentTransaction indicates that the Withdrawal object participating in the Executes association with an object of class ATM represents the transaction currently being processed by the ATM. In other contexts, a Withdrawal object may take on other roles (e.g., the "previous transaction"). Notice that we do not specify a role name for the ATM end of the Executes association. Role names in class diagrams are often omitted when the meaning of an association is clear without them.

In addition to indicating simple relationships, associations can specify more complex relationships, such as objects of one class being *composed of* objects of other classes. Consider a real-world automated teller machine. What "pieces" does a manufacturer put together to build a working ATM? Our requirements document tells us that the ATM is composed of a screen, a keypad, a cash dispenser and a deposit slot.

In Fig. 25.9, the **solid diamonds** attached to the ATM class's association lines indicate that ATM has a **composition** relationship with classes Screen, Keypad, CashDispenser and DepositSlot. Composition implies a *whole/part relationship*. The class that has the composition symbol (the solid diamond) on its end of the association line is the *whole* (in this case, ATM), and the classes on the other end of the association lines are the *parts*—in this case, Screen, Keypad, CashDispenser and DepositSlot. The compositions in Fig. 25.9 indicate that an object of class ATM is formed from one object of class Screen, one object of class CashDispenser, one object of class Keypad and one object of class DepositSlot. The ATM *has a* screen, a keypad, a cash dispenser and a deposit slot. (As we saw in Chapter 9, the *is-a* relationship defines inheritance. We'll see in Section 26.3 that there's a nice opportunity to use inheritance in the ATM system design.)

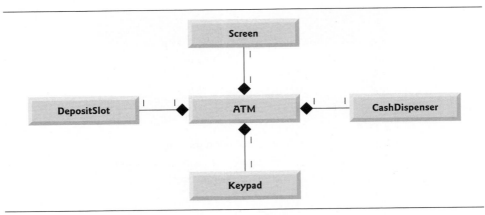

Fig. 25.9 | Class diagram showing composition relationships.

According to the UML specification (www.omg.org/technology/documents/formal/uml.htm), composition relationships have the following properties:

1. Only one class in the relationship can represent the *whole* (i.e., the diamond can be placed on only *one* end of the association line). For example, either the screen is part of the ATM or the ATM is part of the screen, but the screen and the ATM cannot both represent the whole in the relationship.

2. The *parts* in the composition relationship exist only as long as the whole does, and the whole is responsible for the creation and destruction of its parts. For example, the act of constructing an ATM includes manufacturing its parts. Also, if the ATM is destroyed, its screen, keypad, cash dispenser and deposit slot are also destroyed.

3. A *part* may belong to only one *whole* at a time, although it may be removed and attached to another whole, which then assumes responsibility for the part.

The solid diamonds in our class diagrams indicate composition relationships that fulfill these properties. If a *has-a* relationship does not satisfy one or more of these criteria, the UML specifies that **hollow diamonds** be attached to the ends of association lines to indicate **aggregation**—a weaker form of composition. For example, a personal computer and a computer monitor participate in an aggregation relationship—the computer *has a* monitor, but the two parts can exist independently, and the same monitor can be attached to multiple computers at once, thus violating composition's second and third properties.

Figure 25.10 shows a class diagram for the ATM system. This diagram models most of the classes that we've identified, as well as the associations between them that we can infer from the requirements document. Classes BalanceInquiry and Deposit participate in associations similar to those of class Withdrawal, so we've chosen to omit them from this diagram to keep it simple. In Section 26.3, we expand our class diagram to include all the classes in the ATM system.

Figure 25.10 presents a graphical model of ATM system's structure. It includes classes BankDatabase and Account, and several associations that were not present in either Fig. 25.7 or Fig. 25.9. It shows that class ATM has a **one-to-one relationship** with class BankDatabase—one ATM object *authenticates users against* one BankDatabase object. In

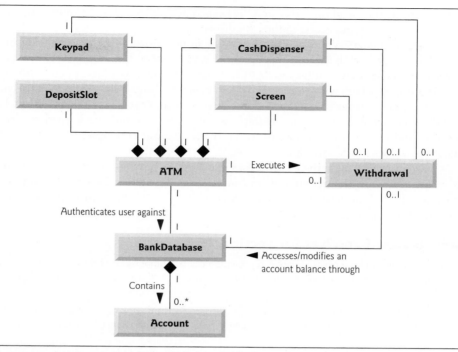

Fig. 25.10 | Class diagram for the ATM system model.

Fig. 25.10, we also model the fact that the bank's database contains information about many accounts—one BankDatabase object participates in a *composition* relationship with zero or more Account objects. The multiplicity value 0..* at the Account end of the association between class BankDatabase and class Account indicates that zero or more objects of class Account take part in the association. Class BankDatabase has a **one-to-many relationship** with class Account—the BankDatabase can contain many Accounts. Similarly, class Account has a **many-to-one relationship** with class BankDatabase—there can be many Accounts stored in the BankDatabase. Recall from Fig. 25.8 that the multiplicity value * is identical to 0..*. We include 0..* in our class diagrams for clarity.

Figure 25.10 also indicates that at any given time 0 or 1 Withdrawal objects can exist. If the user is performing a withdrawal, "one object of class Withdrawal accesses/modifies an account balance through one object of class BankDatabase." We could have created an association directly between class Withdrawal and class Account. The requirements document, however, states that the "ATM must interact with the bank's account information database" to perform transactions. A bank account contains sensitive information, and systems engineers must always consider the security of personal data when designing a system. Thus, only the BankDatabase can access and manipulate an account directly. All other parts of the system must interact with the database to retrieve or update account information (e.g., an account balance).

The class diagram in Fig. 25.10 also models associations between class Withdrawal and classes Screen, CashDispenser and Keypad. A withdrawal transaction includes prompting the user to choose a withdrawal amount, and receiving numeric input. These actions require the use of the screen and the keypad, respectively. Furthermore, dispensing cash to the user requires access to the cash dispenser.

Classes `BalanceInquiry` and `Deposit`, though not shown in Fig. 25.10, take part in several associations with the other classes of the ATM system. Like class `Withdrawal`, each of these classes associates with classes `ATM` and `BankDatabase`. An object of class `Balance-Inquiry` also associates with an object of class `Screen` to display the balance of an account to the user. Class `Deposit` associates with classes `Screen`, `Keypad` and `DepositSlot`. Like withdrawals, deposit transactions require use of the screen and the keypad to display prompts and receive input, respectively. To receive deposit envelopes, an object of class `Deposit` accesses the deposit slot.

We've now identified the initial classes in our ATM system—we may discover others as we proceed with the design and implementation. In Section 25.4 we determine the attributes for each of these classes, and in Section 25.5 we use these attributes to examine how the system changes over time.

Self-Review Exercises for Section 25.3

25.4   Suppose we have a class `Car` that represents a car. Think of some of the different pieces that a manufacturer would put together to produce a whole car. Create a class diagram (similar to Fig. 25.9) that models some of the composition relationships of class `Car`.

25.5   Suppose we have a class `File` that represents an electronic document in a standalone, non-networked computer represented by class `Computer`. What sort of association exists between class `Computer` and class `File`?
    a) Class `Computer` has a one-to-one relationship with class `File`.
    b) Class `Computer` has a many-to-one relationship with class `File`.
    c) Class `Computer` has a one-to-many relationship with class `File`.
    d) Class `Computer` has a many-to-many relationship with class `File`.

25.6   State whether the following statement is *true* or *false*, and if *false*, explain why: A UML diagram in which a class's second and third compartments are not modeled is said to be an elided diagram.

25.7   Modify the class diagram of Fig. 25.10 to include class `Deposit` instead of class `Withdrawal`.

25.4 Identifying Class Attributes

[*Note:* **This section may be read after Chapter 4.**]
Classes have attributes (data) and operations (behaviors). Class attributes are implemented as fields, and class operations are implemented as methods. In this section, we determine many of the attributes needed in the ATM system. In Section 25.5 we examine how these attributes represent an object's state. In Section 25.6 we determine class operations.

Identifying Attributes
Consider the attributes of some real-world objects: A person's attributes include height, weight and whether the person is left-handed, right-handed or ambidextrous. A radio's attributes include its station, volume and AM or FM settings. A car's attributes include its speedometer and odometer readings, the amount of gas in its tank and what gear it's in. A personal computer's attributes include its manufacturer (e.g., Dell, Sun, Apple or IBM), type of screen (e.g., LCD or CRT), main memory size and hard disk size.

We can identify many attributes of the classes in our system by looking for descriptive words and phrases in the requirements document. For each such word and phrase we find that plays a significant role in the ATM system, we create an attribute and assign it to one or more of the classes identified in Section 25.3. We also create attributes to represent any additional data that a class may need, as such needs become clear throughout the design process.

Figure 25.11 lists the words or phrases from the requirements document that describe each class. We formed this list by reading the requirements document and identifying any words or phrases that refer to characteristics of the classes in the system. For example, the requirements document describes the steps taken to obtain a "withdrawal amount," so we list "amount" next to class Withdrawal.

Class	Descriptive words and phrases
ATM	user is authenticated
BalanceInquiry	account number
Withdrawal	account number
	amount
Deposit	account number
	amount
BankDatabase	*[no descriptive words or phrases]*
Account	account number
	PIN
	balance
Screen	*[no descriptive words or phrases]*
Keypad	*[no descriptive words or phrases]*
CashDispenser	begins each day loaded with 500 $20 bills
DepositSlot	*[no descriptive words or phrases]*

Fig. 25.11 | Descriptive words and phrases from the ATM requirements document.

Figure 25.11 leads us to create one attribute of class ATM. Class ATM maintains information about the state of the ATM. The phrase "user is authenticated" describes a state of the ATM (we introduce states in Section 25.5), so we include userAuthenticated as a **Boolean attribute** (i.e., an attribute that has a value of either true or false) in class ATM. The Boolean attribute type in the UML is equivalent to the boolean type in Java. This attribute indicates whether the ATM has successfully authenticated the current user—userAuthenticated must be true for the system to allow the user to perform transactions and access account information. This attribute helps ensure the security of the data in the system.

Classes BalanceInquiry, Withdrawal and Deposit share one attribute. Each transaction involves an "account number" that corresponds to the account of the user making the transaction. We assign an integer attribute accountNumber to each transaction class to identify the account to which an object of the class applies.

Descriptive words and phrases in the requirements document also suggest some differences in the attributes required by each transaction class. The requirements document indicates that to withdraw cash or deposit funds, users must input a specific "amount" of money to be withdrawn or deposited, respectively. Thus, we assign to classes Withdrawal and `Deposit` an attribute `amount` to store the value supplied by the user. The amounts of money related to a withdrawal and a deposit are defining characteristics of these transactions that the system requires for these transactions to take place. Class `BalanceInquiry`, however, needs no additional data to perform its task—it requires only an account number to indicate the account whose balance should be retrieved.

Class `Account` has several attributes. The requirements document states that each bank account has an "account number" and "PIN," which the system uses for identifying accounts and authenticating users. We assign to class `Account` two integer attributes: `accountNumber` and `pin`. The requirements document also specifies that an account maintains a "balance" of the amount of money in the account and that money the user deposits does not become available for a withdrawal until the bank verifies the amount of cash in the deposit envelope, and any checks in the envelope clear. An account must still record the amount of money that a user deposits, however. Therefore, we decide that an account should represent a balance using two attributes: `availableBalance` and `totalBalance`. Attribute `availableBalance` tracks the amount of money that a user can withdraw from the account. Attribute `totalBalance` refers to the total amount of money that the user has "on deposit" (i.e., the amount of money available, plus the amount waiting to be verified or cleared). For example, suppose an ATM user deposits $50.00 into an empty account. The `totalBalance` attribute would increase to $50.00 to record the deposit, but the `availableBalance` would remain at $0. [*Note:* We assume that the bank updates the `availableBalance` attribute of an `Account` some length of time after the ATM transaction occurs, in response to confirming that $50 worth of cash or checks was found in the deposit envelope. We assume that this update occurs through a transaction that a bank employee performs using some piece of bank software other than the ATM. Thus, we do not discuss this transaction in our case study.]

Class `CashDispenser` has one attribute. The requirements document states that the cash dispenser "begins each day loaded with 500 $20 bills." The cash dispenser must keep track of the number of bills it contains to determine whether enough cash is on hand to satisfy withdrawal requests. We assign to class `CashDispenser` an integer attribute `count`, which is initially set to 500.

For real problems in industry, there's no guarantee that requirements documents will be precise enough for the object-oriented systems designer to determine all the attributes or even all the classes. The need for additional classes, attributes and behaviors may become clear as the design process proceeds. As we progress through this case study, we will continue to add, modify and delete information about the classes in our system.

Modeling Attributes

The class diagram in Fig. 25.12 lists some of the attributes for the classes in our system— the descriptive words and phrases in Fig. 25.11 lead us to identify these attributes. For simplicity, Fig. 25.12 does not show the associations among classes—we showed these in Fig. 25.10. This is a common practice of systems designers when designs are being developed. Recall from Section 25.3 that in the UML, a class's attributes are placed in the middle compartment of the class's rectangle. We list each attribute's name and type separated by a colon (:), followed in some cases by an equal sign (=) and an initial value.

Consider the `userAuthenticated` attribute of class `ATM`:

```
userAuthenticated : Boolean = false
```

This attribute declaration contains three pieces of information about the attribute. The **attribute name** is userAuthenticated. The **attribute type** is Boolean. In Java, an attribute can be represented by a primitive type, such as boolean, int or double, or a reference type like a class. We've chosen to model only primitive-type attributes in Fig. 25.12—we discuss the reasoning behind this decision shortly. The attribute types in Fig. 25.12 are in UML notation. We'll associate the types Boolean, Integer and Double in the UML diagram with the primitive types boolean, int and double in Java, respectively.

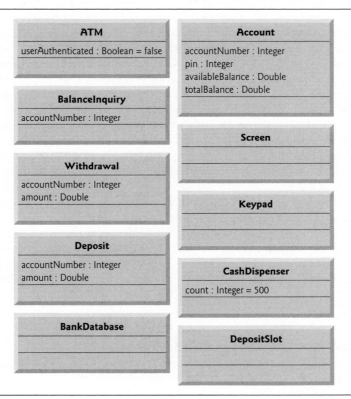

Fig. 25.12 | Classes with attributes.

We can also indicate an initial value for an attribute. The userAuthenticated attribute in class ATM has an initial value of false. This indicates that the system initially does not consider the user to be authenticated. If an attribute has no initial value specified, only its name and type (separated by a colon) are shown. For example, the accountNumber attribute of class BalanceInquiry is an integer. Here we show no initial value, because the value of this attribute is a number that we do not yet know. This number will be determined at execution time based on the account number entered by the current ATM user.

Figure 25.12 does not include attributes for classes Screen, Keypad and DepositSlot. These are important components of our system, for which our design process has not yet revealed any attributes. We may discover some, however, in the remaining phases of design or when we implement these classes in Java. This is perfectly normal.

> **Software Engineering Observation 25.1**
>
> *At early stages in the design process, classes often lack attributes (and operations). Such classes should not be eliminated, however, because attributes (and operations) may become evident in the later phases of design and implementation.*

Figure 25.12 also does not include attributes for class `BankDatabase`. Recall that attributes in Java can be represented by either primitive types or reference types. We've chosen to include only primitive-type attributes in the class diagram in Fig. 25.12 (and in similar class diagrams throughout the case study). A reference-type attribute is modeled more clearly as an association between the class holding the reference and the class of the object to which the reference points. For example, the class diagram in Fig. 25.10 indicates that class `BankDatabase` participates in a composition relationship with zero or more `Account` objects. From this composition, we can determine that when we implement the ATM system in Java, we'll be required to create an attribute of class `BankDatabase` to hold references to zero or more `Account` objects. Similarly, we can determine reference-type attributes of class `ATM` that correspond to its composition relationships with classes `Screen`, `Keypad`, `CashDispenser` and `DepositSlot`. These composition-based attributes would be redundant if modeled in Fig. 25.12, because the compositions modeled in Fig. 25.10 already convey the fact that the database contains information about zero or more accounts and that an ATM is composed of a screen, keypad, cash dispenser and deposit slot. Software developers typically model these whole/part relationships as compositions rather than as attributes required to implement the relationships.

The class diagram in Fig. 25.12 provides a solid basis for the structure of our model, but the diagram is not complete. In Section 25.5 we identify the states and activities of the objects in the model, and in Section 25.6 we identify the operations that the objects perform. As we present more of the UML and object-oriented design, we'll continue to strengthen the structure of our model.

Self-Review Exercises for Section 25.4

25.8   We typically identify the attributes of the classes in our system by analyzing the _____ in the requirements document.
- a) nouns and noun phrases
- b) descriptive words and phrases
- c) verbs and verb phrases
- d) All of the above.

25.9   Which of the following is *not* an attribute of an airplane?
- a) length
- b) wingspan
- c) fly
- d) number of seats

25.10   Describe the meaning of the following attribute declaration of class `CashDispenser` in the class diagram in Fig. 25.12:

```
count : Integer = 500
```

25.5 Identifying Objects' States and Activities

[*Note:* This section may be read after Chapter 5.]
In Section 25.4, we identified many of the class attributes needed to implement the ATM system and added them to the class diagram in Fig. 25.12. We now show how these attributes represent an object's state. We identify some key states that our objects may occupy and discuss how objects *change state* in response to various events occurring in the system. We also discuss the workflow, or **activities**, that objects perform in the ATM system, and we present the activities of BalanceInquiry and Withdrawal transaction objects.

State Machine Diagrams
Each object in a system goes through a series of states. An object's state is indicated by the values of its attributes at a given time. **State machine diagrams** (commonly called **state diagrams**) model several states of an object and show under what circumstances the object changes state. Unlike the class diagrams presented in earlier case study sections, which focused primarily on the system's *structure*, state diagrams model some of the system's *behavior*.

Figure 25.13 is a simple state diagram that models some of the states of an object of class ATM. The UML represents each state in a state diagram as a **rounded rectangle** with the name of the state placed inside it. A **solid circle** with an attached stick (⟶) arrowhead designates the **initial state**. Recall that we modeled this state information as the Boolean attribute userAuthenticated in the class diagram of Fig. 25.12. This attribute is initialized to false, or the "User not authenticated" state, according to the state diagram.

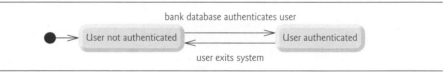

Fig. 25.13 | State diagram for the ATM object.

The arrows with stick (⟶) arrowhead indicate **transitions** between states. An object can transition from one state to another in response to various *events* that occur in the system. The name or description of the event that causes a transition is written near the line that corresponds to the transition. For example, the ATM object changes from the "User not authenticated" to the "User authenticated" state after the database authenticates the user. Recall from the requirements document that the database authenticates a user by comparing the account number and PIN entered by the user with those of an account in the database. If the user has entered a valid account number and the correct PIN, the ATM object transitions to the "User authenticated" state and changes its userAuthenticated attribute to a value of true. When the user exits the system by choosing the "exit" option from the main menu, the ATM object returns to the "User not authenticated" state.

Software Engineering Observation 25.2

Software designers do not generally create state diagrams showing every possible state and state transition for all attributes—there are simply too many of them. State diagrams typically show only key states and state transitions.

Activity Diagrams

Like a state diagram, an activity diagram models aspects of system behavior. Unlike a state diagram, an activity diagram models an object's **workflow** (sequence of events) during program execution. An activity diagram models the **actions** the object will perform and in what *order*. The activity diagram in Fig. 25.14 models the actions involved in executing a balance-inquiry transaction. We assume that a `BalanceInquiry` object has already been initialized and assigned a valid account number (that of the current user), so the object knows which balance to retrieve. The diagram includes the actions that occur after the user selects a balance inquiry from the main menu and before the ATM returns the user to the main menu—a `BalanceInquiry` object does not perform or initiate these actions, so we do not model them here. The diagram begins with retrieving the balance of the account from the database. Next, the `BalanceInquiry` displays the balance on the screen. This action completes the execution of the transaction. Recall that we've chosen to represent an account balance as both the `availableBalance` and `totalBalance` attributes of class `Account`, so the actions modeled in Fig. 25.14 refer to the retrieval and display of *both* balance attributes.

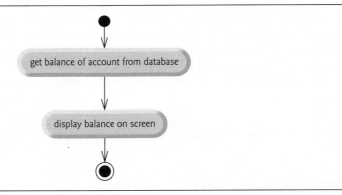

Fig. 25.14 | Activity diagram for a `BalanceInquiry` object.

The UML represents an action in an activity diagram as an action state modeled by a rectangle with its left and right sides replaced by arcs curving outward. Each action state contains an *action expression*—for example, "get balance of account from database"—that specifies an action to be performed. An arrow with a stick ($\rightarrow$) arrowhead connects two action states, indicating the order in which the actions represented by the action states occur. The solid circle (at the top of Fig. 25.14) represents the activity's *initial state*—the beginning of the workflow before the object performs the modeled actions. In this case, the transaction first executes the "get balance of account from database" action expression. The transaction then displays *both* balances on the screen. The solid circle enclosed in an open circle (at the bottom of Fig. 25.14) represents the *final state*—the end of the workflow after the object performs the modeled actions. We used UML activity diagrams to illustrate the flow of control for the control statements presented in Chapters 4–5.

Figure 25.15 shows an activity diagram for a withdrawal transaction. We assume that a `Withdrawal` object has been assigned a valid account number. We do not model the user selecting a withdrawal from the main menu or the ATM returning the user to the main

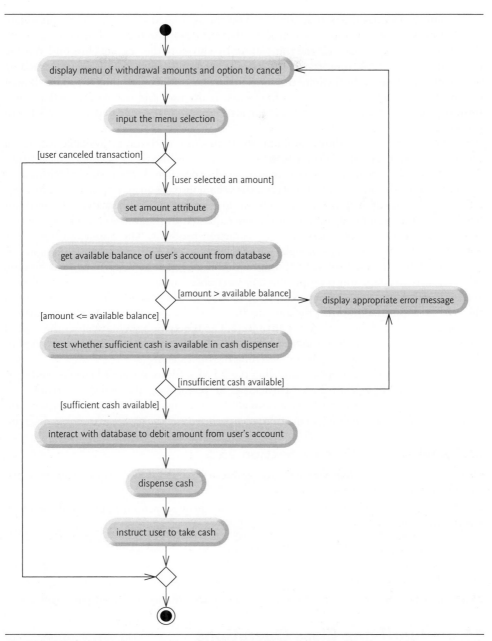

Fig. 25.15 | Activity diagram for a withdrawal transaction.

menu because these are not actions performed by a Withdrawal object. The transaction first displays a menu of standard withdrawal amounts (shown in Fig. 25.3) and an option to cancel the transaction. The transaction then receives a menu selection from the user. The activity flow now arrives at a decision (a fork indicated by the small diamond symbol).

This point determines the next action based on the associated guard condition (in square brackets next to the transition), which states that the transition occurs if this guard condition is met. If the user cancels the transaction by choosing the "cancel" option from the menu, the activity flow immediately skips to the final state. Note the merge (indicated by the small diamond symbol) where the cancellation flow of activity joins the main flow of activity before reaching the activity's final state. If the user selects a withdrawal amount from the menu, Withdrawal sets amount (an attribute originally modeled in Fig. 25.12) to the value chosen by the user.

After setting the withdrawal amount, the transaction retrieves the available balance of the user's account (i.e., the availableBalance attribute of the user's Account object) from the database. The activity flow then arrives at another decision. If the requested withdrawal amount exceeds the user's available balance, the system displays an appropriate error message informing the user of the problem, then returns to the beginning of the activity diagram and prompts the user to input a new amount. If the requested withdrawal amount is less than or equal to the user's available balance, the transaction proceeds. The transaction next tests whether the cash dispenser has enough cash remaining to satisfy the withdrawal request. If it does not, the transaction displays an appropriate error message, then returns to the beginning of the activity diagram and prompts the user to choose a new amount. If sufficient cash is available, the transaction interacts with the database to debit the withdrawal amount from the user's account (i.e., subtract the amount from *both* the availableBalance and total-Balance attributes of the user's Account object). The transaction then dispenses the desired amount of cash and instructs the user to take it. Finally, the main flow of activity merges with the cancellation flow of activity before reaching the final state.

We've taken the first steps in modeling the ATM software system's behavior and have shown how an object's attributes participate in performing the object's activities. In Section 25.6, we investigate the behaviors for all classes to give a more accurate interpretation of the system behavior by filling in the third compartments of the classes in our class diagram.

Self-Review Exercises for Section 25.5

25.11 State whether the following statement is *true* or *false*, and if *false*, explain why: State diagrams model structural aspects of a system.

25.12 An activity diagram models the _____ that an object performs and the order in which it performs them.
  a) actions
  b) attributes
  c) states
  d) state transitions

25.13 Based on the requirements document, create an activity diagram for a deposit transaction.

25.6 Identifying Class Operations

[*Note:* **This section may be read after Chapter 6.**]
In this section, we determine some of the class operations (or behaviors) needed to implement the ATM system. An operation is a service that objects of a class provide to clients (users) of the class. Consider the operations of some real-world objects. A radio's operations include setting its station and volume (typically invoked by a person's adjusting the

radio's controls). A car's operations include accelerating (invoked by the driver's pressing the accelerator pedal), decelerating (invoked by the driver's pressing the brake pedal or releasing the gas pedal), turning and shifting gears. Software objects can offer operations as well—for example, a software graphics object might offer operations for drawing a circle, drawing a line, drawing a square and the like. A spreadsheet software object might offer operations like printing the spreadsheet, totaling the elements in a row or column and graphing information in the spreadsheet as a bar chart or pie chart.

We can derive many of the class operations by examining the key *verbs and verb phrases* in the requirements document. We then relate these verbs and verb phrases to classes in our system (Fig. 25.16). The verb phrases in Fig. 25.16 help us determine the operations of each class.

Class	Verbs and verb phrases
ATM	executes financial transactions
BalanceInquiry	*[none in the requirements document]*
Withdrawal	*[none in the requirements document]*
Deposit	*[none in the requirements document]*
BankDatabase	authenticates a user, retrieves an account balance, credits a deposit amount to an account, debits a withdrawal amount from an account
Account	retrieves an account balance, credits a deposit amount to an account, debits a withdrawal amount from an account
Screen	displays a message to the user
Keypad	receives numeric input from the user
CashDispenser	dispenses cash, indicates whether it contains enough cash to satisfy a withdrawal request
DepositSlot	receives a deposit envelope

Fig. 25.16 | Verbs and verb phrases for each class in the ATM system.

Modeling Operations

To identify operations, we examine the verb phrases listed for each class in Fig. 25.16. The "executes financial transactions" phrase associated with class ATM implies that class ATM instructs transactions to execute. Therefore, classes BalanceInquiry, Withdrawal and Deposit each need an operation to provide this service to the ATM. We place this operation (which we've named execute) in the third compartment of the three transaction classes in the updated class diagram of Fig. 25.17. During an ATM session, the ATM object will invoke these transaction operations as necessary.

The UML represents operations (that is, methods) by listing the operation name, followed by a comma-separated list of parameters in parentheses, a colon and the return type:

operationName(parameter1, parameter2, ..., parameterN) : return type

Each parameter in the comma-separated parameter list consists of a parameter name, followed by a colon and the parameter type:

parameterName : parameterType

Fig. 25.17 | Classes in the ATM system with attributes and operations.

For the moment, we do not list the parameters of our operations—we'll identify and model some of them shortly. For some of the operations, we do not yet know the return types, so we also omit them from the diagram. These omissions are perfectly normal at this point. As our design and implementation proceed, we'll add the remaining return types.

Authenticating a User

Figure 25.16 lists the phrase "authenticates a user" next to class BankDatabase—the database is the object that contains the account information necessary to determine whether the account number and PIN entered by a user match those of an account held at the bank. Therefore, class BankDatabase needs an operation that provides an authentication service to the ATM. We place the operation authenticateUser in the third compartment of class BankDatabase (Fig. 25.17). However, an object of class Account, not class Bank-Database, stores the account number and PIN that must be accessed to authenticate a user, so class Account must provide a service to validate a PIN obtained through user input against a PIN stored in an Account object. Therefore, we add a validatePIN operation to class `Account`. We specify a return type of `Boolean` for the `authenticateUser` and `validatePIN` operations. Each operation returns a value indicating either that the operation was successful in performing its task (i.e., a return value of `true`) or that it was not (i.e., a return value of `false`).

Other *BankDatabase and Account Operations*

Figure 25.16 lists several additional verb phrases for class `BankDatabase`: "retrieves an account balance," "credits a deposit amount to an account" and "debits a withdrawal amount from an account." Like "authenticates a user," these remaining phrases refer to services that the database must provide to the ATM, because the database holds all the account data used to authenticate a user and perform ATM transactions. However, objects of class `Account` actually perform the operations to which these phrases refer. Thus, we assign an operation to both class `BankDatabase` and class `Account` to correspond to each of these phrases. Recall from Section 25.3 that, because a bank account contains sensitive information, we do not allow the ATM to access accounts directly. The database acts as an intermediary between the ATM and the account data, thus preventing unauthorized access. As we'll see in Section 25.7, class `ATM` invokes the operations of class `BankDatabase`, each of which in turn invokes the operation with the same name in class `Account`.

Getting the Balances

The phrase "retrieves an account balance" suggests that classes `BankDatabase` and `Account` each need a `getBalance` operation. However, recall that we created *two* attributes in class `Account` to represent a balance—`availableBalance` and `totalBalance`. A balance inquiry requires access to *both* balance attributes so that it can display them to the user, but a withdrawal needs to check *only* the value of `availableBalance`. To allow objects in the system to obtain each balance attribute individually, we add operations `getAvailableBalance` and `getTotalBalance` to the third compartment of classes `BankDatabase` and `Account` (Fig. 25.17). We specify a return type of `Double` for these operations because the balance attributes they retrieve are of type `Double`.

Crediting and Debiting an *Account*

The phrases "credits a deposit amount to an account" and "debits a withdrawal amount from an account" indicate that classes `BankDatabase` and `Account` must perform operations to update an account during a deposit and withdrawal, respectively. We therefore assign `credit` and `debit` operations to classes `BankDatabase` and `Account`. You may recall that crediting an account (as in a deposit) adds an amount only to the `totalBalance` attribute. Debiting an account (as in a withdrawal), on the other hand, subtracts the amount from *both* balance attributes. We hide these implementation details inside class `Account`. This is a good example of encapsulation and information hiding.

Deposit Confirmations Performed by Another Banking System

If this were a real ATM system, classes `BankDatabase` and `Account` would also provide a set of operations to allow another banking system to update a user's account balance after either confirming or rejecting all or part of a deposit. Operation `confirmDepositAmount`, for example, would add an amount to the `availableBalance` attribute, thus making deposited funds available for withdrawal. Operation `rejectDepositAmount` would subtract an amount from the `totalBalance` attribute to indicate that a specified amount, which had recently been deposited through the ATM and added to the `totalBalance`, was not found in the deposit envelope. The bank would invoke this operation after determining either that the user failed to include the correct amount of cash or that any checks did not clear (i.e., they "bounced"). While adding these operations would make our system more complete, we do *not* include them in our class diagrams or our implementation because they're beyond the scope of the case study.

Displaying Messages
Class `Screen` "displays a message to the user" at various times in an ATM session. All visual output occurs through the screen of the ATM. The requirements document describes many types of messages (e.g., a welcome message, an error message, a thank you message) that the screen displays to the user. The requirements document also indicates that the screen displays prompts and menus to the user. However, a prompt is really just a message describing what the user should input next, and a menu is essentially a type of prompt consisting of a series of messages (i.e., menu options) displayed consecutively. Therefore, rather than assign class `Screen` an individual operation to display each type of message, prompt and menu, we simply create one operation that can display any message specified by a parameter. We place this operation (`displayMessage`) in the third compartment of class `Screen` in our class diagram (Fig. 25.17). We do not worry about the parameter of this operation at this time—we model it later in this section.

Keyboard Input
From the phrase "receives numeric input from the user" listed by class `Keypad` in Fig. 25.16, we conclude that class `Keypad` should perform a `getInput` operation. Because the ATM's keypad, unlike a computer keyboard, contains only the numbers 0–9, we specify that this operation returns an integer value. Recall from the requirements document that in different situations the user may be required to enter a different type of number (e.g., an account number, a PIN, the number of a menu option, a deposit amount as a number of cents). Class `Keypad` simply obtains a numeric value for a client of the class—it does not determine whether the value meets any specific criteria. Any class that uses this operation must verify that the user entered an appropriate number in a given situation, then respond accordingly (i.e., display an error message via class `Screen`). [*Note:* When we implement the system, we simulate the ATM's keypad with a computer keyboard, and for simplicity we assume that the user does not enter nonnumeric input using keys on the computer keyboard that do not appear on the ATM's keypad.]

Dispensing Cash
Figure 25.16 lists "dispenses cash" for class `CashDispenser`. Therefore, we create operation `dispenseCash` and list it under class `CashDispenser` in Fig. 25.17. Class `CashDispenser` also "indicates whether it contains enough cash to satisfy a withdrawal request." Thus, we include `isSufficientCashAvailable`, an operation that returns a value of UML type `Boolean`, in class `CashDispenser`.

Figure 25.16 also lists "receives a deposit envelope" for class `DepositSlot`. The deposit slot must indicate whether it received an envelope, so we place an operation `isEnvelopeReceived`, which returns a `Boolean` value, in the third compartment of class `DepositSlot`. [*Note:* A real hardware deposit slot would most likely send the ATM a signal to indicate that an envelope was received. We simulate this behavior, however, with an operation in class `DepositSlot` that class `ATM` can invoke to find out whether the deposit slot received an envelope.]

Class *ATM*

We do not list any operations for class `ATM` at this time. We're not yet aware of any services that class `ATM` provides to other classes in the system. When we implement the system with Java code, however, operations of this class, and additional operations of the other classes in the system, may emerge.

Identifying and Modeling Operation Parameters for Class *BankDatabase*

So far, we've not been concerned with the *parameters* of our operations—we've attempted to gain only a basic understanding of the operations of each class. Let's now take a closer look at some operation parameters. We identify an operation's parameters by examining what data the operation requires to perform its assigned task.

Consider `BankDatabase`'s `authenticateUser` operation. To authenticate a user, this operation must know the account number and PIN supplied by the user. So we specify that `authenticateUser` takes integer parameters `userAccountNumber` and `userPIN`, which the operation must compare to an `Account` object's account number and PIN in the database. We prefix these parameter names with "user" to avoid confusion between the operation's parameter names and class `Account`'s attribute names. We list these parameters in the class diagram in Fig. 25.18 that models only class `BankDatabase`. [*Note:* It's perfectly normal to model only one class. In this case, we're examining the parameters of this one class, so we omit the other classes. In class diagrams later in the case study, in which parameters are no longer the focus of our attention, we omit these parameters to save space. Remember, however, that the operations listed in these diagrams still have parameters.]

BankDatabase
authenticateUser(userAccountNumber : Integer, userPIN : Integer) : Boolean getAvailableBalance(userAccountNumber : Integer) : Double getTotalBalance(userAccountNumber : Integer) : Double credit(userAccountNumber : Integer, amount : Double) debit(userAccountNumber : Integer, amount : Double)

Fig. 25.18 | Class `BankDatabase` with operation parameters.

Recall that the UML models each parameter in an operation's comma-separated parameter list by listing the parameter name, followed by a colon and the parameter type (in UML notation). Figure 25.18 thus specifies that operation `authenticateUser` takes two parameters—`userAccountNumber` and `userPIN`, both of type `Integer`. When we implement the system in Java, we'll represent these parameters with `int` values.

Class `BankDatabase` operations `getAvailableBalance`, `getTotalBalance`, `credit` and `debit` also each require a `userAccountNumber` parameter to identify the account to which the database must apply the operations, so we include these parameters in the class diagram of Fig. 25.18. In addition, operations `credit` and `debit` each require a `Double` parameter `amount` to specify the amount of money to be credited or debited, respectively.

*Identifying and Modeling Operation Parameters for Class **Account***
Figure 25.19 models class Account's operation parameters. Operation validatePIN requires only a userPIN parameter, which contains the user-specified PIN to be compared with the account's PIN. Like their BankDatabase counterparts, operations credit and debit in class Account each require a Double parameter amount that indicates the amount of money involved in the operation. Operations getAvailableBalance and getTotal-Balance in class Account require no additional data to perform their tasks. Class Account's operations do *not* require an account-number parameter to distinguish between Accounts, because these operations can be invoked only on a specific Account object.

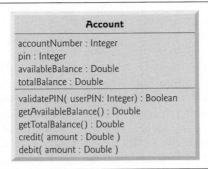

Fig. 25.19 | Class Account with operation parameters.

*Identifying and Modeling Operation Parameters for Class **Screen***
Figure 25.20 models class Screen with a parameter specified for operation display-Message. This operation requires only a String parameter message that indicates the text to be displayed. Recall that the parameter types listed in our class diagrams are in UML notation, so the String type listed in Fig. 25.20 refers to the UML type. When we implement the system in Java, we'll use the Java class String to represent this parameter.

Fig. 25.20 | Class Screen with operation parameters.

*Identifying and Modeling Operation Parameters for Class **CashDispenser***
Figure 25.21 specifies that operation dispenseCash of class CashDispenser takes a Double parameter amount to indicate the amount of cash (in dollars) to be dispensed. Operation isSufficientCashAvailable also takes a Double parameter amount to indicate the amount of cash in question.

Identifying and Modeling Operation Parameters for Other Classes
We do not discuss parameters for operation execute of classes BalanceInquiry, Withdrawal and Deposit, operation getInput of class Keypad and operation isEnvelope-

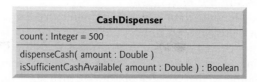

CashDispenser
count : Integer = 500
dispenseCash(amount : Double) isSufficientCashAvailable(amount : Double) : Boolean

Fig. 25.21 | Class `CashDispenser` with operation parameters.

Received of class DepositSlot. At this point in our design process, we cannot determine whether these operations require additional data, so we leave their parameter lists empty. Later, we may decide to add parameters.

In this section, we've determined many of the operations performed by the classes in the ATM system. We've identified the parameters and return types of some of the operations. As we continue our design process, the number of operations belonging to each class may vary—we might find that new operations are needed or that some current operations are unnecessary. We also might determine that some of our class operations need additional parameters and different return types, or that some parameters are unnecessary or require different types.

Self-Review Exercises for Section 25.6

25.14 Which of the following is *not* a behavior?
    a) reading data from a file
    b) printing output
    c) text output
    d) obtaining input from the user

25.15 If you were to add to the ATM system an operation that returns the amount attribute of class Withdrawal, how and where would you specify this operation in the class diagram of Fig. 25.17?

25.16 Describe the meaning of the following operation listing that might appear in a class diagram for an object-oriented design of a calculator:
    `add(x : Integer, y : Integer) : Integer`

25.7 Indicating Collaboration Among Objects

[*Note:* **This section may be read after Chapter 7.**]
In this section, we concentrate on the collaborations (interactions) among objects. When two objects communicate with each other to accomplish a task, they're said to **collaborate**—objects do this by invoking one another's operations. A **collaboration** consists of an object of one class sending a **message** to an object of another class. Messages are sent in Java via method calls.

In Section 25.6, we determined many of the operations of the system's classes. Now, we concentrate on the messages that invoke these operations. To identify the collaborations in the system, we return to the requirements document in Section 25.2. Recall that this document specifies the range of activities that occur during an ATM session (e.g., authenticating a user, performing transactions). The steps used to describe how the system must perform each of these tasks are our first indication of the collaborations in our system. As we proceed through this section and Chapter 26, we may discover additional collaborations.

Identifying the Collaborations in a System

We identify the collaborations in the system by carefully reading the sections of the requirements document that specify what the ATM should do to authenticate a user and to perform each transaction type. For each action or step described, we decide which objects in our system must interact to achieve the desired result. We identify one object as the sending object and another as the receiving object. We then select one of the receiving object's operations (identified in Section 25.6) that must be invoked by the sending object to produce the proper behavior. For example, the ATM displays a welcome message when idle. We know that an object of class Screen displays a message to the user via its display-Message operation. Thus, we decide that the system can display a welcome message by employing a collaboration between the ATM and the Screen in which the ATM sends a displayMessage message to the Screen by invoking the displayMessage operation of class Screen. [*Note:* To avoid repeating the phrase "an object of class…," we refer to an object by using its class name preceded by an article (e.g., "a," "an" or "the")—for example, "the ATM" refers to an object of class ATM.]

Figure 25.22 lists the collaborations that can be derived from the requirements document. For each sending object, we list the collaborations in the order in which they first occur during an ATM session (i.e., the order in which they're discussed in the requirements document). We list each collaboration involving a unique sender, message and recipient only once, even though the collaborations may occur at several different times throughout an ATM session. For example, the first row in Fig. 25.22 indicates that the ATM collaborates with the Screen whenever the ATM needs to display a message to the user.

Let's consider the collaborations in Fig. 25.22. Before allowing a user to perform any transactions, the ATM must prompt the user to enter an account number, then to enter a PIN. It accomplishes these tasks by sending a displayMessage message to the Screen. Both actions refer to the same collaboration between the ATM and the Screen, which is already listed in Fig. 25.22. The ATM obtains input in response to a prompt by sending a getInput message to the Keypad. Next, the ATM must determine whether the user-specified account number and PIN match those of an account in the database. It does so by sending an authenticateUser message to the BankDatabase. Recall that the BankDatabase cannot authenticate a user directly—only the user's Account (i.e., the Account that contains the account number specified by the user) can access the user's PIN on record to authenticate the user. Figure 25.22 therefore lists a collaboration in which the BankDatabase sends a validatePIN message to an Account.

After the user is authenticated, the ATM displays the main menu by sending a series of displayMessage messages to the Screen and obtains input containing a menu selection by sending a getInput message to the Keypad. We've already accounted for these collaborations, so we do not add anything to Fig. 25.22. After the user chooses a type of transaction to perform, the ATM executes the transaction by sending an execute message to an object of the appropriate transaction class (i.e., a BalanceInquiry, a Withdrawal or a Deposit). For example, if the user chooses to perform a balance inquiry, the ATM sends an execute message to a BalanceInquiry.

Further examination of the requirements document reveals the collaborations involved in executing each transaction type. A BalanceInquiry retrieves the amount of money available in the user's account by sending a getAvailableBalance message to the BankDatabase, which responds by sending a getAvailableBalance message to the user's

An object of class...	sends the message...	to an object of class...
ATM	displayMessage getInput authenticateUser execute execute execute	Screen Keypad BankDatabase BalanceInquiry Withdrawal Deposit
BalanceInquiry	getAvailableBalance getTotalBalance displayMessage	BankDatabase BankDatabase Screen
Withdrawal	displayMessage getInput getAvailableBalance isSufficientCashAvailable debit dispenseCash	Screen Keypad BankDatabase CashDispenser BankDatabase CashDispenser
Deposit	displayMessage getInput isEnvelopeReceived credit	Screen Keypad DepositSlot BankDatabase
BankDatabase	validatePIN getAvailableBalance getTotalBalance debit credit	Account Account Account Account Account

Fig. 25.22 | Collaborations in the ATM system.

Account. Similarly, the BalanceInquiry retrieves the amount of money on deposit by sending a getTotalBalance message to the BankDatabase, which sends the same message to the user's Account. To display both parts of the user's account balance at the same time, the BalanceInquiry sends a displayMessage message to the Screen.

A Withdrawal responds to an execute message by sending displayMessage messages to the Screen to display a menu of standard withdrawal amounts (i.e., $20, $40, $60, $100, $200). The Withdrawal sends a getInput message to the Keypad to obtain the user's selection. Next, the Withdrawal determines whether the requested amount is less than or equal to the user's account balance. The Withdrawal can obtain the amount of money available by sending a getAvailableBalance message to the BankDatabase. The Withdrawal then tests whether the cash dispenser contains enough cash by sending an isSufficientCash-Available message to the CashDispenser. A Withdrawal sends a debit message to the BankDatabase to decrease the user's account balance. The BankDatabase in turn sends the same message to the appropriate Account, which decreases both the totalBalance and the availableBalance. To dispense the requested amount of cash, the Withdrawal sends a dispenseCash message to the CashDispenser. Finally, the Withdrawal sends a display-Message message to the Screen, instructing the user to take the cash.

A Deposit responds to an execute message first by sending a displayMessage message to the Screen to prompt the user for a deposit amount. The Deposit sends a get-Input message to the Keypad to obtain the user's input. The Deposit then sends a displayMessage message to the Screen to tell the user to insert a deposit envelope. To determine whether the deposit slot received an incoming deposit envelope, the Deposit sends an isEnvelopeReceived message to the DepositSlot. The Deposit updates the user's account by sending a credit message to the BankDatabase, which subsequently sends a credit message to the user's Account. Recall that crediting funds to an Account increases the totalBalance but not the availableBalance.

Interaction Diagrams

Now that we've identified possible collaborations between our ATM system's objects, let's graphically model these interactions using the UML. The UML provides several types of **interaction diagrams** that model the behavior of a system by modeling how objects interact. The **communication diagram** emphasizes *which objects* participate in collaborations. Like the communication diagram, the **sequence diagram** shows collaborations among objects, but it emphasizes *when* messages are sent between objects *over time*.

Communication Diagrams

Figure 25.23 shows a communication diagram that models the ATM executing a Balance-Inquiry. Objects are modeled in the UML as rectangles containing names in the form objectName : ClassName. In this example, which involves only one object of each type, we disregard the object name and list only a colon followed by the class name. [*Note:* Specifying each object's name in a communication diagram is recommended when modeling multiple objects of the same type.] Communicating objects are connected with solid lines, and messages are passed between objects along these lines in the direction shown by arrows. The name of the message, which appears next to the arrow, is the name of an operation (i.e., a method in Java) belonging to the receiving object—think of the name as a "service" that the receiving object provides to sending objects (its clients).

Fig. 25.23 | Communication diagram of the ATM executing a balance inquiry.

The solid filled arrow represents a message—or **synchronous call**—in the UML and a method call in Java. This arrow indicates that the flow of control is from the sending object (the ATM) to the receiving object (a BalanceInquiry). Since this is a synchronous call, the sending object can't send another message, or do anything at all, until the receiving object processes the message and returns control to the sending object. The sender just waits. In Fig. 25.23, the ATM calls BalanceInquiry method execute and can't send another message until execute has finished and returns control to the ATM. [*Note:* If this were an **asynchronous call**, represented by a stick ($\rightarrow$) arrowhead, the sending object would not have to wait for the receiving object to return control—it would continue sending additional messages immediately following the asynchronous call. Asynchronous calls are implemented in Java using a technique called multithreading, which is discussed in Chapter 21.]

Sequence of Messages in a Communication Diagram

Figure 25.24 shows a communication diagram that models the interactions among system objects when an object of class BalanceInquiry executes. We assume that the object's accountNumber attribute contains the account number of the current user. The collaborations in Fig. 25.24 begin after the ATM sends an execute message to a BalanceInquiry (i.e., the interaction modeled in Fig. 25.23). The number to the left of a message name indicates the order in which the message is passed. The **sequence of messages** in a communication diagram progresses in numerical order from least to greatest. In this diagram, the numbering starts with message 1 and ends with message 3. The BalanceInquiry first sends a getAvailableBalance message to the BankDatabase (message 1), then sends a getTotalBalance message to the BankDatabase (message 2). Within the parentheses following a message name, we can specify a comma-separated list of the names of the parameters sent with the message (i.e., arguments in a Java method call)—the BalanceInquiry passes attribute accountNumber with its messages to the BankDatabase to indicate which Account's balance information to retrieve. Recall from Fig. 25.18 that operations getAvailableBalance and getTotalBalance of class BankDatabase each require a parameter to identify an account. The BalanceInquiry next displays the availableBalance and the totalBalance to the user by passing a displayMessage message to the Screen (message 3) that includes a parameter indicating the message to be displayed.

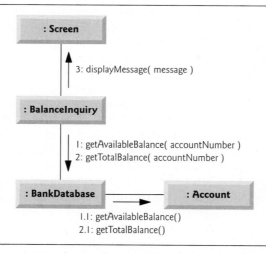

Fig. 25.24 | Communication diagram for executing a balance inquiry.

Figure 25.24 models two additional messages passing from the BankDatabase to an Account (message 1.1 and message 2.1). To provide the ATM with the *two* balances of the user's Account (as requested by messages 1 and 2), the BankDatabase must pass a getAvailableBalance and a getTotalBalance message to the user's Account. Such messages passed within the handling of another message are called **nested messages**. The UML recommends using a decimal numbering scheme to indicate nested messages. For example, message 1.1 is the first message nested in message 1—the BankDatabase passes a getAvailableBalance message during BankDatabase's processing of a message by the same name. [*Note:* If the BankDatabase needed to pass a second nested message while processing message 1, the second message would be numbered 1.2.] A message may be passed only when *all* the nested messages from the previous message have been passed. For example, the BalanceInquiry passes message 3 only after messages 2 and 2.1 have been passed, in that order.

The nested numbering scheme used in communication diagrams helps clarify precisely when and in what context each message is passed. For example, if we numbered the messages in Fig. 25.24 using a flat numbering scheme (i.e., 1, 2, 3, 4, 5), someone looking at the diagram might not be able to determine that BankDatabase passes the getAvailableBalance message (message 1.1) to an Account *during* the BankDatabase's processing of message 1, as opposed to *after* completing the processing of message 1. The nested decimal numbers make it clear that the second getAvailableBalance message (message 1.1) is passed to an Account within the handling of the first getAvailableBalance message (message 1) by the BankDatabase.

Sequence Diagrams

Communication diagrams emphasize the participants in collaborations, but model their timing a bit awkwardly. A sequence diagram helps model the timing of collaborations more clearly. Figure 25.25 shows a sequence diagram modeling the sequence of interactions that occur when a Withdrawal executes. The dotted line extending down from an object's rectangle is that object's **lifeline**, which represents the progression of time. Actions occur along an object's lifeline in chronological order from top to bottom—an action near the top happens before one near the bottom.

Message passing in sequence diagrams is similar to message passing in communication diagrams. A solid arrow with a filled arrowhead extending from the sending object to the receiving object represents a message between two objects. The arrowhead points to an activation on the receiving object's lifeline. An **activation**, shown as a thin vertical rectangle, indicates that an object is executing. When an object returns control, a return message, represented as a dashed line with a stick ($\gg$) arrowhead, extends from the activation of the object returning control to the activation of the object that initially sent the message. To eliminate clutter, we omit the return-message arrows—the UML allows this practice to make diagrams more readable. Like communication diagrams, sequence diagrams can indicate message parameters between the parentheses following a message name.

The sequence of messages in Fig. 25.25 begins when a Withdrawal prompts the user to choose a withdrawal amount by sending a displayMessage message to the Screen. The Withdrawal then sends a getInput message to the Keypad, which obtains input from the user. We've already modeled the control logic involved in a Withdrawal in the activity diagram of Fig. 25.15, so we do not show this logic in the sequence diagram of Fig. 25.25. Instead, we model the best-case scenario in which the balance of the user's account is greater than or equal to the chosen withdrawal amount, and the cash dispenser contains a sufficient amount of cash to satisfy the request. You can model control logic in a sequence diagram with UML frames (which are not covered in this case study). For a quick overview of UML frames, visit www.agilemodeling.com/style/frame.htm.

After obtaining a withdrawal amount, the Withdrawal sends a getAvailableBalance message to the BankDatabase, which in turn sends a getAvailableBalance message to the user's Account. Assuming that the user's account has enough money available to permit the transaction, the Withdrawal next sends an isSufficientCashAvailable message to the CashDispenser. Assuming that there's enough cash available, the Withdrawal decreases the balance of the user's account (i.e., both the totalBalance and the availableBalance) by sending a debit message to the BankDatabase. The BankDatabase responds by sending a debit message to the user's Account. Finally, the Withdrawal sends

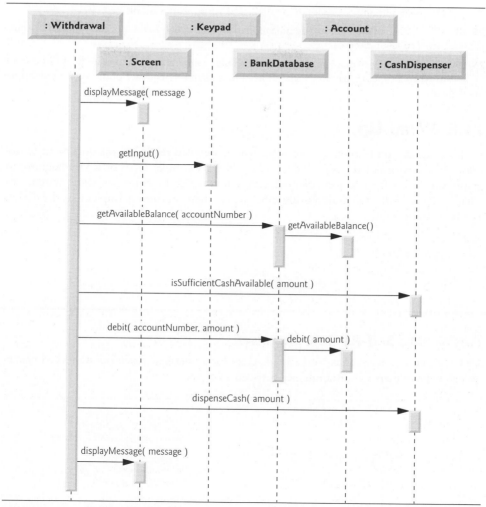

Fig. 25.25 | Sequence diagram that models a `Withdrawal` executing.

a `dispenseCash` message to the `CashDispenser` and a `displayMessage` message to the `Screen`, telling the user to remove the cash from the machine.

We've identified the collaborations among objects in the ATM system and modeled some of them using UML interaction diagrams—both communication diagrams and sequence diagrams. In Section 26.2, we enhance the structure of our model to complete a preliminary object-oriented design, then we begin implementing the ATM system in Java.

Self-Review Exercises for Section 25.7

25.17 A(n) _____ consists of an object of one class sending a message to an object of another class.

    a) association   b) aggregation

   c) collaboration   d) composition

25.18 Which form of interaction diagram emphasizes *what* collaborations occur? Which form emphasizes *when* collaborations occur?

25.19 Create a sequence diagram that models the interactions among objects in the ATM system that occur when a `Deposit` executes successfully, and explain the sequence of messages modeled by the diagram.

25.8 Wrap-Up

In this chapter, you learned how to work from a detailed requirements document to develop an object-oriented design. You worked with six popular types of UML diagrams to graphically model an object-oriented automated teller machine software system. In Chapter 26, we tune the design using inheritance, then completely implement the design as a Java application.

Answers to Self-Review Exercises

25.1 Figure 25.26 contains a use case diagram for a modified version of our ATM system that also allows users to transfer money between accounts.

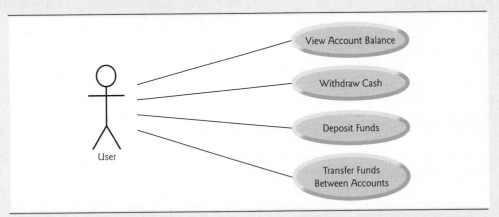

Fig. 25.26 | Use case diagram for a modified version of our ATM system that also allows users to transfer money between accounts.

25.2 b.

25.3 d.

25.4 [*Note:* Answers may vary.] Figure 25.27 presents a class diagram that shows some of the composition relationships of a class `Car`.

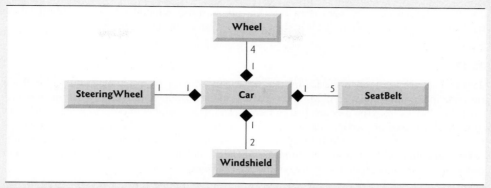

Fig. 25.27 | Class diagram showing composition relationships of a class `Car`.

25.5   c. [*Note:* In a computer network, this relationship could be many-to-many.]

25.6   True.

25.7   Figure 25.28 presents a class diagram for the ATM including class `Deposit` instead of class `Withdrawal` (as in Fig. 25.10). `Deposit` does not access `CashDispenser`, but does access `DepositSlot`.

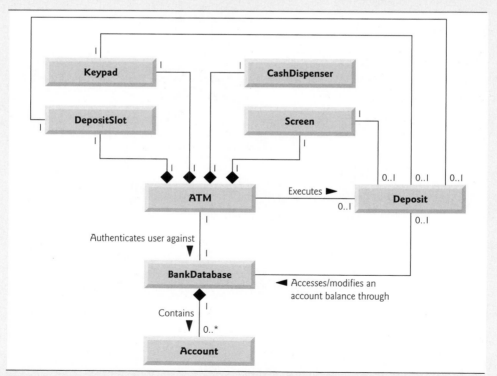

Fig. 25.28 | Class diagram for the ATM system model including class `Deposit`.

25.8   b.

25.9   c. Fly is an operation or behavior of an airplane, not an attribute.

25.10   This indicates that count is an Integer with an initial value of 500. This attribute keeps track of the number of bills available in the CashDispenser at any given time.

25.11   False. State diagrams model some of the behavior of a system.

25.12   a.

25.13   Figure 25.29 models the actions that occur after the user chooses the deposit option from the main menu and before the ATM returns the user to the main menu. Recall that part of receiving a deposit amount from the user involves converting an integer number of cents to a dollar amount. Also recall that crediting a deposit amount to an account increases only the totalBalance attribute of the user's Account object. The bank updates the availableBalance attribute of the user's Account object only after confirming the amount of cash in the deposit envelope and after the enclosed checks clear—this occurs independently of the ATM system.

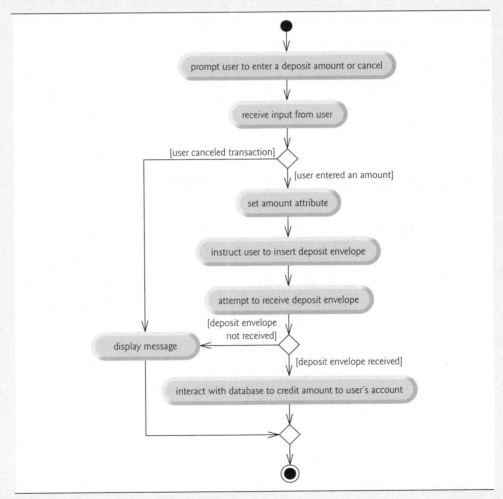

Fig. 25.29 | Activity diagram for a deposit transaction.

25.14   c.

25.15 To specify an operation that retrieves the amount attribute of class `Withdrawal`, the following operation listing would be placed in the operation (i.e., third) compartment of class `Withdrawal`:

```
getAmount() : Double
```

25.16 This operation listing indicates an operation named `add` that takes integers x and y as parameters and returns an integer value.

25.17 c.

25.18 Communication diagrams emphasize *what* collaborations occur. Sequence diagrams emphasize *when* collaborations occur.

25.19 Figure 25.30 presents a sequence diagram that models the interactions between objects in the ATM system that occur when a `Deposit` executes successfully. A `Deposit` first sends a `display-Message` message to the `Screen` to ask the user to enter a deposit amount. Next the `Deposit` sends a `getInput` message to the `Keypad` to receive input from the user. The `Deposit` then instructs the user to enter a deposit envelope by sending a `displayMessage` message to the `Screen`. The `Deposit` next sends an `isEnvelopeReceived` message to the `DepositSlot` to confirm that the deposit envelope has been received by the ATM. Finally, the `Deposit` increases the `totalBalance` attribute (but not the `availableBalance` attribute) of the user's `Account` by sending a `credit` message to the `BankDatabase`. The `BankDatabase` responds by sending the same message to the user's `Account`.

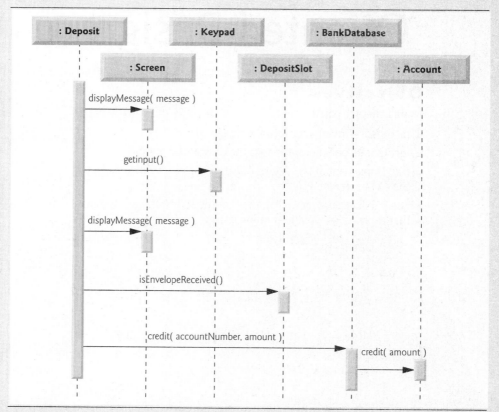

Fig. 25.30 | Sequence diagram that models a `Deposit` executing.

26

ATM Case Study Part 2: Implementing an Object-Oriented Design

Objectives

In this chapter you'll:

- Incorporate inheritance into the design of the ATM.
- Incorporate polymorphism into the design of the ATM.
- Fully implement in Java the UML-based object-oriented design of the ATM software.
- Study a detailed code walkthrough of the ATM software system that explains the implementation issues.

26.1 Introduction

In Chapter 25, we developed an object-oriented design for our ATM system. We now implement our object-oriented design in Java. In Section 26.2, we show how to convert class diagrams to Java code. In Section 26.3, we tune the design with inheritance and polymorphism. Then we present a full Java code implementation of the ATM software in Section 26.4. The code is carefully commented and the discussions of the implementation are thorough and precise. Studying this application provides the opportunity for you to see a more substantial application of the kind you're likely to encounter in industry.

26.2 Starting to Program the Classes of the ATM System

[*Note:* This section may be read after Chapter 8.]

Visibility

We now apply access modifiers to the members of our classes. We've introduced access modifiers public and private. Access modifiers determine the **visibility** or accessibility of an object's attributes and methods to other objects. Before we can begin implementing our design, we must consider which attributes and methods of our classes should be public and which should be private.

We've observed that attributes normally should be private and that methods invoked by clients of a given class should be public. Methods that are called as "utility methods" only by other methods of the same class normally should be private. The UML employs **visibility markers** for modeling the visibility of attributes and operations. Public visibility is indicated by placing a plus sign (+) before an operation or an attribute, whereas a minus sign (–) indicates private visibility. Figure 26.1 shows our updated class diagram with visibility markers included. [*Note:* We do not include any operation parameters in Fig. 26.1—this is perfectly normal. Adding visibility markers does not affect the parameters already modeled in the class diagrams of Figs. 25.17–25.21.]

Navigability

Before we begin implementing our design in Java, we introduce an additional UML notation. The class diagram in Fig. 26.2 further refines the relationships among classes in the ATM system by adding navigability arrows to the association lines. **Navigability arrows**

Fig. 26.1 | Class diagram with visibility markers.

(represented as arrows with stick ($\twoheadrightarrow$) arrowheads in the class diagram) indicate the direction in which an association can be traversed. When implementing a system designed using the UML, you use navigability arrows to determine which objects need references to other objects. For example, the navigability arrow pointing from class ATM to class Bank-Database indicates that we can navigate from the former to the latter, thereby enabling the ATM to invoke the BankDatabase's operations. However, since Fig. 26.2 does *not* contain a navigability arrow pointing from class BankDatabase to class ATM, the BankDatabase cannot access the ATM's operations. Associations in a class diagram that have navigability arrows at both ends or have none at all indicate **bidirectional navigability**—navigation can proceed in either direction across the association.

Like the class diagram of Fig. 25.10, that of Fig. 26.2 omits classes BalanceInquiry and Deposit for simplicity. The navigability of the associations in which these classes participate closely parallels that of class Withdrawal. Recall from Section 25.3 that Balance-Inquiry has an association with class Screen. We can navigate from class BalanceInquiry to class Screen along this association, but we cannot navigate from class Screen to class

BalanceInquiry. Thus, if we were to model class BalanceInquiry in Fig. 26.2, we would place a navigability arrow at class Screen's end of this association. Also recall that class Deposit associates with classes Screen, Keypad and DepositSlot. We can navigate from class Deposit to each of these classes, but *not* vice versa. We therefore would place navigability arrows at the Screen, Keypad and DepositSlot ends of these associations. [*Note:* We model these additional classes and associations in our final class diagram in Section 26.3, after we've simplified the structure of our system by incorporating the object-oriented concept of inheritance.]

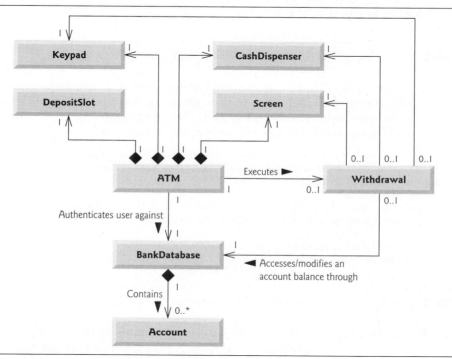

Fig. 26.2 | Class diagram with navigability arrows.

Implementing the ATM System from Its UML Design

We're now ready to begin implementing the ATM system. We first convert the classes in the diagrams of Fig. 26.1 and Fig. 26.2 into Java code. The code will represent the "skeleton" of the system. In Section 26.3, we modify the code to incorporate inheritance. In Section 26.4, we present the complete working Java code for our model.

As an example, we develop the code from our design of class Withdrawal in Fig. 26.1. We use this figure to determine the attributes and operations of the class. We use the UML model in Fig. 26.2 to determine the associations among classes. We follow the following four guidelines for each class:

1. Use the name located in the first compartment to declare the class as a public class with an empty no-argument constructor. We include this constructor simply as a placeholder to remind us that *most classes will indeed need custom construc-*

tors. In Section 26.4, when we complete a working version of this class, we'll add arguments and code the body of the constructor as needed. For example, class Withdrawal yields the code in Fig. 26.3. If we find that the class's instance variables require only default initialization, then we'll remove the empty no-argument constructor because it's unnecessary.

```
1   // Class Withdrawal represents an ATM withdrawal transaction
2   public class Withdrawal {
3      // no-argument constructor
4      public Withdrawal() { }
5   }
```

Fig. 26.3 | Java code for class Withdrawal based on Figs. 26.1–26.2.

2. Use the attributes located in the second compartment to declare the instance variables. For example, the private attributes accountNumber and amount of class Withdrawal yield the code in Fig. 26.4. [*Note:* The constructor of the complete working version of this class will assign values to these attributes.]

```
1   // Class Withdrawal represents an ATM withdrawal transaction
2   public class Withdrawal {
3      // attributes
4      private int accountNumber; // account to withdraw funds from
5      private double amount; // amount to withdraw
6
7      // no-argument constructor
8      public Withdrawal() { }
9   }
```

Fig. 26.4 | Java code for class Withdrawal based on Figs. 26.1–26.2.

3. Use the associations described in the class diagram to declare the references to other objects. For example, according to Fig. 26.2, Withdrawal can access one object of class Screen, one object of class Keypad, one object of class CashDispenser and one object of class BankDatabase. This yields the code in Fig. 26.5. [*Note:* The constructor of the complete working version of this class will initialize these instance variables with references to actual objects.]

```
1   // Class Withdrawal represents an ATM withdrawal transaction
2   public class Withdrawal {
3      // attributes
4      private int accountNumber; // account to withdraw funds from
5      private double amount; // amount to withdraw
6
7      // references to associated objects
8      private Screen screen; // ATM's screen
9      private Keypad keypad; // ATM's keypad
```

Fig. 26.5 | Java code for class Withdrawal based on Figs. 26.1–26.2. (Part 1 of 2.)

```
10      private CashDispenser cashDispenser; // ATM's cash dispenser
11      private BankDatabase bankDatabase; // account info database
12
13      // no-argument constructor
14      public Withdrawal() { }
15   }
```

Fig. 26.5 | Java code for class Withdrawal based on Figs. 26.1–26.2. (Part 2 of 2.)

4. Use the operations located in the third compartment of Fig. 26.1 to declare the shells of the methods. If we have not yet specified a return type for an operation, we declare the method with return type void. Refer to the class diagrams of Figs. 25.17–25.21 to declare any necessary parameters. For example, adding the public operation execute in class Withdrawal, which has an empty parameter list, yields the code in Fig. 26.6. [*Note:* We code the bodies of methods when we implement the complete system in Section 26.4.]

This concludes our discussion of the basics of generating classes from UML diagrams.

```
1    // Class Withdrawal represents an ATM withdrawal transaction
2    public class Withdrawal {
3       // attributes
4       private int accountNumber; // account to withdraw funds from
5       private double amount; // amount to withdraw
6
7       // references to associated objects
8       private Screen screen; // ATM's screen
9       private Keypad keypad; // ATM's keypad
10      private CashDispenser cashDispenser; // ATM's cash dispenser
11      private BankDatabase bankDatabase; // account info database
12
13      // no-argument constructor
14      public Withdrawal() { }
15
16      // operations
17      public void execute() { }
18   }
```

Fig. 26.6 | Java code for class Withdrawal based on Figs. 26.1–26.2.

Self-Review Exercises for Section 26.2

26.1   State whether the following statement is *true* or *false*, and if *false*, explain why: If an attribute of a class is marked with a minus sign (-) in a class diagram, the attribute is not directly accessible outside the class.

26.2   In Fig. 26.2, the association between the ATM and the Screen indicates that:
  a) we can navigate from the Screen to the ATM
  b) we can navigate from the ATM to the Screen
  c) Both (a) and (b); the association is bidirectional
  d) None of the above

26.3   Write Java code to begin implementing the design for class Keypad.

26.3 Incorporating Inheritance and Polymorphism into the ATM System

[*Note:* **This section may be read after Chapter 10.**]

We now revisit our ATM system design to see how it might benefit from inheritance. To apply inheritance, we first look for *commonality among classes* in the system. We create an inheritance hierarchy to model similar (yet not identical) classes in a more elegant and efficient manner. We then modify our class diagram to incorporate the new inheritance relationships. Finally, we demonstrate how our updated design is translated into Java code.

In Section 25.3, we encountered the problem of representing a financial transaction in the system. Rather than create one class to represent all transaction types, we decided to create three individual transaction classes—`BalanceInquiry`, `Withdrawal` and `Deposit`—to represent the transactions that the ATM system can perform. Figure 26.7 shows the attributes and operations of classes `BalanceInquiry`, `Withdrawal` and `Deposit`. These classes have one attribute (`accountNumber`) and one operation (`execute`) in common. Each class requires attribute `accountNumber` to specify the account to which the transaction applies. Each class contains operation `execute`, which the ATM invokes to perform the transaction. Clearly, `BalanceInquiry`, `Withdrawal` and `Deposit` represent *types of* transactions. Figure 26.7 reveals commonality among the transaction classes, so using inheritance to factor out the common features seems appropriate for designing classes `BalanceInquiry`, `Withdrawal` and `Deposit`. We place the common functionality in a superclass, `Transaction`, that classes `BalanceInquiry`, `Withdrawal` and `Deposit` extend.

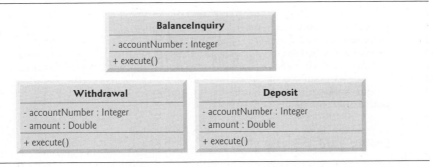

Fig. 26.7 | Attributes and operations of `BalanceInquiry`, `Withdrawal` and `Deposit`.

Generalization

The UML specifies a relationship called a **generalization** to model inheritance. Figure 26.8 is the class diagram that models the generalization of superclass `Transaction` and subclasses `BalanceInquiry`, `Withdrawal` and `Deposit`. The arrows with triangular hollow arrowheads indicate that classes `BalanceInquiry`, `Withdrawal` and `Deposit` extend class `Transaction`. Class `Transaction` is said to be a generalization of classes `BalanceInquiry`, `Withdrawal` and `Deposit`. Class `BalanceInquiry`, `Withdrawal` and `Deposit` are said to be **specializations** of class `Transaction`.

Classes `BalanceInquiry`, `Withdrawal` and `Deposit` share integer attribute `accountNumber`, so we *factor out* this *common attribute* and place it in superclass `Transaction`. We no longer list `accountNumber` in the second compartment of each subclass, because the

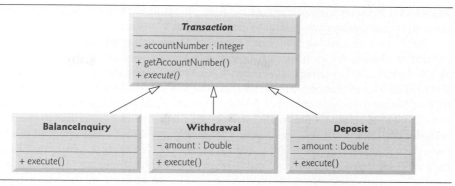

Fig. 26.8 | Class diagram modeling generalization of superclass `Transaction` and subclasses `BalanceInquiry`, `Withdrawal` and `Deposit`. Abstract class names (e.g., `Transaction`) and method names (e.g., `execute` in class `Transaction`) appear in italics.

three subclasses *inherit* this attribute from `Transaction`. Recall, however, that subclasses cannot directly access `private` attributes of a superclass. We therefore include `public` method `getAccountNumber` in class `Transaction`. Each subclass will inherit this method, enabling the subclass to access its `accountNumber` as needed to execute a transaction.

According to Fig. 26.7, classes `BalanceInquiry`, `Withdrawal` and `Deposit` also share operation `execute`, so we placed `public` method `execute` in superclass `Transaction`. However, it does *not* make sense to implement `execute` in class `Transaction`, because the functionality that this method provides *depends on the type of the actual transaction*. We therefore declare method `execute` as `abstract` in superclass `Transaction`. Any class that contains at least one abstract method must also be declared `abstract`. This forces any subclass of `Transaction` that must be a *concrete* class (i.e., `BalanceInquiry`, `Withdrawal` and `Deposit`) to implement method `execute`. The UML requires that we place abstract class names (and abstract methods) in italics, so `Transaction` and its method `execute` appear in italics in Fig. 26.8. Method `execute` is *not* italicized in subclasses `BalanceInquiry`, `Withdrawal` and `Deposit`. Each subclass overrides superclass `Transaction`'s `execute` method with a concrete implementation that performs the steps appropriate for completing that type of transaction. Figure 26.8 includes operation `execute` in the third compartment of classes `BalanceInquiry`, `Withdrawal` and `Deposit`, because each class has a different concrete implementation of the overridden method.

Processing Transactions Polymorphically
Polymorphism provides the ATM with an elegant way to execute all transactions "in the general." For example, suppose a user chooses to perform a balance inquiry. The ATM sets a `Transaction` reference to a new `BalanceInquiry` object. When the ATM uses its `Transaction` reference to invoke method `execute`, `BalanceInquiry`'s version of `execute` is called.

This *polymorphic* approach also makes the system easily *extensible*. Should we wish to create a new transaction type (e.g., funds transfer or bill payment), we would just create an additional `Transaction` subclass that overrides the `execute` method with a version of the method appropriate for executing the new transaction type. We would need to make only minimal changes to the system code to allow users to choose the new transaction type from the main menu and for the ATM to instantiate and execute objects of the new subclass.

The ATM could execute transactions of the new type using the current code, because it executes all transactions *polymorphically* using a general Transaction reference.

Recall that an abstract class like Transaction is one for which you never intend to instantiate objects. An abstract class simply declares common attributes and behaviors of its subclasses in an inheritance hierarchy. Class Transaction defines the concept of what it means to be a transaction that has an account number and executes. You may wonder why we bother to include abstract method execute in class Transaction if it lacks a concrete implementation. Conceptually, we include it because it corresponds to the defining behavior of *all* transactions—executing. Technically, we must include method execute in superclass Transaction so that the ATM (or any other class) can polymorphically invoke each subclass's *overridden* version of this method through a Transaction reference. Also, from a software engineering perspective, including an abstract method in a superclass forces the implementor of the subclasses to override that method with concrete implementations in the subclasses, or else the subclasses, too, will be abstract, preventing objects of those subclasses from being instantiated.

Additional Attribute of Classes **Withdrawal** *and* **Deposit**

Subclasses BalanceInquiry, Withdrawal and Deposit inherit attribute accountNumber from superclass Transaction, but classes Withdrawal and Deposit contain the additional attribute amount that distinguishes them from class BalanceInquiry. Classes Withdrawal and Deposit require this additional attribute to store the amount of money that the user wishes to withdraw or deposit. Class BalanceInquiry has no need for such an attribute and requires only an account number to execute. Even though two of the three Transaction subclasses share this attribute, we do *not* place it in superclass Transaction—we place only features *common* to all the subclasses in the superclass, otherwise subclasses could inherit attributes (and methods) that they do not need and should not have.

Class Diagram with **Transaction** *Hierarchy Incorporated*

Figure 26.9 presents an updated class diagram of our model that incorporates inheritance and introduces class Transaction. We model an association between class ATM and class Transaction to show that the ATM, at any given moment, either is executing a transaction or is not (i.e., zero or one objects of type Transaction exist in the system at a time). Because a Withdrawal is a type of Transaction, we no longer draw an association line directly between class ATM and class Withdrawal. Subclass Withdrawal inherits superclass Transaction's association with class ATM. Subclasses BalanceInquiry and Deposit inherit this association, too, so the previously omitted associations between ATM and classes BalanceInquiry and Deposit no longer exist either.

We also add an association between class Transaction and the BankDatabase (Fig. 26.9). All Transactions require a reference to the BankDatabase so they can access and modify account information. Because each Transaction subclass inherits this reference, we no longer model the association between class Withdrawal and the BankDatabase. Similarly, the previously omitted associations between the BankDatabase and classes BalanceInquiry and Deposit no longer exist.

We show an association between class Transaction and the Screen. All Transactions display output to the user via the Screen. Thus, we no longer include the association previously modeled between Withdrawal and the Screen, although Withdrawal still participates in associations with the CashDispenser and the Keypad. Our class diagram incor-

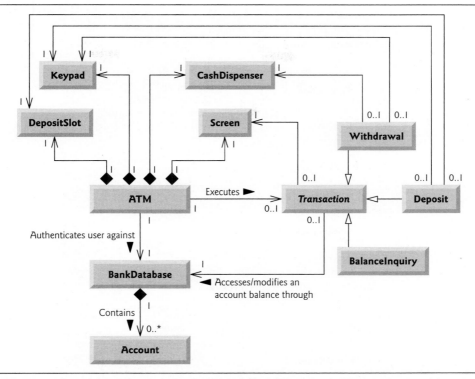

Fig. 26.9 | Class diagram of the ATM system (incorporating inheritance). The abstract class name `Transaction` appears in italics.

porating inheritance also models `Deposit` and `BalanceInquiry`. We show associations between `Deposit` and both the `DepositSlot` and the `Keypad`. Class `BalanceInquiry` takes part in no associations other than those inherited from class `Transaction`—a `BalanceInquiry` needs to interact only with the `BankDatabase` and with the `Screen`.

Figure 26.1 showed attributes and operations with visibility markers. Now in Fig. 26.10 we present a modified class diagram that incorporates inheritance. This abbreviated diagram does not show inheritance relationships, but instead shows the attributes and methods after we've employed inheritance in our system. To save space, as we did in Fig. 25.12, we do not include those attributes shown by associations in Fig. 26.9—we do, however, include them in the Java implementation in Section 26.4. We also omit all operation parameters, as we did in Fig. 26.1—incorporating inheritance does not affect the parameters already modeled in Figs. 25.17–25.21.

Software Engineering Observation 26.1

A complete class diagram shows all the associations among classes and all the attributes and operations for each class. When the number of class attributes, methods and associations is substantial (as in Figs. 26.9 and 26.10), a good practice that promotes readability is to divide this information between two class diagrams—one focusing on associations and the other on attributes and methods.

Fig. 26.10 | Class diagram with attributes and operations (incorporating inheritance). The abstract class name Transaction and the abstract method name execute in class Transaction appear in italics.

Implementing the ATM System Design (Incorporating Inheritance)

In Section 26.2, we began implementing the ATM system design in Java code. We now incorporate inheritance, using class Withdrawal as an example.

1. If a class A is a generalization of class B, then class B extends class A in the class declaration. For example, abstract superclass Transaction is a generalization of class Withdrawal. Figure 26.11 shows the declaration of class Withdrawal.

```
1  // Class Withdrawal represents an ATM withdrawal transaction
2  public class Withdrawal extends Transaction {
3  }
```

Fig. 26.11 | Java code for shell of class Withdrawal.

2. If class A is an abstract class and class B is a subclass of class A, then class B must implement the *abstract* methods of class A if class B is to be a *concrete* class. For example, class Transaction contains abstract method execute, so class Withdrawal must implement this method if we want to instantiate a Withdrawal object. Figure 26.12 is the Java code for class Withdrawal from Fig. 26.9 and Fig. 26.10. Class Withdrawal inherits field accountNumber from superclass Transaction, so Withdrawal does not need to declare this field. Class Withdrawal also inherits references to the Screen and the BankDatabase from its superclass Transaction, so we do not include these references in our code. Figure 26.10 specifies attribute amount and operation execute for class Withdrawal. Line 5 of Fig. 26.12 declares a field for attribute amount. Lines 13–14 declare the shell of a method for operation execute. Recall that subclass Withdrawal must provide a concrete implementation of the abstract method execute in superclass Transaction. The keypad and cashDispenser references (lines 6–7) are fields derived from Withdrawal's associations in Fig. 26.9. The constructor in the complete working version of this class will initialize these references to actual objects.

Software Engineering Observation 26.2

Several UML modeling tools can convert UML-based designs into Java code, speeding the implementation process considerably. For more information on these tools, visit our UML Resource Center at www.deitel.com/UML/.

```
1   // Withdrawal.java
2   // Generated using the class diagrams in Fig. 26.9 and Fig. 26.10
3   public class Withdrawal extends Transaction {
4      // attributes
5      private double amount; // amount to withdraw
6      private Keypad keypad; // reference to keypad
7      private CashDispenser cashDispenser; // reference to cash dispenser
8
9      // no-argument constructor
10     public Withdrawal() { }
11
12     // method overriding execute
13     @Override
14     public void execute() { }
15  }
```

Fig. 26.12 | Java code for class Withdrawal based on Figs. 26.9 and 26.10.

Congratulations on completing the case study's design portion! We implement the ATM system in Java code in Section 26.4. We recommend that you carefully read the code and its description. The code is abundantly commented and precisely follows the design with which you're now familiar. The accompanying description is carefully written to guide your understanding of the implementation based on the UML design. Mastering this code is a wonderful culminating accomplishment after studying Sections 25.2—25.7 and 26.2–26.3.

Self-Review Exercises for Section 26.3

26.4 The UML uses an arrow with a _____ to indicate a generalization relationship.
a) solid filled arrowhead
b) triangular hollow arrowhead
c) diamond-shaped hollow arrowhead
d) stick arrowhead

26.5 State whether the following statement is *true* or *false*, and if *false*, explain why: The UML requires that we underline abstract class names and method names.

26.6 Write Java code to begin implementing the design for class Transaction specified in Figs. 26.9 and 26.10. Be sure to include private reference-type attributes based on class Transaction's associations. Also be sure to include public *get* methods that provide access to any of these private attributes that the subclasses require to perform their tasks.

26.4 ATM Case Study Implementation

This section contains the complete implementation of the ATM system. We consider the classes in the order in which we identified them in Section 25.3—ATM, Screen, Keypad, CashDispenser, DepositSlot, Account, BankDatabase, Transaction, BalanceInquiry, Withdrawal and Deposit.

We apply the guidelines from Sections 26.2—26.3 to code these classes based on their UML class diagrams of Figs. 26.9 and 26.10. To develop the bodies of methods, we refer to the activity diagrams in Section 25.5 and the communication and sequence diagrams presented in Section 25.7. Our ATM design does *not* specify all the program logic and may not specify all the attributes and operations required to complete the ATM implementation. This is a *normal* part of the object-oriented design process. As we implement the system, we complete the program logic and add attributes and behaviors as necessary to construct the ATM system specified by the requirements document in Section 25.2.

We conclude the discussion by presenting a Java application (ATMCaseStudy) that starts the ATM and puts the other classes in the system in use. Recall that we're developing a first version of the ATM system that runs on a personal computer and uses the computer's keyboard and monitor to approximate the ATM's keypad and screen. We also simulate only the actions of the ATM's cash dispenser and deposit slot. We attempt to implement the system, however, so that real hardware versions of these devices could be integrated without significant changes in the code.

26.4.1 Class ATM

Class ATM (Fig. 26.13) represents the ATM as a whole. Lines 5–11 implement the class's attributes. We determine all but one of these attributes from the UML class diagrams of Figs. 26.9 and 26.10. We implement the UML Boolean attribute userAuthenticated in Fig. 26.10 as a boolean in Java (line 5). Line 6 declares an attribute not found in our UML design—an int attribute currentAccountNumber that keeps track of the account number of the current authenticated user. We'll soon see how the class uses this attribute. Lines 7–11 declare reference-type attributes corresponding to the ATM class's associations modeled in the class diagram of Fig. 26.9. These attributes allow the ATM to access its parts (i.e., its Screen, Keypad, CashDispenser and DepositSlot) and interact with the bank's account-information database (i.e., a BankDatabase object).

```java
 1   // ATM.java
 2   // Represents an automated teller machine
 3
 4   public class ATM {
 5      private boolean userAuthenticated; // whether user is authenticated
 6      private int currentAccountNumber; // current user's account number
 7      private Screen screen; // ATM's screen
 8      private Keypad keypad; // ATM's keypad
 9      private CashDispenser cashDispenser; // ATM's cash dispenser
10      private DepositSlot depositSlot; // ATM's deposit slot
11      private BankDatabase bankDatabase; // account information database
12
13      // constants corresponding to main menu options
14      private static final int BALANCE_INQUIRY = 1;
15      private static final int WITHDRAWAL = 2;
16      private static final int DEPOSIT = 3;
17      private static final int EXIT = 4;
18
19      // no-argument ATM constructor initializes instance variables
20      public ATM() {
21         userAuthenticated = false; // user is not authenticated to start
22         currentAccountNumber = 0; // no current account number to start
23         screen = new Screen(); // create screen
24         keypad = new Keypad(); // create keypad
25         cashDispenser = new CashDispenser(); // create cash dispenser
26         depositSlot = new DepositSlot(); // create deposit slot
27         bankDatabase = new BankDatabase(); // create acct info database
28      }
29
30      // start ATM
31      public void run() {
32         // welcome and authenticate user; perform transactions
33         while (true) {
34            // loop while user is not yet authenticated
35            while (!userAuthenticated) {
36               screen.displayMessageLine("\nWelcome!");
37               authenticateUser(); // authenticate user
38            }
39
40            performTransactions(); // user is now authenticated
41            userAuthenticated = false; // reset before next ATM session
42            currentAccountNumber = 0; // reset before next ATM session
43            screen.displayMessageLine("\nThank you! Goodbye!");
44         }
45      }
46
47      // attempts to authenticate user against database
48      private void authenticateUser() {
49         screen.displayMessage("\nPlease enter your account number: ");
50         int accountNumber = keypad.getInput(); // input account number
51         screen.displayMessage("\nEnter your PIN: "); // prompt for PIN
52         int pin = keypad.getInput(); // input PIN
53
```

Fig. 26.13 | Class ATM represents the ATM. (Part 1 of 3.)

```
54          // set userAuthenticated to boolean value returned by database
55          userAuthenticated =
56             bankDatabase.authenticateUser(accountNumber, pin);
57
58          // check whether authentication succeeded
59          if (userAuthenticated) {
60             currentAccountNumber = accountNumber; // save user's account #
61          }
62          else {
63             screen.displayMessageLine(
64                "Invalid account number or PIN. Please try again.");
65          }
66       }
67
68       // display the main menu and perform transactions
69       private void performTransactions() {
70          // local variable to store transaction currently being processed
71          Transaction currentTransaction = null;
72
73          boolean userExited = false; // user has not chosen to exit
74
75          // loop while user has not chosen option to exit system
76          while (!userExited) {
77             // show main menu and get user selection
78             int mainMenuSelection = displayMainMenu();
79
80             // decide how to proceed based on user's menu selection
81             switch (mainMenuSelection) {
82                // user chose to perform one of three transaction types
83                case BALANCE_INQUIRY:
84                case WITHDRAWAL:
85                case DEPOSIT:
86
87                   // initialize as new object of chosen type
88                   currentTransaction =
89                      createTransaction(mainMenuSelection);
90
91                   currentTransaction.execute(); // execute transaction
92                   break;
93                case EXIT: // user chose to terminate session
94                   screen.displayMessageLine("\nExiting the system...");
95                   userExited = true; // this ATM session should end
96                   break;
97                default: // user did not enter an integer from 1-4
98                   screen.displayMessageLine(
99                      "\nYou did not enter a valid selection. Try again.");
100                  break;
101            }
102         }
103      }
104
```

Fig. 26.13 | Class ATM represents the ATM. (Part 2 of 3.)

```
105     // display the main menu and return an input selection
106     private int displayMainMenu() {
107         screen.displayMessageLine("\nMain menu:");
108         screen.displayMessageLine("1 - View my balance");
109         screen.displayMessageLine("2 - Withdraw cash");
110         screen.displayMessageLine("3 - Deposit funds");
111         screen.displayMessageLine("4 - Exit\n");
112         screen.displayMessage("Enter a choice: ");
113         return keypad.getInput(); // return user's selection
114     }
115
116     // return object of specified Transaction subclass
117     private Transaction createTransaction(int type) {
118         Transaction temp = null; // temporary Transaction variable
119
120         // determine which type of Transaction to create
121         switch (type) {
122           case BALANCE_INQUIRY: // create new BalanceInquiry transaction
123             temp = new BalanceInquiry(
124                 currentAccountNumber, screen, bankDatabase);
125             break;
126           case WITHDRAWAL: // create new Withdrawal transaction
127             temp = new Withdrawal(currentAccountNumber, screen,
128                 bankDatabase, keypad, cashDispenser);
129             break;
130           case DEPOSIT: // create new Deposit transaction
131             temp = new Deposit(currentAccountNumber, screen,
132                 bankDatabase, keypad, depositSlot);
133             break;
134         }
135
136         return temp; // return the newly created object
137     }
138 }
```

Fig. 26.13 | Class ATM represents the ATM. (Part 3 of 3.)

Lines 14–17 declare integer constants that correspond to the four options in the ATM's main menu (i.e., balance inquiry, withdrawal, deposit and exit). Lines 20–28 declare the constructor, which initializes the class's attributes. When an ATM object is first created, no user is authenticated, so line 21 initializes userAuthenticated to false. Likewise, line 22 initializes currentAccountNumber to 0 because there's no current user yet. Lines 23–26 instantiate new objects to represent the ATM's parts. Recall that class ATM has composition relationships with classes Screen, Keypad, CashDispenser and DepositSlot, so class ATM is responsible for their creation. Line 27 creates a new BankDatabase. [*Note:* If this were a real ATM system, the ATM class would receive a reference to an existing database object created by the bank. However, in this implementation we're only simulating the bank's database, so class ATM creates the BankDatabase object with which it interacts.]

ATM *Method run*

The class diagram of Fig. 26.10 does not list any operations for class ATM. We now implement one operation (i.e., public method) in class ATM that allows an external client of the class (i.e., class `ATMCaseStudy`) to tell the ATM to run. ATM method `run` (lines 31–45) uses an infinite loop to repeatedly welcome a user, attempt to authenticate the user and, if authentication succeeds, allow the user to perform transactions. After an authenticated user performs the desired transactions and chooses to exit, the ATM resets itself, displays a goodbye message to the user and restarts the process. We use an infinite loop here to simulate the fact that an ATM appears to run continuously until the bank turns it off (an action beyond the user's control). An ATM user has the option to exit the system but not the ability to turn off the ATM completely.

Authenticating a User

In method `run`'s infinite loop, lines 35–38 cause the ATM to repeatedly welcome and attempt to authenticate the user as long as the user has not been authenticated (i.e., `!user-Authenticated` is `true`). Line 36 invokes method `displayMessageLine` of the ATM's `screen` to display a welcome message. Like `Screen` method `displayMessage` designed in the case study, method `displayMessageLine` (declared in lines 11–13 of Fig. 26.14) displays a message to the user, but this method also outputs a newline after the message. We've added this method during implementation to give class `Screen`'s clients more control over the placement of displayed messages. Line 37 invokes class ATM's `private` utility method `authenticateUser` (declared in lines 48–66) to attempt to authenticate the user.

We refer to the requirements document to determine the steps necessary to authenticate the user before allowing transactions to occur. Line 49 of method `authenticateUser` invokes method `displayMessage` of the `screen` to prompt the user to enter an account number. Line 50 invokes method `getInput` of the `keypad` to obtain the user's input, then stores the integer value entered by the user in a local variable `accountNumber`. Method `authenticateUser` next prompts the user to enter a PIN (line 51), and stores the PIN input by the user in a local variable `pin` (line 52). Next, lines 55–56 attempt to authenticate the user by passing the `accountNumber` and `pin` entered by the user to the `bankData-base`'s `authenticateUser` method. Class ATM sets its `userAuthenticated` attribute to the `boolean` value returned by this method—`userAuthenticated` becomes `true` if authentication succeeds (i.e., `accountNumber` and `pin` match those of an existing `Account` in `bank-Database`) and remains `false` otherwise. If `userAuthenticated` is `true`, line 60 saves the account number entered by the user (i.e., `accountNumber`) in the ATM attribute `current-AccountNumber`. The other ATM methods use this variable whenever an ATM session requires access to the user's account number. If `userAuthenticated` is `false`, lines 63–64 use the `screen`'s `displayMessageLine` method to indicate that an invalid account number and/or PIN was entered and the user must try again. We set `currentAccountNumber` only after authenticating the user's account number and the associated PIN—if the database could not authenticate the user, `currentAccountNumber` remains 0.

After method `run` attempts to authenticate the user (line 37), if `userAuthenticated` is still `false`, the `while` loop in lines 35–38 executes again. If `userAuthenticated` is now `true`, the loop terminates and control continues with line 40, which calls class ATM's utility method `performTransactions`.

Performing Transactions

Method `performTransactions` (lines 69–103) carries out an ATM session for an authenticated user. Line 71 declares a local `Transaction` variable to which we'll assign a `Balance-`

Inquiry, Withdrawal or Deposit object representing the ATM transaction the user selected. We use a Transaction variable here to allow us to take advantage of polymorphism. Also, we name this variable after the *role name* included in the class diagram of Fig. 25.7—currentTransaction. Line 73 declares another local variable—a boolean called userExited that keeps track of whether the user has chosen to exit. This variable controls a while loop (lines 76–102) that allows the user to execute an unlimited number of transactions before choosing to exit. Within this loop, line 78 displays the main menu and obtains the user's menu selection by calling an ATM utility method displayMainMenu (declared in lines 106–114). This method displays the main menu by invoking methods of the ATM's screen and returns a menu selection obtained from the user through the ATM's keypad. Line 78 stores the user's selection returned by displayMainMenu in local variable mainMenuSelection.

After obtaining a main menu selection, method performTransactions uses a switch statement (lines 81–101) to respond to the selection appropriately. If mainMenuSelection is equal to any of the three integer constants representing transaction types (i.e., if the user chose to perform a transaction), lines 88–89 call utility method createTransaction (declared in lines 117–137) to return a newly instantiated object of the type that corresponds to the selected transaction. Variable currentTransaction is assigned the reference returned by createTransaction, then line 91 invokes method execute of this transaction to execute it. We'll discuss Transaction method execute and the three Transaction subclasses shortly. We assign the Transaction variable currentTransaction an object of one of the three Transaction subclasses so that we can execute transactions *polymorphically*. For example, if the user chooses to perform a balance inquiry, mainMenuSelection equals BALANCE_INQUIRY, leading createTransaction to return a BalanceInquiry object. Thus, currentTransaction refers to a BalanceInquiry, and invoking currentTransaction.execute() results in BalanceInquiry's version of execute being called.

Creating a Transaction

Method createTransaction (lines 117–137) uses a switch statement to instantiate a new Transaction subclass object of the type indicated by the parameter type. Recall that method performTransactions passes mainMenuSelection to this method only when mainMenuSelection contains a value corresponding to one of the three transaction types. Therefore type is BALANCE_INQUIRY, WITHDRAWAL or DEPOSIT. Each case in the switch statement instantiates a new object by calling the appropriate Transaction subclass constructor. Each constructor has a unique parameter list, based on the specific data required to initialize the subclass object. A BalanceInquiry requires only the account number of the current user and references to the ATM's screen and the bankDatabase. In addition to these parameters, a Withdrawal requires references to the ATM's keypad and cashDispenser, and a Deposit requires references to the ATM's keypad and depositSlot. We discuss the transaction classes in more detail in Sections 26.4.8—26.4.11.

Exiting the Main Menu and Processing Invalid Selections

After executing a transaction (line 91 in performTransactions), userExited remains false and lines 76–102 repeat, returning the user to the main menu. However, if a user does not perform a transaction and instead selects the main menu option to exit, line 95 sets userExited to true, causing the condition of the while loop (!userExited) to become `false`. This `while` is the final statement of method `performTransactions`, so control returns to the calling method `run`. If the user enters an invalid main menu selection (i.e., not an integer from 1–4), lines 98–99 display an appropriate error message, `userExited` remains `false` and the user returns to the main menu to try again.

Awaiting the Next ATM User

When `performTransactions` returns control to method `run`, the user has chosen to exit the system, so lines 41–42 reset the ATM's attributes `userAuthenticated` and `currentAccountNumber` to prepare for the next ATM user. Line 43 displays a goodbye message before the ATM starts over and welcomes the next user.

26.4.2 Class Screen

Class `Screen` (Fig. 26.14) represents the screen of the ATM and encapsulates all aspects of displaying output to the user. Class `Screen` approximates a real ATM's screen with a computer monitor and outputs text messages using standard console output methods `System.out.print`, `System.out.println` and `System.out.printf`. In this case study, we designed class `Screen` to have one operation—`displayMessage`. For greater flexibility in displaying messages to the `Screen`, we now declare three `Screen` methods—`displayMessage`, `displayMessageLine` and `displayDollarAmount`.

```java
 1    // Screen.java
 2    // Represents the screen of the ATM
 3
 4    public class Screen {
 5       // display a message without a carriage return
 6       public void displayMessage(String message) {
 7          System.out.print(message);
 8       }
 9
10       // display a message with a carriage return
11       public void displayMessageLine(String message) {
12          System.out.println(message);
13       }
14
15       // displays a dollar amount
16       public void displayDollarAmount(double amount) {
17          System.out.printf("$%,.2f", amount);
18       }
19    }
```

Fig. 26.14 | Class `Screen` represents the screen of the ATM.

Method `displayMessage` (lines 6–8) takes a `String` argument and prints it to the console. The cursor stays on the same line, making this method appropriate for displaying prompts to the user. Method `displayMessageLine` (lines 11–13) does the same using `System.out.println`, which outputs a newline to move the cursor to the next line. Finally, method `displayDollarAmount` (lines 16–18) outputs a properly formatted dollar amount (e.g., $1,234.56). Line 17 uses `System.out.printf` to output a `double` value formatted with commas to increase readability and two decimal places.

26.4.3 Class Keypad

Class Keypad (Fig. 26.15) represents the keypad of the ATM and is responsible for receiving all user input. Recall that we're simulating this hardware, so we use the computer's keyboard to approximate the keypad. We use class Scanner to obtain console input from the user. A computer keyboard contains many keys not found on the ATM's keypad. However, we assume that the user presses only the keys on the computer keyboard that also appear on the keypad—the keys numbered 0–9 and the *Enter* key.

```java
1   // Keypad.java
2   // Represents the keypad of the ATM
3   import java.util.Scanner; // program uses Scanner to obtain user input
4
5   public class Keypad {
6      private Scanner input; // reads data from the command line
7
8      // no-argument constructor initializes the Scanner
9      public Keypad() {
10         input = new Scanner(System.in);
11      }
12
13      // return an integer value entered by user
14      public int getInput() {
15         return input.nextInt(); // we assume that user enters an integer
16      }
17   }
```

Fig. 26.15 | Class Keypad represents the ATM's keypad.

Line 6 declares Scanner variable input as an instance variable. Line 10 in the constructor creates a new Scanner object that reads input from the standard input stream (System.in) and assigns the object's reference to variable input. Method getInput (lines 14–16) invokes Scanner method nextInt (line 15) to return the next integer input by the user. [*Note:* Method nextInt can throw an InputMismatchException if the user enters non-integer input. Because the real ATM's keypad permits only integer input, we assume that no exception will occur and do not attempt to fix this problem. See Chapter 11, Exception Handling: A Deeper Look, for information on catching exceptions.] Recall that nextInt obtains all the input used by the ATM. Keypad's getInput method simply returns the integer input by the user. If a client of class Keypad requires input that satisfies some criteria (i.e., a number corresponding to a valid menu option), the client must perform the error checking.

26.4.4 Class CashDispenser

Class CashDispenser (Fig. 26.16) represents the cash dispenser of the ATM. Line 6 declares constant INITIAL_COUNT, which indicates the initial count of bills in the cash dispenser when the ATM starts (i.e., 500). Line 7 implements attribute count (modeled in Fig. 26.10), which keeps track of the number of bills remaining in the CashDispenser at any time. The constructor (lines 10–12) sets count to the initial count. CashDispenser has two public methods—dispenseCash (lines 15–18) and isSufficientCashAvailable (lines 21–30). The class trusts that a client (i.e., `Withdrawal`) calls `dispenseCash` only after establishing that sufficient cash is available by calling `isSufficientCashAvailable`. Thus, `dispenseCash` simply simulates dispensing the requested amount without checking whether sufficient cash is available.

```java
1   // CashDispenser.java
2   // Represents the cash dispenser of the ATM
3
4   public class CashDispenser {
5      // the default initial number of bills in the cash dispenser
6      private final static int INITIAL_COUNT = 500;
7      private int count; // number of $20 bills remaining
8
9      // no-argument CashDispenser constructor initializes count to default
10     public CashDispenser() {
11        count = INITIAL_COUNT; // set count attribute to default
12     }
13
14     // simulates dispensing of specified amount of cash
15     public void dispenseCash(int amount) {
16        int billsRequired = amount / 20; // number of $20 bills required
17        count -= billsRequired; // update the count of bills
18     }
19
20     // indicates whether cash dispenser can dispense desired amount
21     public boolean isSufficientCashAvailable(int amount) {
22        int billsRequired = amount / 20; // number of $20 bills required
23
24        if (count >= billsRequired) {
25           return true; // enough bills available
26        }
27        else {
28           return false; // not enough bills available
29        }
30     }
31  }
```

Fig. 26.16 | Class `CashDispenser` represents the ATM's cash dispenser.

Method `isSufficientCashAvailable` has a parameter `amount` that specifies the amount of cash in question. Line 22 calculates the number of $20 bills required to dispense the specified `amount`. The ATM allows the user to choose only withdrawal amounts that are multiples of $20, so we divide `amount` by 20 to obtain the number of `billsRequired`. Lines 24–29 return `true` if the `CashDispenser`'s `count` is greater than or equal to `billsRequired` (i.e., enough bills are available) and `false` otherwise (i.e., not enough bills). For example, if a user wishes to withdraw $80 (i.e., `billsRequired` is 4), but only three bills remain (i.e., `count` is 3), the method returns `false`.

Method `dispenseCash` (lines 15–18) simulates cash dispensing. If our system were hooked up to a real hardware cash dispenser, this method would interact with the device to physically dispense cash. Our version of the method simply decreases the `count` of bills remaining by the number required to dispense the specified `amount`. It's the responsibility of the client of the class (i.e., `Withdrawal`) to inform the user that cash has been dispensed—`CashDispenser` cannot interact directly with `Screen`.

26.4.5 Class `DepositSlot`

Class `DepositSlot` (Fig. 26.17) represents the ATM's deposit slot. Like class `CashDispenser`, class `DepositSlot` merely simulates the functionality of a real hardware deposit slot. `DepositSlot` has no attributes and only one method—`isEnvelopeReceived`—which indicates whether a deposit envelope was received.

Recall from the requirements document that the ATM allows the user up to two minutes to insert an envelope. The current version of method `isEnvelopeReceived` simply returns `true` immediately (line 8), because this is only a software simulation, and we assume that the user has inserted an envelope within the required time frame. If an actual hardware deposit slot were connected to our system, method `isEnvelopeReceived` might be implemented to wait for a maximum of two minutes to receive a signal from the hardware deposit slot indicating that the user has indeed inserted a deposit envelope. If `isEnvelopeReceived` were to receive such a signal within two minutes, the method would return `true`. If two minutes elapsed and the method still had not received a signal, then the method would return `false`.

```
1   // DepositSlot.java
2   // Represents the deposit slot of the ATM
3
4   public class DepositSlot {
5      // indicates whether envelope was received (always returns true,
6      // because this is only a software simulation of a real deposit slot)
7      public boolean isEnvelopeReceived() {
8         return true; // deposit envelope was received
9      }
10  }
```

Fig. 26.17 | Class `DepositSlot` represents the ATM's deposit slot.

26.4.6 Class `Account`

Class `Account` (Fig. 26.18) represents a bank account. Each `Account` has four attributes (modeled in Fig. 26.10)—`accountNumber`, `pin`, `availableBalance` and `totalBalance`. Lines 5–8 implement these attributes as `private` fields. Variable `availableBalance` represents the amount of funds available for withdrawal. Variable `totalBalance` represents the amount of funds available, plus the amount of deposited funds still pending confirmation or clearance.

```
1   // Account.java
2   // Represents a bank account
3
4   public class Account {
5      private int accountNumber; // account number
```

Fig. 26.18 | Class `Account` represents a bank account. (Part 1 of 2.)

```
 6        private int pin; // PIN for authentication
 7        private double availableBalance; // funds available for withdrawal
 8        private double totalBalance; // funds available + pending deposits
 9
10        // Account constructor initializes attributes
11        public Account(int theAccountNumber, int thePIN,
12           double theAvailableBalance, double theTotalBalance) {
13           accountNumber = theAccountNumber;
14           pin = thePIN;
15           availableBalance = theAvailableBalance;
16           totalBalance = theTotalBalance;
17        }
18
19        // determines whether a user-specified PIN matches PIN in Account
20        public boolean validatePIN(int userPIN) {
21           if (userPIN == pin) {
22              return true;
23           }
24           else {
25              return false;
26           }
27        }
28
29        // returns available balance
30        public double getAvailableBalance() {
31           return availableBalance;
32        }
33
34        // returns the total balance
35        public double getTotalBalance() {
36           return totalBalance;
37        }
38
39        // credits an amount to the account
40        public void credit(double amount) {
41           totalBalance += amount; // add to total balance
42        }
43
44        // debits an amount from the account
45        public void debit(double amount) {
46           availableBalance -= amount; // subtract from available balance
47           totalBalance -= amount; // subtract from total balance
48        }
49
50        // returns account number
51        public int getAccountNumber() {
52           return accountNumber;
53        }
54     }
```

Fig. 26.18 | Class Account represents a bank account. (Part 2 of 2.)

The Account class has a constructor (lines 11–17) that takes an account number, the PIN established for the account, the account's initial available balance and the account's initial total balance as arguments. Lines 13–16 assign these values to the class's attributes (i.e., fields).

Method validatePIN (lines 20–27) determines whether a user-specified PIN (i.e., parameter userPIN) matches the PIN associated with the account (i.e., attribute pin). Recall that we modeled this method's parameter userPIN in Fig. 25.19. If the two PINs match, the method returns true; otherwise, it returns false.

Methods getAvailableBalance (lines 30–32) and getTotalBalance (lines 35–37) return the values of double attributes availableBalance and totalBalance, respectively.

Method credit (lines 40–42) adds an amount of money (i.e., parameter amount) to an Account as part of a deposit transaction. This method adds the amount only to attribute totalBalance. The money credited to an account during a deposit does *not* become available immediately, so we modify only the total balance. We assume that the bank updates the available balance appropriately at a later time. Our implementation of class Account includes only methods required for carrying out ATM transactions. Therefore, we omit the methods that some other bank system would invoke to add to attribute availableBalance (to confirm a deposit) or subtract from attribute totalBalance (to reject a deposit).

Method debit (lines 45–48) subtracts an amount of money (i.e., parameter amount) from an Account as part of a withdrawal transaction. This method subtracts the amount from *both* attribute availableBalance and attribute totalBalance, because a withdrawal affects *both* measures of an account balance.

Method getAccountNumber (lines 51–53) provides access to an Account's accountNumber. We include this method in our implementation so that a client of the class (i.e., BankDatabase) can identify a particular Account. For example, BankDatabase contains many Account objects, and it can invoke this method on each of its Account objects to locate the one with a specific account number.

26.4.7 Class BankDatabase

Class BankDatabase (Fig. 26.19) models the bank's database with which the ATM interacts to access and modify a user's account information. We study database access in Chapter 22. For now we model the database as an array. An exercise in Chapter 22 asks you to reimplement this portion of the ATM using an actual database.

```
1   // BankDatabase.java
2   // Represents the bank account information database
3
4   public class BankDatabase {
5      private Account[] accounts; // array of Accounts
6
7      // no-argument BankDatabase constructor initializes accounts
8      public BankDatabase() {
9         accounts = new Account[2]; // just 2 accounts for testing
10        accounts[0] = new Account(12345, 54321, 1000.0, 1200.0);
11        accounts[1] = new Account(98765, 56789, 200.0, 200.0);
12     }
13
```

Fig. 26.19 | Class BankDatabase represents the bank's account information database. (Part 1 of 2.)

```
14      // retrieve Account object containing specified account number
15      private Account getAccount(int accountNumber) {
16         // loop through accounts searching for matching account number
17         for (Account currentAccount : accounts) {
18            // return current account if match found
19            if (currentAccount.getAccountNumber() == accountNumber) {
20               return currentAccount;
21            }
22         }
23
24         return null; // if no matching account was found, return null
25      }
26
27      // determine whether user-specified account number and PIN match
28      // those of an account in the database
29      public boolean authenticateUser(int userAccountNumber, int userPIN) {
30         // attempt to retrieve the account with the account number
31         Account userAccount = getAccount(userAccountNumber);
32
33         // if account exists, return result of Account method validatePIN
34         if (userAccount != null) {
35            return userAccount.validatePIN(userPIN);
36         }
37         else {
38            return false; // account number not found, so return false
39         }
40      }
41
42      // return available balance of Account with specified account number
43      public double getAvailableBalance(int userAccountNumber) {
44         return getAccount(userAccountNumber).getAvailableBalance();
45      }
46
47      // return total balance of Account with specified account number
48      public double getTotalBalance(int userAccountNumber) {
49         return getAccount(userAccountNumber).getTotalBalance();
50      }
51
52      // credit an amount to Account with specified account number
53      public void credit(int userAccountNumber, double amount) {
54         getAccount(userAccountNumber).credit(amount);
55      }
56
57      // debit an amount from Account with specified account number
58      public void debit(int userAccountNumber, double amount) {
59         getAccount(userAccountNumber).debit(amount);
60      }
61   }
```

Fig. 26.19 | Class BankDatabase represents the bank's account information database. (Part 2 of 2.)

We determine one reference-type attribute for class BankDatabase based on its composition relationship with class Account. Recall from Fig. 26.9 that a BankDatabase is composed of zero or more objects of class Account. Line 5 implements attribute accounts—an array of Account objects—to implement this composition relationship. Class BankData-base's no-argument constructor (lines 8–12) initializes accounts with new Account objects. For the sake of testing the system, we declare accounts to hold just two array elements, which we instantiate as new Account objects with test data. The Account constructor has four parameters—the account number, the PIN assigned to the account, the initial available balance and the initial total balance. Recall that class BankDatabase serves as an intermediary between class ATM and the actual Account objects that contain a user's account information. Thus, the methods of class BankDatabase do nothing more than invoke the corresponding methods of the Account object belonging to the current ATM user.

We include private utility method getAccount (lines 15–25) to allow the Bank-Database to obtain a reference to a particular Account within array accounts. To locate the user's Account, the BankDatabase compares the value returned by method get-AccountNumber for each element of accounts to a specified account number until it finds a match. Lines 17–22 traverse the accounts array. If the account number of currentAc-count equals the value of parameter accountNumber, the method immediately returns the currentAccount. If no account has the given account number, then line 24 returns null.

Method authenticateUser (lines 29–40) proves or disproves the identity of an ATM user. This method takes a user-specified account number and PIN as arguments and indicates whether they match the account number and PIN of an Account in the database. Line 31 calls method getAccount, which returns either an Account with userAccount-Number as its account number or null to indicate that userAccountNumber is invalid. If getAccount returns an Account object, line 35 returns the boolean value returned by that object's validatePIN method. BankDatabase's authenticateUser method does not per-form the PIN comparison itself—rather, it forwards userPIN to the Account object's val-idatePIN method to do so. The value returned by Account method validatePIN indicates whether the user-specified PIN matches the PIN of the user's Account, so method authen-ticateUser simply returns this value to the class's client (i.e., ATM).

BankDatabase trusts the ATM to invoke method authenticateUser and receive a return value of true before allowing the user to perform transactions. BankDatabase also trusts that each Transaction object created by the ATM contains the valid account number of the current authenticated user and that this is the account number passed to the remaining BankDatabase methods as argument userAccountNumber. Methods getAvail-ableBalance (lines 43–45), getTotalBalance (lines 48–50), credit (lines 53–55) and debit (lines 58–60) therefore simply retrieve the user's Account object with utility method getAccount, then invoke the appropriate Account method on that object. We know that the calls to getAccount from these methods will never return null, because userAccount-Number must refer to an existing Account. Methods getAvailableBalance and getTotal-Balance return the values returned by the corresponding Account methods. Also, credit and debit simply redirect parameter amount to the Account methods they invoke.

26.4.8 Class Transaction

Class Transaction (Fig. 26.20) is an abstract superclass that represents the notion of an ATM transaction. It contains the common features of subclasses BalanceInquiry, With-drawal and Deposit. This class expands upon the "skeleton" code first developed in Section 26.3. Line 4 declares this class to be abstract. Lines 5–7 declare the class's pri-vate attributes. Recall from the class diagram of Fig. 26.10 that class Transaction contains an attribute accountNumber (line 5) that indicates the account involved in the Transaction. We derive attributes screen (line 6) and bankDatabase (line 7) from class Transaction's associations modeled in Fig. 26.9—all transactions require access to the ATM's screen and the bank's database.

```java
1   // Transaction.java
2   // Abstract superclass Transaction represents an ATM transaction
3
4   public abstract class Transaction {
5      private int accountNumber; // indicates account involved
6      private Screen screen; // ATM's screen
7      private BankDatabase bankDatabase; // account info database
8
9      // Transaction constructor invoked by subclasses using super()
10     public Transaction(int userAccountNumber, Screen atmScreen,
11        BankDatabase atmBankDatabase) {
12
13        accountNumber = userAccountNumber;
14        screen = atmScreen;
15        bankDatabase = atmBankDatabase;
16     }
17
18     // return account number
19     public int getAccountNumber() {
20        return accountNumber;
21     }
22
23     // return reference to screen
24     public Screen getScreen() {
25        return screen;
26     }
27
28     // return reference to bank database
29     public BankDatabase getBankDatabase() {
30        return bankDatabase;
31     }
32
33     // perform the transaction (overridden by each subclass)
34     abstract public void execute();
35  }
```

Fig. 26.20 | Abstract superclass Transaction represents an ATM transaction.

Class Transaction's constructor (lines 10–16) takes as arguments the current user's account number and references to the ATM's screen and the bank's database. Because Transaction is an *abstract* class, this constructor will be called only by the constructors of the Transaction subclasses.

The class has three public *get* methods—getAccountNumber (lines 19–21), get-Screen (lines 24–26) and getBankDatabase (lines 29–31). These are inherited by Transaction subclasses and used to gain access to class Transaction's private attributes.

Class Transaction also declares abstract method execute (line 34). It does not make sense to provide this method's implementation, because a generic transaction cannot be executed. So, we declare this method abstract and force each Transaction subclass to provide a concrete implementation that executes that particular type of transaction.

26.4.9 Class BalanceInquiry

Class BalanceInquiry (Fig. 26.21) extends Transaction and represents a balance-inquiry ATM transaction. BalanceInquiry does not have any attributes of its own, but it inherits Transaction attributes accountNumber, screen and bankDatabase, which are accessible through Transaction's public *get* methods. The BalanceInquiry constructor takes arguments corresponding to these attributes and simply forwards them to Transaction's constructor using super (line 9).

```
 1   // BalanceInquiry.java
 2   // Represents a balance inquiry ATM transaction
 3
 4   public class BalanceInquiry extends Transaction {
 5      // BalanceInquiry constructor
 6      public BalanceInquiry(int userAccountNumber, Screen atmScreen,
 7         BankDatabase atmBankDatabase) {
 8
 9         super(userAccountNumber, atmScreen, atmBankDatabase);
10      }
11
12      // performs the transaction
13      @Override
14      public void execute() {
15         // get references to bank database and screen
16         BankDatabase bankDatabase = getBankDatabase();
17         Screen screen = getScreen();
18
19         // get the available balance for the account involved
20         double availableBalance =
21            bankDatabase.getAvailableBalance(getAccountNumber());
22
23         // get the total balance for the account involved
24         double totalBalance =
25            bankDatabase.getTotalBalance(getAccountNumber());
26
27         // display the balance information on the screen
28         screen.displayMessageLine("\nBalance Information:");
29         screen.displayMessage(" - Available balance: ");
30         screen.displayDollarAmount(availableBalance);
31         screen.displayMessage("\n - Total balance:      ");
32         screen.displayDollarAmount(totalBalance);
33         screen.displayMessageLine("");
34      }
35   }
```

Fig. 26.21 | Class BalanceInquiry represents a balance-inquiry ATM transaction.

Class BalanceInquiry overrides Transaction's abstract method execute to provide a concrete implementation (lines 13–34) that performs the steps involved in a balance inquiry. Lines 16–17 get references to the bank database and the ATM's screen by invoking methods inherited from superclass `Transaction`. Lines 20–21 retrieve the available balance of the account involved by invoking method `getAvailableBalance` of bank-Database. Line 21 uses inherited method `getAccountNumber` to get the account number of the current user, which it then passes to `getAvailableBalance`. Lines 24–25 retrieve the total balance of the current user's account. Lines 28–33 display the balance information on the ATM's screen. Recall that `displayDollarAmount` takes a `double` argument and outputs it to the screen formatted as a dollar amount. For example, if a user's `available-Balance` is 1000.5, line 30 outputs $1,000.50. Line 33 inserts a blank line of output to separate the balance information from subsequent output (i.e., the main menu repeated by class `ATM` after executing the `BalanceInquiry`).

26.4.10 Class `Withdrawal`

Class `Withdrawal` (Fig. 26.22) extends `Transaction` and represents a withdrawal ATM transaction. This class expands upon the "skeleton" code for this class developed in Fig. 26.12. Recall from the class diagram of Fig. 26.10 that class `Withdrawal` has one attribute, `amount`, which line 5 implements as an `int` field. Figure 26.9 models associations between class `Withdrawal` and classes `Keypad` and `CashDispenser`, for which lines 6–7 implement reference-type attributes `keypad` and `cashDispenser`, respectively. Line 10 declares a constant corresponding to the cancel menu option. We'll soon discuss how the class uses this constant.

```java
// Withdrawal.java
// Represents a withdrawal ATM transaction

public class Withdrawal extends Transaction {
   private int amount; // amount to withdraw
   private Keypad keypad; // reference to keypad
   private CashDispenser cashDispenser; // reference to cash dispenser

   // constant corresponding to menu option to cancel
   private final static int CANCELED = 6;

   // Withdrawal constructor
   public Withdrawal(int userAccountNumber, Screen atmScreen,
      BankDatabase atmBankDatabase, Keypad atmKeypad,
      CashDispenser atmCashDispenser) {

      // initialize superclass variables
      super(userAccountNumber, atmScreen, atmBankDatabase);

      // initialize references to keypad and cash dispenser
      keypad = atmKeypad;
      cashDispenser = atmCashDispenser;
   }
```

Fig. 26.22 | Class `Withdrawal` represents a withdrawal ATM transaction. (Part 1 of 3.)

```
25        // perform transaction
26        @Override
27        public void execute() {
28           boolean cashDispensed = false; // cash was not dispensed yet
29           double availableBalance; // amount available for withdrawal
30
31           // get references to bank database and screen
32           BankDatabase bankDatabase = getBankDatabase();
33           Screen screen = getScreen();
34
35           // loop until cash is dispensed or the user cancels
36           do {
37              // obtain a chosen withdrawal amount from the user
38              amount = displayMenuOfAmounts();
39
40              // check whether user chose a withdrawal amount or canceled
41              if (amount != CANCELED) {
42                 // get available balance of account involved
43                 availableBalance =
44                    bankDatabase.getAvailableBalance(getAccountNumber());
45
46                 // check whether the user has enough money in the account
47                 if (amount <= availableBalance) {
48                    // check whether the cash dispenser has enough money
49                    if (cashDispenser.isSufficientCashAvailable(amount)) {
50                       // update the account involved to reflect the withdrawal
51                       bankDatabase.debit(getAccountNumber(), amount);
52
53                       cashDispenser.dispenseCash(amount); // dispense cash
54                       cashDispensed = true; // cash was dispensed
55
56                       // instruct user to take cash
57                       screen.displayMessageLine("\nYour cash has been" +
58                          " dispensed. Please take your cash now.");
59                    }
60                    else { // cash dispenser does not have enough cash
61                       screen.displayMessageLine(
62                          "\nInsufficient cash available in the ATM." +
63                          "\n\nPlease choose a smaller amount.");
64                    }
65                 }
66                 else { // not enough money available in user's account
67                    screen.displayMessageLine(
68                       "\nInsufficient funds in your account." +
69                       "\n\nPlease choose a smaller amount.");
70                 }
71              }
72              else { // user chose cancel menu option
73                 screen.displayMessageLine("\nCanceling transaction...");
74                 return; // return to main menu because user canceled
75              }
76           } while (!cashDispensed);
77        }
```

Fig. 26.22 | Class Withdrawal represents a withdrawal ATM transaction. (Part 2 of 3.)

```
78
79      // display a menu of withdrawal amounts and the option to cancel;
80      // return the chosen amount or 0 if the user chooses to cancel
81      private int displayMenuOfAmounts() {
82         int userChoice = 0; // local variable to store return value
83
84         Screen screen = getScreen(); // get screen reference
85
86         // array of amounts to correspond to menu numbers
87         int[] amounts = {0, 20, 40, 60, 100, 200};
88
89         // loop while no valid choice has been made
90         while (userChoice == 0) {
91            // display the withdrawal menu
92            screen.displayMessageLine("\nWithdrawal Menu:");
93            screen.displayMessageLine("1 - $20");
94            screen.displayMessageLine("2 - $40");
95            screen.displayMessageLine("3 - $60");
96            screen.displayMessageLine("4 - $100");
97            screen.displayMessageLine("5 - $200");
98            screen.displayMessageLine("6 - Cancel transaction");
99            screen.displayMessage("\nChoose a withdrawal amount: ");
100
101           int input = keypad.getInput(); // get user input through keypad
102
103           // determine how to proceed based on the input value
104           switch (input) {
105              case 1: // if the user chose a withdrawal amount
106              case 2: // (i.e., chose option 1, 2, 3, 4 or 5), return the
107              case 3: // corresponding amount from amounts array
108              case 4:
109              case 5:
110                 userChoice = amounts[input]; // save user's choice
111                 break;
112              case CANCELED: // the user chose to cancel
113                 userChoice = CANCELED; // save user's choice
114                 break;
115              default: // the user did not enter a value from 1-6
116                 screen.displayMessageLine(
117                    "\nInvalid selection. Try again.");
118           }
119        }
120
121        return userChoice; // return withdrawal amount or CANCELED
122     }
123  }
```

Fig. 26.22 | Class Withdrawal represents a withdrawal ATM transaction. (Part 3 of 3.)

Class Withdrawal's constructor (lines 13–23) has five parameters. It uses super to pass parameters userAccountNumber, atmScreen and atmBankDatabase to superclass Transaction's constructor to set the attributes that Withdrawal inherits from Transaction. The constructor also takes references atmKeypad and atmCashDispenser as parameters and assigns them to reference-type attributes keypad and cashDispenser.

Class `Withdrawal` overrides `Transaction` method `execute` with a concrete implementation (lines 26–77) that performs the steps of a withdrawal. Line 28 declares and initializes a local `boolean` variable `cashDispensed`, which indicates whether cash has been dispensed (i.e., whether the transaction has completed successfully) and is initially `false`. Line 29 declares local `double` variable `availableBalance`, which will store the user's available balance during a withdrawal transaction. Lines 32–33 get references to the bank database and the ATM's screen by invoking methods inherited from superclass `Transaction`.

Lines 36–76 execute until cash is dispensed (i.e., until `cashDispensed` becomes `true`) or until the user chooses to cancel (in which case, the loop terminates). We use this loop to continuously return the user to the start of the transaction if an error occurs (i.e., the requested withdrawal amount is greater than the user's available balance or greater than the amount of cash in the cash dispenser). Line 38 displays a menu of withdrawal amounts and obtains a user selection by calling `private` utility method `displayMenuOfAmounts` (declared in lines 81–122). This method displays the menu of amounts and returns either an `int` withdrawal amount or an `int` constant `CANCELED` to indicate that the user has chosen to cancel the transaction.

Method `displayMenuOfAmounts` (lines 81–122) first declares local variable `userChoice` (initially 0) to store the value that the method will return (line 82). Line 84 gets a reference to the screen by calling method `getScreen` inherited from superclass `Transaction`. Line 87 declares an integer array of withdrawal amounts that correspond to the amounts displayed in the withdrawal menu. We ignore the first element in the array (index 0) because the menu has no option 0. Lines 90–119 repeat until `userChoice` takes on a value other than 0. We'll see shortly that this occurs when the user makes a valid selection from the menu. Lines 92–99 display the withdrawal menu on the screen and prompt the user to enter a choice. Line 101 obtains integer `input` through the keypad. The `switch` statement at lines 104–118 determines how to proceed based on the user's input. If the user selects a number between 1 and 5, line 110 sets `userChoice` to the value of the element in `amounts` at index `input`. For example, if the user enters 3 to withdraw $60, line 110 sets `userChoice` to the value of `amounts[3]` (i.e., 60). Variable `userChoice` no longer equals 0, so the loop terminates and line 121 returns `userChoice`. If the user selects the cancel menu option, lines 113–114 execute, setting `userChoice` to `CANCELED` and causing the method to return this value. If the user does not enter a valid menu selection, lines 116–117 display an error message and the user is returned to the withdrawal menu.

Line 41 in method `execute` determines whether the user has selected a withdrawal amount or chosen to cancel. If the user cancels, lines 73–74 execute and display an appropriate message to the user before returning control to the calling method (i.e., ATM method `performTransactions`). If the user has chosen a withdrawal amount, lines 43–44 retrieve the available balance of the current user's `Account` and store it in variable `availableBalance`. Next, line 47 determines whether the selected amount is less than or equal to the user's available balance. If it's not, lines 67–69 display an appropriate error message. Control then continues to the end of the do...`while`, and the loop repeats because `cashDispensed` is still `false`. If the user's balance is high enough, the `if` statement at line 49 determines whether the cash dispenser has enough money to satisfy the withdrawal request by invoking the `cashDispenser`'s `isSufficientCashAvailable` method. If this method returns `false`, lines 61–63 display an appropriate error message and the do...`while` repeats. If sufficient cash is available, then the requirements for the withdrawal are satisfied, and line 51 debits amount from the user's account in the database. Lines 53–54 then instruct the cash dispenser to dispense the cash to the user and set cashDispensed to true. Finally, lines 57–58 display a message to the user that cash has been dispensed. Because cashDispensed is now true, control continues after the do…while. No additional statements appear below the loop, so the method returns.

26.4.11 Class Deposit

Class Deposit (Fig. 26.23) extends Transaction and represents a deposit transaction. Recall from Fig. 26.10 that class Deposit has one attribute amount, which line 5 implements as an int field. Lines 6–7 create reference attributes keypad and depositSlot that implement the associations between class Deposit and classes Keypad and DepositSlot modeled in Fig. 26.9. Line 8 declares a constant CANCELED that corresponds to the value a user enters to cancel. We'll soon discuss how the class uses this constant.

```java
1   // Deposit.java
2   // Represents a deposit ATM transaction
3
4   public class Deposit extends Transaction {
5      private double amount; // amount to deposit
6      private Keypad keypad; // reference to keypad
7      private DepositSlot depositSlot; // reference to deposit slot
8      private final static int CANCELED = 0; // constant for cancel option
9
10     // Deposit constructor
11     public Deposit(int userAccountNumber, Screen atmScreen,
12        BankDatabase atmBankDatabase, Keypad atmKeypad,
13        DepositSlot atmDepositSlot) {
14
15        // initialize superclass variables
16        super(userAccountNumber, atmScreen, atmBankDatabase);
17
18        // initialize references to keypad and deposit slot
19        keypad = atmKeypad;
20        depositSlot = atmDepositSlot;
21     }
22
23     // perform transaction
24     @Override
25     public void execute() {
26        BankDatabase bankDatabase = getBankDatabase(); // get reference
27        Screen screen = getScreen(); // get reference
28
29        amount = promptForDepositAmount(); // get deposit amount from user
30
31        // check whether user entered a deposit amount or canceled
32        if (amount != CANCELED) {
33           // request deposit envelope containing specified amount
34           screen.displayMessage(
35              "\nPlease insert a deposit envelope containing ");
```

Fig. 26.23 | Class Deposit represents a deposit ATM transaction. (Part 1 of 2.)

```
36                screen.displayDollarAmount(amount);
37                screen.displayMessageLine(".");
38
39                // receive deposit envelope
40                boolean envelopeReceived = depositSlot.isEnvelopeReceived();
41
42                // check whether deposit envelope was received
43                if (envelopeReceived) {
44                   screen.displayMessageLine("\nYour envelope has been " +
45                      "received.\nNOTE: The money just deposited will not " +
46                      "be available until we verify the amount of any " +
47                      "enclosed cash and your checks clear.");
48
49                   // credit account to reflect the deposit
50                   bankDatabase.credit(getAccountNumber(), amount);
51                }
52                else { // deposit envelope not received
53                   screen.displayMessageLine("\nYou did not insert an " +
54                      "envelope, so the ATM has canceled your transaction.");
55                }
56             }
57             else { // user canceled instead of entering amount
58                screen.displayMessageLine("\nCanceling transaction...");
59             }
60          }
61
62          // prompt user to enter a deposit amount in cents
63          private double promptForDepositAmount() {
64             Screen screen = getScreen(); // get reference to screen
65
66             // display the prompt
67             screen.displayMessage("\nPlease enter a deposit amount in " +
68                "CENTS (or 0 to cancel): ");
69             int input = keypad.getInput(); // receive input of deposit amount
70
71             // check whether the user canceled or entered a valid amount
72             if (input == CANCELED) {
73                return CANCELED;
74             }
75             else {
76                return (double) input / 100; // return dollar amount
77             }
78          }
79       }
```

Fig. 26.23 | Class Deposit represents a deposit ATM transaction. (Part 2 of 2.)

Like Withdrawal, class Deposit's constructor (lines 11–21) passes three parameters to superclass Transaction's constructor. The constructor also has parameters atmKeypad and atmDepositSlot, which it assigns to corresponding attributes.

Method execute (lines 24–60) overrides the abstract version in superclass Transaction with a concrete implementation that performs the steps required in a deposit transaction. Lines 26–27 get references to the database and the screen. Line 29 prompts the user to enter a deposit amount by invoking `private` utility method `promptForDepositAmount` (declared in lines 63–78) and sets attribute `amount` to the value returned. Method `prompt-ForDepositAmount` asks the user to enter a deposit amount as an integer number of cents (because the ATM's keypad does not contain a decimal point; this is consistent with many real ATMs) and returns the `double` value representing the dollar amount to be deposited.

Line 64 in method `promptForDepositAmount` gets a reference to the ATM's screen. Lines 67–68 display a message asking the user to input a deposit amount as a number of cents or "0" to cancel the transaction. Line 69 receives the user's input from the keypad. Lines 72–77 determine whether the user has entered a real deposit amount or chosen to cancel. If the latter, line 73 returns the constant `CANCELED`. Otherwise, line 76 returns the deposit amount after converting from the number of cents to a dollar amount by casting `input` to a `double`, then dividing by 100. For example, if the user enters 125 as the number of cents, line 76 returns 125.0 divided by 100, or 1.25—125 cents is $1.25.

Line 32 in method `execute` determines whether the user has chosen to cancel the transaction instead of entering a deposit amount. If so, line 58 displays an appropriate message, and the method returns. If the user enters a deposit amount, lines 34–37 instruct the user to insert a deposit envelope with the correct amount. Recall that `Screen` method `displayDollarAmount` outputs a `double` formatted as a dollar amount.

Line 40 sets a local `boolean` variable to the value returned by `depositSlot`'s `isEnvelopeReceived` method, indicating whether a deposit envelope has been received. Recall that we coded method `isEnvelopeReceived` (Fig. 26.17) to always return `true`, because we're simulating the functionality of the deposit slot and assume that the user always inserts an envelope. However, we code method `execute` of class `Deposit` to test for the possibility that the user does not insert an envelope—good software engineering demands that programs account for *all* possible return values. Thus, class `Deposit` is prepared for future versions of `isEnvelopeReceived` that could return `false`. Lines 44–50 execute if the deposit slot receives an envelope. Lines 44–47 display an appropriate message to the user. Line 50 then credits the deposit amount to the user's account in the database. Lines 53–54 will execute if the deposit slot does not receive a deposit envelope. In this case, we display a message to the user stating that the ATM has canceled the transaction. The method then returns without modifying the user's account.

26.4.12 Class ATMCaseStudy

Class `ATMCaseStudy` (Fig. 26.24) is a simple class that allows us to start, or "turn on," the ATM and test the implementation of our ATM system model. Class `ATMCaseStudy`'s `main` method instantiates a new `ATM` object named `theATM` and invokes its `run` method to start the ATM.

```
1   // ATMCaseStudy.java
2   // Driver program for the ATM case study
3
4   public class ATMCaseStudy {
5      // main method creates and runs the ATM
6      public static void main(String[] args) {
```

Fig. 26.24 | ATMCaseStudy.java starts the ATM.

```
 7            ATM theATM = new ATM();
 8            theATM.run();
 9        }
10    }
```

Fig. 26.24 | ATMCaseStudy.java starts the ATM.

26.5 Wrap-Up

In this chapter, you used inheritance to tune the design of the ATM software system, and you fully implemented the ATM in Java. Congratulations on completing the entire ATM case study! We hope you found this experience to be valuable and that it reinforced many of the object-oriented programming concepts that you've learned. In the next chapter, we present the Java Platform Module System—Java 9's most important new software-engineering technology.

Answers to Self-Review Exercises

26.1 True. The minus sign (–) indicates private visibility.

26.2 b.

26.3 The design for class Keypad yields the code in Fig. 26.25. Recall that class Keypad has no attributes for the moment, but attributes may become apparent as we continue the implementation. Also, if we were designing a real ATM, method getInput would need to interact with the ATM's keypad hardware. We'll actually read input from the keyboard of a personal computer when we write the complete Java code in Section 26.4.

```
 1    // Class Keypad represents an ATM's keypad
 2    public class Keypad {
 3        // no attributes have been specified yet
 4
 5        // no-argument constructor
 6        public Keypad() { }
 7
 8        // operations
 9        public int getInput() { }
10    }
```

Fig. 26.25 | Java code for class Keypad based on Figs. 26.1–26.2.

26.4 b.

26.5 False. The UML requires that we italicize abstract class names and method names.

26.6 The design for class Transaction yields the code in Fig. 26.26. The bodies of the class constructor and methods are completed in Section 26.4. When fully implemented, methods getScreen and getBankDatabase will return superclass Transaction's private reference attributes screen and bankDatabase, respectively. These methods allow the Transaction subclasses to access the ATM's screen and interact with the bank's database.

```
1   // Abstract class Transaction represents an ATM transaction
2   public abstract class Transaction {
3      // attributes
4      private int accountNumber; // indicates account involved
5      private Screen screen; // ATM's screen
6      private BankDatabase bankDatabase; // account info database
7
8      // no-argument constructor invoked by subclasses using super()
9      public Transaction() { }
10
11     // return account number
12     public int getAccountNumber() { }
13
14     // return reference to screen
15     public Screen getScreen() { }
16
17     // return reference to bank database
18     public BankDatabase getBankDatabase() { }
19
20     // abstract method overridden by subclasses
21     public abstract void execute();
22  }
```

Fig. 26.26 | Java code for class `Transaction` based on Figs. 26.9 and 26.10.

Java Platform Module System

27.1 Introduction[1]

In this chapter, we introduce the **Java Platform Module System (JPMS)**—Java 9's most important new technology. Modularity—the result of **Project Jigsaw**[2]—helps developers at all levels be more productive as they build, maintain and evolve software systems, espe-

---

1. We'd like to thank Brian Goetz, Alex Buckley, Alan Bateman, Lance Anderson, Mandy Chung and Paul Bakker for answering our questions and sharing insights.

2. "Project Jigsaw." `http://openjdk.java.net/projects/jigsaw/`.

cially large systems. College students in upper-level programming courses will want to master modularity for career preparation.

Software Required

Before reading this chapter, install JDK 9 and the chapter's source-code examples as described in the Before You Begin section that follows the Preface. We'll present several module-dependency graphs that were created with an early access version of the NetBeans IDE that includes JDK 9 support:

```
http://wiki.netbeans.org/JDK9Support
```

Other IDE vendors will likely provide similar tools.

What is a Module?

Modularity adds a higher level of aggregation above packages. The key new language element is the **module**—a uniquely named, reusable group of related packages, as well as resources (like images and XML files) and a **module descriptor** specifying:

- the module's *name*,
- the module's *dependencies* (that is, other modules this module depends on),
- the packages it *explicitly* makes available to other modules (all other packages in the module are *implicitly* unavailable to other modules),
- the *services it offers*,
- the *services it consumes*, and
- to what other modules it allows *reflection*.

History

The Java SE Platform has been around since 1995. There are now approximately 10 million developers using it to build everything from small apps for resource-constrained devices—like those in the Internet of Things (IoT) and other embedded devices—to large-scale business-critical and mission-critical systems. There are massive amounts of legacy code out there, but until now, the Java platform has primarily been a monolithic one-size-fits-all solution. Over the years there have been various efforts geared to modularizing Java, but none is widely used.

Modularizing the Java SE Platform has been challenging to implement and the effort has taken many years. *JSR 277: Java Module System* was originally proposed in 2005[3] for Java 7. This JSR was later superseded by *JSR 376: Java Platform Module System* and targeted for Java 8. The Java SE Platform is now modularized in Java 9, but only after Java 9 was delayed until July 2017.

Goals

According to JSR 376, the key goals of modularizing the Java SE Platform are:[4]

- Reliable configuration—Modularity provides mechanisms for explicitly declaring dependencies between modules in a manner that's recognized both at compile

---

3. "JSR 277: Java Module System." https://jcp.org/en/jsr/detail?id=277.
4. "JSR 376: Java Platform Module System." https://jcp.org/en/jsr/detail?id=376.

time and execution time. The system can walk through these dependencies to determine the subset of all modules required to support your app.

- Strong encapsulation—The packages in a module are accessible to other modules only if the module explicitly "exports" them. Even then, another module cannot use those packages unless it explicitly states that it "requires" the other module's capabilities. This improves platform security because fewer classes are accessible to potential attackers. You may find that considering modularity helps you come up with cleaner, more logical designs.

- Scalable Java Platform—Previously the Java Platform was a monolith consisting of a massive numbers of packages, making it challenging to develop, maintain and evolve. It couldn't be easily subsetted. The platform is now modularized into 95 modules (this number will change as Java evolves). You can create custom runtimes consisting of only modules you need for your apps or the devices you're targeting. For example, if a device does not support GUIs, you could create a runtime that does not include the GUI modules, significantly reducing the runtime's size.

- Greater platform integrity—Before Java 9, it was possible to use many classes in the platform that were not meant for use by an app's classes. With strong encapsulation, these internal APIs are truly encapsulated and hidden from apps using the platform. One downside of this is that it can make migrating your legacy code to Java 9 problematic.

- Improved performance—The JVM uses various optimization techniques to improve application performance. JSR 376[5] indicates that these techniques are more effective when it's known in advance that required types are located only in specific modules.

Listing the JDK's Modules

A crucial aspect of Java 9 is dividing the JDK into modules to support various configurations (JEP 200[6]). Using the java command from the JDK's bin folder with the **--list-modules** option, as in:

```
java --list-modules
```

lists the JDK's set of modules (Fig. 27.1), which includes the **standard modules** that implement the Java SE Specification (names starting with java), JavaFX modules (names starting with javafx), JDK-specific modules (names starting with jdk) and Oracle-specific modules (names starting with oracle). Each module name is followed by a *version string*. In this case, we used a JDK 9 early access version, so each module is followed by the version string "@9-ea", indicating that it's a Java 9 early access ("ea") module. The "-ea" will be removed when Java 9 is released.

---

5. Reinhold, Mark. "JSR 376: Java Platform Module System." https://jcp.org/en/jsr/detail?id=376.
6. Reinhold, Mark. "JEP 200: The Modular JDK." http://openjdk.java.net/jeps/200.

java.activation@9-ea	jdk.httpserver@9-ea
java.base@9-ea	jdk.incubator.httpclient@9-ea
java.compiler@9-ea	jdk.internal.ed@9-ea
java.corba@9-ea	jdk.internal.jvmstat@9-ea
java.datatransfer@9-ea	jdk.internal.le@9-ea
java.desktop@9-ea	jdk.internal.opt@9-ea
java.instrument@9-ea	jdk.internal.vm.ci@9-ea
java.jnlp@9-ea	jdk.jartool@9-ea
java.logging@9-ea	jdk.javadoc@9-ea
java.management@9-ea	jdk.javaws@9-ea
java.management.rmi@9-ea	jdk.jcmd@9-ea
java.naming@9-ea	jdk.jconsole@9-ea
java.prefs@9-ea	jdk.jdeps@9-ea
java.rmi@9-ea	jdk.jdi@9-ea
java.scripting@9-ea	jdk.jdwp.agent@9-ea
java.se@9-ea	jdk.jfr@9-ea
java.se.ee@9-ea	jdk.jlink@9-ea
java.security.jgss@9-ea	jdk.jshell@9-ea
java.security.sasl@9-ea	jdk.jsobject@9-ea
java.smartcardio@9-ea	jdk.jstatd@9-ea
java.sql@9-ea	jdk.localedata@9-ea
java.sql.rowset@9-ea	jdk.management@9-ea
java.transaction@9-ea	jdk.management.agent@9-ea
java.xml@9-ea	jdk.naming.dns@9-ea
java.xml.bind@9-ea	jdk.naming.rmi@9-ea
java.xml.crypto@9-ea	jdk.net@9-ea
java.xml.ws@9-ea	jdk.pack@9-ea
java.xml.ws.annotation@9-ea	jdk.packager@9-ea
javafx.base@9-ea	jdk.packager.services@9-ea
javafx.controls@9-ea	jdk.plugin@9-ea
javafx.deploy@9-ea	jdk.plugin.dom@9-ea
javafx.fxml@9-ea	jdk.plugin.server@9-ea
javafx.graphics@9-ea	jdk.policytool@9-ea
javafx.media@9-ea	jdk.rmic@9-ea
javafx.swing@9-ea	jdk.scripting.nashorn@9-ea
javafx.web@9-ea	jdk.scripting.nashorn.shell@9-ea
jdk.accessibility@9-ea	jdk.sctp@9-ea
jdk.attach@9-ea	jdk.security.auth@9-ea
jdk.charsets@9-ea	jdk.security.jgss@9-ea
jdk.compiler@9-ea	jdk.snmp@9-ea
jdk.crypto.cryptoki@9-ea	jdk.unsupported@9-ea
jdk.crypto.ec@9-ea	jdk.xml.bind@9-ea
jdk.crypto.mscapi@9-ea	jdk.xml.dom@9-ea
jdk.deploy@9-ea	jdk.xml.ws@9-ea
jdk.deploy.controlpanel@9-ea	jdk.zipfs@9-ea
jdk.dynalink@9-ea	oracle.desktop@9-ea
jdk.editpad@9-ea	oracle.net@9-ea
jdk.hotspot.agent@9-ea	

Fig. 27.1 | Output of java --list-modules showing the JDK's 95 modules.

JEPs and JSRs of Java Modularity

We discussed what JEPs and JSRs are in the Preface. The Java modularity JEPs and JSRs are shown in Fig. 27.2. We cite these throughout the chapter.

Java Modularity JEPs and JSRs
JEP 200: The Modular JDK (`http://openjdk.java.net/jeps/200`)
JEP 201: Modular Source Code (`http://openjdk.java.net/jeps/201`)
JEP 220: Modular Run-Time Images (`http://openjdk.java.net/jeps/220`)
JEP 260: Encapsulate Most Internal APIs (`http://openjdk.java.net/jeps/260`)
JEP 261: Module System (`http://openjdk.java.net/jeps/261`)
JEP 275: Modular Java Application Packaging (`http://openjdk.java.net/jeps/275`)
JEP 282: `jlink`: The Java Linker (`http://openjdk.java.net/jeps/282`)
JSR 376: Java Platform Module System (`https://www.jcp.org/en/jsr/detail?id=376`)
JSR 379: Java SE 9 (`https://www.jcp.org/en/jsr/detail?id=379`)

Fig. 27.2 | Java Modularity JEPs and JSRs.

Quick Tour of the Chapter

This chapter introduces key modularity concepts you're likely to use when building large-scale systems. Some of the key topics you'll see throughout this chapter include:

- Module declarations—You'll create module declarations that specify a module's dependencies (with the `requires` directive), which packages a module makes available to other modules (with the `exports` directive), services it offers (with the `provides...with` directive), services it consumes (with the `uses` directive) and to what other modules it allows reflection (with the `open` modifier and the `opens` and `opens...to` directives).

- Module-dependency graphs—We'll use the NetBeans IDE's JDK 9 support to create module graphs that help you visualize the dependencies among modules.

- Module resolver—We'll show you the steps the runtime's module resolver performs to ensure that a module's dependencies are fulfilled.

- `jlink` (the Java linker)—You'll use this new JDK 9 tool to create smaller custom runtimes, then use them to execute apps. In fact, many of this book's command-line apps can be executed on a custom runtime consisting only of the most fundamental JDK module—**java.base**—which includes core Java API packages, such as `java.lang`, `java.io` and `java.util`. As you'll see, all modules *implicitly* depend on `java.base`.

- Reflection—*Reflection* enables a Java program to dynamically load types then create objects of those types and use them.[7] These capabilities can still be used, despite Java 9's strong encapsulation, but only with modules that *explicitly* allow it. We'll show how to specify that a module allows reflection with an `open` modifier and the `opens` and `opens...to` directive in a module declaration.

- Migration—The Java platform has been in use for over 20 years, so enormous amounts of non-modularized legacy code will need to be migrated to the modular

---

7. *The Java™ Tutorials*, "Trail: The Reflection API," `https://docs.oracle.com/javase/tutorial/reflect/`.

world of Java 9. Though there are traps and pitfalls due to Java 9's stronger encapsulation, we'll show how the unnamed module and automatic modules can help make migration straightforward. We'll use the `jdeps` tool to determine code dependencies among modules and on pre-Java-9 internal APIs (which are for the most part strongly encapsulated in Java 9). Much pre-Java-9 code will run without modification, but there are some issues that we explain in Section 27.6.

- Services and Service Providers—When you create substantial software systems that fulfill important needs, they can live on for decades. During that time, change is the rule rather than the exception. In Section 10.13, we discussed *tight coupling* and *loose coupling*. It's been proven that *tight coupling* makes it difficult to modify systems. We'll show how to create loosely coupled system components with service-provider interfaces and implementations and the `ServiceLoader` class. We'll also demonstrate the `uses` and `provides...with` directives in module declarations to indicate that a module uses a service or provides a service implementation, respectively.

We'll present the preceding concepts using several larger live-code examples with meaningful outputs, some code snippets, module graphs produced with the NetBeans IDE's **Graph** view of a module declaration and examples of various new commands (like `jlink`) and new options for existing commands (like `javac`, `java` and `jar`). Some additional example-rich sources are:

- Project Jigsaw: Module System Quick-Start Guide—`http://openjdk.java.net/projects/jigsaw/quick-start`

- Mak, Sander, and Paul Bakker. *Java 9 Modularity: Patterns and Practices for Developing Maintainable Applications.* Sebastopol, CA: O'Reilly Media, 2017.

A Terminology Note

The Java Runtime Environment (JRE) includes the Java Virtual Machine (JVM) and other software for executing Java programs. As of Java 9, the JRE is now a proper subset of the Java Development Kit (JDK), which contains all the Java APIs and tools required to create and run Java programs. This chapter uses the terms Java Platform and Java SE Platform synonymously with the JDK.

27.2 Module Declarations

As we mentioned, a module must provide a module descriptor—metadata that specifies the module's dependencies, the packages the module makes available to other modules, and more. A module descriptor is the compiled version of a **module declaration** that's defined in a file named **module-info.java**. Each module declaration begins with the keyword **module**, followed by a unique **module name** and a **module body** enclosed in braces, as in

```
module modulename {
}
```

The module declaration's body can be empty or may contain various **module directives**, including `requires`, `exports`, `provides...with`, `uses` and `opens` (each of which we discuss). As you'll see in Section 27.3.5, compiling the module declaration creates the module descriptor, which is stored in a file named **module-info.class** in the module's root folder. Here we briefly introduce each module directive. You'll see actual module declarations beginning in Section 27.3.3.

27.2.1 requires

A **requires module directive** specifies that this module depends on another module—this relationship is called a **module dependency**. Each module *must* explicitly state its dependencies. When module A `requires` module B, module A is said to **read** module B and module B **is read by** module A. To specify a dependency on another module, use `requires`, as in:

```
requires modulename;
```

Section 27.3.3 demonstrates a `requires` directive.[8]

27.2.2 requires transitive—Implied Readability

To specify a dependency on another module and to ensure that other modules reading your module also read that dependency—known as **implied readability**—use `requires transitive` as in:

```
requires transitive modulename;
```

Consider the following directive from the `java.desktop` module declaration:

```
requires transitive java.xml;
```

In this case, any module that reads `java.desktop` also *implicitly* reads `java.xml`. For example, if a method from the `java.desktop` module returns a type from the `java.xml` module, code in modules that read `java.desktop`, becomes dependent on `java.xml`. Without the `requires transitive` directive in `java.desktop`'s module declaration, such dependent modules will not compile unless they *explicitly* read `java.xml`.

According to JSR 379,[9] Java SE's standard modules *must* grant implied readability in all cases like the one described here. Also, though a Java SE standard module may depend on non-standard modules, it must *not* grant implied readability to them.

Portability Tip 27.1

*Because Java SE standard modules **must not** grant implied readability to non-standard modules, code depending only on Java SE standard modules is portable across Java SE implementations.*

27.2.3 exports and exports...to

An **exports module directive** specifies one of the module's packages whose `public` types (and their nested `public` and `protected` types) should be accessible to code in all other modules. An **exports...to directive** enables you to specify in a comma-separated list precisely which module's or modules' code can access the exported package—this is known as a **qualified export**. Section 27.4 demonstrates the `exports` directive.

---

8. There is also a `requires static` directive to indicate that a module is required at *compile time*, but *optional* at runtime. This is known as an *optional dependency* and is beyond this chapter's scope.
9. Clark, Iris, and Mark Reinhold. "Java SE 9 (JSR 379)." March 6, 2017. `http://cr.openjdk.java.net/~iris/se/9/java-se-9-pr-spec-01/java-se-9-spec.html#s7`.

27.2.4 uses

A **uses module directive** specifies a service used by this module—making the module a **service consumer**. A service is an object of a class that implements the interface or extends the abstract class specified in the uses directive. Section 27.9.3 demonstrates the uses directive.

27.2.5 provides...with

A **provides...with module directive** specifies that a module provides a service implementation—making the module a **service provider**. The provides part of the directive specifies an interface or abstract class listed in a module's uses directive and the with part of the directive specifies the name of the class that implements the interface or extends the abstract class. Section 27.9.6 demonstrates the provides...with directive.

27.2.6 open, opens and opens...to[10,11]

Before Java 9, reflection could be used to learn about all types in a package and all members of a type—even its private members—whether you wanted to allow this capability or not. Thus, nothing was truly encapsulated.

A key motivation of the module system is *strong encapsulation*. By default, a type in a module is not accessible to other modules unless it's a public type *and* you export its package. You expose only the packages you want to expose. With Java 9, this also applies to reflection.

Allowing Runtime-Only Access to a Package
An **opens module directive** of the form

> **opens** *package*

indicates that a specific *package*'s public types (and their nested public and protected types) are accessible to code in other modules at runtime only. Also, all of the types in the specified package (and all of the types' members) are accessible via reflection.

Allowing Runtime-Only Access to a Package By Specific Modules
An **opens...to module directive** of the form

> **opens** *package* **to** *comma-separated-list-of-modules*

indicates that a specific *package*'s public types (and their nested public and protected types) types are accessible to code in the listed module(s) at runtime only. Also, all of the types in the specified package (and all of the types' members) are accessible via reflection to code in the specified modules.

---

10. Buckley, Alex. "JPMS: Modules in the Java Language and JVM." February 23, 2017. http://cr.openjdk.java.net/~mr/jigsaw/spec/lang-vm.html.
11. Gosling, James, Bill Joy, Guy Steele, Gilad Bracha, Alex Buckley, and Dan Smith. "The Java® Language Specification Java SE 9 Edition." Section 7.7.2. February 22, 2017. http://cr.openjdk.java.net/~mr/jigsaw/spec/java-se-9-jls-pr-diffs.pdf.

Allowing Runtime-Only Access to All Packages in a Module

If all the packages in a given module should be accessible at runtime and via reflection to all other modules, you may **open** the entire module, as in

```
open module modulename {
    // module directives
}
```

Reflection Defaults

By default, a module with runtime reflective access to a package can see the package's `public` types (and their nested `public` and `protected` types). However, the code in other modules *can* access *all* types in the exposed package and *all* members within those types, including `private` members. For more information on using reflection to access all of a type's members, visit

```
https://docs.oracle.com/javase/tutorial/reflect/
```

Dependency Injection

Reflection is commonly used with *dependency injection*. One example of this, is an FXML-based JavaFX app, like those you've seen in Chapters 12, 13, 20 and miscellaneous other examples. When an FXML app loads, the controller object and the GUI components on which it *depends* are dynamically created as follows:

- First, because the app *depends* on a controller object that handles the GUI interactions, the `FXMLLoader` *injects* a controller object into the running app—that is, the `FXMLLoader` uses reflection to locate and load the controller class into memory, and to create an object of that class.

- Next, because the controller *depends* on the GUI components declared in FXML, the `FXMLLoader` creates the GUI components objects declared in the FXML and *injects* them into the controller object by assigning each to the controller object's corresponding @FXML instance variable.

Once this process is complete, the controller can interact with the GUI and respond to its events. We'll use the `opens...to` directive in Section 27.7.2 to allow the `FXMLLoader` to use reflection on a JavaFX app in a custom module.

27.2.7 Restricted Keywords

The keywords `exports`, `module`, `open`, `opens`, `provides`, `requires`, `to`, `transitive`, `uses` and `with` are *restricted keywords*. They're keywords only in module declarations and may be used as identifiers anywhere else in your code.

We mentioned in footnote 8 that there is also a `requires static` module directive. Of course, `static` is a regular keyword.

27.3 Modularized Welcome App

In this section, we create a simple `Welcome` app to demonstrate module fundamentals. We'll:

- create a class that resides in a module,
- provide a module declaration,

- compile the module declaration and Welcome class into a module, and

- run the class containing main in that module.

After covering these basics, we'll also demonstrate:

- packaging the Welcome app in a modular JAR file and

- running the app from that JAR file.

27.3.1 Welcome App's Structure

The app we present in this section consists of two .java files—Welcome.java contains the Welcome app class and module-info.java contains the module declaration. By convention, a modularized app has the following folder structure:

> *AppFolder*
>   src
>   *ModuleNameFolder*
>   *PackageFolders*
>   *JavaSourceCodeFiles*
>   module-info.java

For our Welcome app, which will be defined in the package com.deitel.welcome, the folder structure is shown in Fig. 27.3.

Fig. 27.3 | Folder structure for the Welcome app.

The src folder stores all of the app's source code. It contains the module's **root folder**, which has the module's name—com.deitel.welcome (we'll discuss module naming momentarily). The module's root folder contains nested folders representing the package's directory structure—com/deitel/welcome—which corresponds to the package com.deitel.welcome. This folder contains Welcome.java. The module's root folder contains the required module declaration module-info.java.

Module Naming Conventions
Like package names, module names must be *unique*. To ensure *unique* package names, you typically begin the name with your organization's Internet domain name in reverse order. Our domain name is deitel.com, so we begin our package names with com.deitel. By convention, module names also use the reverse-domain-name convention.

At compile time, if multiple modules have the same name, a compilation error occurs. At runtime, if multiple modules have the same name an exception occurs.

This example uses the same name for the module and its contained package, because there is only one package in the module. This is not required, but is a common convention. In a modular app, Java maintains the module names separately from package names and any type names in those packages, so duplicate module and package names *are* allowed.

Modules normally group related packages. As such, the packages will often have commonality among portions of their names. For example, if a module contains the packages

```
com.deitel.sample.firstpackage;
com.deitel.sample.secondpackage;
com.deitel.sample.thirdpackage;
```

you'd typically name the module with the common portion of the package names—com.deitel.sample. If there's no common portion, then you'd choose a name representing the module's purpose. For example, the java.base module contains core packages that are considered fundamental to Java apps (such as java.lang, java.io, java.time and java.util), and the java.sql module contains the packages required for interacting with databases via JDBC (such as java.sql and javax.sql). These are just two of the many standard modules that you saw in Fig. 27.1. The online documentation for each provides a complete list of its exported packages—for the java.base module, visit:

```
http://download.java.net/java/jdk9/docs/api/java.base-summary.html
```

Listing the *java.base* Module's Contents

You can use the java command's --list-modules option to display information from the java.base module's descriptor, including its list of exported packages, as in:

```
java --list-modules java.base
```

Figure 27.4 shows the *portion* of the preceding command's output which lists the java.base module's packages that *any* module can access. You've used several of these packages in the book, including java.io, java.lang, java.math, java.nio, java.time and java.util.

```
exports java.io                      exports java.security.acl
exports java.lang                    exports java.security.cert
exports java.lang.annotation         exports java.security.interfaces
exports java.lang.invoke             exports java.security.spec
exports java.lang.module             exports java.text
exports java.lang.ref                exports java.text.spi
exports java.lang.reflect            exports java.time
exports java.math                    exports java.time.chrono
exports java.net                     exports java.time.format
exports java.net.spi                 exports java.time.temporal
exports java.nio                     exports java.time.zone
exports java.nio.channels            exports java.util
exports java.nio.channels.spi        exports java.util.concurrent
exports java.nio.charset             exports java.util.concurrent.atomic
exports java.nio.charset.spi         exports java.util.concurrent.locks
exports java.nio.file                exports java.util.function
exports java.nio.file.attribute      exports java.util.jar
exports java.nio.file.spi            exports java.util.regex
exports java.security                exports java.util.spi
```

Fig. 27.4 | Partial output of the command java --list-modules java.base. (Part 1 of 2.)

```
exports java.util.stream            exports javax.security.auth
exports java.util.zip               exports javax.security.auth.callback
exports javax.crypto                exports javax.security.auth.login
exports javax.crypto.interfaces     exports javax.security.auth.spi
exports javax.crypto.spec           exports javax.security.auth.x500
exports javax.net                   exports javax.security.cert
exports javax.net.ssl
```

Fig. 27.4 | Partial output of the command java --list-modules java.base. (Part 2 of 2.)

The complete output of the preceding command lists lots of additional information about the java.base module. Figure 27.5 shows some of the remaining output with sample lines from each category of information.

```
...
  uses java.util.spi.CurrencyNameProvider
  uses java.util.spi.ResourceBundleControlProvider
  uses java.util.spi.LocaleNameProvider
...
  provides java.nio.file.spi.FileSystemProvider
    with jdk.internal.jrtfs.JrtFileSystemProvider
...
  exports sun.net.sdp to oracle.net
  exports jdk.internal.jimage to jdk.jlink
  exports sun.net.www.protocol.http.ntlm to jdk.deploy
...
  contains com.sun.crypto.provider
  contains com.sun.java.util.jar.pack
  contains com.sun.net.ssl
...
```

Fig. 27.5 | Partial output of the command java --list-modules java.base showing other categories of information that it displays.

The uses lines, like

```
    uses java.util.spi.CurrencyNameProvider
```

indicate that there are types in the java.base module's packages which use objects that implement various service-provider interfaces. The provides...with

```
    provides java.nio.file.spi.FileSystemProvider
        with jdk.internal.jrtfs.JrtFileSystemProvider
```

indicates that this module's jdk.internal.jrtfs package contains a service-provider implementation class named JrtFileSystemProvider that implements the service-provider interface named FileSystemProvider from package java.nio.file.spi. Section 27.9 shows a substantial example demonstrating that service-provider interfaces and implementations can be used to create *loosely coupled* system components for systems that are easier to develop, maintain and evolve than tightly coupled systems.

The exports...to lines like

```
    exports sun.net.sdp to oracle.net
```

indicate that the java.base module exports a given package (sun.net.sdp) *only to a specified module* (oracle.net). The java.base module has many of these qualified exports. Packages listed in such exports may be read only by the one or more designated modules in the comma-separated list after the keyword to. In the JDK, such qualified exports are used for packages (like sun.net.sdp) containing JDK internal implementations of types that should not be used by developers.

The contains lines, like

```
contains com.sun.crypto.provider
```

specify that the module contains packages that are not exported for use in other modules. Note that contains is not a directive like requires or exports that you can use in your modules. Rather, it's information inserted by the compiler to indicate that a module contains the specified package—the package is not exported for use by other modules. The JVM uses this information to improve performance when it loads classes from those packages at runtime.[12]

27.3.2 Class Welcome

Figure 27.6 presents a Welcome app that simply displays a String at the command line. When defining types that will be placed in modules, every type *must* be placed into a package (line 3).

```
1   // Fig. 27.6: Welcome.java
2   // Welcome class that will be placed in a module
3   package com.deitel.welcome; // all classes in modules must be packaged
4
5   public class Welcome {
6      public static void main(String[] args) {
7         // class System is in package java.lang from the java.base module
8         System.out.println("Welcome to the Java Platform Module System!");
9      }
10  }
```

Fig. 27.6 | Welcome class that will be placed in a module.

27.3.3 module-info.java

Figure 27.7 contains the module declaration for the com.deitel.welcome module. We call modules we create for our own use **application modules**.

```
1   // Fig. 27.7: module-info.java
2   // Module declaration for the com.deitel.welcome module
3   module com.deitel.welcome {
4      requires java.base; // implicit in all modules, so can be omitted
5   }
```

Fig. 27.7 | Module declaration for the com.deitel.welcome module.

---

12. Brian Goetz, e-mail message to authors, March 16, 2017.

Again, the module declaration begins with the keyword `module` followed by the module's name and braces that enclose the declaration's body. This module declaration contains a `requires` module directive, indicating that the app depends on types defined in module `java.base`. Actually, all modules depend on `java.base`, so the `requires` module directive in line 4 is *implicit* in all `module` declarations and may be omitted, as in:

```
module com.deitel.welcome {
}
```

Software Engineering Observation 27.1
Every module implicitly depends on `java.base`. *Writing* `requires java.base;` *in a module declaration is redundant.*

27.3.4 Module-Dependency Graph

Figure 27.8 shows the **module-dependency graph** for `com.deitel.welcome`, indicating that the module reads only the standard module `java.base`. This dependency is indicated in the diagram with the arrow from `com.deitel.welcome` to `java.base`. This graph will be identical regardless of whether you include line 4 in the module declaration.

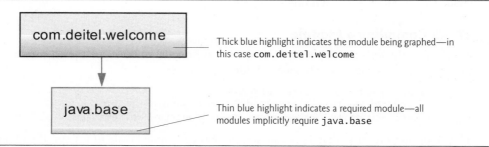

Fig. 27.8 | Module-dependency graph for the `com.deitel.welcome` module.

A module-dependency graph shows dependencies among **observable modules**[13]—that is, the built-in standard modules and any additional modules required by a given app or library module. The graph's *nodes* are modules and their *dependencies* are represented by directed edges (arrows) that connect the nodes. Some edges represent **explicit dependencies** on modules explicitly specified in a module declaration's `requires` clauses (as you'll see in Fig. 27.14). Some edges represent **implicit dependencies** in which one of the required modules in turn depends on other modules (as you'll see in Fig. 27.22). In Fig. 27.8, `java.base` is shown as an explicit dependency, because all modules depend on it.

This graph was produced with an early access version of NetBeans that has JDK 9 support—again, you can learn about this version of the IDE and download its installer from:

```
http://wiki.netbeans.org/JDK9Support
```

In a NetBeans project, when you open a module's `module-info.java` file, you can choose between the **Source** code and **Graph** views. In **Graph** view, NetBeans creates a module-de-

---

13. Bateman, Alan, Alex Buckley, Jonathan Gibbons and Mark Reinhold. "JEP 261: Module System." `http://openjdk.java.net/jeps/261`.

pendency- graph, based on the module declaration. When NetBeans graphs a module, it also graphs that module's dependencies, including the implicit dependency on java.base. Figure 27.8 shows that java.base itself does not have any dependencies.

To create this graph in NetBeans, we performed the following steps:

1. First, we created a WelcomeApp project containing the com.deitel.welcome package.

2. Next, we added the com.deitel.welcome module's module-info.java file by right-clicking the project, selecting **New > Other...**, selecting **Java Module Info** from the **Java** category of the dialog, then clicking **Next >** and **Finish**. The file is added to the project's default package automatically.

3. Finally, we opened module-info.java file, changed the module name from the default provided by NetBeans (the project name) to com.deitel.welcome and switched to **Graph** view.

You can arrange the nodes in NetBeans by dragging them or by right clicking the graph and selecting from various **Layout** options—we chose **Hierarchical**, in which the given module appears at the top and arrows point down to the module's dependencies. You may use **Zoom To Fit** to make the graph fill the available space in the window and **Export As Image** to save an image containing the graph.

27.3.5 Compiling a Module

To compile the Welcome app's module, open a command window, use the cd command to change to this chapter's WelcomeApp folder, then type:

```
javac -d mods/com.deitel.welcome ^
    src/com.deitel.welcome/module-info.java ^
    src/com.deitel.welcome/com/deitel/welcome/Welcome.java
```

The -d option indicates that javac should place the compiled code in the specified folder—in this case a mods folder that will contain a subfolder named com.deitel.welcome representing the compiled module. The name mods is used by convention for a folder that contains modules.

Note Regarding Lengthy Commands in This Chapter

For clarity, we split the preceding command into multiple lines, using line-continuation characters. Many of the commands we use in this chapter's examples are lengthy. This chapter shows the commands in Windows format, with the caret (^) line-continuation character. Linux and macOS users should replace the carets in the commands with the backslash (\) line-continuation character. You can also enter such lengthy commands as a single command without the line continuations.

Welcome App's Folder Structure After Compilation

If the code compiles correctly, the WelcomeApp folder's mods subfolder structure contains the compiled code (Fig. 27.9). This is known as the **exploded-module folder**, because the folders and .class files are not in a JAR (Java archive) file—collection of directories and files compressed into a single file, known as an archive. The exploded module's structure parallels that of the app's src folder described previously. We'll package the app as a JAR shortly. Exploded module folders and modular JAR files (Section 27.3.7) together are **module artifacts**. These can be placed on the **module path**—a list of module artifact locations—when compiling and executing modularized code.[14],[15]

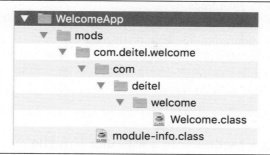

Fig. 27.9 | Welcome app's mods folder structure.

Listing the `com.deitel.welcome` Module's Contents
You can use the java command's `--list-modules` option to display information from the `com.deitel.welcome` module descriptor, as in:

```
java --module-path mods --list-modules com.deitel.welcome
```

The resulting output:

```
module com.deitel.welcome (file:///C:/examples/ch36/WelcomeApp/
mods/com.deitel.welcome/)
   requires java.base (@9-ea)
   contains com
   contains com.deitel
   contains com.deitel.welcome
```

shows that the module `requires` the standard module `java.base` and `contains` the packages `com`, `com.deitel` and `com.deitel.welcome` (each folder is viewed as a package). Though the module `contains` these packages, they are *not* exported. Therefore, its contents *cannot* be used by other modules. The module declaration for this example *explicitly* required `java.base` and the preceding listing included

```
requires java.base
```

If the module declaration had *implicitly* required `java.base`, then the listing instead would have included

```
requires mandated java.base
```

There is no `requires mandated` module directive—it is simply included in the `--list-modules` output to indicate the implicit dependence on `java.base`.

---

14. Reinhold, Mark. "The State of the Module System." March 8, 2016. http://openjdk.java.net/projects/jigsaw/spec/sotms/#module-artifacts.
15. Bateman, Alan, Alex Buckley, Jonathan Gibbons and Mark Reinhold. "JEP 261: Module System." http://openjdk.java.net/jeps/261.

27.3.6 Running an App from a Module's Exploded Folders

To run the Welcome app from the module's exploded folders, use the following command (again, from the WelcomeApp folder):

```
java --module-path mods ^
    --module com.deitel.welcome/com.deitel.welcome.Welcome
```

The **--module-path** option specifies the module path—in this case, the mods folder. The **--module** option specifies the module name and the fully qualified class name of the app's entry point—that is, a class containing main. The program executes and displays:

```
Welcome to the Java Platform Module System!
```

In the preceding command, --module-path can be abbreviated as -p and --module as -m.

27.3.7 Packaging a Module into a Modular JAR File

You can use the jar command to package an exploded module folder as a **modular JAR file**[16] that contains all of the module's files, including its module-info.class file, which is placed in the JAR's root folder. When running the app, you specify the JAR file on the module path. The folder in which you wish to output the JAR file must exist before running the jar command.

If a module contains an app's entry point, you can specify that class with the jar command's **--main-class** option, as in:

```
jar --create -f jars/com.deitel.welcome.jar ^
    --main-class com.deitel.welcome.Welcome ^
    -C mods/com.deitel.welcome .
```

The options are as follows:

- --create specifies that the command should create a new JAR file.

- -f specifies the name of the JAR file and is followed by the name—in this case, the file com.deitel.welcome.jar will be created in the folder named jars.

- --main-class specifies the fully qualified name of the app's entry point—a class that contains a main method.

- -C specifies which folder contains the files that should be included in the JAR file and is followed by the files to include—the dot (.) indicates that all files in the folder should be included.

You can simplify the -create, -f and --main-class options in the preceding command with the shorthand notation -cfe, followed by the JAR file name and main class, as in:

```
jar -cfe jars/com.deitel.welcome.jar ^
    com.deitel.welcome.Welcome ^
    -C mods/com.deitel.welcome .
```

---

16. Bateman, Alan, Alex Buckley, Jonathan Gibbons and Mark Reinhold. "JEP 261: Module System." http://openjdk.java.net/jeps/261.

27.3.8 Running the Welcome App from a Modular JAR File

Once you place an app in a modular JAR file for which you've specified the entry point, you can execute the app as follows:

```
java --module-path jars -m com.deitel.welcome
```

or

```
java -p jars -m com.deitel.welcome
```

The program executes and displays:

```
Welcome to the Java Platform Module System!
```

If you did not specify the entry point when creating the JAR, you may still run the app by specifying the module name and fully qualified class name, as in:

```
java --module-path jars ^
    -m com.deitel.welcome/com.deitel.welcome.Welcome
```

or

```
java -p jars -m com.deitel.welcome/com.deitel.welcome.Welcome
```

27.3.9 Aside: Classpath vs. Module Path

Before Java 9, the compiler and runtime located types via the *classpath*—a list of folders and library archive files containing compiled Java classes. In earlier Java versions, the classpath was defined by a combination of a CLASSPATH environment variable, extensions placed in a special folder of the JRE, and options provided to the javac and java commands.

Because types could be loaded from several different locations, the order in which those locations were searched resulted in brittle apps. For example, many years ago, one of the authors installed a Java app from a third-party vendor on his system. The app's installer placed an old version of a Java library into the JRE's extensions folder. Several Java apps on his system depended on a newer version of that library with additional types and enhanced versions of the library's older types. Because classes in the JRE's extensions folder were loaded *before* other classes on the classpath,[17] the apps that depended on the newer library version stopped working, failing at runtime with NoClassDefFoundErrors and NoSuchMethodErrors—sometimes long after the apps began executing.

The reliable configuration provided by modules and module descriptors helps eliminate many such runtime classpath problems. Every module explicitly states its dependencies and these are resolved *as an app launches*. In Section 27.8.5, we'll show the steps that the JRE's *module resolver* performs at launch time.

Common Programming Error 27.1

The module path may contain only one of each module and every package may be defined in only one module. If two or more modules have the same name or export the same packages, the runtime immediately terminates before running the program.

---

17. "Understanding Extension Class Loading." https://docs.oracle.com/javase/tutorial/ext/basics/load.html.

27.4 Creating and Using a Custom Module

To demonstrate a module that depends on another custom module in addition to standard modules, let's reorganize one of the book's earlier, non-modularized examples. We'll declare Section 8.2's Time1 and Time1Test classes in separate modules, then use class Time1 from the module containing Time1Test. As you'll see, we'll *export* class Time1's package from one module and *require* Time1's enclosing module from a module containing the Time1Test class. Figure 27.10 shows the src folder structure for the app's two modules.

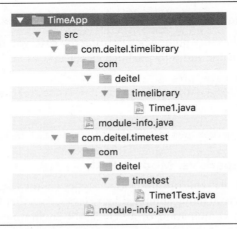

Fig. 27.10 | TimeApp example's src folder structure.

27.4.1 Exporting a Package for Use in Other Modules

As you learned previously, every class that you wish to place in a module *must* be declared in a package. For this reason, we added the package statement in line 3 (Fig. 27.11) to class Time1 (which was originally declared in Fig. 8.1).

```
1   // Fig. 27.11: Time1.java
2   // Class Time1 that will be placed in a module.
3   package com.deitel.timelibrary;
4
5   public class Time1 {
6       private int hour; // 0 - 23
7       private int minute; // 0 - 59
8       private int second; // 0 - 59
9
10      // set a new time value using universal time; throw an
11      // exception if the hour, minute or second is invalid
12      public void setTime(int hour, int minute, int second) {
13          // validate hour, minute and second
14          if (hour < 0 || hour >= 24 || minute < 0 || minute >= 60 ||
15              second < 0 || second >= 60) {
```

Fig. 27.11 | Class Time1 that will be placed in a module. (Part 1 of 2.)

```
16                 throw new IllegalArgumentException(
17                     "hour, minute and/or second was out of range");
18             }
19
20         this.hour = hour;
21         this.minute = minute;
22         this.second = second;
23     }
24
25     // convert to String in universal-time format (HH:MM:SS)
26     public String toUniversalString() {
27         return String.format("%02d:%02d:%02d", hour, minute, second);
28     }
29
30     // convert to String in standard-time format (H:MM:SS AM or PM)
31     public String toString() {
32         return String.format("%d:%02d:%02d %s",
33             ((hour == 0 || hour == 12) ? 12 : hour % 12),
34             minute, second, (hour < 12 ? "AM" : "PM"));
35     }
36 }
```

Fig. 27.11 | Class Time1 that will be placed in a module. (Part 2 of 2.)

com.deitel.timelibrary *Module Declaration*

After placing Time1 in a package, we must declare the module via a module declaration (Fig. 27.12). Line 4 indicates that the module com.deitel.timelibrary exports the package com.deitel.timelibrary. Now the package's public classes (in this case, just class Time1) can be used by *any* module that reads the com.deitel.timelibrary module, provided that the module can be found on the module path, as you'll see in Section 27.4.3.

```
1  // Fig. 27.12: module-info.java
2  // Module declaration for the com.deitel.timelibrary module
3  module com.deitel.timelibrary {
4      exports com.deitel.timelibrary; // package available to other modules
5  }
```

Fig. 27.12 | Module declaration for the com.deitel.timelibrary module.

27.4.2 Using a Class from a Package in Another Module

The app's entry point—class Time1Test (which was originally declared in Fig. 8.2)—also must be packaged for placement in a module (line 3 of Fig. 27.13). In addition, class Time1Test manipulates an object of class Time1, which is declared in a package of another module. For this reason, we import Time1 in line 5.

```
1  // Fig. 27.13: Time1Test.java
2  // Time1 object used in an app.
3  package com.deitel.timetest;
```

Fig. 27.13 | Time1 object used in an app. (Part 1 of 2.)

```
4
5    import com.deitel.timelibrary.Time1;
6
7    public class Time1Test {
8       public static void main(String[] args) {
9          // create and initialize a Time1 object
10         Time1 time = new Time1(); // invokes Time1 constructor
11
12         // output string representations of the time
13         displayTime("After time object is created", time);
14         System.out.println();
15
16         // change time and output updated time
17         time.setTime(13, 27, 6);
18         displayTime("After calling setTime", time);
19         System.out.println();
20
21         // attempt to set time with invalid values
22         try {
23            time.setTime(99, 99, 99); // all values out of range
24         }
25         catch (IllegalArgumentException e) {
26            System.out.printf("Exception: %s%n%n", e.getMessage());
27         }
28
29         // display time after attempt to set invalid values
30         displayTime("After calling setTime with invalid values", time);
31      }
32
33      // displays a Time1 object in 24-hour and 12-hour formats
34      private static void displayTime(String header, Time1 t) {
35         System.out.printf("%s%nUniversal time: %s%nStandard time: %s%n",
36            header, t.toUniversalString(), t.toString());
37      }
38   }
```

Fig. 27.13 | Time1 object used in an app. (Part 2 of 2.)

com.deitel.timetest *Module Declaration*

Because class Time1 is located in a package of the com.deitel.timelibrary module, the module containing class Time1Test (com.deitel.timetest) must declare its dependency on that other module. The module declaration (Fig. 27.14) indicates this dependency with the requires directive (line 4). Without this *and* the exports directive in Fig. 27.12, class Time1Test would not be able to import and use class Time1.

```
1    // Fig. 27.14: module-info.java
2    // Module declaration for the com.deitel.timetest module
3    module com.deitel.timetest {
4       requires com.deitel.timelibrary;
5    }
```

Fig. 27.14 | Module declaration for the com.deitel.timetest module.

com.deitel.timetest *Module-dependency Graph*

Figure 27.15 shows the Time1Test app's module-dependency graph indicating that:

- the module named com.deitel.timetest reads com.deitel.timelibrary and the standard module java.base, and

- the module named com.deitel.timelibrary reads the module java.base.

To create this graph in NetBeans, we performed the following steps:

1. Created a TimeLibrary project containing the com.deitel.timelibrary package and com.deitel.timelibrary's module-info.java file.

2. Created a TimeApp project containing the com.deitel.timetest package and com.deitel.timetest's module-info.java file.

3. Right clicked the TimeApp project's **Libraries** node and selected **Add Project...**, then selected the TimeLibrary project and clicked **Add Project JAR Files**—this adds the TimeLibrary project's modular JAR file to the TimeApp project.

4. Finally, we opened the TimeApp project's module-info.java file in **Graph** view.

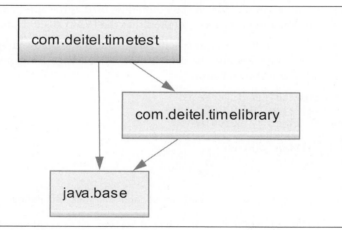

Fig. 27.15 | Module-dependency graph for the com.deitel.timetest module.

27.4.3 Compiling and Running the Example

You must compile both modules before running this app. The com.deitel.timelibrary module must be compiled first, because com.deitel.timetest depends on it. IDEs and other build tools (like Ant, Gradle and Maven) typically can deal with order-of-compilation issues like this for you.

Compiling Module com.deitel.timelibrary

To compile the com.deitel.timelibrary module, open a command window, use the cd command to change to this chapter's TimeApp folder on your system, then type:

```
javac -d mods/com.deitel.timelibrary ∧
    src/com.deitel.timelibrary/module-info.java ∧
    src/com.deitel.timelibrary/com/deitel/timelibrary/Time1.java
```

Compiling Module `com.deitel.timetest`

Next, to compile the `com.deitel.timetest` module, type:

```
javac --module-path mods -d mods/com.deitel.timetest ^
    src/com.deitel.timetest/module-info.java ^
    src/com.deitel.timetest/com/deitel/timetest/Time1Test.java
```

Here we added the option `--module-path` to indicate that the `mods` folder contains modules on which the `com.deitel.timetest` module depends—in this case, we previously compiled the `com.deitel.timelibrary` module into the `mods` folder.

Running the Example

Finally, to run this example, type:

```
java --module-path mods ^
    -m com.deitel.timetest/com.deitel.timetest.Time1Test
```

In this command:

- the option `--module-path` indicates where the app's modules are located, and
- the option `-m` specifies which class should be used as the app's entry point—that is, a class containing the `main` method that the JVM calls to launch the app.

For the `main` class, note that you must specify its module name followed by a slash and its fully qualified class name, because the class is now in a package contained in a module. The program's output is shown below:

```
After time object is created
Universal time: 00:00:00
Standard time: 12:00:00 AM

After calling setTime
Universal time: 13:27:06
Standard time: 1:27:06 PM

Exception: hour, minute and/or second was out of range

After calling setTime with invalid values
Universal time: 13:27:06
Standard time: 1:27:06 PM
```

27.4.4 Packaging the App into Modular JAR Files

In this section, we'll package each app into a modular JAR file then run the app. To package `com.deitel.timelibrary` into a modular JAR file, type:

```
jar --create -f jars/com.deitel.timelibrary.jar ^
    -C mods/com.deitel.timelibrary .
```

To package `com.deitel.timetest` into a modular JAR file, type:

```
jar --create -f jars/com.deitel.timetest.jar ^
    --main-class com.deitel.timetest.Time1Test ^
    -C mods/com.deitel.timetest .
```

Running the App from a Modular JAR File

Once you place an app in a modular JAR file for which you've specified the main class, you can execute the app as follows:

```
java --module-path jars -m com.deitel.timetest
```

The program executes and displays the same output shown in Section 27.4.3.

27.4.5 Strong Encapsulation and Accessibility

Before Java 9, you could use any public class that you imported into your code. Whether you could access the class's members was determined by how they were declared—public, protected, package access or private (as described in Chapters 3–8). Due to Java 9's **strong encapsulation** in modules, public types in a module are no longer *accessible* to your code by default—so public no longer means available to all:

- If a module exports a package, the public types in that package are accessible by *any* module that reads the package's module.

- If a module exports a package to a specific module (via exports...to), the public types in that package are accessible *only* to the specific module and only if that module *reads* the package's module.

- If a module does not export a package, the public types in that package are accessible *only* within their enclosing module.

Once you have access to a type in another module, then the normal rules of public, protected, package access and private apply.

Compilation Error When Attempting to Use an Inaccessible Type

The project TimeAppMissingExports in this chapter's ExamplesShowingErrors folder demonstrates that *explicitly named modules* have *strong encapsulation* and do not export packages unless you *explicitly* list them in exports directives. In this project, we removed the exports directive from the com.deitel.timelibrary's module declaration, then recompiled the module. Next, we tried to recompile the com.deitel.timetest module. The compiler produced the following error message, which indicates that the package com.deitel.timelibrary is not exported and thus is inaccessible:

```
src\com.deitel.timetest\com\deitel\timetest\Time1Test.java:5:
error: package com.deitel.timelibrary is not visible
import com.deitel.timelibrary.Time1;
              ^
  (package com.deitel.timelibrary is declared in module
com.deitel.timelibrary, which is not in the module graph)
1 error
```

Common Programming Error 27.2

When a requires dependency is not fulfilled by an exports clause in another module a compilation error occurs.

27.5 Module-Dependency Graphs: A Deeper Look

Previously, we've shown two module-dependency graphs. Here we continue our discussion of module graphs and show the errors that occur if a module directly or indirectly `requires` itself—known as a cycle.

27.5.1 `java.sql`

Figure 27.16 shows the module-dependency graph for a module named `modulegraphtest` that depends on the `java.sql` module, per the following module declaration:

```
module modulegraphtest {
    requires java.sql;
}
```

NetBeans highlights the module declared by the module declaration (`modulegraphtest`) with a thick blue line. It also highlights `java.sql`, because it's *explicitly* listed in a `requires` directive and `java.base`, because it's implicitly required by all modules. The other modules shown (`java.xml` and `java.logging`) are included in the graph, because `java.sql` depends on them.

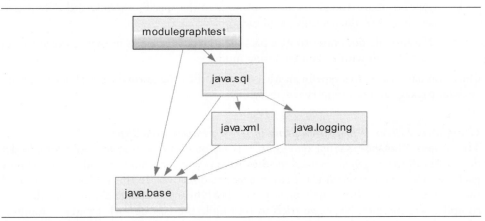

Fig. 27.16 | Dependency graph for a module that depends on `java.sql`.

27.5.2 `java.se`

Figure 27.17 shows the significantly more complex **java.se** module's dependency graph—this is an **aggregator module** that specifies via `requires transitive` all the modules necessary to support Java SE 9 apps. To produce this graph, we first downloaded the JDK 9 source code, as described at

```
http://hg.openjdk.java.net/jdk9/jdk9/raw-file/tip/common/doc/
    building.html
```

We then opened the java.se module's declaration (located in the source-code folder's jdk/src/java.se/share/classes folder) in NetBeans **Graph** view. We rotated the graph 90° for readability. There is also a **java.se.ee** aggregator module, which includes everything in the java.se module and additional Java SE modules with packages that overlap with the Java Enterprise Edition (EE) Platform.

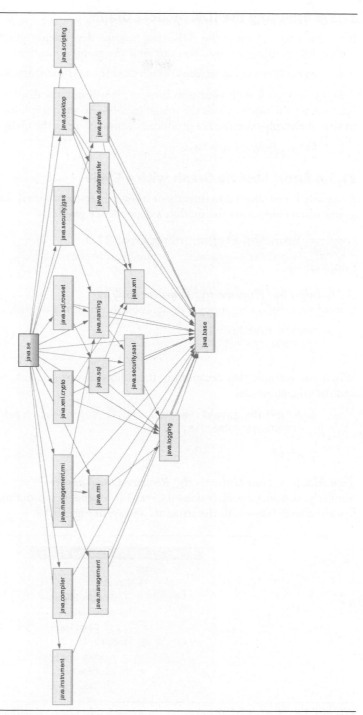

Fig. 27.17 | `java.se` module-dependency graph.

27.5.3 Browsing the JDK Module Graph

It's interesting to look at the JDK's full module-dependency graph. This is the largest of the module graphs we show. You can view the graph on our website at:

```
http://deitel.com/bookresources/jhtp11/ModularJDKGraph.png
```

When you open it with your web browser, it will initially display the complete image in the browser's window. Click the image to zoom in, then scroll horizontally and vertically to view the graph's details. We produced this image using the Graphviz tool available from

```
http://www.graphviz.org/
```

27.5.4 Error: Module Graph with a Cycle

A module is not allowed to directly or indirectly reference itself. Doing so would result in a *cycle* when computing the module's dependency graph.

> **Common Programming Error 27.3**
> *A compilation error occurs if a module graph contains a cycle.*

A Module That (Incorrectly) Requires Itself
Consider the following module declaration in which the module requires itself:

```
module mymodule {
    requires mymodule;
}
```

When you compile this declaration, the following error occurs, indicating a cycle in the module's dependencies:

```
module-info.java:2: error: cyclic dependence involving mymodule
    requires mymodule;
             ^
1 error
```

Two Modules That (Incorrectly) Require One Another
Similarly, consider a project named CircularDependency containing two modules—module1 and module2—with the structure shown in Fig. 27.18.

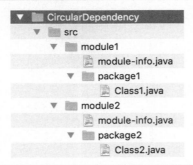

Fig. 27.18 | CircularDependency example's src folder structure.

If the module declarations for these two modules indicate that each module `requires` the other, as in

```
module module1 {
    exports package1;
    requires module2;
}
```

and

```
module module2 {
    exports package2;
    requires module1;
}
```

then, when you compile these modules

```
javac --module-source-path src ^
    --module-path mods -d mods ^
    src/module1/module-info.java ^
    src/module1/package1/Class1.java ^
    src/module2/module-info.java ^
    src/module2/package2/Class2.java
```

the compiler again issues an error indicating a cycle in the module dependencies:

```
src\module1\module-info.java:9: error: cyclic dependence involving
module2
    requires module2;
             ^
1 error
```

Modules in a Cycle Are Really "One Thing"

Ultimately all the modules in a cycle are really one module—not separate modules.[18] While we were writing this chapter, a friend of ours who works for a large organization told us that his group is preparing for Java 9 modularity. He indicated that they have multiple large pre-Java-9 JAR files. Initially they thought they'd make each JAR a separate module, but their JARs turned out to be so interdependent that they've decided to combine them into a single module. This kind of interdependency is what leads to cycles in your design. Ideally, when you modularize a previously monolithic system, you want to break that system into separate modules that are easier to maintain and secure. This can pose significant refactoring challenges in large code bases.

27.6 Migrating Code to Java 9

Many pre-Java-9 apps will run unaltered on Java 9. In fact, as we prepared this book, we tested every app using JDK 9 and they all compiled and ran without issue. In Java 9, all programs are compiled and executed using the module system. Java 9 strongly encapsulates types that are not exported by modules, so it's possible that some apps will fail to compile because types that were accessible to them prior to Java 9 no longer are. For example, there are many pre-Java-9 **internal APIs** that were not meant for use outside the JDK, but were in fact used outside the JDK—many of these are not exported in Java 9 and thus are

---

18. Alex Buckley, e-mail message to authors, March 24, 2017.

inaccessible.[19] If your code uses such internal APIs directly or indirectly, it will fail to compile.

Some internal APIs considered critically important are still available in Java 9. Various JEPs referenced by JSR 379[20] define new public APIs that replace these internal APIs. These internal APIs will eventually be removed.

Software Engineering Observation 27.2

Modularity enables strong encapsulation. Code that is not exported cannot be accessed by other modules.

Error-Prevention Tip 27.1

You can use the jdeps tool (Section 27.6.3) released with Java 8 to locate a type's dependencies or the dependencies for all types in a JAR file. In Java 9, the tool also supports modules. The jdeps option --jdk-internals specifically identifies uses of JDK internal APIs in code. Some pre-Java-9 internal APIs have been placed into packages that are exported in Java 9 and some are now strongly encapsulated. For each internal API that jdeps locates, you can review JEP 260 and update your code accordingly.

Common Programming Error 27.4

JDK 9 hides most pre-Java-9 internal APIs, so pre-Java-9 code that uses them will not compile and run on Java 9.

Java is more than two decades old so there's vast amounts of legacy Java code to migrate to Java 9. The module system provides mechanisms that can automatically place your code in modules to help you with migration.

27.6.1 Unnamed Module

In Java 9, all code is required to be placed in modules. When you execute code that's not in a module, the code is loaded from the *classpath* and placed in the **unnamed module**. This is why we can run some non-modularized code in the modularized JDK, but unfortunately without the benefits of modularization.

The unnamed module:

- *implicitly* exports all of its packages, and
- *implicitly reads* all other modules.

However, because the module is *unnamed*, there's no way to refer to it in a requires directive from a named module, so a named module cannot depend on the unnamed module.

27.6.2 Automatic Modules

There are enormous numbers of preexisting libraries that you can use in your apps. Many of these are not yet modularized. However, to facilitate migration, you can add *any* library's JAR file to an app's module path, then use the packages in that JAR. When you do, the JAR file implicitly becomes an **automatic module** and can be specified in a module

---

19. Reinhold, Mark. "JEP 260: Encapsulate Most Internal APIs." http://openjdk.java.net/jeps/260.
20. Clark, Iris, and Mark Reinhold. "Java SE 9 (JSR 379)." March 6, 2017. http://cr.openjdk.java.net/~iris/se/9/java-se-9-pr-spec-01/java-se-9-spec.html.

declaration's `requires` directives. The JAR's file name—minus the `.jar` extension—becomes its module name, which *must be a valid Java identifier* for use in a `requires` directive. Also, an automatic module:

- *implicitly* `exports` all of its packages—so, any module that reads the automatic module (including the unnamed module) has access to the `public` types in the automatic module's packages.
- *implicitly reads* (`requires`) all other modules, including other automatic modules and the unnamed module—so, an automatic module has access to all the `public` types exposed by the system's other modules.

We demonstrate an automatic module in Section 27.7.

27.6.3 jdeps: Java Dependency Analysis

Another tool to help you migrate your code to Java 9 is the **jdeps command**, which was introduced in Java 8 to help you determine a type's *class* and *package* dependencies. A key use of `jdeps` is to locate dependencies on pre-Java-9 internal APIs that are now strongly encapsulated in Java 9. To determine whether a class has any such dependencies, use the following command on your compiled pre-Java-9 code:

```
jdeps --jdk-internals YourClassName.class
```

or if you have many classes in a JAR file, use:

```
jdeps --jdk-internals YourJARName.jar
```

If this command produces no output, then your class or set of classes does not have any dependence on JDK internal APIs that are no longer accessible.

Error-Prevention Tip 27.2

Check every pre-Java-9 compiled class/JAR file with the `jdeps` *command to ensure that your code does not depend on JDK internal APIs.*

Determining the Modules You Need

Java 9 adds the ability to discover *module* dependencies in Java 9 code. When you're preparing to create *custom* runtimes, you also can use `jdeps` to determine your app's dependencies, so you know which modules to include. For example, this chapter's `Welcome` app depends only on `java.base`. We can confirm that by executing the following command from the `WelcomeApp` folder, which checks the `com.deitel.welcome` module's dependencies:

```
jdeps --module-path jars -m com.deitel.welcome
```

This produces the following output, showing the packages and modules the app uses:

```
com.deitel.welcome
 [file:///C:/examples/ch36/WelcomeApp/jars/com.deitel.welcome.jar]
   requires java.base (@9-ea)
com.deitel.welcome -> java.base
   com.deitel.welcome      -> java.io       java.base
   com.deitel.welcome      -> java.lang     java.base
```

The output shows that our module com.deitel.welcome depends on the java.base module, and that our module specifically uses types from the java.base module's java.io and java.lang packages.

The preceding command may also be written as

```
jdeps jars/com.deitel.welcome.jar
```

In addition, you can use jdeps on a specific .class file, as in:

```
jdeps mods/com.deitel.welcome/com/deitel/welcome/Welcome.class
```

which produces

```
Welcome.class -> java.base
    com.deitel.welcome      -> java.io      java.base
    com.deitel.welcome      -> java.lang    java.base
```

Verbose jdeps Output

If you'd like more details, you can specify the -v (verbose) option as in:

```
jdeps -v jars/com.deitel.welcome.jar
```

which produces:

```
com.deitel.welcome
 [file:///C:/examples/ch36/WelcomeApp/jars/com.deitel.welcome.jar]
    requires java.base (@9-ea)
com.deitel.welcome -> java.base
    com.deitel.welcome.Welcome    -> java.io.PrintStream    java.base
    com.deitel.welcome.Welcome    -> java.lang.Object       java.base
    com.deitel.welcome.Welcome    -> java.lang.String       java.base
    com.deitel.welcome.Welcome    -> java.lang.System       java.base
```

showing precisely which packages, types and modules the app uses. Knowing that the app requires only java.base, we can then use jlink to create a custom runtime containing only that module, which we'll do in Section 27.8.

Using jdeps to Produce DOT Files for Graphing Tools

You can use graphing tools—such as Graphviz (www.graphviz.org) and its web-based version (www.webgraphviz.com)—to produce module-dependency graphs using the DOT graph description language,[21] which specifies a graph's nodes and edges. The jdeps tool can create DOT (.dot) files with the --dot-output option as in:

```
jdeps --dot-output . jars/com.deitel.welcome.jar
```

which produces two .dot files in the current folder (.):

- summary.dot—the description of module com.deitel.welcome's dependencies.
- com.deitel.welcome.dot—the description of module com.deitel.welcome's specific package dependencies.

Figure 27.19 shows the graph we produced by opening summary.dot in a text editor, then copying and pasting its contents

---

21. https://en.wikipedia.org/wiki/DOT_(graph_description_language).

```
digraph "summary" {
  "com.deitel.welcome" -> "java.base (java.base)";
}
```

into the textbox at `webgraphviz.com` and clicking **Generate Graph**.[22]

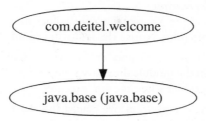

Fig. 27.19 | `Webgraphviz.com` graph based on `summary.dot`

Additional *jdeps* Options

For a complete list of `jdeps` options, visit

```
http://download.java.net/java/jdk9/docs/technotes/tools/windows/
    jdeps.html
```

for Windows or visit

```
http://download.java.net/java/jdk9/docs/technotes/tools/unix/
    jdeps.html
```

for macOS and Linux.

27.7 Resources in Modules; Using an Automatic Module

When the types in a module require resources—such images, videos, XML documents and more—those resources should be packaged with the module to ensure that they're available when the module's types are used at execution time. This is known as **resource encapsulation**.[23] In this section, we'll migrate our non-modularized JavaFX `VideoPlayer` example from Section 20.6 into a module that also encapsulates the app's resources—the FXML file that describes the GUI and its video file that will be loaded and played at execution time. By convention, resources typically are placed in a folder named `res`.

Recall that the original `VideoPlayer` example consisted of the following files all in Chapter 20's `VideoPlayer` folder:

- `VideoPlayer.xml`—The FXML file that describes the app's GUI.

- `VideoPlayer.java`—The `Application` subclass that begins the app's execution.

- `VideoPlayerController.java`—The controller class that responds to the GUIs events and loads the video.

---

22. The `.dot` extension is also used by Microsoft Word document templates. On systems with Microsoft Word installed, open the `jdeps`-produced `.dot` files directly from a text editor.

23. "Java Platform Module System Requirements." `http://openjdk.java.net/projects/jigsaw/spec/reqs/#resource-encapsulation`

- sts117.mp4—The NASA video[24] that the app loads and plays.

- controlsfx-8.40.12—The ControlsFX library containing the dialog class ExceptionDialog. We display an ExceptionDialog if the MediaPlayer encounters any errors.

Reorganizing for Modularization

For the purpose of this example, we reorganized the files into the folder structure shown in Fig. 27.20 to support modules. Notice the following about the structure:

- The files VideoPlayer.fxml and sts117.mp4, which are not Java source code files, are located in the module directory's res folder. These files will be read from the module's res folder when the app executes.

- As required for modularization, we placed the classes VideoPlayer and Video-PlayerController in a package—the folder structure com/deitel/videoplayer corresponds to the package com.deitel.videoplayer.

- As required, we created a module-info.java file in the module's root folder.

In addition, we renamed controlsfx-8.40.12.jar to controlsfx.jar and placed it directly in the VideoPlayer folder's mods subfolder.

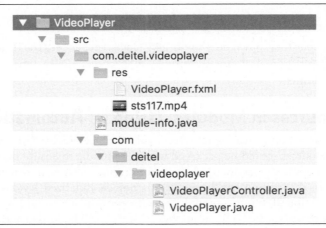

Fig. 27.20 | Modularized VideoPlayer src folder structure.

27.7.1 Automatic Modules

The ControlsFX library we used when developing the VideoPlayer in Section 20.6 was not designed to be a Java module. However, you can add *any* library's JAR file to an app's module path, then use the packages in that JAR. When you do, the JAR file implicitly becomes an **automatic module** and can be specified in a module declaration's requires directives. The JAR's file name—minus the .jar extension—becomes its module name, which *must be a valid Java identifier* for use in a requires directive. This is why we renamed the JAR by removing -8.40.12 from the original filename. Also, an automatic module:

---

24. For NASA's terms of use, visit http://www.nasa.gov/multimedia/guidelines/.

- *implicitly* exports all of its packages—so, any module that reads the automatic module has access to the public types in the automatic module's packages.
- *implicitly reads* all other modules in the app, including other automatic modules—so, an automatic module has access to all the public types exposed by the system's other modules.

Code Changes for Modularization
We made the following code changes:

- VideoPlayer.fxml—We modified the controller class's name to use its fully qualified name com.deitel.videoplayer.VideoPlayerController so that the FXMLLoader can find the controller class.
- VideoPlayer.java—We changed the name of the FXML file to load from "VideoPlayer.fxml" to "/res/VideoPlayer.fxml", which indicates that the FXML file is located in the module's res folder. We also added the package statement

  package com.deitel.videoplayer;

- VideoPlayerController.java—We modified the name of the video file from "sts117.mp4" to "/res/sts117.mp4", which indicates that the video file is located in the module's res folder. We also added the package statement

  package com.deitel.videoplayer;

The rest of the code is identical to what we presented in Section 20.6.

27.7.2 Requiring Multiple Modules

The com.deitel.videoplayer module declaration (Fig. 27.21) indicates that the module requires javafx.controls, javafx.fxml, javafx.media and controlsfx (the automatic module discussed in Section 27.7.1). The module exports the com.deitel.videoplayer package (line 9), because class VideoPlayerController is used by class FXMLLoader (module javafx.fxml) when it creates the controller object and the app's GUI.

```
 1   // Fig. 27.21: module-info.java
 2   // Module declaration for the com.deitel.videoplayer module
 3   module com.deitel.videoplayer {
 4       requires javafx.controls;
 5       requires javafx.fxml;
 6       requires javafx.media;
 7       requires controlsfx; // automatic module for ControlsFX
 8
 9       exports com.deitel.videoplayer;
10       opens com.deitel.videoplayer to javafx.fxml;
11   }
```

Fig. 27.21 | Module declaration for the com.deitel.videoplayer module.

27.7.3 Opening a Module for Reflection

In Fig. 27.21, the opens...to directive (line 10) indicates that the accessible types in the package com.deitel.videoplayer should be available via *reflection* at runtime to types in the javafx.fxml module. As we discussed in Section 27.2.6, this enables the FXMLLoader to locate and load class VideoPlayerController. The FXMLLoader the creates a VideoPlayerController object and *injects* into it references to the GUIs components that the FXMLLoader creates from the app's FXML file. For one module to *open* a package to another module, that package must first be exported (possibly as a qualified export using exports...to).

27.7.4 Module-Dependency Graph

Figure 27.22 shows the com.deitel.videoplayer module-dependency graph. Again, the ones with light blue highlights are explicitly specified in requires directives—except for java.base, which is implicitly required by all modules. The other modules shown are dependencies of the modules specified in the requires directives.

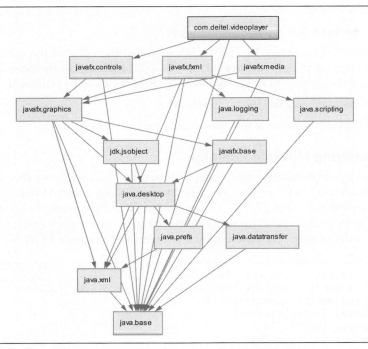

Fig. 27.22 | com.deitel.videoplayer module-dependency graph.

27.7.5 Compiling the Module

To compile the com.deitel.videoplayer module, type:

```
javac --module-path mods -d mods/com.deitel.videoplayer ^
    src/com.deitel.videoplayer/module-info.java ^
    src/com.deitel.videoplayer/com/deitel/videoplayer/*.java
```

Note that we included the --module-path option, because the mods folder contains controlsfx.jar—the automatic module that is required to compile this app.

Copying the Resource Files into the Module

Though some IDEs and build tools will automatically put the module's resources into the compiled module, the preceding javac command does not. Once you've compiled the module, copy the res folder from this project's src/com.deitel.videoplayer folder into the mods/com.deitel.videoplayer folder.

27.7.6 Running a Modularized App

To execute class VideoPlayer from the com.deitel.videoplayer module, type:

```
java --module-path mods ^
    -m com.deitel.videoplayer/com.deitel.videoplayer.VideoPlayer
```

Figure 27.23 shows the app executing on Windows.

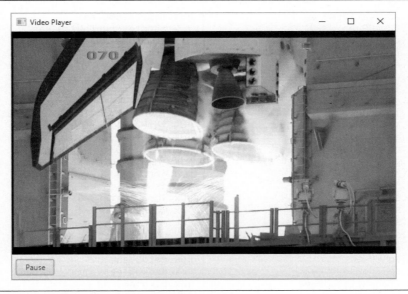

Fig. 27.23 | Modularized VideoPlayer app executing.

27.8 Creating Custom Runtimes with jlink

A new tool in JDK 9 is the **jlink command**—Java's linker for creating custom runtime images.[25] In a custom runtime, you can include just what's necessary for a given app or set of apps to execute. For example, if you're creating a runtime for a device that does not support GUIs, you can create a runtime without the corresponding modules that support Swing and JavaFX. In fact, many of this book's text-only, command-line examples can execute on a runtime that contains only the java.base module.

---

25. Denise, Jean-Francois. "JEP 282: jlink: The Java Linker." http://openjdk.java.net/jeps/282.

27.8.1 Listing the JRE's Modules

With modularization the JRE is a proper subset of the JDK.[26] If you run the command:

```
java --list-modules
```

from the JRE's bin folder, the result contains only the JRE's 73 modules (Fig. 27.24), rather than the full listing of the JDK's 95 modules. This number will change as Java evolves. In Section 27.8.3, we do this on a custom runtime produced with the jlink command—in that case, only the single module bundled with that runtime will be displayed.

> **Software Engineering Observation 27.3**
>
> *You can use the modularized Java platform to conveniently form custom runtimes for smaller capacity devices.*

java.activation@9-ea	jdk.charsets@9-ea
java.base@9-ea	jdk.crypto.cryptoki@9-ea
java.compiler@9-ea	jdk.crypto.ec@9-ea
java.corba@9-ea	jdk.crypto.mscapi@9-ea
java.datatransfer@9-ea	jdk.deploy@9-ea
java.desktop@9-ea	jdk.deploy.controlpanel@9-ea
java.instrument@9-ea	jdk.dynalink@9-ea
java.jnlp@9-ea	jdk.httpserver@9-ea
java.logging@9-ea	jdk.incubator.httpclient@9-ea
java.management@9-ea	jdk.internal.le@9-ea
java.management.rmi@9-ea	jdk.internal.vm.ci@9-ea
java.naming@9-ea	jdk.javaws@9-ea
java.prefs@9-ea	jdk.jdwp.agent@9-ea
java.rmi@9-ea	jdk.jfr@9-ea
java.scripting@9-ea	jdk.jsobject@9-ea
java.se@9-ea	jdk.localedata@9-ea
java.se.ee@9-ea	jdk.management@9-ea
java.security.jgss@9-ea	jdk.management.agent@9-ea
java.security.sasl@9-ea	jdk.naming.dns@9-ea
java.smartcardio@9-ea	jdk.naming.rmi@9-ea
java.sql@9-ea	jdk.net@9-ea
java.sql.rowset@9-ea	jdk.pack@9-ea
java.transaction@9-ea	jdk.plugin@9-ea
java.xml@9-ea	jdk.plugin.dom@9-ea
java.xml.bind@9-ea	jdk.plugin.server@9-ea
java.xml.crypto@9-ea	jdk.scripting.nashorn@9-ea
java.xml.ws@9-ea	jdk.scripting.nashorn.shell@9-ea
java.xml.ws.annotation@9-ea	jdk.sctp@9-ea
javafx.base@9-ea	jdk.security.auth@9-ea
javafx.controls@9-ea	jdk.security.jgss@9-ea
javafx.deploy@9-ea	jdk.snmp@9-ea
javafx.fxml@9-ea	jdk.unsupported@9-ea
javafx.graphics@9-ea	jdk.xml.dom@9-ea
javafx.media@9-ea	jdk.zipfs@9-ea
javafx.swing@9-ea	oracle.desktop@9-ea
javafx.web@9-ea	oracle.net@9-ea
jdk.accessibility@9-ea	

Fig. 27.24 | Output of java --list-modules showing the modules that compose the JRE.

26. Brian Goetz, e-mail message to authors, March 20, 2017.

27.8.2 Custom Runtime Containing Only `java.base`

For the purpose of this example, change to the `WelcomeApp` folder—after creating the custom runtime, you'll execute the `Welcome` app using it. The following command creates a runtime containing only the module `java.base`:

```
jlink --module-path "%JAVA_HOME%"/jmods --add-modules java.base ^
    --output javabaseruntime
```

The commands options are as follows:

- `--module-path` specifies one or more folders in which to locate the modules that will be included in the runtime—in this case, the JDK's `jmods` folder, which contains the modular JAR files for all of the JDK's modules.

- `--add-modules` specifies which modules to include in the runtime—in this case, just `java.base`.

- `--output` specifies the folder in which the runtime's contents are placed—in this case, the folder `javabaseruntime`. This folder will be placed in the folder from which you execute the preceding command (unless you specify additional path information). If the folder already exists, an error occurs.

This runtime can execute an app that depends only on types from the packages in module `java.base`, including many of this book's command-line apps.

Note Regarding the JAVA_HOME Variable

The `JAVA_HOME` environment variable must refer to JDK 9's installation folder on your system—see the Before You Begin section before the preface for information on configuring this environment variable. On Windows, you specify `%JAVA_HOME%` to use `JAVA_HOME`'s value in a command. Linux and macOS users should replace `%JAVA_HOME%` with `$JAVA_HOME`. So, for example, the preceding command on Linux and macOS would be:

```
jlink --module-path "$JAVA_HOME"/jmods --add-modules java.base \
    --output javabaseruntime
```

In either case, if the path contains spaces, place the environment variable in quotes ("").

Executing the Welcome App Using This Custom Runtime

To run the app with the custom runtime, on Windows use:

```
javabaseruntime\bin\java --module-path mods ^
    --module com.deitel.welcome/com.deitel.welcome.Welcome
```

or on macOS/Linux use:

```
javabaseruntime/bin/java --module-path mods \
    --module com.deitel.welcome/com.deitel.welcome.Welcome
```

The program executes and displays:

```
Welcome to the Java Platform Module System!
```

Listing the Modules in a Custom Runtime

Previously we used the command

```
java --list-modules
```

to list all the modules in the JDK. Once you have a custom runtime, you can use the `java` command from the custom runtime's `bin` folder to confirm the modules it includes, as in:

```
javabaseruntime\bin\java --list-modules
```

When executing the custom runtime's `java` command, use \ to separate folder names on Windows and / to separate the folder names on macOS and Linux. The preceding command produces the following output:

```
java.base@9-ea
```

Similarly the following command creates a custom runtime containing only the module `java.desktop` and any other modules on which it depends:

```
jlink --module-path "%JAVA_HOME%"/jmods ^
    --add-modules java.desktop --output javadesktopruntime
```

For this custom runtime, running

```
javadesktopruntime\bin\java --list-modules
```

(again, use forward slashes on macOS and Linux) produces the following output

```
java.base@9-ea
java.datatransfer@9-ea
java.desktop@9-ea
java.prefs@9-ea
java.xml@9-ea
```

27.8.3 Creating a Custom Runtime for the Welcome App

To create a custom runtime containing only the modules `com.deitel.welcome` and its dependencies (in this case, `java.base`), use:

```
jlink --module-path jars;"%JAVA_HOME%"/jmods ^
    --add-modules com.deitel.welcome --output welcomeruntime
```

This creates a custom runtime in the folder `welcomeruntime`. The preceding command specifies multiple folders—`jars` and `%JAVA_HOME%`. On Windows, the path-separator character for lists of folders is a semicolon (`;`). Linux and macOS users should replace the semicolons in the commands with the colon (`:`) path-separator character, as in

```
jlink --module-path jars:"$JAVA_HOME"/jmods \
    --add-modules com.deitel.welcome --output welcomeruntime
```

To see the list of modules included in the custom runtime, on Windows use:

```
welcomeruntime\bin\java --list-modules
```

(again, use forward slashes on macOS and Linux) which produces the following list of modules:

```
com.deitel.welcome
java.base@9-ea
```

27.8.4 Executing the Welcome App Using a Custom Runtime

To run the app with the custom runtime, on Windows use:

```
welcomeruntime\bin\java -m com.deitel.welcome
```

(Again, use forward slashes on macOS and Linux.) The program executes and displays:

```
Welcome to the Java Platform Module System!
```

27.8.5 Using the Module Resolver on a Custom Runtime

When you run a modularized app, the JVM uses a **module resolver** to determine which modules are required at execution time and ensure that their dependencies are satisfied—this is known as the **transitive closure** of those modules. To locate modules, the module resolver looks at the **observable modules**—that is, those built into the runtime (like java.base) and those located on the module path. For a required module that cannot be found, the runtime throws a java.lang.module.FindException.

For a given app and runtime, you can view the steps the module resolver follows to determine module dependencies and ensure that the required modules are available to the program. To do so, include **-Xdiag:resolver option**[27] in the java command, as in:

```
welcomeruntime\bin\java -Xdiag:resolver -m com.deitel.welcome
```

(Again, use forward slashes on macOS and Linux.) This uses the custom welcomeruntime's java command to display the resolver's steps for locating modules, followed by the program's output:

```
[Resolver] Root module com.deitel.welcome located
[Resolver]    (jrt:/com.deitel.welcome)
[Resolver] Module java.base located, required by com.deitel.welcome
[Resolver]    (jrt:/java.base)
[Resolver] Result:
[Resolver]    com.deitel.welcome
[Resolver]    java.base
Welcome to the Java Platform Module System!
```

The module-resolution process for the Welcome app proceeds as follows:

1. First, the resolver locates the app's **initial module**—com.deitel.welcome—containing the app's entry point. The resolver refers to this as the *root module*. This is the root node in the module-dependency graph.

2. Next, the resolver locates java.base, because the com.deitel.welcome module descriptor specifies that com.deitel.welcome requires java.base.

3. Since java.base does not depend on other modules, the dependency graph is now complete and the resolver displays the resulting list of modules required to execute the program.

Next, the program executes and displays its output. If a required module were not found during this process, a java.lang.module.FindException would be displayed in this output and the program would not execute.

27.9 Services and ServiceLoader

In Section 10.13, we discussed "programming to an interface, not an implementation" as a mechanism for creating loosely coupled objects. We'll use these concepts in this section

---

27. Bateman, Alan, Alex Buckley, Jonathan Gibbons and Mark Reinhold. "JEP 261: Module System." http://openjdk.java.net/jeps/261.

as we introduce services and class ServiceLoader, which help you create loosely coupled system components. This can make large-scale systems easier to develop and maintain.

MathTutor App

We'll develop a MathTutor app (consisting of three modules) that supports various types of randomly generated math problems. Rather than hard-coding these into the app, we'll load math problems through a *service-provider interface* that describes how to obtain math problems. We'll then define two *service providers*—classes that implement this interface. One service provider will create addition problems and the other multiplication problems. At runtime, we'll load objects of these service-provider implementation classes and use them. The completed app structure consisting of three modules is shown in Fig. 27.25.

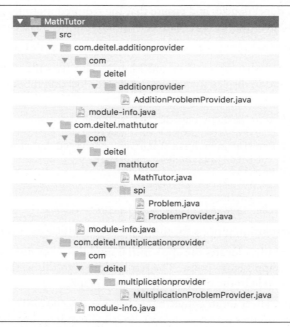

Fig. 27.25 | Folder structure for the MathTutor app's modules.

MathTutor App's Modules

Module com.deitel.mathtutor aggregates two related packages:

- com.deitel.mathtutor: This package contains class MathTutor—a command-line app that displays random math problems to the user, inputs the user's responses and displays whether each response is correct or incorrect.

- com.deitel.mathtutor.spi: This package contains the ProblemProvider service-provider interface and the supporting abstract class Problem, which represents a math problem. Class MathTutor uses ProblemProviders to obtain Problem objects.

Module com.deitel.additionprovider contains a package of the same name in which we declare class AdditionProblemProvider. This implementation of the service-provider interface ProblemProvider generates random addition Problems.

Module com.deitel.multiplicationprovider contains a package of the same name in which we declare class MultiplicationProblemProvider. This implementation of the service-provider interface ProblemProvider generates random multiplication Problems.

How We'll Demonstrate the App

We'll initially run the MathTutor app without placing the service-provider implementation modules on the module path to demonstrate what happens when *no* service providers are found at runtime. Next, we'll "plug in" the module com.deitel.additionprovider on the module path, then re-run the app to demonstrate that we're able to obtain Problems from an AdditionProblemProvider. Finally, we'll "plug in" both the com.deitel.additionprovider and com.deitel.multiplicationprovider modules on the module path, then re-run the app to demonstrate that we're able to obtain Problems generated by both an AdditionProblemProvider and a MultiplicationProblemProvider.

Plug-in Architecture

This "plug-in" architecture using a service-provider interface and multiple service-provider implementations makes the MathTutor app easy to extend. Simply create a module containing a ProblemProvider implementation, then add it to the module path when you run the app. It also makes the app more configurable, because you can choose which modules to include on the module path when you execute the app.

Reliable Configuration

The mechanisms for creating loosely coupled systems like the MathTutor app have been used extensively in Java since its early versions. A key new concept in Java 9—which also applies to modules in general—is *reliable configuration*. For the MathTutor app to be able to display Problems to the user, it must be able to locate and load ProblemProvider implementations. As you'll see, module declarations enable you to specify which service-provider interfaces a module uses and whether a module contains types that implement those interfaces.

27.9.1 Service-Provider Interface

The package com.deitel.mathtutor.spi contains the com.deitel.mathtutor module's service-provider interface ProblemProvider and the supporting abstract class Problem. The final component of this package's name—spi—is commonly used in packages that declare one or more service-provider interfaces. Interface ProblemProvider (Fig. 27.26) declares method getProblem (line 6) that returns a Problem.

```
1   // Fig. 27.26: ProblemProvider.java
2   // Service-provider interface for obtaining a Problem
3   package com.deitel.mathtutor.spi;
4
5   public interface ProblemProvider {
6      public Problem getProblem();
7   }
```

Fig. 27.26 | Service-provider interface for obtaining a Problem.

Abstract class `Problem` (Fig. 27.27) provides the common features of math problems in this example. Each has two `int` operands and an `int` result as well as a `String` representing the operation—the `MathTutor` displays this `String` with each math problem it presents to the user. Class `Problem`'s abstract method `getResult` is overridden in each service-provider implementation's concrete subclass of `Problem`.

```java
1   // Fig. 27.27: Problem.java
2   // Problem superclass that contains information about a math problem.
3   package com.deitel.mathtutor.spi;
4
5   public abstract class Problem {
6      private int leftOperand;
7      private int rightOperand;
8      private int result;
9      private String operation;
10
11     // constructor
12     public Problem(int leftOperand, int rightOperand, String operation) {
13        this.leftOperand = leftOperand;
14        this.rightOperand = rightOperand;
15        this.operation = operation;
16     }
17
18     // gets the leftOperand
19     public int getLeftOperand() {return leftOperand;}
20
21     // gets the rightOperand
22     public int getRightOperand() {return rightOperand;}
23
24     // gets the operation
25     public String getOperation() {return operation;}
26
27     // gets the result
28     public abstract int getResult();
29  }
```

Fig. 27.27 | `Problem` superclass that contains information about a math problem.

27.9.2 Loading and Consuming Service Providers

Class `MathTutor` (Fig. 27.28) is the app's entry point. It provides the logic for locating and loading `ProblemProvider` implementations, then using them to present math problems to the user.

```java
1   // Fig. 27.28: MathTutor.java
2   // Math tutoring app using ProblemProviders to display math problems.
3   package com.deitel.mathtutor;
4
5   import java.util.List;
6   import java.util.Random;
```

Fig. 27.28 | Math tutoring app using `ProblemProviders` to display math problems. (Part 1 of 3.)

```
7    import java.util.Scanner;
8    import java.util.ServiceLoader;
9    import java.util.ServiceLoader.Provider;
10   import java.util.stream.Collectors;
11   import com.deitel.mathtutor.spi.Problem;
12   import com.deitel.mathtutor.spi.ProblemProvider;
13
14   public class MathTutor {
15      private static Scanner input = new Scanner(System.in);
16
17      public static void main(String[] args) {
18         // get a service loader for ProblemProviders
19         ServiceLoader<ProblemProvider> serviceLoader =
20            ServiceLoader.load(ProblemProvider.class);
21
22         // get the list of service providers
23         List<Provider<ProblemProvider>> providersList =
24            serviceLoader.stream().collect(Collectors.toList());
25
26         // check whether there are any providers
27         if (providersList.isEmpty()) {
28            System.out.println(
29               "Terminating MathTutor: No problem providers found.");
30            return;
31         }
32
33         boolean shouldContinue = true;
34         Random random = new Random();
35
36         do {
37            // choose a ProblemProvider at random
38            ProblemProvider provider =
39               providersList.get(random.nextInt(providersList.size())).get();
40
41            // get the Problem
42            Problem problem = provider.getProblem();
43
44            // display the problem to the user
45            showProblem(problem);
46         } while (playAgain());
47      }
48
49      // show the math problem to the user
50      private static void showProblem(Problem problem) {
51         String problemStatement = String.format("What is %d %s %d? ",
52            problem.getLeftOperand(), problem.getOperation(),
53            problem.getRightOperand());
54
55         // display problem and get answer from user
56         System.out.printf(problemStatement);
57         int answer = input.nextInt();
58
```

Fig. 27.28 | Math tutoring app using `ProblemProvider`s to display math problems. (Part 2 of 3.)

```
59          while (answer != problem.getResult()) {
60              System.out.println("Incorrect. Please try again: ");
61              System.out.printf(problemStatement);
62              answer = input.nextInt();
63          }
64
65          System.out.println("Correct!");
66      }
67
68      // play again?
69      private static boolean playAgain() {
70          System.out.printf("Try another? y to continue, n to terminate: ");
71          String response = input.next();
72
73          return response.toLowerCase().startsWith("y");
74      }
75  }
```

Fig. 27.28 | Math tutoring app using `ProblemProvider`s to display math problems. (Part 3 of 3.)

Using ServiceLoader to Locate Service Providers
Lines 19–20

```
ServiceLoader<ProblemProvider> serviceLoader =
    ServiceLoader.load(ProblemProvider.class);
```

create a **ServiceLoader** (package java.util) that loads ProblemProvider implementations. ServiceLoader's static **load** method receives as its argument the Class object representing the service-provider interface's type—ProblemProvider.class is a **class literal** that's equivalent to creating a Class<ProblemProvider> object, as in:

```
new Class<ProblemProvider>()
```

Method load returns a ServiceLoader<ProblemProvider> that knows only how to load ProblemProvider implementations.

There are several ways to get service-provider implementations from a ServiceLoader. In lines 23–24

```
List<Provider<ProblemProvider>> providersList =
    serviceLoader.stream().collect(Collectors.toList());
```

we obtain a List of the available service-provider implementations using ServiceLoader's **stream** method. This returns a Stream<Provider<ProblemProvider>> representing all the available ProblemProvider implementations, if any. Interface Provider (imported at line 9) is a nested type of class ServiceLoader. For each available ProblemProvider implementation, the stream contains one Provider<ProblemProvider> object. Line 24 uses Stream method collect and the predefined Collector defined by Collectors.toList to get the List containing all the available implementations. If that List is empty (line 27) the program displays an appropriate message and terminates.

Using a Service-Provider Interface
If the List contains any service-provider implementations, lines 36–46 use them to display one math problem at a time to the user. Lines 38–39

```
      ProblemProvider provider =
         providersList.get(random.nextInt(providersList.size())).get();
```

randomly select one `Provider<ProblemProvider>` object from the `providersList`, then invoke that object's `get` method to obtain its `ProblemProvider`. Line 42

```
      Problem problem = provider.getProblem();
```

then gets a `Problem` from whichever `ProblemProvider` was selected.

Note the *loose coupling* of the `MathTutor` app and its `ProblemProviders`. The app does not refer in any way to `AdditionProblemProviders` or `MultiplicationProblemProviders` that generate math problems.

27.9.3 uses Module Directive and Service Consumers

Figure 27.29 shows the `com.deitel.mathtutor` module declaration. Note that this module `exports` the package `com.deitel.mathtutor.spi` containing the service-provider interface `ProblemProvider` and its supporting `Problem` class. This enables modules that implement interface `ProblemProvider` to access those types. The new feature in this declaration is the **uses module directive** (line 6). This directive indicates that there is a type in the `com.deitel.mathtutor` module that *uses* objects which implement the `ProblemProvider` interface. Such a module is called a **service consumer**.

```
1  // Fig. 27.29: module-info.java
2  // Module declaration for the com.deitel.mathtutor module
3  module com.deitel.mathtutor {
4     exports com.deitel.mathtutor.spi; // package for provider interface
5
6     uses com.deitel.mathtutor.spi.ProblemProvider;
7  }
```

Fig. 27.29 | Module declaration for the `com.deitel.mathtutor` module.

To be able to consume `ProblemProviders`, the `ServiceLoader` must be able to locate and load their implementations dynamically using Java's *reflection* capabilities. When you run this app, the module resolver will see in the descriptor that this module *uses* `ProblemProvider` implementations and thus is dependent on such providers. It will then search the modules on the module path looking for any modules that provide implementations of this interface. If it finds any such modules, it will add them to the module-dependency graph.

27.9.4 Running the App with No Service Providers

To compile the `com.deitel.mathtutor` module, type:

```
javac -d mods/com.deitel.mathtutor ^
   src/com.deitel.mathtutor/module-info.java ^
   src/com.deitel.mathtutor/com/deitel/mathtutor/MathTutor.java ^
   src/com.deitel.mathtutor/com/deitel/mathtutor/spi/*.java
```

Next, run the app with no `ProblemProvider` implementations on the module path by using the following java command, which places only the `com.deitel.mathtutor` module on the module path:

```
java --module-path mods/com.deitel.mathtutor ^
    -m com.deitel.mathtutor/com.deitel.mathtutor.MathTutor
```

The result is

```
Terminating MathTutor: No problem providers found.
```

27.9.5 Implementing a Service Provider

Next, let's create class `AdditionProblemProvider` (Fig. 27.30), which implements the service-provider interface `ProblemProvider` (line 10). This class's `com.deitel.addition-provider` package will be placed in the `com.deitel.additionprovider` module (Section 27.9.6). We import interface `ProblemProvider` and class `Problem` from the `com.deitel.mathtutor` module's exported package `com.deitel.mathtutor.spi` (lines 7–8). When the `MathTutor` calls an `AdditionProblemProvider`'s getProblem method (lines 14–23), the method creates an anonymous subclass of `Problem` (lines 16–22), passing to `Problem`'s constructor two random int values as the operands and the String `"+"` as the operation. Lines 18–21 override superclass `Problem`'s getResult method to return the sum of the left and right operands.

```java
 1  // Fig. 27.30: AdditionProblemProvider.java
 2  // AdditionProblemProvider implementation of interface
 3  // ProblemProvider for the MathTutor app.
 4  package com.deitel.additionprovider;
 5
 6  import java.util.Random;
 7  import com.deitel.mathtutor.spi.Problem;
 8  import com.deitel.mathtutor.spi.ProblemProvider;
 9
10  public class AdditionProblemProvider implements ProblemProvider {
11     private static Random random = new Random();
12
13     // returns a new addition problem
14     @Override
15     public Problem getProblem() {
16        return new Problem(random.nextInt(10), random.nextInt(10), "+") {
17           // override getResult to add the operands
18           @Override
19           public int getResult() {
20              return getLeftOperand() + getRightOperand();
21           }
22        };
23     }
24  }
```

Fig. 27.30 | `AdditionProblemProvider` implementation of interface `ProblemProvider` for the `MathTutor` app.

27.9.6 provides...with Module Directive and Declaring a Service Provider

Figure 27.31 shows the com.deitel.additionprovider module declaration. Note that this module requires the module com.deitel.mathtutor. Recall from Fig. 27.29 that this module exports the package com.deitel.mathtutor.spi containing the types used in class AdditionProblemProvider. The new feature in this module declaration is the **provides...with module directive**. Lines 6–7 specify that this module

- provides an implementation of interface ProblemProvider—declared in the com.deitel.mathtutor module's com.deitel.mathtutor.spi package

- with class AdditionProblemProvider—declared in this module's com.deitel.additionprovider package.

Such a module is called a **service provider**. The directive's provides part is followed by the name of an interface or abstract class that's specified in a module's uses directive. The directive's with part is followed by the name of a class that implements the interface or extends the abstract class.

```
1   // Fig. 27.31: module-info.java
2   // Module declaration for the com.deitel.additionprovider module
3   module com.deitel.additionprovider {
4      requires com.deitel.mathtutor;
5
6      provides com.deitel.mathtutor.spi.ProblemProvider
7         with com.deitel.additionprovider.AdditionProblemProvider;
8   }
```

Fig. 27.31 | Module declaration for the com.deitel.additionprovider module.

27.9.7 Running the App with One Service Provider

Next, we'll run the app with the AdditionProblemProvider included in the module path. First, compile the com.deitel.additionprovider module, as follows:

```
javac --module-path mods -d mods/com.deitel.additionprovider ∧
   src/com.deitel.additionprovider/module-info.java ∧
   src/com.deitel.additionprovider/com/deitel/additionprovider/ ∧
      AdditionProblemProvider.java
```

Then run the app with the following java command:

```
java --module-path mods ∧
   -m com.deitel.mathtutor/com.deitel.mathtutor.MathTutor
```

The following sample output shows addition problems:

```
What is 9 + 6? 15
Correct!
Try another? y to continue, n to terminate: y
What is 2 + 6? 7
Incorrect. Please try again:
What is 2 + 6? 8
Correct!
Try another? y to continue, n to terminate: n
```

27.9.8 Implementing a Second Service Provider

Class `MultiplicationProblemProvider` (Fig. 27.32) also implements the service-provider interface `ProblemProvider` (line 10). This class's `com.deitel.multiplicationprovider` package will be placed in the `com.deitel.multiplicationprovider` module (Fig. 27.33). Class `MultiplicationProblemProvider` is nearly identical to class `AdditionProblemProvider`, except that line 16 passes the `String` `"*"` for the `Problem`'s operation and the overridden `Problem` method `getResult` returns the product of the left and right operands.

```
1   // Fig. 27.32: MultiplicationProblemProvider.java
2   // MultiplicationProblemProvider implementation of interface
3   // ProblemProvider for the MathTutor app.
4   package com.deitel.multiplicationprovider;
5
6   import java.util.Random;
7   import com.deitel.mathtutor.spi.Problem;
8   import com.deitel.mathtutor.spi.ProblemProvider;
9
10  public class MultiplicationProblemProvider implements ProblemProvider {
11     private static Random random = new Random();
12
13     // returns a new addition problem
14     @Override
15     public Problem getProblem() {
16        return new Problem(random.nextInt(10), random.nextInt(10), "*") {
17           // override getResult to add the operands
18           @Override
19           public int getResult() {
20              return getLeftOperand() * getRightOperand();
21           }
22        };
23     }
24  }
```

Fig. 27.32 | `MultiplicationProblemProvider` implementation of interface `ProblemProvider` for the `MathTutor` app.

Figure 27.33 shows the `com.deitel.multiplicationprovider` module declaration. Again, this module `requires` the module `com.deitel.mathtutor`. Lines 6–7 specify that this module `provides` an implementation of the `ProblemProvider` interface with class `MultiplicationProblemProvider`.

```
1   // Fig. 27.33: module-info.java
2   // Module declaration for the com.deitel.multiplicationprovider module
3   module com.deitel.multiplicationprovider {
4      requires com.deitel.mathtutor;
5
6      provides com.deitel.mathtutor.spi.ProblemProvider with
7         com.deitel.multiplicationprovider.MultiplicationProblemProvider;
8   }
```

Fig. 27.33 | Module declaration for the `com.deitel.multiplicationprovider` module.

27.9.9 Running the App with Two Service Providers

Next, we'll run the app with both the `AdditionProblemProvider` and the `Multiplica-tionProblemProvider` included in the module path. First, compile the `com.deitel.mul-tiplicationprovider` module, as follows:

```
javac --module-path mods ^
    -d mods/com.deitel.multiplicationprovider ^
    src/com.deitel.multiplicationprovider/module-info.java ^
    src/com.deitel.multiplicationprovider/com/deitel/
        multiplicationprovider/MultiplicationProblemProvider.java
```

Then run the app with the following `java` command:

```
java --module-path mods ^
    -m com.deitel.mathtutor/com.deitel.mathtutor.MathTutor
```

The following is a sample output showing both addition and multiplication problems:

```
What is 4 * 8? 20
Incorrect. Please try again:
What is 4 * 8? 32
Correct!
Try another? y to continue, n to terminate: y
What is 3 * 6? 18
Correct!
Try another? y to continue, n to terminate: y
What is 3 + 7? 10
Correct!
Try another? y to continue, n to terminate: y
What is 9 + 3? 12
Correct!
Try another? y to continue, n to terminate: n
```

27.10 Wrap-Up

In this chapter, we introduced Java 9's new Java Platform Module system. We introduced key modularity concepts you're likely to use when building large-scale systems.

You saw that all modules implicitly depend on `java.base`. You created module declarations that specify a module's dependencies (with the `requires` directive), which packages a module makes available to other modules (with the `exports` directive), services it offers (with the `provides...with` directive), services it consumes (with the `uses` directive) and to what other modules it allows reflection (with the `open` modifier and the `opens` and `opens...to` directives).

To help you visualize the dependencies among modules, we showed several module-dependency graphs that we created using the NetBeans IDE's JDK 9 support. We discussed the steps that the runtime's module resolver performs to ensure that a module's dependencies are fulfilled.

You used JDK 9's new `jlink` tool (the Java linker) to create smaller custom runtimes, then used them to execute apps. We discussed the module system's strong encapsulation and showed the steps required to explicitly allow runtime reflection via the `open` modifier or the `opens` and `opens...to` directives in a module declaration.

We discussed the enormous amount of non-modularized legacy code that will need to be migrated to modular Java 9, then showed how the unnamed module and automatic modules can help make migration straightforward. We used the jdeps tool to determine code dependencies among modules and showed how the tool can be used to check for uses of pre-Java-9 internal APIs (which are for the most part strongly encapsulated in Java 9).

Finally, we discussed services and service providers for building loosely coupled systems by using service-provider interfaces and implementations and the ServiceLoader class. We also demonstrated the uses and provides...with directives in module declarations to indicate that a module uses a service or provides a service implementation, respectively. In the next chapter, we discuss various additional Java 9 topics.

Additional Java 9 Topics

Objectives

In this chapter you'll:

- Briefly recap the Java 9 features we've already covered.

- Understand Java's new version numbering scheme.

- Use the new regular-expression `Matcher` methods `appendReplacement`, `appendTail`, `replaceFirst`, `replaceAll` and `results`.

- Use the new `Stream` methods `takeWhile` and `dropWhile` and the new `iterate` overload.

- Learn about the Java 9 JavaFX and other GUI and graphics enhancements.

- Use modules in JShell.

- Overview the Java 9 security-related changes and other Java 9 features.

- Become aware of the capabilities no longer available in JDK 9 and Java 9.

- Become aware of packages, classes and methods proposed for removal from future Java versions.

28.1 Introduction

Just before we published this book, Java Specification Request (JSR) 379: Java SE 9 was released as a draft at:

```
http://cr.openjdk.java.net/~iris/se/9/java-se-9-pr-spec-01/java-se-
    9-spec.html
```

The JSR details the

- features included in Java 9,

- features that have been removed from Java 9, and

- features that are proposed for removal from future Java versions.

Once this JSR is approved as final it will be posted at:

```
https://www.jcp.org/en/jsr/detail?id=379
```

This JSR is a must read for any Java 9 developer. It gives a high-level overview of the breadth and depth of Java 9 and provides links to all the key JEPs and JSRs.

In any new version of a language there are items of immediate benefit to most programmers, items of interest to some programmers and narrow-purpose, specialty topics that limited numbers of developers will use. We divided this chapter into several groups:

- A recap of the Java 9 features we covered in earlier chapters.
- Live-code examples and discussions of additional functionality that will be useful to a wider audience.
- A brief overview of specialty features with references to where you can learn more.
- A list of features removed from JDK 9 and Java 9.
- A list of features proposed for removal from future Java versions.

Developers should, of course, avoid features in the last two groups in new development, and replace uses of those features in old code as it's migrated to Java 9.

28.2 Recap: Java 9 Features Covered in Earlier Chapters

Here we list the Java 9 features already covered in the book and where you can find each:

- Underscore (_) is no longer a valid identifier (Section 2.2). This is one of several features of JEP 213: Milling Project Coin (http://openjdk.java.net/jeps/213).
- Mentioned enhancements to SecureRandom (Section 6.8) per JEP 273 (http://openjdk.java.net/jeps/273).
- As of Java 9, the compiler now issues a warning if you attempt to access a static class member through an instance of the class (Section 8.11).
- Introduced private interface methods (Section 10.11), another feature of JEP 213: Milling Project Coin.
- Mentioned the new Stack-Walking API (Section 11.7) from JEP 259 (http://openjdk.java.net/jeps/259).
- Mentioned that effectively final AutoCloseable variables can now be used in try-with-resources statements (Section 11.12), another feature of JEP 213: Milling Project Coin.
- Overviewed new JavaFX 9 features and other GUI and graphics enhancements (Section 13.8).
- Mentioned Java 9's more compact String representation (Section 14.3), per JEP 254 (http://openjdk.java.net/jeps/254).
- Presented the new convenience factory methods for creating read-only collections (Section 16.14), per JEP 269 (http://openjdk.java.net/jeps/269).
- Chapter 23, Introduction to JShell: Java 9's REPL for Interactive Java, presented detailed, example-driven coverage of the JDK's new jshell tool.
- Chapter 27, Java Platform Module System, presented detailed example-driven coverage of Java 9's new module system.

28.3 New Version String Format

Prior to Java 9, JDK versions were numbered 1.X.0_*updateNumber* where X was the major Java version. For example,

- Java 8's current JDK version number is jdk1.8.0_121 and
- Java 7's final JDK version number was jdk1.7.0_80.

This numbering scheme has changed. JDK 9 initially will be known as jdk-9. Future minor version updates will add new features, and security updates will fix security holes. These updates will be reflected in the JDK version numbers. For example, in 9.1.3:

- 9—is the major Java version number
- 1—is the minor version update number and
- 3—is the security update number.

So 9.2.5 would indicate the version of Java 9 for which there have been two minor version updates and five total security updates (across major and minor versions). For additional details, see JEP 223:

```
http://openjdk.java.net/jeps/223
```

28.4 Regular Expressions: New Matcher Class Methods

Java SE 9 adds several new Matcher method overloads—**appendReplacement**, **appendTail**, **replaceFirst**, **replaceAll** and **results** (Fig. 28.1).

```java
1  // Fig. 28.1: MatcherMethods.java
2  // Java 9's new Matcher methods.
3  import java.util.regex.Matcher;
4  import java.util.regex.Pattern;
5
6  public class MatcherMethods {
7     public static void main(String[] args) {
8        String sentence = "a man a plan a canal panama";
9
10       System.out.printf("sentence: %s%n", sentence);
11
12       // using Matcher methods appendReplacement and appendTail
13       Pattern pattern = Pattern.compile("an"); // regex to match
14
15       // match regular expression to String and replace
16       // each match with uppercase letters
17       Matcher matcher = pattern.matcher(sentence);
18
19       // used to rebuild String
20       StringBuilder builder = new StringBuilder();
21
22       // append text to builder; convert each match to uppercase
23       while (matcher.find()) {
24          matcher.appendReplacement(
25             builder, matcher.group().toUpperCase());
26       }
27
28       // append the remainder of the original String to builder
29       matcher.appendTail(builder);
30       System.out.printf(
31          "%nAfter appendReplacement/appendTail: %s%n", builder);
32
```

Fig. 28.1 | Java 9's new Matcher methods. (Part 1 of 2.)

```
33          // using Matcher method replaceFirst
34          matcher.reset(); // reset matcher to its initial state
35          System.out.printf("%nBefore replaceFirst: %s%n", sentence);
36          String result = matcher.replaceFirst(m -> m.group().toUpperCase());
37          System.out.printf("After replaceFirst: %s%n", result);
38
39          // using Matcher method replaceAll
40          matcher.reset(); // reset matcher to its initial state
41          System.out.printf("%nBefore replaceAll: %s%n", sentence);
42          result = matcher.replaceAll(m -> m.group().toUpperCase());
43          System.out.printf("After replaceAll: %s%n", result);
44
45          // using method results to get a Stream<MatchResult>
46          System.out.printf("%nUsing Matcher method results:%n");
47          pattern = Pattern.compile("\\w+"); // regular expression to match
48          matcher = pattern.matcher(sentence);
49          System.out.printf("The number of words is: %d%n",
50             matcher.results().count());
51
52          matcher.reset(); // reset matcher to its initial state
53          System.out.printf("Average characters per word is: %f%n",
54             matcher.results()
55                 .mapToInt(m -> m.group().length())
56                 .average().orElse(0));
57       }
58    }
```

```
sentence: a man a plan a canal panama

After appendReplacement/appendTail: a mAN a plAN a cANal pANama

Before replaceFirst: a man a plan a canal panama
After replaceFirst: a mAN a plan a canal panama

Before replaceAll: a man a plan a canal panama
After replaceAll: a mAN a plAN a cANal pANama

Using Matcher method results:
The number of words is: 7
Average characters per word is: 3.000000
```

Fig. 28.1 | Java 9's new Matcher methods. (Part 2 of 2.)

28.4.1 Methods appendReplacement and appendTail

The new Matcher method overloads appendReplacement (lines 24–25) and appendTail (line 29) are used with Matcher method find (line 23) and a StringBuilder in a loop to iterate through a String and replace every-regular expression match with a specified String. At the end of the process, the StringBuilder contains the original String's contents updated with the replacements. Lines 13–26 proceed as follows:

- Line 13 creates a Pattern to match—in this case, the literal characters "an".

- Line 17 creates a Matcher object for the String sentence (declared in line 8). This will be used to locate the Pattern "an" in sentence.

- Line 20 creates the `StringBuilder` in which the results will be placed.

- Line 23 uses `Matcher` method `find`, to locate an occurrence of `"an"` in the original `String`.

- If a match is found, method `find` returns `true`, and line 24 calls `Matcher` method `appendReplacement` to replace `"an"` with `"AN"`. The method's second argument calls `Matcher` method `group` to get a `String` representing the set of characters that matched the regular expression (in this case, `"an"`). We then convert the matching characters to uppercase. Method `appendReplacement` then appends to the `StringBuilder` in the first argument all of characters up to the match in the original `String`, followed by the replacement specified in the second argument. Then, the loop-continuation condition attempts to `find` another match in the original `String`, starting from the first character *after* the preceding match.

- When method `find` returns `false`, the loop terminates and line 29 uses `Matcher` method `appendTail` to append the remaining characters of the original `String` sentence to the `StringBuilder`.

At the end of this process for the original `String` `"a man a plan a canal panama"`, the `StringBuilder` contains `"a mAN a plAN a cANal pANama"`.

28.4.2 Methods `replaceFirst` and `replaceAll`

`Matcher` method overloads `replaceFirst` (line 36) and `replaceAll` (line 42) replace the first match or all matches in a `String`, respectively, using a `Function` that receives a `MatchResult` and returns a replacement `String`. Lines 36 and 42 implement interface `Function` with lambdas that group the matching characters and convert them to uppercase `Strings`. Lines 34 and 40 call `Matcher` method `reset` so that the subsequent calls to `replaceFirst` and `replaceAll` begin searching for matches from the first character in `sentence`.

28.4.3 Method `results`

The new `Matcher` method `results` (lines 50 and 54) returns a stream of `MatchResults`. In lines 47–50, we use the regular expression `\w+` to match sequences of word characters then simply `count` the matches to determine the number of words in `sentence`. After resetting the `Matcher` (line 52), lines 54–56 use a stream to map each word to its `int` number of characters (via `mapToInt`), then calculate the average length of each word using `IntStream` method `average`.

28.5 New Stream Interface Methods

Java 9 adds several new `Stream` methods—**takeWhile**, **dropWhile**, **iterate** and **ofNullable** (Fig. 28.2). All but `ofNullable` are also available in the numeric streams like `IntStream`.

```
1   // Fig. 28.2: StreamMethods.java
2   // Java 9's new stream methods takeWhile, dropWhile, iterate
3   // and ofNullable.
```

Fig. 28.2 | Java 9's new stream methods `takeWhile`, `dropWhile`, `iterate` and `ofNullable`. (Part 1 of 3.)

```
4    import java.util.stream.Collectors;
5    import java.util.stream.IntStream;
6    import java.util.stream.Stream;
7
8    public class StreamMethods {
9       public static void main(String[] args) {
10          int[] values = {1, 2, 3, 4, 5, 6, 7, 8, 9, 10};
11
12          System.out.printf("Array values contains: %s%n",
13             IntStream.of(values)
14                      .mapToObj(String::valueOf)
15                      .collect(Collectors.joining(" ")));
16
17          // take the largest stream prefix of elements less than 6
18          System.out.println("Demonstrating takeWhile and dropWhile:");
19          System.out.printf("Elements less than 6: %s%n",
20             IntStream.of(values)
21                      .takeWhile(e -> e < 6)
22                      .mapToObj(String::valueOf)
23                      .collect(Collectors.joining(" ")));
24
25          // drop the largest stream prefix of elements less than 6
26          System.out.printf("Elements 6 or greater: %s%n",
27             IntStream.of(values)
28                      .dropWhile(e -> e < 6)
29                      .mapToObj(String::valueOf)
30                      .collect(Collectors.joining(" ")));
31
32          // use iterate to generate stream of powers of 3 less than 10000
33          System.out.printf("%nDemonstrating iterate:%n");
34          System.out.printf("Powers of 3 less than 10,000: %s%n",
35             IntStream.iterate(3, n -> n < 10_000, n -> n * 3)
36                      .mapToObj(String::valueOf)
37                      .collect(Collectors.joining(" ")));
38
39          // demonstrating ofNullable
40          System.out.printf("%nDemonstrating ofNullable:%n");
41          System.out.printf("Number of stream elements: %d%n",
42             Stream.ofNullable(null).count());
43          System.out.printf("Number of stream elements: %d%n",
44             Stream.ofNullable("red").count());
45       }
46    }
```

```
Array values contains: 1 2 3 4 5 6 7 8 9 10
Demonstrating takeWhile and dropWhile:
Elements less than 6: 1 2 3 4 5
Elements 6 or greater: 6 7 8 9 10

Demonstrating iterate:
Powers of 3 less than 10,000: 3 9 27 81 243 729 2187 6561
```

Fig. 28.2 | Java 9's new stream methods takeWhile, dropWhile, iterate and ofNullable. (Part 2 of 3.)

```
Demonstrating ofNullable:
Number of stream elements: 0
Number of stream elements: 1
```

Fig. 28.2 | Java 9's new stream methods `takeWhile`, `dropWhile`, `iterate` and `ofNullable`.
(Part 3 of 3.)

28.5.1 Stream Methods `takeWhile` and `dropWhile`

Lines 19–30 demonstrate methods `takeWhile` and `dropWhile`, which based on a `Predi-cate` include or omit stream elements, respectively. These methods are meant for use on ordered streams. Unlike `filter`, which processes all of the stream's elements, each of these new methods process elements only until its `Predicate` argument becomes `false`.

The stream pipeline in lines 19–23 takes `int`s from the beginning of the stream while each `int` is less than 6. The predicate returns `true` only for the first five stream elements—as soon as the `Predicate` returns `false`, the remaining elements of the original stream are ignored. For the five elements that remain in the stream, we map each to a `String` and returns a `String` containing the elements separated by spaces.

The stream pipeline in lines 26–30 drops `int`s from the beginning of the stream while each `int` is less than 6. The resulting stream contains the elements beginning with the first one that was 6 or greater. For the elements that remain in the stream, we map each element to a `String` and collect the results into a `String` containing the elements separated by spaces.

Error-Prevention Tip 28.1

Invoke `takeWhile` and `dropWhile` only on ordered streams. If these methods are called on an unordered stream, the stream may return any subset of the matching elements, including none at all, thus giving you potentially unexpected results.

Performance Tip 28.1

According to the `Stream` interface documentation, you may encounter performance issues for the `takeWhile` and `dropWhile` methods on ordered parallel pipelines. For more information, see `http://download.java.net/java/jdk9/docs/api/java/util/stream/Stream.html`.

28.5.2 Stream Method `iterate`

In Section 4.5, we showed a `while` loop that calculated the powers of 3 less than 100. Lines 34–37 show how to use the new overload of `Stream` method `iterate` to generate a stream of `int`s containing the powers of 3 less than 10,000. The new overload takes as its arguments

- a seed value which becomes the stream's first element,

- a `Predicate` that determines when to stop producing elements, and

- a `UnaryOperator` that's invoked initially on the seed value, then on each prior value that iterate produces until the `Predicate` becomes `false`.

In this case, the seed value is 3, the `Predicate` indicates that iterate should continue producing elements while the last element produced is less than 10,000, and the `UnaryOper-ator` multiplies the prior element's value by 3 to produce the next element. Then we map each element to a `String` and collect the results into a `String` containing the elements separated by spaces.

28.5.3 Stream Method `ofNullable`

The new `Stream static` method `ofNullable` receives a reference to an object and, if the reference is not `null`, returns a one-element stream containing the object; otherwise, it returns an empty stream. Lines 42 and 44 show mechanical examples demonstrating an empty stream and a one-element stream, respectively.

Method `ofNullable` typically would be used to ensure that a reference is not `null`, before performing operations in a stream pipeline. Consider a company employee database. A program could query the database to locate all the `Employees` in a given department and store them as a collection in a `Department` object referenced by the variable `department`. If the query were performed for a nonexistent department, the reference would be `null`. Rather than first checking whether `department` is `null`, then performing a task as in

```
if (department != null) {
    // do something
}
```

you can instead use code like the following:

```
Stream.ofNullable(department)
    .flatmap(Department::streamEmployees)
    ... // do something with each Employee
```

Here we assume that class `Deparment` contains a `public` method `streamEmployees` that returns a stream of `Employees`. If `department` is not `null`, the pipeline would `flatMap` the `Department` object into a stream of `Employees` for further processing. If department were `null`, `ofNullable` would return an empty stream, so the pipeline would simply terminate.

28.6 Modules in JShell

In Section 23.10, we demonstrated how to add your custom classes to the JShell classpath, so that you can then interact with them in JShell. Here we show how to do that with the `com.deitel.timelibrary` module from Section 36.4. For the purpose of this section, open a command window and change to the `TimeApp` folder in the `ch36` examples folder, then start `jshell`.

Adding a Module to the JShell Session

The `/env` command can specify the module path and the specific modules that JShell should load from that path. To add the `com.deitel.timelibrary` module, execute the following command:

```
jshell> /env -module-path jars -add-modules com.deitel.timelibrary
|  Setting new options and restoring state.

jshell>
```

The `-module-path` option indicates where the modules you wish to load are located (in this case the `jars` folder in the folder from which you executed JShell). The `-add-modules` option indicates the specific modules to load (in this case, `com.deitel.timelibrary`).

Importing a Class from a Module's Exported Package(s)

Once the module is loaded, you may `import` types from any of the module's exported packages. The following command `import`s the module's `Time1` class:

```
jshell> import com.deitel.timelibrary.Time1

jshell>
```

Using the Imported Class

At this point, you can use class `Time1`, just as you used other classes in Chapter 23. Create a `Time1` object,

```
jshell> Time1 time = new Time1()
time ==> 12:00:00 AM

jshell>
```

Next, inspect its members with auto-completion by typing `"time."` and pressing *Tab*:

```
jshell> time.
equals(            getClass()          hashCode()
notify()           notifyAll()
setTime(           toString()          toUniversalString()
wait(

jshell> time.
```

View just the members that begin with `"to"` by typing `"to"` then pressing *Tab*:

```
jshell> time.to
toString()            toUniversalString()

jshell> time.to
```

Finally, type `"U"` then press *Tab* to auto-complete `toUniversalString()`, then press *Enter* to invoke the method and assign the 24-hour-clock-format `String` to an implicitly declared variable:

```
jshell> time.toUniversalString()
$3 ==> "00:00:00"

jshell>
```

28.7 JavaFX 9 Skin APIs

In Chapter 20, JavaFX Graphics, Animation and Video, we demonstrated how to format JavaFX objects using *Cascading Style Sheets (CSS)* technology which was originally developed for styling the elements in web pages. CSS allows you to specify *presentation* (e.g., fonts, spacing, sizes, colors, positioning) separately from the GUI's *structure* and *content* (layout containers, shapes, text, GUI components, etc.). If a JavaFX GUI's presentation is determined entirely by a style sheet (which specifies the rules for styling the GUI), you can simply swap in a new style sheet—sometimes called a *theme* or a *skin*—to change the GUI's appearance.

Each JavaFX control also has a *skin class* that determines its default appearance and how the user can interact with the control. In JavaFX 8, these skin classes were defined as *internal APIs*, but many developers extended these classes to create custom skins.

Portability Tip 28.1

Due to strong encapsulation, the JavaFX 8 internal skin APIs are no longer accessible in Java 9. If you created custom skins based on these pre-Java-9 APIs, your code will no longer compile in Java 9, and any existing compiled code will not run in the Java 9 JRE.

As part of Java 9 modularization, JavaFX 9 makes the skin classes `public` APIs in the `javafx.scene.control.skin` package, as described by JEP 253:

```
http://openjdk.java.net/jeps/253
```

The new skin classes are direct or indirect subclasses of class `SkinBase` (package `javafx.scene.control`). You can extend the appropriate skin class to customize the look-and-feel for a given type of control. You can then specify the fully qualified name of your skin class for a given control via the JavaFX CSS property **-fx-skin**.

Generally CSS is the easiest way to control the look of your JavaFX GUIs. For precise control over every aspect of a control, including the control's size, position, mouse and keyboard interactions and more, extend `SkinBase` or one of its many new control-specific subclasses in package `javafx.scene.control.skin`.

28.8 Other GUI and Graphics Enhancements

In addition to the changes mentioned in Sections 13.8– and 28.7, JSR 379 includes enhanced image support and additional desktop integration features.

28.8.1 Multi-Resolution Images

Apps often display different versions of an image, based on a device's screen size and resolution. Java 9 adds support for multi-resolution images in which a single image actually represents a set of images and class `Graphics` (package `java.awt`) can choose the appropriate resolution to use, based on the device. For more information, visit:

```
http://openjdk.java.net/jeps/251
```

28.8.2 TIFF Image I/O

The Image I/O framework provides APIs for loading and saving images. The framework supports plug-ins for different image formats, with PNG and JPEG required to be supported on all Java implementations. As of Java 9, all implementations are also required to support the TIFF (also called TIF) format—macOS uses TIFF as one of its standard image formats and various other platforms also support it. For more information on the Image I/O framework, visit:

```
https://docs.oracle.com/javase/8/docs/technotes/guides/imageio/
```

For more information on the new TIFF support, visit:

```
http://openjdk.java.net/jeps/262
```

28.8.3 Platform-Specific Desktop Features

In Java 9, various internal APIs that were used for operating-system-specific desktop integration—such as interacting with the dock in macOS—are no longer accessible due to the module system's strong encapsulation. JEP 272 adds new public APIs to expose this capability for macOS and to provide similar capabilities for other operating systems (such as Windows and Linux). Other features that will be provided include

- login/logout and screen lock/unlock event listeners so a Java app can respond to those events

- getting the user's attention via the dock or task bar with blinking or bouncing app icons and

- displaying progress bars in a dock or task bar.

For more information, visit:

```
http://openjdk.java.net/jeps/272
```

28.9 Security Related Java 9 Topics

It's important for developers to be aware of Java security enhancements. In this section, we provide brief mentions of a few Java 9 security-related features and where you can learn more about each.

28.9.1 Filter Incoming Serialization Data

Java's **object serialization** mechanism enables programs to create **serialized objects**—sequences of bytes that include each object's data, as well as information about the object's type and the types of the object's data. After a serialized object has been output, it can be read into a program and **deserialized**—that is, the type information and bytes that represent the object are used to recreate the object in memory.

Deserialization has the potential for security problems. For example, if the bytes being deserialized are read from a network connection, an attacker could intercept the bytes and inject invalid data. If you do not validate the data after deserialization, it's possible that the object would be in an invalid state that could affect the program's execution. In addition, the deserialization mechanism enables any serialized object to be deserialized, provided that its type definition is available to the runtime. If the object being deserialized contains an array, an attacker potentially could inject an arbitrarily large number of elements, potentially using all of the app's available memory.

JEP 290, Filter Incoming Serialization Data:

```
http://openjdk.java.net/jeps/290
```

is a security enhancement to object serialization that enables programs to add filters that can restrict which types can be deserialized, validate array lengths and more.

28.9.2 Create PKCS12 Keystores by Default

A keystore maintains security certificates that are used in encryption. Java has used a custom keystore since Java 1.2 (1998). By default, Java 9 now uses the popular and extensible

PKCS12 keystore, which is more secure and will enable Java systems to interoperate with other systems that support the same standard. For more information, visit:

```
http://openjdk.java.net/jeps/229
```

28.9.3 Datagram Transport Layer Security (DTLS)

Datagrams provide a connectionless mechanism to communicate information over a network. Java 9 adds support for the Datagram Transport Layer Security (DTLS) protocol which provides secure communication via datagrams. For more information, visit:

```
http://openjdk.java.net/jeps/219
```

28.9.4 OCSP Stapling for TLS

X.509 security certificates are used in public-key cryptography. JEP 249 is a security and performance enhancement for checking whether an X.509 security certificate is still valid. For details, visit:

```
http://openjdk.java.net/jeps/249
```

28.9.5 TLS Application-Layer Protocol Negotiation Extension

This is a security enhancement to the `javax.net.ssl` package to enable applications to choose from a list of protocols for communicating with one another over a secure connection. For more details, visit

```
http://openjdk.java.net/jeps/244
```

28.10 Other Java 9 Topics

In this section, we provide brief mentions of various other features of JSR 379. At the time of this writing during Java 9's early access stage, only limited documentation was available to us. So we concentrated on the information from the JSRs and JEPs. In a few cases, we did not comment on certain new Java 9 features. These include:

- JEP 193: Variable Handles (`http://openjdk.java.net/jeps/193`),
- JEP 268: XML Catalogs (`http://openjdk.java.net/jeps/268`) and
- JEP 274: Enhanced Method Handles (`http://openjdk.java.net/jeps/274`).

28.10.1 Indify String Concatenation

JEP 280, Indify String Concatenation, is a behind-the-scenes enhancement to `javac` that's geared to improving `String` concatenation performance in the future. The goal is to enable such performance enhancements to be developed and added to future Java implementations *without* having to modify the bytecodes `javac` produces. For more information, visit:

```
http://openjdk.java.net/jeps/280
```

28.10.2 Platform Logging API and Service

Developers commonly use logging frameworks for tracking information that helps them with debugging, maintenance and evolution of their systems, analytics, detecting security breaches and more. JEP 264, Platform Logging API and Service, adds a logging API for use by platform classes in the java.base module. Developers can then implement a service provider that routes logging messages to their preferred logging framework. For more information, visit

```
http://openjdk.java.net/jeps/264
```

28.10.3 Process API Updates

Java 9 includes enhancements to the APIs that enable Java programs to interact with operating-system-specific processes without having to use platform-specific native code written in C or C++. Some enhancements include access to a process's ID, arguments, start time, total CPU time and name, and terminating and monitoring processes from Java apps. For more information, visit:

```
http://openjdk.java.net/jeps/102
```

28.10.4 Spin-Wait Hints

Section 21.7 introduced a multithreading technique in which a thread that's waiting to aquire a lock on an object uses a loop to determine whether the lock is available and, if not, waits. Each time the thread is notified to check again, the loop repeats this process until the lock is acquired. This technique is known as a spin-wait loop. Java 9 adds a new API that enables such a loop to notify the JVM that it is a spin-wait loop. On some hardware platforms, the JVM can use this information to improve performance and reduce power consumption (especially crucial for battery-powered mobile devices). For more information, visit:

```
http://openjdk.java.net/jeps/285
```

28.10.5 UTF-8 Property Resource Bundles

Class ResourceBundle (package java.util) enables programs to load locale-specific information, such as Strings in different spoken languages. This technique is commonly used to localize apps for users in different regions. Java 9 upgrades class ResourceBundle to support resources that are encoded in UTF-8 format (https://en.wikipedia.org/wiki/UTF-8). For more information, visit:

```
http://openjdk.java.net/jeps/226
```

28.10.6 Use CLDR Locale Data by Default

CLDR—the Unicode Common Locale Data Repository (http://cldr.unicode.org)—is an extensive repository of locale-specific information that developers can use when internationalizing their apps. Data in the repository includes information on

- date, time, number and currency formatting
- translations for the names of spoken languages, countries, regions, months, days, etc.
- language-specific information like capitalization, gender rules, sorting rules, etc.
- country information, and more.

CLDR support was included with Java 8, but is now the default in Java 9. For more information, visit:

```
http://openjdk.java.net/jeps/252
```

28.10.7 Elide Deprecation Warnings on Import Statements

Many company coding guidelines require code to compile without warnings. In JDK 8, if you imported a deprecated type or statically imported a deprecated member of a type, the compiler would issue warnings, even if those types or members were never used in your code. Java allows you to prevent deprecation warnings in your code via the @Suppress-Warnings annotation, but this cannot be applied to import declarations. For this reason, it was not possible to prevent certain compile-time warnings. JDK 9 no longer produces such warnings on import declarations. For more information, visit:

```
http://openjdk.java.net/jeps/211
```

28.10.8 Multi-Release JAR Files

Even with Java 9's release, many people and organizations will continue using older versions of Java—some for many years. In one session at the 2016 JavaOne conference, attendees were asked which Java versions they were using. Several developers indicated their companies were still using versions as old as Java 1.4, which was released more than 15 years ago.

Library vendors often support multiple Java versions. Prior to Java 9, this required providing separate JAR files specific to each Java version. JDK 9 provides support for multi-release JAR files—a single JAR may contain multiple versions of the same class that are geared to different Java verions. In addition, these multi-release JAR files may contain module descriptors for use with the Java Platform Module System (Chapter 27). For more information, visit:

```
http://openjdk.java.net/jeps/238
```

28.10.9 Unicode 8

Java 9 supports the latest version of the Unicode Standard (unicode.org)—Unicode 8. Appropriate changes have been made to classes String and Character, as well as several other classes dependent on Unicode. For more details, visit:

```
http://openjdk.java.net/jeps/267
```

28.10.10 Concurrency Enhancements

JEP 266, More Concurrency Updates, adds features in three categories:

- Support for reactive streams—a technique for asynchronous stream processing—via class Flow and its nested interfaces. For a reactive streams overview and links to various other resources, visit:

```
https://en.wikipedia.org/wiki/Reactive_Streams
```

- Various improvements that the Java team accumulated since Java 8.
- Additional methods in class CompletableFuture (listed below).

New Methods of Class **CompletableFuture**

Section 21.14 introduced class CompletableFuture, which enables you to *asynchronously* execute Runnables that perform tasks or Suppliers that return values. Java 9 enhances CompletableFuture with the following methods:

- newIncompleteFuture
- defaultExecutor
- copy
- minimalCompletionStage
- completeAsync
- orTimeout
- completeOnTimeout
- delayedExecutor
- completedStage
- failedFuture
- failedStage

For more information on the concurrency enhancements, visit:

    http://openjdk.java.net/jeps/266

and see the online Java 9 documentation for java.util.concurrent (which includes class CompletableFuture's methods) and related packages in the java.base module:

    http://download.java.net/java/jdk9/docs/api/overview-summary.html

28.11 Items Removed from the JDK and Java 9

To help prepare the Java Platform for modularization, Java 9 removed several items from both the platform and its APIs. These are listed in JSR 379, Sections 8 and 9:

    http://cr.openjdk.java.net/~iris/se/9/java-se-9-pr-spec-01/java-se-
        9-spec.html

Removed Platform Features

JSR 379 Section 8 lists the platform changes. These include removal of the Java extensions mechanism. Prior to Java 9, the extensions mechanism allowed you to place a library's JAR file in a special JRE folder to make the library available to all Java apps on that computer. Classes in that folder were guaranteed to load before app-specific classes, so this was sometimes used to upgrade libraries with newer versions. In Java 9, the extensions mechanism is replaced with *upgradeable modules*:

    http://openjdk.java.net/projects/jigsaw/goals-reqs/03#upgradeable-
        modules

Upgradable modules are used primarily for standard technologies that evolve independently of the Java SE platform, but are bundled with the platform, such as JAXB—the Java Architecture for XML Binding. When a new JAXB version is released, its module can be placed in the java command's --**upgrade-module-path**. The runtime will then use the new version, rather than the earlier version that was bundled with the platform.

Removed Methods

JSR 379 Section 9 lists methods that have been removed from various Java classes to help modularize the platform. According to the JSR, these methods were infrequently used, but keeping them would have required placing the packages of the java.desktop module into the java.base module, resulting in a much larger minimal runtime size. This would not make sense, because many apps do not require the java.desktop module's GUI and desktop integration capabilities.

28.12 Items Proposed for Removal from Future Java Versions

The Java Platform has been in use for more than 20 years. Over that time, some APIs have been deprecated in favor of newer ones—often to fix bugs, to improve security or simply because an improved API was added that rendered the prior ones obsolete. Yet, many deprecated APIs—some from as far back as Java 1.2, which was released in December 1998—have remained available in every new version of Java, mostly for backward compatibility.

28.12.1 Enhanced Deprecation

JEP 277

```
http://openjdk.java.net/jeps/277
```

adds new features to the @Deprecated annotation that enable developers to provide more information about deprecated APIs, including whether or not the API is scheduled to be removed in a future release. These enhanced annotations are now used throughout the Java 9 APIs and pointed out in the online API documentation to highlight features you should no longer use and that you should expect to be removed from future versions. For example, everything in the java.applet package is now deprecated (Section 28.12.4), so when you view the package's documentation at

```
http://download.java.net/java/jdk9/docs/api/java/applet/package-
    summary.html
```

you'll see deprecation notes in the package's description and for each type in the package. In addition, if you use the types in your code, you'll get warnings at compile time.

28.12.2 Items Likely to Be Removed in Future Java Versions

JSR 379, Section 10 lists the various packages, classes, fields and methods that are likely to be removed from future Java versions. The JSR indicates that these packages evolve separately from the Java SE Platform or are part of the Java EE Platform specification. According to the JSR, the classes, fields and methods proposed for removal typically do not work, are not useful or have been rendered obsolete by newer APIs.

28.12.3 Finding Deprecated Features

Each page in the online Java API documentation

```
http://download.java.net/java/jdk9/docs/api/overview-summary.html
```

now includes a **DEPRECATED** link so you can view the **Deprecated API** list containing the deprecated APIs:

```
http://download.java.net/java/jdk9/docs/api/deprecated-list.html
```

When you click a given item, its documentation generally mentions why it was deprecated and what you should use instead.

Error-Prevention Tip 28.2

Avoid using deprecated features in new code. Also, if you maintain or evolve legacy Java code, you should carefully study the Deprecated API list and consider replacing the listed items with the alternatives specified in the online Java documentation. This will help en-sure that your code continues to compile and execute correctly in future Java versions.

28.12.4 Java Applets

As of Java 9 the Java Applet API is deprecated, per JEP 289 (`http://openjdk.java.net/jeps/289`). Previously this enabled Java to run in web browsers via a plug-in. Though this API has not been proposed for removal *yet*, it could be in a future Java version. Most popular web browsers removed Java plug-in support due to security issues.

28.13 Wrap-Up

In this chapter, we briefly recapped the Java 9 features covered in earlier chapters, then discussed various additional Java 9 topics. We presented the fundamentals of Java's new version numbering scheme. We demonstrated the new regular-expression `Matcher` methods `appendReplacement`, `appendTail`, `replaceFirst`, `replaceAll` and `results`. We also demonstrated the new `Stream` methods `takeWhile` and `dropWhile` and the new `iterate` overload. We discussed the Java 9 JavaFX changes, including the new `public` skin APIs and other GUI and graphics enhancements. You saw how to use modules in JShell.

We overviewed the Java 9 security-related changes and various other Java 9 features. We discussed the capabilities that are no longer available in JDK 9 and Java 9. Finally, we discussed the packages, classes and methods proposed for removal from future Java versions.

Staying in Contact with the Authors and Deitel & Associates, Inc.

We hope you enjoyed reading *Java 9 for Programmers* as much as we enjoyed writing it. We'd appreciate your feedback. Please send your questions, comments and suggestions to `deitel@deitel.com`. To stay up-to-date with the latest news about *Java 9 for Programmers*, and Deitel publications and corporate training, sign up for the *Deitel® Buzz Online* e-mail newsletter at

```
http://www.deitel.com/newsletter/subscribe.html
```

and follow us on social media at

- Facebook—http://facebook.com/DeitelFan
- LinkedIn—http://bit.ly/DeitelLinkedIn
- Twitter—http://twitter.com/deitel
- YouTube—http://youtube.com/DeitelTV

To learn more about Deitel & Associates' worldwide on-site programming training for your company or organization, visit

    http://www.deitel.com/training

or e-mail deitel@deitel.com. Good luck!

Operator Precedence Chart

Operators are shown in decreasing order of precedence from top to bottom (Fig. A.1).

Operator	Description	Associativity
++ --	unary postfix increment unary postfix decrement	right to left
++ -- + - ! ~ (*type*)	unary prefix increment unary prefix decrement unary plus unary minus unary logical negation unary bitwise complement unary cast	right to left
* / %	multiplication division remainder	left to right
+ -	addition or string concatenation subtraction	left to right
<< >> >>>	left shift signed right shift unsigned right shift	left to right
< <= > >= instanceof	less than less than or equal to greater than greater than or equal to type comparison	left to right

Fig. A.1 | Operator precedence chart. (Part 1 of 2.)

Operator	Description	Associativity
==	is equal to	left to right
!=	is not equal to	
&	bitwise AND	left to right
	boolean logical AND	
^	bitwise exclusive OR	left to right
	boolean logical exclusive OR	
|	bitwise inclusive OR	left to right
	boolean logical inclusive OR	
&&	conditional AND	left to right
||	conditional OR	left to right
?:	conditional	right to left
=	assignment	right to left
+=	addition assignment	
-=	subtraction assignment	
*=	multiplication assignment	
/=	division assignment	
%=	remainder assignment	
&=	bitwise AND assignment	
^=	bitwise exclusive OR assignment	
|=	bitwise inclusive OR assignment	
<<=	bitwise left-shift assignment	
>>=	bitwise signed-right-shift assignment	
>>>=	bitwise unsigned-right-shift assignment	

Fig. A.1 | Operator precedence chart. (Part 2 of 2.)

ASCII Character Set

	0	1	2	3	4	5	6	7	8	9
0	nul	soh	stx	etx	eot	enq	ack	bel	bs	ht
1	nl	vt	ff	cr	so	si	dle	dc1	dc2	dc3
2	dc4	nak	syn	etb	can	em	sub	esc	fs	gs
3	rs	us	sp	!	"	#	$	%	&	'
4	(	)	*	+	,	-	.	/	0	1
5	2	3	4	5	6	7	8	9	:	;
6	<	=	>	?	@	A	B	C	D	E
7	F	G	H	I	J	K	L	M	N	O
8	P	Q	R	S	T	U	V	W	X	Y
9	Z	[	\	]	^	_	'	a	b	c
10	d	e	f	g	h	i	j	k	l	m
11	n	o	p	q	r	s	t	u	v	w
12	x	y	z	{	|	}	~	del		

Fig. B.1 | ASCII character set.

The digits at the left of the table are the left digits of the decimal equivalents (0–127) of the character codes, and the digits at the top of the table are the right digits of the character codes. For example, the character code for "F" is 70, and the character code for "&" is 38.

Most users of this book are interested in the ASCII character set used to represent English characters on many computers. The ASCII character set is a subset of the Unicode character set used by Java to represent characters from most of the world's languages.

Keywords and Reserved Words

Java Keywords				
abstract	assert	boolean	break	byte
case	catch	char	class	continue
default	do	double	else	enum
extends	final	finally	float	for
if	implements	import	instanceof	int
interface	long	native	new	package
private	protected	public	return	short
static	strictfp	super	switch	synchronized
this	throw	throws	transient	try
void	volatile	while		

Keywords that are not currently used

const	goto

Fig. C.1 | Java keywords.

Java also contains the reserved words `true` and `false`, which are `boolean` literals, and `null`, which is the literal that represents a reference to nothing. Like keywords, these reserved words cannot be used as identifiers.

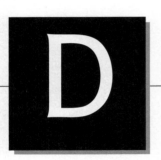

Primitive Types

Type	Size (bits)	Values	Standard
boolean		true or false	
char	16	'\u0000' to '\uFFFF' (0 to 65535)	(ISO Unicode character set)
byte	8	-128 to $+127$ (-2^7 to $2^7 - 1$)	
short	16	$-32{,}768$ to $+32{,}767$ (-2^{15} to $2^{15} - 1$)	
int	32	$-2{,}147{,}483{,}648$ to $+2{,}147{,}483{,}647$ (-2^{31} to $2^{31} - 1$)	
long	64	$-9{,}223{,}372{,}036{,}854{,}775{,}808$ to $+9{,}223{,}372{,}036{,}854{,}775{,}807$ (-2^{63} to $2^{63} - 1$)	
float	32	*Negative range:* $-3.4028234663852886E+38$ to $-1.40129846432481707e-45$ *Positive range:* $1.40129846432481707e-45$ to $3.4028234663852886E+38$	(IEEE 754 floating point)
double	64	*Negative range:* $-1.7976931348623157E+308$ to $-4.94065645841246544e-324$ *Positive range:* $4.94065645841246544e-324$ to $1.7976931348623157E+308$	(IEEE 754 floating point)

Fig. D.1 | Java primitive types.

Notes

- A boolean's representation is specific to each platform's Java Virtual Machine.
- You can use underscores to make numeric literal values more readable. For example, 1_000_000 is equivalent to 1000000.
- For more information on IEEE 754 visit http://grouper.ieee.org/groups/754/. For more information on Unicode, see http://unicode.org.

Bit Manipulation

E.1 Introduction

This appendix presents an extensive discussion of bit-manipulation operators, followed by a discussion of class **BitSet**, which enables the creation of bit-array-like objects for setting and getting individual bit values. Java provides extensive bit-manipulation capabilities for programmers who need to get down to the "bits-and-bytes" level. Operating systems, test equipment software, networking software and many other kinds of software require that the programmer communicate "directly with the hardware." We now discuss Java's bit-manipulation capabilities and bitwise operators.

E.2 Bit Manipulation and the Bitwise Operators

Computers represent all data internally as sequences of bits. Each bit can assume the value 0 or the value 1. On most systems, a sequence of eight bits forms a byte—the standard storage unit for a variable of type byte. Other types are stored in larger numbers of bytes. The bitwise operators can manipulate the bits of integral operands (i.e., operations of type byte, char, short, int and long), but not floating-point operands. The discussions of bitwise operators in this section show the binary representations of the integer operands.

The bitwise operators are **bitwise AND (&)**, **bitwise inclusive OR (|)**, **bitwise exclusive OR (^)**, **left shift (<<)**, **signed right shift (>>)**, **unsigned right shift (>>>)** and **bitwise complement (~)**. The bitwise AND, bitwise inclusive OR and bitwise exclusive OR operators compare their two operands bit by bit. The bitwise AND operator sets each bit in the result to 1 if and only if the corresponding bit in both operands is 1. The bitwise inclusive OR operator sets each bit in the result to 1 if the corresponding bit in either (or both) operand(s) is 1. The bitwise exclusive OR operator sets each bit in the result to 1 if the corresponding bit in exactly one operand is 1. The left-shift operator shifts the bits of its left operand to the left by the number of bits specified in its right operand. The signed right shift operator shifts the bits in its left operand to the right by the number of bits specified in its right operand—if the left operand is negative, 1s are shifted in from the left; otherwise, 0s are shifted in from the left. The unsigned right shift operator shifts the bits in its left operand to the right by the number of bits specified in its right operand—0s are shifted in from the left. The bitwise complement operator sets all 0 bits in its operand to 1 in the result and sets all 1 bits in its operand to 0 in the result. The bitwise operators are summarized in Fig. E.1.

Operator	Name	Description
&	bitwise AND	The bits in the result are set to 1 if the corresponding bits in the two operands are both 1.
|	bitwise inclusive OR	The bits in the result are set to 1 if at least one of the corresponding bits in the two operands is 1.
^	bitwise exclusive OR	The bits in the result are set to 1 if exactly one of the corresponding bits in the two operands is 1.
<<	left shift	Shifts the bits of the left operand left by the number of bits specified by the right operand; fill from the right with 0.
>>	signed right shift	Shifts the bits of the left operand right by the number of bits specified by the right operand. If the left operand is negative, 1s are filled in from the left; otherwise, 0s are filled in from the left.
>>>	unsigned right shift	Shifts the bits of the left operand right by the number of bits specified by the second operand; 0s are filled in from the left.
~	bitwise complement	All 0 bits are set to 1, and all 1 bits are set to 0.

Fig. E.1 | Bitwise operators.

When using the bitwise operators, it's useful to display values in their binary representation to illustrate the effects of these operators. The application of Fig. E.2 allows the user to enter an integer from the standard input. Lines 8–10 read the integer from the standard input. The integer is displayed in its binary representation in groups of eight bits each. Often, the bitwise AND operator is used with an operand called a **mask**—an integer value with specific bits set to 1. Masks are used to hide some bits in a value while selecting other bits. In line 16, mask variable `displayMask` is assigned the value 1 << 31, or

```
10000000 00000000 00000000 00000000
```

Lines 19–28 obtains a string representation of the integer, in bits. Line 21 uses the bitwise AND operator to combine variable `input` with variable `displayMask`. The left-shift operator shifts the value 1 from the low-order (rightmost) bit to the high-order (leftmost) bit in `displayMask` and fills in 0 from the right.

```
1   // Fig. E.2: PrintBits.java
2   // Printing an unsigned integer in bits.
3   import java.util.Scanner;
4
```

Fig. E.2 | Printing the bits in an integer. (Part 1 of 2.)

```
5    public class PrintBits {
6       public static void main(String[] args) {
7          // get input integer
8          Scanner scanner = new Scanner(System.in);
9          System.out.println("Please enter an integer:");
10         int input = scanner.nextInt();
11
12         // display bit representation of an integer
13         System.out.println("\nThe integer in bits is:");
14
15         // create int value with 1 in leftmost bit and 0s elsewhere
16         int displayMask = 1 << 31;
17
18         // for each bit display 0 or 1
19         for (int bit = 1; bit <= 32; bit++) {
20            // use displayMask to isolate bit
21            System.out.print((input & displayMask) == 0 ? '0' : '1'  );
22
23            input <<= 1; // shift value one position to left
24
25            if (bit % 8 == 0) {
26               System.out.print(' '); // display space every 8 bits
27            }
28         }
29      }
30   }
```

```
Please enter an integer:
0

The integer in bits is:
00000000 00000000 00000000 00000000
```

```
Please enter an integer:
-1

The integer in bits is:
11111111 11111111 11111111 11111111
```

```
Please enter an integer:
65535

The integer in bits is:
00000000 00000000 11111111 11111111
```

Fig. E.2 | Printing the bits in an integer. (Part 2 of 2.)

Line 21 determines whether the current leftmost bit of variable value is a 1 or 0 and displays '1' or '0', respectively, to the standard output. Assume that input contains 2000000000 (01110111 00110101 10010100 00000000). When input and displayMask are combined using &, all the bits except the high-order (leftmost) bit in variable input are "masked off" (hidden), because any bit "ANDed" with 0 yields 0. If the leftmost bit is 1, the expression input & displayMask evaluates to 1 and line 21 displays '1'; otherwise, line 21 displays '0'. Then line 23 left shifts variable input to the left by one bit with the expression input <<= 1. (This expression is equivalent to input = input << 1.) These steps are repeated for each bit in variable input. [*Note:* Class Integer provides method **toBinaryString**, which returns a string containing the binary representation of an integer.] Figure E.3 summarizes the results of combining two bits with the bitwise AND (&) operator.

Common Programming Error E.1
Using the conditional AND operator (&&) instead of the bitwise AND operator (&) is a compilation error.

Bit 1	Bit 2	Bit 1 & Bit 2
0	0	0
1	0	0
0	1	0
1	1	1

Fig. E.3 | Bitwise AND operator (&) combining two bits.

Figure E.4 demonstrates the bitwise AND operator, the bitwise inclusive OR operator, the bitwise exclusive OR operator and the bitwise complement operator. The program uses the display method of the utility class BitRepresentation (Fig. E.5) to get a string representation of the integer values. Notice that method display performs the same task as lines in Fig. E.2. Declaring display as a static method of class BitRepresentation allows display to be reused by later applications. The application of Fig. E.4 asks users to choose the operation they would like to test, gets input integer(s), performs the operation and displays the result of each operation in both integer and bitwise representations.

```java
1   // Fig. E.4: MiscBitOps.java
2   // Using the bitwise operators.
3   import java.util.Scanner;
4
5   public class MiscBitOps {
6      public static void main(String[] args) {
7         int choice = 0; // store operation type
8         int first = 0; // store first input integer
9         int second = 0; // store second input integer
10        int result = 0; // store operation result
11        Scanner scanner = new Scanner(System.in); // create Scanner
12
```

Fig. E.4 | Bitwise AND, bitwise inclusive OR, bitwise exclusive OR and bitwise complement operators. (Part 1 of 4.)

```
13          // continue execution until user exit
14          while (true) {
15              // get selected operation
16              System.out.println("\n\nPlease choose the operation:");
17              System.out.printf("%s%s", "1--AND\n2--Inclusive OR\n",
18                  "3--Exclusive OR\n4--Complement\n5--Exit\n");
19              choice = scanner.nextInt();
20
21              // perform bitwise operation
22              switch (choice) {
23                  case 1: // AND
24                      System.out.print("Please enter two integers:");
25                      first = scanner.nextInt(); // get first input integer
26                      BitRepresentation.display(first);
27                      second = scanner.nextInt(); // get second input integer
28                      BitRepresentation.display(second);
29                      result = first & second; // perform bitwise AND
30                      System.out.printf(
31                          "\n\n%d & %d = %d", first, second, result);
32                      BitRepresentation.display(result);
33                      break;
34                  case 2: // Inclusive OR
35                      System.out.print("Please enter two integers:");
36                      first = scanner.nextInt(); // get first input integer
37                      BitRepresentation.display(first);
38                      second = scanner.nextInt(); // get second input integer
39                      BitRepresentation.display(second);
40                      result = first | second; // perform bitwise inclusive OR
41                      System.out.printf(
42                          "\n\n%d | %d = %d", first, second, result);
43                      BitRepresentation.display(result);
44                      break;
45                  case 3: // Exclusive OR
46                      System.out.print("Please enter two integers:");
47                      first = scanner.nextInt(); // get first input integer
48                      BitRepresentation.display(first);
49                      second = scanner.nextInt(); // get second input integer
50                      BitRepresentation.display(second);
51                      result = first ^ second; // perform bitwise exclusive OR
52                      System.out.printf(
53                          "\n\n%d ^ %d = %d", first, second, result);
54                      BitRepresentation.display(result);
55                      break;
56                  case 4: // Complement
57                      System.out.print("Please enter one integer:");
58                      first = scanner.nextInt(); // get input integer
59                      BitRepresentation.display(first);
60                      result = ~first; // perform bitwise complement on first
61                      System.out.printf("\n\n~%d = %d", first, result);
62                      BitRepresentation.display(result);
63                      break;
```

Fig. E.4 | Bitwise AND, bitwise inclusive OR, bitwise exclusive OR and bitwise complement operators. (Part 2 of 4.)

```
64                    case 5: default:
65                        System.exit(0); // exit application
66                }
67            }
68        }
69    }
```

```
Please choose the operation:
1--AND
2--Inclusive OR
3--Exclusive OR
4--Complement
5--Exit
1
Please enter two integers:65535 1

Bit representation of 65535 is:
00000000 00000000 11111111 11111111
Bit representation of 1 is:
00000000 00000000 00000000 00000001

65535 & 1 = 1
Bit representation of 1 is:
00000000 00000000 00000000 00000001

Please choose the operation:
1--AND
2--Inclusive OR
3--Exclusive OR
4--Complement
5--Exit
2
Please enter two integers:15 241

Bit representation of 15 is:
00000000 00000000 00000000 00001111
Bit representation of 241 is:
00000000 00000000 00000000 11110001

15 | 241 = 255
Bit representation of 255 is:
00000000 00000000 00000000 11111111

Please choose the operation:
1--AND
2--Inclusive OR
3--Exclusive OR
4--Complement
5--Exit
3

Please enter two integers:139 199
```

Fig. E.4 | Bitwise AND, bitwise inclusive OR, bitwise exclusive OR and bitwise complement operators. (Part 3 of 4.)

```
Bit representation of 139 is:
00000000 00000000 00000000 10001011
Bit representation of 199 is:
00000000 00000000 00000000 11000111

139 ^ 199 = 76
Bit representation of 76 is:
00000000 00000000 00000000 01001100

Please choose the operation:
1--AND
2--Inclusive OR
3--Exclusive OR
4--Complement
5--Exit
4
Please enter one integer:21845

Bit representation of 21845 is:
00000000 00000000 01010101 01010101

~21845 = -21846
Bit representation of -21846 is:
11111111 11111111 10101010 10101010
```

Fig. E.4 | Bitwise AND, bitwise inclusive OR, bitwise exclusive OR and bitwise complement operators. (Part 4 of 4.)

```java
1   // Fig E.5: BitRepresentation.java
2   // Utility class that displays bit representation of an integer.
3
4   public class BitRepresentation {
5      // display bit representation of specified int value
6      public static void display(int value) {
7         System.out.printf("\nBit representation of %d is: \n", value);
8
9         // create int value with 1 in leftmost bit and 0s elsewhere
10        int displayMask = 1 << 31;
11
12        // for each bit display 0 or 1
13        for (int bit = 1; bit <= 32; bit++) {
14           // use displayMask to isolate bit
15           System.out.print((value & displayMask) == 0 ? '0' : '1');
16
17           value <<= 1; // shift value one position to left
18
19           if (bit % 8 == 0) {
20              System.out.print(' '); // display space every 8 bits
21           }
22        }
23     }
24  }
```

Fig. E.5 | Utility class that displays bit representation of an integer.

The first output window in Fig. E.4 shows the results of combining the value 65535 and the value 1 with the bitwise AND operator (&; line 29). All the bits except the low-order bit in the value 65535 are "masked off" (hidden) by "ANDing" with the value 1.

The bitwise inclusive OR operator (|) sets each bit in the result to 1 if the corresponding bit in either (or both) operand(s) is 1. The second output window in Fig. E.4 shows the results of combining the value 15 and the value 241 by using the bitwise OR operator (line 40)—the result is 255. Figure E.6 summarizes the results of combining two bits with the bitwise inclusive OR operator.

Bit 1	Bit 2	Bit 1 | Bit 2
0	0	0
1	0	1
0	1	1
1	1	1

Fig. E.6 | Bitwise inclusive OR operator (|) combining two bits.

The bitwise exclusive OR operator (^) sets each bit in the result to 1 if *exactly* one of the corresponding bits in its two operands is 1. The third output window in Fig. E.4 shows the results of combining the value 139 and the value 199 by using the exclusive OR operator (line 51)—the result is 76. Figure E.7 summarizes the results of combining two bits with the bitwise exclusive OR operator.

Bit 1	Bit 2	Bit 1 ^ Bit 2
0	0	0
1	0	1
0	1	1
1	1	0

Fig. E.7 | Bitwise exclusive OR operator (^) combining two bits.

The bitwise complement operator (~) sets all 1 bits in its operand to 0 in the result and sets all 0 bits in its operand to 1 in the result—otherwise referred to as "taking the one's complement of the value." The fourth output window in Fig. E.4 shows the results of taking the one's complement of the value 21845 (line 60). The result is -21846.

Figure E.8 demonstrates the left-shift operator (<<), the signed right-shift operator (>>) and the unsigned right-shift operator (>>>). The application asks the user to enter an integer and choose the operation, then performs a one-bit shift and displays the results of the shift in both integer and bitwise representation. We use the utility class `BitRepresentation` (Fig. E.5) to display the bit representation of an integer.

The left-shift operator (<<) shifts the bits of its left operand to the left by the number of bits specified in its right operand (performed at line 27 in Fig. E.8). Bits vacated to the right are replaced with 0s; 1s shifted off the left are lost. The first output window in Fig. E.8 demonstrates the left-shift operator. Starting with the value 1, the left shift operation was chosen, resulting in the value 2.

```java
1   // Fig. E.8: BitShift.java
2   // Using the bitwise shift operators.
3   import java.util.Scanner;
4
5   public class BitShift {
6      public static void main(String[] args) {
7         int choice = 0; // store operation type
8         int input = 0; // store input integer
9         int result = 0; // store operation result
10        Scanner scanner = new Scanner(System.in); // create Scanner
11
12        // continue execution until user exit
13        while (true) {
14           // get shift operation
15           System.out.println("\n\nPlease choose the shift operation:");
16           System.out.println("1--Left Shift (<<)");
17           System.out.println("2--Signed Right Shift (>>)");
18           System.out.println("3--Unsigned Right Shift (>>>)");
19           System.out.println("4--Exit");
20           choice = scanner.nextInt();
21
22           // perform shift operation
23           switch (choice) {
24              case 1: // <<
25                 System.out.println("Please enter an integer to shift:");
26                 input = scanner.nextInt(); // get input integer
27                 result = input << 1; // left shift one position
28                 System.out.printf("\n%d << 1 = %d", input, result);
29                 break;
30              case 2: // >>
31                 System.out.println("Please enter an integer to shift:");
32                 input = scanner.nextInt(); // get input integer
33                 result = input >> 1; // signed right shift one position
34                 System.out.printf("\n%d >> 1 = %d", input, result);
35                 break;
36              case 3: // >>>
37                 System.out.println("Please enter an integer to shift:");
38                 input = scanner.nextInt(); // get input integer
39                 result = input >>> 1; // unsigned right shift one position
40                 System.out.printf("\n%d >>> 1 = %d", input, result);
41                 break;
42              case 4: default: // default operation is <<
43                 System.exit(0); // exit application
44           }
45
46           // display input integer and result in bits
47           BitRepresentation.display(input);
48           BitRepresentation.display(result);
49        }
50     }
51  }
```

Fig. E.8 | Bitwise shift operations. (Part 1 of 2.)

```
Please choose the shift operation:
1--Left Shift (<<)
2--Signed Right Shift (>>)
3--Unsigned Right Shift (>>>)
4--Exit
1
Please enter an integer to shift:
1

1 << 1 = 2
Bit representation of 1 is:
00000000 00000000 00000000 00000001
Bit representation of 2 is:
00000000 00000000 00000000 00000010

Please choose the shift operation:
1--Left Shift (<<)
2--Signed Right Shift (>>)
3--Unsigned Right Shift (>>>)
4--Exit
2
Please enter an integer to shift:
-2147483648

-2147483648 >> 1 = -1073741824
Bit representation of -2147483648 is:
10000000 00000000 00000000 00000000
Bit representation of -1073741824 is:
11000000 00000000 00000000 00000000

Please choose the shift operation:
1--Left Shift (<<)
2--Signed Right Shift (>>)
3--Unsigned Right Shift (>>>)
4--Exit
3
Please enter an integer to shift:
-2147483648

-2147483648 >>> 1 = 1073741824
Bit representation of -2147483648 is:
10000000 00000000 00000000 00000000
Bit representation of 1073741824 is:
01000000 00000000 00000000 00000000
```

Fig. E.8 | Bitwise shift operations. (Part 2 of 2.)

The signed right-shift operator (>>) shifts the bits of its left operand to the right by the number of bits specified in its right operand (performed at line 33 in Fig. E.8). Performing a right shift causes the vacated bits at the left to be replaced by 0s if the number is positive or by 1s if the number is negative. Any 1s shifted off the right are lost. Next, the output window the results of signed right shifting the value -2147483648, which is the value 1 being left shifted 31 times. Notice that the leftmost bit is replaced by 1 because the number is negative.

The unsigned right-shift operator (>>>) shifts the bits of its left operand to the right by the number of bits specified in its right operand (performed at line 39 in Fig. E.8). Performing an unsigned right shift causes the vacated bits at the left to be replaced by 0s. Any 1s shifted off the right are lost. The third output window of Fig. E.8 shows the results of unsigned right shifting the value -2147483648. Notice that the leftmost bit is replaced by 0. Each bitwise operator (except the bitwise complement operator) has a corresponding assignment operator. These **bitwise assignment operators** are shown in Fig. E.9.

Bitwise assignment operators	
&=	Bitwise AND assignment operator.
|=	Bitwise inclusive OR assignment operator.
^=	Bitwise exclusive OR assignment operator.
<<=	Left-shift assignment operator.
>>=	Signed right-shift assignment operator.
>>>=	Unsigned right-shift assignment operator.

Fig. E.9 | Bitwise assignment operators.

E.3 BitSet Class

Class `BitSet` makes it easy to create and manipulate **bit sets**, which are useful for representing sets of `boolean` flags. `BitSet`s are dynamically resizable—more bits can be added as needed, and a `BitSet` will grow to accommodate the additional bits. Class `BitSet` provides two constructors—a no-argument constructor that creates an empty `BitSet` and a constructor that receives an integer representing the number of bits in the `BitSet`. By default, each bit in a `BitSet` has a `false` value—the underlying bit has the value 0. A bit is set to `true` (also called "on") with a call to `BitSet` method **set**, which receives the index of the bit to set as an argument. This makes the underlying value of that bit 1. Bit indices are zero based, like arrays. A bit is set to `false` (also called "off") by calling `BitSet` method **clear**. This makes the underlying value of that bit 0. To obtain the value of a bit, use `BitSet` method **get**, which receives the index of the bit to get and returns a boolean value representing whether the bit at that index is on (`true`) or off (`false`).

Class `BitSet` also provides methods for combining the bits in two `BitSet`s, using bitwise logical AND (**and**), bitwise logical inclusive OR (**or**), and bitwise logical exclusive OR (**xor**). Assuming that `b1` and `b2` are `BitSet`s, the statement

```
b1.and(b2);
```

performs a bit-by-bit logical AND operation between `BitSet`s `b1` and `b2`. The result is stored in `b1`. When `b2` has more bits than `b1`, the extra bits of `b2` are ignored. Hence, the size of `b1` remain unchanged. Bitwise logical inclusive OR and bitwise logical exclusive OR are performed by the statements

```
b1.or(b2);
b1.xor(b2);
```

When `b2` has more bits than `b1`, the extra bits of `b2` are ignored. Hence the size of `b1` remains unchanged.

BitSet method **size** returns the number of bits in a BitSet. BitSet method **equals** compares two BitSets for equality. Two BitSets are equal if and only if each BitSet has identical values in corresponding bits. BitSet method **toString** creates a string representation of a BitSet's contents.

Figure E.10 implements the Sieve of Eratosthenes (for finding prime numbers). We use a BitSet to implement the algorithm. The application asks the user to enter an integer between 2 and 1023, displays all the prime numbers from 2 to 1023 and determines whether that number is prime.

```java
// Fig. E.10: BitSetTest.java
// Using a BitSet to demonstrate the Sieve of Eratosthenes.
import java.util.BitSet;
import java.util.Scanner;

public class BitSetTest {
   public static void main(String[] args) {
      // get input integer
      Scanner scanner = new Scanner(System.in);
      System.out.println("Please enter an integer from 2 to 1023");
      int input = scanner.nextInt();

      // perform Sieve of Eratosthenes
      BitSet sieve = new BitSet(1024);
      int size = sieve.size();

      // set all bits from 2 to 1023
      for (int i = 2; i < size; i++) {
         sieve.set(i);
      }

      // perform Sieve of Eratosthenes
      int finalBit = (int) Math.sqrt(size);

      for (int i = 2; i < finalBit; i++) {
         if (sieve.get(i)  ) {
            for (int j = 2 * i; j < size; j += i) {
               sieve.clear(j);
            }
         }
      }

      int counter = 0;

      // display prime numbers from 2 to 1023
      for (int i = 2; i < size; i++) {
         if (sieve.get(i)  ) {
            System.out.print(String.valueOf(i));
            System.out.print(++counter % 7 == 0 ? "\n" : "\t");
         }
      }
```

Fig. E.10 | Sieve of Eratosthenes, using a BitSet. (Part 1 of 2.)

```
43          // display result
44          if (sieve.get(input)  ) {
45              System.out.printf("\n%d is a prime number", input);
46          }
47          else {
48              System.out.printf("\n%d is not a prime number", input);
49          }
50      }
51  }
```

```
Please enter an integer from 2 to 1023
773
2       3       5       7       11      13      17
19      23      29      31      37      41      43
47      53      59      61      67      71      73
79      83      89      97      101     103     107
109     113     127     131     137     139     149
151     157     163     167     173     179     181
191     193     197     199     211     223     227
229     233     239     241     251     257     263
269     271     277     281     283     293     307
311     313     317     331     337     347     349
353     359     367     373     379     383     389
397     401     409     419     421     431     433
439     443     449     457     461     463     467
479     487     491     499     503     509     521
523     541     547     557     563     569     571
577     587     593     599     601     607     613
617     619     631     641     643     647     653
659     661     673     677     683     691     701
709     719     727     733     739     743     751
757     761     769     773     787     797     809
811     821     823     827     829     839     853
857     859     863     877     881     883     887
907     911     919     929     937     941     947
953     967     971     977     983     991     997
1009    1013    1019    1021
773 is a prime number
```

Fig. E.10 | Sieve of Eratosthenes, using a BitSet. (Part 2 of 2.)

Line 14 creates a BitSet of 1024 bits. We ignore the bits at indices zero and one in this application. Lines 18–20 set all the bits in the BitSet to "on" with BitSet method set. Lines 23–31 determine all the prime numbers from 2 to 1023. The integer finalBit specifies when the algorithm is complete. The basic algorithm is that a number is prime if it has no divisors other than 1 and itself. Starting with the number 2, once we know that a number is prime, we can eliminate all multiples of that number. The number 2 is divisible only by 1 and itself, so it's prime. Therefore, we can eliminate 4, 6, 8 and so on. Elimination of a value consists of setting its bit to "off" with BitSet method clear (line 28). The number 3 is divisible by 1 and itself. Therefore, we can eliminate all multiples of 3. (Keep in mind that all even numbers have already been eliminated.) After the list of primes is displayed, lines 44–49 use BitSet method get (line 44) to determine whether the bit for the number the user entered is set. If so, line 45 displays a message indicating that the number is prime.

Labeled **break** and **continue** Statements

F.1 Introduction

In Chapter 5, we discussed Java's break and continue statements, which enable programmers to alter the flow of control in control statements. Java also provides the labeled break and continue statements for cases in which a programmer needs to conveniently alter the flow of control in nested control statements. This appendix demonstrates the labeled break and continue statements with examples using nested for statements.

F.2 Labeled break Statement

The break statement presented in Section 5.8.1 enables a program to break out of the while, for, do...while or switch in which the break statement appears. Sometimes these control statements are nested in other iteration statements. A program might need to exit the entire nested control statement in one operation, rather than wait for it to complete execution normally. To break out of such nested control statements, you can use the **labeled break statement**. This statement, when executed in a while, for, do...while or switch, causes immediate exit from that control statement and any number of enclosing statements. Program execution resumes with the first statement after the enclosing **labeled statement**. The statement that follows the label can be either an iteration statement or a block in which an iteration statement appears. Figure F.1 demonstrates the labeled break statement in a nested for statement.

```
1   // Fig. F.1: BreakLabelTest.java
2   // Labeled break statement exiting a nested for statement.
3   public class BreakLabelTest {
4      public static void main(String[] args) {
5         stop: // labeled block
6         {
```

Fig. F.1 | Labeled break statement exiting a nested for statement. (Part 1 of 2.)

```
 7                // count 10 rows
 8                for (int row = 1; row <= 10; row++) {
 9                    // count 5 columns
10                    for (int column = 1; column <= 5 ; column++) {
11                        if (row == 5) { // if row is 5,
12                            break stop;   // jump to end of stop block
13                        }
14
15                        System.out.print("* ");
16                    }
17
18                    System.out.println(); // outputs a newline
19                }
20
21                // following line is skipped
22                System.out.println("\nLoops terminated normally");
23            } // end labeled block
24        }
25    }
```

```
* * * * *
* * * * *
* * * * *
* * * * *
```

Fig. F.1 | Labeled **break** statement exiting a nested **for** statement. (Part 2 of 2.)

The block (lines 5–23 in Fig. F.1) begins with a **label** (an identifier followed by a colon) at line 5; here we use the **stop:** label. The block is enclosed in braces (lines 6 and 23) and includes the nested **for** (lines 8–19) and the output statement at line 22. When the **if** at line 11 detects that row is equal to 5, the **break** statement at line 12 executes. This statement terminates both the **for** at lines 10–16 and its enclosing **for** at lines 8–19. Then the program proceeds immediately to the first statement after the labeled block—in this case, the end of main is reached and the program terminates. The outer **for** fully executes its body only four times. The output statement at line 22 never executes, because it's in the labeled block's body, and the outer **for** never completes.

> **Good Programming Practice F.1**
>
> *Too many levels of nested control statements can make a program difficult to read. As a general rule, try to avoid using more than three levels of nesting.*

F.3 Labeled **continue** Statement

The **continue** statement presented in Section 5.8.2 proceeds with the next iteration of the immediately enclosing **while**, **for** or **do...while**. The **labeled continue statement** skips the remaining statements in that statement's body and any number of enclosing iteration statements and proceeds with the next iteration of the enclosing **labeled iteration statement** (i.e., a **for**, **while** or **do...while** preceded by a label). In labeled **while** and **do...while** statements, the program evaluates the loop-continuation test of the labeled loop immediately after the continue statement executes. In a labeled for, the increment expression is executed and the loop-continuation test is evaluated. Figure F.2 uses a labeled continue statement in a nested for to enable execution to continue with the next iteration of the outer for.

```java
1   // Fig. F.2: ContinueLabelTest.java
2   // Labeled continue statement terminating a nested for statement.
3   public class ContinueLabelTest {
4      public static void main(String[] args) {
5         nextRow: // target label of continue statement
6            // count 5 rows
7            for (int row = 1; row <= 5; row++) {
8               System.out.println(); // outputs a newline
9
10              // count 10 columns per row
11              for (int column = 1; column <= 10; column++) {
12                 // if column greater than row, start next row
13                 if (column > row) {
14                    continue nextRow; // next iteration of labeled loop
15                 }
16
17                 System.out.print("* ");
18              }
19           }
20
21        System.out.println(); // outputs a newline
22     }
23  }
```

```
*
* *
* * *
* * * *
* * * * *
```

Fig. F.2 | Labeled continue statement terminating a nested for statement.

The labeled for (lines 5–19) starts at the nextRow label. When the if at line 13 in the inner for detects that column is greater than row, the continue statement at line 14 executes, and program control continues with the increment of the control variable row of the outer for loop. Even though the inner for counts from 1 to 10, the number of * characters output on a row never exceeds the value of row, creating an interesting triangle pattern.

Index

[*Note:* Page references for defining occurrences of terms appear in **bold**.]